INTRODUCTION
TO THE
OLD TESTAMENT

*with a comprehensive review of
Old Testament studies
and a special supplement on the Apocrypha*

by

R. K. HARRISON

*Professor of Old Testament
Wycliffe College, University of Toronto*

WILLIAM B. EERDMANS PUBLISHING COMPANY
GRAND RAPIDS, MICHIGAN

Copyright © 1969 by William B. Eerdmans Publishing Company
All rights reserved
Library of Congress Catalog Card Number 64-22030
PRINTED IN THE UNITED STATES OF AMERICA
ISBN 0-8028-3107-9

First printing, September 1969

Reprinted, July 1982

To My Parents

PREFACE

The present work is an attempt to evaluate the contents of the Old Testament and Apocrypha against the vast background of knowledge that is now available for students of ancient Near Eastern life and culture. The more detailed introduction to the books of the Old Testament is prefaced by seven sections dealing with important areas of Old Testament study; although this procedure results in some repetition throughout the book, it is hoped that it will serve the interests of the beginning student in furnishing a resume of the history of thought in each particular branch of study. The section dealing with the Apocrypha was added at the request of the publishers. Its presence should not be taken to imply that its contents are to be regarded as of equal inspiration or authority with the Old Testament.

Considerable emphasis has been placed upon methodology in an endeavor to permit the Hebrew Scriptures to speak for themselves against their ancient Near Eastern background. Much of what has passed for critical study in this field has in fact consisted largely of the application of *a priori* literary-critical theories, often in apparent isolation from methodological approaches involving archaeology, comparative religion, sociology, history, linguistics, and aspects of the biological and physical sciences. All of these have a part to play in the proper understanding of the Scriptural record, and must now take their place beside literary and textual criticism as valid means to this end. The methodology adopted in this book is inductive, and the writer has been at considerable pains in resisting temptations to "burke any issue," to borrow the quaint Victorian phrase favored occasionally by H. H. Rowley.[1] The conclusions that appear in the book are tentative and amenable to modification in the light of whatever relevant factual information may emerge in the future.

I wish to acknowledge my indebtedness for permission to quote from copyright works to the following: to Dr. G. E. Wright for allowing the use of material contained in various numbers of *The Biblical Archaeologist*; to the University of Chicago Press for permission to reprint sections from

---

[1] H. H. Rowley, *BJRL*, XXXVII (1955), p. 550 n. 3, *et al.*

A. Heidel, *The Gilgamesh Epic and Old Testament Parallels* (1949 edition), D. D. Luckenbill, *Ancient Records of Assyria and Babylonia* (2 volumes, 1926); to Y. Kaufmann, *The Religion of Israel*, translated by Moshe Greenberg (1960); to the American Philosophical Society for their kindness in allowing the use of copyright material in S. N. Kramer, *Sumerian Mythology* (1947 edition), originally published in 1944 in Volume 21 of the Society's *Memoirs*, and to Dr. Kramer himself for his generous consent; and to Princeton University Press for permitting quotations from J. Finegan, *Light From the Ancient Past* (1946), and J. B. Pritchard (ed.), *Ancient Near Eastern Texts Relating to the Old Testament* (1950).

I would like to take this opportunity of thanking those who have been of particular assistance and encouragement in the preparation of this book, including Principal Leslie Hunt of Wycliffe College, and my past and present colleagues, Professors T. W. Harpur, J. Jocz, T. R. Millman, W. Prior, R. F. Stackhouse, and the Rev. Dr. R. A. Ward. I want also to express my gratitude to Mr. J. Freeman of Montreal for his interest in my work; to Mrs. G. G. Simms for typing out portions of the manuscript; to Dr. S. J. Mikolaski for a critical reading of Part Seven; to Mrs. H. Bohne, librarian of Wycliffe College, for her generous help with source materials, and to the Rev. Norman Green, Field Secretary of Wycliffe College for his diligence in correcting the proofs. Finally my thanks are due to the editorial and production staffs of the Wm. B. Eerdmans Publishing Company for their painstaking attention and unfailing courtesy in the making of this book.

—R. K. Harrison

Wycliffe College,
University of Toronto.

CONTENTS

CONTENTS

ABBREVIATIONS

AASOR	*The Annual of the American Schools of Oriental Research*
AAT	L.E.T. André, *Les Apocryphes de l'Ancien Testament* (1903)
AJ	Flavius Josephus, *The Antiquities of the Jews* (1829 edition)
AJA	*American Journal of Archaeology*
AJSL	*American Journal of Semitic Languages and Literatures*
ANE	J.B. Pritchard (ed.), *The Ancient Near East* (1958)
ANET	J.B. Pritchard (ed.), *Ancient Near Eastern Texts Relating to the Old Testament* (1950)
AP	W.F. Albright, *The Archaeology of Palestine* (1949)
APOT	R. H. Charles (ed.), *The Apocrypha and Pseudepigrapha of the Old Testament* (1913), 2 vols.
ARAB	D.D. Luckenbill, *Ancient Records of Assyria and Babylonia* (1926), 2 vols.
ARE	J.H. Breasted, *Ancient Records of Egypt* (1906-07), 5 vols.
ARI	W.F. Albright, *Archaeology and the Religion of Israel* (1955)
BA	*The Biblical Archaeologist*
BACP	Y. Kaufmann, *The Biblical Account of the Conquest of Palestine* (1953)
BANE	G.E. Wright (ed.), *The Bible and the Ancient Near East* (1961)
BASOR	*Bulletin of the American Schools of Oriental Research*
BCIA	L.H. Brockington, *A Critical Introduction to the Apocrypha* (1961)
BCNE	H. Frankfort, *The Birth of Civilisation in the Near East* (1956)
BHI	J. Bright, *A History of Israel* (1959)
BJRL	*Bulletin of the John Rylands Library*
BPAE	W.F. Albright, *The Biblical Period from Abraham to Ezra* (1963)
BZAW	*Beihefte zur Zeitschrift für die Alttestamentliche Wissenschaft*
CAEM	A.L. Perkins, *The Comparative Archaeology of Early Mesopotamia* (1949)
CBQ	*Catholic Biblical Quarterly*
DILOT	S.R. Driver, *An Introduction to the Literature of the Old Testament* (1912 edition)
DJD	D. Barthélemy and J.T. Milik, *Discoveries in the Judean Desert I.* Qumran, Cave I (1955); II Murabba' at (1961)
DOTT	D. Winton Thomas (ed.), *Documents from Old Testament Times* (1958)
EB	*Encyclopedia Biblica* (1899), 4 vols.
EQ	*The Evangelical Quarterly*
ERE	J. Hastings (ed.), *Encyclopaedia of Religion and Ethics* (1911-22), 12 vols.

ET	*The Expository Times*
ETOT	O. Eissfeldt, *The Old Testament, An Introduction* (1965)
FSAC	W.F. Albright, *From the Stone Age to Christianity* (1957 edition)
GBB	C.H. Gordon, *Before the Bible* (1962)
GI	M. Noth, *Geschichte Israels* (1950)
HDB	J. Hastings (ed.), *Dictionary of the Bible* (1911), 5 vols.
HNTT	R.H. Pfeiffer, *A History of New Testament Times* (1949)
HUCA	*Hebrew Union College Annual*
IAAM	H.A. Frankfort, *et al.*, *The Intellectual Adventure of Ancient Man* (1948)
IB	*The Interpreter's Bible* (1952-7), 12 vols.
IBOT	W.O.E. Oesterley and T.H. Robinson, *An Introduction to the Books of the Old Testament* (1934)
ICC	*International Critical Commentary*
IDB	*The Interpreter's Dictionary of the Bible* (1962), 4 vols.
IHANE	R.C. Dentan (ed.), *The Idea of History in the Ancient Near East* (1955)
IOTT	C.H. Gordon, *Introduction to Old Testament Times* (1953)
ISBE	*The International Standard Bible Encyclopedia* (1915), 5 vols.
JAOS	*Journal of the American Oriental Society*
JBL	*Journal of Biblical Literature*
JCS	*Journal of Cuneiform Studies*
JE	*The Jewish Encyclopedia* (1901-1905), 12 vols.
JEA	*Journal of Egyptian Archaeology*
JJS	*Journal of Jewish Studies*
JNES	*Journal of Near Eastern Studies*
JPOS	*Journal of the Palestine Oriental Society*
JQR	*Jewish Quarterly Review*
JRAS	*Journal of the Royal Asiatic Society*
JTS	*Journal of Theological Studies*
KRI	Y. Kaufmann, *The Religion of Israel*, translated by Moshe Greenberg (1960)
LAP	J. Finegan, *Light from the Ancient Past* (1946 edition)
MNHK	E.R. Thiele, *The Mysterious Numbers of the Hebrew Kings* (1965 ed.)
MTA	B. Metzger, *An Introduction to the Apocrypha* (1957)
NBD	*The New Bible Dictionary*
OLZ	*Orientalistische Literaturzeitung*
OTFD	A. Weiser, *The Old Testament: Its Formation and Development* (1961)
OTMS	H.H. Rowley (ed.), *The Old Testament and Modern Study* (1951)
PEF	*Palestine Exploration Fund*
PEQ	*Palestine Exploration Quarterly*
PG	*Patrologia Graeca* (ed. Migne)
PIOT	R.H. Pfeiffer, *Introduction to the Old Testament* (1941)
PJB	*Palästinajahrbuch*
PL	*Patrologia Latina* (ed. Migne)
PTR	*Princeton Theological Review*
RA	*Revue d'assyriologie et d'archéologie orientale*

RB	*Revue Biblique*
RDM	H.H. Rowley, *Darius the Mede and the Four World Empires of the Book of Daniel* (1935)
RHPR	*Revue d'histoire et de philosophie religieuses*
RSL	H.H. Rowley, *The Servant of the Lord and Other Essays on the Old Testament* (1952)
SRA	*Syria, Revue d'Art orientale et d'archéologie*
TAL	C.C. Torrey, *The Apocryphal Literature: A Brief Introduction* (1945)
TH	O.R. Gurney, *The Hittites* (1952)
UC	C.L. Woolley, *Ur of the Chaldees* (1950 edition)
UL	C.H. Gordon, *Ugaritic Literature* (1949)
UP	M. Noth, *Überlieferungsgeschichte des Pentateuchs* (1948)
VDJD	G. Vermès, *Discovery in the Judean Desert* (1956)
VT	*Vetus Testamentum*
WBA	G.E. Wright, *Biblical Archaeology* (1957)
WHAB	G.E. Wright and F.V. Filson, *Westminster Historical Atlas to the Bible* (1953 edition)
WJ	Flavius Josephus, *Wars of the Jews* (1829 edition)
WMTS	M. Burrows, *What Mean These Stones?* (1941)
YIOT	E.J. Young, *Introduction to the Old Testament* (1960 edition repr. 1963)
ZA	*Zeitschrift für Assyriologie und verwandte Gebiete*
ZAW	*Zeitschrift für die alttestamentliche Wissenschaft*
ZDMG	*Zeitschrift der Deutschen Morgenländischen Gesellschaft*

CDC	*Cairo Damascene Covenanters*
1QIsa[a]	St. Mark's Monastery Isaiah Scroll
1QIsa[b]	Hebrew University's Isaiah Scroll
1Q, etc.	The first, etc., Qumran Cave
1QH	The Qumran Hymn Scroll
1QM	The Qumran Military Scroll
1QpHab	The Qumran Habakkuk Commentary
1QS	*The Community Rule* or *Manual of Discipline*
AV	Authorized (King James) Version (1611)
RV	Revised Version (1881)
RSV	Revised Standard Version (1952)
LXX	Septuagint Greek version

AT	*Altes Testament*
ch.	chapter
d.	died
ed.	edition, edited by
E. tr.	English translation (by)
MT	Massoretic text
n.	note
n.d.	no date
pl.	plate

N.F.	*Neue Folge*
NT	New Testament, *Neues Testament*
O.S.	Old series
OT	Old Testament
rev.	revision, revised (by)
tr.	translated (by)
V.F.	*Vierte Folge*

Part One

THE DEVELOPMENT OF OLD
TESTAMENT STUDY

I. THE BACKGROUND—THROUGH THE EIGHTEENTH CENTURY

A. EARLY AND MEDIEVAL CRITICISM

The present survey of the growth and development of Old Testament study can well commence with the observation that, even before the Jews adopted an official formulation of their canon of sacred writings, the Christian Church had accepted the three traditional divisions of the Law, Prophecy, and Writings as constituting Scripture. Although many of the early Christians used the LXX version in preference to the Hebrew, they nevertheless maintained an unswerving stand that these writings possessed an authority of such degree as to be compatible only with divine inspiration and authorship.[1] As such the Scriptures demanded implicit belief and obedience on the part of all those who accepted and venerated them. The teachings of the various Old Testament books were regarded as basically identical in nature, the result of this conclusion being that the principal task concerning the understanding of this teaching was thought to be the presentation of Biblical doctrines in systematic form.

This situation did not last for any length of time, however, for even in the first century of the Christian era there were those who perverted the teachings of Scripture,[2] thereby calling into question the genuineness and authority of the sources. With the rise of Gnosticism in the second century of our era the Church witnessed the first onslaught of destructive criticism, and this, interestingly enough, was directed against the Old Testament. Epiphanius recorded that a certain Simon (whether or not the Simon Magus of Acts 8:10 is unknown) denied the divine source and inspiration of the Law and the Prophets.[3] In the *Clementine Homilies* Simon is cited as having criticized certain anthropomorphic passages in

[1] Cf. *Westminster Confession of Faith*, I:4. Article VI of the *Book of Common Prayer* (1662) was concerned primarily with the sufficiency of the Holy Scriptures for salvation, as was the fifth of the Forty-Two Articles of 1553. Cf. W. H. Griffith Thomas, *The Principles of Theology* (1930), pp. 104ff.

[2] I Tim. 1:19f., 2 Tim. 2:17f. Cf. *The Acts of Paul and Thecla*, XIV, in M. R. James, *The Apocryphal NT* (1924), p. 275.

[3] *PG*, XLI, Col. 292.

the Old Testament.[4] The Ophites, who were the precursors of the Gnostics, scorned the God of the Old Testament as wicked and ignorant,[5] while the Cainites held that their progenitor Cain had been sacrificed in order to appease the wrath of the Demiurge.[6] Among the Gnostics of Syria, the Antiochan Satornilus, who was contemporary with Ignatius (d. ca. A.D. 110), taught that certain of the prophecies were of Satanic origin, while others had come from the lips of angels who, according to Gnostic thought, had created the world.[7] Even Tatian, who is renowned for his compilation of extracts from the Gospels in the form of a single narrative (the *Diatessaron*, or *Harmony of the Gospels—ca.* A.D. 174), held that the Old Testament was the product of an inferior deity.[8]

From Alexandria, which had become a remarkable center of Greek culture and philosophy, the activities of Valentinus led an assault upon the text of the Old Testament. This prominent Gnostic leader, who subsequently propagated his doctrines in Rome, rejected certain parts of the Torah and the Prophets as unauthentic, and altered other portions of the Hebrew text with a view to improving it. To Valentinus was attributed the involved Gnostic theory of the aeon-origin of the universe, which he substituted for the creative activity of the Old Testament deity.[9] Another form of Pentateuchal criticism was furnished by a certain Ptolemy of Italian origin, who taught between A.D. 145 and 180. His arguments, preserved in a letter found among the writings of Epiphanius,[10] raised the basic question as to the origin of the Torah. Ptolemy concluded that the five books attributed to Moses could not possibly have come from one author, but that they were compiled by Moses from sources emanating from God, from Moses himself, and from the Elders.

More serious than the foregoing attacks upon the witness of the Early Church to the authority and authenticity of the Scriptures, however, were the speculations and teachings of the prominent second-century heretic Marcion, the son of a Christian bishop. Arriving in Rome about A.D. 138, he studied under a Gnostic teacher and ultimately developed a complicated intellectual system based upon the concepts of his philosophical dualism. He was the first of many subsequent critics of Biblical writings to apply canons of a subjective nature in the prosecution of his activities. He adopted a literalistic interpretation of the text, and arrived at the conclusion that God was weak, unjust, lacking in prescience, and

[4] *PG*, II, Col. 436.
[5] *PG*, VII, Cols. 675ff., XLI, Cols. 641ff.
[6] *PG*, XLI, Col. 656.
[7] *PG*, VII, Cols. 675ff.
[8] *PG*, VI, Col. 848, XLI, Cols. 831ff.
[9] *PG*, VII, Col. 523.
[10] *PG*, XLI, Cols. 557ff.

essentially fickle.[11] Consequently he ejected the Old Testament completely from his canon of Scripture, which in the end consisted mainly of Pauline material along with an expurgated edition of the Gospel of Luke.[12] His criticisms of the Old Testament cannot be regarded as scientific in any sense of that term, since they were dictated by purely subjective philosophical considerations, but they are of importance in any study of the growth of Biblical criticism generally.

The Nazarites, a Jewish-Christian sect, also denied the Mosaic authorship of the Pentateuch,[13] and according to Epiphanius[14] the Ebionites rejected certain parts of the Torah and in addition manifested a complete disregard for the writings of the prophets. The *Clementine Homilies*,[15] which, though later than the second century in their extant form, were actually the product of the Judaic-Gnostic school, applied subjective and rationalistic principles in their attempts to cast doubt upon the authenticity of certain events mentioned in the Old Testament. Passages which presented obvious difficulties were alleged to have been interpolated by the Devil, and only those parts of Scripture were accepted as genuine which were thought to be in accord with the tenets of this school relating to the creation of the world and men.

The first definite and reasoned attack upon Christianity's claim to be an exclusive and universal religion came from Celsus, a man about whom very little is known. His treatise, *The True Word*, was written about A.D. 180, and it is due largely to the labors of Origen, who refuted the work systematically in his great apologetic document *Contra Celsum*,[16] written about A.D. 249, that scholars have been able to reconstruct his arguments to any significant extent. Although Celsus did not reject the Mosaic authorship of the Pentateuch, he showed only a slight acquaintance with Old Testament history and religion in general. Consequently he disparaged the Jews and ridiculed a great many of their institutions. His entire approach was derogatory, and to him belongs the dubious distinction of assembling most of the arguments which have been levelled against Christianity and the Bible by subsequent generations of rationalists, atheists, and agnostics. In the third century after Christ the mystical philosophy known as Neoplatonism arose to challenge the Christian faith. Porphyry, one of its chief exponents, published an attack on historic Christianity entitled *Against the Christians*, a treatise even

11 *PL*, II, Cols. 263ff.

12 For the Marcionite Prologues to the Pauline epistles see D. de Bruyne, *Revue Benedictine*, XXIV (1907), pp. 1ff.; P. Corssen, *Zeitschrift für die neutestamentliche Wissenschaft*, X (1909), pp. 37ff.

13 *PG*, XLI, Col. 257, XCIV, Cols. 688f.

14 *PG*, XLI, Col. 436.

15 Cf. A. Neander, *Die pseudoclementinischen Homilien* (1818); the 1953 edition of the *Homilies* by A. R. M. Dressel was reproduced in *PG*, II.

16 Cf. *PG*, XI, Cols. 315ff.; H. Chadwick, *Origen: Contra Celsum* (1953), pp. 3ff.

more damaging in its effects than that of Celsus. Porphyry was the first to argue that Daniel was not the work of the prophet to whom tradition had attributed it but was in fact composed in the time of Antiochus IV Epiphanes (175-163 B.C.). He based his conclusions on the premise that Daniel could not have predicted the future in such minute detail, and that therefore the later chapters of the book must have been roughly contemporary with the events described. It is not easy to determine whether Porphyry denied the Mosaic authorship of the Pentateuch or not,[17] but at all events he appeared to accept the historical existence of Moses.

Criticism of the Biblical text of Daniel is also found in the third-century writings of Julius Africanus (*ca.* A.D. 225), who in his *Epistola ad Originem* argued that Susanna could not have formed part of the Hebrew-Aramaic composition attributed to Daniel, since it was originally written in Greek.[18] Certain statements of Jerome (d. A.D. 420) have sometimes been interpreted as implying that Ezra re-edited the Pentateuch,[19] but there seems little doubt that he accepted the orthodox attribution of the Pentateuch to Moses,[20] although he does record that Deuteronomy had been found in the Temple during the reign of Josiah.[21]

A rudimentary form of literary criticism was applied by Theodore of Mopsuestia (*ca.* A.D. 400) to certain books of the Old Testament. He was the first to assign the authorship of certain of the Psalms to the Jews of the Maccabean period. He also rejected the titles of the Psalms, and maintained that they were added during the days of Hezekiah and Zerubbabel. He criticized the book of Job by alleging that the author was not of Hebrew stock,[22] and refused to espouse an allegorical view of the Song of Songs, holding that it was meant to be interpreted literally as an erotic composition.[23]

Questions concerning the text and canon of the Scriptures that had arisen sporadically in the Early Church were dealt with by Cassiodorus (d. A.D. 562) in a work entitled *De Institutione Divinarum Scripturarum*. Although the book was intended to be a compendium of theology, it included several sections on the copying of manuscripts and the general methods to be adopted in a study of the text, as well as a survey of matters relating more particularly to the canon. As such the work constituted a valuable contribution to the beginnings of Biblical

[17] Cf. R. M. Grant, *The Journal of Religion*, XXV (1945), pp. 183ff.
[18] *PG*, XI, Cols. 11f.
[19] Cf. *PL*, XXIII, Col. 199.
[20] *PL*, XXIII, Col. 226.
[21] *PL*, XXV, Col. 17; cf. XXIII, Col. 227.
[22] *PG*, LXVI, Col. 698.
[23] *PG*, LXVI, Col. 699.

criticism as applied specifically to the text of the Hebrew Bible, a discipline which in a later age came to be known as "lower criticism."

Individual authors in subsequent centuries raised certain problems presented by the Old Testament narratives. In the process they contrived to challenge to a greater or lesser degree the traditions of orthodox Christianity about questions of authorship and date of particular books. A number of the difficulties raised in connection with the Pentateuch by some who had already abandoned the Christian faith were collected by Anastasius, a patriarch of Antioch, towards the end of the seventh century in his *Guide*.[24] A similar though more polemical approach was adopted by the ninth-century Jewish rationalist Hiwi al Balkhi, who listed numerous alleged contradictions in the Old Testament.[25]

The tenth and eleventh centuries witnessed a number of critical attacks in Spain upon various parts of the Hebrew Scriptures, one of which was made by Ibn Hazam of Córdova about A.D. 994. He discovered what he considered serious errors in the chronology of the Old Testament, and claimed that much of the Pentateuch was actually the work of Ezra.[26] The motivation for his attack upon the integrity of the Hebrew Scriptures was not impartial, however, for he was concerned to defend the claims of Islam, which for him constituted the true faith. A decade later another writer, Ibn Yashush (*ca.* 1000), maintained that there were a number of post-Mosaic sections in the Pentateuch, but his arguments generally exhibit a good deal of confusion. His opinions were denounced by the celebrated Spanish exegete Ibn Ezra (1092-1167), who himself maintained the existence of several late insertions in the Pentateuch while at the same time regarding these to be compatible with Mosaic authorship. Ibn Ezra was one of the first Biblical scholars to suggest that the last twenty-six chapters of the book of Isaiah might be considerably later than the eighth century B.C., and written by someone other than Isaiah ben Amoz. In the twelfth century the book of Daniel was subjected to further criticism by Hugo of St. Victor, who gave impetus to the view that the latter chapters of that prophecy could only be interpreted in the light of events that transpired within the Maccabean period.[27]

B. The Reformation

While the foregoing inquiries represented the beginnings of a movement towards a more critical examination of the Old Testament writings, they were by no means systematized in nature. Their concern was with a comparatively small number of books in the canon. Nor can it be said

[24] *PG*, LXXXIX, Cols. 284f.
[25] J. Rosenthal, *JQR*, XXXVIII (1947-48), pp. 317ff., 419ff., XXXIX (1948-49), pp. 79ff.
[26] Cf. A. Guillaume, *Prophecy and Divination* (1938), pp. 415ff.
[27] *PL*, CLXXV, Cols. 9ff.

that the Reformation introduced Biblical criticism as such, even though individual Reformers sometimes adopted a standpoint towards certain books in the canon which was not in complete harmony with earlier ecclesiastical traditions. For the most part Martin Luther (1483-1546) confined his critical observations to books in the New Testament canon. Using a primarily theological criterion, Luther excluded four compositions generally considered canonical (Hebrews, James, Jude, and Revelation). According to Luther's standards, writings purporting to be Scriptural stood or fell according to the extent to which they promoted Christ.[28] For obvious reasons this standard could not be applied directly to the Old Testament without some difficulty, and it was largely because of this that Luther never undertook a revision of the Old Testament canon, although he consistently emphasized that the Old Testament itself claimed its fullest meaning in proportion to the extent to which it pointed to the gospel of Christ.[29]

While Calvin (1509-1564) did not go quite as far as Luther in expurgating the New Testament canon, he displayed considerably more interest than the latter in the composition of certain Old Testament books. His studies led him to the conclusion that Joshua and Samuel were not the authors of the books attributed to them, though he was unable to arrive at any firm conclusions as to the actual authors of these writings. Of all the Old Testament books that he expounded in his *Commentaries*, the Song of Songs was the only one he neglected almost completely. He adhered to a high view of the inspiration of Scripture,[30] maintaining the essential spiritual unity of the Old and New Testaments.[31]

An attack upon the Mosaic authorship of the Pentateuch was made by Andreas Rudolf Bodenstein (1480-1541), a contemporary and rival of Martin Luther.[32] Arguing from the fact that Moses could not possibly have written the account of his own death, he proceeded to reject the Mosaic authorship of the entire Pentateuch, since it seemed to him to be composed in the same general style as the obituary passage.

Zwingli (1484-1531) agreed with Calvin in asserting the divine origin of Scripture.[33] But, as an adherent of a rather more radical philosophical rationalism than either Luther or Calvin—an attitude which brought him into conflict with the former—he concentrated upon the practical application of the ethic of Jesus to the social and theological problems of the day, and did not apply his range of talents to a minute exegetical survey of Scripture as Luther and Calvin did. The importance of the Reforma-

---

[28] Luther affirmed that Christ was the *punctus mathematicus sacrae Scripturae*, *Werke* (Weimar ed., 1892), II, p. 439.

[29] *Ibid.*, V, pp. 47ff.

[30] Cf. *Institutes of the Christian Religion*, I, 7, 5.

[31] *Ibid.*, II, 11, 1.

[32] Cf. C. F. Jaeger, *Andreas Bodenstein von Karlstadt* (1856).

[33] *Werke* (ed. M. Schuler and J. Schulthess, 1828-42), III, pp. 156ff.

tion for Biblical criticism lay not so much in a concern for the historical or literary processes involved in the formulation of the Biblical canon as in a continued insistence upon the primacy of the simple grammatical meaning of the text in its own right, independent of any interpretation by ecclesiastical authority.

C. THE SIXTEENTH AND SEVENTEENTH CENTURIES

A more developed critical approach to the Old Testament appeared in the writings of several men who were not professional theologians. One of these was a Roman Catholic lawyer named Andreas Masius (d. 1573), who in a commentary on Joshua supported the earlier view that Ezra and his associates had added certain sections to the Pentateuch, although he did not deny the essential Mosaic authorship of the composition as a whole.[34] Another celebrated lawyer, Hugo Grotius (1583-1645), wrote a series of *Annotationes* on the books of the Bible, of which the sections dealing with the Old Testament were published only a year before he died. Like some earlier critics he dealt principally with the rather more peripheral works in the Old Testament canon, such as Canticles and Ecclesiastes, and adopted a fairly independent standpoint on some of the books he considered. He accepted the Solomonic authorship of the Song of Songs, although he apparently did not subscribe to the allegorical interpretation which saw in it an expression of the relationship between Christ and His Church. He regarded Ecclesiastes as a collection of human opinions on the subject of happiness by someone other than Solomon, backing up his view of a post-Solomonic period of origin by an appeal to the vocabulary of Aramaic portions of the Old Testament, which, he claimed, had the greatest affinity with the text of the Song of Songs. Grotius also assigned the book of Job to a date not earlier than the exile, and in addition he expressed doubts as to the historicity of Esther. His commentaries were of importance in that they espoused the principles adopted by the Reformers in their endeavor to interpret Scripture solely by the application of grammatical rules independently of *a priori* dogmatic assumptions.[35]

A further attempt in the sixteenth century to investigate the questions involving the authorship and date of Old Testament writings was made by the Deistic philosopher Thomas Hobbes (1588-1679). While his examination of Scripture constituted the basis of his search for a source of ultimate authority for the State, the principles which he utilized represented an advance on the approach which had been adopted by Grotius. Using internal evidence as a criterion for determining questions of authorship and date, he concluded that Moses long antedated the Pentateuch in its written form, although he did not deny the Mosaic

---

[34] *Josuae Imperatoris Historia* (1574).
[35] Cf. his remarks on the authority of the Old Testament writings, *De Veritatione Religionis Christianae* (1627), III, sect. 16.

authorship of those sections which were specifically attributed to him.[36] In the main, however, he did not regard the titles of books as a reliable indication of authorship, holding that Joshua and Judges were compiled long after the events which they described. The books of Samuel, Kings, and Chronicles were to him as obviously post-exilic as the writings of Ezra and Nehemiah.

Hobbes, like some of his successors in the field, professed a complete inability to assign a date to the book of Job, and regarded it less as history than as a "Treatise concerning a question in ancient time much disputed, *why wicked men have often prospered in this world, and good men have been afflicted.*" Proverbs, Ecclesiastes, and the Song of Songs were regarded as Solomonic, with the exception of the inscriptions of the latter two. Concerning the book of Jonah, Hobbes remarked:

> ...the Book of Jonas is not properly a Register of his Prophecy...but a History or Narration of his frowardnesse and disputing God's commandments, so that there is small probability he should be the Author, seeing he is the subject of it.

The Jewish philosopher Benedict Spinoza (1632-1677) continued the tendencies of Hobbes, whose work he doubtless knew and utilized, in his *Tractatus Theologico-Politicus*, published anonymously in 1670. Starting from the premise that no speculative or scientific investigation ought to be regarded as putting religion in jeopardy, Spinoza applied such procedural canons as to make his treatise the first significant contribution to the modern discipline of Biblical criticism. His rules for the interpretation of Scripture involved a consideration of the life, character, and aims of each author of the various books as a means of determining the purpose, occasion, and date of writing.[37] Following Ibn Ezra to some extent, Spinoza rejected the Mosaic authorship of the Pentateuch, and appeared to think that all the books from Genesis through 2 Kings were the work of Ezra.[38] He agreed with Ibn Ezra that Job was probably the product of a Gentile author who wrote in a language other than Hebrew, and he assigned dates in the Maccabean period to Daniel, Ezra, Nehemiah, Esther, and Chronicles.

The critical tendencies evident in the writings of Hobbes and Spinoza also appear in the work of a professional theologian named Richard Simon (1638-1712), a Roman Catholic priest who for a number of years was professor of philosophy at Juilly. Lacking the restraints of the Protestant Reformers, whose dictum "*Scriptura sola*" precluded their criticism of such a pre-eminent authority, Simon approached the problem of Biblical criticism from the Romanist standpoint, which maintained that Scripture was merely one source of authority, along with tradition, papal

---

[36] *Leviathan,* III, ch. 33.
[37] *Tractatus Theologico-Politicus,* ch. VII.
[38] *Ibid.,* ch. VIII and following.

pronouncements, and conciliar decrees. Unfortunately this uninhibited approach was not matched by an equal degree of responsibility, for in his *Histoire critique du Vieux Testament* (1678), Simon allowed himself to make some very injudicious statements, including one to the effect that the Christian faith could have sustained itself by tradition alone, without any Scriptural corpus in evidence. Simon abandoned the kind of textual criticism which had been adopted by earlier medieval writers as a methodological procedure, and resorted to the use of literary criticism proper. On the basis of his studies he concluded that the Pentateuch in its extant form could not possibly be the work of Moses, and he declared that the historical books were the result of a long process of compilation and redaction of annals and chronicles by a guild of "public scribes."

Not only did Simon provoke the antagonism of Protestant writers by his sharp attacks upon their principles, but he also aroused vigorous opposition among Roman Catholics, and within a few months after publication his book was ordered to be destroyed. Of those who replied to Simon, the Arminian professor Le Clerc was the most prominent because of his protests that the views of Protestant writers had been accorded unfair treatment. While Le Clerc challenged the theories of Simon regarding the composition of the historical books, his own views, expressed in his *Sentiments de quelques Théologiens de hollande sur l'Histoire Critique du Vieux Testament par R. Simon* (1685), tended to date both the Pentateuch and the historical books of the Old Testament even later than the period assigned to them by Simon himself.

During the seventeenth century a number of introductions to the Bible were written. One of these, published in 1636 by Michael Walther, and entitled *Officina Biblica Noviter Adaperta*, was notable for the manner in which it distinguished between the problems of a general introduction to the Bible and the special consideration that the individual books themselves required. This work was followed by several others that dealt with the canon and text of the Old Testament, including an important treatise by John Leusden entitled *Philologus Hebraeus*, published in 1657, and the celebrated Polyglot Bible of 1657, edited by Bishop Walton of Chester.

D. Source Criticism and Eighteenth-Century Enlightenment

In 1689, an orthodox theologian named Campegius Vitringa suggested in his *Observationes Sacrae* that Moses had had access to ancient sources from the patriarchal period, and that these, along with other information, formed the basis of the Pentateuch. This early attempt at source-criticism was subsequently developed by Jean Astruc (1684-1766), who studied medicine and ultimately taught as a professor in several French universities. Some thirteen years before his death he published anonymously a treatise on the book of Genesis, an event that marked the beginnings of Pentateuchal source-criticism proper.[39] He argued that the material upon which Moses drew had been transmitted over several centuries either orally or in written form, and was of the opinion that the latter type was predominant. Thus Moses compiled Genesis by dividing up these ancient memoirs and reassembling them so as to furnish a continuous narrative.

To substantiate his conclusions Astruc pointed out that Genesis contained duplicate narratives of such events as creation and the Flood, and that God was referred to by the names *Elohim* and *Jehovah*[40] both in Genesis and also in the early chapters of Exodus. By adopting the divine names as a criterion for source-analysis, Astruc was following in the tradition of Witter, who had been the first to suggest that they could be employed for that purpose.[41] Finally he concluded that the compiler had confused the chronological picture of Genesis so that certain events were narrated out of their proper order.

Astruc then went on to claim that this confusion could be resolved by a simple analysis and reconstruction of the Hebrew text, and as a preliminary step towards this goal he isolated all the passages in which God was designated as *Elohim* and placed them in one column (A) of his reorganized text. This he regarded as the original documentary source for the material which it contained, and despite the purely subjective nature of this conclusion he proceeded on this basis to reduce all those passages which spoke of God as *Jehovah* to the content of another underlying document, which he placed in a parallel column (B). Between these he inserted column C, comprising repetitions, chapters 23 and 24 of Genesis, and perhaps chapter 34, and column D, comprising non-Israelite material from various sources, which he divided into nine subsections,[42] some of which he regarded as interpolations.

This kind of analysis seemed to him to answer all the problems posed by the state of the text, and as a result of his researches Astruc felt confident that Moses had actually compiled Genesis on the basis of these four columns, which later copyists had edited and rearranged. He did not merely affirm the substantial Mosaic authorship of the Pentateuch, but he actually went to considerable lengths to defend it.[43] However, the thesis had some disadvantages, for as Young has pointed out,[44] Astruc

[39] *Conjectures sur les mémoires originaux dont il paraît que Moyse s'est servi pour composer le Livre de la Genèse. Avec des Remarques qui appuient ou qui éclaircissent ces Conjectures* (1753).

[40] The latter is a genuine hybrid form of the tetragrammaton יהוה, and not a "mistaken medieval form," as K. Grobel (*IDB*, I, p. 410) has suggested.

[41] H. B. Witter, *Jura Israelitarum in Palaestina* (1711).

[42] E, Gen. 14; F, Gen. 19:29ff.; G, Gen. 22:20-24; H, Gen. 25:12-29; I, Gen. 34; J, Gen. 26:34ff.; K, Gen. 28:6-10; L, Gen. 36:20-31; M, Gen. 39.

[43] Cf. A. Lods, *RHPR*, IV (1924), pp. 109ff., 201ff.

[44] *YIOT*, pp. 118ff.

realized that the divine names were inadequate criteria for a satisfactory analysis of Genesis into its underlying sources, and that they needed to be supplemented by other elements if the process was to be carried out to a proper conclusion. The question could not be settled merely by adducing the presence of subsidiary documents in the extant corpus, for it was found necessary to invoke the existence of textual interpolations so as to reinforce the testimony of the other criteria. This facile, though somewhat arbitrary, analysis of the text into alleged underlying documents misled Astruc and subsequent critics into thinking that the delineation of such material was a comparatively easy task, a notion which later events were to dispel.

The critical methods of Simon were revived some seventy years after the *Histoire Critique* was written, when J. S. Semler (1725-1791), a Protestant professor at Halle, translated the work into German. A moderate Rationalist, Semler adopted the critical procedures outlined by Simon but contrived to produce results which proved to be largely negative in character. Somewhat of a reaction to Semler's methodology appeared in the writings of the poet J. G. von Herder (1744-1803), who in 1783 published his celebrated work on Hebrew poetry entitled *Vom Geist der hebräischen Poesie*. Herder was attracted to the monism of Spinoza insofar as it presented God as an object of satisfaction alike for the feelings and the intellect, and he endeavored to convey this sentiment as he discerned that it was expressed spiritually in the literary structure of Hebrew verse. Despite his attempts to stress the aesthetic and moral elements inherent in Old Testament poetry, however, Herder's theological conclusions were largely speculative in nature, although his critical tendencies were of a unifying and constructive, rather than of an analytical, order. He was one of the first Old Testament scholars to base his observations concerning Scripture upon an acquaintance with the larger background of ancient Near Eastern culture. Further interest in Hebrew poetry was made evident during this same period by the work of Bishop Robert Lowth, who made a pioneer study of the parallelisms and other features of Hebrew poetic structure, and published his findings in a work entitled *De Sacra Poesi Hebraeorum* (1753).

The Age of Enlightenment was characterized by the enthroning of human reason, accompanied by a revolt against external authority. One offshoot of this situation was the claim that the Old Testament ought to be subject to the same principles of careful scrutiny as those applied to secular writings generally. Even more important than this was the feeling that such an investigation should be able to be pursued independently of ecclesiastical authority, religious dogmas, or church traditions of any sort. This attitude crystallized largely as the result of the work of J. G. Eichhorn (1752-1827), a rather conservative Rationalist who had fallen somewhat under the influence of Herder. In the end his activities proved to be directed principally against the rationalists and humanists of his own day, and he set himself to the task of winning back the educated classes to religion.

Eichhorn commenced the long series of modern introductions to the Old Testament writings with his three-volume *Einleitung in das Alte Testament* (1780-1783), a work which earned him the title of "father of Old Testament criticism."[45] Although Eichhorn professed to be affected profoundly by the literary grandeur of the Hebrew Scriptures, he reacted against the position of the Reformers and orthodox theology generally regarding the inspiration and authority of Scripture in his conclusion that the Old Testament displayed more of the character of Hebrew national literature than what might be expected to constitute Holy Scripture as such. Eichhorn extended the criteria postulated by Astruc for documentary analysis of the Pentateuch by suggesting that the means for differentiating between the underlying sources should include diversities of literary style and consideration of words or phrases peculiar to one or the other of the documents previously isolated. However, apart from this his opinions largely corresponded with those traditionally held concerning the nature and content of the Old Testament.

In 1792 a Scottish Roman Catholic theologian named Geddes published a translation of the Pentateuch and the book of Joshua; he followed this in 1800 with a work entitled *Critical Remarks*. In these two compositions Geddes assigned the Pentateuch to the Solomonic period and assumed that it had been compiled by a single redactor or editor from a mass of fragments, some of which antedated Moses. He accepted Astruc's contention that the incidence of the divine names could be employed as a criterion for purposes of discerning two series of fragmentary sources, but rejected the actual delineation of Elohistic and Jehovistic documents which Astruc and Eichhorn had recognized. He anticipated later critical writers by claiming that the book of Joshua belonged properly with the Pentateuch to compose a Hexateuch, and maintained that the same redactor was responsible for the compilation and editing of these six books. Official conservative Romanism was naturally distressed by these rationalistic observations, and Geddes was subjected to stern rebukes by the ecclesiastical authorities.

The fragmentary hypothesis which Geddes had postulated was developed by J. S. Vater, who in his *Commentar über den Pentateuch*, published in 1805, postulated the existence of as many as forty separate fragmentary sources underlying the Pentateuchal writings. He thought that some of these may have antedated Moses, while others obviously belonged to his general era. However, Vater assigned the Pentateuch

---

[45] Cf. T. K. Cheyne, *Founders of OT Criticism* (1893), pp. 13ff., 21ff.

in its final form to the period of the exile. His analysis embraced the entire Pentateuch, unlike those of his predecessors who had for the most part restricted themselves to Genesis.

The rationalistic tendencies of Geddes found another adherent in the person of W. M. L. De Wette, who supported to some extent the fragmentary theory of Pentateuchal origins in his *Beiträge zur Einleitung in das Alte Testament*, published in 1807. He parted company with previous critics in affirming that the earliest portions of the Pentateuch could only be dated from the period of David, and maintained that the different books were compiled by separate redactors who drew upon independent fragmentary sources. De Wette was the first to identify the original legal nucleus of Deuteronomy with the Book of the Law discovered during the reign of King Josiah,[46] an opinion that was to exercise a good deal of influence in subsequent discussions of that subject. De Wette felt that the literary phenomena of Genesis could be explained more readily by recourse to the documentary theory espoused by Astruc and Eichhorn than to its fragmentary counterpart as maintained by Geddes. Accordingly he postulated the existence of an Elohistic type of document as source material for Genesis and the first six chapters of Exodus. Reflecting some of the opinions of Herder, he maintained that much of Genesis was in the nature of epic poetry, a view which was not wholly lacking in support at a later period.[47]

Vater and De Wette were vigorously opposed by a number of scholars who felt convinced of the essential Mosaic authorship of the Pentateuch.[48] What is probably the most devastating attack upon the fragment theory was made by H. Ewald, who in his commentary on Genesis presented strong arguments for the underlying unity of the book on philological and other grounds.[49] While he did not adhere to the traditional view that Moses was the author of Genesis, he assigned the composition of the book to a comparatively early period. Ewald was undoubtedly more constructive in his approach to the literary problems of the Pentateuch than many of his predecessors, and in line with this tendency he proposed a supplementary theory which in nature reflected to some extent the views of De Wette on the composition of Genesis. Ewald maintained that an Elohistic source underlay the composition of the Pentateuch and Joshua, and that it had been supplemented by the addition of older sections such as the Decalogue. At a later time a

[46] In his doctoral thesis, *Dissertatio qua Deuteronomium a prioribus Pentateuchi libris diversum alius cuiusdam recentioris auctoris opus esse demonstratur* (1805), subsequently reprinted in his *Opuscula* (1833).

[47] Cf. O. Pfleiderer, *The Development of Theology in Germany since Kant* (1890), pp. 97ff.

[48] Cf. *YIOT*, pp. 123f.

[49] H. Ewald, *Die Komposition der Genesis kritisch untersucht* (1823).

compilation of sources of a Jehovistic character arose, from which portions were placed in the basic Elohistic document.

Whereas the majority of scholars had maintained that the "Foundation Document" or *Grundschrift* was early, Wilhelm Vatke in his book entitled *Die biblische Theologie wissenschaftlich dargestellt* (1835) followed the trend set by De Wette and roundly declared that a great many sections of the *Grundschrift* could be dated as late as the exile, so that in fact the source was of late rather than of early origin. He anticipated later writers by stating that the Torah was the product of the Hebrew state rather than the basis upon which it was founded, and he went so far as to reconstruct the history of the Israelites on what amounted to an evolutionary pattern.[50]

The supplementary theory postulated by Ewald received some backing from De Wette, who from 1840 adhered to the view that the Elohistic document had been augmented by means of extracts from the Jehovistic document, which, with the Deuteronomic source, made for a threefold redaction of the Hexateuch. In 1843 J. J. Stähelin suggested in his *Kritische Untersuchungen über den Pentateuch* that the early monarchy saw the redaction of the Hexateuch, and that Samuel may have been the responsible agent. He affirmed that the Elohistic source was the most comprehensive of its kind in the Pentateuch, including as it did the bulk of Exodus, Leviticus, and Numbers, and maintained that because of its archaic form it was certainly the earliest of the Pentateuchal sources.

The final form of the supplement theory found expression in the work of J. C. F. Tuch, who in his *Kommentar über die Genesis* (1838), maintained that the Pentateuch was undergirded by two documentary sources which could be distinguished quite readily by their use of the two divine names. The Elohistic document was the basic Pentateuchal source, and was dignified by the name of *Grundschrift*. This was augmented by extracts from the Jehovistic material, which Tuch dated in the Solomonic era. Even this formulation, which seemed to many contemporary scholars to meet the situation quite adequately, came under heavy criticism. J. H. Kurtz in his *Die Einheit der Genesis,* which was published in 1846, raised the question as to why the Elohistic passages, which according to the theory had been written considerably prior to the time when the Jehovistic *Ergänzer* or "supplementer" commenced his scribal activities, presupposed or in other ways referred to the contents of the Jehovistic portions. Although Kurtz subsequently abandoned his position, an answer to this enigmatic situation was never forthcoming from other supporters of the supplement hypothesis.

A further blow at Tuch's view was struck by Ewald, who modified his earlier position to the point of asserting in his *Geschichte des Volkes*

Israel (1843) that there were certain sections of the Pentateuch which did not belong either to the Elohistic, Jehovistic, or Deuteronomic documents. He claimed that these additional sources included a *Book of Covenants*, dating perhaps from the Judges period, a *Book of Origins*, compiled during the Solomonic era, and the work of three narrators, all of whom were prominent in the compilation of the Hexateuch about 500 B.C.

This "crystallization hypothesis," as it is sometimes called, was modified by Hermann Hupfeld, who in his investigation of the sources of Genesis[51] argued that the *Grundschrift* regarded by earlier critics as a unity was in fact the product of two writers, both of whom had employed *Elohim* as the name of God. He further maintained that the second scribe was closer in linguistic peculiarities and style to the Jehovistic author than to the first Elohistic scribe (*die Urschrift*), who distinctly manifested priestly tendencies. There were now four principal sources to be borne in mind in all considerations relating to the compilation of the Pentateuch or Hexateuch: these consisted of a Jehovistic (J) document, an Elohistic (E) compilation, a Priestly (P) source (formerly considered to be part of the "Foundation Document"), and the book of Deuteronomy (D). This theory was formulated as a means of dispensing with the problems raised by the supplement hypothesis, and its appeal depended to a considerable extent upon the successful functioning of a redactor or editor who had been responsible for reducing the four originally separate sources to their present combined form, a process in which a good deal of imagination was required on his part. The anonymous redactor proved to be a very useful ground of appeal when textual obscurities, chronological and topographical difficulties, or other problematical issues of a like nature threatened to make havoc of the theory. In point of fact, many later scholars followed Hupfeld in allotting to the redactor or his colleagues a good deal of responsibility for what they regarded as errors, conflations, confusions, and the like.

While the various theories relating to the origin and composition of the Hexateuch were being promulgated with some degree of consistency, they were being attacked continually by more orthodox scholars on a variety of grounds. One of the most important opponents of the various documentary hypotheses was E. W. Hengstenberg (1802-1869), a brilliant classical student who subsequently specialized in Old Testament studies at Berlin.[52] He quickly acquired a reputation in scholarly circles for disliking every form of rationalism, and throughout his lifetime he was a consistent challenger of Biblical liberalism. His enormous literary output,

---

[51] *Die Quellen der Genesis und die Art ihrer Zusammensetzung von neuen untersucht* (1853).

[52] Cf. F. Lichtenberger, *A History of German Theology in the Nineteenth Century* (1889), pp. 212ff.

some of which was translated into English, included his *Beiträge zur Einleitung in das Alte Testament* (1831-1839), *Die Bücher Mosis und Ägypten* (1841), and *Commentar über die Psalmen* (1842-1847). Others who followed the general tradition of Hengstenberg included M. Drechsler, H. Ch. Havernick, and C. F. Keil. The last collaborated with F. Delitzsch to produce a series of conservative commentaries on the various Old Testament books.

II. THE GRAF-WELLHAUSEN HYPOTHESIS

A. GRAF AND WELLHAUSEN

The decade following the division of the "Foundation Document" by Hupfeld saw a significant return to the position of Vatke, as a result of the work of K. H. Graf.[1] Like Vatke Graf tried to show that the *Grundschrift* was one of the latest rather than the earliest of the proposed documentary sources of the Pentateuch.[2] This view was based substantially upon the opinions of his teacher, Eduard Reuss, who in the summer of 1834 had suggested to his students at the University of Strasbourg that the Elohistic source was not the earliest but the latest of the documents which were thought to underlie the Pentateuch. Graf took up this theory, and maintained that the priestly interests of the "Foundation Document" indicated a date of composition subsequent to the contents of the book of Deuteronomy. As a result he assigned the document to the post-exilic period and associated it with the promulgation of the Law in the time of Ezra. However, he held that Leviticus 18–26, the so-called "Holiness Code," belonged properly to the period of Ezekiel.

With regard to the rest of the Pentateuch Graf adhered to the supplement theory, asserting that the Jehovistic additions were subject to redaction by the editor of Deuteronomy. The criteria upon which Graf based his late dating of the Priestly document were purely subjective in nature, and although his conclusions were challenged on this and other grounds he still clung to his contention that the basic Pentateuchal document was late rather than early. One result of this scholarly activity was to introduce a further branch of criticism to the study of the Old Testament. By attempting to assign dates to the proposed documents, the various writers transcended the bounds of literary criticism as such and moved into the area of historical criticism.

---

[1] It has been thought possible by some that the objections raised to Vatke's late date for the "Foundation Document" and his subsequent reconstruction of Israelite history were in fact a reaction against the obvious Hegelian tendencies of Graf.

[2] Graf, *Die geschichtlichen Bücher des AT: Zwei historisch-kritische Untersuchungen* (1865).

Basic to this approach was a comparison of the date furnished by the literary sources themselves with the events of history as recorded by the Old Testament historical and prophetic writings in an attempt to determine the authenticity and age of the material under study. Unfortunately this useful branch of criticism was dominated almost from the very beginning by the wholly fallacious assumption that, because the more significant regulations were either ignored entirely or at best rather neglected for prolonged periods in the early history of the Israelite nation, they could not possibly have been promulgated in the time of Moses or even in the early monarchy. Such a standpoint was adopted by De Wette,[3] Vatke, and later writers. The fallacy of this position has only been exposed within comparatively recent years with the realization that the peoples of the ancient Near East habitually lived for long periods according to inherited customs and traditions, many of which were frequently quite independent of legal promulgations.[4]

During the general period in which Graf was writing, a further contribution to the study of the problem was made by John William Colenso (1814-1883), who when Bishop of Natal undertook a critical examination of the Hexateuch in a series of seven treatises published between 1862 and 1879 under the general title, *The Pentateuch and the Book of Joshua Critically Examined*. Like Graf he concluded that the principal documentary source claimed by earlier scholars was late in nature, and that it contained purported historical material that was in actual fact anything but historical. He held that the minute ecclesiastical organization depicted in Leviticus and Numbers could only be the work of writers who belonged to a much later age than the Mosaic period, and in accordance with this general tendency he assigned Deuteronomy to a time subsequent to the settlement of the Hebrew tribes in Canaan. He inferred that the Book of the Law discovered during the reign of Josiah was Deuteronomy itself, and concluded that Chronicles had been compiled with the deliberate intention of exalting the priests and Levites.

Colenso's views stirred up a storm of controversy, and for this achievement as well as for other reasons he was deposed from his See and prohibited from preaching in England. However, his opinions had attracted the attention of the Dutch scholar Abraham Kuenen, who came to the conclusion that the prophetic material of Genesis, Exodus, and Numbers was considerably older than the *Grundschrift*. In *De Godsdienst van Israël*, published in 1870, Kuenen lent strength to the theories of Graf in suggesting that the Jehovistic source was basic to the Pentateuch and that it had been supplemented by extracts from an Elohistic document, by the addition of Deuteronomy, which was dated in the period of Josiah, by the legislative material emerging from the exilic era,

---

[3] Developed in his *Beiträge zur Einleitung in das AT* (1806-1807).
[4] Cf. *IOTT*, pp. 238ff.

including the "Law of Holiness," and by the incorporation of the Priestly document, which was assigned to the time of Ezra. Thus the former order of composition in terms of a P E J D arrangement was replaced by a projected J E D P scheme of compilation.

This basic theory was given its classic expression in the work of Julius Wellhausen (1844-1918), who studied theology under Ewald at the University of Göttingen. A man of wide spiritual vision, Wellhausen possessed a brilliant and penetrating mind, the quality of which is perhaps seen most clearly in his work on the text of the books of Samuel,[5] a study that surpassed all others on the subject until the discovery of the Qumran scrolls. Wellhausen followed Vatke in adopting the evolutionary concepts characteristic of the philosophy of Hegel, and was also influenced to some extent by the views of Herder on the Old Testament.[6] He lived in an age when the intellectual climate was dominated by theories of evolution, and, as Hahn has remarked,[7] he occupied a position in the field of Old Testament criticism analogous to that of Darwin in the area of biological science.

Wellhausen at once acknowledged his indebtedness to Graf.[8] By applying the developmental approach of Vatke, a thoroughgoing Hegelian, to the study of Hebrew religious institutions and combining it with the successive arrangement of ritual laws made by Graf, Wellhausen attempted to prove that the connection between the succession of the legal codes and the progressive development of religious practices among the Israelites could only be compatible with a late date for the Priestly document. Wellhausen apparently did not subject the theories of Graf to searching criticism, but developed them to what he deemed to be their logical conclusion. In consequence he regarded the Pentateuch as essentially of composite origin, consisting of a Jehovistic source (J), dated in the ninth century B.C.; an independent Elohistic document (E), coming from the eighth century B.C.; the basic content of the book of Deuteronomy (D), which was assigned to the time of King Josiah (640/39-609 B.C.); and a Priestly source (P), from about the fifth century B.C. According to the process outlined in his book entitled *Die Komposition des Hexateuchs*, published in 1877, the Jehovistic author compiled a narrative document from the sources J and E, and this was supplemented by the addition of Deuteronomy in the time of Josiah. Leviticus 17-26 was added to the Priestly document somewhat after the time of Ezekiel, while the remainder of the priestly material in the Elohistic source was compiled by Ezra. At a subsequent period the

---

[5] *Der Text der Bücher Samuelis untersucht* (1871).

[6] Cf. H. J. Kraus, *Geschichte der historisch-kritischen Erforschung des AT* (1956), p. 248.

[7] *OT in Modern Research* (1954), p. 11.

[8] *Geschichte Israels,* I (1878), pp. 3ff.

entire corpus was revised and edited to form the extant Pentateuch, perhaps by about 200 B.C.

Wellhausen then applied his conclusion that the Mosaic legislation was the basic law code of post-exilic Judaism rather than the starting-point for the development of Israelite religious institutions to a reconstruction of Hebrew religion. Rejecting current theological interpretations in favor of Hegelian principles of causation and evolution, he envisioned the early religious activity of Israel in terms of primitive impulses of an animistic character; consequently, he dismissed as unhistorical the sources which described patriarchal religion as monotheistic in nature. This completely arbitrary action was followed by the affirmation that the history of Hebrew religion could only commence with the beginnings of the peoples themselves. While there is a sense in which the latter is obviously true, Wellhausen failed to see that the religion of the settlement and the earlier Wilderness period had its antecedents in the Hebrew patriarchs; as a result, he asserted that the Israelites emerged on the historical scene as a people no earlier than the time of Moses.[9]

For Wellhausen the adaptation of the Israelites to Canaanite patterns of worship subsequent to the settlement of the tribes in Palestine was a step towards the emergence of a monotheistic faith, and this largely resulted from the activity of the prophets. Wellhausen maintained that prior to the reforms of Josiah there had been no central sanctuary, with the result that sacrifices were offered at various places in Canaan. Ultimately the prophetic teachings concerning monotheism led to the centralization of cultic worship in Jerusalem, an event which provided the impetus for that kind of ritual activity which in the post-exilic period culminated in the formulation of the Priestly Code.[10]

Although Wellhausen had added little or nothing that was specifically new to the critical conclusions of Graf, his method brought to a climax the investigations of earlier liberal scholars and served to show the fundamental difference between the nineteenth-century *Zeitgeist* and the theological exegesis of an earlier age. Wellhausen had contrived to reduce the elements of law, covenant, religion, and history to one comprehensive and controlled scheme, consisting of three major periods of Hebrew historical development in which simple forms evolved into progressively differentiated aspects. His scheme bore all the marks of Hegelian evolutionism, and by its very simplicity and comprehensiveness it commended itself to an age which was endeavoring to resolve the many into the one by means of a single interpretative principle.

So completely did the scheme which Wellhausen elaborated meet the needs of his day that it gained wide acceptance within a very short period of time. In Holland, the views of Wellhausen were disseminated

[9] Wellhausen, *Prolegomena zur Geschichte Israels* (1883), pp. 363ff.
[10] Wellhausen, *Israelitische und jüdische Geschichte* (1897), pp. 110ff.

nthusiastically by Kuenen;[11] in France the aged Reuss propounded
/ith renewed vigor the theories which he had advanced in 1834 when
e affirmed that the basic Elohistic document was in fact the latest of all
hose thought to underlie the Pentateuch.[12]

However, other equally notable scholars were far from being convinced
f the merits of many aspects of the evolutionary position that had been
et out so plausibly by Wellhausen. Eduard Riehm attacked the view
hat the Priestly Code was the latest part of the Pentateuch, observing
hat the Deuteronomic legislation presupposed acquaintance with it.[13]
)illmann placed the Priestly Code considerably prior to Deuteronomy in
erms of development, and assigned the bulk of the Holiness Code, to
vhich he accorded the designation S(inai), to an even earlier date.[14]
¡audissin placed the Law of Holiness in the pre-Deuteronomic period,[15]
vhile Kittel held that the Priestly literature had existed for a prolonged
ime as a document of ecclesiastical law, available only to the priests at
irst but subsequently made public by force of circumstances.[16]

Whereas Dillmann, Kittel, and Baudissin tended towards a mediating
iew of the Priestly material, Franz Delitzsch openly attacked the entire
Vellhausenian scheme in his commentary on Genesis.[17] He held that all
ections of the Pentateuch specifically attributed to Moses in the text
vere in fact from his hand, while other portions of his legal enactments
vere given their final form by priestly circles during the settlement
>eriod. Delitzsch was attracted to the possibility that Joshua was com-
>iled by the author of Deuteronomy from Jehovistic and Elohistic mod-
·ls from details of ecclesiastical arrangement and organization he ar-
;ued for a pre-exilic date for much of the Priestly writings,[18] and stoutly
defended the genuineness of the Decalogue,[19] which even Smend had
·riginally attributed to Moses.[20]

A different form of attack upon the views of Wellhausen came in 1893,
vhen A. Klostermann rejected the developmental hypothesis and re-
>laced it with his own version of the crystallization theory of Ewald and
<nobel. In his work on the Pentateuch he postulated the existence of an
>riginal Mosaic nucleus of law which, because of its liturgical use, was
:xpanded by priestly editors. Although he adhered to the ideas of a

---

[11] *Historisch-Critisch Onderzoek naar het Ontstaan en de Verzameling van de
¡oeken des Ouden Verbonds* (3 vols., 1885-1893).
[12] *L'Histoire Sainte et la Loi* (1879).
[13] *Einleitung in das AT* (1889), I, p. 218.
[14] *Numeri, Deuteronomium und Josua* (1886), pp. 605, 644ff., 660.
[15] *HDB*, IV, p. 88.
[16] *Geschichte der Hebräer* (1888), I, pp. 100ff.
[17] *Neuer Kommentar über die Genesis* (1887), E. tr. 1888.
[18] *Zeitschrift für kirchliche Wissenschaft und kirchliches Leben* (1880), p. 268.
[19] *Ibid.* (1882), pp. 281ff.
[20] *Theologische Studien und Kritiken,* XLIX (1876), p. 643.

Jehovistic and an Elohistic recension, he held that these were united at a comparatively early period,[21] making for a definite pre-exilic origin for the Priestly sources. Like many other scholars he held that Deuteronomy had been added to the Pentateuchal corpus in the time of Josiah of Judah.

B. Wellhausen and His Followers

Despite the weighty criticisms levelled against it, the Graf-Wellhausen hypothesis became very appealing to the younger scholars of the day, since it seemed to furnish the answer to their critical needs with simplicity and conviction. From rather humble textual beginnings the theory had grown through the work of successive thinkers to the point where, under Wellhausen, it had become a precision instrument for examining the rationale of Hebrew history against a background of Hegelian evolutionism. Having developed critical methodology to this point, Wellhausen devoted his time to grappling with the literary analysis of the Gospels, relinquishing the application of his methods to other aspects of Old Testament study to his followers. The challenge was taken up with enthusiasm by such able investigators as Smend, Kautzsch, Stade, Budde, Cornill, and others of like caliber, and within a very short time the volume of literary output based on the Graf-Wellhausen methodology had assumed enormous proportions, virtually stifling other opposing views through sheer bulk. In common with other disciplines of the age, the literary-critical method of Old Testament study claimed the title "scientific," and from this it was only a short step to its being regarded by the followers of Wellhausen as the new orthodoxy.

There can be little doubt that when Wellhausen promulgated his theory of Pentateuchal origins he was endeavoring to develop an instrument for the deeper understanding of Scripture. To him and to his supporters the scholarly activities in which they were engaged were far superior methodologically to the older canons of theological exegesis, which left a great many questions unanswered. More particularly, the humanistic approach of the Enlightenment had liberated Scripture from the confines of Roman Catholic and Lutheran "fundamentalism," and had made the Old Testament in particular a legitimate object of intellectual inquiry. Wellhausen approached his task with a lucid mind and a sympathetic understanding, and his writings conveyed clearly the appreciation he had for the significance of the religious phenomena in the lives of the Hebrew people. Had he continued to apply his principles to parts of the Old Testament other than the Hexateuch, the results of his study might well have been very different from what actually obtained.

[21] *Der Pentateuch* (1893), p. 185.

24

What Wellhausen did not appreciate, however, in handing over his methodology to his disciples, was that the *Zeitgeist* was characterized by profound emotional overtones, so that the critical discipline which he had evolved quickly degenerated in nature to the point where it became the unwitting vehicle for the expression of specific weaknesses implicit in the German national character. In the end it failed to develop into a reliable and objective scientific approach to literary study. It is merely a matter of observation that the writings of contemporary German scholars manifested an egotistical inability to appreciate any standpoint other than the one to which they themselves subscribed, and this tendency was compounded by clearly defined trends towards intellectual aggression and domination, a self-assured ideological superiority, and a general consciousness of the monopoly of truth.

The followers of Wellhausen accepted his intellectual leadership uncritically, as Wellhausen himself confessed to having done with respect to the opinions of Graf concerning the late dating of the Law. The single-minded devotion to detail of these men, combined with their general lack of respect for the opinions of those scholars who were in a minority position, soon rewarded their diligence and application by making Wellhausen's scheme the dominant ideology in the field of Old Testament studies. Ultimately this attitude produced such self-assured results of criticism as the divided authorship of Isaiah and the assigning of the book of Daniel to a Maccabean date.

Influenced in part by considerations of academic patronage, the enthusiasm of the more junior European scholars for the critical methodology resulted in a thoroughgoing application of the Graf-Wellhausen analytical and developmental schemes to nearly every book in the Old Testament canon. All too frequently the basic subjectivity of the method encouraged a wide diversity of opinion upon matters of specific detail, such as the exact delineation of the various proposed documentary sources of the Pentateuch. In certain areas of study its application produced some lamentable extremes of literary analysis against which a subsequent generation was to react. But for the younger scholars, devotion to the literary-critical method brought with it a feeling that it could be developed still further and made more efficient as a result. Accordingly they devoted themselves increasingly to the more technical requirements of analyzing the scope and formation of the documents adduced by earlier scholars, with the result that successive students broke down the basic sources thought to underlie the Pentateuch into even smaller components than Wellhausen himself had done.

So vigorous was this tendency that scholars in Europe became preoccupied to an ever greater extent with the task of isolating and subdividing such elemental categories, and not infrequently they found themselves caught up in involved and ponderous arguments relating to the provenance of isolated verses or sentences. Whereas Wellhausen had endeavored to maintain a view of the panorama of Hebrew history in his delineation of supposed documentary sources, his followers manifested an increasing concern for the analysis of "documents" as an end in itself thus contributing materially to the general sterility of their results.

Even Wellhausen himself, it is reported, became more and more anxious as time went on about the usage to which his methodology was being put and the results which were being obtained,[22] but by that time the movement had gained momentum and reached a stage where it was largely out of control. Before his death in 1918 Wellhausen conceded that the rationalism which he had embraced so avidly in earlier years had made havoc of his own faith in the authority and authenticity of the Old Testament.

Up to this point liberal criticism had emerged as a threefold discipline for the examination of the Hebrew Scriptures. Its aims were the reconstruction of the original text with the greatest degree of accuracy, so as to determine the manner and date of writing of the various books, the establishment of the nature of their underlying sources as far as possible, and the attempt to arrive at some decision relating to questions of authorship of the various compositions in the canon.

The earliest phase of this activity, which in fact antedated the rise of literary criticism, was marked by the growth of textual criticism, the objective of which was to discover to the fullest degree possible the original wording of the documents under study. This constituted an extremely important branch of study, partly because the basic reliability of the Hebrew text was the foundation upon which all other areas of criticism erected their superstructures, and partly because transcriptional errors were considerably more frequent in the days when all manuscripts were copied out by hand than they were after the invention of printing when the manuscript as such was replaced by a book. Since no autograph manuscript of any Old Testament composition has survived, it was rightly deemed important for the Hebrew text to represent as accurate a copy of the original as was possible under the circumstances.

The second branch of criticism was the purely literary kind, which had been given the designation of "higher" by Eichhorn in the preface to the second edition of his *Einleitung* (1787), in order to distinguish it from "lower" or textual criticism. Literary-critical activities included an examination of the sources considered to underlie a particular book or document, as well as some pronouncement on matters relating to the authorship and date of the material. Higher criticism was also concerned to classify literature according to type, with the aim of isolating legal enactments, biographical sections, poetry, prophetic oracles and the like.

[22] See P. J. Wiseman, *New Discoveries in Babylonia about Genesis* (1958), pp. 121f.

The final branch of criticism was due in no small measure to the work of Wellhausen, who by relating literary criticism to the exigencies of his evolutionary view of Old Testament history laid considerable stress upon the necessity for developing historical criticism as a means of determining the historicity and credibility of the events under consideration.

Within a decade of the publication by Wellhausen of the *Prolegomena* in 1883, a large number of histories of Israel, surveys of Old Testament religion, commentaries on various canonical books, and introductions to the Old Testament as a whole appeared under the names of distinguished scholars, the vast majority of whom employed the literary-critical methods made popular by Wellhausen. A high standard of historical and critical investigation was fostered by the appearance of two German commentaries on the Old Testament books, the fifteen-volume *Handkommentar zum Alten Testament* (1892-1903) and the twenty-volume *Kurzer Handkommentar zum Alten Testament* (1897-1904).

A similar series, *The International Critical Commentary on the Holy Scriptures,* made an appearance at approximately the same time in England and the United States under the editorial auspices of S. R. Driver, A. Plummer, and C. A. Briggs. Although the Old Testament section was planned to consist of twenty-six volumes, it was never in fact completed.

C. The Spread of Wellhausen's Method to England and America

While their New Testament counterparts were busily employed in refuting the theories of the Tübingen school, British Old Testament scholars were avidly embracing the views of Wellhausen and his followers in Europe. Chiefly responsible for this trend were A. B. Davidson and W. Robertson Smith. The latter in particular accorded unquestioned orthodoxy to the writings of Wellhausen. Whereas Davidson was primarily a teacher,[23] Robertson Smith was a man of considerable literary ability who wrote extensively in support of the growing literary-critical movement. In 1875 he contributed an important article to the *Encyclopaedia Britannica* which, along with other material, resulted in his trial for heresy and ultimate expulsion from the Free Church College of Aberdeen in 1881. In the same year he published his lectures on *The Old Testament in the Jewish Church,* and in the following year he issued *The Prophets of Israel.* In 1885 he published a monograph dealing with *Kinship and Marriage in Early Arabia,* and four years later his book entitled *The Religion of the Semites* appeared, quickly becoming a classic of the day. Less influential were the writings of T. K. Cheyne, who contributed commentaries on *Micah* (1882) and *Hosea* (1884) to

[23] Cf. H. W. Robinson, *ET*, XLI (1929-1930), pp. 247f.

the Cambridge Bible series, as well as publishing books dealing with the Psalms and the Wisdom Literature.[24] Unfortunately Cheyne fell victim to the practice of excessive textual emendation—a procedure necessary in order to fit certain awkward portions of the Hebrew text into the Wellhausenian evolutionary scheme—and much of what he contributed to the *Encyclopaedia Biblica,* of which he was an editor, must be assessed in the light of this fact.

But by far the most influential figure in the dissemination of Biblical criticism in England was S. R. Driver of Oxford. He succeeded to the Regius Professorship of Hebrew on the death of E. B. Pusey in 1882, supplanting A. H. Sayce, whose election to the chair was vetoed by Gladstone on the ground that Sayce was one of the leading exponents of German criticism at Oxford, and therefore an "unsafe" candidate for the chair.[25] Ironically enough, while Sayce subsequently turned to archaeological investigation and ultimately became a distinguished champion of orthodox belief, it was Driver who made one of the most important contributions to the promulgation of Old Testament criticism in the English language.

Driver had already established his reputation as a scholar with the publication in 1874 of his *Hebrew Tenses,* and after this he set about modifying the extremes of German critical ideology in order to accommodate it to the less radical tastes of the British. The result was his *Introduction to the Literature of the Old Testament,* published in 1891. Although this work was simply no match for the flowing prose and lucid artistry of many of the contemporary German writings, it made up in diligence what it lacked in imagination and originality. Driver's *Introduction* was by far the most influential of his numerous writings;[26] and it served an important function in establishing a pattern of critical orthodoxy which became normative for British scholars. A close if unofficial surveillance was imposed upon potential candidates for positions in the Old Testament field in British universities, and only those who displayed proper respect for the canons of critical orthodoxy were appointed to academic posts. Consequently scholars of a more conservative bent were relegated to comparative obscurity in theological colleges of various denominations and other independent institutions of learning. The bulk of the literary material which emerged from this general

[24] *The Book of Psalms* (1888), *The Origin of the Psalter* (1891), *Job and Solomon* (1887).

[25] Cf. D. E. Hart-Davies, *Biblical History in the Light of Archaeological Discovery since A.D. 1900* (1935), pp. 1ff.

[26] Including his *Notes on the Hebrew Text of the Books of Samuel* (1890), in which he leaned heavily on the work of Wellhausen, and commentaries on *Deuteronomy* (ICC series, 1895), *Daniel* (Cambridge Bible, 1900), *Genesis* (Westminster Commentaries series, 1904), and *Exodus* (Cambridge Bible, 1911).

period consisted of uncritical expositions of German liberal criticism based upon the mediating pattern established by S. R. Driver, with only slight variations on the fundamental theme being countenanced. Such were characteristics of the books by J. E. Carpenter, H. E. Ryle, A. F. Kirkpatrick, W. H. Bennett, J. Strachan, A. T. Chapman, and A. B. Davidson.[27]

Although the tide of literary criticism was running high at the end of the nineteenth century, its onslaught by no means went unchallenged. In 1885 E. C. Bissell attacked the basic presuppositions of the Wellhausenian hypothesis,[28] while in the following year Geerhardus Vos castigated the current scheme of literary analysis, rejected the late date assigned the Priestly material, and claimed substantial Mosaic authorship for the Pentateuch.[29] From a more theological standpoint James Orr made an important criticism of the Wellhausenian hypothesis and censured severely the contemporary efforts at the critical reconstruction of Old Testament history.[30] Orr not only pointed out the essential weaknesses of the application of the analytical method by the more extreme members of the Wellhausen school, but he showed that the method itself was characterized by fundamentally inadequate postulates in a number of important areas. In his refutation of the analytical approach and his defense of orthodox conservatism Orr was not, as Hahn implies,[31] unable to understand the significance of historical research. It is of some interest to note that his penetrating criticisms were never accorded the dignity of an answer, much less an attempt at refutation, by those whose views he challenged. A similar situation obtained in the case of Baxter, who also subjected the methodology of Wellhausen to a searching criticism in the light of Hebrew religious institutions, rejecting the late date accorded to the Priestly sections by critical scholars.[32]

In the meantime the distinguished scholar A. H. Sayce was bringing the developing science of modern archaeology to bear upon some of the more pressing problems of the Old Testament. As a result of his studies he abandoned his earlier support for the German liberal position and became an influential advocate of more traditional views. Outstanding among his many writings were *The "Higher Criticism" and the Verdict of*

---

[27] Carpenter, *The Composition of the Hexateuch* (1902); *The Hexateuch* (with G. Harford-Battersby, 2 vols., 1900), *The Pentateuch* (1900). Ryle, *The Canon of the OT* (1892). Kirkpatrick, *The Divine Library of the OT* (1896), *The Book of Psalms* (1902). Bennett, *A Primer of the Bible* (1897), *The Book of Joshua* (1899). Strachan in *ERE*, IV, pp. 314ff. Chapman, *Introduction to the Pentateuch* (1911). Davidson in the Cambridge Bible commentaries on *Job* (1884), *Ezekiel* (1892), and *Nahum, Habakkuk and Zephaniah* (1896).

[28] *The Pentateuch: Its Origin and Structure* (1885).

[29] *The Mosaic Origin of the Pentateuchal Codes* (1886).

[30] *The Problem of the OT* (1906).

[31] *OT in Modern Research*, p. 23.

[32] *Sanctuary and Sacrifice: A Reply to Wellhausen* (1895).

the Monuments (1894), *Early Israel and the Surrounding Nations* (1899), and *Monument Facts and Higher Critical Fancies* (1904).

Other attacks by conservative writers were directed at the criteria used by critical scholars in their documentary analyses and reconstructions. One such investigation by Dahse examined the criterion of the divine names and showed that it was impossible to maintain that the names of Jacob and Israel were indications of the existence of different literary sources.[33] In a study of the occurrence of the divine names in the LXX Dahse pointed out significant variations from the usage in the Hebrew text, and argued from such inconsistencies to the comparative unsuitability of the divine names as a criterion for documentary analysis. He also emphasized that the cultural and religious conditions depicted in the Old Testament narratives reflected a far more advanced degree of maturity than Wellhausen and his followers were prepared to concede,[34] a position which was to be reinforced by Mesopotamian archaeology some forty years later.

Although Dahse adhered to the view that the literary form of the legal material contained in the Pentateuch was comparatively late, he maintained that the ritual practices which it reflected were considerably older than the form of the laws themselves, since they depicted theological concepts which belonged to an early age.[35] In general he rejected the idea that the beginnings of institutions necessarily had to be simple in form, and with this he jettisoned the evolutionary interpretation of Hebrew religious institutions that was propounded by Wellhausen. But Dahse's appeal to the comparatively advanced nature of other ancient Near Eastern religious and cultural forms, although supported by the archaeological discoveries of the day, fell on deaf ears; for the liberal critics were preoccupied with the analysis of purely internal evidence as supplied by the Hebrew text, and had neither the time nor the taste for archaeology.

In 1912 the English lawyer H. M. Wiener wrote in opposition to the critical scheme of Old Testament study.[36] Like Dahse, Wiener attacked the criterion of the divine names, pointing out the variation of usage between the Massoretic text and the LXX. He maintained the substantial Mosaic authorship of the Pentateuch, although he recognized the existence of certain post-Mosaic sections. In 1908 B. D. Eerdmans commenced a series of studies, subsequently published under the title of *Alttestamentliche Studien I-IV* (1908-14), in which he also rejected the theory that the divine names could be employed as valid criteria for the

---

[33] J. Dahse, *Archiv für Religionswissenschaft*, VI (1903), pp. 305ff. Cf. also his *Textkritische Materialen zur Hexateuchfrage* (1912).

[34] *Alttestamentliche Studien, II: Die Vorgeschichte Israels* (1909), pp. 38ff., *III: Das Buch Exodus* (1910), p. 126.

[35] *Ibid. IV: Das Buch Leviticus* (1912), pp. 143f.

[36] *Pentateuchal Studies* (1912); cf. *ibid., Essays on Pentateuchal Criticism* (1909).

purpose of distinguishing underlying documents. He held that the material as a whole belonged to four different stages of development, of which the earliest was polytheistic and the latest monotheistic. In the post-exilic period the accumulated body of written tradition was re-edited from a monotheistic standpoint and augmented by means of other material to become the extant Pentateuch. At a later period Eerdmans attempted to modify the Wellhausenian reconstruction of Hebrew religious history in his *Godsdienst van Israël*, published in 1930,[37] but his views met with little enthusiasm.

The spread of German critical methods in Old Testament study to the United States occurred at approximately the same time as their acceptance by British scholars. In the forefront of those who acclaimed the new methodology were Francis Brown and C. A. Briggs, who introduced it to Union Theological Seminary in New York City. Both men were eminent Hebrew scholars who cooperated with S. R. Driver in producing the *Hebrew Lexicon of the Old Testament* in 1906, a volume which was based upon the work of the renowned Semitic philologist Gesenius. The early writings of Briggs[38] were not particularly distinguished by their critical acumen as compared with similar European compositions, although in 1893, when he published *The Higher Criticism of the Hexateuch*, he had absorbed the general principles of higher criticism. Like some of his predecessors in the field he had a feeling for the beauty and poetry of the Hebrew Psalter, and in 1886 he contributed a series of articles dealing with the form and structure of Hebrew poetry to the third volume of *Hebraica*, a technical journal founded in 1884 by W. R. Harper, then the President of the University of Chicago. Subsequently this journal became *The American Journal of Semitic Languages and Literatures*. These studies constituted a preparatory step towards the production of his *magnum opus*, the two-volume work, *A Critical and Exegetical Commentary on the Psalms*, which appeared in 1906-07. His *General Introduction to the Study of the Old Testament* was published in 1899.

As was the case with Robertson Smith, Briggs became heavily involved in controversy as a result of his views relating to the Graf-Wellhausen hypothesis; and in 1892 he was tried for heresy by the presbytery of New York. He was subsequently acquitted, but when an appeal was launched before the General Assembly he was suspended from office in 1893. Seven years later he was ordained to the priesthood in the Episcopal Church, where he ministered until his death in 1913.

The critical views prevalent in Europe were also reflected in the commentary *The Genesis of Genesis* (1892) by B. W. Bacon,[39] and in

---

[37] E. tr. rev., *The Religion of Israel* (1947).

[38] *Biblical Study* (1884), *Messianic Prophecy* (1886). See E. G. Kraeling, *The OT Since the Reformation* (1955), p. 294 n. 13.

[39] See also his *The Triple Tradition of Exodus* (1894).

contributions to the *International Critical Commentary* series by G. F. Moore, H. P. Smith, C. H. Toy, W. R. Harper, G. A. Barton, and L. B. Paton.[40] Among others W. H. Green of Princeton Theological Seminary challenged the opinions of Harper, as a result of which a debate appeared in the fifth volume of *Hebraica* (1888) on the entire scope of the Pentateuchal problem. The discussion attained a high standard of literary and academic achievement, and the charitable tone which prevailed throughout was in marked contrast to the acrimony which existed elsewhere. Green was a competent Hebrew scholar who had already issued a reply to the opinions of Bishop Colenso,[41] and had challenged the views espoused in Kuenen's critical study of the Hexateuch[42] in his *Moses and the Prophets* (1883). Green subsequently issued two important works on the Pentateuch in one year,[43] both of which furnished eloquent testimony to the erudition of the author and constituted fundamental challenges to the entire methodological system of Wellhausen and his followers.

[40] Moore, *A Critical and Exegetical Commentary on the Book of Judges* (1895); Smith, *Samuel* (1899); Toy, *Proverbs* (1899); Harper, *Amos and Hosea* (1905); Barton, *Ecclesiastes* (1908); Paton, *Esther* (1906).

[41] *The Pentateuch Vindicated from the Aspersions of Bishop Colenso* (1863).

[42] *Historisch-Critisch Onderzoek naar het Ontstaan en de Verzameling van de Boeken des Ouden Verbonds, I-III* (1885-1893); E. tr. of sect. I, *The Hexateuch* (1886).

[43] *The Unity of the Book of Genesis* and *The Higher Criticism of the Pentateuch* (1895).

III. REACTIONS TO THE GRAF-WELLHAUSEN HYPOTHESIS

A. PHILOLOGY, ARCHAEOLOGY, AND ANTHROPOLOGY

While the limitations of literary criticism were already painfully apparent as a result of the unfortunate excesses of certain European scholars, new sources of knowledge were becoming available for the study of the Old Testament which were themselves demanding a modification of the extreme attitudes reflected by many adherents of the critical position. The decipherment of Mesopotamian cuneiform and Egyptian hieroglyphic scripts made available for purposes of comparative study an enormous number of sources having an important bearing on all periods of Old Testament history. As a result it was becoming increasingly possible to study Hebrew life generally in terms of the larger ancient Near Eastern environment. With the development of archaeology as a scientific discipline a more assured basis was furnished for philology and comparative linguistics as a whole. Important contributions to the study of Semitic languages had already been made by H. F. W. Gesenius, the father of modern Hebrew lexicography, by E. Renan, Friedrich Delitzsch, A. H. Sayce, W. Wright, H. Zimmern, T. Nöldeke, and E. König.[1] These studies were to be enriched and extended by the labors of subsequent generations of scholars.

Most significant of all, however, was the realization that while Semitic philology was a well-grounded subject in its own right, it had an invaluable part to play in constituting one aspect of legitimate critical inquiry for the elucidation of some of the mysteries of the ancient Near Eastern

---

[1] Gesenius, *Hebräisches und Chaldäisches Handwörterbuch* (1812). Renan, *Histoire générale des langues semitiques* (1863). Delitzsch, *Prolegomena eines neuen Hebräisch-Aramäischen Wörterbuchs zum AT* (1886); *Assyrisches Wörterbuch zur gesampten bisher veröffentlichen Keilschriftliteratur* (1887-1890); *Assyrische Grammatik* (1889). Sayce, *Assyrian Grammar for Comparative Purposes* (1872); *Principles of Comparative Philology* (1874); *Introduction to the Science of Language* (1879). Wright, *Lectures on the Comparative Grammar of the Semitic Languages* (1890). Zimmern, *Vergleichende Grammatik der semitischen Sprachen* (1898). Nöldeke, *Die Semitischen Sprachen* (1899). König, *Historisch-Kritisches Lehrgebäude der Hebräischen Sprache* (1881); *Hebräisch und Semitisch* (1901).

environment that various Old Testament books reflect. Since that time comparative linguistics has become an essential adjunct to any serious study of the Old Testament, and has contributed enormously to the modern understanding of traditions, allusions, and practices, which by their very nature were entirely unfamiliar to the occidental mind. With the enrichment of Hebrew philology there came also a more scientific approach to the study of the Hebrew text, making it possible for scholars to come closer to the original autographs and thereby clarifying some of the problems which had arisen during the processes of textual transmission.

Other methods of study relating to the Hebrew Scriptures, which were different from those normally envisaged by philology and archaeology, were also being investigated at this period. It is to the credit of Robertson Smith that attention was first focused on a specifically anthropological approach to the study of Hebrew religion. Although in his *Lectures on the Religion of the Semites* he examined the earliest forms of Hebrew beliefs and rituals from the standpoint, common among anthropologists of his day, that the more developed forms of a religion could best be understood by a detailed study of the primitive or rudimentary phases from which it had evolved, he ultimately parted company with some of the views of Wellhausen by maintaining the cohesiveness and compulsion of social rather than purely personal customs and convictions. Through the study of such ritual institutions as sacrifice Smith endeavored to grapple with the nature of primitive religious belief among the Semites, and concluded that the ideas of atonement and communion were basic concepts of primitive Semitic religion.[2]

A more diversified approach to this same subject was reflected in the writings of Sir James G. Frazer. For many years Frazer collected material relating to the fundamental thought-forms and activities of savage and primitive peoples for the successive editions of his work *The Golden Bough*.[3] In the field of Old Testament studies Frazer attempted to find in the narratives traces of survivals of the most primitive stage of Hebrew religious beliefs,[4] but while the method of analogy and comparison which he utilized frequently did much to illumine the meaning of an obscure passage, he was unable to present his data in the coherent and logical manner characteristic of the work of Robertson Smith. Frazer unfortunately had little or no concept of the religious growth of the Hebrews, so that for the Biblical scholar his attempts to recover the most

[2] *The Religion of the Semites*, pp. 251ff., 312ff.

[3] *The Golden Bough: A Study in Magic and Religion* (1890 ed.), 2 vols., (1900 ed.), 3 vols., (1910-1915 ed.), 12 vols. A one-volume abridgement was published in 1922.

[4] *Folk-lore in the OT: Studies in Comparative Religion* (3 vols., 1918).

34

primitive aspects of belief or ritual procedure were at best somewhat unfruitful, if only because they appeared to be out of proportion in terms of the total picture.

B. FORM-CRITICISM—GUNKEL AND HIS FOLLOWERS

Although these approaches were valuable in attempting to rectify and give proper dimensions to an imbalanced literary criticism, they had less effect upon the excesses of the Graf-Wellhausen school than did the rise of form-criticism. With an increasing number of objections to the results obtained by the exercise of literary criticism, and with decided uncertainty in many quarters about the validity of the proposed solutions, it became clear that a new approach to the problem was a matter of some urgency. Utilizing the conclusions which had emerged from the comparative study of religions, and relating them to the literary products of the Hebrew people, a group of German scholars associated with Hermann Gunkel began an attempt to trace the basic religious ideas of the Hebrews as enshrined in the Massoretic text back to their original oral form. Gunkel laid considerable emphasis upon the importance of the life-situation or *Sitz im Leben des Volkes* as a means of understanding the various extant literary forms, which he subjected to a careful though generally sympathetic criticism.

Gunkel also took pains to compare the religious *motifs* of the Hebrews with the mythological and cultic forms of Mesopotamian, Egyptian, and Hittite religion, so as to determine, if possible, the extent to which the Hebrews had been influenced by the cultures of the ancient Near East. Since Gunkel considered the literature of a people to be in fact the tangible expression of their spiritual history, he deemed it of great importance to be able to penetrate the extant literary form and recover the ultimate sources in terms of oral tradition. In his work on Genesis,[5] which formed an introduction to his larger commentary in the *Handkommentar zum Alten Testament,* he advanced the view that the narratives of Genesis had originally been transmitted orally in the form of independent sagas, which subsequently had become associated with some particular person. The art of the storyteller was later reduced to a literary form of considerable aesthetic value prior to the prophetic period, and collections of these sagas formed the basis of the Jehovistic and Elohistic documents which were ultimately united in their extant form in the Pentateuch.

Gunkel emphasized that his method of literary appreciation was a means of grasping the religious values of the Old Testament, which had been largely obscured as a result of the critical activities of the Graf-

[5] *Die Sagen der Genesis* (1901).

Wellhausen school.[6] However, he also made it clear that the sagas of Genesis were for him basically folklore, like that of any other ancient people, and not necessarily the embodiment of historical fact as such. He deemed his task to be that of uncovering the original oral form of these sagas through an examination of the various types of literary composition in the Hebrew Scriptures in terms of his particular methodology. Though Gunkel claimed allegiance to the Wellhausenian hypothesis his work represented a fundamental criticism of it, since his assertion that the documents were collections of sagas rather than the writings of individual authors had elements in common with the fragmentary hypothesis advocated by Geddes and Vater. Furthermore, Gunkel argued for the antiquity of the original form of the sagas, as opposed to the late dating assigned by the members of the Graf-Wellhausen school.

Reflecting the influence of Herder, Gunkel applied his methodology to the Hebrew Psalms in a series of writings which surveyed the peculiarities of linguistic expression found in the Psalter and estimated the place occupied by these compositions in the stream of Israelite literary history.[7] On the assumption that certain conventions of form had become traditional over many centuries of usage, Gunkel assigned a long history to Hebrew poetry, suggesting that, as with the Genesis sagas, the Psalms had originally existed in an oral form that attained an apogee in the pre-ex ʾic period. Although he had some difficulty tracing the growth of many of his principal literary types (*Gattungen*), owing to the traditional fashion of associating certain forms of composition with specific categories of subject-matter, he was able to find sufficient indications of growth with regard to poetic forms to produce a fruitful classification of the literature as a whole.

Gunkel maintained that the majority of the post-exilic psalms had been composed in virtually their extant form, but he also recognized that many of them contained elements of much older literary compositions. This was a considerable advance upon earlier critical tendencies,[8] which had in general regarded the individual psalms as late rather than early in point of time. Gunkel, however, did not question the assumption commonly espoused by liberal scholars that the Psalter as a unit had been compiled at a late date.

This method of classification by literary types in relation to a characteristic cultural setting has contributed more to the understanding of the Psalter than any other facet of literary-critical activity. The rigorous insistence upon relating Hebrew poetry to the larger background of

[6] *Deutsche Rundschau*, CLXI (1914), pp. 215ff.; see also his *What Remains of the OT? and Other Essays* (1928), pp. 13ff.

[7] *Ausgewählte Psalmen* (1904); *Die Psalmen* in *Handkommentar zum AT* (ed. Nowack, 1926), II, vol. 2; *Einleitung in die Psalmen: Die Gattungen der religiösen Lyrik Israels* (1928-1933), parts I, II.

[8] Cf. Gunkel, *Einleitung in die Psalmen*, pp. 514ff.

ancient Near Eastern literary products resulted in some penetrating liturgical and exegetical insights, and indicated that further information about the origins of Hebrew psalmody would most probably be derived through the comparative study of religion. This situation was made even more clear with the discovery of the poetic material from Ras Shamra (Ugarit) in 1929, some three years before Gunkel died. These tablets, however, required some modification of the *Sitz im Leben des Volkes* approach which Gunkel had adopted, since they indicated that Hebrew poetry did not depend so much upon analogous forms in Egyptian and Babylonian religious texts as upon the literature of Ugarit, which contained a vast number of stylistic forms, phrases, and grammatical expressions in common with the Hebrew.

Another challenge to the Graf-Wellhausen hypothesis resulted from the work of Sievers, who applied the principles underlying his studies on Hebrew poetic meters to the Pentateuch.[9] Sievers intended to demonstrate the validity of the documentary analysis by this means, but in point of fact he returned, like Gunkel, to the fragmentary hypothesis of Geddes and Vater by subdividing the documents of J, E, and P into five, three, and six different sources respectively. As G. Ch. Aalders has pointed out, if Sievers had investigated the meter of the book of Genesis without recourse to the principles of the Graf-Wellhausen school, he would almost certainly have arrived at an entirely different conclusion, positing one principal source supplemented by means of six secondary ones.[10]

The techniques that Gunkel applied to the sagas of Genesis and the contents of the Psalter were employed by his followers to investigate other areas of the Old Testament. Outstanding in this regard was the work of Hugo Gressmann, whose major concern was with the historical writings. Starting from the saga-concept of Gunkel, he postulated the theory that the narrative qualities of the extant historical literature could be related directly to the form of the narrative art as it existed during the oral stage of the source material. From this he was led to the study of the individual narratives in terms of literary types, which in his view was more important than an analysis of the manner in which a book was thought to have been compiled from documentary sources. His study of the historical writings[11] attracted the attention of other scholars. A fragmentation of the historical books resulted from the work of Wiese on Judges[12] and from the studies of Caspari[13] and Rost[14] dealing with the books of Samuel. All of these labored diligently in an attempt to identify the separate sources original to these compositions, from which they be-

---

[9] *Metrische Studien I-III* (1901-1907).
[10] *A Short Introduction to the Pentateuch* (1949), pp. 19f.
[11] *Die älteste Geschichtsschreibung und Prophetie Israels* (1910).
[12] *Zur Literaturkritik des Buches der Richter* (1926).
[13] *Die Samuelbücher* in *Kommentar zum AT* (ed. E. Sellin, 1926), vol. VII.
[14] *Die Überlieferung von der Thronnachfolge Davids* (1926).

lieved the extant documents had been formulated. While the application of form-critical principles was not intended in the first instance as a substitute for the Graf-Wellhausen hypothesis, its growth represented a decided reaction against an excessive preoccupation with the minutiae of literary analysis, and made abundantly clear the importance of certain considerations which fell outside the narrow concern of the Graf-Wellhausen scheme proper.

Although the methods employed by Gunkel and his followers represent a valuable contribution to the problem of determining how the various Old Testament books assumed their present form, there can be little doubt that Gunkel laid a disproportionate amount of emphasis upon what he considered to be the general usage in the matter of ancient literary styles. In this connection it ought to be noticed that the Psalms in particular frequently exhibit a considerable degree of independence from stylized literary conventions in the essentially personal nature of their approach to the problems of the spiritual life. Although it is true that certain literary sources are referred to in the historical writings, which may be taken as being representative of the underlying source material, there is little actual evidence for the contention of critical scholars that these existed for long periods in saga form, or that they were placed in juxtaposition mechanically to constitute a description of a particular period in the life of the nation. Indeed, certain histories, notably Chronicles, show marked indications of the personality of the compiler, who selected his material according to certain predetermined principles in order to present his readers with a particular metaphysical interpretation of the historical process.

C. Early Twentieth-Century Attacks

The period of pure literary criticism as such may be said to have been concluded with two impressive works, Steuernagel's *Lehrbuch der Einleitung in das Alt Testament* (1912), which furnished a comprehensive and sympathetic consideration of the Graf-Wellhausen analytical scheme, and Sellin's *Einleitung in das Alte Testament* (1910), which argued convincingly against it at many points, including the question of the late dating assigned to Hexateuch sources, while at the same time accepting in general outline the developmental hypothesis.

Events took yet another turn just prior to World War I when Rudolph Smend published his work on the Hexateuch.[15] Although he professed adherence to the Graf-Wellhausen analytical patterns, he actually substituted a major modification of the original scheme in developing a theory advanced in 1885 by Charles Bruston. Smend maintained that there were two Jehovistic authors—whom he designated J¹ and J²—whose work

---

[15] *Die Erzählung des Hexateuchs auf ihre Quellen untersucht* (1912); cf. ZAW, XXXIX (1921), pp. 181ff.

was to be found throughout the entire Hexateuch. Whereas he regarded Deuteronomy and the Priestly material as exhibiting numerous additions, he denied that the Elohistic source had been supplemented in any way, and drew attention to the powerful literary execution of the document as a whole, a characteristic which he also attributed to the Jehovistic source.[16]

The suggestion of two Jehovistic authors was adopted by Eichrodt,[17] who undertook an analysis of the patriarchal narratives in order to establish this hypothesis. While his interests were of a primarily theological nature, he was at some pains to demonstrate the fact of growth and development, not merely in the historic beliefs of the Hebrews but also in the manner in which those beliefs had been transmitted and had assumed their definitive form. The theories of Smend and Eichrodt were given their fullest development in the work of Otto Eissfeldt, who in 1922 expounded what in fact was a five-document theory of Hexateuchal origins.[18] He followed the twofold division of the Jehovistic source suggested by Smend, but maintained that J[1] was the older of the two, and constituted a secular collection or "laity-source" (*Laienquelle*) which had originated during the semi-nomadic phase of Israelite history. Such material typified the Rechabite ideal, was uniformly hostile to Canaanite culture and religion, and constituted the polar extremity of the sacerdotal Priestly material. In his analysis Eissfeldt neglected Leviticus and the bulk of Deuteronomy almost entirely, preferring to base his contentions, like Eichrodt, upon the early chapters of Genesis. Such an approach to the problem reflected what has been described as an "atomizing of sources," a tendency which was fostered to some extent by the growth of form-criticism itself.

Persistent attacks upon the Graf-Wellhausen theory had been made from 1899 on by Wilhelm Möller, a scholarly pastor who had once been an ardent supporter of the documentary theory. His most important work, *Wieder den Bann der Quellenscheidung* (1912), subjected the critical hypothesis to a searching examination.[19] In repudiating its general approach to Pentateuchal problems, and arguing both for the unity and the Mosaic authorship of the Pentateuch, Möller explained the two divine names as being in fact indicative of two different functions. Thus *Elohim* was employed when the reference was to the activity of God in nature, whereas the tetragrammaton *YHWH* was used specifically of the God of revelation. Two years later Edward König criticized the Graf-Wellhausen scheme of literary analysis in a book[20] that also took Dahse

---

[16] *Die Erzählung des Hexateuchs auf ihre Quellen untersucht,* pp. 345ff.
[17] *Die Quellen der Genesis* (1918).
[18] *Hexateuch-Synopse* (1922).
[19] See also his *Are the Critics Right?* (1903).
[20] *Die Moderne Pentateuchkritik und ihre neueste Bekämpfung* (1914).

to task for his efforts to show how unreliable the divine names were as criteria for purposes of documentary analysis by comparing their incidence in the Massoretic text and in the LXX.

Although continental European scholars such as Kittel[21] and Gressmann[22] made it clear shortly after the end of World War I that the minutiae of literary-critical research had reached the limits of their usefulness, many British and American scholars continued to follow the patterns laid down by the Graf-Wellhausen school. British liberal scholarship, having erected its superstructure upon the foundation laid by S. R. Driver, was represented by the work of such men as G. B. Gray, J. Skinner, C. F. Burney, A. S. Peake, A. R. S. Kennedy, and G. A. Smith.[23] In the United States the leading advocates of the critical position included P. Haupt, who illustrated the principles of Biblical criticism by means of a gaily colored Polychrome Bible, J. A. Bewer, H. Preserved Smith, who subsequently became embroiled in controversy concerning his critical views, G. F. Moore, C. H. Toy, and C. C. Torrey.[24]

These and other scholars of like persuasion produced their major works in a period when the results of the literary-critical movement appeared to be solidly established for all time. In consequence, certain of the writings which emerged after World War I manifested a degree of arrogance and patronage towards those who adhered to different opinions, an unfortunate reflection on one of the less praiseworthy attributes of the Anglo-Saxon character. English liberal scholars were

[21] ZAW, XXXIX (1921), pp. 84ff.

[22] ZAW, XLII (1924), p. 8.

[23] Gray, *Hebrew Proper Names* (1896); in the *International Critical Commentary* series, *Numbers* (1903), *Isaiah, Chapters 1-27* (1912), and *Job* (with S. R. Driver, 1921). Skinner, *Isaiah I-XXXIX, XL-XLVI* in the Cambridge Bible series (1896-98); *A Critical and Exegetical Commentary on the Book of Genesis* (*ICC*, 1910); *I and II Kings* in the Century Bible series (n.d.); *Prophecy and Religion* (1922). Burney, *Notes on the Hebrew Text of the Books of Kings* (1903); *Israel's Hope of Immortality* (1909); *The Book of Judges* (1918). Peake, *The Problem of Suffering in the OT* (1904); *Job* and *Jeremiah* in the Century Bible series (1904-1911); *A Commentary on the Bible* (1919). Kennedy, *I and II Samuel* in the Century Bible series (n.d.); *The Book of Ruth* (1928). Smith, *Isaiah I-XXXIX, XL-XLVI* in *The Expositor's Bible* (n.d.); *The Book of the Twelve Prophets* (2 vols., 1896); *Deuteronomy* in the Cambridge Bible series (1918); *The Book of Isaiah* (2 vols., 1927).

[24] Haupt, *The Sacred Books of the OT* (1893); *The Book of Nahum* (1907). Bewer, in the *International Critical Commentary* series, *Obadiah and Joel* (1911), *Jonah* (1912); *The Literature of the OT* (1922). Smith, *Inspiration and Inerrancy* (1893); in the *ICC* series, *The Books of Samuel* (1899); *OT History* (1903); *The Religion of Israel: An Historical Study* (1914); for the reply to his critics see his *The Heretic's Defence: A Footnote to History* (1926). Moore, *Judges* (*ICC* series, 1895); *The Literature of the OT* (1928). Toy, *Judaism and Christianity* (1890); *Proverbs* (*ICC* series, 1899). Torrey, *The Composition and Historical Value of Ezra-Nehemiah* (1896); *Ezra Studies* (1910); *The Second Isaiah* (1928).

accustomed to adopt an attitude of condescension towards the views of more conservative writers if they did not ignore their work altogether, and the general impression which one derives from perusing the literature of the period is that of a completely unwarranted confidence in the evolutionary *Zeitgeist* and an uncritical acceptance of the hypotheses advanced by European scholars of the liberal variety.

In the United States there was a stronger and more vociferous group of conservative writers, and these men attacked the liberal position with great vigor and considerable learning, if not always with quite that degree of courtesy which the situation seemed to require. From this onslaught there emerged a continuing debate between what were rather derisively styled as "fundamentalists" and the exponents of the modern liberal approach to the understanding of Scripture. One of the most learned advocates of scholarly conservatism in the United States was Robert Dick Wilson, whose linguistic talents reputedly made him familiar with some forty-five languages and dialects. His *Studies in Daniel* made an attempt to maintain the traditional view of the authorship and date. Although he concentrated his work on Daniel, he wrote a great number of technical articles dealing with the problems of higher criticism generally, in which he frequently challenged the methods employed by the liberal school. The results of his studies were published in 1929[25] and formed an important contribution to the discussion of critical problems.

Despite the optimistic pronouncements of the advocates of literary-critical method, the results obtained by this approach were by no means as assured as many liked to think, and continued criticisms of the Graf-Wellhausen scheme were being made by European scholars as well as English-speaking conservative writers. What was tantamount to a denial that the Priestly Code ever existed as a literary corpus was made by Max Löhr in 1924. Although he recognized the existence of priestly interests in certain portions of the Pentateuchal writings, he advanced the view that Ezra had formulated the Torah from small groups of laws and narratives rather than from extended documentary sources.[26]

Still another attack upon the critical theories regarding the compilation of the Pentateuch was made by Volz, who questioned the unity of Priestly sources in Genesis and who joined with Rudolph in an examination of that book in order to determine the nature of the documentary substructure. They rejected the four-document hypothesis in favor of giving priority to the Jehovistic narrator, and on the basis of independent study they concluded that he had compiled his collection of ancient Hebrew traditions against a background of deep religious insight at some

[25] *A Scientific Investigation of the OT* (1929), rev. E. J. Young (1959).
[26] *Untersuchungen zum Hexateuchproblem, I: Der Priesterkodex in der Genesis,* BZAW, XXXVIII (1924).

410

time in the Solomonic era, welding his sources into one consecutive narrative. As far as Volz and Rudolph were concerned the Elohistic material had never enjoyed an independent existence as a document, and they maintained that those sections of Genesis which were usually assigned to Elohistic sources were either original portions of the Jehovistic narrative or the work of redactors who may have functioned during the time of King Josiah.[27]

This theory failed to gain wide acceptance among scholars. One of the most important reasons for this was that the authors had confined their work to Genesis, with Volz investigating chapters 15–36 and Rudolph studying the Joseph narratives. Feeling that the phenomena of Genesis alone were inadequate as a foundation for a theory involving the reconstruction of the Pentateuch as a whole, Rudolph subsequently extended the theory which he and Volz had adopted so that it embraced the remainder of the Hexateuch.[28] Unfortunately his analysis of the situation was gravely weakened by the fact that he almost completely neglected the corpus of legal material in the Pentateuch in favor of dealing with the narrative sections of the Hexateuch. In his work he again gave prominence to the Jehovistic narrator, and ascribed to his activity those passages and narratives which other scholars had attributed to Elohistic sources. Unlike Volz, however, he did not deny the existence of the Priestly Code, nor did he reject the basic premises of the Graf-Wellhausen analytical scheme.

A further important assault upon the unity of the proposed Genesis Priestly material resulted from the incisive observations of von Rad in 1934.[29] This eminent scholar sought to demonstrate that the P document actually consisted of two independent, although parallel, sources standing in juxtaposition. In his subsequent work, *Das formgeschichtliche Problem des Hexateuchs* (1938), he attempted to show the manner in which the Jehovistic author had unified the previously existing Hebrew literary sources and had given them the perspective of the traditions associated with the Exodus and Sinai on the one hand, and with the narratives of the patriarchal period on the other. The Jehovistic author, according to von Rad, augmented and organized this material in such a manner that the outworking of the divine purpose in history was clearly evident. Von Rad was careful to stress that, in his view, this concept was a marked feature of Israelite corporate existence from its earliest stages, and not a comparatively late development for which post-exilic priestly circles were responsible.

[27] Volz and Rudolph, *Der Elohist als Erzähler, ein Irrweg der Pentateuchkritik?*, BZAW, LXIII (1933), pp. 13ff. For a criticism of their views see *UP*, pp. 23f., and the review by R. E. Wolfe, *JBL*, LX (1941), pp. 417ff.

[28] W. Rudolph, *Der "Elohist" von Exodus bis Josua*, BZAW, LXVIII (1938).

[29] *Die Priesterschrift im Hexateuch* (1934).

D. THE PLACE OF DEUTERONOMY

Perhaps the most damaging assault of all on the Graf-Wellhausen hypothesis was the criticism levelled against the place accorded to Deuteronomy in the evolutionary scheme. For several decades scholars had become accustomed to think in terms of the religious reformation of King Josiah, about 630 B.C., and to insist that the basis of the revival was the centralization of worship in Jerusalem. On such a premise scholars had ventured to attempt something approaching an absolute dating of the various elements making up the Pentateuch,[30] but the hazards attached to this procedure became evident through the work of J. B. Griffiths.[31] A former adherent of the Graf-Wellhausen position, he argued from archaeological and philological considerations that Deuteronomy could not possibly have originated in the days of Josiah. To substantiate this contention he pointed out that scarcely more than three of the twenty-five laws that critical scholars regarded as being peculiar to the Deuteronomic legislation could have had any real significance for the circumstances obtaining in the days of Josiah, and even these three could have originated at an earlier period of Israelite history.

In 1919 Kegel examined the implications of the reformation under Josiah in a work that repudiated the theory that the "Book of the Law" was a recent composition that was being foisted upon the people of Judah by priestly interests, and argued convincingly for its antiquity and the general correctness of the historical narrative describing the event.[32] He also took issue with the critical contention that the purpose of the reformation was to restrict sacrificial worship to the central shrine in Jerusalem, and maintained instead that its primary aim was to remove alien religious practices from the cult itself, with other considerations assuming a secondary place. He insisted further that the newly discovered book must have consisted of the entire Torah rather than the book of Deuteronomy alone, positing an early date for the Law in its complete written form. That the document provoking the reforms of Josiah was in fact the whole Torah seems unlikely, however, as Gordon has indicated,[33] and in all probability comprised only one comparatively small portion of the Law.

In 1920, Kennett assigned a later dating to Deuteronomy than was commonly accepted by liberal scholars of the period, regarding it as a distinct product of the exilic age.[34] According to this view it was compiled by priestly circles in Palestine, and reflected Levitical interests predominantly. However, Kennett failed to account satisfactorily for the

---

[30] E.g. *IBOT*, pp. 57ff.
[31] *The Problem of Deuteronomy* (1911).
[32] *Die Kultus-Reformation des Josia* (1919).
[33] *IOTT*, p. 238.
[34] *Deuteronomy and the Decalogue* (1920); cf. his *OT Essays* (1928).

presence of such influential priestly groups in the ravaged land of Judah during the exilic period, and this unfortunate deficiency must be regarded as a serious flaw in his arguments. Despite this obvious weakness his theory attracted the attention of Hölscher, who in 1922 affirmed his belief that the Deuteronomic legislation could not possibly have originated until after the return from exile, thereby assigning Deuteronomy to a rather later period than Kennett had done.[35]

Hölscher questioned the common identification of the Priestly writings with the law code of Ezra, and completely opposed the views of the Graf-Wellhausen school by regarding Deuteronomy as fundamentally priestly rather than prophetic in character. He urged that the provisions of Deuteronomy were completely unsuited to a theory that placed their origin in the days of Josiah, and concluded that the idealistic nature of the legislation pointed to a time when the Judaean kingdom no longer existed and the people were in subservience to foreign domination. The vigor with which Hölscher proclaimed his convictions was not meant to be anti-critical in intention, but rather to serve as an improvement upon the speculations of the Graf-Wellhausen school. This laudable objective had a somewhat different effect, however, since any attempt to enhance a situation which had already reached the peak of its development was bound to constitute a criticism of it in one manner or another.

An opposite tendency regarding the dating of Deuteronomy became apparent the following year, when Oestreicher denied any connection between Deuteronomy and the reformation of Josiah.[36] He followed Kegel in the assumption that the purpose of the religious revival was the purification of the cultus rather than its centralization at any one shrine, and he emphasized that the reforming activities of Josiah applied to all the shrines in the kingdom of Judah. The result of his speculations was that he dated Deuteronomy well in advance of the age of Josiah. Such an attempt to overthrow the Wellhausenian position by striking what has been spoken of as its "Achilles heel" received powerful support from Staerk. The latter had already subjected Deuteronomy to a more minute analysis than had been customary among the adherents of the Graf-Wellhausen methodology, and had discovered traces of older legislation along with clear indications of editorial activity in successive periods.[37] In 1924 he openly disavowed any connection between Deuteronomy and the legal enactments that promoted the centralization of worship associated with the reforms of Josiah.[38] Like Oestreicher he assigned

---

[35] *Geschichte der israelitischen und jüdischen Religion* (1922), pp. 130ff., also, ZAW, XL (1922), pp. 161ff.

[36] *Das Deuteronomische Grundgesetz* (1923).

[37] *Das Deuteronomium: sein Inhalt und sein literarische Form* (1894). Similar conclusions were reached by J. Hempel, *Die Schichten des Deuteronomiums* (1914).

[38] Staerk, *Das Problem des Deuteronomiums* (1924).

Deuteronomy to a period long prior to the age of Josiah, and in this he was followed by Adam Welch, who advanced cogent arguments for a comparatively early date for the book of Deuteronomy, assigning it to the period of Samuel.[39]

Welch maintained that Deuteronomy consisted of many ancient legal principles which had circulated in the northern kingdom, and had originated as a result of prophetic censures of Baal worship. He insisted that the main point at issue in the book was not the conflict between one shrine and many shrines, but between the depraved Baal religion and the ancestral faith of the Israelites. The Mosaic authorship of Deuteronomy was again urged by Möller, who attempted to demonstrate the way in which Deuteronomy contained allusions to and implied the existence of the remainder of the Pentateuch.[40]

An important contribution to the study of the Deuteronomic problem was made by Edward Robertson, who in a series of studies undertaken between 1936 and 1949[41] maintained that Deuteronomy had been compiled by Samuel from the religious traditions associated with the local shrines prior to the Kingdom period. He emphasized the importance of the Samaritan sources for an understanding of the religious situation existing in Canaan before the time of King David,[42] and in this he was followed by Brinker,[43] who held that Samuel compiled Deuteronomy for the twelve tribes, as contrasted with the Priestly material of the Pentateuch, which he deemed to have originated in religious circles at Gibeon. The essential Mosaicity of Deuteronomy was also supported by an eminent Jewish scholar, J. H. Hertz, who reflected the traditions of Hoffmann[44] and Jacob[45] in his conservative commentary on the Pentateuch,[46] which gained wide scholarly acclaim.

G. von Rad also allied with those who repudiated the idea that Deuteronomy furnished the moral and legal impetus for the reforms of Josiah in a work published in 1947.[47] Using the principles of form-

---

[39] *The Code of Deuteronomy: A New Theory of Its Origin* (1924); see also his *Deuteronomy: The Framework to the Code* (1932) and in ZAW, XLIII (1925), pp. 250ff.

[40] W. Möller, *Rückbeziehungen des 5. Buches Mosis auf die vier ersten Bücher* (1925).

[41] *BJRL*, XX (1936), pp. 134ff., XXV (1941), pp. 182ff., XXVI (1942), pp. 369ff., XXVII (1943), pp. 359ff., XXX (1946), pp. 91ff., XXXIII (1949), pp. 19ff. These were subsequently published under the title *The OT Problem with Two Other Essays* (1950).

[42] *The OT Problem*, pp. 163ff.

[43] *The Influence of Sanctuaries in Early Israel* (1946).

[44] *Die wichtigsten Instanzen gegen die Graf-Wellhausensche Hypothese* (1916).

[45] *Quellenscheidung und Exegese im Pentateuch* (1916).

[46] J. H. Hertz, *The Pentateuch and Haftorahs* (5 vols., 1936; one-volume edition, 1937).

[47] *Deuteronomium Studien* (1947), E. tr., *Studies in Deuteronomy* (1953).

criticism with which he had previously investigated the composition of the Hexateuch, he emphasized that the tradition associated with the giving of the Law on Mount Sinai had been fostered at the religious center of Shechem.[48] It was against this kind of background that Deuteronomy was composed by a group of priests who were anxious to restore and maintain the traditions associated with the cultic center of the Israelite amphictyony.

Despite the diverse nature of the attacks made upon the Graf-Wellhausen theory and the manner in which they were presented,[49] the majority of liberal scholars remained unshaken in their adherence to the principles espoused by the literary-critical school.[50] In his presidential address to the Society for Old Testament Study[51] in 1924, A. S. Peake expressed himself as convinced that the main lines of the critical hypothesis were unassailable.[52] Recognizing that there were still scholars who were discovering new "documents" or sub-documents in various parts of the Pentateuch,[53] and the historical writings,[54] Peake was confident of the essential reasonableness of the moderate critical position.

E. THE LITURGICAL TRADITION—MOWINCKEL AND HIS FOLLOWERS

Peake apparently did not fully appreciate the significance of the researches being undertaken by those scholars who were following the methods laid down by Gunkel[55] and Gressmann in an attempt to trace the development of the units of tradition in a wider area than that of the Pentateuchal writings as such, and to reconstruct the original form of that tradition insofar as it was possible. Prominent in the search for cultic connections in relationship to Hebrew poetry was Sigmund Mowinckel, a brilliant Old Testament scholar, who in a series of studies on the Psalms[56] analyzed and discussed the various literary types before

[48] *Das formgeschichtliche Problem des Hexateuchs* (1938).

[49] Cf. J. E. McFadyen in *The People and the Book* (ed. A. S. Peake, 1925), pp. 183, 218f.

[50] E.g. D. C. Simpson, *Pentateuchal Criticism* (1914), rev. ed., 1924; G. B. Gray, *A Critical Introduction to the OT* (1913).

[51] For a survey of the history of this group see H. W. Robinson (ed.), *Record and Revelation* (1938), pp. 499ff.; G. H. Davies, *The Society for OT Study: A Short History, 1917-1950* (n.d.).

[52] *BJRL*, XII (1928), pp. 72f.

[53] E.g. J. Morgenstern, *HUCA*, IV (1926-1927), pp. 1ff.; R. H. Pfeiffer, *ZAW*, XLVIII (1930), pp. 66ff.; *PIOT*, pp. 159ff.

[54] O. Eissfeldt, *Die Quellen des Richterbuches* (1925); *Die Komposition der Samuelisbücher* (1931); cf. his *Einleitung in das AT* (1934), p. 306; *ETOT*, pp. 281ff.

[55] *Schöpfung und Chaos in Urzeit und Endzeit* (1895); *Genesis in Handkommentar zum AT* (ed. W. Nowack, 1901).

[56] *Psalmenstudien I-VI* (1921-1924).

attempting to interpret them in terms of pre-exilic sanctuary rituals and the like.

Whereas Gunkel had placed considerable stress upon the individual nature of Hebrew religious compositions, Mowinckel related them more consistently to the operation of social forces. He argued that, in ancient Israel, God was enthroned as universal king in a ritual which formed a prominent part of the autumn New Year festival. For him this was the cultic significance of the "enthronement psalms" or *Thronbesteigungs-lieder* (Pss. 47, 93, 97–99, 106:10ff.) that Gunkel had isolated, for which there was already a well-attested prototype from the Babylonian New Year festival.

Mowinckel assigned a date in the early monarchy for the origin of this festival in Israel,[57] but subsequently withdrew it.[58] He also identified an oracular type of Psalm (e.g. Pss. 60:6ff., 75, 82), which he held to have constituted the divine answers to the intercessions of the worshippers as pronounced by the cult-prophets attached to the various sanctuaries.[59] The weakness of his analysis seems to lie in his assumption that each class of Psalm was used for only one ritual occasion in the cults, an idea that led to the extremely questionable conclusion that every Psalm that spoke of God as creator or king was *ipso facto* to be relegated to the New Year enthronement-festival concept, and not to wider or more general circumstances.[60] His association of the prophets with the cultic shrines, however, was an advance upon earlier views,[61] which had generally stressed the denunciation of cult-worship by the prophets.

There seems little doubt on reflection that Mowinckel had been influenced by the opinions of Hugo Winckler, Alfred Jeremias, and Friedrich Delitzsch in his conjectures about the extent to which Israelite cultic worship reflected the Babylonian New Year festival customs. Winckler had suggested that Hebrew thought generally contained little that could be regarded as unique, and that in fact the Israelites were merely participating in a cultural situation common to all the nations of the ancient Near East.[62] Delitzsch developed the "pan-Babylonian" concepts of Winckler and precipitated a storm of controversy with his suggestion that anything of significance in the Old Testament was based upon earlier Babylonian ideas and practices.[63] Despite the attempts of

[57] *Ibid.*, II (1922), p. 204; cf. H. J. Kraus, *Worship in Israel* (1966), pp. 8f.
[58] ZAW, XLVIII (1930), p. 267.
[59] *Psalmenstudien III* (1923), pp. 20ff.
[60] Cf. Gunkel's criticisms, *Einleitung in die Psalmen* (1928-1933), pp. 100ff.
[61] E.g. J. Skinner, *Prophecy and Religion: Studies in the Life of Jeremiah* (1922), pp. 53ff.
[62] *Der alte Orient* (1901), III, pp. 2f.; *Geschichte Israels* (1900), II.
[63] *Babel und Bibel* (1902); cf. W. L. Wardle, *Israel and Babylon* (1925), pp. 301ff.

Jeremias to sustain the theory,[64] it lost favor when archaeologists and students of comparative religion demonstrated the extent to which Egyptian influence was evident in the life and thought of the ancient Hebrews.[65] With the work of Gunkel a more sober and balanced perspective replaced the sweeping generalizations of Winckler and his followers, and the "pan-Babylonian" movement faded into obscurity.

Following Mowinckel, numerous scholars sought to discover the liturgical usage of ancient traditions in other areas of the Old Testament. Thus P. Humbert postulated the theory that the first chapter of Genesis and Psalm 104 were recited ceremonially at an Israelite New Year festival, in accord with a similar Babylonian custom in which the creation epic was read aloud as part of the festive ritual.[66] In a comparable manner J. Pedersen ignored the classical analysis of the early chapters of Exodus for the purposes of his investigation, and treated that material as a literary unit which he thought was used as a cult-legend in the Passover celebrations.[67] So obsessed did some scholars become with the *Sitz im Leben des Volkes* concept that they even assigned an attested liturgical function to the documentary sources that had resulted from the critical studies of the Wellhausenian school, regardless of the fact that the material thus extracted from the Massoretic text furnished not the slightest hint of such a usage.[68]

A final application of the methodology pioneered by Gunkel was to the Pentateuch itself. The various laws enshrined in the Torah were subjected to attempts at classification by Jepsen[69] and Jirku,[70] who, working independently, followed the same general pattern of separating those laws that had demonstrable affinity with other ancient Near Eastern legislation from those that, because of their unique features, could be regarded as specifically Israelite in origin. This distinction was followed by Albrecht Alt, who in a treatise on the origins of Israelite law described the first of these categories as "casuistic" and the second

[64] *Das AT im Lichte des alten Orients* (1904), E. tr., *The OT in the Light of the Ancient East* (2 vols., 1911); *Handbuch der altorientalischen Geisteskultur* (1913).

[65] E.g. L. W. King, *A History of Babylon* (1915), pp. 291ff.; G. Foucart, *Histoire des religions et méthode comparative* (1912), pp. 305ff.; J. H. Breasted, *A History of Egypt* (1905), pp. 371ff., *The Dawn of Conscience* (1933), pp. 368, 384.

[66] Humbert, *RHPR*, XV (1935), pp. 1ff.

[67] Pedersen, *ZAW*, LII (1934), pp. 161ff.

[68] E.g. E. Sellin, *Einleitung in das AT* (1929 ed.), pp. 60f.; P. Humbert, *RHPR*, XII (1932), pp. 1ff. and *Problèmes du livre d'Habacuc* (1944); A. Haldar, *Studies in the Book of Nahum* (1947); I. Engnell, *BJRL*, XXXI (1948), pp. 54ff. and *The Call of Isaiah: An Exegetical and Comparative Study* (1949); A. Bentzen, *JBL*, LXVII (1948), pp. 37ff.; C. Lindhagen, *The Servant Motif in the OT* (1950); J. Lindblom, *The Servant Songs in Deutero-Isaiah* (1951).

[69] *Untersuchungen zum Bundesbuch* (1927).

[70] *Das weltliche Recht im AT* (1927).

as "apodictic."[71] The casuistic or case-law type is the dominant form of law known from the ancient Near East, as illustrated by the Hittite code, which emanates from the middle of the second millennium B.C. in Asia Minor, the Code of Hammurabi, which dates from seventeenth-century B. C. Babylonia, and some other older legislation from Mesopotamia. Because of its consonance with the Babylonian *Sitz im Leben des Volkes*, the "casuistic" group of Israelite enactments was alleged to be the earlier of the two groups isolated. On the other hand, the apodictic or categorical laws emanated from accredited priestly sources, and in consequence it seemed to Alt that they had originally constituted solemn prescriptions uttered in the course of priestly legislative functioning. Their life-situation was therefore religious, as opposed to the secular court-origin of the casuistic legislation.

Mowinckel had already anticipated the observations of Volz with regard to the Elohistic source. The former thought of the growth of that document in terms of an oral process extending over several centuries in the life of the southern kingdom.[72] As far as the promulgation of legalistic material was concerned, Mowinckel suggested that certain groups of legal-ceremonial prescriptions had been recited as a preliminary to ritual observances at the shrines. Allowing for procedural variations, he held that probably more than one decalogue had been in existence, and that, if this had actually been the case, the content might well have exhibited a certain degree of variation in different parts of the country.[73]

In separating the smaller units of Hebrew law from the Priestly Code, Eissfeldt had concluded that they represented the literary product of earlier legislative activity at the local shrines. He also felt that they reached back even further to the stage when they were transmitted simply in the form of oral tradition.[74] Noth developed this general concept to indicate the manner in which Israelite law was thought to have grown through the legislative activities of the priests at the sanctuaries or at the city gates, and related the entire creative process to the Hebrew cultural situation.[75] In a somewhat similar manner Begrich saw the development of the Torah in terms of a process of oral transmission, during which the legal traditions of the Israelite priests were handed down over a period of many generations and enlarged in matters of

---

[71] *Die Ursprünge des israelitischen Rechts* (1934), pp. 12ff.; cf. W. F. Albright, *JBL*, LV (1936), pp. 164ff.

[72] *ZAW*, XLVIII (1930), pp. 233ff.

[73] Cf. Mowinckel, *Le décalogue* (1927), pp. 154ff., also in *ZAW*, LV (1937), pp. 218ff.

[74] *Einleitung in das AT* (1934 ed.), pp. 26ff.; *ETOT*, pp. 212ff.

[75] *Die Gesetze im Pentateuch* (1940); also Köhler, *ZAW*, XXXIV (1914), p. 146.

detail to suit the needs of a developing social and religious economy.[76]

F. HISTORICAL ANTHROPOLOGY

At the beginning of the twentieth century the researches of Tylor,[77] Robertson Smith, and Frazer were modified by an approach that placed less emphasis upon individual primitive psychology and devoted increasing attention to the place that the forces of society as a whole occupied in the formulation of religious beliefs and customs. Wilhelm Wundt was the first to stress the importance of group-experience as a formative influence in the growth of primitive psychology.[78] His theories were developed by Durkheim[79] and his followers, who associated such concepts as *mana*[80] with the dynamics of group life. Lévy-Bruhl pointed to the essential unity of those forces upon which the individual drew for his magical rites, and which at the same time furnished the basis for collective religious functioning, by showing that, for primitive man, causation resulted from the activity of invisible animistic forces which were deemed to be at work in the natural environment.[81]

Praiseworthy as all these theories were, they suffered from the basic defect of the nineteenth-century *Zeitgeist*, namely the endeavor on the part of scholars to explain the incidence of all phenomena in terms of one relatively uncomplicated single feature, process, or principle. In the biological sphere the concepts of organic evolution as expounded by Darwin and Wallace were held to constitute the key to terrestrial and human origins alike, while in the burgeoning realm of psychological study the dominant principle of human motivation was held by Freud to be intimately related to primitive sexual urges buried deep in the unconscious mind. As far as Old Testament studies were concerned, the one basic principle upon which an understanding of the origins of Israelite literature depended had been expounded at length by Graf and

[76] In *Werden und Wesen des AT* (ed. P. Volz, 1936), pp. 63ff. On oral transmission cf. *FSAC*, pp. 64ff., S. Gandz, *Osiris* (1939), VII, pp. 415ff.

[77] *Researches into the Early History of Mankind and the Development of Civilisation* (1865), *Primitive Culture: Researches into the Development of Mythology, Philosophy, Religion, Language, Art and Custom* (1871), and *Anthropology* (1881).

[78] *Völkerpsychologie* (2 vols, 1900-1909).

[79] *Les formes élémentaires de la vie religieuse* (1912), E. tr. J. W. Swain, *The Elementary Forms of the Religious Life* (1915).

[80] R. H. Codrington, *The Melanesians: Studies in Their Anthropology and Folklore* (1891).

[81] Cf. Lévy-Bruhl, *Les fonctions mentales dans les sociétés inférieures* (1910), E. tr. *How Natives Think* (1926); *L'âme primitive* (1923), E. tr. *The Soul of the Primitive* (1928); *La mentalité primitive* (1922), E. tr. *Primitive Mentality* (1923). In *Les Carnets de Lucien Lévy-Bruhl* (1949), published after his death, Lévy-Bruhl abandoned the principal lines of the argument he had expressed in *Les fonctions mentales dans les sociétés inférieures*.

Wellhausen; in the field of anthropology the unifying factor which was popularly alleged to underlie all primitive religious activity was being interpreted by scholars in terms of concepts such as *mana*, magic, tabu, and the like.

The error of this type of approach became evident—to students of anthropology at least—when it was discovered that, as research progressed, it was increasingly impossible to relate the phenomena of primitive life to one comprehensive principle of interpretation. An attempt to remedy the deficiencies of theoretical anthropology was made by Franz Boas,[82] who rejected the idea of primitive culture as a general condition characteristic of all mankind in favor of an approach which studied patterns of culture in specific geographic areas and related them to corresponding cultural phenomena in neighboring localities.

The application of historical method in anthropology to the problems of early Semitic religion was undertaken by S. A. Cook in a series of studies prefacing the third edition of *Lectures on the Religion of the Semites,* by Robertson Smith. Recognizing the close interrelationship that Smith had pointed out between secular and sacred in primitive life, Cook saw that such situations were typified by a remarkable degree of complexity. For him, therefore, the problem did not consist so much of postulating some sort of evolutionary process from comparatively simple to more highly differentiated forms as of making some attempt to assess the significance of individual cultural patterns as they were related to the larger environment of society.[83]

A development of this concept occurred in the work of the so-called "myth and ritual" school under the leadership of the British scholar S. H. Hooke, who has been called the "high priest" of cultic patternism. Basing their conclusions on the theory that there had been a diffusion of one cultural pattern of ritual mythology throughout the religions of the ancient Near East, Hooke and his followers applied the form-critical techniques employed by Mowinckel in an attempt to show that a recognizable set of rituals and myths had been the common property of the various ancient Near Eastern cultures.[84] Although these scholars did not go to the extremes of the "pan-Babylonian" school, they stressed that all mythical conceptions had their origin in cultic rites, and that Hebrew myths and rituals, particularly those connected with sacral kingship and

---

[82] *The Mind of Primitive Man* (1911), *Anthropology and Modern Life* (1932), and in *American Anthropologist,* XXII (1920), pp. 311ff.; cf. A. Goldenweiser, *Early Civilisation* (1922).

[83] Cf. S. A. Cook (ed.), *Lectures on the Religion of the Semites* (1927 ed.), pp. xlvi, 590ff.; his articles in *Cambridge Ancient History* (1923), I, pp. 182ff., and in *The People and the Book* (ed. A. S. Peake, 1925), pp. 42ff.

[84] Hooke (ed.), *Myth and Ritual: Essays on the Myth and Ritual of the Hebrews in Relation to the Cultic Pattern of the Ancient East* (1933), *The Labyrinth: Further Studies in the Relation Between Myth and Ritual in the Ancient World* (1935).

the so-called "enthronement festival," were intimately connected with similar concepts in the thought of other Near Eastern peoples, particularly those of Babylonia.

Hooke endeavored to establish a parallel between the Hebrew pre-exilic Feast of Asiph, or Ingathering, and the Babylonian *akitu* or New Year festival.[85] The latter consisted of a dramatic re-enactment of the role which the king played in community life as the "divine figure," and the ritual patterns involved a representation of the death and resurrection of the god, the deification of the king, the recitation of the creation myth,[86] a ritual battle between the deity and his enemies in which the god emerged victorious, a sacred marriage, a triumphal procession in which the king acted as a substitute for the personage of the deity, and an emphasis upon the importance of the royal personage for communal well-being.[87]

There is evidence for the belief that Babylonian myths were used in conjunction with accredited Mesopotamian rituals of a religious nature, as King showed,[88] but there is almost no ground at all for attempting to discern elements of the Babylonian *akitu* rituals either in the pre-exilic Feast of Ingathering or in its post-exilic counterpart, the three festivals of Tishri, as Snaith has remarked.[89] Thus, in the end the findings of Hooke are just as subjective and just as inadequately grounded as those of Mowinckel.

However, the hypothesis that a pattern of myth and ritual was associated with regnal functions was explored by several other scholars. Following Mowinckel, the general position of the king in relation to the New Year rituals in Jerusalem was examined by Morgenstern,[90] who concluded that the king served as chief priest of the nation. This process was taken a step further by A. R. Johnson,[91] who claimed that there were distinct points of contact between the Israelite New Year festival and the Babylonian *akitu* ceremonies, particularly with regard to the person and function of the king in Israel, whom he alleged to have been regarded as the responsible agent for communal prosperity and the symbol of national virility for the ensuing year. Again, this theory was

[85] For a description of this ceremony see S. A. Pallis, *The Babylonian Akitu Festival* (1926), pp. 250ff.; cf. H. Zimmern, *Das Babylonische Neujahrsfest* (1926).

[86] Cf. Hooke, *The Origins of Early Semitic Ritual* (1938), pp. 16ff.

[87] Cf. Hooke in *Journal of the Manchester Egyptian and Oriental Society*, XIII (1927), pp. 29ff.

[88] *The Legends of Babylon and Egypt in Relation to Hebrew Tradition* (1918), pp. 50f.

[89] In H. W. Robinson (ed.), *Record and Revelation*, p. 260.

[90] In *AJSL*, LV (1938), pp. 1ff., 183ff., 360ff.

[91] A. R. Johnson in *The Labyrinth* (ed. S. H. Hooke), pp. 71ff.; cf. Johnson's article in *ET*, LXII (1950-1951), pp. 36ff.

ased upon pure conjecture, and could not be substantiated at any point
y concrete evidence from the Old Testament.

Hooke subsequently modified his views on cultic patternism in a series
f essays published in 1956, in which he conceded a certain nucleus of
w and custom as uniquely Mosaic, while at the same time viewing the
ulk of Israelite worship and cultic forms in the light of Egyptian and
abylonian ritual and liturgical patterns.[92] In the meantime Cook had
ut the comparative method of anthropological study to better use by
ndeavoring to show that, though many concepts in the Old Testament
arratives could be paralleled by similar ideas in other ancient Near
astern religions, they may well have undergone a process of trans-
ormation and change during the early period of Hebrew history to the
oint where, in their final form, they had acquired a uniquely Israelite
haracter.[93]

A further attempt by Mowinckel to throw light upon the religious
evelopment of ancient Israel utilized the approach of earlier anthropol-
gists in speculating upon the place of magic in religious activity. He
rgued for the influence of pagan magical concepts in Hebrew cultic life
y interpreting the term "evil" in certain psalms of petition as a refer-
nce to the practice of magic. Similarly he held that the rituals of
lessing and cursing found in the Psalter and elsewhere presupposed the
ctivity of magical practitioners. However, as Gunkel pointed out,[94]
Mowinckel was wrong in assuming that magical rites and customs had
urvived for a longer period than that generally indicated by the histori-
al records of the Hebrew people. Hempel[95] adhered to the view that
lthough some of the formulas of malediction and benediction may have
een motivated by considerations of magic in the distant past, their
resence in the religious activities of the Hebrew monarchy suggested
hat they had become orthodox in nature, and that their religious con-
ent was genuine.

G. OLD TESTAMENT SOCIOLOGY

Whereas the comparative study of Near Eastern religions and the
growth of form criticism had been largely concerned with the cultural
oots of characteristic Hebrew religious concepts and with attempts to
elate particular cultic manifestations to the life-situations of social
groups, there was no branch of study readily established which would
onsider the sociological background of Hebrew culture as a uniquely
eligious manifestation. Although one or two authors had written on the

---

[92] Hooke, *The Siege Perilous: Essays in Biblical Anthropology and Kindred
ubjects* (1956), pp. 173ff.
[93] Cook, *The OT: A Reinterpretation* (1936), pp. 88ff.
[94] *Einleitung in die Psalmen* (1928), pp. 196ff.
[95] In *ZDMG*, LXXIX (1925), pp. 20ff.

general subject of social customs among the ancient Israelites,[96] littl
attempt had been made to relate questions of social organization to th
growth of Hebrew religion. The first serious efforts expended in thi
direction were the sociological studies of Max Weber,[97] who employe
the results of the Graf-Wellhausen school to interpret the economi
situation obtaining at an early period of Hebrew history. Weber stresse
the significance of the Covenant as an important agent for insurin
political and social solidarity in the pre-monarchical period and was th
first scholar to speak of the leadership which obtained during the Judge
era as "charismatic" in nature.[98] He also held to the view that the grea
majority of the prophetic protests about social conditions were the resul
of popular accommodation to the existing social, rather than religious
configurations of the native Canaanites.[99] In general he sought to shov
that new perspectives on Hebrew history could be obtained by envisag
ing the development of national life against a background of tension
furnished by the interaction of urban Canaanite organization within th
radically different sociological pattern of family and tribe exhibited b
the Israelites.

This theme was expounded by Adolphe Lods,[100] and to a lesse
extent also by Causse,[101] both of whom emphasized the part that th
prophets played in an attempt to restore the "nomadic ideal" in prefer
ence to the urban civilization of Canaan. But they also made it clear tha
the prophets were more than potential social reformers; they proclaime
high standards of personal morality and made the ethical concept o
righteousness a consideration of paramount importance. Although thi
exposition of the religio-historical situation suffers from the assumption o
the Graf-Wellhausen school that the prophets—particularly those of th
eighth century B.C.—were the first to formulate a doctrine of ethica
monotheism, its general approach was of great value in that it drev
attention to the importance of yet another aspect of the *Sitz im Leber
des Volkes.*

[96] E.g. J. Fenton, *Early Hebrew Life: A Study in Sociology* (1880) and P. J
Baldensperger, *The Immovable East. Studies of the People and Customs of Palestin*
(1913).

[97] Especially his *Gesammelte Aufsätze zur Religionssoziologie* (3 vols., 1920-1921)
E. tr. T. Parsons, *The Protestant Ethic and the Spirit of Capitalism* (1936).

[98] Cf. Weber, *Grundriss der Sozialökonomik* (1922), III, pp. 140ff. He wa
followed in this by A. Alt, *Die Staatenbildung der Israeliten in Palästina* (1930)
pp. 7ff., 16ff.

[99] Weber, *Gesammelte Aufsätze*, III, pp. 120ff., 290ff.

[100] *Israël des origines au milieu du VIIIe siècle* (1930), E. tr. S. H. Hooke, *Israe
from its Beginnings to the Middle of the Eighth Century* (1932); *Les prophète
d'Israël et les débuts du judaisme* (1935), E. tr. Hooke, *The Prophets of Israe*
(1937).

[101] *Du groupe ethnique à la communauté religieuse* (1937).

The most prominent scholar in the United States to give consideration to questions of Old Testament sociology was Louis Wallis, an erudite thinker who owed much of his inspiration to the work of Weber. Over a period of thirty years he published several works dealing with the process by which Hebrew religion was thought to have originated and developed.[102] Like others of his generation Wallis tended to look for a single interpretative principle that could be applied readily to the phenomena of the historical situation in order to resolve them into some sort of consistent pattern. In consequence he inclined to the view that the kind of ethical monotheism that the eighth- and seventh-century B.C. prophets proclaimed was the result of the clash between the economic ideals of settled Canaanite society and the more austere morality of the Hebrew Wilderness code.

In adopting this position Wallis overlooked the fact that Israel's violation of the fundamental provisions of the Sinai Covenant was the real issue at stake in the minds of the prophets, and that questions dealing with social inequality and injustice were merely secondary manifestations of the larger issue. Like others of his day, Wallis erred in failing to take account of the growing body of extra-Biblical evidence, which in his case threw direct light upon the religious and social forms of ancient Canaan.[103] His position with regard to the nature of the local Baals was essentially that of the Wellhausen school, a position that has had to be revised drastically as a result of the archaeological discoveries at Ras Shamra (Ugarit).[104] Perhaps the greatest deficiency in the approach adopted by Wallis was that its author, like so many of his contemporaries, failed to accommodate his own speculations to the evidence furnished by the discoveries of archaeologists.

This deficiency was remedied to a considerable extent by the researches of Graham,[105] although he too was hampered by an uncritical acceptance of the theory that monotheism was the end-result of a slow process of growth from rudimentary theological principles. He rejected Wallis' suggestion that monotheism had emerged from something like a "class struggle" between the sedentary Canaanites and the semi-nomadic Israelites, preferring to consider instead the possibility of a genetic relationship between the Hebrew faith and the Ras Shamra cultus. He thought of the work of the prophets as a regenerating activity, bringing new life to the cultural and religious patterns of Palestine, which had begun to disintegrate somewhat prior to the founding of the monarchy. The new social ideal of such prophetic functioning primarily stressed personal

[102] A Sociological Study of the Bible (1912), God and the Social Process (1935), The Bible Is Human (1942).
[103] Cf. H. G. May in Journal of Bible and Religion, XII (1944), pp. 98ff.
[104] Cf. W. F. Albright in Religion in Life, XXI, No. 4 (1952), pp. 544f.
[105] In Journal of Religion, XIV (1934), pp. 306ff., also his The Prophets and Israel's Culture (1934).

values, according to Graham, and demanded an opportunity for the development of the individual human spirit.[106] As a sociological appraisal of the contribution of the prophets to their own life and times, his researches exhibited remarkable deficiencies, the chief of which was his inability to recognize that the prophets of Israel were not so much social reformers as evangelists, calling men to a new way of life based upon repentance and faith rather than on the amelioration of social evils.

A more successful interpretation of the prophetic situation was furnished by S. W. Baron, who stressed the essentially "chosen" nature of the Israelites as an important element in the unfolding of the divine plan for human history.[107] The destiny of the Hebrew people was to be a "light to the nations," and this was firmly grounded upon an historical monotheism whose original formulation constituted part of the work of Moses. The prophets uttered their oracles in order to call the people back to an observance of their commitments under the Covenant relationship. In process of this they elaborated upon the monotheistic theme found in the Torah. Prominent in their teaching was the assertion that, if the ethical ideals of Sinai were taken to heart, the issues of social justice, which were intimately bound up with the concept of the Covenant, would manifest themselves in the normal behavior of the people.

From a different sociological standpoint the present writer attempted an inquiry as to the extent to which, if at all, the influence of the ancient Egyptian matriarchate could be traced in the social configurations of the early monarchy.[108] The *Sitz im Leben des Volkes* approach virtually demanded an explanation different from those normally tendered for certain facets of the relationships existing between David and Saul, and for such events as the violation of Tamar by her half-brother Amnon (2 Sam. 13:2ff.). Accordingly it was felt that the best way of accounting for these and other apparently peculiar forms of social behavior was to postulate the influence in southern Palestine of a traditional Egyptian sociological phenomenon in which all real property and inheritance generally descended through the female of the line rather than through the male.[109]

Definite traces of matriarchal patterns appear during the period of the early monarchy, but a fuller demonstration is hampered by lack of

[106] Graham, *The Prophets and Israel's Culture*, pp. 86ff.

[107] *A Social and Religious History of the Jews* (3 vols., 1937; rev. ed., 2 vols., 1952).

[108] R. K. Harrison, *EQ*, XXIX (1957), pp. 29ff. and *A History of OT Times* (1957), pp. 143f., 150ff.

[109] For the concept of *Mutterrecht* in Egypt see A. Erman and H. Ranke, *Ägypten und Ägyptisches Leben im Altertums* (1923), pp. 175ff.; J. Černý and T. E. Peet, *JEA*, XIII (1927), pp. 30ff.; J. Černý, *Bulletin de l'Institut Français d'Archéologie Orientale*, XXXVII (1937-1938), pp. 41ff.; A. Gardiner, *JEA*, XXVI (1940), pp. 23ff.; J. Černý, *JEA*, XL (1954), pp. 23ff.

evidence in certain important areas. Thus it is impossible to be sure that the person named Ahinoam, who was married to David (1 Sam. 25:43), was identical with Ahinoam daughter of Ahimaaz and wife of Saul, which is important for the theory of matriarchal descent and the consequent inheritance by David of the Israelite throne. Again, there is some doubt as to the identity of Maachah, daughter of Absalom, who in 2 Samuel 14:27 is called Tamar and in 2 Chronicles 11:21 was known as Maachah, the favored spouse of Rehoboam.[110] However, if the ancient Egyptian matriarchate did in fact exert some influence in Canaan during the immediate premonarchic period, its recognition would help to clarify some of the issues involved in regal succession during the early monarchy.

The social organization of the early settlement period was examined in the light of form-critical procedures by Albrecht Alt and Martin Noth in studies that have exerted considerable influence in the world of Old Testament scholarship. The wide difference in political structure and social configuration between the Palestinian peoples and those of Transjordan in the eleventh century B.C. was pointed out by Alt,[111] who contrasted the various social forms with what he called the "charismatic" leadership in Israel during the period of the Judges,[112] which for him constituted the basic political organizational form among the early Israelites. Alt also held that the apodictic legislation of the Torah, with its reflection of a monotheism characterized by an advanced ethical content, was specifically Israelite in nature, and maintained that much of it could be assigned with confidence to Moses. He further stated that the sociological phenomenon of the "Judges" was in all probability the channel through which such casuistic legal material as that found in the Book of the Covenant (Exod. 21–23) penetrated to Israel.[113] Alt appears to have followed Max Weber in regarding the leadership which obtained during the era of the Judges as "charismatic." In this and other areas he was evidently attempting to relate Israelite institutions to the traditions of the Heroic Age, but he missed the essential point, common to the Mycenaean age and the Judges period, that the Judges were not inspired leaders produced from the proletariat by some kind of divine afflatus, but were in fact accredited members of the aristocracy, from whom leadership invariably came.[114]

Alt and his followers also stressed the comparatively uncomplicated social and political status of early Israel in their studies relating to the organizational system of the tribes. They pointed out that the nation con-

---

110 Cf. 1 Kgs. 15:10; *AJ*, VII, 8, 5; VII, 10, 3.
111 *Die Staatenbildung der Israeliten in Palästina,* pp. 31ff.
112 *Ibid.*, pp. 16ff.
113 Alt, *Die Ursprunge des israelitischen Rechts* (1934), pp. 31ff.
114 Cf. *GBB*, pp. 295ff., also Gordon in *Biblical and Other Studies* (ed. A. Altmann, 1963), p. 12.

sisted of several tribes or "clan-groups," traditionally twelve in numbe
which were bound together by the religious provisions of the Covena
relationship and were associated with a central sanctuary at Shiloh. A
thought of this tribal organization in terms of an amphictyony, followir
the social structures of certain Aegean people; and Noth elaborate
upon this general theme.

Making the Covenant ideal the basis for this kind of social formulatic
in Israel, Noth argued from what he regarded as the original form of th
sources to the conclusion that the tradition of the "twelve" tribes ha
begun in the period of charismatic rule,[115] and that it constituted a
enumeration of an early Hebrew amphictyonic association.[116] In th
area of investigation Noth supported the general historical process ente
tained by Caspari,[117] who had maintained that the Covenant conce
took its rise from a religious league that was in existence prior to th
settlement of Israel in Canaan, while at the same time he made
fundamental to the organization of the amphictyony.[118] These conclu
sions are open to serious criticism on historical and other grounds, an
fail to take sufficient cognizance of the great antiquity of the covenan
form in the Near East. Despite this, however, the work of Alt and Not
proved to be of value in bringing some semblance of order to bear upo
the decidedly confused picture that had emerged of the Judges perio
as the result of critical studies. For liberal scholars in particular th
studies of Alt and Noth succeeded in showing the manner in whic
form criticism had availed to throw light upon the origin and meanin
of important areas in the historical tradition of the Hebrew people, whic
had previously been rejected by advocates of the Graf-Wellhausen hy
pothesis as unhistorical and untrustworthy as sources for purposes c
reconstructing historical sequences.[119]

H. OLD TESTAMENT ARCHAEOLOGY

The discovery of numerous literary artifacts in Mesopotamia, Pale
tine, Egypt, and elsewhere in the Near East during the middle and latte
portion of the nineteenth century had demonstrated beyond question th
immense antiquity of writing, and had also furnished material whic
supplemented and corroborated the historical data of the Old Testamer

---

[115] For the dating of the city-lists in Joshua 15 to the period of Josiah see Al
Kleine Schriften zur Geschichte des Volkes Israel (1953), II, pp. 276ff.

[116] Noth, *Das System der zwölf Stämme Israels* (1930), pp. 39ff.

[117] *Die Gottesgemeinde von Sinai und das nachmalige Volk Israel* (1922), p
15ff., 137f.

[118] Cf. M. Noth, *Zeitschrift für die Deutschen Palästina-Vereins*, LVIII (1935
pp. 185ff.

[119] For a critical evaluation of the school of Alt and Noth see J. Bright, *Earl
Israel in Recent History Writing* (1956), pp. 79ff. For a criticism of the conclusior
regarding the border-lists of the tribes see S. Mowinckel, *Zur Frage nach dokumer
tarischen Quellen in Josua 13-19* (1946).

in certain significant areas. Some of the material made reference to events that were not recorded in the Massoretic text, such as the fact that Ahab was an important military leader in the battle of Qarqar (853 B.C.), and that Jehu had paid tribute to Shalmaneser III rather than oppose him. The dramatic discoveries of Layard at Nineveh[120] had excited wide interest in the nature of Mesopotamian antiquities, and this was sustained by the researches of Sir Henry Rawlinson and J. E. Taylor, who visited Ur and other Babylonian sites from 1849 on.

A decade earlier Rawlinson had translated some two hundred lines of the bilingual inscription of Darius the Great at Behistun, which he had copied at considerable risk to his life when he served as British Representative at Baghdad. When the syllabic nature of cuneiform was recognized by Edward Hincks in 1847, it was merely a question of time before the true values of a great many combinations of wedges were known. The translation of cuneiform took a dramatic step forward with the work of George Smith, an engraver employed by the British Museum, who in the course of his duties recognized and deciphered the celebrated Babylonian Deluge tablets, publishing his results in 1872. From that time on the study of cuneiform was assigned a degree of importance only accorded previously to the language of ancient Egypt, and it remained for the philologists to exploit the situation as fully as possible.

Despite the establishment of the Palestine Exploration Fund in 1865, and the spectacular discovery by Clermont-Ganneau of the famous Moabite Stone,[121] the unearthing of significant archaeological material from Palestinian sources lagged far behind similar activity in other areas of the Near East. A discouragement to Biblical scholars was the fact that the Graf-Wellhausen school mostly ignored the possible effect which extra-Biblical sources might have as a control over the more extravagant use of purely theoretical speculations, an attitude that was still maintained when Winckler[122] so dramatically disproved the contentions of liberal scholars concerning the place which the Hittites occupied in ancient Near Eastern history.[123] What was perhaps even more calamitous was the tendency of European scholars generally to describe such archaeological artifacts from Palestine of which they took cognizance as though they were merely "antiquities."[124]

---

[120] *Nineveh and Its Remains* (2 vols., 1849).

[121] C. S. Clermont-Ganneau, *La Stèle de Mésa* (1887).

[122] *Sonderabzug aus der Orientalistischen Litteratur Zeitung*, Dec. 15, 1906; *Mitteilungen der Deutschen Orientgesellschaft*, XXXV (1907), pp. 1ff.; Winckler and Puchstein, *Smithsonian Report for 1908*, pp. 677ff.

[123] It was left for S. R. Driver (*Modern Research as Illustrating the Bible* [1909]) to correct this tendency.

[124] E.g. W. Nowack, *Lehrbuch der hebräischen Archäologie* (2 vols., 1894); I. Benzinger, *Hebräische Archäologie* (1894; rev. ed., 1927).

Palestinian archaeology as such finally came into its own after World War I with the carefully disciplined pragmatic approach of the American excavators. Chief among these towered the figure of W. F. Albright the foremost Biblical archaeologist of the century, a man who combined prodigious mental capacities with unusual linguistic talents, reputedly being familiar with over twenty-five languages and dialects. As one of his students, John Bright, has remarked, Albright's innumerable contributions to linguistic science, Biblical archaeology, and the entire field of ancient oriental history have enabled him to exercise an influence over Old Testament studies in particular of a more abiding nature than that of probably any other single scholar in the twentieth century.[125]

Albright first went to Palestine in 1919 as a Fellow of the American Schools of Oriental Research. He quickly surpassed his teachers, who included W. J. Phythian-Adams, H. Vincent, and C. S. Fisher. With his emphasis upon careful ceramic study he ushered in a new era of archaeological activity in Palestine, and it was as a result of his unremitting labors that Palestinian archaeology finally attained its majority between 1920 and 1940.[126] In particular, the general pattern of life in the Middle Bronze Age is now well attested, due in no small measure to the efforts of Albright, as is also the broad outline of Biblical chronology. Since Albright is, as one of his pupils has described him, conservative but critically informed,[127] he was able to attract the more conservative students as well as those who, although liberal by training, were aware of the inadequacies of the Graf-Wellhausen categories of method and interpretation, and who wished to pursue a more independent approach to the problems of the Old Testament text. A major effect of the work of Albright has been that all books written before 1940 about the themes of Old Testament history and archaeology must be regarded as obsolete.

Shortly after World War I Kittel[128] and Gressmann[129] suggested that the future course of Old Testament studies would be marked by an increasing use of new material, including the utilizing of archaeology as a method of external control, as well as a study of ancient Near Eastern culture as a whole with a view to determining the true theological outlook of the Old Testament writers. These predictions were borne out to a very large extent by subsequent events, due again in no small measure to the work of Albright and his pupils. Archaeological activity has now furnished a vast amount of material which enables a reasonably precise picture of life in the lands of the Bible to be drawn as far back as

[125] *BANE*, p. 13. A biographical sketch appears in *History, Archaeology and Christian Humanism* (1964), pp. 301ff. A bibliography of Albright's works from 1911 through May 1958 is assembled as Appendix II of *BANE*, pp. 363ff.

[126] *BANE*, pp. 73f.

[127] D. N. Freedman, in *BANE*, p. 203.

[128] ZAW, XXXIX (1921), pp. 84ff.

[129] ZAW, XLII (1924), pp. 1ff.

the Neolithic period, and perhaps even beyond. Comparative studies have resulted in a substantial correlation of Palestinian culture with its counterparts in Egypt, Asia Minor, the Aegean, and Mesopotamia. In consequence the background against which the events narrated in the Old Testament took place has been widened immeasurably since the days of Wellhausen, so that it is now possible to reconstruct entire periods of Old Testament history in a manner unknown to earlier generations of scholars.

Despite the overwhelming nature of much of the evidence, however, there are still some who prefer subjective speculations to control by extraneous factors such as archaeology. Chief among these are the followers of Albrecht Alt, who in particular exercise a studied disregard for the evidence presented by archaeological excavations in relationship to whole periods of time, such as, for example, the Middle Bronze Age (ca. 2100-1550 B.C.), except on those rather rare occasions when some especial facet of the discipline happens to suit their purposes. Such an attitude overlooks the important fact that the present age is no longer one of the "grand design," in which facts must be made to conform to an *a priori* theory of one kind or another, or else be disregarded completely if they prove to be embarrassing to the theoretician.[130]

One of the most important benefits of archaeological studies is that they have given the *Sitz im Leben des Volkes* approach a dimension which could scarcely have been imagined in the days of Gunkel. The evaluation of the many cultural facets evident in the pattern of ancient Near Eastern life will undoubtedly contribute much additional information as linguistic, historical, religious, and other studies progress, and no approach to the problems of the Old Testament can be regarded as legitimate or valid unless it is firmly based upon an appreciation of the contribution which archaeology has to make. It should be observed, however, that the basic function of this latter discipline is to illumine the general background of Old Testament events, and not to "prove" the truth of particular happenings as such. The integrity of Biblical scholarship is now generally such that, given the basic facts, the "truth" can usually be relied upon to follow without undue difficulty. Although there will always be the tendency in some quarters to restrict the study of archaeology to a technical examination of artifacts and stratigraphic levels, there can be little doubt that such major discoveries as those at Mari, Nuzu, Ugarit, and Qumran will emphasize the necessity for comprehensiveness in study rather than the more restricted approach of much earlier writing in the Old Testament field.

[130] Cf. M. Noth, *PJB*, XXXIV (1938), pp. 7ff.; *GI*, pp. 70f.

IV. OLD TESTAMENT SCHOLARSHIP
SINCE WORLD WAR I

A. The 1930s

The rise of particularized methods of Biblical study did not deter independent criticism of the classical scheme of Pentateuchal analysis. In 1931 Wilhelm Möller followed his earlier defense of the Mosaic authorship of the Pentateuch with a spirited challenge to the methodology and general conclusions of the critical school.[1] Umberto Cassuto was another vigorous opponent of the adherents of documentary analysis, and in 1934 he published his criticisms in a work which set out to examine the various problems raised by Genesis.[2] Cassuto argued for the organic unity of this composition, and maintained that it had been written in the later years of King David by a person of some genius who had compiled patriarchal and other earlier narratives to form a homogeneous account of Hebrew beginnings.

Two decades earlier Kyle had applied certain facets of archaeological discovery to the problem of the Pentateuch in an attempt to determine the authorship of the various books. In a work published in 1919 he argued against the documentary analysis by urging that the consistent use of Egyptian words throughout the various alleged documents indicated their essential unity of authorship.[3] A year later he followed up this argument in a further work, in which he again argued that the Egyptian influence evident in the Pentateuchal writings pointed to the Mosaic authorship of the corpus. He took decided issue with the "pan-Babylonian" school in repudiating the suggestion that the Mosaic sacrificial system had either Babylonian or Egyptian origins, and concluded that the Pentateuchal records ought to be read as they stood. He accounted for certain peculiarities adduced by critical scholars on the ground that differences could be attributed to the varieties of the laws

[1] *Die Einheit und Echtheit der fünf Bücher Mosis* (1931). A similar position was adopted by D. B. Macdonald, *The Hebrew Literary Genius* (1933).

[2] U. Cassuto, *La Questione della Genesi* (1934), *The Documentary Hypothesis*, E. tr. Israel Abrahams (1962). Cf. B. Jacob, *Das Erste Buch der Thora* (1934).

[3] *Moses and the Monuments: Light from Archaeology on Pentateuchal Times* (1920), pp. 41ff.

and the usages for which they were intended, and relegated the legal material of the Pentateuch generally to Moses as the responsible author.[4]

A further criticism of Wellhausenism, based upon archaeological evidence, was made by A. S. Yahuda. Following the example of Naville, he began to investigate the data of the Pentateuch in the light of the knowledge furnished by archaeological activity in Egypt. A skilled linguist, Yahuda published in 1929 the results of a decade of research dealing with the influence of the Egyptian language upon the Hebrew of the Pentateuch.[5] His minute and detailed studies, which throw considerable light upon the meaning of obscure phrases in the Joseph narratives, led him to conclude that the literary origin presupposed a cultural milieu in which Hebrews and Egyptians were living together. Yahuda adduced this as a decisive argument for the compilation of the Pentateuch in the days of Moses, or at the latest in the immediate post-Mosaic period. While many of his arguments were based upon solid philological foundations, some of his conclusions went beyond the available evidence, for example, his claim that the Babylonian Deluge story contained distinctive Egyptian elements, which was also the case for the Tower of Babel narrative. Despite this and other similar matters, however, Yahuda made it clear that the influence of Egypt upon the Old Testament narratives was far from negligible, a conclusion that was reinforced by subsequent archaeological discoveries.

On different grounds considerable disfavor was expressed with the Graf-Wellhausen theory by the brilliant Orientalist T. J. Meek, who, in the preface of his *Hebrew Origins*, written in 1936, spoke disparagingly of the analytical theory. In the preface to the second edition, published in 1950, Meek explained that while he did not repudiate it entirely, he took the view that it was far too artificial in nature, a conclusion which had been arrived at by many other critics of the scheme. Meek maintained the existence of a cycle of tradition in the southern kingdom which could approximate to J, and an equivalent cycle for the northern kingdom which was then absorbed into J. However, he expressed uncertainty as to whether the J cycle was ever reduced to written form, and repudiated any attempt to separate the northern from the southern cycle. On this basis Meek preferred to think in terms of a "stratum" hypothesis rather than of a purely documentary one. His views appear to have been of a mediating order, and attracted little attention in the scholarly world.

An important step towards an understanding of the manner in which Genesis was compiled in the light of the ancient Babylonian "life-

[4] *The Problem of the Pentateuch: A New Solution by Archaeological Methods* (1920), p. 284.
[5] *Die Sprache des Pentateuch in ihren Bezeihungen zum Aegyptischen*, I (1929), E. tr. *The Language of the Pentateuch in its Relation to the Egyptian* (1931). Cf. his *The Accuracy of the Bible* (1934).

situation" was made in 1936 by P. J. Wiseman. A British air-commodore of decidedly antiquarian bent, Wiseman examined the literary forms of ancient Babylonian tablets with a view to solving the literary problem of the origin of Genesis. From the existence of colophons, catch-lines, scribal dating, and other devices of antiquity familiar to the Assyriologist, Wiseman argued towards the presence of similar phenomena in the bulk of Genesis. He interpreted the enigmatic phrase "these are the generations of" as in fact constituting a colophon in the text, and pointing to the preceding verses as a complete unit which in cuneiform would have constituted a tablet.[6] He further adduced the presence in the early Genesis narratives of such Babylonian literary mechanisms as scribal attempts at dating, the linking of passages in series, specific titles of sections, and the use of catch-lines.

Wiseman's theory postulated documentary sources for Genesis, although of a completely different nature from those suggested by the adherents of the Graf-Wellhausen school. He stressed the strictly Mesopotamian nature of much of the source-material which he had uncovered, and suggested that it had been combined with the Joseph narratives to form the book of Genesis, presumably under the direct influence of Moses. His approach had the distinct advantage of relating the ancient Mesopotamian sources underlying Genesis to an authentic Mesopotamian life-situation, unlike the attempts of the Graf-Wellhausen school, and showed that the methods of writing and compilation employed in Genesis were in essential harmony with the processes current among the scribes of ancient Babylonia.

From a study of Greek literature F. Dornseiff launched an attack in 1934 upon the validity of using the divine names in the Pentateuch as a criterion for purposes of literary analysis. Referring to the Iliad of Homer, he remarked that the name "Alexandros" was frequently found in association with "Paris," which on the basis of the literary analysis adopted by the Graf-Wellhausen school could serve as a valid criterion for dividing the Iliad up into "Alexandrosist" and "Parisist" sources. He also compared the legal sections interpolated into the historical narratives of the Pentateuch with similar occurrences in ancient Classical literature, notably the *Opera et Dies* of Hesiod. Ridiculing the "paste-and-scissors" method for the compilation of such a majestic work as the Iliad, he also rejected it as a valid method for the literary formulation of the extant Pentateuch. What was perhaps most remarkable of all about his study was that these pronouncements were published in a journal that had been founded by the distinguished advanced critic, Bernhard Stade.[7]

---

[6] *New Discoveries in Babylonia About Genesis* (1936), pp. 45ff.; cf. *GBB*, p. 282.

[7] F. Dornseiff, ZAW, LII (1934), pp. 57ff., LIII (1935), p. 154, LV (1937), pp. 127ff., LVI (1938), pp. 64ff.

On the basis of early excavations at Ras Shamra, the deficiencies inherent in the conclusions of the Graf-Wellhausen school were pointed out by the scholarly conservator of the Paris Louvre, René Dussaud. Remarking on the tremendous importance that the discoveries at the site of ancient Ugarit had for an understanding of Phoenician-Canaanite culture, Dussaud maintained that, in the light of the new evidence, the Graf-Wellhausen hypothesis had assigned too late a date to the alleged sources, and had also greatly underestimated the value of Israelite tradition itself. He concluded his criticisms of the classical analytical scheme by stating that it would need to be subjected to a total revision as a result of the discoveries at Ras Shamra,[8] an opinion which has been amply substantiated since that time. Small wonder, therefore, that J. Coppens could declare that, even for the faithful, the magnificent critical edifice was palpably rocking on its foundations.[9]

In 1930 Mowinckel anticipated somewhat the later conclusions of Volz and Rudolph by maintaining that the Elohistic source belonged properly to Judah rather than to Israel, and that it had existed over several centuries as an oral process rather than as a written tradition in the best sense of that term.[10] He also stated that the Elohistic material did not contain any traditions that were independent of the Jehovistic document; rather, it invariably harked back to the parallel Jehovistic forms in its narration of early traditions. However, by 1937 Mowinckel had taken a different view of the situation, assigning the Flood sections of Genesis to the Elohistic source and the non-Flood material to the Jehovistic author.[11]

Abandonment of the traditional Wellhausenian position was announced in 1931 by Pedersen,[12] who repudiated the Hegelian overtones of the analytical scheme and pointed to the problems involved in the minute delineation of supposed literary sources and the precisions of dating which accompanied the process. Although he granted that certain collections of material could possibly be designated by the sigla J, E, D, and P, these were parallel and variegated sources that could not by their very nature be organized within the framework of some *a priori* evolutionary scheme. Pedersen continued his attack upon the current form of the Pentateuchal theory some three years later in an article that firmly rejected the Wellhausenian analysis of Exodus 1–15, and examined the Passover material in general against the background of cultic history

[8] Dussaud, *Les Découvertes de Ras Shamra (Ugarit) et L'Ancien Testament* (1937), pp. 110ff.

[9] *L'Histoire Critique de l'Ancien Testament* (1938), p. 87.

[10] ZAW, XLVIII (1930), pp. 233ff.

[11] Mowinckel, *The Two Sources of the Predeuteronomic Primeval History (JE) in Gen. i-xi* (1937).

[12] ZAW, XLIX (1931), pp. 161ff.

rather than the principles of literary analysis.[13] Pedersen held that this cult-legend appeared in its earliest form shortly after the Israelite settlement in Canaan, although its extant structure may have been post-exilic.[14]

B. THE UPPSALA SCHOOL

What many scholars consider to be the most devastating attacks by far upon classical Pentateuchal literary criticism have been made by the so-called "Uppsala School" of Sweden. While certain aspects of the work of these Scandinavian scholars have affinity with the British "Myth and Ritual" school (somewhat to the embarrassment of the latter, it is said) and with the concepts of kingship[15] and cultic prophecy advocated by Mowinckel, it cannot be denied that the emphasis of the Uppsala school upon the importance of oral tradition ultimately reaches back to Gunkel. An enthusiastic advocate of the place which oral transmission held in the general growth of the Old Testament corpus was H. S. Nyberg,[16] who claimed that the Graf-Wellhausen theory of origins did despite both to the native Hebrew intuition and to the techniques of those who preserved and circulated the sagas of early Israel. Furthermore, Nyberg and his followers urged that adhering to a belief in the existence of documentary sources as such militated against the reliability and significance of oral tradition. This latter was held to have been preserved by circles or centers of tradition over prolonged periods of time, and remained substantially in this form until after the exile.

This general standpoint was applied to the composition of the prophetical writings by Birkeland,[17] who maintained that the literary fixity of the prophetical compositions was a comparatively late individual phenomenon which represented the literal form of an already crystallized oral tradition. According to his theories, each prophet was surrounded by followers who, after his death, transmitted his utterances orally and reworked them in the light of the traditions that had grown up around the individual concerned. For Birkeland, therefore, it was virtually impossible to be sure that any particular verse contained the *ipsissima verba* of any given prophet,[18] so that final pronouncements on such

[13] ZAW, LII (1934), pp. 161ff.; cf. his *Israel: Its Life and Culture* (1940 ed.), III-IV, pp. 726ff.

[14] For a criticism of the general position of Pedersen see C. R. North, *OTMS*, p. 77.

[15] Cf. I. Engnell, *Studies in Divine Kingship in the Ancient Near East* (1943).

[16] ZAW, LII (1934), pp. 241ff.; see also his *Studien zum Hoseabuche: zugleich ein Beitrag zur Klärung des Problems der alttestamentlichen Textkritik* (1935).

[17] *Zum hebräischen Traditionswesen: die Komposition der prophetischen Bücher des AT* (1938).

[18] Cf. I. Engnell, *Svensk Exegetisk Årsbók* (1947), XII, pp. 94ff., and *The Call of Isaiah* (1949), pp. 54ff.

matters could only be made on a traditio-historical, rather than on a literary-critical basis.[19]

Another prominent scholar who followed the lead of Nyberg was Engnell, who went further than either Volz or Pedersen had done in repudiating both the Wellhausenian evolutionary view of Israelite religion and the documentary hypothesis of Pentateuchal origins itself. Nyberg agreed with Noth in separating the Deuteronomy-Kings corpus from that of Genesis-Numbers, styling the former "P-work" and the latter "D-work." These sigla did not indicate documents in the classical analytical sense, but rather symbolized the circles of tradition which transmitted this material until it ultimately assumed its extant form. Basic to an understanding of this process was a recognition of the role that oral tradition exercised in antiquity.

In this connection Engnell maintained that oral tradition and written fixity were complementary forms of the same general process, which dispensed with anonymous redactors in favor of circles and schools of tradition.[20] He rejected the Graf-Wellhausen scheme of analysis categorically as an anachronistic European interpretation, and repudiated the idea that there ever existed the kind of parallel sources of narrative in the Pentateuch that were fundamental to the speculations of the Wellhausenist school. Engnell followed Dahse and Dornseiff in attacking the criterion of the divine names, and argued from a comparison of the Massoretic text with the LXX that the variation in usage of the divine names in the former was largely due to later processes of unification.[21] Generally he emphasized the reliability of the Massoretic text.

Engnell followed Pedersen in proclaiming that the "Passover-legend" of Exodus 1–15 was the central passage of a Priestly complex which seemed to him to be roughly equivalent to the Priestly source of the Graf-Wellhausen school. This "P-work" enshrined the traditions of the southern kingdom and rested for the most part upon oral tradition, with the possibility that certain sections—notably the legal enactments—had assumed an early written character but were also preserved concurrently in the form of oral statements. The final structure of this tradition was assigned to the period of Ezra and Nehemiah. In much the same way the legal sections of Deuteronomy were assumed to have been in writing at a comparatively early period, and to have mirrored the customs of the northern kingdom more consistently than the "P-work," although by the time the book had assumed its final form in the days of Ezra and

---

[19] For a criticism of this proposed methodological change see J. van der Ploeg, *RB*, LIV (1947), pp. 5ff.

[20] Engnell, *Gamla Testamentet: En traditionshistorisk inledning* (1945), I, pp. 8ff.

[21] *Ibid.*, pp. 191ff. For a demonstration that the Hebrew text is superior to the LXX see J. Skinner, *The Divine Names in Genesis* (1914).

Nehemiah it had begun to exhibit noticeable overtones of the theological standpoint current in Judaea.

The general position established by Nyberg and Engnell was adopted by a number of Scandinavian scholars and applied to various aspects of prophecy,[22] Israelite religion,[23] the Wisdom Literature,[24] and general problems of Old Testament introduction.[25] The approach of the Uppsala scholars and their followers has brought a new outlook to bear upon Pentateuchal studies in particular, but it has come in for a certain amount of criticism.[26] Many of those who stand outside this group have felt that the Uppsala writers have fallen into the same trap as the adherents of the Graf-Wellhausen theory by pushing their method beyond its logical limits. While their emphasis upon oral tradition is of great importance in focusing attention upon one of the ways in which material was transmitted in the ancient Near East, it appears to have been emphasized to the virtual exclusion of writing, which also occupied a prominent position in the preservation and transmission of ancient religious materials in Mesopotamia, Egypt, and elsewhere in the Near East. Engnell in particular appears, as Bright has pointed out,[27] to have substituted one form of source-criticism for another of the same general kind, which can hardly be construed as a telling criticism of the classical documentary hypothesis if imitation is to be considered as the sincerest form f flattery. Quite aside from this, however, is the fact that the Scandinavian scholars appear to have entirely misunderstood the function of oral tradition in the Near East, which was used predominantly for spatial and contemporary dissemination of material, and only incidentally for purposes of transmission over a period of time, since it was the general practice to commit anything of importance to written

[22] E.g. J. Lindblom, *Profetismen i Israel* (1934); S. Mowinckel, *JBL*, LIII (1934), pp. 199ff., *Acta Orientalia*, XIII (1935), pp. 264ff., XIV (1936), p. 319, *JBL*, LVI (1937), pp. 261ff., *Prophecy and Tradition* (1946); A. Haldar, *Associations of Cult Prophets Among the Ancient Semites* (1945), *Studies in the Book of Nahum* (1947); A. S. Kapelrud, *Joel Studies* (1948); G. Widengren, *Literary and Psychological Aspects of the Hebrew Prophets* (1948); C. Lindhagen, *The Servant Motif in the OT: A Preliminary Study to the 'Ebed-Yahweh Problem in Deutero-Isaiah* (1950).

[23] J. Lindblom, *Israels religion i gammaltestamentlig tid* (1936); cf. his *Den gammaltestamentliga religionens egenart* (1935).

[24] J. Lindblom, *Boken om Job och hans lidande* (1940); G. Widengren, *The Accadian and Hebrew Psalms of Lamentation as Religious Documents* (1937); H. Ringgren, *Word and Wisdom: Studies in the Hypostatization of Divine Qualities and Functions in the Ancient Near East* (1947).

[25] A. Bentzen, *Indledning til det Gamle Testamente* (1941), E. tr. rev. as *Introduction to the OT* (2 vols., 1948-1949); G. Oestborn, *Tōrā in the OT. A Semantic Study* (1945) and *Cult and Canon: A Study in the Canonization of the OT* (1951).

[26] Cf. C. R. North, *OTMS*, pp. 77ff.

[27] *BANE*, p. 22.

form shortly after the events concerned had transpired. While written and oral forms of the same material doubtless co-existed for lengthy periods, the latter was never meant to supplant the former or to serve as its antecedent.

C. BRITAIN AND THE UNITED STATES—1930-1950

Except for occasional minor variations upon the main critical theme, British scholars in the decade prior to World War II continued to follow the pattern set by S. R. Driver, nervously depending on one another and on their German mentors. The writings of W. O. E. Oesterley and T. H. Robinson, A. S. Peake, S. A. Cook, W. J. Phythian-Adams, H. W. Robinson, and H. H. Rowley are typical of this period.[28] As events turned out, Rowley was to become the most distinguished Old Testament scholar of the post-war era in Great Britain. A man of profound erudition and wide sympathies, he established a tradition of accuracy and detail in scholarly studies that could well be emulated, not merely by his compatriots in the field of Old Testament writing, but also by other contributors to the general area of the humanities. Along with S. H. Hooke, Rowley was one of the most independent thinkers of his generation, and was largely responsible for an increased emphasis in Britain upon the unity of the Biblical writings.[29]

Contemporary liberal scholarship in the United States was strongly influenced by the writings of C. A. Briggs, C. C. Torrey, J. A. Bewer, A. T. Olmstead, J. M. Powis Smith, and R. H. Pfeiffer.[30] The critical extremes of their speculations were subjected to the moderating influences of the Albright school and others similarly engaged in archaeological activity. This situation was quite different from the one in Britain and Europe, where only a very few scholars in the Old Testament field were at all versed in the disciplines of archaeology, and where, in consequence, there was much more opportunity for men to become susceptible to the vagaries of subjective literary criticism.

[28] Representative works are: Oesterley and Robinson, *Hebrew Religion, Its Origin and Development* (1930), *A History of Israel* (2 vols., 1932), *An Introduction to the Books of the OT* (1934). Peake, *The Servant of Yahweh and Other Lectures* (1931). Cook, *The OT: A Reinterpretation* (1936). Phythian-Adams, *The Call of Israel* (1934). Robinson, *The OT: Its Making and Meaning* (1937), *The History of Israel: Its Facts and Factors* (1938). Rowley, *Darius the Mede and the Four World Empires of Daniel* (1935).

[29] Cf. Rowley, *The Relevance of the Bible* (1941), *The Unity of the Bible* (1953).

[30] American writings include: Briggs, *The Higher Criticism of the Hexateuch* (1897). Torrey, *The Composition and Historical Value of Ezra-Nehemiah* (1896), *Ezra Studies* (1910), *The Second Isaiah* (1928), *Pseudo-Ezekiel and the Original Prophecy* (1930). Bewer, *The Literature of the OT* (1912). Olmstead, *History of Assyria* (1923), *History of Palestine and Syria* (1931), *History of the Persian Empire* (1948). Powis Smith, *The Origin and History of Hebrew Law* (1931). Pfeiffer, *Introduction to the OT* (1941).

The period of World War II imposed severe restrictions upon scholarly activity, although some studies managed to appear in print, particularly in the United States and in a few neutral countries. A few German scholars continued to espouse the classical form of Wellhausenism,[31] studiously ignoring the works of Scandinavian and other writers, and found a degree of fellow-feeling in British circles.[32] Other scholars, however, notably Artur Weiser,[33] were careful to point out the hindrances that political circumstances had imposed upon their contact with scholars of other countries. Despite this unfortunate situation, the post-war German literature in the Old Testament field soon began to show the influence of Scandinavian scholarship. Thus, while von Rad[34] still employed the sigla J, E, D, and P, the age that he assigned to the traditions had a very different relationship to their final written form from that envisaged by the school of Wellhausen. Martin Noth made a concession to the emphasis upon oral tradition by regarding the documents as the crystallization of generations of oral transmission, but apart from this he proceeded along the classical lines of literary criticism, except perhaps for his assertion that the "deuteronomic" history commenced with the book of Deuteronomy and carried on until the exilic period.[35]

The post-war era also witnessed a revival of the attack upon the Graf-Wellhausen position from a variety of sources. In 1943 Oswald Allis urged the acceptance of the substantial Mosaic authorship of the Pentateuch in a careful examination of the issues connected with the traditional liberal position.[36] E. J. Young published his conservative *An Introduction to the Old Testament* in 1949, which subjected scholarly thought in the field to searching scrutiny.[37] F. V. Winnett also made a careful examination of the traditions underlying the Pentateuch, and concluded that Exodus and Numbers drew upon a continuous Mosaic tradition which took its rise in the northern kingdom.[38] When Samaria fell to the Assyrians in 722 B.C., this tradition was transferred to the southern kingdom, where it survived in priestly circles and was revised in accordance with the prevailing national ethos. In the seventh century B.C. the Mosaic tradition was drastically reshaped, according to Winnett, and issued in the form of Deuteronomy. The post-exilic priestly

---

[31] E.g. G. Hölscher, *Die Anfänge der Hebräischen Geschichtsschreibung* (1942); cf. his *Geschichtsschreibung in Israel. Untersuchungen zum Jahvisten und Elohisten* (1952).

[32] E.g. C. A. Simpson, *The Early Traditions of Israel: A Critical Analysis of the Pre-Deuteronomic Narrative of the Hexateuch* (1948).

[33] In the Foreword to the second edition (1949) of *Einleitung in das AT*.

[34] *Deuteronomium-Studien* (1948 ed.), *Das erste Buch Mose, Genesis Kapitel 1-12, 9* (1949).

[35] In his *Überlieferungsgeschichte des Pentateuch* (1948).

[36] *The Five Books of Moses* (1943).

[37] Revised edition, 1960.

[38] *The Mosaic Tradition* (1949).

circles in Jerusalem (P) attempted to harmonize the original Mosaic tradition with its Deuteronomic form, but without success.

Winnett cautioned against the application of the sigla J and E to his Mosaic tradition, although on balance he expressed a preference for J, on the understanding that it be clearly recognized as a product of the northern kingdom, where the national traditions of the Israelites took shape. He interpreted the problems of the Pentateuch historically rather than textually, seeing the key to the situation in an awareness of the fact that the extant form of the tradition reflected the claim of the Jerusalem sanctuary and its priestly officiants to primacy over the "Samaritan" or northern priesthood, a claim that was without foundation. Although this theory did not gain wide acceptance, it is important for the emphasis laid upon the place of the Samaritans in the formulation of the Pentateuchal canon, a matter that had been largely ignored by the Graf-Wellhausen school.

A series of studies made by the Roman Catholic scholar A. van Hoonacker, in which he contrived to accept both the documentary analysis and the Mosaic authorship of the Pentateuch, appeared in 1949.[39] This series was edited by J. Coppens, who himself argued subsequently for the strong impress of the Mosaic character upon the material of the Pentateuch.[40] The Roman Catholic scholar J. Steinmann went considerably further in ascribing to Moses a major part in the assembling and formulation of the religious and historical traditions which underlay the Pentateuch.[41] Additional attempts to reverse the tendencies of classical Wellhausenism by maintaining the literary homogeneity and Mosaic authorship of the Pentateuch were made by Helling[42] and Levy,[43] who adduced fresh arguments in support of their positions.

In 1955 W. J. Martin argued on stylistic and philological grounds for the general Mosaicity of the Pentateuch and attacked one of the basic presuppositions for composite authorship by postulating the presence of an elliptical interrogative in the passage in Exodus 6:3 involving the divine names. Martin pointed to the characteristics that indicated the homogeneous nature of Genesis, and urged the adoption of a methodology based upon a more objective approach to Old Testament problems than had been the case with the activities of the Graf-Wellhausen school.[44] In 1957 G. T. Manley undertook a study of Deuteronomy, in

[39] J. Coppens (ed.), *De Compositione Literaria et de Origine Mosaica Hexateuchi. Disquisitio Historico-Critica* (1949).
[40] *Chronique d'Ancien Testament, Le Problème de l'Hexateuque* (1953); cf. Coppens' article in *Nouvelle revue théologique*, LXV (1938), p. 513: E. tr. in chap. 1 of E. A. Ryan and E. W. Tribbe, *The OT and the Critics* (1942), pp. 11ff.
[41] *Les plus anciennes Traditions du Pentateuque* (1954).
[42] *Die Frühgeschichte des israelitischen Volkes* (1947).
[43] *The Growth of the Pentateuch* (1955).
[44] *Stylistic Criteria and the Analysis of the Pentateuch* (1955), pp. 5ff.

which he rejected the contention of the Uppsala school and its supporters that Deuteronomy shared a common authorship with the Joshua-
Kings literary corpus.[45] In disavowing any connection between the
reforms of Josiah and the origin of Deuteronomy, he held that the author
of the book was someone other than Moses, who related those things that
he had heard and received from others for the benefit of the Israelite
nation. Arguing from the fact that the topographical and geographical
data bore every indication of originality, he thought that the book might
have been written in the time of Eli.

In the second edition of his *Einleitung*,[46] Artur Weiser moved some
little distance away from the theories of Pentateuchal origins associated
with Noth and von Rad. While crediting the supplementary hypothesis
of Volz and Rudolph, the fragmentary theory of Gunkel, and the more
classical documentary concepts of Smend and Eissfeldt with some measure of truth, Weiser acknowledged that each view of the situation had
its own particular limitations. He protested against the atomizing process
that so frequently resulted from literary-critical study by indicating the
impossibility of analyzing literary sources to the last detail, and by showing that the completed Pentateuch consisted of considerably more than
the sum of its respective parts. Weiser related the origin of the literature
to the life-situation of the cult, and recognized that oral tradition may
well have co-existed over long periods with written sources. He inclined
to the belief that the authors of the various sources were in fact individuals, and not circles or schools of tradition as Gunkel had suggested. Because the Pentateuch partook of a quasi-sacramental nature, originating,
as he maintained, in the cult-festivals, the questions of provenance constituted something more than literary-historical problems in the generally accepted sense of that term.

The influence of Mowinckel and Hooke was apparent in the work of
A. R. Johnson, who attempted to demonstrate the functional equality of
priest and prophet in the sanctuary rituals.[47] In Johnson's view the
prophet was the responsible agent for the pronouncing of oracles as well
as for the exercise of his own particular prophetic gifts, which would
include divination and prayer. From the existence of prophetic guilds in
the pre-exilic period Johnson argued that the groups of prophets at
Jerusalem became the guilds of singers mentioned in Priestly writings
and in Chronicles. Unfortunately his treatment of the latter topic suffers
from an inadequate appreciation of the cultural conditions which existed
in pre-exilic Canaan. As Albright has shown,[48] the tradition that em-

[45] *The Book of the Law* (1957).
[46] Published in 1948; rev. E. tr. by D. M. Barton, *The OT: Its Formation and Development* (1961).
[47] *The Cultic Prophet in Ancient Israel* (1944).
[48] *ARI*, pp. 125ff.

phasized the place of music and psalmody in the early days of the Hebrew monarchy has been amply verified by archaeological discoveries.

From these it would appear that the Canaanites had a class of temple personnel, referred to in cuneiform sources as "sarim,"[49] and in the time of David the Hebrew singers were organized in terms of a guild, following Ugaritic patterns. This persisted independently of prophetic activity as such until long after the exile; in consequence, it is not easy to see exactly how the Jerusalem prophetic cults postulated by Johnson could be transformed into singers and musicians. In general the author appeared to convey the impression that the prophets were little more than cultic functionaries, and this is certainly not the view presented by the Old Testament narratives.

D. OLD TESTAMENT SCHOLARSHIP SINCE 1950

The immediate post-war period in Britain witnessed the major contributions of H. H. Rowley,[50] while in the United States the members of the Albright school were resuming their literary productions, along with other scholars whose work had been interrupted by the war. One notable feature of the American scene has been the extent to which Jewish authorities have contributed consistently to Old Testament study, as represented in the writings of T. H. Gaster, H. M. Orlinsky, H. L. Ginsberg, L. Finkelstein, Nelson Glueck, and numerous other scholars.[51]

The impetus given to Roman Catholic Biblical scholarship by the papal encyclical *Divino Afflante Spiritu*, issued in 1943, resulted in increased attention being given to the influence of liberal Protestant Biblical criticism upon the traditional forms of Roman Catholic thought, as well as the extent to which archaeological discoveries had a bearing upon the dogma of the Roman Catholic Church. While some scholars of Roman Catholic persuasion adhered to the traditional position of their church in

---

[49] Cf. C. H. Gordon, *Ugaritic Handbook* (1955), p. 272, No. 1934, cf. No. 1991.
[50] Including *The Rediscovery of the OT* (1944), *The Missionary Message of the OT* (1945), *The Authority of the Bible* (1949), *From Joseph to Joshua: Biblical Traditions in the Light of Archaeology* (1950), *The Growth of the OT* (1950), *The Teach-Yourself Bible Atlas* (1960).
[51] Represented by: Gaster, *Thespis: Ritual, Myth, and Drama in the Ancient Near East* (1950); he also edited *The New Golden Bough* (1959). Orlinsky, *The Septuagint: The Oldest Translation of the Bible* (1949), *Ancient Israel* (1954). Ginsberg, *Ugaritic Texts* (1936), *The Legend of King Keret* (1946), *Studies in Koheleth* (1950). Finkelstein, *The Jews: Their History, Culture and Religion* (1949). Glueck, *The Other Side of the Jordan* (1940), *The River Jordan, Being an Illustrated Account of the Earth's Most Storied River* (1946), *Rivers in the Desert* (1949).

matters of literary criticism,[52] others tacitly adopted theories which were being discarded increasingly by Protestant and Jewish scholars, making for a considerable increase of tension within the dogmatic confines of the Roman ecclesiastical corpus.[53]

A new era of Biblical scholarship was ushered in with the accidental discovery of a manuscript deposit in a cave at the northern end of the Dead Sea. Millar Burrows, an eminent American scholar who had earlier published an important work on Biblical archaeology,[54] was responsible with J. C. Trever for the earliest stages of identification and publication of one section of the Qumran scrolls. When the nature of the discovery was communicated to the world of scholarship, it was immediately recognized as being of the highest importance for Biblical studies. A veritable flood of learned treatises arose in the field, in which contributions by younger English-speaking scholars were a welcome and conspicuous feature. The priceless value of the Qumran Biblical manuscripts for the textual critic became apparent immediately when it was certain that they represented a genuine pre-Christian tradition which in itself had advanced the textual evidence for the Hebrew Old Testament by at least a millennium. Decades of study in this general field had accustomed scholars to the idea of a prolonged interval of time between the period when the latest Hebrew writings were compiled and the date of the extant manuscripts, but with the discovery of the Qumran Biblical scrolls this gap was bridged to an undreamed-of extent.

When Professor E. L. Sukenik reported that none of the scrolls that had come into his possession needed to be dated later than A. D. 70, a furious discussion arose among scholars, who were frankly skeptical of the genuineness and proposed date of the manuscript material, remembering previous hoaxes in the Biblical field. However, the authenticity of the scrolls was placed beyond reasonable doubt when a party of competent archaeologists rediscovered and excavated the cave where the manuscripts had been deposited originally. Since that time a number of manuscript caches have been discovered, revealing a wide range of Biblical and non-Biblical literature associated with a religious community that had occupied the Khirbet Qumran area intermittently from about 150 B.C. to the fall of Jerusalem in A.D. 70. The classification and publication of the many manuscript fragments by an international team of experts commenced a few years after the initial discoveries, and the

[52] E.g. C. Schedl, *Geschichte des AT* (4 vols., 1956); F. Michaeli, *Le livre de la Genèse (Chapitres 1 à 11)* (1957); B. Mariani, *Introductio in libros Veteris Testamenti* (1958); P. O'Connell, *Science of Today and the Problems of Genesis* (1959).

[53] For a study of the Roman Catholic Biblical movement see J. Levie, *The Bible, Word of God in Words of Men* (1962), pp. 40ff., 191ff.

[54] *What Mean These Stones?* (1941).

speed of modern methods of communication enabled the scholarly world to have access to photographic reproductions of numerous manuscripts and fragments within a comparatively short interval of time.

Of the many appraisals that have been made of the Qumran scrolls and their importance for Biblical studies, few have failed to stress their revolutionary effect upon all future approaches to traditional problems. The first decade of study was sufficient to reveal the manner in which the scrolls upheld the general trustworthiness of the Massoretic text, and to throw some light upon the processes which underlay its transmission through the centuries. Scholars of many countries have participated in Qumran studies of various kinds. This has resulted in a staggering output of literature on the subject, which shows no sign of abating at the time of writing. It is safe to say that very few books in the future that deal with the manifold problems of the Old Testament can expect to be immune to the influence of the Qumran scrolls. A brief survey of the manuscripts themselves and the importance of Qumran studies generally for the Old Testament will be undertaken subsequently in the present work.

Of the books published in the second half of the twentieth century that were not immediately concerned with the Dead Sea Scrolls, several ought to be noticed if only for the effect that they have had upon the course of Biblical studies. Of particular importance was the monumental synthesis of Old Testament religious history published in Hebrew by Yehezkel Kaufmann, which was translated and abridged in a one-volume edition by Moshe Greenberg.[55] While Kaufmann generally accepted the conclusions of the Graf-Wellhausen school regarding the isolation of the Pentateuchal sources J, E. D, and P, his views on other matters were in diametrical opposition to those of classic European Biblical criticism. His revolutionary study of the history of Israelite religion was based upon the premise that, although rooted in the advanced cultures of the ancient Near East, the religion of the Hebrews was absolutely different from anything else that was known to the nations of antiquity.

Kaufmann postulated the existence of a monotheistic world-view among the Hebrews from a very early stage, and rejected uncompromisingly the Wellhausenian theory of an evolutionary unfolding faith from primitive beginnings to its culmination in the ethical monotheism of the major prophets. Instead, he maintained that the monotheistic *Weltanschauung* was fundamental to the Hebrew concept of a national culture, and underlay every aspect of it from its very beginning. Although his work was marked by certain Wellhausenian overtones, it had the effect of making a significant break with earlier critical views on the origin and

---

[55] Kaufmann, תולדות האמונה הישראלית: מימי קדם עד סוף בית שני (8 vols., 1937-1956), E. tr. *The Religion of Israel: From Its Beginnings to the Babylonian Exile* (1960).

development of Israelite religion,[56] and laid a foundation for a fresh approach to this extremely important area of Old Testament study.

Many of the vexing problems associated with the chronology of the Hebrew monarchy were afforded a radical solution by E. R. Thiele in 1954.[57] His purpose was to determine the exact methods by which the scribes of antiquity compiled their chronologies, and he commenced his task by assuming that the Massoretic text was basically reliable and correct in its extant form. As a result he was able to trace the presence of accession-year and nonaccession-year methods of scribal computation in the books of Kings and Chronicles, and to relate them successfully both internally and also to certain fixed points in ancient Near Eastern chronology. His procedures, which succeeded where all earlier attempts had failed, claimed the advantage of being firmly grounded upon a methodology appropriate to oriental categories of thinking, a state of affairs which was conspicuously different from that which had obtained in the great bulk of previous attempts to resolve the chronological problems of the Hebrew monarchy.

A new emphasis upon the basic unity of the Hebrew faith found expression prior to World War II in the work of W. Eichrodt,[58] who departed to a considerable extent from the customary method of historical presentation of data and related the various elements of the ancient Israelite faith to one central idea, namely that of the Covenant at Sinai.[59] A similar approach was also adopted by Sellin,[60] who selected as central ideas the basic doctrines of God, man, and salvation, on the ground that they furnished a wider foundation than the Covenant for purposes of demonstrating the unity of Biblical teaching. Sellin interpreted the theology of Israel in a Christocentric manner, an approach that was developed at greater length by Vischer, who in a two-volume work[61] endeavored to present a theological system so formulated as to comprise universally valid eternal truth. A major work written by the Roman Catholic scholar P. Van Imschoot[62] reflected the influence of Köhler and Eichrodt in certain particulars, although it adopted a more

[56] As those expressed, for example, by Oesterley and Robinson in *Hebrew Religion*.

[57] *The Mysterious Numbers of the Hebrew Kings: A Reconstruction of the Chronology of the Kingdoms of Israel and Judah* (1954, rev. ed., 1965).

[58] *Theologie des AT* (3 vols., 1933-1939), E. tr. J. Baker, *Theology of the OT* (vol. 1, 1961).

[59] Cf. L. Köhler, *Theologie des AT* (1935), E. tr. A. S. Todd, *OT Theology* (1957); C. Alves, *The Covenant* (1957); R. de Vaux, *Ancient Israel: Its Life and Institutions* (1962); J. B. Payne, *The Theology of the Older Testament* (1962).

[60] *Alttestamentliche Theologie auf religionsgeschichtlicher Grundlage* (2 vols., 1933).

[61] *Das Christuszeugnis des AT* (2 vols., 1934, 1942), E. tr. *The Witness of the OT to Christ* (vol. 1, 1949).

[62] *Théologie de l'Ancien Testament* (2 vols., 1954, 1956).

dogmatic approach to Old Testament theology, and did not attempt to demonstrate the unity of Hebrew faith in terms of a central idea such as the Covenant. Other authors who dealt with various aspects of Old Testament theology at a slightly later period included N. H. Snaith, Wheeler Robinson, Millar Burrows, Th. C. Vriezen, O. J. Baab, W. A. L. Elmslie, A. R. Johnson, H. H. Rowley, R. C. Dentan, and G. E. Wright.[63]

An English translation of E. Jacob's *Théologie de l'Ancien Testament* (1955) appeared in 1958. In 1957 the first volume of an Old Testament theology by von Rad was published.[64] The English version of an important theological contribution by Mowinckel, originally entitled *Han som kommer*, was issued in 1956,[65] and was notable in that it represented a modification by the author of many of his earlier views on such matters as the Servant of the Lord. In this book Mowinckel also took the stand that the Christian Church was completely justified in finding in the person and work of Jesus Christ the true fulfilment of the Servant prophesies of Isaiah.[66] G. A. Knight attempted a Christian interpretation of Old Testament theological concepts,[67] while J. Jocz stressed the importance of the election of Israel and the place of the nation in the divinely revealed plan of salvation.[68]

The vast increase of archaeological knowledge resulted, among other things, in a renewed interest in the production of numerous treatises on the geography of the Holy Land,[69] thereby bringing older treatments of

---

[63] Snaith, *The Distinctive Ideas of the OT* (1944). Robinson, *Inspiration and Revelation in the OT* (1946). Burrows, *An Outline of Biblical Theology* (1946). Vriezen, *Hoofdlijnen der Theologie van het Oude Testament* (1949), E. tr. *An Outline of OT Theology* (1958). Baab, *The Theology of the OT* (1949). Elmslie, *How Came Our Faith: A Study of the Religion of Israel and its Significance for the Modern World* (1949). Johnson, *The One and the Many in the Israelite Concept of God* (1942), *The Vitality of the Individual in the Thought of Ancient Israel* (1949). Rowley, *The Biblical Doctrine of Election* (1950). Dentan, *Preface to OT Theology* (1950, rev. ed., 1963). Wright, *The God Who Acts: Biblical Theology as Recital* (1952).

[64] *Theologie des AT, I* (1957), E. tr. D. M. G. Stalker, *OT Theology I: The Theology of Israel's Historical Traditions* (1962); II (1965).

[65] E. tr. G. W. Anderson, *He That Cometh* (1956).

[66] Cf. C. R. North, *The Suffering Servant in Deutero-Isaiah* (1948), p. 218.

[67] *A Biblical Approach to the Doctrine of the Trinity* (1957), *A Christian Theology of the OT* (1959), *Law and Grace* (1962).

[68] J. Jocz, *A Theology of Election: Israel and the Church* (1958), *The Spiritual History of Israel* (1961).

[69] E.g. G. E. Wright and F. V. Filson, *Westminster Historical Atlas to the Bible* (1945); L. H. Grollenberg, *Atlas of the Bible* (1956); E. G. Kraeling, *Bible Atlas* (1956); D. Baly, *The Geography of the Bible* (1957); M. du Buit, *Géographie de la Terre Sainte* (2 vols., 1958); H. H. Rowley, *The Teach-Yourself Bible Atlas* (1960); M. A. Beek, *Atlas of Mesopotamia* (1962); C. F. Pfeiffer, *Baker's Bible Atlas* (1962).

the subject[70] abreast of modern knowledge. Other publications dealt with the artistic productions of the ancient Near East,[71] and with the everyday life of the Old Testament world.[72] The works of S. Moscati[73] and C. H. Gordon[74] have thrown a great deal of light upon many facets of ancient Near Eastern culture, while Old Testament scholarship in general has owed a long-standing debt to the editorial labors of individuals such as F. Pohl (*Orientalia* and *Analecta Orientalia*), F. F. Bruce (*The Palestine Exploration Quarterly* and *The Evangelical Quarterly*), G. E. Wright and F. M. Cross (*The Biblical Archaeologist*), de Boer (*Oudtestamentische Studiën*), T. Fish (*The Journal of the Manchester University Egyptian and Oriental Society*), C. J. Bleeker (*Numen*), and many other distinguished scholars who have served in similar capacities.

The English-speaking world has derived particularly great benefit from a profusion of Bible dictionaries, encyclopedias, and commentaries, replacing the older works such as those edited by Hastings[75] and Orr,[76] and reflecting many of the advances in knowledge that are the property of the mid-twentieth century.[77] Besides producing similar

[70] E.g. T. H. Horne, *A Summary of Biblical Geography and Antiquities* (1856); G. A. Smith, *The Historical Geography of the Holy Land* (1894); J. B. Calkin, *Historical Geography of Bible Lands* (1904); F.-M. Abel, *Géographie de la Palestine* (1933).

[71] E.g. H. Frankfort, *The Art and Architecture of the Ancient Orient* (1954); J. B. Pritchard, *The Ancient Near East in Pictures Relating to the OT* (1954); A. Malroux and G. Salles (eds.), *The Arts of Mankind: Sumer* (A. Parrot, 1960), *Nineveh and Babylon* (Parrot, 1961), *Iran, Parthians and Sassanians* (R. Ghirshman, 1962).

[72] E.g. M. S. and J. L. Miller, *Encyclopedia of Bible Life* (1944); E. W. Heaton, *Everyday Life in OT Times* (1956); P. R. Ackroyd, *The People of the OT*; W. Corswant, *A Dictionary of Life in Bible Times* (1960 ed.); R. de Vaux, *Ancient Israel: Its Life and Institutions* (1962).

[73] *Storia e Civilta dei Semiti* (1949), E. tr. *Ancient Semitic Civilisations* (1957); *L'epigrafia ebraica antica 1935-1950* (1951); *L'oriente Antico* (1952); *Oriente in nuovo luce* (1954); *Il Profito dell' Oriente Mediterraneo* (1956), E. tr. *The Face of the Ancient Orient* (1960); *Il predecessori d'Israele* (1956).

[74] C. H. Gordon, *Ugaritic Handbook* (1947), *Ugaritic Literature: A Comprehensive Translation of Poetic and Prose Texts* (1949), *Introduction to OT Times* (1952), *Adventures in the Nearest East* (1957), *The World of the OT: An Introduction to OT Times* (1958), *Before the Bible* (1962).

[75] J. Hastings (ed.), *Dictionary of the Bible* (5 vols., 1911).

[76] J. Orr (ed.), *The International Standard Bible Encyclopedia* (5 vols., 1915).

[77] E.g. M. S. and J. L. Miller, *Harper's Bible Dictionary* (1952); G. A. Buttrick *et al.* (eds.), *The Interpreter's Bible* (12 vols., 1952-1957); G. A. Buttrick *et al.* (eds.), *The Interpreter's Dictionary of the Bible* (4 vols., 1962); J. D. Douglas *et al.* (eds.), *The New Bible Dictionary* (1963); M. Black and H. H. Rowley (eds.), *Peake's Commentary on the Bible* (1962); M. C. Tenney (ed.), *The Zondervan Pictorial Bible Dictionary* (1963); J. Marsh *et al.* (eds.), *The Torch Bible Commentaries* (1949ff.); E. J. Young (ed.), *The New International Commentary on the OT* (1965ff.); W. F. Albright and D. N. Freedman (eds.), *The Anchor Bible* (1964ff.).

works in their own language, German scholars have lent their efforts to a series in English under the editorship of G. E. Wright and others, entitled *The Old Testament Library*,[78] which includes compositions other than purely Biblical commentaries,[79] and in point of fact has drawn heavily upon the noted German series *Das Alt Testament Deutsch*. Notable translations of the Bible embodying new archaeological and theological knowledge have also been conspicuous in the literature of the mid-twentieth century.[80] Yet another outstanding achievement was the publication of a new edition of the Massoretic text by the British and Foreign Bible Society.[81]

One of the most important repudiations of the Graf-Wellhausen theory was made by C. H. Gordon in an article in *Christianity Today*.[82] Gordon, a veteran Near Eastern archaeologist and a brilliant linguistic scholar, stated the reasons which led to his change of outlook from an earlier liberal position,[83] and drew upon parallels in ancient Near Eastern literature to show the complete inadequacy of using the divine names in the Pentateuch as a criterion for documentary analysis. In particular he warned, as others had done, against employing a critical methodology which was out of harmony with the observed facts of the ancient Near Eastern *Sitz im Leben*, and which could only result in the conclusion that little or nothing in the Old Testament was authentic. This extremely important criticism of the Graf-Wellhausen analytical method, reflecting as it does a vast knowledge of oriental life and customs, will of necessity have to be taken into account by all serious students of the Old Testament.

In 1962 Gordon published a valuable contribution to the study of the background common to the Greek and Hebrew civilizations in which he demonstrated that, so far from being totally different from one another, they were actually parallel structures erected upon the same east-Mediterranean cultural foundations.[84] Gordon was concerned not so much with the Hellenistic age, when the union of Greece with other areas of the Near East was an accomplished fact that is now recognized on all sides, but with the "Heroic Age" of Greece and Israel. The period under consideration extended from the beginning of the Egyptian Amarna Age (fifteenth century B.C.) to the tenth century B.C. By reference to

[78] E.g. G. von Rad, *Das erste Buch Mose, Genesis* (1956), E. tr. J. H. Marks, *Genesis* (1961); M. Noth, *Das zweite Buch Mose, Exodus* (1959), E. tr. J. S. Bowden, *Exodus* (1962)

[79] E.g. W. Eichrodt, *Theologie des AT, I* (1959), E. tr. J. Baker, *Theology of the OT, I* (1960).

[80] E.g. *The Revised Standard Version* (1952), *The Bible*, published by the Jewish Publication Society of America (vol. 1, 1963).

[81] Ed. N. H. Snaith (1958).

[82] *Christianity Today*, IV, No. 4 (1959), pp. 131ff.

[83] Already apparent in *UL*, pp. 7f.

[84] *Before the Bible* (1962).

numerous similarities and differences Gordon furnished a convincing account of the extent to which Greek and Hebrew texts alike reflected authentic traditions of the Heroic Age of the eastern Mediterranean during the last half of the second millennium B.C.

Although W. F. Albright attempted to disparage to some extent the conclusions that Gordon arrived at,[85] the latter was equally emphatic as to the validity and importance of his work for Homeric and Old Testament studies alike;[86] and for anyone who is well grounded in both disciplines the facts of the matter are quite evidently on the side of Gordon. Particularly valuable for the whole question of Pentateuchal origins is his insistence upon a maximum of written sources underlying the narratives, as opposed to the general emphasis of liberal orthodoxy, which adheres to the concept of a prolonged period of oral transmission before the written material assumed its final form. This conclusion led Gordon to a rejection of the notion that the Pentateuch was the "work of an editor who pasted together various documents," and an espousal of the view that it was instead the epic of nationhood.[87]

E. THE CURRENT STATUS OF OLD TESTAMENT SCHOLARSHIP

It is a commonplace for those who comment upon the situation in the area of critical analysis from the mid-twentieth century to state that it is far more difficult to assess than was the case with that same movement fifty years earlier.[88] The faith of a great many in the philosophical rationale of critical orthodoxy has undergone a severe testing, as indicated by the comments of Bright in 1960:

> . . . after two total wars and countless other unmentionable horrors, few are left today who would find a melioristic evolution a sufficient explanation of human history—and, by the same token, of Israel's history.[89]

He further pointed out that scholars have recognized increasingly the impossibility of arranging documents in neat chronological progression, or of adducing such documents to support an equally concise picture of the evolution of Israelite religion.[90] Yet he also made it clear that the documentary hypothesis was not the express prerogative of the Graf-Wellhausen school, and that it rises or falls independently of that body of opinion to a large extent. In noting that many scholars still adhered to the classical formulation of documents, thus substantiating to a large extent the predictions of Peake[91] that a "central position" on the matter

---

[85] *Christianity Today*, VII, No. 8 (1963), p. 359.

[86] *Ibid.*, VII, No. 12, p. 580; cf. *IOTT*, pp. 89ff., *HUCA*, XXVI (1953), pp. 84ff.

[87] *GBB*, p. 284.

[88] E.g. G. W. Anderson, *A Critical Introduction to the OT* (1959), p. v.

[89] *BANE*, p. 16.

[90] *Ibid.*, p. 18.

[91] *BJRL*, XII (1928), pp. 28f.

would be adopted, Bright was faced with the same problematical situation as that which confronted Kaufmann under similar circumstances.

The latter wrote:

> Wellhausen's arguments complemented each other nicely, and offered what seemed to be a solid foundation upon which to build the house of biblical criticism. Since then, however, both the evidence and the arguments supporting the structure have been called into question and, to some extent, even rejected. Yet biblical scholarship, while admitting that the grounds have crumbled away, nevertheless continues to adhere to the conclusions. The critique of Wellhausen's theory which began some forty years ago has not been consistently carried through to its end. Equally unable to accept the theory in its classical formulation and to return to the precritical views of tradition, biblical scholarship has entered upon a period of search for new foundations.[92]

Many professional students of the Old Testament, including some scholars of the highest intellectual caliber, have come to the conclusion that it is becoming increasingly impossible to ignore or dismiss the results of honest scholarship and research any longer. Accordingly they have begun to devote themselves to the task of ascertaining as far as is possible the actual facts of the ancient Near Eastern cultural situation, and against such a background are making a strenuous attempt to interpret the literary and other phenomena of the Old Testament.

In this endeavor the initiative appears to the present writer to rest quite clearly with American scholarship, and not least with the members of the Albright school and the followers of C. H. Gordon. The creative period of critical study in Germany has long since terminated, and the naturalism and nihilism of scholars such as Noth militate against any realistic progress towards a more assured methodology. Indeed, if such an emphasis is permitted to continue its influence over German thought, it appears difficult to avoid the conclusion that the products of German Old Testament scholarship will become increasingly of merely antiquarian value and interest, representing the product of an academic backwater far removed from the main stream of thought in the area of Old Testament studies.

The work of Gunkel, along with the insights of the Scandinavian scholars, points towards more fruitful results than could otherwise be expected, although even here a careful rein needs to be kept upon the purely speculative element, the exercise of which has been so conspicuous in European scholarship generally. British writers, who had followed faithfully the mediating views of S. R. Driver, found themselves in the pre-Qumran period the victims of what in economic circles would be known as the law of diminishing returns, and apart from the work of S. H. Hooke and H. H. Rowley were only rescued from this perilous condi-

[92] *KRI,* p. 1.

tion to some limited extent by the activities of the few younger scholars who participated actively in the investigation of the Qumran material.[93]

It seems abundantly clear that all future scholarship must adopt a much more critical attitude towards its theoretical presuppositions, particularly in the light of the increasingly large corpus of information which is now available on almost every aspect of life in the ancient Near East. As wide an acquaintance as possible with the assured facts of the situation would seem to the writer to be a far more desirable prerequisite for scholarship than an indoctrination with *a priori* critical speculations, many of which have been advanced with enthusiasm but never demonstrated conclusively.

If, with C. H. Gordon, one is prepared to go where the facts lead regardless of the consequences this may have for a pietistic approach to past scholarship, one will still encounter difficult problems, but at the very least one will confront them in the assurance that the methodological approach which one has adopted is grounded securely in proper inductive procedures of reasoning, and is not an arbitrary instrument for subjective exercise. This is not an easy path for scholars to follow, however, as Gordon has pointed out,[94] particularly for those who have been trained exclusively in the methods of literary analysis as expounded by the Graf-Wellhausen school. Yet it is just a matter of observed fact that the old foundations have proved grossly inadequate to the situation demanded by the exercise of critical faculties, and, until they are replaced, the superstructure, erected with such enthusiasm by so many diverse hands over a prolonged period, is in incessant danger of collapse, as indicated by the widely divergent state of mid-twentieth-century opinion on the whole question of literary-critical findings.

In the end, therefore, it is a matter of method, and in the view of the present writer it is only when criticism is properly established upon an assured basis of ancient Near Eastern life rather than upon occidental philosophical or methodological speculations that Old Testament scholarship can expect to reflect something of the vitality, dignity, and spiritual richness of the law, prophecy, and the sacred writings.

[93] Especially J. M. Allegro, *The Dead Sea Scrolls* (1956), *The Treasure of the Copper Scroll* (1960), and P. Wernberg-Møller, *The Manual of Discipline* 1957).

[94] *Christianity Today,* IV, No. 4 (1959), p. 134.

Part Two

OLD TESTAMENT ARCHAEOLOGY

I. HISTORICAL SURVEY OF SCIENTIFIC ARCHAEOLOGY

As a scientific discipline, archaeology, which endeavors to evaluate the significance of the material remains of past human activity, is a comparatively new facet of the long interest in and exploration of the lands of the Near East. In this connection, as Albright has pointed out,[1] Palestine has long held a unique position among the countries that are of significance for the Bible student. Not merely did it serve as the place where Judaism and Christianity were nurtured, but for many centuries during the Christian era it was the undisputed geographical locale of Islam.

A. PRESCIENTIFIC ARCHAEOLOGY

1. Pilgrimages. Almost from the earliest days of Christianity it was customary for the devout to make pilgrimages to the Holy Land,[2] possibly in imitation of similar journeys made to Mount Sinai in the Old Testament period. Even though the Crusades halted this expression of interest in sacred sites for some time, it was subsequently permitted to continue, since, among other reasons, the Moslem inhabitants of Palestine found it to be a profitable source of income. Most medieval accounts of journeys to the Holy Land and neighboring countries followed the basic pattern common to travel diaries, whether ancient or modern. It was not until the sixteenth century that the first systematic observations relating to the natural history of Palestine in general, and to its flora in particular, were recorded by Leonhard Rauwolf.[3]

Certain notations concerning archaeological data were preserved in the writings of Pietro della Valle, who travelled in the Near East at the beginning of the seventeenth century,[4] but it was in 1743 that the first systematic plans of sacred locations and copies of inscriptions were published by Bishop Pococke, describing what he had encountered

---

[1] *AP*, p. 23.

[2] For one such account *ca.* A.D. 333, see the Bordeaux Pilgrim's *Itinerary from Bordeaux to Jerusalem*, tr. A. Stewart, *Palestine Pilgrims' Text Society* (1887).

[3] Leonhard Rauwolf, *Aigentliche beschreibung der raiss . . . inn die Morgenländer* (1583).

[4] The first portion of the *Travels,* describing his adventures in Palestine and Turkey, was published in 1650, two years before his death.

during his tour of Palestine and the East.[5] The records of previous pilgrimages were largely superseded, however, by the activities of the Dutch scholar Reland, who collected a great deal of archaeological and topographical information from a wide variety of sources, and in attempting to systematize it furnished the first critical examination of the study of Palestinian antiquities.[6]

2. *Napoleon in Egypt.* Prior to 1798 Near Eastern archaeology had been loosely associated with the pillaging of tombs and with the uncritical admiration of sites that tradition had connected with some of the major events or personalities of the Judaeo-Christian continuum.

That year Napoleon invaded Egypt, including in his entourage about a hundred scholars and artists, who gazed with unconcealed admiration and amazement upon the antiquities of Egyptian culture. Modern archaeology may be said to have its beginnings in the manner in which the Napoleonic scholars and artists copied out hieroglyphic inscriptions, made numerous water-color illustrations, and wrote systematic descriptions of the sites and monuments that they encountered.[7] Some scholars in the post-Napoleonic era published independent works dealing with Egyptian archaeology,[8] so that by the middle of the nineteenth century there was a vast fund of available literary material relating to the antiquities of Egypt.

3. *Surface explorations.* Modern surface exploration of Palestine as such commenced in 1805 with the activities of Seetzen, who travelled extensively in Transjordan and discovered the sites of 'Amman and Gerasa.[9] Nearly twenty-five years later the erudite American scholar Edward Robinson journeyed across Palestine with his companion and student Eli Smith, studying the general topography of the country and identifying many Biblical sites in Judah. Their discoveries included the line of the Third or Agrippan Wall of Jerusalem, the validity of which was subsequently disputed by most of the experts, and which has only been vindicated within recent years.[10]

Widespread interest in the archaeological potential of Mesopotamia was aroused at the beginning of the nineteenth century when C. J. Rich, the resident of the East India Company at Baghdad, explored neighbor-

[5] *A Description of the East and Some Other Countries* (2 vols., 1743-1745).

[6] *Palaestina ex monumentis veteribus illustrata* (1714).

[7] *Description de l'Égypte ou Recueil des observations et des recherches qui ont été faites en Égypte pendant l'expédition de l'armée française, publié par les ordres de sa majesté l'Empereur Napoléon le Grand* (21 vols., 1809-1828).

[8] E.g. J. F. Champollion, *Monuments de l' Égypte et de la Nubie* (4 vols., 1835-1845); K. R. Lepsius, *Denkmäler aus Ägypten und Äthiopen* (12 vols., 1849-1856); A. Mariette, *Voyage dans la Haute-Égypte* (2nd ed., 2 vols., 1893).

[9] *Reisen* (Kruse ed., 4 vols., 1854).

[10] E. L. Sukenik and L. A. Mayer, *The Third Wall of Jerusalem* (1930); cf. *BASOR*, No. 83 (1941), pp. 5ff., No. 89 (1943), pp. 18ff.

ng mounds and recovered numerous cuneiform inscriptions. When the French consular agent at Mosul, Paul Émile Botta, discovered the ruined remains of a palace belonging to Sargon II at Khorsabad (Dur-Sharrukin) in 1843,[11] the resulting wave of enthusiasm for Mesopotamian antiquities saw A. H. Layard commence excavations at Nimrod (Calah) and Nineveh from 1845. Almost immediately the palace of Ashurnasirpal II was uncovered, and the following year excavations there yielded the valuable Black Obelisk of Shalmaneser III,[12] an ancient monument which recorded that Jehu of Israel had been made tributary to the Assyrians. In 1847, while digging at Kuyunjik (Nineveh), Layard uncovered the great palace of Sennacherib, which was almost completely excavated during a second expedition from 1849 to 1851.[13]

As a result of these discoveries, interest in Near Eastern archaeology took a practical turn with the establishment of the Palestine Exploration Fund in 1865. Two years later the PEF sent Charles Warren to Jerusalem as its first representative to conduct excavations there. Although Warren's work was marred by the use of unreliable chronological methods, his ordnance survey of the city and its environs has remained the basis for all subsequent work at the site.[14]

At this time the brilliant French scholar Clermont-Ganneau served with the French Consulate in Palestine, and within a very few years he distinguished himself by announcing the discovery of the celebrated Moabite Stone.[15] This black basalt *stele*, which told of the extent to which Omri (*ca.* 885-873 B.C.) had gained control of northern Moab, had been discovered initially by a German missionary named Klein when visiting ancient Dibon in Moab. The *stele* was sent to the Louvre in Paris in 1870. Under C. R. Conder and H. H. Kitchener a careful survey of western Palestine was made from 1872 to 1877, and this material is still of considerable value to the archaeologist and topographer.[16]

One of the most urgent tasks confronting Egyptian archaeologists was accomplished by the indefatigable labors of J. H. Breasted (1865-1935), who set himself the objective of copying and translating as many inscrip-

---

[11] Subsequently explored intensively by the Oriental Institute of the University of Chicago. Cf. G. Loud, *Khorsabad I, Excavations in the Palace and at a City Gate* (1936), Oriental Institute Publications XXXVIII; G. Loud and C. B. Altman, *Khorsabad II, The Citadel and the Town* (1938), Oriental Institute Publications XL.

[12] A. H. Layard, *Nineveh and Its Remains* (1849), I, p. 282; cf. C. J. Gadd, *The Stones of Assyria* (1936), p. 48.

[13] Layard, *The Monuments of Nineveh* (1853), *A Second Series of the Monuments of Nineveh* (1853), *Discoveries Among the Ruins of Nineveh and Babylon* (1875).

[14] Cf. C. Warren and C. R. Conder, *The Survey of Western Palestine, PEF Memoirs,* "Jerusalem" Volume (1884). For an account of Warren's work see R. A. S. Macalister, *A Century of Excavation in Palestine* (1925), pp. 32ff.

[15] C. S. Clermont-Ganneau, *La Stèle de Mésa* (1887).

[16] Conder and Kitchener, *Map of Western Palestine in 26 Sheets, PEF* (1880).

tions as could be found in Egyptian temples and other monuments. This gigantic task took well over a decade, and involved a good deal of arduous travel.[17] When complete, the material that Breasted had collected furnished scholars and students with an authoritative compilation of historical sources extending from the First Dynasty of Egypt to the time of the Persian conquest.[18]

B. Scientific Archaeology Since Flinders Petrie

1. The spread and development of archaeological techniques. The scientific development of Palestinian archaeology began to make vast strides with the work of the scholarly Flinders Petrie. While excavating the mound of Tell el-Hesi in southwestern Palestine, during the last decade of the nineteenth century, Petrie became aware of the fact that each particular occupational level had its own distinctive pottery, which could be differentiated by means of expert examination from that of earlier and later periods. When he correlated pottery fragments with similar ceramic styles of known date from Egyptian and other deposits, he was able to introduce the principle of ceramic dating-sequences for estimating the age of archaeological strata. Although doubt was cast upon the validity of his dating-criterion at that particular time, it has been amply vindicated by subsequent research and now occupies an extremely important place in all archaeological activity.

Of the many skilled archaeologists who followed Flinders Petrie, mention should be made of the brilliant German scholar Ernst Sellin, who excavated Taanach from 1901 to 1904,[19] and who was associated with Watzinger in an attempt to uncover the secrets of Jericho (Tell es-Sultan) from 1907 to 1909.[20] R. A. S. Macalister investigated several mounds situated in the Judaean Shephelah from 1898 with A. C. Dickie and F. J. Bliss;[21] from 1902 to 1909 he was responsible for the excavations at Gezer (Tell Jezer).[22] G. A. Reisner supervised the first American excavations in Palestine at Samaria between 1908 and 1910 with C. S. Fisher and D. G. Lyon.[23] Reisner's major contribution to the science of archaeology was his introduction of an excavating technique that included the formulation of an elaborate analysis of stratigraphic material, comprehensive recording of all artifacts and other relevant data,

---

[17] See C. Breasted, *Pioneer to the Past* (1943), pp. 78f.

[18] Compiled in his *Ancient Records of Egypt* (5 vols., 1906-1907).

[19] Sellin, *Tell Ta'annek* (1904).

[20] Sellin and Watzinger, *Jericho* (1913).

[21] Macalister, *A Century of Excavation in Palestine*, pp. 47ff.

[22] Macalister, *The Excavation of Gezer* (3 vols., 1912); cf. his *Bible Side-Lights from the Mound of Gezer* (1906).

[23] Reisner, Fisher, and Lyon, *Harvard Excavations at Samaria, 1908-1910* (2 vols., 1924).

careful study of the architectural features of buildings, and an emphasis upon accurate surveying of sites to be excavated.

Meanwhile excavations in Mesopotamia were proceeding apace. From 1899 onwards the *Deutsche Orientgesellschaft* under the direction of R. Koldewey began to uncover the remains of Babylon as it existed in the days of Nebuchadnezzar II.[24] Elaborate fortifications, magnificent temples, carefully planned streets, and waterways gradually emerged from the vast complex of ruins, testifying to the highly developed standard of life in ancient Babylon. Still more important was the discovery of the foundation of Babylonian culture as a result of the work of H. R. Hall and C. L. Woolley at Tell el-Obeid from 1923 on,[25] and the excavations of Chiera and Starr at Nuzu beginning in 1925.[26] The latter was enlarged by the activities of the *Musée du Louvre* working from 1933 under André Parrot at Tell Harari, the site of the ancient city of Mari,[27] where a culture very similar to that at Nuzu flourished during the third millennium B.C.

The spectacular recovery of the ancient Hittite civilization of Asia Minor was another remarkable result of the archaeological activity that flourished at the beginning of the twentieth century. Until that time it had only been possible to hint at the nature and extent of the Hittite empire by studying a few scattered monuments.[28] In 1906 Hugo Winckler began excavating the site of Boghazköy,[29] the ancient Hittite capital, and uncovered a large number of cuneiform clay tablets written in several different tongues. When deciphered some of these revealed at once the splendor and advanced culture of the ancient Hittite empire.[30]

In Palestine, the British mandate established after World War I was favorable to a policy of systematic excavation of sites in the Holy Land. A Department of Antiquities was set up, and was headed by John Gar-

---

[24] Koldewey, *Das Ischar-Tor in Babylon* (1918), *Das wieder erstehende Babylon* (1925).

[25] Hall and Woolley, *Ur Excavations I, Al-'Ubaid* (1927); C. L. Woolley, *Ur of the Chaldees* (1929).

[26] R. F. S. Starr, *Nuzi, Report on the Excavations at Yorgan Tepa near Kirkuk, Iraq, Conducted by Harvard University in Conjunction with the American Schools of Oriental Research and the University Museum of Philadelphia, 1927-1931* (2 vols., 1937-39).

[27] For the early reports see A. Parrot, *SRA*, XVI (1935), pp. 1ff., 117ff., XVII (1936), pp. 1ff., XVIII (1937), pp. 54ff., XIX (1938), pp. 1ff., XX (1939), pp. 1ff.

[28] E.g. the works of W. Wright, *The Empire of the Hittites* (1884); A. H. Sayce, *The Hittites, The Story of a Forgotten Empire* (5th ed., 1910).

[29] Winckler, *Sonderabzug aus der Orientalistischen Litteratur-Zeitung*, Dec. 15, 1906, *Mitteilungen der Deutschen Orientgesellschaft*, XXXV (1907), pp. 1ff.; ·I. Winckler and O. Puchstein, *Excavations at Boghaz-keui in the Summer of 1907* (Smithsonian Report for 1908), pp. 677ff.

[30] For the philological observations of a leading scholar who assisted in the decipherment of the tablets see F. Hrozný, *Die Sprache der Hethiter* (1917).

stang of the University of Liverpool. During the following fifteen years work was undertaken at a number of important Palestinian sites, including Beth-shan (Tell el-Husi) from 1921 until 1933.[31] In 1922 W. F. Albright commenced work at ancient Gibeah (Tell el-Ful), and uncovered the fortress of King Saul.[32] The largest excavation ever undertaken in Palestine began in 1925 at Megiddo (Tell el-Mutesellim) under C. S. Fisher, P. L. O. Guy and G. Loud, continuing until 1939[33] the work that had been initiated by Schumacher and the *Deutsche Orientgesellschaft* in 1903.

In 1929 a discovery of very great significance was made by the French archaeologist C. F. A. Schaeffer at Ras Shamra, the ancient Ugarit, where a rich tomb had been found by accident the previous year. The result of this was the recovery of remains of a highly developed civilization that had flourished in Canaan in the Egyptian Amarna period (fifteenth to fourteenth centuries B.C.), and which claimed close affinities with the culture of the Biblical Hebrews.[34] Without any question the discovery of the remains of ancient Ugaritic society represents one of the major achievements of twentieth-century archaeological activity.

From 1929 to 1936 John Garstang conducted a series of excavations at Jericho continuing the work first begun by Sellin. During these campaigns a number of the stratigraphic problems that the *Deutsche Orientgesellschaft* had confronted were resolved and the tremendous antiquity

---

[31] Cf. A. Rowe, *The Topography and History of Beth-Shan* (1930); G. M. FitzGerald, *Beth-Shan Excavations 1921-23* (1931); A. Rowe, *Beth-Shan, Four Canaanite Temples* (1940); W. F. Albright, *BASOR*, No. 6 (1926), pp. 51ff.; G. E. Wright, *AJA*, XLV (1941), pp. 483ff.; C. C. McCown, *The Ladder of Progress in Palestine* (1943), pp. 151ff.

[32] Cf. Albright, *BASOR*, No. 4 (1924), pp. 51ff.

[33] Cf. G. Schumacher and C. Steuernagel, *Tell el-Mutesellim, I, Fundbericht* (1908); G. Watzinger, *II, Die Funde* (1929); R. S. Lamon and G. S. Shipton, *Megiddo I: Seasons of 1925-34* (1939); G. Loud, *Megiddo II: Seasons of 1935-1939* (1948); H. G. May, *Material Remains of the Megiddo Cult* (1935); R. S. Lamon, *The Megiddo Water System* (1935); P. L. O. Guy and R. M. Engberg, *Megiddo Tombs* (1938); G. Loud, *The Megiddo Ivories* (1939); W. F. Albright, *AJA*, LIII (1949), pp. 213ff.; G. E. Wright, *JAOS*, LXX (1950), pp. 56ff., *BA*, XIII, No. 2 (1950), pp. 28ff.; Y. Yadin, *BA*, XXIII, No. 2 (1960), pp. 62ff.; A. Goetze and S. Levy, *'Atiqot* (1959), II, pp. 121ff.

[34] For the excavation reports up to World War II see C. F. A. Schaeffer, *SRA*, X (1929), pp. 285ff., XII (1931), pp. 1ff., XIII (1932), pp. 1ff., XIV (1933), pp. 93ff., XV (1934), pp. 105ff., XVI (1935), pp. 141ff., XVII (1936), pp. 105ff., XVIII (1937), pp. 125ff., XIX (1938), pp. 193ff., XX (1939), pp. 277ff. For some subsequent studies see R. de Langhe, *Les Textes de Ras Shamra-Ugarit et leurs Rapports avec le Milieu biblique de l'Ancien Testament* (1945), I-II; C. H. Gordon, *Ugaritic Literature* (1949); G. R. Driver, *Canaanite Myths and Legends* (1956); C. F. A. Schaeffer, *Ugaritica* (1956), III; C. Virolleaud, *Le Palais Royal d'Ugarit* (1957), II.

of human occupation of the site was definitely established.[35] Problems raised by the work of Reisner at Samaria (Sebastiyeh) were cleared up by the excavations of Crowfoot, Kenyon, and Sukenik from 1931 to 1935.[36] In 1934 W. F. Albright and J. L. Kelso commenced work on the mound at Bethel.[37] Meanwhile Nelson Glueck had already begun an extensive archaeological survey in Transjordan, during which he located hundreds of sites and established the date of their occupational periods through the study of surface ostraca. In 1937 Glueck cleared a Nabataean shrine at Khirbet et-Tannur, and in the same year he began a series of campaigns which resulted in the discovery of a copper refinery at Ezion-geber (Tell el-Kheleifeh) dating from the Solomonic era.[38]

The Arab-Israeli conflict which followed World War II made the excavation of certain archaeological sites an extremely difficult matter. Despite this, work has been carried on at Beth-yerah (Khirbet Kerak) under B. Mazar, M. Avi-Yonah, Y. Yadin, and others since 1944, at Tirzah (Tell el-Far'ah) in a spasmodic fashion since 1946 under R. de Vaux, and also at other sites.

The spectacular discovery of the Dead Sea Scrolls in 1947, which has been described as one of the most sensational in the entire history of archaeological investigation, prompted a flurry of activity from 1948 in the Khirbet Qumran, Wadi Murabba'at, and Khirbet Mird areas under the direction of R. de Vaux, G. L. Harding, W. L. Reed, and others. Work was resumed at the site of Jericho in 1952 under Kathleen M. Kenyon,[39] one result of which was to assign an occupational history to Jericho reaching back to the seventh millennium B.C. The excavation of the large mound of ancient Hazor (Tell el-Qedah) was begun in 1954 by Y. Yadin,[40] while in 1956 digging was resumed at Shechem (Balatah) by G. E. Wright. As political conditions become increasingly favorable there will be many more opportunities for the excavation of

[35] J. Garstang, *Annals of Archaeology and Anthropology, University of Liverpool* XIX (1932), pp. 3ff., XX (1933), pp. 3ff., XXI (1934), pp. 99ff., XXII (1935), pp. 143ff., XXIII (1936), pp. 67ff.; J. and J. B. E. Garstang, *The Story of Jericho* (1948).

[36] J. W. Crowfoot, K. M. Kenyon, and E. L. Sukenik, *The Buildings at Samaria* (1942).

[37] Albright, *BASOR*, No. 56 (1934), pp. 2ff., No. 74 (1939), pp. 15ff.

[38] For his reassessment see N. Glueck, *BA*, XXVIII, No. 3 (1965), pp. 70ff.

[39] For the earlier reports see *PEQ*, LXXXIV (1952), pp. 62ff., LXXXV (1953), pp. 81ff., LXXXVI (1954), pp. 45ff., LXXXVII (1955), pp. 106ff., LXXXVIII (1956), pp. 67ff., LXXXIX (1957), pp. 101ff.; K. M. Kenyon, *Digging Up Jericho* (1957); also her articles in *BA*, XVI, No. 3 (1953), pp. 46ff., XVII, No. 4 (1954), pp. 98ff., and the volume *Jericho I* (1960).

[40] For preliminary reports see *Israel Exploration Journal*, VI (1956), pp. 120ff., VII (1957), pp. 118ff., VIII (1958), pp. 1ff., IX (1959), pp. 74ff.; *BA*, XXI, No. 2 (1958), pp. 30ff., XXII, No. 1 (1959), pp. 2ff.; Yadin, *Hazor I* (1958), *II* (1960); cf. A. Malamat, *JBL*, LXXIX (1960), pp. 12ff.

Biblical sites, thereby adding significantly to the already impressive accumulation of archaeological data.

2. Radiocarbon dating. Modern nuclear physics made an extremely important contribution to scientific archaeology subsequent to World War II through the development of the carbon-14 system of dating artifacts. This process is based upon the recognition of the fact that every living organism contains a proportion of radioactive carbon. The ordinary carbon present in living creatures is stable, and has an atomic weight of 12. Radioactive carbon, formed in the upper atmosphere through the bombardment of nitrogen-14 atoms by cosmic rays, is unstable in nature and has an atomic weight of 14. It has been discovered that, in practice, oxygen combines with the heavy carbon-14 atom to produce a variety of carbon dioxide, which is then ingested by all living things in a constant proportion of approximately one-trillionth of a gram of carbon-14 to one gram of carbon-12.

When the life of the particular organism terminates, the absorption ceases, and its radioactive carbon content begins to deteriorate at a regular rate in much the same way as radium gradually degenerates to become lead. Since carbon-14, like radium, exhibits a progressive rate of deterioration, the time when the assimilation of the unstable radioactive element ceased can be estimated with a reasonable degree of accuracy by measuring the amount of carbon-14 which remains in the specimen. The half-life of a carbon-14 atom has been estimated to be 5500 years; and in order to compute the age of organic remains it is necessary to reduce the material to carbon by burning, after which the carbon-14 content of the residue is measured by means of a highly sensitive radiation-counter. The first of these machines was developed by Professor W. F. Libby of the University of Chicago, and there are now many others in use in different parts of the world.[41]

As with so many other scientific procedures there is a certain margin of experimental error, sometimes in excess of five per cent. As newer and more sensitive radiation-counters are developed the range of measurement can be expected to be increased considerably, and to be accompanied by a reduction in the margin of error. Tests carried out to date have shown that certain types of organic material lend themselves more readily to carbon-14 dating than others. The carbon-14 technique is also extremely valuable for dating bones which contain a measurable amount of collagen. Sometimes radically wrong readings are furnished when disinterred remains have been allowed to become contaminated by such sources as the radioactive fallout from nuclear explosions, a fact

[41] Cf. W. F. Libby, *Radiocarbon Dating* (1954); K. Rankana, *Isotope Geology* (1954). For a survey of the various scientific methods which aid in archaeological evaluation see L. Bieck, *Archaeology and the Microscope* (1962), D. R. Brothwell and E. S. Higgs (eds.), *Science in Archaeology* (1962), pp. 21ff.

which demonstrates the desirability of independent dating-control on the basis of ceramic and stratigraphic techniques.

C. THE FUNCTION OF ARCHAEOLOGY

One of the principal functions of archaeological activity is to awaken a sense of the vitality of the Hebrew past in the student of Old Testament life and times. This is of great importance for the simple, though frequently unappreciated, reason that the essential message of the Old Testament cannot be fully comprehended without a knowledge of the cultural, religious, historical, and social background of the people to whom the revelation of God was given. Archaeological investigation has brought to light many new facets of Israelite life that had been lost with the passing of the ages and has helped to set Hebrew culture in proper perspective in relation to the trends and currents of ancient Near Eastern life generally. Many details of Hebrew history and religion have been confirmed by the spade of the excavator; yet, the main function of Biblical archaeology is to expose the human environment and furnish a properly accredited background to the study of the ancient Hebrews. It should never be expected to demonstrate the veracity of the spiritual truths implicit in the Old Testament, since archaeology is essentially a human activity and cannot therefore as such confirm theology or open the realm of faith.[42]

Bearing these considerations in mind, however, it can be said at once that the results of archaeological discovery have contributed enormously to the understanding of Biblical history and culture and have gone far towards confirming the veracity of the Old Testament writers. New light has been thrown upon pressing problems of chronology; forgotten languages have been discovered and made intelligible once more, obscure events and ideas have been clarified, and curious social customs set against their correct historical and sociological background. The selective nature of many of the Old Testament records is clearly such that certain occurrences that did not serve the predominantly religious purposes of the various authors to any significant extent were either omitted completely or only mentioned briefly in passing. Recent archaeological discoveries have enabled some of these omissions to be rectified in the interests of a continuous historical picture, while at other points they have furnished much new information on subjects which constituted matters of understatement in the Old Testament.

The character of modern archaeology is such that it can be said to constitute the *sine qua non* of any realistic understanding of ancient man and his world, a fact which is of particular importance for ancient Near Eastern and Biblical studies generally. Unfortunately, however, as with all observed "scientific facts," archaeological data can be sifted and

42 G. W. Van Beek, *IDB*, I, p. 205.

blended to conform to all kinds of preconceived schemes, and not least in the realms of Old Testament history and religion. Against this tendency is the growing realization among scholars that the results of lower criticism and the evidence from excavated sites generally reinforce one another. When a *schema* for the historical development of the Hebrews is formulated on such a basis, it is seen to be considerably closer to the historical orthodox position than any other, including the conjurations of those who postulated the documentary and fragmentary theories of Pentateuchal origins.

The positive values which have accrued for students of the Old Testament as the outcome of archaeological activity in the late nineteenth and the twentieth centuries have included, among others, the confirmation of the Biblical narrative at most points, and this, as R. A. Bowman has remarked,[43] has led to a new respect for the Biblical tradition and a more conservative conception of Biblical history. In this same connection an even more forthright statement, which was subsequently quoted widely, was made by the eminent Biblical archaeologist Nelson Glueck. In a *New York Times* review of *The Bible as History* by Werner Keller, Glueck stated that he had spent many years in Biblical archaeology, and in association with his colleagues had made discoveries confirming in outline or in detail historical statements in the Bible. He was consequently prepared to go on record as stating that no archaeological discovery has ever been made that contradicts or controverts historical statements in Scripture.

Not long after the present writer had published his popularly written *A History of Old Testament Times,* in 1957, a reviewer remarked that the book had been compiled in such a way as to suggest that the Old Testament, as traditionally interpreted, was confirmed by every new archaeological find.[44] Quite aside from the fact that the purpose of the work was to show the extent to which the Biblical self-estimate had been vindicated and supported by the discoveries of the Near Eastern archaeologists, the writer has yet to become acquainted with any single archaeological find which by itself or in conjunction with others specifically and categorically disproves the testimony of the Old Testament to itself in any single area of history or religion, or discredits its basic trustworthiness in the manner in which liberal scholars have been endeavoring to do for many years.

This is not to say, of course, that each newly excavated archaeological site has thrown immediate and convincing floods of light upon one or another of the numerous problems presented to the western mind by the Old Testament narratives. All too often the testimony of artifacts proves to be ambiguous, due to a wide variety of conditions in which the purely

---

[43] In *The Study of the Bible Today and Tomorrow* (ed. H. R. Willoughby, 1947), p. 30.

[44] L. H. Brockington, *JTS,* IX (1958), p. 416.

human element is not infrequently dominant. But when taken as part of a vast cultural complex, such discoveries enrich and enlarge contemporary knowledge of the manifold facets of ancient Near Eastern life, and supply precisely the kind of information that will enable the Old Testament narratives to be interpreted authoritatively against their social, historical, and cultural background.

It is not the purpose of the present review to adduce every possible scrap of evidence in favor of the veracity of the Old Testament narratives and to ignore the problems presented by certain of the excavated sites. At the same time the writer has been at some pains to portray the positive results of archaeological activity as they relate to the Hebrew Scriptures, rather than ignoring them so as to concentrate upon the difficulties raised, an approach that is the favored methodological procedure in certain scholarly circles.

II. THE ARCHAEOLOGY OF EARLY MESOPOTAMIA

On the basis of what is now known one can formulate a remarkably detailed picture of life in ancient Mesopotamia, particularly as it affected the origins of the Hebrew peoples. Archaeological activity in the land of the Tigris and Euphrates has now demonstrated conclusively that culture originated in that general geographical area rather than in Egypt, as was thought during the middle of the nineteenth century. Some of the earliest inhabited sites of Mesopotamia represented by present-day mounds,[1] belong to the Neolithic period (*ca.* 6000-4500 B.C.) of northern Mesopotamia. These include the mound at Nineveh and the *tell* at Tepe Gawra, twelve miles northeast of Nineveh. Professor M. E. L. Mallowan took soundings of the mound at Nineveh in 1931, and at a depth of about ninety feet he uncovered the remains of prehistoric villages. Decayed wood and ashes were mingled with pieces of crude pottery marked by notches and other rough decorative attempts.[2]

The first traces of Chalcolithic (*ca.* 4500-3000 B.C.) culture were unearthed at Tell Halaf in northern Mesopotamia by Baron von Oppenheim just before World War I.[3] Remains such as these are styled Halafian, in conformity with the practice of designating the different cultural stages in terms of the sites where they were originally discovered. The most important feature of the excavations at Tell Halaf was the delicate painted pottery which was unearthed from the lowest levels of the mound. One vase was decorated with the picture of a wheeled vehicle, perhaps a wagon or a chariot, and this represents the earliest known drawing of a spoked wheel. Most experts agree that the design, texture, and temperature-control exhibited by Halafian pottery were unsurpassed in the ancient world.[4]

---

[1] *Tell* (pl. *tulul*), an ancient Babylonian term surviving in modern Arabic. References to both ruined and inhabited mounds occur in Josh. 8:28 and 11:13.

[2] M. E. L. Mallowan, *Annals of Archaeology and Anthropology, University of Liverpool*, XX (1933), pp. 127ff., *Proceedings of the First International Congress of Prehistoric and Protohistoric Sciences, 1932* (1934), pp. 165ff. M. von Oppenheim, *Der Tel Halaf, eine neue Kultur im ältesten Mesopotamien* (1931).

[3] *CAEM*, pp. 16ff.

[4] *FSAC*, p. 90; *LAP*, p. 15 and pl. 1.

The work of C. L. Woolley and H. R. Hall at Tell el-Obeid enabled them to date the earliest Obeid levels about 4000 B.C.[5] A later Obeid stratum (XIII) at Tepe Gawra[6] revealed the existence of three large shrines whose construction was characterized by a series of recessed vertical niches in the walls, an architectural technique that made possible the construction of the Egyptian pyramids many centuries later.[7]

Excavations by Jordan at Uruk[8] brought to light the next cultural phase, known as the Uruk period. The site yielded black, grey, and red ceramic ware that had been made on a potter's wheel. An important discovery was that of the remains of the first Babylonian *ziggurat*,[9] which was about forty-five yards square. Another building at the site was decorated by means of patterned mosaics of flattened clay cones executed in three colors and reminiscent of Obeid patterns.[10] The earliest-known cylinder seal was found at Uruk; this device replaced the decorative button-like stamp seal that was used for identifying property in the earlier Obeid period. The stone cylinder seal was engraved in relief in such a manner that when it was rolled on soft clay surfaces it left a distinctive impression, which in later times was often a matter of some artistic achievement. Uruk culture also produced a rough pictographic script written on clay tablets, which was the precursor of Babylonian cuneiform. The Uruk texts were inscribed in perpendicular columns from left to right, and employed a sexagesimal system of computation that was subsequently enlarged by the Sumerians.[11]

The beginning of the third millennium B. C. at Jemdet Nasr[12] in central Mesopotamia saw the development of an increasingly complex urban life, in which bronze first came into use and the scope of agriculture was extended by the cultivation of wheat, barley, grapes, olives, onions, beans, and other vegetables.[13] Although the cultural expansion of southern Mesopotamia had been hindered initially through the difficulties encountered in attempts to drain the rich alluvial mud of the Tigris-Euphrates delta, the efforts expended in this direction were finally so successful that by the beginning of the third millennium B. C. a range

---

[5] Hall and Woolley, *Ur Excavations I, Al 'Ubaid* (1927).

[6] E. A. Speiser, *BASOR*, No. 65 (1937), p. 8, No. 66 (1937), pp. 3ff.; *CAEM*, pp. 44ff., 162ff.

[7] *BCNE*, pp. 126ff.

[8] The "Erech" of Gen. 10:10. Cf. J. Jordan, *Uruk-Warka nach den Ausgrabungen durch die Deutsche Orient-gesellschaft* (1920); *CAEM*, pp. 97ff.

[9] An artificial mound on which a shrine was erected. The term was often used to include the structure also. Cf. *CAEM*, pp. 110ff.

[10] *BCNE*, p. 55.

[11] A. Falkenstein, *Archaische Texts aus Uruk* (1940), pp. 49, 61; *FSAC*, p. 146.

[12] *CAEM*, pp. 106f., 143ff.

[13] *FSAC*, p. 145.

of crops and vegetables as varied as those of northern Mesopotamia was being grown in the southern part of the country also.

About 4000 B.C. a people of superior intellectual caliber, known as Sumerians after their central area Sumer, occupied the marshy regions of the Tigris-Euphrates delta. Although their place of origin is far from certain, they may have come from the Caucasus, or perhaps from the mountainous regions east of Mesopotamia. They were a swarthy, non-Semitic group, and were characterized by a high degree of cultural attainment and considerable organizational ability. Their advanced religious concepts prompted them to draw up a list of deities and develop theological principles that dominated the religious life of Mesopotamia for many centuries.[14] Remains of articles found in temple storerooms[15] have pointed to the activities of craftsmen who initiated and developed commercial dealings with India, Asia Minor, and Syria in such articles as toilet sets, gold and silver jewelry, decorated pottery, and agricultural implements including plows.

Mesopotamia had always been subject to devastating inundations, and a flood or series of floods was a firmly established part of the early dynastic traditions of Sumeria. Several versions of a flood-narrative were extant in the third millennium B. C., some of which spoke of Shuruppak as the site of the deluge. One fragmentary clay tablet found at Nippur preserved the tradition of that time with an account of the way in which the gods first created mankind and then regretted their having done so, and decided upon the destruction of the human race. The fourth column of the tablet recorded how Enki, the powerful water-deity, revealed the plan of devastation to Ziusudra, the pious king-priest who is the Sumerian counterpart of the Biblical Noah.

The fifth column described the way in which Ziusudra survived the tremendous flood:

> All the windstorms, exceedingly powerful, attacked as one...
> After, for seven days and seven nights,
> The deluge had raged in the land,
> And the huge boat had been tossed about on the great waters...
> Ziusudra opened *a window* of the huge boat...
> Before Utu prostrated himself.
> The king kills an ox, slaughters a sheep...[16]

Late Jemdet Nasr levels at Shuruppak[17] revealed the existence of a large alluvial deposit, while the excavations of Langdon at Kish[18] uncovered a similar stratum measuring some eighteen inches in depth. Lang-

---

[14] S. N. Kramer, *IDB,* IV, pp. 460f.

[15] *BCNE,* p. 67.

[16] S. N. Kramer, *Sumerian Mythology* (1944), pp. 97f.

[17] E. F. Smith, *The Museum Journal,* XXII (1931), pp. 200f.

[18] L. C. Watelin and S. Langdon, *Excavations at Kish IV, 1925-30* (1934), pp. 40ff.; *LAP,* pl. 8.

don described the latter in terms of the flood of Noah,[19] a distinction that was also claimed by Woolley for an eight-foot middle-Obeid alluvial deposit at Ur.[20] What was unfortunate about this situation was that the alluvial levels at Ur and Kish were not contemporary, and that similar deposits at Lagash, Kish, Uruk, and Shuruppak did not correspond with the dating of the Ur stratum. Matters were further complicated when Watelin excavated Kish and uncovered several more alluvial layers, two of which were separated by a nineteen-foot level of debris.[21] When Woolley carried out work on the mound known as Tell el-Obeid, four miles distant from ancient Ur, he failed to find any traces whatever of water-laid strata.

This attempt at correlation furnishes some idea of the difficulties involved in the interpretation of archaeological material, and has even led some scholars to state that the excavations in Mesopotamia have failed to uncover any traces of the Noachian deluge.[22] What is immediately clear is that it is far from easy to associate any one of these deposits at all closely with the flood described in the book of Genesis. Yet it is still a fact that Mesopotamia suffered from cataclysmic inundations at different periods in antiquity. Since the depth of the alluvial levels varied from site to site, it is reasonable to conclude from the available evidence that the deluge recorded in Genesis constituted one such flood of major proportions that occurred in a comparatively localized area.[23] As far as later Semitic tradition was concerned, the inundation was important because it involved the ancestors of the Biblical patriarchs, and unlike other ancient Mesopotamian floods it had a basis in morality.

The excavations of Watelin at Kish uncovered cylinder impressions of Gilgamesh, the legendary hero of Babylonian epic poetry, at levels which were beneath the ones identified by Langdon with the deluge of Genesis.[24] From this it would appear that the Babylonian account of the flood was already known at Kish, which is striking testimony to the antiquity of the tradition. In the light of the evidence available to date it is impossible to state with any degree of certainty either the origin of the Babylonian and Hebrew accounts of the flood or the extent of their interrelationship.[25] From a purely archaeological standpoint the most

19 *JRAS* (1930), p. 603.
20 *UC*, pp. 21ff.; C. L. Woolley, *The Antiquaries Journal*, X (1930), pp. 329ff.
21 L. C. Watelin, *Kish IV* (1934), pp. 42ff.
22 E.g. J. Bright, *BA*, V, No. 4 (1942), p. 58.
23 J. C. Whitcomb and H. M. Morris, *The Genesis Flood* (1961), expounded the view that the Genesis deluge was a universal aqueous catastrophe, and rejected the uniformitarian theories of geology.
24 L. C. Watelin, *Kish IV*, pp. 40ff.
25 In *WBA*, p. 119, the tradition underlying the Flood story is assigned to the end of the Stone Age (*ca.* 4000 B.C.).

that can be said at the time of writing is that the Genesis deluge cannot be associated with any one particular archaeological level.[26]

Similar problems are immediately encountered when attempts are made to recover and identify the ark used by Noah to escape from the worst effects of the Flood. The mountains of Ararat, the traditional resting-place of the ark, can quite possibly be identified with the *Urartu* of Assyrian inscriptions, corresponding to the neighborhood of Lake Van in modern Armenia. However, the other attempts to locate the Biblical Ararat have witnessed archaeological activity in Iranian and Russian territory, as well as that of Turkey. Periodic endeavors have been made to recover pieces of the "original ark,"[27] and even though radiocarbon dating has established the antiquity of some of the fragments brought back from possible locations by travellers and explorers, it is completely illogical to try to identify such pieces with Noah's ark. There is very little likelihood that the ark has survived in any form to the present day, and even if traces of an ancient vessel[28] were recovered from a probable site, there would be no means of knowing with certainty whether or not the fragments were in fact part of the original ark.

The excavations of Woolley at Ur have furnished graphic proof of the advanced nature of the First Dynasty culture. A burial area outside the walls of the primitive city yielded a variety of funerary objects including cups, eapons, tools, and jewelry.[29] The celebrated "royal tombs" of Ur were unearthed at a lower level, and were found to consist of an upper and lower vault constructed from blocks of imported limestone. The body which was entombed in the upper vault was identified from a lapis lazuli cylinder as that of Queen Pu-abi, while an accompanying cylinder seal designated the occupant of the lower tomb as A-bar-gi.

Adjacent burial pits contained the remains of male and female attendants, along with a variety of funerary objects including some beautifully inlaid harps and two statues of goats standing erect before a bush.[30]

---

[26] Among those connecting the Ur alluvial stratum with the Genesis flood are H. Peake, *The Flood: New Light on an Old Story* (1930), p. 114; C. Marston, *The Bible Is True* (1934), pp. 67ff.; S. Caiger, *OT and Modern Discovery* (1938), p. 34; F. Kenyon, *The Bible and Archaeology* (1940), p. 140; A. R. Short, *Modern Discovery and the Bible* (1942), p. 98; A. Rehwinkel, *The Flood* (1951), pp. 47ff., 174ff.; E. F. Kevan, *New Bible Commentary* (1953), p. 84; W. Keller, *The Bible as History* (1956), pp. 48ff. Those rejecting this association include R. L. Harris, *The Bible Today*, XXXVII, No. 9 (1943), pp. 575ff.; B. C. Nelson, *Before Abraham* (1948), p. 108; F. R. Steele, *Eternity*, III (1952), p. 44; M. F. Unger, *Archaeology and the OT* (1954), p. 47; *WBA*, p. 119; J. C. Whitcomb and H. M. Morris, *The Genesis Flood*, pp. 110ff.

[27] Described by A. Parrot, *The Flood and Noah's Ark* (1955), pp. 63ff.

[28] Ancient Mesopotamian craft are figured in *ibid.*, pls. 6 and 7.

[29] *UC*, pp. 74ff. For the suggestion that Ur of the Chaldees was in the region of Harran, as maintained by some nineteenth-century authors, see *GBB*, pp. 287f.

[30] *UC*, pl. 5 (a), 6.

The high degree of contemporary artistic skill was made clear by the recovery of the magnificent golden helmet of Ur, found in the grave of "Meskalam-dug, Hero of the Good Land." It was fashioned from solid gold in the form of a wig, with the locks of hair hammered in relief and engraved in a delicate symmetrical form.[31] From another stone vault came the celebrated "Standard of Ur," a mosaic panel of shell and lapis lazuli depicting the themes of war and peace, and perhaps constituting a banner or standard which was carried in procession on ceremonial occasions.[32]

During the fourth millennium B.C. some Semitic tribes settled in the northern part of the plain of Shinar and began to establish trading relationships with the Sumerians. About 2400 B.C. they became a powerful nation under the vigorous leadership of Sargon of Agade, and were known from that time as Akkadians. Sargon defeated Lugalzaggesi of Sumeria about 2355 B.C., occupied the territory thus gained, and assimilated the bulk of Sumerian culture into his own dynasty. For a short time there was a dramatic revival of the classic Sumerian culture as expressed in the Third Dynasty of Ur (*ca.* 2113-1991 B.C.), during which Ur-Nammu, "king of Sumer and Akkad" erected the massive *ziggurat* at Ur which was excavated by Woolley in 1922.[33] A fragmentary *stele* of the king recovered from the site depicted him as a workman carrying compasses, a pick, and a trowel,[34] while a flying angel gave divine sanction to the work being undertaken.[35] The Third Dynasty terminated in devastation at the hands of Elamite raiders from the north, and for a time Mesopotamia reverted to the ancient city-state system. But under Hammurabi (*ca.* 1728-1686 B.C.), the last king of the First Babylonian Dynasty, the dominance of Babylon was clearly established.

Hammurabi was an outstanding military and political figure, who exerted great cohesive force upon the society of his day. He was responsible, among other things, for the earliest known attempts at townplanning,[36] as well as for the celebrated collection of legal decisions which has become known as the Code of Hammurabi. This landmark of Mesopotamian jurisprudence was first uncovered by J. de Morgan at Susa in 1901 in the form of a black diorite *stele*,[37] having been carried there from its original site by marauding Elamites about 1200 B.C. The *stele*

---

[31] *UC*, pp. 59f.; C. L. Woolley, *The Sumerians* (1928), pl. 9.
[32] C. L. Woolley, *The Sumerians*, pp. 50ff. and pl. 14.
[33] *UC*, pp. 89ff.; *Ur Excavations: V, The Ziggurat and Its Surrounding* (1939).
[34] *LAP*, pl. 20.
[35] *UC*, pl. 10 (a); cf. C. L. Woolley, *The Development of Sumerian Art* (1935), p. 112.
[36] Cf. A. Parrot, *Babylon and the OT* (1958), pp. 68ff.
[37] *LAP*, pp. 48ff. and pl. 22.

was a copy of the original, and on examination was found to contain fifty-one columns of cuneiform.

Hammurabi's Code was based upon earlier legal material from Sumeria that had been adapted to the needs of Babylonian society. A prologue recorded the divine commission that had prompted the work, and this was followed by nearly three hundred prose sections[38] dealing with a wide variety of commercial, moral, social, and domestic matters. Society at that period was divided into three classes, comprising the *awilum* or patrician, the *mushkenum* or free artisan, and the *wardum* or chattel-slave classes. When legal satisfaction of any sort was required, the principle of retaliation in kind (*lex talionis*) was applied in terms of these divisions. The Code makes it clear that a great many kinds of medical and surgical procedures were in common use, and that there were serious attempts made to regulate the activities of the medical practitioners by the prescribing of fee-scales and the enacting of severe punishments in instances of proven malpractice. The construction of houses and public buildings, tax-collection, animal husbandry, river navigation, and many other topics were the subject of legislation in the Code, furnishing an indication of the highly complex nature of contemporary political and social life. Scholars have frequently drawn instructive parallels between the Code of Hammurabi and the Mosaic legislation.[39] In the matter of adultery the Code (Section 129) and the Torah (Lev. 20:10; Deut. 22:22) prescribed capital punishment for both offenders. In Exodus 21:16, as in the Code (Section 14), the kidnapping and selling of a person was punishable by death. Again, the principle of retaliation as enunciated in Exodus 21:23ff., and Deuteronomy 19:21 was identical with that underlying many parts of the Code of Hammurabi (e.g. Sections 197, 210, 230). It is interesting to note that the Mosaic legislation differed from the legal provisions of Hammurabi (Section 142) in refusing to allow women equal rights of divorce with men. While there is a complete absence of a reliance upon magic in the Code of Hammurabi, it is not especially notable for its emphasis upon ethical and spiritual principles, and in general it can be said that the legislation placed a decidedly inferior valuation upon human life than did the Mosaic enactments.

During the days of Hammurabi the Babylonian scribes expanded and rewrote Sumerian literary originals to produce the celebrated creation epic known from its opening words as *Enuma elish* or "When from above. . . ." The finished form of this composition ran to about one thou-

---

[38] *ANET*, pp. 164ff.; *ANE*, pp. 138ff.
[39] E.g. S. A. Cook, *The Laws of Moses and the Code of Hammurabi* (1903); W. W. Davies, *The Codes of Hammurabi and Moses* (1905); W. Eilers, *Die Gesetzesstele Chammurabis* (1932); F. M. Böhl, *King Hammurabi of Babylon in the Setting of His Time* (1940); J. Rapaport, *PEQ*, LXXIV (1941), pp. 158ff.; W. J. Martin in *DOTT*, pp. 27ff.

sand lines of cuneiform written on seven tablets linked in series, and contained many of the familiar religious traditions of Mesopotamia.[40] The sixth tablet described the creation of mankind from the blood of a mythical deity named Kingu, while the concluding tablet established Marduk firmly as the accredited leader of the entire Babylonian pantheon.

Another well-known composition which emerged from the First Babylonian Dynasty was the Epic of Gilgamesh,[41] which, like *Enuma elish,* was first recovered from the ruined palace library of Ashurbanipal (669-627 B.C.) at Nineveh. The Epic described the exploits of the legendary Sumerian king of Uruk early in the third millennium B.C., who became engaged in a search for the "plant of life." The eleventh tablet in the series preserved the Babylonian account of the Deluge, in which Utnapishtim, keeper of the "plant of life," warned Gilgamesh that the gods planned to engulf Shuruppak by means of a devastating flood. Utnapishtim[42] was ordered to construct an ark, and shortly after it was finished a terrible tempest arose:

> Six days and (six) nights
> the wind blew, the downpour, the tempest (and) the flood,
> When the seventh day arrived . . .
> The sea grew quiet, the storm abated, the flood ceased.
> I opened a window and light fell upon my face. . .
> On Mount Nisir the ship landed. . . .[43]

In the days of Rim-Sin of Larsa, an older contemporary of Hammurabi, a group of people arose in Mesopotamia who were referred to frequently in tablets and inscriptions by means of the ideogram SA.GAZ, and elsewhere as Habiru or Hapiri.[44] They were of obscure origin, and did not appear to have had any established role in the society of the day, since they occurred in the cuneiform texts as mercenary soldiers, government employees, musicians, captives, landless troops, domestic servants, and the like.[45] Albright has maintained that there is some philological connection between the Habiru, whom he thinks were more properly designated 'Apiru, and the 'Ibrîm or Biblical Hebrews.[46] While there

---

[40] A. Heidel, *The Babylonian Genesis* (1951 ed.), pp. 8ff.

[41] A. Heidel, *The Gilgamesh Epic and OT Parallels* (1949).

[42] The Semitic Babylonian form of the name *Ziusudra* (Sumerian).

[43] A. Heidel, *The Gilgamesh Epic,* pp. 85f.

[44] The latter may be equivalent to the 'Aperu or 'Apiru of Egyptian inscriptions such as the *stele* of Sethi I (*ca.* 1319-1300 B.C.). Cf. W. F. Albright, *AASOR,* VI (1926), pp. 35f.; A. Rowe, *The Topography and History of Beth-Shan* (1936), pp. 29f.

[45] For a survey of the problems connected with the origin of the Habiru see M. Greenberg, *The Hab/piru* (1955), pp. 3ff.; M. G. Kline, *Westminster Theological Journal,* XX (1957), pp. 46ff.

[46] *FSAC,* p. 240; *BPAE,* pp. 5, 11.

are still some unsolved problems connected with this matter, there seems little valid reason for rejecting the theory that the Hebrews may have been a small ethnic component of the larger Habiru group. At all events, the varied nature of the social units which existed in the second millennium of Mesopotamian history certainly leaves room for such a possibility.

III. THE ARCHAEOLOGICAL BACKGROUND OF THE OLD TESTAMENT

A. PATRIARCHAL HISTORY

With the fall of the Third Dynasty of Ur, a Semitic group known as the Amorites (Amurru) took advantage of the struggle for power between Babylon and Larsa to establish their capital at Mari (Tell Hariri). Under Shamshi-Adad I (ca. 1748-1716 B.C.) they became the dominant military force in the northern part of the country subsequently known as Assyria, and by the eighteenth century B.C. they were so powerful that they virtually monopolized the important public offices in Mesopotamia. The nature of the culture at Mari was brought to light by the excavations of Parrot in 1933,[1] who identified the *tell* by means of a statue from the temple of Ishtar which bore the inscription: "Lamgi-Mari, king of Mari, high-priest of Enlil, dedicated his statue to Ishtar."[2] The excavation of the royal palace at Mari in 1935 furnished convincing proof that Mari had kept abreast of the cultural developments of the day. The palace buildings numbered nearly three hundred, spread over an area of 150 acres.[3] Some of the original bathrooms were found to contain twin terra-cotta baths, beside which were simple covered toilets.[4] Parrot and his colleagues were amazed to discover that the pottery conduits which drained the palace roof were still in working order some three-and-a-half millennia after their installation.[5]

Tablets recovered from the palace archives included correspondence between Zimri-Lim, the last ruler of Mari, and Hammurabi, showing that the military attachés of the former relayed regular intelligence reports to Mari from the court of Hammurabi. One such record spoke of a Mari

---

[1] For the early reports see *SRA*, XVI (1935), pp. 1ff., 117ff., XVII (1936), pp. 1ff., XVIII (1937), pp. 54ff.

[2] G. E. Mendenhall, *BA*, XI, No. 1 (1948), p. 5.

[3] In contrast Jericho was probably not more than 8 acres at this time. Cf. *WBA*, pp. 36f., pl. 11.

[4] Mendenhall, *BA, loc. cit.*, pp. 8f., pl. 5.

[5] A. Parrot, *Mari, une ville perdue* (1935), p. 161.

105

diplomat as saying: "Whenever Hammurabi is occupied with any affair he writes to me, and I go to him wherever he may be. Whatever the affair may be, he tells it to me."[6]

This phase of Amorite history has important bearings upon the origins and traditions of the Biblical patriarchs. In the Balikh valley south of Haran (spelled Harran in the cuneiform texts), the names of certain patriarchal personages were commemorated in the designations of sites such as Serug, Peleg, and Terah.[7] In the Mari texts Nahor occurred as Nakhur, and was referred to as the home of some of the Habiru. By the beginning of the second millennium B.C. the names Abraham, Isaac, Jacob, Laban, and Joseph were in common usage. Abraham appeared in syllabic form as *A-ba-ra-ma, A-ba-am-ra-ma,* and *A-ba-am-ra-am,* while Jacob, written as *Ya-ʿqub-el,* was found as a Palestinian place name by 1740 B.C.[8] The name of Jacob in the form *Ya-ah-qu-ub-il* occurred on tablets from Tell Chagar Bazar in northern Mesopotamia about 1725 B.C.

In second-millennium B.C. texts of Mari an aggressive group of nomads known as the Banu-Yamina were mentioned periodically. These "sons of the right (south)," along with another nomadic group, the Khanu, proved to be very troublesome for the rulers of Mari, and in the end Zimri-Lim managed to slay one of the chiefs of the Banu-Yamina. Some scholars have connected this group with the Benjamites (Gen. 49: 29, cf. Judg. 20:16, 1 Chron. 12:2), though this cannot be definitely established as yet. The Mari term *dawidum,* translated "chieftain," was held by some early interpreters of the texts probably to have constituted the original form of the name David, but subsequent studies have raised objections to this suggestion,[9] and it now appears probable that the word may instead mean "defeat."

The excavations of Chiera, Starr, and others at Nuzu (Yorgan Tepe) and adjacent mounds near Kirkuk in Iraq from 1925 have proved to be of great importance also for an understanding of the patriarchal era. During work at the site of Nuzu some twenty thousand clay tablets, written in a Babylonian dialect with a cuneiform script, were unearthed from the family archives of several villas, and are of significance because on being translated they were found to have preserved a remarkable record of the social and legal structure of the fifteenth-century B.C. Hurrians, who at that time were in control of Nuzu. Although this is somewhat later than the period of the Biblical patriarchs, there is evidence that many of the customs mentioned in the texts had been observed for some centuries previously, and that the Hurrians had been a

[6] Mendenhall, *BA, loc. cit.,* p. 13.

[7] *FSAC,* pp. 236f.; Albright in *JBL,* XLIII (1924), pp. 385ff.; *BPAE,* p. 2; Mendenhall, *BA, loc. cit.,* pp. 15f.

[8] *FSAC,* pp. 237f.; *WBA,* p. 42.

[9] Cf. Mendenhall, *BA, loc. cit.,* p. 17; H. Tadmor, *JNES,* XVII (1958), p. 130; J. J. Stamm, *VT,* suppl. VII (1960), pp. 165ff.

virile part of the population of northern Mesopotamia and Syria from the eighteenth century B.C. Consequently, the tablets throw an interesting light upon the life and times of Abraham, Isaac, and Jacob, setting them accurately against the cultural background of second-millennium B.C. Assyrian society.[10]

The bulk of the cuneiform material excavated concerned family or private life, and some of the texts mentioned the Habiru's contracting for domestic service in wealthy households. One legal document told of the nefarious activities of the mayor, Kush-shiharbe (ca. 1500 B. C.), who was immoral in his private life and corrupt in his attitude towards civic administration. Ultimately the citizens of Nuzu had him arrested and brought to trial, and his misdemeanors were suitably punished.[11] By far the most prominent social institution in ancient Nuzu was the practice of adoption. Contemporary law prohibited the sale of land, probably because it was believed to be held in trust from the gods who were venerated as its sole owners. In consequence adoption was employed as a convenient device for transferring real property from one person to another. The usual procedure consisted in an individual's being "adopted" by one or more families, to whom he usually gave a "filial gift" for the privilege of acquiring title to the lands which he would inherit on the death of the adopting parents.

Not all adoptions were of this kind, however, for it was not uncommon for childless couples to adopt a particular person as a means of perpetuating their estate and family name. Even slaves were adopted for this purpose from time to time, as the Nuzu texts clearly indicate. The obligations associated with adoption entailed the performance of normal filial duties as well as the fulfilment of mourning rites on the death of the parents. The majority of contracts associated with adoption at Nuzu contained a proviso that if a natural son was born to the parents after adoption, their own offspring should have the precedence as the legal heir, and to him should go the terra-cotta household gods (the *teraphim* mentioned in Gen. 31:19).

There can be no doubt that Nuzu society laid great stress upon procreation rather than companionship as the primary purpose of marriage. In consequence, a married woman who proved to be unable to bear children for one reason or another was in an extremely invidious position. The normal marriage contract often made provision for such a contingency by requiring a childless wife to supply her husband with a

---

[10] E. Chiera, *Publications of Baghdad School I-III* (1927-1931); E. R. Lachemann *et al.*, *Excavations at Nuzi I-IV* (1929-1955); C. H. Gordon, *The Living Past* (1941), pp. 156ff.; *IOTT*, pp. 100ff. For some roughly contemporary north-Syrian texts see D. J. Wiseman, *The Alalakh Tablets* (1953); cf. C. L. Woolley, *A Forgotten Empire* (1953), pp. 51ff.

[11] R. H. Pfeiffer and E. A. Speiser, *AASOR*, XVI (1936), pp. 59ff.

concubine by whom he could obtain an heir. One such clause from a Nuzu marriage contract read as follows:

> If Gilimninu (the bride) will not bear children, Gilimninu shall take a woman of N/Lullu-land (whence the choicest slaves were obtained) as a wife for Shennima (the bridegroom).[12]

While certain privileges were thus conferred upon a concubine, the position of the wife in the household was normally protected to the point where the concubine was recognized as being of inferior status in the domestic economy. The rights of the concubine were also safeguarded by an important provision of Nuzu law which made it mandatory for the concubine and her offspring to remain within the family circle. As a consequence of this enactment, any attempt to expel a concubine and her children was regarded in a most serious light. Once again, however, if the legal wife subsequently bore a son to her husband, the child obtained the precedence as the heir to the family fortunes, a situation similar to that at Alalakh (Tell el-'Atshana) in northern Syria at about the same period.

Contemporary Nuzu society permitted a certain degree of latitude to be exercised in connection with the birthright, one of the most treasured possessions of the ancient Semites.[13] Thus it was legitimate for the birthright to be exchanged for something else, or negotiated in any other fashion warranted by the prevailing circumstances. One Nuzu tablet recorded the transfer of inheritance rights to an adopted brother, while another contained the agreement by which a man named Tupkitilla sold his birthright:

> On the day they divide the grove . . . Tupkitilla shall give it to Kurpazah as his inheritance share. And Kurpazah has taken three sheep to Tupkitilla in exchange for his inheritance share.[14]

Against this background of information it is immediately apparent that the patriarchal narratives of Genesis reflect the cultural and social trends of Nuzu society with a remarkable degree of fidelity. It now seems most probable that Terah and his family migrated from the region of Ur during the early part of the nineteenth century B.C., when northern Mesopotamia was largely under Amorite control. The proposals regarding the adoption of Eliezer as the heir-presumptive of Abraham (Gen. 15:2ff.) reflect contemporary practices in Nuzu very closely, as

---

[12] C. H. Gordon, *BA*, III, No. 1 (1940), p. 3.

[13] From 2 Kgs. 2:9 it appears that possession of the birthright carried with it a double portion of the inherited estate, along with other responsibilities (cf. Deut. 21:15ff., 2 Chron. 21:1ff.). This custom obtained both in Mesopotamia and at Alalakh.

[14] Gordon, *BA, loc. cit.*, p. 5.

contrasted with the implications of the divine assurance that Eliezer would in fact not be the true heir of Abraham in the last analysis.[15]

The way in which the childless wife Sarah gave her Egyptian slave Hagar to her husband Abraham as a concubine (Gen. 16:2; see also Gen. 30:3) in order to provide him with an heir (Ishmael) was in full accord with the prevailing local customs in northern Mesopotamia. When Sarah subsequently bore Isaac, the natural son was entitled by law to the rights of primogeniture. As far as Sarah was concerned, the continuing presence of Hagar and Ishmael in the confines of the household constituted a threat to the position of Isaac, who may have been of delicate physical constitution as a child. The apprehension that Abraham felt when Sarah expressed her determination to expel Hagar and Ishmael (Gen. 21:11) was prompted as much by the knowledge that such action was in direct contravention of Nuzu law and social custom as by purely humanitarian considerations. However, it is important in this connection to notice that Sarah's action could have been defended according to the ancient Sumerian code of Lipit-Ishtar (ca. 1850 B.C.),[16] one of the sources underlying the legislation of Hammurabi, which stated that the freedom received by the dispossessed slave was to be considered adequate compensation for the act of expulsion. This piece of legal sophistry was particularly ironic in a patriarchal society, where for a woman membership in a household was essential to her very existence.

The transfer of the birthright from Esau to Jacob (Gen. 25:31), a story which has always sounded a little bizarre to occidental ears, is now seen to mirror contemporary Nuzu social practices, which frequently condoned similar equally uneven transactions. At present it is not possible to say whether the birthright was ever sold to a complete stranger, since all extant transactions deal only with negotiations between members of the same family. Since the birthright was so intimately connected with private family affairs in a patriarchal society, it seems improbable that it would be an element in transactions between strangers, whatever conditions of duress might have prompted such a sale or disposition.

The nature of the relationship between Jacob and Laban has come into decidedly clearer focus as a result of the archaeological discoveries at Nuzu. The adoption of Jacob that Laban entertained apparently took place at a time when Laban had no sons of his own; and, as was usual in those days, he gave his daughters to Jacob for wives when certain stipulated conditions had been met. These included a clause that Jacob would forfeit his inheritance rights if he entered into marriage with other

---

[15] Ibid., p. 2. Cf. Albright, The Archaeology of Palestine and the Bible (1935 ed.), pp. 137ff.
[16] ANET, pp. 159f.

women. A tablet from Nuzu which contained similar provisions read as follows:

> The adoption tablet of Nashwi, son of Arshenni. He adopted Wullu, son of Puhishenni. . . . When Nashwi dies, Wullu shall be heir. Should Nashwi beget a son (the latter) shall divide equally with Wullu but (only) Nashwi's son shall take Nashwi's gods. But if there be no son of Nashwi's, then Wullu shall take Nashwi's gods. And (Nashwi) has given his daughter Nuhuya as wife to Wullu. And if Wullu takes another wife he forfeits Nashwi's land and buildings. . . .[17]

The manner in which Laban asserted his rights as a patriarch (Gen. 31–43) shows clearly that he regarded Jacob as his legally adopted son, not merely as a son-in-law. Within the next two decades it would appear that natural sons were born to Laban (Gen. 31:41), an event that disqualified under Nuzu law the adopted son from receiving and exercising the coveted rights of primogeniture. An attempt to remedy the imbalance may perhaps be seen in the action of Rachel in stealing and hiding the household gods (Gen. 31:19). Such images were normally the property of the natural rather than the adopted son, and their possession could be adduced in support of any claim Jacob might have cared to press to the inheritance of Laban.

From a strictly legal standpoint, Jacob and his family would be judged guilty by contemporary Nuzu society for leaving the household of Laban without first securing permission and a formal patriarchal blessing. Yet it is clear from the narratives that there was also fault on the side of Laban, for his daughters complained that he had treated them as "foreign women" (Gen. 31:15), thereby relegating them to the position normally occupied by household slaves at that period. The entire incident reflects the embarrassment of both parties, and the solution arrived at is eloquent testimony to the ability of oriental peoples to extricate themselves with dignity from an involved and delicate situation.

One feature of Nuzu society noticeable from the texts is the way in which impending death furnished the patriarchal figure with the supreme opportunity for bestowing his blessings, a practice also recorded in the book of Genesis (Gen. 27:27ff., 49:3ff.). Since at that time it was not the custom for written dispositions of property to be made, the death-bed pronouncements recorded in the Nuzu tablets constituted in effect the last will and testament of the dying man, and as such were regarded as legally binding upon all concerned and irrevocable in nature (cf. Gen. 27:33). That these testaments were apt to take strange courses in antiquity, as indeed in more recent times, is illustrated by a particular tablet

[17] Gordon, *BA, loc. cit.,* p. 5.

in which the moribund man "willed" a certain woman as wife to his unmarried son:

> My father, Huya, was sick and lying in bed, and my father seized my hand and spoke thus to me: "My other older sons have taken wives, but thou hast not taken a wife, and I give Zululishtar to thee as wife."[18]

In a subsequent court action the son succeeded in maintaining his right to marry this woman, even though it is highly probable that neither party had been consulted prior to the declaration of patriarchal intention.

During the Mari Age it was customary for the Amorites to ratify covenants or treaties by the sacrifice of an ass. This *khayaram katalum*, as the texts phrased it, was regarded as an essential element in concluding all agreements, whether they were of a business or commercial nature between individuals, or of a more international stature affecting the well-being of different peoples. One of the tablets has preserved a diplomatic communication from a government official to Zimri-Lim (*ca.* 1730-1700 B.C.) of Mari:

> I sent that message to Bina-Ishtar (and) Bina-Ishtar replied as follows: "I have killed the ass with Qarni-Lim and thus I spoke to Qarni-Lim under the oath of the gods: 'If you despise [?] Zimri-Lim and his armies, I will turn to the side of your adversary.'"[19]

A survival of this practice is to be seen in the habits of the semi-sedentary stockbreeders of patriarchal and later times, and it is particularly evident among the descendants of Shechem, who claimed the title "Bene Hamor" or "sons of the ass,"[20] and offered spiritual allegiance to the Canaanite deity Baal-berith or "Lord of the Covenant."

As a result of the recovery of certain Hittite legal texts from Boghazköy, the purchase of the Cave of Machpelah by Abraham (Gen. 23:3ff.) comes into considerably clearer perspective.[21] Ephron the Hittite wished to dispose of the property for an apparently exorbitant price, an offer that Abraham seemed reluctant to entertain. Under ancient Hittite law the one who purchased the entire property of the vendor assumed at the time of transfer certain legal obligations to render feudal services, the nature and extent of which are at present obscure. If, however, only a portion of the property was purchased, these duties were not mandatory. As a result, Abraham expressed interest in only a part of the total estate with a view to avoiding any attendant legal

---

[18] *Ibid.*, p. 8.

[19] G. E. Mendenhall, *BA*, XI, No. 1 (1948), p. 18, XVII, No. 3 (1954), pp. 52f.; M. Noth, *Gesammelte Studien zum AT* (1957), pp. 142ff.

[20] Cf. Josh. 24:32; Judg. 9:4. For other aspects of covenant-making at Mari which illustrate Old Testament practices see M. Noth, *Mélanges Isidore Lévy* (1958), pp. 433ff.

[21] Cf. *GBB*, pp. 29f.

obligations (Gen. 23:9). Ephron declined to accede to this suggestion; for reasons which are not stated in the Genesis narrative he found it to his advantage to dispose of the entire property. Ultimately Abraham agreed to the stated terms, and in accordance with the custom of the day the sale was conducted in public with the purchase price being measured in weighed amounts of silver.[22] The mention of trees in the narrative reflects the Hittite practice of listing the exact number of trees growing on each piece of property sold.[23]

From this brief survey of archaeological material from the second millennium B.C. of Assyrian culture, it will be clear that the patriarchal narratives are set firmly against a contemporary social and cultural background. To talk of Abraham and the Hebrew patriarchs generally as real personages who enjoyed an independent existence is not to beg the entire question as to whether Abraham and the Biblical tradition concerning him is historical, as Jacobsen would imply.[24] Rather, as W. F. Albright has remarked:

> Abraham, Isaac, and Jacob no longer seem isolated figures, much less reflections of later Israelite history; they now appear as true children of their age, bearing the same names, moving about over the same territory, visiting the same towns (especially Harran and Nahor), practising the same customs as their contemporaries.[25]

From an Egyptian tomb at Beni-Hasan has come some indication of the way in which the Semites of the time of Abraham must have dressed. A relief dated about 1900 B. C. depicted a group of semi-nomadic Semites on a visit to Egypt,[26] and showed, among other things, that the men wore beards while the women kept their flowing hair in position by means of clips or bands. Their clothes were multi-colored, and whereas the men wore short skirts and sandals, the women were attired in long dresses which they fastened at the shoulder with a clasp.[27]

The work of Nelson Glueck in the Hashemite Kingdom of Jordan[28] has made it clear that at this time (*ca.* 2000-1700 B.C.) the sites of Dothan, Gerar, Shechem, and Bethel were all inhabited, lending substance to the Genesis tradition that associated the patriarchs with the densely wooded hill country of Palestine (cf. Gen. 13:18; 26:23; 28:10; 33:18; 35:1; 37:17). The political atmosphere of the day is conveyed quite aptly by the story

[22] *IOTT*, p. 111.

[23] Gen. 23:17. M. R. Lehmann, *BASOR*, No. 129 (1953), pp. 15ff. Cf. J. C. L. Gibson, *JNES*, XX (1961), pp. 224ff.

[24] *IDB*, IV, p. 738.

[25] Quoted by G. F. Owen, *Archaeology and the Bible* (1961), p. 120.

[26] *WHAB*, p. 23.

[27] *WBA*, p. 46.

[28] N. Glueck, *The Other Side of the Jordan* (1940), pp. 114ff., *BA*, XVIII, No. 1 (1955), pp. 2ff.; *WMTS*, p. 71.

of Sinuhe, a prominent state official in Egypt who lived in the twentieth century B.C. at a time when southern Syria and Palestine were organized in terms of city-states. The political upheaval which had taken place on the death of the Egyptian pharaoh Amenemhet I made it desirable for Sinuhe to seek asylum in Palestine. His *Tale*[29] described the dangers attached to his crossing of the heavily guarded border and the hardships that he experienced en route to Kedem, where he fell in with an Amorite chieftain of the same kind as Abraham, Laban, and Jacob.

Sinuhe gained the confidence of the Amorites to the point where he ultimately commanded one of their tribes in a series of raids. His account of Amorite life closely resembles that experienced by the patriarchs, while his description of the highlands of Palestine is distinctly reminiscent of Deuteronomy 8:8.

> There were figs in it, and vines,
> More plentiful than water was its wine,
> Copious was its honey, plenteous its oil;
> All fruits were upon its trees.
> Barley was there, and spelt,
> Without end all cattle. . . .[30]

B. THE EXODUS

1. Israel's sojourn in Egypt. The political and social problems of the Egyptian Middle Kingdom period (*ca.* 2000-1776 B.C.) were compounded by an increase in trading relations with the Semitic nomads of Canaan and Arabia, and by the appearance upon the horizon of the Hyksos, a people of mixed Semitic-Asiatic descent.[31] By introducing the horse-drawn iron-fitted chariot and the compound Asiatic bow as military weapons, the Hyksos swept unconquered into the Nile delta about 1715 B.C., and by about 1680 B.C. they had subjugated the people of the Two Lands, a state of affairs that lasted for almost a century-and-a-half.

If elements of the Habiru were involved in some manner with the Hyksos ("chiefs of foreign lands") invasion of Egypt, it would be comparatively easy to understand why the descendants of Jacob were able to thrive in a land which was normally hostile, or at best only tolerant, towards strangers and immigrants. Such a connection between the Avar-

---

29 *ANET*, pp. 18ff.

30 *ARE*, I, Sect. 496. Cf. *ANET*, pp. 19f.; *LAP*, p. 82.

31 For a discussion of Hyksos origins see H. Stock, *Studien zur Geschichte und Archäologie der 13. bis 17. Dynaste Ägyptens* (1942), pp. 19ff.; R. M. Engberg, *The Hyksos Reconsidered* (1939), pp. 4ff.; T. Säve-Söderberg, *JEA*, XXXVII (1951), pp. 53ff.; *FSAC*, pp. 202ff.; W. F. Albright, *Tell Beit Mirsim II*, pp. 27ff. For a description of contemporary weapons see Y. Yadin, *The Art of Warfare in Biblical Lands* (1963), I, pp. 77ff.

is era of Hyksos rule and the patriarchal migration around 1700 B.C. would also throw light on the reference to Joseph's buying up the land for Pharaoh (Gen. 47:13), a procedure that reflected the social disruption in Palestine under Hyksos rule and which resulted in a form of feudalism.[32]

Against such a background it would not be unwarranted to expect considerable local color in the sagas of Joseph. The phrase "overseer over his house" (Gen. 39:4) is a translation of a title used of officers in the houses of Egyptian nobility; the designations "over my house" and "father to Pharaoh . . . lord of all his house . . . ruler throughout all the land of Egypt"(Gen. 41:40; 45:8) correspond exactly to the office of vizier or prime minister of Egypt.[33] One post not mentioned in the Old Testament is that of "Superintendent of the Granaries," an office of considerable importance in a country such as Egypt, where so much depended upon the proper storage and distribution of the grain. Since Joseph exercised these functions, he probably assumed the title also.[34] The suggestion that the office which Joseph held was a high one created especially in a time of emergency does not take adequate cognizance of the fact that Joseph was already very prominent politically before the catastrophes overtook Egypt.

The procedure by which the vizier was invested with a golden chain of office has been illustrated by a mural from the reign of Seti I (*ca.* 1308-1290 B.C.).[35] Riding in chariots was reserved for important state personages, to whom ordinary individuals were required to pay proper respect as the chariots passed. The incidence of periodic famines has been commemorated in inscriptions on tomb walls, as for example at Beni-Hasan (*ca.* 1980 B.C.),[36] and El Kab.[37] The familiar Egyptian "Tale of the Two Brothers,"[38] narrating the attempted seduction of a virtuous man, Bata, by the wife of his older brother, has points of contact with the account of Joseph and the wife of Potiphar (Gen. 39:7ff.), although in other respects it is quite different. In the "Tale," which was invariably related in ancient Egypt for entertainment rather than for moral instruction, the amorous wife made some suggestive remarks to the unfortunate Bata, and then she

> . . .stood up and took hold of him. . .then the lad (became) like a leopard with (great) rage at the wicked suggestion which she had made to him, and she

[32] Cf. Steindorff and Seele, *When Egypt Ruled the East* (1942), p. 88.
[33] *WBA*, p. 53.
[34] K. A. Kitchen, *Tyndale House Bulletin*, No. 2 (1957), pp. 4ff.; cf. W. A. Ward, *Journal of Semitic Studies*, V (1960), pp. 144ff.; J. Vergote, *Joseph en Égypte* (1959), pp. 32ff.
[35] J. A. Thompson, *Archaeology and the OT* (1959), pp. 37f.
[36] Cf. S. L. Caiger, *Bible and Spade* (1936), p. 61.
[37] Cf. R. K. Harrison, *Archaeology of the OT* (1962), p. 38.
[38] *ANE*, p. 12.

was very, very frightened. Then he argued with her, saying, "See here—you are like a mother to me, and your husband is like a father to me...What is this great crime which you have said to me? Don't say it to me again!"[39]

That this general theme was not unknown in other parts of the ancient world is evident from the presence of the Bellerophon story in the eastern Mediterranean texts of the Amarna-Mycenaean age, a narrative describing an adulterous wife who attempts to seduce a virtuous youth and maligns him when she is unsuccessful in her scheme.

Deliverance from Hyksos rule came for the Egyptians about 1560 B.C. When the hated invaders had finally been expelled, all possible traces of Hyksos domination, including public buildings, inscriptions, and the like, were eradicated.[40] During the Nineteenth Dynasty the pharaoh Rameses II moved his capital from Thebes to Tanis (Avaris), and enlarged the city that had been reconstructed by Seti I. Excavations at the site by Montet recovered *stelae* and other artifacts bearing the name of Rameses and his successors.[41] Since contemporary Egyptian texts mentioned that some 'Apiru were employed to drag the huge stones used in temple construction at sites that probably included Pithom and Rameses, it may well be that the narrative in Exodus 1 points to this period of reconstruction under Rameses II. Pithom has been identified with Tell el-Retabeh, and excavations there have uncovered some of the massive brick structures dating from the time of Rameses II in the Nineteenth Dynasty. Since no traces of construction or expansion in the preceding dynasty were evident at the site, it would appear that the Exodus tradition of bondage refers to the forced labor on constructional projects in the days of Rameses II. To this evidence may be added the fact that for two centuries (*ca.* 1300-1100 B.C.) Tanis was known as *Per Re'emasese* or "House of Rameses."[42] In sum this would appear to point to a thirteenth-century B.C. date for the Exodus.

With the discovery of the site of Rameses, the route followed by the withdrawing Israelites on their way to Sinai can be established with reasonable accuracy.[43] Clearly it was important for them to journey southeast to Succoth in order to avoid the heavily fortified frontier post of Zilu, which guarded the "Way of the Land of the Philistines." Thus they could not possibly have taken the northern route out of Egypt, as older scholars mistakenly supposed.[44] It is almost certain that the Israel-

[39] *ANET*, p. 24.
[40] Cf. *ARE*, II, sect. 303.
[41] P. Montet, *Les Nouvelles fouilles de Tanis* (1929-1933).
[42] *WBA*, p. 59.
[43] For a tentative map of the route see *WHAB*, p. 41.
[44] Cf. M. K. Schleiden, *Die Landenge von Sues* (1959); H. K. Brugsch, *L'Exode et les Monuments Égyptiens* (1875); C. S. Jarvis, *Yesterday and Today in Sinai* (1931). A. Gardiner, *JEA*, XIX (1933), pp. 127f., withdrew his earlier objections to the substantial historicity of the Exodus account.

ites crossed over a vast papyrus marsh, the Yam Suph or "Reed Sea,"[45] situated between the Bitter Lakes and the town of Zilu (Thiel), on their way to the Sinai peninsula, where sites such as Elim (Wadi Gharandel), Dophkah (Serabit el-Khadem), and Rephidim have been identified with reasonable certainty. More or less restricted to travel by asses, the wandering Israelites were compelled to keep fairly close to the oases and grazing lands to the southwest of the Dead Sea. This may well explain why the thirty-seven years of wilderness wanderings prior to the entrance into Canaan were actually spent in the region of Kadesh ('Ain Qudeirat—'Ain Qudeis) (Deut. 1:46).

2. *Canaan prior to the conquest.* The study of the history and religion of the Canaanites before the arrival of the Israelites has been considerably enlightened by the recovery of two second-millennium B.C. cultures. The activities of Winckler at Boghazköy (Khattusas) in east-central Asia Minor brought to light the majesty of the ancient Hittites, who made up the first Indo-European migration from the Caucasus region to reach the inland areas of Cappadocia.[46] They intermingled with the native Khatti, whose territory they conquered, and established a number of city-states beginning about 1850 B.C., while the ancient Assyrians were gaining the ascendancy in Mesopotamia. The Old Empire period lasted from about 1800 B.C. to approximately 1600 B.C., at which time internal strife seriously weakened the Hittite nation and led to a revival of Hurrian influence in the old Mitanni kingdom of northern Mesopotamia. The New Empire period began under the leadership of Suppiluliuma (*ca.* 1375-1340 B.C.), and was characterized by friendly relations with Egypt. Of the thousands of clay tablets written in several different languages—including Nesian and some dialects of Luvian—that were recovered from Boghazköy, one diplomatic text contained a greeting from Suppiluliuma to Amenhotep III (Huria) of Egypt as follows:

> Thus hath Suppiluliuma the great king, king of Hatti-land, to Huria, king of Egypt, my brother, spoken: "I am well. With thee may it be well. . .just as thy father and I mutually requested presents, so wilt also thou and I now be mutually good friends. . . ."[47]

By the time Hattusilis III (*ca.* 1275-1250 B.C.) came to the throne, Hittite power had been weakened by intrigue in neighboring confederate states. The Hittite empire finally crumbled under a series of powerful attacks by the "Sea Peoples" from the Aegean, and about 1200 B.C. the Hittites vanished from the historical scene.

---

[45] Cf. G. E. Wright, *IDB*, II, pp. 197ff.

[46] Cf. H. Winckler, *Sonderabzug aus der Orientalistischen Litteratur-Zeitung*, Dec. 15, 1906; *Mitteilungen der Deutschen Orientgesellschaft*, XXXV (1907), pp. 1ff.; H. Winckler and O. Puchstein, *Smithsonian Report for 1908*, pp. 677ff.; A. Götze, *Hethiter, Churriter und Assyrer* (1936), p. 27.

[47] *LAP*, p. 167; J. A. Knudtzon, *Die El-Amarna Tafeln* (1901-1905), I, No. 41.

Cuneiform texts from Boghazköy have demonstrated conclusively the cultural virility of these people, who were once relegated by liberal critics to an insignificant place in ancient Near Eastern history.[48] It is now known that the Hittites were in possession of advanced technological processes for smelting iron for all commercial purposes. They were renowned horsemen, and were the first to manufacture chariots with iron fittings and use them as weapons of war.[49] From the extant Royal Addresses it is evident that the ancient Hittites valued the arts of peace also, for the texts indicate that they had already enjoyed a prolonged tradition of settled court life.[50] The form that their society ultimately adopted seems to have been that of an exclusive caste superimposed upon the indigenous Anatolian Khatti. At an earlier time it had consisted of numerous separate townships governed by bodies of elders.[51]

Legal tablets from Khattusas showed that the Hittites thought in terms of the same general concepts of justice as the ancient Babylonians. Their legal corpus was based on several earlier collections, some of which may indicate stages in the development of a Code.[52] The inviolability of oaths, covenants, and treaties was consistently emphasized, as in other ancient Near Eastern systems of jurisprudence; but in contrast to the codes of Hammurabi and Moses the principle of retaliation was subordinate to that of restitution. One additional feature of Hittite legislative and social enlightenment can be seen in the marked degree of respect accorded to women.[53]

An advanced degree of syncretism characterized Hittite religion, whose pantheon included Sumerian, Akkadian, Egyptian, and native Khatti deities. Unlike their Babylonian counterparts the Hittite shrines were constructed in such a manner as to allow only a select few to observe the rituals of the holy place or *cella*.[54] The temple priests appear to have been occupied predominantly with ritual ministrations to the weather-deity of Hatti, who was known as "King of Heaven, Lord of the Land of Hatti." The cuneiform texts contained occasional references to human sacrifices, but for the most part the offices of the priests were directed towards the propagation of a nature-worship, which included spring rites for the quickening of the earth. Extant tablets indicate very little connection, if any, between the Hittite royal festival and the ceremonies that marked the commencement of the Babylonian New Year.[55]

[48] So, e.g. H. Ewald, *The History of Israel* (1883 ed.), I, pp. 233f., 235.

[49] *TH*, pp. 104f.

[50] *Ibid.*, p. 67.

[51] *Ibid.*, pp. 68f.

[52] *Ibid.*, p. 88.

[53] For Hittite legal texts see F. Hrozný, *Code hittite provenant de l'Asie Mineure* (1922); J. M. P. Smith, *The Origin and History of Hebrew Law* (1931), pp. 246ff.; E. Neufeld, *The Hittite Laws* (1951); *ANET*, pp. 188ff.

[54] *TH*, p. 145, pl. 9.

[55] *Ibid.*, pp. 152ff.

The second of these cultures that flourished in the second millennium B.C. was that of the Canaanites, a culture that was considerably more advanced than its counterpart in Israel during the period following the death of Joshua. The Canaanites made widespread use of Hittite technological developments in the field of iron manufacture, and shared with the Philistines the bulk of the export trade in the metal to Egypt. The actual recovery of ancient Canaanite culture was the result of an accidental discovery at Ras Shamra (Ugarit) in 1928. The site was excavated by Schaeffer the following year, and was found to date from the Neolithic period. Known as Ugarit in the Egyptian Amarna Age, its culture became dominant in Canaan during the fourteenth century B.C., after which it declined under Hittite and Egyptian influence. The tablets that were unearthed had been written in a Hurrian dialect and in an unfamiliar northwest Semitic language, transcribed in an alphabetic rather than a syllabic script, and were closely akin to Phoenician and Biblical Hebrew.[56]

Whereas the ancient Egyptians had employed a combination of syllabic writing (in which each sign represents a syllable) and logographic writing (in which each sign stands for a word) to produce the complicated hieroglyphic script, the Canaanites were the first to utilize the principle of alphabetism in cuneiform, thereby making a break with the syllabics of the Mesopotamians. The alphabet in consonantal form was subsequently transmitted through the Hebrews and the Phoenicians to the Greeks, who modified it, introduced diphthongs, and gave the language its classical form. At a later period the alphabet was modified still further by the Romans. Ancient Ugaritic culture is thus very important in the history of the development of pure alphabetism.[57]

The literature of Ugarit was predominantly mythological, consisting of legends and epic cycles, but the prose texts reflected the highly organized nature of Ugaritic society in describing land-ownership, civic affairs, administration, taxation, diplomatic matters, veterinary medicine, and many other topics.[58] What is of particular significance in these compositions, as far as the student of Scripture is concerned, is their exhibition of grammatical and literary forms that also occur in various parts of the Hebrew Bible, notably the Psalter. This discovery has already done much to clear up the alleged textual anomalies in the Psalms and other poetical writings, indicating that many forms that were previously

[56] Cf. C. H. Gordon, *Orientalia*, XIX (1950), pp. 374ff.; E. A. Speiser, *BASOR*, No. 121 (1951), pp. 17ff.; J. Friedrich, *Scientia*, LXXIV (1949), pp. 220ff.; W. F. Albright, *BASOR*, No. 150 (1958), pp. 36ff.; *FSAC*, p. 39; C. F. Pfeiffer, *Ras Shamra and the Bible* (1962), pp. 15, 25ff.; *BANE*, p. 58.

[57] Cf. *IOTT*, p. 81; D. Diringer, *The Story of the Aleph Beth* (1960), pp. 32ff.; C. H. Gordon, *Ugarit and Minoan Crete* (1965), p. 15.

[58] *ANET*, pp. 129ff.; *ANE*, pp. 92ff.; C. H. Gordon, *Ugaritic Handbook*, pp. 129ff.; *UL*, pp. 11ff.

thought to be corrupt are in fact peculiarities of Canaanite linguistic and grammatical structure whose significance had been forgotten with the passing of the generations and ages. Literary parallelism was a conspicuous feature of Ugaritic poetry, as seen in the citation:

> Lo thine enemies, O Baal,
> Lo thine enemies wilt thou smite.
> Lo thou wilt vanquish thy foes.[59]

which closely resembles the form of Psalm 92:9:

> For behold thine enemies, O Lord,
> For behold thine enemies shall perish.
> All the workers of iniquity shall be scattered.

Further parallels to Hebrew thought can be seen in the description of Baal as the "Rider of the Clouds" (cf. Pss. 68:4; 104:3), who was enthroned in the heavens (cf. Pss. 2:4; 103:19) and hurled down lightnings and thunderbolts (cf. Pss. 18:13; 77:18; 144:6).[60] The references of the Psalmist (Ps. 74:13f.) to "dragons" and "leviathan" may be somewhat reminiscent of the legend cycle of Baal and Anat, in which the marine monster Tannin was invoked for magical purposes.[61] But in this connection there are other considerations which have to be borne in mind, and these will be discussed elsewhere in the present work.

Ugaritic cult-worship as revealed by the cuneiform texts has done much to illumine the Old Testament references to Canaanite religion. The depraved nature of the pagan deities Anat and Astarte is evident in all phases of the poetic cycles from Ugarit. Both these mythical personages were styled "the great goddesses which conceive but do not bear," and the seduction of Anat by Baal was a popular element of contemporary mythology. In one text Anat was depicted as a butcher, slaying young and old alike in a frantic effort of destruction.[62] Asherah, the "creatress of the Gods," was commonly represented to be a nude prostitute called "Holiness," as was also the case in Egyptian cult-worship.[63] There was a recognized homosexual guild (Cinaedus) in the Canaanite temples, and ritual prostitution of both sexes was a commonplace occurrence.

Worship seems for the most part to have been carried out at the altars located on or near the summits of hills. To these "high places" the

---

[59] UL, p. 15; cf. H. L. Ginsberg, Orientalia, V (1936), p. 171; W. F. Albright, Religion in Life, XXI, No. 4 (1952), pp. 542ff.
[60] Cf. A. S. Kapelrud, The Ras Shamra Discoveries and the OT (1965), pp. 30ff.; W. F. Albright, CBQ, VII (1945), pp. 5ff.; T. H. Gaster, Thespis (1949 ed.), pp. 115ff.; W. F. Albright, Religion in Life, XXI, No. 4 (1952), pp. 542f.
[61] UL, p. 49.
[62] UL, pp. 17f.; cf. ARI, pp. 77, 88; BPAE, pp. 16f.
[63] W. F. Albright in The Jews, Their History, Culture and Religion (ed. L. Finkelstein, 1949), I, p. 10; BPAE, pp. 16f.

worshippers brought their offerings of cereals or meat, and the ritual in which they engaged normally included prayer and the presentation of offerings. A sacrificial feast of some kind seems also to have been a general part of the ceremony. The texts indicate that Canaanite sacrificial ritual was more diversified than was the case among the Israelites.[64] The Old Testament narratives speak of specific cult-objects, including the *asherah* and the sacred pillar or *maççebah* as being associated with sanctuary-worship in Canaan. The Ugaritic texts leave no doubt as to the gross sensuality and immorality of the Canaanite cultic rites, and it is sobering to realize that its barbarity and license had a widespread appeal to the contemporary Near Eastern nations.

3. *The conquest of Canaan.* Just before the death of Moses the Israelites crossed into Transjordan, preparatory to an attack on Jericho, a former Hyksos fortress that guarded access to Canaan proper. During the Middle Bronze Age (*ca.* 2100-1500 B.C.) the Hyksos had enlarged Jericho and strengthened its defenses by the addition of a huge embankment. About 1550 B.C. they retreated to Jericho after being expelled from Egypt, but they were unable to make a firm stand against Egypt's armies and lost their fortress by fire. Shortly after this period Jericho was apparently rebuilt on a smaller scale, and fortified by means of a double wall of mud brick, the inner structure following the general lines of the Early Bronze Age wall.

Garstang designated this as "City D," which he held to have been destroyed about 1400 B.C. under the leadership of Joshua.[65] However, the work of Kathleen Kenyon at the site has necessitated some revision of this estimate. She found very few if any purely demonstrable traces of the Joshua period in the mound, and no remains whatever of Late Bronze Age walls. Indeed, the structures which Garstang had ascribed to "City D" were actually found to date from the third millennium B.C., and evidently constituted part of a defensive system erected during that period.[66] As a result, it is at present extremely difficult to make any reliable pronouncement upon the nature and extent of Jericho in the time of Joshua. However, it is certainly in the realm of possibility that the military forces of the Eighteenth Dynasty of Egypt had reduced the once-powerful Hyksos fortress to little more than an outpost after 1600 B.C., although it was still imposing due to its strategic location.[67]

The general picture presented by archaeological excavation at the site is one of thorough desolation at Late Bronze Age levels, so that if these were exposed at the time of Joshua, the following five centuries, during which the site lay uninhabited (1 Kgs. 16:34), would furnish ample

[64] *ARI*, p. 92.

[65] J. and J. B. E. Garstang, *The Story of Jericho*, pp. 135ff.

[66] Cf. K. M. Kenyon, *BA*, XVI, No. 3 (1953), pp. 46ff., XVII, No. 4 (1954), pp. 98ff.; also her *Digging Up Jericho*, pp. 170ff., 259ff.

[67] Cf. *WBA*, p. 79; K. A. Kitchen, *NBD*, pp. 612f.

opportunity for the forces of erosion to obliterate traces of Late Bronze Age strata. It is apparent from other areas of the mound that this may well have been the case, for Jericho's Middle Bronze Age levels were considerably denuded by erosion. Whatever sections of the site were not occupied by the Iron Age settlement of Ahab and subsequent periods have been exposed to erosive forces down to the present day. Thus it can be said that archaeological evidence from Jericho relating to a thirteenth-century B.C. date for the conquest is inconclusive, and it is not too much to suppose that this situation may be one result of the conquest itself.

Excavations at the sites of Ai, Bethel, Lachish, and Debir have furnished important evidence for their destruction in the thirteenth century B.C., and of these only the first presents any real difficulties in the matter of interpretation. Madame Marquet-Krause undertook work at Ai (et-Tell, some thirteen miles northwest of Jericho) in 1933, and showed that the site had been one of the major fortresses in Canaan between 3200 and 2400 B.C. It was destroyed shortly after this time, apparently by Amorite raiders, and seems to have remained uninhabited except for a small village settlement about 1100 B.C.[68] Ai was thus already in ruins at the time when the invading Israelites under Joshua conquered the land, and it may be that its name, which means "ruin," was given to it at that period.

The mention of Ai in the narrative dealing with the conquest of Bethel (Josh. 8:1ff.),[69] a mile-and-a-half distant, probably arose because the *tell* served as an advanced observation and strongpoint for the defenders of Bethel, and not, as Noth suggested,[70] because the entire narrative of the destruction of Ai constituted an aetiological legend introduced in order to account for the significance of the Hebrew term. There can be no doubt that the Biblical description of that aspect of the campaign involving Ai and the surrounding territory intended to convey the impression that the inhabitants of the locality made a firm defensive stand at Ai, and that the invaders subsequently destroyed the site as a means of forestalling any subsequent offensive action by the military forces of Ai and Bethel. This fact, combined with the strategic role which Ai had played prior to 2300 B.C., should constitute sufficient evidence for the existence of this important site, and furnish proper justification for the action taken by the conquering Israelites.

The Biblical account of the battle for Ai and its environs appears to envisage it as an inhabited—or at the very least occupied—site having

[68] *AJA*, LX (1936), p. 158; J. A. Callaway, *RB*, LXXII (1965), pp. 409ff.
[69] Cf. *BPAE*, pp. 29f.
[70] M. Noth, *PJB*, XXXIV (1938), pp. 7ff. Albright, *BASOR*, No. 74 (1939), pp. 15ff., suggested that the ruins of Ai had been associated by a subsequent generation with the destruction of Bethel.

its own ruler. This man, however, was most probably not so much a petty king as a military commander-in-chief whose troops were firmly entrenched in a defensive strongpoint—either of a temporary or a permanent nature—where the Israelites encountered initial resistance. Even when the text is taken as it stands, the narrative exhibits clear military purpose and plan on the part of Joshua, as will be made evident in a subsequent chapter. From an archaeological point of view, as observed above, no completely satisfactory explanation of the situation has been offered to date. It may be that Late Bronze Age levels at the site have been obliterated, as at Jericho, or even that the identification of Ai with et-Tell is incorrect. Certainly more work will need to be undertaken at Ai before the archaeological picture can be regarded as completely clarified.

Excavations at Bethel under W. F. Albright in 1934 revealed that the city had enjoyed considerable prosperity during the Middle and Late Bronze Ages. It was destroyed by a tremendous conflagration during the thirteenth century B.C., as indicated by the huge quantities of charred debris, burnt brick, and ashes that were unearthed at lower Late Bronze Age levels.[71]

Excavations by J. L. Starkey at Lachish,[72] which commenced in 1933, showed that the city had been one of great importance from the beginning of the Middle Bronze Age, and that at the time of Joshua it had attained the status of a Canaanite royal city, controlled by an Amorite governor. The reconstruction of a fragmentary bowl recovered from the site pointed to a thirteenth-century B.C. date for the destruction of the city. The pieces of pottery were inscribed with a notation, possibly made by an Egyptian tax collector, in which the fourth year of a certain pharaoh was mentioned. Despite the absence of a specific name, the script is clearly contemporary with Meneptah (ca. 1224 B.C.); and, since the bowl was broken when the city fell, it would appear that Lachish was destroyed between 1220 and 1200 B.C.[73]

The third stage of the Israelite occupation of Canaan was marked by the destruction of Hazor in Galilee. Garstang made a few soundings at the site (Tell el-Qedah) in 1926, but apart from his work it was nearly thirty years before anything was known from an archaeological standpoint about the Galilee campaign of Joshua. The huge rectangular plateau just to the north of the *tell* proper had been identified by Garstang as an enclosure for Hyksos chariotry, partly because he had been impressed with the huge earthen defensive rampart that stood some fifty feet in height. From 1954 on an expedition from the Hebrew University of Jerusalem under Yigael Yadin began to excavate the mound thoroughly,

[71] Albright, *BASOR*, No. 56 (1934), pp. 2ff.; *AASOR*, Vol. 39 (1968).
[72] Finally identified with Tell ed-Duweir by Albright, *ZAW*, XLVII (1929), p. 3.
[73] Albright, *BASOR*, No. 68 (1937), pp. 23f., No. 74 (1939), pp. 20ff.

and it was not long before something of the extent of ancient Hazor began to be apparent.[74]

The site was first settled about 4000 B.C. The rampart surrounding the enclosure was found to be of Hyksos origin, as Garstang had surmised, but the discovery of a cemetery from the Middle and Late Bronze Ages indicated that the last occupation of the site was in the thirteenth century B.C., and not about 1400 B.C., as Garstang had suggested.[75] Thus it would appear that the Biblical tradition, which relates a rather rapid occupation of Canaan under Joshua, as distinct from a systematic reduction of each strongpoint in the way of the advance, is substantially correct when correlated with the evidence of destruction revealed by the Late Bronze Age levels of various Palestinian sites mentioned in the early chapters of Joshua.

C. THE ISRAELITE KINGDOM

1. United. The political, social, and religious background of the early monarchy has been illuminated to a considerable extent as the result of archaeological excavations at sites associated with the activities of Saul, David, and Solomon. At Gezer, tenth-century B.C. levels yielded the celebrated "calendar," a small tablet of limestone that described the various months of the year and the particular type of agricultural work undertaken at that time:

> His two months are (olive) harvest; his two months are grain-planting; his two months are late planting; his month is hoeing up of flax; his month is barley-harvest; his month is harvest and festivity; his two months are vine-tending; his month is summer fruit.[76]

The excavations of Albright at Gibeah (Tell el-Ful) brought to light a fortress which most probably served as the headquarters of Saul when he was engaged in conflict with the Philistines. The defensive walls reflected Hittite designs, and were similar in character to those of Shechem, Beth-shemesh, and Tell Beit Mirsim in the eleventh to tenth centuries B.C.[77] The remains of pottery vessels and a plow at Gibeah pointed to continuous agricultural activity in the area, and an iron plowpoint in the *tell* was hailed as the earliest datable iron implement found to date in the uplands of Palestine.[78] Albright assigned it to about 1010

---

[74] Y. Yadin, *BA*, XIX, No. 1 (1956), pp. 2ff., XX, No. 2 (1957), pp. 34ff.; Yadin *et al., Hazor I* (1958), pp. 5ff., *II* (1960). Cf. A. Malamat, *JBL*, LXXIX (1960), pp. 12ff.

[75] *Joshua-Judges* (1931), p. 383.

[76] Albright, *BASOR*, No. 92 (1943), pp. 16ff.; *ANET*, p. 320; *DOTT*, pp. 201ff.

[77] Cf. *WMTS*, pp. 141f.

[78] Cf. Albright, *AASOR*, IV (1924), pp. 51f., *BASOR*, No. 52 (1933), pp. 6ff., *AP*, pp. 120ff.; L. A. Sinclair, *BA*, XXVII, No. 2 (1964), pp. 52ff.

B.C., and its presence at Gibeah is an important comment on the monopoly which the Philistines had come to exercise over the manufacture and distribution of iron from about 1100 B.C.

The choice of Jerusalem as a capital for the Davidic kingdom was necessitated as much by political reasons as by geographical considerations. This Jebusite stronghold, built on a site that had been occupied as early as 3000 B.C., had never been conquered by Joshua and his followers, and the native defenders considered it to be impregnable. The city itself was erected upon a limestone promontory known as Ophel, where massive walls, bastions, and gates which go back to Jebusite origins have been discovered.[79] Complications arising from deficient water-supplies had been met in antiquity by means of tunnels similar to those excavated beneath Gezer, Megiddo, and Gibeon, which may have antedated the period of King David by as much as a millennium.[80] One such structure designed to bring water from the spring of Gihon in the Kidron valley southeast of Ophel consisted of a long aqueduct which emptied into the "old pool" just outside the city walls.

To enter Jerusalem by means of such an underground water system would have been a strenuous undertaking by any standards. An alternative access route has been furnished by Albright, who suggested that the word *çinnôr*, which is commonly translated "gutter" or "water-shaft," is in fact a Canaanite term meaning "hook."[81] Thus the reference would imply that David and his followers gained access to the fortress by means of grappling-hooks thrown over the parapets of the walls, and not by a penetration of the underground water-shafts.

Biblical traditions concerning the Solomonic period have been widely confirmed by archaeological discoveries in Palestine and elsewhere. Solomon revised the Egyptian bureaucratic patterns which his father David had adopted,[82] and divided the country into twelve areas for purposes of administration.[83] Taking advantage of Phoenician maritime skills and experience, Solomon built a large fleet of merchant ships for trade with southwest Arabia and Ethiopia. He also accumulated a number of ore-carrying or "Tarshish" ships in order to transport smelted

[79] Cf. G. A. Smith, *Jerusalem*, I (1907), pp. 152ff.; H. Vincent, *Jérusalem Antique* (1917), pp. 187ff.; G. Dalman, *Jerusalem und sein Gelände* (1930), pp. 123ff.; J. Simons, *Jerusalem in the OT* (1952), pp. 64ff. For a survey of the Jerusalem excavations see K. M. Kenyon, *BA*, XXVII, No. 2 (1964), pp. 34ff.

[80] Cf. R. A. S. Macalister, *The Excavation of Gezer* (1912), I, pp. 256ff.; R. S. Lamon, *The Megiddo Water System* (1935).

[81] In *OT Commentary* (ed. H. C. Alleman and E. E. Flack, 1954), p. 149. Cf. H. Vincent, *Jérusalem Antique*, pp. 146ff., also in *RB*, XXXIII (1924), pp. 357ff.; J. Simons, *Jerusalem in the OT*, pp. 168ff.

[82] Cf. J. Begrich, *ZAW*, LVIII (1940-1941), pp. 1ff.

[83] Cf. W. F. Albright, *JPOS*, V (1925), p. 17.

metal from mining areas in the western Mediterranean that had been developed by the Phoenicians.[84]

In the Wadi Arabah Nelson Glueck uncovered the first copper refinery ever found in the Near East. Built for Solomon in the tenth century B.C. by Phoenician workmen who were experienced in the construction of copper furnaces and the refining of ore, it was located at Ezion-geber (Tell el-Kheleifeh) between the hill-country of Sinai and the land of Edom. Its location was ideal, for, standing squarely as it did in the path of the north winds that howled down the Arabah rift-valley, it caught their full force and directed them to the furnace areas where the copper and iron ores were refined. The building in which the latter activity took place presented a blank surface to the prevailing north winds, and the only apertures in its structure were two parallel rows of holes linked by means of air-ducts to form flues. The ore was placed in crucibles above a wood or brush fire, and the air from the flues was then directed on the blaze to produce heat intense enough to smelt the ore. Imports of raw or partly refined material from Sardinia or Spain were augmented by plentiful deposits of copper and iron (cf. Deut. 8:9) in the soft sandstone of this inhospitable region.[85] The presence of numerous slag-heaps adjacent to the buildings indicates that the ore underwent preliminary processing at the site before being transported elsewhere. Adjoining the slag-heaps Glueck discovered the ruins of foundry rooms and the living-quarters of the miners themselves, many of whom were probably slaves. The development of the mining and smelting industry of the Arabah was as important economically in the early monarchy as it was technologically, since it furnished King Solomon with the principal export of his day and added to his immense wealth. As a result he was able to enter into commercial dealings with the Arabian monarchs, including the celebrated Queen of Sheba (Saba), whose position as head of a tribal confederacy in southern Arabia has been largely vindicated from cuneiform sources.

Traces of the ambitious building projects of Solomon have been unearthed at Megiddo and Gezer.[86] At the former site tenth-century B.C. levels yielded the remains of a palace fortified by means of massive walls and defensive towers. A stable compound was unearthed to the southeast of the *tell*, revealing the presence of hitching-posts which also helped to support the roof. Standing beside the posts on the cobblestone

---

[84] For the name "Tarshish" see F. Thieberger, *King Solomon* (1947), p. 206; cf. Albright, *BASOR*, No. 83 (1941), pp. 14ff., *BPAE*, p. 54.

[85] Glueck, *The Other Side of the Jordan*, pp. 50ff.; *BASOR*, No. 90 (1943), pp. 13f. For his revised views cf. *BA*, XXVIII, No. 3 (1965), pp. 70ff.

[86] G. E. Wright, *BA*, XXI, No. 4 (1958), pp. 103f.; Yadin, *Israel Exploration Journal*, VIII (1958), pp. 80ff.; *BA*, XXXIII, No. 3 (1970), pp. 65ff.

floor were several stone mangers.[87] From an examination of the masonry elements of the walls it is clear that earlier Phoenician constructional techniques were amply represented, appearing again in a similar form at Gezer, Lachish, and Ezion-geber.[88]

The rebuilding of the Millo and the extension of the mound of Ophel were part of the spectacular constructional activity which culminated in the erection of the royal palace and the Temple at Jerusalem. Although few actual remains of the Solomonic period are extant in Jerusalem, it is obvious from the style and structure of contemporary buildings that the Temple was a characteristically Phoenician edifice. Examples of a proto-Aeolic pilaster capitol have been recovered from eleventh-century B.C. strata at Samaria and Shechem, as well as from eleventh- and eighth-century B.C. levels at Megiddo. The lilies and palmettes that were used to decorate the temple were familiar *motifs* in Syro-Phoenicia, and cherubim were commonly found in the iconography of western Asia between 1800 and 600 B.C.[89]

2. Divided. The prosperity that was a feature of the kingdom of Israel under Omri (885/4-874/3 B.C.) saw the fortification of the capital city Samaria (modern Sebastiyeh) against possible Syrian attack. The Harvard expedition, which commenced work at the site in 1908 and continued there for two years,[90] was joined by teams from the Hebrew University and the British School of Archaeology in Jerusalem between 1931 and 1935. Of the sixteen levels of occupation at the site, seven have been assigned to the Israelites. Periods I and II, extending over the approximately twenty-eight years of Kings Omri and Ahab, were found to exhibit a high degree of constructional activity. A great many ivory inlays, the earliest of which belonged to the period of Omri, were recovered.[91] They consisted mainly of small panels in relief, and had as their subjects a variety of animals, plants, and winged human figures, reflecting both Egyptian and Phoenician cultural interests. The discovery of the Moabite Stone in 1866, which had been erected by King Mesha of Dibon about 840 B.C., revealed something of the vigor that characterized the rule of Omri. From the inscription it is evident that the latter

---

[87] *WBA*, pl. 85. J. W. Crowfoot, *PEQ*, LXXIII (1940), pp. 143ff., dated the stables in the time of Ahab, whereas Albright, *AJA*, CLIV (1940), pp. 546ff., assigned Stratum IV to the Solomonic period. Yadin, *BA*, XXIII, No. 2 (1960), pp. 62ff., postulated a date in the period of Ahab, with traces from the Solomonic era.

[88] *AP*, pp. 125ff.

[89] *ARI*, p. 216 n. 65.

[90] G. A. Reisner, C. S. Fisher, and D. G. Lyon, *Harvard Excavations at Samaria 1908-1910* (2 vols., 1924).

[91] J. W. and G. M. Crowfoot, *Early Ivories from Samaria* (1938); J. W. Crowfoot *et al.*, *The Objects from Samaria* (1957).

had gained control of northern Moab and was exacting heavy tribute from that land:

> I am Mesha, son of Chemosh...king of Moab, the Dibonite...Omri, king of Israel...oppressed Moab many days because Chemosh was angry with his land. And his son succeeded him, and he also said, "I will oppress Moab...."[92]

Artifacts relating to the period of Shalmaneser III (*ca.* 859-824 B.C.) have furnished independent confirmation of events that took place in the period of Ahab and Jehu. The Monolith Inscription of Shalmaneser gave an account of the battle at Qarqar on the Orontes in 853 B.C., a military engagement not mentioned in the Old Testament. In the text of this inscription, "Ahab the Israelite" was credited by Shalmaneser with the most powerful military elements in the coalition of Israelite and Syrian rulers.[93] The Black Obelisk of Shalmaneser, found by Layard in 1846, recorded the subjugation of Jehu and the amount of tribute which he paid to the Assyrians:

> Tribute of Jehu, son of Omri. Silver, gold, a golden bowl, a golden beaker, golden goblets, pitchers of gold, staves for the hand of the king, javelins, I received from him....[94]

From the time of Jeroboam of Israel (782/1-753 B.C.) came a jasper seal belonging to "Shema, servant of Jeroboam," which was found at Megiddo by Schumacher in 1904.[95] The celebrated Samaritan (or Samarian) ostraca, recovered by the Harvard expedition in 1910, are also dated within this period.[96] These consist of administrative documents recording shipments of wine and oil to Samaria, and throw interesting light upon the social conditions of the age, which came under such intense prophetic censure (Am. 6:6).[97] One such ostracon read:[98]

> In the tenth year. To Shamariah from Beeryam, a jar of old wine.
>
> | Raga, son of Elisha | 2 |
> | Uzzah ... | 1 |
> | Eliba | 1 |
> | Baala, son of Elisha | 1 |
> | Jedayah | 1 |

[92] *HDB*, III, p. 407; *LAP*, p. 157 and pl. 67; *ANET*, pp. 320f.

[93] *ARAB*, I, sect. 611.

[94] *LAP*, p. 173 and pl. 73; *ANET*, p. 281.

[95] *WBA*, p. 110 (a). S. Yeivin, *JNES*, XIX (1960), pp. 205ff., prefers to assign the seal to the time of Jeroboam I.

[96] Cf. J. W. Jack, *Samaria in Ahab's Time* (1929), pp. 37ff.; *ANET*, p. 321; *DOTT*, pp. 204ff.

[97] Cf. B. Maisler, *JPOS*, XXI (1948), pp. 117ff.

[98] Cf. *WBA*, p. 158.

The Assyrian annals of Tiglathpileser III record the nature of the tribute that Menahem of Israel (1 Kgs. 15:19ff.) paid about 740 B.C.:

> As for Menahem, terror overwhelmed him . . . he fled and submitted to me . . . silver, colored woollen garments, linen garments . . . I received as his tribute. . . .[99]

Around 727 B.C. Shalmaneser V, the successor of Tiglathpileser III, besieged Samaria when Hoshea of Israel (732/1-723/2 B.C.) sought to make an alliance with Egypt and refused to pay tribute to Assyria. Before Samaria fell in 722 B.C. Shalmaneser was succeeded by Sargon II (ca. 722-705 B.C.), who reduced Samaria and carried the Israelite tribes into captivity. The Khorsabad Annals furnished this account of the end of the northern kingdom:

> I besieged and captured Samaria, carrying off 27,290 of the people who dwelt therein. Fifty chariots I gathered from among them . . . .[100]

Twenty years later Hezekiah of Judah was faced with a military threat from the Assyrians when Sennacherib invaded Palestine, isolated Tyre, and reduced Joppa, Ekron, and a number of other cities in the Philistine plain. An Egyptian relief force was heavily defeated at Lachish in 701 B.C., and Hezekiah decided to become tributary to Sennacherib in order to gain a brief respite while Jerusalem was made ready for a siege. The principal problem confronting the inhabitants of the capital city was that of the water supply. In order to improve on the earlier Jebusite attempts, Hezekiah had his engineers excavate a tunnel to bring the waters of Gihon into the old city proper. The conduit (2 Kgs. 20:20, 2 Chron. 32:30) that was planned was dug by means of simple hand tools through nearly six hundred yards of solid rock; and terminated just inside the southeastern corner of the city where the pool subsequently known as Siloam was situated. The record of this amazing feat of engineering was preserved for posterity in an inscription on the right-hand wall of the tunnel, some twenty feet from the Siloam entrance. Written in eighth-century B.C. script it reads:

> Now this is the story of the boring through; while the excavators were still lifting up their picks, each towards his fellow, and while there were yet three cubits to excavate, there was heard the voice of one calling to another, for there was a crevice in the rock on the right hand. And on the day they completed the boring-through, the stone-cutters struck pick against pick, one against the other; and the waters flowed from the spring to the pool, a distance of 100 cubits. And a hundred cubits was the height of the rock above the heads of the stone-cutters.[101]

[99] ARAB, I, sect. 816.
[100] ARAB, II, sect. 55; ANET, pp. 284f.
[101] G. A. Barton, Archaeology and the Bible (1946 ed.), p. 475. Cf. LAP, p. 160; DOTT, pp. 209ff.

Sennacherib appears to have been sufficiently gratified by his exploits at Lachish to have had a carved stone panel placed in his palace at Nineveh in order to commemorate the event. It depicted him seated in triumph upon his throne, receiving the spoils of victory,[102] and conveyed no hint whatever as to any catastrophe which his forces might have encountered during the Palestinian campaign, namely the destruction of 185,000 Assyrian troops.

The discovery of a number of inscribed ostraca at Lachish by J. L. Starkey from 1935 has provided dramatic illustration of Jeremiah's portrayal of the last days of Judah.[103] The potsherds were recovered in two groups from the mound at Tell ed-Duweir, the first fifteen in 1935 in the ruins of a small guard-room located just outside the city gate and the remaining three in the same general area three years later. The bulk of the ostraca can be dated from the autumn of 589 B.C., since they belong to the layer of ash representing the final overthrow of Lachish by Nebuchadnezzar. Although the sherds are in a bad state of preservation, with only about one third of the text being reasonably intelligible, they are of great importance philologically, quite apart from their significance for the age of Jeremiah. They consisted for the most part of dispatches written from a military outpost north of Lachish by a person named Hoshaiah to another individual, Joash, who may have been a staff officer at Lachish.

Ostracon III mentions a certain "prophet":

> . . . And it hath been reported to thy servant, saying, "The commander of the host, Coniah, son of Elnathan, hath come down in order to go into Egypt; and unto Hodaviah, son of Ahijah, and his men hath he sent to obtain . . . from him." And as for the letter of Tobiah, servant of the king, which came to Shallum, son of Jaddua through the prophet, saying, "Beware!" thy servant hath sent it to my lord.[104]

Considerable discussion has centered upon the identity of the "prophet," some scholars claiming that an unknown prophet was being referred to, others that the allusion was to Jeremiah himself. Torczyner favors an identification with Uriah of Kiriath-jearim (Jer. 26:20ff.), whose treasonous acts resulted in his extradition from Egypt and execution in

---

[102] A. H. Layard, *Discoveries Among the Ruins of Nineveh and Babylon* (1875), pp. 126ff.; *WBA*, pl. 117.

[103] Cf. H. Torczyner, *Lachish I, The Lachish Letters* (1938), BASOR, No. 70 (1938), pp. 11ff., No. 73 (1939), pp. 16ff., No. 80 (1940), pp. 11ff., No. 82 (1941), p. 24. On the excavations see also O. Tufnell, *Lachish II, The Fosse Temple* (1940), *Lachish III, The Iron Age* (1953), *Lachish IV, The Bronze Age* (1958), *PEQ*, XCI (1959), pp. 90ff.; R. D. Barnett, *Israel Exploration Journal*, VIII (1958), pp. 161ff.

[104] *ANET*, p. 322; *DOTT*, pp. 214f.

Jerusalem.[105] Ostracon VI contains the complaint of a patriotic official alleging that the *sarim* (royal personages or notables) were "weakening the hands" of the people by issuing demoralizing communications.[106] Ironically enough, it was this very accusation that had been levelled against Jeremiah during the days of Zedekiah (Jer. 38:4).

3. *Exiled.* As a result of the discovery in 1956 by D. J. Wiseman of four additional tablets of the Babylonian Chronicle in the archives of the British Museum, it is now possible to fix the precise date for Jerusalem's fall to the Babylonians with reference to an extra-Biblical source. The Babylonian texts make it clear that the city fell on the second of Adar (March 15-16), 597 B.C., and in addition they record that the Egyptians suffered a shattering defeat at Carchemish in 605 B.C., thus enabling the Babylonians to occupy "the whole area of Hatti."[107] A previously unrecorded engagement between the Babylonians and the Egyptians occurred in 601 B.C., in which both sides suffered heavy losses and Nebuchadnezzar was compelled to withdraw to Babylon for one year in order to obtain new equipment for his forces. The following twelve months were spent in exploratory attacks in Syria prior to the campaign against Judah which resulted in the fall of Jerusalem in 597 B.C. The evidence furnished by the Babylonian Chronicle thus confirms the Biblical tradition that Jerusalem collapsed under the Babylonian onslaughts of 597 and 587 B.C.

Conclusive evidence for the presence of Jewish captives in Babylonia has been provided by discoveries near the Ishtar Gate of Ancient Babylon, where several tablets were found that listed the rations of grain and oil allotted to captives in Babylon between 595 and 570 B.C.[108] The list of royal princes included "Yaukin, king of the land of Yahud,"[109] which substantiated the statement in 2 Kings 25:27 that Jehoiakin was a recipient of Babylonian royal bounty. Three stamped jar-handles from Debir and Beth-shemesh[110] bore the words "belonging to Eliakim, steward of Yaukin,"[111] implying that a crown steward was in charge of the royal property between 598 and 587 B.C. A seal impression recovered from

[105] For the unknown prophet identification, see C. H. Gordon, *The Living Past* (1941), p. 189; for Jeremiah, J. W. Jack, *PEQ*, LXX (1938), pp. 165ff.; also H. Torczyner, *The Lachish Letters*, p. 62. Other discussions are found in D. W. Thomas, "*The Prophet*" in the Lachish Ostraca (1946), pp. 7ff.; J. Hempel and L. Rost (eds.), *Von Ugarit nach Qumran* (1958), pp. 244ff.

[106] *ANET*, p. 322.

[107] D. J. Wiseman, *Chronicles of Chaldean Kings (626-556 B.C.) in the British Museum* (1956), pp. 32ff.

[108] R. Koldewey, *Das Wieder Erstehende Babylon* (1925), pp. 90ff. Cf. E. F. Weidner, *Mélanges Syriens offerts à M. René Dussaud* (1939), II, pp. 923ff.

[109] W. F. Albright, *BA*, V, No. 4 (1942), pp. 49f.

[110] *DOTT*, p. 224.

[111] *WBA*, pl. 125; D. J. Wiseman in C. F. H. Henry (ed.), *Revelation and the Bible* (1958), p. 313.

Lachish in 1935 carried the inscription, "to Gedaliah who is over the household," the owner of the seal being without doubt the governor of Judah appointed by Nebuchadnezzar (2 Kgs. 25:23).[112] On the reverse side the impression showed traces of the papyrus document to which it had been originally attached, and which had long since perished. The title "who is over the house" was invariably borne by the chief administrative official next in rank to the king. That the family of Gedaliah had been civil servants for some generations is evident from the fact that both his father and grandfather had occupied important offices in the state.

Archaeological discoveries of the twentieth century have furnished striking confirmation of many previously disputed aspects of the book of Ezra. C. C. Torrey and others maintained that the language of the book was late, and dated it from the third century B.C., after the time of Alexander the Great.[113] This position was seriously weakened with the discovery in 1903 of the celebrated Elephantine papyri at a military colony on an island near Aswan in Upper Egypt.[114] These documents were Aramaic letters written by the Jews of Elephantine between 500 and 400 B.C., when the colony was known as Yeb. Although it was of a military nature, the island's occupants derived a livelihood from trading, stone-quarrying, customs duties, and other administrative functions, in addition to furnishing a garrison. The papyri included legal contracts, deeds, official documents, agreements, diplomatic texts, and private letters. One papyrus was found to be a copy of a letter dispatched by the priests of the Jewish temple at Elephantine to Bagoas, the governor of Judah, complaining that anti-Semitic activity on the part of the Egyptians in 410 B.C. had resulted in the temple's being destroyed, and requesting financial aid in rebuilding it.

Estate transactions were prominently represented in the papyri, which showed that both men and women could engage in business on equal terms. One text contained the names of individuals who had donated gifts to the temple at Yeb, many of whom were women. All business dealings reflected in the contracts and agreements were drawn up in an accredited legal manner and attested by witnesses. They were then sealed and identified as to general content by means of a notation on the outside of the papyrus, following the traditional Babylonian method still in use later in the Persian empire. Quite apart from the way in which the papyri indicate the extent to which Aramaic had become the general

112 *WBA*, pl. 128.
113 Torrey, *The Composition and Historical Value of Ezra-Nehemiah* (1896); *Ezra Studies* (1910).
114 E. Sachau, *Aramaeische Papyrus und Ostraka aus einer juedischen Militaer-Kolonie zu Elephantine* (2 vols., 1911); A. Ungnad, *Aramäische Papyrus aus Elephantine* (1911); A. Cowley, *Aramaic Papyri of the Fifth Century B. C.* (1923). A subsequent group, discovered in 1947 in the archives of the Brooklyn Museum, were published by E. G. Kraeling, *The Brooklyn Museum Aramaic Papyri* (1953). Cf. *ANET*, pp. 222f., 491ff.; *ANE*, pp. 278ff.; *DOTT*, pp. 256ff.

131

language of trade and diplomacy in the Persian period, the texts are important for demonstrating the historicity of Ezra, because they show conclusively that the Aramaic used in that book was characteristic of the fifth century B.C.

The authenticity of the royal decrees in Ezra 1:2ff. and 6:3ff. has also been vindicated by modern archaeological discoveries, against the assertions of older historians who argued that there was no evidence that Cyrus ever made such a decree as recorded there. Others who also denied their authenticity adopted a less radical position by conceding that there may have been some underlying historicity for the material.[115] It is now apparent by comparison with other ancient Near Eastern royal decrees from the Persian period (ca. 539-331 B.C.) that both documents are substantially accurate and authentic.[116] The first was a typical royal proclamation drawn up for utterance in the language of the people who were being addressed, whereas the second was a *dikrona* or official memorandum recording a decision to be implemented by the administrative official concerned. The memorandum was filed in the archives with other government documents once appropriate action had been taken on its contents, and in this connection it is important to note that, according to the Ezra narratives, the decree was discovered in the repository at Ecbatana (Achmetha), where Cyrus is known to have stayed in his first regnal year (538 B.C.).

Some sidelights on the book of Esther have emerged from excavations at Susa from 1851 under Williams and Loftus.[117] A trilingual inscription recovered from the throne room of the palace on the north side of the mound recounts the way in which Artaxerxes II had restored the building during his reign:

> Says Artaxerxes, the great king, the king of kings...the son of king Darius, the son of king Darius Hystaspes: My ancestor Darius built this *apadana* (throne room of the palace) in former times. In the time of Artaxerxes, my grandfather, it was burnt by fire. I have restored it....[118]

Further work at the site by Marcel Dieulafoy from 1884 showed that in the Persian period the city had covered nearly five thousand acres, and

[115] Some of the historians denying that Cyrus made the decree were B. Stade, *Geschichte des Volkes Israel* (1888), II, pp. 122n., 159n.; C. C. Torrey, *The Composition and Historical Value of Ezra-Nehemiah*, pp. 7ff., 55ff.; G. Hölscher in *Die Heilige Schrift des AT* (ed. Kautzsch and Bertholet, 1923), II, pp. 494f.; L. E. Browne, *Early Judaism* (1929), pp. 36ff., 44f. The more moderate group is represented by J. Wellhausen, *Nachrichten von der Gesellschaft der Wissenschaften zu Göttingen* (1895), pp. 169, 175f.

[116] Cf. E. Bickermann, *JBL*, LXV (1946), pp. 244ff.; Albright, *Alexander Marx Jubilee Volume* (1950), pp. 61ff.

[117] W. K. Loftus, *Travels and Researches in Chaldea and Susiana; With an Account of Excavations at Warka, the "Erech" of Nimrod, and Shush, "Shushan the Palace" of Esther*, in 1849-1852 (1857).

[118] I. Price, *The Monuments and the OT* (1925), p. 403.

was divided into four separate areas—the citadel mound, the royal city ("Shushan the Palace"), the residential and business area ("the city Shushan"), and the district of the plain to the west of the river.[119] The palace fortress covered 123 acres, and consisted of the Throne Room or *apadana*, the "House of the King," and the "House of the Women," along with numerous courts, stairways, arches, and terraces. Among the debris removed from the adjacent "King's Gate" Dieulafoy discovered a quadrangular prism on which were engraved the numbers 1, 2, 5, and 6. This "die" (or *pur*, as it was known in its contemporary Assyrian designation) thus explains how Haman was able to "cast lots" for establishing a date on which the Jews would be destroyed, for the Persian method of throwing dice was equivalent to the Jewish custom of "casting the lot."

Additional information relating to fourth-century B.C. Samaria was unexpectedly furnished by the discovery in 1962 of some papyrus documents, consisting of fragments and strips of papyri and several relatively well-preserved rolls.[120] These comprise legal and administrative documents, in which familiar Biblical names such as Sanballat and Nehemiah occur. Neither of these two individuals was the Biblical personage of that specific name, but the fragments have made it possible to reconstruct with a fair degree of certainty the sequence of the governors of Samaria.[121] Even more important, however, is the significance of this material for palaeographical science. As far as the chronology of the third-century B.C. Biblical manuscripts from Qumran is concerned, it is already evident that the dates proposed by Cross for the Exodus manuscript from 4Q (*ca.* 250 B.C.) and the archaic fragment of Samuel (*ca.* 225 B.C.)[122] are definitely minimal, and may need to be revised upwards.

The fourth century B.C. has very few other dated Jewish documents, and material from Babylonia or Egypt that would throw light on the fortunes of the Jewish colonies in those countries is also virtually non-existent. In Palestine, the rise of Arab power in the fifth century B.C. compelled the Edomites to migrate to Judaea, where they became known as Idumeans. They in turn were replaced by the Nabataeans, another Arab group who established a capital at Petra and carved temples and dwellings out of the soft red sandstone of the valley. Strategic areas of their frontier were protected by a series of fortresses, and their distinctive culture has finally become known through the excavation of Nabataean sites.[123]

[119] M. Dieulafoy, *L'acropole de Suse* (4 vols., 1890-1892).
[120] F. M. Cross, *BA*, XXVI, No. 4 (1963), pp. 110ff.
[121] *Ibid.*, p. 120.
[122] *BANE*, pp. 140ff.
[123] N. Glueck, *The Other Side of the Jordan*, pp. 158ff.; J. Starcky, *BA*, XVIII, No. 4 (1955), pp. 84ff.; W. H. Morton, *BA*, XIX, No. 2 (1956), pp. 26ff.; S. Moscati, *The Semites in Ancient History* (1959), pp. 117ff.; S. Cohen, *IDB*, III, pp. 491ff.

IV. THE DEAD SEA SCROLLS

Perhaps the most famous archaeological discovery of all times was the finding of the Dead Sea Scrolls in the Judaean wilderness in the late 1940s. The result of this discovery has been a vast increase of evidence bearing on Biblical studies. No attempt to sketch briefly their nature and significance could properly begin without a passing reference to the remarkable circumstances attending the discovery of the first Qumran cave.[1] Unfortunately, as Cross has remarked, these circumstances have been obscured by time and by the incidence of legendary accretions.[2] The general consensus of opinion, however, has it that the contents of the first Qumran cave (1Q) were discovered accidentally by two Ta'amireh tribesmen who were tending a mixed flock of sheep and goats in the Wadi Qumran area.[3] The elongated jars that the tribesmen found contained decaying rolls of leather instead of the expected coinage and other negotiable treasure, and it was some time, according to informed opinion, before the rolls came into the hands of a dealer in antiquities whose home was in Bethlehem.

During this interval a number of clandestine explorations of caves had apparently been taking place, so that by about 1948 there were two distinct collections of manuscripts from the Qumran area in existence. One of these passed into the hands of the Syrian Metropolitan of Jerusalem, Mar Athanasius Samuel, and included a complete copy of the book of Isaiah, a commentary on the book of Habakkuk, a document dealing with the rules of a religious community, another scroll that could not be unrolled at the time, and a few fragments of manuscripts. The other collection was brought to the attention of the late E. L. Sukenik of

[1] For a survey of the Wadi Qumran and related discoveries see R. K. Harrison, *The Dead Sea Scrolls* (1961). For English translations of the scrolls see T. H. Gaster, *The Dead Sea Scriptures in English Translation* (1956); G. Vermès, *The Dead Sea Scrolls in English* (1962). For a pointed Hebrew version see *Megilloth Midhbar Yehudhah* (ed. A. M. Habermann, 1959). For an early bibliography see W. S. LaSor, *Bibliography of the Dead Sea Scrolls, 1948-57* (1958).

[2] *The Ancient Library of Qumran and Modern Biblical Studies* (1958), p. 5.

[3] Cf. *DJD*, I, pp. 1ff.; G. L. Harding, *PEQ*, LXXXI (1949), pp. 112ff.; W. H. Brownlee, *JNES*, XVI (1957), pp. 236ff.

the Hebrew University of Jerusalem by the dealer in Bethlehem, and steps were taken to acquire the documents for the Hebrew University. This group of scrolls included an imperfect copy of Isaiah, a war document, and a hymnary in several sections.

In 1948 the Syrian Metropolitan allowed the manuscripts in his possession to be taken to the American Schools of Oriental Research in Jerusalem, where J. C. Trever and W. H. Brownlee studied and photographed the material. Their convictions regarding the antiquity of the material were confirmed by W. F. Albright, who after examining a print of part of the Isaiah scroll unhesitatingly declared it to be the "greatest manuscript discovery of modern times." Millar Burrows, who was Director of the American School in Jerusalem in 1948, concurred in this judgment, and on April 11 of that year he made the first announcement of the discovery.[4] Two weeks later Sukenik announced that the Hebrew University also possessed a collection of ancient scrolls of tremendous antiquity.[5]

This state of affairs put G. L. Harding, who was at that time in charge of antiquities in Transjordan and Arab Palestine, in an extremely delicate position, partly because the artifacts had been removed in contravention of Jordanian nationalization legislation, and partly because the problem of rediscovering and excavating the site under properly controlled conditions was now immeasurably more difficult. Meanwhile the scrolls which had been acquired by the Syrian Metropolitan were smuggled to the United States, and were subsequently published by the American Schools of Oriental Research.[6] After indirect negotiations these scrolls were finally purchased for the Hebrew University of Jerusalem in the summer of 1954 for an amount of money in the neighborhood of $250,000.

Due to the strenuous activities of Harding and R. de Vaux, the original Qumran cave was rediscovered in 1949, and despite the fact that they had obviously been preceded by illicit investigators, the archaeologists were able to recover some six hundred fragments of leather and papyrus. Spurred on by the hope of financial gain, the Arabs discovered other caves in 1951 to the southwest of the original Qumran location in what was known as the Wadi Murabba'at area. Material from this site

[4] Cf. G. E. Wright, BA, XI, No. 2 (1948), pp. 21ff.; W. F. Albright, BASOR, No. 110 (1948), pp. 2f.

[5] Cf. the extracts from his diary in E. L. Sukenik and N. Avigad (eds.), 'Oṣar hammegilloth haggenuzoth (1954), p. 20.

[6] M. Burrows (ed.), The Dead Sea Scrolls of St. Mark's Monastery (1950-1951), Vol. I, The Isaiah Manuscript and the Habakkuk Commentary; Vol. II, fasc. 2, Plates and Transcription of the Manual of Discipline. The remaining scroll was unrolled six years later by J. Biberkraut, and proved to be an Aramaic version of parts of Genesis. It was published in 1956 by N. Avigad and Y. Yadin under the title, A Genesis Apocryphon.

included inscribed potsherds, fabric, Greek and Hebrew papyri, along with some documents written by Simon Bar-Kokhba to a certain Joshua ben Galgola. Subsequent discoveries at Qumran and Khirbet Mird brought the number of caves containing artifacts to eleven. In order to simplify identification and reference, the various sites are described in terms of the order of discovery in each particular location. Thus 1Q refers to the first Qumran cave, 2Mu to the second Murabba'at cave, and so on.

Explorations in 1951 on a shelf of rock near the Wadi Qumran uncovered the remains of a community building complete with copious reservoirs fashioned in the rock. As digging progressed it became apparent that the site had been occupied by a religious community from about 110 B.C. to 31 B.C., after which an earthquake (mentioned by Josephus, *AJ*, XV, 5, 2) damaged the building. Occupation was resumed at the beginning of the Christian era and lasted until A.D. 68, when the Romans took over the entire area. During the Second Jewish Revolt (A.D. 132-135) the area was used as a base by the Jewish guerrilla fighters, but at a later time the site became derelict.

The community settlement included the principal building, some 120 feet square, which was situated to the north of the main refectory. An adjoining kitchen was unearthed, and revealed the remains of hundreds of pottery vessels. Other rooms included assembly halls and the community *scriptorium*, which contained writing tables, ink-wells, and benches in fragmentary condition.[7] The recovery of an intact jar that was identical in shape to the remains of those recovered from the first Qumran cave established a decisive link between the scrolls and the people who had lived in the settlement. The site also contained facilities for smelting ore and baking earthenware vessels, indicating that the community was self-supporting. A number of cisterns had been dug into the rocks, and some of them were approached by means of steps, which might indicate that they had been used for baptismal rites or formal lustrations. A cache of coins found in 1955 furnished an almost continuous occupational history of the site from about 140 B.C. to the time of the Second Jewish Revolt against Imperial Rome.[8] A burial ground adjacent to the *khirbeh* showed that members of both sexes had enjoyed membership in the religious community.[9] The austerity of the sect was reflected by the simplicity of the graves and the absence of funerary ornamentation, although these conditions could have resulted from other factors.[10]

---

[7] J. M. Allegro, *The Dead Sea Scrolls* (1956), pp. 88f. and pls. 32-35.

[8] R. de Vaux, *RB*, LXI (1954), pp. 230f. For a plan of the community complex after excavation see *RB*, LXIII (1956), pl. 3; *The National Geographic Magazine*, CXIV, No. 6 (1958), pp. 790f.

[9] *VDJD*, p. 17.

[10] R. de Vaux, *RB*, LX (1953), p. 103.

The scope of the manuscript discoveries affords some indication of the literary interests and religious activities of the Qumran sect. In addition to the Sukenik Isaiah scroll (1QIsa[b]),[11] the War document (1QM), the Thanksgiving Hymns (1QH), the Community Rule (1QS), the Saint Mark's Monastery large Isaiah scroll (1QIsa[a]), and the Commentary on Habakkuk (1QpHab), the community possessed a significant number of extra-canonical writings as well as specifically apocryphal and pseudepigraphal works. The Pentateuch, the Psalms, the prophetic writings, and the book of Daniel were popular with the sectaries, and most of these works have survived in several copies or manuscript portions.

One of the more spectacular finds at Qumran came from 3Q in 1952. It consisted of two oxidized rolls of beaten copper that had been preserved almost by accident when the entrance of the cave, near which they had been placed, had collapsed in antiquity. Some delay occurred while experts in the United States and Britain determined the best method for opening the tightly rolled, eroded copper. Ultimately the two rolls were cut into strips at the Manchester College of Technology in 1956, with an ultimate textual loss of less than five per cent.[12] The two sections of scroll, translated by Allegro, were found to contain directions concerning the locations of treasure hoards, which unfortunately cannot be identified.[13] K. G. Kuhn, who had surmised correctly what the contents of the copper scroll would be before it was unrolled, has suggested that the scrolls may contain a record of the treasures in the Herodian Temple, which was destroyed in A.D. 70.[14]

The excellent state of preservation of the large Isaiah manuscript (1QIsa[a]) is eloquent testimony to the care taken in sealing up the scroll against the time when it could be used once more by the sectaries. The technique of jar-storage most probably originated in ancient Egypt, but it was popular throughout the Near East for many centuries as a convenient means of preserving valuables or documents that were intended for posterity.[15] The Sukenik Isaiah manuscript (1QIsa[b]) had not been fortunate enough to enjoy such a good state of preservation, for when found it was coated with a sticky layer of decayed leather which naturally presented formidable problems for those attempting to restore the text. The manuscripts were written in columnar form in nonmetallic ink, and the letters were suspended for the most part from faintly ruled lines.[16] The fact that so many thousands of fragments were

---

[11] For an explanation of the designations used to refer to the scrolls see R. K. Harrison, *The Dead Sea Scrolls*, p. 29.

[12] J. M. Allegro, *The Dead Sea Scrolls*, pp. 181ff.

[13] J. M. Allegro, *The Treasure of the Copper Scroll* (1960), pp. 33ff.

[14] *Theologische Literaturzeitung* (1956), cols. 541ff.

[15] Cf. Jer. 32:14; *The Assumption of Moses*, I, 18; J. M. Allegro, *The Dead Sea Scrolls*, pp. 78f.

[16] *DJD*, I, p. 39. Cf. S. A. Birnbaum, *VT*, I (1951), pp. 97f.

discovered or eventually acquired through purchase from Arab sources has created an enormous amount of work for the international committee engaged in restoring, editing, and publishing the Qumran texts. Though this task is proceeding with regularity, it will be many years before the work will be completely satisfactory.

The world of Hebrew scholarship received with decidedly mixed reactions the news that the manuscripts in the possession of Professor Sukenik were to be dated not later than A.D. 70. Some were frankly skeptical that the latest Hebrew manuscripts at that time (from the eighth and ninth centuries A.D.) could have been antedated by almost a millennium as the result of a single discovery. Others were suspicious of fraud or forgery, remembering that eminent scholars had been thus victimized in previous generations. At once an acrimonious debate concerning the authenticity and dating of the scrolls sprang up among several eminent scholars who, unfortunately, had not had the opportunity of first-hand acquaintance with the discoveries. In England the early date assigned on palaeographic and other grounds by Albright, Burrows, Sukenik, and Trever was challenged by G. R. Driver, who in turn was immediately taken to task by S. A. Birnbaum, an eminent British palaeographer. In the United States, the chief protagonist was Solomon Zeitlin, the distinguished co-editor of the *Jewish Quarterly Review*, who promptly denounced the manuscripts as forgeries, envisaged the entire proceedings in terms of a gigantic hoax, and assigned a medieval date to the extant documents.[17]

Admittedly the whole situation was unfortunate at the time, since it was complicated by the lack of proper corroborating evidence from Qumran, but this situation has now been remedied by further discoveries. As a result there is substantial scholarly agreement that the scrolls emerged from a period beginning about 250 B.C. and ending

---

[17] Driver's views are found in *The Times* of August 23, 30, and September 22, 1949 (cf. R. Eisler's *Times* article of September 8, 1949), and in *The Hebrew Scrolls from the Neighbourhood of Jericho and the Dead Sea* (1951), pp. 30ff. For Birnbaum's views see *BASOR*, No. 113 (1949), pp. 33ff., No. 115 (1949), pp. 20ff.; *PEQ*, LXXXI (1949), pp. 140ff.; *JBL*, LXVIII (1949), pp. 161ff. Since then Driver has reduced his original dating by several centuries, now holding them to be approximately contemporary with the New Testament writings (*The Judaean Scrolls* [1963]). Zeitlin has written in *JQR*, XXXIX (1948-49), pp. 171ff., 235ff., 337ff., XL (1949-50), pp. 57ff., 291ff., 373ff., XLI (1950-51), pp. 1ff., 71ff., 247ff., XLII (1951-52), pp. 133ff., XLIII (1952-53), pp. 72ff., 140ff., XLIV (1953-54), pp. 85ff., XLV (1954-55), pp. 1ff., 83ff., 174ff., XLVI (1955-56), pp. 1ff., 116ff., XLVII (1956-57), pp. 745ff., XLVIII (1957-58), pp. 71ff., 243ff., XLIX (1958-59), pp. 1ff., 221ff., LI (1960-61), pp. 156ff., 265ff. Persistent rumors that Dr. Zeitlin has abandoned his militant position on the dating of the scrolls are unfounded: in private correspondence with the author he has reaffirmed his stand that the documents are medieval in date, and that they have no value for either the Old or New Testament.

just before the fall of Jerusalem in A.D. 70. Burrows dated the earliest Qumran fragments to about the third century B.C., a decision which may now need to be revised upwards, and assigned 1QIsaᵃ and 1QS to about 100 B.C. He held that 1QpHab was written in the last quarter of the first century B.C.,[18] and that 1QH, 1QM, and 1QIsaᵇ, along with the *Genesis Apocryphon*, were written in the first half of the first century B.C. Carbon-14 dating furnished a range of 168 B.C. to A.D. 233.[19] Generally this has confirmed the dates arrived at by Albright,[20] Birnbaum,[21] and Sukenik[22] on other grounds.

To a considerable extent the nature of the community (*yaḥad*) which had apparently deposited the manuscripts in the Qumran caves was evident from the contents of the scrolls themselves, particularly from 1QS, the document that enshrined the rules of the brotherhood. It is apparent that the sect consisted of a group of priests and laymen living a communal life of strict dedication to God. Specific requirements had to be met by those desiring to participate in the way of life followed by the sectaries (1QS, I:1-15), and all members of the community were required to renew their pledge of obedience to the discipline of the fellowship at an annual ceremony (1QS, II:19-25). Under the leadership of elders and priests the sectaries engaged in constant Biblical study and in a sacramental type of worship (1QS, V:1-IX:26), the aim of which was to foster the growth of personal holiness, justice, equity, and mercy that was in accord with the nature of God as manifested in the ancient Hebrew Scriptures (cf. 1QS, V:3f.).

The sectaries laid great emphasis upon the study of the Law, and their documentary legacy makes it clear that they regarded themselves as the remnant of the true Israel, awaiting patiently the establishing of divine rule upon earth. As Brownlee has commented, the brotherhood had its birth in Biblical interpretation, because God had revealed the mysteries of prophecy to the Righteous Teacher (1QpHab, VII:3ff.).[23] This individual had founded the Qumran brotherhood, and the members felt that their eternal destiny was inextricably bound up with fidelity to his person and precepts (1QpHab, VIII:1ff.), for his very presence and activity implied the near approach of the Messiah. But apparently he was killed by the Wicked Priest (1QpHab, XI:4f.), the leader of his spiritual enemies, who in turn was overtaken by divine retribution.

The Habakkuk Commentary compiled by the sect spoke cryptically of the Kittim as its temporal enemies, under whom the Righteous Teacher

---

[18] For a date *ca.* 64 B.C., see *VDJD*, p. 84.

[19] M. Burrows, *BASOR*, No. 122 (1951), pp. 4ff., No. 123 (1951), pp. 24ff.; cf. O. R. Sellers, *BA*, XIV, No. 1 (1951), p. 29.

[20] *BASOR*, No. 118 (1950), p. 6.

[21] *BASOR*, No. 115 (1949), p. 22.

[22] *Megilloth Genuzoth*, I, pp. 14f.

[23] W. H. Brownlee, *BA*, XIV, No. 3 (1951), pp. 54f.

may have been put to death. The Qumran covenanters envisaged them as agents of divine anger in the last days of the age. As such they were proud and ferocious, the unconquerable scourge of nations and kingdoms, who made a practice of venerating their standards and other weapons of war. Considerable speculative effort has been expended in an attempt to determine the identity of the Kittim. In late Jewish authors the name was used cryptically of any victorious power, and in consequence scholars have identified them variously with the forces of Antiochus IV Epiphanes,[24] the Seleucid[25] or Roman[26] armies in the time of Alexander Jannaeus (103-76 B.C.), the military power of the Roman period proper,[27] some aggressive group in the period of the First Jewish War (A.D. 66-70),[28] or the Crusaders of the medieval period.[29]

A reference in the Habakkuk Commentary to the Kittim sacrificing to their weapons (1QpHab, VI:4f.) might perhaps be an allusion to the Romans, who venerated their "eagles" in sacrificial rites.[30] If this identification is correct, the Commentary may have had in mind the period which ended with the capture of Jerusalem under Pompey in 63 B.C. There are several unsolved problems associated with the identity of the individuals and groups mentioned in the Habakkuk Commentary, and final judgment will have to be deferred until more conclusive evidence is forthcoming.

From 4Q came a mutilated manuscript which assisted considerably in

[24] So B. Reicke, *Studia Theologica*, II, fasc. I (1949), pp. 45ff., later he abandoned this position in *Handskrifterna Fran Qumran* (1952); G. Lambert, *Nouvelle Revue Théologique*, LXXIV (1952), pp. 259ff.; H. H. Rowley, *The Zadokite Fragments and the Dead Sea Scrolls* (1952), pp. 62ff.; A. Michel, *Le Maître de Justice après les documents de la Mer Morte* (1954), pp. 232ff.

[25] Those maintaining this view included R. de Vaux, *RB*, LVII (1950), pp. 428f., LVIII (1951), pp. 442f.; M. Delcor, *Les Manuscrits de la Mer Morte: Essai sur le Midrash d'Habacuc* (1951), pp. 56ff., see also his article in *Revue de l'Histoire des Religions*, CXLII (1952), pp. 129ff.

[26] Cf. J. van der Ploeg, *Bibliotheca Orientalis*, VIII (1951), pp. 9f.; M. H. Segal, *JBL*, LXX (1951), pp. 131ff.; W. H. Brownlee, *BA*, XIV, No. 3 (1951), p. 63; D. Barthélemy, *RB*, LIX (1952), pp. 207ff.

[27] Cf. A. Dupont-Sommer, *Revue de l'Histoire des Religions*, CXXXVII (1950), pp. 129ff. *Aperçus préliminaires sur les manuscrits de la Mer Morte* (1950), p. 40; R. Goosens, *La Nouvelle Clio*, I-II (1940-50), pp. 336ff., 634ff., III-IV (1951-52), pp. 137ff.; K. Elliger, *Studien zum Habakuk-Kommentar vom Toten Meer* (1953), pp. 226ff.; F. F. Bruce, *Second Thoughts on the Dead Sea Scrolls* (1961), pp. 71ff.

[28] So J. Teicher, *JJS*, II (1951), pp. 67ff., III (1952), pp. 53ff.; R. Tournay, *RB*, LVI (1949), pp. 204ff.; G. Vermès, *Ephemerides Theologicae Lovanienses*, XXVII (1951), pp. 70ff.; compare his *Cahiers Sioniens* (1953), pp. 3ff.

[29] Cf. P. R. Weis, *JQR*, XLI (1950-51), pp. 125ff.; S. Zeitlin, *JQR*, XLI (1950-51), pp. 251ff.

[30] H. H. Rowley, *PEQ*, LXXXVIII (1956), pp. 102ff.; R. Goosens, *La Nouvelle Clio*, III-IV (1951-52), pp. 137ff.; *WJ*, VI,6,1.

attempts to identify the Qumran sect itself. This fragment was found to have affinity with an ancient Jewish work dated between the tenth and twelfth centuries A.D., which had first been discovered in 1896 in the *genizah* or storage room of a Cairo synagogue. Published in 1910,[31] this Zadokite composition, commonly styled the *Cairo Damascene Covenanters* (CDC), narrated the fortunes of certain dispossessed Jerusalem priests who had migrated to Damascus during a reform movement in Judaism and had established a monastic sect under the leadership of a "Righteous Teacher." The fragments from 4Q contained parts of CDC. These were supplemented by some other manuscript pieces from 6Q. On the basis of this and additional evidence many scholars have identified the sect of CDC with the Qumran fellowship, and have placed the Damascus migration just prior to the first century B.C.[32]

The Qumran sectaries have also been closely associated with the Essenes, about whom much was written at the beginning of the Christian era. Pliny described one such settlement near the Dead Sea in his *Natural History* (V, 15); Philo commented on their devotional procedures and general manner of life.[33] Josephus[34] and Hippolytus[35] also wrote descriptions of varying length on Essene customs. From these accounts it would appear that the Essenes pursued a communal existence in isolated places, working on the land and exercising themselves in devotions that included synagogue worship, private study, and prayer. They abstained from marriage on the ground that wives were a hindrance to the pursuit of their spiritual ideals. One Essene sect, however, condoned marriage, not for the sake of pleasure or companionship, but as a means of insuring the perpetuation of the community. Under normal conditions membership in Essene groups could be entered into by those who approached the sect with a view to voluntary renunciation of secular life. The Essenes seem to have been pacifist by nature, and did not indulge in animal sacrifice.

---

[31] S. Schechter (ed. and transl.), *Documents of Jewish Sectaries* (2 vols., 1910), Vol. I, *Fragments of a Zadokite Work*. Cf. *APOT*, II, pp. 785ff.; S. Zeitlin, *The Zadokite Fragments* (*JQR* Monograph Series No. 1, 1952); C. Rabin, *The Zadokite Documents* (1954).

[32] Cf. H. H. Rowley, *The Zadokite Fragments and the Dead Sea Scrolls*, p. 3. Scholars who interpreted "Damascus" literally included M. H. Segal, *JBL*, LXX (1951), pp. 131ff.; J. T. Milik, *Ten Years of Discovery in the Wilderness of Judaea* (1959), pp. 90f.; cf. R. de Vaux, *RB*, LXI (1954), pp. 235f.; C. T. Fritsch, *JBL*, LXXIV (1955), pp. 173ff. T. H. Gaster, *The Dead Sea Scriptures in English Translation*, pp. 4, 101 n. 23, thinks the term symbolical, while F. M. Cross, *The Ancient Library of Qumran and Modern Biblical Studies*, p. 82, holds it to be a "prophetic name" for the Qumran desert.

[33] *Quod Omnis Probus Sit Liber*, written *ca.* A.D. 10; *Hypothetica*, XI.

[34] *WJ*, II, 8, 2; *AJ*, XVIII, 1, 5.

[35] *The Refutation of All Heresies*, IX, 13ff., in *The Ante-Nicene Fathers* (1886), V, pp. 134f.

Most scholars have followed Milik in identifying the Qumran sect with one or more of the contemporary Essene groups. While there are obvious points of similarity, there are equally important differences between the two religious bodies. The Essenes were mostly celibates, unlike the Qumran sectaries who admitted women into their fellowship and appear to have had married residents at the community site. Whereas the Essenes tended to spiritualize the sacrificial system, the Damascus group certainly indulged in animal sacrifices (CDC, XIII:27, XIV:2), and the absence of specific instructions in 1QS could be taken as implying that sacrifices were to be carried out in accordance with the normal provisions of the Torah. Whatever interpretation may ultimately be placed upon the Qumran Military Scroll, there can be no doubt whatever that the Qumran sectaries were far from being pacifist by nature or inclination. Again, whereas some of the Essenes not infrequently worked in neighboring villages, the Qumran brotherhood isolated itself from all contact with the outside world. In view of these objections alone it should be clear that the brotherhood at Qumran can only be designated as Essene in the most general sense.[36]

Another cave group known as the Magharians is mentioned in the writings of the tenth-century Jewish sectary Kirkisani, who placed it chronologically somewhat after the Sadducees but prior to the Christian era.[37] This sect is also mentioned by two Moslem writers, Al Biruni (973-1048) and Shahrastani (1071-1153), the latter placing its origin in the first century B.C. The fact that the Qumran covenanters flourished about this time and that they hid their sacred writings in a cave might perhaps indicate some connection between them and the Magharians. The discovery of a rock-dwelling containing books near Jericho about A.D. 800 was mentioned in a Syriac letter from the Nestorian Patriarch of Seleucia, Timotheus I (A.D. 726-819) to Sergius, the Metropolitan of Elam.[38] The cave in question could perhaps have been 1Q, and if this were to be the case it would seem that the cave-sectaries of Kirkisani were identical with the Qumran society. It must be said, however, that actual proof of a connection between the two groups is lacking at the time of writing.[39]

The Therapeutae, who flourished in Egypt about 200 B.C., also bore a superficial resemblance to the fellowship at Qumran. Philo described the Therapeutae as recluses who devoted their efforts to prayer, meditation,

---

[36] Cf. C. T. Fritsch, *The Qumran Community* (1956), p. 110; W. H. Brownlee, *The Dead Sea Manual of Discipline* (*BASOR*, suppl. stud. X-XII, 1951), p. 4; R. Marcus, *JBL*, LXXIII (1954), p. 161; C. Rabin, *Qumran Studies* (*Scripta Judaica*, II, 1957), pp. 59f., 69f.

[37] Cf. L. Nemoy, *HUCA*, VII (1929-30), pp. 363f.

[38] G. R. Driver, *The Hebrew Scrolls from the Neighbourhood of Jericho and the Dead Sea*, pp. 25f.

[39] H. H. Rowley, *The Zadokite Fragments and the Dead Sea Scrolls*, pp. 24f.; L. Nemoy, *JQR*, XLII (1951-1952), p. 127.

and the study of their sectarian documents, only assembling for community worship of a quasi-sacramental nature on the sabbath day or on specifically designated holy seasons. This group admitted women to their fellowship, and wrote commentaries and poetry, much in the manner of the Qumran sectaries, as an essential part of their devotional exercises.[40]

The flood of literature that has emerged following the discovery of the Dead Sea Scrolls is eloquent testimony to the importance which scholars have attached to this remarkable phase of archaeological activity. No work dealing with the Bible generally can now be regarded with any seriousness if it fails to take into account the significance of the Qumran discoveries for its own particular area of study. The vast and highly diversified nature of the subject as reflected by the enormous current bibliography presents its own special problems, but despite this there can be absolutely no doubt whatever as to the revolutionary nature of its impact upon the discipline of theology in general and upon Biblical studies in particular. Although no final pronouncements on many of the problems that have arisen may be possible at the present stage of knowledge, it is already abundantly clear that a great deal of what was formerly accepted as fact will stand in need of radical revision, as will become evident in subsequent chapters of the present work. Again, much that was known in earlier days has been amply confirmed, thus furnishing a more secure basis for future advances in the field of Biblical scholarship.

[40] *De Vita Contemplativa* (Loeb Classical Library Translation), IX, pp. 113ff.

Part Three

ANCIENT NEAR EASTERN CHRONOLOGY

I. CHRONOLOGY FROM ADAM TO ABRAHAM

A. GENEALOGIES AND KING-LISTS

Despite the enormous amount of information available for the modern scholar as the result of historical and archaeological research, formidable difficulties are involved in any attempt to draw up an internally coherent scheme of chronology for any one of the various cultures that flourished in the ancient Near East. There is still an insufficiency of primary source materials for such a task, and the situation is further complicated because some of the necessary information already available is amenable to different interpretations. In the past no comprehensive system of Near Eastern or specifically Biblical chronology has proved entirely satisfactory in matters of detail: frequently it has happened that adjustments to the scheme of dating have been required because of new archaeological or other discoveries, and an already precarious balance has been upset.

Extra-Biblical sources are naturally of very great importance when they furnish fixed dates, and it is often in the light of such material that schemes of Biblical dating have to be modified. Where events in Biblical and extra-Biblical sources can be synchronized to a very narrow range, it is possible to utilize the results in order to establish a framework around which a specific chronology can be built. Fixed points of this nature have been formulated for Babylonian and Assyrian chronology on the one hand, and for Egyptian dating-sequences on the other. Against such vertical patterns it has been possible to establish horizontal synchronisms for certain of the other Near Eastern nations of antiquity, including Israel, so as to form a reasonably assured grid upon which the chronologies of these peoples can be imposed.[1] It must be stressed, however, that the chronologies of Babylonia and Egypt are themselves by no means completely assured in matters of detail, so that certain aspects of the larger picture will need to be modified for some time to come in the light of an expanding knowledge of ancient Near Eastern life and times.

[1] D. N. Freedman, *BANE*, p. 203.

What is probably the earliest, and undoubtedly the most celebrated, attempt at a chronological system in the English-speaking world was furnished by Archbishop James Usher (or Ussher) in the seventeenth century.[2] Taking the genealogies of the Bible as descriptive of strict lineal succession in the sense in which a modern genealogy would be understood, Usher reckoned backwards, computing the dates of the era of the patriarchs on the basis of the figures mentioned in the Massoretic text of Genesis (5:3ff., 7:11ff., 10:1ff., 11:10ff.), concluding that the world was created in 4004 B.C. This chronology, based upon a wealth of archiepiscopal erudition, was accepted without much question at the time, and on the authority of some unknown individual it was incorporated into the margins of reference editions of the Authorized Version of the Bible, which had been published in 1611. While it still continues to occupy this position to the present in some editions of the King James Version, it has no warrant for being there other than tradition.

The system devised by Usher depended inferentially upon the supposition that the Old Testament genealogies did not omit any names, and that the periods of time mentioned in the text were consecutive, assumptions that have been proved to be entirely gratuitous. A careful comparison of the genealogies contained in 1 Chronicles with their counterparts in the historical books will be sufficient to show that on occasions names have been omitted in certain lists. For example, the LXX has retained *Kainan* in Genesis 11:13, whereas the Massoretic text omits it. The situation is further complicated when one realizes that the figures given for the ages of many of the individuals mentioned in the Massoretic text do not agree with the corresponding records in other versions such as the LXX and the Samaritan Pentateuch. Several examples will be sufficient to illustrate this tendency. The age of the patriarch Adam at the birth of Seth was given as 130 years by the Massoretic text and the Samaritan Pentateuch, but this figure was enlarged by a century in the LXX. Kenan was said by the Massoretic text and the Samaritan Pentateuch to have been 70 years of age at the birth of his successor Mahalalel, whereas the LXX again extended this statement by 100 years. However, the LXX agreed with the Massoretic text in stating that Jared was 162 years old when his son was born, compared to the 62 years reported by the Samaritan Pentateuch. In contrast, all three versions agreed in assigning ages of 50 and 100 years respectively to Noah and Shem at the birth of their successors. For the remainder of the lines of these patriarchal figures there is a tendency on the part of the LXX to shorten the period, whereas the Samaritan Pentateuch exhibits close agreement with

[2] J. Usher, *Annales Veteris et Novi Testamenti* (1650-1654); cf. *MNHK*, pp. 228ff., 252f.

the Massoretic text in all cases except those of Jared, Methuselah,[3] and Lamech.

A careful examination of the list of ante- and post-diluvian patriarchs in Genesis indicates that the compilation exhibits a conventional and schematic structure which contains two units of ten names each (if Kainan is included from the LXX). This pattern is similar to the genealogy in Matthew 1, where the generations extending from Abraham to Jesus were reduced to three basic units of fourteen names each. Oriental chronological computation is discussed in Part 5, pp. 295ff.

A comparison of the Massoretic text with the LXX and the Samaritan Pentateuch leaves little doubt that the Hebrew text is the original, constituting the foundation upon which the other versions have built. Presumably in an attempt to introduce some sort of chronological balance into the lives of the earlier patriarchs, the LXX added 100 years to the respective ages of these individuals at the time when their successors were born. For the latter part of their lives the LXX subtracted proportionate periods so as to bring the total life-span of each patriarch into general accord with the figures furnished by the Massoretic text. The Samaritan Pentateuch, on the other hand, tended to shorten the lives of the antediluvian figures and lengthen those of the post-diluvians. According to the chronology of the LXX, Methuselah survived the Flood by some 14 years, whereas the Massoretic text dated his demise in the year in which the Flood occurred (Gen. 7:23). The Samaritan Pentateuch appears to have indicated the commencement of a new era in human affairs with the activities of Noah and his sons by implying that Jared, Methuselah, and Lamech all died in the year of the Flood, presumably as a result of the cataclysm. The low figures furnished by the Massoretic text for the chronology between Arpachshad and Nahor would seem to account for the rather unusual fact that all the patriarchs from Noah to Terah were alive when Abraham was born. The texts of the LXX and the Samaritan Pentateuch, on the other hand, record that all the ancestors of Abraham had died well in advance of his journey to Canaan at the age of 75.

Both the LXX and the Samaritan Pentateuch avoid the sharp decline in the ages of the post-diluvians at the birth of their successors by adopting the device of adding a century to most of the figures contained in the Massoretic text. By this means their records achieve something like parity with the dates assigned in the Hebrew Scriptures for the ante-

---

[3] Though this name and the מתושאל of Gen. 4:18 were both rendered Μαθουσάλα by the LXX, there is no reason to assume that the two names represent the same person.

diluvian patriarchs generally. Table 1 will assist in illustrating some of the matters raised in the foregoing discussion.

TABLE 1: EARLY PATRIARCHAL GENEALOGIES

Name	Age at birth of successor			Balance of life			Total years		
	MT	LXX	Sam. P.	MT	LXX	Sam. P.	MT	LXX	Sam. P.
Adam	130	230	130	800	700	800	930	930	930
Seth	105	205	105	807	707	807	912	912	912
Enosh	90	190	90	815	715	815	905	905	905
Kenan	70	170	70	840	740	840	910	910	910
Mahalalel	65	165	65	830	730	830	895	895	895
Jared	162	162	62	800	800	785	962	962	847
Enoch	65	165	65	300	200	300	365	365	365
Methuselah	187	167	67	782	802	653	868	969	720
Lamech	182	188	53	595	565	600	777	753	653
Noah	500	500	500	450	450	450	950	950	950
Shem	100	100	100	500	500	500			600
Arpachshad	35	135	135	403	430	303			438
Kainan		130			330				
Shelah	30	130	130	403	330	303			433
Eber	34	134	134	430	370	270			404
Peleg	30	130	130	209	209	109			239
Reu	32	132	132	207	207	107			239
Serug	30	130	130	200	200	100			230
Nahor	29	79	79	119	129	69			148
Terah	70	70	70				205	205	145

As de Vries has pointed out, the enormously long ages assigned to the Genesis antediluvians finds a striking analogy in the extended lives of the Sumerian kings prior to the great flood of the late Jemdet Nasr period at Shuruppak.[4] This list of kings, known as the Weld-Blundell prism,[5] was apparently completed during the prosperous Third Dynasty of Ur, and furnished the names of eight kings in chronological succession.

[4] S. J. de Vries, *IDB*, I, pp. 581f.
[5] Published by S. Langdon, *Oxford Editions of Cuneiform Texts* (1923), II. For a critical edition of the king-list using subsequently discovered sources see T. Jacobsen, *The Sumerian King List* (1939), *Assyriological Studies XI, Oriental Institute;* cf. *ANET*, pp. 265f.; C. L. Woolley, *The Sumerians*, p. 21.

TABLE 2: EARLY SUMERIAN KING-LIST

City	Ruler	Regnal years
Eridu	Alulim	28,800
	Alalgar	36,000
Badtibira	Enmenlu-Anna	43,200
	Enmengal-Anna	28,800
	Dumuzi	36,000
Larak	Ensipazi-Anna	28,800
Sippar	Enmendur-Anna	21,000
Shuruppak	Ubar-Tutu	18,600

Total 241,200

Whatever the epic or schematic principles underlying such a composition, it is evident that they are not wholly consistent internally, since the earliest kings are ascribed reigns of the most exaggerated length. This king-list appeared in a later form in writings of Berossus, a priest of Marduk in Babylon under Antiochus I (281-261 B.C.). He extended the list to include two other royal personages, and nearly doubled the sum of their individual reigns (Table 3).

TABLE 3: REVISED SUMERIAN KING-LIST (Berossus)

Ruler	Regnal years
Alorus	36,000
Alaparos	10,800
Amelon	46,800
Ammenon	43,200
Megalaros	64,800
Daos (Daonos)	36,000
Euedorachos	64,800
Amempsinos	36,000
Otiartes	28,800
Xisouthros	64,800

Total 432,000

Xisouthros was the ruler when the great flood descended, according to Berossus. The names are obviously Greek in form, and it may be that some confusion has resulted, with Amelon and Ammenon perhaps being corrupt forms of the cognomen Enmenlu-Anna. What is more probable,

151

however, is that there is some connection between the tradition which underlay the record of Berossus concerning the ten antediluvian kings and that which recorded the existence of ten patriarchs from Adam to Moses.[6] Both forms appear to be schematic, and related to definite chronological sequences whose significance or importance may have been interpreted numerically. To what extent the two sources refer to the same area of Mesopotamia and the same general period, however, is difficult to determine.

It would seem evident that while the numbers assigned to the ages of the patriarchs in Genesis had real meaning for those who were responsible for their preservation in the first instance, they cannot be employed in a purely literal sense as a means of computing the length of the various generations mentioned in the text. Nor is it satisfactory to assume that the various names are those of dynasties or peoples, rather than of individuals, since certain of the narratives regard those mentioned as individual personages and narrate their exploits in the form of a summary. Unfortunately there is as yet no absolute date for an event in the secular history of Babylonia to which the doings of these patriarchal figures can be related for purposes of chronological control. The best that can be done under such circumstances is to assign the historical background of the narratives in question to one or other of the cultural periods established as a result of archaeological discoveries in Mesopotamia.

B. Cultural Periods of Early Mesopotamia

In any attempt to establish a sequence of Old Testament chronology it must always be remembered that the Bible was not designed primarily as a textbook of history or culture; hence, it can hardly be expected to present a carefully formulated and internally consistent pattern of chronological sequences as understood by the occidental mind. In some of the earlier sources from Mesopotamia it is apparent that dates, numbers, and the general computation of time follow certain symbolic configurations whose ratio and overall significance were evidently quite clear to the ancient writers employing them, but whose meaning is completely unknown to the modern western mind. There are still other occasions when the Biblical writers employed dates and numbers as a means of illustrating profound spiritual concepts that they were endeavoring to promote, for example, in connection with the triumphant Exodus of Israel from Egypt. Again, although there are some demonstrable omissions and conflations present in Old Testament sequences of chronology, there are also a great many accurately dated events as well as clear indications of order and arrangement in the succession of individuals,

[6] G. A. Barton, *Archaeology and the Bible* (1937), p. 320.

state officials, and the like, making for a high degree of reliability once the basic pattern of computation is understood.

One unfortunate difficulty which stands in the way of attempts to establish an assured sequence of chronology for the Old Testament is the fact that the various books and sources were not dated in terms of one particular era, as can be done with events which occur in the Christian age, for example. The point of departure for a given historical period in early Mesopotamian life is quite different in many respects from its equivalent at a much later date in the history of that area. Again, the system of chronological computation in Judah during the days of Jeremiah differed in certain important respects from that which was employed by contemporary Babylonian scribes. A good many of the dates and allusions to time-sequences in the Old Testament are of a comparative nature, being frequently related to the reign of a particular king (e.g. 2 Kgs. 15:32) or to some unusual physical phenomenon such as an earthquake (Am. 1:1, Zech. 14:5). Only occasionally did the writers refer to an event like the Exodus, which for them marked the commencement of a new era alike of faith and history (Judg. 11:16, 26, 1 Kgs. 6:1).

As a result of discoveries that archaeologists have made at various sites, it is now possible to envisage the earliest inhabitants of the Near East in terms of Stone Age settlements. In Mesopotamia, the body of a Stone Age baby estimated to have died 75,000 years ago was discovered in the Shanidar Cave, located some 50 miles northeast of Mosul. The skeletons found in the caves of Mount Carmel and elsewhere in the neighborhood of Galilee are of great importance because they indicate the way in which anthropological considerations can contribute materially to the formulation of chronological sequences in critical areas. The deposits were dated in the general period known as Levalloiso-Mousterian, between 150,000 and 120,000 years ago.[7] Upon examination they proved to constitute the remains of a Paleolithic group in which the characteristics of neanthropic man (*Homo sapiens*) and paleoanthropic man (*Homo neanderthalensis*) were so intermingled as to represent a hybrid race.[8] As Albright has pointed out, these discoveries would seem to indicate that *Homo sapiens* entered Europe from the southwest, driving Neanderthal man before him and subsequently interbreeding freely with the various Neanderthaloid types then in existence.[9]

---

[7] D. A. E. Garrod and D. M. A. Bate, *The Stone Age of Mount Carmel: Excavations at the Wady el-Mughara* (1937), I; T. D. McCown and Sir Arthur Keith, *The Stone Age of Mount Carmel: The Fossil Human Remains from the Levalloiso-Mousterian* (1939), II.

[8] G. H. R. von Koenigswald, *Meeting Prehistoric Man* (1956), pp. 71, 206. Cf. Sir Arthur Keith, *New Discoveries Relating to the Antiquity of Man* (1931), pp. 173ff.; J. P. Hyatt, *The Journal of Bible and Religion*, XII (1944), pp. 232ff.

[9] *AP*, pp. 56f.

153

The characteristic Mesolithic period of Palestine was represented by deposits dated about 8000 B.C., and styled Natufian by Dorothy Garrod. From skeletons recovered from various sites in Palestine, as well as from a slightly later period at Helwan in Egypt, it is apparent that the Natufians had certain points in common with the predynastic Egyptians. They were slender in build and were little more than five feet in height. Natufians are usually credited with introducing agricultural activity to the Near East. The discovery of a wide range of flint artifacts has indicated that they obtained some of their food through the cultivation of crops such as millet, which was harvested by means of flint sickles and subsequently ground to a rough consistency in stone mortars. Although these enterprising peoples belonged technically to a pre-pottery phase, they displayed artistic skill in the carving of small images and the fashioning of animal bones to form beads, pins, pendants, and other ornaments. The position of the skeletons indicated that the Natufians generally buried their dead in the contracted manner of predynastic peoples of Egypt, with the arms folded across the chest and the knees drawn up under the chin.[10] It was during this general period that the dog is thought to have been domesticated.

Neolithic culture was characterized in Palestine by successive early occupations of Jericho, one of the most ancient inhabited sites in the entire Near East. The excavations of Kathleen Kanyon have confirmed Garstang's findings of a definite pre-pottery phase in the cultural history of Jericho during which characteristic flint artifacts were made. This was followed, prior to 5000 B.C., by a period in which the manufacture of pottery was a pronounced feature of cultural activity, along with an established flint industry.[11] In the pre-pottery period Neolithic man began to live in villages composed of primitive dwellings clustered around a central shrine. The best representative of this phase in Palestine is found at Jericho, where the houses and shrines were made from small, rounded mud bricks or beaten earth. The shrine was designed in such a manner that it had an outer and an inner chamber of considerable size, and normally contained animal figurines and cult-objects of a sexual nature.[12]

In northern Mesopotamia the village-settlements unearthed at Nineveh, at Tepe Gawra some twelve miles to the northeast, and at Tell Hassuna, a few miles south of modern Mosul, are the best representatives of Neolithic culture discovered to date, and they exhibit the characteristic prehistoric forms. The lowest levels at Tepe Gawra revealed the existence of a delicate decorated ceramic ware, some of which was found in

[10] *AP*, pp. 59ff.

[11] Kenyon, *Digging Up Jericho* (1957), pp. 51ff.

[12] *AP*, pp. 62f. For a survey of the archaeological chronology of Palestine from the Neolithic to the Middle Bronze Age see W. F. Albright in *Relative Chronologies in Old World Archaeology* (ed. R. W. Erich, 1954), pp. 28ff.

association with Neolithic skeletons.[13] This culture of northern Mesopotamia and the Assyrian uplands probably antedates the fifth millennium B.C., thus making the construction of houses and the invention of pottery matters of great antiquity. In Syria this variety of primitive village-culture is found in the lowest levels at Tell ej-Judeideh in the plain of Antioch.[14] In Palestine it is represented at Jericho.[15] In Egypt the Neolithic settlers seem to have been active somewhat before 5000 B.C., as indicated by the remains of occupational levels at Deir Tasa, Merimdeh, Beni-Salameh, and in the Fayyum.[16]

The Chalcolithic or "copper-stone" period (ca. 4500-3000 B.C.), which succeeded the Neolithic, saw the flowering of the first major culture of antiquity. Its best representative site is Tell Halaf, but similar deposits have been found at Carchemish, over 100 miles west of Tell Halaf, at Tell Chagar Bazar, some 50 miles east of Tell Halaf, at Tepe Gawra, and in other areas.[17] To the same period belongs the Badarian culture of ancient Egypt, where serious attempts were made to cultivate grain and to bring certain animals under domestication. There are some indications that the Badarian economy was influenced to a certain extent by the trade-relations they had with other peoples. One example of this tendency may be seen in the fact that the Badarians used eye-paint made from powdered green malachite, a substance which in all probability had been imported from the Sinai peninsula. The Badarians were also familiar to some extent with the malleable properties of copper, although it is doubtful that they actually understood the principles underlying the fusion of metals. Excavation of their burial-sites has shown that they interred their dead in a sleeping position, and that they deposited food offerings and other objects in the graves.[18]

[13] E. A. Speiser, *Asia*, XXXVIII (1938), p. 543, *BASOR*, No. 66 (1937), p. 18, No. 70 (1938), pp. 6f.

[14] R. J. Braidwood, *Mounds in the Plain of Antioch, An Archaeological Survey* (1937), pp. 6f.; C. W. McEwan, *AJA*, XLI (1937), pp. 10f.

[15] G. E. Wright, *The Pottery of Palestine from the Earliest Times to the End of the Early Bronze Age* (1937), pp. 7ff., 107.

[16] For Deir Tasa, see G. Brunton, *Antiquity, A Quarterly Review of Archaeology*, III (1929), pp. 456ff.; for Merimdeh, Beni-Salameh, V. G. Childe, *New Light on the Most Ancient East* (1935), pp. 58ff., H. Ranke, *JAOS*, LIX, No. 4 (1939), suppl. p. 8; for the Fayyum, G. Caton-Thompson and E. W. Gardner, *The Desert Fayyum* (2 vols., 1934), H. J. Kantor in *Relative Chronologies in Old World Archaeology*, p. 3; Kantor dated the Fayyum culture around 4250 B.C.

[17] Cf. M. von Oppenheim, *Der Tell Halaf, eine neue Kultur im ältesten Mesopotamien* (1931); M. E. L. Mallowan and J. C. Rose, *Prehistoric Assyria, The Excavations at Tell Arpachiyah, 1933* (1935), pp. 17ff., 104f.

[18] G. Brunton and G. Caton-Thompson, *The Badarian Civilisation* (1928), pp. 20ff.

The successors to the Badarians were Amrateans of Upper Egypt, with whom commenced the real beginnings of the predynastic period (*ca.* 4500-2900 B.C.). An essentially sedentary people, they are thought to have been the first to attempt the systematic cultivation of the fertile Nile valley. In the Nagada I phase of Upper Egyptian culture they expanded along the entire length of the Nile River. From excavations at Amratean sites it is evident that these early peoples engaged in the weaving of flax and the manufacture of a wide range of small copper tools and implements. Representations of animals and men on pottery objects interred with the dead may perhaps reflect the beginnings of magic in primitive Egyptian life.[19]

Under the Gerzeans, who succeeded the Amrateans, there came an expansion of trade with Mesopotamia and India. Cast metal implements unearthed at Gerzean sites show that they had mastered the art of casting tools and weapons. At this period totemistic symbols were becoming increasingly associated with the villages and towns, and the place of magic was further indicated by distinct evidences of ritual procedure at the time of interment. The rich were buried in graves that had been lined with mud bricks, and at one site walls were found decorated with a mural painting.[20]

The corresponding Palestinian culture was named Ghassulian, after the site where it was first discovered. Excavations at Teleilat Ghassul, just north of the Dead Sea in the vicinity of Jericho, uncovered traces of painted pottery at Chalcolithic levels. The houses from this period were of mud brick construction, and their plastered walls were adorned with well-executed mural paintings.[21]

In Mesopotamia, the most clearly defined culture of the prehistoric period was that uncovered at al 'Ubaid, four miles northwest of Ur. This phase, which is also represented at a number of other ancient Mesopotamian sites, including Erech (Uruk), Ur, and Eridu, can be dated approximately 4000 B.C. Whereas domestic architecture as such exhibited little if any significant advance upon its counterpart in the Halafian period, the 'Ubaid phase is notable for the construction of three shrines found at Tepe Gawra whose architectural features dominated the style of Mesopotamian temples for many centuries. While 'Ubaid culture generally tended towards preserving the self-sufficiency of the Neolithic economy,[22] the presence in contemporary deposits of beads made from amazonite and lapis lazuli points to contact with central Asia and India,

[19] V. G. Childe, *New Light on the Most Ancient East,* pp. 69ff.

[20] J. E. Quibell, *Hierakonpolis,* II (1902), pp. 20f.

[21] A. Mallon, R. Koeppel, and R. Neuville, *Teleilat Ghassul I, Compte rendu des fouilles de l'Institut Biblique Pontifical, 1929-1932* (1934); N. Glueck, *BASOR,* No. 97 (1945), pp. 10f.

[22] V. G. Childe, *What Happened in History* (1942), p. 74.

where such stones were in use as ornaments at that time.[23] The pottery of the al 'Ubaid culture reflects the influence of the Persian highlands, and its appearance can be taken as marking the first attempts at colonizing the southern area of Mesopotamia.[24]

The Uruk phase, which is usually dated towards the end of the fourth millennium B.C., saw the emergence of a new people who exhibited distinctive elements of civilization as prominent marks of their culture. These included engraved cylinder seals, temples constructed of stone rather than of sun-dried mud bricks, sculpture in the round, and writing on clay.[25] The Uruk period was continued in central Mesopotamia towards the end of the fourth millennium B. C. at the site of Jemdet Nasr.[26] Bronze implements discovered there indicated that the Chalcolithic period proper in Mesopotamia was terminating, and that it was being replaced by the Bronze Age. Sculpture in stone was a marked feature of the Jemdet Nasr phase, and the recovery of clay tablets inscribed with a semi-pictographic form of writing made it clear that significant advances upon the achievements of the Uruk period had been made in this area of cultural activity. Such ancient sites as Kish and Shuruppak were most probably founded at this time.The Jemdet Nasr era is so close to recorded history and to the king-lists of Mesopotamia that it can be assigned approximately to a date of 3000 B.C. Some scholars have divided up the chronological sequence in greater detail, designating the latter part of the Uruk phase as Protoliterate A-B or Early Protoliterate, and the early Jemdet Nasr period as Protoliterate C-D or Late Protoliterate, but the basic dating is not seriously affected by such classifications.[27]

The Uruk culture contained numerous elements that foreshadowed in many respects the achievements of the first historical civilized community in southern Mesopotamia. This latter was known as Sumeria, the home of a vigorous people who entered the marshy delta region about 4000 B.C. Between this time and the beginning of the Early Dynastic period, about 2800 B.C., the Sumerians attained to cultural supremacy, and laid the foundations of social organization and behavior in such a manner as to exert a lasting influence over all subsequent Mesopotamian civilizations. The Early Dynastic period came to an end with the rise of the First Dynasty of Ur, during which four kings reigned for a total period of 177 years, according to the king-list. A small limestone tablet

---

[23] E. Mackay, *The Indus Civilisation* (1935), pp. 170, 191ff.

[24] S. Piggott, *Prehistoric India* (1952), p. 55.

[25] *LAP*, pp. 19ff.

[26] E. Mackay and S. Langdon, *Report on Excavations at Jemdet Nasr, Iraq* (1931).

[27] E.g. A. L. Perkins, *CAEM*, pp. 97ff. A. Parrot, *Archéologie mésopotom'enne*, II (1953), pp. 272ff., prefers to use the term "Predynastic," whereas A. Moortgat, *Die Entstehung der sumerischen Hochkultur* (1945), pp. 59ff., employed "Early Historic" for the Protoliterate period, commencing about 3300 B.C.

unearthed by Woolley at Tell el-Obeid dated *ca.* 2700 B.C. proved to be contemporary with the First Dynasty of Ur. It read:

> A-Anne-pada, king of Ur, son of Mes-Anne-pada, king of Ur, has built this for his Lady Nin-kharsag.[28]

This discovery proved to be extremely important for the chronology of this period, for it confirmed the claim of the Sumerian king-list that Mes-Anne-pada was the monarch who had founded the First Dynasty.[29] Equally significant was the light that it shed upon the unusually long reign of 80 years attributed to him, by showing that in all probability his son and successor, whose name was very similar, had somehow been dropped from the king-list and that his reign had been added to that of Mes-Anne-pada, making a total of 80 years. The revised king-list would thus read as in Table 4.

TABLE 4: REVISED SUMERIAN KING-LIST

Ruler	Regnal Years
Mes-Anne-pada ⎫ A-Anne-pada ⎭	80
Meskiag-Nanna	36
Elulu	25
Balulu	36

Total 177

In ancient Egypt, the expansion of community life during the Gerzean period proved to be one of the most important factors contributing to the development of the predynastic era. Towards the end of this phase, about 2900 B.C., two powerful states known as Upper and Lower Egypt came into being. Their unification under Menes of Thinis is generally taken to be the beginning of the Egyptian Protodynastic period (*ca.* 2900-2760 B.C.). The foundations of the Old Kingdom era were laid by the pharaohs of the First and Second Dynasties in the twenty-ninth to the twenty-seventh centuries B.C., and with the rise of the Third Dynasty, *ca.* 2700 B.C., there emerged the Old Kingdom period proper.[30] The Old

[28] *UC*, pp. 72f.
[29] Woolley dated the First Dynasty "Royal Cemetery" at Ur *ca.* 3500-3200 B.C. (*Ur Excavations II, The Royal Cemetery* [1934], p. 223), but this has been criticized for being too high by V. Müller, *JAOS*, LV (1935), pp. 206ff., and H. Frankfort, *JRAS* (1937), pp. 332ff. W. F. Albright has suggested a date of *ca.* 2500 B. C., *BASOR*, No. 88 (1942), p. 32, *AJA*, XLVII (1943), p. 492.
[30] Cf. Albright, *BASOR*, No. 119 (1950), p. 29.

Kingdom lasted for about 500 years, and was the classical period of Egyptian culture. During this time the pyramids were built, the religion of the country assumed its normative character, and the impact of Egyptian life upon the outside world was enhanced by expanding trade relations with the Orient. The glory of the Old Kingdom period waned about 2200 B.C. at the end of the Sixth Dynasty, and from the Seventh to the Eleventh Dynasties (ca. 2200-1989 B.C.) a succession of weak pharaohs proved unable to maintain a vigorous central government. This phase, generally known as the First Intermediate period, ended with the beginning of the Twelfth Dynasty under Amenemhet I, ca. 1989 B.C.

During the twenty-fourth century B.C., the inhabitants of Mesopotamia witnessed the rise to power of Sargon of Agade, who established the Old Akkadian period (ca. 2360-2180 B.C.) with the defeat of Lugalzaggesi of Sumeria and the incorporation of his territory into a Semitic realm. Under Naram-Sin, grandson of Sargon, this empire extended from central Persia to the Mediterranean, and when it was at its height it fell into the hands of the Gutians of Caucasia, ca. 2180 B.C. A revival of Sumerian culture at Lagash, about 2070 B.C., coincided with a decline in Gutian influence, and upon their downfall the magnificent Third Dynasty of Ur, marking the Neo-Sumerian period (ca. 2113-1991 B.C.), arose. Its founder Ur-Nammu was remarkable for his encouragement of literary activity during this period, and in particular for his law code, which is one of the oldest known from Mesopotamia.[31] This cultural revival also flourished at Lagash under the ensi Gudea, a viceroy associated with one of the kings of the Third Dynasty.[32] Although the revival continued under Dungi (Shulgi), Bur-Sin, and their successors, the end of Sumerian culture was close at hand, and its demise occurred with the period of the Elamite and Amorite invasions (ca. 1960-1830 B.C.), during which Ur was sacked[33] and Mesopotamia saw the beginnings of the Old Babylonian period (ca. 1830-1550 B.C.).

The most important single individual of this era, a man whose dates have been revised by scholars from time to time, was Hammurabi, the last great ruler of the First Dynasty. Attempts to identify him on the basis of information contained in Genesis 14 resulted in the association of him with Amraphel, king of Shinar, by many nineteenth-century scholars.[34] C. P. Tiele and W. H. Kosters rejected this identification, and F. Hommel held that Amraphel was the father of Hammurabi.[35] At the

---

[31] S. N. Kramer, *Orientalia*, XXIII (1954), pp. 40ff. and *From the Tablets of Sumer* (1956), pp. 47ff.

[32] *ARI*, p. 224.

[33] Cf. S. N. Kramer, *Lamentation Over the Destruction of Ur* (1940), *Assyriological Studies XII, Oriental Institute*, p. 57.

[34] E.g. T. K. Cheyne, *EB*, I, col. 159, who dated him *ca.* 2250 B.C.

[35] Tiele and Kosters, *EB*, I, col. 733; Hommel, *Geschichte Babyloniens und Assyriens* (1885), pp. 123ff.

same time some scholars were identifying Arioch of Ellasar (Gen. 14:1, 9) with Rim-Sin of Larsa, or with Warad-Sin (Eri-Aku), a king of Larsa dated by Rogers about 2172-2160 B.C.[36] On the basis of the Babylonian king-lists Rogers assigned a date of 2130-2087 B.C. to the reign of Hammurabi,[37] and a date of 2160-2099 B.C. to his contemporary Rim-Sin of Larsa. It is worthy of note that the name Arriwuk occurred in some tablets from Mari as the designation of the fifth son of Zimri-Lim of Mari, ca. 1750 B.C., and perhaps constitutes a parallel form of the Old Testament "Arioch."[38]

In the light of the discoveries at Mari, a date of 2150 B.C. for Hammurabi appears too high. Some of the diplomatic correspondence from the Mari palace archives consisted of messages that passed between Hammurabi and Zimri-Lim, the last king of Mari, who appears to have come to power after Shamshi-Adad I of Assyria (ca. 1748-1716 B.C.) had sent his son Yasmah-Adad to govern Mari on a temporary basis.[39] The Mari documents spoke of Shamshi-Adad I as an Amorite contemporary of Hammurabi, which brings him into the latter part of the Mari Age. On the basis of this important evidence it is now possible to date Hammurabi about 1728-1686 B.C. with reasonable confidence.[40] At present it is extremely difficult to arrive with any degree of certainty at the identity of King Amraphel of Shinar, but it is now evident that he was not the same person as Hammurabi of Babylon.[41]

The beginning of the Middle Bronze Age (ca. 2100-1550 B.C.) saw the rise of another important group, the Hittites, who can be fitted reasonably well into the chronological sequences so far established. A little after 2000 B.C. several groups of Indo-European origin began to move along the northern portion of the Fertile Crescent towards Asia Minor. They mingled freely with the earlier native population of Anatolia who spoke a non-Indo-European language known as Hattic or Proto-Hittite, and in succeeding centuries they built up an empire which covered vast tracts of territory in Anatolia and Syria.

[36] Cf. T. G. Pinches, HDB, I, p. 148. This identification was rejected by L. W. King, The Letters and Inscriptions of Hammurabi (1898-1900), I, pp. xxv, xxvi, xlix. For the dating of Warad-Sin, see Rogers, History of Babylonia and Assyria (1915), II, p. 84.

[37] Ibid., I, p. 516. On the basis of the Nabonidus Inscription he dated Hammurabi ca. 2075 B.C. (ibid., pp. 492f.).

[38] Cf. M. Noth, VT, I (1951), pp. 136ff.

[39] A. Poebel, who published the Khorsabad List of Assyrian kings recovered from the palace of Sargon II, dated Shamshi-Adad I from 1726-1694 B.C., JNES, I (1942), pp. 247ff., 460ff., II (1943), pp. 56ff.

[40] W. F. Albright, BASOR, No. 88 (1942), pp. 28ff., AJA, XLVII (1943), p. 492; BHI, p. 52.

[41] W. F. Albright, JPOS, VI (1926), p. 179. Cf. his articles in Journal of the Society for Oriental Research, X (1926), p. 232 and in JPOS, I (1921), p. 71; also E. A. Speiser, AASOR, XIII (1933), p. 45n.; R. de Vaux, ZAW, LVI (1938), p. 231 and RB, LV (1948), p. 331.

In Genesis 10:15 the offspring of the eponymous progenitor Heth were included in the list of nations of which the population of Canaan was composed. How far these people were connected with the Anatolian Hatti or the later Indo-European invaders is difficult to determine.[42] Part of the confusion has arisen from the fact that the movement of the Indo-European groups into Anatolia was only one part of a great migratory upsurge at the beginning of the second millennium B.C., a later phase of which witnessed the entrance of the Hebrew patriarchs into Palestine.

Another aspect of this movement of peoples was the migration of the Hurrians from an Indo-European source into Upper Mesopotamia, coinciding roughly with the invasion of Anatolia by the peoples who were subsequently known as the Hittites. However, these non-Semitic Hurrians (or Horites, as they are called in Genesis 14:6 and elsewhere) spread westward and penetrated into central Canaan[43] where they were well established in the patriarchal age.[44] Their greatest accomplishment in the political realm was the establishing of the Mitanni empire, whose capital was situated in the Middle Euphrates valley. During the second millennium B.C. the Mitanni dominated the region later known as Assyria, and in the Amarna period they held the balance of power between the Hittites, the Assyrians, and the Egyptians. Thereafter the influence of the Mitanni declined, and they succumbed to the Hittites about 1370 B.C. at the height of the New Empire period and were subsequently absorbed into the Hittite domain.[45]

The history of the Hittites as a military and political force falls into two major divisions. The Old Empire period began with the regime of Pitkhanas, king of Kussar, about 1800 B.C., although later Hittite rulers preferred to trace their ancestry back to the ancient King Labarnas.[46] Under Tudhaliyas I (ca. 1740-1710 B.C.) and his successors the Old Empire flourished for about a century and a half. The strength of earlier days diminished, however, under Mursilis I (ca. 1620 B.C.), due primarily to internal strife.

The New Empire period began with the reign of Tudhaliyas II (ca. 1460-1440 B.C.), but it was only under the influence of Suppiluliuma (ca. 1375-1340 B.C.) that Hittite power became a major factor once again in the Near East. A century later, further internal dissension combined with the invasions of the Aegean "Sea Peoples" to bring about the downfall of the Hittite empire about 1200 B.C., probably during the reign of Suppiluliuma II.

The foregoing synchronisms have been arrived at largely as the result

---

[42] Cf. E. O. Forrer, *PEQ*, LXVIII (1936), pp. 190ff., LXIX (1937), pp. 100ff.

[43] Cf. E. A. Speiser, *AASOR*, XIII (1933), pp. 13ff., *JAOS*, LXVIII (1948), pp. 1ff.; B. Landsberger, *JCS*, LVIII (1954), p. 59.

[44] E. A. Speiser, *IDB*, II, pp. 665f.

[45] F. F. Bruce, *The Hittites and the OT* (1948), pp. 17f.

[46] *TH*, pp. 19f.

of comparative study of archaeological, linguistic and anthropological data. While there may well be modifications in certain matters of detail as more information concerning the Hittites becomes available to scholars, the general outlines of Hittite history appear reasonably assured.

An analysis of the conclusions arrived at in the foregoing discussion can now be presented for convenience in Table 5.

TABLE 5: EARLY CHRONOLOGY

Approx. Date B.C.	Mesopotamia	Palestine	Syria-Asia Minor	Egypt
Before 100,000	Shanidar Cave baby	Palean-thropus palestinensis.		
Before 8000	Paleolithic period (Old Stone Age)			
8000-6000	Mesolithic period (Middle Stone Age) Natufian			
6000-4500	Neolithic period (New Stone Age)			
	Tepe Gawra Nineveh Tell Hass-una	Jericho (pre-pottery and pottery Neolithic)		
4500-3000	Chalcolithic period			
4500-2900				Predynastic
	Tell Halaf Tell el-Obeid Uruk	Jericho III Ghassulian		Fayyum A Deir Tasa Badari Amratean Gerzean
3300-2800	Proto-literate phase Jemdet Nasr			
3200-2000	Early Bronze Age			
2900-2700				Protodynastic period
2800-2360	Early dy-nastic period		Ancient Hatti	
2700-2200				Old Kingdom
2360-2180	Old Akkadian period			
2200-1989				First Intermediate period
2180-2070	Gutian phase			
2060-1950	Neo-Sumerian revival Ur III			
2100-1550	Middle Bronze Age			
2000-1780		Seminomadic incursions		Middle Kingdom

162

Approx. Date B.C.	Mesopotamia	Palestine	Syria-Asia Minor	Egypt
1960-1830	Elamite-Amorite invasions	Patriarchs		
1830-1530	Old Babylonian period			
1800-1600			Hittite Old Empire	
1780-1570				Second Intermediate period
1728-1686	Hammurabi			
1570-1150				New Kingdom
1500-1200	Late Bronze Age			
1460-1200			Hittite New Empire	

The traditions of Genesis, which associated the ancestors of the later Israelites with the nomadic and semi-sedentary peoples who traversed the Fertile Crescent towards the end of the second millennium B.C. and the early centuries of the first millennium B.C., have been strikingly confirmed by linguistic and other data uncovered by archaeological excavations in Mesopotamia. This activity has also made it possible with a high degree of confidence to assign the patriarchal narratives of Genesis to the Middle Bronze Age (ca. 2100-1550 B.C.) for their origin and formulation. As a result, scholars are now able to relate the patriarchal tradition of a migration from Harran to a roughly contemporary eruption of Amorite military and cultural activity in the civilized areas of northern Mesopotamia. Such widely divergent sources as the texts from Mari and Nuzu, and Middle Kingdom Egyptian writings such as the Execration Texts and the Tale of Sinuhe can be adduced in order to illuminate the social and political conditions then prevailing in Palestine.

Despite this encouraging situation, however, it has proved impossible in the light of presently available evidence to assign precise dates to the individual Hebrew patriarchs, or to associate them with any detailed chronological scheme amenable to control by means of extra-Biblical sources. While the literary form of certain portions of the Biblical material presents difficulties, it is not necessary to suppose, with Freedman,[47] that its completed form was the culmination of a long process of oral transmission, since it is highly probable from the literary structure of the elements which constitute the narratives themselves that the material was committed to writing not long after the activities of the individuals named.

[47] BANE, p. 204.

II. THE CHRONOLOGY OF ISRAEL'S EARLY HISTORY

A. THE PATRIARCHS—GENESIS 14

The nature of the genealogical scheme associated with the patriarchs in Genesis 14 has raised important problems of Old Testament chronology. As has been observed above, the association of Amraphel, king of Shinar (Gen. 14:1), with Hammurabi of Babylon led scholars in the first two decades of the twentieth century to assign Hammurabi to a period as early as 2123-2081 B.C.[1] In 1928 S. H. Langdon and J. K. Fotheringham placed the reign of Hammurabi *ca.* 2067-2025 B.C.[2] and gave impetus to a movement that resulted in a progressively later dating for the period of Hammurabi. Thureau-Dangin reduced the dating by more than half a century to *ca.* 2003-1961 B.C;[3] Pirot brought it still lower to *ca.* 1947-1905 B.C.[4] Evidence from Mari led to the general conclusion that the earlier dates were much too high,[5] and when Thureau-Dangin published evidence in 1937 that Shamshi-Adad I was contemporary with the earlier portion of the reign of Hammurabi, Albright suggested a date for the accession of the latter at *ca.* 1870 B.C, which in turn was criticized by Parrot as being too low.[6]

Two years later, however, Albright again revised his conclusions on the basis of new evidence from Mari published by Sidney Smith and reduced his earlier date by some 70 years, assigning Hammurabi to *ca.*

---

[1] Supported by W. F. Albright, *RA*, XVIII (1921), p. 94; S. A. Cook, *Cambridge Ancient History* (1924), I, p. 154; L. W. King, *A History of Babylon from the Foundation of the Monarchy to the Persian Conquest* (1919), pp. 106ff.

[2] Langdon and Fotheringham, *The Venus Tablets of Ammizaduga* (1928), pp. 66f. They were supported by D. Sidersky in A. Wertheimer, J. de Somogyi, and S. Löwinger (eds.), *Dissertationes in honorem Dr. Eduardi Mahler* (1937), pp. 253ff. and A. G. Shortt, *Journal of the British Astronomical Association*, LVII (1947), p. 208.

[3] *RA*, XXIV (1927), pp. 181ff.

[4] L. Pirot, *Supplément au Dictionnaire de la Bible* (1928), I, cols. 7ff.

[5] Cf. G. Contenau, *Manuel d'Archéologie orientale*, IV (1947), pp. 1804ff.

[6] F. Thureau-Dangin, *RA*, XXXIV (1937), pp. 135ff.; cf. C. F. Jean, *RA*, XXXV (1938), pp. 107ff. W. F. Albright, *BASOR*, No. 69 (1938), pp. 18f. A. Parrot, *SRA*, XIX (1938), p. 184.

1800-1760 B.C.[7] The same year Smith reduced his date even further to *ca.* 1792-1750 B.C., a conclusion that Ungnad had arrived at quite independently at the same time.[8] With Poebel's publication of the Khorsabad king-list in 1942 and the dating of Shamshi-Adad I to 1726-1694 B.C., Albright reduced his own dating still further to 1728-1686 B.C.[9] This accorded generally with the conclusions of Neugebauer, who had argued that the Venus astronomical observations required the date of 1792-1750 B.C. or 64 years earlier or later for Hammurabi's reign.[10] A date of 64 years later (1728-1686 B.C.) corresponds to that arrived at by Albright; and this general consensus was further reinforced by the independent investigations of Cornelius, who employed the materials preserved by Berossus to date Hammurabi *ca.* 1728-1686 B.C.[11] Two years later Cornelius raised his dating by one year.[12]

This system, which places the First Dynasty of Babylon *ca.* 1830-1530 B.C., as opposed to other higher dates, is now known as the "low" chronology, and its sequences have been adopted by many scholars. Because of the extremely technical and complex questions involved, it is not surprising that other authorities have disagreed with the conclusions arrived at by Albright and Cornelius. Sidney Smith rejects the "low" chronology, preferring instead to adhere to his own system of dating.[13] Mallowan, arguing from the stratigraphic evidence of Cretan archaeological discoveries, feels that reducing the accession date of Hammurabi to 1728 B.C. raises other chronological difficulties.[14] These might even affect the chronologies of several nations of antiquity, a fact that Gurney recognized in following the dating of Smith rather than that of Albright in establishing the sequences of Hittite chronology.[15]

---

[7] S. Smith, *The Antiquaries Journal*, XIX (1939), pp. 45ff. W. F. Albright, *BASOR*, No. 77 (1940), pp. 25f.

[8] S. Smith, *Alalakh and Chronology* (1940), pp. 10ff. Smith's dating was adopted by M. Noth, *Zeitschrift des deutschen Palästina-Vereins*, LXV (1942), p. 15. Ungnad dated Hammurabi *ca.* 1791-1748 B.C. Cf. his articles in *Mitteilungen der altorientalischen Gesellschaft*, XIII, No. 13 (1940), p. 17, and *Orientalia*, XIII (1944), pp. 83ff. In *Archiv für Orientforschung*, XIII (1940), pp. 145f., Ungnad had assigned a somewhat earlier date to Hammurabi (*ca.* 1801-1759 B.C.). D. Sidersky independently dated the Babylonian ruler *ca.* 1848-1803 B.C. Cf. *RA*, XXXVII (1940), pp. 45ff.

[9] A. Poebel, *JNES*, I (1942), pp. 247ff., 460ff., II (1943), pp. 238, 357ff. W. F. Albright, *BASOR*, No. 88 (1942), pp. 28ff.

[10] *JAOS*, LXI (1941), p. 59.

[11] Cornelius, *Klio*, XXXV (1942), p. 7.

[12] *Forschungen und Fortschritte*, XX (1944), p. 75.

[13] *AJA*, XLIX (1945), pp. 18ff. Albright attempted to justify his position against Smith's arguments in *BASOR*, No. 99 (1945), p. 10 n.; see also *Bibliotheca Orientalis*, V (1948), p. 126.

[14] *Iraq*, IX (1947), pp. 4n., 86n.

[15] *TH*, p. 217.

As a result there is a wide divergence of scholarly opinion regarding the date that is to be assigned to the First Dynasty of Babylon.[16] At one extreme is a date *ca.* 1900 B.C., proposed by Landsberger,[17] which appears prohibitively high. A somewhat lower sequence proposed by Goetze, Sidersky, and Thureau-Dangin would date the First Babylonian Dynasty about 1848-1806 B.C.[18] A "middle" chronology would place it *ca.* 1792-1750 B.C.[19] The "low" dating of Cornelius and Albright was supported by Bright,[20] Van der Waerden, and initially by Rowton, as has been observed above. An "ultra-low" sequence of dating, which places the First Babylonian Dynasty about 1704-1662 B.C., was advocated by Böhl and followed by Schubert and Weidner.[21]

[16] With respect to the dating of Hammurabi, the position of Albright and Cornelius was followed by de Vaux, *RB*, LIII (1945), p. 335, Rowton, *Iraq*, VIII (1946), pp. 94ff., O'Callaghan, *Aram Naharaim, A Contribution to the History of Upper Mesopotamia in the Second Millennium B.C.* (1948), pp. 6ff., and others. C. F. A. Schaeffer, who had suggested an eighteenth- or seventeenth-century date, *Ugaritica* (1939), p. 18n., later inclined towards a date between 1800 and 1700 B.C., in *SRA*, XXV (1946-1948), p. 187. E. Cavaignac, while allowing for a date of 1728 B.C. as a possible alternative, placed the date for the beginning of Hammurabi's reign at 1720 B.C., *RA*, XL (1945-1946), p. 22. R. Weill disputed the results of Cornelius in *Chronique d'Egypte*, XLI (1946), p. 42; F. M. Th. Böhl expressed some hesitation, preferring to state only that the greater part of the reign of Hammurabi ought to be dated subsequent to 1700 B.C., *Mededeelingen der Koninklijke Nederlandsche Akademie van Wetenschappen, Afd. Letterkunde*, IX, No. 10 (1946), pp. 341ff. and *Bibliotheca Orientalis*, I (1944), pp. 57ff. Mediating positions between Smith and Albright were adopted by Van der Meer (*ca.* 1778-1736 B.C.), *Jaarbericht Ex Oriente Lux*, IX (1944), pp. 143f., and Kramer, who stated that his date of 1750 B.C. for the beginning of Hammurabi's reign was merely a compromise that might well need adjustment, *AJA*, LII (1948), p. 163n. Subsequently, Van der Meer proposed an even later date for Hammurabi, *ca.* 1712-1670 B.C., with an addition of up to twenty years, *The Chronology of Ancient Western Asia and Egypt* (1947), pp. 13, 22. B. L. Van der Waerden assigned greater mathematical probability to the dates offered by Cornelius and Albright than to those of Smith and Ungnad, *Jaarbericht Ex Oriente Lux*, X (1945-1948), pp. 414ff. In 1958 Rowton, who had earlier preferred the lower dates, *JNES*, X (1951), pp. 184ff., revised his position and advocated the higher dating of Smith, *JNES*, XVII (1958), pp. 97ff.

[17] *JCS*, VIII (1954), pp. 31ff., 47ff., 106ff.

[18] Goetze, *BASOR*, No. 122 (1951), pp. 18ff., No. 127 (1952), pp. 21ff., No. 146 (1957), pp. 20ff.; Sidersky, *RA*, XXXVII (1940), pp. 45ff.; Thureau-Dangin, *Mémoires de l'Académie des Inscriptions et Belles Lettres*, XLIII, pt. 2 (1942), pp. 229ff.

[19] Supported by Albright, *BASOR*, No. 77 (1940), pp. 20ff., Rowton, *JNES*, XVII (1958), pp. 97ff., Smith, *Alalakh and Chronology* (1940), *AJA*, XLIX (1945), pp. 1ff., and Ungnad, *Mitteilungen der altorientalischen Gesellschaft*. XIII, No. 3 (1940), p. 17.

[20] *BHI*, p. 42.

[21] K. Schubert, *Wiener Zeitschrift für die Kunde des Morgenlandes*, LI (1948-1952), pp. 21ff. E. Weidner, *Archiv für Orientforschung*, XV (1945-1951), pp. 85ff.

In the light of these considerations the majority of scholars have favored a date for the patriarchal age at a later rather than an earlier period of the Middle Bronze Age, placing the origin of the traditions in the seventeenth and sixteenth centuries B.C. rather than in the twentieth and nineteenth centuries. The enigmatic character of Genesis 14 presents one of the chief obstacles to a fuller understanding of the archaeological sequences, and this difficulty can only be removed by additional informative excavations in Mesopotamia, preferably at sites hitherto unexplored. Some scholars have employed the genealogical records associated with the patriarchs in attempting a reasonably assured dating of the events of the patriarchal age. Preferring to regard the chronology of this period as clear and unambiguous, they have dated the patriarchs in the Late Bronze Age, and have based their estimates upon certain references (Exod. 6:16, 18, 20; cf. Gen. 46:26) which would imply that the sojourn in Egypt only lasted for two or three generations at the most. Thus Gordon, arguing from the fact that Egypt was known as the "land of Rameses" (Gen. 47:11) when Jacob went there as an old man, concluded that this event took place during the Amarna period.[22] Since Moses was apparently a grandson of Kohath, son of Levi, who accompanied Jacob into Egypt, he could well have been born before Joseph died, thus spanning the gap between the entrance of Israel into Egypt and the birth of Moses by a single lifetime.

Bowman and Rowley have also dated the patriarchal era in the Late Bronze Age, making the Amarna period the background for the narratives of Joseph rather than the Hyksos setting that the majority of scholars have assumed to have been the case.[23] Part of the difficulty which these scholars are attempting to face consists in the prolonged interval of time between the patriarchs themselves and those who made up the generation of the Exodus, about which the Bible records little or nothing. While genealogies have always constituted an important means of reckoning for oriental peoples, they should not be employed in this instance to the exclusion of the Biblical figures with which they come into conflict. According to Genesis 15:13, the offspring of Abraham were to be afflicted in a foreign land for 400 years, while Exodus 12:40, 41 recorded the stay of the Hebrews in Egypt as 430 years. The LXX of the latter passage allotted a 430-year period to cover the sojourn of the patriarchs in Palestine as well. For this last period Genesis (12:4; 21:5; 25:26; 47:9) allotted a span of 215 years, thus reducing proportionately

[22] *IOTT*, pp. 75, 102ff.; *JNES*, XIII (1954), pp. 56ff.

[23] R. A. Bowman, *JNES*, VII (1948), pp. 68f. Rowley, *From Joseph to Joshua* (1950), pp. 109ff., *RSL*, pp. 273f., 290. Other scholars who assign the entry into Egypt to the Amarna Age include W. C. Wood, *JBL*, XXXV (1916), pp. 166f., C. F. Burney, *Israel's Settlement in Canaan* (1918), pp. 87ff., R. Kittel, *Geschichte des Volkes Israel* (1923), I, p. 336, and T. J. Meek, *Hebrew Origins* (1960 ed.), pp. 18f.

the amount of time spent in Egypt. The Hebrew text of Exodus 12:40 is preferable to the LXX reading, since the following verse clearly indicates that the "selfsame day" constituted the 430th anniversary of the time when Jacob and his family first entered Egypt, thus assuring a lengthy stay in that land.

The principal difficulty that besets the approach of Rowley and Gordon is the assumption, based on the genealogical tables, that there were only three generations between the patriarchal period and the time of the Exodus. This supposition may well be entirely gratuitous since there are reasons for believing that the genealogical record of Exodus 6:16ff., which, of course, can hardly cover 430 years if taken strictly at face value, has been drawn up in terms of the operation of specific principles of selectivity, a procedure commonly adopted by oriental peoples. It is curious that Rowley, who has inveighed so frequently against those who are inclined to accept Biblical statements literally, should be scornful of those who posit the existence of gaps in the chronology of this passage, and should attempt to maintain a closed genealogy.[24] It is merely a matter of record that Egyptian king-lists pass over centuries at a time without formal indication or explanation of the fact. Again, other ancient Near Eastern regnal lists occasionally omit the names of particular individuals, as for example in the case of King Halparutas II of Gurgum in southeastern Asia Minor, who in his genealogy named his father and great-grandfather, but omitted the name of his grandfather, who is listed in the more complete genealogy of Halparutas III.[25]

B. THE SOJOURN IN EGYPT

These considerations are of considerable importance when attempts are made to interpret the chronological scheme of Exodus. Although Moses is regarded as the son of Amram and Jochebed, it is almost certain that the term "son" should in this instance be regarded as the equivalent of "descendant." That Moses was their offspring, though rather considerably removed, seems indicated by the fact that the parents of Moses were not named in the detailed account of his infancy, and also that Amram and his three brothers had several descendants within a year of the Exodus itself (Num. 3:27f.). Although Moses appeared in the fourth generation from Jacob, through Levi, Kohath, and Amram (Exod. 6:20; 1 Chron. 6:1ff.), Bezaleel his contemporary was in the seventh generation from Jacob, through Judah, Perez, Hezron, Caleb, Hur, and Uri (1 Chron. 2:18ff.). His younger contemporary Joshua appeared in the twelfth generation from Jacob, through Joseph, Ephraim, Beriah, Rephah, Resheph, Telah, Tahan, Laadan, Ammihud, Elishama,

[24] *From Joseph to Joshua*, pp. 72f., 78.

[25] The kings of Malatya frequently omitted the father, naming only the grandfather; cf. T. C. Mitchell, *NBD*, p. 457.

and Nun (1 Chron. 7:23ff.). These comparisons would seem to indicate that the genealogy of Moses has been abbreviated.

Furthermore, the sons of Kohath gave rise to the clans of the Amramites and the others mentioned in Numbers 3:27, who numbered 8,600 males within a year of the Exodus. This would be a rather improbable situation, to say the least, unless Amram and his brothers had lived considerably prior to the time of Moses.[26] From this it seems legitimate to assume that the genealogical tables upon which Gordon and Rowley have based their arguments did not in fact preserve detailed and complete information with regard to ancestry prior to the conquest period. It is well known that early genealogies frequently pass directly from the name of the father to that of the clan.[27] Thus, in effect the Exodus reference states that Moses was the descendant of Amram of the clan of Kohath, of the tribe of Levi; hence it preserves only the general designation of clan and tribe.[28]

If the tradition of a prolonged Israelite stay in Egypt, perhaps based upon the Avaris era, has some validity in fact, it still presents certain difficulties when attempts are made to assign a date to Abraham, the ancestor of the later Hebrew peoples. Like Hammurabi, with whom he was once regarded as contemporary, Abraham has sometimes been assigned to the latter part of the twentieth century B.C.[29] Others have maintained a seventeenth-century B.C. date for Abraham.[30] Albright at first followed Kraeling's seventeenth-century dating; then he assigned Abraham to the period between 1800 and 1600 B.C.; and subsequently to a date not earlier than the nineteenth century B.C. In 1942 he returned to a seventeenth-century B.C. date for the patriarchs, but seven years later he dated the migration from Ur to Harran in the twentieth and nineteenth centuries B.C.[31]

There is at present no conclusive evidence that can be adduced for an accurate dating of Abraham or his immediate descendants; the best that can be done is to assign them to the Middle Bronze Age without further

[26] Cf. H. S. Gehman, *The Westminster Dictionary of the Bible* (1944), p. 153; K. A. Kitchen and T. C. Mitchell, *NBD*, p. 214.

[27] Cf. *WBA*, p. 50 n. 5.

[28] D. N. Freedman, *BANE*, p. 206.

[29] Among scholars holding this view are P. E. Dhorme, *RB*, XL (1931), pp. 506ff., G. E. Wright, *BASOR*, No. 71 (1938), p. 34, and Millar Burrows, *WMTS*, p. 71.

[30] These include E. G. H. Kraeling, *Aram and Israel* (1918), p. 32, A. Jirku, *ZAW*, XXXIX (1921), pp. 152ff., 313f., and *Geschichte des Volkes Israel* (1931), pp. 61ff., and F. M. Th. Böhl, *ZAW*, XLII (1924), pp. 148ff. Earlier (*ZAW*, XXXVI [1916], pp. 65ff.), Böhl had placed Abraham much later, *ca.* 1250 B.C. At first W. F. Albright followed Kraeling's dating, *AJSL*, XL (1923-1924), pp. 125ff., *BASOR*, No. 14 (1924), p. 7, *AASOR*, VI (1926), p. 62.

[31] *JPOS*, VI (1927), p. 227, *The Archaeology of Palestine and the Bible* (1932), p. 137, *BASOR*, No. 88 (1942), p. 35, *AP*, p. 83, *FSAC*, p. 200, *BPAE*, p. 2.

specification, so as to maintain a reasonable degree of flexibility in the chronology. Placing the patriarchal migrations and the patriarchs themselves later than the sixteenth century B.C. appears unsatisfactory from an historical point of view.

The narratives and their peculiar nomenclature are closely paralleled by the texts of the early second millennium B.C. The stories of Laban and Jacob are in harmony with the political and social conditions in Upper Mesopotamia both before and after the eighteenth century B.C., when the population of that area was predominantly Amorite. At a later period the region had succumbed to the Mitanni, while Palestine and portions of Syria were firmly established as Egyptian spheres of influence. Subsequently the decline of the Mitanni left Upper Mesopotamia torn between the political ambitions of the Hittites and the increasing power of resurgent Assyria.

Again, the Palestinian setting of the patriarchal narratives is strictly that of the Middle Bronze Age, and not of the later Egyptian Empire period. As Bright has pointed out, the patriarchs wandered in the central mountainous area, in the south, and in Transjordan, meeting no city-kings except those of the Jordanian plain (Gen. 14:1ff.), Melchizedek, king of Jerusalem (Gen. 14:18), and the ruler of Gerar on the coastal plain (Gen. 20:2ff; 26:1ff.). This description is in full accord with the sparsely settled nature of Middle Bronze Age Palestine.[32] Shechem (Gen. 33:18ff.; 34:2ff.) appeared to be in the hands of a tribal confederacy during the patriarchal period, while Hebron, founded "seven years before Zoan in Egypt" (Num. 13:22) was at that time known by its original name of Kiriath-arba (Gen. 23:2; 35:27; the reference in Gen. 13:18 is an explanatory gloss). Since Tanis-Avaris-Zoan was rebuilt by the Hyksos prior to 1700 B.C., the patriarchs would have to be dated even earlier than that time. It is interesting to note that the patriarchal figures never encountered any Egyptians in Palestine, which is consistent with the political situation during the Middle Kingdom period of Egyptian history, and also with the subsequent Hyksos era, when Egyptian control of southern Canaan was non-existent, but out of harmony with the conditions of the turbulent Amarna Age as reflected in the Tell el-Amarna tablets, when local rulers, aided by elements of the Habiru, were engaged in self-aggrandizement or in the complete repudiation of Egyptian overlordship.

Although it is impossible to say with complete confidence precisely when Jacob and his family migrated to Egypt, the general conditions reflected in the Biblical narratives would favor an entry during the Hyksos regime. Although Semites had access to Egypt during all periods of Egyptian history, the eclipse of a strongly nationalistic rule by the alien Hyksos would seem to furnish the most appropriate conditions for

[32] *BHI*, p. 70.

the rise to power of a talented Semite such as Joseph. Against this conclusion must be set the fact that, since the Biblical sources apparently do not present a uniform view of the length of time during which Jacob and his descendants stayed in Egypt, it is obviously impossible to reckon backwards from a presumed date of the Exodus in order to arrive at a suitable time for the arrival of Joseph in Egypt. Furthermore, though it may be attractive to suppose that the pharaoh under whom Joseph rose to prominence was of Hyksos origin, and the ruler who did not recognize his work or reputation was of native Egyptian ancestry, there is to date absolutely no proof for such a position. As is so frequently the case with historical descriptions of aspects of other cultures in widely differing ages, it is highly probable that the comparatively uncomplicated narratives that deal with the Egyptian sojourn of Israel actually conceal a much more involved and complex state of affairs than might appear from a casual reading of the material. Despite all of this, however, it seems best on the evidence available to relate the work of Joseph to the general period of Hyksos rule in Egypt.[33] The political and social conditions reflected in the Genesis narratives suit the Hyksos regime admirably, as Kitchen has shown,[34] whereas they do not by any means conform as closely to the conditions obtaining during the Late Bronze Age.

At this juncture it may be advantageous to devote a little closer attention to the chronology of ancient Egypt in order to supplement what has been said previously on this subject. Although Egyptian chronology, like its Babylonian counterpart, has been revised from time to time, the general picture appears rather more stable than that of early Mesopotamian history. Despite the fact that scholars have been unable to agree upon a precise chronology for Egypt prior to the Saitic revival (663-525 B.C.), the area of disagreement on dates within the Old Testament period is not particularly wide, and can frequently be reduced to the extent of a single generation. This situation is due partly to the fact that the Egyptians preserved their king-lists and annals, thus furnishing valuable source material for chronological study.[35] Another factor is the literary activities of Manetho, an Egyptian priest who lived in the third century B.C. On the basis of various available sources Manetho compiled a history of Egypt in which he listed the pharaohs by dynasties, at first thirty and subsequently thirty-one, a classification that has proved so convenient that it has been retained to the present.

---

[33] In this connection it is interesting to note that Archbishop Usher should have assigned a date of 1728 B.C. for the arrival of Joseph in Egypt, *Annales Veteris Testamenti*, pp. 1f., 6, 14; cf. *WMTS*, p. 72, *BHI*, p. 74.

[34] *NBD*, pp. 342, 657ff.

[35] Herodotus (II, 77) comments that "the Egyptians. . .are the most careful of all men to preserve the memory of the past, and none. . .have so many chronicles."

Unfortunately comparatively little has survived from his work, and even those portions of king-lists and other citations which are extant have obviously suffered in process of transmission.[36]

The rulers of the first two dynasties were listed on small ivory tablets, whereas the annals of the first six dynasties were recorded at somewhat greater length in antiquity on the celebrated Palermo Stone, dated about 2400 B.C.[37] This source gives the names of nine rulers in Lower Egypt, probably supplemented by others on a lost portion of the stone, which doubtless contained a list of Upper Egyptian rulers also. The First and Second Dynasties are usually assigned by scholars to the Protodynastic period, about 2900-2760 B.C.,[38] the dates furnished by older chronologies being generally too high.[39]

The position adopted here is that of the "low" chronology, so called from the dates assigned to the early dynasties of Egypt in terms of synchronisms and agreements with a comparably low dating for the First Dynasty of Babylon. The Old Kingdom period, embracing the Third to the Sixth Dynasties, has been dated ca. 2700-2200 B.C., though the chronological studies of Scharff and Moortgat have reduced this date by a period of fifty or more years. The Seventh to Eleventh Dynasties have been assigned to the period ca. 2200-1989 B.C., with some slight variations connected with the beginning of the succeeding Middle Kingdom period.[40]

The dating of the Twelfth Dynasty was placed by Scharff and Moortgat at 1991-1778 B.C.; Edgerton dated it 1989-1776 B.C. R. A. Parker and W. F. Albright varied slightly from the latter estimate, assigning it to a

[36] Cf. W. G. Waddell, *Manetho* (1940), H. W. Helck, *Untersuchungen zu Manetho und den Ägyptischen Königslisten* (1956), pp. 10ff.

[37] *LAP*, pl. 27.

[38] Cf. A. Scharff and A. Moortgat, *Ägypten und Vorderasien im Altertum* (1950), pp. 25ff.; H. Stock, *Studia Aegyptiaca II* (*Analecta Orientalia* 31, 1949); W. F. Albright, *BASOR*, No. 119 (1950), p. 29; P. van der Meer, *Orientalia Neerlandica* (1948), pp. 23ff.

[39] J. H. Breasted, *The Conquest of Civilisation* (1938), pp. 64f., dated the union of the Two Lands which commenced the First Dynasty ca. 3400 B.C. Cf. his *The Dawn of Conscience* (1934), p. 10. This constituted a significant reduction of the estimate of Champollion (5867 B.C.) and Petrie (4777 B.C.). J. A. Wilson, *The Culture of Ancient Egypt* (1956), p. 43, dated the beginning of the First Dynasty ca. 3100 B.C., and in *IDB*, II, p. 44, ca. 3000 B.C.

[40] A. Scharff and A. Moortgat dated the Eleventh Dynasty ca. 2052-1991 B.C., H. Stock, *BASOR*, No. 119 (1950), p. 29, placed it ca. 2040-1991 B.C. Cf H. E. Winlock, *JNES*, II (1943), pp. 249ff., W. C. Hayes, *The Sceptre of Egypt, Part I* (1953), pp. 34ff. For the dating of the early Egyptian Dynasties see also É Drioton and J. Vandier, *Les peuples de l'Orient Méditerranéen, II: L'Égypte* (1952)

date of 1991-1786 B.C.[41] The Second Intermediate period, embracing the Thirteenth to the Seventeenth Dynasties, can be placed in the period from *ca.* 1776 B.C. to 1570 B.C.[42] The brief revival of Egyptian power under Neferhotep I (*ca.* 1740-1729 B.C.), who attempted to restore Egyptian control of Byblos and dispossess the occupying Amorite forces, may perhaps furnish a valuable synchronism between Egypt and Mesopotamia. This will be particularly the case if the Amorite ruler, known in the Egyptian texts as Enten (Antina), is to be identified with Yantin-ammu, whose name occurs in tablets recovered from Mari.[43]

The New Kingdom period, consisting of the Eighteenth to Twentieth Dynasties, was instituted by Khamosis (*ca.* 1580 B.C.) and continued with the rule of Amosis (*ca.* 1570-1546 B.C.), flourishing after the expulsion of the Hyksos.[44] The chronology of the Eighteenth Dynasty usually follows that drawn up by Borchardt, revised by Rowton and Albright, which assigns a date of *ca.* 1570-1310 B.C. for that period.[45] There is some variation of opinion about the dates of certain pharaohs within the New Kingdom period, for example that of Thutmosis III (*ca.* 1490-1435 B.C.).[46] Dating of the Nineteenth Dynasty (*ca.* 1310-1200 B.C.) also allows some diversity of opinion, but the differences here are minor.[47]

Egyptian historical sources from the New Kingdom period include numerous contemporary inscriptions of pharaohs, often containing the dates of regnal years, as well as similar inscriptions of their officials. The latter not infrequently included genealogical tables in their records, a practice which seems to date back at least to the twentieth century B.C. The earliest extant representative of this genealogical tradition is that of Ukhhotep, count of the fourteenth Upper Egyptian nome in the reign of the pharaoh Amenemhat II, *ca.* 1925 B.C., roughly contemporary with

[41] W. F. Edgerton, *JNES*, I (1942), pp. 307ff. Cf. L. H. Wood, *BASOR*, No. 99 (1945), pp. 5ff. R. A. Parker, *The Calendars of Ancient Egypt* (*Studies in Ancient Oriental Civilisation*, No. 26, 1950), pp. 63ff. Cf. his article in *Encyclopedia Americana* (1962), X, pp. 14b ff. W. F. Albright, *BASOR*, No. 127 (1952), pp. 27ff. For a general survey of this period see H. E. Winlock, *The Rise and Fall of the Middle Kingdom in Thebes* (1947).

[42] Cf. W. F. Albright, *JPOS*, XVI (1935), pp. 222ff.

[43] W. F. Albright, *BASOR*, No. 99 (1945), pp. 9ff.

[44] For the chronology of the reign of Amosis I see W. F. Albright, *BASOR*, No. 68 (1937), p. 22 n. 2.

[45] L. Borchardt, *Die Mittel zur zeitlichen Festlegung von Punkten der ägyptischen Geschichte und ihre Anwendung* (1935), pp. 87ff. M. B. Rowton, *BASOR*, No. 126 (1952), p. 22. W. F. Albright, *BASOR*, No. 118 (1950), p. 19. Cf. *BASOR*, No. 88 (1942), p. 32 and W. F. Edgerton, *AJSL*, LIII (1936-1937), pp. 188ff. For a popular survey of the New Kingdom period see G. Steindorff and K. C. Seele, *When Egypt Ruled the East* (1957 ed.).

[46] Cf. R. A. Parker, *JNES*, XVI (1957), pp. 39ff.

[47] Cf. M. B. Rowton, *JEA*, XXXIV (1948), pp. 57ff., A. Malamat, *JNES*, XIII (1954), pp. 233f., and W. F. Albright, *AJA*, LIV (1950), p. 170.

the period suggested by many scholars for Abraham. From the tomb-chapel of Ukhhotep was recovered a complete list of his forbears and predecessors in office, along with the names of their wives. The record, which appears to be in chronological order, dates back to about 2500 B.C., and extended over a period of some 600 years.[48] The genuineness of the document is attested by the differing styles of the names recorded.

Perhaps the most remarkable of the king-lists from the New Kingdom period is the celebrated Turin papyrus, which catalogued the names of almost all the rulers of Egypt from the earliest times down to what is probably the period of Rameses II (ca. 1290-1224 B.C.). Another, though rather restricted measure of chronological control, is to be found in the mention of lunar dates and the rising of Sirius (Sothis), the Dog-Star, in Egyptian texts of the Middle and New Kingdom periods.[49] There are also definite links with other elements of ancient Near Eastern chronology, particularly regarding synchronisms with kings of western Asia, which are extremely valuable in arriving at approximate dates for both individuals and eras.[50]

C. THE DATE OF THE EXODUS

At the beginning of the twentieth century the majority of scholars of all schools dated the Exodus towards the end of the thirteenth century B.C., although some rejected the Biblical evidence in favor of a twofold entrance to Palestine at widely separated times.[51] Thus Albright identified the tribe of Joseph with the Habiru, and maintained that they were in Palestine about 1400 B.C., while other tribes, particularly the descendants of Judah, left Egypt under the leadership of Moses early in the reign of Rameses II.[52] Meek conflicted completely with Biblical tradition in taking the view that Joshua long antedated Moses.[53] He associated the attack on the central uplands under Joshua with the encroachments of the Habiru during the Amarna period, and placed the settle-

[48] A. M. Blackman, Rock Tombs of Meir, III (1915), pp. 16ff., and pls. 10, 11, 29, 33:1, 35:1, 36:1, 37:1, 2; L. Borchardt, Die Mittel zur zeitlichen Festlegung von Punkten der ägyptischen Geschichte und ihre Anwendung, pp. 112ff.

[49] Cf. R. A. Parker, JNES, XVI (1957), pp. 39ff.; J. A. Wilson, The Culture of Ancient Egypt, p. 61.

[50] Cf. P. van der Meer, The Chronology of Ancient Western Asia and Egypt (Documenta et Monumenta Orientis Antiqui, II, 1947); R. B. Rowton, Iraq, VIII (1946), pp. 94ff.; H. J. Kantor in R. W. Erich (ed.), Relative Chronologies in Old World Archaeology, pp. 7ff.; A. Scharff and A. Moortgat, Ägypten und Vorderasien im Altertum, pp. 35ff.

[51] Cf. A. H. Sayce, The Early History of the Hebrews (1897), pp. 158ff.; E. L. Curtis, HDB, I, p. 398.

[52] W. F. Albright, BASOR, No. 58 (1935), pp. 10ff. He was followed by Burrows, WMTS, p. 79, Wright, WHAB, pp. 39f., and Finegan, LAP, pp. 105ff.

[53] T. J. Meek, Hebrew Origins, pp. 21ff. Cf. BASOR, No. 61 (1936), pp. 17ff.; cf. G. A. Danell, Studies in the Name Israel in the OT (1946), p. 44n.

ment of Judah later than the occupation of the central highlands. The tribes led by Moses subsequently entered Canaan from the south about 1200 B.C., making for an interval of at least a century between Moses and Joshua.[54] Such a view is adequately refuted by the fact that, although the Biblical narratives can perhaps be made to support a twofold entry into Canaan—even though it is made clear that the initial attack in the south was abortive in nature—there is absolutely no textual evidence whatever for a twofold Exodus, a point that even Albright conceded.[55]

The beginning of the twentieth century also witnessed a significant change of opinion in favor of a fifteenth-century B.C. date for the Exodus.[56] This was reinforced by the discoveries of Garstang at Jericho, particularly by his statement that the city had fallen prior to 1400 B.C., which appeared to confirm the chronological statement of 1 Kings 6:1, and place the Exodus in the middle of the fifteenth century B.C.[57] This dating-sequence was accepted immediately by many scholars, some of them regarding it enthusiastically as a signal vindication of the general accuracy of the Biblical narratives.[58] Even though T. H. Robinson claimed confidently that, with a very few exceptions, Old Testament scholars had abandoned the Nineteenth Dynasty date, the facts proved to be otherwise.[59]

The question cannot be settled simply by an appeal to the book of Kings in the light of an arbitrary dating for the fall of Jericho. More recent excavations have cast considerable doubt upon the methods and conclusions of Garstang at Jericho, and the entire question of the date when Jericho fell has been shown to be in fact far from settled. Even Garstang modified his original date to one occurring between 1400 B.C. and the accession of Akhenaton (*ca.* 1370-1353 B.C.), which Albright subsequently lowered to between 1360 and 1320 B.C., and later to about 1300 B.C., finally concluding that the Exodus occurred in the latter part

---

[54] For a criticism of this view see H. H. Rowley, *From Joseph to Joshua*, pp. 141ff.

[55] *JBL*, XXXVII (1918), pp. 138ff.

[56] E.g. J. Orr, *The Problem of the OT* (1909), pp. 422ff.; T. E. Peet, *Egypt and the OT* (1922), p. 121; J. W. Jack, *The Date of the Exodus* (1925).

[57] Garstang, *Joshua-Judges* (1931), p. 146.

[58] T. H. Robinson, *History of Israel* (1931), I, p. 80; A. S. Yahuda, *The Accuracy of the Bible* (1934), pp. 116ff.; L. Dennefeld, *Histoire d'Israël* (1935), pp. 64ff.; S. L. Caiger, *Bible and Spade* (1936), pp. 68ff.

[59] Robinson, *ET*, XLVII (1934-1935), p. 54. Scholars holding to the Nineteenth Dynasty date included Jirku, *Geschichte des Volkes Israel*, pp. 67ff., Vincent, *RB*, XLI (1932), pp. 264ff. and XLIV (1935), pp. 583ff., Barton, *Archaeology and the Bible* (1933), pp. 41f., Albright, *BASOR*, No. 58 (1935), pp. 10ff., Lavergne, *Chronologie Biblique* (1937), p. 48, Noth, *Die Welt des AT* (1940), p. 173, Burrows, *WMTS*, p. 79, Gordon, *The Living Past* (1941), pp. 36f., Finegan, *LAP*, pp. 105ff., and others.

of the fourteenth century or the early years of the thirteenth century B.C.[60]

The diversity of opinion on this matter is further illustrated by Vincent, who proposed a date of between 1250 and 1200 B.C. for the fall of Jericho.[61] Although Schaeffer and de Vaux tended to agree with Vincent, this date has been rejected by Wright as being too low.[62] Bearing in mind the conclusions of Kathleen Kenyon that it is at present impossible to state with certainty the date when Jericho fell,[63] it would seem from the available evidence that a date in the middle of the thirteenth century B.C. is required for the crossing of the Jordan.[64]

This conclusion is supported by the evidence of the Meneptah *stele* the nature of which demands the presence of Israel in Canaan about 1200 B.C. Furthermore, as Glueck has shown, the detour that the Israelites were compelled to make around Edom and Moab (Num. 20:14ff.; 21:4ff.) would, if the narratives are to be regarded as historical, rule out a date prior to the thirteenth century B.C. for the Exodus, since these two kingdoms had not been established before that time.[65] The general testimony of archaeology, although rather ambiguous in certain areas, seems to point to a date in the latter part of the thirteenth century B.C. for the destruction of sites such as Debir, Lachish, and Eglon, if the latter probably can be identified with Tell el-Hesi. The date of the fall of Lachish was assigned to a period not later than 1260 B.C. by Starkey, and to about 1231 B.C. by Albright, who subsequently reduced his date to *ca.* 1221 B.C., whereas Noth and Vincent inclined to a somewhat earlier time.[66]

[60] Garstang's original date is given in *Palestine Exploration Fund Quarterly Statement* (1930), p. 132; his revised suggestion *ibid.* (1936), p. 170. Cf Albright. *BASOR*, No. 58 (1935), p. 13. No. 74 (1939), p. 20; *AP*, pp. 108f.; *AJA*, XXXIX (1935), p. 40; *BPAE*, pp. 14ff.

[61] L.-H. Vincent, *RB*, XXXIX (1930), pp. 403ff., XLI (1932), pp. 264ff., XLIV (1935), pp. 583ff., XLVIII (1939), p. 580.

[62] C. F. A. Schaeffer, *Stratigraphie Comparée et Chronologie de l'Asie Occidentale [IIIe et IIe millenaires]* (1948), pp. 129ff., held that City D was destroyed by fire at the end of the thirteenth century B.C. Cf. R. de Vaux, *ZAW*, LVI (1938), p. 237; G. E. Wright, *BASOR*, No. 86 (1942), p. 33; J. Bright, *BHI*, pp 112f.

[63] K. M. Kenyon, *BA*, XVII, No. 4 (1954), pp. 98ff., and her *Digging Up Jericho* (1957), pp. 262f.

[64] Cf. W. F. Albright in H. C. Alleman and E. E. Flack (eds.), *OT Commentary* (1948), p. 141.

[65] Glueck, *BASOR*, No. 55 (1934), pp. 3ff., No. 86 (1942), pp. 14ff., No. 90 (1943), pp. 2ff.; *BA*, X, No. 4 (1947), pp. 77ff.

[66] J. L. Starkey, *Palestine Exploration Fund Quarterly Statement* (1934), p. 174 Starkey modified his conclusion three years later, favoring then a period towards the end of the Nineteenth Dynasty, *ibid.* (1937), p. 239. For the date of 1231 B.C see Albright, *BASOR*, No. 68 (1937), p. 24, No. 74 (1939), p. 21; cf. *AJA* XXXIX (1935), pp. 139ff. For the date of 1221 B.C., Albright, *FSAC*, p. 255 cf. G. E. Wright, *JNES*, V (1946), p. 111. For earlier dating, Noth, *PJB* XXXIV (1938), p. 16, Vincent, *RB*, XLVIII (1939), p. 419n.

Certain problems have been posed by the narratives concerning the destruction of Bethel and Ai, the former, according to Albright, being overthrown in the first half of the thirteenth century B.C. or possibly a little earlier.[67] A similar date for the destruction of Ai-Bethel was accepted in a guarded fashion by Burrows and Wright, both of whom expressed uncertainty as to the nature of Ai in the time of Joshua.[68] Ai, which is usually, though not uniformly,[69] identified with et-Tell near Bethel, is supposed to have been in ruins from ca. 2000 to ca. 1200 B.C.[70] This has led some scholars to declare that the account of its capture was fictitious,[71] while others assumed that the narrative of an earlier destruction of the site had been transferred to the time of Joshua.[72] Still others have suggested that the confusion arose through associating Ai with the neighboring site of Bethel,[73] or that Ai may have been a temporary fortified outpost of Bethel during the days of Joshua.[74]

Excavations at Hazor by Yigael Yadin have shown that the last Canaanite city to be erected on the site was destroyed in the thirteenth century B.C., which is in conformity with the narratives of Joshua 11:10ff.[75] The general date to be assigned to the conquest of Canaan will naturally vary somewhat, according to whether the Exodus is dated in the first or second half of the thirteenth century B.C. If the Biblical tradition is to be regarded as substantially accurate, the beginning of the conquest can be dated about 1235 B.C., or slightly later,[76] on the assumption that the Exodus occurred in the thirteenth rather than the fifteenth century B.C.

D. THE JUDGES

The chronological tradition of the period of the Judges presents some difficulties. Over against the larger schematic pattern which established

[67] BASOR, No. 57 (1935), p. 30, No. 58 (1935), p. 13; cf. No. 74 (1939), p. 17.

[68] WMTS, p. 76; WHAB, pp. 39f.

[69] F. G. Kenyon, The Bible and Archaeology (1940), p. 190; J. Simons, Jaarbericht Ex Oriente Lux, VI (1939), p. 156, IX (1944), pp. 157ff.

[70] Cf. J. Marquet-Krause, SRA, XVI (1935), pp. 325ff.; L.-H. Vincent, RB, XLVI (1937), pp. 231ff. Cf. BASOR, No. 56 (1934), pp. 2ff.

[71] Such a view is held by R. Dussaud, SRA, XVI (1935), p. 351, W. J. Phythian-Adams, Palestine Exploration Fund Quarterly Statement (1936), pp. 141ff., A. Alt, Werden und Wesen des AT (1936), pp. 20ff.

[72] E.g. W. F. Albright, BASOR, No. 74 (1939), p. 17, M. Noth, PJB, XXXI (1935), pp. 7ff., XXXIV (1938), p. 14n.

[73] W. F. Albright, BASOR, No. 56 (1934), p. 11; WHAB, p. 40; WMTS, p. 76.

[74] L.-H. Vincent, RB, XLVI (1937), pp. 258ff.

[75] Y. Yadin, BA, XIX, No. 1 (1956), pp. 2ff., XX, No. 2 (1957), pp. 34ff., XXI, No. 2 (1958), pp. 30ff., XXII, No. 1 (1959), pp. 2ff.; Y. Yadin et al., Hazor I, An Account of the First Season of Excavations, 1955 (1958); II, (1960).

[76] FSAC, pp. 278f.; WBA, pp. 69ff.

a period of 480 years, or 12 forty-year generations, between the time of the Exodus and the construction of the Solomonic Temple is a series of smaller computations throughout the Judges and the two books of Samuel, in which periods of 20, 40, and 80 years were allotted to various judges and oppressors of the Israelites. In the light of the statistics preserved in the book of Judges, the total for the period of charismatic rule in Israel is 410 years, as shown by Table 6:[77]

TABLE 6: THE JUDGES

Judge or Deliverer	Oppressor	Scripture reference, Judges	Duration
	Cushan-Rishathaim	3:8	8
Othniel		3:11	40
	Eglon	3:14	18
Ehud		3:30	80
	Jabin	4:3	20
Deborah and Barak		5:31	40
	Midianites	6:1	7
Gideon		8:28	40
Abimelech		9:22	3
Tola		10:2	23
Jair		10:3	22
	Ammonites	10:8	18
Jephthah		12:7	6
Ibzan		12:9	7
Elon		12:11	10
Abdon		12:14	8
	Philistines	13:1	40
Samson		15:20; 16:31	20

When this figure of 410 years is added to a forty-year period for the Wilderness wanderings (a tradition which, as Freedman has pointed out, must contain a chronological factor[78]), and is supplemented by an indeterminate period for Joshua and the Elders (Judg. 2:7), a forty-year interval for the ministry of Eli (1 Sam. 4:18), a period in excess of twenty years for the charismatic leadership of Samuel (1 Sam. 7:2, 15), another interval of indeterminate length for the rule of Saul (1 Sam. 13:1),[79] a period of forty years during which David reigned (1 Kgs. 2:11), and four years at the beginning of the Solomonic regime until the Temple was constructed, the result is a total considerably in excess of 554 years.

[77] After H. H. Rowley, *From Joseph to Joshua*, p. 87.
[78] *BANE*, p. 266 n. 14. Cf. A. E. Cundall, *Judges* (1968), pp. 28ff.
[79] Cf. Acts 13:21. See S. R. Driver, *Notes on the Hebrew Text of the Books of Samuel* (1913), p. 97, for discussion of this passage.

However, there is no *a priori* reason why the compiler of Judges should have felt it desirable to make his computations agree with the figure represented by 1 Kings 6:1. Nor is it necessary to suppose that the reference in Kings is not original, and is less preferable than the lower LXX reading, a position which was adopted by Wellhausen,[80] since the figure is clearly schematic. The continuity of this pattern is evident in the fact that Kings gives an additional period of the same length for the total reigns of the kings of Judah from the fourth year of Solomon to 597 B.C., with the addition of a half-century to cover the time from the destruction of the Temple to its reconstruction after the Exile.[81] As J. W. Jack has pointed out, this can hardly be accidental, and the contrived nature of the chronological scheme may in fact indicate that the reference itself is a post-exilic insertion.[82] On the other hand, Rowley has dismissed arguments against the originality of the reference in 1 Kings, and has shown that attention is not focused upon the second period of 480 years in the way in which it is on the earlier one.[83]

For those who accept a fifteenth-century B.C. date for the Exodus, the chronology of the Judges period need not be subjected to the same degree of compression as for those who posit an extent of some 200 years (*ca.* 1200-1000 B.C.) between Joshua and David. On the basis of an early date for the Exodus it would be possible to assign Joshua and the Elders to a period about 1407-1383 B.C., and to place the Judges in succession with the exception of Samson, so that they would then be dated according to Table 7.

TABLE 7: THE JUDGES

Judge	ca. B.C.
Othniel	1376-1336
Ehud	1320-1240
Deborah and Barak	1240-1200
Gideon	1197-1157
Abimelech	1157-1154
Tola	1154-1131
Jair	1131-1109
Jephthah	1089-1083
Ibzan	1083-1076
Elon	1076-1066
Abdon	1066-1058
Samson	1071-1051

[80] *Die Composition des Hexateuchs und der historischen Bücher des AT* (1899), pp. 264f.

[81] C. F. Burney, *Notes on the Hebrew Text of the Book of Kings* (1903), pp. 59f.

[82] *The Date of the Exodus* (1925), p. 204.

[83] *From Joseph to Joshua*, p. 90.

Such a system of dating fails to take account of the possibility that, whether the Judges were tribal heroes or national leaders, it is quite possible that their careers were sometimes contemporaneous and not generally in continuous succession, as a casual perusal of the narratives in Judges might seem to imply.

In all questions of chronology it is important to remember that oriental modes of reckoning are reflected by the Hebrew text. In general, ancient scribes did not draw up synchronistic lists in the modern fashion, but instead recorded each series of rulers and reigns separately. If synchronisms were desired for any particular purpose they were normally supplied from sources different from the king-lists or historical narratives, which had been compiled with other intentions in view. The lack of cross-references between those Judges who may have been contemporaries can be paralleled closely by a similar state of affairs in Sumerian, Old Babylonian, and ancient Egyptian history, indicating that special methods of compilation and computation were evidently employed in drawing up Judges, in which the forty-year pattern was a prominent element.[84]

Although the problems of chronology cannot be solved completely without more detailed information, a recognition of the customs of the ancient scribes, taken together with the archaeological findings that require an interval of some 230 years between Joshua and David, should go far towards resolving most of the difficulties arising from a strictly literal interpretation of the figures in Judges. There is thus no need to invoke a chronological scheme that rests upon the succession of High Priests, as Wellhausen did, or an elaborate pattern that arbitrarily ignores certain aspects of the Biblical dating and reduces awkward chronological sequences, as suggested by Garstang.[85]

[84] D. N. Freedman, *BANE*, pp. 207f.; K. A. Kitchen and T. C. Mitchell, *NBD*, p. 216.

[85] J. Wellhausen, *Prolegomena to the History of Israel* (1885), p. 230. Cf. A. Gampert, *Revue de théologie et de philosophie*, V (1917), p. 246. J. Garstang, *Joshua-Judges*, pp. 55ff.

III. OLD TESTAMENT HISTORY—
THE MONARCHY AND AFTER

A. Kings of Israel and Judah

The chronology of the period of the Israelite monarchy, especially the divided kingdom, deals with much more exact numbers than that of an earlier period. These figures are based on official records that are catalogued in a manner more amenable to the western mind. The historical sources for the rise and development of the monarchy[1] are of very great value; many of them are contemporaneous, or nearly so, with the events described.[2] The chronological pattern of these narratives probably has more in common with the synchronistic chronicles of Babylon than with the king-lists of Egypt.[3] The recorded figures exhibit some variation, due partly to attempts at synchronistic dating with foreign monarchs as well as with events in Israel and Judah. A further problem resides in the calendrical basis for the figures given in the Hebrew text, in view of the fact that the Israelites employed at least two calendars during prolonged periods of their history: a Nisan calendar commencing in the spring, and a Tishri calendar beginning some six months later in the autumn.[4]

The Gezer calendar, as translated by Albright, which is closely associated with the various seasons of the agricultural year, dates from the period of the early divided monarchy, and would imply that the Tishri year was probably introduced not later than the time of Solomon.[5] There seems little doubt, however, that the spring or Nisan calendar is the more primitive, being attested in considerably earlier sources (Exod. 12:2; 13:4; 23:15; 34:18). This tradition of a dual calendar usage need occasion no particular surprise among occidentals: in the modern busi-

---

[1] Cf. M. Noth, *Überlieferungsgeschichtliche Studien I* (1943), pp. 61ff.

[2] *BHI*, p. 163.

[3] Cf. W. F. Albright, *BASOR*, No. 100 (1945), pp. 16ff.

[4] Cf. J. Morgenstern, *HUCA*, I (1924), pp. 13ff., X (1935), pp. 1ff., XX (1947), pp. 1ff., XXI (1948), pp. 365ff.

[5] W. F. Albright, *BASOR*, No. 92 (1943), pp. 16ff.; cf. R. A. S. Macalister, *The Excavation of Gezer* (1912), II, pp. 24ff.

ness world it is common for a fiscal and civil calendar to exist together without coinciding and in religious circles the ecclesiastical calendar and the civil one co-exist, but are related to different calendrical bases and patterns.

Further problems arise from the fact that the Hebrew chroniclers employed two different systems for computing regnal years. As described by Thiele, an ante-dating pattern, popular in Egypt and used by the scribes of Israel until about 789 B.C., reckoned the accession year twice, partly as the terminal year of the dead king and partly as the first year of his successor, while a post-dating or accession-year scheme of computation thought of the new reign as commencing with the beginning of the first month of the following New Year, a method current in Assyria, Babylon, and Persia. According to the latter system, any given year of a reign is always one year lower than its counterpart in the ante-dating or nonaccession-year scheme. Thus the first year of an accession-year pattern would correspond to the second year of the ante-dating form of chronological computation. It is obviously important for the scholar to know precisely which system has been employed at any given time, and whether that system has continued without change or modification throughout the period under study.[6]

The majority of the older chronologists computed the regnal years of the Hebrew kings in terms of a Nisan-to-Nisan year,[7] although Kleber used a Tishri-to-Tishri calendar for establishing his chronology of the Israelite kings.[8] Mowinckel and Morgenstern assumed that both Israel and Judah adopted a Tishri-to-Tishri calendar for the purpose of reckoning regnal years, while Begrich maintained that a Nisan-to-Nisan basis of computation was adopted at a later period, perhaps as a result of pressure exerted by the religious traditions.[9] From the evidence of I Kings 6:1, 37 it would appear that the Tishri-to-Tishri year was the basis of reckoning in the days of Solomon, although the months in Kings and elsewhere were reckoned from Nisan, irrespective of whether the year itself was begun in the spring or the autumn.[10] The totals arrived at invariably reflect the inclusive system of calculation, in which fractions

[6] *MNHK*, pp. 16ff. Cf. *Zondervan Pictorial Bible Dictionary* (1963), pp. 168ff.

[7] E. g. C. F. Keil, *Commentary on the Book of Kings* (1857), I, p. 206, W. J. Beecher, *The Dated Events of the OT* (1907), pp. 11ff., J. Lewy, *Mitteilungen der vorderasiatische-aegyptischen Gesellschaft*, XXIX, No. 2 (1924), pp. 2ff.

[8] *Biblica,* II (1921), pp. 15ff.

[9] S. Mowinckel, *Acta Orientalia*, IX (1941), pp. 175ff. J. Morgenstern, *Occident and Orient* (Gaster Anniversary Volume, 1936), pp. 439ff., and in *HUCA*, X (1935), pp. 1ff. J. Begrich, *Die Chronologie der Könige von Israel und Juda und die Quellen des Rahmens der Königsbücher* (1929), pp. 70ff.

[10] 1 Kgs. 8:2; 2 Kgs. 25:25; Exod. 12:2; Lev. 23:5; 24:27; Num. 9:1, 5; 28:16; 29:1, 7; Jer. 41:1, 8; 2 Chron. 5:3; 7:10; 29:3; Ez. 6:19; Neh. 1:1, *et al.*

of units were incorporated as though they were full units of the group under consideration.

Synchronisms with events recorded in extra-Biblical sources are naturally very important in establishing dates for the various rulers of Israel and Judah. Thus it is a matter of record that Shishak of Egypt invaded Jerusalem in the fifth year of Rehoboam (1 Kgs. 14:25; 2 Chron. 12:2); that Shalmaneser III fought a battle at Qarqar on the Orontes in his sixth year (853 B.C.) against Ahab and Benhadad; that Tiglathpileser III besieged Damascus and received tribute from Menahem of Israel (2 Kgs. 15:19) and subsequently from Jehoahaz (2 Kgs. 16:7ff.); and that Sennacherib attacked Jerusalem in the fourteenth year of King Hezekiah (2 Kgs. 18:13; Isa. 36:1). Since most of these events are mentioned in cuneiform annals, there is a firm measure of control extant for the corresponding periods of Hebrew history.

Synchronisms within the lists of the kings of Israel and Judah present problems when compared with the recorded lengths of the reigns themselves. As Thiele has pointed out, if a chronology is established in terms of the length of reign, the synchronisms do not coincide, and *vice versa*.[11] Scholars have frequently been forced to choose between the two, with results which have failed to do proper justice to the situation. Thus Wellhausen, Ewald, Bleek, Stade, and others ultimately concluded that the chronological records of the Hebrew kings were of no value whatever for the construction of an accurate chronology.[12] By contrast, other scholars have declared that, despite certain transcriptional and other errors, both the synchronisms and the lengths of the individual reigns are basically accurate, and that the data on which the Biblical records were constructed are sufficiently reliable to make an adequate chronology.[13]

Attempts to establish a chronology for the Hebrew kings have usually fallen into two distinct patterns. On the one hand the figures of the Massoretic text have been followed closely, usually by conservative scholars, in independence of contemporary Near Eastern chronology. This has resulted in a system that, for the early Hebrew kings, is at least fifty years longer than the chronology of neighboring nations would allow. As opposed to this "high" dating, other scholars have introduced a "low" chronology which surmounts the difficulty of the additional half-

[11] *MNHK*, p. 9.

[12] J. Wellhausen, *Jahrbücher für deutsche Theologie*, XX (1875), pp. 607ff. H. Ewald, *The History of Israel* (1876), I, pp. 206ff., II, pp. 20ff., 297ff. F. Bleek, *Einleitung in das AT* (1878), pp. 263ff. B. Stade, *Geschichte des Volkes Israel* (1889), I, pp. 88ff., 558ff.

[13] F. Rühl, *Deutsche Zeitschrift für Geschichtswissenschaft*, XII (1894), pp. 44ff.; *PIOT*, pp. 393ff.; *MNHK*, pp. 14f.

century by disregarding the computations of the Massoretic text to some extent in favor of synchronisms with the known chronology of other ancient Near Eastern peoples. While the latter is perhaps a more desirable course of action for the occidental methodologist, it must be remembered that the Biblical material was probably quite accurate originally, and that the lack of mechanical agreement between the figures of the Massoretic text and the synchronized events of contemporary Near Eastern history is most probably due either to alterations of the text in process of transmission, to the operation of now-unknown scribal principles of computation and reckoning, or to both factors.[14]

Whatever the chronological reconstruction of the monarchy, it has generally been found necessary to leave a margin of one or two years for the various reigns, and greater precision cannot be expected until further and more detailed chronological material is available. The reign of David has been assigned to ca. 1001/00-961/60 B.C., and the fact that its length is a compound figure implies that David actually ruled for forty years. Solomon was co-regent with David for a short period prior to his own accession, which can be dated about 961 B.C., from a synchronistic reference to Hiram, king of Tyre, in Josephus,[15] or 962 B.C., as proposed by Rowton.[16] If Solomon is credited with the full forty years allowed to him by the Massoretic text, his rule would terminate about 922 B.C.

A dating-sequence that places David and Solomon a decade earlier has been urged by some scholars[17] as a corrective to the theory of Albright, which was based on an incorrect interpretation of a reference to a lunar eclipse of a premonitory nature allegedly occurring in the reign of Takeloth II of Egypt, which apparently did not take place at all.[18] Thus the dates that Albright suggested for Shishak (ca. 935-915 B.C.) and the beginning of the Twenty-Second Dynasty should be raised by some ten years, making the commencement of the dynasty of Shishak about 945 B.C. and his invasion of Palestine, preserved in relief on a wall at Karnak, about 925 B.C.[19] This in turn would place the death of Solomon at approximately 931/30 B.C., and his accession at ca. 971/70 B.C. The date for the latter is thus somewhat later than the sequences suggested by T. H. Robinson, H. R. Hall, H. P. Smith and R. Kittel, who assigned it to 976 B.C., about 975 B.C., 973 B.C., and 972

---

[14] Cf. R. Kittel, *History of the Hebrews* (1896), II, pp. 235f.

[15] *AJ*, VIII, 3, 1. Cf. *Contra Apionem*, I, 126.

[16] M. B. Rowton, *BASOR*, No. 119 (1950), pp. 20ff. Cf. *ARI*, p. 130.

[17] E.g. K. A. Kitchen and T. C. Mitchell, *NBD*, pp. 217ff.

[18] W. F. Albright, *BASOR*, No. 130 (1953), pp. 4ff., No. 141 (1956), pp. 26f.; cf. R. A. Caminos, *The Chronicle of Prince Osorkon* (1958), pp. 88f.

[19] Cf. *ARE*, IV, sect 712ff., M. Noth, *Zeitschrift des Deutschen Palästina-Vereins*, LXI (1938), pp. 227ff., *VT*, suppl. vol. IV (1957), pp. 57ff.

B.C. respectively.[20] Coucke, Jirku, and Lusseau and Collomb assigned the accession of Solomon to the year 971 B.C.[21]

As Thiele has shown, there are good reasons for believing that the scribes employed a nonaccession-year system of computation in Israel, whereas for the kings of Judah an accession-year system, following the Babylonian pattern, was used in chronological reckoning with the exception of the rulers from Jehoram to Joash, where a nonaccession-year scheme was adopted.[22] It also seems highly probable that about the time of Amaziah of Judah, the scribes of Israel began to reckon in terms of an accession-year pattern, along with the scribes of Judah, who appear to have been using it somewhat prior to the days of Jehoram. There is some evidence also for the existence of co-regencies, and this is frequently to be found in the double datings furnished by the Hebrew scribes. Thus the accession of Joram (Jehoram) of Israel was dated in the second year of Jehoram the son of Jehoshaphat king of Judah (2 Kgs. 1:17) on the one hand, and in the eighteenth year of Jehoshaphat king of Judah (2 Kgs. 3:1) on the other. This points to a co-regency existing between Jehoshaphat and his successor Jehoram, which was mentioned subsequently in Kings (2 Kgs. 8:16).

As far as the possibility of interregna in Israel and Judah is concerned, there does not appear to be any evidence at all to indicate that such periods ever existed during the divided monarchy in either the northern or the southern kingdom. One other point in the matter of methodology is worthy of mention at this juncture. When the scribes of one kingdom synchronized the reign of their king with that of a neighboring ruler, they naturally employed their own system of computation for both monarchs, and did not use the foreign scheme for the foreign king.

The foregoing principles, as developed and illustrated by Thiele, are soundly established upon a correct ancient Eastern methodology, and when applied to the lists of kings found in the Massoretic text reflect a pattern of internal consistency as well as a substantial degree of harmony with the chronologies of neighboring kingdoms. By relating the Hebrew king-lists to cross-references in such invaluable sources as the Assyrian *limmu* or eponym lists[23] and the canon of Ptolemy,[24] it is possible to

[20] T. H. Robinson, *A History of Israel* (1934), I, p. 463; H. R. Hall, *The Ancient History of the Near East* (1936), p. 516; H. P. Smith, *OT History* (1911), p. 499; R. Kittel, *Geschichte des Volkes Israel*, II, p. 271.

[21] V. Coucke in *Supplement au Dictionnaire de la Bible* (ed. L. Pirot and A. Robert), I, col. 1247; A. Jirku, *Geschichte des Volkes Israel*, p. 146; H. Lusseau and M. Collomb, *Manual d'Études bibliques: II, Histoire du peuple d'Israël* (1945), p. 867.

[22] *MNHK*, pp. 17ff.

[23] A. Ungnad in *Reallexikon der Assyriologie* (ed. E. Ebeling and B. Meissner, 1938), II, pp. 412ff.; G. Smith, *The Assyrian Eponym Canon*, pp. 28, 42ff.

[24] F. K. Ginzel, *Handbuch der mathematischen und technischen Chronologie* (1906), pp. 138ff.; J. Hontheim, *Zeitschrift für katholische Theologie*, XLII (1918), pp. 463ff., 687ff.

secure certain synchronisms. The earliest of these is during the reigns of Ahab and Jehu of Israel and the period of Shalmaneser III of Assyria, which assists in insuring two fixed dates in Hebrew chronology. Thus it is now possible to state that the year 853 B.C. saw the death of Ahab and the accession of Ahaziah, and to observe that the death of Joram and the accession of Jehu occurred in 841 B.C.[25]

First Kings 14:25 records another important synchronism, dating the invasion of Judah by Shishak in the fifth year of the rule of Rehoboam. Unfortunately it is not easy to ascertain the corresponding year in the reign of Shishak, since the evidence furnished by Egyptian records in relation to this matter is somewhat ambiguous. According to Albright the reign of Shishak was to be dated *ca.* 935-915 B.C., as was observed above, making for a probable date of *ca.* 918 B.C. for the invasion of Judah.[26] The tentative chronological scheme at which Albright arrived, however, was based on the assumption that many of the numbers relating both to synchronisms and lengths of reigns became corrupt in process of transmission. However, once they had received the imprimatur of the "great work of the Deuteronomist" the numbers in the text were transmitted with "astonishing accuracy."[27] Instead of following the comparatively simple system of computation that he conceded to have existed in the recording of Hebrew regnal years, Albright found it necessary to resort to a series of complicated adjustments which in the end did not harmonize with the Biblical evidence. This is a rather arbitrary procedure, to say the least, especially in view of the fact that Thiele has solved the problem in an eminently satisfactory manner by employing ancient Near Eastern methodology and relating it to the evidence furnished by the Massoretic text. Not even an appeal to the chronology of the kings of Tyre can sustain the arguments of Albright, as Thiele has demonstrated.[28]

One or two modifications may be suggested for the pattern established by Thiele in connection with his objection to the synchronisms of the twelfth year of Ahaz and the accession of Hoshea of Israel (2 Kgs. 17:1), the equating of the third year of Hoshea with the accession of Hezekiah of Judah (2 Kgs. 18:1), and the correlating of the fourth and sixth years of the reign of Hezekiah with the seventh and ninth years of Hoshea (2

---

[25] *MNHK*, pp. 50, 66. D. N. Freedman, *BANE*, p. 210; W. F. Albright, *BASOR*, No. 100 (1945), pp. 19, 21. Cf. A. T. Olmstead, *JAOS*, XXXIX (1915), pp. 344ff., XLI (1921), p. 374, *History of Assyria* (1923), pp. 134ff.; H. R. Hall, *The Ancient History of the Near East*, p. 449; T. H. Robinson, *A History of Israel*, I, p. 296.

[26] W. F. Albright, *BASOR*, No. 130 (1953), pp. 4ff., No. 141 (1956), pp. 26f.; and followed by Bright, *BHI*, pp. 174 n. 26, 183 n. 43, 190 n. 61, 208 n. 15, 209 n. 1, 213 n. 14, 263 n. 31, 263 n. 32.

[27] W. F. Albright, *BASOR*, No. 100 (1945), p. 19 n. 12.

[28] E. R. Thiele, *VT*, IV (1954), pp. 188ff., *MNHK*, pp. 120ff., 181ff.

Kgs. 18:9f.).[29] Thiele assumed that these were years of sole reign, leaving a period of twelve or thirteen years[30] for which no proper place could be found in his chronological scheme. The mystery attaching to this situation is dispelled, however, when it is realized that these references simply continue the pattern of co-regencies established in the cases of Asa and Jehoshaphat, Jehoshaphat and Jehoram, Amaziah and Azariah, Azariah and Jotham, and Jotham and Ahaz. Thus Ahaz was co-regent with Jotham for a period of about twelve years (*ca.* 744/3-732 B.C.), while Hezekiah was co-regent with Ahaz from 729-716/15 B.C., and Manasseh was co-regent with Hezekiah from 696/95-687/86 B.C. There is nothing especially unusual about such a situation: there is a precedent in the example of David and Solomon.

The identity of the various Benhadads of Damascus mentioned in the Old Testament presents certain problems for chronology. The first of these, Benhadad I, who is styled "son of Tabrimmon, son of Hezion, king of Aram" (1 Kgs. 15:18), was described in identical terms in the inscription on the Melqart *stele*, which can be dated by epigraphy between 875 and 825 B.C.[31] It was in the thirty-sixth year of the divided monarchy that Baasha of Israel attacked Judah (2 Chron. 16:1ff.), making it necessary for Asa to seek the assistance of Benhadad I of Aram. This would imply that Benhadad I was already ruler of Damascus by about 895 B.C., or even slightly earlier.[32]

The Benhadad who opposed Ahab (1 Kgs. 20:1ff.) from about 874/3-853 B.C. died by the hand of Hazael in the days of Joram (*ca.* 852-841 B.C.). Hazael then succeeded Benhadad about 843 B.C., and was firmly in control of the Damascene regime when he was mentioned in the annals of Shalmaneser III of Assyria in 841 B.C.[33] The question which arises is whether this Benhadad is in fact to be identified with the Benhadad who was an ally of Asa. Albright accepted this identification, followed by Unger, Bright and others, and assigned a possible date of about 850 B.C. for the Melqart *stele* on the basis of the style of lettering employed.[34] However, the reference of 1 Kings 20:34 would seem to imply that Omri had been defeated in battle at an earlier period by a Benhadad who was the father of Benhadad, the contemporary of Ahab.

---

[29] Cf. *MNHK*, pp. 122ff.; 182ff.

[30] *MNHK*, pp. 120ff.; cf. Thiele in *A Stubborn Faith* (ed. E. C. Hobbs, 1956), pp. 39ff.

[31] Cf. W. F. Albright and L. della Vida, *BASOR*, No. 87 (1942), pp. 23ff., No. 90 (1943), pp. 30ff.; M. Black in *DOTT*, pp. 239ff.

[32] Cf. *MNHK*, pp. 57ff.

[33] M. F. Unger, *Israel and the Aramaeans of Damascus* (1957), p. 75.

[34] *Ibid.*, pp. 59ff., 141f.; Albright, *BASOR*, No. 87 (1942), p. 27; *BHI*, p. 221.

This latter Benhadad was referred to in the annals of Shalmaneser III for 853 B.C.[35] and 845 B.C.[36] under the name Adad-idri (Hadadezer).

On the basis of this evidence, any attempt to posit a single Benhadad who ruled for the lengthy period from about 900-843 B.C. would seem to be somewhat arbitrary. Two distinct individuals appear to be involved, and as such may be assigned reigns of *ca.* 900-860 B.C. and *ca.* 860-843 B.C. respectively. A third Benhadad was the son of Hazael who murdered Benhadad II (2 Kgs. 8:15), and fought against Shalmaneser III in 841 B.C. He was the contemporary of Jehoash of Israel, and was mentioned on the contemporary *stele* of Zakir, king of Hamath and Lu'ash.[37]

Of a rather different nature is the apparent discrepancy between the twenty years of reign credited to Pekah in 2 Kings 15:27 and the seven or eight years, terminating in 732/31 B.C., accorded to him by the Assyrian Eponym Chronicle. In this instance careful attention should be given to the tradition underlying the Biblical record, which indicates that the reign of Pekah was reckoned from 752 B.C., the year following the death of Jeroboam II. This may well imply that during the troubled period in which Zachariah, Shallum, and Menahem ruled over Israel, Pekah had seized control of Gilead, and had built up a kingdom in Transjordan which threatened the security of Israel. If such was actually the case, the chronology in Kings recorded the entire period of his rule, including that over Israel succeeding Pekahiah.

The annals of Sargon of Assyria show that the fall of Samaria occurred in 722 B.C.[38] Assyrian retribution upon Israel occurred as a result of an attempted conspiracy on the part of Hoshea with "So, king of Egypt." This enigmatic Egyptian ruler has been variously identified with Osorkon IV (*ca.* 727-716 B.C.) and with one of the rulers of the Delta region, Tefnakht (*ca.* 727-720 B.C.). The Egyptian commander of 720 B.C., mentioned in cuneiform records, was originally thought to have been named Sib'e, but as Borger has shown, the name should actually have been read as Re'e, a form which cannot be related to "So."[39] It may be that "So" was an abbreviated form of Osorkon in the same manner that "Sese" was a shortened version of Rameses. On the other hand, it may be, as Yeivin has suggested, a Hebrew transcript of the Egyptian word for "vizier," making "So" a high official under Osorkon IV.[40]

---

[35] D. J. Wiseman, *DOTT*, pp. 46ff.

[36] *ANET*, p. 280, *ARAB*, I, sect. 658ff.

[37] M. Black, *DOTT*, 242ff.

[38] Cf. *ANET*, pp. 284f.; *MNHK*, pp. 141ff.; Tadmor, *JCS*, XII (1958), pp. 22ff., 77ff.

[39] J. Borger, *JNES*, XIX (1960), p. 53.

[40] S. Yeivin, *VT*, II (1952), pp. 164ff.

A chronological table from the division of the monarchy to the fall of the northern kingdom will summarize much of the foregoing discussion:

TABLE 8: THE MONARCHY TO 722 B.C.

ISRAEL	JUDAH	Albright[41]	Thiele	Proposed Chronology
Jeroboam I		922-901	931-910	931/30-910/09
	Rehoboam	922-915	931-915	931/30-913
	Abijah	915-913	913-911	913-911/10
	Asa	913-873	911-870	911/10-870/69
Nadab		901-900	910-909	910/09-909/08
Baasha		900-877	909-886	909/08-886/85
Elah		877-876	886-885	886/85-885/84
Zimri		876	885	885/84
Tibni			885-880	885/84-880
Omri		876-869	885-874	885/84-874/73
	Jehoshaphat	873-849	873-848	873/72-848
Ahab		869-850	874-853	874/73-853
Ahaziah		850-849	853-852	853-852
Jehoram		849-842	852-841	852-841
	Jehoram	849-842	853-841	853-841
Jehu		842-815	841-814	841-814/13
	Ahaziah	842	841	841
	Athaliah	842-837	841-835	841-835
	Joash	837-800	835-796	835-796
Jehoahaz		815-801	814-798	814/13-798
Joash		801-786	798-782	798-782/81
	Amaziah	800-783	796-767	796-767
Jeroboam II		786-746	793-753	793-753
	Azariah	783-742	791-740	792/91-740/39
	Jotham	750-735	750-732	750-732/31
Zechariah		746-745	753-752	753-752
Shallum		745	752	752
Menahem		745-738	752-742	752-742/41
Pekahiah		738-737	742-740	742/41-740/39
Pekah		737-732	740-732	752-740/39
	Jehoahaz	735-715	735-715	735-716/15
Hoshea		732-724	732-723	732/31-723/22

It is possible to work out dates to within a year for the southern kingdom from the time of Hezekiah until the capture of Jerusalem by the Babylonians. A synchronism with Assyrian history has enabled scholars

[41] *BASOR*, No. 100 (1945), pp. 16ff.

to establish a date of 701 B.C. for the attack of Sennacherib on Jerusalem, which the Biblical records placed in the fourteenth year of Hezekiah (2 Kgs. 18:13; Isa. 36:1).[42] Thus his accession would occur in 716/15 B.C., having regard to the fact that he had been co-regent with Ahaz from 729 B.C. Such a precise synchronism indicates that the underlying Assyrian and Hebrew sources were based upon an absolute chronology. It is a remarkable testimony to the accuracy of both the Assyrian and the Hebrew records, in view of the fact that the preceding point of synchronism between Hebrew and Assyrian records had occurred a century and a half earlier in their respective chronologies.

Although the accession date of Hezekiah can now be considered established, other aspects of his reign present certain difficulties for chronology. The fall of Samaria (722 B.C.) occurred during the sixth year of his reign (2 Kgs. 18:10), whereas the invasion of Judah in 701 B.C. occurred in the fourteenth year of the same monarch. However, these events become compatible on the assumption that Hezekiah was co-regent with Ahaz from about 729 B.C., and that he succeeded to sole rule about 716 B.C. Thus the two apparently different dates would be recorded in terms of the beginning of the co-regency and from the commencement of his reign as sole monarch respectively. Although Hezekiah was credited with a twenty-nine-year rule, certain questions have been raised as to its actual duration. From 2 Kings 19:35-36 it would appear that the last recorded event of his reign was the deliverance of Jerusalem from the Assyrians under Sennacherib in 701 B.C. However, another reference in Kings (2 Kgs. 19:9; cf. Isa. 37:9) to Tirhakah, the ruler of Ethiopia, has given rise to the view that Judah was invaded by Sennacherib a second time about 688 B.C.

Many scholars have maintained that the mention of Tirhakah is an anachronism, and that the statement in 2 Kings 19:37 implies that Sennacherib died shortly after his return to Nineveh. On this basis they have postulated a subsequent unsuccessful Assyrian campaign against Jerusalem between about 689 and 686 B.C.[43] Tirhakah, equated with the pharaoh Taharqa of the Twenty-Fifth Dynasty of Egypt, reigned for a period of twenty-six years, ca. 690-664 B.C. If he commanded the Egyptian forces that Sennacherib defeated at Eltekeh in 701 B.C. while besieging Jerusalem, he was obviously not the pharaoh at that period, but only the commander of the army.[44] The Kawa temple inscriptions seem to imply that Tirhakah was only twenty years old when he came from Nubia to Lower Egypt as co-regent for six years with his brother Shebitku about 690/89 B.C., which would indicate that he was only nine

[42] E. Schrader, *The Cuneiform Inscriptions and the OT* (1885), I, pp. 307ff.
[43] Following the suggestion of Albright, *JQR*, XXIV (1933-1934), pp. 370f., *BASOR*, No. 130 (1953), pp. 8ff., No. 141 (1956), pp. 23ff.
[44] *BHI*, p. 283.

190

years of age in 701 B.C.[45] On the basis of this interpretation, Albright, Bright, and others have assumed that the contact between Tirhakah and the Assyrians must be dated to about 689 B.C., and consequently have felt that the hypothesis of a second Assyrian attack against Hezekiah suited the chronology rather better than otherwise.

In the first instance it should be noted that the theory of Macadam, which placed the birth of Tirhakah about 709 B.C., making it impossible for him to have led troops against Sennacherib and the Assyrians in 701 B.C., has been refuted by Leclant and Yoyotte, who have shown that Tirhakah could have been as old as twenty-two years by 701 B.C., and thus able to lead military forces in the field.[46] Furthermore, the usually accepted six-year co-regency period has been proved to be incorrect as the result of the studies of Schmidt.[47] The title of Tirhakah as "king of Ethiopia" would relate to a period from about 690 B.C. or later, constituting a prolepsis so as to make the situation perfectly clear to readers of the Biblical account.

If a second Assyrian campaign is postulated for about 687 B.C., there are two major difficulties to be faced. The first is that the Old Testament narrators have conflated descriptions of two separate campaigns into one account, a theory for which there is absolutely no evidence in the Hebrew text. The second requires a military campaign by Sennacherib and the Assyrian forces which is nowhere mentioned in the extant Assyrian annals or the Babylonian Chronicles. Although it is impossible to be absolutely precise on this matter at the present time, it is not unduly out of harmony with the facts of the situation to suppose that the Biblical records were actually describing a single campaign of Sennacherib against Hezekiah in 701 B.C.[48]

As far as the closing years of the southern kingdom are concerned, extra-Biblical sources have furnished a precise date of 605 B.C. for the accession of Nebuchadnezzar II and the battle of Carchemish.[49] Nebuchadnezzar actually ascended the throne of Babylon on September 6, 605 B.C. (cf. 2 Kgs. 24:12; 25:8), although the first official year of his reign commenced with the following New Year, in accordance with

[45] Cf. M. F. L. Macadam, *The Temples of Kawa* (1949); J. M. A. Janssen, *Biblica*, XXXIV (1953), pp. 23ff.

[46] Macadam, *op. cit.*, I, pp. 18ff. J. Leclant and J. Yoyotte, *Bulletin de l'Institut Français d'Archéologie Orientale*, LI (1952), pp. 17ff.

[47] G. Schmidt, *Kush*, VI (1958), pp. 121ff.

[48] Cf. W. Rudolph and A. Alt, *PJB*, XXV (1929), pp. 59ff.

[49] D. J. Wiseman, *Chronicles of Chaldean Kings (626-556 B.C.) in the British Museum* (1956). Cf. J. P. Hyatt, *JBL*, LXXV (1956), pp. 277ff.; H. Tadmor, *JNES*, XV (1956), pp. 226ff.; E. R. Thiele, *BASOR*, No. 143 (1956), pp. 22ff.; Albright, *BASOR*, No. 143 (1956), pp. 27ff.; D. N. Freedman, *BA*, XIX, No. 3 (1956), pp. 50ff.

Babylonian custom.[50] As Wiseman has shown, the Babylonian capture of Jerusalem can be dated with complete accuracy from cuneiform sources to March 15/16, the second day of the month Adar, in 597 B.C.[51] On this basis the reign of Jehoiakim can be assigned to 609-597 B.C., and the rule of Jehoiachin to a three-month period at the beginning of 597 B.C. After this date there are certain difficulties connected with the computation of the Hebrew civil year and the years of Zedekiah and Nebuchadnezzar II.

The first year of Zedekiah must evidently be regarded as 597 B.C., with his regency terminating in 587 B.C., according to the pattern of calculation for the years of the captivity as found in Ezekiel.[52] In such an event the second attack on Jerusalem occurred in 587 B.C., and not a year later as Thiele has suggested.[53] Gedaliah was appointed chief administrator of Judah by Nebuchadnezzar in 587 B.C., and continued in this office until he was murdered about 582 B.C. by a refugee officer.

The chronology of the kingdom of Judah from the time of Hezekiah to the death of Zedekiah is related to the foregoing discussion in Table 9.

TABLE 9: CHRONOLOGY OF JUDAH

Ruler	Albright	Thiele	Proposed Chronology
Hezekiah	715-687	715-686	716/15-687/86
Manasseh	687-642	696-642	697/96-643/42
Amon	642-640	642-640	643/42-641/40
Josiah	640-609	640-608	641/40-609
Jehoahaz II	609	608	609
Jehoiakim	609-598	608-597	609-598
Jehoiachin	598	597	598-597
Zedekiah	598-587	597-586	597-586

B. The Captivity and Return from Exile

1. *Darius the Mede.* Although the general chronology of the exilic period is well established, the attempt to identify Darius the Mede necessitates certain adjustments in matters of detail. For those who, with Rowley, assume that Darius the Mede is a "fictitious creature," there is no real problem of chronology involved.[54] However, those who dismiss

---

[50] So Jer. 52:28f., which follows the Babylonian accession-year system of computation.

[51] D. J. Wiseman, *Chronicles of Chaldean Kings,* pp. 32ff.

[52] Cf. Albright, *BA,* V, No. 4 (1942), pp. 49ff.

[53] *MNHK,* pp. 169ff.; cf. Thiele, *BASOR,* No. 143 (1956), pp. 26f.

[54] H. H. Rowley, *Darius the Mede and the Four World Empires of the Book of Daniel* (1935), p. 59.

the historicity of Daniel 6 have to cope with what they regard as confusions on the part of the second-century B.C. author of the work in the matter of Neo-Babylonian and Persian chronology.[55] These scholars hold to the view that the person who wrote Daniel confused the fall of Babylon in 539 B.C. with that of 520 B.C. under Darius I Hystaspes (522-486 B.C.), made that monarch the predecessor instead of the successor of Cyrus the Great (539-530 B.C.), assumed that Xerxes (486-465/64 B.C.) was the father rather than the son of Darius I, and assigned Darius to Median rather than to Persian ancestry.

If, however, the suggestion of Whitcomb is accepted that Darius the Mede can be identified with Gubaru, the governor of Babylon under Cyrus, the chronology of the period can be settled without undue difficulty.[56] The edict of Cyrus, which was promulgated in 538 B.C., has been shown to be substantially historical as a result of modern archaeological discoveries, and constitutes one of the earliest acts of Cyrus after establishing the Persian empire.[57] The chronology of this period is generally accepted as recorded in Table 10.

TABLE 10: THE PERSIAN EMPIRE

Ruler	Date B.C.
Cyrus	539-530
Cambyses	530-522
Darius I	522-486
Xerxes I	486-465/64
Artaxerxes I	464-423
Darius II	423-404
Artaxerxes II	404-359
Artaxerxes III	359/58-338/37
Arses	338/37-336/35
Darius III	336/35-331

2. *Ezra and Nehemiah.* The most pressing problem for Biblical chronology during this period involves the work of Ezra and Nehemiah, and turns in particular upon the date when Ezra commenced his work in Jerusalem. Of the three current positions adopted on this question the traditional view holds that Ezra was sent to Jerusalem in 458 B.C. on the instructions of Artaxerxes I (464-423 B.C.).[58] The precise position

[55] So J. A. Montgomery, *Daniel* (*ICC* series, 1927), p. 65; R. H. Charles, *A Critical and Exegetical Commentary on the Book of Daniel* (1929), pp. 145f.; *DILOT*, pp. 498ff.; *PIOT*, p. 757.
[56] J. C. Whitcomb, *Darius the Mede* (1959), pp. 5ff. Cf. Albright, *JBL*, XL (1921), p. 112n.; D. J. Wiseman, *NBD*, pp. 293f.
[57] Cf. R. de Vaux, *RB*, XLVI (1937), pp. 29ff.; W. F. Albright, *Alexander Marx Jubilee Volume* (1950), pp. 61ff.
[58] Cf. J. Stafford Wright, *The Date of Ezra's Coming to Jerusalem* (1947), pp. 5ff.

which Ezra held in the Persian administration (cf. Ez. 7:6) has been a matter of some debate, but it most probably corresponded to the office of Secretary of State for Jewish Affairs.[59] At all events, his mission to Jerusalem had as its ultimate objective the proper observance of the Jewish law on the part of the returned community. After an initial period of activity Ezra dropped out of sight, presumably because he returned to Persia with a report which dealt with the situation in Judaea, and only reappeared in 444 B.C. in association with the work of Nehemiah in Jerusalem.

The second view, which is held by many scholars at the present, takes issue with the traditional standpoint and reverses the positions of Ezra and Nehemiah in the chronological scheme. According to this theory it was Nehemiah who came to Jerusalem about 445 B.C., and Ezra who arrived in 398 B.C., following the death of Nehemiah. This opinion lays claim to support from three passages of Scripture. Ezra 9:9 speaks of a city wall in the time of Ezra, whereas the wall was apparently constructed only by Nehemiah. Ezra 10:1 mentions a large assembly of people in Jerusalem, as opposed to Nehemiah 7:4, which indicates that the city was even then sparsely populated. A final citation (Ez. 10:6) mentions Johanan, son of Eliashib, as the contemporary of Ezra. According to Nehemiah 12:22-23, Johanan was the grandson of Eliashib. From the papyri discovered at Elephantine it also appears that Johanan was High Priest in 408 B.C., thus making Ezra later than Nehemiah on this basis. The view that Ezra was to be dated about 398 B.C. in the seventh year of Artaxerxes II was first propounded tentatively by Vernes and developed by Van Hoonacker over a period of thirty-five years.[60] This theory was contested vigorously by all German scholars except Hölscher, who also rejected it subsequently.[61] However, it found support among a number of French and English scholars, who felt that such a view satisfied the need for the reconstruction of events in the late fifth and early fourth centuries B.C.[62]

A third theory regarding the relative position of Ezra and Nehemiah was proposed by Albright, who had wavered for some time between the opinions of Van Hoonacker and the view that, while Ezra should be

---

[59] H. H. Schaeder, *Iranische Beiträge*, I (1930), pp. 14ff., *Esra der Schreiber* (1930), pp. 39ff.

[60] M. Vernes, *Précis d'Histoire juive* (1889), p. 582n. Cf. Van Hoonacker, *Le Muséon*, IX (1890). pp. 151ff., 317ff., 389ff.; *RB*, IV (1895), pp. 180ff., X (1901), pp. 5ff., 175ff.; *Une communauté Judéo-Araméenne à Éléphantine en Égypte, aux VIᵉ et Vᵉ siècles avant J. C.* (1915), pp. 19ff.; *RB*, XXXII (1923), pp. 481ff., XXXIII (1924), pp. 33ff.

[61] G. Hölscher in *Die Heilige Schrift des AT* (ed. Kautzsch and Bertholet, 1910), II, pp. 451f.; cf. *ibid.* (1923 ed.), II, pp. 491ff., 500f.

[62] For a partial bibliography see *RSL*, pp. 133ff., as corrected and supplemented in *BJRL*, XXXVII, No. 2 (1955), pp. 549f.

dated after Nehemiah, both belonged to the period of Artaxerxes I rather than Artaxerxes II.[63] This theory attempted to compromise between the Biblical tradition that the work of Ezra and Nehemiah overlapped and the opinions of Van Hoonacker and his supporters that Ezra followed Nehemiah. Albright finally arrived at a date of 428 B.C. for the beginning of the work of Ezra, taking the reference to the "seventh" year (Ez. 7:7) as haplography for "thirty-seventh," a literary device which he supposed had been undertaken in order to avoid a threefold repetition of the Hebrew letter שׁ and which had the effect of placing Ezra in the thirty-seventh year of Artaxerxes I.[64] While this date is alleged to be more in harmony with the situation in Jerusalem towards the end of the fifth century B.C. as reflected in the Elephantine papyri, it is still simply a fact that the number proposed by Albright can command absolutely no textual support, as Freedman has rightly observed, and thus it can hardly be employed as a valid basis for argument.[65]

Not all the objections that have been marshalled against the traditional position are quite as persuasive as their advocates have been led to believe. The nature of the wall which was in existence when Ezra arrived in Jerusalem has been one of the prime points at issue in the general debate, and the situation allows for a significant difference of opinion. The word in question, gādhēr, occurs nowhere else in Ezra and Nehemiah, and in other instances of its occurrence in the Old Testament it is used of a fence surrounding a vineyard (Ps. 80:13; Isa. 5:5) or a wall of stones without mortar (Num. 22:24; Prov. 24:31; Ezek. 42:7, 10) of varying height.[66] Consequently it has been suggested that the wall of Ezra 9:9 was not a completed city wall[67] but perhaps the kind of preliminary structure which was mentioned in the letter to Artaxerxes (Ez. 4:12), and which was subsequently abandoned (Ez. 4:21ff.; Neh. 1:3).[68] It is at least possible that this "wall" may have even preceded the visit of Ezra to the city by a few years, and have constituted an unsuccessful attempt by the returned community to furnish some sort of physical protection for the dwellers in Jerusalem.

[63] Cf. FSAC, p. 324.

[64] W. F. Albright in The Jews, Their History, Culture, and Religion (ed. Finkelstein, 1949), I, p. 64 n. 133. Cf. The Archaeology of Palestine and the Bible (1932), pp. 169ff., 218f.; BPAE, p. 112 n. 193.

[65] D. N. Freedman, BANE, p. 213.

[66] Cf. H. Kaupel, Biblische Zeitschrift, XXII (1934), pp. 89ff.; A. Fernández, Biblica, XVI (1935), pp. 82ff., XVIII (1937), pp. 207f.; H. Kaupel, Biblica, XVI (1935), pp. 213f.

[67] W. M. F. Scott, ET, LVIII (1946-47), pp. 263ff.; cf. C. T. Wood, ET, LIX (1947-48), pp. 53f.

[68] J. Stafford Wright, The Date of Ezra's Coming to Jerusalem, p. 18. On the walls of Nehemiah see M. Avi-Yonah, Israel Exploration Journal, IV (1954), pp. 239ff. On their position see L.-H. Vincent, Jérusalem de l'Ancien Testament (1954), I, pp. 237ff., pl. LXI; B. Mazar, BA, XXXIII, No. 2 (1970), pp. 49ff.

The argument that Jerusalem was apparently heavily populated in the time of Ezra (Ez. 10:1) but much less so during the period of Nehemiah (Neh. 7:4) turns largely on the nature of local circumstances. Whereas Nehemiah appears to have been concerned with the actual dwelling-places of the inhabitants of Jerusalem, it is clear from Ezra 10:7ff. that the congregation that assembled to hear the words of Ezra was drawn from a larger area than that of the city and its immediate environs, and which may in point of fact have been coextensive with the terrain occupied by the returned exiles.[69]

In any event this is not a particularly cogent argument for the priority of Nehemiah, which has been urged on an additional ground, namely the fact that the name of Nehemiah precedes that of Ezra in Nehemiah 12:26. For Albright, who followed Van Hoonacker on this point, this constituted the most decisive passage in favor of a Nehemiah-Ezra chronological sequence.[70] However, as Rowley has shown, the verse in question need indicate no more than that the chronicler assumed that Ezra and Nehemiah were contemporaries, and in consequence it need carry little weight as an argument for a later date for the period of Ezra.[71]

The references to Nehemiah as the contemporary of Eliashib the High Priest (Neh. 3:1, 20, 21; 13:4, 7)—whereas the son (or descendant) of Eliashib, a man named Johanan (Jehohanan) was contemporary with Ezra— onstitute a more serious objection to the traditional standpoint. According to Nehemiah 12:22, 23, Johanan was in fact the grandson of Eliashib, and as shown by the Elephantine papyri occupied the office of High Priest in Jerusalem in 408 B.C.[72] Thus the high priesthood of his grandfather must have occurred some thirty years earlier, placing Nehemiah towards the middle of the fifth century B.C.[73] A subsequent reference (Neh. 13:28) indicates that Joiada, the son of Eliashib and the father of Johanan, had become High Priest, which in turn might suggest a date of about 432 B.C. for Nehemiah.

In this connection it is important to avoid the assumption that Johanan was High Priest in the time of Ezra, since this is not warranted by the Hebrew text of Ezra 10:6. If, as Josephus claimed, Joiakim was the High Priest when Ezra visited Jerusalem, there would be good reason for the lack of mention of Johanan in this capacity.[74] It may be, as Schofield has suggested, that the situation which involved the family of Joiada, the son of Eliashib, led to the High Priest's being deposed in favor of Johanan.[75]

[69] However, 1 Esdras 8:88 (92), parallel to Ez. 10:1, reads ἀπό Ἱερουσαλήμ instead of the Massoretic text מישׂראל.

[70] Albright, *JBL*, XL (1921), p. 121; Van Hoonacker, *RB*, X (1901), p. 197.

[71] *RSL*, p. 144; *BJRL*, XXXVII, No. 2 (1955), p. 550 n. 4.

[72] Cf. A. Cowley, *Aramaic Papyri of the Fifth Century B.C.* (1923), pp. 111ff.; *ANET*, p. 492.

[73] H. H. Rowley, *BJRL*, XXXVII, No. 1 (1955), pp. 176f.

[74] *AJ*, XI, 5, 5; cf. Neh. 12:10.

[75] J. N. Schofield, *The Religious Background of the Bible* (1944), p. 167.

However, considerable caution is called for in any discussion of the activities of Johanan, since the latter was a widely used name at that period, and this fact must constitute yet another element which contributes to the uncertainty and confusion surrounding this particular phase of Hebrew history. That Nehemiah may have been mentioned before Ezra in one particular passage (Neh. 12:26) has actually little bearing upon the larger chronological problem, since it appears fairly obvious that Nehemiah would in any event have taken precedence in his own memoirs in his capacity as civil governor of Judaea.

While the chronological situation for the period of Ezra and Nehemiah is far from complete, due as much to the lack of corroborative extra-Biblical sources as to any considerations of dislocation or disarrangement within the text itself, there seems to be little justification for abandoning the traditional order of Ezra and Nehemiah for a sequence which is beset with at least as many problems of chronology. As Bright has cautiously concluded, it appears best to avoid a dogmatic approach in the light of the available evidence.[76] Hence it is possible to envisage the traditional sequences of chronology as being at least as probable as any other.

3. *Intertestamental chronology.* After the death of Alexander the Great (331-323 B.C.), the chronology of the Greek period (331-65 B.C.) and subsequent times presents few difficulties for events in the Old Testament. Table 11 summarizes the situation for Syria and Egypt up to the death of Antiochus VII.

TABLE 11: THE GREEK PERIOD

Syria	Egypt	Date B.C.
	Ptolemy I	323-285
Seleucus I		312-281
	Ptolemy II	285-247
Antiochus I		281-261
Antiochus II		261-246
	Ptolemy III	247-222
Seleucus II		246-226/25
Seleucus III		226/25-223
Antiochus III		223-187
	Ptolemy IV	222-205
	Ptolemy V	205-182
Seleucus IV		187-175
	Ptolemy VI	182-146
Antiochus IV		175-163
Antiochus V		163-162
Demetrius I		162-150
Antiochus VII		139-129

[76] *BHI*, p. 376.

In 198 B.C. Palestine passed out of Egyptian control and came under the jurisdiction of the Syrian rulers. Syrian domination continued until 63 B.C., when Pompey established Roman rule in Palestine and made Judaea a protectorate. The chronology for this particular period, taken to 4 B.C., is given by Table 12.

TABLE 12: FROM THE MACCABEES TO HEROD

Event	Date B.C.
Maccabees in Judaea	167-140
Judas Maccabaeus	166-161
Jonathan Maccabaeus	160-143
Dead Sea Community	ca. 150
Simon Maccabaeus	143-135
John Hyrcanus I	135-104
Aristobulus I	104/03
Alexander Jannaeus	103-76
Hyrcanus II and Salome	76-67
Hyrcanus II and Aristobulus II	67-40
Pompey	63
Herod the Great	40-4

Part Four

THE OLD TESTAMENT TEXT AND CANON

I. THE HISTORY OF HEBREW WRITING

The study of the Hebrew text in its own right is a matter of great importance, since the judgments that are made by scholars in this field are basic to all other areas of Old Testament investigation. As a discipline textual criticism is independent of the history and early growth of the Scriptural writings, as well as of the formation of the canon.[1] The primary concerns of this study are the transmission of the text, the rise and development of revisions, the nature and scope of scribal activities during the process of transmission, the incidence of vocalization, and the emergence of the Massoretic text.

The ultimate aim of the textual critic is to recover the text of Scripture as nearly as possible in its original form. However, this laudable objective cannot always be realized, for none of the original drafts of the Old Testament compositions has survived, and the copies that exist have of course been subjected both to the frailty of human nature and the ravages of the centuries. There are undoubtedly numerous instances in which the original text will never be known, and many others in which cogent arguments can be adduced for the adoption of one of several plausible variants.

Contrary to the contentions of Wellhausen, who maintained, against archaeological evidence already available in his day, that writing did not appear among the Hebrews until the early monarchy, they had the means of producing written records at their disposal from very early times. From at least 3100 B.C. in the ancient Near East, writing was regarded as one of the high-water marks of culture and human progress. Writing may have been developed originally by the Sumerians in order to meet their administrative and economic needs,[2] although there appear to have been even earlier forms of written communication. At any rate, the cuneiform Sumerian corpus of logograms, syllabic signs, and determinatives was adopted and expanded by the Akkadians during the first half of the third millennium B.C. as a vehicle for expressing their own Semitic language. In the second millennium it was taken over with

[1] B. J. Roberts, *The OT Text and Versions* (1951), p. 1.
[2] R. J. Williams, *IDB*, IV, p. 909.

201

some modifications by the Horites and Hittites, and in the first half of the first millennium B.C. it also became the literary medium of communication of the Urartians of Armenia, following well-established Near Eastern patterns of linguistic expression. In addition, the Mesopotamian system of cuneiform writing also influenced the development of two other scripts, namely, the Old Persian syllabic and the alphabetic script of Ras Shamra.[3]

During the neo-Assyrian period (900-612 B.C.) the Aramaic language, written in a cursive alphabetic script, was also employed in parts of Mesopotamia, as is indicated by the presence of certain Aramaic notations on some cuneiform tablets.[4] However, the origin of Aramaic, in which some sections of the Old Testament (Dan. 2:4-7:28; Jer. 10:11; Ezra 4:8—6:18, 7:12-26) were written, antedates this period by many centuries. It may be that the influence of proto-Aramaic was enhanced in the third millennium B.C. by the nomadic invaders from the north-Arabian deserts who are mentioned in Assyrian inscriptions from the time of Tiglathpileser I onwards,[5] with whom the Pentateuch (Gen. 24:3ff.; 25:20; 28:2ff.; Deut. 26:5) associated the ancestors of Israel. By the twelfth century B.C. such groups were established in communities all along the Tigris and Euphrates from the Persian Gulf to northern Syria, and southward through Palestine into northern Arabia.[6]

What is perhaps the oldest extra-Biblical specimen of Aramaic may well be the Melqart *stele*,[7] dated in the ninth century B.C. Somewhat later are the inscriptions from Zenjirli, one of which mentions Tiglathpileser III, dating from the eighth century B.C. In addition to the Aramaic notations on Assyrian and Babylonian tablets mentioned above, an important contribution to the history of the Aramaic language comes from the fifth-century B.C. colony of Jewish mercenaries stationed on the island of Elephantine in the Nile near Aswan.

[3] On the development of writing see J. H. Breasted, *AJSL*, XXXII (1916), pp. 230ff.; R. P. Dougherty, *JAOS*, XLVIII (1928), pp. 109ff.; H. Jensen, *Die Schrift in Vergangenheit und Gegenwart* (1935); J. G. Février, *Histoire de l'Écriture* (1948); H. Tur-Sinai, *JQR*, XLI (1950-51), pp. 83ff., 159ff., 277ff., G. R. Driver, *Semitic Writing: From Pictograph to Alphabet* (1944, rev. ed. 1954); D. Diringer, *The Alphabet* (1948), *The Story of the Aleph Beth* (1960); I. J. Gelb, *A Study of Writing* (1952).

[4] Cf. J. H. Stevenson, *Assyrian and Babylonian Contracts with Aramaic Notes* (1902).

[5] A. Jeffery, *IDB*, I, p. 186. Cf. J.-R. Kupper, *Les Nomades en Mésopotamie au Temps des Rois de Mari* (1957), pp. 147ff., 196; M. McNamara, *Verbum Domini*, XXXV (1957), pp. 129ff.; A. Dupont-Sommer, *VT* suppl. I (1953), pp. 40ff.; S. Moscati, *The Semites in Ancient History* (1959), pp. 66f.

[6] R. A. Bowman, *IDB*, I, pp. 191f.

[7] *ANET*, p. 501; *DOTT*, pp. 239ff.; M. Dunand, *Bulletin du Musée de Beyrouth*, III (1941), pp. 65ff.; W. F. Albright, *BASOR*, No. 87 (1942), pp. 23ff.

Earlier scholars were accustomed to divide Aramaic, which is actually a general term employed to describe a number of Semitic dialects closely related to Hebrew, into an eastern and a western group. It was also formerly assumed, in the absence of indications to the contrary, that western Aramaic was of late origin. By employing this as a criterion, Driver and others assigned a late date to Daniel.[8] Utilizing subsequent evidence, however, R. D. Wilson showed the fallacies of this argument, pointing out that the alleged distinction between eastern and western forms of Aramaic did not exist in the pre-Christian period.[9] The presence of Aramaic elements in the cuneiform compositions from Ras Shamra, as illustrated particularly by the consonantal shift from *z* to *d* in the relative pronoun and elsewhere, attests further to the antiquity of the tongue. Consequently, it is no longer possible to argue for a later date for a given composition on the basis of Aramaic words and expressions in it.

In the light of subsequent studies[10] it now appears more desirable to divide the development of Aramaic into four periods: (1) *Old Aramaic*, the language of the north-Syrian inscriptions, dating from the tenth to the eighth centuries B.C.; (2) *Official Aramaic*, which was widely used in the Assyrian (*ca.* 1100-605 B.C.), Neo-Babylonian (605-539 B.C.), and Persian (539-331 B.C.) periods; (3) *Levantine Aramaic*, which probably came into prominence in Syria and Palestine after 721 B.C.; and (4) *Palestinian Jewish Aramaic proper*, which in New Testament times consisted of several dialects (cf. Matt. 26:73). Of particular importance for the text of the Aramaic sections of the Old Testament, as well as for the dating of the books in which they occur, is the Official Aramaic, which apparently was the *lingua franca* in the government offices of the Assyrians. Official Aramaic became popular because it was better known outside Mesopotamia than the native cuneiform and because it was of a simple and quite static nature.

In consequence a good deal of care has to be exercised when attempts are made to date Old Testament documents in which Aramaic is found in view of the prolonged usage which the language enjoyed. The incidence of Aramaisms frequently indicates an early rather than a late date, as exemplified in Genesis 31:47 by the Aramaic name (יְגַר שָׂהֲדוּתָא) given by Laban to the stone heap that Jacob designated by the corre-

---

[8] *DILOT*, pp. 502f., following Th. Nöldeke, *ZDMG*, XXI (1867), pp. 183ff., XXII (1868), pp. 443ff., XXIV (1870), pp. 85ff., XXV (1871), pp. 129f., *Die Semitische Sprachen* (1899), pp. 35ff., in *EB*, I, col. 282; C. H. H. Wright, *A Comparative Grammar of the Semitic Languages* (1890), pp. 15f. Against this see G. L. Archer, *A Survey of OT Introduction* (1964), pp. 125ff.

[9] R. D. Wilson, *A Scientific Investigation of the OT* (1926), pp. 105ff., *Biblical and Theological Studies by the Members of the Faculty of Princeton Theological Seminary* (1912), pp. 261ff. Cf. H. H. Rowley, *JRAS* (1933), pp. 777ff.

[10] Cf. H. L. Ginsberg, *AJSL*, L (1933), pp. 1ff., LII (1935), pp. 95ff.; R. A. Bowman, *JNES*, VII (1948), pp. 65ff.; J. Kutscher, *EB* (1955), I, col. 584ff.

sponding Hebrew form (גלעד). Among other traces of early Aramaic structures in the area of Paddan-aram[11] during the second millennium B.C. are those materials contained in Egyptian texts from the New Kingdom period (1570-1150 B.C.), which followed the Aramaic rather than the Canaanite form when speaking of Aram-naharaim.[12]

Although Official Aramaic was comparatively static in nature, it nevertheless underwent considerable orthographic modification in the fifth century B.C. Such procedures were not uncommon in antiquity, as can be illustrated by the *Instruction of the Vizier Ptahhotep*,[13] written about 2400 B.C. in Old Egyptian[14] and revised by 1900 B.C. to include predominantly Middle Egyptian grammatical forms. Resultant "late" words or spellings of proper names merely date the particular scribal revision in which they occur, and not the manuscript itself, a point apparently not appreciated by H. H. Rowley in his criticism of Wilson.[15] Thus as Rosenthal has pointed out, the criteria that liberal scholars adduced as evidence for the late date of Daniel and Ezra are nothing more than the result of a process of modernizing in spelling which was carried out in the fifth century B.C.[16]

There can no longer be any doubt from archaeological sources that writing was a feature of life in Syria and Palestine from the earliest occupational periods. Certainly by the time of Moses there were several well-established means of linguistic expression for purposes of transmitting written communications. From the evidence presented by the Tell el-Amarna letters it is clear that Imperial Akkadian was the *lingua franca* of the age. In pharaonic Egypt the native tongue had been written in hieroglyphic pictographs from a period just prior to 3000 B.C., and shortly thereafter it was represented also by means of hieratic script, a non-pictorial, cursive form of hieroglyphic employed by scribes for purposes of rapid writing. The Canaanites of the Late Bronze Age (*ca.* 1500-1200 B.C.) employed a native cuneiform language, Ugaritic, which has very close affinities with Biblical Hebrew, as well as a linear alphabetic variety of writing. The latter is best exemplified in a *stele* from Balu'ah in ancient Moab, and although the script is badly weathered it is perhaps the same as that occurring on stone and bronze tablets unearthed at Gebal (the Byblos of the Greeks and the Gubla of the Akkadians). These "pseudo-hieroglyphic" inscriptions, as they have been designated, have not yet been read satisfactorily. They are thought to

---

[11] Cf. W. F. Albright, *Archiv für Orientforschung*, VI (1931), p. 218 n. 4.

[12] I. J. Gelb, *Hurrians and Subarians* (1944), p. 74.

[13] *ANET*, pp. 512ff.; cf. *FSAC*, p. 79.

[14] Cf. G. Fecht, *Die Habgierige und die Maat in der Lehre des Ptahhotep* (1958), pp. 49f.

[15] Rowley, *The Aramaic of the OT* (1929), pp. 23ff.

[16] F. Rosenthal, *Die Aramäische Forschung* (1939), p. 676; cf. K. A. Kitchen, *NBD*, p. 58.

date from a period between the eighteenth and fifteenth centuries B.C.

About twenty-five inscriptions recovered in 1904 from the turquoise mines of Serabit el-Khadem in the Sinai peninsula, which in antiquity were controlled by the Egyptians, have demonstrated that for some time prior to the period of Moses an early form of alphabetic script existed, variously named proto-Sinaitic, early Canaanite, and proto-Phoenician. These inscriptions were discovered by Sir Flinders Petrie, who dated them about 1500 B.C.[17] Albright deciphered the inscriptions in 1947 and traced their origin to the use of an alphabetic script by Semitic slaves brought in from Canaan to work the turquoise mines in the days of Thotmes III.[18] Other scholars, however, have expressed a preference for a date in the Middle Kingdom rather than in the Empire (New Kingdom) period. Nevertheless, for the present a date of about 1500 B.C. seems quite acceptable. The inscriptions are generally regarded as containing letters derived from Egyptian hieroglyphs, although the number of different signs, possibly a little more than thirty, indicates that the script is of a non-Egyptian alphabetic character. Potsherds found at Gezer, Lachish, Beth-shemesh, and Hazor, which bear analogous signs, may well constitute a witness to the widespread use of the script in Palestine during this period.

In summary it can be said that by 1500 B.C. the alphabet, as distinct from cuneiform writing and Egyptian hieroglyphs, came into use in Syria and Palestine, perhaps out of a need to find a less complicated form of writing than those in vogue at the time. Far from being illiterate, therefore, the inhabitants of the Syria-Palestine area were making use of at least five systems of writing during the Late Bronze Age.

While there are some gaps in present knowledge concerning the development of the Palestine linear script, it would seem that the Sinaitic variety was followed closely by that of Ugarit. A later stage of the proto-Canaanite can be discerned in a number of inscriptions from Byblos, Beth-shemesh, and Lachish, dated between the thirteenth and twelfth centuries B.C.[19] These latter serve to link the proto-Sinaitic inscriptions[20] with the tenth-century B.C. Phoenician material from Byblos on the sarcophagus of Ahiram (*ca.* 1000 B.C.). The proto-Phoenician script was apparently adopted between the eleventh and tenth centuries B.C. by the Aramaeans, who introduced *matres lectionis* (literally "mothers of reading"), the use of certain letters to indicate the

[17] W. F. M. Petrie and C. T. Currelly, *Researches in Sinai* (1906), pp. 129ff.

[18] Cf. *AP,* pp. 188f., also *BASOR,* No. 110 (1948), pp. 6ff.; F. M. Cross, *BASOR,* No. 134 (1954), pp. 15ff.

[19] Cf. R. H. Pfeiffer, *AJA,* XLI (1937), pp. 643f.; J. W. Flight in E. Grant (ed.), *Haverford Symposium on Archaeology and the Bible* (1938), pp. 114ff.

[20] Cf. J. T. Milik and F. M. Cross, *BASOR,* No. 134 (1954), p. 9.

presence of final long vowels, a feature that appeared from the ninth century B.C. on in Moabite and Hebrew texts. In Hebrew, for example, ו, י and ה, were used to indicate ū, ī, and ā, respectively. Eighth-century B.C. Aramaic inscriptions developed this device further to indicate medial long vowels, and ultimately 'aleph was employed on rare occasions as a vowel-letter. Hebrew script, both lapidary (inscribed on stones) and cursive, was a descendant of the Phoenician, and remained constant in the number and phonic value of its letters.

Although the evidence is too scattered both chronologically and geographically for a detailed palaeographic and epigraphic study, it is sufficient to indicate that the early Hebrew alphabet was constant throughout the millennium of its usage, dating from the Gezer calendar in the tenth century B.C.[21] Thus Diringer concluded that hardly any of its letters changed its form so radically during that time that a layman could mistake its identity, a phenomenon which is probably unique in the history of ancient writing.[22] The cursive script that many Old Testament writers would have employed at an early period was no doubt that found on the inscribed arrowheads and other smaller sources from about 1000 B.C.[23] The earliest group of texts is that from Samaria, assigned to the reign of Jeroboam II, and exhibits a clear flowing script which is quite obviously the work of professional scribes.[24] Word-dividers were commonly utilized in Aramaic, Moabite, and Hebrew inscriptions, and in the case of the Samaritan corpus the unvocalized words were separated by means of small strokes or dots. The script was very similar to that of the Siloam inscription, and by the time that the Lachish ostraca were written it had developed only slightly in form.

Unlike the Hebrew, the Aramaic script exhibited a degree of individual development from about 1000 B.C. The texts recovered from Arslan Tash and Tell Halaf indicate that there was still a close resemblance between the Phoenician linear script and the Aramaic character as late as 850 B.C. In the seventh century B.C. the increasingly cursive style was evident in the inscription on the Bar-Rekub *stele*,[25] on clay tablets, and on a papyrus letter sent from Philistia to Egypt about 604 B.C.,[26] which was written in a more archaic hand than many of the Elephantine papyri. In these texts it is common to discover archaic and late Aramaic forms existing side by side, as in Jeremiah 10:11.

[21] W. F. Albright, *BASOR*, No. 92 (1943), pp. 16ff.

[22] D. Diringer, *BA*, XIII, No. 4 (1950), p. 84.

[23] Cf. J. T. Milk, *BASOR*, No. 143 (1956), pp. 3ff.

[24] *ANET*, p. 321; *DOTT*, pp. 204ff.; *WBA*, p. 158; Y. Yadin, *Studies in the Bible* (1960), pp. 9ff.

[25] J. B. Pritchard, *The Ancient Near East in Pictures* (1954), p. 460.

[26] D. J. Wiseman, *Chronicles of Chaldean Kings (626-556 B.C.) in the British Museum* (1956), p. 28; *DOTT*, pp. 251ff.

By the late third century B.C. a semi-formal script had emerged in Persian Aramaic, similar in character to the Aramaic scripts of Palmyra and Nabataea, which seem to have come into vogue about this period.[27] Early in the second century B.C. modified forms of the Aramaic characters, which by that time had diverged considerably from the Phoenician, were adopted by the Jews, the first stages of which can be seen in the Nash Papyrus, *ca.* 150 B.C., and this was subsequently known as "square" character. Phoenician forms continued in use for some time, however, being found frequently on coins from the second century B.C. to the second century A.D., and surviving in some of the Dead Sea Scrolls. In a more elaborate fashion the Phoenician characters were perpetuated in the script utilized by the Samaritans. The use of special final forms for certain letters in the Aramaic "square" script can be traced back to some Egyptian papyri of about 300 B.C., but at first such letters were not commonly employed.

The formal Hebrew character developed quickly during the Herodian period (30 B.C.-A.D. 70), and after that time its progress could be traced by means of dated commercial and legal documents.[28] The manuscripts and fragments from Qumran and the Wadi Murabba'at exhibited a variety of scripts ranging from Palaeo-Hebrew to the formal and cursive hands of Early Jewish, with some Greek and Latin scripts in addition. Until vowel signs were developed after the fifth century A.D. there was no attempt made to indicate the vocalization of the Hebrew consonants, aside from the use of the *matres lectionis.* Neither a Palestinian nor a Babylonian system of supralinear vowels met with quite the success accorded to the Tiberian method, which was introduced at the end of the eighth century of our era. This was subsequently adopted as the best system for pointing the Hebrew text, and is still employed in modern Hebrew Bibles.

Writing materials varied considerably, to some extent depending upon climate and local conditions. Since stone was relatively scarce in Mesopotamia, cuneiform inscriptions on this substance were restricted to royal texts or *stelae* such as that bearing the Code of Hammurabi. Clay tablets were the commonest vehicles of written communications in Mesopotamia for many centuries, whereas in Egypt it was papyrus which claimed this distinction from about 3000 B.C. Because of the abundance of stone in Egypt it was customary to carve hieroglyphic texts on *stelae* and on the walls of innumerable temples and tombs. Metal was much less commonly used as writing material than either stone or clay, although cuneiform inscriptions in Sumerian, Akkadian, and Old Persian have been discovered on objects made of gold, silver, copper, and bronze. Gold is men-

---

[27] D. J. Wiseman, *NBD*, p. 1349.
[28] F. M. Cross, *BANE*, pp. 136ff.

tioned in Exodus 28:36 as a writing-surface; stone is also referred to several times in the Old Testament in this connection (Exod. 24:12; 34:1; Deut. 4:13; 27:2f.; Josh. 8:32; Job 19:24). The use of broken pottery as writing material was widespread throughout the ancient Near East, although potsherds were of limited value to the Mesopotamians, since they could only be utilized for a script like Aramaic, which was written with pen and ink rather than with a stylus. Wood in one form or another was also employed as a means of receiving writing (Num. 17:2f.; Ezek. 37:16f.; cf. Isa. 8:1; 30:8; Hab. 2:2), as were leather and parchment.

The use of tanned animal skins for purposes of writing dates back to the early third millennium in Egypt, and lasted until the Arab conquest in the seventh century A.D. It is very possible that the prophecies of Jeremiah were written upon a leather scroll (Jer. 36:4, 23) (as were some of the Qumran Scriptures), although papyrus may have been employed on that occasion. This latter may be indicated by the fact that the deed of purchase signed by the prophet (Jer. 32:10ff.) was undoubtedly a papyrus document of the kind found at Elephantine, and also by the use of *chartion* (36:2, 4, 6, 14—LXX chapter 43) and *chartēs* (Jer. 36:23—LXX chap. 43) in the LXX version of Jeremiah 36, both of which denote a sheet of papyrus. Although hides were tanned by the Hebrews (cf. Num. 31:20; 2 Kgs. 1:8), the Old Testament itself does not mention writing on leather. However, the Talmud preserved an ancient tradition that the Mosaic Torah was written upon the hides of cattle.[29] According to Josephus, the Pentateuchal manuscript from which the LXX was translated was written upon leather, although there is little evidence for such a statement.[30]

The widespread use of Egyptian papyrus in Syria long before the time of the early Hebrew monarchy can be appreciated from the report of Wen-Amon, an Egyptian official who had been sent on a journey to Byblos about 1100 B.C. Among other matters contained in his report to the authorities of the temple of Amon at Karnak[31] is a reference to five hundred rolls of papyrus that had been delivered to the Syrian ruler in partial payment for a load of timber required for the ceremonial barge of Amon.

In the light of all available evidence there is absolutely no ground for regarding the Old Testament references to writing in the time of Moses (Exod. 17:14; 24:4; 39:14, 30; Deut. 27:3; 31:24; cf. Josh. 18:4ff.) as anachronisms, in the manner favored by many adherents of the Wellhausenian theories. It is clear that at any period from the time of Moses

[29] *Maccoth*, 5.
[30] *AJ*, XII, 2, 11; cf. the *Letter of Aristeas*, III, 176.
[31] *ANET*, pp. 25ff.

onwards, the ancient Hebrews were capable of producing their own written records. Indeed, it will be shown in a subsequent chapter that there are excellent reasons for thinking that the bulk of Genesis was brought from Mesopotamia in the form of written tablets, and supplemented by the addition of the narratives concerning Joseph. Although there is no explicit statement in the Old Testament to the effect that Moses was literate, the references to his writing activities would seem to leave little doubt as to the facts of the case. As one who was presumably educated in court circles, Moses would be familiar with Egyptian writing and literary methods, and in all probability with Akkadian cuneiform, which from the beginning of the Amarna Age had constituted the official language of diplomacy in Egypt.

The foregoing discussion shows that peoples of the same cultural background as the Hebrews were literate from the fourth millennium B.C. onwards, though naturally not uniformly so. From the second millennium B.C. throughout the ancient Near East men were being trained in schools not only as scribes for business and professional purposes, but also as expert copyists. It seems improbable that from the time of Moses onwards the Hebrews should have been significantly less advanced than their contemporaries in this respect (cf. 2 Sam. 8:17), or that they were less scrupulous in the transmission of their sacred texts than were the Egyptians or the Mesopotamians.[32] Indeed, the prolonged Hebrew tradition of reverence for the text of Scripture indicates that the opposite was in fact the case (cf. Deut. 4:2; Jer. 26:2).

On this basis it is no longer necessary to assume that an extended period of oral transmission is a necessary prerequisite to the written form of many if not all of the Old Testament documents, as is common in liberal circles.[33] Modern scholars have largely misunderstood the purpose and function of oral transmission in the ancient Near East. The firm tradition of the Mosaic period, as well as of ancient peoples other than the Hebrews, was that any events of importance were generally recorded in written form quite soon after they had taken place. Some notable incidents were perpetuated in song and story also, doubtless for many centuries, but the principal purpose of oral transmission was the dissemination of the pertinent information to the people of the day and age in which the events occurred. Only as one generation was succeeded by another did the various elements represented by oral transmission approach anything like a sequence in time. Consequently it is entirely fallacious to assume, as many modern scholars have done, that an oral form of a narrative was the necessary and normal precursor of the written stage. There can be little doubt that in many cases both oral and

[32] Cf. W. J. Martin, *The Dead Sea Scroll of Isaiah* (1954), pp. 18f.
[33] Cf. E. Neilson, *Oral Tradition* (1954); B. S. Childs, *Memory and Tradition in Israel* (1963).

written traditions existed side by side for lengthy periods.[34] While one
tradition may have been reinforced or corrected by reference to the
other on specific occasions, the two were certainly free to pursue an
independent if not an entirely unrelated course.

[34] H. S. Nyberg, ZAW, LII (1934), pp. 241ff. and *Studien zum Hoseabuch*
(1935), pp. 7f., however, held that little of the Old Testament was in fixed written
form until the post-exilic period.

II. THE OLD TESTAMENT TEXT

A. The Transmission of the Hebrew Text

1. Pre-Massoretic developments. Although great care was taken by the Jews in the preservation and transmission of their Scriptures, it is important to notice that the details of the text were not standardized at the time when the canon of the Old Testament took its final form. The manuscripts from Qumran have shown that in the immediate pre-Christian period there were several types of text in circulation, some with readings different from those in the traditional Massoretic text. During the first two centuries or so before the time of Christ, the responsibility for preserving and transmitting the Hebrew text that later came to be known as Massoretic devolved upon the ancient scribes, or *Sopherim*, designated in this manner according to the Talmud,[1] because they counted scrupulously the letters in the Torah. In the immediate pre-Christian period the Jewish authorities gave a great deal of thought to the preservation of the Old Testament text in as pure a form as possible, a concern prompted as much by the existence of manuscript variants as by differences between the Hebrew and LXX texts. Their concern was brought into clear focus as a result of controversy with the Christians, which made it important for them to have a standard Biblical text not merely as an assured basis for theological polemic but also for the discovery of the divine will as revealed in the very words of the Scriptures themselves.

During the second century the movement for establishing an authoritative text of the Hebrew Bible gained momentum, largely through the enthusiasm of the notorious anti-Christian Rabbi Aqiba (d. *ca.* A.D. 132). More than his contemporaries he realized how important the existence of a fixed text of Scripture was for Jewish apologetics, as well as for Halakic and Haggadic exegesis. To him was credited the saying that "the accurate transmission (*massoreth*)of the text is a fence for the Torah."[2] He developed the verbal exegetical method of his teacher

---

[1] *Qiddush.* 30a; B. J. Roberts, *The OT Text and Versions*, p. 31; G. L. Archer, *A Survey of OT Introduction*, pp. 54f.
[2] *Pirqe Abot* III, 17.

Nahum of Gimzo, with whom he studied for twenty-two years, and utilized it to discover hidden truths and spiritual meanings in apparently unimportant Hebrew particles. The elaborate methods of Rabbi Aqiba were reflected in the work of Aquila, a pagan from Sinope, who first embraced Christianity and then at a later time became a Jew. About A.D. 130 Aquila prepared a new literal Greek version of the standard Hebrew text, undertaken with only little regard for either Greek syntax or idiom. Quite apart from its literary deficiencies it incurred the anger of Christians because it departed from the tradition of the LXX in preferring "young woman" for "virgin" in Isaiah 7:14.

Even though there was most probably a standardization of the Hebrew text in the time of Rabbi Aqiba, the resultant Scriptures still contained many divergent readings, variations in orthography, and the like. The scribes who functioned at this time indicated by means of certain marks those passages in the text about whose soundness they were in doubt. At a fairly early period the text was divided into sections, either according to logical breaks in the narrative or on the basis of passages used for liturgical readings. The subdivision of Biblical books into verses took place under the scribes also, although the current chapter divisions are comparatively recent in origin.[3]

2. *The work of the Massoretes.* The work of the scribes came to an end about the beginning of the sixth century after Christ, and in their place arose the Massoretes. Although scholars have argued about the correct spelling,[4] the name itself went back to Mishnaic times[5] (as has been seen in Aqiba's epigram above) and carried with it the general sense of a transmitted tradition. The Massoretes were the custodians of the sacred traditional text, and were active from about A.D. 500 to 1000. They continued and completed the objectives of the *Sopherim* and the rabbis by definitely fixing a form of the Hebrew text, which subsequently became known as Massoretic. Accordingly they concerned themselves with the transmission of the consonantal text as they had received it, as well as with its pronunciation, on the basis that the text itself was inviolable and every consonant sacred.

---

[3] C. D. Ginsburg, *Introduction to the Massoretico-Critical Edition of the Hebrew Bible* (1897), p. 25; cf. G. F. Moore, *JBL*, XII (1893), pp. 73ff.

[4] For the oscillation between *maśśorāh* and *māśorāh* see Bergsträsser, *Hebräische Grammatik* (1918), p. 15, H. H. Rowley, *JTS*, XLII (1941), p. 26, B. J. Roberts, *The OT Text and Versions*, pp. 40ff., P. Kahle, *Historische Grammatik der Hebräischen Sprache* (ed. Bauer and Leander, 1922), pp. 71ff., H. L. Strack, *Realencyklopädie für protestantische Theologie und Kirche* (1896-1909), XII, pp. 393ff., H. Wheeler Robinson, *The Bible in its Ancient and English Versions* (1940), pp. 26ff.

[5] *Sheqal.* VI, 1; *Pirqe Ab.* I, 1; III, 14.

The detailed statistical work that the Massoretes undertook on each book included the counting of verses, words, and letters, establishing the middle of a book (a procedure which was useful in the case of bifid, or two-part, compositions), noting peculiarities of style, and other similar matters. This information was included in the *Massorah finalis* or concluding notes, with which each book of the Massoretic Bible concluded, and it is printed in this way in modern versions of the text. Some of the observations of the Massoretes which were connected with unusual transcriptional forms of certain letters of the alphabet may, as Pfeiffer has observed,[6] have been based upon critical tendencies. The Massoretes replaced the earlier oral transmission of such textual peculiarities by means of Massorah marginals, or marginal notes, written either on the side (*Massorah parva*) or in larger form in the top and bottom margins (*Massorah magna*) of the manuscript. The material of the concluding notes is similar in character to that of the marginal notes, and contains such information as the number of sections, verses, and words in the particular book, along with aids for memorizing these facts.

Since it was the avowed aim of the Massoretes to transmit the Hebrew text in a form unchanged from that which they had received, they left the sacred consonants entirely untouched. But where their training and experience persuaded them that corrections or improvements could be made to passages that contained corruptions, they recorded the amended form by means of a marginal note, a procedure that avoided any alteration of the inviolable written text. The preferred reading was known as *Q're*, meaning "that which is to be read," as contrasted with the sacred consonantal text, the *K'thibh* or "written" Scripture. The *Q're* on occasions may have constituted a genuine variant reading, since it is by no means unusual for copyists to supply such material in the process of their work. On the other hand there are many instances of Massoretic marginal readings that can only be described as conjectural. Although scholars differ in their computations, it has been estimated that there are about five thousand variations in the Massoretic text, of which some three thousand five hundred are orthographic.[7]

At first the Massorah was transmitted orally, but by the sixth century the activities of different Massoretic schools in endeavoring to fix the text and its pronunciation led to the custom of accentuation and vocalizing by means of vowel "points." Shortly after the beginning of the tenth century the Babylonian and Palestinian systems of placing the vowels above and between the consonants gave way to the Tiberian method of placing the vowel points under the Hebrew consonants (with the excep-

[6] *PIOT*, p. 83; cf. K. Albrecht, ZAW, XXXIX (1921), pp. 160ff.
[7] *PIOT*, p. 93.

tion of one vowel sign).[8] The latter system, which was adopted by the western Massoretes, was an elaborately designed and carefully regulated method, which in certain instances required that the conditional pronunciation of specific words be corrected according to its rules.[9]

While the Tiberian vocalization is not infrequently considered to be characterized by a mechanical inertness, it should be remembered that some of its artificiality may have been occasioned by the work of subsequent grammarians, who subordinated the flexibility of the system familiar to the Massoretes of Tiberias to the interests of grammatical schematizing. The fact that there are evidences of numerous inconsistencies and irregularities in the pointing appears to indicate the existence of a degree of liberty that was lost when the Massoretic tradition came to an end in the twelfth century.

The western Massoretes did not exhibit complete harmony among themselves, however, and in the first half of the tenth century two principal Massoretic families flourished in Palestine, that of ben Asher and that of ben Naphtali. Each family prepared a standard copy of the Massoretic Bible, whose minor textual differences[10] have no bearing upon the meaning of the passages concerned. Five generations of the family of ben Asher worked on the Hebrew text,[11] of whom the most famous were ben Asher himself and his son Aaron. The former copied a codex of the prophets in A.D. 895, and furnished it with vowel points and a *Massorah*. This celebrated manuscript is now in the Qaraite synagogue in Cairo. Aaron ben Moshe ben Asher was responsible for providing the pointing and a *Massorah* for a complete Biblical codex written by an unknown Massorete at the beginning of the tenth century, a copy of which was kept in the Sephardic synagogue at Aleppo. A subsequent copy of the ben Asher text was made about A.D. 1010 in Cairo by Samuel ben Jacob, and this important manuscript of the whole Hebrew Bible is in Leningrad.

[8] On the contribution of the Babylonian and Palestinian schools, see Ginsburg, *op. cit.*, pp. 197ff.; P. E. Kahle, *Masoreten des Ostens* (1913), *Theologische Studien und Kritiken*, LXXXVIII (1915), pp. 399ff., *Masoreten des Westens* (1927), I, pp. 23ff., II (1930), pp. 66ff., ZAW, XLVI (1928), pp. 113ff., *Theologische Rundschau*, V (1933), pp. 227ff., *The Cairo Geniza* (1947), pp. 44ff.; R. Gordis, *The Biblical Text in the Making: A Study of the Kethib-Qere* (1937), pp. 70ff.; B. J. Roberts, *The OT Text and Versions*, pp. 53ff.

[9] On the problem of pronunciation, see Kahle, *Masoreten des Westens*, I, pp. 43ff.; W. E. Staples, *AJSL*, XLIV (1928), pp. 6ff.; A. Sperber, *HUCA*, XII-XIII (1937-1938), pp. 103ff.; Kahle, *The Cairo Geniza*, pp. 88ff.; E. F. Sutcliffe, *Biblica*, XXIX (1948), pp. 112ff.

[10] Ginsburg, *op. cit.*, pp. 241ff.; S. H. Blank, *HUCA*, VIII-IX (1931-1932), pp. 229ff.; Kahle, *Masoreten des Westens*, II, pp. 45ff.; L. Lipschütz, *Ben-Ascher—Ben-Naftali. Der Bibeltext der tiberienischen Masoreten* (1937).

[11] Kahle, *The Cairo Geniza*, p. 55; M. H. Goshen-Gottestein, *Biblical and Other Studies* (1963), pp. 80ff.

The family of ben Naphtali is not quite as well known, since the text that they sponsored did not gain particular favor, and is only preserved in part.[12] The Reuchlin codex of A.D. 1105 at Karlsruhe is one of the best representatives of the ben Naphtali approach to the problems of the Hebrew text. A major contribution to the virtual oblivion of their efforts was the decree of Maimonides (d. A.D. 1204) in the twelfth century that the text and vocalization of the ben Asher manuscripts were to be regarded as standard from that time on.

The ben Asher text, influenced by that of ben Naphtali, fixed the pronunciation more exactly by means of the accentual system, although it was unable to exclude completely certain foreign influences which affected the vocalization. This resulted in differences between the ben Asher manuscripts and what later came to be the official text of the Old Testament. It was only during the fourteenth century of our era that the process of mutual assimilation was completed.[13] Its result was the Hebrew *textus receptus* of the late Middle Ages, a text of mixed character that formed the basis of most manuscripts of the Hebrew Bible. It was found in the medieval rabbinic Bibles, which contained the Aramaic Targums and the commentaries of such authoritative rabbis as Kimchi, Rashi, Ibn Ezra, and others, in addition to the text.

The first printed editions[14] of parts of the Hebrew Bible were issued in 1477, perhaps at Bologna; the first complete Bible appeared in Soncino in 1488, followed three years later by a second in Naples, and in 1494 by a third in Brescia. The first Rabbinic Bible was produced by Felix Pratensis and published in Venice by Daniel Bomberg in 1516-1517. It served as the basis for the second Rabbinic Bible, the four-volume work of Jacob ben Chayyim in 1524-1525, also published by Bomberg. The importance of this work was recognized almost immediately, for it furnished a revised text based upon the study of earlier manuscripts and editions. Although the resultant text was decidedly eclectic in character, it was accepted as virtually standard and remained authoritative through the nineteenth century. Subsequent Rabbinic Bibles (published in Venice in 1546-48, 1568, and 1617-19) followed the ben Chayyim text, but the Buxtorf edition, published in Basel in 1611, as well as the one issued in 1618, contained a hybrid type of text based on ben Asher and the Complutensian Polyglot, which was issued under papal sanction at Complutum in 1514-1517.

The urge to draw upon texts that antedated that of ben Chayyim was evident in the first critical edition of the Bible issued in 1720 by J. H. Michaelis, who consulted manuscripts containing variants from the popularly accepted text. Collections of variants were made in 1776 by

---

12 D. R. Ap-Thomas, *A Primer of OT Text Criticism* (1947), p. 13.
13 O. Eissfeldt, *Einleitung in das AT* (1934), p. 706.
14 Cf. C. D. Ginsburg, *op. cit.*, pp. 779ff.

Kennicott, and in the eighteenth and nineteenth centuries by J. B. de Rossi, Baer and Delitzsch. In the twentieth century a critical text was issued by C. D. Ginsburg.[15] The textual revision by J. Athias and J. Leusden in 1661-67 of the manual edition of J. Buxtorf, published in 1611 and based upon the ben Chayyim and Complutensian Polyglot texts, was perpetuated in the widely circulated editions of A. Hahn (1832, 1833, 1868) and M. Letteris of Vienna (1852). The latter was adopted as its text by the British and Foreign Bible Society, who reprinted it from 1866 onwards. A nineteenth-century critical edition of the Old Testament text (which was never completed) was edited by Haupt and published in the United States.[16] It exhibited a variety of colors in its pages as a means of distinguishing the various literary sources that the proponents of the Graf-Wellhausen analytical method claimed to have isolated from the various books. The Hebrew text was printed in an unvocalized form, and was accompanied by critical notes.

The first two editions of the Kittel Hebrew Bible were based generally upon the ben Chayyim text, but furnished variant readings from the ancient versions along with some conjectural emendations.[17] In the third edition Paul Kahle printed the ben Asher text in its purest form, along with a critical apparatus giving variant readings.[18] This return to the ben Asher text was of great importance in the history of the study of the Massoretic tradition, and its validity was confirmed in the Snaith edition of the Hebrew Bible, about which more will be said subsequently.

3. *The Qumran texts.* Until the discovery of the Dead Sea Scrolls in 1947, the critical study of the Old Testament text was hampered by the fact that the earliest Hebrew manuscripts only went back to about A.D. 900.[19] The discovery in 1890 of a number of ancient manuscripts in the scroll-depository or *genizah* of the Old Synagogue in Cairo did not prove to be as significant as was first thought.[20] Some of the manuscripts recovered from this cache contained supralinear punctuation, but the high estimates of their value for the vocalized Massoretic text were diminished somewhat when it was discovered that there was a marked

---

[15] B. Kennicott, *Vetus Testamentum Hebraicum cum variis lectionibus*, 2 vols. (1776-78); J. B. de Rossi, *Variae lectiones Veteris Testamenti ex immensa manu scriptorum editorumque codicum congerie haustae*, 4 vols. (1784-88), *Scholia critica in Veteri Testamenti libros seu supplementa ad varias sacri textus lectiones* (1798); S. Baer and F. Delitzsch, *Textum Masoreticum accuratissime expressit e fontibus Masorae variae illustravit* (1869); C. D. Ginsburg, *The OT, Diligently Revised according to the Massorah and the Early Editions, With the Various Readings from Manuscripts and the Ancient Versions*, 4 vols. (1926).

[16] P. Haupt, *The Sacred Books of the OT* (1894-1904).

[17] R. Kittel, *Biblia Hebraica* (1906-12).

[18] R. Kittel-P. Kahle, *Biblia Hebraica* (1937).

[19] The most important are described by Ginsburg, *Introduction to the Massoretico-Critical Edition of the Hebrew Bible,* pp. 469ff.

[20] Cf. P. E. Kahle, *The Cairo Geniza,* pp. 1ff.

lack of consistency in vocalization. This factor, as well as the almost complete absence of variation from the traditional consonantal text, showed that at the time the manuscripts were written the vocalization was of secondary importance to the accurate transmission of the text. Some of the Biblical manuscripts may date from a little earlier than the ninth century although it is far from easy to establish a date for many of the scrolls.[21]

So bleak were the prospects of getting any nearer to the original Hebrew autographs that F. G. Kenyon wrote in 1939:

> There is, indeed, no probability that we shall ever find manuscripts of the Hebrew text going back to a period before the formation of the text which we know as Massoretic.[22]

This discouraging prospect was changed dramatically by the unexpected discovery of the scrolls in the Qumran caves. When arguments concerning the authenticity and date of the materials had subsided, it became obvious that the Biblical scrolls and fragments had at one blow advanced the extant textual sources by a millennium, and as such made the manuscripts of priceless value both for the textual critic and the palaeographer.[23] The identity of the sect that had preserved this material became somewhat less of a problem when it was found that a mutilated manuscript from 4Q had affinities with an ancient Jewish work known as the Zadokite Document, dated between the tenth and twelfth centuries after Christ, and first discovered in the *genizah* of the Old Synagogue at Cairo in 1876.

The Biblical manuscripts from Qumran have unquestionably confirmed the general tradition regarding the tremendous care exercised in the transmission of the Hebrew Scriptures, and have made it evident that much more respect must be accorded to the Massoretic text than had previously been the case in some quarters. Early studies of the Qumran scrolls showed that they followed the tradition of the Massoretes more consistently than that of the LXX Greek,[24] and contained reflections of ancient sources in the matter of spelling and name-forms.[25]

---

[21] For arguments against dating any manuscripts earlier than about the first half of the ninth century see J. L. Teicher, *JJS*, I (1949), pp. 156ff., II (1950), pp. 17ff.

[22] F. G. Kenyon, *Our Bible and the Ancient Manuscripts* (1939), p. 48.

[23] Cf. S. A. Birnbaum, *The Qumrân (Dead Sea) Scrolls and Palaeography* (1952).

[24] Cf. C. Kuhl, *VT*, II (1952), pp. 307ff.; R. Barthélemy, *RB*, LX (1953), pp. 18ff.; K. Elliger, *Studien zum Habakuk-Kommentar vom Toten Meer* (1953), pp. 78ff.; F. M. Cross, *BASOR*, No. 132 (1953), pp. 15ff.; R. de Vaux, *RB*, LX (1953), pp. 268ff.; P. Kahle, *Theologische Literaturzeitung*, LXXIX (1954), pp. 82ff.; J. Muilenburg, *BASOR*, No. 135 (1954), p. 32; S. Loewinger, *VT*, IV (1954), pp. 155ff.; M. Burrows, *The Dead Sea Scrolls* (1955), pp. 304ff.

[25] Cf. M. Burrows, *JBL*, LXVIII (1949), pp. 204ff.; D. Beegle, *BASOR*, No. 123 (1951), pp. 26ff. For a study of superior readings in 1QIsa^a, see W. H. Brownlee, *The Meaning of the Qumrân Scrolls for the Bible* (1964), pp. 216ff.

The orthography of the large Isaiah scroll (1QIsaᵃ) has certain phonetic characteristics that are less prominent in the Massoretic text, and point to some degree of deviation from the tradition of the immediate pre-Christian period. Compared with the received text it is particularly marked by *scriptio plena* forms, by the full suffix endings of the second- and third-person masculine plural and the second-person masculine singular, and also in certain verbal forms. While some scribal corrections are noticeable in the scroll, they had the effect of bringing the text, rather than the spelling of particular words, into line with the Massoretic tradition, although not uniformly so.

It appears that 1QIsaᵃ furnished a contemporary phonetic spelling designed to make the reading of the Hebrew text considerably easier without at the same time actually altering the time-honored pronunciation. This contrasted with the procedures adopted in the fragmentary Sukenik scroll (1QIsaᵇ), which followed the older form of spelling employed prior to the destruction of the Second Temple. There are numerous textual divergences in 1QIsaᵃ from the Massoretic tradition, and while some may perhaps constitute improvements upon the *textus receptus*, others are quite clearly the result of textual error and corruption.[26] Of the thirteen readings adopted in the RSV on the basis of the text of 1QIsaᵃ, five of them are entirely without support from other ancient versions. The 1QIsaᵇ scroll contained a few readings that disagreed with the Massoretic text, and it is interesting to note that two of them (1QIsaᵇ 53:11, 12) reinforce the LXX tradition as against that of the Massoretes. Even more notable is the fact that 1QIsaᵃ also followed the reading preserved by the LXX in both these passages, since such a circumstance might well point to the possibility of error in the transmission of the Massoretic text itself. Apart from the two instances mentioned above there are nine other textual divergences in 1QIsaᵇ, all of which appear capable of explanation on grounds other than that they constitute genuine variants. The list collated by Loewinger[27] contained about three hundred alleged divergences, but most of these were concerned with the insertion of the consonants (ו) and (י), a phenomenon that has already been noticed in connection with some of the manuscripts from the Cairo *genizah*.

Quite aside from their importance in reflecting the transitional phases of Hebrew orthography,[28] the Qumran Biblical scrolls are of great value for indicating how Hebrew was pronounced just prior to the Christian era. This has been a matter of considerable discussion in scholarly

[26] Cf. M. Burrows, *BASOR*, No. 111 (1948), pp. 16ff., No. 113 (1949), pp. 24ff.
[27] S. Loewinger, *VT*, IV (1954), pp. 155ff.
[28] Cf. M. Burrows, *The Dead Sea Scrolls*, pp. 109ff.

218

circles,[29] since nobody can be absolutely certain as to precisely how the various tongues of antiquity were enunciated, and any information that contributes to the elucidation of this matter is certainly welcome. In another direction the scrolls have demonstrated the incorrectness of those views, long current in scholarly circles, which maintained that Hebrew had become a dead language prior to the second century B.C., since the manuscripts show conclusively that Hebrew persisted in some areas as a living language, despite the fact that most Palestinian Jews spoke Aramaic in one dialect form or another.[30]

Earlier studies in the relationship between the Hebrew text and the LXX[31] received considerable stimulation from the discoveries at Qumran,[32] particularly when fragments of 1 Samuel recovered from 4Q showed that the manuscript represented the same general tradition as that of the Hebrew text underlying the LXX version.[33] The divergences from both the Massoretic and Greek texts indicated that the fragments preserved a number of original readings that were not represented in either the Massoretic or Greek traditions.[34] Thus the 1 Samuel text from 4Q contained the phrase, "he shall become a *nazir* for ever" in 1 Samuel 1:22, a clause that had been lost to both the Hebrew and the Greek by haplography, a form of scribal omission common in antiquity in which a letter, syllable, or word is written only once when it should be written more than once. Such material is of immense importance for the history of the Old Testament text, since it points to a stage of development prior to the standardization of the literary tradition.

From the evidence presented by the Qumran discoveries it appears that there were at least three distinct types of Biblical text in circulation among the Jews of the Second Commonwealth.[35] This development,

---

[29] Cf. B. J. Roberts, *The OT Text and Versions*, pp. 47ff.; M. L. Margolis, *AJSL*, XXVI (1910), pp. 62ff.; E. A. Speiser, *JQR*, XVI (1925-26), pp. 343ff., XXIII (1932-3), pp. 233ff., XXIV (1933-4), pp. 9ff.; E. Brønno, *Studien über hebraische Morphologie und Vokalismus auf Grundlage der Mercatischen Fragmente der zweiten Kolumne der Hexapla des Origenes* (1943); P. E. Kahle, *The Cairo Geniza*, pp. 86f.

[30] Cf. M. Black, *NT Studies*, III (1957), pp. 305ff.

[31] Cf. J. Fischer, *Zur LXX Vorlage im Pentateuch* (1926); G. Bertram, *Theologische Rundschau*, III (1931), pp. 283ff., X (1938), pp. 69ff., 133ff.; F. X. Wutz, *Systematische Wege von der LXX zum hebräischen Urtext* (1937); J. Ziegler, *ZAW*, LIX (1944), pp. 107ff.; H. M. Orlinsky in H. R. Willoughby (ed.), *The Study of the Bible Today and Tomorrow* (1947), pp. 144ff.; I. L. Seeligmann, *The LXX Version of Isaiah* (1948); P. Katz, *Theologische Zeitschrift*, V (1949), pp. 1ff.

[32] Cf. D. Barthélemy, *RB*, LX (1953), pp. 18ff.; P. Kahle, *Theologische Literaturzeitung*, LXXIX (1954), pp. 82ff.; H. S. Gehman, *VT*, III (1953), pp. 141ff., IV (1954), pp. 337ff.; J. W. Wevers, *Theologische Rundschau*, XXII (1954), pp. 85ff., 171ff.

[33] F. M. Cross, *BASOR*, No. 132 (1953), pp. 15ff.

[34] Cf. J. M. Allegro, *The Dead Sea Scrolls* (1956), pp. 57ff.

[35] Cf. W. F. Albright, *Samuel and the Beginnings of the Prophetic Movement* (1961), p. 11.

which already has done much to shake the foundations of traditional literary criticism, depending as it did upon a standard "fixed" text, has made it clear that the Massoretic form was representative of only one body of Hebrew literary tradition. Even the Torah existed in a number of textual forms, contrary to the views held by some scholars of an earlier generation, as has been demonstrated conclusively by the fragments of the Pentateuch recovered from 4Q.[36]

B. THE RESTORATION OF THE HEBREW TEXT

1. The Samaritan Pentateuch. In addition to the Qumran scrolls and fragments, valuable as they are, other sources are also available for the task of restoring the text of the Old Testament. Of great importance in this respect is the Samaritan Pentateuch, which is unquestionably derived from a very ancient textual source. The Samaritans were regarded by the Jews as the descendants of Mesopotamian expatriates whom Sargon had settled in and around Samaria after the collapse of the northern kingdom in 722 B.C. (2 Kgs. 17:24ff.). Other colonists were subsequently introduced to the community by Esarhaddon and Ashurbanipal (cf. Ez. 4:2, 10). Whatever knowledge of Judaism they possessed was dismissed by the Jews as being rather coincidental and certainly superficial, and in consequence they were regarded as being at best only one degree removed from the Gentiles. The Samaritans themselves held quite a different theory of their origins, tracing their descent from those Israelites who had remained loyal to God when the Ark of the Covenant was deposited at the rival shrine of Shiloh (Judg. 18:1) instead of being placed on Mount Gerizim, which they claimed was its true location.[37] The infamy of constructing a second temple on an incorrect site was perpetrated by Ezra, who in the Samaritan view falsified the sacred text and thereby persuaded the returning exiles to erect the second temple in Judaea.

Quite obviously both views have elements in their favor. The Biblical account of the exchange of population after the fall of Samaria is supported in its general content by the Assyrian annals,[38] although it is quite probable that the time sequences indicated in 2 Kings have been compressed somewhat as the narrative now stands. In point of fact the colonization seems to have taken place over a number of years and under successive Assyrian rulers. Thus the Hamathites were probably only transported to Samaria after Sargon had suppressed an uprising in Hamath in 721 B.C., while the Cutheans may well have arrived in Samaria under Ashurbanipal rather than under Shalmaneser V.

[36] F. M. Cross, *BASOR*, No. 141 (1956), pp. 9ff.
[37] Cf. T. H. Gaster, *IDB*, IV, p. 191; J. Macdonald, *The Theology of the Samaritans* (1964), p. 17.
[38] *ARAB*, II, sect. 55.

Against this it should be pointed out that there is much to support the Samaritan claim to be an ancient Jewish sect, despite the fact that their testimony to this effect frequently appeared in an exaggerated form. Whereas Sargon only displaced 27,290 people, a contemporary record from Hebrew sources (2 Kgs. 15:19)[39] placed the number of wealthy landowners at 60,000, while the Chronicler (2 Chron. 34:9) spoke of a "remnant of Israel" still resident in Ephraim and Manasseh about a century later, in the period of Josiah (640-609 B.C.). This would seem to imply that on the fall of Samaria the artisans and peasants were left behind, and it was with these that the Mesopotamian immigrants evidently intermarried to produce the mixed population that subsequently took the name of Samaritans. On such a view, therefore, the enmity between the Jews and the Samaritans which became so marked at a later period was actually nothing more than a perpetuation of the ancient animosity which had existed between Judah and Israel.

As Gordon has shown,[40] there is considerable evidence for the theory that the principal shrine for Hebrew worship should have been located in Samaritan territory rather than in Judaea. Joshua 8:30ff.[41] records that after the fall of Ai, Joshua erected a shrine on Mount Ebal, and at its consecration one half of the people assembled nearby while the other half gathered on the twin peak of Mount Gerizim, which stood at the other side of a narrow pass. It is significant to realize that the shrine that Joshua built on Mount Ebal was the only one to be erected in accordance with the specific instructions of Moses (Deut. 27:4). The importance of the site may be adjudged from the order which Moses gave that the Law should be inscribed upon the stones of the altar there (Deut. 27:8), and that the penalties which would follow breaches of the Law should be proclaimed solemnly from the slopes of Mount Ebal (Deut. 11:29; 27:13; Josh. 8:33f.). It appears probable that Moses intended the center of Hebrew devotion to be located on Mount Gerizim, as the Samaritans insisted, and not at Jerusalem, which was a Jebusite stronghold until the time of David. As a matter of record, the capital of the united nation was chosen with political rather than religious considerations in view, while the Temple itself was an adjunct to the royal palace, and not in itself a primary structure.

Despite their own traditions involving Mount Gerizim and the first return from exile, the Samaritans offered to assist in rebuilding the post-exilic Temple in Jerusalem (Ez. 4:2). However, these "adversaries of Judah and Benjamin" were rebuffed by Zerubbabel; and with the coming of Ezra and Nehemiah the tensions increased considerably. The Samaritans, being of mixed ancestry, felt the weight of the religious

---

[39] Cf. R. Brinker, *The Influence of Sanctuaries in Early Israel* (1946), p. 214.
[40] *IOTT*, pp. 132f.
[41] Cf. G. F. Moore, *Judaism* (1927), I, pp. 25f.

reforms under Ezra; and the situation reached a climax when Nehemiah expelled the grandson of the High Priest, who had married the daughter of Sanballat (Neh. 13:8, 28, 30).[42] Josephus recounts a similar incident, making Sanballat responsible for the construction of the Samaritan temple on Mount Gerizim.[43] Sanballat was one of the chief opponents of Nehemiah, and according to the Elephantine papyri was the governor of Samaria in 407 B.C. If Josephus' story is true (a circumstance which is discounted by most modern scholars),[44] it may either be a distinct though similar narrative,[45] or the result of misunderstanding on the part of Josephus of several of the details, which appears more likely. However, he was doubtless correct in dating the construction of the Samaritan temple about 330 B.C.[46]

The Samaritans had their own version of the Hebrew Pentateuch, the only canonical material that they acknowledged, which they regarded as contemporary with the origins of the sect itself. Their text was independent of Jewish tradition. From the Judaistic point of view it could be thought most probably to have arisen with the return of a deported Hebrew priest whose task was to instruct the newly established inhabitants of Samaria in the Law of God, after a plague of lions had terrorized them (2 Kgs. 17:26ff.). The Samaritans' claim that their oldest Pentateuchal manuscript goes back to Abishua, the great-grandson of Aaron (1 Chron. 6:3f.), is obviously exaggerated; but the canon of the Samaritan Pentateuch long antedated the schism at the time of Nehemiah, since it constituted the Bible of the Samaritan community both before and after that period.[47]

The conservative nature of the group, combined with the tenacity with which they adhered to their particular theological standpoint,[48] resulted in the preservation of the contents of their Bible very much as it was from the beginning. Since the Samaritan community, of which a few

[42] For the continuing relations between Jews and Samaritans see J. A. Montgomery, *The Samaritans* (1907), pp. 71ff.; cf. M. H. Segal, *Asaf Anniversary Volume* (1953), p. 412.

[43] *AJ*, XI, 7, 2; XI, 8, 2ff. Cf. H. H. Rowley, *BJRL*, XXXVIII (1956), pp. 166ff.

[44] H. Willrich, *Juden und Greichen vor der makkabäischen Erhebung* (1895), p. 6; A. H. Sayce, *HDB*, IV, p. 391; F. Vigouroux, *Dictionnaire de la Bible* (1912), V, col. 1443; G. F. Moore, *Judaism*, I, p. 24; E. Sellin, *Geschichte des israelitisch-jüdischen Volkes* (1932), II, p. 169; M. Noth, *The History of Israel* (1960), p. 354.

[45] The view that there were two Sanballats was supported, among others, by H. Petermann in J. J. Herzog (ed.), *Real-encyclopädie für protestantische Theologie und Kirche* (1860), XIII, p. 366; W. F. Albright, *JBL*, XLI (1920), p. 122; M. Gaster, *The Samaritans: Their History, Doctrines and Literature* (1925), p. 30; C. C. Torrey, *The Second Isaiah* (1928), pp. 457f., *JBL*, XLVII (1928), pp. 380ff.; W. F. Lofthouse, *Israel after the Exile* (1928), pp. 33, 235f.

[46] Cf. L. E. Browne, *Ezekiel and Alexander* (1952), pp. 3, 22ff.

[47] Roberts, *The OT Text and Versions*, p. 188.

[48] Cf. J. Macdonald, *The Theology of the Samaritans* (1963), pp. 40ff.

families still survive in the neighborhood of Nablus, was neither large nor widely dispersed, the possibility of the incidence of textual corruptions and recensional divergences was always at a minimum. Thus, aside from deliberate alterations to the archetypal text, the Samaritan Pentateuch bears witness to one of the ancient text-forms of the Hebrew Pentateuch, which was current at least as early as the fifth century B.C., and which may possibly go back as far as the period of the undivided monarchy.

There is naturally considerable doubt about who was responsible for modifying the text of the Hebrew Pentateuch upon which the Samaritans drew for their belief that divine worship should be held on Mount Gerizim alone, since there are evidences that a similar tradition among the Hebrews themselves was subsequently expunged.[49] However, in other respects it is abundantly clear that the Samaritan scribes altered the text of the Pentateuch to suit their own historical and theological interests. In order to enhance the prestige of Mount Gerizim, they added a lengthy interpolation after the Decalogue in Exodus 20:17 and Deuteronomy 5:21, consisting in the main of material from Deuteronomy 11:29f. and 27:2-7, in which "Mount Gerizim" was substituted for "Mount Ebal." Disregarding geographical considerations the Samaritans changed the reference in Deuteronomy 11:30 from "over against Gilgal" to "over against Shechem." Dogmatic interests were responsible for the alteration of the familiar Deuteronomic phrase "the place which the Lord your God will choose" so that the verb read "has chosen," a device achieved by the omission of the initial consonant.[50] Other changes were orthographic and grammatical and did not affect the meaning of the words, such as the use of the *matres lectionis* and the elimination of some unusual constructions and anthropomorphisms.

The antiquity of the archetype appears evident from the confusion found in the oldest extant manuscript between the consonants ר and ד, and also between the letters מ and נ, a situation that would normally not have arisen in a post-exilic archaizing type of script. Confusion of this sort is much more likely to have occurred in the very early angular Sidonian characters, in the letter-forms of the Moabite Stone, or in the Siloam inscription from the time of Hezekiah. Word-dividers in the Samaritan Pentateuch were of a kind commonly employed in early Aramaic, Moabite, and Hebrew inscriptions, which points to an early date for the prototypal manuscript. The Samaritans evidently did not enunciate their gutturals. This may constitute a dialectical peculiarity indicating that their pronunciation dated from the time of Ahab and his successors in Israel, when the non-guttural Phoenician was popular in

---

49 Cf. E. Meyer, *Die Israeliten und ihre Nachbarstämme* (1906), pp. 543ff.; C. C. Torrey, *Ezra Studies* (1910), pp. 321ff.; G. M. Mackie, *HDB*, II, pp. 160f.
50 *PIOT*, p. 102; E. König, *HDB*, V, p. 70.

the northern kingdom[51] as opposed to the Judaean dialect preserved in the Massoretic text. According to some estimates the fixation of the Samaritan Pentateuch in its ornate archaizing script took place in the first century B.C., [52] but Greenberg, among others, preferred a date in the fourth century B.C.[53] The style of the letters is akin to Palaeo-Hebrew script, and the extant manuscripts of the Samaritan Pentateuch show that this ancient version possessed a developed vocalization and an unusual form of paragraph division.[54]

Although there are some indications of a process of textual refinement, it seems reasonably clear that the Samaritans did not possess a body of professional scribes as such at any given period in antiquity. This fact is apparent from the nature of the variations, which are hardly compatible with serious textual study. According to the estimate of Kahle, the Samaritan Pentateuch differed from the Massoretic text in some 6,000 instances, and of these it agreed with the LXX as against the Massoretic text in 1,900 occurrences.[55] Whether the Samaritan Pentateuch has preserved a better reading than the Massoretic text in all cases is very doubtful, even though Kahle was of the opinion that the Samaritan version constituted the best-preserved text of the Hebrew Pentateuch.[56] Probably the most assured readings are those in which the Samaritan Pentateuch is supported by the LXX and by the Greek text underlying certain New Testament passages (Acts 7:4, 32; Heb. 9:3, 4).[57]

As has been noted above, many of the changes in the text of the Samaritan Pentateuch are either willful, accidental, or the product of a misunderstanding or ignorance of grammar and syntax. Of a rather different nature is the tradition concerning the chronology of the genealogies in Genesis, particularly chapters 5 and 11, where the Samaritan Pentateuch presents a record that is independent of both the Massoretic text and the LXX. It would seem that each one of these three texts represents a different recension of the original Hebrew, and at present there is no means of determining which one of the three is either original or correct. Josephus appeared to prefer the LXX chronology

[51] Cf. A. Sperber, *HUCA*, XII-XIII (1937-38), pp. 151f.

[52] *FSAC*, pp. 345f.; F. M. Cross, *The Ancient Library of Qumran and Modern Biblical Studies* (1961), p. 172.

[53] M. Greenberg, *JAOS*, LXXVI (1956), pp. 161ff. Cf. B. D. Eerdmans, *The Religion of Israel*, p. 236.

[54] Cf. E. Robertson, *Catalogue of the Samaritan Manuscripts in the John Rylands Library at Manchester* (1938), cols. xxi and following; cf. his *Notes and Extracts from the Semitic Manuscripts in the John Rylands Library, III. Samaritan Pentateuch Manuscripts* (1937).

[55] P. E. Kahle, *Theologische Studien und Kritiken*, LXXXVIII (1915), pp. 399ff.; cf. A. Sperber, *HUCA*, XIV (1939), pp. 161ff.

[56] P. E. Kahle in H. Bauer and P. Leander, *Historische Grammatik der Hebräischen Sprache*, p. 73.

[57] Cf. P. E. Kahle, *The Cairo Geniza*, pp. 144ff.

over that of the Massoretic text, while the Samaritan form was adopted by the *Book of Jubilees* and in Acts 7. The opinion that all three texts were in circulation among the Jews during the pre-Christian period has received support from the Qumran discoveries. Each one may have represented the tradition of some specific locality or scribal school. The vitality and persistence of the Samaritan version was emphasized by the recovery from the caves of the Wadi Qumran of a fragment of Exodus, in which the Samaritan text was written in Hebrew script.[58]

While the peculiar readings of the Samaritan Pentateuch can usually be accounted for by scholars, its agreements with the LXX against the Massoretic text are more difficult to explain. It seems quite probable that both the Samaritan Pentateuch and the LXX reached back to a Hebrew textual tradition that differed from that of the Massoretes in significant areas, since in those instances where the Samaritan Pentateuch and the LXX coincide, the text is usually preferable to that preserved by the Massoretes. A Greek translation of the Samaritan Pentateuch, known as the *Samaritikon*, was cited by Origen in his *Hexapla*, and it is now known that this translation was made from the Samaritan text by translators who were familiar with the text of the LXX and even employed it on occasions.[59] This material may perhaps constitute the source of some of the readings common to the Samaritan Pentateuch and the LXX, though in general it must be remarked, as Kenyon has observed,[60] that there is no satisfactory proof that either the LXX or the Samaritan Pentateuch was corrected from the other; thus, their independent evidence is extremely difficult to explain except, perhaps, on the basis of a Hebrew textual tradition or traditions other than that of the Massoretes. It may be that when corrections to the Hebrew and Samaritan Pentateuchs had to be made, an Aramaic targum was employed for the purpose,[61] due to the close similarity between the Samaritan dialect and the Aramaic language. But this suggestion too is beset with problems, for there are considerable internal differences between all known manuscripts of the Samaritan-Aramaic targum as well as divergent views regarding its origin.[62]

Quite aside from other considerations, there are numerous traces in the LXX of the influence of the Aramaic targums, making the problem of the agreements between the Samaritan Pentateuch and the LXX one of considerable complexity. It seems clear that, despite the antiquity of the archetype and the attempts of certain modern scholars to reinstate the

[58] Cf. P. W. Skehan, *JBL*, LXXIV (1955), pp. 182ff.; J. M. Allegro, *The Dead Sea Scrolls*, pp. 68f. and pl. 23.

[59] Roberts, *The OT Text and Versions*, pp. 194f.

[60] *Our Bible and the Ancient Manuscripts*, p. 51.

[61] Cf. L. Goldberg, *Das Samaritanische Pentateuchtargum, eine Untersuchung, seine handschriftlichen Quellen* (1935).

[62] Cf. P. E. Kahle, *The Cairo Geniza*, pp. 36ff.

Samaritan Pentateuch,[63] the text of this version must be employed with great care in any attempt to improve upon the readings of the Massoretic text.[64]

2. Aramaic targums. Another valuable source for the study of the Hebrew Old Testament is furnished by the Aramaic targums. "Targum" is a Hebrew word, not occurring in the Old Testament, used to describe an Aramaic paraphrase or interpretative rendering of some portion of the Old Testament. The targums became necessary in the post-exilic period, when Aramaic gradually replaced Hebrew in importance as the spoken language. With the increasing value placed upon Scripture, particularly the Torah, as the basis of faith and a guide to proper living, it became urgent that the ancient writings be rendered in a way that the common people could understand. Thus there grew up in the synagogues the custom of furnishing an oral Aramaic translation as a companion to the portion which had been read from the Torah. Written translations were frowned upon, however, as the Jerusalem Talmud indicates,[65] in an evident desire to avoid any ostensible parity between the original text and a rendering into the vernacular.

This practice of paraphrastic explanation may possibly date back to the time of Nehemiah, since the Hebrew word פֹרָשׁ in Nehemiah 8:8, which is generally translated "clearly," more probably means "with interpretation," as the RSV footnote indicates. At all events, the custom was well established long before the birth of Jesus Christ. The official synagogue interpreter was known in the Jerusalem Talmud as *methurgeman,* and his paraphrase was designated *targum,* from the verb *targēm,*

---

[63] E.g. J. Bowman, *BJRL,* XXXIII (1951), pp. 211ff., XL (1958), pp. 298ff.; *Annual of Leeds University Oriental Society, I* (1959), pp. 43ff.; *PEQ,* XCI (1959), pp. 23ff.

[64] Enthusiasm greeted the first copy of the Samaritan Pentateuch that reached Europe in 1616 through Pietro della Valle, after its discovery in Damascus. Morinus' account of it (1623) claimed that it was in every way superior to the Massoretic text, and his opinion was quickly adopted by many scholars (cf. Kenyon, *Our Bible and the Ancient Manuscripts,* p. 50). The text was first printed in the *Paris Polyglot* (1632), after which it enjoyed considerable popularity, although dissident scholarly opinions were expressed with increasing frequency as to its value for textual criticism. In 1815 Gesenius (*De Pentateucho Samaritani origine, indole et auctoritate commentatio philologico critica*) demonstrated conclusively the superiority of the Massoretic text; subsequently the Samaritan Pentateuch began to decline in importance. Von Gall's five-volume critical edition of 1914-1918 (*Der Hebräische Pentateuch der Samaritaner*) was of limited value for scholarly purposes, as it drew upon only a comparatively small number of late medieval manuscripts. Earlier editions had been published by Walton in the *London Polyglot* (1675), Kennicott (*Vetus Testamentum Hebraicum cum variis lectionibus,* 2 vols., 1776-1780), and Blayney (*Pentateuchos Hebraeo-Samaritanus charactere Hebraeo-Chaldaico editus cura et studio Beniamini Blayney,* 1790). Some authorities have preferred Blayney's edition to that of Von Gall; cf. C. W. Dugmore, *JTS,* XXXVI (1935), pp. 131ff.

[65] *Megill.* IV, 1.

"to translate." While these renderings were oral, there are good grounds for holding that they soon acquired a degree of fixity, so that when they were ultimately committed to writing there was an adequate amount of traditional material available for the use of the Jewish scribes. Because the targums were originally oral, there is no single standard version, and this results in considerable divergences when targumic material is quoted by ancient authorities. It is thought probable that traces of early written targums can be seen to underlie the quotation from Psalm 22:2 in Matthew 27:46 and Mark 15:34,[66] as well as in one instance that occurs in Ephesians 4:8, corresponding to the targum of Psalm 68:19. The Babylonian Talmud mentions a targum to Job that was current in the days of Gamaliel I;[67] this is perhaps the same as that recovered from 11Q. Aside from this material from the first century after Christ, the earliest targums were probably committed to writing in the fifth century. At the present, targums exist for the Pentateuch, the Prophets, and part of the Writings, with the notable exceptions of Daniel, Ezra, and Nehemiah.

The most familiar of the three targums to the Pentateuch is the revised recension known as targum Onkelos, which is an Official Aramaic version of the Hebrew text. The identity of the author has been a matter of considerable discussion from early times,[68] with the Babylonian Talmud claiming him as a proselyte of the first century of our era,[69] whereas the Jerusalem Talmud confused him with Aquila,[70] the author of a Greek version of the Old Testament. Whatever his true identity, it seems probable that he produced his work about A.D. 145. This targum was conservative, adhering closely to the original Hebrew. Perhaps it was because of this very tendency that it acquired an authoritative position among contemporary Jews. The oldest targum to the Pentateuch is the so-called Palestinian Pentateuch targum, written in the kind of idiomatic Aramaic that was used in Palestine as early as the first century of the Christian era. It was formerly known only through fragments, but within recent years it has been identified in its entirety in a Vatican manuscript, Codex Neofiti I, an edition of which is in preparation at the time of writing.[71]

The official targum to the Prophets bore the name of Jonathan ben Uzziel, who, according to Jewish tradition, was a disciple of Hillel in the first century of the Christian era. Just as Onkelos furnished an official recension for the Pentateuch, Jonathan endeavored to produce a stand-

---

[66] Cf. A. Wikgren, *Journal of Religion*, XXIV (1944), pp. 89ff.
[67] *Shabb.* 115a.
[68] Cf. E. Silverstone, *Aquila and Onkelos* (1931), pp. 122ff.; Kahle, *The Cairo Geniza*, p. 117.
[69] *Megill.* III, 1.
[70] *Megill.* I, 11.
[71] Cf. A. D. Macho, *Estudios bíblicos*, XV (1956), pp. 446f.

ard form for the Prophets. He was more interpretative than Onkelos, however, although he was stricter in his rendering of the historical books of Joshua, Judges, Samuel, and Kings than of the Latter Prophets. Of some interest is the theological tendency to interpret certain passages messianically, particularly Isaiah 53.[72] One of the early Palestinian or "Jerusalem" targums to the Pentateuch was erroneously attributed during the fourteenth century to the activities of Jonathan, and is still frequently referred to as "pseudo-Jonathan." It was a rather fanciful composition which utilized the incidents contained in the original text as a vehicle for the folk legends which had grown up around the personages and circumstances of the narratives.

It is quite likely that, of the extant targums on the Hagiographa, none is older than the fifth century of the Christian era, and many of them are considerably later. Most probably they were originally composed for purposes other than public use in the synagogues or schools, since there was by that time no particular need for Aramaic translations.

Although the targums are useful both for the light which they shed upon traditional Jewish interpretations and the manner in which such activities were undertaken, they are of limited value for the textual critic because of their uncertain witness to the general Massoretic tradition. Unless the divergences of the targums are confirmed by readings from other versions it is frequently the case that they merely reflect targumic characteristics, and do not in fact testify to the presence of corruptions in the Hebrew text. Furthermore, there is no critical edition of the targums available,[73] a deficiency that constitutes a serious obstacle to textual study.

3. *The versions.* Since the Massoretic text cannot be regarded as the original form of the Hebrew, it is necessary to appeal to other sources in addition to the Hebrew variants in order to ascertain if possible what the original Hebrew text really read at disputed points. Valuable assistance in this direction is provided by versions, or translations from the Hebrew into another language. These are of great importance in any attempt to assess the nature of the Hebrew text, since they were often based upon traditions that were somewhat different from, and frequently more primitive than, the one preserved by the Massoretes.

a. The Septuagint. By far the most important version of the Old Testament is the LXX or Alexandrian Version, since it was associated by tradition with the activities of the Jewish community at Alexandria in Egypt. The origin of the name "Septuagint" (in full, "Interpretation of the Seventy Men [or Elders]") is unknown. Originally it applied only to the Pentateuch as rendered into Greek. A legendary explanation is found

[72] Cf. C. R. North, *The Suffering Servant in Deutero-Isaiah*, p. 11.
[73] For available editions see B. J. Roberts, *The OT Text and Versions*, pp. 212f.

in a letter written about 100 B.C., purporting to be from a certain Aristeas to his brother Philocrates during the reign of Ptolemy II Philadelphus (285-247 B.C.).[74] This document related how the monarch, having been persuaded by his librarian to secure a translation of the Hebrew prophecies for the royal library, appealed to the High Priest at Jerusalem, who responded by sending seventy-two elders to Alexandria with an official copy of the Law. Over a period of seventy-two days these men made a complete translation of the Torah, working independently during the day and comparing their results in the evening so as to arrive at a rendering that would be satisfactory to all concerned. This translation was then read to the Jewish community amid scenes of great enthusiasm, and was subsequently presented to the king. This story was embellished both by Jewish and Christian writers to the point where, in the fourth century, it was firmly believed that the translation comprised the entire Hebrew Bible, and that each scribe, working independently, had produced a rendering which was identical with those of his collaborators.[75] A fragment from the writings of an Alexandrian Jewish philosopher named Aristobulus, whose work is generally attributed to the period 170-150 B.C., was preserved by Eusebius and Clement of Alexandria, and dealt with the supposed origins of the LXX.[76] According to Aristobulus, portions of the Hebrew Scriptures relating to Israelite history had been translated into Greek at an earlier period, but by contrast the entire Torah was rendered into Greek in the reign of Ptolemy II Philadelphus through the efforts of Demetrius of Phalerum. Less plausibly, he claimed that Homer, Hesiod, Pythagoras, Socrates, and Plato were familiar with portions of the Pentateuch.

The most that can be said assuredly about these traditions is that about 250 B.C. the Torah was translated into Greek at Alexandria, either as a means of impressing and converting the heathen,[77] or of supplying the expatriate Jews in Alexandria with a Scriptural version in the vernacular[78] for purposes of worship or private study. This constituted the original LXX; the remainder was translated in piecemeal fashion. The canonical books had been rendered into Greek a little before 117 B.C., for they are referred to by the grandson of Ben Sira in the Prologue to Ecclesiasticus. The Apocrypha was completed at the beginning of the Christian era and interspersed among the canonical books. Finally the name "Septuagint" was extended to cover the entire corpus of translated material. This name, derived from the Latin *septuaginta*, meaning "sev-

---

[74] *APOT*, II, pp. 83ff.

[75] H. B. Swete, *An Introduction to the OT in Greek* (1900), pp. 13f.

[76] Eusebius, *Praep. Evang.* XIII, 12; Clement, *Strom.* I, 22, 148.

[77] Philo, *Vita Mosis*, II, 5f.; cf. J. Juster, *Les Juifs dans l'empire romain* (1914), I, p. 253.

[78] So F. Buhl, *Kanon und Text des AT* (1891), pp. 114f.; H. B. Swete, *An Introduction to the OT in Greek*, p. 19.

enty," hardly coincides with the tradition of seventy-two translators preserved in the *Letter of Aristeas*, and it may be that the term either arose or gained currency because of some popular association with the "seventy elders" of Exodus 24:1 and 9, with the seventy members of the Sanhedrin, or with the seventy apostles mentioned in the ministry of Christ (Lk. 10:1).[79]

While the evidence from Qumran[80] makes it obvious that the LXX had a long and involved prehistory, it seems unlikely that underlying the LXX there was a rendering of the Hebrew into Greek letters, as Wutz proposed.[81] Undoubtedly there were in existence transliterations of the Hebrew text into the Greek alphabet, analogous to the Samaritan Pentateuch, as an initial step towards helping Hellenistic Jews who could not follow the Hebrew script to understand the portions that were read aloud in the synagogues.[82] While the LXX does in fact employ Greek transliterations on occasions, particularly in the case of names, it is improbable that the LXX utilized such transcriptions to any significant extent. Thackeray suggested that the earliest portion of the Old Testament to be translated into Greek was the Torah, and that this was followed by Isaiah, parts of Samuel and Kings, the remainder of the Prophets, and finally by the Writings.[83] The balance of Samuel and Kings was thought to have been added by a later translator from Ephesus, whose Greek style resembled that of Theodotion.

Questions concerning the existence and nature of a "proto-LXX" have been raised by the fact that quotations from Greek sources in the New Testament writings and in the work of Josephus and Philo do not correspond verbally with the present LXX text.[84] This circumstance has been taken as implying that there were a number of early Greek texts in existence prior to the work of the LXX translators. Accordingly Kahle suggested that the *Letter of Aristeas* referred, not to a new translation, but to a revision of certain renderings already in existence in order to produce a standard Greek Bible for the benefit of Jews in the Hellenistic Diaspora.[85] Kahle styled this collection of renderings a "Greek targum," and pointed out the diversity of readings which it embraced. For him

[79] Cf. H. M. Orlinsky, *The Septuagint: The Oldest Translation of the Bible* (1949), p. 4.

[80] Cf. F. M. Cross, *BASOR*, No. 132 (1953), pp. 15ff., No. 141 (1956), pp. 9ff.; *IB*, XII (1957), pp. 655ff.

[81] Cf. F. X. Wutz, *ZAW*, XLIII (1925), pp. 115ff., *Die Psalmen textkritisch untersucht* (1925), *Die Transkriptionen von der Septuaginta bis zu Hieronymus* (1933), and *Systematische Wege von der LXX zum Hebräischen Urtext* (1937).

[82] H. M. Orlinsky, *JQR*, XXVII (1936-37), p. 140 n. 10.

[83] H. St. John Thackeray, *ISBE*, IV, pp. 2722ff. and *The Septuagint and Jewish Worship* (1921).

[84] For a survey of the problem see H. H. Rowley, *JQR*, XXXIII (1943-44), p. 497.

[85] Cf. Kahle, *The Cairo Geniza*, pp. 132ff.

the LXX as used by the Christian Church was not necessarily the one mentioned in the *Letter of Aristeas*, but was more probably one of the current translations into Greek, which the Christian Church ultimately adopted as its canonical Greek version of the Hebrew Old Testament. By this time the term "Septuagint" had been expanded to include the entire Old Testament and Apocrypha, whereas for Aristeas it had merely signified the Pentateuch. This view was developed by Sperber, who postulated the existence of a transitional period when Greek was used both for transcription and translation purposes to help the Hellenistic Jews of Egypt to read the Hebrew Scriptures.[86] This situation gave rise to sporadic attempts at translation, leading to the existence of at least two Greek renderings of the Old Testament which can be identified from quotations in the New Testament, whose writers regularly employed Greek versions instead of the Hebrew for their citations.

Although these theories may well throw important light upon the transmission of the text they are extremely difficult to demonstrate with facts, as Orlinsky has pointed out,[87] particularly where the postulate of at least two original and independent Greek renderings of the Hebrew Bible is concerned. Such arguments are rendered even less valid if, as some New Testament scholars suggest, it can be shown that many of the quotations in New Testament writings were derived originally from an Aramaic source or sources, or perhaps even from oral traditions, from memory, or from private translations. Again it should be observed that, while there are a few significant disagreements between manuscripts of the LXX, there are very many more agreements of such a character to indicate beyond reasonable doubt that the various manuscripts belong to the same family. Furthermore, the kind of variant to which Kahle appeals can more probably be accounted for as revisions of a basic LXX text than as remnants of rival translations or back-readings from New Testament authors.

It should be remembered, of course, that there is no definite proof that the early Christian Church ever regarded any particular Greek Old Testament text as standard,[88] and that, as the evidence from Qumran indicates, there was a good deal of freedom in the use of textual types during the immediate pre-Christian period. Yet in the days prior to Origen there was in existence a form of text which constitutes the LXX version, as made evident by the Chester Beatty papyri and the Scheide papyri.[89] While there are certain differences in New Testament usage, there is no doubt that of all the Greek versions the LXX was employed

---

[86] A. Sperber, *Orientalische Literaturzeitung*, XXXII (1929), cols. 533ff. and in *JBL*, LIX (1940), pp. 193ff.

[87] H. M. Orlinsky, *JBL*, LIX (1940), pp. 530f.

[88] B. J. Roberts, *IDB*, IV, p. 590; D. W. Gooding, *NBD*, pp. 1259f.

[89] Cf. Roberts, *The OT Text and Versions*, pp. 148f.

predominantly and that it enjoyed independent existence in the period just prior to the time of Christ.

The language of the LXX is by no means the normal Hellenistic Greek as represented by the papyri of Egypt and other sources, any more than is its counterpart in the New Testament. Even the most idiomatic renderings reflect certain obvious Hebraisms, and there are a great many passages which are little better than transliterations of the Hebrew. In numerous respects the Greek rendering of the Pentateuch is superior to the remainder of the work, and this may well indicate the degree of esteem in which the Pentateuch was held by the translators. Although the finished form of the Pentateuch exhibits a great many variations from the original, with some omissions and displacements in Exodus and Numbers, the parent LXX text corresponds largely to the Massoretic Hebrew. However, the divergence of the LXX text in some of the historical books, notably Samuel, as indicated by the fragments from Qumran,[90] points to the existence of a Hebrew text-type or types different from that of the Massoretes. This departure may have been encouraged by the fact that, outside the Pentateuch, some books appear to have been divided between two or more translators who were working simultaneously. Other books were translated at different times by persons who employed divergent methods and vocabulary; as a result, there is reasonably good *Koine* Greek in sections of Isaiah, Joshua, and 1 Maccabees, moderate Greek in Chronicles, the Psalter, Jeremiah, Ezekiel, the Minor Prophets, and parts of Kings, and very literalistic Greek in Judges, Ruth, the Song of Solomon, and some other sections of Kings. On occasions the translators showed no scruples about interpreting the text to make it conform to their own theological predilections, as with Judges 9:9, where the translation was altered in LXX Codex Vaticanus to enable men to "glorify God."

Wholesale adjustments are found in Jeremiah, where the LXX text was only about seven-eighths as long as that of the Hebrew, and in Job, where the LXX text was augmented from the version of Theodotion to correspond roughly to the length of the Hebrew. The text of Esther appears in two forms in the Greek Bible, one of which is the ordinary LXX and the other the recension of Lucian. Both of these contain interpolations which have no parallels in the Hebrew. The LXX translation of Daniel was so free that it was replaced about the first century of our era with a translation that is generally attributed to Theodotion, although it may well antedate him. The problem of the relationship between the LXX and the Hebrew text of Ezra, Nehemiah, and Chronicles is complicated by the presence of the apocryphal books of 1 and 2 Esdras. From these brief remarks it will be evident that the LXX as

---

[90] F. M. Cross, *BASOR*, No. 132 (1953), pp. 15ff.

a whole is of decidedly uneven quality, and although there are many instances in which it may well point to a more primitive reading than that contained in the Massoretic text, its use requires considerably more caution than might be apparent from the views of certain enthusiastic advocates of the LXX.

b. Other Greek versions. During the second century after Christ a few non-LXX Greek revisions of the Old Testament were undertaken in an attempt to reflect the contemporary Hebrew text. The first of these was Aquila's, produced about A.D. 130. It adhered firmly to the Massoretic tradition, and rejected in particular the witness of the LXX. Its author was a Hellenist who had become a convert to Judaism. His work was widely quoted by the patristic writers and also by some rabbinic authorities. Extant citations of his version were published from 1859,[91] augmented from palimpsests recovered from the *genizah* of the Old Synagogue in Cairo.[92] Owing to its extreme literalness and fidelity to the Massoretic text, this version met the need of the Greek-speaking Jews for a new Greek rendering of their Scriptures. Aquila translated the Hebrew with almost mechanical accuracy, and this procedure led to a version which was far removed from the Greek idiom. He was violently anti-Christian, and did not hesitate to render certain messianic passages in a manner widely different from that in the LXX, the treasured version of the Christian Church. In spite of this tendency, however, his fidelity to the Hebrew text won for his work the respect of such patristic authorities as Origen and Jerome. As may well be imagined, the translation was marked by many peculiarities, not least of which was the consistent imposition of Hebrew grammatical and syntactical structures upon the Greek. According to Reider, while Aquila followed the Massoretic text closely, he diverged from it on an average of once in three verses.[93] The identification of Aquila (who is not to be confused with the Aquila of Acts 18:2 *et al.*) with Onkelos (see above p. 227) is supported in part by marked resemblances between their translations.

Half a century later another rendering of the Old Testament in Greek was produced by a contemporary of Aquila named Theodotion, a proselyte who hailed from Asia Minor.[94] He used for his version a Hebrew text that was considerably closer to the Massoretic text than was the parent of the LXX, and as a result the book of Job exceeded the LXX rendering

---

[91] F. Field, *Origenis Hexaplorum quae supersunt; sive Veterum Interpretetum Graecorum in totum Veterum Testamentum Fragmenta* (2 vols., 1867-74).

[92] F. C. Burkitt, *Fragments of the Books of Kings According to the Translation of Aquila* (1897); C. F. Taylor, *Hebrew-Greek Cairo Genizah Palimpsests from the Taylor—Schechter Collections* (1901); cf. Kahle, *The Cairo Geniza*, p. 13.

[93] Cf. J. Reider, *JQR*, IV (1912-13), pp. 321ff., 577ff., VII (1915-16), pp. 287ff.

[94] For the priority of Theodotion over Aquila see H. M. Orlinsky, *JQR*, XXVI (1935-36), p. 143 n. 14.

233

by about one-sixth. His translation was more idiomatic than Aquila's, and was esteemed more highly by the Christians than by the Jews of that period. Theodotion's version of Daniel actually came to replace the old LXX rendering of that prophecy, a circumstance that is usually attributed to the influence of Origen.

A third Greek version dating from the end of the second century or the beginning of the third century A.D. was that made by Symmachus, who according to Christian tradition was a Jewish convert to Ebionite teaching. Fragments of this translation have survived in portions of the *Hexapla* and in the writings of patristic and rabbinic authors. Apparently the author made use of earlier Greek versions, but on the whole he exhibited a decided preference for the work of Aquila. He followed rabbinic exegetical customs in attempting to remove many of the Old Testament anthropomorphic expressions, and the result of his labors was an independent translation of the Old Testament into decidedly better Greek than that of either Aquila or Theodotion.

Manuscript discoveries in the Wadi Murabba'at caves have brought these versions into prominence again within recent years. Of particular interest was the recovery of a leather scroll in Greek containing fragments of the minor prophets Jonah, Micah, Nahum, Habakkuk, Zephaniah, and Zechariah.[95] Barthélemy dated the manuscript from the end of the first century after Christ, and found that it constituted a revision of the LXX from the pre-Christian era and was similar to that which formed the basis of the renderings by Aquila, Theodotion, and Symmachus. This scroll would thus indicate that in the second century of the Christian era there was current among both Christians and Jews a common textual form acceptable to both parties, which was itself a revision of the earlier LXX translation.[96]

Prior to the work of Origen, several Greek versions existed side by side, some of which are known only from fragments of the *Hexapla*.[97] This great work was compiled by Origen in an attempt to bring some sort of order to the rather chaotic textual situation of his day. His revision of the Greek Old Testament, which was completed by about A.D. 245, contained six parallel columns representing respectively the Massoretic text, the Hebrew text transliterated into Greek letters, the version of Aquila, the translation of Symmachus, his own revision of the LXX, and the translation of Theodotion. For the Psalter he also furnished the versions which he named *Quinta*, *Sexta*, and *Septima*, the first two of

---

[95] Cf. D. Barthélemy, *RB*, LX (1953), pp. 18ff., 85f.; P. E. Kahle, *Theologische Literaturzeitung*, LXXIX (1954), cols. 82ff.; J. M. Allegro, *The Dead Sea Scrolls*, pp. 178f. For a detailed refutation of the views of Kahle see Barthélemy, *Les Devanciers d'Aquila*, VT suppl. X (1963).

[96] B. J. Roberts, *IDB*, IV, p. 583.

[97] Cf. B. J. Roberts, *The OT Text and Versions*, p. 127.

which, according to Kahle,[98] he had discovered in Jewish *genizahs*. Taking the current Hebrew text as his basis, he proceeded with his revision by choosing from all the available Greek manuscripts those readings which accorded most closely with the Hebrew. Where his text was deficient in relationship to the Hebrew he inserted appropriate sections derived mainly from the version of Theodotion, and marked by critical signs. Those portions of his text containing readings that were absent from the Hebrew were retained, but were marked by means of other critical signs employed according to the usage of Aristarchus (third century B.C.). Finally, those passages in the Greek Bible that did not follow the order of the Hebrew[99] were rearranged so as to accord with the Massoretic pattern, and, incidentally, the corresponding columns of Aquila and Symmachus.

It is probable that the last four columns of the *Hexapla* were subsequently issued independently in a form known as the *Tetrapla*.[100] Since it lacked the Hebrew sections, it was a more manageable work. Against the view of Orlinsky that the *Tetrapla* was not a separate four-column work but only a variant designation of the *Hexapla*,[101] it should be noted that the text of the *Tetrapla* contained emended errors of translation and corrections of textual corruptions in the LXX,[102] which would indicate that it was a later work with, ostensibly, a separate existence.

By any standards the *Hexapla* was a monumental accomplishment. The original manuscripts, which were seldom copied owing to their size, were kept for safety in Caesarea, and were probably destroyed when that city was overrun by the Arabs in A.D. 638. The fifth column of the *Hexapla*—the LXX—was copied the most frequently of any, for it was highly esteemed from the beginning of the fourth century and given wide circulation in Palestine through Eusebius and Pamphilius.[103] Al-

---

[98] *The Cairo Geniza*, p. 164; cf. H. M. Orlinsky, *JQR*, XXVII (1936-37), pp. 137ff.

[99] E.g. Exod. 35-40; 1 Kgs. 4-11, 20-21; Jer. 25-50.

[100] Cf. Eusebius, *Hist. Eccl.*, VI, 16; *PIOT*, p. 109.

[101] *BA*, IX, No. 1 (1946), p. 27 n. 10.

[102] Cf. O. Procksch, *ZAW*, LIII (1935), pp. 240ff., LIV (1936), pp. 61ff.; O. Pretzl, *Byzantinische Zeitschrift*, XXX (1930), pp. 262ff.

[103] The Hexaplaric text of Genesis 31 to Judges 21, marked with the Aristarchean critical signs, was contained in the fourth/fifth-century Codex Colberto-Sarrauianus, parts of which are in Leningrad, Paris, and Leyden. Hexaplaric readings were also recorded as notes in the margins of Codex Marchalianus (sixth century) and Codex Coislinianus (seventh century) and in several cursives of the medieval period. Hexaplaric fragments were incorporated into the Sixtine edition of the Greek Bible by Petrus Morinus; see J. Reider, *JQR*, V (1913-14), p. 330. The same material was published by Drusius in 1622 and Lambertus Bos in 1709. A more comprehensive collection was made by de Montfaucon in *Origenis Hexaplorum quae supersunt, multis partibus auctiora quam a Flaminio Nobilio et Joanne Drusio edita fuerint* (vol. II, 1713); this was superseded by Field's *Origenis Hexaplorum quae supersunt; sive Veterum Interpretetum Graecorum in totum Veterum Tesamentum*

though Origen's recension of the LXX constituted a landmark in textual study, it did not dispossess other forms of the LXX text. In Syria and Asia Minor a recension prepared by the Antiochene presbyter Lucian of Samosata (d. A.D. 312) enjoyed great esteem for a considerable time. Lucian appears to have revised the Hexaplaric text at least in part by combining variants into conflated readings, substituting synonyms for certain LXX words, and imposing a more polished literary style on the LXX. While the resultant text of the Prophets was of generally poor quality, that of the historical books is of particular value, being frequently based upon a Hebrew text superior to the one preserved by the Massoretes. Paul de Lagarde edited what he believed to be something approximating to the Lucianic text of the LXX, and regarded his work as constituting a step further back into the involved history of the LXX.[104] However, he appears to have overlooked the possibility that Lucian may actually have possessed a type of text containing better Hebrew readings, or that he may have arrived at his renderings with the aid of an earlier non-LXX form of translation. Thus the Lucianic version may possibly be another Greek rendering of a variant Hebrew original, at least in part, and not a strict revision of the Alexandrian text as such.[105]

In Egypt a third recension was in common use, prepared by Hesychius of Alexandria (d. A.D. 311).[106] Although this revision is mentioned by Jerome in the *Prologus Galeatus*, little is known either about the reviser or the procedure upon which his work was based. Contrary to most scholars, Kahle and Sperber held that the texts of Lucian and Hesychius were not revisions of the LXX, but instead constituted independent translations.[107] Sperber also maintained that as late as the time of Origen there were two different translations of the Old Testament into Greek that were circulating separately and were known as "Septuaginta."[108] However, since the principal materials available for the reconstruction of the Lucian and Hesychian recensions are to be found mainly in

Fragmenta (2 vols., 1867-74), which, although restricted to poor copies and collations of manuscripts, was a work of great importance. The only remnants of a transmission of the *Hexapla* in manuscript form are the "Mercati fragments," which were discovered by Cardinal Mercati in Milan at the end of the nineteenth century in a palimpsest manuscript. It contained portions of the Psalter from the last five columns of the *Hexapla*. A representative portion of Psalm 45 (LXX) was published by Klostermann in 1896 (ZAW, XVI, pp. 334ff.; cf. Kahle, *The Cairo Geniza*, p. 88).

104 P. de Lagarde, *Librorum Veteris Testamenti canonicorum pars prior graece edita* (1883).

105 Cf. G. F. Moore, AJSL, XXIX (1913), pp. 37ff.

106 Cf. Eusebius, *Hist. Eccl.*, VIII, 13; A. Sperber, JBL, LIV (1935), pp. 73ff.

107 Kahle, *Theologische Studien und Kritiken*, LXXXVIII (1915), pp. 410ff. Sperber, JBL, LIV (1935), pp. 75ff.

108 JBL, LIX (1940), p. 279.

patristic citations, there would seem to be inadequate manuscript evidence for making too forthright a claim for these versions as independent renderings of the LXX.

Attempts at a critical reconstruction of the LXX, insofar as this is possible, are based upon manuscripts of the Greek Bible. A major classification of such material was begun by Rahlfs,[109] which was superior to its precursors, although it was not absolutely exhaustive. The earliest manuscript material is fragmentary, and consists of scraps of papyrus dated between the second and fourth centuries after Christ. One of the oldest extant LXX manuscript fragments is the Rylands papyrus, discovered in 1917 and published in 1936 as *John Rylands Library Papyrus Greek 458*.[110] It contained Deuteronomy 23:24—24:3; 25:1-3; 26:12, 17-19; 28:31-33, and was written in a fine book-hand of the second century B.C.[111] This text preceded the revisions of Aquila, Symmachus, and Theodotion by some three centuries, and the later recensions by five centuries. It is thus an extremely important witness to the nature of the early LXX text. Other valuable papyrological material includes the Chester Beatty papyri,[112] the Freer Greek manuscript at Washington, and the Berlin Genesis.[113] Of the great uncial manuscripts containing both the Old and New Testaments the most important is the fourth-century Codex Vaticanus, to which portions of the Scheide Biblical papyri are related textually.[114] Although it is by far the best extant copy of the LXX and constitutes the basic text of the editions of the Greek Bible currently in use, a study of the manuscript makes it clear that there is a striking lack of uniformity in the quality of the text itself. For Judges it furnished an Egyptian version made early in the fourth century,[115] while for Daniel, Ezra, Nehemiah, and Chronicles it followed the translation of Theodotion.[116] Though the text of Codex Vaticanus does not belong properly to the Hexaplaric recension, there are numerous instances in which it has obviously been corrected from it.[117] Another

[109] *Verzeichnis der griechischen Handschriften des Alten Testaments für das Septuaginta-Unternehmen aufgestellt* (1914).

[110] C. H. Roberts, *Two Biblical Papyri in the John Rylands Library, Manchester* (1936).

[111] F. G. Kenyon, *The Text of the Greek Bible* (1949 ed.), pp. 41f.

[112] F. G. Kenyon, *The Chester Beatty Biblical Papyri* (1933-7), fasc. i-vii, *Our Bible and the Ancient Manuscripts*, pp. 64ff.; A. C. Johnson, H. S. Gehmann, and E. H. Kase, *The John H. Scheide Biblical Papyri* (1938).

[113] H. A. Sanders and C. Schmidt, *The Minor Prophets in the Freer Collection and the Berlin Fragment of Genesis* (1927); H. A. Sanders, *Facsimile of the Washington Manuscript of the Minor Prophets in the Freer Collection* (1927).

[114] Cf. H. S. Gehmann, *JAOS*, LVIII (1938), pp. 92ff.; J. Ziegler, *ZAW*, LX (1945-8), pp. 76ff.

[115] G. F. Moore, *A Critical and Exegetical Commentary on the Book of Judges* (1903), p. xlv.

[116] C. C. Torrey, *Ezra Studies*, pp. 66ff.

[117] F. C. Burkitt, *JTS*, X (1909), p. 445.

important uncial from the fourth century is Codex Sinaiticus, discovered in 1844 by Tischendorf and ultimately purchased in 1933 from Russia by the British government.[118] Much of the Old Testament is missing from this manuscript, and according to Noth it may never have existed in a complete form.[119] Fragments of the Pentateuch are followed by portions of Chronicles, Ezra, Nehemiah, and several of the prophetical works. In general the text of Codex Sinaiticus is similar to that of Vaticanus, to which it is not greatly inferior.

A more complete uncial is that known as Codex Alexandrinus, an early fifth-century manuscript preserved in the British Museum. This uncial has far fewer gaps than Codex Sinaiticus, omitting in the main portions of Genesis, 1 Samuel, and the Psalter.[120] It exhibits an independent type of text that was revised according to the *Hexapla*, although there are some scholars who maintain that it represents a distinct translation of the LXX and not just a corrected form.[121] Another great uncial, the palimpsest known as Codex Ephraemi Rescriptus, now in Paris, was probably originally written in the fifth century, but only parts of the Old Testament have survived, amounting in all to some sixty-four leaves. Other uncial and minuscule codices contain only limited sections of Old Testament material.[122]

c. Latin versions. In any attempt to establish the text of the LXX it is important to utilize a number of other ancient versions from the early

[118] *The Mount Sinai Manuscript of the Bible* (1934). British Museum.
[119] *Die Welt des AT* (1940), p. 216.
[120] F. G. Kenyon, *The Text of the Greek Bible*, pp. 49, 82.
[121] Cf. A. Allgeier, *Die Chester Beatty Papyri zum Pentateuch* (1938), p. 35.
[122] For a history of the printed texts of the Greek Bible see H. B. Swete, *An Introduction to the OT in Greek*, pp. 171ff. Among these texts are the Complutensian Polyglot (1514-1517); the Aldine edition (1518-1519), based on manuscripts in Venice; the Sixtine edition (1587), based on Codex Vaticanus. This was reproduced substantially in the Walton *London Polyglot* (1654-1657), the *Vetus Testamentum Graecum Cum Variis Lectionibus* (ed. R. Holmes and J. Parsons, 5 vols., 1798-1827), the editions by Tischendorf from 1850 on, and in several others. J. E. Grabe published an edition of Codex Alexandrinus in Oxford between 1707 and 1720. Paul de Lagarde undertook a new edition of the LXX (1882), but this so-called "Göttingen Septuagint" was actually an attempt to restore the recension of Lucian in its original form. After Lagarde's death (1891), his work was carried on, with important modifications, by Rahlfs and his school at Göttingen. Seven volumes of this planned sixteen-volume work have appeared since 1926. Rahlfs' edition is based on that of Holmes and Parsons and the *Larger Cambridge Septuagint* (ed. A. E. Brooke, N. McLean, H. St. J. Thackeray, 1906ff.), both of which follow Codex Vaticanus, as did H. B. Swete's three-volume edition published between 1887 and 1907. Distinct from this project is Rahlfs' *Septuaginta* (2 vols., 1935), a convenient edition of the LXX whose value is somewhat limited by the eclectic nature of the text, which was based primarily upon Codices Vaticanus, Sinaiticus, and Alexandrinus, with selections from other sources provided in a small critical apparatus.

Christian period, which were translated from the Greek into a variety of European and Oriental languages in order to meet the needs of the inhabitants of countries where Greek was not spoken. One of the most prominent of these versions is the Old Latin, which originated with the work of Pope Victor (*ca.* A.D. 190), and was soon firmly established in North Africa with the writings of Tertullian (A.D. 160-230) at Carthage. In this region Latin supplanted Greek as the language of the Christian Church, as it did also in the northern provinces of Italy.[123] Presumably the first Latin translations of the LXX came into existence in the second half of the second century, although nothing is known about their origins. There are citations from these early Latin renderings in Tertullian and Cyprian (d. A.D. 258), although these differ in important areas. However, the first Latin translations of the LXX are of great significance because they go back to the text as it existed prior to the revisions of the third and fourth centuries, and therefore furnish valuable evidence for the reconstruction of the LXX text. Latin interpreters of the Greek were not wanting either in second-century southern Gaul or third-century Rome, and their activities led Augustine to complain about the "*infinita varietas*" of Latin translations and variant readings.[124]

The Old Latin or "Itala"[125] version of the Old Testament was probably made in Africa, and fragments of this material, recovered principally from patristic citations, were collected and published by Sabatier.[126] The Lyons manuscript of the Pentateuch was published in three volumes in 1881.[127] The presence of an Old Latin recension in Lyons indicates that there was a European Old Latin family as well as an African one, though whether the former was an independent version or merely a revision of the latter is unknown. The European Old Latin furnished a more polished rendering than its African counterpart and had apparently been revised with reference to the LXX text. The most significant section of the Old Latin is the Psalter, which was commonly employed in ecclesiastical liturgies.

The vocabulary of the Old Heptateuch was studied by Billen;[128] fragments of the Pentateuch at Munich were edited by Ziegler.[129] A sixth-century palimpsest at Würzburg containing fragments of the Pen-

---

[123] H. F. D. Sparks in H. Wheeler Robinson (ed.), *The Bible in its Ancient and English Versions*, p. 101.

[124] *De Doct. Christ.* II, 11.

[125] Cf. F. C. Burkitt, *The Old Latin and the Itala* (1896), p. 5 and *JTS*, XI (1910), pp. 260ff.

[126] P. Sabatier, *Bibliorum Sacrorum Latinae versiones antiquae, seu Vetus Italica et caeterae* (3 vols., 1739-49).

[127] U. Robert, *Pentateuchi versio latina antiquissima e codice Lugdunensi* (1881); cf. H. A. A. Kennedy, *HDB*, III, pp. 47ff.

[128] A. V. Billen, *The Old Latin Texts of the Heptateuch* (1927).

[129] L. Ziegler, *Bruchstücke einer vorhieronymianischen Übersetzung des Pentateuch* (1883).

tateuch and some passages from the Prophets was published by Ranke in 1871.[130] The task of making a comprehensive collection of Old Latin texts was begun by Fischer in 1949,[131] who based his collection principally upon the work of Denk. While there are many instances in which the Old Latin furnishes a source for the pre-Origen LXX, it is generally conceded to be of only limited value in the criticism of the Massoretic text.

The Vulgate, a revision of the Old Latin undertaken by Jerome at the behest of Pope Damasus in A.D. 383, was an attempt to remedy the chaotic textual situation that had arisen from the manifold contemporary interpretations of the LXX.[132] Jerome commenced his work with a revision of the Old Latin Psalter, which on completion in A.D. 383 was incorporated forthwith into the Roman liturgy by Pope Damasus.[133] A second edition based upon the *Hexapla* became known as the *Psalterium Gallicanum*, because it was first adopted in Gaul. Jerome then revised the remainder of the Old Testament books, but apart from the Psalter and a recension of Job only fragments of Proverbs, Ecclesiastes, and Canticles have survived. The remaining books apparently disappeared before they were published.

The translation was far from uniform, and although Jerome adhered to the Hebrew he frequently followed the LXX, Aquila, Symmachus, and Theodotion, particularly where the original presented doctrinal difficulties for Christians.[134] Despite these efforts his translations from the Hebrew were declared heretical by Rufinus (d. A.D. 410), and their necessity questioned by Augustine (d. A.D. 430). Even when his work received the sanction of Gregory the Great (d. A.D. 604), the text was treated with a noticeable lack of care, so that it required successive revisions during the medieval period.[135] It is apparent that even greater caution is required when the Vulgate is employed for purposes of textual criticism than is the case for many other ancient versions.

d. Syriac versions. After the LXX, the oldest and most important rendering of the Hebrew Scriptures into other languages is the Syriac version. This translation, used by the Syriac Church, has been described since the ninth century by the term *Peshitta* or "simple." It must not be confused with the Syro-Hexaplaric version. Like the LXX it was the

---

[130] E. Ranke, *Par palimpsestorum Wirceburgensium Antiquissimae Veteris Testamenti Versionis Latinae Fragmenta* (1871).

[131] B. Fischer, *Vetus Latina, die Reste der altlateinischen Bibel nach Petrus Sabatier neu gesammelt und herausgegeben von der Erzabtei Beuron* (1949).

[132] Cf. H. J. White, *HDB*, IV, pp. 872ff.

[133] The authorship by Jerome of the *Psalterium Romanum* was contested by D. de Bruyne, *Revue Bénédictine*, XLII (1930), pp. 101ff., but accepted by A. Allgeier, *Biblica*, XII (1931), pp. 447ff.

[134] Cf. F. Stummer, *Einführung in die Lateinische Bibel* (1928), pp. 99ff.

[135] *Ibid.*, pp. 125ff.

product of many hands, and it is possible that some portions of the Old Testament translations reached back to pre-Christian times, although many scholars have maintained that the version itself was Christian in origin.[136] There is at present no direct information about the date of the translation or the authors of the work. This circumstance is hardly surprising, since details concerning the origin of the Syriac version were unknown as early as the time of Theodore of Mopsuestia (d. A.D. 428). It seems probable, however, that some earlier Jewish translations were utilized in the compilation of the work, since the Syrian Christian Church contained many Jewish members. Further evidence for this is found in the way that the translation of Chronicles paraphrases freely and avoids anthropomorphisms in a manner characteristic of the targums. Nöldeke went so far as to affirm that the Peshitta of Chronicles was in fact a Jewish targum,[137] but this cannot be proved.

Kahle has conjectured that the Old Testament, or at least some portions of it, were translated into Syriac for the benefit of the Jewish royal family of Adiabene in the middle of the first century of the Christian era.[138] Whatever the date of origin, it seems probable that the Pentateuch was the first portion to be translated; and it was subsequently revised to constitute the present Syriac Pentateuch. Linguistic affinities between the Palestinian Aramaic targum and the Syriac version of the Pentateuch possibly indicate that the Peshitta Pentateuch originated in a district where eastern Aramaic, of which Syriac is a dialect, was spoken, and which had some contact or relationship with Jerusalem.[139] The most probable region would be that of Adiabene, a province of Syria situated east of the Tigris, which was converted to Judaism about A.D. 40. Since the Palestinian Aramaic targum, written in the dialect of Judaea, was in use in Palestine at that period, it appears quite probable that it was transposed into the Syriac dialect spoken in Adiabene. Further examination indicates that manuscripts of the Peshitta Pentateuch existed at an early period in two recensions, one literal and the other more like a targum. According to Barnes the literal translation was the older, since the Syriac Church authorities were more familiar with that type of text.[140] However, this view appears inadequate when it is remembered that the Syrian Fathers such as Aphraates and Ephraem did not always quote the literal rendering. It is therefore

---

[136] E.g. F. Buhl, *Kanon und Text des AT*, p. 187; E. König, *Einleitung in das AT*, p. 122; *PIOT*, p. 120. This view was opposed by F. C. Burkitt, *EB*, IV, col. 5025; J. Bloch, *AJSL*, XXXV (1919), pp. 215ff.; A. Baumstark, *Geschichte der syrischen Literatur* (1922), p. 18; Kahle, *The Cairo Geniza*, p. 180; A. Bentzen, *Introduction to the OT*, I, pp. 72f.; C. Peters, *Le Muséon*, XLVIII (1935), pp. 1ff.

[137] T. Nöldeke, *Die Alttestamentliche Litteratur* (1868), p. 263.

[138] *The Cairo Geniza*, pp. 179ff.

[139] Cf. A. Baumstark, *ZDMG*, XIV (1935), pp. 89ff.

[140] *JTS*, XV (1914), p. 38.

considered more likely that a targum was revised during the second century in order to bring it into conformity with the ancient Hebrew text.

The Peshitta can scarcely be described as a homogeneous piece of translation, varying as it does from literal to paraphrastic renderings. Proverbs and Ezekiel are distinctly reminiscent of the targums, while the Psalter is translated in a free fashion, and along with Isaiah and the Minor Prophets shows clearly the influence of the LXX.[141] Job was translated from the original Hebrew, and is unintelligible in parts due to corruptions in textual transmission and the influence of other versions. Chronicles, as has been noted, is paraphrastic in character, and according to Fraenkel was translated by Jews in Edessa in the third century and added as a supplement along with the contents of the Apocrypha.[142]

The oldest surviving manuscript of the Peshitta dates from about A.D. 464, and there are several extant sixth-century manuscripts of the Psalms and Isaiah. The most important manuscript, Codex Ambrosianus, which comprises the entire Old Testament, is in Milan. This manuscript, which uses the western Syriac form of the text, was published in a photo-lithographic edition by Ceriani in 1874.[143] Other Syriac translations include a Jerusalem rendering of the Old and New Testament made in the sixth century, of which only a few fragments of the Old Testament have survived. It was evidently made from the LXX, and was intended for the religious worship of the Palestinian-Syriac Melchite Church. The language was Palestinian Aramaic, written in Syriac characters. A translation of the entire Bible from Greek into Syriac was commissioned about A.D. 508 by Philoxenus of Mabbug, but no Old Testament portions other than fragments of the Psalter have survived. According to Baumstark, the latter were based on a Lucianic recension of the text of Isaiah.[144]

Another Syriac version of the Old Testament was made in A.D. 617 at the request of the Patriarch Athanasius by Paul, bishop of Tella. It followed the text of the LXX column of the *Hexapla* with slavish exactness, and is known as the Syro-Hexaplaric version. It retained the Hexaplaric signs in marginal notes, and supplied readings from Aquila, Symmachus, and Theodotion. Some fragments of the Syro-Hexapla were collected by Lagarde[145] to supplement earlier manuscripts, particularly the edition published by Ceriani in 1874. Within recent years a number

[141] Cf. W. E. Barnes, *JTS*, II (1901), p. 197.

[142] S. Fraenkel, *Jahrbücher für Protestantische Theologie* (1879), pp. 508ff., 720ff.

[143] A. M. Ceriani, *Translatio Syra Pescitto Veteris Testamenti* (1874).

[144] A. Baumstark, *Geschichte der syrischen Litteratur*, pp. 144f.

[145] *Bibliothecae Syriacae I. Veteris Testamenti Graeci in sermonem Syriacum versi fragmenta octo* (1892).

of new fragments of this recension were discovered among some manuscripts in London.[146] The Syro-Hexapla is not merely of value for restoring the Hexaplar text of the LXX, but also for recovering the original LXX text of Daniel. No complete scientific edition of the Syriac Old Testament exists as yet, although critical texts of certain canonical books such as the Psalter, Isaiah, Canticles, and Ezra have been published. The main edition of the Peshitta was prepared by a Marcionite, Gabriel Sionita, for inclusion in the 1645 *Paris Polyglot*, but unfortunately it was based upon inadequate manuscript sources. This text was followed in the Walton *London Polyglot* of 1657, and also by Lee in the 1821 and later editions published by the British and Foreign Bible Society under the title *Vetus Testamentum Syriace*. The Urmia edition, representing the eastern Syriac text, was published in 1852, and in many instances followed the readings of Nestorian manuscripts.

From about A.D. 300 on numerous translations of the LXX into different vernacular dialects appeared among the Coptic Christians of Egypt, the Ethiopic Church, the Armenians, and the Arabs. These versions were subsequently revised and expanded and became in turn the basis of later translations as the need was dictated by missionary expansion and other considerations.

[146] M. H. Goshen-Gottestein, *Biblica*, XXXVI (1955), pp. 162ff.

III. TEXTUAL CRITICISM

A. SEMITIC PHILOLOGY

Within recent years important aids to textual criticism have been furnished by inscriptional and manuscript discoveries. These include valuable proto-Hebrew Ugaritic texts, northwest Semitic documents of the Late Bronze and Early Iron Ages, ostraca such as those from Lachish, Aramaic papyri from the fifth century B.C., and, of course, the Dead Sea Scrolls. Archaeological material of this sort is of immense value in studying the history of the Hebrew language against its northwest Semitic background.[1] The dramatic advances that have been made possible by recent dicoveries can be appreciated in the light of the complaint by Gesenius, who in the fifth edition (1822) of his *Hebräische Grammatik* noted a total lack of historical data for the earlier stages of the development of the language. Even a century later, the Bauer-Leander *Historische Grammatik der Hebräischen Sprache* showed that little progress in the historical understanding of the language had taken place, despite the decipherment of the Phoenician inscriptions by Gesenius and the important contribution made by the 1907 edition of the Tell el-Amarna tablets.[2]

Some light was thrown upon the nature of early Hebrew in 1926, when Bauer collected and published all the personal and geographical names from Old Babylonian documentary sources that had been held to reflect a west-Semitic speech.[3] In the same year Sethe published his decipherment of the celebrated "Execration Texts," inscribed in Egyptian upon vases suitable for smashing.[4] Aside from the implications of this material for processes of sympathetic magic, it has been observed that among the names of potential rebel vassals listed on the vases are about thirty Palestinian and Syrian chieftains, mentioned in conjunction with the

---

[1] Cf. W. L. Moran, *BANE*, pp. 54ff.

[2] J. A. Knudtzon, *Die El-Amarna Tafeln* (vol. I, 1907, vol. II, 1915).

[3] T. Bauer, *Die Ostkanaanäer, Eine philologisch-historische Untersuchung über die Wanderschicht der Sogenannten "Amoriter" in Babylonien* (1926).

[4] K. Sethe, *Die Ächtung feindlicher Fürsten, Völker und Dinge auf altägyptischen Tongefässscherben des mittleren Reiches* (1926).

244

territory over which they ruled. All appeared to be of the same type, and reflected substantially the same language as that studied by Bauer in connection with the cuneiform sources.[5] They are generally regarded as having come from the period between 1925 and 1875 B.C.[6]

Similarly inscribed figurines were found at Sakkarah from a slightly later period,[7] and on examination proved to be identical linguistically with the earlier texts published by Sethe. More than thirty northwest Semitic names, mostly of females, were contained in the Hayes list published by Albright,[8] and assigned to the eighteenth century B.C. While these 150 or so personal names from Syria and Palestine in the period 1900-1700 B.C.[9] may not appear particularly significant in themselves, they are of great value, since they are substantially the same as those found in the more abundant cuneiform sources. The orthographic principles governing Egyptian transcriptions were laid down in the fundamentally important treatise *The Vocalization of the Early Egyptian Syllabic Orthography* by W. F. Albright (1934). This threw additional light upon early Canaanite designations of individuals and places.

Study of the history of northwest Semitic was unexpectedly enriched by the tablets excavated at Mari from 1933,[10] as well as by similar material from Alalakh[11] and Tell Chagar Bazar,[12] which contained invaluable information for the study of philology and grammar. The Mari texts in particular furnished hundreds of personal and geographical names, and through deviations in vocabulary and idiom from the current Babylonian these have supplied material of great importance for estimating the nature of northwest Semitic speech in the patriarchal period. Considerable diversity of opinion exists in connection with this particular subject,[13] and there is a pressing need for an authoritative synthesis of the material now available.

As with the Amarna tablets, it was a chance discovery that led to the excavations at the site of ancient Ugarit. While the native Amorite speech of Mari was similar to, though not identical with, the Hebrew of

---

[5] W. L. Moran, *BANE*, p. 56.

[6] Cf. G. Posener, *Princes et pays d'Asie et de Nubie* (1940), pp. 31ff.; W. F. Edgerton, *JAOS*, LX (1940), p. 492 n. 44; Albright, *BASOR*, No. 88 (1942), p. 32.

[7] Posener, *op. cit.*, pp. 40ff.

[8] *JAOS*, LXXIV (1954), pp. 222ff.

[9] For studies see Albright, *JPOS*, VIII (1928), pp. 223ff., *BASOR*, No. 81 (1941), pp. 16ff., 30ff.; J. Simons, *Handbook for the Study of Egyptian Topographical Lists Relating to Western Asia* (1937); M. Noth, *Zeitschrift des Deutschen Palästina-Vereins*, LXV (1942), pp. 9ff.

[10] For early reports see *SRA*, XVI (1935), pp. 1ff., 117ff., *et al.*; for transliterations and translations of texts, *Archives royales de Mari* (1950-54), I-VI; for a bibliography to 1950, *Studia Mariana* (1950), pp. 127ff.

[11] Cf. C. L. Woolley, *Alalakh* (1955); D. J. Wiseman, *The Alalakh Tablets* (1953).

[12] Cf. C. J. Gadd, *Iraq*, VII (1940), pp. 35ff.

[13] W. L. Moran, *BANE*, p. 57.

the patriarchal period, the language of the Ugaritic texts consisted of a Hurrian dialect and a previously unknown northwest Semitic tongue closely akin to pre-Mosaic Hebrew. The importance of the archaic Canaanite dialect for the writings of the Old Testament, and particularly the Psalms, was immediately apparent, as has been observed in an earlier chapter. The contribution of this material to the study of Hebrew grammar was of great value also, for it was soon realized that the Massoretic text had preserved peculiarities in Canaanite grammar and speech-forms, whose nature and significance had passed into oblivion after the close of the Amarna Age, and which had been regarded as textual corruptions by the critical scholars of the nineteenth century. Not the least benefit for the grammarian is the information which this ancient literary corpus has furnished with regard to the problems connected with the Hebrew verbal system.[14]

Although the professional student of Hebrew palaeography and epigraphy cannot boast of a wealth of material such as is available in cuneiform, he does possess many hundreds of inscriptions that have made available a fund of new knowledge of enormous value for a study of the Old Testament text. Many of the inscriptions on stone were written in various dialects of Canaanite[15] as well as in north-[16] and south-Arabic, and their importance for the history of the north-Semitic alphabet has been shown previously. Equally valuable were the discoveries of inscribed ostraca at Samaria and Lachish.[17] The former comprised administrative documents recording shipments of wine and oil to Samaria in the time of Jeroboam II, and contained numerous personal names and place-designations, some of which also appeared in the Old Testament. The latter are of value for the textual critic because of the incidence of scribal errors, the use of the *scriptio defectiva* rather than the fuller forms of the Massoretic tradition, the presence of a dot as a word-divider, and the fact that the language of the ostraca is to all intents and purposes the kind of classical Hebrew familiar from the Old Testament writings.

[14] *Ibid.*, pp. 61ff.

[15] Cf. J. W. Flight in *Haverford Symposium on Archaeology and the Bible* (ed. E. Grant), pp. 114ff.; A. M. Honeyman, *OTMS*, pp. 264ff.

[16] Cf. F. V. Winnett, *BASOR*, No. 73 (1939), pp. 3ff.; W. F. Albright, *BASOR*, No. 66 (1937), p. 30.

[17] For Samaria see W. F. Albright, *PEF Quarterly Statement* (1936), pp. 211ff., *BASOR*, No. 73 (1939), p. 21; D. Diringer, *Le inscrizioni antico-ebraiche palestinese* (1934), pp. 21ff.; *ANET*, p. 321; *DOTT*, pp. 204ff. For Lachish see H. Torczyner, *The Lachish Letters* (1938); J. W. Jack, *PEF Quarterly Statement* (1938), pp. 165ff.; K. Elliger, *PJB*, XXXIV (1938), pp. 30ff., *Zeitschrift des Deutschen Palästina-Vereins*, LXII (1939), pp. 63ff.; J. Hempel, *ZAW*, LVI (1938), pp. 126ff.; R. de Vaux, *RB*, XLVIII (1939), pp. 181ff.; D. W. Thomas, *JTS*, XL (1939), pp. 1ff.; Albright, *BASOR*, No. 82 (1941), p. 21.

When the antiquity of the Qumran scrolls was demonstrated to the satisfaction of the majority of scholars, the palaeographers and textual critics realized that they had in their possession materials which at once advanced textual sources to a completely unexpected extent. The large manuscript of Isaiah (1QIsaᵃ) proved of particular value in this connection, since it differed in certain respects from the Massoretic text, including the wider use of the *matres lectionis* and the preservation of some readings not found in the Massoretic tradition but supported by the LXX and other ancient versions. Subsequent studies of the Qumran Biblical material[18] have shown something of the extent to which these documents testify independently to the traditions lying behind the Massoretic form, and have furnished powerful support for the general trustworthiness of the Massoretic text. In addition to earlier materials, the palaeographer now has at his disposal a variety of scripts including palaeo-Hebrew, early Jewish, and Greek hands, written both in formal and cursive styles. There is thus a significant corpus available for purposes of typological analysis and for fixing absolute dates within the relative systems furnished by such analyses.

As with many other aspects of Biblical study, much of the groundwork of palaeographical method was laid by Albright, whose analysis of the Nash Papyrus constituted a model of its kind.[19] Palaeographic study of the Qumran material led to conclusions as to the date of the materials from 1Q, which were subsequently confirmed by carbon-14 dating of linen scraps from the same source.[20] In a reply to certain critics of advanced palaeographic methods, Birnbaum furnished an excellent conspectus of the science.[21] Presently he is in process of issuing his major work on Hebrew palaeography, an attempt to deal with the various

[18] E.g. F. M. Cross, *JBL*, LXXIV (1955), pp. 147ff.; P. W. Skehan, *CBQ*, VIII (1955), pp. 38ff., XXII (1960), pp. 47ff., *VT*, suppl. IV (1957), pp. 182ff.; H. M. Orlinsky in *A Stubborn Faith* (ed. E. C. Hobbs, 1956), pp. 117ff., *JBL*, LXXVIII (1959), pp. 26ff.; Cross, *The Ancient Library of Qumran and Biblical Studies* (1958), pp. 179ff.; M. Martin, *The Scribal Character of the Dead Sea Scrolls* (2 vols., 1958); B. J. Roberts, *BJRL*, XLII (1959), pp. 132ff.; W. J. Brownlee, *The Meaning of the Qumran Scrolls for the Bible*, pp. 5ff.

[19] *JBL*, LVI (1937), pp. 145ff.; cf. G. Margoliouth, *JE*, VIII, pp. 304, 312; N. Peters, *Die älteste Abschrift der zehn Gebote, der Papyrus Nash* (1905).

[20] Albright, *BASOR*, No. 118 (1950), p. 6; J. C. Trever, *BASOR*, No. 113 (1949), p. 23, *Smithsonian Report* (1953), pp. 425ff.; S. A. Birnbaum, *BASOR*, No. 115 (1949), p. 22; E. L. Sukenik, *Megilloth Genuzoth*, I, pp. 14f. These methods were contested by Kahle, *Die hebräischen Handschriften aus der Höle* (1951), p. 22 *passim;* J. L. Teicher, *JJS*, II (1951), pp. 67ff.; O. H. Lehmann, *PEQ*, LXXXIII (1951), pp. 32ff.; E. R. Lacheman, *JQR*, XL (1949-1950), pp. 15ff.

[21] S. A. Birnbaum, *The Qumran Scrolls and Palaeography. BASOR*, Suppl. Stud. 13-14 (1952).

phases through which Hebrew scripts have passed, which is expected to become definitive in its field.[22]

Within recent years comparative Semitic philology has gone hand in hand with the Qumran discoveries in increasing scholarly confidence in the substantial trustworthiness of the Massoretic tradition. In the light of the fuller information that scholars now possess concerning northwest Semitic languages generally, it has become apparent that much of the zealous emendation of the Hebrew text undertaken by adherents of the Graf-Wellhausen theories on what was the flimsiest of ground or no ground at all can no longer be justified on a philological basis, or any other, for that matter. As Thomas has pointed out, what were formerly imagined to be impossible Hebrew forms can now be explained quite satisfactorily by comparison with some other Semitic tongue.[23]

The foundations of modern Semitic philology were laid in the nineteenth century by the monumental labors of several scholars, among them Gesenius, who deciphered the Phoenician alphabet, and Rödiger, who studied the Minaeo-Sabaean alphabet. Among the numerous subsequent studies are included works on grammar, lexicons, and studies of the Amarna tablets.[24]

---

[22] *The Hebrew Scripts* (vols. I, II, 1954). Other valuable contributions to the field have been made by Cross, *JBL*, LXXIV (1955), pp. 147ff., *BANE*, pp. 133ff.; N. Avigad, *Scripta Hierosolymitana*, IV (1957), pp. 56ff.; and Milik, *DJD*, II, pp. 67ff.

[23] In *Record and Revelation* (ed. H. W. Robinson, 1938), p. 400; *OTMS*, p. 242.

[24] Gesenius' *Hebräisches und Chaldäisches Handwörterbuch* first appeared in 1812; Rödiger published the fourteenth to twenty-first editions of Gesenius' Grammar between 1845 and 1872. An edition of Gesenius' lexicon was published by F. Buhl in 1915, entitled *Hebräisches und Aramäisches Handwörterbuch über das AT*. Other nineteenth-century contributions included F. Delitzsch, *Prolegomena eines neuen Hebräisch-Aramäischen Wörterbuch zum AT* (1886), *Assyrisches Wörterbuch zur gesampten bisher veröffentlichen Keilschriftliteratur* (1887-90), and *Assyrische Grammatik* (1889); A. H. Sayce, *Assyrian Grammar for Comparative Purposes* (1872), *Principles of Comparative Philology* (1874), and *Introduction to the Science of Language* (1879); W. Wright, *Lectures on the Comparative Grammar of the Semitic Languages* (1890); H. Zimmern, *Vergleichende Grammatik der semitischen Sprachen* (1898); Th. Nöldeke, *Die Semitischen Sprache* (1899); E. Kautzsch, *Grammatik des Biblisch-Aramäischen* (1884); K. Marti, *Kurzgefasste Grammatik der Biblisch-Aramäischen Sprache* (1896); E. König, *Historisch-kritisches Lehrgebäude der Hebräischen Sprache* (vol. I, 1881, vol. II, 1897) and *Hebräisch und Semitisch* (1901); and P. de Lagarde, *Uebersicht über die im Aramäischen, Arabischen und Hebräischen übliche Bildung der Nomina* (1889). Early twentieth-century studies included Delitzsch, *Philologische Forderungen an die hebräische Lexicographie* (1917); H. Torczyner, *Die Entstehung des semitischen Sprachtypus* (1906); Brockelmann, *Grundriss der vergleichenden Grammatik der semitischen Sprachen* (1908); and D. O'Leary, *Comparative Grammar of the Semitic Languages* (1923). The linguistic form of the Tell el-Amarna tablets was studied by F. Böhl, *Die Sprache der Amarnabriefe* (1909), and F. Ebeling, *Das Verbum der El-Amarna-Briefe* (1910). Numerous Hebrew and Aramaic grammars and lexicons have appeared, among them G. Dalman, *Grammatik des Jüdisch-Palä-*

Taken together all these works—earlier and later—have shown that the Massoretic text, although admittedly faulty at certain points, is a remarkable testimony to scribal fidelity in the transmission of the Hebrew Scriptures, and in general constitutes a witness whose reliability is of a deservedly high degree.[25] While it is now apparent that there were several types of Hebrew text circulating in the pre-Christian period, it is evident that some of the supposed departures from the Massoretic text exhibited by ancient versions such as the LXX are not as real as they purport to be. Sometimes a translation may exhibit certain variations from the traditional meaning of the Hebrew words in a manner that seems to suggest that the translators were working from a divergent Hebrew text. However, comparative philological studies can frequently trace such idiosyncrasies to their source and demonstrate that the divergence in question is more apparent than actual.[26] No scholar would deny, of course, that there are important divergences between the Massoretic text, other pre-Christian texts, and the ancient versions, in which

---

stinischen Aramäisch (1905); Brown, Driver, and Briggs, A Hebrew and English Lexicon of the OT (1906); H. L. Strack, Grammatik des Biblisch-Aramäischen (1921); A. B. Davidson, Hebrew Grammar (rev. ed., 1921); H. Bauer and P. Leander, Historische Grammatik der hebräischen Sprache (vol. I, 1922); P. P. Joüon, Grammaire de l'Hébreu Biblique (1923); W. B. Stevenson, Grammar of Palestinian Jewish Aramaic (1924); Bauer and Leander, Grammatik des Biblisch-Aramäischen (1927); Leander, Laut- und Formenlehre des Ägyptisch-Aramäischen (1928); and L. H. Gray, Introduction to Semitic Comparative Linguistics (1934). A number of treatises have been published dealing with particularized aspects of Semitic speech, e.g. E. König, Stilistik, Rhetorik, Poetik in Bezug auf die biblische Litteratur komparativisch dargestellt (1900); S. Landesdorfer, Sumerisches Sprachgut im AT (1916); A. Jirku, Die Wanderungen der Hebräer (1924). In 1940 Zorell and Semkowski began the publication of their Lexicon Hebraicum et Aramaicum Veteris Testamenti; this was followed in 1948 by the outstanding Lexicon in Veteris Testamenti Libros of Köhler and Baumgartner. G. R. Driver began his important contributions to philological study in 1920; for a select bibliography of these see Hebrew and Semitic Studies Presented to G. R. Driver (ed. D. W. Thomas and W. D. McHardy, 1963), pp. 191ff. In Germany M. Noth's Die Israelitischen Personennamen im Rahmen der gemeinsemitischen Namengebung (1928) superseded all previous works on the subject of Israelite personal names from philological, semantic, and other standpoints. Interest in Semitic philology has been sustained through such studies as Z. S. Harris, Grammar of the Phoenician Language (1936) and Development of the Canaanite Dialects (1939); C. F. A. Schaeffer, Ugaritica (from 1939); R. de Langhe, Les Textes de Ras Shamra-Ugarit et leurs rapports avec le milieu biblique de l'Ancien Testament, I-II (1945); and C. H. Gordon, Ugaritic Grammar (1940) and Ugaritic Handbook (1947); as well as the manifold contributions of Noth, Albright, Winton Thomas, Margolis, Orlinsky, and many other scholars.

[25] Cf. D. W. Thomas, The Recovery of the Ancient Hebrew Language (1939), p. 37.

[26] D. W. Thomas in OTMS, pp. 242f.

readings superior to those of the Massoretes have been preserved. Even conjectural emendation of the Hebrew is a legitimate discipline when carried out under properly controlled conditions, and not as an arbitrary exercise designed to furnish textual support for some conjectural scheme.

B. MODERN EDITIONS OF THE HEBREW BIBLE

At the beginning of the twentieth century the study of Old Testament textual criticism was in decline, and it remained in this condition for the next few decades.[27] Orlinsky[28] correctly laid much of the blame for this unfortunate situation on Rudolf Kittel's celebrated *Biblia Hebraica*. This work, issued in 1906 and 1912, was based on the ben Chayyim text, and superseded both Oort's *Textus Hebraici emendationes quibus in Vetere Testamento Neerlandice vertendo* (1900), which was popular at that time in parts of Europe, and the earlier Hebrew editions of A. Hahn (1832) and M. Letteris (1852), the latter being the text used by the British and Foreign Bible Society (1866). The Kittel Bible tacitly emended the ben Chayyim text, and furnished footnotes that contained conjectural emendations and variant readings from ancient sources such as versions. The critical apparatus received high praise from scholars such as S. R. Driver, though this, characteristically, was tempered with some caution.[29] Very soon, however, as Orlinsky has remarked,[30] scholars began to regard the apparatus as more sacred and authoritative than the Massoretic text itself, and where choice was involved they tended to accept the emendations in preference to the Hebrew text. A third edition of *Biblia Hebraica* was published by Paul Kahle in 1937, based upon what Kahle regarded as the purest form of the ben Asher text, the Leningrad manuscript B 19a, dated A.D. 1008. Different scholars contributed a critical apparatus containing selected variant readings from manuscripts and the ancient versions, but unfortunately this collection of notes was only a slight improvement upon its predecessors.[31]

---

[27] This state of affairs prompted complaints by scholars of the caliber of Rowley, *Society for Old Testament Study Book List*, X (1955), p. 640, and Orlinsky, *BANE*, p. 114, that little interest was shown in textual criticism proper, apart from such occasional articles as M. L. Margolis, *Proceedings of the American Philosophical Society*, LXVII (1928), pp. 187ff.; J. Reider, *HUCA*, VII (1930), pp. 285ff.; Orlinsky, *BA*, IX, No. 2 (1946), pp. 22ff., and in *The Study of the Bible Today and Tomorrow* (ed. H. R. Willoughby), pp. 141ff.

[28] *BANE*, p. 114.

[29] *Notes on the Hebrew Text of the Book of Samuel* (1913), p. xxxv n. 6.

[30] *BANE*, p. 114.

[31] Orlinsky in *The Study of the Bible Today and Tomorrow*, p. 151; *BA*, IX, No. 2 (1946), pp. 24ff.

The first important scholar to criticize this curious situation was C. C. Torrey, who made a scathing attack on the methods used to amass this apparatus.[32] Torrey's views were shared by Montgomery, who in his *Critical and Exegetical Commentary on the Book of Daniel* (1927) ignored the apparatus completely. These opinions were also elaborated by Margolis, who made it clear that the Kittel critical apparatus was completely unreliable for scholarly purposes.[33] Orlinsky also took the same stand in 1934, and has continued his criticisms of this collection of material since that time.[34] Ziegler and Katz have been equally forthright in their warnings as to the complete inadequacy of the Kittel apparatus.[35]

Ignoring these weighty criticisms, the Privilegierte Württembergische Bibelanstalt published in 1951 an introduction by Würthweim to the critical apparatus of the Kittel Hebrew Bible, and this work was translated into English six years later.[36] Criticisms of the German version were rejected quite calmly in the foreword to the English edition, indicating that at least some English and continental European scholars were satisfied with an inadequate and incorrect critical apparatus. Quite obviously, any attempt at textual criticism that employs such a faulty device can only produce indifferent, if not absolutely incorrect, results.

In contrast, textual studies in the LXX version have not been hampered to the same extent by a poor critical apparatus, although Margolis[37] claimed to have discovered errors in the apparatus of the *Larger Cambridge Septuagint*, and also in the edition by H. B. Swete. The recovery of Hebrew and Greek Biblical materials from Qumran has stimulated interest in the restoration of the original Greek text of the LXX, the one from which, according to Lagarde, all existing manuscripts and recensions of the Greek Old Testament arose. This theory received support from scholars such as Albright, Margolis, B. J. Roberts, Marcus, Allgeier, Orlinsky, and others.[38] Although the principles laid down by

---

[32] *The Second Isaiah* (1928), pp. 214f.

[33] *AJSL*, XXVIII (1912), p. 3; cf. H. M. Orlinsky, *Max Leopold Margolis: Scholar and Teacher* (1952), pp. 34ff.

[34] *JQR*, XXV (1934-35), pp. 271ff.; cf. his statements in *JBL*, LXIII (1944), p. 33, LXIX (1950), p. 153 n. 5, *JQR*, XLIII (1952-53), pp. 330, 340, *BANE*, pp. 114ff., and *A Stubborn Faith* (ed. E. C. Hobbs), pp. 117ff.

[35] J. Ziegler, *ZAW*, LX (1944), pp. 108ff. P. Katz in *The Background of the NT and its Eschatology* (ed. W. D. Davies and D. Daube, 1956), pp. 176ff., *VT*, IV (1954), pp. 222f.; for a bibliography see J. W. Wevers, *Theologische Rundschau*, XXII (1954), pp. 86, 90.

[36] *Der Text des AT, eine Einführung in die Biblia Hebraica von Rudolf Kittel* (1951): E. tr. P. R. Ackroyd, *The Text of the OT; an Introduction to Kittel-Kahle's Biblia Hebraica* (1957).

[37] *JBL*, XLIX (1930), pp. 234ff.

[38] Cf. Orlinsky in *Max Leopold Margolis: Scholar and Teacher*, p. 43n.

Lagarde were challenged by Kahle and Sperber,[39] these scholars have themselves been criticized by Orlinsky, Katz, Cross, and others.[40]

According to the hypothesis that Lagarde postulated concerning the archetype of the Scriptures, the Jews possessed a standard authoritative text of the Hebrew Bible from the early part of the second century of the Christian era that was based upon a single master scroll and constituted the text upon which all subsequent medieval manuscripts of the Hebrew Bible depended.[41] Lagarde was followed by Gordis and Orlinsky among others,[42] but his opinions failed to secure firm scholarly support, probably because his theory was overstated. At the same time it has been recognized from the evidence presented by the Qumran texts that at the end of the first century after Christ a uniform Hebrew tradition had begun to appear and that despite textual differences it was handed down in a remarkably consistent form from that time onwards.

Whereas early reports on the textual relationship between the Qumran Hebrew scrolls and the LXX tended to emphasize the agreement of the Hebrew, particularly 1QIsaᵃ, with the LXX as against the Massoretic text, subsequent research disclosed that the Wadi Qumran material did not in fact diverge in favor of the LXX as frequently as had at first been supposed.[43] Recent studies in this and other aspects of textual research have gone far towards showing that the LXX has, with the Massoretic text, acquired very considerable respect as a source for the recovery of the pre-Massoretic Hebrew in disputed areas, although, as has been stated above, the LXX still needs to be used with considerable care.[44]

[39] Kahle in *Theologische Studien und Kritiken*, LXXXVIII (1915), pp. 432ff. and *The Cairo Geniza*, pp. 174ff.; Sperber in *JBL*, LIV (1935), pp. 73ff. and *Studien zur Geschichte und Kultur des Nahen und Fernen Ostens* (ed. W. Heffening and W. Kirfel, 1935), pp. 39ff.; cf. his statements in *HUCA*, XIV (1939), pp. 153f., XVII (1943), pp. 293ff., and *PIOT*, p. 79.

[40] Orlinsky, *JAOS*, LXI (1941), pp. 81ff., *BANE*, p. 121; Katz, *Theologische Zeitschrift*, V (1949), pp. 1ff., *Studia Patristica*, I (1957), p. 353; Cross, *The Ancient Library of Qumran and Modern Biblical Studies*, p. 170 n. 13.

[41] P. de Lagarde, *Anmerkungen zur griechischen Uebersetzung der Proverbien* (1863), pp. 1ff.; cf. Orlinsky, *On the Present State of Proto-Septuagint Studies* (1941), p. 84; W. Robertson Smith, *The OT in the Jewish Church* (1892), p. 57 n. 2.

[42] Gordis, *The Biblical Text in the Making: A Study of the Kethibh-Qere*, pp. 44ff.; Orlinsky, *JAOS*, LXI (1941), pp. 84ff.

[43] Cf. J. Muilenburg, *BASOR*, No. 135 (1954), pp. 32f.; M. Burrows, *More Light on the Dead Sea Scrolls*, pp. 144ff.; P. W. Skehan, *BASOR*, No. 136 (1954), pp. 12ff. and *VT* suppl. IV (1957), pp. 148ff.

[44] Among recent studies are Orlinsky, *The LXX, The Oldest Translation of the Bible* (1949); I. Soisalon-Soininen, *Die Textformen der Septuaginta-Übersetzung des Richterbuches* (1951); D. H. Guard, *The Exegetical Method of the Greek Translators of the Book of Job* (1952); H. S. Gehman, *VT*, III (1953), pp. 141ff., IV (1954), pp. 337ff.; J. W. Wevers, *Theologische Rundschau*, XXII (1954), pp. 85ff.,

Since the publication of the third edition of *Biblia Hebraica* one or two noteworthy attempts have been made to issue an authoritative text of the Hebrew Bible. In 1933 the British and Foreign Bible Society decided to publish a new text to replace the worn-out plates of the Letteris Bible. The editing of it was given to N. H. Snaith, who consulted certain Spanish Hebrew manuscripts in an attempt to come as close as possible to the true ben Asher tradition. The publication of the text was delayed by World War II and its aftermath until 1958. A brochure issued at that time by the British and Foreign Bible Society[45] stated that the text was based upon the first hands of certain Spanish Hebrew manuscripts in the British Museum, together with the Shem Tob manuscript from the library of the late David Sassoon. The work was not a revision of the Letteris text, nor was it connected in any way with the ben Chayyim text that had been edited for the Bible Society by C. D. Ginsburg in the first decade of the 1900s. Following the policy of the Society, the Bible contained no footnotes or apparatus apart from the official Massoretic notes. Although the text was not based upon that of Kahle to any significant extent, the conclusions at which Snaith arrived supported the contentions of Kahle concerning the true nature of the ben Asher tradition.

An edition of the Old Testament that was corrected on the basis of the Massorah of ben Asher was published under the title *Hebrew Bible: Jerusalem Edition* in 1953. Associated with the late M. D. Cassuto, who died two years before the publication of the work, it was not so much a new Bible as a photographic reproduction of the 1908 Ginsburg edition, to which some corrections had been added on the basis of textual notes left behind by Cassuto at his death. The choice of the Ginsburg text was unfortunate—particularly for a scholar such as Cassuto who had an unrivalled first-hand knowledge of the ben Asher codex—because Ginsburg had frequently been influenced by the number rather than by the quality of the manuscripts which supported important variant readings in the text. Compounding this unhappy situation was the hurried and careless technical work of the printer, which resulted among other things in an irregular number of lines per page and in numerous misprints. Since the notes made by Cassuto himself were based upon the Letteris edition of the Hebrew Bible, the finished work presented certain confusing aspects for students of the text.

171ff.; D. W. Gooding, *Recensions of the LXX Pentateuch* (1955); O. Eissfeldt, *Einleitung in das AT* (1956 ed.), pp. 822ff.; G. Zuntz, ZAW, LXVII (1956), pp. 124ff., *Classica et Mediaevalia*, XVII (1956), pp. 183ff.; G. Gerleman, *Studies in the LXX: Proverbs* (1956); H. M. Orlinsky, *BANE*, pp. 117ff.; F. M. Cross, *The Ancient Library of Qumran and Modern Biblical Studies*, pp. 168ff.

45 For similar material see VT, VII (1957), pp. 107ff.

An edition of the complete Hebrew Bible known as the *Koren-Jerusalem Bible* was issued in 1962, preceded in 1959 by the publication of the Torah in Israel and the United States. In announcing this work, Dr. Haim Gevaryahu, chairman of the Israeli Society for Biblical Research and director of the World Jewish Bible Society, remarked that it was the first edition of the Hebrew Bible ever to be set, printed, and published in Jerusalem. Furthermore, this was the first time in over four centuries that Jews had undertaken to print and publish a Hebrew Bible. The text appears to differ only slightly from that of the Massoretes, although there are occasional variations in matters of spelling and punctuation.

In 1955, through the persistence of M. Goshen-Gottestein, the Hebrew University of Jerusalem undertook to place the textual study of the Old Testament on an entirely new basis by abandoning the eclectic character of the Kittel Bible and furnishing all the available evidence, whether valuable or not, for the purpose of recovering the genuine original Hebrew insofar as that objective was possible. This Bible was planned, like the *Biblia Hebraica*, to consist of two parts, the text and an apparatus, each of which was to be a scientific product in its own right. A large part of the Aleppo codex, believed destroyed in 1948 during Arab riots at Aleppo, is now in Israel, and has become available for scholarly study. The editors of the Hebrew University Bible believe that the codex is the original manuscript produced by Aaron ben Asher and recommended by Maimonides. Since only about two-thirds of this venerable source escaped destruction during the riots, it will be necessary for the editors to rely upon other ancient manuscripts that are as close as possible to the Aleppo codex. When completed this magnificent enterprise will present the purest variety of the traditional text in its most scientific form, and will furnish a full critical apparatus to replace the highly selective ones found in editions of the Kittel Bible.

C. SCRIBAL ERRORS IN TRANSMISSION

The account of the manner in which the Massoretic tradition was transmitted makes it apparent that there were times when scribal interference with the text was undertaken in accordance with theological presuppositions or liturgical requirements. These emendations must be differentiated from pure scribal error, however, since they constitute part of the legitimate historical development of the text. Nevertheless, the Massoretic scribes were aware of the fact of accidental textual corruption. One trace of their attempts to preserve the sacred text from error can be seen in the elongated form of the five *literae dilatabiles* (ת, ם, ל, ה, א) and some other consonants, which were lengthened in shape in order to fill vacant space at the ends of lines and thus avoid incorrect repetition of syllables or words.

In the light of present knowledge concerning the conditions under which the ancient scribes made copies of Biblical manuscripts, it is nothing short of miraculous that so few mistakes were made in the transmission of the text. For the most part the errors that do exist fall into definite categories of transcriptional error, which can also be recognized in other ancient works. Although a full discussion of types of scribal error is outside the scope of the present work,[46] the principal varieties can be described briefly as follows.

Purely scribal mistakes in copying the text arose at an early period when the Canaanite script was still in use, and resulted from confusion between consonants that exhibited a similar archaic form. Such mistakes usually involved the consonants *beth* and *daleth* (Gen. 9:7), *kaph* and *mem* (2 Kgs. 22:4), *'aleph* and *daleth* (2 Chron. 22:10), *nun* and *pe* (1 Chron. 11:37). When the square Aramaic script was introduced, confusion between ד and ר (Gen. 41:3, 19), ה and ח (Isa. 13:2), י and ו (Isa. 30:4), ה and ת (Ps. 49:15), and other consonants became increasingly common. Other instances of this kind may possibly be due to textual peculiarities in the parent manuscripts, and may not represent actual scribal error at all.

The absence of word-division in the Canaanite and early Aramaic scripts frequently led to corruptions of the text. Thus in Isaiah 2:20 the word for "to the moles" (לחפרפרות) was wrongly divided in the Massoretic tradition to comprise two words, "to a hole of rats" (לחפר פרות). A common scribal mistake arises when the consonant ו, occurring at the end of a verb, is attached erroneously to the beginning of the next word as though it were the conjunction "and" (1 Sam. 14:21). In Joel 2:1-2 an incorrect sentence-division assigned the words "for it is near" to the end of verse one rather than to the beginning of verse two, as the metrical structure requires. The introduction of the *matres lectionis* occasioned considerable textual variation, which was, however, minor. Occasionally such consonants appeared in a wrong context (e.g. Num. 21:1; 1 Sam. 10:5; Jer. 2:25), and when copied by the Massoretes produced a pointing that varied from the original as it might be reconstructed from ancient versions.

Distinct from the foregoing, which arose primarily from a misunderstanding of the text, are those corruptions which involved a definite alteration, whether accidental or deliberate, of the Hebrew consonants. The rearrangement of letters known as metathesis involves the reversing of their proper position, as in the Hebrew of Psalm 49:12, where the Massoretic text reads קרבם ("their inward parts") instead of the obvious

---

[46] Cf. A. Geiger, *Urschrift und Übersetzungen der Bibel* (1857); F. Perles, *Analekten zur Textkritik des AT* (1895); F. Delitzsch, *Die Lese- und Schreibfehler im AT* (1920). J. Kennedy in *An Aid to the Textual Amendment of the OT* (ed. N. Levison, 1928), should be used with caution.

form קברם ("their grave"). Transposition of consonants can be seen in Amos 6:2, where the Hebrew reads, "*Is their* border wider than *your* border?", thus supplying the wrong answer. Quite clearly the respective suffixes of the two nouns have been transposed accidentally, with the result that *your* must be read for *their* and *vice versa*. The acrostic form of Nahum 1:6 transposes the first two words, so that the second must be regarded as actually coming first in order to supply the ו needed for the acrostic.

Errors of confusion can be subdivided into *aural* and *visual* classes, depending on whether the scribe was writing from dictation or from sight. Aural errors are those in which the scribe substitutes one letter for another similar one on the basis of sound (e.g. 1 Sam. 2:16; 1 Kgs. 11:22); in visual errors consonants of like form are confused (e.g. Isa. 14:4). Conjectural emendation, or the restoration of the Hebrew or Greek text to a state that, in the opinion of the scribe, conveyed the best sense, was resorted to in cases of lacunae or gaps in the exemplar, or where the faded ink made the reading illegible. Quite frequently the general sense of the context left little doubt as to what was intended, although in at least one instance the inadequacy of this procedure can be demonstrated from internal evidence. Apparent illegibility of the text in 2 Samuel 22:33 led the scribe to emend the line to read, "God is my refuge," influenced possibly by verse two of the chapter. However, the duplicate form of the verse in Psalm 18:32 makes it clear that the original read, "God was girded with power," a reading that is supported by the versions.

An interesting variant arising from wrong word-division and pointing can be seen in Amos 6:12, where the Massoretic text reads, "Does one plow with oxen (*babbᵉqarim*)?" This obviously gives an answer that was not intended, and some versions, such as the AV and RV, have accordingly inserted the word "there" in order to make some sort of sense. Clearly the copyist read two words as one, so that the Hebrew should have been divided up into *bᵉbhaqar yam* ("with an ox [the] sea") to read, "Does one plow the sea with an ox?" Less sophisticated alterations are found in Jeremiah 27:1, where "Jehoiakim" should read "Zedekiah," as indicated by the context and as corrected by several ancient versions. Abbreviated forms frequently led to error also, as in Isaiah 5:19, where the consonant ה representing the Divine Name, was absorbed into the preceding word.

Another common scribal addition to the text is that of *dittography*, in which the copyist wrote a letter or an entire word twice instead of once. Thus initial consonant כ in the word for "thy garment" found in the Massoretic text of Isaiah 63:2 should be omitted on such grounds, and the text of Ezekiel 48:16 should be similarly amended to omit the second "five." Scribal glosses were commonly employed in antiquity to explain rare words in the text, as in Isaiah 51:17, 22, where the word כום

("cup") was inserted in order to convey the proper meaning of the unfamiliar קבעת, a Ugaritic term meaning "libatory vessel." Scribal corrections made in the margins of manuscripts were sometimes incorporated into the text, and this may explain the phrase "an evil divine spirit" in 1 Samuel 18:10, where "evil" may have been intended as a marginal improvement upon or correction of "divine."

Where there are apparently unnecessary words in the text, their presence may point to the readings of two different manuscripts or groups. This may possibly underlie the awkward rendering in 1 Samuel 28:3, where the phrase "in his city" appears to be a variant of "in Ramah" which was incorporated into the narrative, presumably on the authorship of an independent manuscript source. A more developed form of this situation consists of the conflation or blending of different accounts of the same incident, as in Zechariah 12:2, where the mention of "Judah" and "Jerusalem" seems to have combined two sets of textual possibilities.

Scribal omissions can be posited in all instances in which the Massoretic text is shorter than the original appears to have been, and each of these mistakes seems to have been unintentional. The resultant losses vary from the omission of a single letter, as in 2 Samuel 22:41, where the meaningless תתה should read נתתה ("thou hast given")—as in the duplicate section in Psalm 18:41—to the omission of the phrase "let us go into the field" after the Massoretic reading, "And Cain said unto his brother Abel . . ." in Genesis 4:8, which was retained by several ancient versions.

Haplography, or the failure to repeat a letter, syllable, or word, can be contrasted with instances of *homoiosis,* where the same or similar letters or words are accidentally repeated. In Genesis 32:23, *hû'* should read *hahû',* "on that night"; in Judges 20:13 the word *b'nê* should precede "Benjamin" to read, "And the Benjamites were not willing." Haplography is also commonly found in cases of similarity between the last consonants of two words or the last words of two phrases, and is known as *homoioteleuton.* This phenomenon occurs when the eye of the scribe jumps across the contents of a section enclosed between identical or closely related words, and can be seen in 1 Samuel 14:41, where it is evident from the ancient versions that an entire section has been omitted.[47] Similar examples of the loss of a passage between identical words can be seen in 1QIsaᵃ 4:5f.; 16:8f.; and 23:15.

D. THE ROLE OF THE TEXTUAL CRITIC

While the avowed aim of the textual critic is to recover the original Hebrew form, it must always be remembered, as Winton Thomas has

[47] D. R. Ap-Thomas, *A Primer of OT Text Criticism,* pp. 40f.

pointed out,[48] that this objective is essentially ideal, and in actual fact cannot be attained to a large extent. Indeed, the very concept of an "original Hebrew" raises certain pressing theoretical and practical questions, even if it is granted that at least some of the Old Testament documents existed at one time in a single textual form. Aside from the strictly ben Asher manuscript, it is at least possible that even the Massoretic text itself was never completely free from mixed readings. However, the pressing need for the textual critic is to come to grips with the pre-Massoretic text, hypothetical though this may be from some points of view. For this purpose he will find the Massoretic tradition an indispensable starting-point for assessing the text-types from Qumran on the one hand and those underlying the ancient versions on the other.

Textual critics have generally proceeded on the principle that the more ancient the document is, the greater is its authority. This dictum must be modified by the realization that, given two manuscripts of different antiquity, the older one may have been copied from a comparatively recent and inferior exemplar, while the other may reach back to a considerably earlier and better text. Furthermore, the character of the text as it occurs in different manuscripts must also be borne in mind, since particular copyists have been known to be amenable to certain typical errors.[49] Again, it should be recognized that the incidence of divergences might not necessarily indicate textual corruption so much as the existence of variant textual forms, especially insofar as peculiarities of dialect are involved.[50] Textual corruptions can also be eliminated by comparative means, although it must be remembered here that sheer numerical preponderance can never be decisive in itself. No matter how many representatives there may be of the same archetype, they can obviously count as only one witness to the nature of the text.

As has been noted earlier, the Qumran discoveries have enhanced the prestige of the LXX considerably in matters of textual criticism. Some of the Qumran scrolls occasionally agree with the LXX against the Massoretic text in places where the LXX was thought to paraphrase and be unsupported by any Hebrew tradition. Even here, however, it must be urged that the readings of the Biblical scrolls from Qumran need not necessarily be good ones simply because they may antedate or differ from those of the Massoretic text. Merely to compare individual LXX readings with their counterparts in the traditional Hebrew text can lead to an unbalanced view of the essential worth of the LXX version. It is true, of course, that the Qumran discoveries have lent considerably more stature to the historical books of the LXX, but, as with all translations of the Hebrew, it has become apparent that the attitudes and techniques of

---

[48] *OTMS*, p. 259.
[49] Cf. J. Hempel, *ZAW*, XLVIII (1930), pp. 191ff.
[50] Cf. B. J. Roberts, *JJS*, I (1949), pp. 147ff.

the translators need to be studied carefully before the superiority of a part or the whole of their work is conceded. Such controls have placed the LXX in a rather different light from that of an earlier period, and in the future will insure that the proper precautions are taken in its use.

It seems most probable that all future critical reconstructions of the text will be rather eclectic, with each variant reading being judged upon its merits in the light of all the available textual evidence. While this procedure obviously involves a certain degree of subjectivity, it will be controlled to a large extent by the vast body of knowledge that is now available from such disciplines as epigraphy, lexicography, and comparative linguistics. If on examination it is found that either the Samaritan Pentateuch or the LXX, for example, offers a better rendering than that of the Massoretic Hebrew, the textual critic will be governed accordingly. He will also be sufficiently instructed in his discipline to avoid the mistaken view espoused by some contributors to the critical apparatus of the *Biblia Hebraica* that a divergent LXX reading, when retranslated into Hebrew, necessarily represents the "original" pre-Massoretic Hebrew. Textual emendation will still be necessary, but this procedure can no longer be undertaken in the spirit of gay abandon that characterized some areas of Old Testament scholarship in earlier generations. The textual critic is in some respects a responsible interpreter of the text, particularly in those places where the Hebrew is badly corrupted. He will, however, subject himself to those controls that safeguard the integrity of the Hebrew text and the versions, and such tentative emendations as are suggested will be given their proper place in the critical apparatus, and will not be presented to the unsuspecting reader as an authoritative rendering of the text.

However inviting and relatively harmless his work may be thought to be as a discipline, the textual critic will not be content with merely producing as perfect a restoration as possible of the one complete, though textually faulty, Hebrew recension that has been handed down by tradition. If the doctrine of inspiration means anything at all for the written Word of God, it surely refers to the original autographs, since subsequent copyists, however gifted or diligent, were not themselves inspired. The true objective of the textual critic, therefore, should be the restoration of the Hebrew to the point where it is as near as possible to what the original author is deemed to have written. Such an endeavor will confront all the present difficulties of the Massoretic text with every device of modern scholarship, and will make full and proper use of those ancient translations that are known to have been based upon Hebrew exemplars of one family or another. The exercise of the purely subjective factor will itself be governed by adequate controls, and the end-result will constitute an impressive attempt to reconstruct a genuine pre-Christian Old Testament text, thus making the ancient Word of God more intelligible to its modern readers.

IV. THE OLD TESTAMENT CANON

A. The Growth of the Canon

The study of the Old Testament canon can properly commence with the observation that all the major world religions have as their legacy a collection of writings that the devout regard as the word of God to a greater or lesser extent, and therefore as containing authoritative norms for faith and practice. Not all adherents of the various religious faiths existing in the modern world maintain that their Scriptures are necessarily inspired, but in any event they normally regard them as enshrining the highest degree of religious authority. The Hebrew Scriptures, emerging as they did over a lengthy period of time and from widely diverse circumstances, constituted the official collection of Jewish religious literature. Portions of this material were originally oral, and represented the communication of revealed truth from God to man. Some historical sections were in written form from the beginning, and there is no doubt that certain portions of the Hebrew Scriptures co-existed in written and oral forms for prolonged intervals.

To speak of a "canon" of Scripture is to employ the Greek term κανών in one of its special senses. The word itself was derived from such Semitic cognates as the Assyrian *qanû*, the Ugaritic *qn*, and the Hebrew *qaneh*. These were borrowed in turn from the Sumerian GI-NA, which originally meant a "reed" (Job 40:21). In this sense the term passed into Greek, Latin, and other languages to indicate something of a reed character or structure. In a figurative sense it implied anything straight and upright, and in Greek it was used, among other things, to describe a rule, standard, paradigm, model, boundary, chronological table, and a tax assessment. The Greek and Latin Church Fathers applied the word κανών in a general sense to Biblical law, an ideal or exemplary man, articles of faith, Church doctrines, a catalog or list, a table of contents, and an index of saints.[1] It is possible that Origen may have used the designation "canon" in the sense of the divinely inspired books of Scripture, although there is no direct evidence that it was applied to the Bible

---

[1] Cf. A. Souter, *Text and Canon of the NT* (1912), pp. 154ff.

as such any earlier than *ca.* 352, when Athanasius (d. A.D. 373) used it in this precise sense in the *Decrees of the Synod of Nicea,* No. xviii.

The earliest designation of the books of the Old Testament as the "holy books" or "holy writings" occurred in the work of Josephus, *ca.* A.D. 100. For him the essential characteristic of canonical Scripture was that it constituted divine pronouncements of unquestioned authority that originated within the prophetic period and were therefore under divine inspiration. It was also to be distinguished from every other form of literature because of its intrinsic holiness; the number of canonical writings was strictly limited, and its verbal form was inviolable.[2] These views were completely in accord with the pronouncements of official Judaism as they were ultimately crystallized in the Talmud. While in Greek usage the term κανών appears at first to have denoted the catalog of sacred literature as such, the Latin Fathers employed the designation for Scripture itself, thus indicating that this literary corpus vested with divine authority constituted the rule for faith and life.

Although the Jews of the immediate pre-Christian period venerated their national literature, and in particular regarded the Torah as the authoritative guide to godly living, they were somewhat indiscriminate in their acceptance of material that could be considered as "holy writ." The nearest approach to the idea of canonicity was expressed in the Mishnah,[3] where it was stated that those writings which accorded with such a concept "render the hands unclean." The meaning of this phrase is at best rather uncertain, and numerous explanations have been adduced for it. It may have been intended to insure greater caution against the profanation of the sacred scrolls by careless handling, but it seems more likely that, regarding the sacrosanct nature of the canonical writings, it described a situation whereby contact with such scrolls demanded ritual ablutions after handling in order that conditions of ceremonial purity might be maintained.[4] The term was ultimately extended to include all the writings in the canonical list determined by the rabbinic authorities, thereby distinguishing such compositions from non-canonical works.[5]

While there is a distinct sense in which it can be asserted that it was Christian theism that specifically related the ideas of inspiration and authority to the concept of Biblical canonicity, using the latter term to embrace the writings of the New Testament as well as those composi-

---

[2] *Contra Apionem,* I, 38ff.; cf. Hölscher, *Kanonisch und Apokryph* (1905), p. 4; S. Zeitlin, *Proceedings of the American Academy for Jewish Research,* III (1932), pp. 121ff.

[3] *Yad.* III, 5.

[4] Cf. G. F. Moore, *Judaism,* III, pp. 65ff.; S. Zeitlin, *An Historical Study of the Canonization of the Hebrew Scriptures* (1933), p. 19; M. Haran, *Tarbiz* (1956), XXV, pp. 245ff.; cf. *Yad.* IV, 6; *Zab.* V, 12; *Shabb.* 13*a*, 14*a*.

[5] Cf. L. Blau, *Zur Einleitung in die Heilige Schrift* (1894), pp. 21, 69ff.

tions which were venerated by the Jews, it must never be forgotten that later Jewish tradition also adopted the view that every word of Holy Writ was inspired by the divine Spirit. In each instance this Spirit was believed to have rested upon a prophet, and in consequence every Old Testament book was attributed to the activity of a prophetic author. For the Christian the use of the term "Old Testament canon" signifies that the Old Testament is to be regarded as a closed collection of books, inspired by the Spirit of God (2 Tim. 3:15), having a normative authority, and valid as the rule for faith and life. The final provision is important for the Christian, since it serves to emphasize the unity of the revelation in both Testaments, and also witnesses that there are important aspects of the Old Testament self-disclosure of God in history that are binding upon both Christians and Jews for all time. This is in direct contravention of the view, popular in some quarters, which asserts that the Christian ethic can commence with the Sermon on the Mount rather than with the events on Mount Sinai and earlier phases of Hebrew covenantal history.

In any discussion of the Old Testament canon it is of importance to distinguish between that of the Hebrew Bible and its counterpart in other versions of Scripture. The degree of difference in the idea of a canon of sacred writings can be seen by reference on the one hand to the Samaritan version, in which only the Pentateuch was accorded canonicity, and on the other to the LXX, which included the writings known as the Apocrypha. Furthermore, while in many versions the books listed were generally the same as those of the Old Testament canon, the order and number were apt to differ considerably, as was the length of certain of the compositions. The Hebrew canon comprises twenty-four books arranged in three major divisions which are designated the Law, the Prophets, and the Writings respectively. By contrast, the various Christian Bibles, following the general pattern of the Greek and Latin versions, recognized thirty-nine books as canonical, dividing Samuel, Kings, Chronicles, and Ezra-Nehemiah into two books each, and regarding the Minor Prophets as twelve separate works.

The very fact that the canon exists at all in its present form is a striking testimony to human activity and cogitation under divine guidance. Unfortunately it is virtually impossible to be more specific than this about the processes by which the Old Testament canon, or parts of it, became acknowledged as authoritative. While the Bible legitimately ought to be allowed to define and describe canonicity, it has in point of fact almost nothing to say about the manner in which holy writings were assembled, or the personages who exercised an influence over the corpus during the diverse stages of its growth. Historical investigation is no more fruitful in uncovering significant information about the activities of synods or other authoritative bodies with regard to the formation of the Old Testament canon than any other form of study. For the Hebrew Scriptures, however, this circumstance need not occasion particular surprise, since they are of a self-authenticating character, and do not derive their authority either from individual human beings or from corporate ecclesiastical pronouncements. As Ridderbos has pointed out,[6] the various books possessed and exercised divine authority long before men ever made pronouncements to that effect. Ecclesiastical councils did not give the books their divine authority, but merely recognized that they both had it and exercised it.

The concept of a divine norm or rule reaches far back into Hebrew history. Adam, Noah, and Abraham received specific commandments from God that served as their rule of faith and life, and which were enshrined in written form at an early period. During the Mosaic age specific collections of laws were put into writing, as indicated by the formulation of the Book of the Covenant (Exod. 24:4ff.) and the composition of the essentials of Deuteronomy (Deut. 31:9ff.). The latter was of particular importance, because it was placed in close proximity to the highly sacred Ark of the Covenant to constitute the divine witness to the people. Its position was an indication of the sacredness and divine authority attaching to this legal code, which was required to be read in the presence of the nation (Deut. 31:11). To insure equity in Israel, the king was to be given a copy of it, and he was to regulate his decisions according to its contents (Deut. 17:18ff.). Even a revered figure such as Joshua was commanded to adhere to its precepts (Josh. 1:8).

In subsequent periods of Hebrew history the Mosaic Torah was considered to be the divine rule for faith and life (1 Kgs. 2:3; 2 Kgs. 14:6), and the people were urged continually to obey its injunctions. In this connection the prophets played an important role, for they reminded their hearers that the misfortunes and calamities that overtook them were divine judgments for disobedience of the Law, and made it clear that further infractions could only result in drastic punishment. While the prophets urged deference to the Law, and frequently based their own utterances upon its doctrinal themes, they also regarded the words that they themselves spoke under the influence of the divine afflatus as of equal authority with the Torah, arising as they did from the same inspirational source. Popular disregard of their pronouncements was held to bring an equal measure of divine wrath upon the heads of the offenders as did disregard of the Law.

The exalted position that the Torah occupied in Hebrew national life as the standard for faith and practice is reflected in the attitude adopted by the Old Testament writers towards their sources. Unlike many authors in other nations and at different periods, the Hebrews treated their source material with profound respect, preferring to copy the sections

---

[6] *NBD*, p. 187; cf. E. J. Young in *Revelation and the Bible* (ed. Carl F. H. Henry), p. 157.

that they needed as literally as possible rather than quoting them freely from memory. Because their sacred literature was an essentially vital and relevant corpus, and because it still had to attain to the degree of fixity that became a concomitant of canonicity, it was possible for the ancient Hebrews to interpolate additional material into their writings, to replace one law by another when altered circumstances made such a procedure necessary,[7] or to engage in whatever revisions were considered desirable and proper at the particular time.

The belief that God could reveal His will by means of a holy book was thus an early and indelible feature of Israelite religious life. This concept did not originate, as Eissfeldt imagined,[8] from a belief in the word of an inspired person—the *torah* of the priest or the utterance of the prophet— so much as from the fact that what the inspired individual said constituted the *verba ipsissima* of God, and was accepted as such even though its implications were not always taken to heart. By uniform tradition the early normative communications of God to Israel took the form of laws, which were committed to writing by and large within the contemporary situation. On two occasions Israel solemnly pledged herself to obey the Book of the Law that God had given through Moses, first during the reign of Josiah (2 Kgs. 23:2ff.; 2 Chron. 34:30ff.), subsequent to the discovery of an ancient legal code of unknown content, second during the period of Ezra and Nehemiah (Ez. 7:6, 14; Neh. 8:1ff.), when the "Book of the Law" comprised at the very least a part of the Pentateuch.

It is impossible in the light of present knowledge to state with any degree of certainty exactly when the Pentateuch was finished in its extant form, although there seem to be substantial grounds for thinking that it was virtually complete by the death of Samuel.[9] What can be said, however, is that from the very beginning of its existence high authority was attached to its contents, and as a result it is little wonder that it became the first major section of the Hebrew Scriptures to be accorded unquestioned acceptance prior to subsequent formal canonicity. It is evident that the Torah in general, and Deuteronomy in particular, goes back in principle to an early period of Israelite life from the presence of a formula of imprecation warning against adding anything to its contents or detracting from it in any way (Deut. 4:2; 12:32). So specific a command, which is reflected only once in other parts of the Old Testament (Prov. 30:6), was employed in a considerably more elaborate form at the end of the laws of Hammurabi,[10] where impreca-

---

[7] For such modifications compare Num. 26:52-56 with 27:1-11, 36:1-9; Num. 15:22-31 with Lev. 4:1ff.

[8] *Einleitung in das AT*, p. 615.

[9] Cf. R. Brinker, *The Influence of Sanctuaries in Early Israel*, pp. 216ff., 224.

[10] *ANET*, pp. 178f.

tions were directed at any who would endeavor to alter the law. Hammurabi's law was codified under the stated patronage of the deity Shamash and mediated by a great leader of the state to the people, who were given due warning to pay careful heed to its contents. As far as Hebrew religious tradition was concerned, the fundamental precepts of the Mosaic Torah were manifested to Israel through the agency of a divinely appointed leader of the populace. Thus the idea of a revealed, authoritative, and mediated written code was by no means novel both before and during the Mosaic era. The fact and existence of the Mosaic Torah at an early period furnished the foundations for all subsequent religious writing in Israel, and as such supplied one element of the concept of canonicity.

It may be, as Bentzen has suggested,[11] that another germinal aspect relating to the formation of a canon of Scripture is what von Rad has called the "historical *credo* of Israel"[12] as it occurs in certain types of Old Testament literature.[13] Some caution should be urged in entertaining this idea, however, since it would be comparatively easy to assume that such a *credo* constituted the skeletal form that was subsequently clothed by the religious traditions of an Israelite "amphictyony" and enriched by the "laws of the state." It must be remembered, accordingly, that the *credo*, if it can be legitimately conceived of as such, was only one element in a tradition that was already rich in literary material (as will be argued subsequently in the present work) and had as its authoritative written foundation the legislation given to Moses on Mount Sinai.

It is clear, therefore, that the Torah did not only mark the beginning of a body of national literature (a fact that, in the event, is rather incidental to more pressing spiritual considerations) but also constituted the normative expression of the divine will for the Hebrew people. By its very nature it established a basis for doctrine and life upon which subsequent expositors of revealed religion leaned heavily. So deeply rooted were the traditions as to the antiquity and sanctity of the Mosaic enactments that the term "Torah" was applied not only to the first five books of the developing canon, but also to the entire corpus of the Hebrew Scriptures at a later period. This designation, which occurs in 2 Esdras 19:21, and in John 10:34 under the form *nomos*, arose from the belief, popular in rabbinic circles, that the Prophets and the Writings were to be included in the Torah, since Holy Writ in its entirety constituted the Word of God. Since, however, "Torah" was the title of the first and principal section of the Biblical writings, it is also conceivable that it

---

[11] *Introduction to the OT*, I, p. 24.

[12] G. von Rad, *Das Formgeschichtliche Problem des Hexateuchs* (1938), pp. 3ff.

[13] Exod. 15:1ff.; Deut. 26:5-9 (cf. 6:20-24); Josh. 24:2-13; Ps. 136:1ff.

265

was transferred to the entire collection as a means of indicating its inspiration and canonicity.

The second major section of the canon, the Prophets, was commonly subdivided into two parts. These were the "Former Prophets," consisting of the books of Joshua, Judges, Samuel, and Kings, and the "Latter Prophets," which comprised Isaiah, Jeremiah, Ezekiel, and the Twelve. The authority that the Former Prophets acquired is readily understandable when it is realized that these writings describe the manner in which the provisions of the Covenant agreement were applied to the conditions in the land of Canaan. As chronicles of the relationships between God and His people, these documents were without doubt drawn up by individuals of official standing in Israel, and so in many respects would have a secular as well as a religious authority.

By their very nature the compositions of the Latter Prophets were held to be authoritative from their earliest appearances, although initially, at least, the number of those who venerated them as writings whose tenor and spirit were akin to that of the Torah was probably quite small. Almost certainly their authority was enhanced greatly when the predictions of disaster that many of them contained found fulfillment in the exile, and the victims of that catastrophe were forced to think of other aspects of the prophetic message. That the individual prophets themselves felt that they stood in a firm and unified spiritual tradition can be seen from the manner in which they ascribed authority to their predecessors either by quoting from their utterances, alluding to incidents in the Torah (e.g. Jer. 4:4; 5:15, 17; 11:4), or rebuking the nation for not listening to previous prophecies (Zech. 1:4ff.; Hos. 6:5). Undoubtedly some of this material was set down in written form during the lifetime of most if not all of the individuals concerned, as were the prophecies of Jeremiah. If the reference in Daniel 9:2 to "the books" is to a collection of prophetic writings, as seems most probable, it would imply that these works were regarded as having divine authority, and were thus akin to the Pentateuchal compositions.

The third major division of the canon, known as the Writings or Hagiographa, comprised eleven compositions of diverse character emanating from various facets of Hebrew life. The collections of psalms that formed the basis of the Psalter were important both for private and public devotions and for their associations with the sanctuary and the cultus and the revered name of David, the traditional father of Hebrew psalmody. In the same manner, the connecting of the proverbs with Solomon and the growth of the Wisdom Literature from the utterances and traditions of the Hebrew sages led to the acceptance of important elements of this division of the canon as constituting authoritative moral and spiritual pronouncements that participated fully in the divine spirit expressed in the Torah. Historical and prophetic writings such as those attributed to Daniel, Ezra, and Nehemiah were also accepted as being in keeping with the religious tenor of other aspects of the national literature, as were the Chronicles, which were compiled with a specific theological standpoint in view. These and other books were regarded properly as holy writings because of their association with the cultus, the national history and tradition, and revered personages of the past. If the Prophets can be said to have derived some of their authority from their consonance with the teachings of the Torah, the Writings did also, springing as they did from the very warp and woof of the Hebrew spiritual fabric.

There are some grounds for assuming the antiquity of a twofold rather than a threefold division of the canon, in which the Old Testament Writings were subsumed under the second major section because of the similarity of some of the compositions to the works of the prophets, with the result that the canon was simply thought of in terms of the Law and the Prophets. References in certain of the Qumran scrolls, to be mentioned subsequently, indicate that the sectaries themselves thought in terms of a twofold division, as did some of the copyists of later LXX manuscripts.

The foregoing outline of the conjectured growth of a canonical corpus of Old Testament writings is, of course, general and is based in part upon the rather scanty internal information that the Old Testament furnishes with regard to the assembling and the relationships of the various canonical books. From the purely Jewish standpoint there is a distinct sense in which the concept of canonicity can only have been crystallized and implemented when there were sufficient works in the corpus of Hebrew literature from which a selection could be made, since not all Hebrew writings were accorded canonicity. As far as the historical books were concerned, the finished product alone rather than the underlying sources constituted the preferred choice. In the sense that they were incorporated in some manner into the final production the sources themselves could be considered canonical, but the most obvious reason for the overall attitude consisted in the comparative availability of the extant work as contrasted with that of the source material. Public acceptance was thus one important criterion of canonicity. The feelings of the readers regarding canonicity were governed, of course, by the considerations of essential consonance with the spirit of the Torah and the other factors referred to above.

B. Speculation About the Canon

The completed Jewish canon consisted of twenty-four books as follows: five of the Pentateuch, eight books of the Prophets—Joshua, Judges, Samuel, Kings, Isaiah, Jeremiah, Ezekiel, the Minor Prophets, and eleven Writings—Psalms, Proverbs, Job, Song of Solomon, Ruth, Lamentations, Ecclesiastes, Esther, Daniel, Ezra, and Chronicles. From the Greek translation by Aquila it is seen that Samuel and Kings formed one book each; the Twelve were also known as a single work in the time of Ben Sira (Ecclus. 49:10). The division of the Prophets into "Former" and "Latter" was evidently introduced by the Massoretes. Later Jewish tradition gave great prominence to the activity of prophets in the formulation of the canon of Scripture, and held that every word of Holy Writ was inspired by the Spirit of God. Because this Spirit was believed to have rested in every case upon a prophet, it followed that the authorship of such Biblical books ought to be attributed to prophetic functioning.

1. Baba Bathra. The classical passage for the sequence of the books in the Babylonian *Baba Bathra* 14b proceeded on this assumption, discovering the prophetic author either in the titles or the sequence of the works themselves. Thus Moses, Joshua, Samuel, Ezra, and the Prophets were credited with having written the compositions attributed to them; in addition Moses was regarded as the author of Job, whose hero was held to have been his contemporary. The last eight verses of the Pentateuch were thought to have been composed by Joshua. Samuel was given credit for the authorship of Judges and Ruth. Jeremiah was believed to have written Kings and Lamentations, and Ezra the scribe was regarded as the author of Chronicles. There was thus an unbroken chain of prophets from Moses to Malachi, into which company David and Solomon were also placed. The Psalms were credited as a whole to David, while Proverbs, Canticles, and Ecclesiastes were assigned to the literary activity of Solomon. Esther alone was not attributed a prophetic author, but this omission was more apparent than real since Jewish tradition venerated Mordecai as a prophet contemporary with Haggai, Zechariah, and Malachi and he was held to have prophesied at the time of Darius I. In any event, the position of Esther was safeguarded by the tradition that the Great Synagogue had numerous prophets among its members, who took upon themselves the right to have the Esther scroll written down.[14] Quite clearly, then, one dominant criterion of canonicity for the ancient Jews was the attribution of a work to prophetic authorship, so that a composition such as Ecclesiasticus, in which the identity of the author was known to be non-prophetic, presented absolutely no problems as far as canonicity was concerned.

In summary, from the Jewish standpoint only those works which could properly claim prophetic authorship had a legitimate right to canonicity, and out of this corpus there was a decided preference for finished works rather than for source material of prophetic origin. The relationship of the particular author to the theocracy was also an important determining consideration.[15] Moses was naturally a towering figure in the Old Testament economy generally, since he occupied a pre-eminent position as the faithful servant of God (cf. Num. 12:1ff.). In virtue of being as-

[14] Cf. *Yom.* 80a; *Shabb.* 104a; *Megill.* 2a.
[15] Young in *Revelation and the Bible,* pp. 165f.

268

sumed as the author of the Pentateuch as a whole, and the real contributor of a significant amount of its contents, his literary products formed the foundation on which the entire Old Testament corpus was based.

Although the second section of the Hebrew canon, the Prophets, comprised material written by men standing within the spiritual tradition of Moses, these individuals were nevertheless inferior in stature to the great lawgiver himself. In the theocracy, therefore, their position in the affections of the Jews is shown by the division that incorporated their writings into a second major group of sacred literature, different in content from the Torah but akin in moral and spiritual quality. Although there are some respects in which the attribution of prophetic stature to certain of the authors of compositions in the Hagiographa imposes a strain upon the concept of prophetism, it may well be that the writers concerned were thought of in the ancient Hebrew sense as mediators between God and the nation, or as representatives of God in their capacity as spokesmen to the people (cf. Exod. 4:16; 7:1; Deut. 18:15ff.). At all events they appear to have been accorded a position of considerable importance in the traditions of the Israelites, quite aside from being regarded as inspired by the Holy Spirit of God. Perhaps it was this that led to a twofold division of the canon into the Law of Moses and the Prophets, in which some, if not all, of the compositions subsequently designated by the technical term *K^ethubhim* or "Writings" were included.

Whatever the motivation governing the curious and sometimes rather uncritical kind of rabbinic speculation in matters of Scripture, the threefold division of the canon was well established in the early Christian era. The New Testament makes it clear that the canon familiar to Jesus Christ was identical with the one which exists today. None of the Apocrypha or Pseudepigrapha is ever cited by name, much less accorded the status of Scripture, whereas Daniel is specifically quoted as a prophetic composition in Matthew 24:15. The three chief divisions were enumerated in Luke 24:44 as the Law, the Prophets, and the Psalms. Usually the New Testament writers only mentioned the first two sections (cf. Matt. 5:17; Lk. 16:16), but quite obviously they included the Hagiographa with the Prophets just as the Talmudic teachers did (due perhaps to the lack of a current technical term for the Hagiographa).

From the words of Jesus in Matthew 23:35 and Luke 11:51, it can be inferred that Chronicles was regarded as the last book in the Hebrew canon at that time. The murder of Abel is recorded in the first canonical writing (Genesis); that of Zechariah is contained in the final book of the Hebrew Scriptures (2 Chronicles 24:20). Of course no chronological order is intended to be conveyed by the words of Jesus, since innocent blood was shed after the killing of Zechariah (Jer. 26:23). The reference in Matthew could possibly be to the prophet Zechariah, who was the son of Berechiah (Zech. 1:1), although there is no independent evidence to the effect that he was martyred. Alternatively, some have supposed that

269

the reference is to the martyrdom of Zechariah the son of Jehoiada (2 Chron. 24:20-22), and that the error of the father's name was due either to the Evangelist himself, or, since it does not occur in the best manuscript of Luke, to the addition of a copyist.

Further evidence of a threefold division of the canon is provided by Josephus,[16] who enumerated five books of Moses, thirteen prophetical writings, and four books of hymns to God and precepts for human behavior. Probably Josephus arrived at the number thirteen for the second division of the canon by including Ruth with Judges and Lamentations with Jeremiah, and regarding the Minor Prophets as a unified book in the manner current in the time of Ben Sira. A threefold canon of Scripture was also given attestation in the writings of Philo, particularly in his *Contemplative Life*, written about A.D. 40.[17] Although some doubt was thrown on the genuineness of this work by nineteenth-century scholars, there is, as Cohn has demonstrated,[18] no substantial ground for such an attitude. Philo mentions by title the Law, the Prophets, the Psalms and other books, but does not refer to Ezekiel, Daniel, or the five Megilloth (Canticles, Ruth, Lamentations, Ecclesiastes, and Esther) in his extant works. But Philo's failure to name these books cannot be taken as proof that they were not in his canon of Scripture, for as Blau has pointed out,[19] the silence of Philo concerning Ezekiel is most probably accidental, since even Ben Sira mentioned the book attributed to that prophet. Consequently, there seems no good ground for questioning the assertion of Siegfried[20] and others that the canon known to Philo was essentially the same as that current at the present time.

An even earlier attestation of the threefold division is to be seen in the Prologue to Ecclesiasticus, dated about 132 B.C., in which specific mention was made of the Law and the Prophets (or prophecies) as well as "the others which follow after them." Since the author of the Prologue stated that his grandfather Jesus ben Sira, the compiler of Ecclesiasticus *ca.* 190 B.C., had long given himself to a careful study of the "law and the prophets and the other books of the fathers," it is legitimate to assume that this threefold division went back at least to the beginning of the second century B.C. A reference in 2 Maccabees, which was extant by about the middle of the first century of the Christian era and may have been compiled as early as 100 B.C., spoke of the founding of a library by Nehemiah, who "gathered together the books concerning the

---

[16] *Contra Apionem*, I, 8.
[17] *De Vita Contemplativa*, II, 475.
[18] *Einleitung und Chronologie der Schriften Philo's* (1899), p. 37.
[19] *JE*, III, p. 146.
[20] *Philo* (1875), p. 61. Cf. H. E. Ryle, *The Canon of the OT* (1904), pp. 158ff.

kings and the prophets, and those of David, and the epistles of the kings concerning holy gifts" (2 Macc. 2:13f.).

The Torah was not mentioned in this collection, since its wide circulation made references to it unnecessary. However, there can be no doubt about the second part of the canon, which was unmistakably specified by "books concerning the kings," that is, Joshua, Judges, Samuel, and Kings, and by "the prophets," namely, Isaiah, Jeremiah, Ezekiel, and the Minor Prophets. Since the Hagiographa had not at that time received its technical designation, the contents were referred to as "those of David," that is, the Psalms, using as a title the first and most important book of the collection. But if the expression "the books of the kings concerning holy gifts" indicates the royal letters mentioned in Ezra and Nehemiah,[21] then the Hagiographa as a whole would seem to be implied by reference to the Psalms and Ezra-Nehemiah-Chronicles as the first and last books respectively.

As mentioned above, the classical definition of the sequence of canonical Hebrew Scriptures was the *baraitha* or unauthorized gloss in the Talmudic tractate *Baba Bathra*. There are reasons for believing that the gloss is of second-century B.C. origin, for at that time there was considerable discussion as to which books of Scripture belonged to the same section, and therefore were to be written in one roll. With the exclusion of interpolated comments[22] the *baraitha* is as follows:

> The order of the prophets is Joshua, Judges, Samuel, Kings, Jeremiah, Ezekiel, Isaiah, the Twelve (Minor Prophets). That of the Kethubhim is Ruth, Psalms, Job, Proverbs, Ecclesiastes, Song of Solomon, Lamentations, Daniel, the roll of Esther, Ezra, Chronicles.
>
> Who wrote the books? Moses wrote his book, the section about Balaam, and Job; Joshua wrote his book and the last eight verses of the Torah; Samuel wrote his book, Judges, and Ruth. David wrote the Psalms at the direction of the Ten Ancients, namely through Adam [Ps. 139:16; Ps. 92?], Melchizedek [Ps. 110], Abraham [Ps. 89], Moses [Pss. 90-100], Heman [Ps. 88], Jeduthun [Ps. 62, Ps. 77?], Asaph [Pss. 50, 73-83], and the three sons of Korah [Pss. 42, 49, 78, 84, 85, 88]. Jeremiah wrote his book, the Book of Kings, and Lamentations; king Hezekiah and his council wrote Isaiah, Proverbs, Song of Solomon, and Ecclesiastes; the men of the Great Synagogue wrote Ezekiel, the Twelve Prophets, Daniel, and Esther. Ezra wrote his book and the genealogy of Chronicles down to his own period. Nehemiah completed it.

From the fact that Moses is mentioned as the author of the Torah it may be gathered that the five books of the Law were originally designated in the collection to which the gloss referred. However, because of the familiarity of the Jews with the Torah through contemporary synagogue usage, it could well have been regarded as comprising a single

---

[21] For the view that they were letters from the Persian kings relating to gifts for the Temple see G. Ch. Aalders, *Oud-testamentische Kanoniek* (1952), p. 31.

[22] For the full form, translated from G. A. Marx—G. Dalman, *Traditio Rabbinorum Veterrima* (1884), see H. E. Ryle, *The Canon of the OT*, pp. 284ff.

work whose component parts needed no specific enumeration. Since the gloss does not specify the books according to their origin, succession, and age, it can only have considered the order of the Biblical writings insofar as they belonged to the same section of the canon. Yet it seems clear from the gloss that the "Former Prophets" had been credited with a fixed sequence of considerable antiquity concerning which there was no doubt in the minds of the rabbinical authorities. This was evidently occasioned by the way in which the writings from Joshua to Kings carried on the narrative of Hebrew history from post-Mosaic times (cf. 2 Macc. 2:13). The order of the "Latter Prophets" was irregular, and in the majority of manuscripts the only uniformity occurred in the placing of the Twelve Minor Prophets at the end of the list of books. According to Ginsburg there were no fewer than eight varying sequences of the Hagiographa.[23]

The *baraitha* in its fuller form is certainly a curious piece of writing, containing as it does some strange and occasionally impossible traditions regarding the composition of certain books of the Hebrew canon. While it has often been held to have had an important bearing upon the history of the canon, its contents demonstrate that it can throw no light at all upon the processes by which the canon achieved its final form. The unusual order of Jeremiah, Ezekiel, and Isaiah was explained by Talmudic authorities on the basis of a principle of internal consistency. Kings ended with destruction, and as such was appropriately succeeded by the prophecy of Jeremiah, which began and concluded with desolation also. Despite the fact that Ezekiel commenced with destruction, it ended with consolation, while all of Isaiah consisted of a consoling theme. In this way destruction appropriately followed upon destruction, and consolation upon consolation. This explanation is patently artificial, and it seems most probable that the prophetical books were actually arranged according to their size, a principle that appears to have been followed also in the accumulation of Mishnaic treatises.

2. *Apocrypha, Septuagint, and patristic sources.* It seems highly improbable that there was ever any specific enumeration of the books of the canon in Jewish literature generally. Early estimates were apt to vary somewhat; Second Esdras gives the number as twenty-four,[24] whereas Josephus computed the number as twenty-two.[25] In his preface to Samuel and Kings, Jerome mentions twenty-two books, but he finally arrived at a total of twenty-four, whereas Origen adhered to the number suggested by Josephus.[26] Since both Origen and Jerome studied under

[23] *Introduction to the Massoretico-Critical Edition of the Hebrew Bible* (1897), p. 7.

[24] 2 Esdr. 14:44ff. Variant readings (94, 204, 84, 974) agree in containing the number "4."

[25] *Contra Apionem*, I, 8.

[26] In Eusebius, *Hist. Eccl.*, VI, 25.

Jewish teachers, it appears probable that the synagogue authorities themselves were somewhat undecided on the matter. The *baraitha* seems to favor twenty-four books, if Ruth formed one roll along with Judges or Psalms, and if Lamentations was included with Jeremiah on another roll, thus making twenty-two rolls but twenty-four books. The latter number was mentioned specifically in some Midrashic passages, and according to Strack[27] it was also known in antiquity in certain non-Jewish circles.

Scholars generally assume the arrangement of the books as given in *Baba Bathra* to be essentially the original one, and that of the LXX to be secondary. This view is by no means undisputed, however. Although the antiquity of the threefold division of the canon is never seriously questioned, it is obviously difficult to ascertain the order and contents of a section referred to as "the prophets" (Lk. 24:44), for example. In this general connection some reference may be made again to Origen and Josephus. The latter stated that the number of sacred books received by the Jews was twenty-two, which he distinguished from other works and enumerated as the five books of Moses, thirteen compositions in which the prophets described Hebrew history from the immediate post-Mosaic period to the reign of the Persian monarch Artaxerxes I, and four books containing hymns of praise and regulations for social behavior.[28] It seems reasonably certain that Josephus combined Ruth and Lamentations with Judges and Jeremiah respectively in his computation, as suggested above, and that in so doing he was following a well-established Palestinian tradition.

Origen, who also held that the Jews accepted twenty-two books as their Scriptural canon, showed considerably greater conformity to the order of the LXX in his enumeration of the canonical writings than did Josephus and some rabbinical authorities.[29] However, he did not follow the LXX listing slavishly, and there are significant differences between the two. It is at least reasonable to conclude from Origen's testimony that the order of the canon in *Baba Bathra* did not command unquestioned assent in Palestine during that period.[30] From the evidence presented by the Qumran texts it would seem probable that there were several different forms of the canon in existence by the first century of the Christian era, which is in harmony with the rather fluid picture of the pre-Massoretic text as indicated by the Qumran scrolls.

Any assessment of the LXX canon of the Old Testament must note that the Greek manuscripts exhibit significant differences, both in the

---

[27] In J. J. Herzog (ed.), *Real-Encyklopädie für Protestantische Theologie und Kirche* (1896), IX, p. 757.

[28] *Contra Apionem*, I, 8.

[29] In Eusebius, *Hist. Eccl.*, VI, 25.

[30] Cf. A. Jepsen, ZAW, LXXI (1959), pp. 114ff. and *Theologische Literaturzeitung*, LXXIV (1949), pp. 65ff.

number of the books that they contain and the order in which they are arranged. Such a situation would appear to reflect an earlier Palestinian Jewish tradition, and indicate the secondary nature of the LXX canon. It is of significance that Philo followed the Jewish rather than the Alexandrian tradition in his estimate of the content of Scripture. It would seem that the differences between the Hebrew and the LXX canons lie not so much in a wider interpretation of the canon by the Alexandrian Jews because they thought in terms of a much broader view of inspiration, as in the fact that the Jews in Alexandria (and the Diaspora generally) did not distinguish as sharply between the canonical and non-canonical works as their Palestinian counterparts did. Had they done so it is highly probable that the early Christian Church would have looked a little more critically at the excess of the Hebrew canon that they used in the LXX version.

A criticism of the originality of the Hebrew order was made by Katz,[31] who maintained that the earliest attestation of the Hebrew selection of books was related to the period of the reconstitution of Judaism after the destruction of the Temple. He further claimed that the evidence for twenty-four as the number of Old Testament canonical books was scanty, and that twenty-two was the proper and correct total as known in Palestine. In order to disprove the originality of the Hebrew order of books, he maintained that the arrangement Ezra-Nehemiah-Chronicles was artificial, a position that, in the view of the present author, is extremely difficult to justify, even if the Chronicler is considered to be someone other than Ezra. As has been remarked above, it is quite likely that in early times several forms of the canon existed side by side, preserving the same threefold division but varying to some degree in content. The fact that the Old Testament books were written down on separate rolls would contribute to this diversity and indeed would serve as a hindrance to the appearance of a fixed order of books. The canon of the LXX evidently reflected this general state of affairs, and perpetuated it in some ways, thus showing its dependence upon the traditions of the Palestinian Jews.

Although neither the *baraitha* nor the Hellenistic Jews of Alexandria can furnish proper information relating to the compilation of the Hebrew canon, it is interesting to note that for many centuries the view was current that the canon of the Old Testament was formulated and completed within the lifetime of Ezra. This tradition drew for its Biblical foundation upon Ezra and Nehemiah (cf. Ez. 7:10, 25; Neh. 8:1ff.; 9:3), and was given currency not merely by *Baba Bathra*, which credited Ezra with the compilation of his own book and the genealogy of Chronicles to his own time, but also to some extent by the opinions of Josephus. About

[31] *Zeitschrift für die Neutestamentliche Wissenschaft*, XLVII (1956), pp. 191ff.

274

A.D. 95 Josephus recorded that the history of the origin of the world up to the reign of Artaxerxes I had been described in the Jewish holy writings, and added that although the story had subsequently been carried towards his own time, this latter material did not deserve the same confidence on the part of the reader, since the succession of the prophets was not fixed accurately.[32] From this statement it can be inferred with great probability that during the lifetime of Ezra the historical books of the Old Testament, and perhaps some portions of the Hagiographa as well, were circulating in their extant form.

Second Esdras, a Jewish apocalyptic composition whose central section seems to have been written by an unknown Jew at the end of the first century of the Christian era, preserved the tradition that in the thirtieth year after the destruction of Jerusalem (557 B.C.) Ezra was inspired to dictate ninety-four books to five scribes within a period of some forty days. Of this corpus twenty-four books were to be made available for general perusal, while the remaining seventy, evidently consisting of apocalyptic material, were to be restricted to the wise men (2 Esdr. 14:18ff.). Presumably the twenty-four books were the same as those mentioned by other writers—with Ruth and Lamentations as separate works which had been incorporated, for various reasons, with Judges, Psalms, or Jeremiah. Another apocryphal work, 2 Maccabees (ch. 2:13ff.), contains a letter purporting to have been written by Palestinian Jews to the Hellenistic Jews of Alexandria. This epistle mentions the nature of the library said to have been assembled by Nehemiah. If it is genuine, it would be dated 165 B.C., but many scholars have denied its authenticity and assigned it to the first century B.C. While these passages may be nothing more than attempts to project into the age of Ezra and Nehemiah certain tendencies that were only evident at a later period, it must not be forgotten that the middle of the fifth century B.C. was a time when considerable interest was shown in the codification of Hebrew sacred literature. On the other hand, neither the Talmud nor Josephus specifically credits Ezra with a special function in the formulation of the Old Testament canon, even though *Baba Bathra* mentions his literary activity.[33] The tradition that ascribes to Ezra an important role in the creation of the Old Testament canon only appears to go back with certainty as far as the account in 2 Esdras, and the nature of this material is such that it is difficult to ascertain its historical value. Despite this fact it may well be that the narrative was based upon a genuine tradition of collection and assemblage of Scriptural materials in the fifth century B.C., whether by Ezra, Nehemiah, or some of their followers. In the same way it is at least possible that an historically reliable tradition is at the root of the information furnished by 2 Macca-

---

[32] *Contra Apionem*, I, 8.
[33] Cf. E. Bickermann, *RB*, LV (1948), p. 398.

bees. Whatever may be the facts of this situation, it is simply a matter of record that little is known about the development of the canon in the period immediately following the time of Ezra and Nehemiah. As has been observed previously, Ben Sira knew of the threefold division of the Old Testament canon, and attached high authority to the various sections. He was familiar with at least some of the Writings, though to what extent he was conversant with all of them is uncertain. In the narratives about the Maccabees there are numerous references to the sacred books of the Jews,[34] although it is impossible in the nature of the case to be certain as to the extent to which such a corpus corresponded to the Old Testament canon.

By the time of Christ, it would seem, the Old Testament existed as a complete collection. The evidence presented by the New Testament writers indicates that the Old Testament as a whole was referred to as "the Scriptures"[35] or "the Scripture"[36] at that period to designate a familiar and unified group of inspired and authoritative writings. In particular, the specific designation of "Old Testament" was applied by the primitive Church to this corpus of Holy Writ to convey the sense of a completed assemblage of Scriptural compositions (2 Cor. 3:14). New Testament authors commonly alluded to the Scriptures in terms of two categories—the Law and the Prophets. Support for this position has been provided by the discoveries from Qumran, where in four instances the Community Rule or Manual of Discipline (1QS, I:3; VIII:13ff.) and the Zadokite Fragment (CDC, V:21; VII:15ff.) referred to the Old Testament writings in precisely the same two categories. That this twofold canon included all the present works appears obvious from the fact that the Qumran community cited most of the Old Testament books, including those later classified in the third section of the canon. On this evidence alone there would seem to be considerable ground for a theory of the antiquity of a twofold division of the Old Testament canon.

Naturally it is impossible to determine in detail the contents of the canon in the time of Christ, although, as has been mentioned above, one reference (Matt. 23:35, Lk. 11:51) would imply that the canon terminated with Chronicles at that time. The fact that Esther, Ecclesiastes, Canticles, Ezra, Nehemiah, Obadiah, Nahum, and Zephaniah are not cited by New Testament authors does not in itself indicate that these compositions were not considered to constitute part of the Old Testament at that particular period, since being quoted in the New Testament is not a necessary condition of canonicity for an Old Testament book.

If this assemblage of sacred writings was substantially the same in the days of Jesus Christ as it is at the present, such a canon was "closed"

---

[34] E.g. 1 Macc. 1:56f., 4:30, 7:41, 12:9.
[35] Matt. 26:54; John 5:39; Acts 17:2, et al.
[36] John 2:22; Acts 8:32, et al.

more by common consent and popular acceptance than by formal decree on the part of the rabbinic or early Christian authorities. In connection with this latter concept an appeal has sometimes been made to the work of the "men of the Great Synagogue," who were referred to in the Talmud.[37] Unfortunately it is far from clear as to precisely who these men were. According to some theories they belonged to a generation that included Haggai, Zechariah, Daniel, and Esther, a view that Ryle repudiated as "ignorant tradition."[38] In the view of Elias Levita (d. A.D. 1549), these men, along with Ezra, united in one volume the twenty-four books of the canon, which until that time had circulated separately, and classified them in three divisions, determining the order of the Prophets and the Sacred Writings.[39]

Although Levita's arrangement differs from the order listed in *Baba Bathra*, his view gained currency in the sixteenth century, and for the next two hundred years was accepted as orthodox. From the middle of the seventeenth century, however, the nature of the "Great Synagogue" was disputed, and in the nineteenth century Kuenen argued strongly that the "Synagogue" was none other than the great assembly at Jerusalem described in Nehemiah 8:1ff., which pledged itself to the acceptance of those conditions enunciated by Ezra the scribe from the ancient Jewish law.[40] On the basis of the available evidence[41] it would seem that if such a body of men as was envisaged in *Baba Bathra* actually existed, its activity was confined to the period of Ezra and that it extended to only four books, not the entire Old Testament canon. When it is said that they "wrote" Ezekiel, the Twelve Prophets, Daniel, and Esther, what is meant is clearly that they were engaged in editing such works, probably with a view to incorporating them into a sacred canon.

3. *The "Council of Jamnia."* It has also been suggested that pronouncements that defined the limits of the Old Testament canon were made by a formal council of Jewish authorities held towards the end of the first century after Christ at Jamnia or Jabneh. Desirable though such an event might have been, it is far from certain that there ever was a Council or Synod of Jamnia in the strictest sense. To speak of such a body as though it was responsible for closing the Old Testament canon

---

[37] *Bab. Bath.* 14b, 15a.

[38] *The Canon of the OT*, p. 290.

[39] E. Levita, *Massoreth Hammassoreth* (1867 ed.), p. 120; cf. A. Bentzen, *Introduction to the OT*, I, p. 27.

[40] Kuenen in K. Budde (ed.), *Gesammelte Abhandlungen* (1894), pp. 161ff. He was followed, among others, by W. Robertson Smith, *The OT in the Jewish Church* (1881), pp. 156ff., 168f.; *DILOT*, p. vii; K. Budde, *EB*, I, cols. 654f. The tradition was defended by C. H. H. Wright, *The Book of Koheleth, Commonly Called Ecclesiastes* (1883), pp. 475ff.; S. Krauss, *JQR*, XI (1898-99), pp. 347ff.

[41] Cf. E. Bickermann, *RB*, LV (1948), pp. 397ff.

by fixing its limits as they had been arrived at by A.D. 90 is to beg the entire question, as Moore has pointed out.[42] As far as the facts of the situation are concerned, very little is known about the supposed Synod of Jamnia. After Jerusalem was destroyed by the forces of Titus in A.D. 70, Rabbi Johanan ben Zakkai obtained permission from the Romans to settle in Jamnia, where he proposed to carry on his literary activities. The location soon became an established center of Scriptural study, and from time to time certain discussions took place relating to the canonicity of specific Old Testament books including Ezekiel, Esther, Canticles, Ecclesiastes, and Proverbs.[43] There can be little doubt that such conversations took place both before and after this period, and it seems probable that nothing of a formal or binding nature was decided in these discussions, even though, as Rowley had indicated,[44] the various debates helped to crystallize and establish the Jewish tradition in this regard more firmly than had been the case previously.

If it is questionable as to how far one can speak correctly of the Council of Jamnia, it is even more doubtful if the participants in the discussions were actually concerned with the problem as to whether certain books should be *included* in the canon of Scripture or not. Rather, as Young has pointed out,[45] the conversations seem to have centered upon the question as to whether specific books should be *excluded* from what was to be regarded as the Scriptural corpus. Certain compositions were generally accepted as inspired and authoritative, even though they reflected the Jewish tradition in a somewhat peculiar fashion: Esther did not mention the Divine Name; Ecclesiastes seemed partly Epicurean to some authorities and out of harmony with contemporary Jewish philosophy; and the Song of Songs, though credited to Solomon, appeared to be nothing more than a composition dealing with the vagaries of human passion and physical love.

The fact is that the works under discussion were already accorded canonical status in popular esteem, so that, as Stafford Wright has stated,[46] the "Council" was actually confirming public opinion, not forming it. The conversations that took place were strictly academic, and in consequence it is very questionable if the doubts that they raised in connection with certain compositions actually represented the general attitude of the populace as a whole to any significant extent. Certainly Ezekiel, to mention but one topic of dispute, must have been accepted as Scripture long before the rabbis of Jamnia undertook to examine its status. It ought to be concluded, therefore, that no formal pronounce-

---

[42] *Judaism,* I, pp. 83ff.; cf. W. W. Christie, *JTS,* XXVI (1925), pp. 347ff.
[43] Cf. *Yad.* III, 5; G. Lisowsky, *Jadajim* (1956), pp. 9, 57.
[44] *The Growth of the OT* (1950), p. 170.
[45] *Revelation and the Bible,* p. 160.
[46] *EQ,* XIX, No. 2 (1947), pp. 93ff.

ment as to the limits of the Old Testament canon was ever made in rabbinic circles at Jamnia.

4. *Modern theories.* The manuscript discoveries at Qumran provide little information about the origin and limits of the Old Testament canon. The library of the sectaries included numerous religious compositions other than those normally accepted by the Jews, but as far as the content of the Hebrew canon is concerned, the only work missing in the early discoveries was Esther.[47] One reason for this omission from the Qumran collection of scrolls may be that it was deliberately rejected by the sectaries.[48] On the other hand, the absence of the manuscript could be entirely a matter of chance, and the book may yet be discovered in the fragments which at the time of writing have still to be examined and evaluated.

As far as the available evidence goes, it is clear that while the Old Testament does not furnish any significant information about the manner in which the canon arose, or the extent of the Prophets and the Writings at any given period of their history, it does bear testimony to the existence from early times of an authoritative literature to which appeal was made in varying ways and which, with subsequent additions, was venerated as Holy Writ. This vague internal testimony has been more than offset by the precision of modern critical scholarship, which has furnished a number of theories as to the growth and content of the Old Testament canon. These views have generally emphasized the concept of the Biblical canon in terms of purely human acceptance of a national literature, taking no particular cognizance of the divine inspiration or authority of the canonical writings.

Such approaches are a product of their age in the sense that, for the most part, they are firmly wedded to the outlook and tenets of the Graf-Wellhausen school. Thus Ryle[49] maintained that a Hebrew national literature was in existence long before there was any canon as such. While the latter was assembled in three successive stages, due notice had to be taken of the literary antecedents of the various books, the redaction to their extant form, and finally the elevation of these works to a position in the national canon of Scripture. For Ryle, as for all liberal scholars, the Pentateuch in its finished form was the end-product of a prolonged period of growth during which various supposed documents were brought together and edited. When Ezra read what Ryle and others thought to be the Pentateuch in the presence of the assembled multitude, this Law was acknowledged as binding upon the people and was deemed canonical as a result. However, such a canon was inade-

[47] F. M. Cross, *BASOR*, No. 141 (1956), pp. 9ff., 56ff.

[48] So H. L. Ginsberg in *Israel: Its Role in Civilisation* (ed. M. Davis, 1956), p. 52.

[49] *The Canon of the OT*, pp. 29ff.

quate, for considerable interest had been aroused during the time of Nehemiah in preserving the utterances of the prophets. These books were subsequently canonized perhaps between 300 and 200 B.C., possibly as a result of the threat which Hellenistic culture was posing to traditional Judaism. When the prophetic portion of the canon was closed, other writings such as Ecclesiastes were assembled, and their popularity during the Maccabean period led to their being recognized as authoritative. Ryle maintained, with some others,[50] that the entire collection was deemed canonical by about A.D. 100, and related this activity to the Council of Jamnia.

A modification of this view appeared in the work of Hölscher, who thought that one mark of canonicity consisted in the fact that the very holiness of the books distinguished them from every other form of literature, a suggestion made considerably earlier by Josephus. Hölscher[51] did not subscribe to the idea of a threefold canonization of Scripture, but suggested instead that the concept of the canon arose because Greek culture and the growth of Greek literature presented a serious challenge to the religious traditions of Judaism. Equally pressing was the widespread dissemination of Jewish apocryphal material, so that in being compelled to separate the genuine from the spurious the Jewish religious authorities were forced to accept the idea of a canon of Scripture. The Torah was highly venerated from the seventh century B.C., but even when it had reached its final form about the end of the fourth century B.C. it was still not accorded canonicity. The same situation existed for the Prophets, which in the opinion of Hölscher were added periodically to the larger corpus up to the middle of the second century B.C. The testimony of Ben Sira could not be regarded as evidence that the prophetical canon was closed by that time,[52] but instead served to indicate the particular works which had come to be regarded with special veneration by about 190 B.C. For Hölscher, proof that the idea of a canon had not arisen at that time was furnished by the fact that Ben Sira could speak of himself as the latest of all the Biblical writers (Ecclus. 33:16), and deck out his utterances in the style of the ancient prophets.[53] Plausible as the latter objection sounds, it does not explain precisely why Ecclesiasticus failed to gain acceptance into the Old Testament canon, nor does it recognize the fact that Ben Sira was not standing in the tradition of the prophets, but of the ancient Hebrew sages.

[50] E.g. Wellhausen, *Einleitung in das AT,* pp. 550f.; F. H. Woods, *HDB,* III, p. 614; K. Budde, *EB,* I, cols. 671f.

[51] *Kanonisch und Apokryph,* pp. 4ff.

[52] This view was adopted by F. Buhl, *Kanon und Text des AT* (1891), p. 12, Ryle, *The Canon of the OT,* p. 113, and others.

[53] Hölscher, *Kanonisch und Apokryph,* p. 20.

A similar view of the formation of the canon was adopted by Oesterley and Robinson,[54] who acknowledged their indebtedness to Hölscher, and maintained that the concept of relative holiness provoked the idea of a canon of Scripture. The feeling that some books were more holy than others could not, in their view, have arisen all at once. Indeed, it was only gradually and by general consent that certain works came to have a special sanctity attached to them.[55] Oesterley and Robinson followed Hölscher again in maintaining that there had never been three successive stages in which the principal collections of books were in turn recognized as canonical in the strictest sense. For them the fixing of the Biblical canon was a piecemeal affair, and was governed in part by the spread of Hellenism and the impact of Jewish apocryphal literature upon the nation. The canon was supposed to have been formulated finally about A.D. 100, and when completed was recognized by the Jews as binding and authoritative. But, as Anderson has pointed out,[56] a theory of this sort seems to attribute too much to an assembly whose very existence has been questioned, and for which the evidence is neither precise nor complete. Any denial of a threefold stage in the organization of the canonical Hebrew Scriptures must take cognizance of the veneration associated with the Law on the part of both Jews and Samaritans, and the fact that, for the latter, the Torah alone was canonical. This is not to say, however, that a more detailed tripartite division of Holy Writ did not ultimately emerge from a clarification in definition and usage of a corpus of Scripture which was in general thought of in terms of two preponderant sections, the Law and a collection of prophetical writings.

According to Bentzen,[57] the reading of the Law in the time of Ezra and Nehemiah probably signified the introduction of the form of the Torah which was current in Babylonian Jewish circles at that particular period. Basing his views upon the critical analysis of the Pentateuch he maintained that even if the latter was not complete, comparatively little could have been lacking. In any event, the idea of a normative lawbook occurred as early as the reform of King Josiah in 621 B.C., a time which was of particular importance for the formation of the idea of a holy written law. Even earlier, however, was the ancient concept of law as given by a god, and also, following von Rad,[58] the ancient *credo* of Israel.[59] Nevertheless, these ideas did not lead to the fixed concept of a canon, the oldest portion of which was established when the various

[54] *IBOT*, pp. 5ff.

[55] *Ibid.*, p. 2.

[56] *A Critical Introduction to the OT* (1959), p. 13.

[57] *Introduction to the OT*, I, pp. 22f.

[58] *Das Formgeschichtliche Problem des Hexateuchs*, pp. 3ff.

[59] A similar position was adopted by G. W. Anderson, *A Critical Introduction to the OT*, p. 13.

alleged strata of the Pentateuch were unified in the post-exilic period. For Bentzen the prophetic section of the Old Testament canon commenced when Isaiah (8:16) imposed upon his disciples the obligation to be the bearers and preservers of his words, and when Jeremiah instructed his secretary Baruch to commit his prophecies to writing. The exile was of great importance in that it sealed the prophetic utterances with the stark confirmation of history. The post-exilic prophets, who stood in the tradition of their predecessors (cf. Zech. 1:4; 7:7), had their writings regarded as canonical somewhat before 200 B.C., while the Hagiographa, the most vaguely defined portion of the canon, was probably complete by the time the prologue to Ecclesiasticus was written. Plausible as this theory may appear, it unfortunately fails to take account of the fact that the Samaritans venerated the Torah as canonical from at least the time of Ezra and Nehemiah, if not indeed considerably earlier, and that it was the Jewish and not the Babylonian form of the Law that they accepted as authoritative. Again like many another liberal scholar, Bentzen assigns too late a date to many of the writings in the Prophets and the Hagiographa, and thus finds it necessary to consider the Synod of Jamnia important in the fixing of the Old Testament canon.

A modification of the views expressed by Ryle occurred in the writings of R. H. Pfeiffer.[60] He maintained that the first instance of canonization in human history occurred when Deuteronomy, discovered during the reign of King Josiah, was venerated as the Word of God and respected as a norm for human behavior. But apart from this, other literary works in Israel were being combined and edited about 650 B.C. to comprise a national epic. A century later the canonized Deuteronomy was interpolated into the corpus of this material, with the result that the latter also came to be regarded as canonical. About 200 B.C. the so-called "Priestly document" was inserted into this combined work, and it also attained to canonicity as a result. Unhappily this theory not merely reflects all the weaknesses associated with the developmental theory of Pentateuchal origins, but assumes quite gratuitously and without any evidence that the lawbook recovered from the Temple in the time of Josiah actually constituted the book of Deuteronomy, a position for which there is not the slightest factual justification. Even a casual reading of the text will be sufficient to indicate that the finding of the Temple scroll was in fact the rediscovery of an already authoritative book, of which both Josiah and Hilkiah had heard previously, but which had been lost. Pfeiffer maintained an inadequate view of the concept of canonicity, as would seem evident from his assertion that a book could apparently exist from 650 to 550 B.C. as a mere national epic, and then suddenly span the gap separating the secular from the sacred to become the Word of God. Furthermore, Pfeiffer's assumption that the Jewish scribes would incor-

---

[60] *PIOT*, pp. 50ff.; *IDB*, I, p. 503.

porate non-canonical material with that which was deemed canonical reflects a fundamental misunderstanding of the entire Jewish attitude towards Scripture.

Critical authors have been apt to maintain that the Law, in part or whole, attained to canonical status through the activities of Ezra and Nehemiah.[61] Since, however, Ezra was described as an "adept scribe in the Law of Moses" (Ez. 7:6), it is apparent that the Mosaic enactments had already become an object of professional study in their own right prior to his time. Furthermore, the whole purpose of Ezra in going up to Jerusalem with the permission of Artaxerxes was to insure that the precepts of the Law were carried out. Ezra 7:14, 23, 25, 26 shows clearly that the Law was already in existence, and that its commands required the wholehearted obedience of the people. There is consequently no evidence whatever that Ezra, in virtue of his position in the community, was about to impart to certain already existing religious writings of the Hebrews a degree of moral and spiritual authority that they had not possessed at an earlier time.

In the same way it is incorrect to see Nehemiah 8—10 as an account of the canonization of Scriptural writings.[62] The "book of the Law of Moses" that Ezra read at the request of the people, which resulted in a solemn act of religious renewal, owed its authority to the fact that it was an ancient document believed to have constituted material revealed by God to Moses. Rather than being an occasion on which the opinions of men were given in such a way as to assign canonical stature to a written composition by common resolve, it demonstrated that it was the inherent authority of the book itself that, when properly received, subjected the assembled throng to the judgment of God and recalled the populace to the observance of the ancient religious precepts.

If these considerations apply to Ezra and Nehemiah, they are of equal force for the "men of the Great Synagogue" and the Council of Jamnia—assuming that the latter was a properly constituted body. What these groups did, if anything, was to approve as canonical works that which had for long been venerated as authoritative. Even though doubts had arisen concerning Ecclesiastes and the Song of Solomon, the weight of tradition was such that they were included in the corpus of Scripture without undue difficulty.

The fundamental issue that divides liberal scholars from their more conservative counterparts appears to be their rejection of inspiration as the ultimate determining principle of the extent of the Old Testament canon. For liberal scholars the formation of the Scriptural corpus was nothing more than a type of human activity in which certain books were

[61] E.g. S. Zeitlin and S. Tedesche, *The Second Book of Maccabees* (1954), p. 113.

[62] So Ryle, *The Canon of the OT*, pp. 80ff.

regarded as canonical because they had demonstrated their pragmatic value in religious usage. However, such a theory has to face the fact that, although works such as Ecclesiasticus and 1 Maccabees had undoubted value for Judaism, they failed to secure a place in the canon of Scripture. Even if the concept of conformity to the spirit and ideals of the Torah is held to be the determining factor in the formation of the canon, as is commonly maintained by some writers, the problem still needs to be taken one stage further back by accounting for those principles which resulted in the canonization of the Law.

In contradistinction to the liberal outlook, the available evidence supports the position that the Old Testament writings, being divinely inspired, were consequently authoritative and were accepted as such from the period of their initial appearance. The Spirit of God that inspired these compositions also worked in the hearts and minds of the chosen people to testify to them that the writings were in fact the divine Word. It was this witness, in conjunction with the conscious human response, that was evidently the ultimate determining agent in the formulation of the canon. Had the question of canonicity merely rested upon purely academic decisions without an acknowledged concept of inspiration, it is impossible to see how the Jews could ever have come to accept the Old Testament books as being of divine authority. If considerations of positive affectivity had been dominant in the process of endeavoring to arrive at some form of canonical delineation it is very doubtful that more than a fraction of the extant canon would ultimately have proved to be acceptable, since the majority of the Old Testament compositions were severely critical of the ancient Hebrews in one way or another.

There is little doubt that matters relating to inspiration were responsible for furnishing at least some of the criteria by which certain compositions were assigned by the rabbinic authorities to the third division of the Hebrew canon. As has been noticed earlier, Jewish tradition maintained that all the Old Testament authors were prophets. Not all the contributors to the K‘thubhim or Sacred Writings could claim this distinction, however; for example, Daniel was a statesman rather than a classic mediator between God and a theocratic nation. His position in the third division of the canon was apparently justified by the fact that works in the K‘thubhim were deemed to have been written by individuals who were not prophets in the strictest sense of the word, but who nevertheless wrote under divine inspiration.[63]

It has been already observed that numerous questions were raised at different times among rabbinic authorities concerning the canonicity of certain highly esteemed compositions. In particular, discussion centered

[63] Cf. N. Schmidt, JE, III, p. 152; R. L. Harris, Zondervan Pictorial Bible Dictionary (1963), p. 145.

upon Ezekiel, Esther, and the three works attributed popularly to Solomon—Proverbs, Ecclesiastes, and Canticles. The opposition to Ezekiel was only temporary, and apparently arose because the priestly nature of the program outlined in the concluding nine chapters of the prophecy was thought to be in conflict with the tenor of the Pentateuch. Those who questioned its suitability for inclusion in the canon wished to prevent its use as authoritative Scripture, but the work was ultimately rehabilitated by the labors of a certain Hananiah ben Hezekiah ben Garon, who "spent three hundred jars of oil to release it."[64]

Tannaite scribes of the second century B.C. were eager to include the Esther scroll in the canon of Scripture, and in the end the issue turned upon the question as to whether or not the work actually constituted a revealed composition. If the latter proved to be the case and the book was found to have proceeded from other than divine inspiration, it could not properly be given a place in the list of Scriptural writings.[65] Despite considerable uncertainty on the matter,[66] it was ultimately agreed, with Rabbi Simeon (150 B.C.), that Esther "defiled the hands," and as such it was deemed canonical. The opposition to Proverbs was comparatively slight, and was based for the most part upon apparent internal inconsistencies. Similar objections were levelled against Ecclesiastes,[67] although in this case it was felt that the quasi-Epicurean tone of the book was out of harmony with the religious traditions of Judaism.[68] The canonicity of Ecclesiastes was supported, among others, by the followers of Hillel, while the most vigorous opposition apparently came from the strict school of the Shammaites.[69]

According to Rabbi Simon ben Menasya, the Song of Solomon "defiled the hands," since it was inspired by the Holy Spirit of God.[70] Regarding this work it can be said in general that it does not appear to have evoked any specific statement to the contrary. That there was prolonged, and perhaps acrimonious, discussion concerning Canticles, however, is apparent from the drastic step taken by Rabbi Aqiba about A.D. 100 to rehabilitate the Song in his celebrated pronouncement that "he who, for the sake of entertainment, sings the Song as though it were a profane song, will have no share in the future world."[71] There can be little doubt that the popularity of works such as Esther, Ecclesiastes, and

---

[64] Cf. *Shabb.* 13b; *Men.* 45a.
[65] Cf. *Yom.* 29a; *Megill.* 7a.
[66] Cf. *Sanhed.* 100a; *Megill.* 19b.
[67] *Shabb.* 30b.
[68] *Levit. Rabb.* XXVIIIff.
[69] Cf. H. Graetz, *Koheleth* (1871), p. 149.
[70] *Tosef. Yad.* II, 14.
[71] *Sanhed.* 101a; *Megill.* 7a.

Canticles in connection with Jewish feast days furnished powerful support for their claim to canonicity.

While certain books were the subject of periodic discussion in this regard, there was no controversy at all in connection with the books of the Apocrypha, for everyone was agreed that they were non-canonical.[72] The reason appears to have been that the works themselves simply gave no evidence whatever of having been divinely inspired. As Green and others have pointed out, some of these writings contain egregious historical, chronological, and geographical errors, quite apart from justifying falsehood and deception and making salvation dependent upon deeds of merit.[73] Although the books of the Apocrypha can quite obviously claim to possess much that is in harmony with the spirit of the canonical compositions, there are numerous instances in which they diverge sharply from the latter.

The lengthy processes by which the canon of the Old Testament arrived at its present form cannot be traced with anything approaching exactitude, and only the most general of principles can be enunciated reasonably satisfactorily. Without doubt the element of divine inspiration was a profoundly important consideration for the Jews, particularly in the immediate pre-Christian period. Equally true is the fact that, from its beginnings, the Pentateuch was considered authoritative because it contained the divine revelation to Moses, and as a direct result it was regarded as the standard to which other writings were to be related.[74] The Torah must obviously have possessed what amounts to canonical authority long before it was accorded such by the Hebrews, otherwise the nation of Israel would have been under no obligation to accept its precepts as the norm for moral and spiritual behavior. The fact of this recognition was thus the effect rather than the cause of the "canonical" status associated with the Torah from early times. It is apparent from the evidence presented by the Samaritan Pentateuch that the Torah commanded a high degree of veneration even prior to the early post-exilic period, and that during the time of Ezra and Nehemiah its authority was accepted anew by the nation.

As far as the prophetic literature is concerned, the evidence is even more scanty, for there is no record in the Old Testament either of formal recognition or acceptance by the people of any of the works contained in the second and third divisions of the Hebrew canon. The fact that some portions of the Hagiographa are older than certain of the prophecies might imply that the second division of the canon remained "open" until

[72] Cf. L. Ginzberg, *JBL*, XLI (1922), pp. 115ff.
[73] W. H. Green, *General Introduction to the OT, The Canon* (1899), pp. 195f.
[74] Cf. G. Wildeboer, *The Origin of the Canon of the OT* (1895), p. 97.

much of the Hagiographa was in existence. Whether this was actually the case or not, the determining principle of canonicity for the Jewish religious authorities appeared to be that of divine inspiration. Even here there are certain difficulties in interpretation, however, for the medieval scholars were accustomed to assert that the three divisions of the canon corresponded to three degrees of inspiration. The highest of these was that of Moses, who communicated directly with God: the second was that attributed to the prophets, who wrote by the spirit of prophecy; while the lowest was that of the other writers, who were inspired by the Holy Spirit of God.[75] Such a differentiation is, of course, completely unsupported by the Scriptures themselves. The prophets believed that they stood firmly in the Mosaic tradition and that their own words possessed equal moral and spiritual authority with the pronouncements of the great lawgiver. Furthermore, the alleged distinction between the spirit of prophecy and the Holy Spirit is purely imaginary.

While the "men of the Great Synagogue" and the Council of Jamnia may possibly have played some small part in the growth of the canon in its final stages, there is insufficient evidence to show that their disputations resulted in any significant fixing of its limits. If the views of those liberal writers who regard the canon as having been "closed" about A.D. 100 are unacceptable because their dating is far too late, the theories of those conservative scholars who would place the closing of the Old Testament canon about 400 B.C.[76] are equally improbable, simply because such a date appears to be too early. In all its essentials the canon was most probably complete by about 300 B.C., and while discussion concerning certain component parts was continued well into the Christian era, the substance of the canon as it existed a century-and-a-half after the time of Ezra and Nehemiah remained unaffected by these controversies.

Supplementary Literature

Blau, L. *Masoretische Untersuchungen.* 1891.

———. *Zur Einleitung in die Heilige Schrift.* 1894.

Fritsch, C. T. *The Anti-Anthropomorphisms of the Greek Pentateuch.* 1943.

Fürst, J. *Der Kanon des Alten Testaments nach den Überlieferungen in Talmud und Midrasch.* 1868.

[75] F. Buhl, *Canon and Text of the OT* (1892), pp. 37f.
[76] So E. B. Pusey, *Daniel the Prophet* (1891), p. 294; W. H. Green, *General Introduction to the OT, The Canon*, pp. 38, 78, 117; J. H. Raven, *OT Introduction*, p. 33.

Kahle, P. *Der Hebräische Bibeltext seit Franz Delitzsch.* 1961.

Lofthouse, W. F. *The Making of the Old Testament.* 1915.

Loisy, A. *Histoire critique du texte et des versions de la Bible.* 2 vols., 1893-1895.

Margolis, M. L. *The Hebrew Scriptures in the Making.* 1922.

Price, I. M. *The Ancestry of our English Bible.* Rev. ed. 1956.

Ryle, H. E. *Philo and Holy Scripture.* 1895.

Tyle, R. H. *The Canon of the Old Testament.* 1904.

Part Five

OLD TESTAMENT HISTORY

Part Five

OLD TESTAMENT HISTORY

I. THE STUDY OF OLD TESTAMENT HISTORY

A. History and Historiography

In its most comprehensive sense history may be said to furnish a description of phenomena in process of continuous change: of all that has happened in human life and in natural life. Such a definition provides a proper basis for both the activities of the historian of science and of the chronicler of various phases of human endeavor. Thus anything that changes in any way, that happens or appears to happen, falls within this broad purview.

In a more restricted sense the concept of history involves a controlled, scientific, descriptive consideration of certain facets of this universal process of change. As a result, history has frequently been thought of in a twofold sense: first, a study of chronological and literary forms as a record of events, and secondly, in possibly a more dynamic manner, as the events themselves, implied, for example, by the expression "makers of history." In the former sense its predominant concern is the basic aims of inquiry and statement; in the latter its appeal to the sense of drama in the human personality has occasionally resulted in the interpretation of processes and movements—sometimes in the absence of specifically written narratives—in terms that have come close to epic proportions.[1]

It may well be this tendency that has led to the familiar charge that historians are chiefly concerned to record only events that result from the activities of the "history-makers," and consequently ignore or treat inadequately large areas of cultural and social development that would be very important to one writing from a different standpoint. In the best sense of the term, the objective of history, as a branch of research or inquiry in the field of the humanities, is the investigation of human activities in a given period or periods of the past[2] with a view to discerning the nature and significance of man's achievements.[3]

---

[1] The writings of chroniclers from Herodotus to the nineteenth-century English historians furnish ample illustration of this attitude.

[2] Cf. R. G. Collingwood, *The Idea of History* (1946), p. 9.

[3] The term ἱστορία was first employed by the sixth-century B.C. Ionians to describe their search for knowledge in the widest sense. It was used at that time to convey the basic impression of inquiry or investigation into a subject in order to obtain

The modern scientific approach to historiography distinguishes two phases in the work of the historian. First, there is a period of investigation in which the facts are ascertained as carefully and accurately as scientific method will permit. Second, there is a descriptive task, involving the presentation of an interpretation of the material accumulated in a systematized, acceptable literary form. This stage inevitably brings aesthetic considerations to bear upon the finished product. Unlike many earlier authors modern historiographers have managed to avoid a heavy reliance upon subjective descriptions of sources far removed from the original events, and they now possess an important array of valuable ancillary tools in such sciences as linguistics, philology, sociology, anthropology, and archaeology.

As Albright has pointed out, the task of the historian is by no means complete when he has accumulated a vast store of properly authenticated historical data.[4] There must be at least some mental reflection upon the problems posed by historical events if the material collected by painstaking research is to become history in the most genuine sense of the word. This, in the last analysis, is a philosophical exercise,[5] which may often be characterized by legitimate moral overtones, for life tends to move in recognizable configurations, thus demanding from the histori-

---

specific information or knowledge (Herodotus, *Hist.*, II, 118). This understanding of the term led Aristotle to designate his *Natural History* by the expression Aἱ περὶ τῶν ζῴων ἱστορία which the natural historian Theophrastus (*ca.* 320 B.C.) imitated in entitling his work 'Η φυτῶν ἱστορία. The knowledge that was obtained as a result of pursuing an investigation was also described as ἱστορία by Herodotus (*Hist.*, I, 1; II, 99) and Hippocrates (*Vet. Med.*, XVI). The earliest use of the word in the sense of a narrative, history, or written account of an individual inquiry can also be traced to Herodotus (*Hist.*, VII, 96; cf. Aristotle, *Rhet.*, I, 4, 13; *Poet.*, IX, 1). By the fourth century B.C. the word ἱστορικός (narrator) had replaced to a large extent the earlier ἱστορέων (inquirer after knowledge), and in the writings of Aristotle (e.g. Poet., IX, 2) it was employed as a substantive to mean "a historian." In Plutarch (*Themist.*, XIII) the phrase τὰ ἱστορικά was interpreted as "histories." Polybius (*ca.* 170 B.C., II, 62, 2) utilized ἱστοριόγραφος, an expanded form of the earlier Greek term, to designate a "writer of history" in the sense of one who pursued inquiry into historical facts; Plutarch (II, 898A) distinguished between this function and that of the narrator (συγγραφεύς) himself. From this it is clear that history as a branch of scientific research activity commenced properly with the work of Herodotus in the secular field. This distinguished writer of antiquity was both narrator and historian. With Aristotle came the application of ἱστορία to the finished literary product enshrining the data accumulated during a prolonged search for knowledge instead of to the inquiry antecedent to the written result. Since that time *historia* has universally been accepted as a form of literature.

4 *FSAC*, p. 82.

5 Thus provoking Voltaire's comment, "Il faut écrire l'histoire en philosophe." Cf. H. Butterfield, *Christianity and History* (1949), pp. 28ff.; C. A. Beard in H. Meyerhoff (ed.), *The Philosophy of History in Our Time* (1959), pp. 142ff.; G. J. Renier, *History, Its Purpose and Method* (1950), p. 253.

an certain conclusions that will necessarily transcend to some extent the data themselves.

Modern historiography has rejected the assumption that the actuality of history can be identical with, or even closely akin to, that of the physical world. History therefore cannot properly be regarded as an exact science, even though it may employ scientific techniques in the execution of its objectives. Yet it can quite legitimately be deemed to constitute a valid interpretation of human affairs, and as such the historian's opinion is an inevitable factor in the larger picture. Since he is dealing with the activities of a species whose character is based in morality, he has every right to include moral considerations in his estimate of the human situation.

The problem of historical interpretation was met in the late nineteenth and early twentieth centuries by such widely divergent approaches as those of Marx and Lenin, Oswald Spengler, and Arnold Toynbee. Marxism rejected the Hegelian notion that the causal force in history subsisted in the process itself, supplying history with its own meaning. For Marxist materialism the only reality was matter in motion, and the Hegelian dialectic was no longer regarded as furnishing the metaphysical clue to the significance of history. Marx conceived of historical processes as having definite meaning and an attainable goal, which would be realized dialectically and would be characterized by material and economic progress in an emerging classless proletariat.

Spengler was an able advocate of the nineteenth-century view that natural law was the valid framework of reference for historians, but he departed from the optimistic evolutionary concepts of progress popular with historians of that century generally and emphasized that decay and doom were the inescapable fate of all civilizations. Spengler maintained that every culture passed through a quasi-biological cycle of birth, progress, and ultimate degeneration,[6] an approach that led him to adopt a concept of naturalistic determinism that was the antithesis of the Kantian and Hegelian notion of progress and freedom as the goals of history. Although Spengler emphasized the importance of the cultural contribution that each epoch of history made to its successors, his failure to comprehend the meaning of history correctly arose from his substitution of a biological metaphor of society for the dynamics of historical processes.

Arnold Toynbee grappled with the problems posed by the forces of cultural change in a significantly different manner by appealing to the *élan vital* of Henri Bergson for a clue to the puzzle as to why civilizations should rise and fall. Starting from the general premise that a definite

---

[6] O. Spengler, *Der Untergang des Abendlandes* (1920), I, p. 153.

forward or upward movement is discernible in history,[7] he adduced a theory that implied that civilizations flourish as long as they meet the challenges confronting them with adequate responses. Despite the attractive development and presentation of this theory, it has failed to answer why there should be a particular time in the history of every culture when a challenge is no longer able to be met successfully, so that degeneration results.

The foregoing represent different reactions to the positivistic German school whose interpretative principles were established through the writings of L. von Ranke, Th. Mommsen, and E. Meyer in the nineteenth century. For those men the task of the historian lay in reconstructing as accurately as possible a picture of what actually took place in the past. Ranke was concerned to let the facts speak for themselves—"*wie es eigentlich gewesen*"—in apparent unawareness that facts so frequently need to be interpreted if they are to be at all meaningful historically. Yet although positivistic method has led in some quarters to a cult of scientific historicism, its emphasis upon accurate verification of facts and classification of data is of supreme importance for any branch of historical study. While it is true to say that it is virtually impossible to envisage a philosophy of history without postulating some sort of generally purposive evolutionary process, it must also be realized that such an outlook is at best only theoretical, and need not correspond to the facts of a situation in a given age or time. Frequently the kind of evolutionary development assumed to be normative by biologists like Darwin is neither completely valid for their own discipline nor for other fields of study to which the principle may be applied.

Any holism that purports to see a continuous and progressive development in the unfolding stream of world history from the comparatively simple existence of primitive peoples to the complexities of modern civilization requires a certain manipulation of the facts. Geological studies have shown conclusively that the flora and fauna in existence at the beginning of each new era occurred in their most developed and highly differentiated forms, and subsequently degenerated through the successive periods of the era until they approached extinction, a situation that was quite the opposite of the process contemplated by philosophically minded nineteenth-century biologists. In the ancient Near East the culture of the Sumerians apparently came on the historical scene in a fully developed form and exerted a vast influence in Mesopotamia before succumbing to the incursions of the Akkadians and Elamites. An even more spectacular example of this tendency is furnished by the culture of ancient Egypt, which burst upon the scene in full flower at the

---

[7] A. Toynbee, *A Study of History* (1934), I, p. 196; III, p. 216. For a survey of this approach see W. F. Albright, *History, Archaeology and Christian Humanism* (1964), pp. 241ff.

beginning of the Old Kingdom period (2700-2200 B.C.) and gradually degenerated (apart from such notable revivals as that experienced at the beginning of the New Kingdom period, 1570-1150 B.C.) until its grandeur was lost irretrievably in the Ptolemaic period.

The most instructive scheme of interpretation is always a servant rather than a master. Particular caution must be exercised whenever any attempt is made to adduce a philosophical interpretation of sequences that can be touted as valid for all civilizations in all ages. Too frequently such approaches are strictly the product of the western mind, and the application of their categories to ancient oriental civilizations is not necessarily valid and in specific instances decidedly untrue. As Albright has wisely remarked, historical and sociological configurations are less rigid than those of the physical sciences, so that the mechanical principles applicable to the latter must be related to the former more as analogies rather than as rigorous demonstrations.[8] Only in this sense is it possible for terms such as "continuum," "operational method," "integration," and the like to be employed, and always on condition that the limitations of this type of procedure are fully recognized. Thus it is of vital importance for the historian to be acutely aware of the need for a proper methodology. If the information upon which he relies cannot survive critical examination of its accuracy, it is clearly not an adequate basis for his general principles. The historian must be determined to face the implications of *all* the available evidence, whether or not it conflicts ultimately with any of his predetermined theories. Too much of what has been allowed to pass as history in recent years has actually consisted of ingenious attempts to arrange factual data so as to make them conform to some preconceived *schema*. This tendency has been as noticeable in the field of Old Testament study as in the writings of Spengler and Toynbee.

B. SEMITIC HISTORIOGRAPHY

Since modern occidental methods of historical interpretation may present decided problems when imposed upon oriental cultures, particularly those of antiquity, it is probably wise to consider the historical outlook and methods of compilation of the Near Eastern cultures on their own terms also, lest the historiographical attempts of antiquity unwittingly be assessed in terms of the scientific methods of more recent times, with equally unfortunate results. The Sumerians were the first peoples who not merely made history, but actually recorded it. Basic to their cultural concepts were the associated ideas of *nam* and *me* (approximating roughly to "essence" and "dynamism"),[9] the activities of

[8] *FSAC*, p. 117.
[9] Cf. E. A. Speiser, *IHANE*, p. 37; T. Jacobsen, *JNES*, V (1946), p. 139 n. 20, approximates *me* to *modus operandi*.

which underlay all cultural functioning. Unfortunately it is at present impossible to determine the role these factors played in the Sumerian idea of history. However, this should not necessarily be taken as an indication that these ancient Mesopotamians were oblivious to the happenings of the past, for the eager manner in which they recorded all kinds of details concerning occurrences in former times furnishes clear indications to the contrary. For the Sumerians history was the very warp and woof of life as manifested in a temporal continuum of past, present, and future events, so that the process of historical appreciation was a matter of personal experience of life rather than the analysis of sources or the formulation of principles. Fortunately for purposes of control, the available source material recurs at different stages of Mesopotamian civilization. It consists of such direct historical references as king-lists,[10] chronicles,[11] and annals, along with literary compositions based upon historical happenings that had been overlaid with myth and legend. Dated bricks, official inscriptions commemorating the erection of palaces and temples,[12] and foundation deposits were also available for those who were interested in the study of the past. The latter sources proved to be of especial value to Babylonian monarchs of a subsequent era who were possessed of antiquarian tastes, as Ashurbanipal (669-627 B.C.) and Nabonidus (556-539 B.C.).

One reason that has been adduced for the preoccupation of later rulers with Mesopotamian antiquities is that they desired to learn how to interpret the present and the future in the light of past experience.[13] This objective was no doubt aided greatly by the extremely conservative attitude adopted towards the traditional values of ancient Mesopotamia. The profoundly superstitious outlook of these peoples virtually demanded that the course of terrestrial events should be governed by antecedent celestial decisions, a prominent feature in their myths and legends. In this sense, therefore, history was of a theocratic order, although, as the mythological cycles indicate, the latter was not absolute, since divine authority was not infrequently modified by other considerations.[14]

Like the Mesopotamians, the ancient Egyptians had no single term for "history" or the "idea of history." Nevertheless, they were at least as

---

[10] See the Weld-Blundell prism, probably written during the Third Dynasty of Ur; S. Langdon, *Oxford Editions of Cuneiform Texts* (1923), II; G. A. Barton, *The Royal Inscriptions of Sumer and Akkad* (1929); T. Jacobsen, *The Sumerian King List*. Assyriological Studies XI (1939).

[11] The Weidner Chronicle recounts the first two post-diluvian dynasties at Kish and Uruk and the Akkadian dynasty of Sargon I; H. G. Guterbock, ZA, XLII (1934), pp. 47ff.

[12] It is not easy to see how Collingwood, *The Idea of History*, p. 11, can dismiss these as lacking "the character of science," since they expressed the facts of the situation as the ancient Sumerians knew them.

[13] *IHANE*, pp. 48f.

[14] *IHANE*, pp. 55f.

interested in the record of their national past as were the Mesopotamians.[15] Events deemed worthy of being handed down to posterity were carefully preserved by royal command, and some of these records reach back into the predynastic period (4500-2900 B.C.). The earliest of these sources is a fragment dating from *ca.* 2550 B.C., made long after the particular events themselves.[16] One portion of this is the celebrated Palermo Stone, a diorite monument that no doubt originally contained lists of the rulers over the two predynastic kingdoms of Upper and Lower Egypt, which were subsequently united under Menes of Thinis at the beginning of the Protodynastic period (*ca.* 2900-2760 B.C.).[17]

The famous Turin papyrus of Kings,[18] written about the thirteenth century B.C. and comprising a list of more than three hundred kings of Egypt, was of unusual interest because its compilers had attempted to trace the rulers back to the celestial deities from whom they were popularly supposed to have descended. Four other shorter king-lists, dating from the New Kingdom period, seem to have preserved a genuine collection of names from the particular epochs with which they dealt.[19] Several genealogical lists, covering many generations and varying considerably in size, have also been dated from the latter part of the dynastic period. To the extent that the references to individuals can be verified from other contemporary sources, the contents of the genealogies appear to be reasonably accurate as they now stand.

Along with the Narmer Palette, which was recovered in 1898 from the temple at Hierakonpolis,[20] the macehead excavated from the same site,[21] and the royal annals of the Old Kingdom period, there are numerous smaller tablets of ivory and wood that contain a wide variety of observations of a historical character. From the Old Kingdom period also came the pyramids, which in every sense of the term can be held to constitute monuments to the historicity of the rulers whose corpses they were designed to protect. Numerous inscriptions recovered from the walls of private tombs have also preserved a wealth of autobiographical material, some of which goes back to a very early period of Egyptian life.

Despite the abundance of historical source-data, the Egyptians do not appear to have manifested too much concern for historiography itself, for

---

[15] Cf. Herod. *Hist.*, II, 77.

[16] Cf. J. T. Shotwell, *The History of History* (1939), I, p. 79.

[17] *LAP*, pp. 70, 74, and pl. 27; Finegan, *Handbook of Biblical Chronology* (1964), pp. 77ff.

[18] Published in 1938 by G. Farina, *Il papiro dei re;* cf. A. Gardiner and J. Černý, *The Turin Canon of Kings* (1952).

[19] *IHANE*, pp. 7ff.

[20] J. E. Quibell, *Hierakonpolis* (1900), I, p. 10 and pl. 29.

[21] *Ibid.*, pp. 8f. and pl. 26B; II (1902), pp. 40f.

no histories have survived from the dynastic period.[22] It was only in the time of Manetho (third century B.C.) that any systematic attempt at historical formulation was undertaken, and even so the result was less in the tradition of Egyptian historical interest than in the Greek view of the significance of events. Although the myths and religious texts make clear their subservience to the deities, there seems in general to have been a less developed sense of dependence upon theocratic rule among the ancient Egyptians than was the case in Mesopotamia. This tendency may have been due in part to the greater stability of the Egyptian temperament[23] and the decidedly static quality of their general world-view, which was one result of their comparative geographic isolation. The ancient Egyptians had never laid claim to a tradition of migration to the land of the Nile; and because they considered themselves to have been the original inhabitants of the terrain, they proudly assumed the title of "men," a situation that reflected with some distaste upon their heterogeneous neighbors to the west, the east, and the south.

One serious drawback to a study of Egyptian history generally is that the treasury of source material, abundant though it frequently is, fails to furnish a consistently illuminated picture of ancient Egyptian times and events. While those intervals of national history that have been well represented by extant records tend quite naturally to occupy the attention of historians, the areas that are deficient in such testimony have been unduly neglected in historical study. An additional obstacle which stands in the way of a proper interpretation of events in ancient Egypt is the fact that the great majority of the historical monuments erected in that country and duly inscribed with a record of happenings were actually intended as official propaganda for transmitting to posterity that projection of the glory and power that the pharaohs thought proper for the occasion. As such they are not really the kind of material upon which an objective historical study ought to be based, a situation which has caused not a little embarrassment among unwary exponents of the Egyptian past. As with other ancient Near Eastern countries, it must also be remembered that in Egypt a great many crises of revolution, inner strife, political intrigue, and military defeats in foreign wars were either passed over in silence or else were interpreted in such a manner that the monuments conveyed impressions that were thoroughly distorted and invariably manipulated so as to reflect creditably upon the Egyptians themselves.

Like other peoples in the ancient world, the Egyptians had no fixed method for reckoning the passing of the years and ages. Events that they wanted to record in chronological order were usually associated with particular regnal years of the pharaohs, although in the earliest period

22 *IHANE*, p. 20.
23 *IAAM*, pp. 39ff.

these were not counted. As in ancient Babylonia, specific years were styled in terms of outstanding events that had occurred in them, so that one year came to be designated as "the year of fighting and smiting the northerners." This clumsy method was gradually superseded by a simpler one in which the reckoning was related to the regnal year, so that an event became dated in a particular year of a specific pharaoh. Finally, the priests compiled detailed lists of kings in which their names and either the designations or, later, the numbers of their regnal years were entered, and it is highly probable that these archives constituted the basis of the king-lists and the historical tables preserved by Manetho.

Important as the attempts of the Babylonians and Egyptians were in the recording of ancient Near Eastern life and times, they were far surpassed by the creative genius of the Hittite history-writers. Cuneiform sources from Boghazköy indicate clearly that the Hittites were supreme in the area of historiography in their day, and were only surpassed by the Hebrews and the Greeks. C. H. Gordon believes that these two nations emerged as the historians of the western world because they began their historiographic activities on a substratum of Hittite culture. He has remarked:

> It is no accident that Herodotus, the Father of History, came from Anatolia. The seeds of historical writings were planted by the Hittites back in the second millennium throughout their sphere of influence, spanning Halicarnassus and Zion.[24]

While the sources available for determining the idea of history among the ancient Hebrews are of an accredited literary nature, they are quite unlike the cuneiform and hieroglyphic inscriptions of Babylonia and Egypt. At least one Moabite ruler has a royal inscription; the Hebrews possessed none. In fact, there is almost nothing that approximates to a Hebrew inscription with the possible exception of the Siloam inscription and the Lachish and Samarian ostraca. Despite this lack of official records, however, there were a great many other sources in existence upon which the writers of the Old Testament books were able to draw. Some of this material was of considerable antiquity, and includes sagas, poems, historical narratives, genealogical tables, and certain legal formulations, many of which preserved in one way or another the characteristic Hebrew concepts of divine purpose and destiny in history.

The annals that underlie Kings and Chronicles are late in comparison with their Mesopotamian and Egyptian counterparts, and they point to the didactic nature of most Old Testament historical narratives. This resulted largely from the general Hebrew attitude that events were essentially *sub specie aeternitatis*. This religious approach is particularly

[24] *GBB*, p. 97.

prominent in Chronicles, where the ontological significance of the divine commonwealth is presented against an historical framework. For the ancient Hebrews the history that they, as the covenant people, experienced consisted inevitably of more than a mere series of rather coincidental occurrences or "happenings" (*Geschehen*). While history for them included the elements of "events" and "facts"[25] that underlie the categories described by German scholars as *Historie* and *Geschichte*, there was also a transcendent spiritual factor that the ancient Hebrew prophets and historians recognized consistently and associated with the outworking of the Covenant provisions towards a planned goal.

The Hebrew idea of history, therefore, was ultimately a theological one, and as such has frequently been spoken of by scholars as "sacred" or "salvation" history (*Heilsgeschichte*). However, since the Old Testament conveys the general impression of incompleteness in relation to the historical process, and points for its culmination to something beyond itself, the use of the term *Heilsgeschichte* as strictly applicable to Old Testament history is not altogether satisfactory. The predominant concern of the Old Testament was for the nature and manifestation of the divine revelation in and through Israel, but even so it is evident from the Hebrew understanding of history that the process of salvation was far from being accomplished when the extant works were formulated. Consequently the term *Heilsgeschichte* can only find its fullest meaning in the New Testament world-view where the atoning work of Christ gave the greatest degree of ontological significance to the dictum, "salvation is of the Jews" (John 4:22).

Since ancient Semitic historiography was influenced considerably by cultural attitudes and activities among others, the histories of these ancient peoples can be approached most satisfactorily when they are examined from the standpoint of the writers and their environment.[26] Elementary though this observation may appear, the facts of the case are that it is frequently far from easy for the occidental scholar to make such an approach, particularly if his training has been weighted heavily with literary-critical procedures and principles. However, there are still significantly large areas of the world where the attitudes and customs of nations and groups have undergone little fundamental change since the Late Bronze Age, despite the attempts of western nations to impose modern technology upon them. It is therefore instructive to realize, for example, that a good deal of light can be thrown upon the outlook and behavior of the ancient Semites by observing the way of life of the modern Bedouin Arab or the Turkish tribesman.[27]

[25] C. R. North, *IDB*, II, p. 608, has distinguished between these terms by defining a fact of history as an event together with the interpretation accompanying its recollection or recording. Cf. B. Albrektson, *History and the Gods* (1967).

[26] Cf. R. G. Collingwood, *The Idea of History*, pp. 163, 282ff.

[27] Cf. *IOTT*, p. 106 n. 10.

In much the same manner, an appreciation of the sociological importance of such ancient institutions as the matriarchate will go far towards unravelling some of the mysteries implicit in narratives that depicted life in the early Hebrew monarchy. Attention has already been called to the importance of epigraphic material which, when integrated into the larger historical picture by means of stratigraphic, typological, and other forms of evaluation, can furnish very significant corroborative evidence. While it is important to avoid confusing the two concepts of history—as that which has happened and that which has been written down about what has happened—it should be remarked that it is not necessary for the facts furnished by internal evidence to be corroborated at all stages by the external evidence of archaeology and the like before they can be accepted as valid.

What must be examined with consistent care, however, is the manner in which the facts available to the historian have actually been reported. It is now realized that the ancient Near Eastern peoples approached the handling of their material far differently than do modern occidental chroniclers. The scribes of antiquity frequently—though not invariably—compiled their material towards the end of a particular sequence rather than at intervals during it,[28] and in ancient Sumeria the scribes always made more than one copy of any given composition.[29] Poetic material of varying kinds was often transmitted orally over long periods of time, frequently related to written forms of epics and similar works. The ancients valued prose sources such as genealogies, since they preserved a record of past events like those of their modern counterparts in such widely diverse cultures as the modern Bedouin Arab, the inhabitants of Hawaii, the Malagasy people, and others.[30]

The use of numbers among the ancient Near Eastern nations varied sharply from current occidental practice. In contrast to the detail and precision of the West, the numbers employed in literary sources and inscriptions were generally exaggerated greatly. One example of this tendency can be furnished by the Sumerian king-list known as the Weld-Blundell prism,[31] which attributed reigns of completely disproportionate length to eight kings who reigned in Eridu, Badtibira, Larak, Sippar, and Shuruppak.[32] It may well be that on occasion the scribes of Near Eastern antiquity utilized numbers in a symbolic, schematic, or epic fashion, which is decidedly at variance with common occidental

---

[28] This is particularly noticeable in the case of the Egyptian medical texts, such as the Ebers, Hearst, Kahun, Greater Berlin, and Edwin Smith papyri. However, it did not occur to the same extent in Babylonia.

[29] S. N. Kramer, *Sumerian Mythology* (1961), p. 23.

[30] Cf. *FSAC*, p. 72; *IOTT*, pp. 103f.

[31] Cf. *ANET*, pp. 265f.

[32] Cf. C. L. Woolley, *The Sumerians* (1928), p. 21.

practice.[33] Particularly noticeable in oriental compositions is the custom of exaggerating victories in the annals, probably an attempt to magnify the achievements of the rulers and peoples thus commemorated.[34] Conversely, an entirely different attitude was adopted towards defeat: all mention of the calamity was usually omitted. Apparently, therefore, the numerical references in ancient Near Eastern annals generally ought not to be assumed to be factually accurate or "reliable" in the usual occidental sense. Where parallel accounts occur in the Old Testament narratives, these can often furnish a useful measure of control on the records of pagan annalists, although such control is naturally by no means absolute.

Written and oral traditions existed side by side in antiquity, the former often serving as an aid to memory rather than as a substitute for it.[35] Since verse form is generally considered more satisfactory than prose structures for oral transmission, a good deal of the material handed down from generation to generation must have had some basis in poetic formulation. Scholars now recognize that both the prose and poetry of the Old Testament may be related to a limited extent to epic antecedents, and sometimes even modeled upon such structural patterns.[36] Furthermore, it is of some significance to note that the historiography of the Hebrews drew in part on the epic and dramatic forms of ancient Babylonia and Homeric Greece. For example, Old Testament historical writers frequently reconstructed the events of past days in the form of verbatim utterances, a characteristic epic device. One of the best examples of this tendency is seen in the speech of the Assyrian officer in 2 Kings 18:17-35, which occurs in a particularly dramatic historiographical expression, and lends added suspense to the narrative.

C. MODERN SCHOLARS AND OLD TESTAMENT HISTORY

It may be instructive to survey the attitudes of modern western scholars to the historical narratives of the Old Testament with a view to determining the extent to which they thought that the latter could be regarded as constituting an authentic record of the time. Prior to the period of Wellhausen, orthodoxy held that the Biblical accounts were divinely inspired and inerrant in consequence. Interest in Old Testament history as such did not begin until the seventeenth century when Archbishop J. Usher published his *Annales Veteris et Novi Testamenti*

[33] For symbolic interpretation see the attribution of 110 years, the Egyptian ideal of a full and fruitful life (cf. *ANET*, p. 414 n. 33), to Joseph (Gen. 50:26) and Joshua (Josh. 24:29; Judg. 2:8). A schematic interpretation is probable with the numerical reference in 1 Kgs. 6:1. For the epic approach cf. *IOTT*, pp. 293f.
[34] Compare the account of Sennacherib's siege of Jerusalem *ca.* 701 B.C. (*ARAB*, II, sect. 240) with the Biblical narrative in 2 Kgs. 18:14.
[35] *FSAC*, p. 64.
[36] Cf. *IOTT*, pp. 290f.

(1605). The chronological sequences which Usher propounded were subsequently associated with the text of the Authorized Version—though quite without authority. About seventy-five years later J. B. Bousset published his work entitled *Discours sur l'histoire universelle* (1681), and in 1716 the celebrated treatise of H. Prideaux was issued in two volumes under the title *The Old and the New Testaments Connected in the History of the Jews and Neighbouring Nations*.

English Deism produced at least one apologetic work dealing with the subject of Old Testament history: in 1727 S. Shukford wrote *The Sacred and Profane History of the World Connected*. On the continent M. F. Roos published his *Einleitung in die biblische Geschichte* in 1700, which furnished a good historical survey of the Israelites. The following century saw the rise of rationalism, and with it the publication of a work by L. Bauer in 1800 entitled *Geschichte der hebräer Nation*. H. Ewald set the tone of Old Testament historical writing for the nineteenth century with the publication in 1843 of his monumental five-volume *Geschichte des Volkes Israel*. What undoubtedly constituted the standard work of the advanced critical school in Europe was Wellhausen's *Geschichte Israels*, published in 1878, and known as *Prolegomena zur Geschichte Israels* after 1883. The position that he adopted was widely imitated, and its adherents included B. Stade (*Geschichte des Volkes Israel*, 1881), K. H. Graf (*Die geschichtlichen Bücher des Alten Testaments*, 1886), C. Piepenbring (*Histoire du Peuple d'Israël*, 1898), and C. H. Cornill (*Geschichte des Volkes Israel*, 1898). A more moderate account of Hebrew history was furnished by R. Kittel in his three-volume work *Geschichte des Volkes Israel*, published from 1888.

The rise of the nineteenth-century critical school, with its emphasis upon literary analysis and its evolutionary view of Hebrew origins, brought with it an extremely skeptical evaluation of the Old Testament historical narratives. Part of this was due to the Wellhausenian pattern of documentary analysis, which imposed a considerable gap between the form of the narratives and the events that they purported to describe, and part to the principles followed by the members of the Wellhausenian school, which did not permit them to regard the documents as reliable sources for the history of the times they chronicled. Since extra-Biblical archaeological data were deemed too scanty to be worthy of notice, and since comparatively little was known at that time about Near Eastern life in the second millennium B.C., the historians who had fallen under the influence of Wellhausen were thrown back upon the evolutionary philosophy of Hegel. Even when Hegelianism lost its appeal, the basic principle that the faith of Israel had its origins in rudimentary forms, which slowly and demonstrably progressed to the higher forms of belief culminating in monotheism, continued to be repeated tirelessly by the faithful adherents of liberalism. This position necessarily demanded a complete reconstruction of the history of Israel, in which the early traditions were relegated to the realm of myth and legend, the historicity of the patriarchs was denied, the campaigns of Joshua dismissed as fundamentally unhistorical, and the beginnings of Hebrew historiography assigned to a comparatively late period in the growth of the monarchy.

With the availability of much new archaeological information providing a good control for assessing the value and trustworthiness of the Biblical narratives, one might expect that a fundamental change in attitude towards the long-held evolutionary concepts of Hebrew history would have taken place by now among scholars. In point of fact, however, as Bright has stated, the major treatises dealing with Old Testament history still adhere to much the same developmental pattern as that cherished by an earlier generation.[37] This has been reinforced by a general uncritical acceptance of what many nineteenth- and early twentieth-century scholars liked to call "the most assured results of Biblical criticism." Even those who have acknowledged the antiquity and substantial historicity of the tradition underlying the documentary sources that they profess to recognize have been slow to afford such a development its proper place in their scheme of historiography.

Perhaps the most serious objection that can be levelled against contemporary writers in the field of Old Testament history is that so many have failed or have been reluctant to take into proper account those assured archaeological discoveries that are now available to scholars. Such was the case with the two-volume history written by Oesterley and Robinson, which, as Orlinsky has pointed out, did not make adequate use of factual archaeological material in existence at the time of writing, a deficiency that remained uncorrected in subsequent re-issues.[38] Equally guilty was A. Lods, whose two volumes on the historical background of Israelite life betokened a grave ignorance of important areas of archaeological discovery.[39] Not a few European scholars have run afoul of this unfortunate tendency, and reviewers of their work have been quick to comment on this fault. However, there is no excuse for this failure: while it may be perfectly legitimate for a scholar to propound views that issue from the standpoint of critical methodology, it is unscientific for him to ignore vitally important sources of information relating to his subject, whether they result in a modification of his basic position or not. A scholar who persists in this kind of procedure cannot command very much confidence among his colleagues.

Whereas at the end of the nineteenth century one of the most pressing questions of debate among Old Testament historians was the nature of

[37] *Early Israel in Recent History Writing* (1956), pp. 23f.
[38] W. O. E. Oesterley and T. H. Robinson, *A History of Israel* (2 vols., 1932); H. M. Orlinsky, *Ancient Israel* (1954), p. 178.
[39] A. Lods, *Israel from its Beginnings to the Middle of the Eighth Century* (1932) and *The Prophets and the Rise of Judaism* (1937).

the progression from polydaemonism to monotheistic faith in the experience of ancient Israel, the situation had changed by the middle of the twentieth century to the point where scholars were concerned to grapple with the entire question of the origins of Israel. Consequently the whole area of early traditions and methods by which they can be evaluated most effectively has been under constant examination in recent years, particularly by Albright and Noth. Part of the difficulty that liberal scholars invariably have to meet lies in their self-imposed assumption that the traditions in their extant written form are comparatively late. Although there are good reasons for believing that this view is in many respects erroneous, it is a necessary concomitant of the scheme of literary analysis as understood and practiced by Wellhausen and his successors.

What is needed, therefore, is a reliable methodological approach that will bridge the gap between the Biblical events and the extant written form of the narratives describing them, if the writing is not contemporary with the event or nearly so. Basic to any historiographical method for Alt and Noth is the Wellhausenian scheme of literary analysis, assisted by a rigorous application of the results of form-historical study. By this means they feel best equipped to trace the blocks of tradition that they have isolated to their most primitive form, after which they can begin to describe the manner in which the narrative may be thought to have assumed its normative state.[40]

40 Thus Noth devoted the opening sections of *UP* to a careful exposition of the classical documentary theory of Pentateuchal origins, whose tenets he accepted. He then utilized an investigation of the tradition-history or *Überlieferungsgeschichte* of the Pentateuch on the assumption that the underlying sources had experienced a long history of transmission in one form or another before assuming their extant character. On the basis of the five distinct areas of tradition that he isolated according to the principles of form-criticism, Noth concluded that the traditions of the patriarchs had developed and been transmitted independently of the other Pentateuchal narratives, and that originally they had dealt with Jacob as the principal figure. Integral to the procedure of recognition and isolation of traditional elements were the *Haftpunkt*—the place from which the tradition was transmitted or with which it was originally associated—and the *Ortsgebundenheit*—the adherence of traditions to specific localities. One feature of the Alt-Noth school is the way in which the concept of aetiology, the analysis of stories purporting to account for ancient names or customs, has been employed as a means of identifying what are alleged to be accretions of the legendary in orally transmitted material; for the function of aetiology in historical tradition, see W. F. Albright, *BASOR*, No. 74 (1939), pp. 12ff. On this basis the narratives dealing with the meeting of Jacob and Esau at Mahanaim (Gen. 32:6ff.), or the wrestling at Penuel (Gen. 32:24ff.), are aetiological and therefore secondary material (*UP*, p. 104). While Noth, unlike Wellhausen, concedes that the patriarchs were historical personages and not mere eponyms, he has placed them on the desert fringe of Canaan rather than in a cultured Mesopotamian setting. Again, although he admits that Moses is historical, Noth seems to think that he had nothing to do with the Exodus or Wilderness wanderings, but rather was associated with a grave tradition (*Grabstradition*) in

While the methodology of the Alt-Noth school includes an insistence upon a rigorous examination of literary sources, it has largely resulted in what Bright has described as a "totally negative evaluation of the historical worth of the early traditions of Israel and . . . a surprising reluctance to call upon the results of archaeology in a measure to fill the void thus created."[41] There can be no doubt that the position maintained by this school is backed up by scholarly diligence and great erudition. An unfortunate weakness in their methodological procedures, however, is the fact that they are immediately ineffective for anyone who does not accept the documentary or phase-analyses of Alt and Noth. Because archaeological evidence is decidedly subordinated to *a priori* considerations, literary or otherwise, a grossly inadequate view of the Hebrew *Sitz im Leben des Volkes,* or life-situation, results. Their assessment fails from a purely theological standpoint, as Bright has indicated, to account for the phenomenon of Israel's being the "people of the faith." Furthermore, their historical estimate is primarily subjective.

When tested by normal procedures of interpretation, the archaeological material from the Middle Bronze Age points to certain social and historical configurations that Alt and Noth are unprepared to accept. Since for them all other material seems to be subordinated to theoretical considerations, it is not easy to see how their rather nihilistic position represents any significant advance upon the evolutionary hypotheses of Wellhausen. Despite the attention that the efforts of Alt and Noth to interpret the early historical traditions of Israel command, their position must be rejected as an invalid methodology, if for no other reason than that one of its basic presuppositions is in error. As C. H. Gordon has

---

Transjordan (*UP*, pp. 186f.). Interest in this suggestion was quickened in 1962 with the discovery of a pyramid-like structure by a South American archaeological team excavating to the south of 'Amman in Jordan. According to Julio Ripamonti, the leader of the expedition, the walls of the building were about 140 feet high and nearly 95 feet wide, thus representing the largest single building unearthed to date in either Canaan or Transjordan. It was dated to the Late Bronze Age, about 1250 B.C. On examination it was found to consist of an inner building, adjacent to which were twelve small chambers. Ripamonti associated the structure with the burial of Moses, and thought that it may have marked the place where he died. He further suggested the possibility that the twelve chambers represented the traditional number of the tribes of Israel. While this discovery remains to be evaluated at the time of writing, it is not impossible that a cenotaph was erected in Transjordan by the Israelites to commemorate the historical Moses prior to the occupation of the Promised Land. Although Alt and Noth have demonstrated a considerably greater awareness of the nature and significance of archaeological discoveries than did Wellhausen and his more immediate successors, the use to which they have put this information is generally of a decidedly negative character. This is perhaps understandable, since for them much of the tradition has little if any historical value, and therefore there does not seem to be any point in invoking evidence to support it (e.g. *GI*, pp. 70f.).

[41] J. Bright, *Early Israel in Recent History Writing,* p. 55.

remarked, the material available must dictate the method to be employed;[42] and, as a result, it is difficult to repose any confidence in an approach to historiography which, on the basis of rigid *a priori* considerations, is unwilling to consider the total evidence at hand.

A much more satisfactory approach to the problems of Hebrew historiography has been provided by W. F. Albright, the foremost Biblical archaeologist of the twentieth century, who has brought an enormous amount of erudition and experience to bear upon a critical examination of the problems in hand. Under his influence the course of Old Testament studies has taken an entirely new turn, and his prodigious scholarly output from the decade following World War I is eloquent testimony to the virility of his attack upon outstanding difficulties. He has utilized as fully as possible the more adequate controls furnished by archaeological discoveries, and has included philology, sociology, anthropology, and other disciplines in his methodology. His work and that of his students is characterized by a high degree of academic competence combined with a charitable understanding of positions with which they find themselves unable to agree. Though Albright himself and some of his followers appear to concur in a kind of documentary analysis of the Pentateuch that has affinities with that propounded by Wellhausen, they are quick to recognize the breakdown of the classical pattern of source-analysis as the primary means of reconstructing Hebrew history and religion, and are willing to avail themselves of other cognate areas of information.

The significance of this approach is that its methodology is still largely valid even for those, such as the present writer, who reject the Wellhausenian literary analysis of Pentateuchal material, since this analysis, or something very much akin to it, is no longer vital to the success of the method of history-writing. In this sense Albright's approach is unlike the position adopted by Alt and Noth, whose disregard of important areas of evidence vitiates the validity of a great many of their conclusions. An excellent example of the method favored by the Albright school has been furnished by Bright, whose *History of Israel*, published in 1959, grapples with the problems of Hebrew origins and development in a remarkably satisfying manner, furnishing what is by far the best history of Israel since the work of Kittel. Bright marshals as much of the evidence as possible in executing his task, evaluates it critically and presents a coherent pattern that differs radically in significant areas from the history of Noth, written a decade earlier. Bright's book gained early acceptance as the standard English-language history of Israel, and although it must be used with caution at some points, it constitutes in general an important step forward in this area of Biblical study.

[42] *IOTT*, pp. 17f.

II. PROBLEMS OF OLD TESTAMENT HISTORY

On the basis of the foregoing remarks it is possible at this point to consider the historical background of significant periods of Hebrew history and the problems associated with them, utilizing for the purpose as much of the available material as is possible. It will be evident from the following survey that the contention of Wellhausen and his followers that the record of events in the Old Testament is basically tendentious, and consequently requires objective analysis, can no longer be sustained in the light of the facts. As professional students of the ancient Near East acquire even more information about the life and times of ancient cultures in the Biblical world, it becomes increasingly apparent that the Old Testament is a substantially accurate record of events based upon accredited historiographical procedures. That certain tendencies appear in the historical writings from time to time is well recognized, as is the fact that any history worthy of the name must exhibit specific emphases and points of view, whether it is an ancient composition or a modern work. This, incidentally, is one of the reasons for the superiority of ancient Hittite historiography over the dull cataloging and gross exaggeration of comparable Egyptian and Mesopotamian sources.

Perhaps a more serious objection to the approach of the Wellhausenian school is that their methodology, subjective as it was, constituted an entirely inappropriate medium for those precise purposes of objective analysis that they were at such pains to stress. Even more unfortunate is the failure of those who still subscribe to a greater or lesser extent to the methodology of Wellhausen to realize that the literary-critical naturalistic approach can never begin to do adequate justice to the grandeur of Hebrew history and religion as presented in the pages of the Old Testament.[1] In those areas where the writer indulges in a spiritual or metaphysical interpretation of events, it is made abundantly clear that the course of human affairs generally is under divine control, a proposition that cannot be accepted by those whose outlook is rigidly governed by *a priori* positivistic categories.

[1] Cf. *ARI*, p. 3.

308

That there are apparent inconsistencies and contradictions in ancient Hebrew life as recorded in the Old Testament narratives would scarcely be denied by anyone. Yet it is also true that equal inconsistencies and alleged discrepancies can be documented from virtually every period of human history, and not the least by any means from the modern age. As far as the ancient Near East is concerned, scholarly studies and archaeological discoveries have now advanced the corpus of knowledge concerning life in Bible lands to the point where it is far more correct to speak of "problems" in Biblical history or chronology than to think in terms of "contradictions." The one really acceptable methodology for the study of ancient Hebrew history and culture will embrace as full an understanding as possible of the Near Eastern *Sitz im Leben des Volkes* of antiquity and will then set the narratives of Hebrew life and times against this larger factual background with great caution. Only when this is done with all the care and restraint of modern Biblical scholarship will the true nature of Hebrew historiography become apparent to the contemporary mind, and the authors of the Old Testament be revealed as purposeful and responsible men.

A. THE PATRIARCHAL NARRATIVES

Although some scholars have found no historical value in the patriarchal narratives, assuming with Wellhausen that Abraham, Isaac, and Jacob were either eponymous ancestors of clans or at most purely mythical figures,[2] others have begun to realize that the Genesis narratives can no longer be dismissed as mere Canaanite myths or legends.[3] While certain tribal names were treated in Genesis as designations of individuals, following general Semitic custom, and fitted into a genealogical sequence, it has been discovered impossible to carry through to a logical conclusion the theory that in the patriarchal traditions the experiences represented as being individual were actually personifications of group life, since Abraham, for example, conveys every impression of strict and distinct individuality.

It is true, of course, that there is to date no independent confirmation from extra-Biblical sources of the patriarchal narratives as they now stand, and equally true that there is much that will never be known about this particular phase of human history. Yet enough has been discovered by examining the archaeological sequences occurring in the Bronze Age to require a far more sympathetic evaluation of the Genesis tradition than was the case among earlier generations of scholars. This evaluation is based on objective study of the situation rather than on

---

[2] Wellhausen, *Prolegomena zur Geschichte Israels* (1895), pp. 322ff.; B. Stade, *Geschichte des Volkes Israel* (1887), I, pp. 145ff.; cf. E. Meyer, *Die Israeliten und ihre Nachbarstämme* (1906), pp. 249ff.

[3] E.g. E. Dhorme, *La Religion des Hébreux nomades* (1937), p. 69.

purely subjective considerations. All lines of evidence indicate that the cultural milieu of the patriarchal sagas[4] can be placed with complete confidence in the Bronze Age, and in particular within a period extending from 2000 to 1500 B.C.[5] Against a background of an advanced Mesopotamian civilization, the beginnings of Hebrew tradition were associated with the name of Abraham.[6] With the discoveries of texts at Mari and Nuzu has come the realization that the names current in the narratives of the patriarchs were of common occurrence, particularly in Amorite circles, both in Mesopotamia and Palestine in the second millennium B.C.[7] Thus "Abraham," under the syllabic forms *A-ba-am-ra-ma* and *A-ba-am-ra-am*, was in current usage considerably before the sixteenth century B.C., and may have occurred also in the Egyptian Execration Texts.[8] The Mari letters mentioned the city of Nahor, home of Rebekah, under the name Nakhur, which in the eighteenth century B.C. was ruled by an Amorite prince.[9] In an eighteenth-century B.C. Egyptian list the names Asher and Issachar have been found in cognate form.[10] The Nuzu texts, which mirrored the traditions and social customs of a predominantly Horite (Hurrian) group flourishing in northeastern Mesopotamia during the fifteenth century B.C., have thrown particular light upon patriarchal traditions that previously had been deemed inexplicable.[11] For example, the narrative dealing with the sale of the Cave of Machpelah to Abraham, which was assigned by the nineteenth-century critics to the latest of the Pentateuchal documents, is now known to have followed very closely the procedures laid down by Hittite law in cases of land transactions,[12] and is early rather than late in origin. The culture

---

[4] Terms such as "saga" and "tradition" occurring in the present work are used without prejudice as to the historical nature of the material under discussion.

[5] Among the many sources of information are included *FSAC*, pp. 236ff.; R. de Vaux, *RB*, LIII (1946), pp. 321ff., LV (1948), pp. 321ff., LVI (1949), pp. 5ff.; *LAP*, pp. 54ff.; H. H. Rowley, *BJRL*, XXXII (1949), pp. 3ff., reprinted in *The Servant of the Lord and Other Essays* (1952), pp. 271ff.; *WBA*, pp. 40ff.

[6] W. F. Albright, *JBL*, LVIII (1939), pp. 91ff.; *FSAC*, pp. 154f. For the view that Abraham was a merchant prince living in a north-Mesopotamian city see C. H. Gordon in D. W. Thomas and W. D. McHardy (eds.), *Hebrew and Semitic Studies presented to Godfrey Rolles Driver* (1963), p. 77; *GBB*, pp. 287f., in *JNES*, XVII (1958), pp. 28ff., and in A. Altmann (ed.), *Biblical and Other Studies* (1963), p. 8.

[7] *BHI*, p. 70.

[8] W. F. Albright, *BASOR*, No. 83 (1941), p. 34, No. 88 (1942), p. 36; cf. Albright in *JBL*, LIV (1935), pp. 193ff.; J. A. Wilson, *The Culture of Ancient Egypt* (1956), pp. 156f.

[9] Cf. G. E. Mendenhall, *BA*, XI, No. 1 (1948), p. 16.

[10] W. F. Albright, *JAOS*, LXXIV (1954), pp. 227ff.

[11] Cf. C. H. Gordon, *BA*, III, No. 1 (1940), pp. 1ff.; R. T. O'Callaghan, *CBQ*, VI (1944), pp. 391ff.; E. A. Speiser, *JBL*, LXXIV (1955), pp. 252ff.; A. E. Draffkorn, *JBL*, LXXVI (1957), pp. 216ff.

[12] M. R. Lehmann, *BASOR*, No. 129 (1953), pp. 15ff.; cf. *ANET*, p. 191.

and political milieu of the second millennium B.C. in Mesopotamia is also reflected by the migrations of the patriarchs, which were characteristic of many such contemporary movements along the length of the Fertile Crescent.

Despite the admission of Albright[13] that sporadic domestication of the camel might have gone back several centuries before the end of the Bronze Age, there are still writers who assume that the few references to camels in the patriarchal sagas (Gen. 12:16; 24:64) are anachronistic.[14] Prior to their full-scale domestication in the twelfth century B.C., camels were used to a limited extent as beasts of burden, a fact that is evident from their mention (GAM.MAL) in an eighteenth-century B.C. cuneiform list of fodder for domestic animals, discovered at Alalakh in northern Syria.[15] In addition, the excavations of Parrot at Mari uncovered the remains of camel bones in the ruins of a house belonging to the pre-Sargonic era (ca. 2400 B.C.).[16] A relief at Byblos in Phoenicia, dated in the eighteenth century B.C., depicts a camel in a kneeling position, thus indicating the domestication of the animal in Phoenician circles some centuries prior to the Amarna Age.[17] Albright's objection that the animal depicted on the relief had no hump and could not therefore be considered a camel was refuted by de Vaux, who pointed out that there was a socket on the back to which the hump and its load had been attached separately.[18] Other evidence for the early domestication of the camel consists of a jawbone recovered from a Middle Bronze Age tomb (ca. 1900-1600 B.C.) at Tell el-Farah,[19] and cylinder seals found in northern Mesopotamia, dating from the patriarchal era and depicting riders seated upon camels.[20] The foregoing ought to be sufficient to refute the commonly held view that references to camels in Genesis are "anachronistic touches" introduced to make the stories more vivid to later hearers.[21]

The same may be said, to a less demonstrable extent, about the allegation that the occurrence of Philistines in the patriarchal narratives

13 FSAC, p. 165; cf. J. P. Free, JNES, III (1944), pp. 187ff.

14 BHI, p. 72; BANE, p. 204; cf. R. Walz, ZDMG, CI (1951), pp. 29ff., CIV (1954), pp. 45ff.

15 D. J. Wiseman and A. Goetze, JCS, XIII (1959), pp. 29, 37; D. J. Wiseman, The Alalakh Tablets (1953), No. 269:59; S. Moscati, Rivista degle Studi Orientali, XXXV (1960), p. 116; cf. W. G. Lambert, BASOR, No. 160 (1960), p. 42.

16 A. Parrot, SRA, XXXII (1955), p. 323.

17 P. Montet, Byblos et l'Égypte (1928), p. 91 and pl. 52.

18 W. F. Albright, JBL, LXIV (1945), p. 288; R. de Vaux, RB, LVI (1949), p. 9 n. 4f.

19 Ibid., p. 9 n. 8. Cf. C. H. Gordon in Biblical and Other Studies, p. 10.

20 The Tell Halaf sculptured relief (LAP, p. 55 and pl. 25) is far from being "one of the earliest known representations of the camel." For the early domestication of the camel in India see M. Wheeler, The Indus Civilisation (1953), p. 60.

21 BHI, p. 72; K. A. Kitchen, NBD, pp. 181ff.

is also anachronistic.[22] While it is true that a significantly large body of Philistines settled in Palestine (a name that itself is derived from "Philistine") about 1187 B.C., after being repulsed by Rameses III in a naval battle, there are good reasons for believing that the Philistines were active in Canaan at a considerably earlier period. If the term is extended, as it can be quite legitimately, to include the Minoans and other Aegean peoples with whom the Philistines were connected, it must then be remembered that there is conclusive evidence of an expansion of Aegean trade in the Middle Minoan II period (ca. 1900-1700 B.C.), which left behind objects of Aegean manufacture at such places as Ugarit, Hazor, Lachish, and Abydos in Egypt. This commercial thrust alone would be sufficient to bring a number of pioneering Philistine trading-groups into Canaan and Syria, and the fact that they were most probably small in number during the patriarchal period would account for a general lack of mention in the annals of larger states. In this latter connection it is improbable that the members of such a mixed group as the Aegean peoples would be distinguished at all carefully by name in the Middle Minoan period, particularly since they were not in the cultural and military ascendency that was the case in the twelfth century. Nevertheless there are records of Philistine activity in the Near East at this period, including an eighteenth-century B.C. Mari text recording that a certain king of Hazor in Palestine sent gifts to Crete (Kaptara).[23] Pottery from the Middle Minoan period has been recovered from Ras Shamra (Ugarit), from Hazor, and in Egypt from Abydos and Memphis, all of which date between 1900 and 1600 B.C.[24] This is clear evidence for close contact between Aegean groups and the peoples of Palestine during the patriarchal period, a phenomenon that does much to explain why the Philistine settlements in Canaan experienced no linguistic difficulties when dealing with the native inhabitants.[25] It should also be remembered that ancient scribes frequently substituted current designations for earlier names when revising literary works, and it may be that at least some instances of the usage of "Philistine" in Pentateuchal material may be the result of this influence. Whether this was actually the case or not, there can be no doubt that the Philistines were active in Palestine and Egypt during the Middle Bronze Age.

From the standpoint of topography, the patriarchal sagas agree in essence with what is known about Middle Bronze Age life in Canaan also. Genesis represents the patriarchs as semi-nomadic herdsmen or

[22] E.g. B. W. Anderson, *Understanding the OT* (1957), p. 46 n. 3; *BHI*, p. 73, *et al.*

[23] A. Pohl, *Orientalia*, XIX (1950), p. 509.

[24] For Ras Shamra, see C. F. A. Schaeffer, *Ugaritica*, I (1939), pp. 54ff.; for Hazor, Y. Yadin *et al.*, *Hazor II* (1960), p. 86 and pl. 115; for Egypt, H. J. Kantor in *Relative Chronologies in Old World Archaeology* (ed. R. W. Erich), pp. 10ff.

[25] *IOTT*, p. 108.

shepherds. In this connection it is important to note that the places mentioned as visited by Abraham are situated in an area whose annual rainfall is between ten and twenty inches. This is admirably suited to the requirements of sheep,[26] and substantiates the ancient tradition of the sagas in this regard. Furthermore, the patriarchs were associated by the narratives with sites in the densely wooded hill-country of Palestine (cf. Gen. 13:18; 26:23; 28:10; 33:18; 35:1; 37:17). As the investigations of Glueck in the Hashemite Kingdom of Jordan have demonstrated, Dothan, Shechem, Gerar, and Bethel were all inhabited between 2000 and 1700 B.C.[27] Hebron was founded "seven years before Zoan in Egypt,"[28] that is to say, about 1725 B.C., and while the exact age of Beersheba is uncertain, the wells at the site are unquestionably of great antiquity.

Evidence for an earlier rather than a later period of activity for Abraham has been furnished somewhat indirectly by considerations relating to the destruction of Sodom, Gomorrah, and the other "cities of the valley." Their sites may with great probability be located south of el-Lisan ("Tongue") peninsula in the southern part of the Dead Sea. Sodom itself may have been situated near the southern end of the valley, and had its name preserved in Jebel Usdum ("Mount of Sodom"), a mountain along the southern end of the west side of the Dead Sea about five miles long and more than 700 feet high, composed predominantly of crystalline salt. Further evidence supporting the suggested location has been provided by the site of Bab edh-Dhra', situated about five miles from and about five hundred feet above the shore of the Dead Sea southeast of el-Lisan. It had apparently been a pilgrimage place, and since no other traces of human habitation have been uncovered in this general region, it can be concluded that the homes of those who formerly frequented Bab edh-Dhra' must have come from what was once known as the Vale of Siddim. The presence of fertile fields around the mouths of the streams that flow into this southeast part of the Dead Sea lends credence to the belief that the entire area was one of great fertility in antiquity. The date of the catastrophe that overtook Sodom and the neighboring cities in the valley can be estimated roughly with reference to the pottery found at Bab edh-Dhra'—which indicated that the site had been frequented by pilgrims and others between 2300 and about 1900 B.C. The cessation of visits to Bab edh-Dhra' would most probably coincide with the destruction of Sodom and Gomorrah, since it was from the "cities of the valley" that the pilgrims

---

[26] N. Glueck, *BA*, XVIII, No. 1 (1955), p. 4.

[27] Glueck, *The Other Side of the Jordan* (1940), pp. 114ff. and *BA*, XVIII, No. 1 (1955), pp. 2ff.; *WMTS*, p. 71.

[28] Num. 13:22. Its original name may have been Kiriath-arba (Gen. 23:2; 35:27), hence the explanatory gloss of Gen. 13:18.

and other visitors came. The corollary to this is that evidence is here provided that Abraham was living about the end of the twentieth century B.C.

While the patriarchal narratives obviously need to be examined with care against the known background of contemporary life and times before they are used as sources for the history of the period, there can be little serious doubt on the basis of such an examination that the traditions they preserve are substantially historical. If, as many liberal scholars have assumed, the materials were transmitted orally, they may, as Albright has pointed out, have been subjected to processes of refraction and selection of elements suited for epic narrative, and this could well have ignored considerations of strict chronology.[29] But if, on the other hand, these materials have been transmitted as written texts on tablets, some of which were linked in series, they stand in the same general tradition as the Mari, Nuzu, and Alalakh sources, and in consequence they must be accorded a similar degree of historicity.

As has been noted in part three, some of the chronological problems associated with this general period are extremely complex, and there is at the time of writing no noticeable measure of scholarly agreement concerning them. Genesis 14 used to be utilized as a means of setting Abraham within the context of world history, but, although this material is now regarded by many scholars as constituting an ancient historical source, its significance for the chronology of the patriarchal period is still enigmatic in many respects.[30] However, the total picture presented by all the available evidence places the events of the sagas between the twentieth and sixteenth centuries B.C., and not in the Late Bronze Age of the sixteenth to thirteenth centuries B.C.

In discussing above the topography of the patriarchal narratives, it was noted that the pattern was consistent with the situation in the Middle Bronze Age rather than in other periods such as that of the Egyptian Empire (ca. 1570-1200 B.C.), when Palestine was an Egyptian dependency. Despite this assertion, however, it is impossible to say with certainty precisely when the ancestors of the later Israelites actually went down to Egypt and subsequently endured humiliating bondage. Nevertheless, some of the customs mentioned in Genesis 34-50 are particularly characteristic of the Second Intermediate period of Egyptian history (ca. 1776-1570 B.C.), during which the land was under the control of the invading Hyksos. Certain of the names prevalent in early Israelite circles, particularly in the tribe of Levi, reveal a connection with Egypt.[31] The antiquity of the tradition associated with the

[29] FSAC, pp. 68f., 72.
[30] BHI, pp. 75f.
[31] T. J. Meek, AJSL, LVI (1939), pp. 113ff.; J. G. Griffiths, JNES, XII (1953), pp. 225ff. The attempts of Noth, UP, pp. 178f., to dismiss this evidence are unconvincing.

names of the midwives attending Hebrew women in Egypt (Exod. 1:15) is confirmed by the fact that Shiphrah appears as a name in an eighteenth-century B.C. slave-list, and Puah occurs as a proper name in the Ugaritic texts.[32] A papyrus document dated about 1785 B.C. describes the prison system of the period, and on the *verso*, probably written some fifty years later, are listed 79 servants in an Egyptian household, of whom forty-five were Asiatics bearing characteristic west-Semitic names such as Menahem and Shiprah.[33] Finally, it is significant that Egyptian texts refer to the presence of captive 'Apiru in the land during the Empire period, who apparently had been brought as slave laborers to Egypt as early as the time of Amenophis II (*ca.* 1435-1414 B.C.), if not earlier, and among whom would almost certainly have been elements of the later Israelites.[34]

The local color of the narratives recounting the career of Joseph seems to accord with a period when Asiatic invaders dominated Egypt rather than with a time when native Egyptians were exercising rule over their own land. Under normal conditions the ancient Egyptians were never particularly tolerant towards politically ambitious foreigners in their midst, since they regarded their high offices of state as the perquisite of the Egyptian noble families. If, however, an enterprising and talented Semite such as Joseph had the political backing of the Hyksos conquerors, there would be little to prevent his rise to prominence in the land.[35] The Joseph narratives indicate that the territory of Goshen was near the Egyptian capital of Avaris, and that the Hebrews had ready access to the royal court, which would suit the conditions of Hyksos rule quite well. Further evidence of a connection between the patriarchal migration to Egypt and the Avaris era may be seen in the reference to Joseph's buying up land for the pharaoh during the famine years (Gen. 47:13ff.), a procedure that displaced the old landed nobility and created a new class of serfs. This reflects closely the social upheaval in Palestine during the Hyksos regime.[36]

B. The Date of the Exodus

There is no extra-Biblical evidence relating directly to the fact of the Exodus, but it is clear that a belief so firmly rooted in the religious tradition of Israel can hardly be explained in terms other than that this

---

[32] W. F. Albright, *JAOS*, LXXIV (1954), p. 229.

[33] W. C. Hayes, *A Late Middle Kingdom Papyrus in the Brooklyn Museum* (1955); K. A. Kitchen, *NBD*, p. 658.

[34] M. Greenberg, *The Hab/piru*, pp. 56f. For the mention of the Habiru in certain Egyptian texts see *ANET*, pp. 22, 247, 255, 261.

[35] H. M. Orlinsky, *Ancient Israel*, p. 33.

[36] Cf. G. Steindorff and K. C. Seele, *When Egypt Ruled the East* (1942), p. 88. The name "Hyksos" occurred in the Egyptian Execration Texts as early as 1960 B.C. in the form *hekau khasut*. For their Palestinian origin see A. Alt, *Die Herkunft der Hyksos in neuer Sicht* (1954), pp. 26ff.

stupendous liberating act of God occurred in reality. The precise spot where the *Yam Suph* was crossed cannot be identified with certainty,[37] but as Bright has commented, the specific location was as little central to the faith of Israel as is that of the tomb of Christ to the Christian faith.[38]

Attempts to establish a chronology for the Exodus have resulted in some of the most perplexing problems in the entire panorama of Hebrew history, as has been noted in an earlier chapter. Two principal views of the situation have arisen, one of which envisages a date in the fifteenth century B.C., while the other assigns the Exodus to the thirteenth century B.C. What is interesting about this diversity of opinion is that both positions can be supported to some extent from the Biblical narratives themselves. The earlier date furnishes problems for the chronology of the patriarchal period, for by applying the literal statements of Genesis it would appear that a period of 250 years elapsed between the arrival of Abraham in Canaan and the migration of Jacob to Egypt. If the statement that Israel was in Egypt for 430 years (Exod. 12:40) is to be considered independently of the Hyksos movement, it would place the entry of the patriarchs into Canaan some 645 years before the Exodus, giving a date for the birth of Abraham (cf. Gen. 12:4) about 2161 B.C. This event would have thus occurred somewhat before the founding of the Third Dynasty of Ur (*ca.* 2060-1950 B.C.), and judged by the trend of migratory movements in Mesopotamia subsequent to the twentieth century B.C. such a date seems to be a little early.

Genesis 15:13 predicted that the descendants of Abraham would be afflicted in a strange land for 400 years, a figure that was extended in Exodus 12:40 to 430 years.[39] The Massoretic reading in the latter reference is to be preferred to the LXX variant, which regards the 430 years as covering the patriarchal sojournings in Palestine as well as in Egypt, since the "selfsame day" (Exod. 12:41) at the end of this long interval of time was the anniversary of the entrance of Jacob and his family into Egypt. It would thus seem that a period of four hundred and thirty years ensued between the entry of Jacob into Egypt and the departure of the Israelites under Moses. The genealogy that appears to reduce the stay in Egypt to only two or three generations (Exod. 6:16ff.) was probably compiled under the influence of those principles of abbreviation and selectivity that seem to have governed other genealogies (e.g. Gen. 5 and 11).[40]

---

[37] Cf. M. Noth in *Festschrift Otto Eissfeldt* (ed. J. Fueck, 1947), pp. 181ff.; H. Cazelles, *RB*, LXII (1955), pp. 321ff.; *WBA*, pp. 60ff.

[38] *BHI*, p. 112.

[39] On the interpretation of the period as a conventional expression for an *era*, cf. C. H. Gordon, *New Horizons in OT Literature* (1960), p. 13.

[40] Cf. K. A. Kitchen and T. C. Mitchell, *NBD*, p. 214.

The fifteenth-century B.C. date for the Exodus can also be supported on arguments based on the chronological note in 1 Kings 6:1, stating that Solomon commenced building the Temple in the 480th year after the departure from Egypt. If this construction is to be dated about 961 B.C., the Exodus would thus have taken place *ca.* 1441 B.C. If this sequence is meant to be taken literally, it is a powerful argument for a fifteenth-century date.[41] However, while such a figure represents the unanimous testimony of the manuscripts, it can be questioned on other grounds, particularly when it is examined against the background of oriental symbolism.[42] The number 480 can be resolved into units of twelve generations of forty years each. A double cycle or *motif* may be involved in consequence, having the effect of relating the concept of a generation to each of the twelve tribes. If, however, the symbol of forty years as constituting a generation is reckoned more realistically in terms of the period extending from the birth of the father to the birth of his son, a figure of twenty-five years would be a more appropriate estimate for a generation, yielding about 300 years and bringing the Exodus into the mid-thirteenth century B.C.

Symbolic numerical configurations are a recognized element in oriental historiography. The New Testament genealogy of Jesus Christ found in Matthew 1:17 is divided into three sections of fourteen generations each. These extend from the time of Abraham to David, from David to the period of the Babylonian captivity, and from the deportation to the birth of Jesus.

In the same way, by placing the Exodus some four hundred and eighty years prior to the building of the Temple in Jerusalem, there emerges a pattern of twelve generations of High Priests between the erecting of the wilderness Tabernacle, which prefigured the Temple, and the actual construction of the Temple by Solomon. Again, another period of 480 years, or twelve generations of forty years each, extends between the building of the First Temple and its restoration under Zerubbabel. With reference to the 430 years of Exodus 12:40, another period of 480 years emerges by adding the fifty years between the building of the Bethel altar by Jacob (Gen. 28:18; 35:1ff.) and his descent into Egypt, thus furnishing a twelve-generation interval between the erection of the first altar and the commencement of formal worship in the Tabernacle. Quite clearly a systematized approach of this kind indicates that considerations other than those of purely literal chronology are in view.

Further support for a fifteenth-century date for the Exodus was adduced from the excavations of Garstang at Jericho, for, as has been

---

[41] J. W. Jack, *The Date of the Exodus* (1925), pp. 200ff.
[42] B. Couroyer, *L'Exode* (1952), p. 11.

observed earlier, he believed that he had uncovered conclusive evidence of destruction under Joshua, which he dated a little prior to 1400 B.C.[43] The city in question was the fourth in a series that Garstang identified alphabetically at different archaeological levels, beginning about 3000 B.C. City "D" was believed to have been constructed *ca.* 1500 B.C., and to have flourished for approximately a century before being destroyed. From the fact that diplomatic contact between Jericho and Egypt appeared to have ceased under Amenhotep III (*ca.* 1405-1368 B.C.), Garstang formed the opinion that the Exodus had occurred in the reign of the pharaoh Amenhotep II (*ca.* 1436-1414 B.C.).

These conclusions now have to be modified as a result of the work undertaken at Jericho since 1952 by Kathleen M. Kenyon.[44] Her discoveries have confirmed the belief that the city was one of the oldest occupational sites in the entire Near East, going back to the seventh millennium B.C., but they have also made it clear that the walls of City "D" belong properly to the third millennium B.C., about 2300 B.C. They apparently constituted part of a contemporary defensive complex, and as such have no relevance for the conquests of Joshua. Ceramic remains recovered from graves in the area indicated that Jericho was occupied considerably later than 1400 B.C., though it is not wholly clear by whom. It is unfortunate that most of the thirteenth- and twelfth-century levels of the mound have been removed by the local inhabitants or eroded by natural forces. As a result it is virtually impossible for archaeologists to determine with any accuracy the nature and extent of Jericho during this general period.

Although at the beginning of the twentieth century most scholars, liberal and conservative alike, dated the Exodus in the thirteenth century B.C., the discoveries of Garstang at Jericho, and the construction that he imposed upon them, stimulated interest in a fifteenth-century date to the point where other archaeological material was adduced as evidence for an early Israelite departure from Egypt. One such source consisted of a group of clay tablets from Tell el-Amarna. In 1887 a peasant woman, rummaging around in the ruins of el-Amarna, the site of the once-proud city of Akhenaton, had discovered about 370 tablets written in Babylonian cuneiform.[45] When translated they were found to deal with a wide range of social, personal, and political matters, including a series of diplomatic communications from Babylonian, Mitanni, and other rulers to Amenhotep III (*ca.* 1405-1368 B.C.) and Akhenaton (*ca.* 1370-1353 B.C.). About one hundred and fifty of the texts originated in Palestine, and the nature of their contents has enabled scholars to achieve a great

[43] J. Garstang, *Joshua-Judges* (1931), p. 146.

[44] For a survey of work at the site up to 1956 see R. K. Harrison, *The Churchman*, LXX, No. 3 (1956), pp. 157ff.; cf. K. M. Kenyon, *Digging Up Jericho* (1957).

[45] Cf. W. M. F. Petrie, *Tell el Amarna* (1894); J. A. Knudtzon and O. Weber, *Die El-Amarna Tafeln* (1915); S. A. B. Mercer, *The Tell el-Amarna Tablets* (1939).

deal of insight into the state of Palestine prior to the arrival of the Israelites.

Most of the Palestinian texts complained to the Egyptian authorities that the Habiru were overrunning the territory and occupying several of the walled cities in southern Canaan. One of these letters, requesting immediate aid from the Egyptian army, read as follows:

> To the king, my lord, say. . .The whole land of the king has revolted. There is not one governor that is loyal. . . . The Habiru are capturing the fortresses of the king . . . the Habiru are taking the cities of the king. . . .[46]

Particularly poignant was the plea of Abdi-Hiba, governor of Jerusalem, in a letter to the pharaoh Akhenaton, in which he begged for assistance against the marauding Habiru, stressing that continued Egyptian control of southern Canaan was in the balance:

> Let the king. . .send troops against the men who transgress against the king, my lord. If troops are provided (here) this year, then the lands. . .will (still) belong to the king, my lord; if there are no archers, the lands of the king, my lord, will be lost. . . .[47]

This material was interpreted in some academic circles as an account of the conquest of Joshua, written by those administrative officials in southern Palestine who were loyal to the Egyptian regime,[48] an assumption that rested in part on the equating of the Habiru with the invading Hebrews under Joshua.

A more critical reading of the tablets, however, shows that during the Amarna period the Canaanite princes, who had increased greatly in numbers, were endeavoring to obtain their liberty and expand the territory of their city-states by employing mercenary troops to overthrow their neighbors. It was for help against these semi-nomadic marauders, named SA.GAZ or Habiru in the texts, that the loyal princes were appealing to Egypt; and they were not requesting military reinforcements in order to fend off attacks by the Israelites under the leadership of Joshua. Since as few as fifty, or in one instance, ten, soldiers were thought necessary for the purposes of strengthening the defense of loyal strongpoints, the situation appears to have been one of internecine strife rather than invasion by a powerful united enemy.

Furthermore, in the light of other archaeological discoveries it does not seem possible to equate the Habiru with the Hebrews. The term "Habiru" is most probably west-Semitic, and may originally have denoted a social class rather than an ethnic group, although there is a variety of opinion on this matter. The Habiru were mentioned as early as the Third

---

[46] G. L. Robinson, *The Bearing of Archaeology on the OT* (1941), p. 58; cf. *ANET*, pp. 262ff.; *LAP*, pp. 98ff.

[47] Cf. J. A. Knudtzon, *Die El-Amarna Tafeln*, No. 286, lines 55ff.; *ANET*, p. 488.

[48] H. R. Hall, *The Ancient History of the Near East* (1926), p. 409.

Dynasty of Ur, and in the second millennium B.C. they were widely distributed through the ancient Near East. In Ugaritic texts they were designated by the term *'prm*,[49] and seemed to be of a heterogeneous ethnic background, as, indeed, was the case elsewhere. Hittite texts mentioned the Habiru as a social group somewhat above the slave class but not free citizens in the fullest sense of the term. Nevertheless, some texts from Mari and Alalakh convey the impression that the Habiru manifested certain attributes characteristic of an ethnic group, and in the Amarna tablets they are depicted as a separate ethnic entity bearing west-Semitic names.[50]

Albright has maintained that their designation was more properly 'Apiru, a form closely related philologically to 'Ibhrîm, the Biblical Hebrews, which also appears in the Egyptian texts.[51] There are other scholars, however, who have identified the Hebrews and the Habiru, but have disclaimed any connection between the Habiru and the 'Apiru—making, in the end, for a very complex situation.[52] From the available evidence it would seem that, while the 'Apiru were basically semi-nomads of the Near Eastern desert areas who lived and worked under sedentary conditions at various times, it is incorrect to think of all 'Apiru as Hebrews although they may, and perhaps did, include elements of the Hebrews.[53]

If the Habiru mentioned in the letter of Abdi-Hiba to Akhenaton were in fact the Hebrews of the conquest period under Joshua, it would be reasonable to expect some correspondence between the names of the Canaanite princes that occurred in the Amarna texts and the Palestinian chiefs mentioned in the Old Testament narratives, which—unfortunately for the theory of an early dating—is not the case. In point of fact, it would seem that the Amarna tablets and the Joshua narratives portray two quite different social and political settings. In the cuneiform texts the local Canaanite rulers were exploiting the disturbed political conditions of the time as a means of gaining their freedom, using bands of 'Apiru or Habiru mercenaries to that end. In the Joshua narratives, however, the Canaanite city-states were already independent and were

[49] Ch. Virolleaud, *BASOR*, No. 77 (1940), p. 32.

[50] Cf. J. Bottéro, *Cahiers de la Société asiatique*, XII (1954), pp. 10ff.; Greenberg, *The Hab/piru*, pp. 3ff.

[51] W. F. Albright, *The Archaeology of Palestine and the Bible* (1935), pp. 206f.; cf. *FSAC*, p. 240; *BASOR*, No. 77 (1940), p. 33; *Vocalisation of the Egyptian Sullabic Orthography* (1934), p. 42, VII. B. 4; *ARI*, p. 200 n. 8. Cf. T. J. Meek, *Hebrew Origins* (1960 ed.), pp. 11ff.

[52] Cf. H. H. Rowley, *From Joseph to Joshua* (1950), pp. 45ff.

[53] C. de Wit, *The Date and Route of the Exodus* (1960), p. 11. Cf. *BHI*, pp. 124f.; M. Noth, *Festschrift Otto Procksch* (1934), pp. 99ff.; J. Lewy, *HUCA*, XIV (1939), pp. 587ff., XV (1940), pp. 47ff.; E. Dhorme, *Revue de l'Histoire des Religions*, CXVIII (1938), pp. 170ff.; J. W. Jack, *PEQ* (1940), pp. 95ff.; H. H. Rowley, *PEQ* (1942), pp. 41ff.

in a position to make a coalition in order to oppose the advance of the invading Hebrews.

Because of this it appears difficult to reconcile the situation relating to the Habiru of the Tell el-Amarna tablets with the conquering activities of the Biblical Hebrews under the leadership of Joshua, and at the present it would seem unwise to make a positive identification of the Hebrews with either the Habiru, the 'Apiru, or both. It should also be noted that, although the origins of Israel were extremely complex, including the "mixed multitude" of Egypt, the Kenites of the Sinai peninsula, and the Gibeonites of the time of Joshua, the nucleus of Israel at the period of the Exodus consisted of the tribes or descendants of Jacob, who could trace their lineage back to him without any difficulty, and that any 'Apiru or Habiru who happened to be included in the larger number were present originally on a rather incidental basis.

Those scholars who supported a thirteenth-century B.C. date for the Exodus rested their theories in part upon the reference in Exodus 1:11 that implied that elements of the Hebrews were in bondage when the cities of Raamses and Pithom were being rebuilt or enlarged, thus making Seti I (ca. 1308-1290 B.C.) or Rameses II (ca. 1290-1224 B.C.) the pharaoh of the oppression. Excavations at the site of Tanis-Avaris by Montet revealed the reconstruction of the city under Seti I, while the presence of statues, *stelae*, and other artifacts bearing the names of Rameses II and his successors testified to the vigor of the New Kingdom period.[54] Contemporary Egyptian texts mention that some 'Apiru were employed to drag the huge blocks of masonry used at Avaris and at other sites for the construction of temples and public buildings.[55]

It is highly probable that many Hebrews who remained behind in Egypt during the Nineteenth Dynasty, long after the Hyksos had been expelled, were similarly organized into gangs of forced-laborers, and these would certainly include the ancestors of the later Israelites. That there were 'Apiru in Egypt as late as the time of Rameses IV is apparent from a contemporary inscription dated about 1160 B.C.[56] If there is any connection at all between the 'Apiru and the Hebrews, this need only mean that not all of the Hebrews in Egypt went out with Moses, or that other Hebrews settled in Egypt subsequent to the time of the Exodus.[57] A link with the Amarna era was furnished by the discovery of a *stele* recording that the city had been founded some four hundred years prior to the erection of the monument itself. Since the

---

[54] P. Montet, Les nouvelles fouilles de Tanis (1929-33).

[55] Cf. WMTS, pp. 74f.

[56] Cf. J. A. Wilson, AJSL, XLIX (1933), pp. 275ff.; B. Gunn, AASOR, XIII (1933), p. 38 n. 93.

[57] T. J. Meek, Hebrew Origins, p. 35; WMTS, p. 274.

monument has been dated about 1320 B.C., it points to a date for the establishment of the capital city of the Hyksos about 1720 B.C.[58]

The tradition preserved in Exodus that government store-cities were erected by the use of forced Israelite labor has been largely confirmed independently by excavations in Egypt. An ancient site in the Wadi Tumilat, Tell el-Retabeh, supposed to have been Raamses by Petrie who excavated it originally, is now known to have been Pithom.[59] Work at the site has uncovered some of the massive brickwork erected in the time of Rameses II, and since no traces of Eighteenth Dynasty construction or expansion were evident, it would appear that the Exodus tradition of forced labor referred to the days of Rameses II.

Tanis-Avaris, the Hyksos capital in the Nile delta,[60] was renamed the "house of Rameses" (*Per Re'emasese*) and bore this designation for two centuries (*ca.* 1300-1100 B.C.).[61] Its positive identification by Montet made it clear that the store-cities were not constructed under Thotmes III or Queen Hatshepsut—as was once thought—and designated by their later rather than by their earlier names.[62] If the Exodus tradition is to be taken at its face value, therefore, it would imply that Rameses II was the pharaoh of the oppression, and that the Exodus took place in the thirteenth century B.C.

On the basis of the Avaris era, scholars saw a connection between the Hyksos invasion of Egypt and the Hebrew occupation of the land of Goshen in the Nile delta area, as recorded in Exodus 12:40, which gave a 430-year sojourn for Israel in a foreign land. This usage was further alleged from the reference in Numbers 13:22 stating that Hebron was built seven years before Zoan (Avaris), and once again the Avaris period was employed as a medium for dating-sequences.[63] On this basis the Exodus would have occurred some 430 years after the founding of Avaris-Tanis, or about 1300 B.C.

One important Egyptian source precludes a date very much beyond 1220 B.C. for the entry of the victorious Israelites into Canaan. This is the celebrated *stele* from the time of Meneptah (*ca.* 1224-1216 B.C.), which dated from the fifth year of his reign. It was discovered by Flinders Petrie in 1895 in the ruined temple of Meneptah in western Thebes, and consisted of a lengthy court poem describing the victories of

---

[58] *WMTS*, pp. 72, 75.

[59] Pithom was identified in 1883 with Tell el-Mashkuta by E. Naville, *The Store-City of Pithom* (1885), but the "store-chambers" which he claimed to have discovered proved on subsequent examination to be fortress emplacements.

[60] Cf. A. H. Gardiner, *Ancient Egyptian Onomastica* (1947), I, pp. 169ff.

[61] *FSAC*, p. 255.

[62] P. Montet, *Le Drame d'Avaris* (1940), pp. 18ff.; cf. S. Caiger, *Bible and Spade* (1936), pp. 66ff.

[63] R. M. Engberg, *The Hyksos Reconsidered* (1939), p. 49, has observed that this assertion has never been tested archaeologically.

Meneptah over Libya and the eastern Asiatic lands including Palestine. The *stele* described graphically the terror and submission of the neighboring peoples:

> The princes are prostrate, saying: Salaam!
> There is not one who holds up his head among the Nine Bows;
> Since the Libyans are defeated, the land of the Hittites is pacified.
> Canaan is plundered with every evil;
> Askalon is conquered; Gezer is held;
> Yenoan is made a thing of naught;
> Israel is destroyed: it has no seed-corn;
> Palestine has become a widow for Egypt.
> All lands are united in peace. . . .[64]

The name "Israel" was written on the *stele* with the determinative symbol that denotes "people" rather than "land" or "territory," which would imply sedentary occupation of western Palestine.[65] However, it is conceivable that this is a transcriptional error, since the *stele* contains other similar mistakes.

As Burrows has pointed out, some scholars experienced difficulty in interpreting the evidence of the Meneptah *stele,* which shows that Israel experienced a defeat under Meneptah about 1230 B.C., partly because they assigned too late a date for the Exodus itself.[66] For them the *stele* showed that the Israelites were already in Canaan when they should still have been wandering about in the Sinai peninsula. This led to efforts to show that only a portion of the Israelite people had gone into Egypt, and that the *stele* referred to the remainder who had never left Palestine in the first place.[67] While it may well be that the sojourn in Egypt and the events of the Exodus are most properly associated only with a limited group, as described principally in the Biblical narratives, there are good reasons for believing that all the tribes may have been in Canaan prior to 1230 B.C.

The work of Nelson Glueck in the Hashemite Kingdom of Jordan has shown that southern Canaan was in the middle of a nomadic upheaval during the Third Dynasty of Ur. The Middle Bronze Age sites that he excavated afforded convincing evidence of large-scale abandonment and destruction of towns and cities.[68] Before the end of the twentieth century the material culture of the area declined, and sporadic raids by marauding nomads from the east and south precipitated a decline in the density of human settlement. After 1850 B.C. an interruption of sedentary occupation of southern Transjordan resulted in the replacement of inhabitants of walled cities by semi-nomadic tribes, a state of affairs that

---

[64] W. Spiegelberg, *Zeitschrift für Aegyptische Sprache*, XXXIX (1896), pp. 1ff.
[65] *FSAC*, pp. 255f.
[66] *WMTS*, p. 274.
[67] Cf. T. J. Meek, *Hebrew Origins*, p. 31.
[68] N. Glueck, *The Other Side of the Jordan*, pp. 114ff.

lasted about five centuries.[69] No subsequent attempt to settle in walled towns was evident until about 1300 B.C.,[70] which would suggest that the Israelite victories over the Ammonites in Transjordan did not occur until after that time.

If a date *ca.* 1300 B.C. is assigned to the Exodus, the traditional period of the Wilderness wanderings would be sufficient to bring the Israelites into northern Moab a little before the middle of the thirteenth century B.C. Excavations at Lachish, Bethel, Debir, and Hazor have shown clear traces of destruction at thirteenth-century levels, indicating the rapidity of the Israelite advance as described in Joshua. It would seem therefore that the invasion of Canaan by the Hebrews was neither a typical irruption of tent-dwelling nomads who continued to pursue a semi-sedentary way of life long after the first invasion, nor was it a matter of gradual infiltration and assimilation, as many modern scholars have thought.

The highly complex nature of the problems associated with the dating of the Exodus may be conveniently summarized in terms of three distinct theories. The first, based upon the work of Garstang at Jericho, would date the fall of that city between 1400 and 1385 B.C.,[71] associate the Habiru of the Amarna letters with the invading Israelites under the leadership of Joshua, and interpose a century or more between the fall of Jericho and the overthrow of Bethel, Lachish, Debir, and Hazor. The second, following a thirteenth-century B.C. dating-sequence, would maintain that the Exodus took place shortly after 1290 B.C.,[72] and that this was followed by the invasion of Moab and Canaan a little prior to 1250 B.C. Computations of this sort are based in general upon the Avaris era. The third hypothesis, advanced by Rowley and supported to a large extent by Gordon,[73] would place the Exodus after the middle of the thirteenth century B.C. and the conquest at the end of that century. Such a view has the decided disadvantage of disrupting earlier chronological sequences to the point that the patriarchs appear on the historical scene somewhat later than the patriarchal period.

Each of the foregoing positions suffers from obvious disadvantages,[74] and serves to show the enormous amount of care that must be exercised

[69] Cf. W. F. Albright in *The Jews: Their History, Culture and Religion* (ed. L. Finkelstein, 1949), p. 5.

[70] Cf. N. Glueck, *BASOR*, No. 55 (1934), pp. 3ff., *AASOR*, XIV (1934), pp. 1ff., XVIII-XIX (1939), p. 268. These conclusions were confirmed by Albright at Tell Beit Mirsim, *AASOR*, XII (1932), pp. 52ff., XVII (1938), pp. 76ff., and by Sellers at Beth-zur. Cf. O. R. Sellers, *The City of Beth-zur* (1931), pp. 9ff.

[71] J. and J. B. E. Garstang, *The Story of Jericho* (1940), pp. 120ff.

[72] Cf. *FSAC*, pp. 255ff.

[73] H. H. Rowley, *BJRL*, XXII (1938), pp. 243ff., and in *IDB*, II, p. 752; cf. C. H. Gordon, *IOTT*, p. 131.

[74] *WMTS*, p. 79. For the view that the destruction of the "cities of the valley" substantiates an early rather than a late date for Abraham see J. P. Harland, *IDB*, IV, p. 397.

in any attempt to interpret and correlate archaeological data with a view to elucidating and establishing the larger historical pattern. The solution that appears to present the fewest difficulties would seem to envisage a period of time covered by the Late Bronze Age and the Nineteenth Egyptian Dynasty, with the actual Exodus occurring about 1280 B.C.

C. Joshua and Judges

The dating-sequences that a scholar accords to the Exodus from Egypt transpose their own peculiar difficulties into the period of Joshua and Judges, as might well be expected. Those who assign a fifteenth-century B.C. date to the event note that the fall of Jericho was preceded by the Israelite occupation of Moab, which according to Jephthah (Judg. 11:26) extended over a period of three hundred years. By assigning a date of about 1100 B.C. to Jephthah, it was thus possible to place the initial occupation of Moabite territory at 1400 B.C. The attack of Joshua on Debir (Josh. 10:38f.) was interpreted in terms of the destruction of its inhabitants only, the fall of the city proper being considered to have been the work of Israelite forces under Othniel, the nephew of Caleb (Judg. 1:11ff.). Similarly, the final overthrow of Canaanite culture in Hebron was assigned to the period of the Judges (Judg. 1:10).

One of the chief difficulties with the thirteenth-century date of the Exodus espoused by Albright lies in the fact that Joshua apparently had no connection with the fall of Jericho, which by implication had been in ruins for at least fifty years before he crossed the Jordan.[75] However, one can only assume that the destruction of Jericho preceded the circuit of Edom and the invasion of Moab if he rejects some of the archaeological evidence and reverses the order of the Biblical record, which Albright regards in general as substantially historical. Since the archaeological findings at Jericho are at best somewhat inconclusive, the date of its fall ought not to be made the dominant consideration in determining either the date of the Exodus or the settlement in Canaan, although it is of some importance for the traditional Biblical record, which clearly regards Jericho as having immense strategic significance.

That the chronologies in the book of Joshua and Judges are sources of considerable difficulty has already been noted in part three. Attacks made by Noth and Möhlenbrink on the historicity of the conquest narratives have been subjected to devastating criticisms by Albright, who has maintained that the actual course of events followed more closely the sources underlying the Biblical tradition than modern attempts at reconstruction.[76] The first eleven chapters of Joshua present

75 W. F. Albright, *BASOR*, No. 58 (1935), p. 18.
76 M. Noth, *PJB*, XXXIV (1938), pp. 7ff. and *Kleine Schriften zur Geschichte des Volkes Israel* (1953), I, pp. 176ff.; K. Möhlenbrink, *ZAW*, LVI (1938), pp. 238ff.; W. F. Albright, *BASOR*, No. 74 (1939), pp. 11ff.

the traditional view of a rapid succession of forays in southern Canaan, followed by the liquidation of native opposition in the north. The remainder of the book and the first chapter of Judges, however, might convey an impression of a more piecemeal type of conquest, which on some occasions was actually reconquest, accomplished in part by individual tribes independently of the leadership of Joshua.

Some scholars who associated the Habiru incursions into Palestine with the Israelite overthrow of Jericho and the invasion of the hill-country of Ephraim under Joshua concluded that there must have been two distinct settlements in Palestine, perhaps separated by as much as a century and a half.[77] On the one hand was the settlement of the northern or Israelite group occurring from about 1400 B.C.; on the other was the southern or Judaean occupation, thought to have commenced by about 1200 B.C. The Biblical writers, it was maintained, foreshortened and dovetailed the two conquest narratives into one another as the achievement of a single people, a process that would account for the resultant confusion and inconsistency in the Biblical narratives.[78]

Examples of this tendency were adduced from the description of the reduction of Debir (Kiriath-sepher, identified with Tell Beit Mirsim), which in Joshua 10:38f. is attributed to the celebrated Israelite leader, whereas elsewhere (Josh. 15:15; Judg. 1:11ff.) its conquest is regarded as being the work of Othniel. The first 21 verses of Judges attribute the conquest of the south to Judah, whereas verses 22-36 record that northern Canaan was conquered by the Israelite tribes under Joshua. In point of fact, however, the confusion is less real than apparent, for Judges, while summarizing the conquest and occupation of Canaan, shows the extent to which the native inhabitants had been left in possession of their cities and had become resurgent after the death of Joshua. Thus it was necessary for the tribes of Judah and Simeon to advance south against the Canaanites (Judg. 1:4ff.) and overthrow Bezek, following this by attacks upon Hebron and Debir, which had been reoccupied since their destruction in the time of Joshua (Josh. 10:36, 39). Attempts to take Jerusalem from Jebusite control (Judg. 1:21) were not successful, although the attack against Hormah resulted in victory (Judg. 1:17), as did the campaign against the three Philistine cities (Judg. 1:18f.), despite the fact that in the latter case the cities were not held because of Philistine military superiority. The Joseph tribes were forced to reoccupy Bethel (Judg. 1:22ff.), which had revolted; and at this point further Israelite efforts to eradicate the native inhabitants failed. No more cities were taken (Judg. 1:27ff.), and the tribe of Dan was actually evicted from its allotted territory (Judg. 1:34) by the Amorites.

[77] T. J. Meek, *Hebrew Origins*, pp. 21f.
[78] Cf. C. F. Burney, *Israel's Settlement in Canaan* (1921), pp. 3ff.

Thus if a clear view of the conquest period is to be obtained, it is important to distinguish between the events that characterized it and those that occurred after the death of Joshua, when a resurgence of the native Canaanite population took place. The conquest can be illustrated by the facts of archaeological exploration at sites such as Bethel, Lachish, Debir, Hebron, Gibeah, and Hazor, which show clearly that these places were occupied or destroyed in the latter part of the Late Bronze Age. If this destructive activity is to be correlated with the campaigns of Joshua as outlined in the Biblical sources (Josh. 11:16ff.), it would appear that the land as a whole was occupied with comparative rapidity by the Israelite invaders, although not all of the fortified strongholds, including a belt of Canaanite resistance separating the northern and southern tribes, were reduced at that time (cf. Josh. 13:1).

There can also be little doubt from the findings of the excavators that many of the sites were later reoccupied by the dispossessed Canaanites, and subsequently changed hands a number of times in the period from the thirteenth to the eleventh centuries. As Wright has stated, the Biblical version of the campaigns of Joshua reflected success in attacking certain key royal Canaanite cities, but also portrayed the prolonged period of struggle for possession of the land, a situation in evidence for a considerable time after the death of Joshua.[79] As has been mentioned previously, a good deal of discussion has centered upon the problems raised by the narratives dealing with the Israelite conquest of Bethel and Ai in particular, and to a lesser extent with the role of Shechem in the conquest period.

The Biblical account seems to have envisaged Ai as an inhabited site with its own ruler, or at the very least as a defensive point—whether temporary or permanent—manned by troops under the control of a commander-in-chief, where the Israelites encountered initial opposition. The severity of this opposition is indicated by the reference in Joshua 8:33ff., in which a party of thirty thousand men, a number that may have been inflated according to ancient scribal traditions, was sent out to ambush "the city" from the west, while, according to verse 12, a second group of five thousand men was also dispatched to capture the site. Quite apart from the immediate problem raised by the size of the numbers mentioned, it seems clear that the narrative is not just a redactional version of one attack upon Ai, but that it does in fact describe the activities of two distinct ambush parties. The question then arises as to why the military tactics on that occasion should have required such an enormous force of soldiers for such an apparently limited objective. Surely from some points of view it would be more plausible for the thirty thousand men to be sent to Bethel while the five thousand were engaged in reducing the opposition at Ai.

[79] G. E. Wright, *JNES*, V (1946), pp. 105ff.

A rather clearer view of the situation can be obtained by an appreciation of the military exigencies that confronted both Joshua and the enemy commander of both Bethel and "the ruin" (Ai). Since the latter was so prominent in the narratives, it seems most probable that it was a strongpoint that controlled the eastern approaches to Bethel, overlooking as it does the valleys to the north and south. Since Bethel is in a reverse-slope position and Ai in a forward-slope position, any defending commander could be expected to move his principal defensive point forward to the ruin of Ai so as to take advantage of the terrain, and leave his reserve units in Bethel, along with the civilian population. This tactical move would doubtless be influenced by the presence of an established ridgeway track running from Ai to Bethel and making communication over the distance of less than two miles a matter of comparative ease.

The Israelite base camp was located north of Bethel and Ai in "dead ground" beyond the valley, which contained seasonal *wadis* (Josh. 8:11, 13). However, this location presented certain problems, so that even with as many as forty thousand troops at his disposal it must have occurred to Joshua that it would be inadvisable to attack Bethel only to leave his flank and rear guard open to a strong enemy force at Ai. On the other hand he must have realized that he could hardly attack the ruin itself without being observed from some considerable distance, thereby losing the element of surprise. The latter consideration was the more pressing, since a strong Israelite task-force had already been decisively thrown back at Ai (Josh. 7:2ff.). Accordingly Joshua seems to have decided to gain as much tactical advantage as possible under such conditions by surreptitiously placing large bodies of troops near Ai and Bethel, with the apparent intention of drawing the enemy defense by engaging in a decoy frontal attack and subsequently withdrawing, as though he was repeating his previous tactical mistake (Josh. 8:14f.). Thus it was necessary for the larger ambush of thirty thousand men (accepting these figures at their face value for the sake of the immediate discussion) to leave the base camp some thirty-six hours before the battle and move into position, unobserved and concealed, to the west of the ruin. In order to allow an adequate amount of time for this maneuver, the troops were allotted two nights to reach their appointed station (Josh. 8:9, 13). The smaller ambush of about five thousand men would experience considerably less difficulty in moving to the west of Bethel, and as a result they only needed to be dispatched on the eve of the battle (Josh. 8:12). Having briefed the ambushes, Joshua bivouacked in the valley north of Ai in full view of the enemy (Josh. 8:11ff.), leading the officer in command of the force stationed at the ruin to think that the Israelites were on the point of repeating their earlier mistaken tactics. Unaware of the ambush, the reserve troops in Bethel who witnessed the mock flight of the Israelites took off after them in hot pursuit (Josh. 8:15ff.). When the signal was given by Joshua, the thirty thousand soldiers arose to take the pursuing enemy forces in the rear, while the five thousand were left to sack and burn Bethel (Josh. 8:19f.).

This reconstruction of events is based upon the evidence afforded by the text, and takes note of the fact that "the city" and "the ruin" are apparently used interchangeably. Since the two words differ by only one consonant in the Hebrew (העיר and העי), there is an understandable degree of confusion in their specific application to Bethel as the city and to Ai as the ruin. In Joshua 8:12 it becomes necessary to read "Beth-aven" for "Bethel," with the eastern text K*thibh* and the Lagarde edition of the LXX (cf. Josh. 7:2), and at the end of the same verse the Massoretic K*thibh* must be preferred to the Q*re*. The presence of textual confusion in this verse is clearly indicated by the LXX, which has a shorter rendering, but in any case the suggested reading accords with the general sense of the military maneuver, and resolves any clash which might seem to be suggested in Joshua 8:9.

As far as Shechem is concerned, the difficulties are of a different order, and are related in part to the fact that Joshua has nothing to say about the conquest of central Palestine, which is a rather unexpected situation in view of the importance that the region assumed in subsequent Israelite history. The presence of Joshua at the covenant ceremonies celebrated at Shechem, which in early times was the capital of the region and the locale at which the tribes gathered (Josh. 8:24, 30ff.), has led many scholars to conclude that Shechem was at that time under the control of Hebrews who had either never been in Egypt in the first place and therefore did not take part in the Exodus, or that they had been part of an earlier exodus somehow connected with the movements of Hyksos after they had been expelled from Egypt about 1570 B.C. Some writers have even seen the Shechem area as the place where the later differences that arose between Israel and Judah originated. Be that as it may, it is clear from the Tell el-Amarna tablets that the district around Shechem was for at least a century before the time of Joshua in firm control of a military group that paid little heed to the Egyptian pharaoh and many of the petty Canaanite kings who had pledged him their loyalty. It has also been long a matter of recognition that in Genesis 34 there is a tradition of an early Hebrew relationship with Shechem that need not have been modified to any significant extent by the events of the sojourn in Egypt and the Exodus. Certainly the tradition of Joshua 24, in which the Israelite leader sealed the covenant with a united nation at a city which he had not had to reduce previously, would be explicable if there were already in existence at Shechem a mixed Canaanite and Hebrew group of clans, united in a covenant relationship and preserving the memory of an association with the Israelite movement.

329

Excavations conducted at el-Jib, identified with ancient Gibeon, between 1956 and 1959 uncovered the remains of a culture that goes back at least to Late Bronze Age IIb strata (1300-1200 B.C.), and was also well represented in Iron Age levels.[80] Subsequent excavations revealed the presence of five distinct occupational levels dating from about 2800 B.C. to approximately 100 B.C. While certain other sites may present problems in any attempt to correlate the conquest period archaeologically, the findings at el-Jib have at least shown that the occupational situation at Gibeon in the early days of the conquest was that represented in the book of Joshua (ch. 9:21ff.).

There can be little question that the accounts of the military campaigns furnished by the narratives of Joshua are selective. It may well be within the bounds of possibility that some of the battles that occurred during this important period were not included in the final form of the conquest tradition, perhaps because they were considered rather incidental to the general purpose of the author or compiler, namely, to demonstrate that the Israelites had finally occupied the land promised to their ancestors. There seems to be no valid reason for assigning the career of Joshua preserved by tradition to the realm of myth and legend, since all that the original authors were doing was giving the bulk of the credit for the victories in Canaan to their accredited military hero. Exactly the same device is employed by traditionist and historiographer alike in the present age, where, in some senses, the detailed and observed facts of the case might well point to other conclusions. All available evidence indicates that it was Joshua who was the strategic figure in the entire military scheme of things, and that under his inspired leadership the conquest of Canaan was accomplished, a feat that was to be remembered in subsequent times in something approaching epic terms.

Although the general trend of archaeological discovery has made a thirteenth-century B.C. date for the Exodus and conquest a matter of the highest probability, it has raised issues of chronology that affect the Judges period in particular. On the basis of the reference in 1 Kings 6:1 to the fourth year of Solomon, a figure of just under 400 years is obtained for the period covered by Joshua and the Elders, Judges, and Saul. If, however, the beginning of the conquest is assigned to about 1240 B.C. on archaeological grounds, a period of only 230 years or so intervenes between the military activities of Joshua and the accession of David, ca. 1010 B.C. Some scholars have attempted to shorten the Judges period by assuming that the narratives dealt with the exploits of more or less contemporary local heroes rather than with a chronological succession of national leaders, and as a result they have been able to compress the events between the time of Joshua and the rise of Saul into a period of

[80] Cf. J. B. Pritchard, *VT*, suppl. vol. VII (1960), pp. 1ff.

about one hundred and fifty years. Some caution should be urged with respect to the view that the Judges may have been nothing more than local heroes, since while their activities may have been confined to some specific area of the Promised Land, the deliverance that they achieved was certainly regarded by the book of Judges as being national in scope. No doubt at least some of the Judges and the crises with which they dealt were contemporary in incidence, and not strictly successive in point of time as might appear from a superficial reading of Judges.[81] The real problem lies not so much in this area, however, as in the methods of computation and compilation which were employed by the ancient Near Eastern scribes.

The difference between 400 or more years and 230 years, both of which are at least arguable possibilities in terms of occidental reckoning, is not nearly as important as the principles of compression or omission that ultimately dictated the form of the Old Testament narratives dealing with this and other similar periods of time. In antiquity the scribes normally tabulated each series of rulers and reigns separately, and did not compile synchronistic lists in the manner of current occidental chroniclers. The lack of cross-references between contemporaries in the period of the Judges can be paralleled by similar omissions for the history of Dynasties XIII to XVII in the Egyptian Turin Papyrus of Kings. In this Egyptian source, a total of some 450 regnal years has to be aligned to a period of about 216 years between ca. 1786 and 1570 B.C., a situation that illustrates the problems raised and the methods employed to resolve them.

Mesopotamian annals and Egyptian king-lists illustrate the tendency of ancient scribes and chroniclers to foreshorten historical sequences[82] and make selective use of data by exercising principles of omission and other methods of control over the sources. There seems therefore to be no valid reason for supposing that a different methodology was applied in general to a composition such as Judges. On the other hand, it is important for those grounded in occidental traditions of precise numerical expression to realize that the actual numbers as such—whether they occur in Biblical or extra-Biblical sources—need not be called into question, since they may well be accurate in themselves as they now stand. What is significant, however, is the manner in which these numbers were interpreted by the ancient scribes, a consideration that must always be borne in mind by modern readers. From the standpoint of the latter, however, it is obvious that the historical period in question presents difficulties both of chronology and of historical detail, and these cannot be resolved completely without fuller information.

[81] K. A. Kitchen and T. C. Mitchell, NBD, p. 216.
[82] Cf. J. E. McFadyen, ET, XXXVI (1924-25), pp. 103ff.

331

It would not be amiss to mention at this juncture the so-called amphic-tyonic relationship of the Israelite tribes after the period of the immedi-ate territorial occupation of Canaan. The term "amphictyony" was de-rived from the twelve-tribe sacral leagues of the early centuries of the first millennium B.C. in Greece and Italy. This classical concept was applied by Noth and Alt to the organization of the Israelite tribes by Joshua at Shechem near Mount Gerizim (cf. Deut. 11:29; 27:12), where an association of the tribes was established around a central sanctuary, as a means of unifying their religious and political activity.[83] This arrange-ment was held by these scholars to be similar to the somewhat later amphictyonies such as the twelve-member Etruscan League of Voltum-na, or the Greek League of Delphi, which functioned on much the same basis.

Despite the persuasive arguments of Noth and Alt, there is some doubt as to whether such an amphictyony ever existed in Canaan in quite this manner. In the first place, one ought to be able to see such an institution reflected in the social structure of the Philistine occupation of southern Palestine, since these peoples were already grouped into a confederacy for purposes of self-protection. There seem only to have been five major cities, however, with which were associated numerous smaller settlements (1 Sam. 6:18), which certainly does not conform to the overall classical Aegean picture of an amphictyony. The Philistines would certainly be expected to be organized in such a configuration, since their Aegean background could well have given them at least some degree of familiarity with it. This contention would still have validity, even though in its developed form the amphictyony was slightly later than the general period under discussion, since the very existence of the Philistines as a group depended to no small extent upon some such compact social structure. Even though the geography of southern Canaan was favorable to this kind of organization, there is no evidence that the Philistines were grouped in the amphictyonic pattern of Aegean nations. According to the Biblical sources they lived in five independent cities ruled over by lords or governors who acted in concert for the good of the nation as a whole, and were able to overrule dissident or im-prudent decisions made by an individual governor (1 Sam. 29:1ff.).

In actual fact it is more probable that the associations of twelve-member tribes originated in Semitic rather than in Greek circles. Traces of early groups of this kind can be seen in Genesis, where there are enumerated twelve Aramaean tribes (Gen. 22:20ff.), the twelve Ishma-elite tribes (Gen. 25:13ff.), and the twelve tribes of Edom (Gen. 36:10ff.). It is well known that the *motif* of configuration in terms of six or twelve is of Sumerian, and not Greek, origin. Further traces of

---

[83] M. Noth, *Das System der zwölf Stämme Israels* (1930), pp. 39ff. A. Alt, *Kleine Schriften zur Geschichte des Volkes Israel*, I, pp. 278ff.

federations among neighbors of the Israelites, based upon the number six rather than twelve, can also be seen in the six sons of Keturah and in a list of Horite clans (Gen. 36:20ff.). The idea of a central shrine around which houses and other buildings were grouped represented the earliest attempts at social organization in Mesopotamia, as is indicated by the archaeology of the Mesopotamian Neolithic period. It is only a comparatively small step from this basic Semitic concept to the organization of the twelve tribes around a central sanctuary, and subsequently to the Greek amphictyony, which was established on the basis of an accredited religious authority. As represented in Judges, the association of Israelite tribes was at best of a loosely knit variety, and dependent in a significant measure upon the Philistine economy, due to the technological inferiority of the Hebrew peoples.

Although the Hebrews were without a formally organized government like those of neighboring lands, it must not be presumed on that account that the only authority that the Judges claimed was of a moral or spiritual order. This opinion is an incorrect conclusion from the suggestion of Alt that leadership in the period of the Judges was based solely upon acknowledged possession of charismatic gifts. As C. H. Gordon has shown, the Judges were not elevated to positions of leadership simply because they were thought to display inspirational qualities or certain mystic attributes of personality.[84] It is now evident from the nature of Mycenaean kingship and its counterpart among the Hebrews that the Judges followed the pattern familiar in Aegean circles of appointment or selection from the ruling class. While it was possible for inspiration alone to elevate the more inferior members of the aristocracy, it is never recorded as having descended upon those individuals whose fathers were of a lowly and non-aristocratic status in the Heroic Age. Thus, while Jephthah was the son of a woman who occupied a decidedly inferior position in the social scale, he was actually an aristocrat from the side of his father Gilead, whose status conferred upon him the privilege of membership in the warrior class or גבורי חיל.[85] In spite of the kind of leadership that the Judges provided, however, the forces that operated on the side of internal disruption during this period were as serious a menace as the Philistines, Amalekites, or Midianites, for the geographical structure of the country favored territorial groupings and the resultant perpetuation of distinctive dialects, local customs, and special political attitudes.

Even when the central Tabernacle was definitely established at Shiloh, there were a number of other shrines in existence with which groups or alliances of tribes were associated from time to time. Thus the central shrine could not have exercised the cohesive force predicated of those

[84] *GBB*, pp. 295ff.
[85] C. H. Gordon, *Christianity Today*, VII, No. 12 (1963), p. 579.

associated with Mediterranean amphictyonies. The very fact that there were so many places where religious veneration was in evidence seems yet another reason for doubting whether there was in fact any twelve-tribe amphictyony of the kind envisaged by Alt and Noth in existence at this period. It should also be observed that the renewal of the Covenant (Josh. 24:1ff.) was a feature of the Wilderness wanderings (Deut. 27:1ff.), and did not take its rise from Greek configurations. It would therefore seem prudent, with Bright, to relate the origin of the social structure of the Israelite tribes to Sinai rather than to Greek political or religious patterns of organization.[86] Alt and his followers are undoubtedly correct in their attempts to bring the social structure of the Joshua-Judges period within the traditions of the Heroic Age, but against this it has to be noted that the concept of "twelveness" was depicted by the narratives of Joshua and Judges as a normal outgrowth of the kind of tribal system that functioned during the period of the Wilderness wanderings, making it much more probable that the organization of Israel in Canaan subsequent to the conquest was of independent origin.

D. THE MONARCHY

With the commencement of the Iron Age about 1200 B.C., problems of historiography and general chronology become much less confused. The humble beginnings of the kingdom under Saul have been amply illustrated by the excavations of Albright at Gibeah. The rustic simplicity of the buildings unearthed and the presence of cultivated land in the area point to the limited nature of the regal power, and furnish a striking contrast to the wealth and military vigor of subsequent times. The Biblical traditions that associate David with music and psalmody have also been verified from archaeological sources. These indicate that Palestine had been noted for its musical attainments for a number of centuries before the time of David. The Beni-Hasan tableau, which can be dated about 1900 B.C., depicts visiting Palestinian nomads walking behind their animals in Egypt to the accompaniment of a lyre,[87] while inscriptions on Egyptian monuments dated some 350 years later refer to examples of Canaanite music.[88]

The religious poetry of the Ugaritic texts has been shown to have close affinities with the phraseology of the Hebrew Psalms.[89] From the same sources come references to a class of Temple personnel designated by the term *sarim*,[90] who exercised functions similar to those of the Hebrew singers during the monarchy and later times. Some of the servants of

[86] *BHI*, pp. 145f.
[87] *LAP*, p. 83.
[88] *ARI*, pp. 125ff.
[89] J. H. Patton, *Canaanite Parallels in the Book of Psalms* (1944).
[90] C. H. Gordon, *Ugaritic Handbook* (1955), p. 272, No. 1934; cf. No. 1991.

David, who were designated in 1 Kings 4:31 (cf. 1 Chron. 2:6) by the term אֶזְרָח meaning "aboriginal" or "native sons," and who possessed Canaanite names such as Heman, Chalcol, and Darda, were engaged in various forms of musical activity. As such they were described by the phrase "sons of Mahol," a Hebrew term closely related to the Greek ὀρχήστρα, used of a semi-circular area in which the Greek chorus danced,[91] and meaning "members of the orchestral guild." A further reflection of this musical interest became apparent when Megiddo was excavated and the treasure room of the royal palace was uncovered. From this area was recovered a plaque inlaid with ivory, depicting a royal personage seated on a throne. He was drinking from a small bowl, and was being entertained by a court musician who stood before him plucking the strings of a lyre.[92]

The report of the Egyptian envoy Wen-Amon about 1080 B.C. furnishes graphic illustration of the manner in which trade and commerce were expanding in Palestine at that period.[93] With the large-scale domestication of the camel about the twelfth century B.C. there came a significant growth in the volume of the import and export trade in the country. Tribes such as Dan and Asher participated in maritime activity (cf. Judg. 5:17), and the general widening of Mediterranean trade was such that merchant shipping was organized into convoys in order to afford better protection against pirates, freebooters, and other raiders.[94] Archaeological excavations in different Mediterranean lands have confirmed the Biblical traditions that speak of the maritime activity characteristic of the days of Solomon, and the part which Phoenician shipbuilders played in it, a matter that has been noted in an earlier chapter.

It may well have been the threat posed by the technological advances of the Solomonic period to the domestic economy of Arabia which prompted the visit of the Queen of Sheba (Saba) to Jerusalem. Older historians were consistently accustomed to assign this regal personage to the area of myth and legend, but this was because comparatively little was known at that time about the history of the Sabaeans. Originally nomads, these people had become sedentary by the time of Solomon,[95] and had established a kingdom in the region of modern eastern Yemen. As such they exercised a good deal of control over the caravan-routes

---

[91] Cf. Plato *Apol.* 26E.

[92] *WBA*, p. 94.

[93] *ANET*, pp. 25ff.

[94] B. Maisler, *BASOR*, No. 102 (1946), p. 10.

[95] *ARI*, pp. 132ff.; W. F. Albright, *BASOR*, No. 128 (1952), p. 45, *JBL*, LXXI (1952), pp. 248f.; G. W. van Beek, *BA*, XIV, No. 1 (1952), pp. 5f.; R. L. Bowen and F. P. Albright, *Archaeological Discoveries in South Arabia* (1958). pp. 215f. For the history and archaeology of southern Arabia see G. W. van Beek, *BANE*, pp. 229ff., and *BASOR*, No. 151 (1958), p. 16.

between northern India, Mesopotamia, and Palestine. When Solomon acquired control of the northern end of the trading-routes and sought to extend this to the frontier areas of Transjordan also, he posed an immediate threat to the economic interests of southwestern Arabia in particular. The situation was aggravated even further by the expansion of his maritime trade, which brought serious competition to the overland caravan-routes for the first time. It was the urgency of this matter that prompted a Sabaean queen to undertake an arduous journey of about twelve hundred miles by camel. Although the oldest Sabaean inscriptions only go back as far as the eighth century B.C., it is known from cuneiform sources that queens governed large tribal confederacies in northern Arabia from the ninth to the seventh centuries B.C., and that they largely dropped out of the historical picture in southern Arabia after the sixth century B.C.[96] There would therefore seem to be no valid reason for dismissing the account of the visit made by the Sabaean queen to Solomon as legendary (1 Kgs. 10:1ff.).[97]

The unsettled nature of conditions in Palestine following the death of Solomon depicted by the Biblical narratives has also been reinforced by archaeological discovery. The invasion of the country by Shishak I of Egypt in 925 B.C. was part of a larger military campaign designed to restore the fortunes of Egypt in the Near East, a fact made clear by the Shishak inscription on the temple walls at Karnak. With typical oriental exaggeration this inscription depicted the victorious Egyptian pharaoh leading the Asiatic peoples to a state of slavery.[98] A fragment of a *stele* from the period of Shishak was unearthed at Megiddo, and showed the extent of his conquest in the Negeb and Transjordan regions.[99]

While Shishak was busily occupied in subjugating Palestine, the Aramaean dynasty of Damascus was increasing in vigor after rather humble and uncertain beginnings. According to 1 Kings 15:18ff. the succession of rulers was traced back to "Hezion, king of Syria," and this lineage was largely confirmed in 1940 by the discovery of the inscribed *stele* of Benhadad I at a site in Syria some five miles north of Aleppo.[100] Unfortunately this artifact failed to identify the individual described as "Rezon, son of Eliadah," who according to 1 Kings 11:23f. attacked and occupied Damascus in the Solomonic period and subsequently established a Syrian dynasty. The name Rezon has been thought to be a

[96] J. A. Montgomery, *Arabia and the Bible* (1934), p. 180. For an untechnical account of explorations in southern Arabia see W. Phillips, *Qataban and Sheba* (1955).

[97] Cf. E. Ullendorff, *BJRL*, XLV (1963), pp. 486ff.

[98] M. Noth, *Zeitschrift des Deutschen Palästina-Vereins*, XLI (1936), pp. 227ff.; cf. B. Mazar, *VT*, suppl. vol. IV (1957), pp. 57ff.

[99] W. F. Albright, *AASOR*, XXI-XXII (1943), p. 29 n. 10.

[100] Cf. M. Dunand, *Bulletin du Musée de Beyrouth*, III (1941), pp. 65ff.; W. F. Albright, *BASOR*, No. 87 (1942), pp. 23ff., No. 90 (1943), pp. 30ff.

corruption of Hezion, the *Hadyan* of the Benhadad *stele,* or, alternatively, a title meaning "prince."

Before the *stele*[101] was discovered, it was customary to distinguish at least three Damascus rulers named Benhadad. The first was an ally of Asa when Baasha of Israel attacked Judah (2 Chron. 16:1ff.); the second was his son, identified with Hadadezer (Adadidri) (1 Kgs. 20:34), who fought against Shalmaneser III between 853 and 845 B.C.; the third, the son of the Hazael who murdered Benhadad II (2 Kgs. 8:15), fought against Shalmaneser III in 841 B.C. It was one of these persons who left the Melqart *stele,* and the usual attribution is to Benhadad I.[102] Since the *stele* is mutilated and the patronymic is lost, it is difficult to be certain either about the mention or the identity of Rezon, or even about the attribution of the *stele* to Benhadad I. The general position adopted by the Albright school[103] was to subsume the three individual Benhadads under one name, Benhadad I, and to assign a forty-year period (*ca.* 880-842 B.C.) to his reign.[104] If the Benhadad of Ahab and Joram is the same individual as the Benhadad of King Asa, he would have reigned for approximately fifty-seven years, *ca.* 900 to 843 B.C., which, though not without parallel, would certainly be rather unusual. If, however, Benhadad I died about 860 B.C., his successor, Benhadad II (Adadidri), would then be contemporary with Ahab. From the style of the script Albright assigned a median date of about 850 B.C. for the *stele,* but this estimate is at best rather tentative, and is certainly not an assured basis for identifying three Benhadads as a single person. For the present, therefore, the evidence furnished by the Melqart *stele* must be regarded as inconclusive in this matter.

Independent testimony to the events that occurred in the reign of Menahem of Israel (752-742/41 B.C.) has been furnished by Assyrian sources. The cuneiform annals of Tiglathpileser III, an enterprising leader who usurped the Assyrian throne about 745 B.C. and instituted a series of campaigns against Syria and Palestine, recorded the manner in which King Menahem (2 Kgs. 15:17ff.) was compelled to become tributary to the Assyrian regime.[105] The head of this resurgent kingdom, who was known to the Israelites as Pul, though probably originally named Pulu,[106] appeared subsequently on the Israelite scene as an ally of Ahaz of Judah (732/31-716/15 B.C.) in the face of an attack upon the latter by a Syrian-Israelite coalition (2 Kgs. 16:7). Tiglathpileser III marched

---

101 *DOTT*, pp. 239ff. and pl. 15; *ANET*, p. 501.

102 W. F. Albright, *BASOR*, No. 87 (1942), pp. 23ff.

103 Cf. M. Unger, *Israel and the Aramaeans of Damascus* (1957), pp. 59ff., 141f.

104 So *BHI*, p. 221. For views supporting the existence of three Benhadads see M. Vogelstein, *Fertile Soil* (1957), pp. 7ff.; J. Gray, *I and II Kings* (1963), pp. 374f.

105 *ARAB*, I, sect. 816.

106 Cf. E. R. Thiele, *JNES*, III (1944), p. 156.

against the alliance, captured Galilee, placed Damascus under siege, occupied the Philistine plain and took a large number of prisoners.[107] Further Assyrian inroads occurred about 727 B.C. under Shalmaneser V (727-722 B.C.), the successor of Tiglathpileser III, and under Sargon II (722-705 B.C.), when Samaria refused to pay tribute to Assyria. Samaria fell in 722 B.C.,[108] not in 721 B.C. as Bright states,[109] and its collapse was described in the usual graphic terms in the Khorsabad annals.[110]

To the present, no archaeological discoveries have provided conclusive evidence for the captivity of Manasseh in Babylon (2 Chron. 33:10ff.). However, cuneiform sources have preserved a reference to a visit which he made to Nineveh about 678 B.C. at the command of Esarhaddon:

> I summoned the kings of Syria and those across the sea—Baalu, king of Tyre, Manasseh, king of Judah. . .Musurri, king of Moab. . .twenty kings in all. I gave them their orders. . . .[111]

Contrary to the argument that Manasseh could not have visited Babylon at that time in any case because it was in ruins is the fact that, according to cuneiform records, Esarhaddon rebuilt Babylon following its destruction at the hands of Sennacherib.[112] The name "Manasseh, king of Judah" appears on the prism of Esarhaddon,[113] and also on the prism of Ashurbanipal,[114] as part of a list of twenty-two tributaries of Assyria. A parallel to the Chronicles account of the captivity of Manasseh is furnished by the capture and subsequent release of Necho, pharaoh of Egypt, by Ashurbanipal, as preserved on the Rassam cylinder.[115] Since a revolt in support of Shamash-Shum-Ukin, the governor of Babylon who posed a serious military threat to Assyrian power, occurred during the reign of Manasseh, it may well be that the latter was involved to some extent in a move to overthrow Assyrian rule in the Near East.[116]

E. CAPTIVITY AND RETURN

The historicity of the Babylonian captivity of Judah has been amply verified from archaeological sources, a fact that demonstrates the incorrectness of those views that maintained that there was neither a significant exile nor a great return.[117] Excavations at Lachish, Debir, Beth-

---

[107] *ARAB*, I, sect. 801f.; 2 Kgs. 15:29ff.
[108] *MNHK*, pp. 121ff.; H. Tadmor, *JCS*, XII (1958), pp. 22ff., 77ff.
[109] *BHI*, p. 258.
[110] *ARAB*, II, sect. 55; *ANET*, pp. 284f.
[111] *ARAB*, II, sect. 690.
[112] *ARAB*, II, sect. 646f.
[113] *ANET*, p. 291.
[114] *ANET*, p. 294.
[115] *ANET*, p. 295.
[116] Cf. *ANET*, pp. 297ff.
[117] So C. C. Torrey, *Ezra Studies* (1910), *The Chronicler's History of Israel* (1954); S. A. Cook in *The Cambridge Ancient History* (1925), III, pp. 394ff.

shemesh, Beth-zur, and other sites have shown conclusively that there was an almost complete break in the urban life of the southern kingdom of Judah consequent upon the Babylonian incursions, which terminated in 581 B.C. Pottery remains recovered from contemporary levels have indicated the existence of a phase that preceded the more developed Persian ceramic types of the fifth century B.C. From the Palestine Shephelah have come stamped jar-handles dating between 598 and 587 B.C., while excavations at Lachish, Tell en-Nasbeh, and artifacts recovered from the site of the Ishtar Gate in Babylon have furnished conclusive proof of the devastation and depopulation of Judah and the presence of Jewish exiles in Babylon from 597 B.C. on.[118]

The New Empire period (612-539 B.C.) of Babylonia presents certain problems of identification and historicity that have long been a source of discussion. One of these involves the relationship between Nabonidus and Belshazzar in the light of certain statements in Daniel. Nabonidus, the last king of Babylon (556-539 B.C.), was of priestly lineage; his mother was probably the high priestess of Sin, the moon-deity.[119] Nabonidus was a man of considerable culture, who restored the temple of the moon goddess at Ur and maintained a small museum of antiquities in the temple precincts, part of which came to light when Woolley's excavations unearthed its foundations.[120] Nabonidus also instructed his emissaries to collect ancient inscriptions and other similar artifacts from various locations in Mesopotamia, and was responsible for the compilation of a chronology of Babylonian rulers.

The priests of Marduk, patron deity of Babylon, resented many of the religious innovations that Nabonidus introduced, and regarded his revival of long-forgotten rites and ceremonies as bordering upon impiety. Before commencing a series of campaigns in Cilicia and Syria about 554 B.C.,[121] he made Bel-shar-uṣur (Belshazzar) his *maru restu*, or firstborn son, regent of the empire; and about 552 B.C. he transferred his royal residence to the oasis of Teima in the Arabian desert, southeast of Edom. Whether his reasons for this change were religious or commercial is difficult to say with certainty.[122] At all events he remained there for

---

[118] For the Shephelah see *DOTT*, p. 224; H. G. May, *AJSL*, LVI (1939), pp. 146ff.; W. F. Albright, *JBL*, LI (1932), pp. 77ff.; for Lachish *WBA*, pl. 128; *DOTT*, pp. 223f.; for Tell en-Nasbeh *DOTT*, p. 222; for the Ishtar Gate R. Koldewey, *Das Wieder Erstehende Babylon* (1925), pp. 90ff.; W. F. Albright, *BA*, V, No. 4 (1942), pp. 49ff.

[119] Cf. *Recueil Édouard Dhorme. Études bibliques et orientales* (1951), pp. 325ff. This view was opposed, among others, by J. Lewy, *HUCA*, XIX (1945-46), pp. 405ff.

[120] *UC*, pp. 153, 156f.

[121] W. F. Albright, *BASOR*, No. 120 (1950), pp. 22ff.; *ANET*, p. 305.

[122] Cf. R. P. Dougherty, *JAOS*, XLII (1922), pp. 305ff., *AJA*, XXXIV (1930), pp. 296ff.; W. F. Albright, *BASOR*, No. 82 (1941), p. 14; J. Lewy, *HUCA*, XIX (1945-46), pp. 434ff.; C. C. Torrey, *JAOS*, LXXIII (1953), pp. 223f.

about ten years, and erected lavish buildings after the Babylonian manner.[123] Nabonidus was apparently so preoccupied with affairs at Teima that he neglected to visit Babylon in order to observe the New Year festival, an important event that formed the climax of the annual Babylonian cultic rites. Such dereliction of duty was sacrilegious, to say the least, and appears to have contributed to the increasing state of tension and unrest which was current in the empire.[124]

The reference in Daniel 5:30 to Belshazzar as the last king of Babylon can now be understood against this background. Belshazzar was unique in Babylonian antiquity as an example of a crown prince who was officially recognized as co-regent. Two extant legal documents recording oaths taken by the life of Nabonidus the king, and Bel-shar-uṣur the crown prince, dating to the twelfth and thirteenth years of Nabonidus, are without parallel in cuneiform sources.[125] The fact that Belshazzar was mentioned in Daniel 5:18 as a "son" of Nebuchadnezzar is in full accord with Semitic usage, which frequently employed the designation "son" as synonymous with "descendant." Nitocris, mother of Belshazzar, was apparently the daughter of Nebuchadnezzar,[126] thus making Belshazzar his grandson by strict lineal reckoning.

Although the official dating of documents from this period employs the regnal years of Nabonidus, Daniel most probably dates events by reference to the years of co-regency (Dan. 7:1; 8:1). An inscription from Harran assigned a ten-year period for the Arabian exile of Nabonidus,[127] and this, along with other sources, would imply that the royal personage (Dan. 5:30) who was killed in 539 B.C. was in fact Belshazzar. The position of Daniel as "third" in the political echelon is now shown to be correct, and indicates that he was a prominent officer of state (Dan. 5:16, 29). The result of all this is that earlier assertions by critical scholars to the effect that Belshazzar was unhistorical[128] have been shown to be entirely erroneous, and to have been advanced on the basis of an imperfect knowledge of the historical situation. Equally invalid are the objections of Rowley to the designation of Belshazzar as a ruler of the Neo-Babylonian empire, a situation which he described as "a grave

[123] *LAP*, p. 190.
[124] For cuneiform sources from this period see S. Smith, *Babylonian Historical Texts Relating to the Capture and Downfall of Babylon* (1924), pp. 27ff., 98ff.
[125] A. L. Oppenheim, *IDB*, I, pp. 379f.
[126] R. P. Dougherty, *Nabonidus and Belshazzar* (1929), pp. 59ff., 194.
[127] C. J. Gadd, *Anatolian Studies*, VIII (1958), pp. 35ff.
[128] E.g. F. W. Farrar, *The Book of Daniel* (1895), pp. 54ff. Cf. H. Ewald, *A History of Israel* (1880), V, p. 52, who identified Belshazzar with Nabonidus, and A. H. Sayce, *The Higher Criticism and the Monuments* (1895), pp. 526f., who denied a familial relationship between Belshazzar and Nebuchadnezzar. A summary of the evidence for the historicity of Belshazzar is contained in J. A. Montgomery, *A Critical and Exegetical Commentary on the Book of Daniel* (1927), pp. 66ff.

340

historical error."[129] Cuneiform sources have shown that Belshazzar was associated with Nabonidus in governing the kingdom, but in a subordinate capacity, for they speak of him specifically as *mar sharri* or "son of the king," and never as *sharru* or "king."

The other important problem of identification concerns what Rowley has styled "the fiction of Darius the Mede," a man who, according to Daniel 5:30, 31, came to power after the death of Belshazzar.[130] Since Darius the Mede is not mentioned outside the Old Testament narratives, and since the cuneiform inscriptions do not record the existence of any king between Nabonidus-Belshazzar and the accession of Cyrus, the historicity of Darius the Mede has been denied by many liberal scholars, and the accounts concerning his reign have been held to be a conflation of confused tradition.[131] But because these narratives bear all the marks of accredited historical writing, other scholars have taken them as genuine products of the period, particularly since there is a noticeable lack of historical material from the Neo-Babylonian age that might otherwise invalidate such an approach, or at the least introduce considerable modifications.

The discovery of one of the Nabonidus texts at Harran, inscribed in Babylonian cuneiform, referred to the "king of the Medes" in the tenth year of the reign of Nabonidus (546 B.C.). D. J. Wiseman identified this ruler with Cyrus the Persian, assuming that he used the title "king of the Medes" in addition to the more customary designation of "king of Persia, king of Babylonia, king of the lands."[132] Thus Wiseman would translate Daniel 6:29 as "in the reign of Darius, even in the reign of Cyrus the Persian."[133] While Cyrus was related to the Medes through his mother Mandane, it was the custom of the Achaemenid kings to trace their lineage to Persian origins in the victories of Achaemenes over Sennacherib in 681 B.C. Thus the reference to the "seed of the Medes" (Dan. 9:1) must imply that the paternal ancestry of Darius was Median. This, as Rowley has pointed out, would not describe Cyrus the Persian accurately.[134] Again, Cyrus is nowhere spoken of as the "son of Ahasuerus," being in actual fact the son of Cambyses, king of Anshan (Elam).

Arguing from cuneiform sources, Winckler, Riessler, and Boutflower equated Darius the Mede with Cambyses, the son of Cyrus, a procedure that elicited from Rowley the observation that it was "the only effort to harmonise the Book of Daniel with known history that can claim the

129 *JTS*, XXXII (1931), pp. 12ff.
130 *RDM*, p. 59.
131 *Ibid.*, p. 175; cf. *IOTT*, p. 286.
132 *Christianity Today*, II, No. 4 (1957), pp. 7ff.
133 *DOTT*, p. 83; cf. D. J. Wiseman, *Notes on Some Problems in the Book of Daniel* (1965), pp. 12ff.
134 *RDM*, p. 17.

slightest plausibility."[135] Boutflower argued that in the first year of Cyrus after the fall of Babylon, Cambyses stood in the same relationship to his father as Belshazzar had done to Nabonidus, and that Cambyses was subsequently appointed by Cyrus as the successor of Belshazzar. However, Dubberstein showed that several of the tablets dated to the first year of Cambyses had suffered from confused scribal dating-systems, and deduced that Cyrus had made Cambyses co-regent just prior to leaving for what proved to be his final campaign in 530 B.C. Thus Cambyses was not known as "king of Babylon" at a time shortly after the city fell to Cyrus, and therefore could hardly be identified with Darius the Mede. Indeed, as Dubberstein pointed out, to postulate a dual reign at the commencement of the rule of Cyrus rather than at the end is completely unsupported either by the cuneiform texts or by tradition.[136]

Whitcomb has proposed a more acceptable alternative solution to the problem, also based upon cuneiform sources.[137] He noted that the majority of translations of the Nabonidus Chronicle made since the time when it was first published by T. G. Pinches[138] have failed to distinguish between two separate individuals, Gubaru and Ugbaru, mentioned in lines 15 to 22 of Column III of the Chronicle, and instead have identified them with the Gobryas mentioned by Xenophon.[139] The translation by Sidney Smith, published in 1924,[140] however, made such a distinction and suggested that the chronicler intended to differentiate between Ugbaru of Gutium and Gubaru, the former being the Gobryas of Xenophon, who died after the fall of Babylon; whereas the latter was subsequently appointed by Cyrus as governor of southern Babylonia.

Whitcomb has suggested very plausibly that Ugbaru, the governor of Gutium, was the one who led the Persian troops to victory in Babylon in 539 B.C. and died some three weeks after this event, possibly from wounds. Gubaru was then appointed governor of Babylon and the region beyond the river by Cyrus, a position which he appears to have held for at least fourteen years,[141] and was mentioned in the book of Daniel under the designation of Darius the Mede. This theory has the undoubted merit of being based upon an accurate reading of the Nabonidus Chronicle rather than on secondary sources, and makes it clear that at

[135] H. Winckler, *Altorientalische Forschungen* (1899), 2. Reihe, II, p. 214; P. Riessler, *Das Buch Daniel erklärt* (1902), pp. xiv, 53; C. Boutflower, *JTS*, XVII (1916), pp. 48ff., and *In and Around the Book of Daniel* (1923), pp. 142ff.; *RDM*, p. 12.

[136] W. H. Dubberstein, *AJSL*, LV (1938), p. 419.

[137] J. C. Whitcomb, *Darius the Mede* (1959), pp. 5ff.

[138] In *Transactions of the Society of Biblical Archaeology*, VII (1882), pp. 139ff.

[139] *Cyropaed.* IV, 6; VII, 5, 26ff.

[140] *Babylonian Historical Texts Relating to the Capture and Downfall of Babylon*, p. 121.

[141] A. T. Olmstead, *History of the Persian Empire* (1948), pp. 56, 71.

the very least the whole problem connected with Darius as an accredited historical personage has to be re-opened, whatever the nature of his true identity may ultimately prove to be.

Although Rowley brought a good deal of learning to bear upon his efforts to show the fundamentally unhistorical nature of Darius the Mede, his labors were largely vitiated by the fact that he based his arguments upon inaccurate and unreliable secondary sources. As a result, when writing of Gobryas, he had in mind, as Whitcomb has shown,[142] not only a combination of the Gubaru and Ugbaru mentioned in cuneiform sources, but also the Gobryas of Herodotus[143] and Xenophon, and the "Gaubaruva, son of Mardonius a Persian" in the Behistun Inscription. Clearly such a composite character never existed in history, but this is very different from saying that therefore Darius the Mede is unhistorical also.

Failure to note that the translation by Pinches contained certain inaccuracies leading to the identification of a single, so-called Gobryas in the Nabonidus Chronicle[144] resulted in the fact that many scholars tried to relate Darius the Mede with such a Gobryas and also with the individual mentioned by Herodotus and Xenophon. This view can be traced to its earliest phases in a period long before the Nabonidus Chronicle was known to exist, being first represented in the writings of Des-Vignoles and subsequently expounded, among others, by Babelon, Pinches, Wright, R. D. Wilson, and Albright.[145] When the translation by Sidney Smith distinguished accurately between Ugbaru and Gubaru, it became apparent for the first time that two different persons were being described, thereby making it possible for Gubaru to be identified without undue difficulty with Darius the Mede.

The historicity of events mentioned in such compositions as Ezra and Nehemiah has been substantially vindicated by archaeological discoveries also, as is the case with many other periods of Hebrew history. Whereas older authors frequently argued that there was no evidence to indicate that Cyrus ever made a decree about 538 B.C. of the kind mentioned in Ezra 1:2ff.; 6:3ff.,[146] subsequent researches have enabled

---

142 J. C. Whitcomb, *Darius the Mede*, p. 26.

143 *The Persian Wars* III, 70ff.

144 As perpetuated, for example, by A. L. Oppenheim, *ANET*, p. 306.

145 A. Des-Vignoles, *Chronologie de l'histoire sainte et des histoires étrangères qui la concernent depuis la Sortie d'Égypte jusqu'a captivité de Babylone* (1738), II, pp. 517ff. E. Babelon, *Annales de philosophie chrétienne*, N.S. (1881), IV, pp. 680f. T. G. Pinches, *HDB*, I, p. 559. C. H. H. Wright, *Daniel and His Prophecies* (1906), pp. 135ff. R. D. Wilson, *PTR*, XX (1922), pp. 177ff. W. F. Albright, *JBL*, XL (1921), p. 112n.

146 E.g. W. O. E. Oesterley and T. H. Robinson, *A History of Israel*, II, pp. 75, 81; cf. M. Noth, *GI*, pp. 306f.

343

scholars to show beyond doubt that the edict of Cyrus was genuine,[147] and to estimate the effect which its promulgation had upon the captive elements in the Babylonian population. According to Ezra 6:1ff., the second decree, a *dikrona* or memorandum of a royal decision, was discovered in the archives at Achmetha (Ecbatana), where Cyrus is known to have stayed for a time during 538 B.C., his first regnal year.

The most serious problem connected with this period, however, is perhaps not one of historicity as much as of chronology, and deals with the general order of events as reflected in Ezra and Nehemiah. Part of the difficulty lies in the fact that these works have passed through certain phases of transmission, which has resulted in the availability for study of slightly different recensions. In the main, however, the problem turns upon the actual time when Ezra came to Jerusalem, since the dating of Nehemiah's activity does not present quite the same degree of difficulty. The traditional view that Ezra preceded Nehemiah, arriving in Jerusalem in 458 B.C., with Nehemiah coming upon the scene as civil governor in 445 B.C. in order to rebuild the walls and resolve certain economic difficulties, was first challenged by A. van Hoonacker,[148] who rearranged the Biblical text in an attempt to straighten out what seemed to him to be a thoroughly confused picture of events. Van Hoonacker advocated the view that Nehemiah preceded Ezra.[149] There is little

---

[147] Cf. H. H. Schaeder, *Ezra der Schreiber* (1930); R. de Vaux, *RB*, XLVI (1937), pp. 29ff.; E. Bickermann, *JBL*, LXV (1946), pp. 244ff.

[148] A. Van Hoonacker, *Le Muséon*, IX (1890), pp. 151ff., 317ff., 389ff., *RB*, IV (1895), pp. 186ff., X (1901), pp. 5ff., 175ff., XXXII (1923), pp. 481ff., XXXIII (1924), pp. 33ff.

[149] In this he was followed, among others, by M. J. Lagrange, *RB*, V (1908), pp. 343ff., IV O.S. (1895), pp. 193ff.; L. W. Batten, *A Critical and Exegetical Commentary on the Books of Ezra and Nehemiah* (1913), pp. 28ff.; W. E. Barnes, in *The People and the Book* (ed. A. S. Peake, 1925), pp. 293f.; V. Coucke, in *Supplément au Dictionnaire de la Bible* (ed. L. Pirot and A. Robert, 1928), I, cols. 1269f.; W. L. Wardle, in *Record and Revelation* (ed. H. W. Robinson, 1938), p. 127; and H. Daniel-Rops, *Histoire sainte: le peuple de la Bible* (1943), pp. 348ff., 455. The complexity of the situation can be illustrated by the manner in which the views of W. F. Albright have been modified from time to time. In 1921 he inclined to the views of Van Hoonacker, *JBL*, XL (1921), pp. 104ff.; in 1932 he adopted the opinion expressed earlier by Kosters, *Het Herstel van Israël* (1893), pp. 124ff., that Ezra belonged properly to the 32nd year of the reign of Artaxerxes I Longimanus (464-423 B.C.), *The Archaeology of Palestine and the Bible*, p. 219. In the first edition of *FSAC*, p. 248 (1940), he reverted to the standpoint of Van Hoonacker; in the second edition six years later, p. 336, he once more adopted the view of Kosters, although he assigned Ezra to the 37th year of Artaxerxes; cf. Albright, *BA*, IX, No. 1 (1946), pp. 10ff.; cf. J. A. Bewer, *The Literature of the OT* (1922), p. 281. In 1950 he still adhered to this position, in *The Jews: Their Culture, History and Religion* (ed. L. Finkelstein), I, pp. 53, 64; cf. *FSAC* (1957 ed.), p. 324, *BPAE*, pp. 90, 112 n. 193. At no time, however, did these opinions go unchallenged, and despite the assertions of Albright, *FSAC*, p. 324, and others that this position represented the consensus of scholarly thought, it was vigorously opposed by such authorities as Sellin, *Geschichte des israelitisch-jüdischen Volkes*

doubt that the rather confused historical tradition in Ezra and Nehemiah has conceded a degree of legitimacy to both standpoints, and in some quarters has led to more confident claims than the state of the evidence would seem to warrant, thus meriting the caution urged by Noth in this regard.[150]

Certain objections to the traditional view that have been described as "well-nigh insuperable"[151] are not quite as serious as some scholars have imagined. Olmstead has shown that the conditions of travel in the Persian empire about 458 B.C. were by no means as unsafe as has been alleged by those who oppose the priority of Ezra over Nehemiah.[152] Furthermore, the immediate task of Ezra as depicted in the book bearing his name was not to proclaim the binding nature of a new law-book[153] as much as to regulate the religious life of the returned community on the basis of a long-established tradition enshrined in the Torah. If by the "failure" of his mission there is meant the absence of initial success, then the inability of Ezra to organize the life of the theocracy in terms of the precepts of the Law on his first visit to Jerusalem is not quite as unbelievable as Bright would suppose.[154] To attribute such a result to personal deficiencies on the part of Ezra ignores an important reciprocal factor, namely the moral turpitude of the Jews in Judaea, whose norms of behavior he was endeavoring to regulate. In point of fact the activities of Ezra anticipated a situation that occurred under Nehemiah in 433 B.C., under strikingly parallel circumstances. Accordingly it would be no more correct to imply that the initial reforms of Nehemiah failed because abuses arose during his temporary absence from 433 B.C. than it would be to regard the first mission of Ezra as a failure simply because the old conditions that he had attempted to suppress showed signs of resurgence during his absence from Jerusalem. It may well be, of course, that Ezra had aroused local antagonism because of a promise of success rather than failure in his mission, and one explanation of his departure from Judaea could be that his political enemies had managed to secure his recall. A more probable alternative, however, is simply that at the end of a two-year period of duty Ezra returned to the central

---

(1932), II, pp. 134ff.; Kittel, *Geschichte des Volkes Israel* (1923), III, ii, pp. 567ff.; Eissfeldt, *Einleitung in das AT* (1934), p. 597; Weiser, *Einleitung in das AT* (1939), pp. 246ff.; R. de Vaux, in *Supplément au Dictionnaire de la Bible*, IV, cols. 765f.; J. Stafford Wright, *The Date of Ezra's Coming to Jerusalem* (1947); and E. J. Young, *An Introduction to the OT* (1949 ed.), pp. 369ff. To cite additional authorities on this whole question would merely serve to emphasize the wide divergence of opinion that has arisen in this particular area of Old Testament study.

[150] *GI*, p. 277.
[151] *BHI*, p. 377.
[152] A. T. Olmstead, *History of the Persian Empire*, p. 306.
[153] J. Stafford Wright, *The Date of Ezra's Coming to Jerusalem*, p. 26.
[154] *BHI*, p. 378.

administrative bureau in his capacity as Secretary of State for Jewish Affairs in order to present to his Mesopotamian superiors a report on the situation in Judaea.

Arguments for a reversal of the traditional chronology based upon certain passages in Nehemiah (e.g. 12:26, 47) cannot properly be used for purposes of demonstrating chronological sequences, since in his capacity as *tirshatha* or civil governor it would be natural for Nehemiah to give precedence to his own activities when compiling his memoirs. Equally important for the traditional view is the observation of Gordon that an impractical religious enthusiast, such as Ezra was depicted to have been, would need the forceful administrative backing of a disciplined person of the caliber of Nehemiah in order to offset the mistakes and inadvertencies of too enthusiastic an approach to the contemporary social and religious scene.[155] In the last resort it must be realized that no chronological reconstruction is completely free from difficulties, as will be observed subsequently, and this is due in part to the rather confused nature of the Biblical narratives and the lack of specific extra-Biblical confirmation for the date of Ezra. However, it appears to the present writer to be unwise for scholars to jettison the traditional position in matters of chronology in order to adopt one beset with even more uncertainty.

There are very few Jewish documents indeed that can be dated in the fourth century B.C., and the situation is made worse for the historian by the fact that neither Egyptian nor Babylonian sources furnish any information about their Jewish colonies, as contrasted with the state of affairs existing in the late fifth century. It is known, however, that in the late Persian period the Jewish state was recognized by the Persians as a religious commonwealth[156] that, like its north-Syrian counterpart of Hierapolis, was permitted to levy its own temple taxes and issue its own silver coinage based upon the *darkemon* standard mentioned in 1 Chronicles 29:7.[157] Seal impressions have been recovered from jars of this period, and although some of the wording is obscure, it would seem to indicate that the jars were employed for the purpose of collecting some sort of levy.[158]

According to Hecataeus of Abdera, there was a movement of thousands of Jews to Egypt as voluntary immigrants and mercenaries during the reign of Ptolemy Lagi, about 300 B.C. This proved to be a most impor-

---

[155] *IOTT*, p. 270n.

[156] *BHI*, p. 394.

[157] The "daric," known to the Jews from the post-exilic period at least (Ez. 2:69; 8:27; Neh. 7:70f.), as employed here indicates that the current monetary term equivalent to the Davidic amount was being used by the Chronicler.

[158] N. Avigad, *JPOS*, XIV (1934), pp. 178ff., *BASOR*, No. 53 (1934), pp. 20ff., No. 109 (1948), pp. 21f., No. 148 (1957), pp. 28ff., *Israel Exploration Journal*, VII (1957), pp. 146ff.

tant step in the process of Hellenizing the Jews subsequent to the conquests of Alexander the Great. This tradition was shown to be substantially correct by the excavations of Sellers at Beth-zur in 1931, where a coin was discovered bearing the name of Hezekiah, in all probability the high priest mentioned in this connection by Hecataeus.[159] As the *Letter of Aristeas* indicates,[160] it is most probable that Ptolemy I had brought many Jews back as prisoners from one or more of his military exploits in Palestine,[161] and this would help to account for the presence of so many Jews in Egypt during this general period. Be that as it may, the existence of a large Jewish community led ultimately to the translation of the Scriptures into Greek, a task that commenced with the rendering of the Torah into the vernacular in the third century B.C. The result of this activity was a version that opened the way for more adequate communication between Jews and Gentiles, and which for many in the primitive Christian Church constituted Scripture *par excellence*.

This historical panorama of the Seleucid period is well attested by a variety of sources, as is the era of the Roman domination of Palestine from 63 B.C. Important historical sidelights have been thrown upon this age by the discoveries in the neighborhood of the Wadi Qumran, and these testify in part to the turbulence and unrest that characterized this phase of Jewish history. Its close was marked in A.D. 70, when the Jewish Commonwealth was overthrown by the armies of Imperial Rome.

[159] Cf. O. R. Sellers and W. F. Albright, *BASOR*, No. 43 (1931), pp. 2ff.; A. T. Olmstead, *JAOS*, LVI (1936), pp. 243f.; F. M. Abel, *RB*, XLIV (1935), pp. 577f.

[160] Cf. vss. 4, 12.

[161] Pseudo-Aristeas, writing in the second third of the second century B.C., used considerably older material. Cf. E. Bickermann, *Zeitschrift für die Neutestamentliche Wissenschaft*, XXIX (1930), pp. 280ff.; M. Hadas, *Aristeas to Philocrates* (1951), pp. 98f.

Part Six

OLD TESTAMENT RELIGION

I. THE EVOLUTIONARY HYPOTHESIS

Prior to the nineteenth century, such study as was expended upon the subject of Old Testament religion tended to deal with the various elements of the Hebrew faith as units of one institutional corpus. This great body of belief took its rise under Moses at Sinai and was influenced over the centuries by a number of factors, many of them being of an adverse, pagan nature. A prolonged declension from the monotheistic ideals of the Torah led ultimately to divine retribution upon Israel in the Babylonian exile. On returning to Judaea, the Jewish people were found to be purged of all idolatrous tendencies, and for the remainder of the Old Testament period they followed a theocratic pattern of life, to a greater or lesser degree, according to the rituals and ceremonies of the ancient law.

With the rise of the Positivist approach under Auguste Comte (1798-1857), there came an emphasis upon the application of historical method to the study of religion. In part this constituted a reaction against some of the early nineteenth-century speculations about the nature of religion in general. Comte and his followers were concerned with real facts, as opposed to the abstractions of metaphysics or what they regarded as the figments of theological speculation. Their methodology was founded upon the premise that positive science explains natural phenomena in terms of verifiable laws of succession and resemblance, and they repudiated any suggestion that natural events could be understood by such theological devices as the intervention of supernatural beings in the stream of history, or the mutual relationships of hypostasized concepts. Although this type of view is open to serious criticisms, the Positivists attracted the attention of many learned individuals who had previously entertained grave doubts about the intellectual integrity of theological attitudes such as those that characterized Roman Catholicism.

Consequently the scholars who were affected by this naturalistic approach began to study the data of the various religions against the more factual background of their culture and history. This method bore increasing fruit as literary and archaeological sources shed new light on ancient faiths. In studying a given religion, Positivist historians made it

351

their dominant concern to familiarize themselves with all its facets; and, consistent with their view that historical processes were entirely naturalistic, they rejected any alleged supernatural causation. Because religion for them was thus but one manifestation of human culture, all faiths and creeds could be studied on the same general level; and the religion of the Old Testament could be compared with other similar expressions of the human spirit in the ancient Near Eastern world and examined in terms of the same methodological attempt to trace origins, stages of growth, environmental influences, and the like.

A. WELLHAUSEN'S STUDY OF OLD TESTAMENT RELIGION

The study of Old Testament religion took a somewhat different turn as a result of Julius Wellhausen's speculative ideas about the development of Hebrew history. Starting from the Positivist premise that religion was merely an offshoot or product of human cultural activity, he applied the evolutionary philosophical concepts of Hegelianism to a study of the faith of Israel. On the view that little could be known for certain with regard to Hebrew history and religion prior to the beginning of the monarchy, Wellhausen rejected the idea that the Torah as a whole was the starting-point for the history of Israel as a community of the faith. Instead, he adopted a naturalistic view of its origins and development and assumed that the Law constituted primarily a priestly program of religious observances for post-exilic Judaism. True to Hegelian principles, normative Judaism was regarded as a synthesis that resulted from the dialectic of the pre-prophetic Israelite faith (thesis) and the prophetic reaction to that faith (antithesis). Thus on this view the religion of the Old Testament evolved gradually through the phases of popular, prophetic, and priestly belief and practice. At the other end of the historical process, Wellhausen posited the kind of naturalistic origin for Hebrew religion that was also accorded to other faiths of antiquity, particularly to those existing in primitive societies. This procedure involved the use of metaphors of growth and development culled from biological sources, which assumed that the most primitive of the Hebrew religious notions were to be found in the earliest datable sections of the Old Testament while the more advanced concepts could be discovered in passages that emerged from a considerably later period in the chronological sequence.

Looking at primitive society in much the same way as the Positivists did, and being aware of some of the findings in the area of comparative religion, Wellhausen discerned among the Hebrews traces of such typical primitive phenomena as animism, totemism, tabu, polydaemonism and ancestor worship. These facets of religious activity he assigned to the area of patriarchal religion, and held that they were normative during the pre-monarchical period. The eighth- and seventh-century prophets applied themselves to this situation in an attempt to raise the level of religious appreciation to the point where monolatry (the worship of one of a number of available gods) was replaced by henotheism (belief in one god without denying the existence of others). The exile purified Hebrew faith and removed lingering idolatrous elements, so that ethical monotheism, the crown of the religious edifice, was the attested result. This reconstruction of various alleged stages in the development of Hebrew religion gave great prominence to the prophets, but at the same time it detracted from the significance of the events at Sinai and the religious activities of an even earlier period.

Since almost nothing was known of the life and times of the patriarchs at that point, there was little to prevent Wellhausen from assuming that patriarchal religion was scarcely more than crude superstition. Wellhausen, Robertson Smith, and Stade had investigated other aspects of Semitic religion, particularly the customs and beliefs of the pre-Mohammedan Arabs, as a means of illustrating the religious usages of the primitive period of Hebrew history.[1] On the basis of their findings they attributed certain of the phenomena of primitive religion to the pre-Mosaic period.

For Wellhausen the earliest stages of Hebrew religion represented in the Pentateuch furnished clear indications of animism, a term coined by E. B. Tylor to express the belief cherished in primitive society that every object having sufficient innate activity to affect the behavior of an individual was animated by a life and will of its own.[2] Such objects included running water, rolling stones, and waving tree branches[3]—though in some instances movement was not necessary in order for the object to receive attention.[4] Old Testament examples of this alleged tendency included the terebinths of Moreh (Gen. 12:6), Mamre (Gen. 13:18; 18:1), and Shechem (Gen. 35:4), the maççebhah or large stone mentioned in Joshua 24:26 and Judges 9:6, the tamarisk trees of 1 Samuel 22:6 and 1 Kings 13:14, and a great many references to wells and springs of water (e.g. Gen. 14:7; Num. 21:17f.; Josh. 18:17; Judg. 15:18f.).

A slightly later stage of development for Wellhausen consisted in polytheism, the belief in a multiplicity of male and female goddesses. He devoted the first 68 pages of his Reste Arabischen Heidentums to cataloging the names of ancient Arab deities along with their functions, and on

---

[1] J. Wellhausen, Reste Arabischen Heidentums (1887); W. Robertson Smith, Lectures on the Religion of the Semites (1889); B. Stade, Geschichte des Volkes Israel (1886), I, pp. 358ff.; cf. C. G. Montefiori, Lectures on the Origin and Growth of Religion as Illustrated by the Religion of the Ancient Hebrews (1892).

[2] Primitive Culture: Researches into the Development of Mythology, Philosophy, Religion, Language, Art and Custom (1903 ed.), I, pp. 23, 425; cf. J. B. Noss, Man's Religions (1949), pp. 17f.

[3] Cf. J. G. Frazer, The Golden Bough (1927), I, p. 208, II, p. 172; E. O. James, ERE, XII, p. 708a; E. S. Hartland, ERE, XI, p. 864a.

[4] R. H. Codrington, The Melanesians (1891), p. 183.

this basis he was able to associate polytheistic tendencies with such Old Testament concepts as place names connected with God (*El*, Josh. 15:11; 19:14; 2 Kgs. 14:7, *et al.*), the Baals (Num. 25:3; 32:8; Judg. 3:3, *et al.*), sanctuaries (Num. 21:28; Deut. 32:13; 2 Kgs. 17:9; Jer. 7:31, *et al.*), or elements of pagan Canaanite religion (Judg. 3:7; 1 Kgs. 15:13; 2 Kgs. 21:7, *et al.*).

Wellhausen envisaged an even more advanced stage of primitive religion in totemism. The term *totem* is strictly North American Indian in origin, but it is used by anthropologists and students of primitive religion to signify the belief that the members of a clan or tribe are related to some group of plants or animals in a rather impersonal manner.[5] In their examination of the Old Testament Wellhausen and his followers detected totemistic remnants in such personal and place names as Simeon (hyena?), Rachel (רחל, ewe), Caleb (כלב, dog), Shaalbim (שעלבים, foxes), and Eglah (עגלה, calf)[6] in addition to certain references that implied the existence of animal-cult worship as a survival of an earlier totemistic phase (e.g. Isa. 66:3, 17; Jer. 2:27; Ezek. 8:10). A totemistic interpretation was also accorded to personal names that incorporated elements of divine designations such as *El* or *Yah*, on the ground that the individuals who possessed such names believed themselves to be descended from a god, just as the members of a clan that bore the name of an animal thought that they were the offspring of that particular totem animal.

From the study of primitive religions Wellhausen found that tabu was closely associated with totemism. The imposition of tabus[7] is almost universal among primitive peoples; inherent bans exist involving sacred personages, rituals, and ceremonies, a wide variety of non-religious activities including parturition and death, and sometimes even specific objects or places.[8] Wellhausen found many parallels for these attitudes in ancient Near Eastern life, including sacred persons and consecrated things. Ideas of "holiness" and "uncleanness" constituted important tabus among ancient Semitic peoples.[9] Robertson Smith saw particularly close parallels between the varieties of prohibited food in Leviticus and the tabus relating to diet which occurred among heathen Semites general-

---

[5] W. Robertson Smith, *Kinship and Marriage in Early Arabia* (1903 ed.), p. 219; E. S. Hartland, *ERE*, XII, pp. 406b-407; E. Durkheim, *The Elementary Forms of the Religious Life* (1926), pp. 88ff.; J. B. Noss, *Man's Religions*, pp. 24f., 26.

[6] B. Stade, *Geschichte des Volkes Israel*, I, pp. 398, 409; G. B. Gray, *Hebrew Proper Names* (1896), pp. 86ff.

[7] *Tabu* is a Polynesian word meaning "marked off." Cf. R. R. Marett, *The Threshold of Religion* (1909), p. 127.

[8] J. B. Noss, *Man's Religions*, pp. 15f.

[9] Cf. S. A. Cook in W. Robertson Smith, *Lectures on the Religion of the Semites* (1927 ed.), pp. 548ff.; M. Jastrow, *Die Religion Babyloniens und Assyriens* (1912), II, pp. 896f., 933ff.

ly.[10] However, it should be noted that Old Testament tabus dealt with more than the rules concerning food laid down in Leviticus 11:1ff. and Deuteronomy 14:7ff. They embraced a number of other considerations in religious and secular affairs, and if violated they required some kind of purificatory ceremony in order to restore the individual to favor with God (cf. Lev. 6:27ff.; 11:32ff.; 1 Sam. 21:4ff., 2 Sam. 11:4).

A further development of totemism and tabu was seen by Wellhausen and his school in ancestor worship. For them the totem-ancestor gradually developed into a human ancestor, and subsequently into a divine being.[11] In the Old Testament, ancestor worship was naturally contemplated in terms of mourning customs for the departed and the sanctity of burial sites (cf. Gen. 23:1ff.; 35:8; Josh. 24:32, *et al.*), as well as tribal or personal names such as Baal-gad (Josh. 11:17; 12:7; 13:5), which contained the name of the deity. Scholars of that period also detected traces of ancestor worship in the existence of the "teraphim" or "household-gods" (Gen. 31:19, 30; 1 Sam. 19:13, 16). By connecting this ancient Semitic term with the Hebrew רפאים or "shades of the departed," they propounded the theory that the teraphim represented defunct ancestors,[12] who were venerated superstitiously by the living.

These early stages of spiritual growth, thought to be discernible in both primitive religions and the worship of the pre-Mosaic period, gave way to the more localized tribal god of the pre-prophetic period in Israel, and ultimately—through the work of the prophets—to the ideals of ethical monotheism, which were held to be the final stage of Hebrew religious development. Like many other scholars since his time, once Wellhausen had formulated his evolutionary theory to his own satisfaction—based though it was on only a small part of the evidence—he displayed a complete indifference towards subsequent anthropological or archaeological discoveries, even though they demanded a substantial modification of his original position.[13] Instead, he continued to propound his views as though his conclusions were final and irrevocable. In this mental frame of egotistical inflexibility he was followed slavishly by his adherents, with the possible exception of Kittel, who employed Posi-

---

[10] W. Robertson Smith, *Lectures on the Religion of the Semites* (1889), pp. 218ff., *Kinship and Marriage in Early Arabia*, p. 311.

[11] Cf. Wellhausen, *Reste Arabischen Heidentums*, pp. 183ff.; Stade, *Geschichte des Volkes Israel*, I, pp. 387ff.; G. Hölscher, *Geschichte der Israelitischen und Jüdischen Religion* (1922), pp. 24ff.; S. A. Cook in W. Robertson Smith, *Lectures on the Religion of the Semites* (1927 ed.), pp. 508ff., 544ff.

[12] F. Schwally, *Das Leben nach dem Tode* (1892), pp. 358ff.; C. Piepenbring, *Histoire du Peuple d'Israël* (1898), p. 28. For the connection with necromancy see W. O. E. Oesterley, *Immortality and the Unseen World. A Study in OT Religion* (1921), pp. 125ff.

[13] H. F. Hahn, *OT in Modern Research*, p. 86. For the archaeological material available for Wellhausen and his school see H. V. Hilprecht, *Explorations in Bible Lands during the Nineteenth Century* (1903).

tivist categories of approach along with the results of the most recent archaeological discoveries to probe into the origin and growth of the Hebrew people. One immediate effect of Kittel's work was to clarify the religious as well as the historical background of the Old Testament peoples, giving prominence to the patriarchal age as the period when Hebrew religious activities took their rise.

B. REACTIONS AND MODIFICATIONS

The high development of Semitic Babylonian civilization even long before the patriarchal period implied that the religious ideas that could have been brought to bear upon Abraham, Isaac, and Jacob were far more complex than Wellhausen had ever imagined. Accordingly it was necessary to take this new material into account when estimating the nature and origin of the Hebrew faith. This was undertaken by the brilliant Orientalist Hugo Winckler, who was the first to publish a critical edition of the Tell el-Amarna tablets.[14] Subsequently he endeavored to interpret the life of the ancient Near East during the fifteenth and fourteenth centuries B.C.[15] Unfortunately Winckler was unable to exercise proper control over his sources, with the result that his findings furnished an inaccurate picture of Near Eastern culture during the Amarna Age.

Winckler formulated what soon became known as the "pan-Babylonian" theory, which assumed that all the oriental peoples of antiquity had subscribed to concepts about the nature of the universe and man that were dominated by the religious ideas of the Babylonians. From this position it was only a short step to the claim that a great many of the cultural and religious forms that occurred in the Old Testament were in fact dependent on this ancient intellectual and spiritual corpus, a position that Winckler adopted in the second volume of his *Geschichte Israels*, published in 1900. The furor over this theory[16] was overshadowed by the controversy that flared up two years later when Friedrich Delitzsch took the "pan-Babylonian" theory of Winckler a dramatic step further. In his celebrated *Babel und Bibel*, published in 1902, Delitzsch propounded the view that anything of significance in the cultural and religious life of the Hebrews had been derived from Babylonian sources, and that there was little or nothing original about the spirituality of the Old Testament generally. The theories espoused by Delitzsch met with sharp opposition from Egyptologists, who at that time were fully per-

[14] H. Winckler, *Der Tontafelfund von El-Amarna* (2 vols., 1889-90), *Die Tontafeln von Tell el-Amarna* (1896).

[15] H. Winckler, *Das alte Westasien* (1899).

[16] Cf. S. A. Fries, *Moderne Darstellungen der Geschichte Israels* (1898), pp. 11ff.; O. Weber, *Mitteilungen der vorderasiatischen Gesellschaft*, XX (1915), pp. 13ff.; L. W. King, *History of Babylon* (1915), pp. 291ff.; S. A. Cook in *The People and the Book* (1925), pp. 58ff.

suaded that human culture had taken its rise in the Land of the Two Kingdoms.[17] Under the onslaught of criticism the theory subsided, being maintained only by Jeremias.[18] Nevertheless Delitzsch's work had one profoundly important benefit to Old Testament study, namely, it compelled all future investigators of Hebrew history to consider their subjects against the larger background of ancient Near Eastern life and thought.

As far as the followers of Wellhausen were concerned, the theories of Winckler and Delitzsch ran counter to all received concepts of the progressive unfolding of spirituality from rudimentary beginnings. What could not be denied, however, was the fact that even the archaeological evidence of the day pointed unmistakably to an advanced cultural and religious milieu in Babylonia that antedated the patriarchal period considerably. As Hahn has pointed out, the only escape from such a dilemma was to attempt to discover the particular elements of thought and behavior that could have been taken over by the ancient Hebrews from neighboring cultures, and to ascertain the extent to which these specific derivations had affected the nature and growth of Hebrew religion.[19]

It was clear that the methodology adopted by Winckler, Delitzsch, and Jeremias was inadequate for this task, and several years elapsed before Hermann Gunkel, an outstanding exponent of the religio-historical approach, attacked the problem once more. By bringing the comparative method to bear upon the issues of historical criticism, and by attempting to interpret the Old Testament religious concepts on their own terms, the excesses of the "pan-Babylonian" school were avoided and better control was obtained over Near Eastern archaeological material. Old Testament ideas were treated seriously in their own right, and Gunkel maintained that once they had been traced in outline through the Hebrew sources they could then be compared and contrasted with their counterparts in other oriental literary sources.[20] This method proved to be a further criticism of the Wellhausen school, for it emphasized the origin and growth of the fundamental religious concepts rather than the provenance and formulation of alleged documentary sources, and the subordination of the development of Hebrew faith to theories of philosophical and biological evolutionism.

Important also in this connection was the work of Gressmann, who took pains to point out the relationship of Hebrew religious thought to the mythological and eschatological patterns found in ancient Near

[17] Cf. W. L. Wardle, *Israel and Babylon* (1925), pp. 302ff.

[18] A. Jeremias, *Das AT im Lichte des alten Orients* (1904) and *Handbuch der altorientalischen Geisteskultur* (1913).

[19] H. F. Hahn, *OT in Modern Research*, p. 91.

[20] H. Gunkel, *Die Religionsgeschichte und die alttestamentliche Wissenschaft* (1910).

Eastern literature. Although Gressmann did not abandon entirely the methods and results of the Wellhausen school of literary criticism, he followed Gunkel[21] in maintaining that the mythological concepts apparent in prophetic eschatological passages were most probably the result of early contact between Babylonia and the Hebrews, and did not emerge from the exile period as Wellhausen and his followers had suggested.[22] Gressmann drew more consistently upon Egyptian sources for the origin of Hebrew religious concepts than had others before him, and although he did not actually prove that the cultural influences upon which Hebrew religious ideas were allegedly based were early, he made it clear that they could certainly be considered earlier rather than later in incidence, in contrast to what the Wellhausen school held.

More conservative scholars disapproved of the extent to which the religio-historical school envisaged the influence of ancient pagan cultures upon the development of Hebrew religion. Thus Reischle and Clemen cautioned against the tendency to overlook the distinctive features of Hebrew religion in favor of detecting pagan elements within the larger structure.[23] In particular they urged the intrinsic value of those aspects which were peculiar to the religious activities of the Hebrews, especially in view of the fact that the faith of Israel had survived those of her pagan neighbors. Some of these criticisms were unfortunately rather beside the point, for as Gunkel showed, the purpose of the religio-historical method of study, when properly applied, was to bring into sharp relief the greatness of Old Testament religion.[24] There can be no doubt, however, that Gunkel thought that certain portions of the Hebrew literature borrowed Babylonian myths directly, for example, in the accounts of creation and the Flood, although he contended, like many other scholars since his time, that in the process the elements characteristic of Babylonian polytheism had been removed and the finished product given a distinctive monotheistic cast.

A more emphatic rejection of the evolutionary development of Hebrew religion as expounded by Wellhausen and his adherents came from Paul Volz. A conservative member of the religio-historical school, Volz argued from the Mosaic authorship of the Decalogue to the fact that the precepts of ethical monotheism, attributed by Wellhausen to the general exilic period, were in fact promulgated by Moses to the Hebrews at

[21] H. Gunkel, *Schöpfung und Chaos in Urzeit und Endzeit* (1895), pp. 135ff., *Deutsche Rundschau*, CXV (1903), pp. 267ff.
[22] H. Gressmann, *Der Ursprung der israelitisch-jüdischen Eschatologie* (1905), pp. 238ff.
[23] M. Reischle. *Theologie und Religionsgeschichte* (1904), pp. 50ff.; C. Clemen, *Die religionsgeschichtliche Methode in der Theologie* (1904), pp. 20ff.
[24] H. Gunkel, *Deutsche Literaturzeitung*, XXV (1904), pp. 1100ff.

Mount Sinai.[25] He based his views in part on the comparative study of ethical sections in the Egyptian *Book of the Dead*,[26] which can be dated at least to the beginning of the Amarna Age, and also on a series of Babylonian incantation tablets which were compiled between 1500 B.C. and 1150 B.C.[27] Since such ethical material was already extant somewhat prior to the Mosaic period, Volz saw no intrinsic difficulty in attributing the ethical monotheism of the Decalogue to the work of Moses.

A similar position was maintained by Baentsch, who argued from what he thought was an innate monotheism in the ancient texts of Babylonia—speculative though he admitted this form to be—to a general tendency towards monotheism among the peoples of the ancient Near East.[28] This phenomenon was also present among the Hebrew tribes, who were subsequently welded into a spiritual unit by the events consequent upon the Sinai revelation, and who at that time espoused a genuine monotheistic faith. Despite such well-attested Egyptian 'monophysitic' tendencies as the "solar monotheism" of the Old Kingdom period and its revival under Amenhotep IV during the Amarna Age,[29] it is doubtful that monotheism was ever implicit in the religious movements of the orient to the degree that Baentsch assumed. Nevertheless, his arguments concerning the nature of Mosaic monotheism are not, as Hahn has implied, inadequate because he did not accommodate his theories to the accepted canons of contemporary historical criticism.[30] The fact that the mixed multitude of the Hebrews may have manifested somewhat more than a semi-sedentary phase of culture when they entered Palestine need not imply that they consistently incorporated the better developed cultural facets of Canaanite civilization, including the "advanced legislation" of the local communities, into their own way of life as a means of spiritual progression, as the Wellhausen school had supposed. Although the Hebrews were evidently inferior technologically at the commencement of the settlement period, as archaeological discoveries in Palestine have demonstrated, the superiority of their ethic, derived from the

---

[25] P. Volz, *Mose: ein Beitrag zur Untersuchung über die Ursprünge der israelitischen Religion* (1907), pp. 60ff.

[26] As J. H. Breasted, *Development of Religion and Thought in Ancient Egypt* (1959 ed.), pp. 293f., has pointed out, no *Book* as such existed between 1500 and 1100 B.C., but rather a collection of papyrus mortuary texts which were collated subsequently. The section entertained by Volz was the *Negative Confession* in chapter 125.

[27] The celebrated deprecatory spells of "burning," known as the Series *Shurpū*. For the date see A. Schott, *Die Vergleiche in den akkadischen Königinschriften* (1926), ZDMG, LXXXII (1928), p. lvii; W. von Soden, ZDMG, LXXXIX (1935), pp. 156ff.; *FSAC*, pp. 288ff.

[28] *Altorientalischer und israelitischer Monotheismus* (1906), pp. 30ff.

[29] Cf. *IAAM*, pp. 8f., 65f.

[30] *OT in Modern Research*, p. 101.

events at Sinai, was made the source of appeal time after time by prophetic figures from the period of Samuel onwards, particularly on those occasions when the orgiastic polytheism of the pagan Canaanites was a point at issue. If further proof were needed, the antiquity of Tabernacle worship as the religious focus of the Sinai revelation, to be discussed subsequently, and its perpetuation in the Solomonic Temple, points to the distinctiveness and virility of Hebrew monotheism in the midst of unprepossessing environmental circumstances. Though it is well known that there was a great degree of religious and social fusion between the Canaanites and the Israelites, it is faulty historical criticism to suggest that the Hebrew faith advanced to monotheism by way of the pagan rituals of Canaan.

The work of Rudolf Kittel, which represented a significant modification of the position adopted by Wellhausen, was nonetheless not as conservative in outlook as that of Baentsch. Kittel did not subscribe to the view that Moses taught a "genuine monotheism," although he recognized certain historical elements in the Mosaic traditions. On the basis of careful study of what was known at that period about Canaanite culture, he deduced that there may have been some tendency towards monotheism implicit in the religious thought of Canaan.[31] Starting with the worship of El as a supreme being at the pagan shrines, Kittel argued towards an analogous form of devotion during the patriarchal period as the basis for the later Mosaic concepts of the nature and function of deity. This, however, was not the ethical monotheism of the later prophets, but was at best a form of monolatry which failed to emphasize the uniqueness of the divine character. Although he differed from the Wellhausen school in recognizing that a declension from the high levels of Mosaic religion occurred at the beginning of the settlement period, he nevertheless subscribed to the belief that the ethical monotheism of the prophets evolved from the monolatry of Moses.[32]

A similar cautious position was adopted by Ernst Sellin, a brilliant contemporary of Kittel.[33] He, too, parted company with the Wellhausen approach to the extent of placing in an earlier age certain religious ideas that literary-critical orthodoxy had assigned to a much later period. At the same time he left room for the possibility of growth and development within the corpus of Israelite spirituality, which he dated from the Mosaic era. Following Hegelian methodology to a certain degree, Sellin, like Kittel, saw the enrichment of rudimentary Mosaic teaching through the interaction of the advanced spirituality of the Hebrew religious leaders on the one hand, and the continued declension of popular

---

[31] R. Kittel, *Geschichte des Volkes Israel* (1912 ed.), I, pp. 187ff.

[32] *Ibid.*, pp. 549ff.

[33] E. Sellin, *Alttestamentliche Religion im Rahmen der andern altorientalischen* (1908).

360

religion on the other. From this emerged a developing synthesis of religious belief that culminated in the advanced ethical teachings of the prophets.

The attempts that Kittel and Sellin made to emphasize the persistence of Mosaic ideals among minority religious groups during the settlement period and the monarchy served as an effective counterbalance to the stress laid by the critical school upon the presence of demonstrable Canaanite evidence in Hebrew religious life. Equally important was their insistence that significant aspects of the faith of Israel were to be considered as early rather than late. But unlike Volz or Baentsch, they did not quite appear to possess a view of the advancement of contemporary civilization that would have enabled them to assign distinctive monotheistic elements to the faith of Moses. In this respect, however, they were reasonably consistent, since by accepting the dating-sequences assigned by the Wellhausen school to the Mosaic Torah they could hardly do more than attribute a very small amount of the Pentateuch to the great Hebrew leader himself, or regard the monotheistic elements as other than prophetic in origin.[34]

---

[34] Subsequent studies of OT religion were based largely on the developmental theories of the Wellhausen school, although such a forthright exponent of the literary-critical methods as Gustav Hölscher, *Geschichte der israelitisch-jüdischen Religion* (1922), tended to follow Kittel and Sellin in emphasizing the *Sitz im Leben des Volkes* of the ancient Near East, and in attributing certain facets of Hebrew history to a comparatively early period. In the English-speaking world the views of Wellhausen were popularized by such writers as Addis, *Hebrew Religion* (1905); H. Wheeler Robinson, *The Religious Ideas of the OT* (1913); J. P. Peters, *The Religion of the Hebrews* (1914); G. A. Barton, *The Religion of Israel* (1918); H. P. Smith, *The Religion of Israel* (1914); R. L. Ottley, *The Religion of Israel* (1926); and others.

II. RECENT STUDIES IN HEBREW RELIGION

A. The Ras Shamra Texts

Following the lead of Kittel and Sellin, scholars began to look for further traces of Canaanite religious influence during the settlement period and the monarchy upon the faith of Israel. Unfortunately, extra-Biblical sources available to these scholars were extremely sparse, and inscriptions that were available from Syria prior to World War I added very little to what was already known. Anthropological speculations based in part upon the nature of ruined Canaanite shrines proved to be of limited value in determining the character of Canaanite religion.[1]

However, an entirely new and unexpected source of information concerning the culture of ancient Canaan came to light with the discovery in 1929 of a great many cuneiform tablets at Ras Shamra, the Ugarit of the Amarna Age, on the coast of northern Syria. The first tablets were published in 1930 by C. F. A. Schaeffer, and were found to have been written in two languages, one a Hurrian dialect and the other an ancient Canaanite tongue closely resembling pre-Mosaic Hebrew. In the eleven campaigns at the site prior to World War II,[2] many hundreds of tablets were unearthed whose contents placed the culture of ancient Canaan in an entirely new perspective.[3] Since it is no longer possible to discuss the religion of early Israel without reference to Phoenician-

[1] Cf. S. A. Cook, *The Religion of Ancient Palestine in the Second Millennium B.C.* (1908); W. C. Wood, *JBL*, XXXV (1916), pp. 1ff., 163ff.

[2] For early reports see part two, section I, footnote 34 (p. 90); R. de Vaux, *RB*, XLVI (1937), pp. 526ff.; A. Bea, *Biblica*, XIX (1938), pp. 435ff., XX (1939), pp. 436ff.; a bibliography is found in C. F. A. Schaeffer, *Ugaritica: Études relatives aux découvertes de Ras Shamra* (1939), I, pp. 153ff.

[3] Cf. C. F. A. Schaeffer, *The Cuneiform Texts of Ras Shamra-Ugarit* (1939); R. de Langhe, *Les textes de Ras Shamra-Ugarit et leurs rapports avec le milieu biblique de l'Ancien Testament* (2 vols., 1945); C. H. Gordon, *Ugaritic Handbook* (1947), sect. II, pp. 129ff.; G. R. Driver, *Canaanite Myths and Legends* (1956); C. F. A. Schaeffer, *Ugaritica*, III (1956); J. Gray, *The Legacy of Canaan* (1957); H. L Ginsberg, *ANET*, pp. 129ff.

Canaanite[4] cult-worship, a short résumé of the discoveries at Ugarit is desirable.

The sacrificial and ritual texts have furnished the most satisfactory guide to the names of the Ugaritic deities, although an assessment of their interrelationship has been hampered by the extraordinary fluidity of function and individuality of the gods mentioned in the tablets. Thus it is not always easy to ascertain the extent to which specific deities were related to one another mythologically, or even to determine whether they were consistently male or female at specific times—a confusion which contrasts curiously with the gods of the Hittite, Babylonian, and Egyptian pantheons.

The Canaanite generic term for deity was *'el*, probably from an original *'ilum;* and, according to the customs obtaining in the Amarna Age, the gods were designated as members of a class or guild by the terms *'elim* or *Bene 'el*. The supreme deity of the Phoenician-Canaanite pantheon was known as El, that is *the* god, corresponding to *El 'Elyon* or *El Shaddai* in the patriarchal age of Hebrew history. El was at best a rather obscure figure—probably more so than the Egyptian Re or the Sumero-Akkadian Anu—and he was generally depicted as inhabiting a remote area of the cosmos known as the "Source of the Two Deeps," from which he supplied life-giving water to the earth.[5] He was known by the titles "father of man" (*abū adami*) and "father of years" (*abū shanima*), and on a *stele* found at Ras Shamra, he was depicted with hands outstretched in blessing over the ruler of Ugarit.[6]

The consort of El was the goddess Asherat (Ashirat), known to Israelite tradition as Asherah, a deity who was also worshipped by the Amorites and southern Arabians. Although the role of El was generally inactive, one of the myths depicts his seduction of two women, who were banished to the desert once they had given birth to their children, named "dawn" (*Shahru*) and "sunset" (*Shalmu*).[7] The active figure of the Canaanite pantheon was Baal (Haddu), offspring of El and Asherat; he was venerated as the overlord of rain and storm.[8] As the acknowledged king of the gods his titles included the names Aliyn (the Pre-

---

[4] For the cultural unity of these peoples see W. F. Albright, *Studies in the History of Culture* (Waldo Gifford Leland Volume, 1942), pp. 11ff., and the revised form in *BANE*, pp. 328ff.; C. Virolleaud, *Annales de l'Université de Paris*, VIII (1933), pp. 397ff.

[5] The word for deep is תהום, as in Gen. 1:2 *et al.* Note the importance of the water-deity Ea in Babylonian cosmogony and the place of the Nile in Egyptian life; cf. R. Dussaud, *Revue de l' Histoire des Religions*, CIV (1931), pp. 358f.

[6] *LAP*, pl. 60.

[7] Compare the Akkadian *sheru*, Hebrew שׁחר, "dawn"; Akkadian *shalam shamshi*, "sunset."

[8] Compare the eminence of the weather-god Hatti in the Hittite pantheon.

vailer)[9] and Zabul (Earthly Lord),[10] the former occurring with great frequency in Ugaritic poetry. He was also known as the "Son of Dagon," who was the chief deity of Ashdod (1 Sam. 5:1ff.),[11] and who was honored at shrines in Ugarit and the Gaza region (cf. Judg. 16:23).

Fertility goddesses played a far more important part in the cultus at ancient Ugarit than anywhere else in the Near East. As represented in the mythological texts, the relationships existing between Anath, Asherah, and Astarte (Ashtaroth) were particularly complex. The primary function of all three was sexual or procreative, although their warlike attributes were considered almost equally important. A thirteenth-century B.C. Egyptian text spoke of Anath and Astarte as "the great goddesses who conceive but do not bear," but at Ugarit they were regarded sometimes as virgins (*batulu*, Heb. בתולה) and on other occasions as mothers of all life.[12]

Ritual prostitution was a notable feature of Phoenician-Canaanite cultic worship, which frequently functioned at the lowest levels of moral depravity. As a sacred prostitute the goddess bore the title "the holiness of . . . ," in which the word *qudshu* was employed to denote dedication to the service of a deity.[13] The militant, even bloodthirsty, character of the Canaanite goddess Anath is made clear from the cuneiform sources, which represent her on occasions as wallowing fiendishly in human blood.[14] Asherah, who bore the title "She Who Walks in the Sea,"[15] was also referred to by the appellation *qudshu* in the Amarna Age, and was spoken of as the consort of Baal. Canaanite deities were generally depicted in human form, although some artistic representations conceived of them as birds or animals.

The Canaanite goddesses had as their major responsibility the fecundity of animals and man and this function was enshrined in the form of a myth that purported to account for the cyclic pattern of natural forces. Thus Baal, representing rain and vegetation, was killed every spring by Mot (Death) or by the "Devourers," who then dominated the climatic situation during the parched months from April to the end of October. In the autumn, the warrior-consort of Baal overcame death in a vicious struggle, and restored Baal to life. Virility overtook the land in early spring when Baal mated with either Anath or Ashtoreth.

[9] Cf. W. F. Albright, *BASOR*, No. 70 (1938), p. 19.

[10] Cf. Albright, *JPOS*, XII (1932), pp. 191f., XVI (1936), pp. 17f.

[11] *Dagon* is probably a corruption of *Dagan*, an ancient Akkadian vegetation deity; cf. *ARI*, p. 74.

[12] Cf. M. Burrows, *BASOR*, No. 77 (1940), pp. 6f.

[13] Cf. *Mélanges syriens offerts à M. R. Dussaud* (1939), I, p. 118 n. 2; *BASOR*, No. 78 (1940), pp. 26f.

[14] Cf. *Baal Epic* II, 7ff.; *UL*, pp. 17f.; C. Virolleaud, *La déesse 'Anat* (1938), pp. 13ff.; J. Aistleitner, *ZAW*, LVII (1939), pp. 205ff.; *FSAC*, pp. 233f.

[15] *ARI*, pp. 77f.

As Gordon has pointed out,[16] however, it must not be assumed that Baal can be identified with the Dying God, whether Tammuz or some other deity, as earlier anthropologists thought.[17] The Canaanite myths do not contain an annual cycle of death and revival on the part of Baal, but instead represent him as a fertility deity rather than as a seasonal deity. Furthermore, Baal was not necessarily integral to the fertility rituals, for he is not mentioned in one text dealing with the inauguration of a seven-year fertility cycle.[18]

It will be apparent from the foregoing considerations that the primary concern of Canaanite worship was that of insuring the fertility of the land, of flocks and herds, and of the human populace. Male and female prostitution were commonly practiced under the guise of religion at the various centers of worship.[19] The bulk of Canaanite religious activity was carried out at the "high places," where there were sacrificial altars (cf. 1 Sam. 9:12; 1 Kgs. 3:4). The best example of such an altar is found at Megiddo and dates from about 1900 B.C.[20] In the immediate vicinity of this altar were considerable quantities of animal bones comprising the remains of sacrifices which had been offered at this popular "high place."

Objects of religious veneration which were used in Canaanite cult-worship included the sacred post or 'asherāh, which may have been a wooden emblem or image connected with the goddess Asherah.[21] This cult-object was associated with stone pillars or maççebhôth, which were quite possibly intended as representations of Baal or El. Excavations at various Palestinian sites have uncovered small altars of incense of the kind common in Canaan after 1100 B.C. They were made of limestone and carried projections or "horns" on each corner. The earliest of these was found at Megiddo in a shrine of the Israelite period dated in the early tenth century B.C.[22]

From Palmyra in northern Syria came an altar of incense with the term hamman inscribed on it, revealing the original use of the artifact.[23] A well-preserved Canaanite temple unearthed at Lachish in thirteenth-century B.C. levels appeared to have been destroyed by the Israelites while still in use as a sanctuary.[24] Despite the fact that the walls furnished evidence of having sustained heavy damage by fire, they were in sufficiently good condition to make it clear that they had originally

---

[16] UL, pp. 3f.
[17] J. G. Frazer, The Golden Bough, II, pp. 118f.; IV, pp. 5ff.
[18] Text 52, UL, pp. 58ff.
[19] Cf. FSAC, pp. 234f.
[20] G. E. Wright, BA, XII, No. 2 (1950), p. 31, pl. 6.
[21] ARI, p. 78.
[22] WBA, p. 114.
[23] Thus the reading "altar of incense" should be substituted for "sun image" in Lev. 26:30; 2 Chron. 14:5 and 34:4, 7; Isa. 17:8 and 27:9; and Ezek. 6:4, 6.
[24] Cf. Sir Charles Marston, The Times, July 8, 1939.

been plastered and equipped with benches or shelves for storing sacrificial offerings. At the front of the building the archaeologists excavated a raised platform which may originally have accommodated an idol, and perhaps a small sacrificial altar in addition. To the rear of the temple were clearly defined areas for storage, as well as small apartments for the priests, a feature commonly found in the larger shrines. Debris from the sacrifices revealed the presence of many bones from birds and animals, all of them taken from the right front leg of the species.

While this custom reflects the provisions of Levitical law (Lev. 7:32) concerning the peace offerings, which provided that the right shoulder should become the perquisite of the priest, with the remainder presumably being consumed by the assembled worshippers at a festal meal, it should not be thought that the Levitical provisions were comparatively late enactments incorporated into Hebrew religion from pagan sources, or that the temple uncovered at Lachish was in fact an accredited Israelite shrine. As Albright has pointed out, the upper portion of the right foreleg was prescribed specifically by Assyro-Babylonian sacrificial rituals, indicating that the preference for this particular part of the animal was general throughout ancient western Asia,[25] and therefore can hardly be denied to the culture of the Hebrews at a comparatively early period. The almost complete absence of burned bones at the site of the Canaanite temple at Lachish pointed to the fact that the sacrificial meal had been boiled (cf. 1 Sam. 2:12ff.). From a study of the Ugaritic texts it is apparent that Canaanite sacrificial rituals were much more diversified than those among the Israelites, and a far wider range of animals was employed as offerings. These included bullocks, small cattle and birds, wild bulls, stags, fallow deer, and wild goats.[26]

So far comparatively few idols of any size have been unearthed in Syria or Palestine, which contrasts sharply with the situation in other areas of the ancient Near East. However, engravings of deities on stone have come to light, as well as small metal images of male gods, which are referred to in the Old Testament (e.g. Lev. 19:4; Ps. 106:19; Isa. 30:22; Hab. 2:18). Containers of incense and pottery models of pigs, bulls, and birds were commonly associated with Canaanite worship, as were cult-objects such as lilies (representing sex-appeal) and serpents, which were symbolic of fertility. A center dedicated to the worship of Anath was excavated at Gebal (Byblos), an extremely important site in ancient Phoenicia, which was noted for its fertility rites and ceremonial prostitution. Plaques recovered from Ras Shamra depicted the nakedness and fecundity of this same goddess. Terra-cotta figurines of Astarte have been unearthed at a great many sites throughout Palestine, and they invariably portray a naked woman with exaggerated sexual features.

[25] *FSAC*, p. 236.
[26] *ARI*, p. 92.

As was the case in ancient Near Eastern society generally, the Canaanite priesthood played an important part in the organization and control of social life at Ugarit. The king was the head of the community-state, which was organized along theocratic lines. Following Mesopotamian custom, certain of the priests were assigned to full-time duty with the military forces as staff astrologers. Such priests were required to furnish a prognosis for battles upon examination of various parts of sacrificial animals in accordance with the normal priestly procedures. On occasions the course of events in a battle was such that it required a fresh opinion on the basis of a further consideration of the omens, making the position of staff astrologer one of great importance for the fortunes of Ugarit.[27] The priestly hierarchy as a whole was controlled by a "chief of the priests" or *rabbu kahinima* in the fourteenth and thirteenth centuries B.C.[28]

Despite various references in the Old Testament to human sacrifice in the Heroic Age and later times (cf. Judg. 11:31ff.; 2 Kgs. 3:26f.; Mic. 6:7), including the Moloch rituals (cf. Lev. 18:21; 20:1ff.; Jer. 7:29ff.; Ezek. 16:20ff.; 23:37ff.; Am. 5:26) and the remains of child-sacrifices discovered by Garstang under the foundation stones of the gates of ancient Jericho, there is no indication from the Ugaritic texts that human sacrifice was either peculiarly acceptable to the deity, or that it was even practiced to any significant extent in the cultus. This is important in view of the testimony by Roman writers that the Carthaginians, who had migrated from northwest Canaan in the ninth century B.C. and later periods, practiced human sacrifice consistently until the fall of Carthage.[29]

It seems quite evident that the Canaanites shared with the Hebrews and other Semites the belief that, when a person died, he went to a place beneath the earth known as Sheol or "the pit." Here he continued in some sort of vague, shadowy existence in company with the "shades" of those who had preceded him. Thus it is not surprising to find that Canaanite burial customs were similar to those of the Hebrews, the Hittites, and other neighboring nations, with the notable exception of Egypt. Members of a family normally shared a common burial place, as was also the case in Hebrew patriarchal times.[30] With them were interred weapons, jewelry, pottery containers, and other objects thought to be needed in the underworld. When recovered from burial sites, such

---

[27] *IOTT*, p. 82.

[28] *ARI*, p. 108.

[29] Cf. L. Poinssot and R. Lantier, *Revue de l'Histoire des Religions*, LXXXVIII (1923), pp. 32ff.; S. A. Cook, *The Religion of Ancient Palestine in the Light of Archaeology* (1930). For the origins of human sacrifice see E. Meyer, *Geschichte des Altertums* (1909 ed.), I, ii, p. 345; E. A. Westermarck, *The Origin and Development of the Moral Ideas* (1906), I, pp. 434ff.

[30] Cf. the Cave of Machpelah, Gen. 25:9; 49:31; 50:13.

artifacts have proved to be of immense value in contributing to an understanding of contemporary social and religious customs in ancient Canaan.

B. STUDIES OF THE UGARITIC TEXTS

Although it was clear almost from the very beginning that the discoveries at Ras Shamra would require radical revision of the Wellhausenian evolutionary scheme of Hebrew religious development in important areas, the writers of that time tended to treat the subject much as Wellhausen himself had done. Thus Oesterley and Robinson, in their *Hebrew Religion: Its Origin and Development*, originally written in 1930 and subsequently revised in an enlarged edition in 1937, followed the classical liberal theories in assuming that the growth of Hebrew religion passed from a primitive state, associated with the patriarchs, through a phase in which the tribal deity was localized in the pre-prophetic era, and culminated in the highest stage of development, that of the cosmic monotheism of the latter part of Isaiah.[31]

These authors reflected the pattern of critical orthodoxy so faithfully that G. E. Wright was prompted to complain that one-fourth of their book was given over to the description of the supposed animistic and magical background of Israelite religion. "Yet we now know that...the authors are dealing neither with patriarchal nor with pagan religion of the day, but chiefly with Stone Age survivals and relics."[32] In addition, the section dealing with the religion of Canaan[33] treated the Ras Shamra discoveries in a most inadequate fashion, and seemed blissfully unaware of the tremendous importance of the Ugaritic cuneiform sources for the Amarna period as a whole. Other writers such as Jack and Hooke drew attention to similarities and differences in Canaanite and Hebrew religious rituals, but they also failed to appreciate the extent to which the discoveries constituted a criticism of the orthodox Wellhausenian position.[34] As the study of the Ugaritic material progressed, the character of certain aspects of Canaanite religion came into clearer focus. Of considerable importance in this connection was the nature of the deity El. Although some scholars had noted a monotheistic tendency in the Ugaritic worship of El,[35] following to a certain extent the position adopted by Baentsch and in a more modified form by Kittel, it soon

[31] A similar position was adopted by I. G. Matthews, *The Religious Pilgrimage of Israel* (1947), pp. 7ff.

[32] Wright, *The OT Against Its Environment* (1950), p. 12 n. 6.

[33] Oesterley and Robinson, *Hebrew Religion: Its Origin and Development*, pp. 170ff.

[34] J. W. Jack, *The Ras Shamra Tablets* (1935); S. H. Hooke, *The Origins of Early Semitic Ritual* (1938).

[35] E.g. Jack, *The Ras Shamra Tablets*, p. 13.

became evident that Canaanite cult-worship was crude, orgiastic, and polytheistic in character.[36] No longer could it be regarded as having exerted a direct influence upon the wilderness religion of the Hebrews, but it was instead seen as the indigenous faith of Canaan for some time before the Hebrew occupation of the Promised Land.[37]

Attention was also drawn to the fact that certain of the mythological patterns contained in the Ras Shamra literature were reflected to a limited degree in various parts of the Old Testament.[38] Thus the references to the monster Leviathan (Job. 3:8; 41:1ff.; Pss. 74:14; 104:26; Isa. 27:1; Ezek. 29:3ff.)[39] and the dragon Rahab (Job 9:13; 26:12; 38:8ff.; Pss. 87:4; 89:10; Isa. 30:7; 51:9), the female monster of chaos closely allied mythologically with Leviathan, were seen to have been derived from Canaanite literary sources rather than from Babylonian myths, as Gunkel and others had supposed. In the rush of claims for a direct influence of Ugaritic religious forms upon their Hebrew counterparts it was not noticed that early Hebrew tradition was entirely free from such Canaanite influence, which is indicated by the fact that in the Hebrew account of world-beginnings there is no narrative describing a conflict between the Creator and a dragon. Although the curbing of the unruly forces of chaos at the creation is depicted in Genesis poetically in terms that, under certain conditions, could perhaps be applied to Rahab (cf. Job 9:13; 26:12; 38:8ff.), the general imagery in the Old Testament narratives was invariably transferred from the creation setting current in Babylonia to the narrative of the redemption of Israel from Egypt (cf. Ps. 89:10; Isa. 51:9), with the result that the term "Rahab" became synonymous with that country (Ps. 87:4; Isa. 30:7; cf. Ezek. 29:3). Again, it should be observed that although there is an undeniable literary and linguistic relationship between the cuneiform sources from Ugarit and many sections of the Hebrew Bible, it remains true that the characteristic mythological forms of the ancient Near East found no place in Old Testament literature. As Gordon has remarked, the mythology of Canaan constituted little more to the Hebrew writers than a literary background upon which to draw for poetic images.[40]

The Ras Shamra texts were also considered to give support for Sigmund Mowinckel's theories about the presence of a cultic myth underlying an annual New Year enthronement of God as King in Jerusalem, on the

---

[36] R. Dussaud, *Revue de l'Histoire des Religions*, CIV (1931), pp. 353ff.; J. A. Montgomery, *JAOS*, LIII (1933), pp. 101ff.; *ARI*, pp. 71ff.

[37] W. Baumgartner, *Theologische Zeitschrift*, III (1947), pp. 81ff.; *FSAC*, p. 271.

[38] Cf. T. H. Robinson in S. H. Hooke (ed.), *Myth and Ritual* (1933), pp. 172ff.

[39] For comparison with the Ugaritic *lotan* see C. F. Pfeiffer, *EQ*, XXXII (1960), pp. 208ff.

[40] *IOTT*, p. 82.

analogy of the Babylonian *akîtu* festival.[41] This suggestion had been followed principally by Schmidt, and received development and modification by S. H. Hooke and his followers, who attempted to prove that certain clearly defined myths and rituals had been the common property of the ancient Near East.[42] These scholars endeavored to show that what had been the spring festival in Mesopotamia was adapted to the cultural milieu of the Hebrews so as to constitute the three main festival occasions of unleavened bread, the feast of weeks, and the festival of tabernacles. In support of this theory they adduced the fact that at different places in Mesopotamia the *akîtu* festival was celebrated at various times during the year, particularly in the spring and autumn.[4] The Myth and Ritual school associated with Hooke assigned particular importance to an enthronement rite as it was thought to have obtained during the Hebrew monarchy, since the figure of the king was central in the ritual act that renewed the unity of the people with its kingly deity. But, as Pedersen had pointed out, certain of these ideas were at variance with the concepts that Israel entertained concerning its kingship.[4] Considerations of this nature, combined with the realization that there were decided limits to the knowledge of what constituted pre-exilic ritual practices among the Hebrews, led many to conclude that Hooke and his followers had greatly exaggerated the importance and influence of Mesopotamian religious *motifs* upon the cultic practices of the Hebrews, and had adhered too closely to the subjective thinking of Mowinckel in attempting to make the facts conform to their theories.

A similarly cautious approach was adopted by Hvidberg in a study of certain of the cuneiform sources from Ras Shamra.[45] He concluded that while in some areas of Palestine, and possibly in northern Israel, the degree of religious syncretism had become such that God was mourned ritually as dead and then greeted as risen in the manner associated with the Baal fertility ceremonies, the Old Testament furnished absolutely no evidence for this idea. What was in fact celebrated were the saving acts

---

[41] Cf. S. Mowinckel, *Psalmenstudien II. Das Thronbesteigungsfest Jahwäs und der Ursprung der Eschatologie* (1922), pp. 200ff.; *RHPR*, LX (1926), p. 409; K. H. Ratschow, *ZAW*, LIII (1935), pp. 176ff.; A. S. Kapelrud, *Norsk Teologisk Tidsskrift*, XLI (1940), p. 57. For a study of divine kingship as the unifying factor of mankind and the world of nature see H. Frankfort, *Kingship and the Gods: A Study of Ancient Near Eastern Religion as the Integration of Society and Nature* (1948).

[42] H. Schmidt, *Die Thronfahrt Jahves* (1927); S. H. Hooke (ed.), *Myth and Ritual* (1933), *The Labyrinth* (1935), and *The Origins of Early Semitic Ritual* (1938). For a formulation of this theory see *Myth and Ritual*, pp. 1ff.

[43] *Myth and Ritual*, pp. 46f.; cf. S. A. Pallis, *The Babylonian Akîtu Festival* (1926), pp. 27ff.

[44] J. Pedersen, *Israel: Its Life and Culture*, p. 442; cf. O. Eissfeldt, *ZAW*, XLVI (1928), pp. 81ff.; C. R. North, *ZAW*, L (1932), pp. 8ff.

[45] F. F. Hvidberg, *Graad og Latter i det Gamle Testamente* (1938), pp. 115ff.

of God on behalf of His people, and the thing that was renewed was the Sinaitic Covenant. It remained for C. H. Gordon to point out that the texts from Ras Shamra said nothing about any annual death and resurrection of Baal,[46] and that the notion that the agricultural year in Canaan was divided into a fertile and sterile season was false. Since Baal was thus not indispensable as far as fertility rituals were concerned, he is to be considered a seasonal rather than a fertility deity.[47]

The Scandinavian scholar Ivan Engnell argued from traces of divine kingship that he observed in the ancient Near Eastern nations other than Israel to the view that the king as a cultic figure was identical with the dying and resurrected vegetation deity and also with the creator-god. For Engnell the process of religious syncretism was accomplished with penetrating thoroughness in the early monarchy, and was still evident at a much later period.[48]

An attack upon certain of the presuppositions of both the Scandinavian scholars and the Myth and Ritual school was made by N. H. Snaith, who in a study of the so-called "enthronement psalms" renounced the idea that they were in any way connected with the New Year festival, and related them instead to sabbath worship, assigning them to a distinctly post-exilic date.[49] In a subsequent treatise on the New Year festival itself he repudiated the suggestion that the festival was held twice each year, and stated flatly that there was no Old Testament evidence for associating the New Year feast with divine kingship.[50] He was critical of the way in which Mowinckel had reconstructed Hebrew ritual to accord with the Babylonian *akitu* ceremonies, and denied that the kings of Israel ever acted as substitutes for the deity in cultic rites.

Although there might well be some difference of opinion as to the date of the "enthronement psalms," there can be little doubt that Snaith was correct in pointing out the distinctive nature of the Hebrew festivals. It is noteworthy in this connection that the Old Testament feasts did not adopt the ancient Near Eastern pattern of confessional and purificatory rites followed by joyous ceremonies,[51] since the seasonal festivals of the Hebrews differed radically in origin, purpose, and nature. In Mesopotamia and Ugarit the cultic rites were intended in part to honor the gods of the pantheon, so as to insure the fertility of the land for another year. For the Hebrews the festive seasons constituted a manifestation of divine beneficence and demonstrated that God was the supreme provider for the needs of His people, who acknowledged His gifts with gratitude.

---

[46] On one occasion only was he killed (Text 67:II) and was subsequently revived (Text 49:III).

[47] *UL*, pp. 4f.

[48] *Studies in Divine Kingship in the Ancient Near East* (1943).

[49] *Studies in the Psalter* (1934).

[50] *The Jewish New Year Festival* (1947).

[51] T. H. Gaster, *Thespis* (1961 ed.), pp. 26ff.

Whereas in the pagan cultic rites people approached the deity superstitiously and called attention to their needs, the seasonal feasts of the Hebrews proclaimed the reverse of this process, and showed that the divine Creator was working consistently for the requirements of His creatures, for whom He was morally responsible.

There can be little denial of the fact that attempts to see traces of enthronement and vegetation rites in various portions of the Old Testament have led to extreme and even fanciful interpretations of the Hebrew text. Morgenstern envisaged 2 Samuel 15:30ff. in terms of David in his role as the deity of the annual crop leading a solemn procession up the Mount of Olives, where he would stay according to the cultic rite for the seven-day feast of unleavened bread, which was followed immediately by the New Year.[52] Then with the resurrection of the deity accomplished, the king would return in solemn procession to his capital and reascend the throne.

That this is a completely forced and unrealistic interpretation of what actually transpired on that occasion is immediately apparent on a plain reading of the text. Far from participating in a solemn religious festival, David was fleeing from his capital for his life because he was on the point of being usurped as king by his rebellious son Absalom. The sound of the trumpet (2 Sam. 15:10) had no connection whatever with the *shôphār* heralding the beginning of a festival, but was the signal that would climax many months of treachery and intrigue. The entire event bore all the characteristics of a political coup, and the turbulent emotion that marked the flight of David across the Wadi Kidron to Jericho and the Jordan fords were completely removed from the atmosphere of a Hebrew festal occasion.

C. W. F. ALBRIGHT

The work of W. F. Albright has done much to clarify certain of the issues in the study of Hebrew religion. After surveying the various religious systems of the ancient Near East, he concluded that the deities that made up the pantheons of Babylonia, Egypt, Anatolia, and Canaan were personified universal natural forces which functioned in a designated sphere or manner.[53] The reflection of these peoples upon the cosmic activities of a high god led almost immediately to their belief in his universal dominion, a tendency particularly noticeable in Egyptian thought, although it was not completely absent from Mesopotamian literature.[54] Once men had recognized that the many and various deities were simply manifestations of a single god, Albright argued that it was only a comparatively short step to some kind of henotheism, where the

[52] J. Morgenstern, *IDB*, III, p. 545.
[53] *FSAC*, pp. 192, 213; cf. *JBL*, LIX (1940), pp. 102ff.
[54] *FSAC*, pp. 214f.

worshipper focused his adoration on a single deity.[55] He traced two specific stages by which the Mesopotamians moved towards an empirical monotheism,[56] though he observed that such monotheistic tendencies were partial or ineffective. In Egypt, however, he maintained that monotheism had been achieved by about 1400 B.C., when the universal sun-god Amun-Re was divested of mythological accretions and revered as the only deity.[57] However, in this connection it must be remembered that the so-called monotheism of Akhenaton comprises nothing more than the selection of the solar disc as the prime power within nature.

Albright denied that there was any substantial basis for an "El" monotheism among the pre-Mosaic western Semites, and envisaged Moses as monotheistic in the sense that he taught "the existence of only one God, the creator of everything, the source of justice...who has no sexuality and no mythology, who is human in form but cannot be seen by human eye and cannot be represented in any form. . . ."[58] Even though Albright admitted to being hampered in dealing with the subject by the fact that the literary sources were comparatively late in origin[59]— an obstacle furnished by an uncritical acceptance of the Graf-Wellhausen postulates—he felt that the tradition was sufficiently well attested both by the Hebrew Bible and by the nature of second-millennium B.C. religion in the Near East to be considered essentially historical.[60]

Albright's view was a decided advance upon the position of Sellin, who had attributed to Moses only a germ of the ethical monotheism that was represented by the teaching of the Hebrew prophets. It also marked a distinct break with liberal orthodoxy in that it took the historical traditions of the Old Testament much more seriously than had been the case previously. Naturally his views aroused opposition among those who preferred to think that the Old Testament record of the Hebrew past could not be regarded as history in the generally accepted sense, and who were thus unable to think of the Biblical narratives as other than warped or tendentious accounts of remote traditions and events.[61]

There can be little question, however, that Albright presented strong arguments for what he considered to be Mosaic monotheism, and although it would be gratifying to have still more evidence than is available, it remains true that the situation that Albright has depicted represents substantially the religion of the Mosaic age.

---

[55] P. 192.
[56] P. 217.
[57] P. 219.
[58] P. 272; cf. *JBL*, LIX (1940), pp. 91ff.
[59] *FSAC*, p. 257; cf. T. J. Meek, *JBL*, LXI (1942), p. 34.
[60] *ARI*, p. 96.
[61] Cf. the criticisms of M. Burrows, *JQR*, XXXIII (1942-43), pp. 475f.; W. Eichrodt, *Theology of the OT* (1961), I, p. 221 n. 1.

D. YEHEZKEL KAUFMANN

By far the most important treatise since the time of Wellhausen to deal with the origin and nature of Hebrew religion was the eight-volume work published by Yehezkel Kaufmann between 1937 and 1956.[62] In it he adopted a position diametrically opposed to that of Wellhausen and the German school of Biblical criticism, asserting that Israelite monotheism did not at all evolve slowly out of crude polytheism through the concerted efforts of a priestly caste, but was from the very beginning a characteristic of the people of Israel under the religious guidance of Moses. This position was all the more surprising because Kaufmann accepted the principles of higher criticism as such, although he protested against the arbitrary delineation of sources and supported the strictures of the Uppsala school against the "debaucheries of literary criticism."[63] Thus he was in general accord with the consensus of earlier critical opinion that Deuteronomy belonged to the time of Josiah,[64] although he criticized the liberal view that Joshua and Judges contained little or no authentic historical information, stressing that the city-lists in Joshua reached back to the very days of the conquest and settlement.[65] By applying somewhat of the same literary and historical criticism as that favored by the Graf-Wellhausen school, Kaufmann argued from a comparison of the various legal codes to the fact that the Priestly legislation antedated its Deuteronomic counterpart instead of elaborating upon its contents, and thus stood nearer in time to the Jehovistic-Elohistic sources.[66] In addition he also maintained that the Priestly sources reflected an age when the "congregation of Israel" was a military rather than an ecclesiastical body, and concluded that its ideology was independent of prophetic teaching,[67] pointing instead to a period of origin that antedated many of the other Pentateuchal sources.

Kaufmann expressly rejected the conventional Wellhausenian views of the origins of Hebrew monotheism. He maintained that Israelite religion was an original and indigenous product whose monotheistic *Weltanschauung* had no antecedents in ancient near Eastern paganism (*KRI*, p. 2). For Kaufmann Hebrew monotheism was not so much a theological dogma nurtured carefully in prophetical circles over several generations, but an idea that was absolutely basic to the national culture of the Hebrews, which it permeated from the very beginning. While historical relations could be traced between paganism and Israelite religion, the latter

---

[62] Y. Kaufmann, תולדות האמונה הישראלית: מימי קדם עד סוף בית שני. Translated and abridged by M. Greenberg, *The Religion of Israel: From Its Beginnings to the Babylonian Exile* (1960).

[63] *BACP*, pp. 2f.

[64] Cf. *KRI*, pp. 172ff.

[65] *BACP*, pp. 24f.

[66] Cf. *KRI*, pp. 167ff., 175ff.

[67] Y. Kaufmann, ZAW, XLVIII (1930), pp. 23ff., LI (1933), pp. 35ff.

was never genuinely polytheistic in nature. Kaufmann maintained that the Old Testament narratives conceived of pagan gods in a different manner from that current among the votaries of Near Eastern deities, so that where alien gods were mentioned in the text in company with the God of Israel, it was the latter alone who was consistently depicted as an active divine Being (pp. 10f.). Thus when the Hebrew God did battle with the "gods of the nations," the objects of His wrath were idols, and not militant foreign deities (pp. 12f.).

Pentateuchal prohibitions against pagan religions generally depicted them in terms of mere fetishism, whether the underlying sources were early or late, and hence prohibited the manufacture of alien deities and the worship of such material objects. Where prohibitions against the veneration of beings other than the God of Israel were recorded (Exod. 22:19; Lev. 17:7; cf. *KRI*, pp. 63ff.), the point at issue was not that foreign active deities were mentioned, but rather that specifically Israelite divine beings and demons were being envisaged. Any mention of alien gods in the Pentateuch was invariably a reference to idols and nothing more (p. 18). Since this was so, the non-involvement of the Old Testament writers with the mythological materials (pp. 20, 60ff.) and polytheism of pagans required a fresh examination of the conventional notions of Israelite idolatry and, by implication, the general character of Hebrew monotheism itself.

As encountered in the Old Testament literature, the concept of idolatry included magic, divination, idol cults, necromancy, and other manifestations of pagan religion. For Kaufmann the question of Israelite idolatry turned upon whether God was worshipped in Israel as just one of many deities, whether He was associated with a mythological pantheon, or whether Hebrew idolatry was of a genuinely syncretistic variety (pp. 137f.). On the basis of an examination of the sources, Kaufmann concluded that the popular form of idolatry did not constitute a genuine polytheism, but was instead a "vestigial idolatry," comparable to the rather superstitious belief in amulets, spells, and other semi-magical influences that persist in certain levels of monotheistic faith to the present day (p. 142). The popular type of idolatry depicted in the prophetical literature consisted of a magical, fetishistic, non-mythological veneration of imported images along with a certain amount of private cult-worship. On the basis of the readiness of the Hebrews to eradicate Baal worship from their midst on request, Kaufmann claimed that in the popular religious consciousness there was always the underlying conviction that the Lord was God (p. 145). At the same time there lurked in Israel the lingering suspicion that images and cultic rites could lay legitimate claim to a degree of magical efficacy. In sum, Israelite idolatry was to be construed as a vulgar phenomenon characterized by fetishistic, magical, and ritualistic elements, which, because of the lack of a basic pagan mythology, never attained to the level of a cultural force among the Hebrews (pp. 147f.).

Historical monotheism, as interpreted in terms of the Divine Name, a prophetic mission, and the struggle of the nation with idolatry, was not characteristic of the patriarchal period, when none of these elements occurred in the Hebrew records (p. 222). Even the people of Israel who constituted the real bearers of historical monotheism did not inherit their faith from the patriarchal age in the strictest sense, for it was under Moses that the monotheistic concept came into being, at which time there occurred the beginnings of religious tension between Israel and the pagan world. Since the basic concept of Hebrew religion had no roots in paganism, Moses must have been the first to originate it (p. 225). But although Israelite religion was fundamentally different from every other variety of pagan cultic worship, the fact that it was born in the midst of thriving alien cultures virtually assured some degree of influence by Near Eastern paganism. For Kaufmann, however, Hebrew religion was not governed so much by the environmental background of antiquity as by the fact that, in process of incorporating certain pagan materials into its religious corpus, the faith of Israel generated a fresh spirit and a new ethos never contemplated by paganism. It surpassed the monotheistic tendencies of Egypt and Babylonia in that it postulated the existence of a God who transcended nature, whose will was supreme in the universe, who was free from bondage to myth and magic, and was not subject to matters of compulsion or fate (pp. 226f.), rather than merely reducing the arithmetic number of available deities.

This high view of deity, accompanied by the sense of mission fostered by the Sinai Covenant, provided a powerful stimulus towards unity among the Israelite tribes during the time of Joshua. For Kaufmann this underlay the entire conquest period, which he thought of as a unified movement, carried out by a confederation of tribes who were consciously following a national plan of conquest (p. 245). This same preconceived scheme also formed the background to the tribal battles described in the early chapters of Judges. As evidence, Kaufmann adduced the fact that the eras of the conquest and settlement were singularly free from inter-tribal territorial disputes, despite the chaos and internecine strife of the Judges period.

At this time secular authority was vested in the "primitive democracy" of the Elders, a survival of the inter-tribal group of Elders that had arisen during the days of Moses and Joshua (p. 256). The specifically spiritual direction which that age took was the responsibility of those religious figures who emerged periodically to emphasize the fact that the God of Sinai continued to rule His people through His appointed messengers. Kaufmann denied that the Judges were local heroes who were subsequently given national status by the editor of the book of Judges (p. 257), arguing from the general absence of a distinction between

376

national and local events to the possibility that a local deliverance could well have assumed the proportions of national relief. Equally emphatic was his rejection of the view that temples and priesthoods alike were taken over by the Israelites from Canaanite precursors in the land despite the religious syncretism of the period. Israelite temples did not antedate the Hebrew patriarchs, and the sanctity of particular locations from that time arose from the revelations given by God to the ancestors of the Israelites when they were aliens in Canaan.

Kaufmann traced four distinctive phases in the historical development of Hebrew religion. The first, constituting the age of Moses, Joshua, and their generation, was non-idolatrous. This was succeeded by an idolatrous interlude which lasted throughout the Judges period, and was followed by a third phase of loyalty to God in the early monarchy. From the time of Solomon there was a second prolonged interval of an idolatrous nature, culminating in the exile (p. 260). The monarchy was thought of as the direct successor to the "apostolic kingdom of God," operative from the time of Moses, and the somewhat different traditions concerning the way in which Saul was elected to kingship (cf. 1 Sam. 7; 8; 10:17ff.; 12) were held to reflect faithfully an aspect of the contemporary historical situation (p. 264). The involvement of Solomon in the cultic rites of his pagan shrines marked the turning-point of the religious and political fortunes of the monarchy, and subsequent historians raised the vestigial idolatry, which had always persisted among the vulgar, to the level of national sin so as to account for the political decline which followed the days of Solomon (p. 270).

The extent to which the Baal cult constituted a vital danger to the ethos of Hebrew religion was depreciated by Kaufmann (pp. 274f.), who also dissociated the prophetic orders (בני נביאים) that arose after the time of David from the ecstatic figures who appeared in the narratives connected with the work of Samuel. He followed the general pattern of critical opinion in maintaining that the lasting historical significance of Josiah's reform constituted an important step towards the priestly concept of a book of Torah as the regulating medium of national life (p. 290), an ideal that was to become normative with the formulation of the Pentateuch in the post-exilic period (p. 448).

There can be little question that, particularly for the formative period of Hebrew religion, the researches of Kaufmann constitute an extremely important contribution that will richly repay careful study. But while it presents a challenging criticism to certain facets of the traditional liberal interpretation of the origin and development of Hebrew religion, it is still based to a large extent upon the evolutionary premises of the Graf-Wellhausen school, particularly as regards literary sources. Perhaps it is this curious degree of contrast which has led at least one critic to describe the methodology of Kaufmann as eccentric.[68] On the other hand he appears to be following what can be considered a basically legitimate procedure in attempting to interpret the religious symbols of the Hebrew world from within, rather than in examining them in the light of pagan models and counterparts insofar as these existed.[69] As C. H. Gordon has remarked in another connection, by reading *out of* texts it is possible for scholars who understand the general content to derive much more from the sources than comparativist scholars who read so much *into* them.[70]

Nevertheless there is a certain unconscious inconsistency in the general approach adopted by Kaufmann towards his source materials. Concerning the period of the conquest, for example, he stresses that his views "do not flow from the assumption that the stories of the Bible are historical reports"[71] and that "the events of the Conquest are shrouded in a mist of legend."[72] Yet his conclusions as to the course of events are almost identical with what is narrated in Joshua. Precisely what happened to the unhistorical and legendary elements in the process has not been stated. The main difficulty undoubtedly resides in the fact that, while Kaufmann was able to detach himself intellectually from certain propositions of the Graf-Wellhausen school regarding the development of Hebrew religion and suggest some radically different views, he was not in effect weaned from the basic evolutionism of that body of theorists.

The literary strata that Kaufmann has distinguished in the Old Testament look remarkably like the sources that the Graf-Wellhausen school purported to uncover, with the possible exception of the early Near Eastern materials in Genesis.[73] Even if Kaufmann had preferred to avoid the Graf-Wellhausen categories of literary analysis, which he apparently did not, he could have followed the lead of those scholars who utilized the methods of form-criticism in their studies. But aside from noting that Genesis constituted a stratum in itself, whose material was, on the whole, most ancient, Kaufmann does not appear to have applied form-critical techniques to the sources under study.

Kaufmann, like Alt and Noth, is remarkably selective—to say the least—in his consideration of the archaeological evidence for the pre-exilic period. Because he pays little or no attention to this extremely important source of information, he tends to present the conquest in terms of a concerted onslaught by a unified and highly coordinated Israelite task-force under the leadership of one gifted commander. A careful reading of Joshua will make it plain that even the Biblical material falls somewhat short of this exalted conception, while a consid-

[68] J. Bright, *Early Israel in Recent History Writing*, p. 73.
[69] *KRI*, p. 3.
[70] *UL*, p. 4 n. 1.
[71] *KRI*, p. 247 n. 3.
[72] *BACP*, p. 91.
[73] *KRI*, p. 208.

eration of the archaeological evidence relating, for example, to the fall of
Jericho and Ai, gives some indication of the complexity of the problem in
a way that Kaufmann was unable to entertain. It is this precise lack of
attention to archaeological matters that, in the view of the present
writer, led to an inadequate assessment of the character and extent of
Canaanite Baal worship, and a resultant deficiency in the estimate of its
pervasive influence in Hebrew life.

The dissatisfaction of Kaufmann with the general dating-scheme assigned by traditional liberalism to the Pentateuch and the earlier historical books was reflected by his attempts to redate them in accordance
with the principles of criticism upon which he proceeded.[74] Thus he
maintained the Priestly material was more ancient than the Deuteronomic composition,[75] although the latter contained some very early passages and was divisible on grounds of style into "early" and "late" forms.
He criticized the Graf-Wellhausen school for their complete indifference
to the cuneiform literature of Mesopotamia extant in their day, which if
considered would have placed Israelite religious origins in proper perspective by relating them to Assyrian rather than to the much later
Bedouin culture.[76]

Kaufmann assigned the composition of Joshua to the beginning of the
Judges era and held that it was compiled from such sources as the *Book
of Yashar*, the city- and border-lists of that period, and priestly material
including, among other items, a list of Levitical cities. Though Joshua
and Judges bear the marks of Deuteronomic editing, he rejected any
suggestion that they belonged properly to the time of Josiah, and
maintained that only the legislation in Deuteronomy that referred to the
unification of the cult could be dated in the seventh century B.C.
Kaufmann denied any trace of Deuteronomic redaction in Samuel, and
argued from the presence of a reference to cultic unification in 1 Kings
3:2 to the fact that the book was compiled after the reign of Josiah. By
implication the absence of allusions to unification of the cult in Joshua,
Judges, and Samuel (except for an explanatory gloss in Josh. 9:27)
showed that they dated from an earlier period.

The redating of the historical books in this manner is certainly at
variance with the general position adopted by liberal orthodoxy, and
accordingly has come under considerable criticism. While many scholars
now concede that there are very ancient sources in Deuteronomy, few
would follow Kaufmann in his suggestion that there existed an "early"
and a "late" form of Deuteronomy, differentiated on purely stylistic
grounds. Furthermore, on any basis, it is incorrect to state that the book

[74] *KRI*, pp. 153ff.
[75] Cf. *ZAW*, XLVIII (1930), pp. 32ff.; *BACP*, pp. 3f.; *VT*, IV (1954), pp.
307ff.; *KRI*, pp. 175ff.
[76] *KRI*, p. 205 n. 16.

that was found in the Temple at the time of Josiah was Deuteronomy "as has long been recognized."[77] In point of fact there is not a shred of evidence for this view. The precise nature of the code is uncertain, and in all probability it constituted only a small section of the Mosaic law, which may have incorporated some of the ancient Passover material.

By abandoning considerations of style in favor of internal evidence,[78] Kaufmann has certainly cast doubt upon the efficacy of the former as one of the traditional elements of literary criticism, and for this alone his work has been received with misgivings by liberal scholars. However, his use of internal evidence is hampered partly by an indifference to archaeological data and also by the necessity for a continual reference to the general trends of liberal criticism, from which he is not by any means weaned. This results in some rather bizarre attempts to demonstrate the authenticity and reliability of the Biblical narratives by relating them to his own canons of interpretation and criticism, a procedure that does not endear him to either liberal or conservative scholars.

[77] *KRI*, p. 208.
[78] *BACP*, p. 7.

III. INFLUENCES ON THE RELIGION
OF THE HEBREWS

A. THE METHODOLOGICAL APPROACH

Some attempt must now be made to reconstruct in outline the nature of Hebrew religious activity from the earliest periods on in the light of what is known about such phenomena in primitive cultures, bearing in mind the results of archaeological activity in the Near East. It is now generally recognized by scholars that the methodological approach adopted by Wellhausen in his evaluation of the growth of Hebrew religion left much to be desired. As indicated elsewhere, Wellhausen was strongly influenced by the pronounced Hegelianism of Vatke; and taking his cue from biological concepts current in the evolutionism of his day, he concluded that if monotheism was the highest form of Hebrew faith, it must have emerged at the latest phase of development. Similarly, those sections of the Old Testament that could be regarded as early must contain the most primitive traces of religious activity, sometimes barely distinguishable from pure superstition. In complete contrast to the Biblical view, which attributed monotheism to the earliest of the Hebrew ancestors, Wellhausen saw the mature faith of Israel as an outgrowth of the animistic and totemistic trends of patriarchal worship, which slowly evolved into monotheism under the influence of the literary prophets. In conformity with this theory, any comparatively advanced theological concepts found in "early" narratives were relegated to the activities of editors during the prophetic and subsequent periods.

As was the case with the Wellhausenian theories of literary criticism, the criteria by which the development of Israelite religion was judged would certainly have been greatly modified—perhaps even abandoned completely in some areas—if Wellhausen had paid greater attention to the evidences of ancient Near Eastern culture as revealed by the archaeological activity of his day. Wellhausen made some concessions to comparative study by surveying the nature of primitive Bedouin religion. But he made his fundamental error in thinking that Hebrew culture generally arose from comparatively late Bedouin origins and in rejecting the archaeological evidence of social and religious activity in the civilizations of Mesopotamia and Egypt, which he deemed irrelevant for the

381

history of Israelite religion. It seems unfortunate, to say the least, that such a pioneer in the field of Old Testament scholarship should have been content to erect his theoretical formulations on only a portion of the available evidence, particularly when the cuneiform sources from Mesopotamia and the hieroglyphic inscriptions from Egypt were already being studied by scholars with reference to the religion of the Hebrews. As the result of a much wider acquaintance with Near Eastern archaeology, it is now possible to say, with Kaufmann, that the prehistory of Israelite religion is not to be sought in primitive or Bedouin sources, but in the mellowed civilizations of the ancient Near East.[1]

Again, it is extremely doubtful that it is justifiable to apply the metaphors of growth and progress that Wellhausen borrowed from biological sources to religious phenomena. Comparative studies in the area of religious development have shown clearly that "primitive" and "advanced" conceptions of deity can co-exist in the mind of any one individual without apparently being mutually exclusive.[2] Furthermore, the way in which Wellhausen thought of the growth of Israelite religion from rudimentary beginnings to an advanced monotheism is completely contrary in significant areas to the Old Testament interpretation of its own history. This attitude of course requires that the Biblical narratives be taken at something like face value, a procedure that is still anathema to many liberal scholars, or at best is regarded as fraught with danger for all save the most wary. At the risk of repudiating the evolutionism of an earlier phase of Old Testament scholarship, however, it should be observed that the Old Testament narratives saw the historical process as anything but an ordered and progressive development like that contemplated by Wellhausen. Instead, the Old Testament writers consistently thought of their history as a dynamistic confrontation of humanity by the divine Word against a background of revealed monotheism.

Fundamental to this activity was the reminder that, as a supremely moral Being, God would judge the nation for its lack of fidelity to the terms of the Sinaitic Covenant, and that, if the nation persisted in its reprobate ways, it would be rejected as the social instrument of divine revelation to the world. Complementary to this, however, was the self-consistency of God, which required that He should not utterly cast off the people with whom He was bound by the Covenant relationship, but rather that He should purify and re-create them as a unified instrument for conveying His blessing to mankind. To the objection that these conclusions represent the shape into which Hebrew historical material was cast by later scribes and interpreters, it must merely be said that such a view results from an uncritical acceptance of *a priori* evolutionary

---

[1] *KRI*, p. 221.
[2] Cf. I. Engnell, *Gamla Testamentet*, I, p. 111; E. O. James, *The OT in the Light of Anthropology* (1934), pp. 83ff., *Comparative Religion* (1938), p. 11.

and literary-critical theories of sources, which require the appearance of ethical monotheism at the end, rather than at the beginning or during the middle of the process. Modern scholarship is no longer able to sustain the sharp contrast between the Prophets and the Law that was commonly asserted by the older school of liberal criticism.

Whatever may be thought of the difference in degree between the monotheistic outlook of the Mosaic period and the corresponding teaching contained in the prophetical writings, there can be little doubt, as Anderson has stated, that the latter was already in large measure implicit in the older faith.[3] One unfortunate result of the application of growth-metaphors to Old Testament study is the common misunderstanding that requires the subject always to be appraised in terms of an ascending series of values. The dynamistic interpretation of history that the Old Testament narratives contained meant that, as a result of the mighty acts of God, the elect people were challenged to reconsider the significance of their Covenant relationship to Him. This standpoint, as Wright has indicated, cannot easily be accommodated to a single metaphor such as that of growth.[4] The plain fact is that history cannot be viewed either as a collection of chance occurrences or as a chain of mechanically related happenings. Historical sequences are composed, rightly or wrongly, of a vast complex of interacting social, political, and religious patterns that are in continuous flux. As such they cannot be compressed into the framework of a strictly deterministic theory, nor can they be interpreted satisfactorily in terms of so rigid a method as that of Hegelian dialectic,[5] useful though these approaches may be for certain phases of historical investigation.

B. ANIMISM

Recent investigation shows that the interpretation of the earliest phases of Hebrew religion in terms of animism, polydaemonism and the like, which was basic to the Hegelian-Wellhausenian concept,[6] requires considerable modification. It is now evident from the comparative study of ancient Near Eastern literature and from archaeological sources that animism disappeared from the oriental world centuries before the Hebrew patriarchs appeared upon the historical scene. As Wright indicated in his criticism of the developmental theme expounded by Oesterley and Robinson, the animism and polydaemonism which were thought to have characterized the religious activities of the patriarchs and their pagan contemporaries were in fact survivals from the Neolithic period.[7] Just as

[3] *OTMS*, p. 290.
[4] *The OT Against Its Environment*, p. 11.
[5] *ARI*, p. 3.
[6] *FSAC*, p. 88.
[7] *The OT Against Its Environment*, p. 12 n. 6.

is the case with the perpetuation of ancient elements in more modern religions, it is now regarded as extremely doubtful that the true meaning of these remnants was appreciated at all during the later stages of their existence, so that their continued survival was predominantly the result of religious conservatism.

These considerations have been brought into clearer perspective as a result of archaeological activity in Mesopotamia, where accredited temples dating from the end of the fifth or the beginning of the fourth millennium B.C. have been unearthed from the 'Ubaid period at sites such as Tepe Gawra, Eridu, and Uruk. The earliest Chalcolithic shrines at Tell Halaf consisted of a single circular chamber, whereas somewhat later structures were comparable to those of the pre-pottery Neolithic phase at Jericho, with a rectangular anteroom built into the main structure. From these ruins were recovered rough models of domestic animals, as well as a number of human figurines which generally depicted the nude female body with exaggerated sexual organs in a manner similar to that encountered among the Aurignacians and other cave-dwellers.[8]

Pre-pottery Neolithic levels at Jericho yielded a building that appears to have been a shrine. Among other relics it contained some plastic studies of groups of human beings, each containing what seems to have been a father, mother, and child.[9] These artifacts alone should suggest that an animistic phase had long since passed, a conclusion that is reinforced by the highly developed polytheism that characterized the religions of Egypt and Mesopotamia in the third millennium B.C. The Mesopotamians of this period had already applied categories of personality to the great cosmic powers that dominated their pantheon, and were worshipping them in temples that were regarded as the earthly residence of the deities.[10] In Egypt, the authoritarian head of the pantheon was the creator and sun-deity Re, whose cult had flourished in Lower Egypt prior to the First Dynasty and had influenced the conception of kingship in that area.[11] In Canaan, the supreme being was the deity El, whose offspring Baal wielded executive power among gods and men alike. Thus the stage of Hebrew religious formulation represented by the patriarchal period must be related to a comparatively sophisticated cultural situation, far different from the primitive superstitions that Wellhausen associated with the early Bedouin tribes.

Modern anthropological research has also demonstrated the antiquity of human belief in "High Gods," whose powers were considered to be

---

[8] *FSAC*, p. 132.
[9] *FSAC*, p. 135; *LAP*, p. 122.
[10] T. Jacobsen in *Encyclopedia of Religion* (ed. V. Ferm, 1945), pp. 770f.
[11] Cf. G. Roeder, *Urkunden zur Religion des alten Ägypten* (1915), p. 108.

universal.[12] In ancient Mesopotamia the adherents of polytheism described their reactions to the universe and their deities in what has been called "mythopoeic" language.[13] By viewing happenings as individual events, they personalized the qualities and will of the phenomena with which they were confronted, and cloaked their essential truth by means of a literary structure approaching the form of a myth, or better still, of an allegory. Since natural occurrences were understood in terms of human experience, the confrontation of man by environmental forces involved a mode of cognition far transcending that normally accorded animism in primitive cultures.

For the Babylonians this premise found its logical conclusion in the *akîtu* festival, a yearly re-enactment of a ritual designed to secure for the participants an identification with the ruling powers of the cosmos, and an assurance that the life of society was once again in harmony with the activities of nature.[14] Even in its earliest form, such a religious expression represented a much more advanced stage than was implied by the animistic concepts of Wellhausen. There may be some ground for the belief that, as Hooke suggested, an animistic phase of Mesopotamian religion can be seen in the Babylonian preoccupation with the spirits of the deceased, and perhaps also in connection with the amulets and clay figurines recovered by archaeologists from Babylonian sites.[15] However, it should be noted that, in connection with the latter, the "teraphim" were apparently related in some manner to rights of primogeniture in cultures such as those of Mari and Nuzu, and this may well indicate other than purely animistic origins.[16]

There seems to be little doubt that alleged remnants of animism discovered in Hebrew religion by some modern writers have been greatly exaggerated, if not actually misinterpreted. Although it is true that in the religion of Israel, as with the faith of other peoples, there may be a number of primitive survivals whose precise origin defies explanation, an attempt to construct from their incidence what might be regarded as a system of early Hebrew religion is no more valid than it would be to apply the same process to the known religions of Near Eastern antiquity. The accredited animistic traces that may be discerned in these systems belong to the remote past, and as far as the sophisticated culture of the patriarchal period in Mesopotamia is concerned, it is probable that the original meaning of most animistic survivals had even then been long obscured with the passing of time.

[12] E.g. W. Schmidt, *High Gods in North America* (1933), pp. 129ff., *Der Ursprung der Gottesidee* (1926-34), I, pp. 632ff., V, pp. 473ff.
[13] T. Jacobsen, *IAAM*, pp. 8ff.
[14] *Ibid.*, pp. 199f.
[15] S. H. Hooke, *Babylonian and Assyrian Religion* (1953), p. 23.
[16] *IOTT*, p. 117.

Even though it may be agreed that such Old Testament place names as En Mishpat and En-gedi indicated important sources of water, it is surely going beyond the available evidence to suggest that they constituted oracle-wells or that they were subsequently venerated as sites where a divine revelation had been given. In Palestine, where copious supplies of fresh water are seldom assured, any well is an important location, and the idea of "decision" inherent in the ancient name "En Mishpat" need commemorate nothing more than the kind of pastoralist agreement that took place between Abraham and Lot (Gen. 13:7ff.).

Certainly there are no real grounds for thinking that the patriarchs named such sites against a background of animistic superstition, since it is quite probable that they took over the traditional designations from the Canaanites in the first instance, and subsequently renamed them. The attempt to explain the name Beer-Sheba as "well of seven spirits" is fanciful, and Driver was correct in associating the name with the plurality of wells in that district.[17] The true significance of the designation, which means "well of the oath" (Gen. 21:31), was amply illustrated by Robertson Smith, who showed that the Hebrew term "to swear" (שׁבע) means literally "to come under the influence of seven things."[18]

Similar misinterpretations may well apply to sites associated with the names of trees, such as Elon Moreh or Elon Meonenim. The first of these was apparently a familiar landmark in Shechem, and from the reference in Genesis 12:6 it would seem to have derived its name from Canaanite sources. If the tree in question was in fact an evergreen, its value as a shady resting-place in the heat of the day will be immediately evident to any who have travelled in Palestine. The fact that Abraham here received a divine manifestation and later erected an altar to mark the site is coincidental, since he also received other revelations at locations unconnected with trees, and which were also marked by means of wayside altars. In connection with the second, or "diviner's terebinth," mentioned in Judges 9:37, the reference is again to Canaanite origins, and although it may be that apostate Israelites of the Judges period participated in soothsaying at that site, there is no factual evidence for such a supposition, or for the view that the location, which is unknown, had any connection, animistic or other, with the worship of the patriarchal period.

A similar criticism may be levelled against the kind of theory maintained by Robertson Smith in connection with the well addressed in the poetic fragment in Numbers 21:17f.[19] Arguing from late Bedouin counterparts, he held that the well was being venerated as the embodi-

---

[17] G. A. Smith, *EB*, I, col. 518, following A. von Gall, *Altisraelische Kultstätten* (1898), pp. 44ff.; S. R. Driver, *The Book of Genesis* (1904), p. 215.

[18] *Lectures on the Religion of the Semites*, p. 182.

[19] *Ibid.*, p. 169 n. 3; cf. H. Gressmann, *Mose und seine Zeit* (1913), pp. 349f.

ment of a supernatural force.[20] In point of fact, the stanza that commemorated the occasion when an underground source of water was
successfully tapped need have no more significance than that attached to
the rejoicing which takes place in modern times when an arduous effort
of excavation for a water supply is similarly rewarded. This little section
of poetry appears to be of the same general kind as the vintage lyrics
sung by those who were treading out the grapes at the harvest season
(cf. Isa. 16:10; Jer. 25:30). The fact that this fragment occurred in a
poetic section should be sufficient warning against mistaking for animism
what may probably be nothing more than poetic license. Since the
ancient Egyptians regularly personified a wide range of objects without
at the same time assigning to them the structure of divinity,[21] it may
well be that the original author of the passage in Numbers was following
precisely the same literary practice, thereby testifying indirectly to the
antiquity of the composition.

Equally suspect is the assertion, commonly found among an earlier
generation of interpreters of early Hebrew religious tendencies, that a
reference to activity related in some manner to trees indicates a clear
survival of animism. Thus a person such as Deborah the prophetess, who
dispensed judgment for Israel from the shade of a palm tree in the hill-
country of Ephraim (Judg. 4:4f.), or King Saul, who held court under a
pomegranate tree (1 Sam. 14:2), received inspiration not from the
balanced exercise of ratiocinative activity but from the rustling of the
leaves above, and this was thought to indicate the nature of the decision
to be given. The inadequacy of such a view is immediately apparent
from the fact that there is no suggestion anywhere in the Old Testament
that prophets or prophetesses were unable to function in the absence of
certain material concomitants. The staff of Moses constituted the symbol
of his authority and was not the source of his inspiration or power. In the
same way, the mantle of Elijah was a characteristic of the man himself,
and when it was assumed by Elisha it merely constituted a token of the
fact that the inheritance of the first-born (cf. 2 Kgs. 2:9) was henceforward to typify his prophetic activities. The literary sources make it clear
that Deborah was a stern adherent of the Sinai Covenant, who never
countenanced the paganism of the indigenous population for one moment. Similarly, the early days of the reign of Saul were completely
devoid of idolatry, as the narratives that describe the period indicate,
and it was only at the very end of his life, when under acute stress and
beset by a serious psychotic condition, that he indulged in an activity
which he had previously banned from his kingdom (1 Sam. 28:3ff.).

[20] Cf. Oesterley and Robinson, *Hebrew Religion: Its Origin and Development*, p.
38.
[21] *IAAM*, p. 41.

For these and other similar occurrences in the Old Testament there would seem to be a much simpler and more logical explanation. In the countries of the Near East, an outdoor situation is much more tolerable in the shade of a leafy tree than in the heat of a burning sun, a scorching desert wind, or even the doubtful shelter of a tent-doorway. Indeed, it is almost impossible to overestimate the value of trees in that part of the world, a fact that appears to have been impressed upon the minds of its ancient inhabitants, judging from the appreciative references to trees in the Bible and other Near Eastern literature. Unfortunately, simple explanations of this kind seldom commend themselves to those who are determined to find evidence in the written sources for preconceived notions or *a priori* theories in connection with the alleged animistic and polydaemonistic background of patriarchal and early Hebrew religion generally.

C. TOTEMISM

The success of Robertson Smith's attempts to accommodate totemistic concepts to the growth of early Hebrew religion was questioned from the time that his *Kinship and Marriage in Early Arabia* appeared in print. Two of his most noteworthy critics were Lagrange and König, who pointedly repudiated any suggestion that any remnants of totemism could be found in the Old Testament narratives.[22] It must be admitted that the gravest deficiency of a theory of a totemistic stage in Hebrew religious development was its imperfect understanding of the nature and distribution of totemism in primitive religions. Although totemism occurs in such widely diverse parts of the world as North America, Australia, and Africa, it cannot on that account be regarded as a universal stage of religious development.[23] From variations of procedure with respect to the venerated animal or plant species in various parts of the world, it would appear that in some instances totemism is a social custom rather than a religious one. Generally speaking, anthropologists incline to the belief that, where totemism flourishes, it fosters the growth of more advanced spiritual concepts by lending a degree of religious sanction to interpersonal obligations and tribal loyalties.

The Wellhausenian school did not realize fully that the fact that animals were sometimes associated mythologically or otherwise with the gods of a national religion did not necessarily prove that such a religion had passed through a totemistic phase. For them it was comparatively simple to point to the place of animals in the cults of Egypt and Greece, without at the same time appreciating that such a phenomenon need only indicate a primitive animal worship. The religion of ancient

---

[22] M. J. Lagrange, *Études sur les Religions sémitiques* (1903), pp. 112ff.; E. König, *Geschichte der alttestamentlichen Religion* (1924), pp. 72ff.

[23] G. Galloway, *The Philosophy of Religion* (1914), p. 97.

Egypt in particular was taken as a prime example of developed totemism, especially since all the early deities were associated with some
specific plant or animal that constituted the visible aspect of social
unity.[24] Yet when the literary sources of ancient Egypt were studied
carefully, it became apparent that nothing comparable to the totemism
of Australia, North America, or Africa had ever existed in Egypt.

As Frankfort has pointed out, the characteristic features of totemism,
such as the claim of descent from the totem, its sacrifice among certain
tribes so as to provide a ceremonial feast for the clan, and the insistence
upon exogamy, the prohibition of marriage within the clan, cannot be
discovered in Egyptian sources.[25] Although early Egyptian religion
might have possessed the basic attitudes from which some form of totemism or fetishism could have emerged, it seems more probable that it was
in fact simple animal worship, since in Egypt the animal as such appears
to have possessed enormous religious significance, regardless of its specific
nature. This contention is reinforced by the consideration that during
those periods when religion passed through phases of decadence, animal
worship came very much to the fore in Egypt, as evidenced by the
numerous cemeteries filled with mummified cats, crocodiles, dogs, bulls,
and other animals.

If there are grounds for questioning the existence of a genuine totemistic phase in the religious development of ancient Egypt, there are
even more reasons for disputing its existence in Mesopotamia. Whereas
most early Egyptian name-deities were associated in some manner with
an animal or plant, there is virtually no trace of this phenomenon in
early Mesopotamian religion. The names of a few Sumerian deities such
as Shagan, the serpent-god, and Gud, the bull-deity, reflected some
vague linking of animals and gods,[26] but in the main the Sumerian
deities were anthropomorphic in character.[27] Whether one studies the
Sumerian spiritual tradition or its modification by the later Babylonians,
the religion of Mesopotamia conveys the impression of having appeared
in a comparatively advanced stage of development from the time of its
inception. Certainly it contains nothing that would correspond strictly to
a totemistic phase as part of that process of growth.

In the light of these observations it would appear very unlikely that
specifically totemistic survivals can be demonstrated in the Old Testament. Having regard to the elements necessary for proof of the existence
of totemism in any race or culture,[28] it must be observed at once that
nowhere in the Old Testament does the concept that the members of a

---

[24] J. Černý, *Ancient Egyptian Religion* (1952), pp. 19ff.
[25] H. Frankfort, *Ancient Egyptian Religion* (1961 ed.), p. 9; cf. *FSAC*, pp. 178f.
[26] *ARI*, p. 27.
[27] *FSAC*, pp. 192f.
[28] W. Robertson Smith, *Kinship and Marriage in Early Arabia*, p. 219.

particular stock have been derived from the blood of an eponym animal appear. Nor is there any evidence of the belief that the members of a clan with an animal name such as Simeon (*hyena?*) were actually the offspring of the totem animal. Despite the elaborate explanations that G. Buchanan Gray offered for the origin of proper names among the ancient Hebrews,[29] the fact is that very little is known for certain about the process. In view of the absence from the Old Testament writings of the two most important elements in any totemistic system, namely, the claim of descent from the totem and its ceremonial sacrifice among certain tribes, it seems improbable that clan names became in certain cases personal designations "with the break-up of the totem clan system" as Gray suggested.

Biblical records from the patriarchal period indicate that certain individuals were likened to animals with regard to temperament or characteristic attitudes; these included Judah (Gen. 49:9), Issachar (Gen. 49:14), Dan (Gen. 49:17), Naphtali (Gen. 49:21), and Benjamin (Gen. 49:27). In the same way others were compared with the behavior of water, such as Reuben (Gen. 49:4), or with a spreading tree beside a well, as in the case of Joseph (Gen. 49:22). When Hagar received an announcement from the divine messenger, she was promised that her son Ishmael would be "a wild ass of a man" (Gen. 16:12), a complimentary designation indeed, since the wild ass had its habitat in the desert areas and as such was the choicest beast of the entire hunt.[30] In each instance the emphasis appears to have been on the character or physical attributes of the animal or plant concerned and has no reference, overt or explicit, to either animism or totemism. Again, however, a plain reading of the text in the light of the social customs of that remote age will hardly satisfy those who are determined to find evidence for their theories in the Old Testament narratives.

D. TABU

It is possible to adduce from Semitic sources a number of usages that might fall under the heading of tabu, such as lists of animals associated with certain deities.[31] However, it is a mistake to suppose that similar lists in Leviticus (11:2ff.) and Deuteronomy (14:4ff.) reflected a primitive tabu against human consumption of sacred animal species. In these Biblical sources the concern was essentially a dietetic and hygienic one, of a kind completely unique and entirely lacking in other ancient Near Eastern literature. Before the forbidden species were enumerated there was set forth the general principle by which those deemed suitable for human consumption could be recognized empirically. There was no need

[29] *Hebrew Proper Names*, pp. 85ff.
[30] *IOTT*, p. 105.
[31] Cf. M. Jastrow, *Die Religion Babyloniens und Assyriens*, II, pp. 896f., 933ff.

for either magic or priestly counsel in this matter, and when the list is examined in the light of modern medical science it is seen to be of a remarkably advanced nature, embodying fundamental principles of health and human well-being.

Those species that were prohibited are liable to parasitic infection of various kinds, and as such are unsuitable for food, particularly where the danger of epidemic disease is an ever-present reality.[32] The attempt made by Robertson Smith to relate the Levitical prohibitions to pagan tabu concepts by stating that "the unclean creatures therefore are the divine animals of the heathen; such animals as the latter did not ordinarily eat or sacrifice"[33] is vitiated by the observation that the clean species in the Levitical lists were also prominent in the religious veneration of pagan cult-worship, showing that considerations other than those of tabu were being envisaged by the ancient author.

E. ANCESTOR WORSHIP

Since the time of Wellhausen the extent to which traces of ancestor worship can be detected in the Old Testament has been a matter of much controversy. In the main, those who supported this position related it to a totemistic phase, in which the totem-ancestor gradually developed into a human progenitor who subsequently became divine.[34] On the other hand there were scholars who disputed the interpretation of the data adduced in support of ancestor worship, and maintained that the evidence admitted of a different explanation. Thus Vincent argued from the available archaeological material that the care for the dead, rather than a cult-worship of the deceased, was the prepossessing concern of the relevant Old Testament narratives.[35]

Margoliouth conceded that the importance of practices relating to the dead had been greatly exaggerated, and stated flatly that there was no ground for assuming that ancestor worship was the only or even the chief religion of pre-Mosaic Israel.[36] Kautzsch, following Carl Gruneisen, denied that traces of a primitive ancestor worship could be found in the Old Testament, and pointed out that the mourning customs

[32] Cf. A. R. Short, *The Bible and Modern Medicine* (1953), pp. 40ff.; R. K. Harrison, *IDB*, II, pp. 543f.

[33] W. Robertson Smith, *Kinship and Marriage in Early Arabia*, p. 311.

[34] Cf. R. Goldhizer, *Culte des Ancêtres chez les Arabes* (1885), p. 15 *passim*; B. Stade, *Geschichte des Volkes Israel*, I, pp. 387ff.; *Biblische Theologie des AT* (1905), I, pp. 104ff.; J. Wellhausen, *Reste Arabischen Heidentums*, pp. 183ff.; G. Hölscher, *Geschichte der Israelitischen und Jüdischen Religion* (1922), pp. 24ff.; S. A. Cook in *Lectures on the Religion of the Semites*, pp. 508ff., 544ff.; S. A. Cook, *The Religion of Ancient Palestine in the Second Millennium B.C. in the Light of Archaeology and Inscriptions* (1908), pp. 57ff.

[35] A. Vincent, *Canaan d'après l'Exploration Récente* (1907), pp. 288ff.

[36] G. Margoliouth, *ERE*, I, p. 449.

belonged to different grades of thought, with some of them defying all attempts at explanation.[37]

Oesterley enumerated the mourning practices which he regarded as indicative of the remnants of ancestor worship among the Hebrews, including the cutting of the hair, the wearing of sackcloth, baring of the feet, fasting, and the like.[38] What he did not make clear was that, when the Hebrew prophets were inveighing against mourning customs, they were in fact condemning specific Canaanite elements such as laceration.[39] Pentateuchal sources regarded both contact with the dead and formal mourning itself as occasioning ritual or ceremonial defilement. Levitical law permitted the Aaronic priesthood to mourn by rending the clothing, weeping, and allowing the hair to flow freely (Lev. 21:1ff.), but these privileges were forbidden to the High Priest (Lev. 21:10f.). Both priests and people were prohibited from lacerating bodily tissues, trimming off the corners of the beard and the sides of the head, eating tithes as an act of mourning, or offering them on behalf of the dead (cf. Lev. 21:5; 29:27f.; Deut. 14:1; 26:14), all of which were associated with heathen Canaanite worship. Weeping and lamentation, the use of ashes, and the wearing of sackcloth were not prohibited by Hebrew ceremonial law.

The use of tribal or personal names in which an element of the designation of deity occurred is not necessarily an indication of a prior stage of ancestor worship, as some scholars have imagined. While the origin of certain of these names in the Hebrew Bible is unknown, others clearly reflect an association with a theophany or some other significant event. Thus Ishmael, meaning "God hears," was significant to Hagar because of the assurance it carried that God had heard her cry of affliction (Gen. 16:10), and despite the fact that the generic designation "El" formed part of the name, it carried no connotation whatever of the divinity of any ancestor. Even compound forms such as Baal-gad (Josh. 11:17; 12:7; 13:5) designated territory which had been named jointly in honor of the Canaanite storm-deity and the god of Fortune (cf. Isa. 65:11), and had no reference whatever to intermediate human ancestors.

An equally indiscriminate use of evidence is that by Oesterley and Robinson, who argued from the association of altars with the general location of the burial places of Sarah (cf. Gen. 13:18; 18:1; 23:1), Deborah (Gen. 35:8), and others to the postulate that, among ancient peoples, if the grave of an ancestor was a sanctuary, it meant that the

---

[37] E. Kautzsch, *HDB*, extra vol., p. 614; C. Gruneisen, *Der Ahnenkultus und die Urreligion Israels* (1900).

[38] W. O. E. Oesterley, *Immortality and the Unseen World*, pp. 141ff.

[39] For Ugaritic epic parallels cf. *DOTT*, p. 130.

ancestor was being worshipped.[40] This is by no means the case, for it surely indicates that the god of the sanctuary was the foremost object of worship, and that the dead were interred in the locality precisely because it had sacred associations. Thus the deceased members of the family were by implication committed into the care of the deity, and if anything of a more developed nature is to be understood by such activity, the tendency of thought is not so much a reflection of ancestor worship as a groping of the human mind towards some concept of life after death.

In general it may be observed that there is an all-too-common confusion between respect for the departed and a cult of ancestor worship in the minds of certain scholars. Many peoples, both ancient and modern, indulge in burial customs whose significance can be easily and inadvertently misinterpreted, and it is particularly unfortunate when contemporary tendencies and attitudes are projected into the past in an attempt to explain ancient customs. In this connection the contribution of archaeology serves as an important corrective. Although there are many instances where it can throw no light whatever upon archaic attitudes, there are others where it serves to clarify the issue for the occidental mind. One of these is connected with the teraphim as alleged survivals of ancestor worship. From archaeological data it is evident that in the patriarchal period the teraphim were small portable idols the possession of which indicated, among other things, inheritance rights.[41]

F. THE LIMITATIONS OF THESE INFLUENCES

Any attempt to assess the nature of pre-Mosaic religion will need to take cognizance of the much wider range of evidence in the comparative study of religion than was available for Wellhausen and his immediate followers. There will probably be few who would dispute the view expressed by Waterhouse that Tylor made a "brilliant guess" in formulating the concept of animism as one of the most primitive stages of religion.[42] On the other hand there will be those who will urge that Tylor was much too comprehensive and speculative in his conjectures, and that the application of his theories to Semitic religion by Robertson Smith was too rigid, and went beyond the available evidence. More recent study has shown that any dynamistic or animistic phase which may have existed in

[40] W. O. E. Oesterley and T. H. Robinson, *Hebrew Religion: Its Origin and Development*, p. 100.

[41] C. H. Gordon, *IDB*, IV, p. 574, *BA*, III, No. 1 (1940), pp. 1ff.; *IOTT*, pp. 116f.; A. E. Draffkorn, *JBL*, LXXVI (1957), pp. 216ff.

[42] E. S. Waterhouse, *The Dawn of Religion* (1936), p. 31.

ancient Near Eastern life had ended centuries before the patriarchal period commenced, as has been observed earlier.

Furthermore, the concept of animism as understood classically has been modified significantly with regard to the nature of Mesopotamian and Egyptian religion. Elements of life that were personified have been shown to represent the counterpart of an emotional or dynamic reciprocal relationship in which the "I" of selfhood was confronted not by an "it," but by a "Thou" of the phenomenal world. The scope of this relationship can be gathered from the remark of Wilson to the effect that it is difficult to think of any phenomenon with which ancient man might not have had a "Thou" relationship, as exemplified by Egyptian scenes and texts.[43] Or, as Frankfort himself commented, "Primitive man simply does not know an inanimate world. For this very reason he does not 'personify' inanimate phenomena nor does he fill an empty world with the ghosts of the dead, as 'animism' would have us believe."[44] No longer is it merely a question of human behavior's being affected by anything that possessed such innate activity as to suggest that it was animated by its own life and motivating force. Now it is clear that the initiative lay with man, who tended to personalize phenomena, and in the process of confrontation assigned categories of individuality and will to the manifold aspects of life surrounding him.[45]

If it is increasingly difficult to interpret pre-Mosaic religion in terms of animism, it is even more so in terms of totemism, for which there appears to be very little warrant in the early Biblical narratives. As far as the theory of an underlying phase of ancestor worship is concerned, the available evidence lends itself to more than one interpretation, and as a result the extent of its influence in early Israelite religion is very questionable. Although the elements of tabu and polytheism that marked ancient Near Eastern religious life are reflected in varying degrees in the Old Testament records, this is not to say that the restrictions upon Hebrew life established by religious sanction were derived in principle or content from Near Eastern sources, nor that Israelite religion had at one time passed through a polytheistic stage.

Though there may be aspects of early Hebrew religious life that present certain similarities to animism, it seems fairly assured in the light of more recent study that they were not understood by the ancients in the sense attributed to them by the Wellhausenian school. Indeed it is probable that many of the ancient ritual practices of Mesopotamia and Egypt had long outlived their original

[43] J. A. Wilson, *IAAM*, p. 41
[44] *IAAM*, pp. 5f.
[45] *ARI*, p. 27.

394

significance before the patriarchs appeared on the historical scene, a point that has been mentioned above. In the view of what is known about the highly developed cultural forms of Near Eastern antiquity, it seems best to conclude with Kaufmann that the "initial level [of Israelite religion] was not magical, totemistic, animistic, or demonistic; it originated among developed theistic religions."[46]

[46] *KRI*, p. 221.

IV. THE HISTORY OF OLD TESTAMENT RELIGION

A. THE RELIGION OF THE PATRIARCHS

Although the narratives of the Pentateuch convey the impression that the Hebrew patriarchs followed a monotheistic religious tradition, it is made evident in Joshua 24:2 that they were involved in Mesopotamian polytheism to some extent at least.[1] Certainly the Biblical narratives lend no support to the idea that Abraham originated the idea of monotheism, or that he established a monotheistic cult within the framework of his own society. Instead, Abraham was portrayed as the ancestor of that nation which was destined to become monotheistic. Although much is known about the religious practices and beliefs of the contemporary Mesopotamians, little detailed material concerning patriarchal religion is forthcoming from the Genesis narratives. This is rather unfortunate, since they constitute the only records of patriarchal faith and practice, although certain other elements of the corpus can be illustrated from contemporary Mesopotamian sources.

The patriarchs were clearly depicted as objects of divine revelation (Gen. 12:1, 7; 15:1), who were convinced of the necessity for a personal faith-relationship with the Deity. Once this had been established, the patriarchs could look confidently to their God for protection and sustenance throughout life (Gen. 15:4ff.; 17:1ff.; 28:11ff.). On receipt of divine guidance they had no option but to obey the revealed will of God (Gen. 22:3ff.). Circumcision was adopted as a religious rite to mark out specifically those who were included in the Covenant relationship. This act appears to have had a particular significance in designating the ancestors of Israel as a distinctive unit, since it is known that, unlike the Egyptians, the ancient inhabitants of Babylonia and Assyria did not practice the rite.[2] The closeness of their relationship with the Deity caused the patriarchs to commemorate divine beneficence in the names of certain of their offspring, or in the designations of specific localities where a revelation had been given (Gen. 16:11, 14; 32:30; 35:15). The

---

[1] Contrary to J. Muilenburg, *IB*, I, p. 296, who assigned patriarchal religion to a Canaanite milieu.

[2] J. P. Hyatt, *IDB*, I, p. 629.

pattern of worship during the patriarchal age included sacrifice and the offering of prayer to God (Gen. 12:8; 26:25).

The emphasis upon the special quality of the relationship between the individual patriarchs and the Deity seems to have been preserved in the particular names for God that were a feature of this period. As Bright has indicated, the religion of the patriarchs was quite different in character from the paganism of the surrounding nations.[3] The personal deity of the clan-chief was the god of the entire clan, as illustrated by such archaic titles for God as the "Shield" of Abraham (cf. Gen. 15:1; 31:53), the "Kinsman" of Isaac (Gen. 31:42),[4] and the "Champion" of Jacob (Gen. 49:24). As Alt has shown, the deliberate choice of God by each successive generation of patriarchs represents an extremely ancient religious concept that is thoroughly consistent with the Biblical tradition.[5] The place of the deity as the "father" or "brother" of the worshipper was also enshrined in such personal names as Abiram ("the Exalted One is my father"), Abimelech ("the King is my father"), and Ahiram ("the Exalted One is my brother"). It was to such a deity that the clan members, following the lead of the patriarchal head, gave supreme if perhaps not always complete devotion.

Hebrew personal names containing some appellation of deity and clan have been paralleled by a similar usage in Mesopotamia during the Old Akkadian period (ca. 2360-2180 B.C.) and in the Amorite names occurring between 2100 and 1600 B.C.[6] Albright has concluded that the pre-Mosaic religion of the Hebrews envisaged the deity in terms of mountain-imagery. For example, the name El Shaddai may have meant originally "the god of the mountains."[7] Albright interprets this against the general Mesopotamian background of the patriarchs, where among the Amorites the mountain-deity Hadad, associated with winds and storms, was a venerated member of the pantheon. However, he also recognized that the God of the patriarchs was not restricted to one particular locality, but to a family that stood in a special relationship of obedience and faith to Him and whose interests He was pledged to protect.[8] Thus, whatever the pagan antecedents of El Shaddai and other analogous terms may have been, if any, there was for the patriarchs no concept of nature-religion as such and no hint that the deity had ever been displaced from an association with a specific locality in favor of a

[3] J. Bright, *IDB*, II, p. 561.
[4] Cf. *FSAC*, p. 248.
[5] Cf. A. Alt, *Der Gott der Väter* (1929), pp. 40ff.; W. F. Albright, *JBL*, LIV (1935), pp. 188ff.
[6] *FSAC*, pp. 243ff.
[7] *FSAC*, pp. 245f.
[8] Cf. B. W. Anderson, *IDB*, II, p. 412; H. G. May, *JBL*, LX (1941), p. 113, *The Journal of Bible and Religion*, IX (1941), pp. 155ff.

connection with a particular social group, in the manner in which Alt had thought of the growth of primitive tribal religion.[9]

Although Albright is probably correct in asserting that there was no "El-monotheism" current among the early western Semites, there is no evidence for his contention that early Hebrew popular religion was organized in terms of a triad of father, mother, and son, after the Neolithic pattern of plastic statues in triads.[10] At no time in patriarchal religion was there the slightest hint of a female component of deity, and the same is true of the period of the Sinai Covenant. Though the God of the Hebrews might be associated with several titles, there was never any suggestion as to plurality or multiplicity in the personage of the Deity. Insofar as plural forms occurred in Hebrew names for God or in titles relating to the Godhead, they were not so much vestigial remains of an earlier stage of polytheism as grammatical structures designed to emphasize the majesty of the God who was being described. Although Alt tended consistently to associate the primitive deity with a particular locality, he was nevertheless correct in assuming that the divine appellations compounded with "El" in the patriarchal narratives were genuinely pre-Israelite in nature.[11] The antiquity of this practice in west-Semitic religion has been further illustrated by the presence in Ugaritic literature of the titles *Elyon, Olam,* and *Ro'i* as designations of deity.

The traditions that underlie the religious attitudes of the patriarchs can thus be seen to be of great antiquity. In essence their faith involved a sense of personal relationship with the Deity, an awareness that implicit obedience to the divine will was an essential element in the continuity of that relationship, and a degree of spiritual insight that enabled them to assess the nature and significance of the divine promises. Vivid though the patriarchal experience of God appears to have been, it is very doubtful if it can be described consistently as a "real blood relationship between a family or clan and its god" as Albright has done.[12] Albright's language is reminiscent of the attempts of other scholars to establish a totemistic phase in Hebrew religion, an approach which he has repudiated elsewhere.[13] The only blood relationship that existed between a worshipper and the Deity during the patriarchal period was strictly poetic, as represented in certain of the proper names discussed above; and this situation did not hold good for all families or clans by any means. Although the patriarchs worshipped the same deity under a variety of names, he was no mere local numen but the patron of the clan. Despite alleged monotheistic tendencies in the second-millennium

9 Alt, *Der Gott der Väter,* p. 33.
10 *FSAC,* pp. 173, 247.
11 Alt, *Der Gott der Väter,* pp. 49ff.
12 *FSAC,* p. 249.
13 *FSAC,* p. 93.

B.C. religious life of Mesopotamia, it does not seem possible to describe the patriarchs as anything more than monolatrists.

B. THE RELIGION OF MOSES

The origin of historical monotheism must thus be considered in the light of those events which occurred in the Mosaic era. The Biblical sources for this period have been assigned a much greater degree of historicity within recent years than was formerly the case in some scholarly circles. Unfortunately it is still true that others are hampered by an uncritical acceptance of the Wellhausenian dictum that Pentateuchal sources are relatively late and represent a long tradition of oral transmission. Be that as it may, there can be little doubt that Moses established the religious system of Israel, and that the uniform witness of Old Testament tradition to this fact is reliable.

Equally certain is the form of the Divine Name יהוה, which was revealed to Moses. Although this tetragrammaton is often thought to have been pronounced *Yahweh*, following Greek transcriptions such as those of Clement of Alexandria and Theodoret, the fact is that the original pronunciation is unknown, and all attempts to reconstruct it have so far proved conjectural.[14] A shorter form of the Divine Name may have circulated either as "Yah," "Yahu," or "Yo," and although some have thought that one or another of these may have been earlier than the tetragrammaton, the presence of the latter in ancient poetic fragments of the Old Testament as well as in extra-Biblical material such as the Moabite Stone seems to imply that the four-letter form was the original. Attempts to show that the sacred name was known before the time of Moses by adducing as evidence Akkadian personal names such as *Yaum-Ilu* (Mine is the god), or the alleged presence of "Yo" in one of the texts from Ugarit[15] have been unsuccessful to date.

The Kenite hypothesis, which suggested that Moses learned of the Divine Name through marriage into the family of Jethro (Exod. 2:15ff.) and subsequent initiation into the Midian cult of *YHWH*, has certain elements in its favor, but it lacks decisive evidence in terms of the text. In the first instance it is clear that the God of Israel was explicitly the God of the patriarchs, and not exclusively of their Kenite cousins. Secondly, the traditional translation of the revelation of the name *YHWH* in Exodus 6:2f. is open to certain objections. As W. J. Martin has shown, it is possible that the patriarchs did in fact know the name *YHWH*, assum-

---

[14] On this general problem see W. F. Albright, *JBL*, XLIII (1924), pp. 370ff., XLIV (1925), pp. 158ff., XLVI (1927), pp. 175ff., LXVII (1948), pp. 379f.; G. R. Driver, *ZAW*, XLVI (1928), pp. 7ff.; O. Eissfeldt, *ZAW*, LIII (1935), pp. 59ff.; J. Obermann, *JBL*, XLVIII (1949), pp. 301ff.; J. Gray, *JNES*, XII (1953), pp. 278ff.; G. R. Driver, *JBL*, LXXIII (1954), pp. 125ff.; D. Goitein, *VT*, VI (1956), pp. 1ff.; *FSAC*, pp. 258ff.

[15] C. Virolleaud, *La déesse 'Anat* (1938), pp. 97f. and pl. XIII.

ing that there was an elliptical interrogative present in the verse.[16] The passage in question would thus read, "I suffered myself to appear to Abraham, to Isaac, and to Jacob, as El Shaddai, for did I not let myself be known to them by my name *YHWH?*"

An alternative suggestion has been made by J. A. Motyer, who retranslated the verse as follows: "And I showed myself to Abraham, to Isaac, and to Jacob in the character of El Shaddai, but in the character expressed by my name Yahweh I did not make myself known to them."[17] This interpretation is important in recognizing the dynamic character of nomenclature as understood by the peoples of the ancient Near East, where names were so frequently connected with specific functions or with facets of personality. Furthermore, it does not deny to the patriarchs the knowledge of the name *YHWH*, but merely prohibits them from appreciating the significance of what the name implied. As Davidson long ago pointed out, the author of Exodus 6 did not mean to deny that the tetragrammaton was older than Moses or unknown before his day.[18] What he was attempting to show was that it had no divine authorization prior to the Mosaic period, but that in speaking to Moses God appropriated it and authorized it as part of His fuller self-manifestation. Even in its present state the Hebrew text makes it clear that the name *YHWH* was old, since it does not say, "My name *YHWH* was not known to them," but "as to my name *YHWH*, I was not known by them," or "as to my name *YHWH* I did not become known to them." On these grounds alone there would seem to be room for the view that the patriarchs knew of the name *YHWH*, without at the same time being aware of its significance.

The provenance and meaning of the tetragrammaton have been the subject of repeated philological discussion for many decades. Numerous scholars adhered to the view that a causative interpretation of the verb-stem הוה was the only one to supply the real sense of the term. Against those who objected that a causative connotation was too abstract a concept for that period of historical development, Albright pointed out quite properly that such an idea can be illustrated amply from the pre-Mosaic texts of Mesopotamia and Egypt.[19] However, more recent philological research has made it clear that the name is in fact a regular substantive word in which the root הוה is preceded by the preformative י. As a proper noun the tetragrammaton is thus the designation of a Person and stands in contrast to such titles as *El Shaddai* and *El Elyon*.

[16] W. J. Martin, *Stylistic Criteria and the Analysis of the Pentateuch* (1955), pp. 18ff. For examples of this form see P. Joüon, *Grammaire de l'Hébreu Biblique* (1923), p. 495.

[17] *The Revelation of the Divine Name* (1959), pp. 11ff.

[18] *The Theology of the OT* (1904), p. 68.

[19] *FSAC*, p. 260.

Among the ancient Semites the concept of a "name" had a real bearing upon the functions and personality of the individual involved. While *YHWH* was in fact the God of the patriarchs (Exod. 3:15), His newly revealed name involved a considerably wider ideological setting. God was soon to be understood by the fledgling nation of Israel as a living Person who by virtue of the Covenant of Sinai was in intimate moral and spiritual relationship with those who accepted and obeyed His revealed precepts. Unlike other oriental deities He stood alone, without consort or offspring, and was not restricted to any one geographical location, but was the controller of all cosmic forces. While the Covenant was consistently related by tradition to the Sinai region, there was no special cult associated with this particular location, as was the case in Canaan and elsewhere. Attempts to regard *YHWH* as a derivation from an original volcanic deity are unconvincing, since there are no volcanoes, extinct or active, anywhere in either Sinai or Midian. As Morgenstern showed, the language of the Old Testament theophanies is so frequently drawn from weather phenomena, fire, earthquakes, and the like, that the imagery must properly be connected with the divine glory rather than with a localized volcano.[20]

Basic to the Mosaic religious tradition was the anthropomorphic conception of God that represented the divine personality in a manner suggesting human form to the individual worshipper. Equally emphatic, however, were the aniconic strictures emerging from the Mosaic period, which flatly prohibited the representation of deity in tangible form. So basic was this enactment to the whole of Hebrew religious tradition that almost no images or idols that can possibly be identified as representations of *YHWH* have been excavated from archaeological sites in Palestine, a situation which is truly remarkable in view of what the Old Testament writers had to say about the prevalence of idolatry in certain periods of Hebrew history.

The Covenant at Sinai was the logical extension of the revealed personality of God, since it incorporated Israel into the larger scope of divine activity and furnished her with a sense of election and mission. The personal relationship between a god and his people, inherent in the name *YHWH*, was thus made characteristic of Hebrew religion by the contractual nature of the Covenant. It drew the Israelites within the scope of the mighty divine acts, and gave them a sense of historical perspective and destiny that was unique among the nations of the ancient Near East. It also revealed the Deity as a supremely moral and ethical Being, beneficent towards His obedient people yet manifesting Himself as a jealous and wrathful God when the principles of the Covenant relationship were threatened by apostasy. As a righteous Deity, *YHWH* regulated the social and spiritual life of His people, and de-

[20] ZA, XXV (1910), pp. 139ff., XXVIII (1913), pp. 15ff.

manded that the relationships of Hebrew community life should b governed by dynamic concepts of equity and morality. The idea of Torah or body of doctrine of an authoritative order can be attribute with complete confidence to the period of Moses, since as Erman ha shown, the followers of the Aten cult in Egypt used the term *sbayet* ("teaching" to designate the traditional corpus of knowledge or instructio in a manner closely allied to the later Latin *doctrina*.[21]

The extent to which Moses can be regarded as a true monotheist ha been a subject of much discussion among scholars. As was observe earlier, any animistic phase that may have been present in ancient Nea Eastern religion had long since been transcended in the patriarch period,[22] while empirical unitary tendencies in the thought of the Mesc potamians concerning their deities had been in existence from at leas the fourth millennium B.C.[23] Ringgren detected two processes in th thought of the ancient Mesopotamians concerning the nature and func tioning of the deities in their pantheon. Arguing from a primitive belie in "High Gods," he postulated a process of separation in which certai qualities of an original High God, such as his truth and righteousness were split off, personified, and venerated as divine. Complementary t this process in some respects was a tendency towards unification, where by different deities could be regarded as manifestations of a suprem Being who had absorbed their characters and functions.[24]

Despite this, however, as has been observed above, the Hebrew patr archs can hardly be described as monotheists in the generally accepte sense of the term. Furthermore, it has to be recognized that much of th discussion regarding monotheism has been colored by Hellenic rathe than Semitic categories of thought. It is also important to notice, a Anderson has indicated, that Hebrew monotheism is not to be traced t any particular characteristic, but rather to an entire complex of factor inherent in the religion of the Mosaic age.[25] While Moses was no regarded as specifically rejecting all other gods, this attitude was certain ly implicit in his belief that there was only one existent deity, the creato of the world, who exercised control over both the processes of natur and the fortunes of man. In that sense Albright could speak of th religion of Moses as monotheistic, taking care, however, to distinguis such a faith from the monotheistic connotations of the Maccabean an

---

[21] A. Erman, *Die Religion der Ägypter* (1934), pp. 121f. On the etymology o *Torah* see G. Oestborn, *Tōrā in the OT*, pp. 4ff.

[22] G. E. Wright in H. R. Willoughby (ed.), *The Study of the Bible Today an Tomorrow* (1947), p. 90.

[23] *FSAC*, p. 177.

[24] H. Ringgren, *Word and Wisdom* (1947), pp. 20ff.

[25] B. W. Anderson, *OTMS*, p. 291.

Christian eras.[26] In the view of the present writer there seems little justification for not attributing monotheism to Moses, although care should be taken not to understand that concept in a speculative Hellenic sense. A more accurate designation of the situation might well be framed in terms of an empirical ethical monotheism.[27]

C. THE TABERNACLE AND CANAANITE INFLUENCES

Considerable modification of the critical position adopted by Wellhausen with regard to the Tabernacle is now required as the result of recent archaeological study. In his *Prolegomena* Wellhausen took the view that the wilderness Tabernacle was nothing more than the idealization of the Temple. As such, the narratives describing it were historical fiction, and even the intrinsic possibility of the existence of such a structure was a matter of the gravest doubt. In this position he was followed by other scholars,[28] who regarded it generally as the work of some post-exilic priestly compiler, or else as a late idealization of a considerably less complex tent in terms of the Solomonic structure.[29] This opinion, however, was by no means uniform, for as long ago as 1919 Lammens explored late Arabic sources much as Wellhausen had done, and argued from the presence of the old-Arabic *qubbah* to the possibility of some kind of palladium or tent-shrine in the Mosaic period.[30] This view was subsequently adopted by Morgenstern, who showed that, among the Arabs of the pre-Mohammedan period, images or cult-objects of the tribal deity were kept in a small tent normally made of red leather, which was sometimes carried into battle in order to arouse the patriotic instincts of the warriors.[31] An Aramaic inscription from Palmyra contained the word *qubbah*, which was intended as a designation of some kind of sacred tent;[32] bas-reliefs and terra cottas from that area depicted what seem to be portable tent-shrines of the kind carried by camels. On this basis the *qubbah* would appear to have been in use among the Palmyrenes in the early centuries of the Christian era. Although these parallels were comparatively late, Cross and Bright felt sufficient confidence in the ancient tradition preserved by this evidence

---

[26] *FSAC*, pp. 271f. For criticisms of his position see T. J. Meek, *JBL*, LXI (1942), p. 34; M. Burrows, *JQR*, XXXIII (1942-43), pp. 475f.

[27] Cf. H. H. Rowley, *The Rediscovery of the OT*, p. 88; *ET*, LXI (1949-50), pp. 333ff.

[28] E.g. A. Bentzen, *Introduction to the OT* (1948-49), II, p. 34; R. H. Pfeiffer, *Religion in the OT* (1961), p. 77f.

[29] K. Galling, *Exodus* (1939), pp. 128ff.

[30] H. Lammens, *Bulletin de l'Institut Français d'Archéologie Orientale*, XVII (1919), pp. 39ff.

[31] J. Morgenstern, *HUCA*, V (1928), pp. 81ff., XVII (1942-43), pp. 153ff., XVIII (1943-44), pp. 1ff., *The Ark, the Ephod and the "Tent of Meeting"* (1945); cf. E. Nielsen, *VT*, suppl. vol. VII (1959), pp. 61ff.

[32] H. Ingholt, *Berytus* (1936), I, pp. 85ff.

to assign a tent-shrine to the Davidic period, and Albright held that it was captious to refuse a Mosaic date to the Ark of the Covenant and the Tabernacle, since they were of desert origin and in any event foreign to sedentary Canaanite custom.[33]

It should be noted, however, that the nomadic Arabic parallels adduced above are comparatively late and that much earlier evidence for prefabricated religious structures is now available. As Cross has shown,[34] the fragmentary Phoenician histories of Sanchuniathon, dating from the seventh century B.C., referred to a portable shrine drawn by oxen, and a bas-relief dating from the period of Rameses II about 1285 B.C. showed the tent of the divine king deposited in the middle of the Egyptian military encampment.[35] The cultic use of a tabernacle was familiar to the people of Ugarit, as attested by one of the texts that spoke of King Krt practicing certain rituals in a tent,[36] despite the fact that, as Gordon has pointed out, his was an age of roofed houses.[37] Gordon himself adduced this evidence against the idea that the Biblical Tabernacle was a retrospective adaptation of the Temple to pre-Solomonic times as maintained by the Wellhausenian school. The Ugarit sources may well indicate that the Canaanite deity El could have had some such portable shrine as a regular feature of his cult in the Amarna Age,[38] and if this was actually the case it would reflect the practices of a prior nomadic phase in Canaan.

Examples of even earlier prefabricated structures from Egypt have been collected by Kitchen,[39] the most outstanding of which was the splendid portable bed-canopy of Queen Hetepheres I dated about 2600 B.C.[40] It consisted of beams at the top and bottom which were separated by means of vertical rods and corner posts on three sides of a rectangle. The beams and rods were fitted together by means of tenon joints in such a manner that it could be erected and dismantled very quickly, as with the Hebrew Tabernacle. In addition, the structure was overlaid with gold leaf, and had hooks for the hanging of draperies. The prevalence of such canopies in ancient Egypt between 2850 and 2200 B.C. has been indicated by a number of sculptures from the Fourth, Fifth, and Sixth Dynasties in tomb-chapels[41] as well as by the recovery

[33] F. M. Cross, *BA*, X, No. 3 (1947), pp. 45ff. *BHI*, pp. 146f. *FSAC*, p. 266.
[34] *BA*, X, No. 3 (1947), pp. 55, 60f.
[35] Ch. Kuentz, *La Bataille de Qadech* (1928-34), pls. 34, 39, 42.
[36] *The Legend of Krt*, 159; *UL*, pp. 66ff.
[37] *UL*, pp. 5f.
[38] Cf. W. F. Albright, *BASOR*, No. 91 (1943), pp. 39ff., No. 93 (1944), pp. 23ff.
[39] K. A. Kitchen, *The Tyndale House Bulletin*, Nos. 5-6 (1960), pp. 8ff.
[40] Cf. W. S. Smith, *The Art and Architecture of Ancient Egypt* (1958), pls. 30a, 34; L. Cottrell, *The Lost Pharaohs* (1950), p. 128, fig. 23.
[41] G. A. Reisner and W. S. Smith, *A History of the Giza Necropolis* (1955), II, p. 14.

of canopy poles in fragmentary condition from a royal tomb of the First Dynasty at Saqqara.[42]

An analogous specifically religious structure, dating from the third millennium B.C. in Egypt, was the "Tent of Purification," to which the bodies of deceased royalty and high court officials were taken for ritual purification before and after the processes of embalming. As depicted in the scene from the walls of Old Kingdom tombs, these portable buildings were made from a framework of vertical pillars linked by means of horizontal bars, and surrounded by hangings of cloth.[43]

From the Eighteenth and Nineteenth Dynasties, the period of the sojourn of the Israelites in Egypt, come other illustrations of the ancient tabernacle principle. At Karnak, Tuthmosis III erected a stone structure about 1470 B.C. in the huge temple of Amun, which was in effect a replica of a large tent-shrine supported on the traditional wooden pillars.[44] From the tomb of Tutankhamun, about 1340 B.C, was found a complete set of four prefabricated coverings overlaid with gold leaf, which were placed concentrically over the coffins of the dead king.[45] These rectangular shrines were carefully fitted together by means of mortice and tenon joints and assembled in the royal burial chamber.

In view of this evidence there seems to be no adequate reason for denying the existence of a structure such as the Tabernacle to the Hebrews of the Mosaic period. Against the older objection that the Hebrews of that era did not possess the skills necessary for fabricating a structure comparable to that described in Exodus,[46] it need only be remarked that the Egyptians placed a high value upon Semitic craftsmanship in precious metals when it came to exacting tribute from subjugated areas of Syria and Palestine, as illustrated by a number of tomb-scenes.[47]

In their turn the discoveries at Ras Shamra have necessitated a drastic revision of the views of traditional Wellhausenism with regard to the evolutionary nature of Canaanite religion.[48] No longer is it permissible

---

[42] W. B. Emery, *Great Tombs of the First Dynasty* (1949), I, p. 58, fig. 30.

[43] As pictured in A. M. Blackman, *Rock Tombs of Meir* (1952), V, pls. 42, 43.

[44] J. Lange and M. Hirmer, *Egypt: Architecture, Sculpture, Painting in 3000 Years* (1956), pls. 137, 138, 139.

[45] As pictured in P. Fox, *Tutankhamūn's Treasure* (1951), pls. 18, 21.

[46] So S. R. Driver, *The Book of Exodus* (1911), pp. 426f.; A. H. McNeile, *The Book of Exodus* (1917), p. lxxxi.

[47] D. J. Wiseman, *Illustrations from Biblical Archaeology* (1958), p. 34, fig. 29.

[48] Much of the reason why Wellhausen repudiated the Biblical tradition concerning such cultic objects as the Ark of the Covenant and the Tabernacle lay in the fact that they did not conform to his idea of how the cult developed. It would be permissible to argue, as Wellhausen and his followers did, towards a rigid unilinear development of Hebrew religious institutions if it were also possible to grant the validity of the *a priori* evolutionary concepts of Hegelianism. Unfortunately Wellhausen based his theories on the developmental *Zeitgeist* of the nineteenth

to conceive of Baal in a developmental fashion as a spirit that became associated with a particular locality and ultimately came to discharge the functions of a vegetation deity. In the same way, a careful study of the Baal epic and other literary sources from Ugarit has made it evident that it is impossible to regard the title "Baal" as a generic name for a host of local deities each of which exercised jurisdiction over an allotted extent of territory.

It has now become plain that Baal was accorded the status of a "High God" in the cult-worship because of his prominence in the Canaanite pantheon. He was in fact venerated as a cosmic deity who wielded executive power, and who was worshipped in various communities under his own name or under the designation Hadad, the god of wind and storm.[49] Descriptions of Canaanite religion prior to the discovery of the Ugaritic material which pictured it as a primitive form of nature-worship having little or nothing in the way of a priesthood or organized ritual, are now known to be completely inadequate. The Ras Shamra literary material has shown that, while Canaanite religious beliefs and practices exhibited an appalling depravity, the cult possessed an elaborate pantheon that compared favorably with those of the Babylonians, Egyptians, or Hittites, and was characterized by a highly organized priesthood which functioned at a great many temples and shrines throughout Canaan. Some indication of the virility of this degenerate religion can be

---

century, and reinforced his arguments from biological concepts like those fostered by Darwin and Wallace. A closer comparison of historical processes indicates that, instead of pursuing an unfaltering unilinear course, they are apt to swing with an oscillatory movement that is sometimes as vigorous as it is unpredictable; cf. *ARI*, pp. 107f., 204 n. 37. Again, arguments from the field of biological study would be valuable as analogies, provided that the biological concepts themselves were completely assured. Unfortunately the Darwinian theory of organic evolution is as replete with incorrect premises and faulty conclusions as is the Graf-Wellhausen theory of Pentateuchal origins. Thus Darwin assumed that his self-motivating, self-developing scheme of organic evolution known as "Natural Selection" would demonstrate conclusively that organisms became progressively more complex and highly differentiated as a result of slow, almost imperceptible variations over a prolonged period of time. However, as Haldane has pointed out, the usual course followed by an evolving line has been one of degeneration; *The Causes of Evolution* (1932), p. 167. The fallacy of the Darwinian unilinear developmental hypothesis was demonstrated conclusively by Leo Berg, who assembled a vast amount of evidence from zoology, botany, and palaeontology to show that the development of organisms was based on law, not on chance variation as Darwin had assumed, and that it progressed by violent leaps, major mutations and paroxysmal movements rather than by slow and almost unnoticeable variations; *Nomogenesis* (1926), pp. 19 *et al.* In the light of this evidence alone it merely remains to be said that, although it may have been considered valid in the nineteenth century for one unproved empirical hypothesis to invoke a related but equally undemonstrated conjectural theory for support, such a procedure can no longer be entertained methodologically in the light of a far vaster range of knowledge.

[49] *ARI*, pp. 73f.; *BPAE*, pp. 26f.; *FSAC*, pp. 230f.

gathered from the fact that certain aspects of its rituals even succeeded in infiltrating the highly conservative religions of Egypt and Babylonia, where they were identified with their local cultic counterparts. Despite the fundamental importance of the Ugaritic discoveries both for establishing the true nature of Canaanite cult-worship and for providing an instructive background to the religion of the pre-exilic Hebrews, there are still some writers, such as Kaufmann, who tend to minimize or underestimate the basic depravity of Canaanite religion.

As Albright has shown, the traditions concerning the nature of Hebrew cultic personnel have been complicated by certain entirely gratuitous assumptions.[50] The orthodox Wellhausenian view was that, since the place that the High Priest occupied in the cultic activity of the monarchy was comparatively insignificant, there was in fact no High Priest in the period of the Judges, and Biblical statement to the contrary reflected the editorial extrapolation and theological interests of a much later period.[51] It is now known that the ancient Egyptians assigned great importance to the position of High Priest both during and after the fifteenth century B.C. In the Twenty-First Dynasty, the highest officials of the country under the pharaoh included the High Priest of Amun of Karnak, and the Viziers for Upper and Lower Egypt;[52] in the time of Hatshepsut, the Vizier for Upper Egypt was also the High Priest of Amun. At Ugarit, the cultus was headed by a High Priest during the Amarna Age, and he carried the designation of *rabbu kahinima* or "chief of the priests."[53] In view of the latter circumstance it hardly appears necessary to derive the Hebrew word כהן or "priest" from Arabic sources as Wellhausen did, since the term was most probably of Canaanite origin.[54] The fact that the Biblical writings purporting to come from the Judges period spoke only of the High Priest as "the priest" is merely a reflection of Akkadian usage, as Albright has pointed out.[55] In reality the figure of the High Priest is far removed from the Wellhausenian concept of a royal personage who mirrored the functions of the post-exilic religious leaders, for it reflects instead the conditions of the military encampment of the wilderness period, which was subservient to the authority of Moses, not of Aaron.[56] There is thus no reason for denying the priest at Shiloh the eminence attributed to him by the Biblical narratives, nor is there

[50] *ARI*, pp. 107f.
[51] W. Robertson Smith and A. Bertholet, *EB*, III, cols. 3837ff.
[52] Cf. G. Lefebvre, *Histoire des Grands Prêtres d'Amon de Karnak jusqu'à la XXIe Dynastie* (1929); G. A. Reisner, *JEA*, VI (1920), pp. 28ff., 73ff.
[53] *FSAC*, p. 282.
[54] Cf. G. B. Gray, *Sacrifice in the OT* (1925), p. 183; A. Haldar, *Associations of Cult Prophets Among the Ancient Semites* (1945), pp. 162ff.
[55] *ARI*, p. 108.
[56] *KRI*, pp. 184ff.

407

adequate ground for refusing to consider the Tabernacle as essential to Hebrew religious activity during the Judges period.[57]

Indeed, as Albright has remarked, the only reason for the Well-hausenian school's consistent disregard or rejection of the straightforward Biblical account of the central Tabernacle at Shiloh was that it did not fit into their theory of the progressive centralization of the cult.[58] It is true, of course, that there was a comparative lack of emphasis upon the office of the High Priest during the monarchy, but when the kingdom collapsed with the exile, the High Priesthood rose once again to a position of prestige. While recognizing the problems associated with the origin of the Levites, Albright concluded that they had first a functional, and subsequently a tribal significance.[59] He also accepted the historicity of Aaron, and held that there was no adequate reason for not considering Zadok in the Aaronic line, in contrast to the opinion of Rowley,[60] who regarded Zadok as a Jebusite priest of the pre-Davidic Jerusalem sanctury of Nehushtan.

D. The Sacrificial System

No discussion of the religion of Israel would be complete without some mention of the sacrificial system. Scholars have adduced many parallels from neighboring peoples in an attempt to explain Israelite sacrifice. Robertson Smith employed pre-Islamic nomadic Arab sources to reconstruct a theoretical "Semite" for whom the sacrificial meal, involving some kind of communion with the deity, constituted the original sacrificial form.[61] The "pan-Babylonian" school, which flourished at the turn of the twentieth century, looked to the higher civilization of Mesopotamia for the origin of sacrifice, and stressed the developed ritual of propitiatory sacrifice which was practiced there,[62] apparently unaware that the Babylonian rituals lacked the moral and religious characteristics of expiation found in Hebrew sacrifice. Theories of Canaanite origin for the Hebrew rituals were favored by Dussaud, who discovered parallels in the Carthaginian sacrificial tariffs and, more particularly, in the Ugaritic

---

[57] Cf. Josh. 18:1; 1 Sam. 2:22, *et al.*

[58] *FSAC*, p. 282.

[59] *ARI*, pp. 109f.; cf. T. J. Meek, *Hebrew Origins* (1960 ed.), pp. 121ff.; R. de Vaux, *Les Institutions de l'Ancien Testament* (1960), II, pp. 195ff.

[60] *JBL*, LVIII (1939), pp. 113ff.

[61] W. Robertson Smith, *Encyclopaedia Britannica* (1886), XXI, pp. 32ff., *Lectures on the Religion of the Semites* (1894 ed.), pp. 54, 256, 360, following J. Wellhausen, *Prolegomena to the History of Israel* (1885), pp. 62ff.

[62] Cf. P. Haupt, *JBL*, XIX (1900), p. 61; H. Winckler, *Religionsgeschichtlicher und Geschichtlicher Orient* (1906), pp. 20ff.; J. Jeremias, *EB*, IV, col. 4120; A. Jeremias, *The OT in the Light of the Ancient East* (1911), II, p. 49.

texts.[63] With the publication of this material the so-called Myth and Ritual school stressed the sedentary background even more firmly, and the result was a developed pattern of myth and ritual centered in the person of the king.[64]

The first serious suggestion in critical circles that the beginnings might go back as far as the nomadic patriarchs was made by Alt, who argued from Nabataean and Palmyrene Arab veneration of the "gods of the fathers" to the principle that the patriarchs had engaged in a form of monolatrous worship of clan-deities expressed syncretistically by the phrase "the god of Abraham, the god of Isaac, and the god of Jacob."[65] Whereas Maag thought that the *zebhaḥ* or sacrificial communion meal predominated at that time, Vriezen maintained that the *'ōlāh* or burnt offering was more common, a position supported to some extent by Genesis 22:7.[66] When Jacob journeyed to Egypt (Gen. 46:1) he offered slain sacrifices (זבחים), probably of an expiatory variety; and subsequent generations were called to similar sacrifice in the wilderness (Exod. 5:3), which necessitated the use of animal victims and which was differentiated from the kind offered by the Egyptians (Exod. 8:26).

In contrast to the current trends in Old Testament scholarship, which have placed little emphasis upon the personality or work of Moses in relationship to the origin of the developed sacrificial system in the Pentateuch, the uniform witness of Biblical tradition saw the entire pattern of cultic sacrifice as divinely imposed through the agency of Moses. In addition to the three festive occasions prescribed in the Book of the Covenant (Exod. 23:15f.), a number of others were entertained as part of Israelite life, and some of these celebrations (e.g. Judg. 6:25ff.; 11:30ff.; 1 Sam. 1:3) were evidently of non-Mosaic origin. A wealth of detail surrounds the legislation for sacrificial offerings in the Mosaic code, but for practical purposes they could be divided into two groups, animal and vegetable.

Flour, cakes, parched corn, and libations of wine for the drink offerings constituted the normal vegetable sacrifices and were frequently offered in conjunction with the thanksgiving made by fire (Lev. 4:10-21; Num. 5:11; 28:7-15). Acceptable animals were unblemished oxen, sheep, and goats, not under eight days old and not normally older than three

---

[63] R. Dussaud, *Le sacrifice en Israël et chez les Pheniciens* (1914), p. 7; cf. S. Langdon, *JBL*, XXIII (1904), pp. 80ff.; Dussaud, *Revue de l'Histoire des Religions*, CVI (1932), pp. 285ff., *Les découvertes de Ras Shamra et l'Ancien Testament* (1937), pp. 109ff.

[64] S. H. Hooke, *Myth and Ritual* (1933), pp. 1ff., *The Origins of Early Semitic Ritual* (1938).

[65] A. Alt, *Der Gott der Väter*, pp. 67ff.; cf. V. Maag, *VT*, suppl. vol. VII (1960), pp. 131ff.; cf. H. H. Rowley, *Worship in Ancient Israel* (1967), pp. 14f.

[66] V. Maag, *VT*, VI (1956), pp. 14ff.; T. C. Vriezen, *An Outline of OT Theology* (1958), p. 26; cf. R. J. Thompson, *Penitence and Sacrifice in Early Israel outside the Levitical Law* (1963), p. 66, *NBD*, pp. 1114f.

years. In cases of poverty, doves could be offered as a sacrifice (Exod. 12:5; Lev. 5:7; 9:3f.), but wild animals and fishes were not acceptable, and human sacrifice was expressly prohibited (Lev. 18:21; 20:25). The offerings were presented to the officiating priests in the outer court of the sanctuary, but occasionally were sacrificed elsewhere (Judg. 2:5; 1 Sam. 7:17). In all such ritual procedures, whether animal or vegetable, the worshipper had to present himself in a state of ritual purity (Exod. 19:14). During animal sacrifice the worshipper identified himself with his offering by laying his hand upon it and dedicating it to the purposes of atonement through vicarious sacrifice, subsequent to which the blood was sprinkled near the altar. On the Day of Atonement the collective sins of inadvertence on the part of the nation were confessed and forgiven, and on that occasion only the priest entered the Most Holy Place. The Hebrew sacrificial system was intended only for sins of inadvertence, accident, ceremonial defilement, and the like, and there could be no atonement for transgressions committed in a spirit of sheer obduracy (Num. 15:30). A more detailed survey of the various kinds of sacrificial offerings and the prescriptions concerning them will be undertaken subsequently in the present work.

E. THE RELIGION OF THE MONARCHY

The period of the Judges, which saw continuous national idolatry characterized by an alarming degree of Canaanite religious infiltration, was followed by an abrupt change in the pattern of Hebrew religious life. Throughout the reigns of Saul and David, and for the early part of the Solomonic regime, there emerged a period of loyalty to the Deity of the Sinaitic Covenant in which serious attempts were made to suppress the idolatrous practices of Canaanite cult-worship. The Davidic dynasty was confidently expected to usher in a new era of Israelite life of an enduring quality (2 Sam. 7:5ff.), because it was firmly rooted in loyalty to the God of the Covenant.

Probably the most characteristic religious feature of the period was the erection of the Temple at Jerusalem in the early days of Solomon. From the available evidence there can be no doubt that Phoenician skill was drawn upon heavily in the design and building of the Temple, although the general pattern of the wilderness Tabernacle was basic to the structure. Similar sanctuaries, reflecting strong Phoenician influence and built between 1200 and 900 B.C., have been unearthed in different parts of northern Syria, particularly at Tell Tainat (Hattina). Columns such as the two free-standing pillars known as Jachin and Boaz were a common architectural feature in Syrian shrines of the first millennium B.C., and at a later time they occurred in Assyrian and western Mediterranean temples also. The copper laver of the wilderness period (Exod. 3:17ff.) was replaced by an elaborate metal basin fashioned from bronze, and resting upon four groups of four bronze oxen oriented in terms of the compass points. There are reasons for thinking that the basin had mythological associations, and it may be that the removal of the oxen from the pedestal by Ahaz (2 Kgs. 16:17) was an attempt to repudiate these connections with paganism.[67] The cherubim or winged sphinxes, made from olive wood and overlaid with gold leaf, were a characteristic Syro-Phoenician decoration, while the latticed windows placed near the ceiling of the Holy Place were also a feature of Phoenician architecture.

The tradition that associated music and psalmody with the Davidic age generally has been verified by archaeological discoveries, which show decisively that for centuries previously the people of Palestine had been renowned for their musical interests. Palestinian nomads on a visit to Egypt were depicted in the Beni Hasan tableau as walking behind their animals to the accompaniment of music.[68] Other Egyptian sources from 1550 B.C. refer to examples of Canaanite music,[69] while Ugaritic texts are replete with religious poetry, some of it being distinctly parallel in phraseology to the Hebrew Psalter. From the same sources come references to a class of temple personnel known as "sarim,"[70] who closely resembled the Hebrew singers of the monarchy and later periods. The Biblical writings indicate that some of the servants of David who functioned in this manner possessed Canaanite names, for example, Chalcol and Darda (1 Kgs. 4:31; 1 Chron. 2:6). They bore the designation "Sons of Mahol," that is to say, members of the orchestral guild, and were regarded as native Canaanites.[71] Excavations at Megiddo uncovered one plaque inlaid with ivory, showing a royal personage seated on a throne and drinking from a small bowl. His attendants included a musician, who stood before him plucking the strings of a lyre.[72]

With the later days of Solomon came a resurgence of Canaanite idolatry, and when the kingdom began to function as two separate units, the breach between the religious life of the north and south was accentuated. According to references in Kings, the initiator of idolatry in the north was Jeroboam ben Nebat, who set up golden calves in Bethel and Dan, instituted a non-Levitical priesthood, and appointed a new festival to be celebrated in the eighth month (1 Kgs. 12:26ff.; 14:9). The denunciation of the calves by Ahijah, the prophet from Shiloh, is not a late and biased viewpoint as some would imagine,[73] but a contemporary judgment that saw in the infamous calves the establishing in the north of a

---

[67] Cf. *ARI*, pp. 148f.; *KRI*, p. 268.

[68] *LAP*, p. 83.

[69] *ARI*, pp. 125ff.

[70] C. H. Gordon, *Ugaritic Handbook* (1955), p. 272, No. 1934; cf. No. 1991.

[71] *ARI*, p. 210 n. 96. The term אזרח in Exod. 12:19, 48; Num. 9:14; 1 Kgs. 5:11, *et al.* means "aboriginal," "a native of the place."

[72] *WBA*, p. 94.

[73] So *KRI*, p. 270.

counterpart to Egyptian bull-worship as a means of rivalling the spiritual influence of the Temple in Jerusalem.

It has been suggested by certain scholars that Jeroboam was governed to some extent by the cultic traditions of the Canaanites, Arameans, and Hittites in formulating his own religious patterns. Albright has shown that these peoples invariably depicted their deities as seated on a throne borne on the backs of animals or standing upright on such beasts.[74] On this basis the calves made by Jeroboam may perhaps have been winged, and as such may merely have constituted variant forms of the cherub. Consequently, this suggestion continues, they were only the vehicle of deity and not an actual representation of the god.[75] Insofar as he adopted this motif, Jeroboam intended the bulls to represent the pedestal upon which the invisible deity stood, rather than constituting objects of veneration in themselves, although they may have ultimately been regarded as such.

This theory appears plausible enough at first sight in view of the introduction of Canaanite cult-objects, fertility grove rituals, high places for pagan deities, and other forms of gross idolatry into the religion of the northern kingdom. However, it is important to note that Jeroboam I was under no illusions regarding the nature of the images that he had fashioned, for he spoke of them as "thy gods, Israel, which brought thee up out of the land of Egypt" (1 Kgs. 12:28) and deliberately offered sacrifices to the calves as deities in Bethel (1 Kgs. 12:32). That other Israelites adopted precisely the same attitude towards the calves is made plain by Hosea, who said of the Samarian idol, "A workman made it; it is not God" (Hos. 8:6). These considerations, which reflect different phases of contemporary opinion in Israel on the subject, seem much nearer to the facts than the speculations of Albright and his followers.

The basic reason for contemporary denunciations of the religious practices current in the northern kingdom (1 Kgs. 13:1ff.; 14:14ff.) is that bull-worship encouraged the syncretism of *YHWH*-veneration with the depraved fertility cult of Baal, and as such posed a serious threat to the entire ethic of the Sinai Covenant. As far as the religion of the northern kingdom was concerned, the royal cult instituted by Jeroboam set the pattern for all successive reigns. As the memory of the Sinai Covenant and its implications became progressively diminished, the dissolute cultic exercises of Canaan gained a stranglehold upon the worship of the northern kingdom. Society disintegrated increasingly, and with the perversion of justice came a whole host of social iniquities.[76]

[74] *FSAC*, pp. 299f.; cf. *WBA*, pl. 97.
[75] Cf. H. Th. Obbink, ZAW, XLVII (1929), pp. 268f.
[76] J. Bright, *IDB*, II, p. 565; *BHI*, pp. 241ff.

F. The Prophets and Later Judaism

To a lesser extent the southern kingdom of Judah suffered from the oscillation between periods of religious laxity that encouraged Canaanite idolatry, and the attempts to institute a thoroughgoing reformation of national worship. The rise of the literary prophets marked a resurgence of the Covenant faith, and brought a new vitality to the old religious tenets. As Bright has correctly observed, these prophets are not to be described, as has often been done, in terms of great spiritual pioneers who discovered ethical monotheism.[77] On the contrary, it is now clear that they were heirs to a spiritual tradition that was already centuries old. Their attacks upon the social and religious abuses of the day were made in the light of the Covenant provisions that themselves were firmly rooted in the historical past of the nation. The eighth- and seventh-century B.C. prophets added nothing that was specifically new and distinctive to the traditional *Torah* or "teaching," but instead concentrated upon a re-examination or a fresh interpretation of Mosaic tenets. In this way it was possible for the empirical ethical monotheism of the Mosaic age to be proclaimed in an elaborated form with vigor and conviction by the prophet Isaiah, who made explicit for his day that which was already implicit in the older religious tradition.[78]

As the last days of Judah approached, it fell to the prophets to meditate upon the process of divine justice. Jeremiah held no hope for the nation since the provisions of the Covenant had been broken. He rejected outright the superstitions of popular religion, which clung blindly to the permanence of the Jerusalem Temple and the dynasty of David (Jer. 7:1ff.; 21:12ff.), claiming instead that God had renounced His Temple and abandoned the sinful nation to its doom. While Jeremiah rejected the official cult, he prepared the people for the ordeal of spiritual survival in Babylonia without tangible cult-objects by insistence upon character and motive in relation to both worship and life (Jer. 4:4). He maintained that, by an act of divine clemency and grace, a new and purified people would emerge from the ordeal of exile, upheld spiritually by the promise of a New Covenant (Jer. 31:31ff.), and freed from the destructive claims of a pagan faith.

The non-sacrificial type of worship that Jeremiah had contemplated became a reality among the exiled Jews in Babylonia. Under the uncompromising leadership of Ezekiel they were directed to a rigid monotheism and a high standard of personal and social morality. It was due in no small measure to the efforts and example of Ezekiel that pagan practices ceased to all intents and purposes among the Jews in Babylonia, whereas their Egyptian counterparts, who had disregarded the warnings of Jeremiah, continued to indulge in syncretistic observances of a distinctly

[77] J. Bright, *IDB,* II, p. 566.
[78] Cf. G. W. Anderson, *OTMS,* p. 290.

pagan character. Since the Babylonian Jews were unable to participate in the worship of the cultus as in former days, the exile marked an important turning-point in their religious development. Open-air meetings by the Kabar irrigation-canal replaced gatherings in the Temple and its precincts; a non-sacrificial worship emphasized confession, fasting, prayer, and the reading of the Law, and initial improvisations were developed to the point where the faithful community aimed at as great a spiritual differentiation from the pagan Babylonians as was possible. With the development of house-gatherings and the increased importance attached to the knowledge and observance of the Torah, there was laid the basis for subsequent synagogue-worship, an institution that owes its origin to the diligence of Ezekiel.[79]

With the return from exile and the building of the Second Temple came the growth of Judaism proper. It assumed the characteristic form of a theocracy, in which the divine will was proclaimed to the commonwealth through the mediation of the priesthood. The emphasis upon the Covenant, the Torah, and other distinctively Jewish institutions was of material assistance in repudiating the incursions of Hellenism, although at the same time it stimulated tension between the particularistic and universalistic insights of the ancient faith. Careful attention to ritual requirements in worship was held to constitute an invaluable safeguard against any further infiltrations of paganism, although none of the post-exilic prophets ever suggested that correct ritual performances could be regarded as an acceptable substitute for proper moral and spiritual attitudes.

Characteristic of developed Judaism was the emphasis laid upon the keeping of the Torah. To clarify obscurities in the written Law to make it more applicable to certain tangible situations, there grew up a corpus of oral law which gradually acquired a degree of veneration comparable to that assigned to the Mosaic enactments. This traditional law was also employed to safeguard the provisions of the Torah proper, lest they be broken through ignorance or inadvertence. For Judaism, the Law exemplified the ideal concept of a people dedicated to the service of God. While cultic rites never lost their prominence in the post-exilic period, the emphasis in religious activity shifted to the point where Judaism became a religion of the book,[80] in which the highest degree of virtue subsisted in the study and observance of the written Law (cf. Pss. 1:2; 19:7ff.; 119:1ff.). It is this aniconic character, so typical of the age of Moses and so lacking in subsequent eras, recaptured by the stern disciplines of the exile and fostered during the turbulent post-exilic period, which has been perpetuated over the centuries since the dispersion of ancient Judaism to form such a prominent feature of contemporary Jewish faith.

[79] R. K. Harrison, *A History of OT Times* (1957), pp. 197ff.
[80] J. Bright, *IDB*, II, p. 570.

Part Seven

OLD TESTAMENT THEOLOGY

I. THE HISTORY OF OLD TESTAMENT THEOLOGY

A. PRIOR TO THE EIGHTEENTH CENTURY

Until the beginning of the eighteenth century, Old Testament theology was subsumed under the wider study of Christian dogmatic theology. The progressive unfolding of divine truth in the Old Testament was viewed in the light of the Christian dispensation; the Law was considered a shadow of good things to come (Heb. 10:11). Consequently, theological interpretations of the Old Testament tended to presuppose the conclusions of Christian dogmatists and were confined mainly to looking to the Hebrew Scriptures for support or confirmation of the particular concepts under consideration.

While the earliest Christians cherished the text of the Old Testament, particularly in its Greek form, as their Bible, they tended to interpret it along apocalyptic lines.[1] Because of the far-reaching differences between the oriental Semitic mind and the culture of the Hellenistic world, the early Christians recognized that not all the concepts expressed in the Old Testament were in absolute harmony with the outlook of the nascent Christian era.[2] This divergence of standpoint received fresh emphasis when the works of the Law were set in contradistinction to the character of divine grace, as in the theology of Paul. Further accentuation of this distinction came from the increasing spread of the Christian Church into the Gentile world. Nonetheless, the primitive Christians were committed to a loyal acceptance of the Old Testament teachings because of their adherence to the concept of the verbal inspiration and inerrancy of both its Hebrew and Greek texts.

A further problem arose when heretical doctrine began to make an impact on Christian thought. Marcion's repudiation of the Old Testament led a great many Christians to minimize the alleged differences between the two Testaments, and to explain the Old Testament in a symbolic or allegorical manner. When this procedure was ridiculed by the Gnostics it became necessary to emphasize the Incarnation as the

---

[1] E. Stauffer, *Die Theologie des NT* (1947), pp. 2ff.
[2] Cf. R. M. Grant, *Interpretation,* V (1951), pp. 186ff.

focal point in the revealed scheme of divine salvation. This approach saw the Mosaic covenant and the redemptive act of Christ on Calvary as marking appropriate stages in the historical process. Thus Irenaeus was able to balance the different emphases of the Old and New Testaments and at the same time insist upon the fundamental unity of the divine plan for the salvation of humanity.[3]

The rise of this kind of apologetic made it increasingly difficult for the Christian Church to treat the Old Testament as an object of legitimate historical study. The dogmaticians needed the allegorical method of Old Testament interpretation for attacks upon Gnosticism and pagan doctrines in general. This method was carried to its greatest point of development by the Alexandrian school of exegetes, who under Philonic influence strove to discover in the Old Testament all the Christian dogmas in allegorical or figurative form. Clement of Alexandria stressed the existence of hidden truths behind the literal verbal forms;[4] Origen argued from the presence of discrepancies and textual difficulties to the presence of an underlying spiritual truth.[5]

At Antioch a divergent form of interpretation arose in opposition to that of Alexandria. Following the tradition of Bishop Theophilus, who flourished about A.D. 180, the Antiochene school studied the grammar and syntax of the Hebrew and Greek texts, and eschewed the allegorical method in favor of a literal interpretation of the Scriptural writings. In consequence the Antiochene expositors gained a much more balanced insight into the historical nature of the Old Testament revelation. Under Diodorus of Tarsus (A.D. 330-392), close attention was given to the study of Israelite history with a view to discerning the genuine meaning of the extant text, and this tradition was continued to a greater or lesser degree in the writings of Theodore of Mopsuestia and John Chrysostom.

In the west, Jerome was influenced to a considerable extent by the Antiochene school, as exemplified by his interest in the original text of the Old Testament that his task of translating the Scriptures required. Although this period of ecclesiastical history was not characterized by historical criticism,[6] Jerome followed the Antiochenes in attempting to study the text of Scripture from an accredited historical standpoint. With that school he also acknowledged the existence of typological meanings that transcended the bare form of the words themselves.

When Augustine broke with Manichaean canons of Scriptural interpretation, he adopted the allegorical methods popular in Alexandria. Like Jerome he displayed little interest in critical or historical problems.

---

[3] *Adv. Haer.* IV, 9, 2.
[4] *Strom.* VI, 15, 125ff.
[5] *De Princip.* IV, 2, 9; IV, 3, 1ff.; cf. K. Grobel, *IDB*, II, pp. 719f.
[6] Cf. R. M. Grant, *Journal of Religion*, XXV (1945), pp. 183ff.

Although he was primarily concerned with theological issues, he did not attempt to systematize the doctrinal themes of Scripture. However, he made a concerted effort to envisage the theology of history in Books XV-XVII of his celebrated treatise *The City of God*, but this was undertaken more from the standpoint of the apocalyptic interpretation of an earlier generation than from considerations of historical reality.[7]

Although the way in which the early patristic writers used the text of the Bible was in many senses quite different from that of modern expositors, there can be no doubt that they were Biblical theologians in the best sense of the term. For the most part the Fathers adhered to the Scriptures as a textbook of revealed truth, whose propositions could be used to support their own doctrinal inferences. They accepted the inspiration of Scripture without, however, propounding any particular theory of inspiration.[8] Quite frequently they stated that the Logos or the Spirit spoke through the various authors, but in the main the patristic writers were content to acknowledge the existence of both divine and human agencies without formulating any concept of their interrelationship. Perhaps it was because of the fact of inspiration that the Fathers were prepared to find such depths of mystery in the Bible. Certainly for them there was nothing accidental or irrelevant in the Scriptural record, nothing inherently absurd or trivial, and nothing that could be regarded as unworthy of God himself. The common belief of the Fathers that the Old Testament was in principle a Christian book led to their widespread use of the theory of prefiguration, which for them reinforced the unity of the Biblical revelation. The Old Testament was not so much a "schoolmaster unto Christ" as it was a foreshadowing of spiritual realities that were subsequently to be displayed openly, and therefore Christ was the key that would unlock all the Scriptures. Upon this theoretical basis the exegesis of the Old Testament was undertaken by writers such as Origen, Jerome, Chrysostom, and Augustine. Despite the excesses that resulted from this kind of approach, the Fathers held firmly to the conviction of the primacy and sufficiency of Scripture for both the divine revelation and the salvation of humanity.

During the medieval period the Old Testament was frequently the ground of appeal when Scriptural support was required for the theocratic concept of the Church. A great many Old Testament passages were employed to sustain the dogmas of medieval ecclesiasticism, a purpose to which the exegesis of the text was completely subordinated.[9] Such an approach opened the entire field of Old Testament doctrine to gross subjectivism; and this situation was abruptly challenged by Martin Luther, who emphatically repudiated any suggestion that the interpretation of

---

[7] Cf. E. Jacob, *Theology of the OT* (1958), pp. 15f.
[8] H. E. W. Turner, *The Pattern of Christian Truth* (1954), pp. 260ff.
[9] H. Pope in *St. Thomas Aquinas* (ed. A. Whitacre, 1924), pp. 125ff.

419

Scripture was the prerogative of the pope.[10] However, Luther's theological position allowed him to hold certain books of the Biblical canon in greater esteem than others, and he tended to regard the Old Testament as having been superseded to a large extent, although he was quick to adduce its message in support of the New Testament gospel. Certain of his commentaries on the Old Testament showed that he was well aware of the importance of historical method in the study of Scripture, but despite this recognition he was apparently unable to see in the Old Testament writings anything approaching progression in the content of divine revelation.

Calvin, on the other hand, was convinced that a developing revelation was enshrined in Scripture, although his views had nothing in common with the tenets of a much more modern process-theology. He held that the promise to Adam was the dawning of that bright light that illumined the world at the Incarnation.[11] While agreeing with Luther in preferring the "superior excellence of the New Testament" to that of the Old,[12] Calvin linked the two closely together to present a unified dispensation characterized by the proclamation of the law and the gospel. Although he recognized the presence of typological material in certain of the Old Testament rites, Calvin generally avoided the allegorical method of interpretation in consonance with his belief that the natural and obvious meaning of Scripture was in fact the true one. His pre-eminence as an expositor lay in his expressed purpose to subordinate philological, historical, and other considerations to the one aim of discovering and expounding the divine message as contained in the text.

The progressive character of revelation also received emphasis in the works of another Reformed theologian, Johannes Cocceius (1603-1669), a celebrated Hebrew philologist.[13] He was one of the leading exponents of Covenant theology, and in his *Summa Doctrinae de Foedere et Testamento Dei* (1648) he maintained that the relationship between God and man was as much covenantal in nature before the fall as after it. The *foedus naturale* existed prior to the human fall from grace; and it was succeeded by the *foedus gratiae*, the fulfilment of which necessitated the coming of Christ in the flesh. In consequence the Covenant of grace was unfolded both historically and spiritually, with the result that the destiny of old Israel found its logical conclusion in the growth of the Christian Church. While Cocceius invoked an extensive typology in order to arrive at these conclusions, his approach gave a new direction to Biblical study by showing that it was no longer legitimate to suppose

[10] *Werke*, VI, pp. 388ff.

[11] *Institutes*, II, 11, 20.

[12] *Ibid.*, II, 11, 12.

[13] His most valuable work in this field was his *Lexicon et Commentarius Sermonis Hebraici et Chaldaici* (1669).

420

that the Old Testament was merely a repository of proof-texts for the support of ecclesiastical dogmas. Instead, the Bible as a whole was to be considered as a legitimate object of study in its own right, and as a source that could inform—not merely support—the Christian faith.

The work of J. A. Bengel (1687-1752), the greatest Biblical exegete of the eighteenth century, marked a further stage in the development of an historical interpretation of Scripture. Although his major works were concerned with the New Testament, Bengel stressed the continuity of the Old and New Covenants, holding to the view that Scripture contained a unified dispensational scheme grounded in the history of ancient Israel, which looked for its fulfillment in the mission of the Christian Church. Bengel maintained an independent attitude towards the dogmatic orthodoxy of his time, and arrived at his theological conclusions by applying grammatico-historical rules to the text of Scripture.

A revival of interest in Biblical studies in Germany resulted from the Pietist movement within the Lutheran Church, which gained impetus towards the end of the seventeenth century. The forerunners of Pietism included the theosophic mystic Jakob Boehme (1575-1624) and Johann Arndt (1555-1621). More directly, it arose as a result of the work of Philip Jacob Spener (1635-1705), who combined the Lutheran emphasis on Biblical doctrine with the Reformation appeal for vigorous Christian living. His proposals were embodied in his *Pia Desideria,* or *Earnest Desires for a Reform of the True Evangelical Church* (1675), which maintained that the life of the Church would be enriched by an emphasis upon conversion and sanctification rather than by a mere correctness of doctrine. Although Pietism had waned by the middle of the eighteenth century, its individualistic emphasis helped to prepare the way for new and more radical modes of thought.[14]

B. THE RISE OF RATIONALISM

The influence of European rationalism upon the study of Scripture also assisted in liberating it from the impediments of medieval dogmatism, and in its own way made possible a further stage of development in the growth of Biblical theology as an independent entity. The break with medievalism came with the formulation of a distinction between dogmatic and Biblical theology in 1787 in an academic lecture by Johann Philipp Gabler entitled *Oratio de justo discrimine theologiae biblicae et dogmaticae regundisque recte utriusque finibus.* Whereas dogmatic theology consisted of definite propositions that were held to be delivered by authority and drew upon Scripture for support,[15] Biblical theology, as depicted by Gabler, was considered as an historical science whose pur-

14 For the influence of Pietistic theologians see A. Ritschl, *Geschichte des Pietismus* (1886), III, pp. 62f.
15 Cf. H. Martensen, *Christian Dogmatics* (1866), p. 1.

pose was to describe what the writers of the Old and New Testaments thought concerning divine things.

Biblical theology became from that time on an academic discipline in its own right, but the influence of German rationalism upon its growth was such that the native genius of the ancient Hebrews was seldom permitted to penetrate the rigid and artificial mold imposed upon it by rationalistic philosophy. Although there is a sense in which the rationalist movement can be said to have assisted in the objective and methodical study of the Old Testament writings, the ancient Hebrew Scriptures were generally the object of hostile criticism imposed less by an examination of the sources against an oriental background than by the accepted canons of European philosophical speculation. Typical of this approach was Bauer's *Theologie des Alten Testaments* (1796), which, although it purported to trace the development of religious concepts from the earliest days of the Hebrew people to the beginning of the Christian era, merely succeeded in furnishing a depreciatory evaluation of certain Biblical themes, shaped predominantly by the belief that the pure truth of Scripture had to be disentangled from the local and temporal disguises that it had assumed in the text.

A more historical approach, accompanied by a somewhat greater insight into the essential content of Biblical theology, became evident in the work of De Wette,[16] who based his methodology upon the rationalistic principles expounded by Eichhorn, Geddes, and Vater. De Wette's outlook demonstrated an independence of rationalism at least to the extent that he was able to adopt a more flexible view of historical evolution.[17] At the same time he adduced criticisms of Kantian skepticism concerning metaphysical issues. De Wette followed the contemporary historical pattern, which had come to regard the exile as the division between Hebraism and Judaism; and he was rationalistic in his approach to the extent that he desired to separate dogma from the outmoded forms in which the Bible, and particularly the Old Testament, presented it. De Wette recognized that the Old Testament recorded the history of the Hebrew theocracy and noticed a difference between the Mosaic revelation and its implementation at a later period. He accorded only a limited degree of canonicity to the Old Testament, however, and conceded that the nature of life and thought presented in it was largely strange to the western world.

The theological writings of Schleiermacher—especially his two-volume *Der Christliche Glaube nach den Grundsätzen der Evangelischen Kirche* (1821)—did not recognize De Wette's demand that the Old Testament

[16] W. M. L. De Wette, *Lehrbuch der Christlichen Dogmatik, I: Biblische Dogmatik des Alten und Neuen Testaments* (1813).

[17] O. Pfleiderer, *The Development of Theology in Germany Since Kant and Its Progress in Great Britain Since 1825* (1890), pp. 77ff.

e interpreted in a strictly historical manner. Instead Schleiermacher mphasized the points of divergence between the Old and New Testaents. For Schleiermacher the former was largely polemical, and he ccorded inspiration as commonly understood only to the messianic rophecies. He took the view that the best elements of Old Testament hought, such as monotheism, could also be discovered in Greek philosphy, and he maintained that Christian doctrine would only benefit when he practice of adducing Old Testament proof-texts was abandoned.

A more serious treatment of Hebrew history and religious thought took lace in the writings of Hegel,[18] who in his categorizing of the three eligions of spiritual individuality regarded the Jewish faith as that of xaltedness (*Erhabenheit*). Judaism was not an accident of history, as chleiermacher supposed, but a necessary component in the developent of Christianity, which Hegel regarded as the "absolute religion." Iegelian evolutionism was synthesized with the critical findings of Eichorn and De Wette by Wilhelm Vatke, who in 1835 published the most laborate treatise to that time on the development of Old Testament eligion.[19] Half a century later Wellhausen acknowledged his debt to 'atke's work, declaring that it was the most significant attempt ever nade to understand ancient Israel in strictly historical categories. Vatke naintained the basically unhistorical character of the Mosaic society, nd saw in the Torah the product of a state that was already in xistence. Deuteronomy was held to be one result of the religious reormation initiated by Josiah, and the latest portions of the Pentateuch vere thought to have emerged from the exilic period. Vatke held that he religion of the Hebrews evolved from comparatively primitive and nhistorical beginnings into the monotheistic faith that characterized the eligion of Judaism.

Equally typical of Hegelian idealistic thought was B. Bauer's treatise n the problem of Old Testament revelation.[20] He interpreted religion in erms of divine self-consciousness, which was in the process of evolution o more highly differentiated levels. Its fullest development could only e attained when all obstacles to growth were overcome, at which time he content of the history of revelation would become apparent. Since eligion was essentially historical, it too passed through various stages in n ascending pattern, and this was motivated by the degree of antithesis hat any particular stage of religious development exhibited in relationhip to the ultimate goal.

[18] Especially in his posthumous *Philosophy of Religion*. Cf. K. Fischer, *Geschichte der neueren Philosophie* (1909), VIII, 2, pp. 985f.

[19] W. Vatke, *Die Biblische Theologie wissenschaftlich dargestellt, I, Die Religion des AT nach den kanonischen Büchern entwickelt* (1835).

[20] B. Bauer, *Kritik der Geschichte der Offenbarung, I, Die Religion des AT* (1838).

From Hengstenberg, a contemporary of Schleiermacher at Berlin, came a reaction against the higher critical views of Eichhorn and De Wette, with their concomitant unorthodox theological interpretations. In his study of Christology he adhered firmly to traditional views of the authority of Scripture.[21] While recognizing current theories of the origin and growth of the Hebrew Scriptures, he repudiated vigorously the various divisive theories of the critical school. Although he anticipated later Biblical theologians in his stress upon the fundamental unity of the two Testaments, his meticulous rebuttal of the arguments commonly raised against the Mosaicity of the Pentateuch were out of harmony with the critical tastes of the day; and consequently his theological views were largely ignored outside his own immediate circle.

Within the same general tradition, however, was the work of Hofmann,[22] a New Testament scholar who developed his position against the background of the Old Testament. His purpose was to justify the inspiration and authority of the Bible by the use of historical method rather than by dogmatic pronouncement, and he envisaged the entire Old Testament in terms of "redemptive history" or *Heilsgeschichte*. Hofmann viewed each area in the historical process as carrying within itself the seed of the subsequent period, which it anticipated. For him history and prophecy were intimately related, and he reflected the Hegelian outlook in the course of his maintaining that Jesus Christ was the goal of history. Thus his "history of salvation" constituted an accredited historical process that developed through progressive stages until it attained its terminal phase in the Incarnation of Jesus Christ. Consequently, human salvation was firmly rooted in history, and this demonstration provided a stable foundation upon which a theology of the Old Testament could be erected.

The pattern of the historical presentation of revealed religion that Hofmann had established was continued with marked success by Oehler. In 1845 he published a historical *Prolegomena* as a foundation for his posthumous *Theologie des Alten Testaments* (1873) which quickly became a classic. Like Hofmann, Oehler reflected Hegelian influence in his view that life was a continuum in which the earlier stages could only be understood in terms of the final phase of the entire process. Although he rejected the traditional Christian interpretation of the Old Testament, Oehler held that the Hebrew Scriptures were preparatory to the New Testament and could only be explained ultimately in the light of the Incarnation and Atonement. Oehler maintained that the Old Testa-

---

[21] E. W. Hengstenberg, *Christologie des AT* (3 vols., 1829-35); E. tr. R. Keith, *Christology of the OT* (1836-39). A similar position was maintained by H. A. C. Hävernick, *Vorlesungen über die Theologie des AT* (1848).

[22] J. C. K. von Hofmann, *Weissagungen und Erfüllungen im AT und NT* (2 vols., 1841-44) and *Der Schriftbeweis* (1852).

ment recorded the historical process by which God reconciled the world to Himself; and in consequence his Old Testament theology was basically a theology of history, demonstrating God's progressive manifestation to the world, which ultimately aimed at recapturing for man the pristine spiritual fellowship with God and the gift of eternal life. With this laudable aim in view Oehler proceeded according to a strictly historical interpretation. He refused to assign to the Old Testament authors concepts that had been imposed upon them by later Christian interpreters; yet he viewed the content of their thought as an essential contribution to the growth of Christianity, in which the historical process of revelation culminated. Despite the subjectivity that must inevitably accompany such an approach, Oehler was correct in emphasizing the importance of proper historical method and in rejecting some of the more eccentric interpretations of the Old Testament that had been popular since the time of the Alexandrian school.

Three years before Oehler died, an important contribution to the methodology of Old Testament theological study was made by Diestel, who suggested that the best approach to this problem would be to combine three lines of inquiry which had previously been pursued either singly or in inadequate combination.[23] The first of these was an approach from the purely historico-cultural perspective seeking to set Israel firmly against her Near Eastern background. For Diestel this by itself had resulted in an imbalanced evaluation of Hebrew religious worth. The second involved applying a philosophy of religion in order to estimate the nature and extent of Hebrew spiritual growth. This method had previously been clouded with a good deal of subjectivism. Third, Diestel urged that the eternal verities of Israelite religion should be studied in the light of the *Heilsgeschichte* presented in the Old Testament writings. Diestel's methodological synthesis envisaged the fullest revelation of God in Jesus Christ, and, by implication, the conscious activity of God in human history. He was firm in his insistence that obscurities and apparent discrepancies must not be allowed to interfere with the attainment of the soundest possible historical and spiritual evaluation of the divine self-revelation through ancient Israel, arrived at by using all the means at the disposal of scholarship.

Diestel was far ahead of his time in proposing such a method, for it was nearly three-quarters of a century before scholars began to heed his advice and apply his principles. The Biblical writers of his day were for the most part obsessed with the evolutionary and literary-critical concepts that were to blossom with the work of Graf and Wellhausen. Already the developmental approach was being applied to Old Testament theology in a manner that reduced it to a study of the history of

[23] L. Diestel, *Geschichte des AT in der Christlichen Kirche* (1869).

Hebrew religion,[24] although Schultz followed Oehler in emphasizing th unified nature of the Old Testament as a preparation for the coming (the divine kingdom on earth.[25] The barrenness of eighteenth-centur Old Testament studies began to bear its scant fruit at this time in th increasingly secularized approach to Hebrew history as reflected, fc example, in the writings of Ewald.[26] Curiously enough, the theologic: speculations of Ewald tended to revert to the ecclesiasticism of an earli(age.[27] He maintained that the Bible was but one means of coming t know the divine revelation, and that the fellowship of the Christia Church and the personal practice and experience of the fear of Go were equally valid sources. The Bible was the supreme source (revelation for the Christian Church, but it was merely a means to an en and as such should not be overestimated. In the usual Hegelian mann(Ewald discerned progress in the religious ideas of the Old Testamen and his highest praise for the ancient Hebrew Scriptures was the fa(that they were indispensable to the New Testament revelation. Howeve his general views served to subordinate the Bible to the Christia Church and to individual spiritual experience, as Kraeling has ind cated.[28] As far as Old Testament theology was concerned, his approac came perilously close to the scholastic attitude that regarded the O Testament as a legitimate source of proof-texts to support dogmat pronouncements.

Although Wellhausen's views concerning the nature and developmei of Hebrew religion had great influence on contemporary theological est mates of the Old Testament, not all scholars regarded the development: process in quite the same manner. The moderate critic Ernst Sell stressed that it was in the Mosaic period that the characteristic Hebre religious institutions originated, and he urged that correspondingly le: emphasis should be placed upon the supposed emergence of religiou concepts in the exile and later periods.[29] In conjunction with Kittel he modified the Wellhausenian conception that Hebrew religion ha developed through the popular, prophetic, and priestly stages respe(

[24] E.g. A. Kayser, *Die Theologie des AT im ihrer Geschichtlichen Entwicklu dargestellt* (1886). The 1903 edition, revised by K. Marti, was retitled simp *Geschichte der israelitischen Religion.* Cf. C. Piepenbring, *Théologie de l'Anci Testament* (1886).

[25] H. Schultz, *Alttestamentliche Theologie: Die Offenbarungsreligion auf ihr vorchristlichen Entwicklungsstufe* (1896).

[26] H. Ewald, *Geschichte des Volkes Israel* (5 vols., 1843-55).

[27] H. Ewald, *Die Lehre der Bibel von Gott oder Theologie des Alten und Neu Bundes, I, Die Lehre vom Wort Gottes* (1871).

[28] *The OT Since the Reformation* (1955), p. 86.

[29] E. Sellin, *Beiträge zur israelitischen und jüdischen Religionsgeschichte* vols., 1896); *Die alttestamentliche Religion im Rahmen der andern altorientalisch* (1908).

[30] R. Kittel, *Geschichte des Volkes Israel, II: Das Volk im Kanaan* (1895).

tively, to stress that different levels of religious insight had existed at the same time among the Israelites, and went on to show the nature of the religious conflicts that resulted from this situation. August Dillmann supported the theological position of Oehler and Schultz,[31] but in general the trend among European scholars of that period was to depict the development of Old Testament religion in intimate relationship to the history of the Hebrew people.[32]

The historical standpoint was also prominent in the posthumous work of A. B. Davidson, who denied that there was a theology as such in the Old Testament, and preferred instead to treat his subject as the "history of the religion of Israel as represented in the Old Testament."[33] For Davidson the Old Covenant was not so much a foreshadowing of the New as the introduction of the divine kingdom in embryonic form. The purpose of Old Testament theology, as he saw it, was to exhibit the organic development of the religious life that God sought to stimulate in His ancient people. The truths contained in the Old Testament about the divine kingdom were manifested in terms of the history and religious institutions of Israel. These, however, did not necessarily prefigure the birth of the Christian Church, although the latter constituted the climax of the Old Testament revelation. Davidson's work suffered more than similar treatises on Old Testament theology because it was posthumous. In the earlier part of the book he rejected the traditional division of his subject into theology, anthropology, and soteriology, but at a later stage he accepted this pattern as the basis for formulating his study.[34] Whether this was due to poor editorial work by S. D. F. Salmond (as Porteous has suggested),[35] to the confused state of the manuscript sources left by Davidson, or to the fact that the later adoption of the traditional division represented a substantial change in the opinions of the author, is impossible to say.

C. RECENT STUDIES

It is noteworthy that for the next two decades a theological interpretation of the Old Testament was precluded by the constant emphasis upon the study of Hebrew religious history, and only a very limited number of works succeeded in presenting the religious concepts of the Old Testa-

---

[31] A. Dillmann, *Handbuch der alttestamentlichen Theologie* (1895).

[32] E.g. B. Stade, *Geschichte des Volkes Israel* (2 vols., 1887), *Biblische Theologie des AT, I* (1905); R. Smend, *Lehrbuch der Alttestamentlichen Religionsgeschichte* (1893); E. Riehm, *Alttestamentliche Theologie* (1889); R. V. Foster, *OT Studies: An Outline of OT Theology* (1890); W. H. Bennett, *The Theology of the OT* (1896).

[33] A. B. Davidson, *The Theology of the OT* (1904), p. 11.

[34] *Ibid.*, pp. 30ff.; cf. pp. 12ff.

[35] *OTMS*, p. 315; cf. H. Wheeler Robinson, *ET*, XLI (1929-30), p. 247.

ment as such.[36] A reaction to the critical position towards Old Testa
ment theology came in 1922 with the work of König, a brilliant Hebrais
and long-time opponent of the Wellhausen school.[37] He took a high view
of the reliability of the Old Testament sources, and brought to bear upon
his task the exact historical and grammatical procedures for which he
was renowned. While he did not adhere to the current evolutionary
interpretation of Hebrew history, he did follow the customary pattern of
describing the history of Hebrew religion, after which he dealt systemati
cally with the dominant concepts that helped to shape the Israelite
nation. He firmly rejected anything that seemed to him to savor of
allegorical exegesis, and sought instead for explanations in harmony with
a rational and historical interpretation of the text.

Rudolf Kittel had already called for a systematized presentation of the
religious values of the Old Testament in a theological rather than a
purely historical context, and this challenge was taken up by Steuer
nagel, who in the Marti *Festschrift* attempted to resolve the confusion
between Old Testament theology as such and the history of Old Testa
ment religious concepts, arguing that the former was necessary in order
to comprehend the significance of the data supplied by the latter.[38] A
short article by Otto Eissfeldt in 1926 warned of the inherent dangers in
compounding the historical investigation of Israelite religion with the
view that the faith of the Old Testament was essentially a matter of
divine revelation, as was being attempted by the proponents of dialectic
theology.[39] For him the study of Old Testament theology was a perfect
ly legitimate exercise in itself, although it would be conditioned by the
religious approach of the individual scholar. Eissfeldt explained the
tension between the historical and theological attitudes towards the
investigation by stating that the former constricted the breadth and
depth of the revelation amenable to faith, whereas the latter imposed
limitations upon the diverse nature of the historical data. There were
thus two approaches to the subject: the historical attitude, which was
basically one of inquiry and knowledge, and the outreach of faith, which
saw in the Old Testament writings the true religion of divine revelation.
Since he held that it was impossible to demonstrate revelation as such
within the realm of historical events, it was obviously necessary to keep
both approaches to the problem quite separate. Consequently, the study
of Old Testament theology must be undertaken in a systematic manner

[36] E.g. M. Hetzenauer, *Theologia Biblica, I: Vetus Testamentum* (1908); R. F
Girdlestone, *OT Theology and Modern Ideas* (1909); H. Wheeler Robinson, *Th
Religious Ideas of the OT* (1913); A. C. Knudson, *The Religious Teaching of th
OT* (1918); C. F. Burney, *Outlines of OT Theology* (1920).

[37] E. König, *Theologie des AT kritisch und vergleichend dargestellt* (1922).

[38] Kittel, ZAW, XXXIX (1921), pp. 84ff.; Steuernagel, BZAW, XLI (1925
pp. 266ff.

[39] ZAW, XLIV (1926), pp. 1ff.

rather than in the form of a purely historical presentation so as to present the living truth implicit in the Hebrew Scriptures. The Christian writer, however, need not feel under any obligation to find each central Old Testament theme fulfilled in the New Testament, and where Old Testament concepts did not find such fruition, their literary sources could then be regarded as co-equal in the matter of authority with the New Testament writings.

Unfortunately, Eissfeldt's important contribution ignored the fact that revelation is inextricably connected with the historical process as its given sphere of operation. Therefore any imposed dichotomy between historical investigation and theological interpretation is basically false, if for no other reason than that it would remove faith from the immanent historical situation in a manner completely foreign to the Old Testament *Heilsgeschichte*. If Eissfeldt were correct in insisting upon separating faith and knowledge, Old Testament theology would assume a purely confessional character, a situation that would immediately impose severe restrictions upon the acceptability of the findings. In order for Old Testament theology to have any validity at all as an accredited discipline, it could not be hampered by such limitations. An additional disadvantage to applying Eissfeldt's kind of approach is that the same sort of subjective evaluation that brought such confusion and chaos to the findings of the Graf-Wellhausen school would almost certainly be rampant in the field of Old Testament theology. In sum, if the recommendations of Eissfeldt were followed, two independent branches of study would emerge, one of which would examine the manifold data of Old Testament religion objectively, in a manner acceptable to scholars of any religious persuasion, and the other which would be a purely confessional presentation of Old Testament truths arranged systematically.[40]

In 1929 Walter Eichrodt published an article in which he also devoted some attention to the demands of dialectical theology for something in excess of a mere historical investigation of the phenomena of Hebrew religion.[41] However, he went further than Eissfeldt in asserting that it was the scholar's responsibility to expose the structure of Old Testament religion and demonstrate the interrelationship of its component parts so as to uncover those elements which were constant in Old Testament religion. Eichrodt was aware of the extent to which subjective factors operated in historical research, and he felt that the philosophy of history of the Christian Old Testament student ought to have the New Testament revelation as its goal, so that the principles of selectivity employed by the research worker would be governed accordingly.

Within the next few years a number of books dealing with Old Testament theology were published in Europe. In 1933 Sellin followed

---

[40] Cf. G. von Rad, *Theologische Blätter,* XV (1936), pp. 30ff.
[41] *ZAW,* XLVII (1929), pp. 83ff.

the classical pattern, first rejected and then adopted by Davidson, of dealing successively in his study with the doctrines of theology, anthropology, and soteriology.[42] For Sellin such an investigation of the Old Testament was part of the larger discipline of Christian theology, and accordingly he traced the progress of the religious current from the time of Moses until it reached its highest point of development in the revelation of Jesus Christ. Three years later Köhler followed the same basic pattern, but found that the concept of divine kingship served to unify the Old Testament writings.[43] His treatment was more comprehensive than Sellin's and was notable for the opinion that revelation in the Old Testament constituted a progressive unfolding of many and varied truths, and did not merely consist of one body of doctrine.

W. Eichrodt parted company with the traditional arrangement of doctrinal material.[44] His contribution was important because it seized upon a much-neglected theme, the Covenant, as the central concept from which the basic unity of outlook exhibited in the Old Testament writings derived its impetus. In distinction from the members of the Graf-Wellhausen school, Eichrodt ascribed the Covenant concept to Moses,[45] and asserted that it exercised a consistent influence over all other aspects of Old Testament religion. For Eichrodt, God was not merely the sovereign deity of the Israelite monarchy, but One who by a definite agreement had incorporated the Hebrew people into the Kingdom of God. In his attempt to describe the fundamental unity of Old Testament religion Eichrodt did not neglect the possibility of historical development in Old Testament belief, and stressed that the very incompleteness of the Old Testament at certain stages pointed to the emergence of the New Testament revelation in Christ. However, he regarded the connection between the two Testaments as neither accidental nor purely historical. Rather it was an organic connection resulting from the activity of the one God whose kingdom was founded on the law, prophecy, and the gospel. Eichrodt was doubtless correct in thinking that the Old Testament was not particularly amenable to systematic treatment, and although he only applied his unifying principle to the first volume of the triad, he made it clear that the spiritual values of the Old Testament could be interpreted in terms of religious institutions historically evaluated.

[42] E. Sellin, *Alttestamentliche Theologie auf religionsgeschichtlicher Grundlage*, II: *Theologie des AT* (1933).

[43] L. Köhler, *Theologie des AT* (1935), E. tr. A. S. Todd, *OT Theology* (1957). Cf. Köhler in *Theologische Rundschau*, VII (1935), pp. 255ff., VIII (1936), pp. 55ff., 247ff.

[44] W. Eichrodt, *Theologie des AT*, I (1933), II (1935), III (1939); cf. his *Man in the OT* (1951).

[45] Cf. *JBL*, LXV (1946), pp. 205ff.

Of a very different nature was the work of Wilhelm Vischer, which made no secret of its attempt to discern Christian doctrine in the Old Testament.[46] Vischer's approach had much in common with the historical method, but he tended to look for a typological interpretation as a means of revealing the eternal significance of the material for both Testaments. He attempted to systematize the "eternal truth" of the Old Testament as the foundation for the New Testament revelation of God in Christ, and his work is much the best representative of this school of thought.

The theme that Old Testament religion was in fact a developing living relationship between God and man that was completed with the coming of Christianity had been expounded by Baumgärtel, and was dealt with briefly by Lindblom in an Old Testament symposium.[47] The latter maintained that the concept of deity held by the Hebrews was so unique and central to their faith that it differentiated it from the religions of the surrounding nations. Having compared the Old Testament idea of God with contemporary pagan concepts of deity, Lindblom related it organically to the New Testament doctrine of God. Despite obvious differences in the two ideas, he maintained that much of the Old Testament material regarding God had specific value for the Christian Church, and his emphasis upon the purposiveness of the divine nature led him to the conclusion that God was guiding the world to a specific goal in history.

In the same symposium Artur Weiser stressed the importance of discerning the original meaning of the Old Testament through careful exegesis.[48] The dynamic view of reality evident in the Hebrew Scriptures was bound up with a degree of encounter or some movement that involved a decision of faith. The very nature of this experience precluded a formal systematization of concepts by the Hebrews in terms of a "doctrine" of God. The task of the Old Testament exegete was to relate the existence and the destiny of modern man to analogous situations occurring between men and God in Hebrew history. While the sense of progress towards a goal would be identical, the Christian had the decided advantage of a fuller revelation of the divine nature and will.

The general philosophy of revelation was discussed by Wheeler Robinson in 1938, and was followed by an examination of the characteristic doctrines of God, man, sin, grace, and the judgment of history, from Old Testament sources.[49] A posthumous work by the same author was pub-

---

[46] W. Vischer, *Das Christuszeugnis des AT, I* (1934), *II* (1942); E. tr. of vol. I, *The Witness of the OT to Christ* (1949).

[47] F. Baumgärtel, *Die Eigenart der alttestamentlichen Frömmigkeit* (1932). J. Lindblom in *Werden und Wesen des Alten Testaments* (ed. P. Volz, F. Stummer and J. Hempel, 1936), pp. 128ff.

[48] *Ibid.*, pp. 207ff.; cf. Weiser, ZAW, LXI (1945-48), pp. 17ff.

[49] *Record and Revelation* (1938), pp. 303ff.; cf. his *Redemption and Revelation in the Actuality of History* (1942), pp. 95ff.

lished in 1946, which had been intended as a prolegomenon to a project-ed volume on Old Testament theology, and which developed certain lines of approach indicated by Davidson's *Theology of the Old Testament.*[50] The period between World Wars I and II had witnessed a searching re-evaluation of liberal humanism in Europe and elsewhere. In consequence a number of books emerged that sought to show in varying ways that the essential message of the Old Testament was still strictly relevant to the troubled twentieth century of the Christian era. Those who endeavored to furnish an interpretation of Old Testament theology did so predominantly in terms of the permanent ideas of the Hebrew Scriptures, tacitly abandoning the realm of pure historical criti-cism as largely irrelevant for the purposes in view. The result of this was an increased emphasis upon the nature and relevance of the "abiding values" of the Old Testament for the modern reader.[51]

At the beginning of World War II the Roman Catholic theologian Paul Heinisch pursued the classical dogmatic themes in a systematized account of Old Testament theology.[52] Subsequent publications in Eng-lish continued to stress the relevance of the Old Testament for the modern age, and under the influence of neo-orthodoxy they endeavored —with varying degress of success—to relate the theological interpretation of specific areas of the Old Testament to the original day and age, then to the period covered by the entire Bible, and finally to the culmination of the divine revelation in Jesus Christ.[53] Characteristic of the neo-orthodox movement was the conviction that the pattern of the divine purpose for mankind was unfolded gradually by means of specific creative experiences in the stream of historical events,[54] whose logical culmination occurred in the New Testament.[55]

[50] Robinson, *Inspiration and Revelation in the OT.*

[51] E.g. S. A. Cook, *The OT: A Reinterpretation* (1936); *The "Truth" of the Bible* (1938); H. H. Rowley, *The Relevance of the Bible* (1942); G. E. Wright, *The Challenge of Israel's Faith* (1944); R. B. Y. Scott, *The Relevance of the Prophets* (1944); R. Calkins, *The Modern Message of the Minor Prophets* (1947); C. A. Simpson, *Revelation and Response in the OT* (1947); A. G. Hebert, *The Authority of the OT* (1947); G. P. Baker, *The Witness of the Prophets* (1948); W. A. L. Elmslie, *How Came Our Faith: A Study of the Religion of Israel and Its Significance for the Modern World* (1949).

[52] P. Heinisch, *Theologie des AT* (1940); E. tr. W. G. Heidt, *Theology of the OT* (1955).

[53] Cf. H. Cunliffe-Jones, *The Authority of the Biblical Revelation* (1945).

[54] Cf. H. Wheeler Robinson, *Record and Revelation in the Actuality of History*, pp. 304ff.

[55] Cf. W. J. Phythian-Adams, *The Call of Israel* (1934), *The Fulness of Israel* (1938), *The People and the Presence* (1942); C. H. Dodd, *History and the Gospel* (1938); F. G. Lankard, *The Bible Speaks to Our Generation* (1941); H. Wheeler Robinson, *Redemption and Revelation in the Actuality of History* (1942); H. H. Rowley, *The Rediscovery of the OT* (1946); C. H. Dodd, *The Bible Today* (1946); W. A. Smart, *Still the Bible Speaks* (1948); B. W. Anderson, *Rediscovering the Bible* (1951).

Another posthumous work on Old Testament theology was that of Otto Procksch, which represented the final stage of much earlier study by the author.[56] Following Hofmann he adopted a Christocentric attitude towards history, and like Sellin distinguished the permanent elements of Hebrew thought from the more transient ones in the light of the yardstick supplied by the Christian gospel. Procksch began with a history of Israelite religion, and followed this by a more systematized grouping of concepts in which the divine Covenant was associated in a threefold manner with the people of Israel, with mankind, and ultimately with the world.[57] A similar emphasis upon the fundamental unity of the Old and New Testaments was made by Vriezen, who stressed the importance of the Christocentric interpretation of the Old Testament narratives.[58]

Two American publications issued just after World War II continued the theme of the unity of Scripture. Millar Burrows wrote a manual of practical theological studies on the whole Bible, which, although it did not furnish a particularly vigorous picture of Hebrew religion, at least succeeded in expounding the most important concepts against a background of their original context and significance.[59] The other work, by Otto Baab, recognized the existence of stages of development in Hebrew religion, but regarded these as constituting aspects of the fundamental unity of religious experience in the community of Israel.[60] The major doctrines were discussed in the order commonly employed in dogmatic theology, and in the process Baab was careful to point out the importance of personal spiritual insight for the understanding of Old Testament doctrines.[61]

A reflection of the attitudes of Eichrodt appeared in the writings of another American scholar, R. C. Dentan, who utilized the neo-orthodox concept of revelation to relate the history and ideology of Old Testament religion to that of the New Testament.[62] A British writer, N. W. Porteous, in a survey of Old Testament theological writings since the time of Davidson, observed that a theology of the Old Testament will not attempt to obscure the fact that Christ did not merely decode the Old Testament but fulfilled it.[63] Any endeavor to use the word "theology" for

---

[56] O. Procksch, *Theologie des AT* (1950); cf. his study in *Neue kirchliche Zeitschrift*, XXXVI (1925), pp. 485ff., 715ff.

[57] W. Eichrodt, *Theologie des AT*, I, p. 6n., borrowed this pattern from Procksch.

[58] Th. C. Vriezen, *Hoofdlijnen der Theologie van het Oude Testament* (1949).

[59] M. Burrows, *An Outline of Biblical Theology* (1946).

[60] O. J. Baab, *The Theology of the OT* (1949).

[61] Cf. Baab in *The Study of the Bible Today and Tomorrow* (ed. H. R. Willoughby, 1947), pp. 401ff.

[62] R. C. Dentan, *Preface to OT Theology* (1950, rev. ed., 1963).

[63] *OTMS*, p. 344; the survey is found on pages 311ff.

433

a history of human beliefs about God would fail to bring out the fullest sense implicit in the term.[64]

In a book published in 1952, G. E. Wright appeared to reflect von Rad's theory, which saw the Hebrew recognition of divine acts in their history in terms of a confession or *Heilsgeschichtliches Credo*.[65] For Wright, Old Testament faith comprised a recital of such "mighty acts" as the deliverance at the Red Sea and the Covenant event at Sinai. While he showed that the basic beliefs of the Old Testament were given meaning for the early Christian Church through typological means, he adopted a very conservative attitude towards the use of typology generally, preferring to restrict it to what was envisaged by the New Testament authors. This approach appears to have the double demerit of reviving an outmoded form of Biblical dogmatic theology, and making the ancient Hebrew faith confessional in nature. Old Testament religion is to all intents and purposes reduced to a series of thankful reminiscences concerning past historical events, and on this basis would seem to take little cognizance of such important themes as soteriology or divine judgment. Equally unfortunate is the apparent inability of Wright to think of the divine election of Israel as integral to the concept of the Covenant. But in any event, theology as recital is much too restricted to do proper justice to the manifold facets of Old Testament thought concerning the divine nature and purpose. Supremely for Hebrew tradition it was the metaphysic of Sinai that gave meaning and purpose to history, and not *vice versa*. As Fichte remarked in a somewhat different connection, "only the metaphysical can save; never under any circumstances the historical."[66] Certainly the Old Testament writings make it clear that recollection of the characteristic divinely motivated saving events served to

---

[64] Problems connected with Old Testament theology were also discussed in European works that were not specifically theological in character. In a study of the literary strata of the prophetic character of Deuteronomy, H. Breit outlined some of the principal ideas occurring in the book; *Die Predigt der Deuteronomisten* (1933). G. von Rad attempted a similar task in his discussion of the Hexateuchal priestly material, *Die Priesterschrift im Hexateuch* (1934). Noth examined the theological character of Pentateuchal law in *Die Gesetze im Pentateuch: ihre Voraussetzungen und ihr Sinn* (1940). Three years later Von Rad gave a broad consideration to some of the issues involved in formulating a theology of the Old Testament; *Theologische Literaturzeitung*, LXVIII (1943), col. 225, cf. in *Werden und Wesen des AT*, pp. 138ff. He maintained that the Old Testament writings constituted a testimony to continuous divine action in history, and emphasized the *kerygma* of the prophetic utterances. The importance that he assigned to prophecy and its fulfilment can be gauged from the fact that he was in agreement with the limited use of typology in this connection. The seeming nihilism of Noth was reflected in his *Geschichte und Gotteswort im AT* (1950), in which he adduced historical difficulties confronting those who attempted a thorough treatment of Old Testament theology.

[65] G. E. Wright, *God Who Acts: Biblical Theology as Recital* (1952); cf. *IB*, I, pp. 354ff.

[66] Quoted by E. Brunner, *Offenbarung und Vernunft* (1941), p. 394.

furnish a perspective for faith, and never at any time constituted the form or content of faith itself. However, Wright was correct in maintaining that the variety of thought occurring in the Old Testament was unified by the overall concern for the meaning of historical events and the place of Israel within the stream of history. What he does not seem to have made clear, however, is that there is a distinct sense in which the objective written record is at once a description and an interpretation of many of the historical events that it narrates. The Old Testament theologian, therefore, must be prepared to deal alike with the "event-concept" and the "written-concept," and if the latter is rejected or attenuated on the basis of nineteenth-century "objective historicism," the former is immediately open to a great deal of subjective speculation.

A similar emphasis upon the "acts of God" was made in 1955 by Edmond Jacob,[67] who maintained that the faith of the Old Testament was not centered upon concepts of Deity as such, but upon appreciation of and response to the actions of God in history. Jacob adopted a threefold division of his subject which dealt successively with the divine nature and attributes, the activity of God in history and human life, and the concepts of sin, redemption, eschatology, and the consummation of divine activity in history. His work was based upon a moderate critical position, but perhaps because of its inherent assumptions it failed to emphasize the place of the Covenant in the religious life of the nation, and also neglected the status of the cult in Israelite faith generally. It should be said that his presentation suffered from the deficiencies common to those scholars who have based their interpretation of Old Testament religion upon divine acts rather than on Biblical thought as such.

An approach to Old Testament theology from the standpoint of Pauline soteriology was undertaken by F. Baumgärtel in 1952, who held that the Christian gospel was the ultimate standard by which the Old Testament ought to be judged theologically.[68] Employing an objective historical method of interpretation, he claimed that the character of the Old Testament was that of promise rather than prophecy, the expectation being realized in Jesus Christ. The modern Christian, Baumgärtel affirmed, could not utilize typology as the Early Church did in order to make the Old Testament relevant, but instead he ought to relate himself to the Old Testament *Heilsgeschichte* from the standpoint of his experience of Christ. Forgiveness through the Cross presupposed the divine judgments on sin depicted in the Old Testament. Although Baumgärtel made a valiant attempt to bring the theology of the ancient Hebrew

---

[67] E. Jacob, *Théologie de l'Ancien Testament* (1955); E. tr. A. W. Heathcote and P. J. Allcock, *Theology of the OT* (1958).

[68] F. Baumgärtel, *Verheissung: Zur Frage des evangelischen Verständnisses des AT* (1952); cf. in *Theologische Literaturzeitung*, LXXVI (1951), cols. 257ff., and in *Geschichte und Altes Testament, Albrecht Alt zum 70. Geburtstag* (1953), pp. 13ff. Cf. J. Bright, *The Authority of the Old Testament* (1967), pp. 72f.

Scriptures beyond the bounds of mere historicism into the present ex
perience of the individual Christian, he failed to give an adequate plac
to the strictly prophetic element in the Old Testament writings, particu
larly where such passages were of a messianic character.

A major work on Old Testament theology from the standpoint o
Roman Catholicism was published in 1954 by Van Imschoot.[69] The plar
of his book reflected the influence of Köhler and Eichrodt, particularly i
the first volume, which dealt with the nature and attributes of Deity, the
concept of election, and the character of the Covenant relationship. The
second volume was concerned with the doctrine of man, and discussec
his origin, nature, destiny, and duties. The author managed to avoid the
deficient views of sin and its consequences that are apparent in the
theological writings of Köhler and von Rad. Van Imschoot rejectec
Köhler's opinion that the cultus was a human attempt at self
redemption, characterizing it instead as an aspect of human duty
towards God. Van Imschoot does not appear to have been as successfu
as Eichrodt in presenting the essential unity of Israelite faith, despite hi:
emphasis upon the Covenant relationship. Although his work constitutec
a careful synthesis of Biblical material it suffered from certain of the
deficiencies associated with dogmatic methodology.

A comprehensive study of Old Testament theology based on the
general approach of Alt and Noth was published in 1957 by von Rad.[70]
This masterly application of form-critical method to the problems of Olc
Testament theology was based on the presupposition that the principa
task at hand was the reiterating of the historical character of the Hebrew
faith as the witness of ancient Israel, itself a creation of the amphictyony, to the mighty acts of God. In so doing von Rad repudiated the
Israelite "world of faith" envisaged by Eichrodt in favor of retelling in its
historical form the Old Testament *Heilsgeschichte*. For von Rad the
Hexateuch came into being from an arrangement in confessional form o
various groups of traditions that were largely contradictory and conflicting. The figure of Moses emerged but dimly, since the traditions abou
the normative founder of Hebrew faith were held to be far from easy tc
reconcile with one another.

Von Rad accorded separate treatment to the prophetic writings, because the message contained in them not only presupposed the earlie
historical traditions but involved other issues as well. For him the entire
consideration turned upon the assertion that the soteriological concept:
enshrined in the older traditions had proved inadequate, and in consequence would subsequently be replaced by a fresh series of divine
"mighty acts." Von Rad discussed the nature of the prophetic utterances

[69] P. Van Imschoot, *Théologie de l'Ancien Testament*, I (1954); II (1956).

[70] *Theologie des AT, I, Die Theologie der geschichtlichen Überlieferungen Israels*
(1957); E. tr. *OT Theology*, I (1962); II (1965).

generally in relationship to the idea of revelation, and followed this by a treatment of the individual prophets and their teachings. The second volume ended with a section dealing with problems of interpretation and the use of the Old Testament narratives in the books of the New Testament.

Von Rad's work was characterized by a pronounced authoritarian tone, an arbitrary subjectivity of judgment, and a distinct reluctance to consider other points of view on the subject of Old Testament theology. Von Rad conveyed the impression that other approaches than his own were unhistorical because they resulted in a static theological picture, and did not furnish the concept of an ongoing revelation in the stream of historical encounter. The kind of form-criticism that he employed might well raise serious questions as to its validity, especially where it led the author to treat primary elements of the narrative as though they were secondary. For example, it is difficult to see how, if in fact the creation narrative is to be regarded as a secondary element, it can be connected realistically with the *Heilsgeschichte* on his theory.

An even more formidable objection to his general methodology is the question whether the concept of *Heilsgeschichte* is, after all, the best category for exercising control of the source material in any interpretation of Old Testament thought. Again, serious objections must be raised with respect to the claim that the earliest Jehovistic faith was given its normative expression in terms of "short historical creeds." Although it is a commonplace of the Alt and Noth school to emphasize the importance of the amphictyony and to relate the beginnings of Israel to this type of ancient social organization, the shortcomings of a view that deliberately flouts the uniform tradition of Israel regarding its origins must be apparent even to the most casual reader. In any event it is far from certain, as Kaufmann has shown, that the political organization of the Hebrews during the settlement period corresponded to the type of Greek social structure envisaged by Alt and Noth.[71]

Von Rad displayed the kind of insight necessary for producing a true theology of the Old Testament in his determination to show that such a theology was related to the history of the divine acts of salvation. His crucial error, however, consisted in using the critically reconstructed testimonies of Israel to such deeds as the foundation for his theology. Surely a genuine Old Testament theology can only be possible when the ancient Hebrew Scriptures are recognized as constituting nothing less than the oracles of God. For von Rad, however, a sufficient basis for theology was furnished by the witness of Israel to what it believed to be the historic acts of divine mercy. While the presentation that von Rad furnished was generally consistent with the form-critical principles adopted, there must remain grave doubt as to the validity of the methodology upon which the work was based.

[71] *KRI*, p. 256.

The most notable British contribution to Old Testament theology since the time of Davidson was made in 1959 by G. A. F. Knight, who stands firmly in the orthodox liberal tradition of esteem for the Old Testament as the Word of God but insistence on a thoroughgoing reconstruction of the literature along critical lines as a necessary preliminary to theological assessment.[72] Knight exhibits traces of the influence of von Rad and Wright in seeing the "God Who Acts" supremely at work on behalf of His people during the Exodus and the exile. His approach is marked by distinct anthropological overtones that emphasize the pictorial images of the Hebrew mind and show their continuity of expression in the New Testament. Knight seems to assign a position of secondary importance to the Sinai Covenant, and almost completely neglects the covenant associated with Abraham. He prefers to stress the living nature of God rather than attempt a more formal examination of the divine attributes, in the conviction that God was ever active on behalf of His people Israel so as to secure their ultimate salvation and the concomitant blessings for the world.

Knight views with disfavor the Christological interpretation of certain passages of the Old Testament to the exclusion of others, since for him the Hebrew Scriptures as a whole are messianic. Thus a Christian theology of the Old Testament is meaningless without the person of Jesus Christ as its culmination. Though Knight presents his case with considerable erudition, his conclusions are rather vague, and he seems to stress the reality of the Israelite religious experience without giving proper attention to those divine attributes that afforded permanent meaning to that experience. Rather curious is his statement that God "became one flesh with Israel,"[73] which has distinctly Christian overtones, and cannot be demonstrated from the Hebrew Scriptures themselves.

To the present writer Knight seems to display an inadequate appreciation of the extent to which Israelite religious life constituted failure rather than success in its experience of God, a deficiency that is hardly balanced by the statement that Christ was the perfect embodiment of the true Israel, the union of divine and human, however correct the latter might be. In common with some other modern authors Knight pays comparatively little attention to the Temple cultus and its elaborate ritual, and as a result it is hardly surprising that his treatment of the entire question of sacrifice is completely inadequate. It is unfortunate that Knight passes over the nature of the divine attributes so casually, since not merely were these of fundamental importance for the great Hebrew prophetic figures, but, indeed, for the very ethos of the nation of Israel. Any serious attempt to come to grips with a theology of the Old Testament must include a discussion of the attributes of God, particular-

---

[72] G. A. F. Knight, *A Christian Theology of the OT* (1959).
[73] *Ibid.*, p. 205.

ly in the light of the fact that the "wholly other" concept of the neo-orthodox theologians has gone far towards making God quite obscure.

The earlier contributions of Muilenburg to the history and content of ancient Hebrew religion are reflected in a work published in 1961.[74] Like Knight and other liberal writers, Muilenburg's thought presupposes the acceptance of the results of European critical scholarship with a concomitant rearrangement of the Hebrew literature to conform to the precepts of the Wellhausen school. At the same time his inquiry is moderate and well disciplined within this context, emphasizing that the primary responsibility of the scholar is to ascertain the original meaning of the particular passage under study without being unduly influenced by subsequent historical or doctrinal developments. For the Christian, however, the history and religion of ancient Israel find their logical continuation and fruition in the New Covenant. Accordingly, while an evaluation of isolated passages may afford some insight into the divine activity through Israel, the fullest significance of Old Testament faith can only be appreciated as a result of contemplating a linear movement of Biblical thought culminating in the atoning work of Jesus Christ.

Muilenburg was able to avoid many of the difficulties arising from a standpoint that emphasized human religious experience rather than divine revelation. Thus he consistently depicts God as a real Person who transcended human conceptions of Himself, and emphasizes the Covenant as the motivating factor in all considerations of ethical behavior. His general conclusions are the result of careful scholarly inquiry, and his work constitutes one of the most adequate representations of the moderate critical approach to the problems of ancient Hebrew faith.

American conservative scholars who addressed themselves to the theology of the Old Testament include J. H. Raven, who in 1933 issued a work which, while it appeared to deal primarily with Hebrew religion, did in fact constitute an accredited Biblical theology.[75] The book was deficient, however, in that it only considered developments up to the period of Manasseh. The conservative traditions of Princeton Theological Seminary were continued by O. T. Allis of Westminster Theological Seminary, who in 1945 published an anti-dispensational study of the prophetic writings,[76] and also by the works of E. J. Young.[77] While the theological writings of John Murray dealt with Biblical doctrines in the wider sense, they included considerations of more specific Old Testa-

---

[74] His earlier contributions are found in *The Vitality of the Christian Tradition* (ed. G. F. Thomas, 1945), pp. 1ff., and in *IB*, I, pp. 291ff. These were reflected in his *The Way of Israel: Biblical Faith and Ethics* (1961).

[75] *The History of the Religion of Israel* (1933).

[76] *Prophecy and the Church* (1945).

[77] *My Servants the Prophets* (1952); *Studies in Isaiah* (1954); *The Study of OT Theology Today* (1958).

ment themes.[78] Similar to these were the theological studies of G. Vos, who dealt with the major areas of Old Testament theology without actually considering all the doctrines generally envisaged by orthodox dogmatic theology.[79]

Aside from works devoted primarily to the problems encountered in Old Testament theology, a number of semantic studies have enriched the general discipline in important areas of detail.[80] Valuable contributions have been made by German authors in the Kittel *Theologisches Wörterbuch zum Neuen Testament,* which, although it was not concerned specifically with Old Testament concepts, dealt in varying degrees with the Hebrew antecedents of certain Christian doctrines.[81]

Certain of the principles upon which the Kittel *Wörterbuch* was based met with heavy criticism from James Barr,[82] who argued from the standpoint of sound linguistic method that the nature and function of language should not be the victim of unscientific lexicographical speculation. Barr accused contemporary writers in the general field of Biblical theology of uncritical procedures, pointing specifically to the disputed area of the relationship between the Biblical languages and Biblical thought. In particular he focused attention on the problems raised by the kind of semantic approach that ascribed to the Biblical writers a thought-structure based on areas of meaning assigned to specific words. As a necessary preliminary to sound etymological study for Biblical theology, he asserted, it was of paramount importance for Scriptural *statements* to be relied upon, rather than isolated Biblical *words.* In questioning the linguistic presuppositions and methods of Biblical theologians, Barr showed the dangers inherent in an incautious use of the traditional distinctions between Greek and Hebrew modes of thought,[83] maintaining that such contrasts were not infrequently employed *a priori.*

---

[78] *The Covenant of Grace* (1953); *Redemption, Accomplished and Applied* (1955); *The Imputation of Adam's Sin* (1959).

[79] *Biblical Theology* (1948).

[80] One of the most important of these works was N. Glueck's *Das Wort hesed im alttestamentlichen Sprachgebrauch als menschliche und göttliche gemeinschaftsgemässe Verhaltungsweise,* BZAW, XLVII (1927). The trend that he established was followed in the writings of Dodd, *The Bible and the Greeks, I: The Religious Vocabulary of Hellenistic Judaism* (1935); J. Pedersen, *Israel: Its Life and Culture* (vols. I, II, 1926; III, IV, 1940); J. J. Stamm, *Erlösen und Vergeben im AT: eine begriffsgeschichtliche Untersuchung* (1940); A. R. Johnson, *The One and the Many in the Israelite Conception of God* (1942) and *The Vitality of the Individual in the Thought of Ancient Israel* (1949); N. H. Snaith, *The Distinctive Ideas of the OT* (1944); and G. Oestborn, *Tōrā in the OT: A Semantic Study* (1945).

[81] Some of the Biblical studies have been issued separately in English in the series entitled *Bible Key Words.*

[82] *The Semantics of Biblical Language* (1961).

[83] *Ibid.,* pp. 8ff.

440

In consequence the linguistic evidence was generally made to conform to a particular philosophical or theological assumption.[84] This all-too-familiar Wellhausenian pattern raised the question as to whether the interests of Old Testament theologians would not be served more adequately by an emphasis upon the differences between the Old Testament as such and its ancient Near Eastern environment.

In pointing to scholars whose observations on Biblical languages and thought had not been grounded in a proper method of linguistic analysis, Barr called attention to the misuses of etymologies in general[85] and to the underlying presuppositions of the Kittel *Wörterbuch* in particular.[86] His predominant complaint was that the authors of various articles tended to read into Scripture certain theological concepts that could not properly be deduced from the actual linguistic form of the text itself.[87] He also criticized the preoccupation of the *Wörterbuch* with the history of ideas rather than with the specific meanings of words,[88] resulting in the treatment of ordinary semantic criteria as something approaching developed theological concepts. As a corrective he urged the grouping of terms by related semantic fields rather than by roots, and their comparison with synonyms and antonyms[89] as well as the study of phrases or sentences, rather than the individual words, as the true vehicles of theological concepts.[90] Furthermore, he maintained that such presuppositions as eschatology or *Heilsgeschichte* should be subordinated to proper linguistic discipline so as to avoid the common tendency of loading the etymological history of a term with theological significance. In short, the meaning of Hebrew words in the Old Testament was to be determined by their use and context, not by their etymology.

Barr made no secret of the fact that he adopted a functional view of linguistic expression, and that his emphasis upon proper semantic method was designed to bring long-overdue canons of discipline to the study of Biblical terms.[91] While he conceded that many of the conclusions at which Biblical theologians had arrived were correct, he affirmed that the methods that they had utilized in this endeavor were not.

---

[84] *Ibid.*, pp. 23 *passim*.

[85] *Ibid.*, pp. 111ff.; as examples of improper methodology, T. Boman, *Das hebräische Denken im Vergleich mit dem Griechischen* (1954 ed.); E. tr. *Hebrew Thought Compared with Greek* (1960); J. Pedersen, *Israel, I-II* (1920), *III-IV* (1934), E. tr. *Israel: Its Life and Culture* (1926, 1940).

[86] Barr, *op. cit.*, pp. 206ff.

[87] E.g. Weiser, πίστις, VI, pp. 182ff.; W. Foerster, κτίζω, III, pp. 102ff.

[88] Barr, *op. cit.*, pp. 209, 229ff.

[89] *Ibid.*, p. 235.

[90] *Ibid.*, pp. 249, 265f.; cf. L. Bloomfield, *Language* (1933), pp. 27ff.

[91] *Op. cit.*, pp. 263ff.

Whether linguists generally will be in agreement with the position of Barr is naturally a matter of some doubt, linguistic debate being what it is. There can be little question, however, that this brilliant and determined attack upon poor methodology in Biblical linguistic studies will go far towards removing the obscurities and uncritical generalities so commonly associated with the exposition of leading Biblical ideas.

II. PRINCIPLES OF INTERPRETATION

A. The Basis of Old Testament Theology

From the foregoing discussion it is evident that a satisfactory theology of the Old Testament is far from an easy accomplishment.[1] Historical perspective and method in this field did not come into their own until the nineteenth century,[2] and were accompanied by what was regarded as an objective historicism, which, however, rejected the idea of an established written revelation of a final character. This turn of events was unfortunate since Biblical theology was immediately at the mercy of subjective and arbitrary forms of interpretation, which in a great many cases proved to be little more than philosophies of religion. On balance there would seem to be very little to choose between this situation and that which obtained at the height of the medieval period with regard to the theological interpretation of the Old Testament. It is true, of course, that the approaches and emphases were quite different in many respects, but the abuse of the Scriptural text was a feature common to both.

Although the neo-orthodox theologians redressed the imbalance to some extent by stressing the uniqueness of the history itself, they abandoned the traditional view of revelation as the communication to man of divine truth involving the moral and spiritual categories of life in favor of relating the unfolding of the divine purpose through specific experiences of encounter in the history of the chosen people. Although it is true that ordinary historical phenomena constitute part of the vehicle of revelation, there are dangers implicit in the assumption that a satisfactory theology can be built upon certain arbitrarily chosen manifestations of God in history. First of all, the theological presuppositions of the particular author will lead to a sharp difference of opinion as to precisely what constitutes a "saving act," and which of those thus available for discus-

---

[1] For some of the problems connected with Biblical and OT theology generally see E. Ebeling, *JTS*, VI (1955), pp. 210ff.; J. D. Smart, *The Interpretation of Scripture* (1961); J. van der Ploeg, *Une théologie de l'Ancien Testament est-elle possible?* (1962).

[2] Cf. A. Richardson, *The Bible in the Age of Science* (1961), pp. 49ff.

sion are to be taken as exemplifying the purpose of God in history. Clearly the approach adopted in this regard by a Jewish writer will differ radically from that of a Christian. Secondly, the view of a deity who acts in a voluntaristic manner is an essentially Greek one, and can be employed subjectively to associate events that have no organic connection with one another. As E. G. Kraeling has pointed out, there are many who will feel that any grouping of "saving acts" should be limited to the Incarnation, Crucifixion, and Resurrection of Jesus Christ, and that the Old Testament writings in general should be deemed prophetic of the work of the Saviour.[3]

Although it has brought a reaffirmation of many important principles, such as the priority of revelation over reason, the neo-orthodox movement generally has suffered from certain unresolved internal tensions. These are reflected in writings involving Old Testament theology. Following Schleiermacher, who maintained that God imparted life rather than dogma, and that He could not be known as He is in Himself but only in relationship to the existence of the individual human being, writers such as Kierkegaard called for a resolute individual commitment to the truth of a quality that would completely transform the whole of existence. From one point of view this position represented a salutary reaction against formal orthodoxy and shallow liberalism, but in other respects it resulted in a tendency to dispose its adherents towards a doctrine of revelation whose locus consisted in an immediate existential response to encounter, and not in an objective Scriptural content.[4]

Existential truth, as envisaged by Kierkegaard and his followers, may well be dominant in the transformation of concrete individual experience, but at the same time it is important to recognize that the source of truth is neither in mortal experience nor in human reason, but in a rational and objective divine revelation embodied in the Scriptures.[5] For this reason it is important to note, as Rowley has insisted, that an Old Testament theology should be based firmly upon Biblical thought rather than upon particular events in the history of Israel. Such a theology will avoid the dichotomy that Eissfeldt saw between faith and knowledge, for faith will have the same active character as knowledge; and it will lead to a proper appreciation of the spiritual issues involved without impairing the objective historical nature of knowledge. The vast majority of writers in this field have recognized that the Old Testament has a meaning that far surpasses its more immediate significance as the national literature of the ancient Hebrews; and if there are absolute and transcendent spiritual values in the Old Testament, it is surely legitimate for them to be grasped by the exercise of faith in a manner that does not

---

[3] *The OT Since the Reformation*, p. 280.

[4] C. F. H. Henry in *Baker's Dictionary of Theology* (1960), p. 459.

[5] Cf. G. H. Clark in *Revelation and the Bible* (ed. C. F. H. Henry, 1958), pp. 29ff.

compromise the historical situation. The trend of modern studies has been such that it is now no longer necessary to follow the older critical concept that the earlier stages of Old Testament thought were necessarily the most primitive. Instead, a new emphasis has been given to the substantial and unified nature of the corpus of Hebrew belief existing from comparatively early times. Anthropomorphic expressions, which were once regarded as typical of a rudimentary theological outlook, can now be esteemed symbolically as constituting rich and deep insights into the character of the Deity, expressed in a way to afford them the greatest permanence.

B. INTERPRETATIVE APPROACHES

The question as to what principles of interpretation are to be applied to the Old Testament writings will naturally be of some concern in the formulation of an Old Testament theology. Certain approaches are common to the Bible and other ancient literature, while others concern the Scriptural writings exclusively as the unique record of divine revelation in and through Israel. The interpretation of specific events or writings was, of course, a common feature of ancient life, and found a comparable place in the pages of the Old Testament. Thus the interpretation of dreams was recorded on occasions,[6] as well as the exposition of an older passage in one of later date (Jer. 31:29f. expounded in Ezek. 18:2ff.). On a general basis the various Biblical documents and any parts into which they can properly be subdivided must be studied not merely in their immediate verbal context but also against the background of the occasion, the place, and the human situation to which they belong.[7] This requires an understanding of the historical and geographical setting of ancient Near Eastern life—on its own terms and not those of artificial *a priori* postulates—and a firm grasp of the structure and literary idioms of the Biblical languages and their Near Eastern counterparts, as well as an appreciation of the kind of literature under study. The interpretation will naturally vary as the source material is found to be allegory, poetry, prophecy, or apocalyptic. The last named especially calls for the application of special rules of interpretation. An understanding of the historical background of the Old Testament will prevent the interpreter from applying the canons of Christian morality to the social and religious activities of the Middle and Late Bronze Ages. The significance of the prophetic movement will not be appreciated most fully until the religious, social, and political movements in contemporary Near Eastern nations are familiar to the interpreter. Mention should be made again of

---

[6] Gen. 40:8ff.; 41:1ff.; Dan. 2:36ff.; 4:19ff.; cf. E. L. Ehrlich, *Der Traum im AT* (1953).

[7] F. F. Bruce, *NBD*, p. 567.

the importance of the geographical setting[8] and the general *Sitz im Leben* of the ancient Hebrews as revealed by modern archaeological discoveries.[9]

1. Early exegetical approaches. In a more restricted sense the interpretation of the Old Testament involves not merely the separate documents or writings as such, but for the Jewish scholar their place in the entire corpus of Hebrew literature, and for the Christian their interpretation as part of the Bible. In emphasizing that sense of unity and internal harmony in Scripture that enables each part to be interpreted in the light of the whole, the Christian Church was merely applying a principle familiar to Jewish teachers. Traditionally the latter conceived of the Prophets and the Sacred Writings to a large extent as commentaries on the Torah.[10] Medieval Jewish exegetes developed a fourfold theory of interpretation, consisting of the *peshat* or obvious literal meaning of the text, the *remes* or allegorical significance, the *derash*, a meaning to be obtained by applying certain methodological rules, and the *sod* or mystical meaning of the text.

Christian patristic interpretation in Alexandria was influenced by the Biblical expositions of Philo in the direction of undertaking a massive allegorization of the text as a means of ascertaining the mind of the inspiring Spirit of God. In this way much in the Bible that was unacceptable to the intellect or unpalatable to the conscience could be regarded as proper and legitimate. This was as much a theological method as an attitude of faith, for as has been observed above, the Fathers generally were unable to regard anything in Scripture as useless. The Antiochene school, in contrast, paid much more attention to the historical sense of the text, and, while not rejecting the allegorical method completely pursued a more realistic exegetical course. Medieval Christian interpreters could either work on a twofold basis involving the literal historical and the mystical spiritual sense, or in a still more highly differentiated fourfold form parallel to the Jewish canons of exegesis: the *literal* connotation of the Biblical record, the *allegorical* interpretation that deduced doctrine from narrative passages, the *moral* understanding that held lessons for behavior and life, and the *anagogical* sense that found heavenly meanings in earthly facts. On such a basis the word *water* could mean literally a colorless liquid, allegorically baptism by water, moral purity, or anagogically eternal life in the celestial Jerusalem.[11]

---

[8] Cf. J. M. Houston, *Journal of the Transactions of the Victoria Institute,* LXXXV (1954), pp. 62ff.

[9] Cf. L. Köhler, *Der Hebräische Mensch* (1953); E. W. Heaton, *Everyday Life in OT Times* (1956); P. R. Ackroyd, *The People of the OT* (1959); R. de Vaux, *Ancient Israel, Its Life and Institutions* (1962), *et al.*

[10] Cf. J. Weingreen, *BJRL,* XXXIV (1951), pp. 166ff.

[11] F. F. Bruce in *Baker's Dictionary of Theology,* p. 293.

Emphasis upon grammatico-historical exegesis and the primacy of the literal sense of Scripture characterized the Reformation period. Luther began in the old hermeneutic tradition of allegory, but later counselled interpreters against all but the most cautious use of allegorical method. Protestant interpretation generally was governed by the Reformation attitude that Scripture was amenable to a simple literal meaning and that it could never be subservient to a purely human authority.[12]

2. *Modern approaches.* Some modern interpreters have argued from the New Testament use of the Old Testament to establish four basic principles of interpretation.[13] These consist of the *historical*, which regards the Old Testament as an authentic and reliable chronicle of events, the *propositional*, in which Old Testament statements are either fulfilled in the New Testament or employed as a basis for doctrine or conduct, the *homological*, a mathematical concept employed to express the identity or correspondence between Old Covenant and New Covenant situations,[14] and the *illustrational*, in which historic material is employed to reinforce truth and emphasize moral lessons. These principles may be contrasted with such spurious approaches as the superstitious,[15] the rationalistic, the mythological, and the allegorical.

The latter raises the problem as to whether secret senses of Scripture can be said to exist independently, or whether they are valid only by derivation or implication from a primary sense. One form of allegorization which has experienced some degree of revival in the twentieth century is that of *typological* interpretation.[16] This involves the tracing of parallels or correspondences between the two Testaments in order to discern the fundamental meaning of the Old Testament passage in terms of its New Testament equivalent. In the primitive Church typology was employed in general to demonstrate the Old Testament prefigurations of the Christian dispensation, and as such was prophetic and Christocentric in nature.[17] If typology is to be employed at all as a method of interpretation[18] it should follow the cautious approach exhibited by the New Testament writers, who invariably saw the earliest stages in the Biblical demonstration of divine redemption as foreshadowings of later phases. By this means some of the more eccentric allegorical interpreta-

---

[12] Cf. B. Ramm, *Protestant Bible Interpretation* (1953).

[13] Cf. E. F. Kevan in *Revelation and the Bible*, pp. 285ff.

[14] Cf. F. W. Farrar, *The History of Interpretation* (1886), p. 218; W. J. Phythian-Adams, *The Way of At-one-ment* (1944), pp. 10f.; A. G. Hebert, *The Authority of the OT*, p. 219.

[15] Cf. Farrar, *The History of Interpretation*, p. 107.

[16] G. W. H. Lampe and K. J. Woollcombe, *Essays on Typology* (1957); Cf. W. A. Irwin, ZAW, LXII (1950), p. 6; R. Bultmann, *Theologische Literaturzeitung*, LXXV (1950), pp. 205ff.; C. Westermann (ed.), *Essays on OT Hermeneutics* (1963).

[17] W. Broomall in *Baker's Dictionary of Theology*, pp. 533f.

[18] Cf. H. H. Rowley, *The Changing Pattern of OT Studies* (1959), pp. 27f.

tions that arose in the patristic period and were perpetuated by subsequent generations will be avoided.

Any historically oriented Old Testament theology must somehow grapple with the problem of the ultimate meaning of Old Testament history. The standpoint of the author will naturally have considerable bearing upon the conclusions arrived at, but the issue will be particularly problematical for Jewish scholars. The list of those who have showed revived interest in the dynamic Biblical concepts of divine transcendence, of man under sin and grace, and of God as the Lord of History include few Jewish scholars. The neo-orthodox movement did at least serve their interests to the point where it was able to make portions of the Old Testament relevant to the needs of modern man, and this in itself was no small undertaking. But it has been largely unsuccessful in stimulating among Jewish scholars the counterpart to a "theology of crisis," and this is all the more surprising in view of the appalling tribulations suffered by European Judaism. Even Martin Buber concentrated more upon the history of religious thought in Israel than in formulating a theology of the divine-human encounter in Hebrew religion.[19]

a. Heilsgeschichte. For Jewish as for Christian scholars, the *Sitz im Leben* approach, though extremely valuable for historical and cultural investigation, is disappointing in its inability to do much more than point to its own situational context, which has only an indirect bearing upon the great doctrinal themes of the Old Testament revelation. Even more frustrating for Jewish writers must be the greatly overworked concept of *Heilsgeschichte*, which purports to discover the ultimate meaning of history in terms of a specific series of events. The "salvation" expressed by this idea can hardly be said to have been achieved within the period of Old Testament history, either actually or ideally, and if *Heilsgeschichte* can have any meaning at all for Jewish scholars, it must be at best rather potential and tentative. Christian theologians have enjoyed a considerably greater advantage in this respect, for they have been able to perceive in the Person of the Incarnate Christ the climax of the divine purpose of human redemption. While this supreme point of revelation to man was historically oriented in a manner analogous to that of the Torah and prophecy, it partook in a special way of the character of eschatological fulfilment. From its inception the Christian Church accepted the new revelation as being in organic connection with the old though transcending and consummating it. Christian tradition has consistently emphasized that the Old Testament finds its fullest meaning and expression in terms of the work of Christ as a specific and unique redemptive act. This latter transferred to a universalistic setting the divine revelation that had been given earlier to a particular community

---

[19] M. Buber, *Das Kommende, I: Das Königtum Gottes* (1932), *The Prophetic Faith* (1949); cf. *Ich und Du* (1923), pp. 10ff., 25.

and thus the Christian Church was made the supreme organ of divine witness. In fulfilling the Law and prophecy it was the function of Jesus Christ to create a people for Himself, the spiritual heirs and successors of Old Israel, and through them to usher in the final stages of the *Heilsgeschichte*. Insofar as an existential aspect can be demonstrated, Old Testament theology as such will have value for Jewish scholars. But an understanding of the Old Testament as an end in itself can hardly do justice to the great covenantal theme of the prophet Jeremiah (31:31ff.) and its continuation by Ezekiel (34:25ff.; 37:26), or to the concept of the emergent Mighty Ruler (Ps. 103:19; Isa. 40:10) as Messiah and Divine Servant (Isa. 9:6f.; 42:1ff.; 52:13ff.), to the outpouring of the Divine Spirit (Joel 2:28ff.) or the creation of new heavens and a new earth (Isa. 65:17).[20] In all of these there is latent the promise of activity that never actually came to fruition in the Old Testament period, but which for the Christian are essential elements in the fuller concept of *Heilsgeschichte*.

The manner in which the term *Heilsgeschichte* has been employed by certain neo-orthodox writers calls for some caution in its use. As "holy history," the "history of salvation," or "saving history," the word would appear to describe an accredited Biblical situation with a certain accuracy. There are few who would question the assertion that Scripture constitutes a record of happenings set in an historical framework, which for the Christian interpreter moved towards a specific climax within the stream of history and time. Though there is a sense in which any event in history can be attributed generally to divine working, it is important to recognize that the great saving acts of Hebrew history were of a special character, wrought for the benefit of a particular people. A genuine *Heilsgeschichte* will have as its overall consideration the relationship between God and man, but always with a specific concept of redemption in view. The perceptive scholar will take pains to distinguish between redemption and salvation as theological concepts, and will be aware that neither were realized within the period of Old Testament history. An approach of this kind will also recognize the existence of human sin, from which man needs to be redeemed, as well as the accomplished fact of the redemption itself in terms of the atoning work of Jesus Christ.

Quite obviously a purely historical kind of investigation can scarcely do justice to a situation that is basically theological in nature, as neo-orthodox scholars have recognized. Thus any accredited "salvation history" must have the topics of sin and redemption firmly established as central themes in the history of the Hebrew people. Through them it

---

[20] This deficiency is illustrated in the work of Samuel Sandmel, *The Hebrew Scriptures: An Introduction to Their Literature and Religious Ideas* (1963), p. 193, who rather helplessly concluded that the "Suffering Servant" was a "stray poem that quite unaccountably came to be included in the Book of Isaiah."

must relate these concepts to human history as a whole. In this way the basic concern of the Old Testament will be paramount, and will not ultimately be subsumed under what may be considered to be a more urgent task, namely that of reconstructing and rewriting the historical material according to some specific analytical scheme, as von Rad and others have done. While method is of great importance in any constructive endeavor, especially in the field of Old Testament theology, it must always remain the servant of the scholar, and not his master.

Neo-orthodox writers have further complicated the situation regarding the understanding of *Heilsgeschichte* by making a distinction between *Geschichte* and *Historie*. For these authors the supra-temporal or supra-historical realm is more properly described as *Geschichte*, which makes it possible for certain situations normally regarded by orthodox theologians as falling within time and space to be interpreted as purely parabolic or spiritual in nature. Thus for Barth, the resurrection of Jesus Christ is not to be understood historically in the traditional sense, but as a supra-temporal *Geschichte*, belonging to the realm of faith and as such outside purely factual or scientific demonstration.[21] In the same manner the Old Testament narrative of the fall of man into sin is to be assigned to the supra-historical area, and not regarded in the orthodox sense of *Historie*. This standpoint is in diametric opposition to the consistent witness of both Judaism and Christianity, which insist that man fell *in* time rather than *into* it. *Heilsgeschichte* should narrate the various aspects of the divine revelation to men against a strictly historical background, assessing objectively the acts of God on behalf of mankind, and seeing the climax of human redemption in the work of Christ on the Cross. There is a distinct sense in which *Heilsgeschichte* must always remain a limited and incomplete concept, having regard to the eschatological aspects of salvation in Christ.

b. Myth, saga, and legend. The neo-orthodox assumption that certain portions of the Scriptural narratives are supra-historical or nonhistorical has been accompanied by the widespread use of terms such as saga, legend, and myth in an attempt to assign proper character to particular parts of the Old Testament. Barth appears to have distinguished between myth on the one hand, and saga or legend on the other, by regarding myth as hostile to the substance of the Biblical testimony, whereas legend, even when its historical character was a matter for debate, is not necessarily in opposition to the witness of Scripture.[22] Brunner, however, utilized the term "myth" for those categories that Barth described as legend.

The recovery of much of the literature that was widely circulated in the ancient Near East has disproved the assertion of W. Robertson Smith

---

[21] K. Barth, *Kirchliche Dogmatik*, IV, 1, pp. 331ff.; IV, 2, pp. 118ff.
[22] Cf. K. Barth, *Kirchliche Dogmatik*, I, 1, pp. 368ff.

that, strictly speaking, mythology was no essential part of ancient religion.[23] It is now known that scientific and philosophical categories of thought were long antedated by myth-forms, and that the inhabitants of the Near East in antiquity utilized what has been called "mythopoetry" as a substitute for abstract logical thinking.[24] Old Testament critical scholars had for generations pointed to what they considered to be the mythological nature of certain portions of the Hebrew Scriptures, and although the extent to which Israelite literature was influenced by these modes of thought has proved debatable, it seems difficult to imagine on purely rational grounds that the Old Testament writings could remain completely untouched by mythological tendencies in the ancient Near East. The extent to which this is apparent in the Old Testament has been estimated by T. H. Gaster in terms of direct parallels to pagan myths, allusions to gods and ancient heroes, and the use of poetic imagery.[25] Ugaritic texts have illustrated the manner in which natural forces such as the wind[26] and thunder[27] were employed in the literary expressions current in the Amarna Age. The concept of the sun as winged (Mal. 4:2) was familiar from Egyptian usage.[28] References to demonic figures such as Lilith (Isa. 34:14) and Resheph (Hab. 3:5; cf. Job 5:7) reflect Canaanite folklore in an analogous manner. Allusions to epics of ancient deities have been seen in hints found in various parts of the Old Testament relating to a primordial revolt in heaven (cf. Ps. 82:6; Isa. 14:12ff.), or in references to astral bodies (Job 38:31f.; Am. 5:26).

In all the foregoing instances, however, the mythological content as such is so attenuated as to justify the conclusion that it was merely employed as dead verbal imagery whose origins were even then almost completely forgotten. A more direct parallel to pagan mythological ideas has been envisaged in the scattered references to divine conflict with some kind of monster, variously named Leviathan (Job 3:8; Ps. 74:14; Isa. 27:1),[29] Rahab (Job 9:13; 26:12f.; Ps. 89:10; Isa. 30:7; 51:9f.), Tannin, i.e. "Dragon" (Job 7:12; Ps. 74:13; Isa. 27:1; 51:9), Yam, i.e. "Sea" (Job 7:12; Ps. 74:13; Isa. 51:10; Hab. 3:8), and Nahar, i.e. "River" (Ps. 93:3; Hab. 3:8). This has been held to constitute the Hebrew version of the Ugaritic myth dealing with the victory of Baal over the dragon Yam, the spirit of rivers and streams,[30] a theme paralleled in the Mesopotamian narrative of the conflict between Marduk and Tiamat, in

---

23 *The Religion of the Semites*, p. 19.

24 *IAAM*, pp. 7f.

25 *IDB*, III, pp. 481ff.

26 Cf. T. H. Gaster, *Thespis* (1961 ed.), p. 168.

27 Cf. F. Rück in Hommel *Festschrift* (1917), pp. 279ff.

28 Cf. B. Perring, *Archiv für Orientforschung*, VIII (1933), pp. 281ff.; V. Christian, *ibid.*, IX (1934), p. 30.

29 Cf. G. R. Driver in *Studi orientalistici (Levi della Vida Festschrift)*, I (1956), pp. 234ff.

30 T. H. Gaster, *Thespis*, pp. 153ff.; *UL*, text 137, p. 14.

the old Hittite story of the struggle between the storm-deity and the dragon Illuyankas,[31] in the Sumerian myth narrating the triumph of Ninurta over the monster Asag,[32] in the fight between Horus of Beḥdet and the "Caitiff,"[33] and other similar Near Eastern legends.[34]

When those Old Testament passages which are commonly cited as references for these myths are examined carefully, they fall into two distinct groups. The first category preserves pagan folklore concerning monsters, a feature that has remained a consistent part of the tradition of more modern peoples. Such references are to be found principally in the poetical writings and in Isaiah. The second category, also predominantly poetical, has as its primary purpose not so much the preservation of ancient mythology as the demonstration of divine superiority over every aspect of nature and life. The fact that an extant vocabulary was utilized in this connection merely shows that there was never any new or specific terminology of divine revelation. The difference between Israelite and pagan usage consisted supremely in the manner in which traditional terminology and thought-forms were interpreted. In this connection it will be readily observed that pagan myths and deities were frequently held up as the object of ridicule among the Hebrews, and served as symbols of all that was alien to the true Hebrew genius.[35]

It further appears evident that where pagan myths were reflected in the Psalms and in the prophetic writings, they had already been subjected to a considerable process of what might be described as demythologizing. In at least one dramatic instance (Ps. 74:12ff.) the language of myth was employed to refute conclusively the very beliefs that had been responsible for the rise of myth-forms, and to assert the absolute sovereignty of God. Again, in Isaiah 51:9ff., which is rich in poetic imagery of all kinds, the mythology of the ancient Near East was applied both to the Exodus from Egypt and to the projected return from exile to demonstrate the supreme power of God as exemplified in mighty acts of restoration. In Amos 9:3 Leviathan is depicted as the servant of God rather than His enemy (cf. Ps. 104:26), indicating a similar transformation of a pagan mythological concept. It would appear, then, that where

[31] Cf. ANET, pp. 125f.

[32] S. N. Kramer, Sumerian Mythology (1961), pp. 78ff.

[33] Cf. A. Blackman and H. W. Fairman, JEA, XXI (1937), pp. 26ff., XXVIII (1942), pp. 32ff., XXIX (1943), pp. 3ff.

[34] For the principal Egyptian texts see ANET, pp. 2ff.; for Akkadian myths, ANET, pp. 60ff.; DOTT, pp. 3ff.; for Ugaritic myths, ANET, pp. 129ff., UL, pp. 9ff., DOTT, pp. 128ff. Cf. IAAM, pp. 50ff., 157ff., S. H. Hooke (ed.), Myth, Ritual and Kingship (1958); E. O. James, Myth and Ritual in the Ancient Near East (1958); J. R. Clarke, Myth and Symbol in Ancient Egypt (1959); T. H. Gaster, Thespis (1961).

[35] Thus the text of Hosea 8:6 can now be understood to mean, "Who is the bull-deity El? He is the one made by an artisan, and is not a god at all," replacing the meaningless מישראל ("from Israel," AV, RV; "in Israel," RSV) by מי שר אל.

the language of myth was countenanced in the Old Testament writings, it carried with it a very different meaning for the Hebrews than for the pagan nations of the Near East. As a literary phenomenon, the usage of mythological allusions is widespread in many later cultures, and the fact that such references might appear in literary productions is no indication that the writer is necessarily committed to any underlying theology, or that he does more than merely approve of the suitability of the allusion as part of the process of human communication.[36]

In any event, the Old Testament passages which appear to reflect the myths of the ancient world are of a poetic and highly figurative nature, making a literal interpretation of them both unwise and unwarranted. The "leviathan" of Job 41:1ff. is ultimately nothing more than a crocodile, and as such can hardly be considered a primeval foe of Jehovah. The conflict of Isaiah 27:1 is a future one, and "leviathan" is either the Assyrian or the Babylonian empire, or possibly both. In Isaiah 30:7, "Rahab" is explicitly Egypt, an illusion which is repeated elsewhere. In point of fact there is never once any clear statement in the Old Testament that the foes of Jehovah were regarded as mythological deities of any kind whatsoever.

By far the most challenging area of myth has been that connected with the early chapters of Genesis, which has been a matter of concern for both Old Testament scholars and neo-orthodox theologians. The recovery of Mesopotamian creation and flood narratives persuaded many writers that the Genesis accounts were comparatively late compositions, stripped by post-exilic priestly interests of their Babylonian paganism, and presented in a demythologized form as the accredited Hebrew tradition of the creation and deluge. However, further study of the situation has shown that these conclusions represented an over-simplification of the entire matter, and that in actual fact the problems of interrelation are infinitely more complex than the earlier scholars imagined. To no small degree what is involved is the occidental understanding of the oriental concept of myth. Unfortunately western understanding in this case has been dominated by the classical Greek mythological forms, which were marred by highly personified and individualized ideas of a distinctly static nature. Scholars assumed, quite erroneously, that the Greek understanding of myth was characteristic of ancient Near Eastern attitudes as a whole in this matter; however, the situation was entirely different, for the peoples of Mesopotamia and Egypt regarded everything in the world of nature as pulsating with life; and they regularly distinguished these natural forces as personal simply because they had experienced a direct encounter with them. For the superstitious inhabitants of Mesopotamia in particular and to a certain extent for the Egyptians, it was evident from the beginning that man was

[36] Cf. *IOTT*, pp. 81f.; D. F. Payne, *Genesis One Reconsidered* (1964), p. 14.

swamped by the interaction of prodigious natural forces with which he had to coordinate his activity if he was to survive. Thus to apply the concept of personification as encountered in the Greek myths to Mesopotamian mythology is misleading, since the deities and other supernatural entities of the latter were nothing more than the forces of nature as experienced personally. Their very existence depended entirely upon the presence and activity of natural phenomena, and although later literary developments in the legendary cycles tended to assign a greater degree of individuality to the deities than the situation warranted, the fact remains that even at the highest level the gods of Mesopotamia seldom if ever gained a true personality independent of the functioning of natural forces.[37] While some Greek philosophers, notably Thales and the Milesians, held that everything was "full of gods," they were merely describing a vague pantheism which bore no real relationship either to the Homeric heroes, to the cosmological speculations of the sixth-century B.C. Ionian thinkers generally, or to the contemporary revival of religious thought, which revered the personifications of those subterranean powers allegedly responsible for the sustaining and renewing of vegetable life.

c. Creation and fall. It is significant that to the present no Canaanite cosmogonic myths have been discovered. There can be little doubt, however, that such material would have followed the dominant pattern established by the Sumerians and adopted by the Babylonians and other peoples of the ancient Near East. Even Egyptian cosmogonic mythology, peculiar as it was to the local scene, conformed to the same basic concepts expressed by the Sumerians and Babylonians. What is of importance for the student of Mesopotamian cosmogony, however, is that the myths show no concern with creation in the accredited sense at all. An underlying monistic concept pervades all these writings that deal with creative activity, which in general describes in mythological form the evolution of an ordered cosmos from a primeval chaos. In a manner that was never clearly explained, the creator-deities emerged from the chaos, managed to conquer it and formulate it into some sort of order, and manipulated the process to the point where man finally appeared at the end, being especially for the Sumerians almost an afterthought of divine creativity.

The similarities between *Enuma elish* and the creation narratives in Genesis can be summarized by saying that both commence with something analogous to a watery chaos and conclude with the Creator in repose, and the sequence of creative events follows the same general order. However, it is a scientific axiom that in all questions of comparison the differences are more important than the similarities, and in the light of this principle it is apparent that a comparison furnishes no real

---

[37] Cf. *ARI*, pp. 91f.

parallels between the Genesis creation narratives and *Enuma elish.* At one period it was customary among critical scholars to stress the similarities between the deluge narrative of the Gilgamesh Epic and its counterpart in the Biblical writings, with the inference that there were similar parallels in the Genesis creation narratives and *Enuma elish.*[38] Aside from the fact that this assumption is completely unwarranted by the nature of the evidence, such an attitude failed to realize that the Genesis Flood narrative was dealing essentially with the problem of certain events within historic time, and did not have as its immediate concern the composition of legendary poetic material. While there are few who would question the ultimate Mesopotamian background of the Biblical creation and deluge narratives, the relationship of either or both to extant Mesopotamian mythological cycles such as *Enuma elish* or the Epic of Gilgamesh is very much an open question.[39]

The Genesis narratives of human creation and fall used to be described as myths because of their alleged desire to explain aetiologically the reason for existing human customs and attitudes, the behavior of serpents, and similar phenomena.[40] But subsequent research has shown that the subjects of myth among ancient Near Eastern peoples were the essential powers of the universe as experienced personally, and not questions of human custom or the behavior of certain animal species. The prime concern of the Mesopotamians of antiquity was to insure that they remained firmly on the side of those powers that had brought order from chaos, with the expectation that such a favorable state of affairs would continue to exist. Where the form of myth served its supreme purpose was in narrating in a memorable way the universal facts of life to which man had to adjust himself. Thus, as Frankfort has pointed out, the myths of the ancient Near East recounted events in which the people who formulated them, and indeed their successors, were involved to the extent of their entire existence.[41] Although they were products of the imagination, they were not mere fantasy, and as such must be distinguished carefully from legend, saga, fable, and fairy tale.

The Mesopotamian myths presented their images and imaginary actors with a compelling authority that perpetuated the essential reality of the I-Thou relationship. For the Babylonians, myth constituted a form of poetry that transcended mere poetic function and proclaimed a complex truth. Acts of reasoning inherent in myth-form were designed to bring

---

[38] S. R. Driver, *Genesis* in Westminster Commentaries (1926 ed.), p. 30. H. Zimmern and T. K. Cheyne, *EB,* I, col. 938, *et al.;* cf. A. Richardson, *Genesis I-XI* (1953), pp. 17f.

[39] Cf. A. Heidel, *The Babylonian Genesis* (1951), p. 139; J. V. Kinnier Wilson, *DOTT,* p. 14; G. von Rad, *Genesis* (1961), p. 48.

[40] S. R. Driver, *Genesis,* p. 36; H. Gunkel, *Die Schriften des AT* (1911), p. 65; S. Mowinckel, *He That Cometh,* p. 11.

[41] *IAAM,* p. 7.

about a recognition of the truth that they sought to proclaim, and where ritual behavior was involved it merely served to illustrate and exemplify the basic concepts of reality underlying the visible drama.[42] The imagery of such myth must consequently never be confused with allegory, since it constituted the cloak of authoritative truth. Nor could it ever be separated from the thought-content, for the very important reason that the imagery was basic to the form in which the experience had become actualized, whether that form was dramatized or presented as simple poetry. Fundamental to the character of myth was the recognition of its underlying, essential truth by the initiated or the faithful, as opposed to its irrationality for the critical, unsympathetic, or skeptical observer.

The Biblical narratives of the creation and fall of man are particularly good examples of material that partakes of the basic character of ancient Mesopotamian myth. In an even wider sense they reflect the concern of the oriental mind regarding the communication of essential truth, namely to safeguard by every possible means that which is most precious, and protect it from the skeptical gaze of the profane by cloaking it in story form. If the structure of the story form was perpetuated in a way that led to a rejection of both the form and the content by the undiscerning, the basic truth embedded in it would at least have been protected from ridicule. The principle underlying this attitude was crystallized by Isaiah (6:9f.), and repeated by Jesus Christ in connection with the parabolic method (Matt. 13:14ff.; Mark 4:12; cf. John 12:40 and Acts 28:26f.).

Yet despite the fact that the narratives of creation exhibit the same attitude towards the presentation of truth as their Mesopotamian counterparts, they cannot properly be regarded as myths in themselves. Their precise origin is a matter of considerable speculation, and while some would suggest that they constituted "demythologized" Mesopotamian material, others would assert that they were unique products of the Hebrew religious spirit. Since a careful comparison with pagan mythology reveals only the most casual parallels between Mesopotamian and Hebrew accounts of creation, and in view of the fact that none of the characteristic elements of the Babylonian myths appears in the Genesis narratives, it would seem unwise to employ the term "myth" in order to describe the Biblical accounts of creation, the fall, and so on, especially in view of the fact that the concept of myth is misleading for the occidental mind because of Greek influences ascribing implicit untruth to myth. As has been remarked, this is the exact opposite of what the ancient inhabitants of Mesopotamia envisaged in their myth-forms.

The inadequacy of the term "myth" as descriptive of the Biblical presentation of faith was demonstrated by G. E. Wright, who em-

[42] *IAAM*, p. 8.

456

phasized the difference between the Biblical material and the polytheistic compositions of the ancient Near East.[43] He pointed out that the Old Testament narratives were historical accounts whose traditions were taken seriously in the presentation of the faith of Israel. There was no question of adjusting life to a divine cosmic pattern typical of polytheism, and furthermore, the Old Testament literature was not unreal in the sense that it was separated from the stream of normal human life. While the Biblical writers showed a distinct interest in nature, they did not regard it as necessarily constituting the life of God, who was invariably considered as an independent Being. As distinct from the gods of Mesopotamian and Egyptian polytheism, the God of the Hebrews demonstrated His personality and sense of purpose by means of significant continuous acts in history. Man himself was a creature of God, furnished with a sense of destiny and cautioned to formulate the pattern of his life within the context of divine promise and fulfilment in history. Thus the Old Testament can never be regarded as a typical mythology in part or in whole, because it proclaimed God as the Lord of History in contradistinction to the polytheistic patterns that made life and history in general dependent upon the rhythm of natural forces. The sense of historical movement that the Hebrews possessed was based upon the Covenant concept, and related metaphysical dynamism to specific events and periods within the temporal continuum of Israelite life. As such it is diametrically opposed to myth, which in its classical occidental form is timeless and static, and therefore unsuitable for use in connection with Old Testament material.

The general problem of terminology in this regard was discussed by B. S. Childs, who felt that the definition of myth in terms of aesthetic, historical, form-critical, or philosophical categories was inadequate, and proposed that it should be construed in phenomenological terms.[44] This suggestion would seem to be hampered by certain difficulties from a terminological standpoint, if not an existential one. Richardson was considerably nearer the truth of the matter when he spoke of such material as symbolic and partaking of the nature of parable.[45] Unfortunately such a definition fails to convey the dynamic content inherent both in ancient Near Eastern mythology and in the Genesis narratives of the creation and fall. The present writer prefers to regard them as "religious drama," using the noun in the sense entertained by the Homeric verb $\delta\rho\acute{a}\omega$, in which activity was the paramount concern. This definition helps to preserve the form which is essential to the content, without at the same time casting any doubt, historical or otherwise, upon the basic truths en-

[43] WBA, pp. 102f.
[44] B. S. Childs, Myth and Reality in the OT (1960); cf. R. A. F. MacKenzie, Faith and History in the OT (1963), pp. 61ff.
[45] Genesis I-XI, pp. 27ff.

shrined in the narratives themselves. Certainly to follow the lead of Reinhold Niebuhr and other theologians, who apply to the early material in Genesis the concept of myth as a symbolical representation of nonhistorical truth, is to beg the entire question, and to ignore the distinct possibility that the so-called "myth" was for the ancient Hebrews an account of what were actually thought to have been the historical facts of the case.

It was to the credit of the neo-orthodox theologians that they repudiated the puerile view of the fall that regarded the Genesis account as a conglomeration of narrative material merely designed to explain certain circumstances of human society and animal behavior. However, they were unable to accept the concept of the fall as an historical event, a matter upon which Barth in particular was quite evasive.[46] Instead, they insisted that existential method was incompatible with the view of the fall as an occurrence in the remote past, maintaining that it was something that everyone commits. For this reason it was of paramount theological importance for anyone who was prepared to take a realistic view of human nature. For neo-orthodox thinkers the tradition of the New Testament as enshrined in Augustine and Calvin invited a conflict with modern scientific opinion.

By taking note of the attitude of neo-orthodox scholars generally towards the theological and historical problems of the Old Testament, one can find certain anomalies in their position. By emphasizing the subjective nature of the religious experience, neo-orthodoxy is in constant danger of minimizing the objective reality or "givenness" of the revelation itself. No one would deny the importance of an existential relationship with God, which was just as fundamental for the ancient Hebrew as it is for the modern Christian. On the other hand, it must also be recognized that human experience in this regard can never be considered to be coterminous with the objective revelation itself. As far as the fall is concerned, neo-orthodoxy has sought to existentialize the matter by asserting that it is something committed by everybody. This presumably would refer to conscious life and activity, which in turn involves the exercise of free choice. If, therefore, it is possible to share in the fall of man, it should be equally possible to resist participation in the sin of Adam through the equal exercise of such choice, unless *homo sapiens* is the victim of a rigid determinism. From this it would follow that man is able to assist in his own salvation by becoming to a considerable extent his own savior, a position far removed theologically from both the Old and New Testament teachings.

[46] Cf. E. Brunner, *Der Mensch im Widerspruch* (1937), p. 78n. For an orthodox analysis of Brunner's thought see P. K. Jewett, *Brunner's Concept of Revelation* (1954); see also C. Van Til, *The New Modernism, An Appraisal of the Theology of Barth and Brunner* (1946), *The Defence of the Faith* (1947); E. J. Carnell, *The Case for Orthodox Theology* (1962).

There are obvious overtones of Pelagianism in such an inadequate doctrine of man, for if there is neither transmitted corruption nor an implicit sense of guilt in human nature, there would appear to be no absolute necessity for the existence and operation of divine grace. What neo-orthodox theologians have failed to grasp clearly is that by the very act of birth the individual is placed immediately on the side of fallen humanity, and that this is a circumstance upon which individual choice has absolutely no bearing. Modern scientific studies in the realm of human personality have reinforced the Biblical conclusion that man is characterized by a typical egocentric orientation and that this is a transmitted feature of the species. On this matter the Biblical testimony is illuminating in pointing to a time when this condition did not obtain.

The Biblical and Augustinian doctrine of human fall involving an empirical event can never be regarded as scientifically obsolete, since science cannot make a final pronouncement upon it for lack of the kind of evidence with which the descriptive sciences deal. While neo-orthodox writers have rightly stressed the revelational character of the early narratives of Genesis, they have also denied the basically historical nature of revelation by refusing to consider the events that the narratives described as having in fact occurred in a time-space dimension. One would suspect that many exponents of this view have stumbled in characteristic occidental fashion over the form of the early Genesis accounts, confusing the issues of an historic fall with the narrative structure in which that truth was conveyed. As P. K. Jewett has pointed out, this "event-ness" is not simply the form of revelation but actually constitutes the revelation itself, with man falling, not into history, but in it.[47]

In the view of the present writer, to relegate the fall to the shadowy realm of a supra-temporal *Geschichte* or *Urgeschichte* is to adopt an unrealistic standpoint towards one of the most compelling and characteristic features of *homo sapiens* and to remove any substantial foundation for a doctrine of man that does justice to the Old Testament narratives. One unfortunate product of the neo-orthodox attitude towards the fall has been the embarrassing anomaly whereby the disobedience of the first Adam has been existentialized out of history, and the obedience of the Second Adam emphasized as a fact in time and held necessary to all true Christian faith.[48] Since there is a good deal of diversity in the theological pronouncements of representative writers in the neo-orthodox movement, and a certain inevitable distortion or modification of their views by their followers, the reader will recognize that the forego-

[47] In *Revelation and the Bible*, p. 49.
[48] P. K. Jewett in *Baker's Dictionary of Theology*, p. 377.

ing comments are rather general, and in certain particular circumstances might not be applicable to the opinions of some writers.

Any view of the primal history of *homo sapiens* as recorded in Genesis is almost certain to encounter some difficulty with the religious drama that constitutes the indispensable form of the narrative. That it contains what might appear to the occidental mind as bizarre elements that in reality were designed as safeguards for the inner truths has been noted earlier. What is seldom observed, however, is the presence in this and other Biblical narratives of a characteristic Near Eastern literary idiom known to modern scholarship as *merismus*, the relating of antonymic pairs as polar extremes to describe the totality of a particular situation, for example, the ancient Egyptian expression "evil-good," which meant "everything."[49]

Thus in the narrative of the fall, the phrase literally translated "good and evil" as applied to the Tree of Knowledge (Gen. 2:10) should be rendered more properly in a manner recognizing the inherent concept of *merismus*. Unfortunately the conservative nature of Biblical translations is generally such as to perpetuate traditional renderings, however inappropriate they may be in the light of subsequent discovery and research. Even A. M. Honeyman, in a discerning study of *merismus* in Biblical Hebrew, was influenced by tradition in this particular instance.[50] To be true to the idiom, therefore, the "tree" should be envisaged as the "tree of the entire range of moral knowledge." In the light of this the subtlety of the temptation becomes more evident. What was in fact offered to woman was an opportunity to know the entire moral sphere as God does, that is to say, intuitively. Aside from the gross deception involved, the temptation was the kind of flattering appeal to the alleged intuitive qualities of the female that few women would be able to resist. Unfortunately for mankind, the privilege of knowing the range of moral experience invariably carries with it certain harsh realities.

What applies to the narrative idiom in the description of the fall is also true in a rather wider sense of the whole question of evil. Thus it is no longer seen as necessary to envisage elements of an Iranian or other form of dualism when considering the relationship of evil to the Creator, as in Isaiah 45:7. If, as Temple has stated,[51] the most promising philosophies of religion are apt to come to grief upon this question,[52] it is also true that many theologies experience difficulties in ascribing the creation of evil to the Deity, save, perhaps, when dualistic tendencies are contemplated. There can actually be no question that the ancient Hebrews

[49] C. H. Gordon, *Archiv Orientální*, XVIII (1950), p. 202 n. 7.
[50] A. M. Honeyman, *JBL*, LXXI (1952), pp. 11ff.
[51] W. Temple, *Nature, Man and God* (1935), p. 356.
[52] A. M. Fairbairn, *The Philosophy of the Christian Religion* (1903), pp. 94f.

were firmly monistic in outlook, and could embrace such diverse concepts as peace and evil in a manner that depicted them as polar opposites in a comprehensive scheme of existence for which the one true God was ultimately responsible. Thus the emphasis was not upon the creation of evil as a specific metaphysical category; it was instead upon the totality of existence, of which evil constituted only one aspect. This understanding of the situation is obviously of great importance for any exposition of Old Testament theological concepts.

III. THE AUTHORITY OF SCRIPTURE

A. Revelation

One of the great merits of neo-orthodoxy was that it repudiated the nineteenth-century liberal Protestant view of man in many of its facets and dethroned reason as the supreme arbiter of human life, giving priority instead to the concept of divine revelation. However, the movement fell short of the implicit Biblical view that revelation can be subordinated into the categories of general and special. Barth in particular was quite emphatic as to the inadmissibility of the former on the ground that it set up a second source of divine revelation alongside that of Christ. Brunner, on the other hand, upheld the concept of general revelation, maintaining that this did not destroy the image of God in the manner envisaged by Barth. Richardson dissented from both Barth and Brunner in repudiating their view that a saving revelation was to be found only in the Judeo-Christian tradition.[1] He maintained that general as well as special revelation partook of the nature of salvation, but that the former had become distorted through human sin and egocentric preoccupation, making the latter a spiritual necessity. However he denied the possibility of a simple continuity between general and special revelation, since the latter was a qualitatively new kind of existence. Richardson did not support the orthodox view that special revelation consisted of the disclosure of supernatural knowledge, but regarded it instead as the power to apprehend those spiritual truths communicated by means of general revelation.

As far as the Biblical evidence is concerned, the idea of general revelation as that contained in nature (cf. Pss. 19:1ff.; 29:3ff.), history, and conscience was supported on empirical grounds by Paul (cf. Acts 17:27ff.; Rom. 1:26f.; 2:14f.) to show that fallen man could not claim complete exemption from the revelation of God. While no one would suggest that the existence of the God of Israel could be deduced by means of formal logical reasoning on the basis of an empirical examination of the cosmos, the possibility of a general revelation to mankind

---

[1] *Christian Apologetics* (1947), pp. 127ff.

462

needs more than a passing thought if only because modern archaeological discoveries have shown the sophisticated nature of fourth-millennium B.C. life in Mesopotamia, and the concomitant highly developed concepts of a personal deity.

Special or particular revelation complements the distortion of any general manifestation of the nature and character of Deity by focusing attention upon divine redemption through the medium of the historical process, culminating in the work of Jesus Christ. Generally speaking, however, the Bible correlated general and special revelation by showing that the divine λόγος was both Creator and Redeemer, and by introducing special revelation to stress the guilt of humanity. Divine revelation was intimately bound up with the written word of God, which the Christian Church traditionally regarded as in itself constituting a form of revelation. Neo-orthodox writers have protested vigorously against the latter identification, preferring instead to regard Scripture simply as a witness to revelation, and to think of Jesus Christ alone as the Word of God. This attitude is completely unsupported by both Old and New Testaments, which emphasize the concept of divine revelation in the form of rational ideas (cf. Isa. 8:1; Jer. 18:5ff.; Hos. 2:1ff.; 1 Thess. 2:13), and which in any event distinguish between the λόγος of God as the Incarnate Word, and the ῥῆμα, which is the epistemological word of Scripture.

As one result of the neo-orthodox emphasis upon supernatural revelation in terms of a special divine disclosure, the whole question of the nature of revelation has assumed a position of central importance in theological discussion.[2] While it is ultimately the nature of the Christian revelation which is at issue, it is obvious that what the Old Testament has to contribute to this matter is basic to all other considerations. At the risk of some repetition, it should be remarked that the earliest Christian views concerning revelation proclaimed the self-disclosure of God in the Hebrew Scriptures. In the Early Church this attitude was enlarged to include the canonical writings of the New as well as of the Old Testament as constituting the tangible record of divine utterances bearing witness to the nature and purpose of Deity. The medieval insistence upon supplementing and authenticating the Scriptures by means of the *ecclesia docens* was repudiated by the Reformers, who held that, under the Holy Spirit, Scripture was self-authenticating and self-interpreting. Luther stressed the importance of approaching Old Testament doctrines against a background of sympathetic experience before undertaking any

---

[2] Cf. D. M. Baillie, *The Idea of Revelation in Recent Thought* (1956), pp. 1f.; H. D. McDonald, *Theories of Revelation. An Historical Study, 1860-1960* (1963); H. Schuster, *Offenbarung Gottes im AT* (1962).

interpretation of the narratives, emphasizing the importance of personal trust or *fiducia* in the Biblical revelation.[3]

With the seventeenth century a liberal humanism arose that reflected the tradition of the ancient Greek Sophists in elevating man and his reason as the sole standard of judgment and the final authority for faith. With the period of the Enlightenment in the following century this rationalistic subjectivism came into full flower, and with Kant there was formulated the denial of any factual knowledge involving the supra-sensible. The liberal theological interests of Schleiermacher sought to ransom Christianity from complete rationalism by introducing the concept of a mystical subjectivism, which, as far as Old Testament theology was concerned, was limited to the examination of certain human feelings or emotional reactions involving religious phenomena. For Schleiermacher, revelation was not a disclosure of fundamental truth from God to mankind, but at best represented the progress of humanity towards a consciousness of God. Under the impact of nineteenth-century evolutionism the Wellhausen school jettisoned the supernaturalism implicit in the outlook of the Hebrews in favor of a religious record rewritten in terms of the naturalistic principle of monolinear evolution.[4]

When the confident anthropocentrism of the nineteenth century went into eclipse, largely as the result of World War I, the vacuum began to be filled by the rise of the neo-orthodox movement proper and the dialectical theology of crisis associated with Barth. Against a background of existential method, the adherents of this position sought to resolve the problem of authority in religion by reasserting the priority of revelation over reason in theology, but doing so without becoming involved in what was regarded as orthodox obscurantism. Their concept of inspiration and the nature of the *kerygma* prevented them from identifying the words of Scripture with the Word of God, since its human dimension made the Bible fallible and liable to error. This standpoint has led many theologians to reject, in part or in whole, the orthodox concept of Scripture as the divine communication to the Biblical writers of unique and otherwise inaccessible truths about the divine nature and purpose, and to think of revelation as the process by which God directed the historical sequences recorded in the Biblical narratives, and made individuals aware by one means or another of His existence and activity. Concomitant with this has been the abandonment of the traditional view that the Biblical revelation was largely propositional in character. This has led many scholars to the conclusion that the Bible is most adequately thought

[3] Cf. M. Reu, *Luther and the Scriptures* (1924), pp. 24ff.; B. B. Warfield, *Calvin and Calvinism* (1931), p. 83; J. Kostlin, *The Theology of Luther* (1897), II, p. 252.

[4] J. I. Packer in *Revelation and the Bible*, p. 92.

of as a fallible human response to revelation, and not as revelation in the sense of the communication of abstract moral and spiritual truths.

The majority of theological writers who do not observe the canons of orthodox thought on the question of revelation have envisaged two major foci in which man is confronted authoritatively and directly by revelation. The first is found in the sequence of historical events by which God disclosed Himself to the original witness of the "mighty acts," an emphasis that is of interest to those scholars who are primarily concerned with Biblical history.[5] The second "moment of revelation" consists in the repeated encounter in which the content of the original revelation is mediated to, and appropriated by, successive generations of the faithful; and this aspect is of primary concern to the writers in the fields of apologetics and systematic theology.[6] A further group of scholars, predominantly British, insist upon divine initiative in the matter of revelation without adopting the conclusions of Barth and Brunner, and in general deny that Scripture as such constitutes revealed truth.[7]

An ardent adherent of the naturalistic approach to the question of revelation in the Old Testament was W. A. Irwin. In a composite work published in 1947, he viewed religion as in the last analysis a social process, and as such identifiable with the divine working in human hearts everywhere, an activity that constantly urged mankind to higher

[5] E.g. C. H. Dodd, *History and the Gospel* (1938); H. Wheeler Robinson, *Redemption and Revelation in the Actuality of History* (1940), *Inspiration and Revelation in the OT* (1946); A. Simpson, *Revelation and Response in the OT* (1947); G. E. Wright, *God Who Acts* (1952); S. Mowinckel, *The OT as Word of God* (1959).

[6] E.g. K. Barth, *Kirchliche Dogmatik*, I, 1, p. 2, E. tr. *The Doctrine of the Word of God* (1956); F. W. Camfield, *Revelation and the Holy Spirit* (1934); J. Baillie and H. Martin (eds.), *Revelation* (1937); J. Baillie, *Our Knowledge of God* (1939); E. Lewis, *A Philosophy of the Christian Revelation* (1940); H. R. Niebuhr, *The Meaning of Revelation* (1940); Reinhold Niebuhr, *Moral Man and Immoral Society* (1932), *The Nature and Destiny of Man* (1941); E. Brunner, *The Divine-Human Encounter* (1944), *Revelation and Reason* (1947); N. F. S. Ferré, *Faith and Reason* (1946); R. Niebuhr, *Faith and History* (1949); P. Tillich, *Systematic Theology, I* (1953).

[7] These included John Oman, *Grace and Personality* (1925), *Vision and Authority* (1929), and *The Natural and the Supernatural* (1931); W. Temple, *Nature, Man, and God* (1934); J. Y. MacKinnon, *The Protestant Doctrine of Revelation* (1946); Alan Richardson, *Christian Apologetics* (1947); and D. D. Williams, *What Present-Day Theologians Are Thinking* (1952) and *Interpreting Theology 1918-1952* (1953). Treatments of the question of revelation from an orthodox standpoint were published by J. Orr, *Revelation and Inspiration* (1910); B. B. Warfield, *Revelation and Inspiration* (1927); John Murray *et al.*, *The Infallible Word* (1946); Louis Berkhof, *Reformed Dogmatics: Introduction* (1932); T. Engelder, *Scripture Cannot Be Broken* (1944); L. S. Chafer, *Systematic Theology* (1948); Geerhardus Vos, *Biblical Theology* (1948); and C. F. H. Henry, *Remaking the Modern Mind* (1948), *The Protestant Dilemma* (1948), and (ed.) *Revelation and the Bible* (1959).

goals.[8] Divine revelation was thus fully human and natural, and to be connoted only in terms of universal divine process. A special revelation in Israel could only be countenanced in the sense that the Bible stands supreme in the exaltation of its knowledge of God, in the nobility of its vision of human duty, and in its power to stimulate the imagination with a vision of possibilities that lie open to the human spirit. This attempt to minimize the supernatural experience of God, so prominent throughout Old Testament history, enshrined the worst features of philosophical naturalism by being aligned to a concept of evolutionary meliorism, and by refusing to treat the primary source material on its own terms. The logical outcome of such an unscientific procedure can only be the loss of a credible divine Word, and, indeed, of the concept of God Himself. If one commences a consideration of revelation from an anthropocentric standpoint, it is difficult to see how one can possibly avoid losing the essence of what historic Christianity has connoted by the general term, namely an activity of God.

Although neo-orthodoxy has performed a valuable service in emphasizing the reality of sin, its interpretation of revelation in terms of selective historical events, fallible records, and encounter with God can only end in subjectivism and in a mystical interpretation of Scripture that fails to do justice to the Biblical view of itself as the words and acts of God revealed through a controlled redemptive history and recorded in written form to constitute an authoritative basis for human thought concerning the divine. There is an avowed Schleiermacherian influence evident in the thought of most neo-orthodox writers, and this fact makes for obvious internal difficulties in their consideration of revelation. Not the least of these is the attempt to erect some superstructure of the supra-rational upon the foundations of philosophical rationalism. It is not easy to see how such theological writers can claim that they have substituted the Biblical conception of the Deity for the liberal Protestant one while still retaining the liberal understanding of Scripture as fallible, and remain consistent methodologically.[9]

While neo-orthodoxy in full flood denied the possibility of an authoritative verbal revelation as such, a matter of grave doubt for such writers as Brunner and Tillich, the tide has now turned to the point where it is no longer possible for scholars to dismiss out of hand the orthodox doctrine of Scripture as the Word of God on the ground that a revelation in words is not possible.[10] The fact of the matter is that the revelation of a personal Deity can only be properly effected through the medium of

[8] W. A. Irwin in H. R. Willoughby (ed.), *The Study of the Bible Today and Tomorrow* (1947), pp. 259ff.

[9] Cf. J. Lowe in *The Interpretation of the Bible* (ed. C. W. Dugmore, 1944), p. 113.

[10] Cf. V. Taylor, *The Person of Jesus Christ in NT Teaching* (1958), pp. 246ff.; A. M. Ramsey, *Durham Essays and Addresses* (1957), p. 32.

466

personal communication, the most characteristic form of which is verbal. While the order and functioning of nature and the events of history may be appealed to as valid means of revelation, they are at best inadequate in comparison to the proclamation of the divine word through law, prophecy, and the person of Jesus Christ. Furthermore, it should be noticed that according to uniform Biblical tradition, the revelation enshrined in the written records is substantially propositional in nature. Finally, on *a priori* grounds, there is no reason, as Reid has pointed out, why a divine disclosure such as that represented by the Biblical writings should not have the character of a body of divinely guaranteed truths.[11]

B. INSPIRATION

While a place has been found in modern theology for supernatural revelation, the same cannot be said for the concept of supernatural inspiration that would give validity and authority to the written record of the divine revelation. The orthodox doctrine of inspiration was formulated in the Early Church from Scriptural allusions to the work of the Holy Spirit in connection with the testimony of Scriptural writings (cf. Matt. 22:43; John 14:26; 2 Tim. 3:16; 2 Pet. 1:21 *et al.*). This attitude was in general harmony with that of contemporary Judaism, which adhered to a high view of inspiration, especially towards the Torah. For the Early Church, however, the objective inspiration of the written record was matched by a subjective enlightening of the human understanding, the latter being a peculiar function of the Holy Spirit. This conception helped to guard against any association with pagan ideas regarding inspiration, which tended to depreciate the human element and interpret inspiration as a purely psychological phenomenon.[12]

The Church Fathers accepted the inspiration and authority of the Scriptures as self-evident, and gave proper recognition to the place of the human element in the corpus of the Biblical writings generally. During the medieval period a high doctrine of inspiration was maintained, although the authority of Scripture was minimized considerably when the Bible was considered as only one source of Church doctrine. In repudiating this development, the Reformers reasserted the traditional view that God alone was the true author of Scripture, a matter that was particularly emphasized by Calvin.[13] Reformed theologians of the seventeenth century, while upholding the teaching of the Reformers regarding inspiration, tended to subsume the personality of the human author under that of the divine.[14] They also pushed the

---

11 *The Authority of Scripture* (1957), pp. 162f.
12 Cf. Plato, *Ion*, 533.
13 *Institutes*, I, 7, 2ff.
14 G. W. Bromiley in *Revelation and the Bible,* p. 213.

doctrine of verbal inspiration to extremes by insisting upon the inspired nature of the Massoretic pointing system, and made inerrancy the increasing basis of their doctrine of inspiration.

The rationalistic attacks upon the literary and historical material of Scripture, common in the following century, involved a rejection of the classic concept of inspiration to a greater or lesser degree, and a restatement of the situation in terms of conformity to the concepts of pure reason. The influence of Kant led to the subjective postulates of Schleiermacher, who subordinated the divine element to the human and understood inspiration as the activity of the common spirit of the faithful, which because of its intrinsic nature could bestow equal inspiration upon any great spiritual composition.[15] The mysticism of Schleiermacher, compounded by the influence of Hegel, who separated faith from reason, and Ritschl, who distinguished sharply between the scientific and the religious, provided a fertile soil from which the various forms of liberalism subsequently sprang.

Of the neo-orthodox writers Brunner in particular was hostile to the idea of verbal inspiration, which for him had deified the "letter" of the Bible to the point of imprisoning the Spirit between the covers of a book.[16] Brunner maintained that the prophetic utterances of the Old Testament came closest to the concept of verbal inspiration, though such a theory had clearly been demolished by higher criticism and evolutionary science.[17] Biblical infallibility was precluded on the ground of alleged errors and contradictions in the Scriptural narratives, which would point in general to a degree of restriction upon the activity of the Holy Spirit in the matter of inspiration. While Barth was less vehement than Brunner in his views on verbal or plenary inspiration, he too rejected the orthodox viewpoint in his attempt to formulate a concept of Biblical authority.[18]

In venturing to define the concept of inspiration, modern theologians do so with some hesitation, and on occasions with frank misunderstanding of what is involved. Thus some authors speak of "degrees of inspiration"—when probably they should be thinking of progressive revelation—oblivious to the fact that inspiration does not admit of degrees, any more than morality, honesty, and similar concepts do. In this connection it should be noted that the Bible as a whole, and not least the Old Testament, never enunciates any principle for distinguishing between those parts which are inspired, and therefore authoritative for faith and doctrine, and any ostensibly uninspired portions, which would conse-

[15] Schleiermacher, *Der christliche Glaube nach dem Grundsätzen der evangelischen Kirche* (1821-22), II, pp. 409ff.
[16] *Revelation and Reason* (1947), p. 145.
[17] *Ibid.*, pp. 133, 286f.
[18] Cf. Barth, *Zwischen den Zeiten* (1925), III, pp. 215ff.

quently not possess binding authority upon Jew or Christian. Other writers have tended to confuse the idea of Biblical inspiration with the divine illumination of the human mind that enables the revealed truths to be appropriated.[19] Even those who criticize the terms "verbal" and "plenary" as means of describing inspiration are not always clear as to what is to be understood by them.

Accordingly it should be recognized that the concept of the inspiration of Scripture must be evaluated in the light of what the Bible teaches about the term "inspiration." The text that constitutes the *locus classicus* of the doctrine occurs in 2 Timothy 3:16, which in the AV was translated, "All Scripture is given by inspiration of God...," a rendering that was modified in the RV to follow Tyndale in reading, "Every Scripture inspired of God...."[20] The point at issue is the interpretation of the Greek word θεόπνευστος, a term that occurs nowhere else in Scripture. The sense of the word is passive rather than active, and the implicit movement is outwards rather than inwards. Thus the adjective speaks of being "out-breathed" rather than "in-breathed," so that to speak of Scripture as θεόπνευστος means that God has breathed out Scripture as part of His creative activity, not that it is "breathed-into" by God, or that it is inspiring, true though the latter may be in other connections. Because of the absence of the verb "to be" in the Greek, the way in which Tyndale construed the clause has found wide approval among liberal writers.[21] Even a casual glance at the Greek, however, will be sufficient to indicate that the first three words constitute a clause that embodies its own separate idea, and this is linked up with the development of that concept by means of the conjunction "and." This is a common Greek construction, and when translated should be rendered so as to indicate an elliptical verb "to be," as was done in the AV.

As against the complaint of Brunner that διδασκαλία should properly be rendered "teaching" rather than "doctrine,"[22] it must be remembered that the Latin word *doctrina* signified both teaching and doctrine, without prejudice as to the nature of either. Paul was making it clear that the sacred writings were God-breathed, and therefore valuable for both life and faith. On such a basis orthodoxy has understood inspiration to describe in a general manner the influence of the Holy Spirit upon the minds of certain individuals, making them media for the communication of revelation. With regard to Scripture itself, the term was employed

---

[19] E.g. J. Baillie, *The Idea of Revelation in Recent Thought*, p. 66.

[20] πᾶσα γραφὴ θεόπνευστος καὶ ὠφέλιμος πρὸς διδασκαλίαν ..., where the adjective θεόπνευστος is in the predicative position. To translate καὶ here as "also" is inadmissible, since it constitutes the simple conjunctive particle "and." Cf. J. N. D. Kelley, *A Commentary on the Pastoral Epistles* (1964), pp. 202f.

[21] So S. Mowinckel, *The OT as Word of God*, p. 23.

[22] E. Brunner, *Revelation and Reason*, p. 9n.

469

actively to denote the means by which Scripture was produced, and passively to describe the inspired nature of the Biblical material.[23]

The method by which the written testimonies were produced under divine inspiration has frequently been misunderstood. As a result the views of some conservative scholars have been caricatured by more liberal writers.[24] Accordingly it should be made clear that nowhere does the Bible even countenance a concept of mechanical dictation or automatic writing, let alone propound it. Such an idea of divine inspiration belongs strictly to Philo, to the Talmud, and to some of the early Christian Fathers such as Augustine. But even Augustine was careful not to obliterate the human element so obviously necessary in any understanding of inspired writing.[25] It was only in the seventeenth century that continental Reformed dogmaticians began to incline to a theory of dictation,[26] but this tendency was certainly never a part of the theological scene in England, nor was it characteristic of Protestant theology generally.[27] Of the nineteenth-century writers in English, only Cunningham used the concept of "dictation," and at that in a metaphorical and carefully qualified sense.[28] The basic inspirational idea was modified by the term "plenary" in the writings of Lee and Orr, while Strong sought to clarify the meaning of inspiration by the use of the expression "dynamical inspiration."[29] Where other orthodox theological writers entertained the doctrine of verbal inspiration, they did so in a manner that disclaimed completely any mechanical delineation of the method of inspiration, and allowed proper scope for the spontaneous expression of the individual personality in the process of writing.[30] What

[23] J. I. Packer, *NBD*, p. 564.

[24] Cf. E. Brunner, *Revelation and Reason*, pp. 127f.; G. Hebert, *Fundamentalism and the Church of God* (1957), p. 56; A. Richardson, *Chamber's Encyclopaedia* (1959 ed.), p. 114; J. Huxtable, *The Bible Says* (1962), pp. 64ff.

[25] Cf. *De Consensu Evang.* II, 12; R. Preus, *The Inspiration of Scripture* (1955), pp. 53ff.

[26] Cf. H. Heidegger, *Corp. Theol.* II, 34; W. Bucan, *Inst. Theol.* I, 4, 2.

[27] J. I. Packer, *Fundamentalism and the Word of God: Some Evangelical Princ'ples* (1958), p. 79.

[28] W. Cunningham, *Theological Lectures* (1878), pp. 349ff.

[29] W. Lee, *The Inspiration of the Holy Scriptures* (1857), pp. 21ff.; J. Orr, *Revelation and Inspiration*, p. 211; A. H. Strong, *Systematic Theology* (1949 ed.), pp. 208ff.

[30] This attitude was represented by such scholars as C. Wordsworth, *The Inspiration of the Bible* (1861), p. 5; C. Hodge, *Systematic Theology* (1873), I, pp. 156f.; W. B. Pope, *Compendium of Christian Theology* (1879 ed.), I, 171, 183; C. H. Waller, *Authoritative Inspiration* (1887), pp. 200f.; H. C. G. Moule, *Veni Creator* (1890), pp. 53f.; B. B. Warfield, *The Inspiration and Authority of the Bible* (1951 ed.), pp. 153ff., 173n. J. M. Gray specifically rejected the mechanical view of inspiration as a tenet of American conservative belief, *The Fundamentals* (1917 ed.), II, 16; British scholars in the evangelical area never adhered to it at any time, and even repudiated it, as Hebert conceded, *Fundamentalism and the Church of God*, p. 56.

both British and American conservative writers were concerned to safeguard was the fact of inspiration, and not any particular theory as to the method by which it was achieved.

In any consideration of the nature and fact of inspiration it would seem the course of wisdom to refrain from going beyond what the Bible itself has to say concerning this extremely important doctrine. It appears evident from the reference in Second Timothy that inspiration did not terminate with the individuals responsible for the composition of the Scriptural writings, as maintained by many liberal thinkers,[31] but in the written end-product of their inspiration. For the prophets of the Old Testament period, divine revelation was basically verbal, but was accompanied on occasions by certain visionary concomitants which, as Köhler has recognized, also constitute verbal revelation.[32]

Great caution should be urged at this point, however, against reading into the Biblical concept of inspiration ideas derived from the Latin term *inspiratio*. While there is no explicit denial that a divine accentuation or heightening of the native human abilities of the individual prophet took place in certain instances, the Old Testament as a whole does not teach that such was a general preliminary to prophetic pronouncements. In ways that obviously differed according to the personality of the individual involved, the authors of the various Scriptural writings were used by God to produce the message that He desired to communicate through them to mankind.[33] Until more is known about the psychology of the Hebrew prophetic consciousness, it appears unwise to add to the statement that the kind of inspiration under which the Biblical authors produced their writings did not detract from the exercise of the human personality, but instead brought the creative faculties of the individual composers into particular focus for their task. Their sense of responsibility extended to the factual accuracy of their material, and in this connection it should be noted that many of the alleged errors in Scripture are nothing more than misinterpretations of the oriental scene by the western mind, or are the product of sheer ignorance of facets of ancient Near Eastern life on the part of modern scholars.

In the view of the present writer, the usage of terms such as "verbal" and "plenary," although they are meant to safeguard the fact of inspiration, tends to obscure the issue in the minds of many thinkers, and in some instances these words introduce actual confusion into the concept.

---

[31] Cf. S. Mowinckel, *The OT as Word of God*, pp. 25f.

[32] L. Köhler, *OT Theology* (1957), p. 103.

[33] Cf. G. H. W. Lampe, *IDB*, II, p. 714. For a Roman Catholic treatment of the doctrine of Biblical inspiration see J. Levie, *La Bible, Parole Humaine et Message de Dieu* (1958), E. tr. S. H. Treman, *The Bible, Word of God in Words of Men* (1962); J. L. McKenzie, *Myths and Realities: Studies in Biblical Theology* (1963), pp. 37ff.

Perhaps the safest course would be to speak simply of the inspiration of Scripture, without introducing any other kind of qualification that could be taken as pointing to some opinion as to the mode of inspiration which the situation clearly does not warrant.

Brunner was correct in assuming that the closest analogy to verbal inspiration is in the prophetic experience of revelation.[34] This does in fact characterize inspiration proper as the process by which God stirred His chosen servants to communicate His salvation, and to preserve it for posterity in written form. Scripture thus constitutes written revelation in precisely the same way as the prophetic oracles consisted of spoken revelation. Again it should be observed that the Old Testament narratives relating to divine self-disclosure in "redemptive history" are not merely human testimony to divine revelation, but actually constitute the essence of the revelation itself. Just as the prophetic experience of the divine afflatus validated and certified the truth of that aspect of the divine mind and will that the servants of God were concerned to communicate, so the concept of inspiration may be taken in general terms as a guarantee of an essential harmony, whether involving meaning or fact, between the mind of God and the words of men as contained in the Biblical narratives.

Neo-orthodox writers have generally taken pains to clarify their conviction that the "Word of the Lord" cannot be identified with the totality of the Scriptural corpus. Consequently they have stressed that while Scripture contains the divine Word, it ought not to be regarded as consisting of the Word of God *in toto*. That this is rather an artificial approach to the question of Biblical inspiration was pointed out by Griffith Thomas, who wrote:

> It is sometimes said that the Bible *is* the Word of God, while at other times it is said that the Bible *contains* the Word of God. These are both true, if held together, though either alone is liable to misapprehension. If we only say the Bible *is* the Word of God, we are in danger of forgetting that it contains the words of men also, many of which are not true in themselves, though the record that they were spoken is true and reliable. If, on the other hand, we limit our belief to the phrase, the Bible *contains* the Word of God, there is the opposite danger of not knowing which is God's Word and which is man's, an entirely impossible position. The Bible *is* the Word of God in the sense that it conveys to us an accurate record of everything God intended man to know and learn in connection with his will. The Bible *contains* the Word of God in the sense that in it is enshrined the Word of God which is revealed to us for our redemption.[35]

While it is true that the setting of the divine proclamations in past ages was a deliberate element in the self-revelation of God, it is important to note, as Ellison has pointed out, that the Scripture as a record is not in

---

[34] E. Brunner, *Revelation and Reason,* p. 122 n. 9.
[35] W. H. Griffith Thomas, *The Principles of Theology* (1930), p. 119.

itself life-giving.[36] From this standpoint it cannot be regarded as the agent of revelation *per se*, for the simple reason that it is never more than an instrument to be used by the Holy Spirit of God in order to make the revelation contained in Scripture personal to the believer.

C. INFALLIBILITY AND INERRANCY

The concepts of inerrancy[37] and infallibility have frequently been applied by conservative writers to the Scriptural narratives in order to indicate the completeness of inspiration and authority. Some would argue strongly, however, that to set up inerrancy as the basis of a doctrine of inspiration is in their view open to the serious objection that the demonstration of inaccuracies, errors, or inconsistencies, whether actual or alleged, immediately involves the rejection of the idea of inspiration as well as that of inerrancy. Such an objection was the basis of Dewey Beegle's attempt to relate inspiration to an errant Scripture on the premise of a subjective definition of revelation.[38] As a prime indication of error in the original text of the Old Testament he adduced the reign of Pekah of Israel, who according to 2 Kings 15:27 ruled for twenty years, but whose actual reign, based on Assyrian sources, lasted probably not more than eight years.[39]

While at first sight there appears to be a serious discrepancy in the Biblical text at this point by comparison with extra-Biblical sources, a number of considerations have to be borne in mind. First, any computation of regnal years must be made according to the practices current in the appropriate period of ancient Near Eastern life. Second, not all of the factors that led the chronologist to assign a twenty-year rule to Pekah may be evident from a reading of the Biblical narrative. Third, the temptation to identify Pekah with his precursor Pekahiah must be resisted in the interests of an honest attempt to ascertain and do justice to the facts of the case. From the Assyrian Eponym Chronicle it is clear that the reign of Pekah terminated in 732/31 B.C., and that on the basis of the death of Pekahiah in 740/39 B.C., the rule of Pekah over Israel did in fact last not more than eight years.

On the other hand, 2 Kings 16:1 states explicitly that Ahaz began to reign in the seventeenth year of Pekah. This need present no problem, however, when it is remembered that Ahaz was co-regent with Jotham his father from 744/43 B.C. until 732/31 B.C., the year in which Pekah died, becoming the senior partner in this alliance in 735 B.C., the event to which the Kings reference most probably alludes. What is significant

---

[36] H. L. Ellison, *EQ*, XXVI (1954), pp. 213f.

[37] This is not a "modern doctrine" as some liberals, e.g. A. G. Hebert, *The Authority of the Old Testament* (1947), p. 98, have supposed, being in fact orthodox Church teaching until the seventeenth century.

[38] D. M. Beegle, *The Inspiration of Scripture* (1963).

[39] *ARAB*, I, sect. 816; cf. *MNHK*, pp. 119ff.

for the computation of the Pekah regime is the fact that the king reckoned his years from 752 B.C., that is to say, the year following the death of Jeroboam II. Since Pekah was an adjutant in the army of Pekahiah, king of Israel, 742/41-740/39 B.C., and quite possibly of Gileadite stock,[40] it may well have happened that in the period of unrest following the death of Jeroboam II he seized power in Gilead and established firm control over that part of Transjordan. If this was actually the case, it would go far towards explaining the insecurity of Menahem and the intervention of Tiglathpileser III, to whom Pekah fell victim. While the Old Testament narratives make no specific mention of Pekah as the head of a Gileadite monarchy from 752 B.C., the tradition by which he reckoned his dates from the year after the death of Jeroboam II is of considerable significance in this regard. As Curtis has pointed out, such a Gileadite regime would, when computed with the accession of Pekah to the throne of Israel in 740/39 B.C., enable him to lay claim to a total reign of twenty years, as recorded in Kings.[41] Probably the best explanation of the situation is that the period of his reign consisted of partly usurped years. That such a practice was not unknown in the Near East is indicated by the fact that in the Raameside records of Egypt, Haremhab, ca. 1300 B.C., usurped the regnal years of Akhenaton and certain of his successors.

To regard the Old Testament statement as a factual error, in the manner of Beegle, constitutes a vast oversimplification of the problem, which is certainly amenable to a very different solution. As has been observed previously, so many of the alleged errors in the Biblical record are the product of occidental ignorance of ancient Near Eastern life and customs, rather than the work of the original authors. This is one reason why conservative scholars deprecate the confident pronouncements concerning errors which are sometimes made. As Thiele has so clearly shown, there is no adequate reason to doubt that the chronologists of the Old Testament were honest individuals who were as much concerned for the accuracy of their facts as for the characteristics of the various rulers whose reigns were duly recorded. Again it needs to be observed that, in the realm of historical phenomena in particular, archaeological discoveries have shown beyond reasonable doubt the amazing accuracy of the Old Testament material as compared with other historical sources in antiquity.

To the present writer, two basic issues are involved in the question of infallibility. The first is whether in fact the concept of infallibility is really a concomitant of inspiration or not. Some have pointed out that the term itself is not Biblical in nature, and was not especially prominent in the theology of the Reformers. It can be applied most properly only

[40] H. B. MacLean, *IDB*, III, p. 709; cf. S. J. De Vries, *IDB*, I, p. 593.
[41] J. B. Curtis, *JBL*, LXXX (1961), pp. 362f.; similarly J. Gray, *I and II Kings: A Commentary* (1963), pp. 63f.

to the prophetic and apostolic writings as the authoritative revelation of God which culminated in the work of Jesus Christ and as authentic records of that revelation. In the last resort, however, infallibility is the characteristic of the Divine Author of Scripture and then, by derivation, of the writings of which Scripture is composed.

The second issue concerns the true meaning of infallibility. This will need careful examination if it is not to go beyond what the Bible actually claims for itself in this regard. Here Scripture makes it explicit that its testimony to the saving revelation and redemption of God in Christ is reliable, and that it furnishes an authoritative norm of faith and conduct for the believer. It shows that the Word of God achieves its intended objective, and at the same time serves as a medium through which the Holy Spirit, by whom it has been given, can speak to mankind. In an inspired Scripture, therefore, it would seem logical to expect infallibility as here defined to be a normal constituent element.

IV. PROBLEMS IN OLD TESTAMENT THEOLOGY

A. The Covenant

The attempt by Eichrodt to demonstrate the essential unity of Israelite faith by relating it to the central concept of the Covenant brought a welcome emphasis to bear upon what is surely one of the most characteristic facets of Hebrew religious life. The idea of a covenant as a bond linking two parties by agreement has been demonstrated archaeologically from the second millennium B.C. in the ancient Near East.[1] The Hebrew ברית probably goes back to the Akkadian word *birîtu*, signifying a bond or fetter, while the Hebrew expression כרת ברית, meaning literally "to cut a covenant," has been found in two instances on the Qatna texts, which probably date from the fifteenth century B.C. One tablet containing this expression consisted of an agreement in which a number of men contracted to enter into the service of one another and discharge certain obligations. The other instance occurred on a tablet that listed the rations of food to be received by the men who had thus contracted for service.[2] These contracts were doubtless inspired by the agreements made between cities and states during the Mari Age,[3] which in turn depended upon earlier Sumerian originals.

Second-millennium B.C. covenants among the Hittites have been shown to consist of suzerainty and parity agreements.[4] In the former only the inferior party was bound by an oath, whereas in the latter both sides were under an obligation to abide by the oath which sealed the agreement. In the suzerainty treaty, which, according to Mendenhall, was the principal form, the vassal did not only have to take an oath, but had also to profess his faith in the integrity and magnanimity of the overlord. Such legal undertakings between a great king and a vassal normally commenced with a preamble in which the instigator of the covenant was

---

[1] Cf. D. J. McCarthy, *Treaty and Covenant, A Study in Form in the Ancient Oriental Documents and in the OT* (1963).

[2] W. F. Albright, *BASOR*, No. 121 (1951), pp. 21f.

[3] Cf. G. E. Mendenhall, *BA*, XI, No. 1 (1948), p. 18.

[4] G. E. Mendenhall, *BA*, XVII, No. 3 (1954), pp. 50ff.; reprinted as *Law and Covenant in Israel and the Ancient Near East* (1955); cf. Mendenhall in *IDB*, I, pp. 714ff.

identified and his credentials established.[5] This was followed by an outline of the historical relations between the parties entering into the agreement (cf. Exod. 20:2; Josh. 24:2f.), with proper stress upon the integrity of the overlord and his graciousness towards his vassal (Deut. 7:7).[6] Then followed the description of the obligations to be imposed upon and accepted by the vassal, and this normally included a prohibition against the latter's engaging in foreign alliances (cf. Exod. 20:3; 34:14; Josh. 24:14). A further provision stipulated that the document should remain in the deposit of the vassal and be read publicly at intervals, in order to remind him of the nature of the obligations undertaken (cf. Exod. 25:16, 21; Deut. 31:9ff.; Josh. 24:26; 1 Kgs. 8:9). A concluding portion normally listed the deities as witnesses and enumerated the blessings or curses that would occur according as the covenant was kept or violated (cf. Exod. 23:20ff.; Lev. 26:3ff.; Deut. 27:12ff.). In Joshua 24:22 the Israelites replaced the heathen deities as witnesses; cf. Isaiah 1:2; Hosea 2:21f.; and Micah 6:2. The remarkable parallels to the Covenant relationship between God and Israel set the Sinai agreement firmly and authentically against a second-millennium B.C. milieu, and do not require a date for the Covenant outside the Heroic Age.

The significance of the Hebrew Covenant, however, can only be understood most fully against the background of the Old Testament itself, for while the idea of an agreement between two responsible contracting parties is implicit in the Sinai Covenant, the contract itself clearly involves a dispensation of grace and promise for the future.[7] The first reference to a covenant in the Old Testament is the agreement with Noah before the Flood (Gen. 6:18ff.). The nature of an Old Testament covenant is shown clearly by the post-diluvian pact with him. In this instance, as in others, the approach was initiated by God but the benefits were universal and unconditional. The Abrahamic Covenant contained the same concept of divine dispensation, but interpreted it more narrowly to include the promises connected with the inheritance of Canaan, the multiplying of the offspring of Abraham, and the general assurance of divine support for the people. In the latter regard, however, the Covenant exhibited certain particularistic features, such as the exclusion of Ishmael (Gen. 17:18ff.) and the restriction of the blessing as issuing through the offspring of Abraham rather than being given to all mankind. Yet as in the Hittite suzerainty treaties, the overlordship and supremacy of God were made quite evident at the commencement, and the responsibility for keeping the provisions of the agreement was placed squarely upon Abraham and his offspring. In these circumstances it

---

[5] Cf. Exod. 20:1f., Josh. 24:2; M. G. Kline, *Treaty of the Great King* (1963), pp. 10ff.

[6] Cf. *ANET*, p. 204.

[7] Cf. J. Murray, *The Covenant of Grace* (1953), p. 31.

should be noted that the unilateral bestowal of divine grace and the human obligation to observe the conditions set out in the Covenant are complementary rather than mutually exclusive factors. There is a pronounced spiritual element underlying the entire contractual procedure, which if entertained seriously would demand a high degree of consecration and single-mindedness from the human participants. Certain other concomitant features indicate the great antiquity of the Abrahamic Covenant, as Mendenhall has shown, which serve to place it firmly within the pre-Mosaic era.[8]

As a result of activities of the Wellhausen school, the Mosaic Covenant was regarded as a form of tribal religious relationship in which the deity was little more than the symbol of the tribe itself. On this basis it was affirmed that it was only with the eighth-century prophets that a sense of awareness of the ethical content of this relationship developed, and this was followed in the immediate pre-exilic period with the enunciation of the Covenant concept proper in the thought of the prophet Jeremiah. As the result of modern archaeological discoveries, however, it is now possible to place the Mosaic Covenant confidently against the background of the Late Bronze Age. It is important to notice further in this connection that there was an avowed social and political aspect to the Covenant relationship as well as a purely religious one. The concept of the Sinai agreement would be virtually meaningless were it not for the fact that the religious and ethical norms that it contained were designed to produce a reciprocal action in strictly social terms. Not merely were the adherents bound together in loyalty to the Deity, but they were linked by the Covenant relationship as the *people* of God. It was at this juncture that they received a unique identity. They became the specific medium of divine revelation in "saving history," and at the same time they received a missionary vocation as the divine witnesses to the surrounding pagan nations.[9] Quite aside from its religious implications, the Covenant furnished a distinctive form and structure for the social life of the Israelite community. Yet in all this it must never be forgotten that it was the religious nature of the Covenant that furnished its characteristic uniqueness.

Basic to the continuance of the relationship was the demand that divine holiness should be the governing factor in Israelite life (cf. Lev. 19:2; Deut. 6:4). This holiness would be made apparent in the continuing obedience of the religious community to the commands of God, and would constitute the means by which the Covenant agreement would continue to function for the blessing and prosperity of Israel (Lev.

---

[8] *IDB*, I, p. 718.

[9] For H. H. Rowley, *Israel's Mission to the World* (1939), pp. 2ff., this "wider vision" was to be interpreted predominantly in terms of post-exilic religious developments.

478

26:3ff.). Disobedience, whether in the form of passive negligence or active rebellion, constituted an act of sin that could speedily undermine the entire Covenant relationship if it assumed communal proportions. In this sense von Rad was correct in asserting that the individual was so closely identified with the group that when he committed an act of sin it had repercussions throughout the entire community.[10] However, it should be observed that sin belongs properly to the category of the sacred rather than the social, and that it constitutes an affront to and an assault upon the holiness of God. The weakness of the presentation by von Rad in this area of Old Testament theology is his deficient view of sin, characterized by his reluctance to consider man as a fallen creature. This attitude was shared by many contemporary German scholars, who were influenced by the philosophical speculations of Nietzsche.

Although the theological concepts of the Old Testament do not lend themselves with particular readiness to attempts at systematization, as Eichrodt conceded, there can be little doubt that the Covenant idea must be given an important place in any formulation of the unity of Scripture. The New Testament clearly envisaged a continuation of the Covenant tradition of the Old Testament, and the supreme expression of this tendency is found in the Last Supper (Matt. 26:28; Mark 14:24; Lk. 22:20; 1 Cor. 11:25), where the New Covenant was thought of in terms of the atonement for human sin by Jesus Christ on Calvary. Not merely is Christ therefore the mediator and surety of the New Covenant; there is a very real sense in which He Himself constitutes the New Covenant. However, it must again be emphasized that in any study of the Old Testament concept of the Covenant it is of prime importance to envisage the idea in its own terms. Where continuity with the New Testament is at issue, the interpreter should avoid strenuously any explanation that depends upon a Greek or western background of thought or practice. This unfortunately was not seen clearly by J. B. Payne, who in a comprehensive and unusual study of the Covenant from a conservative standpoint preferred to employ the term "testament" in the Graeco-Roman sense of a last will and testament as the structure for his work.[11] He restricted the idea of a covenant to the relationship that existed between man and God prior to the fall, and he maintained that such a situation was more marked by a synergistic quality than subsequent dispositions of divine grace. Despite the erudition and painstaking work of the author, it is fallacious to assume that the word $\delta\iota\alpha\theta\eta\kappa\eta$ in Hebrews 9:15ff. was being employed exclusively in the western sense of a last will and testament, for as such it is inappropriate as a general description of divine dealings with men.

[10] G. von Rad, *Theologie des AT, I*, pp. 216ff.
[11] *The Theology of the Older Testament* (1962).

B. THE MESSIAH

No survey of Old Testament theology would be complete without some attention being devoted to the concepts of the Messiah and the Servant of the Lord. The idea of an "anointed one" occurred frequently in the writings of the Old Testament, and was not by any means restricted to the ruler of the last days. Frequently it pointed to the ruler over Israel or Judah during the monarchy; in the Pentateuch it was occasionally applied to the High Priest in the exercise of certain of his ritual functions (Lev. 4:3ff.; 6:15 *et al.*). The title "the Lord's Anointed" was applied to Saul (e.g. 1 Sam. 24:6), David (2 Sam. 19:22), Zedekiah (Lam. 4:20), and to the Davidic king (e.g. 1 Sam. 2:35; Hab. 3:13), as well as to a non-Israelite figure, Cyrus of Persia (Isa. 45:1). The central figure of Jewish apocalyptic expectation was specifically associated with the term in Daniel 9:25f. As F. F. Bruce has indicated, the reference to Cyrus is helpful in adducing some of the more prominent elements of the Old Testament messianic concept.[12] Cyrus was described as a man chosen by God (Isa. 44:28) to accomplish a purpose of redemption for the chosen people (Isa. 45:11f.) and to bring judgment upon the enemies of God (Isa. 45:1ff.), over whom he was to be given the dominion. In all this he was not acting on a basis of individual responsibility, but as the agent of God Himself. While functioning in a secular sense, as indeed some of the anointed kings of Israel did (e.g. Jehu, 1 Kgs. 19:16), he was at the same time a distinct soteriological figure, which is characteristic of the most developed concepts of the Messiah.

The antiquity and nature of the messianic expectation have been a matter of considerable debate among scholars, influenced not a little by the views of the participants concerning facets of Old Testament literary criticism. By way of observation it should be noted that the messianic concept of the Hebrews, like certain other Old Testament eschatological emphases, has no proper counterpart in ancient Near Eastern culture. The messianic expectation was linked normatively with the house of David, which consummated the promises contained in the final blessing of Jacob (Gen. 49:9f.).[13] The prophecy of Nathan (2 Sam. 7:12ff.; cf. Ps. 89:3ff.) furnished religious sanction for the permanence of the Davidic dynasty, and employed it as an additional assurance of redemption within the framework of the Covenant, consistent with its provisions. Although the Hebrew kingship did not carry any of the significance for religious life that was so commonly found in contemporary Near Eastern thought, the ideas of king and Messiah were associated on occasions to the point where the royal Psalms could speak of the ruler as the adopted

---

[12] *NBD*, pp. 811f.

[13] On Shiloh see E. Jenni, *IDB*, III, p. 362; N. K. Gottwald, *IDB*, IV, p. 330.

son of God (Ps. 2:7), as the one who insured law and justice in Israel (Ps. 72:1ff.) and brought divine blessing to the people (Ps. 72:6ff.), and as the victor over all his enemies (Ps. 21:9ff.), who ruled over the whole earth for ever (Pss. 21:5; 72:5ff.). Although phraseology of this kind did not actually deify the ruler, there can be little disagreement that it was distinctly reminiscent of similar Babylonian utterances. Thus there was a firm basis in the monarchy for the expectation of an eschatological figure to whom the characteristics glowingly attributed to the earthly David could easily be transferred (cf. Ezek. 34:23).

According to Mowinckel, the figure of the Messiah was originally political, commencing with the adoption by Israel of the Canaanite model of kingship, suitably modified and transformed to align itself readily to the Hebrew covenant ideal.[14] The Israelite king was held to be superhuman and divine, reflecting Canaanite patterns of kingship,[15] and as the anointed of God he received special gifts of wisdom. Since, in the opinion of Mowinckel, the true ideal of kingship never became an actuality in Israel, there emerged the expectation that an anointed one of God would ultimately arise. In this sense the Messiah is an eschatological figure who belongs properly to the "last days." Since all the indisputable messianic passages in the Old Testament writings regard the collapse of the Davidic monarchy as historical fact, the Messiah must be a creation of the post-exilic period, and cannot logically be posited in pre-exilic documents that might otherwise be regarded as predicting his emergence. Those passages of the Old Testament belonging to the monarchy that appear to be messianic must be regarded as addressed to the reigning monarch of the day, and therefore devoid of proper eschatological significance.

This rather circular and certainly highly subjective form of reasoning has been challenged in part by Knight, who questioned whether the rulers mentioned in Kings could ever have been thought of as addressed in the kind of language employed in the royal Psalms.[16] Careful study shows that, in point of fact, a messianic pattern similar to that accorded to Cyrus emerges from the royal Psalms. Thus the king meets with world opposition (Pss. 2:1ff.; 110:1), but is victorious through the power of God (Pss. 45:3ff.; 89:22f.; 2:6ff.; 18:46ff.; 110:1f.) and establishes a universal domain (Pss. 2:8ff.; 18:43ff.; 72:8ff.; 110:5f.) characterized by peace (Ps. 72:7) and prosperity (Ps. 72:16). This king is the enemy of the oppressor and the protector of the poor (Ps. 72:2f.) and righteous (Ps. 72:7). His rule is everlasting (Pss. 21:4; 45:6; 72:5), as are his name (Ps. 72:17) and his memory (Ps. 45:17); and he is the recipient of perpetual blessing from God (Ps. 45:2). More specifically he is heir to the

---

[14] *He That Cometh*, pp. 4ff.
[15] *Ibid.*, p. 59.
[16] *A Christian Theology of the OT*, pp. 300f.

covenant of David (Ps. 89:28ff.) and the priesthood of Melchizedek (Ps. 110:4), as well as being the son of God (Pss. 2:7; 89:27), seated at the right hand of the Father (Ps. 110:1), and divine in nature (Ps. 45:6). Even the most exalted flight of poetic fancy could scarcely have envisaged the monarchs of Israel and Judah in such terms, particularly since Kings and Chronicles were apt to evaluate the behavior of certain of those notable figures in a distinctly critical manner from time to time.

It would appear, therefore, that some lofty spiritual ideal was being expressed by such sentiments as those found in the royal Psalms. Furthermore, it should be noted that the messianic concept in Israel contained other motifs that cannot be traced back directly to the royal ideal. Aside from the rather obscure promise of a ruler for Judah in the blessing of Jacob, there is the mystic connotation of a paradise situation in which the redemption of fallen man was promised through the activity of a soteriological figure of ancient origin (cf. Gen. 3:15, RSV; Job 15:7ff.; Ezek. 28:2; Mic. 5:2). More particularly the ideas of the mysterious birth of the Messiah (Isa. 7:14; Mic. 5:2f.) and the peace of paradise (Isa. 11:6ff.) have nothing whatever to do with the association of the king and the Messiah. Therefore it would seem imprudent to follow Mowinckel in rejecting all those messianic passages that do not define the Messiah in the most rigid eschatological sense; and it is instead legitimate, with Vriezen, to regard as messianic all those prophecies of the Old Testament that placed an individual in a position of prominence as a savior and deliverer.[17] On this basis it would be possible to regard Messiah as the antitype of the "first Adam" and also of Moses (cf. Deut. 18:15ff.).

The annunciation formula in Isaiah 7:14 concerning the birth of a Messiah has been illumined to some extent by a wider understanding of its ancient Near Eastern setting. It has been described by Engnell as a "divine-royal formula," which in pagan mythology was commonly associated with the announcement of the birth of a child to the gods.[18] A declaration of birth similar to that in Isaiah is also found in connection with Hagar (Gen. 16:11) and Sarah (Gen. 17:19). At Ras Shamra an annunciation to the goddess Nikkal was phrased:

> tld btl [t   "A virgin will give birth . . .
> hl ǵlmt tld b[n   A damsel will bear a son . . ."[19]

As Hammershaimb pointed out, ǵlmt, the equivalent of the Hebrew עלמה, was a designation for the mother-goddess, or, better still, the queen who subsequently gives birth to the royal heir.[20] What is impor-

[17] An Outline of OT Theology, pp. 350ff.

[18] Studies in Divine Kingship in the Ancient Near East (1943), p. 133.

[19] C. H. Gordon, Ugaritic Handbook, text 77, line 7.

[20] Studia Theologica, III (1951), p. 128; cf. C. H. Gordon, Journal of Bible and Religion, XXI (1953), p. 106; E. R. Lacheman, ibid., XXII (1954), p. 43.

tant to notice, however, is that this term refers to Nikkal before her marriage took place, not after it. Thus, it would appear that in Canaanite usage *btlt* and *ǵlmt* were virtually synonymous;[21] and the former constituted the standard designation in the mythological texts for Anat as a virgin (*btlt 'nt*).[22] Although *ǵlmt* was not a technical designation denoting a *virgo intacta,* for which (as Gordon has pointed out)[23] no term existed in the ancient Near East, it is of some significance to observe that it never occurred in the cuneiform Canaanite texts as a description of a married woman. This fact is important in view of the appeal by Mowinckel to the *Legend of Keret,* in which he understood the *ǵlmt* to be the wife of Keret, thus making the עלמה of Isaiah other than a virgin.[24] A careful reading of the text, however, shows that the wife of Keret is consistently described after her marriage as "lady Hry" (*m't ḥry*) and "your wife" (*a'tk*), but never as *ǵlmt.* Clearly the Ras Shamra texts lend no support to those who claim that the Hebrew עלמה can be used of a married woman.[25] Against those who maintain that the Hebrew language has a completely unmistakable word for "virgin," namely בתולה and that if "virgin" had been meant in Isaiah's annunciation formula this word would have occurred there, it merely needs to be remarked that among the seven occurrences of עלמה in the Old Testament, there is not one instance where the word was clearly used of a woman who was not a *virgo intacta,* whereas in Joel 1:18, a בתולה is said to be weeping for the *husband* of her youth.

Messianic figures in the Old Testament include the Branch (Jer. 23:5; 33:15), the Seed of the Woman (Gen. 3:15), and the Son of Man (Dan. 7:1ff.), but by far the most prominent was the Servant of the Lord in Isaiah. Not only was this Servant charged with responsibility towards a covenant people in bondage (Isa. 42:18ff.), but he was also given a mission to the Gentiles (Isa. 42:1ff.). While Cyrus would constitute the instrument of deliverance who would liberate and restore the faithful remnant, it was the Servant who would bring that remnant back to God (Isa. 49:1ff.). The Servant was designated by the name Israel (Isa. 49:3) simply because the nation as a whole had foregone any right to the use of that exalted title. The distinction between the Servant and the nation was then made clear (Isa. 49:14ff.), and the faithful Israelites were

[21] E. J. Young, *Studies in Isaiah* (1955), p. 167; cf. Mowinckel, *He That Cometh,* p. 114.

[22] C. H. Gordon, *Ugaritic Handbook,* Texts 6:19; 49:II:14; III:22f.; IV:45; 128:II:27.

[23] *Ugaritic Manual* (1955), I, p. 249b.

[24] S. Mowinckel, *He That Cometh,* pp. 113f.

[25] As maintained by Kimchi (cf. L. Finkelstein, *The Commentary of David Kimhi on Isaiah* [1926], p. 49); K. Marti, *Das Buch Jesaja* (1900), p. 76; B. Duhm, *Das Buch Jesaia,* p. 75, and many subsequent commentators. Cf. R. D. Wilson, *PTR,* XXIV (1926), p. 316.

urged to adopt his piety and dedication as their model for living. The act of salvation—national and universal—which the Servant was to achieve (Isa. 51:1ff.), involved his life in society and his substitutionary death (Isa. 53:1ff.), followed by his exaltation. On the basis of this accomplishment Israel would be called to enter the New Covenant (Isa. 54:1ff.), and the salvation wrought by the work of the Servant would be made available to all those in need (Isa. 55:1ff.).

Few topics in Old Testament theology have been discussed more widely than the question of the identity of the Divine Servant, and few have been less amenable to a consensus of scholarly opinion.[26] Prior to the nineteenth century the Christian Church interpreted Isaiah 53 as a messianic prophecy. For the first three hundred years of the Christian era the Church commonly identified the Servant with the righteous—whether on an individual or collective basis—before the standard messianic interpretation became general.[27] When European scholars such as Semler, Koppe, and Eichhorn denied Isaiah's authorship of chapters forty and following, they gradually forsook the concept of a Davidic Messiah in favor of interpreting the Servant as the entire nation of Israel.[28] This tendency was not uniform, however, for J. C. R. Eckermann regarded the Servant as the ideal Israel, on the ground that there was a clear difference between the state and its citizens.[29] This view was subsequently adopted by Vatke and Ewald, being expounded to foster the expectation that the spiritual Israel would be instrumental in the restoration of the moribund mortal Israel.[30] Samuel Davidson followed Ewald in abandoning the traditional messianic interpretation and identifying the Servant with the ideal Israel.[31] In this he was supported by Cheyne, A. B. Davidson, and S. R. Driver.[32] The principal difficulty attached to this view was that it was completely unable to explain how an ideal Israel could die for the sins of an actual Israel as part of a redemptive scheme.

The theory that the Servant constituted the faithful minority within the large nation was first suggested by Paulus, and given considerable

[26] Cf. A. Causse, Israël et la vision de l'humanité (1924), p. 54; RSL, p. 3.
[27] Cf. C. R. North, The Suffering Servant in Deutero-Isaiah (1948), pp. 9ff.
[28] J. S. Semler, Abhandlung von freier Untersuchung des Canons (1771-75); J. B. Koppe, D. Robert Louth's Jesaias neu übersetzt nebst einer Einleitung und critischen philologischen und erläuternden Anmerkungen mit Zusätzen und Anmerkungen (1779-81); J. G. Eichhorn, Allgemeine Bibliothek der biblischen Litteratur (1794). Cf. J. L. McKenzie, Second Isaiah (1968), pp. xliiiff.
[29] Theologische Beyträge (1790).
[30] W. Vatke, Die Religion des AT, I (1835). H. Ewald, Die Propheten des Alten Bundes (1840).
[31] An Introduction to the OT (1863), III, pp. 62ff.
[32] T. K. Cheyne, Isaiah Chronologically Arranged (1870), pp. 176, 181; A. B. Davidson, OT Prophecy (1903), pp. 437ff.; S. R. Driver, Isaiah: His Life and Times (1888), p. 179.

prominence by Knobel and Kuenen.[33] On this view the task and glory of the Messiah were to be transferred during the exile to a section of the Israelite community, which would atone for the sins of the nation and thereby achieve its redemption. Unfortunately this interpretation also failed to show how a portion of the people could die in exile in order to atone for the iniquities of Israel as a whole and effect justification for the people of God. Other attempts to account for the identity of the Divine Servant associated him with the prophetic order in some manner, or with a particular historical individual such as Hezekiah, Isaiah himself, Jeremiah, or some unknown personage.[34]

[33] H. E. G. Paulus, *Philologischer Clavis über das AT für Schulen und Akademien. Jesaias* (1793); A. Knobel, *Der Prophet Jesaia* (1843); A. Kuenen, *The Prophets and Prophecy in Israel. An Historical and Critical Enquiry* (1877).

[34] For the prophetic order, see W. Gesenius, *Der Prophet Jesaja* (1821); G. M. L. De Wette, *Opuscula theologica: Commentatio de morte Jesu Christi expiatoria* (1830); J. C. K. Hofmann, *Weissagung und Erfüllung im A und NT* (1841). For Hezekiah, see K. F. Bahrdt, *Die Kleine Bibel, I* (1780). For Isaiah, C. F. Staüdlin, *Neue Beiträge zur Erläuterung der biblischen Propheten* (1791). For Jeremiah, B. Duhm, *Die Theologie der Propheten* (1875). For an unknown personage, H. Ewald, *Die Propheten des Alten Bundes* (1840). Delitzsch' celebrated "pyramid theory," *Biblical Commentary on the Prophecies of Isaiah* (1890 ed.), p. 236, saw the concept of the Servant as having its lowest level rooted in the entire nation of Israel. In a more developed sense it envisaged a spiritual rather than an actual Israel; and at its highest point it represented the person of the Redeemer-Messiah. Cheyne, *The Prophecies of Isaiah* (1880), and G. A. Smith, *The Book of Isaiah* (1890), approved this idea; however, it was resisted by a number of European scholars, who still sought to identify the Servant with some historical personage. Duhm abandoned his association of the Servant with Jeremiah, *Die Theologie der Propheten*, pp. 287ff., for one regarding the Servant as an unknown Teacher of the Law who died of leprosy, *Das Buch Jesaja übersetzt und erklärt* (1892), pp. 278ff. Bertholet, in maintaining a diverse authorship of the four Servant oracles, thought that the Servant was the martyred scribe Eleazar, who met death at the hands of Antiochus Epiphanes; *Zu Jesaja 53: Ein Erklärungsversuch* (1899); cf. 2 Macc. 6:18ff. Ernst Sellin proposed no less than four theories of the personage of the Servant, successively identifying him with Zerubbabel, *Serubbabel: Ein Beitrag zur Geschichte der messianischen Erwartung und der Entstehung des Judentums* (1898); Jehoiachin, *Studien zur Entstehungsgeschichte der jüdischen Gemeinde nach dem babylonischen Exil. I. Der Knecht Gottes bei Deuterojesaja* (1901); Moses, *Mose und seine Bedeutung für die israelitisch-jüdische Religionsgeschichte* (1922); and Deutero-Isaiah, *Neue Kirchliche Zeitschrift*, XLI (1930), pp. 73ff., 145ff.; cf. ZAW, LV (1937), pp. 177ff. This last identification was supported by H. M. Orlinsky, *The So-Called "Suffering Servant" in Isaiah 53* (1964), pp. 8ff. Rudolf Kittel associated the Servant with an anonymous contemporary of Deutero-Isaiah, *Der Prophet Jesaja erklärt von Dr. August Dillmann* (1898), *Zur Theologie des AT. II. Jesaja 53 und der leidende Messias im AT* (1899), *Gestalten und Gedanken in Israel* (1925). Weir held to an identification with Cyrus, *Westminster Review*, CLXIX (1908), pp. 309ff. Still in favor of a collective interpretation of messianic functions, however, were Budde, *Die sogenannten Ebed-Jahwe Lieder und die Bedeutung des Knechtes Jahwes in Jes. 40-55; Ein Minoritätsvotum* (1900); Giesebrecht, *Beiträge zur Jesajakritik* (1890), pp. 146ff.; and A. S. Peake, *The Problem of Suffering in the OT* (1904) and *The Servant of Yahweh* (1931).

The most serious treatment of the view that the Servant was in fact Deutero-Isaiah was undertaken by Mowinckel, who denied the collective interpretation and maintained that there was a sharp distinction between the Servant as represented in the four oracles on the one hand, and in surrounding material on the other.[35] In the latter the Servant was in fact the nation of Israel, whereas in the oracles the active missionary vocation of the Servant pointed, among other indications, to his essential individuality. This "autobiographical" theory encountered considerable difficulty with the fourth Servant oracle (Isa. 52:13-53:12).[36] Other difficulties Mowinckel disposed of by resorting to the favorite critical device—textual emendation. The view that the author propounded appeared to make the prophetic figure describe his own sufferings and death in anticipation of these events, a feature that failed to win the approval of some scholars who followed Mowinckel in other aspects of the theory. For them it was more preferable to suppose that the fourth oracle had been composed by a disciple of the prophet shortly after his death.[37] Even Mowinckel was compelled to modify his original view, for in 1931 he advanced the opinion that the oracles composed by Deutero-Isaiah had been assembled by his disciples who themselves were the authors of the material assigned by critical scholars to Trito-Isaiah. Furthermore, the Servant oracles were neither written by Deutero-Isaiah nor originally included in the first edition of his oracles.[38] According to Mowinckel the Servant had already met his death before the songs were completed, and while he did not formally deny the possibility that the Servant was Deutero-Isaiah, he came to recognize that he might well be a purely futuristic personage.[39] Concerning such a view it needs only to be remarked that such a tentative and internally inconsistent theory will hardly carry lasting conviction, and not least because it requires a forced and artificial interpretation of the Hebrew text if it is to be the least valid.

In a broadly messianic interpretation of the Servant, Nyberg, a member of the Scandinavian school, thought of him as a supra-individual figure belonging alike to the past, present, and future.[40] For him the Servant concept contained religious elements from Ras Shamra, the Tammuz liturgy, and the history of Israel, and reflected both individual

[35] S. Mowinckel, *Der Knecht Jahwäs* (1921).

[36] For scholarly opinion as to the scope of the oracles see *RSL*, p. 6 n. 1.

[37] E.g. P. Volz, *Jesaia II übersetzt und erklärt* (1932), pp. 149ff.

[38] Cf. S. Mowinckel, ZAW, XLIX (1931), pp. 87ff., 242ff., *Acta Orientalia*, XVI (1938), pp. 1ff., 40ff.

[39] Cf. *He That Cometh*, pp. 228f.; C. R. North, *Scottish Journal of Theology*, III (1950), pp. 363ff.

[40] H. S. Nyberg, *Svensk Exegetisk Årsbok*, VII (1942), pp. 5ff.

and collective characteristics.[41] A similar position was reached by another Scandinavian scholar, Ivan Engnell, who while stressing the presence of mythological elements in the Servant oracles, pointed out their regal background and claimed that the term "Servant" was actually a royal title.[42] He agreed with Mowinckel in recognizing that insofar as the Servant was an individual, he was essentially a figure of the future. Although the Servant was not a direct prediction of Jesus Christ, he was nevertheless basically a messianic figure.

Any attempt to derive the Servant concept from pagan Canaanite or Babylonian religious sources is open to the serious objection that the Servant of the Lord as envisaged in Isaiah was a strictly Israelite development for which there are no proper points of connection with the cult of a dying and rising deity. This is all the more certain since the larger context inveighed consistently against pagan idolatry, which was uniformly treated with contempt and scorn.[43] Furthermore, as Young has shown, the theological ideas underlying the concept of the Servant are radically different from any analogous material at Ras Shamra.[44]

Modern supporters of the traditional messianic interpretation of the Servant have relied to some extent upon the masterly expositions of Fischer.[45] Roman Catholic scholars who have adhered to this position included Feldmann, Condamin, and Van Hoonacker.[46] In the Dutch Reformed Church the messianic concept of the Servant was urged by Schelhaas and Edelkoort among others.[47] In a penetrating survey of the vast literature connected with the discussion of the identity of the Servant in Isaiah, C. R. North concluded that the idea moved from the nation of Israel to an individual and pointed forward to Jesus Christ, in whom the expectation was subsequently realized,[48] a position which had elements in common with that of J. van der Ploeg.[49] H. H. Rowley discerned a greater degree of oscillation in the Servant concept than North was prepared to allow, making the idea of a corporate personality a

---

[41] Cf. W. A. Irwin, *The Prophets and Their Times* (1941), pp. 234f.; J. P. Hyatt, *JNES*, III (1943), pp. 79ff.

[42] I. Engnell, *Svensk Exegetisk Årsbok*, X (1945), pp. 31ff.; *BJRL* (1948), pp. 54ff.; cf. G. Oestborn, *Tōrā in the Old Testament*, pp. 56ff.; S. Mowinckel, *Studia Theologica*, II (1949), pp. 71ff.; A. R. Johnson in S. H. Hooke (ed.), *The Labyrinth* (1935), pp. 99f.

[43] *RSL*, p. 43.

[44] E. J. Young, *Westminster Theological Journal*, XIII (1950-51), pp. 19ff.

[45] J. Fischer, *Isaias 40-55 und die Perikopen vom Gottesknecht* (1916), *Das Buch Isaias übersetzt und erklärt, II. Teil: Kapitel 40-66* (1939).

[46] F. Feldmann, *Der Knecht Gottes in Isaias Kap. 40-55* (1907), *Das Buch Isaias übersetzt und erklärt* (1926); A. Condamin, *Le Livre d'Isaïe: Traduction critique avec notes et commentaires* (1905); A. van Hoonacker, *Het Boek Isaias* (1932).

[47] J. Schelhaas, *De lijdende Knecht des Heeren* (1933); A. H. Edelkoort, *De Christusverwachting in het Oude Testament* (1941).

[48] C. R. North, *The Suffering Servant in Deutero-Isaiah* (1948).

[49] J. van der Ploeg, *Les Chants du Serviteur de Jahvé* (1936).

preferable interpretation.[50] For him the idea of the Servant developed from the thought of Israel as the Servant of God to the concept of an individual Servant of a supreme spiritual quality without at the same time sacrificing the basic theme of Israel as the Servant. His conclusions, however, were to a large extent those of the traditional messianic interpreters.

Mention should be made of the mythological view of the Servant advocated early in the twentieth century by Gressmann and Gunkel.[51] According to this theory the fourth Servant song was to be understood in terms of the Adonis-Tammuz cult, being based on one of the ritual songs of the dying and rising deity. For Gressmann the Servant was neither the nation of Israel nor any historical individual, while Gunkel showed that the Servant as described in Isaiah far surpassed any of the notable figures in previous Israelite history. However, despite their appeals to the Tammuz liturgies, neither Gressmann nor Gunkel was able to establish a connection between the nature-myths and the Biblical sources.[52] This is scarcely surprising, since the monotheism of Isaiah would never have countenanced such origins or affiliations, nor admitted to any consonance between the atoning death of the Servant and the periodic ritual demise of the Babylonian Tammuz deity, which bore no atoning significance. Although a few scholars subsequently professed to see elements of the Adonis-Tammuz cult in the Servant oracles, the mythological view of the Servant attracted few advocates after the time of Gressmann.[53]

Some justification for the vast and complex literature dealing with the Servant of the Lord is immediately apparent upon even a casual reading of the Servant oracles. In the first of these (Isa. 42:1-4) the Servant was recognized as the one who had been divinely chosen and empowered by the Spirit to bring true religion to the nations of the world, a task in which he would persist until it was accomplished. The second oracle (Isa. 49:1-6) portrayed the Servant as recognizing his divine call from birth and his consequent preparation for his exalted task. He constituted the Israel in whom God would be glorified, and his work was that of illuminating the Gentiles so as to make the divine salvation universal. In the third oracle (Isa. 50:4-9 or 50:1-11) the speaker, who was presumed to be the Servant, described his daily contact with God and proclaimed his confidence in divine vindication, despite the fact that his immediate task presented certain difficulties. The final oracle (Isa. 52:13–53:12)

---

[50] *RSL*, pp. 23, 54ff.; C. R. North, *op. cit.*, p. 216.

[51] H. Gressmann, *Der Ursprung der israelitisch-jüdischen Eschatologie* (1905), *Der Messias* (1929); H. Gunkel, *Die Religion in Geschichte und Gegenwart* (1912), III, cols. 1540ff.

[52] Cf. W. W. Graf Baudissin, *Adonis und Esmun* (1911), p. 424.

[53] E.g. F. M. Th. Böhl, *De "Knecht des Heeren" in Jezaja 53* (1923), pp. 24ff.; G. H. Dix, *JTS*, XXVI (1925), pp. 241ff.; S. Mowinckel, *ZAW*, XLIX (1931), pp. 256f.

described the promised exaltation of the Servant, which, however, would be preceded by violence culminating in the death of the Servant and his burial with the wicked.

In such a composite picture it is possible to see individual, collective, actual, and ideal elements at one and the same time, which makes for no small difficulty in interpretation. A fully collective theory of the Servant must face the objection that the character of the Servant depicted in Isaiah is radically different from that of Israel as found elsewhere in the Old Testament. Purely individual interpretations of the Servant, whether as an historical personage such as Jehoiachin, Uzziah, or Cyrus, or as an unknown contemporary of the prophet are also inadequate on the ground that the description of the Servant was most probably not intended as the portrait of any one individual.[54] The Servant was represented as an anonymous yet ideal figure, and was clearly not meant to be identified with the nation of Israel, which was admittedly imperfect (Isa. 53:6). While the theory of a corporate personality, as advanced by Eissfeldt and Wheeler Robinson, attempted to take a comprehensive view of the functions ascribed to the Servant by assuming that the concept could pass readily from nation to individual and *vice versa*, it failed to give adequate precision to the character of the Servant as an emergent and ultimately established individual by being unable to distinguish clearly between Israel and the Servant.[55]

One variation of the traditional messianic interpretation has envisaged the Servant as the future Messiah depicted in the role of the pre-exilic king, who was thought to have suffered certain ritual chastisements as part of an annual enthronement liturgy. In this sense the king was the representative and perhaps even the embodiment of the people over whom he ruled, and through his ritual "sufferings" the people were "redeemed" on an annual basis.[56] Such a theory fails to take account of the fact that the Hebrew kings were never considered to be the embodiment of their subjects, and does not recognize the consistent religious tradition of Israel in the matter of redemption and atonement, whose ritual performances were entirely a matter for the priests, not the king. National forgiveness was amply provided for under the law in the Day of Atonement ceremonies, and nowhere is there any suggestion that this annual "redemption" was connected with the position or function of the ruler. An even more serious objection to such an approach is that at

---

[54] E.g. R. Kittel, *Geschichte des Volkes Israel*, III, pp. 222ff.; W. O. E. Oesterley and T. H. Robinson, *Hebrew Religion: Its Origin and Development*, pp. 303ff.

[55] O. Eissfeldt, *Der Gottesknecht bei Deuterojesaja* (1933); H. Wheeler Robinson, *The Cross of the Servant* (1926).

[56] Cf. H. Zimmern in E. Schrader (ed.), *Die Keilinschriften und das AT* (1903), pp. 384ff.; L. Dürr, *Ursprung und Ausbau der israelitisch-jüdischen Heilands-erwartung. Ein Beitrag zur Theologie des AT* (1925), pp. 134ff.

489

present nothing that can be considered as real evidence has been adduced in support of an annual enthronement festival in Israel.

There appears to be no adequate reason for maintaining that the traditional messianic interpretation is wedded to an excessively mechanical doctrine of inspiration, as North and others have implied.[57] In the first instance the picture of the Servant is sufficiently indistinct to admit of differences between the Servant and Jesus Christ the Messiah. Secondly, the Servant is not the only messianic figure in Isaiah, the problem here being compounded by a wholly arbitrary division of the prophecy into numerous segments of greatly diverse chronology, and for which there is no textual warrant or evidence whatever.

Furthermore, there are no grounds for supposing that the prophet was completely unaware of the significance of the Servant oracles, although it seems equally clear that their deepest implications escaped both the immediate writer and the Israelite nation as a whole. Even when the oracles were illumined by the life and work of Jesus Christ, there were still many who professed an inability to perceive the meaning of these passages in relationship to Christ as Messiah. Whatever may be the nature of the interpretation that is ultimately assigned to these enigmatic sections in Isaiah, the fact remains that the mission of the Servant received its fullest and most distinctive expression in the atonement of Christ on Calvary. Or as North has remarked, "On all hands it is agreed that whoever was the original of the Servant, none except Christ was its fulfilment."[58]

In a study of the way in which messianic prophecy came to its fruition, F. F. Bruce held that the words of Isaiah 55:3 as quoted in Acts 13:34 marked the link between the Davidic line and the person of the Servant.[59] This latter was originally Israel after the flesh, but in becoming an individual realized in his own self the ideal Israel. In the person and work of Jesus Christ the Davidic Messiah and the Servant became one. This view rests to some extent upon the observations of Delitzsch, and has the advantage of preserving the organic continuity between the Old and New Testaments. It also serves to show that, despite differences that inevitably arise over the interpretation of the Servant in the prophecy of Isaiah, the Christian can do no better than follow the example of one of the earliest evangelists of the primitive Church, and in taking the Servant oracles, begin to preach Jesus from them.[60]

Despite the limitations of the foregoing survey of Old Testament theological studies, enough has been said to indicate the interest of

---

[57] C. R. North, *The Suffering Servant in Deutero-Isaiah*, p. 207.

[58] C. R. North, *IDB*, IV, p. 294.

[59] F. F. Bruce, *The Sure Mercies of David* (1954); cf. H. L. Ellison, *The Servant of Jehovah* (1953).

[60] R. S. Cripps in L. W. Grensted (ed.), *The Atonement in History and in Life* (1929), p. 93; cf. the criticism in E. J. Young, *Studies in Isaiah* (1955), p. 103.

scholars in developing the field as an area of investigation in its own right. The problems presented by such an undertaking are as numerous as they are fascinating, and if the mind of the ancient Hebrew writers is to be interpreted correctly it is of the utmost importance that scholars should approach their task against a background of sound ancient Near Eastern methodology, and not that of occidental speculative philosophy. As H. H. Rowley has remarked, writers who discover in the text what they themselves bring to it, instead of first finding what the text was intended to mean and then perceiving what it has come to mean, are a peril to themselves and to their readers alike.[61] A properly accredited theology of the Old Testament must be based firmly upon the revealed Word of God, and not merely constitute some kind of commentary upon the faith or knowledge of a particular author. When scholars are prepared to submit to the authority of the Old Testament Scriptures and study them on their own terms, the spiritual message of these ancient writings will emerge in all its clarity and grandeur to furnish an all-important corrective for the distorted outlook of mortal man.

[61] *RSL*, p. ix.

Part Eight

THE PENTATEUCH

I. THE STUDY OF THE PENTATEUCH

The first major division of the Hebrew canon consisted of the five books with which the English Bible commences. It had long been associated in the ancient Jewish mind with the legislative activities of Moses, and in post-exilic times the corpus was known as the "Torah" or Law. This proper noun was derived from the Hebrew root ירה, one of whose meanings is "to teach." The Torah was a manual of direction or guidance, and this usage was in full accord with the emphasis that tradition had placed upon the legal element dominant in this body of writings. It did not minimize the importance of the historical or narrative sections of the Torah, however, for it was recognized that such material constituted the essential temporal setting for the legislation itself.

The fundamentally legal character of the Torah can be appreciated from the many references in the Bible to the "law of God" (Neh. 10:28f.), the "book of Moses" (Ez. 6:18; Neh. 13:1; Mk. 12:26), the "Law" (Josh. 8:34; Ez. 10:3; 2 Chron. 14:4; Lk. 10:26), the "book of the law of Moses" (Josh. 8:31; 23:6; 2 Kgs. 14:6; Neh. 8:1),[1] and other analogous expressions. The Torah was first described as "Pentateuch" in the commentary by Origen on the Fourth Gospel,[2] although it is possible that this designation, from the Greek words πέντε ("five") and τεῦχος ("scroll"),[3] may have been employed by the Hellenistic Jews of Alexandria as early as the first Christian century to correspond to the Talmudic description of the Torah as חמשה חומשי תורה ("the five fifths of the Law"; cf. *Sanhed.* 28a). In Latin Tertullian employed "Pentateuch" as a proper name in his disputes with the Marcionites.[4]

The Hebrew title of each of the five books is simply the initial word of that work; the English title is derived from the Greek (by way of the Latin), and indicates the initial subject of each book. Apart from Numbers, the Greek titles were used by Philo, who attests to the division of the Pentateuch into five sections, as does Josephus. Such a partitioning was familiar to those who made the LXX translation of the Torah about 250 B.C., and this in itself reflects a tradition of considerable antiquity.

---

[1] Cf. *YIOT*, p. 39.
[2] *PG*, XIV, col. 444.
[3] Τεῦχος originally meant "implement," but was subsequently used of a case for carrying papyrus rolls, and later for the roll itself.
[4] *PL*, II, col. 282.

The division of the Torah into five parts was doubtless prompted as much by the nature of the subject matter as by the fact that the leather scrolls that were available in earlier times would each probably only accommodate about one-fifth of the whole Pentateuch.

As Pfeiffer has pointed out, it should be noted that the Pentateuch is a single work in five volumes, not a collection of five different books.[5] There is a further sense in which it can be regarded as the first stage of a nine-volume work, that is to say, Genesis to Kings, that described Hebrew history and religious institutions from the creation to the events immediately consequent upon the fall of Jerusalem in 587 B.C. Thus, as Weiser has shown, after placing the creation of the earth in a universal setting, the Pentateuch describes the manner in which Israel came into existence as a people, and presents the fundamental traditions of the Hebrews up to a point prior to their entrance into the Promised Land.[6] According to this pattern the individual books can be summarized roughly as follows:

    I. Primeval History with a Mesopotamian Background, Gen. 1–11
    II. History of the Patriarchs, Gen. 12–50
    III. The Oppression of Israel and Preparations for the Exodus, Exod. 1–9
    IV. The Exodus, Passover, and the Arrival at Sinai, Exod. 10–19
    V. The Decalogue and the Covenant at Sinai, Exod. 20–24
    VI. Legislation Relating to the Tabernacle and Aaronic Priesthood, Exod. 25–31
    VII. The Idolatrous Violation of the Covenant, Exod. 32–34
    VIII. The Implementation of Regulations Concerning the Tabernacle, Exod. 35–40
    IX. The Law of Offerings, Lev. 1–7
    X. The Consecration of the Priests and Initial Offerings, Lev. 8–10
    XI. The Laws of Cleanliness, Lev. 11–15
    XII. The Day of Atonement, Lev. 16
    XIII. Laws Concerning Morality and Cleanliness, Lev. 17–26
    XIV. Vows and Tithes, Lev. 27
    XV. Numberings and Laws, Num. 1–9
    XVI. The Journey from Sinai to Kadesh, Num. 10–20
    XVII. Wanderings to Moab, Num. 21–36
    XVIII. Historical Retrospect to the Wilderness Period, Deut. 1–4
    XIX. Second Speech, with an Hortatory Introduction, Deut. 5–11
    XX. Collected Statutes and Rights, Deut. 12–26
    XXI. Cursing and Blessing, Deut. 27–30
    XXII. The Accession of Joshua and Death of Moses, Deut. 31–34

---

[5] *PIOT*, p. 129.
[6] *OTFD*, pp. 70f.; cf. *PIOT*, pp. 130ff.

Aside from the books of Genesis and Deuteronomy, which present certain special problems, the division of the Hebrew text into the present five books hardly accords with the structure of the material itself. Were the latter to be divided at Exodus 19 and Numbers 10 respectively, the contents would fall into three convenient categories consisting of the history of Israel up to the Sinai period, the revelation at Sinai itself, and the departure from the peninsula towards the plains of Moab.

A. Antecedents of the Developmental Hypothesis

There is no reason to doubt that by the time of Ezra the Pentateuch was considered to be the authoritative revelation of God to Moses, and the norm for faith and morals. Since that time it has been traditional for Judaism, Islam, and Christianity to accept Moses not merely as the mediator of the divinely revealed laws (Exod. 18:13ff.; 31:18; 34:28, et al.), but also as the author of the entire Pentateuch. Such ancient writers as the compiler of Ecclesiasticus (24:23), Philo, Josephus, and the Mishnaic and Talmudic authorities accepted without question the Mosaic authorship of the Torah.[7] The only question that arose was in connection with the passage relating to the death of Moses (Deut. 34:5f.), and in this connection Philo and Josephus affirmed that Moses described his own death, whereas the Talmud credited Joshua with having composed eight verses of the Torah, presumably the closing section of Deuteronomy.

So rigid did tradition become concerning Mosaic authorship of the Pentateuch that to deny it was, for some Jews at least, tantamount to excluding oneself from Paradise.[8] This attitude was attacked in the early Christian era by sectarians of different religious standpoints.[9] Second Esdras 14:1-48 describes a story telling how the lost Torah, along with other books, were dictated by Ezra under divine inspiration to five secretaries during a forty-day period.[10] Views of this kind influenced some orthodox Christian theologians to the point that Jerome, for example, seems to have vacillated between Moses and Ezra as the author of the Pentateuch.[11] The Nazarenes denied the Mosaicity of the work, as did Celsus and Ptolemy, who also questioned its literary unity, while the *Clementine Homilies* held to the radical view that the Pentateuch consisted of a corrupt and deviate transcript of the oral pronouncements of Moses.

The existence in the text of certain scribal glosses indicating an interval of time between the period of the writer and that of Moses (e.g.

---

[7] Philo, *Vita Mosis*, III, 39; Josephus, *AJ*, IV, 8, 48; Mishnah, *Pirqe Ab.* I, 1; Talmud, *Bab. Bath.* 14b.

[8] Cf. A. Westphal, *Les sources du Pentateuque* (1888), I, p. 25.

[9] Cf. H. Holzinger, *Einleitung in den Hexateuch* (1893), pp. 11f., 25ff.

[10] Cf. *APOT*, II, pp. 542ff., 620ff.

[11] Cf. *PL*, XXIII, col. 227; XXV, col. 17.

Gen. 12:6; 13:7; 32:33; Deut. 3:14; 34:6 *et al.*) led certain medieval Jewish scholars to question the Mosaic authorship of the Pentateuch as a whole. On such a basis Ibn Ezra (1088-1167) recorded that a certain Rabbi Isaac (perhaps Isaac of Toledo, 982-1057) had dated Genesis 36:31 in the reign of Jehoshaphat, a view that he himself denounced. The medieval Roman Catholic commentator A. Du Maes, in a work entitled *Josuae Imperatoris Historia*, published in 1574, maintained that the Pentateuch had been compiled by Ezra the scribe from ancient written sources, basing his views mostly upon the incidence of later scribal names for such ancient sites as Laish and Kiriath-arba (Gen. 14:14; Deut. 34:1; Gen. 13:18; 23:2, *et al.*).

The possibility that subsequent scribal additions had been made to the Mosaic Pentateuch was recognized by the Spanish Jesuit commentator B. Pereira in his work on Genesis (1594-1600); and similar views were held by J. Bonfrère a quarter of a century later. The philosopher Thomas Hobbes in his *Leviathan* (1651) adopted the position of Du Maes, although he credited Moses with all that the Pentateuch claimed for him. The apparent discrepancies and anachronisms that had perplexed certain medieval Jewish exegetes also troubled the philosopher Benedictus de Spinoza, who in his *Tractatus Theologico-Politicus* (1670) concluded that Ezra had compiled the history of his nation, utilizing a mass of ancient written material including some by Moses, and that he himself had interpolated Deuteronomy, which according to Spinoza comprised the legal code promulgated by Ezra.

The speculations of Spinoza may be said in some senses to have ushered in the period of critical study of the Pentateuch, which commenced in earnest with the divisive theories of authorship proposed by the Roman Catholic author Richard Simon in 1678 and the Arminian Jean Le Clerc in 1685, an era when much of Old Testament scholarship was confined to critical study of the Pentateuch. A comprehensive survey of the various trends of thought in this area has been provided in part one of the present work; hence, it will be sufficient at this point to recapitulate the development of literary criticism in brief outline.

The first attempt at a documentary theory of Pentateuchal origins came in 1753, when the French physician Jean Astruc published his speculations anonymously in a work that maintained that Moses had compiled Genesis from two principal ancient *"mémoires"* and a number of shorter documents.[12] He identified the two main sources from the non-interchangeable use of the divine names יהוה (Jehovah), and אלהים (deity); and, according to the developed form of his theory, the sections that employed the latter belonged to an A source and those in which the

---

[12] *Conjectures sur les mémoires originaux dont il parait que Moyse s'est servi pour composer le Livre de la Genèse. Avec des Remarques, qui appuient ou qui éclaircissent ces Conjectures.*

former occurred came from a B source. This formulation was sufficient, in Astruc's view, to account for the repetitions and alleged discrepancies that some earlier critics had observed, but it is important to note that Astruc did not deny the Mosaic authorship of Genesis, and actually went to some lengths to defend it. He also recognized something that the majority of his critical successors failed to acknowledge, namely, that the divine names could not be utilized successfully as criteria for the purpose of analyzing the entire Torah.

Astruc's work with the A and B sources convinced him that the divine names were inadequate for dividing Genesis into supposed *"mémoires,"* and he was not slow to point out that certain passages, such as Genesis 14, did not fit in any sense into a documentary analysis. In order to complete his work he found it necessary to invoke the presence of remnants of ten sources of Midianite or Arabian origin in addition to his A and B material, and when even these insertions proved to be insufficient to meet his critical needs he was compelled to discover the existence of certain textual "interpolations."[13]

The abiding merit of this approach is that in asserting that Moses may have utilized written memoirs for the purpose of compiling Genesis, Astruc doubtless correctly assessed the facts of the case. His fundamental error lay in his subjective estimate of the nature and extent of the underlying source material and his ignorance of the principles by which documents and books were compiled in the ancient Near East. He may well have been aware of the latter to some extent, however, for he was careful to insist that his basic criteria, the divine names, were unsuitable for purposes of analyzing the book of Genesis into documents.

One would think that the difficulties of Astruc's approach to the problems associated with the compilation of Genesis would have made it sufficiently clear to any possible successors in the field that critical reconsideration of Astruc's methods was needed. But this was not the case, and nothing daunted, a German scholar named J. G. Eichhorn published a three-volume *Einleitung* (1780-83), in which he expanded the views of Astruc into an early form of the classic documentary theory. Although he claimed independence of Astruc, Eichhorn's fundamental approach was essentially the same as that which had been adopted by the French physician. He finally abandoned his earlier views as to the Mosaic authorship of the Pentateuch, divided Genesis and Exodus 1-2 into sources designated J(ehovistic) and E(lohistic), and held that they had been edited by an unknown redactor.

Following the trend made popular by Eichhorn, the Scottish Roman Catholic priest Geddes investigated the *"mémoires"* identified by Astruc and between 1792 and 1800 developed the fragmentary hypoth-

[13] Cf. H. Osgood, *The Presbyterian and Reformed Review*, III (1892), pp. 83ff.; A. Lods, *Jean Astruc et la critique biblique au XVIIIᵉ siècle* (1924).

esis of Pentateuchal origins. The theory maintained that the Torah had been compiled by an unknown redactor from numerous fragments that had originated in different circles, one Elohistic and the other Jehovistic, and that it had probably attained its final form in Jerusalem during the reign of Solomon. In this hypothesis Geddes was followed by J. S. Vater, who endeavored to trace the growth of the Pentateuch from over thirty fragments, and to a lesser extent by W. M. L. De Wette, who maintained that much of the legal material was comparatively late in nature, not earlier than the time of David.[14] De Wette also followed Jerome in identifying Deuteronomy with the legal code recovered from the Temple during the reign of King Josiah.

The emphasis by De Wette upon one basic document supplemented by numerous fragments was developed in 1831 by H. Ewald, who, in a review of J. J. Stähelin's *Kritische Untersuchungen über die Genesis* (1830), maintained that the chief Pentateuchal document was the Elohistic source, which carried the narrative from the creation up to the beginning of the settlement under Joshua, and that this was supplemented by the Jehovistic narrative, whose compiler was also the final redactor of the material as a whole. At a later period Ewald abandoned this "supplementary theory," and asserted that the Pentateuch contained fragments that did not go back either to J, E, or Deuteronomy.

B. THE MODERN THEORY OF PENTATEUCHAL ORIGINS

The modern form of the theory of Pentateuchal origins in terms of underlying documentary sources came with the work of Hupfeld, who sought to remedy the difficulties of the "supplementary hypothesis" by introducing even more supplements. In his *Die Quellen der Genesis und die Art ihrer Zusammensetzung von neuen untersucht* (1853), he maintained that the J passages constituted a continuous document rather than supplements to an earlier E source and that the Elohistic material was itself composite and consisted of the original Elohist (E[1]) and the later Elohist (E[2]). The three documents were assembled in their present form, according to Hupfeld, by a redactor whose individualistic approach to his task itself occasioned many of the "difficulties" in the Pentateuch. A year later, when E. Riehm published his *Die Gesetzgebung Mosis im Lande Moab* (1854), a work that sought to demonstrate the independent character of Deuteronomy, the four principal documents of the liberal school had been isolated and dated in the order E[1], E[2], J, and D.

The developmental hypothesis took a step forward with the work of K. H. Graf, who adopted the suggestion of E. G. Reuss, J. F. L. George, and W. Vatke that the Levitical legislation was later than the date as-

---

[14] J. S. Vater, *Commentar über den Pentateuch* (1802-1805). W. M. L. De Wette, *Beiträge zur Einleitung in das AT* (1807).

signed to Deuteronomy, and that it could not have arisen any earlier than the exilic period. Consequently he affirmed that the source designated E^1 and known as P(riestly Code) by modern liberal scholars, was the latest rather than the earliest of the documents that underlay the Pentateuch. This conclusion involved a change in the earlier order E^1 E^2 J D, and set the stage for a debate as to whether the correct chronological sequence was EJDP (E^2JDE^1) or JEDP. When Abraham Kuenen, who had (in part at least) worked independently of Graf, published his *De Godsdienst van Israel* (1869-70), he assured the success of the Graf JEDP sequence, which also found support in the work entitled *Das Vorexilische Buch der Urgeschichte Israels*, published in 1874 by August Kayser.

It was left to Julius Wellhausen in his *Die Composition des Hexateuchs* (1876-77) to bring this hypothesis to its highest point of development. In this work and subsequent publications he held that the earliest parts of the Pentateuch came from two originally independent documents, the Jehovist and the Elohist. The former was dated about 850 B.C. and came from religious circles in the southern kingdom; the latter supposedly emanated from the northern kingdom about 750 B.C. The two were combined by an unknown redactor or editor (R^{JE}) about 650 B.C. Wellhausen regarded Deuteronomy as a product of the period of Josiah, about 621 B.C., and maintained that it was added to the existing corpus by yet another editor (R^D) about 550 B.C., to make a group of Pentateuchal material equivalent to JED. The Priestly Code, which was supposed by the literary theorists to have been compiled between 500 and 450 B.C. by priestly authors, was then presumably added by another anonymous redactor (R^P) to the already existing material to produce JEDP by about 400 B.C.; and the Pentateuch in its extant form emerged about 200 B.C.

Most of the larger critical introductions to the Old Testament will furnish the student with an overwhelming mass of data relating to the contents of these supposed documents. While it is not the intention of the present author to reproduce this kind of material, it may well be useful at this juncture to present a brief outline of what these alleged sources have generally been held to contain.

The Jehovistic narrative (J), postulated as dating from the ninth century B.C., is thought to have had its rise in Judah, partly because of references to territorial expansion in Genesis (Gen. 15:18; 27:40) and partly because of the general ascendancy of Judah as depicted in the source material isolated (cf. Gen. 49:8ff.). In this alleged document can be found narratives dealing with events which occurred between the time of the creation and the entry of Israel into Canaan. The literary style is deemed to constitute an outstanding example of epic composition, worthy of the tradition of Homer. Like that of other proposed Pentateuchal source documents, the extent of J has always been a matter

501

of some dispute, and this factor has precluded a firm determination of its date. The J source is held by its proponents to be intensely nationalistic in outlook, and shows particular interest in recording the activities of the Hebrew patriarchs. From a theological standpoint it is alleged to be notable for its anthropomorphic representation of the deity, who frequently assumed quasi-human form and communed with men.

The Elohistic source (E) is generally dated a century later than J by advocates of the Graf-Wellhausen theory, and its Ephraimite origin has been postulated on the basis of the omission of the stories of Abraham and Lot, which had to do with Hebron and the cities of the valley, and also because of the special emphasis thought to be given to Bethel and Shechem (Gen. 28:17, 31:13, 33:19f.). A further reason for postulating a northern origin for this material lies in the prominence given to the activities of Joseph, the ancestor of the northern tribes of Ephraim and Manasseh. This alleged document is supposed to contain less continuous narrative than J, and in any event it is thought to be more fragmentary. Theologically it is held to be of interest on account of its religious and moralistic emphases, an outstanding example of this being the command to sacrifice Isaac (Gen. 22:1ff.) as a means of teaching the patriarch Abraham that true sacrificial offering is an inward, motivated affair, and not a matter of external ritual.

The alleged Deuteronomic document (D) corresponds in large measure to the canonical book of Deuteronomy. Fundamental to the approach of the Graf-Wellhausen school was the view that the law-book discovered in the time of Josiah (2 Kgs. 22:3ff.) comprised at least part, if not actually the whole, of Deuteronomy. Attention was drawn to the correspondence between D and the trend of the religious reformation promulgated under Josiah, particularly with regard to the centralization (2 Kgs. 23:4ff.; Deut. 12:1ff.) and purification (2 Kgs. 23:4ff.; Deut. 16:21f.; 17:3; 18:10f.) of the cultus. D embodied a religious philosophy of history that formulated the terms of divine blessing and judgment and demonstrated the necessity for a pronounced sense of social justice under the provisions of the Covenant relationship. For the critical school, D comprised a collection of exhortations and legal enactments compiled during the apostasies of Manasseh and combined editorially with J and E after the time of Josiah.

The Priestly Code (P) was regarded as a compilation of legal and ceremonial material derived from various periods of Israelite history, and codified in such a manner as to organize the legal structure of the post-exilic Jewish theocracy. While P was held to contain certain narrative sections, it was thought to be more concerned with the mechanics of genealogies and the origins of ritualistic or legalistic practices and concepts than with the direct recording of events. The highly detailed nature of much of its contents, as with the description of the Tabernacle (Exod. 25:1-27:21), along with the complex ritual and legal material which it preserved, has been taken as an indication of the fact that the source had its origins in the post-exilic period. The theological outlook of the P document envisaged God as utilizing the legislation for a means of grace, in that the concepts of holiness and ceremonial purity would serve as a vehicle for conveying divine blessing to Israel.

The evolutionary approach of the Graf-Wellhausen school proved extremely attractive to the naturalistic tendencies of the contemporary theological mind. Largely through the writings of W. Robertson Smith and S. R. Driver, the Graf-Wellhausen scheme of documentary analysis gained widespread acceptance in the English-speaking world. For many years it was venerated as axiomatic for scholarly faith and practice in the Old Testament field, and any individual who was sufficiently imprudent either to criticize it or attempt to reject it ran the risk of being scorned by his fellows and consigned to academic oblivion. It is only within recent times that archaeological and other discoveries have forced upon scholars the necessity for adopting a much more critical approach to the general Wellhausenian position, and have made radical assessments of it an increasingly frequent outcome.

Documentary analysis of the materials in the earlier portions of the Hebrew canon of Scripture did not stop with the work of Wellhausen, however. Following a suggestion made in 1883 by Karl Budde, an attempt was made by Rudolf Smend to formulate a different kind of documentary hypothesis.[15] He maintained the existence of two Jehovists, J^1 and J^2, regarding them as two parallel authors whose literary activity was in evidence throughout the Hexateuch. While he believed that D and P were marked by numerous additions or supplements, he insisted upon the unity of the Elohistic source. The material that Smend had described as J^1 was identified by Otto Eissfeldt as a "Lay Source" (L) or *Laienquelle*, because it stood in marked contrast to the Priestly document and emphasized the nomadic ideal in opposition to the Canaanite way of life.[16]

Morgenstern purported to discover a Kenite document (K), which supposedly dealt with certain biographical details in the life of Moses and described the relations between Israel and the Kenites.[17] Following the same general trend, R. H. Pfeiffer thought that he detected the existence of a non-Israelite source in Genesis, which he designated S (South or Seir).[18] He maintained that it differed materially from the "Lay Source" identified by Eissfeldt, and also from J^1, being restricted to Genesis and being characterized by its own special concerns. The division of the Priestly material by von Rad into two principal segments, P^A

---

[15] *Die Erzählung des Hexateuchs auf ihre Quellen untersucht* (1912).
[16] O. Eissfeldt, *Hexateuch-Synopse* (1922), p. 5 *passim; ETOT*, pp. 191ff.
[17] J. Morgenstern, *HUCA*, IV (1926-27), pp. 1ff.
[18] *PIOT*, pp. 141, 159ff.; *ZAW*, XLVIII (1930), pp. 66ff.

and P^B,[19] was an offshoot of the atomizing tendencies that were given expression in the writings of B. Baentsch, who in his commentary on Leviticus in the Nowack *Handkommentar* series (1903) professed to find no fewer than seven main sources of P, and the activity of at least two redactors.

Although the minute dissections of the literary-analytical school had fallen into disfavor to a large extent by the 1920's, C. A. Simpson flouted current trends in England by continuing to pursue conjectural documentary sources through the Hexateuch with all the fervor of a bygone era of stylistic analysis.[20] In defiance of the fundamental criticisms levelled against his methods by Rowley[21] and others, Simpson published his *Composition of the Book of Judges* (1957), in which he continued to employ his subjective techniques.

But perhaps the credulity of the faithful was most heavily taxed in 1958 by the continued insistence of Eissfeldt upon the presence of the L document in Genesis.[22] For him, even the most complete documentary hypothesis should leave room for isolated fragments, and on this basis it was clearly his duty to gather up these solitary elements and combine them, willy-nilly, into another document related to the J source. It apparently did not occur to Eissfeldt that the very fact of their isolation—assuming for the moment that these fragments are as genuine as the literary analysts would have their readers believe—militated against their ever having either constituted a documentary unity or having manifested such a character. In order to suit the purposes of a doctrinaire analysis, these fragments were dragooned with characteristic Teutonic precision into yet another "document," and presented for the approval of Old Testament scholarship as a whole. The comparative lack of enthusiasm with which this latest source has been received is a sufficient judgment upon its validity.

Part one of the present work has described the manner in which conservative scholars attacked the various divisive hypotheses of Pentateuchal origins. In 1847, F. W. Hengstenberg published an English version of his masterly work on the Pentateuch under the title *Dissertations on the Genuineness of the Pentateuch,* and he was followed in some of his conclusions by Drechsler.[23] H. Ch. Havernick, C. F. Keil, H. M. Wiener, E. Naville, W. Möller, J. Orr, and many others championed the Mosaic authorship of the Pentateuch in one way or another, while

[19] G. von Rad, *Die Priesterschrift im Hexateuch* (1934).

[20] C. A. Simpson, *The Early Traditions of Israel: A Critical Analysis of the Pre-Deuteronomic Narrative of the Hexateuch* (1948).

[21] H. H. Rowley, *The Society for Old Testament Study Book List* (1949), p. 34.

[22] O. Eissfeldt, *Die Genesis der Genesis. Vom Werdegang des ersten Buches der Bibel* (1958), an expanded form of his article on Genesis in *IDB,* II, pp. 366ff.; *ETOT,* pp. 191ff.

[23] M. Drechsler, *Die Einheit und Echtheit der Genesis* (1838).

among liberal scholars, some of the conclusions of the analytical school, particularly with respect to the dating of the Priestly Code, were hotly contested by A. Dillmann, H. L. Strack, W. W. Graf Baudissin, and E. König, as well as in the earlier writings of R. Kittel.

More recently the methodology of the nineteenth-century liberal Protestants of Germany has come under attack by R. D. Wilson, O. T. Allis, G. Ch. Aalders, E. J. Young, G. T. Manley, C. H. Gordon, and numerous others.[24] In a rather different way the classic documentary theory of Pentateuchal composition has been the object of sustained criticism by a group of Scandinavian scholars including Pedersen, Engnell, Haldar, Nyberg, Bentzen, and others. By drawing heavily upon comparative studies they have managed to make considerably more room than was the case previously for a recognition of the fact of oral transmission alongside that of documentary sources, and in general they have stressed the great reliability of material passed along by word of mouth.

The "traditio-historical" approach of the Swedish school has proved unacceptable to many liberal writers because in their view it over-emphasizes the role of oral tradition and places too little stress upon literary analysis.[25] Accordingly, scholars such as Widengren[26] and Mowinckel[27] have sought in their teachings to modify the importance that Nyberg, Birkeland, and others had attributed to the place of oral tradition, an undertaking in which they were only partially successful. Important criticisms of the Wellhausenian methodology were also made by Hermann Gunkel and Hugo Gressmann, who were primarily responsible for the development in the field of literary criticism of the form-critical method or *Gattungsforschung*. Their objections to the positions adopted by the Wellhausen school included accusations of lack of vision and disregard of the archaeological and psychological discoveries that alone augured for historical reality.[28]

C. GENERAL PRESUPPOSITIONS OF THE GRAF-WELLHAUSEN HYPOTHESIS

Because the Graf-Wellhausen theory of Pentateuchal origins has exerted a profound influence for a prolonged period over the minds of Old Testament scholars, however, a fairly close look should be taken at its fundamental postulates and energizing factors. At the outset it must be recognized that far more was involved in the Wellhausenian presentation

---

24 R. D. Wilson, *A Scientific Investigation of the OT* (1926), reprinted, with annotations by E. J. Young (1959); O. T. Allis, *The Five Books of Moses* (1943); G. Ch. Aalders, *A Short Introduction to the Pentateuch* (1949); E. J. Young, *Introduction to the Old Testament* (1949, rev. 1958, 1960); G. T. Manley, *The Book of the Law* (1957); C. H. Gordon, *Christianity Today*, IV, No. 4 (1959), pp. 131ff.

25 Cf. G. W. Anderson, *Harvard Theological Review*, XLIII (1950), pp. 239ff.

26 *Literary and Psychological Aspects of the Hebrew Prophets* (1948).

27 *Prophecy and Tradition* (1946).

28 Cf. J. Coppens, *The OT and the Critics* (1942), p. 71.

than mere considerations of documentary analysis. The Graf-Wellhausen school based its critical studies upon a philosophical evolutionary theory that had a great deal in common with the speculations of Hegel. Against such an evolutionary *Zeitgeist* the advocates of critical theories of Pentateuchal analysis developed a monolinear view of Hebrew history that followed a pattern similar to that formulated by Darwin with respect to biology. Commencing with humble beginnings in animism and primitive culture, Hebrew history as they saw it progressed little by little to its climax in the post-exilic period. The religion of Israel was thought to have advanced in a similar fashion from the simple sacrifices on family altars in the settlement period to the vastly more complex liturgical celebrations of the Priestly Code, the latter being assigned by the members of the Graf-Wellhausen school generally to some point in the later post-exilic era.

Behind this disarmingly simple view of progress was a powerful emotional force grounded upon two suppositions. The first comprised that peculiar facet of the western outlook that assumes that it is both possible and desirable to resolve the complexities of a given situation by reducing the "many to the one," as Socrates endeavored to do with the Greek gods of his own day. As a result one should attempt to posit a single interpretative principle for some branch of study or for the whole of phenomena represented by contingent existence. The second premise was that, as a consequence of the material and intellectual advances of the late eighteenth and early nineteenth centuries, it was possible to conceive of humanity as progressing steadily and relentlessly towards advanced goals of social, cultural, and ultimately spiritual development.

In the light of subsequent events, both presuppositions have been proved to be completely erroneous. The "glimpses of ultimate reality" that fall within the purview of any given individual are invariably fragmentary, occasional, and of extremely short duration. Neither in biology nor in any other field, whether within the descriptive sciences or out of them, is it even remotely possible to fasten upon a single potentially interpretative concept and make it the definite standard by which everything else is to be judged. Those who have followed Darwin in the biological field in endeavoring to make "evolution" such an interpretative principle for organic life have received unexpected setbacks as the general area of scientific knowledge has widened. Thus it is now recognized from geological studies that progress occurs by spasms or leaps, and not by the slow, scarcely perceptible procedures of improvement or differentiation postulated by Darwin and his followers. As regards the optimistic views current at the end of the nineteenth century concerning the inevitable material, intellectual, and moral progress of the species *homo sapiens,* numerous sociological, theological, and other studies have made it abundantly apparent that technological development and social uplifting have not been accompanied by a corresponding degree of maturity in the human spirit, and that ultimately the outlook for the human race is best expressed in negative and deteriorative, rather than in positive and progressive terms.

All of this, of course, was not apparent to the nineteenth-century pundits of evolutionary philosophy. So absolutely assured were they of their opinions that even their methodology was subordinated to doctrinaire considerations, a procedure that has proved in other circumstances to be as disastrous in its results as it is ill-advised in theory. As far as the Graf-Wellhausen school of literary criticism was concerned, the methods it adopted were for the most part in complete accord with the spirit of the age. What they did not perceive, unfortunately, was that their procedures were founded less upon scientific discipline than upon the emotional upsurge of contemporary rationalism.

In particular, the methodology of the European critical scholars exhibited many of the flaws and weaknesses of the German national character, tendencies that are seen most clearly in the approach of Wellhausen himself. This gifted scholar was clearly obsessed by a resolute desire to prove his thesis—once he found a clue in the work of previous thinkers—by every possible means, including the maximum exercise of native ingenuity and imagination, and the assembling and forcing into service of anything that might pass for evidence or function as some kind of proof of his contentions. If Wellhausen was at all aware of the dangers inherent in this kind of methodology he certainly made no attempt to rectify them, and he may even have consoled himself with the *ad verecundiam* argument that other great minds had utilized exactly the same approach.

In company with others, Wellhausen exhibited that remarkable characteristic of the German mind which consists in the ability to arrive at definitive conclusions on the basis of only part of the total evidence, accompanied by a distinct reluctance to introduce anything more than the slightest theoretical modifications even when much more complete evidence—the nature of which requires substantial changes in the theory as a whole—is available. More remarkable still is the ability of the German mind to utilize the resultant hypothesis and its earlier supporting evidence as a means of refuting—to its own satisfaction at least—both the later evidence and the modifications of the original formulation that it demands. Thus the theoretical position that has been adopted initially becomes virtually sacrosanct, however flimsy its foundations may subsequently be discovered to be. After all this it is a matter of personal honor to engage in its defense and to esteem it as the only possible and legitimate explanation of the phenomena under consideration.

To this gross error of dogmatic statement of conclusions on an extremely inadequate basis of factual evidence, Wellhausen and his followers added the contemporary rationalistic prejudices against the supernatural. Historically, as has been observed previously, the Graf-Wellhausen school adopted a rather skeptical and positivistic approach consistent with the spirit of Hegelian philosophy. On the basis of such an *a priori* evolutionism all facts were made to conform to the theory of literary analysis, in an exaggerated emphasis upon the concept of unilinear development.[29] All social, religious, and institutional phenomena were made to fit into a given mold, and this frequently involved an unabashed emendation or excision of portions of the Hebrew text when particular passages proved hostile to the general theory, or a thoroughgoing reconstruction of historical processes, based upon nothing more substantial than the most subjective of considerations.

Like so many other positivists, Wellhausen and his followers assumed that analogies between mechanistic materialism and aspects of the descriptive sciences were in fact the same thing as scientific method. This tendency, along with a remarkable facility for committing the gross logical fallacy of begging the question, made for further grave weaknesses in the methodological system of the Graf-Wellhausen school. In fairness to the historical development of this situation, however, it should be observed that within recent years most liberal writers have spared their readers the embarrassment attached to the claim that their literary-critical method is scientific. Whether this has resulted from a genuine insight into the theoretical position adopted, or merely from the assured belief that there can no longer be any serious question as to the scientific nature of their procedures, is difficult to ascertain. What can be remarked, however, is that in properly accredited scientific research the investigator is first confronted by a mass of facts that he is required to study carefully and subsequently to classify and categorize in accordance with the best traditions of his discipline. This process in itself involves many revisions, particularly as new knowledge becomes available while the work is proceeding.

By adopting canons of inductive reasoning, which involves arguing from what is known to what is unknown, the research worker gradually builds up in his mind some kind of theoretical explanation of the known facts. The hypothesis thus resulting may well be highly tentative and imperfect at the best, and should it happen that it requires substantial modification somewhat later as the result of the impact of what T. H. Huxley once called "one ugly little fact," the truly scientific investigator will make whatever changes are demanded by the situation, even if he is compelled to begin his research *de novo* to all intents and purposes. To commence the task of investigation with an *a priori* theoretical position; to organize the available material into conformity with this approach; and to manipulate or transform any obdurate facts to the point where, at worst, they will not entirely overthrow the basic postulates, is the very

---

[29] Cf. *FSAC*, p. 84; Albright, *History, Archaeology and Christian Humanism* (1964), pp. 136f.

antithesis of scientific method. Thus for the Wellhausenian and other analogous schools of literary criticism that depend upon the *a priori* deductive approach to pretend to those who are not nourished upon the humanities that their methodology is scientific is to invite nothing less than derision and ridicule for their pains. Equally serious was the manner in which the school of Wellhausen could accept previously expressed opinions in a completely uncritical fashion. Thus Wellhausen was able to write: "I learned through Ritschl that Karl Heinrich Graf placed the law later than the prophets; and, almost without knowing his reasons for the hypothesis, I was prepared to accept it."[30]

The ability that German scholars generally exhibited in rationalizing their way out of awkward situations was only matched by their utter self-confidence and peremptoriness. Despite the significantly wide divergence of opinion in critical circles, Wellhausen could write in the most categorical manner about anything upon which he chose to make a pronouncement. With supreme arrogance the critical savants designated their findings as constituting "the most assured results of Biblical scholarship," as "showing incontrovertibly" or as "demonstrating conclusively." The fact that such findings were based upon the flimsiest of what could be styled as evidence did not disturb the confident investigators for one moment.

Whatever else may be adduced in criticism of Wellhausen and his school, it is quite evident that his theory of Pentateuchal origins would have been vastly different (if, indeed, it had been formulated at all) had Wellhausen chosen to take account of the archaeological material available for study in his day, and had he subordinated his philosophical and theoretical considerations to a sober and rational assessment of the factual evidence as a whole. While he and his followers drew to some extent upon the philological discoveries of the day and manifested a degree of interest in the origins of late Arabic culture in relation to Semitic precursors, they depended almost exclusively upon their own view of the culture and religious history of the Hebrews for purposes of Biblical interpretation.

Wellhausen took almost no note whatever of progress in the field of oriental scholarship, and once having arrived at his conclusions, he never troubled to revise his opinion in the light of subsequent research in the general field. He ignored completely such vastly important discoveries as the Tell el-Amarna tablets, even though Hugo Winckler had made the texts readily available in a critical edition. Even as late as 1893 the faithful followers of Wellhausen were still propounding his dictum that, since writing was only utilized about the time of David, Moses could not possibly have written the Pentateuch even if he had wanted to.[31]

[30] *Prolegomena to the History of Israel* (1885), p. 3.
[31] So H. Schultz, *OT Theology* (1893), I, p. 25.

That this bizarre postulate could even have been suggested seriously, let alone accorded axiomatic status by Wellhausen and his disciples, can only be accounted for by assuming an irresponsible and wanton neglect of a body of archaeological evidence that was already enormous while Wellhausen was formulating his critical theories. The process of agglomeration began with the copying in 1765 of some trilingual inscriptions from Persepolis by the Danish scholar Carsten Niebuhr,[32] and continued with the labors of H. C. Rawlinson from 1835 on. The decipherment of Akkadian resulted from the activities of French scholars under Botta at Khorsabad from 1842 and at Nineveh and Nimrud under Layard from 1845 on. Sumerian inscriptions on bricks and tablets from sites such as Nippur, Erech, and Larsa were described by Rawlinson from 1855 on, and the language was deciphered as the result of pioneer studies by Hincks and Oppert.

This linguistic material was supplemented by such actual sources as the Rosetta Stone, discovered in 1789, the Behistun Inscription, transcribed in 1835 by Rawlinson, the Kuyunjik tablets unearthed at Nineveh from 1845 on, the Black Obelisk of Shalmaneser III, found in 1846, and the Monolith Inscription issuing from the same period, the excavations at Susa from 1852 and 1864, the discovery of the Moabite Stone in 1868, and other material, the nature of which attested invariably to its great antiquity. This corpus comprised part of the evidence that Wellhausen ought to have taken into account when he was formulating his hypothesis. Unfortunately, however, his preoccupation with the subjective literary analysis of the Pentateuch and his disregard for anything that might interfere in any way with the development of his thesis precluded an objective examination of this sort of evidence. As a result, his theory was unbalanced and prejudiced heavily in favor of purely arbitrary and subjective considerations from the very beginning.

Subsequent adherents of the Graf-Wellhausen theory of Pentateuchal origins stood firmly in the tradition established by the great master. For them the Old Testament narratives were replete with confused repetition of events, characterized by gross historical, topographical, and other errors in the text, and overlaid with a tissue of pagan mythology of such a sort as to require the attention of highly skilled analytical minds before the real trend of events could be outlined at all satisfactorily. Later research, however, has revealed that a great many of these objections were more artificial than real, and depended for their veracity upon the basic assumptions of the liberal school, which, as has been mentioned above, were gravely deficient from the very outset.

For example, one of the many objections raised against the historical reliability and integrity of the Pentateuch dealt with an alleged conflict of tradition in regard to the place where Aaron died. According to one of

---

[32] Cf. S. N. Kramer, *Sumerian Mythology* (1961), pp. 3ff.; *FSAC*, pp. 32ff.

the sources that scholars purported to identify, he died on Mount Hor (Num. 20:22; 21:4; 33:33; Deut. 32:50), but according to a "different" tradition he died at Moserah (Deut. 10:6). A careful reading of the text shows that in point of fact there is absolutely no conflict in the tradition concerning the death of Aaron at all. The word מוסרה in Deuteronomy 10:6 means "chastisement," thus describing the place of his death in terms of a value judgment. This allusion makes it clear that his decease on Mount Hor constituted a reproof for the trespass at Meribah (Num. 20:24; Deut. 32:51), and that, like Moses, he was excluded from the Promised Land because of his rebellion against God. The two supposedly conflicting traditions are thus in complete harmony, and preserve the facts that Aaron died on Mount Hor while the people encamped below in mourning. In order to mark this sad occasion, which, with his own exclusion from the Promised Land, lay heavily upon the mind of Moses (Deut. 1:37; 3:23ff.), the incident and the camp-site were designated Moseroth (Num. 33:31; Deut. 10:6).

In an attempt to elucidate the route taken by the wandering Israelites as they approached Edomite and Amorite territory in preparation for their assault upon Canaan (Num. 21:10ff.), E. G. Kraeling was "quite surprised" to find himself further to the south at the River Arnon,[33] primarily because he assumed, quite without warrant, that the Hebrew term הפסגה was actually the name of a mountain, following the fashion in critical circles. He was thus reduced to the normal expedient of identifying and separating "early" and "late" narrators, and of attempting to reconcile and harmonize their testimonies so as to present a constructive interpretation of the situation. In point of fact there is no reason whatever for assuming that there was ever just one single place named "Mount Pisgah." On each occasion when the term *Pisgah* occurs in the Hebrew text it is accompanied by the definite article, showing that it was not a single identifiable location but rather a common noun. Derived from a root which in later Hebrew meant "to cleave," and represented as such in the LXX, the term described a ridge crowning a hill or mountain which, when viewed from beneath, presented an uneven outline. It thus meant "the elevated ridge," and as such was applied to various sites in Palestine, and not to one specific mountain. It can be noted here that the documentary analysis of Pentateuchal written sources is particularly weak in its attempts to interpret the Wilderness wanderings of the Israelites, a matter that will be considered subsequently.

Quite aside from being beguiled and misled by a faulty methodology, liberal scholars have contrived to make their own difficulties in process of supporting the Graf-Wellhausen critical position. Thus H. H. Rowley, in his attempt to present an authoritative basis for what he held to be the Maccabean dating of the book of Daniel, employed inferior secondary

---

[33] *Rand McNally Bible Atlas* (1956), p. 122.

sources comprising translations of the Nabonidus Chronicle[34] as a means of building up a composite image of a "Gobryas."[35] Rowley then employed his "Gobryas" to demolish theories suggesting the identification of Darius the Mede with Gobryas, and by direct implication rejected the historicity of Darius the Mede. This example rested, as Whitcomb has pointed out,[36] upon the assumption that "Gobryas" was not only a combination of the persons named Gubaru and Ugbaru in the cuneiform sources, but also the "Gobryas" of Herodotus and Xenophon and the "Gaubaruva, son of Mardonius a Persian" in the Behistun Inscription. Had Rowley based his studies upon more reliable translations, and especially upon the cuneiform of the Nabonidus Chronicle, he would have become aware of the fact that Gubaru and Ugbaru, who were mentioned in connection with the fall of Babylon in 539 B.C., were regarded as two distinct individuals in the Chronicle. This simple distinction, properly pursued, would have led to an entirely different formulation of his views regarding the identity of Darius the Mede, a task which, in the event, was left for J. C. Whitcomb to accomplish. Unfortunately for the speculations of Rowley on this particular question, his methodological error was as elementary as it was egregious.

Although the foregoing may well have been an honest mistake, the same cannot be said for certain ambivalent tendencies which have marred liberal criticism over the years. Thus it is curious, to say the least, that many scholars are perfectly content to allow the validity of evidence from Josephus concerning the fact that Jaddua was High Priest during the time of Alexander the Great,[37] and hence assign a date between 350 and 250 B.C. for the work of the Chronicler, but are completely unwilling to recognize from the same source the correctness of the testimony to the fact that the book of Daniel was in its completed form by 330 B.C.[38]

While many of the European adherents of the Graf-Wellhausen hypothesis have modified their views to the extent of recognizing that the results of literary criticism in its apogee were rather arid and sterile, there is little evidence at the time of writing that they are willing to part serious company with the documentary theory of Pentateuchal origins in its present form. Thus, in a recent compendium of material dealing with Old Testament interpretation, C. Westermann's *Essays on Old Testa-*

---

[34] I.e., other than the translation of Sidney Smith, *Babylonian Historical Texts Relating to the Downfall of Babylon* (1924).

[35] H. H. Rowley, *Darius the Mede and the Four World Empires in the Book of Daniel* (1935), pp. 20ff.

[36] J. C. Whitcomb, *Darius the Mede: A Study in Historical Identification* (1959), p. 26; cf. D. J. Wiseman, *NBD*, pp. 293f., *Notes on Some Problems in the Book of Daniel* (1965), pp. 9ff.

[37] *AJ*, VI, 7, 2; XI, 8, 5.

[38] *AJ*, XI, 8, 5.

ment Hermeneutics (1963), Zimmerli could recognize only the barest elements of originality in the patriarchal narratives, which for him had been heavily reinforced by material dating from the pre-conquest period, and had been largely rewritten by the "Yahwist" to stress the emergent element of promise.[39] But another contributor to the volume, Hesse, could hardly go as far as that, for he asserted that while the Old Testament envisaged Abraham as the bearer of the promise and the tried and true man of faith, "we cannot accept this witness from the Old Testament without further ado, because we know that this Abraham never existed in this way."[40] In harmony with traditional German critical authoritarianism, Hesse never troubled to inform his readers as to the nature and content of his special fount of knowledge concerning Abraham.

In the same work Walter Eichrodt continued to perpetuate the old attitude of radical criticism in his statement that the historical material of the Old Testament is highly stylized and cannot be accepted at face value, since for him and his fellow-critics, "Old Testament history has received in essential points a quite different aspect from that which it could have had for a generation untouched by the historical work of the last two centuries."[41] Here again Eichrodt is only prepared to consider the witness of the Old Testament to itself after the text has been thoroughly reworked according to the canons of classical literary criticism, and appears unwilling to recognize the substantial gains made towards the rehabilitation of the traditional text of the Old Testament historical material as the result of modern archaeological, linguistic, historical, and other research.

Much of the credit for a return to the view that the Old Testament is an authentic document of religious history must go to the archaeologically oriented school of W. F. Albright. Through rigorous emphases upon linguistics and archaeology, this renowned scholar has contributed more to the accumulating fund of knowledge concerning Old Testament life and times than any other individual in the field. To some extent Albright has broken with the traditions of Wellhausen, particularly since 1940, in his insistence on the primacy of archaeology in the broad sense as a method of control, as well as upon the substantial historicity of the patriarchal tradition and the precedence of oral tradition over written literature.[42] Yet while he has claimed a greater sympathy towards the Mosaic traditions now than previously, he has asserted that the oldest document in the Old Testament that has survived in approximately its

[39] Pp. 90ff.
[40] P. 298.
[41] P. 232.
[42] *FSAC*, p. 2.

original form is the Song of Deborah,[43] a pronouncement that has a curious Wellhausenian ring about it. Such a statement is certainly remarkable, to say the least, in view of the known antiquity of writing in Near Eastern cultures, as well as the fact that the processes of writing *per se* are referred to nearly forty times in the Pentateuch alone.

That Albright actually holds to the documentary analysis of the Pentateuch, albeit modified to some extent by the emphasis upon oral tradition as found in the form-critical school, is apparent from his attempts at dating the "Pentateuchal documents."[44] He has maintained in this connection that J and E were transmitted separately, being written down not later than 750 B.C.; that Deuteronomy was written in the time of Josiah, not as a pious fraud (contrary to the views of some Wellhausenians) but as an earnest attempt to recapture and express the Mosaic tradition, and that the Priestly Code is almost certainly not pre-exilic. Like many other liberal scholars he handicaps himself when dealing with the question of Mosaic monotheism by the quite gratuitous assumption that "all our literary sources are relatively late. . .and that we must depend on a tradition which was long transmitted orally."[45]

In spite of his professed objectivity, it is difficult to believe that Albright is, by and large, following the direction to which the facts point. With one breath he can adhere in broad principle to the Graf-Wellhausen theory, and with another he can state quite confidently that the foundations of literary criticism have been seriously undermined by the manuscript discoveries from 4Q.[46] While still supporting a somewhat modified Graf-Wellhausen position he can abandon the "developmental character" of Old Testament history in favor of the unity of tradition implied by the records. Unfortunately, however, in postulating the existence of "divergences from basic historical fact,"[47] Albright commits precisely the same error as that characteristic of the nineteenth-century critical writers, who interpreted the traditional data in accordance with their own peculiar philosophy of history. While it is important to realize, as Burrows has pointed out,[48] that the accuracy of the history and the truth of the interpretation must not be confused, it is equally necessary to emphasize the accredited historical character of much of the material that, in critical circles, has hitherto been explained away in terms of myth, legend, folk-lore, and empirico-logical thought.

Although Albright has been in advance of many liberal thinkers in recognizing that most prophecies are actually anthologies of oracles or

[43] *Recent Discoveries in Bible Lands* (1956), p. 90.
[44] *FSAC*, pp. 250f.
[45] *FSAC*, p. 257.
[46] *Samuel and the Beginnings of the Prophetic Movement* (1961), p. 11.
[47] *Archaeology and the Religion of Israel* (1955), p. 176.
[48] *WMTS*, p. 5.

sermons,[49] he has insisted upon placing the prophecy of Isaiah in a special category, in that for him it contains extraneous material. This view is an obvious concession to the critical speculations of the Graf-Wellhausen school, and is absolutely incapable of being substantiated either by internal or external evidence. By contrast, the situation is quite different in the case of the book of Jeremiah, in which there seem to be distinct traces of extraneous matter (e.g. Jer. 52:1ff.).

The followers of Albright naturally share his ambivalence in matters of historical and theological interpretation. Thus it is possible for F. M. Cross and J. Bright to assign an early date to the Tabernacle, a position that is eminently justified in the light of the archaeological evidence;[50] but at the same time they expound a somewhat modified Graf-Wellhausen critical position. This is a curious anomaly, to say the least, for according to classical literary criticism the Tabernacle emerged from priestly sources and was widely regarded as a completely idealistic reverse projection of the later Temple into the remote past. Yet neither Cross nor Bright appears to recognize that the views which they hold regarding the date of the Wilderness Tabernacle constitute such a fundamental criticism of the Graf-Wellhausen position as to amount to its rejection in one cardinal area of its development.

Pursuing the lead afforded by these facts, it would appear possible that if the theory is vulnerable in this vital area, it may well be deficient in other important respects also. Unfortunately, Albright and his followers, while doubtless recognizing the compelling force of this kind of logic, are apparently unwilling to jettison the traditions of Graf and Wellhausen and strike out independently along a new line of investigation, following the direction in which the facts point. Judging once more from their writings, the members of the Albright school would seem to have as little real sympathy for supernaturalism in the Old Testament as did Alt and his followers.[51]

Of all the criticisms levelled against the Graf-Wellhausen hypothesis in recent years, by far the most significant was that published by C. H. Gordon in 1959.[52] This renowned archaeologist and Near Eastern scholar rejected what he described as "the badge of interconfessional academic respectability" largely on the ground of archaeological evidence. His conclusions were stimulated by a comparison of the eleventh tablet of the Gilgamesh Epic with the Genesis account of the construction of the ark. He became impressed with the absurdity of assigning the Genesis description to the Priestly Code and to the era of the Second Temple, as

---

[49] *FSAC*, p. 275.
[50] F. M. Cross, *BA*, X, No. 3 (1947), pp. 55ff.; Bright in *BHI*, pp. 146f.
[51] O. T. Allis, *Christianity Today*, III, No. 17 (1959), p. 9.
[52] C. H. Gordon, *Christianity Today*, IV, No. 4 (1959), pp. 131ff.

the Graf-Wellhausen school did, without doing precisely the same for the remarkably similar Gilgamesh Epic account of the ark.

Consequently he was able to argue that the pre-Abrahamic traditions of the book of Genesis, such as that involving the Deluge, were not in fact late Priestly Code material at all. Instead, he concluded that they were pre-Mosaic, and that it was extremely difficult to single out any detail that was attestably late. This had been clear for some time from the evidence presented by Sumerian and Akkadian cuneiform sources, and was made certain by the texts recovered from Ras Shamra (Ugarit), where whole literary themes, as well as specific phrases, occurred in tablets of pre-Mosaic date. Such a position represented a crystallizing of earlier tendencies in the thought and writings of Gordon,[53] and led him to separate the real literary sources of the Pentateuch from the spurious ones advanced by the Graf-Wellhausen school.

From his studies of Ugaritic material Gordon became aware of the high degree of culture in Canaan prior to the emergence of the Hebrews as a sedentary people, and as a result he was able to reject quite readily the notion advanced by earlier literary critics that the formative stages of Israelite religion and society were essentially primitive. Gordon suggested as a conclusion to his article that subsequent Old Testament studies could only be based most satisfactorily upon an exacting and accreuited scientific methodology in which the spurious and imaginary would be rejected in favor of the genuine and factual, and the *a priori* deductive system of classical liberalism replaced by an inductive approach that would pursue with resolution any specific direction indicated by the facts of the situation.

Enough has been said in relationship to the general criticism of the Graf-Wellhausen methodology and its doctrinaire exercise by generations of scholars to demonstrate the fundamental weaknesses of such an approach. It can only be a matter for the deepest regret that the methods of literary criticism were formulated without any but the most casual reference to the actual characteristics of contemporary Near Eastern literature insofar as it was available to scholars, since in a great many areas it exhibits remarkable similarities to the writings of the ancient Hebrews. What is quite certain is that, in any new methodology that may be adopted by scholars in the future, the compositions of ancient Near Eastern nations must be utilized as an external control over subjective theories of literary origins of Biblical material.

D. Criteria of the Graf-Wellhausen Hypothesis

1. YHWH and Elohim. Against the background of the foregoing discussion it is now possible to take a more detailed look at the criteria that were held to validate the Graf-Wellhausen theory in the minds of its

---

[53] Cf. *UL,* pp. 6f.

adherents. As has been observed in preceding pages, the earliest criterion to be employed in isolating the alleged underlying documentary
sources of the Pentateuch was the variant usage of the divine name, with
YHWH (יהוה, Eng. Jehovah) used exclusively in one document and
Elohim (אלהים) in the other. In refuting the validity of this procedure it
can be said at once that no other religious document from any of the
ancient Near Eastern cultures can be shown to have been compiled in
this manner. The Gilgamesh Epic, for example, incorporates older material, particularly in the Deluge story, but it is neither desirable nor
possible to attempt to analyze the Epic into underlying "documentary"
sources on the basis of a variation in the usage of the divine names.
Were one to undertake this procedure there would emerge as many
theoretical documents as the number of deities mentioned in this ancient
cuneiform composition.

The inadequacy of using the divine names YHWH and Elohim as
criteria for distinguishing supposed documents in the Pentateuchal corpus can be further demonstrated by using as a control another characteristically Semitic body of material, the Koran. While this is many centuries removed historically from the composition of the Pentateuch, there
can be little serious doubt that, as Albright has pointed out, the transmission of the Hebrew Torah must have resembled that of the Tradition
(ḥadîth) in Islam.[54] Many years ago, in his study of the divine names
in the Koran, R. D. Wilson showed that certain suras of the Koran
preferred the designation of God as Allah (e.g. IV, IX, XXIV, XXXIII),
whereas others employed Rab (e.g. XVIII, XXIII, XXV); in precisely
the same way that portions of Genesis favored YHWH (e.g. 7:1ff.; 11:1ff.;
18:1–19:28), whereas others used Elohim (e.g. Gen. 1:1–2:3; 6:9ff.;
17:2ff.) as the divine name.[55] Yet in spite of the existence in the Koran
of exactly the same kind of criterion as that employed by the European
literary critics for the formulation of their theory of Pentateuchal origins,
there is absolutely no support whatever among Islamic scholars for a
documentary approach to studies of the Koran on the basis of difference
in usage between Allah and Rab.

In any question of the relative occurrences of YHWH and Elohim as
criteria for determining the presence of underlying documentary sources,
the evidence of textual criticism both from the Pentateuch of the
LXX version and from the Qumran manuscript fragments has to be
taken into consideration. The LXX version of the Torah exhibits a
greater variation in the use of the divine names than that apparent in
the MT. This situation would suggest, among other things, that if the
translators of the LXX Pentateuch knew about the existence of the

---

[54] FSAC, p. 258. For the origin and authenticity of the Islamic Tradition see J.
Fueck, ZDMG, XCIII (1939), pp. 1ff.
[55] R. D. Wilson, PTR, XVII (1919), pp. 644ff.

alleged documents underlying the finished structure of the Law, they were not influenced to any significant extent by those considerations that, according to the Graf-Wellhausen theory, had determined the activities of the anonymous redactors of the various manuscript sources. On the contrary, they had evidently prepared the LXX version of the Law against a background of obvious freedom of choice from whatever families of manuscripts were available for the task of translation.

That there were at least three distinct families of Hebrew manuscripts in existence in the pre-Massoretic period has been demonstrated convincingly as a result of the manuscript discoveries at Qumran, and in particular from the fragments recovered from 4Q, thereby confirming the opinion that there was considerably more variety in the text of early Pentateuchal manuscripts than was the case with the MT itself. Since the latter has traditionally been used as the basis of documentary analysis in view of the fact that it was regarded as the "fixed" text, it is interesting to speculate as to what might have happened to the entire Graf-Wellhausen theory had one or more pre-Massoretic texts been available for the use of nineteenth-century literary critics. The answer has in fact been supplied to a large extent by Albright, who, as mentioned above, has stated that the fragmentary manuscripts recovered from 4Q have already seriously undermined the foundations of detailed literary criticism.

It will be recalled from earlier discussion that the use of the divine names as a criterion for literary analysis had been attacked in a number of quarters at the end of the nineteenth century. Notable in this connection were Dahse and Wiener, both of whom called attention to variations in the LXX text, and argued from this to the fact that it is impossible to be certain of the usage of the names *YHWH* and *Elohim* in the original Hebrew text. According to their view, the incidence of the divine names in the MT and the LXX ought to be uniform if the premises upon which the documentary theory was based were to be considered valid, and as such the names occurring in the LXX ought to be just as reliable a criterion for documentary analysis as those found in the MT. Skinner attempted to meet this argument by endeavoring to show on grounds of textual criticism that the MT was more reliable than the LXX in this matter, and it must be observed that, while his efforts met with some success, he failed to come to grips with the fundamental issues raised by Dahse and Wiener.[56] What is even more unfortunate is the fact that his arguments have been gravely weakened by the textual evidence from Qumran, which shows that it was eminently possible for the translators of the LXX version to have had several manuscript families of the Pentateuch at their disposal, whose nature and contents

---

[56] J. Skinner, *The Divine Names in the Book of Genesis* (1914).

were by no means identical in all respects with those of the Massoretic tradition.

The difficulties encountered by critics in employing the single names for deity are multiplied greatly when the use of a compound such as *YHWH-Elohim* (Gen. 2:4–3:24) is considered. According to the Graf-Wellhausen theory, a conflation of J and E sources into JE was held to account for this phenomenon. This in itself posed a difficult problem for the critical scholars who propounded this explanation, since it involved a combining of the divine names that in theory were supposed to furnish the vital clues to the existence of separate documents. This embarrassing situation was made more acute by the realization that, with characteristic independence of the strict Massoretic tradition, the LXX version contained many more instances of this combination than are apparent in the Hebrew (e.g. Gen. 4:6, 9; 5:29; 6:3, 5). Turning from the Scriptures to "control" material, it is now known that there is ample evidence for the use of compound names for deities in Ugaritic, Egyptian, and Greek literature. Thus, as Gordon has shown, it was a commonplace at Ugarit for deities to have compound names allotted to them.[57] One god was known as Qadish-Amrar, another Ibb-Nikkal, another Koshar-Hasis, and so on. Quite obviously the multiplicity of divine names in the Pentateuch must be evaluated against such a background, particularly in view of the close literary relationship that has been shown to exist between Ugaritic and Biblical Hebrew. On the basis of such comparisons it is apparent that, by themselves, *YHWH* and *Elohim* need not imply dual authorship in any given chapter of the Pentateuch any more than the incidence of Baal and Haddu would in a Ugaritic myth.

Probably the most familiar example of this tendency in antiquity can be seen in the combined name Amon-Re, the god who became the great universal deity as a result of Egyptian conquests during the Eighteenth Dynasty.[58] Amon, it will be recalled, was the ramheaded deity of the capital city Thebes; and Re was revered as the old universal sun-god. The fusion of the religious universalism associated with Re and the political leadership in the Thebes of Amon underlies the fact of the compound name "Amon-Re" as a single entity. The *stele* of Ikhernofret (*ca.* 1800 B.C.) goes considerably further than a great many other Egyptian sources in the matter of multiple divine names, for it offers no fewer than four different names and epithets of the god Osiris, both singly and in combination, in harmony with contemporary practices in this matter.

As Gordon has pointed out, scholars can do much to account for the combination of the elements in *YHWH-Elohim* by suggesting, for example, that the multiple form can be explained in terms of the equation

[57] *GBB*, p. 160; *UL*, p. 6.
[58] J. Černý, *Ancient Egyptian Religion* (1952), pp. 38, 61f.

"*YHWH* equals *Elohim*."[59] But when the view is seriously propounded that *YHWH-Elohim* is the result of documentary conflation, it becomes as impossible to accept this contention as it is to argue that Amon-Re emerged as a designation because certain scribes combined an "A" document with an "R" document. Even a cursory examination of Egyptian religion shows just how widespread was the custom of describing deities in terms of compound names. To give one more example only, in some localities of ancient Egypt the sun-deity Re was also known as Sobek-Re, the crocodile-god, while at Elephantine he was identified with Khnum, who appeared as a ram, and was known as Khnum-Re.[60]

As far as Greek culture is concerned, classical scholars have long been familiar with the reference in Herodotus to Themistocles' attempt to extort money from the Andrians by informing them that he came with two persuasive deities named "Persuasion-and-Necessity."[61] The Andrians refused to pay, however, on the ground that they were saddled with certain impecunious deities whose names were "Poverty-and-Impotence." The parallel with the religious traditions of Ras Shamra can be seen when it is observed that the names of the Ugaritic deities are able to be written with the conjunction "and," as with "Qadish-and-Amrar," "Koshar-and-Hasis," and so on. Exactly the same phenomenon occurred in the Greek combinations "Kratos-Bia-te" and "Kratos kai Dike," the personified forms of strength and might, in the writings of Aeschylus.[62]

The phenomenon of coupled or compound names is thus well attested in Near Eastern antiquity. Precisely what the combination *YHWH-Elohim* was intended to signify, however, is open to some question. Whereas *Elohim* designated the idea of deity in a general sense, *YHWH* constituted a specific divine name, and if the former was used as a universal name for God, it is possible that *YHWH* was meant to indicate the more restricted Deity of the Covenant. It may also be that the close association and interchange of the two designations in the Pentateuch points to an attempt on the part of the author or authors to emphasize the ideas associated with each name.[63] Certainly these and similar problems pertaining to the incidence of the divine names in the Torah have shown their inadequacy as criteria for the whole process of documentary analysis.[64] If this actually constituted the cornerstone of the Graf-Wellhausen hypothesis, as the writings of liberal critics indicate, it is clearly a most fragile structure upon which to build.

2. *Multiple names.* Other criteria employed in attempts to outline or recover the underlying documents or "hands" in the Pentateuch have

[59] C. H. Gordon, *Christianity Today*, IV, No. 4 (1959), p. 133.
[60] Cf. H. Frankfort, *Ancient Egyptian Religion* (1961), p. 20.
[61] *Hist.*, VIII, 111.
[62] *Prom. Solut.*, 12; *Choeph.*, 244.
[63] Cf. I. Engnell, *Gamla Testamentet* (1945), I, pp. 194ff.
[64] Cf. *YIOT*, pp. 140ff.

included double names for individuals, racial groups and places, as well as multiple divine names.[65] Thus the incidence of Reuel as an alternative designation of Jethro was held to point to the presence of different documentary sources, as was the use of Canaanites as a variant form of Amorites, or Horeb as an alternative description of the location of Sinai. The falsity of multiple names as a criterion for the differentiation of underlying documentary sources may be attested from even the most casual perusal of the "control" material emanating from the ancient Near East. There are literally hundreds of examples from Egypt of variant personal names, as with the military commander designated Sebekkhu, who was also known as Djaa. With reference to such usages involving groups, Kitchen has called attention to the Manchester Museum *stele* from the time of Sesostris III (*ca.* 1800 B.C.), in which Djaa described his single Palestinian enemy by no fewer than three terms: *Mntyw-Sst* (Asiatic bedouin), *Rtnw* (Syrians), and '*Amw* (Asiatics).[66]

In early Old Testament narratives the terms "Amorite" and "Canaanite" were frequently used either interchangeably, or else in the form of double designations or "pairs." In a wide sense the word "Canaanite" could describe the hinterland of the Syro-Palestinian coast, and in consequence it could be used of Syria-Palestine in general. The dispersed families of the Canaanites (Gen. 10:15ff.) also included the Hittites, Jebusites, Amorites, Hivites, and Girgashites, who lived in an area extending from Sidon to Gaza, then inland to the southern Dead Sea region, and thence northwards to Lasha, a site of uncertain location. This broad designation also appeared in the fourteenth-century B.C. Amarna tablets, in which the kings of Babylon and elsewhere occasionally employed "Canaan" to describe the Syro-Palestinian territories under the military control of Egypt. In the narrow sense, "Canaanite" was regarded as the equivalent of "merchant" (Job 41:6; Isa. 23:8; Ezek. 17:4; Zeph. 1:11), a usage reflected on a *stele* from the time of Amenophis II (*ca.* 1440 B.C.).[67] The term "Amorite" was also employed in both a wide and a restricted sense in antiquity, the former being the virtual equivalent of "Canaanite" (Gen. 10:15f.; Num. 13:17ff.; Josh. 24:15, 18), while the latter was used to describe the Amorites more specifically as part of the population of the hill-country of Palestine (Num. 13:29; Josh. 5:1; 11:3). On the basis of such evidence it is clearly incorrect to regard these and other double designations as indications of diverse authorship, for the use of the terms in this way is entirely out of harmony with the external records, which themselves are not characterized by underlying "hands," and do not admit of any such literary analysis.

[65] E.g. *DILOT*, p. 119; O. Eissfeldt, *Einleitung in das AT* (1956 ed.), p. 217; *ETOT*, pp. 182ff.
[66] K. A. Kitchen, *NBD*, p. 349; *Ancient Orient and Old Testament* (1966), p. 123.
[67] Cf. *ANET*, p. 246; B. Maisler, *BASOR*, No. 102 (1946), p. 9.

As regards place names of a dual character, the triumphal paean found on the celebrated Israel *stele* of Meneptah (*ca.* 1224-1216 B.C.) described Egypt variously as *Kmt* and *T'-imri'*,[68] while Memphis was designated by three terms, *Mn-nfr, 'Inb-ḥd* and *'Inb*.[69] It is important to realize that these and many similar examples that could be cited from monuments and other texts are from sources which have absolutely no literary pre-history extending beyond the immediate period of their composition, so that the possibility of "hands" and underlying documentary sources is completely precluded.

A study of Near Eastern writings shows that the considerations that apply to the literary prehistory of *stelae* and similar inscriptional sources are also valid for compositions on papyrus or ostraca, which have had a prolonged history of transmission. Since none of this "control" material was compiled according to the methods elaborated by the Graf-Wellhausen school, it seems only proper to conclude that the composition of the Pentateuch followed contemporary scribal and compilatory patterns, and was not the result of redactional manipulation of artificial documentary sources.

3. *Gattungsforschung.* While form-criticism of the *Gattungsforschung* variety may theoretically be a valid means of isolating laws, poems, and the like,[70] any explorative technique of this kind must always be subordinated to sound knowledge concerning ancient literary phenomena as a whole, otherwise the exponents will simply fall into precisely the same methodological error as that committed by the Graf-Wellhausen school. In point of fact, such a contention appears to have constituted the basic criticism brought against the form-critical school of Gunkel and Gressmann by Sidney Smith, who rightly protested against the arbitrary demolition of prophetical writings into tiny portions to conform to rigidly classified types of literature.[71]

The fact that scholars now possess first-hand, datable, contemporary and comparative material with which to exercise objective control over the forms of Old Testament literature as well as over the different varieties of literary criticism, has made possible a closer inspection of the recording and transmissional methods employed by the scribes of Near Eastern antiquity. In both Mesopotamia and Egypt scribes were educated to a high degree of literary proficiency, and were renowned for their consistent accuracy in recording and copying.[72] An Egyptian religious papyrus from about 1400 B.C. carried a certification to the effect that the scribes regarded the book in its extant written form as complete

68 *ANET*, pp. 376ff.
69 K. A. Kitchen, *Ancient Orient and Old Testament,* p. 124.
70 So *BHI*, pp. 63f.
71 S. Smith, *Isaiah XL-LV* (1944), pp. 6ff.
72 Cf. *FSAC,* pp. 78f.

from beginning to end, having been copied, revised, compared, and verified sign by sign.[73] If this was the case in Mesopotamia and Egypt, there is no warrant for the assumption that the Hebrews were any less careful or accurate in the matter of their own sacred writings.

Equally well attested is the fact that ancient Near Eastern scribes occasionally revised the grammar and spelling of the ancient texts with which they were dealing, with the intent of making the meaning of specific passages as clear as possible to the reader. Such an unexceptionable practice is of great antiquity, and has been followed faithfully, if sometimes unobtrusively, down to the present time in revisions of sacred literature. Whereas modern changes are apt to be slight, alterations were both minor and thoroughgoing in antiquity. Thus, as Kitchen has shown, the celebrated "Instruction" of Ptah-hotep, originally compiled in terse Old Egyptian about 2400 B.C., was supplied some five hundred years later with extensive grammatical revisions in Middle Egyptian.[74] Despite this activity it is still possible to distinguish clearly between the "received text," which is Middle Egyptian in linguistic character, and the textual form of the original work which emerged from the Old Kingdom period. In the *Tale of Sinuhe*, which unquestionably dates from the Twelfth Dynasty and for which there are numerous manuscripts dating from *ca.* 1800 B.C. to *ca.* 1000 B.C., a thirteenth-century copy substituted a Late Egyptian negative, *bw*, for the Middle Egyptian *n* in one passage, and a Late Egyptian loan-word *ym* (sea) for the Middle Egyptian term *nwy* (waterflood) in another. Such "late" words merely serve to date the particular manuscript of the *Tale of Sinuhe*, and have no bearing upon determining the period of its original composition.

This pattern of scribal revision is very important for the study of those Old Testament passages that contain allegedly "late" words, since it shows that only the text of the particular manuscript is comparatively late. As such the incidence of a "late" word is irrelevant as an argument against an earlier date of composition of the section under consideration. Along with revisions of spelling and the inclusion of glosses on the text, the scribes of antiquity frequently replaced an earlier proper name by its later form. This latter phenomenon may well account for such apparent anachronisms as the mention in the Pentateuch of the "way of the land of the Philistines" (Exod. 13:17), at a time when the Philistines had yet to occupy the Palestinian coastal region in any strength.

Egyptian scribes also allowed certain terms to appear sporadically in ancient sources, such as the Pyramid Texts of ca. 2400 B.C., then permitted the usage of such words to lapse for some centuries, and ultimately revived them at a very late date, sometimes two millennia after the original usage of the terms. In ignorance of this now well-

---

[73] J. Černý, *Paper and Books in Ancient Egypt* (1952), p. 25 n. 131.
[74] K. A. Kitchen, *NBD*, p. 350.

attested custom, nineteenth-century literary critics assumed that words that were rare or of supposedly late date could be employed as criteria for establishing the comparative lateness of the passage or material in which they occurred. However, using the same criteria, the Sixth Dynasty pyramids of Egypt (*ca.* 2400 B.C.) would have to be post-dated by two millennia, simply because words found in their inscriptions do not recur until the Graeco-Roman period. What the critics failed to realize is that the Old Testament passages containing "demonstrably late" words could also be interpreted as actually enshrining evidence attesting to the earliest use of these terms. As Kitchen has remarked, where such critical methods are so obviously inapplicable to texts of the Biblical period emerging from the closest neighbors of Israel, the most serious misgivings about the validity of a vast amount of current Old Testament literary criticism must be raised; and these are raised on purely literary grounds well attested by tangible objective data without any recourse to theological predispositions or considerations.[75]

A common contention of the critical school to the effect that short passages must necessarily be early and *vice versa* has been disproved by reference to ancient Near Eastern literary sources. The Egyptian *Admonitions of Ipuwer*, dating as early as 2000 B.C., contained lengthy tirades against the inequities of contemporary society and the shortcomings of the central administration, showing that long pronouncements were by no means unknown in the pre-patriarchal period.[76] Similarly, Sidney Smith cited lengthy sequences from Babylonian oracles that stood in the same general literary tradition, thereby making it evident that the length of a passage has no necessary bearing upon its date.[77]

As remarked above, many of the supposed anachronisms of the Pentateuch can be explained on the basis of successive scribal revisions that had the effect of bringing the text up to date in certain areas. In Genesis 40:15, the reference to Canaan as the land of the Hebrews is clearly the result of this kind of activity, which is seen again, for example, in the use of the name Dan (Gen. 14:14; Deut. 34:1), the reference to the Israelite monarchy (Gen. 36:31), the description of Moses as a prophet of Israel (Deut. 34:10), and the use of the phrase "unto this day" (Gen. 32:32; Deut. 3:14; 34:6), as well as the various scribal glosses that furnished the later forms of earlier place names (Gen. 14:8, 15, 17; 16:14; 23:2; 35:6). There is, however, nothing inherently anachronistic about the mention of a "king" in Deuteronomy 17:14, as Weiser alleges,[78] since the passage in question is a foretelling of events still to take place, and not a record of past occurrences.

[75] *Ibid.*
[76] *ANET*, pp. 441ff.
[77] S. Smith, *Isaiah XL-LV*, p. 8 n. 47.
[78] *OTFD*, p. 72.

One of the commonest critical grounds for positing differences of authorship subsisted in the doublets or repetitions, with their variant forms, that are to be found on occasions in the Old Testament text. But as C. H. Gordon has pointed out, such repetitions were typical of ancient Near Eastern literature, as illustrated profusely from Babylonian, Ugaritic, and even Greek compositions.[79] In the Koran, which is of considerably later date, although strictly Semitic in tradition, there are scores of examples of repetition dealing, among other things, with the teaching of Mohammed on the unity of God and the condemnation of unbelievers. Every *sura* of the Koran commences with the words "In the name of the merciful and gracious God," and the degree of duplication and repetition in the work can be gauged from the fact that, out of one hundred and fourteen *suras*, seventy-seven condemn the unbelievers directly by name, while many of the remainder do so by implication. As far as the Biblical world is concerned, the tastes of the times called for duplication, as illustrated by the way in which both Joseph and Pharaoh had prophetic dreams in duplicate, while in a later period the dismay of the prophet Jonah was described in two separate stages, each accompanied by a question from God (Jon. 4:4, 9). The consonance of this kind of material is such that it would be petulant to go so far as to suggest that it arose from several different sources.

One particular type of duplicate is of especial interest because of the extra-Biblical collateral material now available. Judges 4 furnishes the prose account of the victory of Deborah; the poetic form occurs in the following chapter. Because the two accounts contain variations in matters of detail, it has long been argued by critical scholars that the poetic version was older than the prose account, on the ground that verse-form is supposedly "much better adapted for oral transmission than is any kind of prose."[80] However, to presume to pronounce in favor of a disparity in age or provenance between two such accounts on the basis of the nature or style of the literary vehicle is entirely specious. Study of "control" material makes it clear that in ancient Egypt, historic events were sometimes recorded simultaneously in prose and poetic versions, and that not only was provision made for the major differences appropriate to the two literary media, but also that, on occasions, a third version of a pictorial nature was made in order to celebrate the event. In approaching such questions as those relating to the authorship and date of the two accounts in Judges 4 and 5, therefore, it is of far greater importance for the student to be aware of scribal usages in ancient Near Eastern society than to be beguiled by the subjective speculations of the

<hr/>

[79] C. H. Gordon, *Christianity Today*, IV, No. 4 (1959), p. 132; cf. J. Pedersen, *Israel I-II* (1926), p. 123; J. Muilenburg, *VT suppl. III* (1953), pp. 97ff.; W. H. Brownlee, *The Meaning of the Qumrân Scrolls for the Bible* (1964), pp. 258f.

[80] *FSAC*, p. 66.

occidental scholarly mind, which have issued in a logical but totally unrealistic system of interpretation. It might also be opportune to observe at this juncture that for millennia it has been a common practice for Semitic orientals to memorize long genealogical tables as a means of establishing their ancestry and marking the passing of the various generations. Although this material does not appear in poetic form in the Old Testament, the Semitic mind had experienced little difficulty in mastering it and transmitting it over many generations, thus throwing some doubt on the common belief that poetry is a more suitable vehicle than prose for such a purpose.

4. Stylistic variations. As contrasted with more recent trends, the early critical analyses of the Pentateuch made much of differences in literary style, which, it was alleged, could be recognized readily from the text and could be taken as indicating the existence of underlying "hands" or documents. In the minds of some scholars considerations of style became so completely subjective as to be virtually worthless, and even the more responsible exponents of the art of literary analysis exhibited considerable confidence in their use of style as a means of determining the existence of source material, even though some of them, such as Driver,[81] confused literary "characteristics" with analytical "criteria." When, however, this methodological approach is subjected to examination by comparison with extra-Biblical "control" material from the Near East, it becomes apparent that the critical procedures of the nineteenth-century scholars are completely absurd, since it is now known that a great many oriental writings of antiquity exhibit precisely the same literary phenomena.

Thus Kitchen has shown that the biography of the Egyptian general Uni, dated in the Sixth Dynasty about 2300 B.C., contains flowing narrative (the J and E of the critical school) in those sections where his various state activities and his campaigns are described, while at intervals he employed two stereotyped refrains to indicate the recognition by the pharaoh of his successive accomplishments (corresponding roughly to P_1 and P_2). In addition, his biography included the victory-paean that he and his army chanted during their return from the Palestinian campaign (a special H, or hymnal, source). This work was carved in stone at the specific request of Uni, and there is absolutely no possibility that the final form was developed through or during any literary prehistory by means of a number of documents.[82] This is clear from the fact that the events the biography contains fell within the adult career of one specific individual, and that the work itself was commissioned, composed, written, and executed in stone within a period of a few months at the most. Equally clearly there cannot possibly be any "hands" underlying its

[81] *The Book of Genesis* (1920 ed.), pp. vii ff.
[82] K. A. Kitchen, *NBD*, p. 349.

style, which merely varies with the nature of the subjects under immediate consideration, and in any event is made to conform to canons of literary suitability. This is but one example from dozens of available Egyptian and other texts, occurring from the last three millennia B.C., a corpus of material that is invaluable for the light it throws upon the compositional techniques of Near Eastern scribes in particular.[83]

5. *The Tabernacle.* A few other difficulties confronting adherents of the Graf-Wellhausen theory may be mentioned briefly at this juncture. The Tabernacle, which was confidently assigned to a post-exilic date and held to have been based upon late Temple practice, can hardly have been later than the monarchy, since it lacked such important features of pre- and post-exilic worship as singers, a point that Wellhausen apparently failed to notice. The geography of the Wilderness wanderings, with its wealth of detail, contrasts strangely with the rather general character of the references to the geography and topography of Canaan, which would be quite remarkable had the narratives of the wanderings been composed in the manner in which critical scholars have suggested. In particular, the fact that there are no specific references or allusions to Jerusalem in the Pentateuch would be unthinkable in any alleged source emanating from the southern kingdom in the ninth century B.C.

This in turn leads to the question whether Jerusalem was ever intended to play a dominant role in the centralization of cult-worship, and raises issues concerning the real reason for the composition of Deuteronomy, which according to critical theories of an earlier generation was supposed to have been written in order to promote the centralization of worship. Again, the fact that certain passages in Deuteronomy presuppose a knowledge of portions of the so-called Priestly Code[84] compiled, in the view of the theorists, at a much later date than Deuteronomy, presents awkward problems for the exponents of the classical documentary theory to which they have yet to address themselves satisfactorily.

6. *The Samaritans.* One of the more disconcerting pieces of evidence with which the critical school has had to deal in attempting to formulate late dates for certain sources has been that presented by the Samaritan Pentateuch. Most commonly the nineteenth-century liberal writers either ignored the existence of this document,[85] or else, where they tried to come to grips with the problem, they furnished at best a poor and unsatisfactory explanation of the situation.[86] Occasionally a very garbled

---

[83] Cf. C. H. Gordon, *HUCA*, XXVI (1954-55), p. 67; *UL*, p. 6.

[84] Compare Deut. 22:9-11 and Lev. 19:19; Deut. 24:14 and Lev. 19:13; Deut. 25:13-16 and Lev. 19:35; Deut. 28 and Lev. 26; Deut. 12 and Lev. 17, *et al.* Lev. 11 is also earlier than Deut. 14:3-21.

[85] E.g. F. H. Woods, *HDB*, II, pp. 363ff. It was described by E. König in *HDB Extra Volume* (1904), pp. 68ff.

[86] E.g. E. Nestle, *The New Schaff-Herzog Encyclopedia of Religious Knowledge* (1908), II, p. 130.

story by Josephus[87] was quoted to the effect that Sanballat, who was regarded as a contemporary of Alexander the Great, had sent his son-in-law, Manasseh, to Samaria to function as High Priest. The scholars who mentioned this story assumed that Manasseh had taken the Torah with him, and that this subsequently came to constitute the Samaritan Scriptures. However, according to Josephus, this Manasseh was also the grandson of Eliashib, the High Priest in the time of Ezra and Nehemiah, and may perhaps have been alluded to in Nehemiah 13:28. Aside from other considerations, however, Josephus said nothing about a lawbook's having been taken by Manasseh to Samaria; and in any event, this Manasseh lived a century later than Nehemiah, when the division between the Jews and Samaritans had become consolidated.

While the origins of the Samaritans have traditionally been connected with events somewhat subsequent to the fall of Samaria (2 Kgs. 17:24ff.), it must be remembered that this is based on a Judaean account, which as Macdonald has pointed out constitutes something quite different from what the Samaritans themselves believed about their origins and the existence and nature of the "First Kingdom" in the time of Joshua.[88] In their *Chronicles* the followers of Uzzi, the Samaritan High Priest in the early monarchy period, were said to have been taken into captivity at the time when Samaria fell, and to have come back to Mount Gerizim in the First Return under their High Priest Seraiah some years later. The precise date is unknown, and while the Samaritan *Chronicles* tend to confuse it with the Second Return, roughly contemporary with that of the Judaean exiles under Zerubbabel, it was most probably the situation described in 2 Kings 17:24ff.

According to Samaritan tradition, there was a famine in Canaan after the fall of Samaria in 722 B.C., and the hardships of this experience, combined with the incidence of a plague of lions, prompted the remaining inhabitants to ask the king of Assyria to send back to Palestine those who had previously cultivated the land in the northern kingdom. The Assyrian ruler, who was not mentioned by name, requested the Samaritans, who at that time were living in Harran, to return to Canaan. For their part, according to the tradition, they insisted that they could only insure divine favor if the true worship of God was restored to Mount Gerizim. The king agreed to assist them in this matter, with the result that they returned to Canaan, apparently with other pagan colonists, rebuilt the ruined sanctuary on Mount Gerizim that had been given its traditional site by Joshua, and never thereafter departed from the Prom-

[87] *AJ*, XI, 8, 2; cf. R. Brinker, *The Influence of Sanctuaries in Early Israel* (1946), pp. 217f.

[88] J. Macdonald, *The Theology of the Samaritans*, pp. 14ff.; cf. H. H. Rowley in B. W. Anderson and W. Harrelson (eds.), *Israel's Prophetic Heritage* (1962), pp. 208ff.

ised Land, as the existence of a few Samaritan families at the present day near Nablus indicates.

On this view the breach between Samaritans and Judaeans occurred, not in the time of Ezra, but in the days of Eli, who took it upon himself to establish an apostate sanctuary of God at Shiloh, despite the clear prescription of the Law that true worship was to be carried on at Mount Gerizim.[89] The Judaean account in Kings denied the antecedent history claimed by the Samaritan tradition, and regarded them as descendants of the colonists whom Shalmaneser of Assyria is said to have brought from Cutha, Babylon, Hamath, and elsewhere in Mesopotamia to repopulate the land after the fall of Samaria in 722 B.C. From a study of the *Annals* of Sargon and from a reference in Chronicles to a "remnant of Israel" (2 Chron. 34:9) it would appear that after 722 B.C. the local population of Samaria comprised the remainder of the native Israelites in addition to the foreign colonists from Mesopotamia. Evidently other Judaean sources, particularly the prophets (cf. Isa. 11:12f.; Jer. 23:5f.; 31:17ff.; Ezek. 37:16f.), either did not know of, or else ignored, the tradition that Samaria was an impure admixture of pagan Mesopotamians and surviving northern Israelites.[90]

What is known, however, is that in the time of Ezra the Samaritans stated that they had been using the method of sacrifice to God as prescribed in the Torah as far back as the days of Esarhaddon of Assyria (Ez. 4:2). Whether stated deliberately in this manner or not, the Samaritan claim would seem to support the Judaistic tradition that the Samaritans were worshippers of the God of the Hebrews by the seventh century B.C. Samaritan faith and practice was based upon the Torah alone, and this fact, along with other elements in their tradition, would suggest that their Pentateuch, whose canon is identical with that of the Hebrew Torah,[91] was in its extant form by that time at the very latest. This naturally raises questions as to the date of the Samaritan Pentateuch and also brings up the problem of the relationship between it and the MT and similar texts. As has been observed in an earlier chapter, most scholars followed Gesenius with regard to the latter in his conclusion that the Samaritan Pentateuch was a secondary version of the MT.[92] Among those who did not hold to this opinion was Pfeiffer, who suggested that the Samaritan Pentateuch may in fact represent a version as

---

[89] T. H. Gaster, *IDB*, IV, p. 191.

[90] M. Gaster, *The Samaritans: Their History, Doctrines and Literature* (1925), pp. 12ff.

[91] For differences of text see Ch. Heller, *The Samaritan Pentateuch: An Adaptation of the Massoretic Text* (1923); J. Montgomery, *The Samaritans: The Earliest Jewish Sect* (1907), p. 286.

[92] Cf. M. Gaster, *The Samaritans: Their History, Doctrines and Literature*, pp. 102, 133.

529

old as the MT.[93] Paul Kahle also placed an increased emphasis upon the nature of the Samaritan Pentateuch in his study of their Scriptures.[94]

More recently the Samaritan Qumran manuscript 4QEx[a] has demonstrated the antiquity of the text and the degree of constancy with which it was transmitted without, however, pronouncing upon the priority of its text over that of the Massoretic tradition.[95] In addition, the great antiquity of the Samaritan recension has been increasingly emphasized as the result of photographic examination of the Abisha' scroll at Nablus.[96] It is difficult to see precisely how the Samaritan text can constitute a relatively late branch of tradition separating from the main Jewish line and going back at its earliest to Hasmonaean times, as Cross has maintained.[97] Such an argument, which rests upon precarious palaeographic grounds,[98] has been rightly criticized by Rowley.[99]

There are certain clear indications within the text of the Samaritan Pentateuch itself that it is of pre-exilic origin. It is written in the angular script, rather than the Jewish "square" or Aramaic character, and it exhibits some confusion between the letters "d" and "r," which are also quite similar in form in the later Aramaic script, and between "m" and "n." This confusion could hardly have originated in the post-exilic scripts, and obviously goes back to the early angular Phoenician prototype or to such inscriptions as that on the *stele* of Mesha or that of the Siloam tunnel. An interesting feature of the Samaritan tongue was that none of its gutturals was pronounced at all in the Pentateuch, which would indicate that their enunciation dated from the time of Ahab and his successors, when the non-guttural Phoenician dialect was popular in Israel.

Jewish tradition has preserved the important fact that the Pentateuch was originally written in the angular script, and that Ezra was the instigator of a change into the square variety of character so as to make it differ from the Samaritan form of script.[100] As Gaster has pointed out, the only reason for so drastic a step could have been to break completely with tradition and to eliminate the Samaritan text from circulation among the Jews.[101] Such a change could not have occurred later than the time of Ezra, and may even have happened at an earlier period, as adduced from many instances in the LXX translation that are clearly due to the use of a manuscript written in square characters.

---

[93] *PIOT*, pp. 101ff.

[94] P. E. Kahle, *The Abisha' Scroll of the Samaritans* (1953).

[95] Cf. P. W. Skehan, *JBL*, LXXIV (1955), pp. 182ff.

[96] Cf. P. Castro, *Sefarad* (1953), pp. 119ff.; R. E. Moody, *Boston University Graduate Journal*, X (1957), pp. 158ff.

[97] F. M. Cross, *The Ancient Library of Qumran* (1961), p. 172.

[98] *FSAC*, p. 336.

[99] H. H. Rowley, *Men of God* (1963), p. 272.

[100] *Sanhed.* 21b. Cf. R. Brinker, *The Influence of Sanctuaries in Early Israel*, pp. 221f.

[101] M. Gaster, *The Samaritans: Their History, Doctrines and Literature*, p. 28.

Evidence of this kind would argue strongly against the supposition that the Samaritans acquired their text from Ezra, since it is clear from the separation of the scripts that the Samaritan Pentateuch was already in existence in his day, and had been for some considerable time previously. If these considerations are disregarded it becomes increasingly impossible to explain precisely why the Jews should have received the Pentateuch from Ezra in a comparatively late script, while the Samaritans, who are alleged to be only borrowers and imitators, preserved the older and more original script. On the basis of this and other evidence[102] it is impossible to accept the hypothesis that the Samaritans acquired their Pentateuch from Manasseh after his expulsion from Jerusalem by Ezra, the alleged compiler of the document. There can be no doubt that the Pentateuch had been in the possession of the Samaritans for a great many generations prior to the visit of Ezra to Jerusalem. Since it would not have been possible at any time during the period of religious schism and political division between the northern and southern kingdoms to promulgate any body of legislation of a kind that both parties could have adopted without any recriminations, it can only be concluded that the Pentateuch must have been in existence in written form prior to the political rift between the northern and southern tribes.

If this reflects what actually transpired, the very latest date that could be assumed for the compilation of the Torah in its present form would be some period prior to the death of Solomon. In the view of the present writer the Pentateuch was in fact in substantially its extant form by the time the prophet Samuel died, but whether this is the case or not, the evidence for an early dating of the Law as furnished by the Samaritan Pentateuch militates decisively against the Graf-Wellhausen documentary hypothesis of Pentateuchal origins, since according to the latter neither D nor P had yet been written when the Samaritan Pentateuch was already in its final canonical form.

E. A Proper Methodological Approach to Pentateuchal Studies

It is only fair to recognize in a study such as the present one that the Graf-Wellhausen theory has come under increasingly vigorous assault within recent years, even in critical circles, and that more and more liberal scholars are expressing serious doubts about its validity at many important points. Some of these are able to see that such alleged sources as J, E, D, and P can no longer be regarded as points on the dateline, but ought to be interpreted preferably as streams of tradition, in the flow of which there is both old and new material.[103] There can therefore be said to be a real sense in which current liberal attempts to grapple with

---

[102] Cf. R. Brinker, *The Influence of Sanctuaries in Early Israel*, p. 222.
[103] So G. H. Davies, *IDB*, IV, p. 503.

the problems of the Old Testament have diverged to a considerable extent from the confident criticism of former years.

That this is only true in a very limited respect, however, is borne out by the fact that there has yet to be a large-scale abandonment of the Graf-Wellhausen methodology and its faulty presuppositions. Many scholars undoubtedly cling to this hypothesis, inadequate as it has been shown to be, simply because they lack a suitable, ready-made replacement. Indeed, H. H. Rowley has, on more than one occasion, stated his own willingness to abandon it, provided that a more satisfactory hypothesis is adduced to replace it.[104] The present writer can only speak for himself in expressing the earnest hope that the scholarly world will not have to endure yet another supposedly "scientific" hypothesis that purports to explain the origins of Old Testament literature. What is required is a thoroughgoing attempt to replace any and all developmental hypotheses by a correct methodology grounded firmly upon an assured foundation of knowledge concerning the manifold facets of ancient Near Eastern life, which, in setting the Biblical writings in proper historical and cultural perspective, will furnish authoritative information as to scribal customs and usages in the realm of ancient literary activity.

Instead of approaching the Old Testament literature with the *a priori* supposition that it is replete with error, internal contradictions, unhistorical material, and gross textual corruptions, the application of a proper methodology will require a careful examination of the Hebrew text in the light of what is now known about the divergent streams of life in the ancient Near East from at least the third millennium B.C. That this trend is already being reflected in the work of some scholars has been indicated by Orlinsky, who wrote: "More and more the older view that the Biblical data were suspect and even likely to be false, unless corroborated by extra-biblical facts, is giving way to one which holds that, by and large, the Biblical accounts are more likely to be true than false, unless clear-cut evidence from sources outside the Bible demonstrates the reverse."[105]

The enormous amount of available comparative material from Near Eastern sources has made it very evident that in the field of Old Testament studies very little can be taken as absolutely settled, and least of all the much-touted "assured results of Biblical criticism" that emerged from the last century. Indeed, it is now apparent that much of what passed for "scientific research" in the Victorian and subsequent eras will have to be re-investigated entirely, this time from a properly based

---

[104] E.g. in his review of F. V. Winnett, *The Mosaic Tradition* (1949) in *JTS*, I (1950), p. 195; *Theology Today*, V (1948), p. 124; *The Growth of the OT* (1950), p. 46.

[105] H. M. Orlinsky, *Ancient Israel* (1954), p. 8.

methodological approach, rather than from an emotional or ideological standpoint.[106]

Whatever the numerous and grave faults of their methodology, the classical contributors to the development of the Graf-Wellhausen hypothesis were undoubtedly masters of their craft. Although their approach was dominated to a disproportionate extent by Hegelian presuppositions, they generally managed to express their findings in language that, if not infrequently authoritarian in tone, was nonetheless direct and unequivocal in its intention. Even in translation the writings of most nineteenth-century German scholars are characterized by a degree of clarity and even elegance that has long departed from the scene of Old Testament studies, having been replaced to a large extent by a technical jargon that includes such dubious and frequently misunderstood terms as "sacral kingship," "amphictyony," and the like.

In view of the grave shortcomings of the Graf-Wellhausen approach to the problems of the Pentateuch, and to the Old Testament in general, any new study will need to be based firmly upon an accredited methodology that will utilize the vast quantities of control material now available to scholars throughout the world, and will argue inductively from the known to the unknown instead of making pronouncements from a purely theoretical standpoint that bears only a slight relation to some of the known facts. For those who regard the Scriptural narratives as self-authenticating, such a procedure will be scarcely necessary or desirable. In this connection, however, it should be noted that the application of a proper methodology is not, *per se*, inimical to any doctrine of the inspiration and authority of Scripture. Rather, it constitutes an attempt to replace an incorrect and faulty method of approach by one that is based upon a thorough knowledge of the cultural *milieux* from which the various parts of Scripture emerged, or to which they can be related, as a

---

[106] As has been noted, the inadequacies of the analytical-literary method when applied to the writings of Classical Greek authors such as Homer have long since been recognized by scholars in the field (cf. J. A. Scott, *The Unity of Homer*, 1921; *GBB*, pp. 218f.), who have shown that the procedure was based upon inconsequent reasoning and false statistics (cf. W. J. Martin, *Stylistic Criteria and the Analysis of the Pentateuch*, 1955, pp. 6ff.).

Precisely the same result has occurred regarding the work of Omar Khayyam. Sixty years of meticulous research by literary experts resulted in the verdict that Omar had actually written very little poetry indeed, and that the quatrains of later poets had been foisted upon this semi-legendary character. One distinguished German scholar actually went so far as to state that the name of Omar Khayyam ought to be eradicated from the history of literature. Manuscript discoveries just prior to 1950, however, brought a radical change to this situation, for one manuscript, dated 1207, some 75 years after the death of the poet, was found to contain 252 quatrains, and this appears to constitute only a selection from a larger corpus, pointing unquestionably to the fact that Omar Khayyam was actually a poet of considerable stature (A. J. Arberry, *The Listener*, September 21, 1950, pp. 382ff.).

means of understanding as fully as possible the meaning and significance of the divine revelation.

It is equally important that such an approach not be construed as a means of solving the problems associated with the origins, nature, and development of the cultural and religious traditions of Israel merely by relating them to, and perhaps attempting to derive them from, the ethnic religions of the ancient Near East in a manner that would appear to emphasize superficial similarities and minimize or ignore entirely the fundamental and essential divergences. It is an axiom of the descriptive sciences that, in all questions of comparison, differences are more significant than similarities, and this principle will also be borrowed by any correctly grounded methodology of Old Testament study.

Such an attitude will recognize that the Old Testament does, in fact, contain "error" in the sense that numerous examples of accredited scribal mistakes of different kinds can be discerned from an examination of the Hebrew.[107] These and other similar errors are the property of every age, and one function of textual criticism is to call attention to their existence so that due notice can be taken of them in translation or in attempts to recover a genuine pre-Christian text of the Old Testament.

An accredited methodology will avoid the atomizing or fragmentizing of Biblical narratives, and in rejecting such "sources" as J, E, D, P, H, and L as spurious will instead concentrate upon the nature and provenance of the genuine sources that underlie certain of the Old Testament writings. The early chapters of Genesis, rather than being dismissed as legendary or mythical, will actually be seen to be Mesopotamian in character, and will be examined accordingly against their appropriate literary and cultural background. The real source material of the Pentateuch and other writings will be seen in such cited material as the "Book of the Generations of Adam" (Gen. 5:1), the "Book of the Wars of YHWH" (Num. 21:14), the "Book of Jashar" (Josh. 10:13; 2 Sam. 1:18), the "Book of the Covenant" (Exod. 24:7; 2 Kgs. 23:2 et al.), the many documentary sources underlying the books of Kings and Chronicles, and so on. In particular it will also be recognized that a creative individual such as Moses could, like Homer, work with the matrix of the tradition to select his subject matter from earlier and contemporary sources, reshape it, and fashion it into a masterpiece of enduring literary and spiritual value.

---

[107] To cite but one of several such examples, there is an obvious case of scribal confusion between the letters ר and ד in 2 Samuel 8:13, where ארם should be emended to אדם. A clear transcriptional error is apparent in 2 Kings 7:6, where the original text evidently read "Musurites," which has been preserved as "Egyptians" (מצרים). Another mistake is the mention of Jehoiakim in Jeremiah 27:1, instead of Zedekiah, who is obviously indicated by the general context. For further examples of scribal errors in transmission see part four, section III-C above.

Taking the Old Testament on its own terms against a background of collateral material from the ancient Near East also requires a recognition of the fact that written and oral material are both early phenomena. The oral never appears consistently before the written in the ancient Near East, and the evidence furnished by secular sources shows that both forms frequently co-existed for lengthy periods of time. While some sections of the Old Testament probably circulated in oral form before being committed to writing, the high literacy of the ancient Near East points, as Gordon has shown, to a maximum of written sources lying behind the Scriptural narratives.[108]

The specific usage of ספר (book) in this connection is to be understood strictly in terms of a written document, since the word was never employed in relationship to oral material. Again, the very concept of law (tôrāh) needs to be interpreted against an oriental background rather than that of ancient Rome, as was common in early critical circles. Even in Mesopotamia, where codified law was an early and familiar concept, the law-courts did not cite the codes in handing down decisions, but instead functioned in accordance with custom, precedent, and accepted tradition, a point that has still not been grasped by some occidental scholars. As Gordon has indicated,[109] the kind of law reflected in the Homeric writings is designated themistes (Odyssey, XVI, 403), and indicates the sum total of oracles by which the gods regulated society. This has much in common with the Hebrew idea of Torah, since even a casual reading of the Pentateuch shows that there is comparatively little which can be called law in the strictest sense of that term. The spirit of Torah actually subsists in the oracles which God delivered to Moses, and as such is in full accord with the traditions of the Heroic Age.

While even the most restrained variety of modern literary criticism tends to fragment the material under investigation, a correct methodological approach will never lose sight of the fundamental unity of such classic compositions as the Pentateuch. As Gordon has remarked, this document, for all its diversity, was considered to be an integral whole by both Jews and Samaritans for many centuries.[110] If it is broken down into its component parts typologically, it appears to be a patchwork quilt of badly stitched sources, telling as it does about the cosmos, litigation, war, social institutions, sacrifice, agriculture, and a variety of other topics.

In this connection, however, it is important to notice that such subjects were also worked into the composition of the celebrated Shield of Achilles,[111] a fact that again mirrors accurately the literary and cultural

---

[108] GBB, p. 283.
[109] GBB, pp. 248f.
[110] GBB, pp. 281f.
[111] The cosmos, Iliad, XVIII, 483ff.; social institutions, XVIII, 490ff.; sacrifices, XVIII, 558ff.

traditions of the period extending from the fifteenth to the tenth century B.C. Since the Torah was the supreme guide of conduct and life for the ancient Hebrews, it was necessary for this work to cover all those aspects of existence that they would encounter, and the totality of this experience must accordingly be matched by a holistic view of the Pentateuch.

An examination of the narrative material from such a standpoint shows not merely that the various parts have been arranged in chronological order as a single work in five volumes, but that the Pentateuch is actually a part of a tightly organized group of literary material that extends from Genesis to 2 Kings. In this *schema* the Torah exercises a fundamentally important role as the epic of nationhood, whose two constituent parts were the patriarchal and Exodus sequences. In the former the land of Canaan was promised to the forefathers of Israel and was actually acquired by them to some limited extent. In the latter, the way was opened for their descendants, the true inheritors of the Promised Land, to return and take formal possession of it.

While it is inappropriate methodologically to compare the Pentateuch with the Iliad as literature, since they are, of course, entirely different types of compositions, it is important at the same time to observe that both works served much the same purpose for their readers. For the Greeks, the Homeric writings constituted Scripture *par excellence*, and were venerated as the divinely inspired guide for life. In precisely the same fashion the ancient Hebrews looked for advice and help to the divine revelation given to the people through Moses, a situation that once again reflects the general ethos of the Heroic Age.

Enough has been said to make it clear that a proper methodology will regard the whole as something more than the sum of its parts, and that it will eschew the fragmenting of the material under study in favor of what might be called an "inductive holism." Fundamental to this methodology, as has been observed previously, is the setting of the literature under scrutiny against its proper historical, religious, and cultural background in Near Eastern antiquity, the isolation of major and minor parallels, and the singling out of special details within the fabric of the whole for specific study.

To the task of elucidation will be brought all the available resources of philology, archaeology, and other related disciplines in a resolute determination to go where the ascertained facts lead, regardless of whether particular theories, in part or in whole, stand or fall in the process. Such observations as are made will need to be checked continually against existing and newly discovered facts alike, and if necessary revised in the light of the evidence at hand. Only when these safeguards have been exercised will the work of the scholar remain unimpeded by imposing but faulty hypothetical systems, and his results be grounded firmly on a factual basis.

The following estimate of the Pentateuch is an attempt to envisage the work holistically as an organic body of material subject to processes of growth, codification, and editing within the Mosaic period. It takes cognizance both of the fact of post-Mosaic additions and also the tradition that accorded early veneration to the Torah as the normative guide for the life of the nation. It must be emphasized that, contrary to the views of some scholars, the Mosaic Torah is not the codification of the priestly cult, for the admixture of historical narrative, Levitical rules, and specifically moral and ethical principles furnishes convincing evidence of more than a purely cultic concern. The true spirit of the Torah is to be found not so much in the strict concept of law as in the oracles that God spoke to Moses.[112] It is this factor that transcends the purely local and historic interpretation of the enactments at Sinai, and by removing the faith of Israel from a strictly tribal context has given the divine revelation through Moses a universal applicability.

In view of certain scholarly trends to relegate Moses to a minor position in the development of the characteristic Hebrew faith and assign instead the beginnings of the true Israelite ethos to some sort of amphictyonic situation in the settlement period, it should be pointed out that ancient Hebrew tradition unanimously credits Moses with a substantial place in the mediation of the Law and is wholly opposed to any concept that would place the beginnings of national historic, moral, and spiritual tradition at some point during or subsequent to the occupation of Canaan under Joshua. However, Hebrew tradition itself must be assessed critically, particularly in view of the fact that among the rabbis the figure of Moses had achieved the eminence accorded to a superman, and that in character he was quite unlike the harassed, frequently frustrated, yet consistently energetic man of God depicted in the Pentateuchal writings. Any estimate of the person and work of Moses must be entertained within the strict limits of the Pentateuchal data and related to the contemporary ancient Near Eastern life-situation. In particular it is of fundamental importance to avoid the emotional overtones that have become attached to the words "Moses" and "Mosaic" since the advent of literary criticism, and which have resulted in such extreme positions as the denial of the very existence of Moses on the one hand, or the attributing to him of every word and syllable of the Pentateuch on the other.

The present study will have made it clear that, aside from any other considerations, Moses played a highly original role in the revelation of the divine nature and will to nascent Israel, as well as in the task of sifting and correlating earlier northwest Semitic and specifically Israelite legalistic concepts and behavioral practices. From the very beginning of the tradition Moses was specifically credited with such portions of the

---

[112] *GBB*, pp. 248f.

text as the judgment against Amalek (Exod. 17:14), the Book of the Covenant (Exod. 20:22–23:33, along with the Decalogue), the restoration of the Covenant (Exod. 34:27, referring to Exod. 34:10-26), an itinerary (Num. 33:1ff., referring to the source underlying Num. 33:3-40), the bulk of Deuteronomy referring to the renewal of the Covenant and the reinforcement of its laws, and the two poetic sections that concluded Deuteronomy.

The concentration in one man of the ability to write historical narrative, to compose poetry, and to collate legal material is by no means as unique as earlier critical writers were wont to assume. As Kitchen has pointed out, an illustration of this kind of ability from ancient Egypt at a period some seven centuries prior to the time of Moses has been furnished in all probability by Khety (or Akhtoy), son of Duauf, a writer who lived in the time of the pharaoh Amenemhat I (ca. 1991-1962 B.C.).[113] This versatile individual apparently combined the functions of educator, poet, and political propagandist, and wrote the *Satire of the Trades* as a text for use by students in the scribal schools. He was probably commissioned to give literary form to the *Teaching of Amenemhat I*, which was a political pamphlet popular in the Eighteenth to Twentieth Dynasties as an exercise to be copied by schoolboys.[114] In addition, he may have been the author of a popular *Hymn to the Nile*,[115] which with the foregoing works was also frequently copied out by scribes.[116] Quite clearly, then, it is by no means inherently impossible for a talented individual to have engaged during the Amarna period in the kind of literary activity traditionally ascribed to Moses.

Of course it must always remain a matter of conjecture as to precisely how many laws were original with Moses, and how many, particularly as reflected in the book of Deuteronomy, must be considered against four centuries of sedentary Israelite life in the Goshen region and against the period of occupation of Transjordan by two-and-a-half tribes prior to the death of Moses. Equally uncertain is the actual extent to which Moses recorded personally the written material credited to him. It may well be that the presence of third person pronouns in various sections of the Mosaic enactments indicate that these sections were dictated. Quite possibly many of the small or isolated sections in the Hebrew text were committed initially to the priests for safekeeping, and only at a later period were the manuscript pieces assembled into some sort of mosaic and joined together into a roll.

[113] K. A. Kitchen, *NBD*, p. 849.
[114] *ANET*, pp. 418f.
[115] *ANET*, pp. 372f.
[116] Cf. A. Gardiner, *Hieratic Papyri in the British Museum, Third Series* (1935), I, pp. 40ff.; G. Posener, *Littérature et Politique dans L'Égypte de la XII° Dynastie* (1956), pp. 4ff., 19 n. 7, 72f.

While in the view of the present writer leather would be the preferred material for preserving the enactments, it should be noted that good papyrus, when available, made for quite sturdy and durable documents. Thus a sheet from the criminal register of the prison at Thebes was used at different times over a period of seventy years, and in the end still served adequately to record a bequest to servants.[117]

It is now abundantly evident from the many comparative sources available to scholars that detailed codes such as those found in the Pentateuchal writings are by no means anachronistic, as was commonly imagined by an earlier generation of literary critics. Nor is it any longer either necessary or desirable to assign the origin of many of the Mosaic enactments to the eighth or seventh centuries B.C.[118] Instead, Pentateuchal legislation must now be examined against a background of a common intellectual and cultural heritage,[119] from which an understandable similarity of antecedents naturally emerges. The uniqueness of the Hebrew enactments then becomes apparent in the realization that striking differences point to an absence of direct borrowing on the part of the Hebrews.[120]

If the vitality of the divine revelation to man is to be appreciated properly, it is important to avoid the temptation to regard the Mosaic legislation as an essentially static corpus, and instead see it as an organic collection of material subject to certain controlled processes of growth and modification. Thus it is quite possible that in the post-Mosaic period some of the enactments were altered somewhat to suit changing circumstances, a process that is perfectly legitimate in any culture, and which does not in any sense vitiate the provenance of the original legislation. No doubt some of the duplications and inconsistencies in Pentateuchal law of which Hahn speaks[121] were due, not to the rise of separate though parallel cultic regulations, as he and many other liberal writers suppose, but to the deliberate attempt on the part of the responsible authorities, whether priestly or other, to adapt the traditional legislation to the point where new conditions of life would be properly accommodated. This doubtless underlies the situation whereby the provisions of Numbers 26:52-56 relating to inheritance were modified by the circumstances detailed in Numbers 27:1-11 and Numbers 36:1-9, or where the regulations for an offering to cover sins of ignorance or inadvertence (Lev. 4:2-21) were changed by the provisions of Numbers 15:22-29. Again, it is of importance to note the witness of the text to the fact that

117 K. A. Kitchen, *The Tyndale House Bulletin,* No. 2 (1957), pp. 1ff., Nos. 5-6 (1960), p. 18.
118 Cf. J. Bright, *BANE,* pp. 22f.
119 Cf. T. J. Meek, *Hebrew Origins,* pp. 49ff.
120 *Ibid.,* p. 69.
121 *OT in Modern Research,* p. 32 n. 58.

some later additions were made to the Book of the Covenant in the time of Joshua (Josh. 24:26).

When compilation of this living legal corpus was being contemplated, a unitary objective was achieved by reference to the general chronological order of events, a natural and useful device under the circumstances. However, as will be observed later, the compiler, whether Moses or someone else, frequently took the opportunity of inserting other relevant material when two rolls needed to be joined together. Some such insertion would almost certainly have been made while the smaller units were in process of being assembled, as appears to be the case in the section of enactments of Exodus 19:1–23:33, where the skillful blend of legal and historical material nullifies critical attempts to break down the material into such entirely imaginary sources as J and E. Even when a particular book was in substantially its final form long after the time of Moses, there would still be occasion for alterations or additions. This again is in full accord with the general literary traditions of the ancient Near East, where the scribes regularly revised ancient literary and other documents by removing obvious archaic grammatical and orthographical forms and making such additions as the immediate situation required.[122]

The use of the term "code" with reference to the Mosaic enactments should not be interpreted as meaning that Moses was the promulgator of some kind of civil legislation for Israel. From the outset the nation was intended to be a holy people, and, as will be pointed out below, the relationship in form and structure of a document such as Deuteronomy to the Near Eastern treaties of the second and first millennium B.C. demonstrates that Israel was bound in a spiritual vassal-union with God, the great King. Because God was an essentially moral and ethical Being, the essence of the Covenant relationship was to be manifested at that exalted spiritual level. The treaty obligations were specifically intended to be normative for all areas of the national life, since they were formulated on the basis that the very fact of day-to-day living under the provisions of the Covenant itself constituted a profound religious experience. For this reason, if for no other, it is not too much to suggest that the Pentateuchal ideal derives, not so much from the *Sitz im Leben des Volkes* of the settlement period, but from the mediatorial office and specific *doctrina* of Moses as the recipient of revelation.

The emphasis in the present work that the Pentateuchal material was in written form at an earlier rather than a later period has been entertained deliberately, partly as a safeguard against the views of the "oral-traditionists," who so frequently misinterpret the evidence from the ancient Near East, and partly because the witness of contemporary life in the ancient Near East fully substantiates such a possibility. As Kitchen

[122] *FSAC*, p. 79.

has pointed out, the uniform testimony of oriental literary practice demanded that matters that were considered important or were required to be recorded for posterity should be written or inscribed in permanent form, and not left to the care of bards and campfire romancers.[123]

In the view of the present writer, almost the entire body of Pentateuchal material could have been easily extant in practically its present form by the late Joshua period. No doubt the passing of time brought certain editorial activities to bear upon the Hebrew text in the form of explanatory glosses, insertions, and revisions of language and spelling, consistent with the practices of Babylonian, Egyptian, and other Near Eastern scribes. Even when cognizance has been taken of this situation, there appears to be no substantial ground for denying that the Pentateuch in virtually its extant form was in existence by the time of Samuel.

The Pentateuch is a homogeneous composition in five volumes, and not an agglomeration of separate and perhaps only rather casually related works. It described, against an accredited historical background, the manner in which God revealed Himself to men and chose the Israelites for special service and witness in the world and in the course of human history. The role of Moses in the formulation of this literary corpus appears pre-eminent, and it is not without good reason that he should be accorded a place of high honor in the growth of the epic of Israelite nationhood, and be venerated by Jews and Christians alike as the great mediator of the ancient Law.

[123] *NBD*, p. 850.

II. THE BOOK OF GENESIS

A. NAME AND OUTLINE

While Genesis is an anonymous work, as are the other four books of the Pentateuch, its attributive author is Moses. However, to what extent he wrote any of its contents, with the possible exception of all or part of the Joseph narratives, is unknown. In attributing Mosaic authorship to the Pentateuch as a whole, conservative scholars have pointed out that the Torah in its entirety must not necessarily be assumed to have been the work of his own hands, any more than any of the *stelae* of antiquity were the product of direct activity on the part of their attributive authors. Some writers, such as Young,[1] have not precluded the possibility that the writer drew on earlier written sources, but in general the ascription of Mosaicity to the Pentateuch implies its historicity and its formulation by Moses under divine inspiration, with the supposition that later editors may have revised the contents somewhat in accord with the traditions of the ancient Near Eastern scribes.[2]

The Jews designated Genesis according to its initial word, בְּרֵאשִׁית which is almost always incorrectly translated in English by the phrase "In the beginning."[3] In Talmudic times the work was known as the "Book of the Creation of the World," while the English title "Genesis" was actually derived from the LXX rendering of Genesis 2:4a, "This is the book of the γενέσεως of heaven and earth," and from the subsequent headings (Gen. 5:1; 6:9; 10:1; 11:10; 11:27; 25:12; 25:19; 36:1; 36:9; and 37:2), the nature of which will be dealt with shortly.

On the basis of the extant Hebrew text the book can be analyzed as follows:

I. Prehistory: the Creation Record, 1:1–2:3
II. The Story of Man, 2:4–11:26

---

[1] *YIOT*, pp. 42ff.

[2] R. D. Wilson, *A Scientific Investigation of the OT* (1959 ed.), pp. 48ff. For a refutation of the theory that the arrangement of the Pentateuch arose by adaptation to a triennial synagogue lectionary cycle, see J. R. Porter in *Promise and Fulfillment* (ed. F. F. Bruce, 1963), pp. 163ff.

[3] E. A. Speiser, *Genesis* (1964), p. 3, has "When God set about. . . ." A more accurate rendering would be "By way of beginning. . . ."

III. The Choice of Abraham, 11:27–23:20
IV. The Choice of Isaac, 24:1–26:35
 V. The Choice of Jacob, 27:1–36:43
VI. The Choice of Judah; the Joseph Narratives, 37:1–50:26

B. תולדת AND THE ORIGINS OF GENESIS

According to the Graf-Wellhausen documentary hypothesis of Pentateuchal origins, Genesis assumed its present form through various editorial processes that saw a combination of elements of J, E, and P sources into a continuous document. In the view of those who advocate the "traditio-historical" approach to the problem of Pentateuchal compilation, Genesis arose through the preservation of "cycles of tradition" that grew up in various areas in oral form. These "traditions" developed around focal events such as the Passover and other similar occurrences significant for the religious life of the nation and found expression in the rituals and liturgies of the Israelites. In the more moderate forms of both these views there is no necessary attempt to deny historicity to the material involved, even though most of the scholars who support these approaches would prefer to attribute general rather than specific historicity to the subject matter.

The present writer does not support either of these positions, and prefers to examine the problem of the compilation of Genesis against a background of ancient Near Eastern literary activity. It should be observed as a general principle that there may well be quite a number of sources designated in the Old Testament writings which have not actually been recognized as such by most modern scholars. Genesis appears to be a case in point, with the clue to the underlying sources being provided, not by the incidence of the divine names or the presence of supposed duplicate narratives, but by the phrase translated "these are the generations of," an expression that has perplexed a great many scholars, and regarded by the exponents of the classic documentary theory as a characteristic of the Priestly Code.

In order to appreciate the significance of the Hebrew term תולדת, it will be necessary to examine briefly the nature and format of cuneiform communications in the ancient world. Clay was the preferred material upon which the wedge-shaped symbols were impressed, and the resultant tablets, which could contain a wide range of literary material, varied in size and shape from a tiny square to a large cylinder. The general style of a tablet furnished some indication as to its contents; and as far as single tablets were concerned the material communicated usually consisted of letters, contracts, invoices, business correspondence, genealogical tables, and the like. Generally speaking individual tablets were not made too large, partly because of the sheer weight of the clay and more particularly because a large tablet would be more likely to break than a smaller one.

It was the normal practice in Near Eastern antiquity for single communications of this kind to commence with some sort of title, followed by the body of the text, and then a colophon, which would sometimes contain, among other things, a hint as to the identity of the scribe or owner of the tablet and the date when the tablet was written. The imprint of a button or cylinder seal upon the clay tablet helped to identify the owner of the communication. If a more lengthy communication required more than one tablet, the proper sequence of the series was preserved by a system of titles, catch-lines, and numbering. The title was normally taken from the opening words of the tablet, and these were frequently repeated at the end of each subsequent tablet, being followed by the serial number of that particular tablet. The catch-line attempted to insure the continuity of the narrative by repeating the first few words of the following tablet at the end of the previous tablet, so that, if a series of tablets became disarranged, there could be no doubt as to which word or words were to be read immediately after the conclusion of a tablet. This practice is still followed in some modern legal documents, and occurs also in the Hebrew Bible, where on the bottom left-hand margin the first word or two of the following page is to be found.

The colophon, which concluded the individual tablet or the series, normally contained the name of the scribe or the owner of the tablet, as has been remarked above, and frequently it also included some attempt at dating. In addition, it often embodied the title given to the narrative, and if the tablet was part of a series it furnished the serial number and a statement as to whether the tablet did or did not conclude the series.

That the expression "these are the generations of" is a distinguishing phrase of Genesis has long been recognized by adherents of the Graf-Wellhausen theory, as well as by more conservative scholars. S. R. Driver affirms that

> . . .the narrative of Genesis is cast into a framework, or scheme, marked by the recurring formula *"these are the generations* (lit. begettings) *of"* . . .the entire narrative as we now possess it is accommodated to it.[4]

While Ryle could state that the phrase bore a close relation to the structure of the Priestly Code in Genesis, he rejected the subdivision of the book on the basis of this formula, although on entirely subjective grounds.[5] Other commentators of widely varying schools of thought, however, divided Genesis up into sections that commenced with the phrase.[6]

[4] S. R. Driver, *The Book of Genesis* (1904), p. ii; *DILOT*, pp. 6f.
[5] H. E. Ryle, *The Book of Genesis* (1914), pp. xi-xii.
[6] So Spurrell, Lenormant, Skinner, Carpenter, Bullinger, Lange, Keil, Wright, and others.

But while scholars were agreed as to the importance of the expression, they appear to have misunderstood entirely both its usage and its significance for the literary origins of Genesis. The reason for this is quite simple, for as Wiseman has pointed out, many of the sections in Genesis commence, as is frequently the case in ancient documents, with a genealogy.[7] This practice led scholars to associate the phrase "these are the generations of" with the genealogical list in those cases where such a register of individuals followed; hence they assumed, quite without warrant, that the phrase was being employed as a preface or introduction. Thus Driver could consider it as belonging properly to a genealogical system, implying that the person to whose name it was prefixed was of sufficient importance as to make a break in the genealogical series. For Driver it also indicated that the person named, along with his descendants, would form the subject of discussion in the ensuing section until another name was reached that could be considered prominent enough to form the commencement of a new passage.

This assertion, however, is completely contrary to the facts, for an examination of the evidence in relation to the latter part of the statement would indicate that Abraham, the most prominent person in Genesis, ought certainly to have been named in connection with the phrase under discussion. Yet curiously enough, while other lesser individuals were mentioned in the various records in this manner, there is not one instance where the phrase "these are the generations of Abraham" occurs in the Hebrew text. Furthermore, the phrase does not by any means always belong to a genealogical list, since in certain cases there is no addendum of such tabular material.

What is evident, however, is that the principal facts concerning the individual involved have been recorded *before* the incidence of the phrase in question, and that they are not recorded after its occurrence. Thus when the expression "These are the generations of Adam" (Gen. 5:1) occurs, nothing more is stated about Adam apart from a mention of his age at death. Again, the record that follows the sentence "These are the generations of Isaac" (Gen. 25:19) is not so much a history of Isaac, son of Abraham, as a chronicle of events that occurred in the lives of Jacob and Esau. Still further, after the phrase "These are the generations of Jacob" (Gen. 37:2), the narrative deals with the story of Joseph, and mentions Jacob only in a rather incidental manner as the unfolding of the events warranted. This peculiarity has been a source of perplexity and embarrassment to the vast majority of commentators schooled in the critical methods of Gráf, Kuenen, and Wellhausen, and in view of the fact that the phrase quite clearly does not constitute an introduction or preface to the history of a person, as is commonly imagined, it is of some importance to determine its precise meaning.

[7] *New Discoveries in Babylonia About Genesis* (1958), p. 46.

The Hebrew for "generations" in the expression under discussion is תולדת, and not the ordinary Hebrew word דור, which is translated "generations" over one hundred and twenty times in the older English versons. דור corresponds to the word "generations" as implied by common English usage, and can refer to a past (Isa. 51:9) or future (Exod. 3:15) period, a class of people (Deut. 32:5), or to the heirs of a covenant (Gen. 17:7, 9). תולדת occurs ten times in Genesis in such a manner as to lend itself to the division of the material associated with it into eleven sections, each being styled "the generations of . . . ." It also occurs in isolation from a stereotyped phrase in Genesis 10:32; 25:13; 36:9 and elsewhere in the Old Testament.

The word originated in the Hebrew root ילד, "to bear," "to beget," which doubtless accounts for the English rendering "generation." But from the time of the Hebrew lexicographer Gesenius it has been apparent from Old Testament usages of the word that it means a "history," "narrative," or "genealogical record" of a family or some other such social unit. As has been observed above, the LXX has rendered the term by γενέσεως, and it is of some interest to the Christian student to note that the expression βίβλος γενέσεως 'Ιησοῦ Χριστοῦ, "the book of the genealogy of Jesus Christ" in Matthew 1:1 reflects closely the Hebrew phrase ספר תולדת אדם, "book of the genealogy of Adam" in Genesis 5:1. The Hebrew word was used regularly for the collection of Jewish traditions concerning the life of Jesus, and in modern times it has formed part of the title of Yehezkel Kaufmann's eight-volume history of Israelite religion.

Thus the term תולדת is used to describe history, and more particularly in Genesis, at all events, of family history in its origins. Quite clearly, therefore, the phrase "these are the generations of" points back to the beginnings of the family history, and not forward to its later development through a line of descendants. In this connection it is of some interest to note that the phrase that occurs in Genesis 2:4 obviously points back to the narrative of the creation of the cosmos contained in the preceding chapter. It could not refer to the narrative that follows, since that section contains no reference whatever to the creation of the heavens. As Wiseman has commented, the phrase is only appropriate as a concluding sentence, so that most commentators, notwithstanding their usual interpretation of the phrase, made the story of creation terminate with it.[8] Had they but perceived that all such sections of Genesis conclude with this formula, they would have possessed the key to the composition of the book. As it was, the majority of scholars found themselves in serious methodological difficulties in their assumption that the expression "these are the generations of" was employed in all the remaining instances as an initial, rather than a terminal phrase.

[8] *Ibid.*, p. 48.

On only two occasions in Genesis does a genealogical list follow the expression in the absence of intervening words, and yet here both lists are quite complete even without its use. While the formula is not necessarily connected with a genealogical table, in almost every instance a list of immediate descendants is given before the phrase occurs in the Hebrew text. It is therefore obvious that the formula did not constitute a preamble to a genealogical table, but that it was in fact an ending of such a list. Notice should also be taken of the mention of ספר, translated "book," in Genesis 5:1, where the reference can only be to a written "record" on a clay tablet, and also of the LXX version of Genesis 2:4, which reads, "This is the book of the origins of the heavens and the earth."

A final point in connection with the significance of תולדת is that in at least some cases the person mentioned in connection with the phrase might well have been the owner, or possibly the writer, of the tablet in question, if Mesopotamian scribal practices are actually in evidence in the manner suggested. Thus in Genesis 6:9, the phrase "These are the generations of Noah" does not necessarily mean "This is the history involving Noah," since it is primarily the succeeding section that describes the activities of this individual. Instead, the expression could well be interpreted as meaning "This is the history written (or possessed) by Noah," which once more would be in full accord with ancient Near Eastern literary practices. Again, in Genesis 10:1, the mention of the sons of Noah implies that the preceding record of family history was in their possession, a practice that can be documented extensively from family archives recovered from Nuzu, Mari, and elsewhere in ancient Mesopotamia.

In Genesis 11:27, the reference to the "generations of Terah" contains little information about that individual except that he was the son of Nahor. Quite evidently it was intended to indicate that Terah either wrote, or else had compiled for him, the list of his ancestors found in verses 10 to 27. The excavations at Mari have shown the extent to which genealogical tables were treasured in antiquity as a means of establishing pedigree and for other social purposes, so that there is nothing inherently impossible in the action of Terah in this regard.

C. THE SOURCES OF THE BOOK

The foregoing discussion can be summarized, therefore, by stating that the term תולדת can be held to indicate the presence of a colophon in the text, and to constitute part of the concluding sentence of each section, thereby pointing back to a narrative already recorded. Accordingly it is eminently possible to regard its incidence as indicating the presence of a genuine Biblical source in the text.[9] It is not by any means accidental

[9] Cf. C. H. Gordon, *Christianity Today*, IV, No. 4 (1959), p. 133.

that much of the material in which the phrase under consideration occurs was either of Mesopotamian provenance or was written under the influence of Mesopotamian culture. Accordingly the present writer feels justified in following Wiseman in the assertion that Genesis contains in the first thirty-six chapters a series of tablets whose contents were linked together to form a roughly chronological account of primeval and patriarchal life written from the standpoint of a Mesopotamian cultural milieu.[10]

1. *The Eleven Tablets.* Such a view is based upon the conviction that this approach alone does the fullest justice to the literary phenomena of much of Genesis, particularly in the light of what is now known regarding the antiquity of writing, the diverse nature of literary communications in the Near East during the second millennium B.C., and the special characteristics of contemporary scribal techniques. The tablets that may be isolated will be seen to have a title, a residuum of textual matter, and a colophon, along with certain additional features to be noted subsequently. The sources can be described briefly as follows:

Tablet 1: Gen. 1:1–2:4. The origins of the cosmos
Tablet 2: Gen. 2:5–5:2. The origins of mankind
Tablet 3: Gen. 5:3–6:9a. The histories of Noah
Tablet 4: Gen. 6:9b–10:1. The histories of the sons of Noah
Tablet 5: Gen. 10:2–11:10a. The histories of Shem
Tablet 6: Gen. 11:10b–11:27a. The histories of Terah
Tablet 7: Gen. 11:27b–25:12. The histories of Ishmael
Tablet 8: Gen. 25:13–25:19a. The histories of Isaac
Tablet 9: Gen. 25:19b–36:1. The histories of Esau
Tablet 10: Gen. 36:2–36:9. The histories of Esau
Tablet 11: Gen. 36:10–37:2. The histories of Jacob

Apart from Tablets one and two, which deal with the origins of the cosmos and mankind respectively, and do not contain proper names in their colophons, there appears to be no event recorded in which the person or persons named could not have written either from personal knowledge or from other reliable sources. Furthermore, where individuals are mentioned by name in the colophons, the history recorded in the various sections isolated above and identified with suggested tablets ceases in all instances prior to the death of the person named at the conclusion of the tablet. The present writer is of the opinion that the foregoing classification of material represents the genuine literary sources underlying the first thirty-six chapters of Genesis.

[10] Wiseman, *op. cit.*, pp. 53ff.; cf. his *Creation Revealed in Six Days* (1958), pp. 46f.

On closer examination the first postulated tablet (Gen. 1:1–2:4) bears the title "God created the cosmos," interpreting the phrase "the heavens and the earth" as a *merismus* form, and this title is repeated in the colophon (Gen. 2:4). There is no series number associated with the latter; the colophon contains no personal or other names, and there is no catch-line linking it with the second suggested tablet (Gen. 2:5–5:2), which deals with the origins of mankind. The abruptness of the transition from Genesis 2:4 to the following verse might indicate that the original title of the second proposed tablet had either been lost in antiquity, or else had been deliberately removed in process of editing. Be that as it may, the colophon of this source contained no proper name and no evidence of ownership. It is just possible that the scribe who wrote the tablet attempted to convey the antiquity of his material by using the phrase, "in the day that God created mankind" (Gen. 5:1), a circumstance that may also be true for the expression "when they were created" in Genesis 2:4. In the light of the critical theories common in an earlier generation, which repeatedly asserted the influence of Mesopotamian traditions over those of the Hebrews, it is significant to note that more recent appraisals now limit this as far as the material covered by the first two tablets is concerned to a possible three points, including the initial waters and the divine respite after the creation of man.

Tablet three, as isolated above (Gen. 5:3–6:9a), bears the title "And man," narrates his descent, and mentions Noah, who is named in the colophon (Gen. 6:9a), perhaps in his capacity as owner of the source. The title of Tablet four (Gen. 6:9b–10:1) is "Shem, Ham and Japheth," and the text deals with the Flood and its aftermath. This material is terminated by the colophon in Genesis 10:1, where the allusion to the period "after the Flood" may perhaps constitute a scribal attempt at dating. The title of the tablet, it will be noted, is repeated in the colophon. Tablet five (Gen. 10:2–11:10a), is apparently entitled "The sons of Japheth," and deals with the Table of Nations and the Babel incident. It is concluded by the colophon, "These are the generations of Shem."

Tablet six (Gen. 11:10b–11:27a) is comparatively brief, and is entitled simply "Shem." It contains the genealogical list of Terah, and mentions his death, along with the fact that Nahor lived on until Abram was seventy-five years old. If the reference in Genesis 11:26, which recorded the age of Terah, was actually a scribal attempt at dating, then according to the Samaritan Pentateuch it was written just one year after the last chronological event mentioned in it, namely the death of Nahor. The repetition of "Abram, Nahor, and Haran" before and after the colophon formula indicates that the phrase constitutes a catch-line, and conforms to the usual scribal procedure of repeating the first words of the subsequent tablet after the last line of its precursor.

Tablets six and seven are thus linked in series, with the latter (Gen. 11:27b–25:12) forming a lengthy account of the life of Abraham and concluding with his death. The title of the tablet is apparently "Abram, Nahor, and Haran," and the text can presumably be dated by the reference to Isaac dwelling at Beer-lahai-roi (Gen. 25:11). These family histories were evidently in the possession of Ishmael, brother of Isaac, and seem to be closely linked with the brief contents of Tablet eight (Gen. 25:13–25:19a), as indicated by the colophon. The events recorded in Tablets seven and eight ceased just prior to the death of Isaac, who was mentioned either as the possible writer or else as the owner of the tablets. He survived Ishmael by some fifty-seven years, according to the text, and presumably came into possession of the family records on the death of his brother.

The title of Tablet nine (Gen. 25:19b–36:1) is apparently "Abraham begat Isaac," and the narrative content deals at length with the relationship between Jacob and Esau, and with subsequent events in the life of Jacob up to the death of Isaac. Possibly the reference to his interment constitutes a scribal attempt at dating, but whether this was actually the case or not, the histories were clearly of Edomite origin, as the explanatory gloss in Genesis 36:1 would indicate. Tablet nine was followed closely by Tablet ten (Gen. 36:2–36:9), a fragmentary record also from Edomite sources and dealing with the descent of Esau. There is little doubt that Pfeiffer was correct in postulating the existence of a "South" or "Seir" source in Genesis,[11] but owing to his improper methodological approach to the literary problems of Genesis he was only able to isolate a few relevant fragments, and he included in his S^1 and S^2 much that had no connection whatever with Mount Seir.

Quite evidently Tablets nine and ten belonged to such a "source," as did the final text, Tablet eleven (Gen. 36:10–37:2), part of which Pfeiffer attributed to S^1. Genesis 36:31, placed at the commencement of a list of Edomite kings, is obviously a post-Mosaic editorial or scribal comment. It could only have been written at a time when Israel had a king, since it is not a theoretical anticipation of the possibility of kingship, as in Deuteronomy 17:14ff., but evidently originates in the reality of an Israelite kingdom. As such it may well represent editorial activity on the part of the prophet Samuel. Immediately before the colophon in Genesis 37:2 is the statement that Jacob was living in the land of Canaan, and this can be taken as evidence for the time and place of the composition of Tablet eleven. Within a few years Jacob had moved into the land of Egypt, but this reference points to his place of abode when his historical record was closed. Jacob had obviously returned to the south country and taken up his residence in Hebron, where his father Isaac was living.

11 *PIOT,* pp. 159ff.

It can hardly be mere coincidence that the material discussed so far has been preserved in so characteristically an ancient Near Eastern fashion. As with all similar ancient literature, these tablets constituted highly valuable sources for the delineation of patriarchal origins, and it is a testimony to their antiquity and to the esteem in which they were held that they have survived in the Hebrew text in something which in all probability approximates to their original form, a circumstance that makes it possible for them to be recovered by means of the application of an accredited methodology. Precisely who was responsible for editing this material is, of course, unknown, but since another such tablet can be recovered from the text of Numbers (perhaps Num. 1:1–3:1), it seems legitimate to suppose that the redactional activity was by and large the work of Moses.

In view of the overwhelming support given by Near Eastern literary traditions for the recovery of such clearly indicated underlying sources, it can only be a matter of considerable regret that some eminent orientalists have refused to follow the course indicated by the facts in their translations of Genesis. Thus T. J. Meek rendered תולדת in Genesis 2:4 by the expression, "the following are the origins of the heavens," thus completely misunderstanding the significance of the original.[12] In the same manner E. A. Speiser treated the colophon of Genesis 5:1 as though it were a heading.[13] While this may have been due in part in his translation to sheer considerations of format, it still remains the case that the reader would have no inkling whatever of the real character of the constituent source, being invited instead to relate the composition of Genesis to the outworn traditions of the literary-critical school. Like other thoroughgoing advocates of the Wellhausenian position, Speiser could hardly be expected to adopt a format that would belie his convictions with regard to the origin and nature of the Pentateuchal writings. Meek, however, was in an entirely different category, since he consistently professed independence of any given literary-analytical scheme.[14] It can only be concluded, therefore, that he was either unaware of the significance of the evidence, or else that he, like many other scholars, refused to go where the facts of the matter led.

2. *The Joseph narratives.* The remainder of Genesis deals with the Joseph narratives (Gen. 37:2b–50:26), the Egyptian background of which has been so well attested by scholars as to make further comment

[12] *Genesis* in *The Complete Bible: An American Translation* (ed. J. M. Powis Smith and E. J. Goodspeed, 1939), p. 2.

[13] *Genesis,* p. 39 and elsewhere; but cf. p. 280, where תולדת is specifically related to what precedes.

[14] T. J. Meek, *Hebrew Origins* (1960 ed.), p. xi.

unnecessary.[15] Most probably this material was still in oral form when
Moses was alive, and it may be that it was he who reduced it to writing
in magnificent literary Hebrew. Quite possibly Moses was responsible for
substituting leather for the Amarna Age tablet-form vehicle of communication.[16] In this general connection it should be noted that whereas in
certain instances in the Pentateuch Moses was directed to inscribe the
divine revelation upon durable material such as stone (Exod. 34:28), it
is probable that the more durable leather came to be employed at this
period by the Hebrews as writing material in general preference to
papryus, used extensively in all periods of Egyptian history.[17] Quite
aside from the Jewish tradition that the Torah should always be written
upon leather, since this was apparently the original material vehicle of
its transmission, the passage in Numbers 5:23f. only makes the fullest
sense if leather was the material which the people were using at that
time.

If it is correct to assume that the major part of Genesis was transmitted by means of cuneiform tablets, it is comparatively easy to imagine the process by which it was ultimately compiled, given the existence
of a Joseph story comparable to the *Tale of Sinuhe*, whether it was a
written Egyptian document or an oral Hebrew tradition.[18] A person such
as Moses would have been eminently suited to the task of assembling
ancient records and transcribing them in edited form as a continuous
record on a leather or papyrus roll. Given this basic·document, it would
be well within the realm of possibility to envisage the activity of scribes
of later generations in matters of textual revision, the incorporating of
marginal comments, or the bringing up to date of certain chronological
material (e.g. Gen. 36). For while it is important to affirm the general
literary fixity of the material as a whole, it is also necessary to allow
sufficient freedom for accredited scribal activity to operate in a customary manner at later stages, in consonance with the traditions evident
in ancient Near Eastern literary sources.

There can be no real question as to the immense antiquity of the
source material that is to be found in Genesis. Evidence for this includes
the large number of Babylonian words that occur in the earlier part of
the book, the topographical references, such as those relating to Sodom
and Gomorrah (Gen. 10:19),[19] and the number of glosses required to
bring ancient names up to date (e.g. Gen. 14:2, 3, 7, 8, 15, 17; 16:14;

---

[15] Cf. K. A. Kitchen, *The Tyndale House Bulletin*, Nos. 5-6 (1960), pp. 4ff.,
NBD, pp. 344ff., 656ff.; C. H. Gordon, *The World of the OT* (1958), p. 139; P
Montet, *L'Égypte et la Bible* (1959); J. Vergote, *Joseph en Égypte* (1959).

[16] On the use of leather in Egypt see A. Shorter, *JEA*, XX (1934), p. 34; cf. A
Scott, *JEA*, XIII (1927), p. 239.

[17] Cf. J. S. Wright, *EQ*, XXV (1953), p. 7.

[18] Cf. J. S. Wright, *How Moses Compiled Genesis. A Suggestion* (1946).

[19] Cf. J. P. Harland, *IDB*, IV, pp. 395ff.

23:2; 35:19). Primitive geographical expressions such as the "south country" (Gen. 20:1; 24:62) and the "east country" (Gen. 25:6), which were used in the days of Abraham, never recurred in the Old Testament narratives as a description of the countries adjoining the south and east of Palestine, since these regions subsequently acquired familiar and well-defined designations. Archaeological discoveries at Mari, Nuzu, Boghazköy, and elsewhere have been of particular value in furnishing abundant literary materials for an understanding of the narratives concerning the Hebrew patriarchs and the conditions of life that existed in Palestine and Egypt during the Amarna Age and the Hyksos periods.[20]

D. THE MATERIAL OF GENESIS

By definition Genesis is the Book of Origins, the great introduction to the drama of human redemption. The prologue is cast in universal terms suitable to the subject-matter, and depicts the creative activity of God in fashioning the cosmos and placing man upon the earth. The universality of sin is depicted, along with the fact that, as rebellion against God, it must always stand under divine judgment, a situation exemplified by the account of the Deluge. The rise of Abraham, the first of the two major emphases of the Pentateuchal writings, is associated with covenantal relationships, and the stage is thus set for the occurrence of the second great concern of the Torah, namely the deliverance of Israel from Egypt in the dramatic event of the Exodus.

1. Creation and fall. Considerations of space preclude anything more than the briefest of comments upon the fascinating material contained in the early chapters of Genesis. (The relationship of the concept of "myth" to this corpus has already been discussed in part seven.) A very common obstacle to the understanding of Genesis 1 is the notion that the chapter is "at variance with the scientific account of the beginning of the world."[21] In point of fact, however, there are surprising consonances with scientific discoveries and theories,[22] a situation that is all the more amazing since Genesis 1 was never meant to constitute a scientific document in the accepted occidental sense.

The general pattern of creative progress can be easily illustrated by reference to geological discoveries, which, of course, are infinitely more detailed in their descriptions of phenomena. Although Genesis only deals with the major divisions of geological time, there is still in evidence a remarkable degree of parallelism with the findings of geology, a fact that cannot be ignored in any assessment of the material at hand. Earlier generations of Biblical scholars were accustomed to point out,

---

[20] Cf. H. H. Rowley, *BJRL*, XXXII (1950), pp. 44ff., reprinted in *RSL*, pp. 269ff.
[21] D. W. Cleverley Ford, *A Key to Genesis* (1951), p. 1.
[22] A. R. Short, *Modern Discovery and the Bible* (1949), pp. 89ff.; B. Ramm, *The Christian View of Science and Scripture* (1954), pp. 221ff.

frequently with great restraint,[23] that the unscientific nature of the cosmology in Genesis 1 was evident in such matters as the mention of "grass" immediately after the emergence of land from the primeval oceans and prior to the creation of the heavenly bodies. In explaining this phenomenon it must first be noted that the standpoint of the first chapter of Genesis is an ideal geocentric one, as though the writer were actually upon the earth at that time and in a position to record the developing phases of created life as he experienced them. From such a standpoint the heavenly bodies would only become visible when the dense cloud-covering of the earth had dispersed to a large extent, subsequent to the formation of an atmosphere (רקיע). Secondly, the importance of the position assigned to the emergence of vegetation has been greatly increased by the discovery that animal life could not have been sustained until there was an adequate amount of vegetation to supply the requisite atmospheric oxygen through the process of photosynthesis. The mechanisms of photosynthesis are still imperfectly understood, but in general it involves the replacement of carbon dioxide in the air as one result of the interaction of sunlight on the green pigment chlorophyll present in leaves, grass, trees, and other vegetable matter.

Since the first chapter of Genesis is clearly not intended to comprise a scientific document—if only because of its sheer untechnical language—it is obviously undesirable to posit concordist theories of the relationship between the creation narratives and the findings of modern descriptive science. Having said this, however, it is necessary to remind the reader that the phases of development recorded in Genesis 1 are by no means as unaligned with the findings of modern science as was supposed by earlier writers on the subject. What is of primary importance for the Biblical student as well as for the scientist is to realize that the Genesis narrative must be interpreted from the standpoint of its anonymous author before pontifications are made as to when it is and is not "scientific."

The reference to the irrigation-canals of Pishon and Gihon (Gen. 2:11) makes it clear that the activity of earliest man was contemplated against a background of Mesopotamian irrigation culture, a fact which places the beginnings of the race considerably nearer to historic time than many writers have imagined hitherto. The two stories of creation (Gen. 1:1–2:4a; Gen. 2:4b-25) are typical of ancient scribal practices, as has been observed previously, but in this connection it should be noted that they are not duplicates, as many scholars have imagined. In point of fact they are not even strict repetitions of one another, for the first presents a general description of the creative situation as a whole while the second discusses one specific aspect of it, namely man in his physical

---

[23] Cf. H. E. Ryle, *The Book of Genesis* (1914), p. 12; S. R. Driver, *The Book of Genesis*, pp. 21f.

environment, and relates it to particular geographical considerations. If two separate tablets are involved here, as has been suggested above, the phenomenon of repetition would point to the preservation of two traditions relating to human origins, one dealing in cosmological generalities and describing the earth in relation to the universe, while the other focused more direct attention upon *homo sapiens* in his geographical surroundings, and involved the use of what the author prefers to style "religious drama" in recounting the mystery of the creation of woman. Despite related elements, the two passages in question can hardly be held to be either duplicate narratives or even genuine parallels in the commonly accepted sense, for the first account speaks in completely general terms, while the second deals from a rather different standpoint with a single locality and a specific pair of individuals.

From the time when George Smith first introduced the Gilgamesh Epic to English readers, it was commonly assumed that the original material underlying Genesis 1 as a whole was the Babylonian Creation Epic known as *Enuma elish*,[24] even though Wellhausen himself could discover no mythological ingredients in Genesis 1 save for chaos,[25] a view that his followers either repudiated or ignored. A more careful study of similarities and differences, however, has made it evident that resemblances between the Babylonian and Israelite cosmogonies are not as close as had been imagined previously.[26] So distinct has been the reaction that some scholars have even gone so far as to declare the probability that the Babylonian epic has no connection of any kind or at any point with the corresponding material in Genesis, and that each is *sui generis*.[27] Although it seems hardly possible to make such positive claims at the present, Heidel's conclusion that the relationship between the two sources is once again an open question is certainly quite proper.[28]

The Genesis narrative dealing with the creation of woman has invariably been misrepresented in such versions as those which translate the Hebrew word צלע as "rib." The word carries a number of meanings, and in Genesis 2:21f., the situation is somewhat obscured by the form of the "religious drama" in which the creative act is cast. Here צלע evidently means "an aspect of the personality," and not a skeletal rib, as commonly imagined. Even though the statement "bone of my bone and flesh of my flesh" might appear to imply such a rendering, a literal bone is not

---

[24] G. Smith, *The Chaldean Account of Genesis* (1876); cf. his piece in *Transactions of the Society of Biblical Archaeology*, II (1873), pp. 213ff. For other versions of Babylonian creation myths see A. Heidel, *The Babylonian Genesis* (1951), pp. 61ff.

[25] J. Wellhausen, *Prolegomena to the History of Israel*, p. 298.

[26] Cf. H. E. Ryle, *The Book of Genesis*, p. xxxii; G. von Rad, *Genesis*, p. 48.

[27] J. V. Kinnier Wilson in *DOTT*, p. 14; cf. D. F. Payne, *Genesis One Reconsidered* (1964), pp. 10ff.

[28] A. Heidel, *The Babylonian Genesis*, p. 139.

intended to be understood, since the removal of the צלע from man was not accompanied by a corresponding extraction of flesh. Instead, the phrase is simply meant to demonstrate the organic and spiritual unity of the subdivided species, which is further reflected in the play on words involving "man" (איש) and "woman" (אשה). The dramatic form of the narrative thus conceals the spiritual equation "Man = male + female," teaching that the personality of an individual of the species *homo sapiens* can only be most fully expressed when it is complemented in proper and compatible marital unity by that of another individual of the opposite sex. The comment in Genesis 2:24 exemplifies the Biblical ideal of monogamic marriage, and may well be an editorial comment added by Moses and designed to inculcate the uniqueness of a relationship which binds a man even more closely to his wife than to his parents. This ancient passage is thus as important for the doctrine of man as it is for the Biblical teaching concerning marriage.

It can be noted in general that there is no close extant mythological parallel to the material to be found in Genesis 2, even though certain of the details are not unique to the Biblical narrative. For example, the Sumerian story of Enki and Ninhursag seems to have had some sort of paradise background, and there is a minor reference to a "rib," but aside from these possible features there are very few other resemblances.[29] By way of conclusion it can be remarked with Engnell that neither Genesis 1 nor 2 stands alone, for while the two chapters have their individual teaching, they are integral to the book as a whole and, indeed, to the entire Pentateuch.[30]

The "religious drama" that describes the pristine rebellion of man against God (Gen. 3:1-24) contains certain resemblances to Babylonian sources such as the Adapa myth, which deals with a squandered opportunity for gaining immortality, but despite this fact it does not contain such extremely important *motifs* as the serpent.[31] This Genesis narrative manifests examples of *merismus* (Gen. 3:5, 22; cf. Gen. 2:9) which, as mentioned earlier in the present work, are of very great importance in any attempt to understand the meaning and spiritual significance of the drama. Thus the "tree of the knowledge of good and evil" is actually the symbol for the entire range of moral knowledge or experience. The subtlety of the temptation that confronted Eve lay in the opportunity presented to her of being able, without apparent effort, to intuit all experience in the manner in which God would seem to do. By any standards of comparison this latter is no mean feat, and when related through processes of flattery and deception to the alleged intuitive

29 Cf. S. N. Kramer, *History Begins at Sumer* (1958), pp. 193ff.

30 I. Engnell in M. Noth and D. W. Thomas (eds.), *Wisdom in Israel and in the Ancient Near East* (1955), p. 109.

31 Cf. *ANET*, pp. 101ff.; S. G. F. Brandon, *Creation Legends of the Ancient Near East* (1963), pp. 126ff.

capacities of a woman it presented an overwhelming temptation for the female not merely to dominate the male, contrary to the intention of the Creator, but also to emulate divine activity in terms of the apperception of experience.

The passage that mentions the Nephilim (Gen. 6:1-4) has, by common consent of the literary-critical school, been dismissed as myth and has been subjected to such implausible explanatory crudities as the suggestion that the Nephilim were actually "fallen angels."[32] To relegate such an ancient section to the realm of myth or legend as popularly understood by liberal scholars is to preclude immediately the possibility of any rational interpretation of the text, and to miss entirely the invaluable anthropological insights into the interrelation of *homo sapiens* and pre-Adamic species which the passage contains, and which are amenable to those scholars who are equipped to pursue them.

2. *The Flood, Babel, and the nations.* A number of versions of a deluge story have been discovered among the cuneiform documents excavated at various Near Eastern sites. A Sumerian tablet from Nippur, dated about 2000 B.C., told of a pious king-priest named Ziusudra who was warned about an approaching deluge from heaven, which he was able to avoid by building a boat.[33] This story evidently had literary antecedents in earlier centuries, and occurred in Akkadian versions from both Babylonia and Assyria in more than one form. The best known of these is contained in the eleventh tablet of the Gilgamesh Epic, and this demonstrates certain affinities with its Sumerian precursor, including a dependence upon Sumerian liturgical sources.[34] In the Gilgamesh Epic the survivor, Utnapishtim, informed Gilgamesh, the legendary king of Uruk, of the way in which the powerful water-deity Ea had warned him of the coming inundation, and how he had constructed a boat in the contemporary fashion in order to preserve himself, his family and his possessions, as well as certain local fauna. The flood lasted for seven days, and the boat finally came to rest upon Mount Nisir in northwestern Persia. These cuneiform accounts exhibit points of contact with the Biblical narrative, and these may be explained either by common reference to an actual original or historical event, or by the fact that a standard method of escaping from the worst effects of the devastating flash-floods of Mesopotamia was being described in mythological or epic fashion. Attempts on the part of literary-critical scholars to discern in the Hebrew text the presence of what they regard as duplicate accounts of the Flood encounter serious difficulties,[35] and can hardly be taken with

---

[32] J. Skinner, *A Critical and Exegetical Commentary on the Book of Genesis* (1910), pp. 139ff., for the theories and literature.

[33] Cf. A. Heidel, *The Gilgamesh Epic and OT Parallels* (1949 ed.), pp. 103f.; S. N. Kramer, *Sumerian Mythology* (1944), pp. 97f.

[34] *The Gilgamesh Epic and OT Parallels*, pp. 85f.

[35] E.g. *IBOT*, p. 27.

much seriousness, as Aalders has pointed out.[36] The literary style, the standpoint of the writer, and the internal consistency of the narrative all indicate the fundamental unity of the Deluge narrative, and stand united in the face of attempts to disprove the integrity of the material. All endeavors to relate the Flood to some specific archaeological period have proved inconclusive at the time of writing, and can be illustrated by reference to the various levels of water-laid clay as excavated at Ur, Kish, Uruk, Farah, and elsewhere.[37] Most of the alluvial strata uncovered at these sites were evidently occasioned by river-flooding of unusual severity, and if the Genesis Deluge was actually one of these serious local floods it would have occurred after 4000 B.C., the general date assigned to the earliest of the alluvial levels found at Ur.

If, as seems probable, the Biblical Deluge was a comparatively local affair, the natural concern of Noah and his family would be for the preservation of only the most immediate fauna of the neighborhood in the ark, thus precluding some of the fanciful interpretations of the situation as furnished by artists and others. No certain geological evidence of the Flood is known, and consequently there is no ground for the belief that the Genesis Deluge covered the entire world. Much of the evidence cited in support of the latter theory can be explained either in terms of the history of the structure of mountains or else as the vestiges of glacial activity in the so-called Quaternary Ice Age and its associated geological changes. There is, however, no definite evidence of this at hand, and any attempt to relegate the events described in Genesis to a flood in an actual historical period must be regarded, for the present at least, as tentative.

In the light of the geographical knowledge that is now known to have existed in the second millennium B.C., it is no longer necessary to assume a date of composition for the Table of Nations (Gen. 10:2-32) either as early as the monarchy (for the so-called J source) or as late as the post-exilic period (for the Priestly Code). In point of fact, the absence of Persia from this Table would be extremely difficult to explain if the list had been largely compiled and edited to its extant form by priests who owed their return from exile and their presence in Judaea to the religious policy of the Persian regime. The scope of the Table of Nations depends to some extent upon the interpretation of "earth" in Genesis 10:32, which can either be "the whole world" in a comprehensive sense, the "known world" in a more restricted manner, or else some specific "country." While most expositors prefer to think of אֶרֶץ in verse 32 as implying "the known world," the fact that many of the names in the Table are as yet unidentified would indicate that a wider estimate of

[36] G. Ch. Aalders, *A Short Introduction to the Pentateuch*, pp. 45ff.

[37] Cf. A. Parrot, *The Flood and Noah's Ark* (1950), pp. 50ff.; R. K. Harrison *Archaeology of the OT* (1962), pp. 9f.

the situation than that available to modern scholars fell within the purview of the ancient scribes.

Identifications in the list dealing with the descendants of Japheth that have received general, though not exclusive, scholarly assent include Gomer (*Cimmerians*), Ashkenaz (*Scythians*), Madai (*Medes*), Javan (*Ionians*), and Dodanim (*Rhodes*). Similar identifications from the list of Ham include Cush (*Ethiopia*), Sheba (*Saba*), Mizraim (*Egypt*), Caphtorim (*Cretans*), Heth (*Hittites*), and Hivites (*Hurrians*). A few accepted identifications from the list of Shem include Elam, Asshur (*Assyria*), Sheba, and Aram (*Aramaeans*).

The Table of Nations is unquestionably of ancient origin, partly because of its literary form but principally on account of its contents. It is quite possible, however, that the latter were subjected to slight scribal revision from the time of Moses onwards, since such peoples as the Cimmerians, Scythians, Philistines, and Medes do not appear in written documents until after the end of the second millennium B.C. On the other hand, these peoples obviously existed as tribes or racial groups long before they appeared in extant records, as for example with the peoples of southern Arabia, who only occur in written documents in the first millennium B.C., but who are known to have existed prior to that time. Certainly the Philistines were familiar as one group that lived in Palestine during the patriarchal period, even though they were augmented significantly by waves of immigrants at a considerably later time.

The narrative dealing with the construction of a city and a high tower at a site later known as Babel (Gen. 11:1-9) has an obviously Babylonian background, and this, combined with the fact of its early date, probably accounts for the incident being mentioned nowhere else in the Old Testament. Interpreters have generally assumed that the city, like the tower (Gen. 11:8), was incomplete at the dispersion of the population, and that the tower (מִגְדָּל) was intended to be a staged structure such as the *ziggurats* of Babylonia, which were first developed in the early third millennium B.C. While there is no archaeological evidence to date that would confirm the existence of a city at Babylon prior to the First Dynasty (*ca.* 1800 B.C.), Babylonian tradition, along with a text of Sharkalisharri, king of Agade about 2250 B.C., which mentioned his restoration of the *ziggurat* at Babylon, would seem to point clearly to the existence of an earlier sacred city on the site.[38] The name "Babel" was explained by popular etymology in terms of a similar Hebrew root בָּלַל to imply "confusion" or "mixing." Babel thus constituted a synonym for the confusion provoked by the linguistic differences that were part of the divine punishment for the attitude of human pride displayed in the construction of the city and the tower.

[38] D. J. Wiseman, *NBD*, p. 116.

Attempts to locate the site of the tower of Babel have been made for many centuries, but with indifferent success. Some scholars have identified it with the *ziggurat* at Babylon that had been given the Sumerian name Etemenanki ("The Building of the Foundation-platform of Heaven and Earth"), and whose present site is a pit, Es-Sahu, as deep as the original *ziggurat* was high. Other authorities have identified Babel with the ruins of a staged tower still in evidence at Borsippa (Birs Nimrud), some seven miles south-southwest of Babylon. This view is improbable for the reason that the structure involved is almost certainly from the Neo-Babylonian period. Yet another identification places the tower of Babel at Dūr-Kurigalzu (Aqar Quf), west of Baghdad, but this again is unlikely since the city was only constructed there about 1400 B.C. All that can be said on the matter with certainty is that the Biblical narrative bears all the marks of a reliable historical account of the construction of buildings that have not yet been traced.

Occidental interpreters of this narrative have not infrequently thought of the building of the *ziggurat* in terms of medieval European attempts to glorify God by the construction of a massive cathedral. Such a view rests upon a fundamental misunderstanding of what the ancient Mesopotamians had in mind when they were building their *ziggurats*. Excavations have shown that such a structure constituted the logical development of the small central shrine around which the other houses in the primitive village-settlements of the Chalcolithic period were grouped. It was intended to be the equivalent of a mountain, that is to say, an eminence of the earth with its characteristic concentration of life-giving forces. As such the *ziggurat* furnished a suitable setting for divine life and power to be manifested by creating precisely those conditions under which proper communion with God would be possible. This, however, did not entail the veneration of a transcendent deity, as in Christianity, but rather a sense of community with an essentially immanent god.

3. *The Mesopotamian coalition of Genesis 14.* To the present, archaeological discoveries have been unable to furnish conclusive information regarding the members of the Mesopotamian coalition that fought against the kings in the cities of the plain (Gen. 14:1ff.). Certain difficulties exist in connection with the identification both of Amraphel and the territory over which he ruled. The MT, the Samaritan Pentateuch (Gen. 14:1), the LXX, and the Syriac versions all designate him clearly as "king of Shinar," but the Samaritan Pentateuch (Gen. 14:9), the targums and the Qumran *Genesis Apocryphon* specifically record that he was king of Babel. Shinar was the country in which the great Babylonian cities of Erech and Akkad were located (Gen. 10:10), and was situated in a plain in which early migrants had settled and had founded the city and *ziggurat* of Babel (Gen. 11:2). The LXX interpreted "Shinar" (Heb. שִׁנְעָר) to mean "Babylonia" or "the land of Babylon," following the traditions of Genesis 10:10.

On philological and other grounds it is improbable that "Shinar" can be equated with "Sumer" or southern Babylonia, as some scholars have proposed. It is also interesting to note that, although the Syriac term Sen'ar designates the environs of Baghdad, no earlier name for Babylon which might correspond with "Shinar" has yet come to light. Albright suggested that the land over which Amraphel ruled might have been the west-Semitic Sangār in Syria, known to the Egyptians of the Amarna period by that name and appearing in the Tell el-Amarna tablets in the Akkadian form Shankhar.[39] However, a Syrian location for the kingdom seems unlikely, since the narrative of Genesis 14 appears to envisage Mesopotamia as the general area from which Amraphel came. Perhaps the reference is to the district of Singhar in Upper Mesopotamia, although this cannot now be known for certain.

The discovery at Susa in 1901 of the famous Code of Hammurabi led many contemporary scholars to identify Amraphel with that renowned Akkadian ruler. However, they were confronted almost immediately with some pressing philological problems which proved difficult to resolve. The "l" at the end of Amraphel was a particular matter of contention, with some scholars maintaining that it was in fact the Akkadian determinative particle "ilu" or "god." This view is improbable since in cuneiform the determinative symbol invariably precedes the name with which it is associated. If the "l" is linked with the following Hebrew word מֶלֶךְ ("king") as other scholars suggested, it destroys the sense of the phrase, which is clearly a standardized literary expression.

Other indecisive approaches to the problem included the theory that the Hebrew form 'amrāphel was actually a scribal error for 'mrphi (Ammurapi; Hammurabi), or that it was a compressed transcription of the Akkadian title Ammurapi-ili ("Hammurabi is my god"). Such arguments tend to posit corruptions of the text for which there is no factual evidence, and at the best they are philologically unconvincing. There would therefore appear to be no sound reason for maintaining the identification of Amraphel and Hammurabi, particularly as it remains unsubstantiated by Mesopotamian history as such.

Chedorlaomer, an ancient Elamite king who led the Mesopotamian coalition against the resurgent kings of Sodom, Gomorrah, and the other cities of the valley, is equally obscure as an historical person in extra-Biblical sources. The *Genesis Apocryphon* agreed with the pseudepigraphical *Book of Jubilees* (XIII:22) in naming Chedorlaomer as the leader of the invading Mesopotamian confederacy, but this opinion may well be dependent upon purely Biblical sources. Despite extensive investigation into the early phases of Elamite history, the names of a number of the founders of Elamite dynastic power are still unknown.

[39] Cf. *ANET*, pp. 243, 247.

The LXX form of the name is *Chadollogomor,* which implies a vocalization which is rather different from that of the Massoretes, and points to the assimilation of "r" with "l" and the pronunciation of "o" as "gho," making *Codorlaghomer.* Written in cuneiform, the Elamitic version would most probably have comprised a combination of *Kutir* (or *Kudur*), meaning "servant," and the term *Lagamar,* which appears in several Elamite texts as a divine name. The element *Kutir* (or *Kudur*) was a common Elamite word, and occurred regularly in Elamite proper names, as for example in *Kutir-Naḫḫunte. Kutir* (or *Kudur*)-*Lagamar* would thus comprise a genuine Elamitic construction meaning "servant of (the god) Lagamar," a title which could be borne quite legitimately by a ruler.

To the present, however, no individual bearing the specific name Kutir (or Kudur)-Lagamar has been recognized from extra-Biblical records of any kind. Cuneiform tablets have yielded the name of an Elamite monarch, Kudur-KU.MAL, which is now read as Kutir-nahuti (the Sumerian KU.MAL being the equivalent of the Babylonian *nāḫu*), and have spoken of him as the conqueror of Babylon. Perhaps he is to be equated with Kutir-Naḫḫunti I of Elam, who ruled about 1625 B.C., and some scholars, including Albright, have identified him with the Chedorlaomer of Genesis 14.[40]

This view, however, involves both philological and historical difficulties. It is possible to argue philologically that the form Naḫundi is the equivalent of the west-Semitic word *La'mr* (*La'nd*), but the latter with its alternative suggests the probability of confusion between the final ר and ד in the ancient Hebrew script. Quite aside from this, however, the absence of proper controls from Elamite cuneiform sources makes such an approach somewhat precarious. Historically the above identification requires a late date for Abraham, which is contrary to the evidence provided by the fate of the cities of the valley.[41]

The approximate date of the catastrophe which overtook Sodom, Gomorrah, and neighboring sites may be conjectured from the evidence supplied by pottery remains discovered at Bab edh-Dhra'. This festival site appears to have been frequented from about 2300 B.C. to about 1900 B.C., and the cessation of such visits may have coincided with the destruction of Sodom and the other cities of the valley, from which the worshippers apparently came on pilgrimages to the site. The evidence of Genesis 14 thus furnishes the important corollary that Abraham was living about 1900 B.C., or near the end of the twentieth century B.C., since he was in the vicinity when the cities perished.

[40] Albright, *BASOR,* No. 88 (1942), pp. 33ff.
[41] Cf. W. F. Albright, *BASOR,* No. 14 (1924), pp. 5ff., *AASOR,* VI (1924-25), pp. 58ff.; J. P. Harland, *BA,* V, No. 2 (1942), pp. 17ff., VI, No. 3 (1943), pp. 41ff., and in *IDB,* IV, pp. 395ff.

Suggestions by earlier Assyriologists to the effect that Chedorlaomer could well be identified with a person named Kudur-laḫ(gu)mal, who was mentioned in several late Babylonian legends, were based in part on the assumption that the Tudḫul(a) named in one of the sources was in fact "Tidal king of nations" (Gen. 14:1). While the name Tid'al can almost certainly be identified with the Hittite name Tudḫalia, it is as impossible to be sure that the "nations" over which Tidal ruled were Hittite, or even Hurrian, peoples as it is to identify Tidal himself with any degree of assurance or to place him firmly within a given chronological situation. Of the four or five Hittite kings who bore the name Tudḫalia, all except the first one date from between 1400 and 1200 B.C., and therefore lived long after the date entertained for Abraham in the present work. Tudḫalia I lived about 1740 B.C., which is still too late for the time of Abraham on the evidence furnished by the destruction of Sodom and Gomorrah. It is known, however, that in the early second millennium B.C., Asia Minor and northern Syria were not political unities, but were divided up among various small states and groups. Quite possibly, therefore, Tidal may have been an early Tudḫalia who governed a federation of Hittite and Hurrian groups on the borders of southeast Asia Minor and northern Syria, perhaps about the nineteenth century B.C.[42]

4. The patriarchal narratives. The extent to which the patriarchal narratives have been illumined by the recovery of second-millennium B.C. cultural remains from Mari, Nuzu,[43] and Alalakh has been dealt with elsewhere in the present work. Accordingly it merely remains to observe that the avowed reluctance of contemporary German scholars such as Noth and von Rad to credit these narratives with a firm background of historicity is due entirely to their disinclination to face up to the implications of the archaeological evidence. No serious methodological approach to the patriarchal era can possibly afford to dispense with or neglect the evidence for the nature and vitality of second-millennium B.C. society in northern Babylon and Syria. There can be no doubt that the archaeological evidence recovered to date has brought an inestimable wealth of detail to bear upon the patriarchal narratives, and has set the traditions relating to Abraham, Isaac, and Jacob against a properly accredited background of second-millennium B.C. social life. As Albright has remarked, in no case are these patriarchal stories mere reflections of the life of Israel in the divided monarchy, as used to be maintained by most

---

[42] Cf. D. J. Wiseman, *NBD*, p. 1276.
[43] For Nuzu see C. H. Gordon, *The Living Past* (1941), pp. 156ff.; *IOTT*, pp. 100ff.; H. H. Rowley, *BJRL*, XXXII (1950), pp. 76f.; *BHI*, pp. 60ff. For Alalakh see D. J. Wiseman, *The Alalakh Tablets* (1953).

of the literary critics.[44] Instead, they actually go back almost a thousand years to the Middle Bronze Age.

One of the more serious misinterpretations of the Hebrew text in favor of advancing evidence for the presence of a supposed "duplicate" account can be seen in connection with the story of Joseph. Critical scholars generally have long argued for the presence of two different sources underlying the text, one of which (Gen. 37:25, 28b) recorded that Joseph was sold by his brothers to an Ishmaelite caravan which took him to Egypt, while the other (Gen. 37:28a, 36) narrated that the Midianites took Joseph from the dry cistern in which he had been placed on the advice of Reuben, and subsequently sold him to Potiphar.[45] However, the apparent contradictions can be cleared up quite readily by a proper understanding of the circumstances involved. In Egypt, the Midianites, or, more properly, Medanites (as in the Hebrew of Gen. 37:36), sold Joseph to Potiphar, who was said to have obtained him from the Ishmaelites (Gen. 39:1). While the caravan from Gilead was predominantly Ishmaelite, it also included Midianites. The latter were found in parts of Transjordan from Moab to Edom, and were linked to Abraham through Midian, son of the concubine Keturah (cf. Gen. 25:1ff.). They were desert-dwellers who were associated with both the Ishmaelites and the Medanites. It is important to notice that there is a certain degree of overlapping in the use of the terms "Medanites" and "Midianites," as also in the case of "Midianite" and "Ishmaelite." The latter is made explicit in Judges 8:24, which identified Midianites and Ishmaelites; and with regard to the former it should be observed that both Medan and Midian were spoken of as being the sons of Abraham by Keturah (Gen. 25:2; cf. 1 Chron. 1:32).

As Kitchen has pointed out,[46] the use of multiple terms in narratives is not indicative of disparate documents, but is characteristic of ancient Near Eastern stylistic usage. Evidence for an analogous occurrence of three terms within a few lines of narrative can be adduced from the *stele* of the Egyptian Sebekkhu (*ca.* 1850 B.C.), who referred to the one general enemy which he confronted on his Palestinian campaign as *Mntyw-Sst* ("Asiatic bedouin"), *Rntw ḥst* ("vile Syrians") and *'mw* ("Asiatics"). Since this source was commissioned by one man and executed as a unit, a matter that has been observed previously, there can be absolutely no question as to the possibility of underlying separate documents. In the narrative of Genesis 37:28, the word "they" refers, not to the Midianites, but to the brothers of Joseph, who were taxed with the

[44] Albright, *Religion in Life*, XXI, No. 4 (1952), p. 542.

[45] Cf. *DILOT*, pp. 17f.; H. E. Ryle, *The Book of Genesis*, p. 356; T. H. Robinson in *The People and the Book* (ed. A. S. Peake, 1925), pp. 153ff.; *IBOT*, p. 29; G. von Rad, *Genesis*, p. 348; A. S. Herbert, *Genesis 12-50* (1962), p. 124; E. A. Speiser, *Genesis*, p. 291.

[46] K. A. Kitchen, *NBD*, p. 657; *Ancient Orient and Old Testament*, p. 123.

deed (Gen. 45:5) when Joseph ultimately revealed his true identity to them.[47]

* * * * *

Genesis, the book of beginnings, introduces the readers to the great drama of redemption. The first eleven chapters of the book may be regarded as the prologue, which is cast in universal terms. The drama proper commences with the rise of Abraham, whose position in relationship to the subsequent Israelite nation constitutes one of two principal themes upon which the Pentateuch is built. In the prologue the reader is furnished with an account of the creation of the world and of man, the incidence of sin as a universal concept, and the corollary that by definition it must always stand under divine judgment. The character of the Deity as holy and righteous is complemented by evidence of grace and mercy, one result of which is that a remnant of sinful humanity survived the drastic punishment meted out to the wicked in the Flood.

The divine answer to the iniquity of man appears in the personage of Abraham, who exemplified the moral and spiritual ideals demanded by the Creator from those who would aspire to fellowship with Him. In the drama of salvation the descendants of Abraham had a vital role to play, for they would ultimately constitute an elect and covenanted group whose responsibility it would be to witness to their pagan neighbors concerning divine mercy, grace, and power. The process by which the offspring of Abraham attained to the status of election, which comprised the second major theme of the Pentateuch, is the concern of Exodus.

On the whole the text of Genesis has been preserved in good condition, a fact that may be attributed to the degree of veneration in which the Torah was held, and the resultant care taken in the transmission of the text. In a document such as Genesis, which draws on extremely ancient sources, there are naturally some problems of interpretation and construction, such as those presented by Genesis 4:7; 14:14; 41:8; and others. Versions such as the Samaritan Pentateuch and the LXX occasionally preserve what appears to be a better reading than that found in the MT, as in Genesis 4:8; 29:34; 38:3; 47:21; 50:26; and a few others.

Supplementary Literature

Alt, A. *Der Gott der Väter.* 1929.
Böhl, F. M. Th. *Das Zeitalter Abrahams.* 1930.
Chaine, J. *Le Livre de la Genèse.* 1948.
Eichrodt, W. *Die Quellen der Genesis.* 1916.
Finn, A. H. *The Creation, Fall, and Deluge.* No date.
Kidner, D. *Genesis.* 1967.
Robast, K. *Die Genesis.* 1951.

---

[47] Cf. B. Jacob, *Das erste Buch der Tora, Genesis* (1934), pp. 706f.; G. Ch. Aalders, *A Short Introduction to the Pentateuch,* pp. 48f.; J. H. Hertz, *The Pentateuch and Haftorahs: Genesis* (1929), p. 316.

III. THE BOOK OF EXODUS

A. NAME AND OUTLINE

The second book of the Torah was given its name from the opening words ואלה שמות ("and these are the names"), which were sometimes shortened by the Jews to שמות ("names"). It was the LXX that designated the work according to its principal theme, Ἔξοδος (Exod. 19:1), and this was followed by the Vulgate (*Exodus*) and the English versions.

Exodus serves as a connecting link between the narratives of Genesis and the subsequent legislative material of the Pentateuch. It deals with the fortunes of the Hebrews after the propitious times of Joseph, and its principal concern is with the events leading up to, and immediately following, the Exodus from Egypt. Although the narratives appear to be set against the background of the Avaris era, the chronological picture is outlined in only the most general terms, consistent with the Hebrew treatment of history as a sequence of events and not a series of dates.[1]

The book can be analyzed as follows:

I. The Hebrews in Bondage and Preparation for Their Deliverance, ch. 1-12
 A. Preliminary genealogy, 1:1-6
 B. The bondage in Egypt, 1:7-22
 C. The childhood of Moses, 2:1-10
 D. Biography of Moses, 2:11–4:26
 E. The afflicting of the Israelites, 4:27–6:13
 F. Genealogical table, 6:14-27
 G. Moses and Aaron before Pharaoh, 6:28–7:25
 H. The plagues of Egypt, 8:1–11:10

II. The Exodus and the Journey to Mount Sinai, ch. 13–19
 A. Institution of the Passover, 12:1-28, 43-50
 B. Final plague and withdrawal from Egypt, 12:29-42, 51
 C. Ordinances concerning firstlings and unleavened bread, 13:1-16
 D. Preliminaries to departure from Egypt, 13:17-22

---

[1] W. J. Martin, *NBD*, p. 404.

E. Triumph of the Exodus, 14:1-31
F. Song of Moses to Israel, 15:1-21
G. The Wilderness of Shur, 15:22-27
H. The Wilderness of Sin, 16:1-33
I. Editorial comment, 16:34-36
J. Events at Rephidim, 17:1-16
K. Jethro and Moses, 18:1-27
L. Moses at Sinai, 19:1-25; 20:18-21

III. Legislation Given to the Israelites at Sinai, ch. 20–40

A. The Decalogue, 20:1-17
B. The Covenant Code, 20:22—23:33
C. Ratification of the Covenant, 24:1-8
D. Moses returns to Sinai, 24:9-18
E. Specifications of the Tabernacle, 25:1–27:21
F. The ministry and ritual of the Tabernacle, 28:1–31:11, 18
G. Sabbath enactment, 31:12-17
H. The idolatry of the golden calf, 32:1-35
I. Moses meets with God at Horeb, 33:1-23
J. A second recording of the Covenant, 34:1-35
K. A short sabbath enactment, 35:1-3
L. Offerings for the sanctuary, 35:4—36:38
M. Construction of Ark and Tabernacle furniture, 37:1–38:31
N. Preparation of priestly garments, 39:1-43
O. The Tabernacle erected, 40:1-33
P. The guiding cloud, 40:34-38

B. Compilation and Authorship

According to the tenets held by the members of the critical school, the authorship of Exodus was to be conceived of in terms of the hypothetical documents J, E, and P,[2] to which Eissfeldt added his "Lay" source,[3] as has been remarked above. Although Pfeiffer could doubtless have adduced some evidence for the presence of his "S" or "Southern" source in Exodus, he did not pursue it beyond Genesis. All critical reconstructions, of course, imply oral transmission of the material—a position that is quite remarkable in view of the repeated references to writings and records—and go on to postulate a prolonged interval of time between the occurrence of the events and the writing, despite the evidence of the ancient world to the contrary. An equally common critical presupposition involved the view that the customs and rites

---

[2] So A. H. McNeile, *The Book of Exodus* (1937), p. ii; *DILOT*, pp. 22ff.; *OTFD*, pp. 99ff.
[3] *Einleitung in das AT* (1956 ed.), pp. 230ff.; cf. *IDB*, II, p. 370, *ETOT*, pp. 194ff.

contained in Exodus were antedated and represented as having already been propounded and put into operation in the Mosaic age.[4]

To support a view of the essentially fraudulent nature of such a composition it was also a commonplace procedure in critical circles to remark that the narrators enriched the narrative material from their own imagination, with the result that the traditions acquired a miraculous element in the centuries that intervened between the original events and the times in which the composers of the various sources lived.[5] The unlikely event of Moses' being an historical figure in any acceptable sense of that term was coupled with assertions as to his complete lack of ability to write down a series of moral precepts such as that which is found in the Decalogue. Particular criticisms were also directed at the Tabernacle, whose historicity was uncompromisingly rejected by all followers of Wellhausen.

Those who supported the Mosaicity of Exodus were generally ready to admit that it was not by any means written as a continuous narrative; that there may well be indications of editorial activity, some perhaps emerging from the post-Mosaic era, and that quite probably the earliest portion of the book to be committed to writing after the Decalogue and the Covenant Code was the Song of Moses and Miriam (Exod. 15:1-21). It is also well within the bounds of possibility that there were later insertions in the Covenant Code (a matter which will be considered subsequently) and apparent dislocations of the text. Conservative scholars also recognized that archaeological discoveries have furnished evidence for the antiquity of the Tabernacle concept, in direct contradiction to the Wellhausenian view, and that the narratives of the Wilderness wanderings present some perplexing problems of fact and interpretation for the members of the critical school.

Furthermore the critical hypothesis, which unfortunately does not rest upon quite as substantial a basis of argument as Eissfeldt[6] and others have supposed, contains some curiously self-contradictory elements in relationship to Exodus. As Martin has pointed out, it is strange that P, which according to literary-critical theory was written from a priestly standpoint, does so little in the book to enhance the status of the priesthood.[7] Instead it is Moses, the political leader, who remains the great hero, while the one who allows the people to lapse into idolatry is Aaron, the priest, whom Moses rebukes for his infidelity and whom he subsequently reinstates. This, as the narratives of Exodus make clear, was not the only lapse on the part of the leader of the priestly cult. Furthermore, if the whole corpus of material was arranged in such a

---

[4] E.g. S. R. Driver, *The Book of Exodus* (1918), p. lxv.

[5] McNeile, *The Book of Exodus*, p. cxii.

[6] *Einleitung in das AT*, p. 288.

[7] W. J. Martin, *NBD*, p. 405.

manner as to furnish an ideal picture of the theocracy as it was supposed to have existed in the Mosaic age,[8] it can only be observed that, in the light of the stubbornness and intractability of the people, the entire project miscarried to an alarming degree.

The view that Moses was the substantial author of Exodus is based partly upon the fact that making a direct recording of happenings is alleged to have been the regular custom of Moses, and this tradition is in complete harmony with what is now known about the transmission of events by scribes in Near Eastern antiquity. Thus it would appear from Exodus 17:14 that Moses recorded the battle with Amalek immediately after the event. The "book" thus produced would correspond to the "annals" of Egypt and other ancient Near Eastern nations, in which, by ancient custom, all events worthy of note were recorded. The most accessible, and doubtless the preferred, material available in the Wilderness for making such records would be leather. In Exodus 24:4 Moses is said to have written "all the words of the Lord" in a manner suggesting that he transcribed the contents of the Decalogue and the so-called Covenant Code as he remembered them onto some kind of durable material. In addition, in Exodus 34:27, Moses was given a similar, though rather different, set of regulations, and on that occasion he was instructed to commit them to writing, presumably while he was still in the Sinai region.

The actual process by which the extant book of Exodus was compiled is, of course, entirely unknown, but in the light of ancient Near Eastern scribal practices it may have taken somewhat of the following form. The compiler, whether Moses himself or some such individual as Joshua or Eleazar who undertook the task either while Moses was still alive or immediately after his death, would have as a basic source-residuum the Decalogue and the Book of the Covenant, the latter perhaps being somewhat shorter than its extant form; the Song of Moses and Miriam, the various ordinances concerning sabbath observance, and the sources dealing with the specifications for the Tabernacle, the detailed contents of which would seem to indicate that they were already in written form at a very early period. Whatever elements of this corpus were still in oral form would be written down at that time, and the sources assembled into some kind of order with the aim of covering the general sequence of events rather than conforming to a precise chronological order or pattern.

The dominant theme of the document was, of course, the deliverance from Egypt in the supreme event of the Exodus, but in order to preserve the pattern of internal coherence the compiler or compilers evidently thought it necessary to introduce material that would constitute a brief prelude to the account of the Exodus itself. This section, which com-

[8] Driver, *The Book of Exodus*, p. xii.

prises Exodus 1:1-17, served to establish the identity of the enslaved Israelites, thereby sequentially linking the Joseph narratives in Genesis with the bondage in Egypt and introducing the personage of Moses the deliverer. Quite possibly one section of the scroll that contained Exodus ended at this point, and before another one began with the narrative of events in Egypt, a list dealing principally with the family tree of Moses and Aaron was inserted so as to ground these two important individuals in the history of the Hebrew people.[9]

In some respects it might have been better from a sheer narrative standpoint if the section containing the names in Exodus 6:14-27 had been inserted after Exodus 4:26, although even in its present position the continuity of the narrative as a whole is far from being seriously disturbed. Quite possibly Exodus 6:10-13 and 6:28–7:7 point to the place where one roll ended and another began. This may be adduced from the similarities between them, which would make it possible for the second roll to be read intelligibly yet independently of its immediate precursor. A somewhat similar situation may be said to exist in the relationship of 2 Chronicles 36:22f. to Ezra 1:1-3a, where the former is utilized as an elaborate "catch-line" in the accredited Mesopotamian manner so as to insure the continuity of the narrative.

What appears to have been a new section of scroll carried on the story of Exodus 12:28, where there is a possible dislocation of the text. Exodus 12:43-50 may well have come immediately after Exodus 12:28, so as to preserve the general order of events relating to the institution of the Passover. This would then be followed chronologically by the final plague and the departure from Egypt, as recorded in Exodus 12:29-42, 51. It is possible that Exodus 12:42 is an editorial comment added by a later hand during processes of revision, and may perhaps date from the time of Samuel. Exodus 13:1-16, which deals with ordinances concerning firstlings and unleavened bread, also seems to be out of place in relation to the strict order of events, but while the passage in question may not have been communicated to Moses at the precise moment that its insertion into the extant composition might suggest, it was clearly important priestly material, and as such was associated intimately with the text of the Passover enactment. As Stafford Wright has commented, the historian has to decide continually whether to arrange his history by subjects or in a strict chronological order, and frequently he is forced to compromise between the two in his finished narrative.[10] So in this instance, a number of Passover regulations of early date were inserted into a gap in the story.

Perhaps another roll of the history commenced with Exodus 13:17-22, which narrated the preliminary movement of the Israelites away from

[9] J. S. Wright, *EQ*, XXV (1953), p. 12.
[10] *Ibid.*, p. 13.

Egyptian territory. As with the previous proposed roll, it commenced with an introductory section covering much of the same ground as Exodus 12:37-41 in order to preserve the general sequence of events. The narrative then continued to the giving of the Decalogue at Sinai (Exod. 20:1-17), but to what extent it is possible to say that this passage marked the conclusion of another section of leather scroll is unknown. What can be asserted, however, is that the contents of Exodus 20:22—23:33 once existed as a separate document, the so-called Covenant Code, or else were extant in conjunction with the Decalogue, since in Exodus 24:4 Moses wrote down "all the words of the Lord," presumably in order to formulate the record of the Covenant that had been instituted at that time.[11]

There seems little doubt that, in view of the fundamental importance for Hebrew faith and destiny of the events at Sinai, Moses intertwined history and laws in his narratives from the very beginning. Nor can it be reasonably objected that this procedure was entirely accidental, since it was of obvious importance for the revelation of God to be firmly grounded in temporal events, and for the faith of Israel to be regulated in terms of moral and social legislative concepts. The most that can be said concerning the length of this proposed section of the Exodus is that it may have concluded either about Exodus 19:25 or Exodus 20:18-21. It is not outside the bounds of possibility, however, that the latter was the introduction to a new section of the scroll. The narrative of chapter 24:1-8 concerning the ratification of the Covenant is closely associated with the Decalogue and the Book of the Covenant for obvious reasons, but whether Exodus 24:9-11 also belongs to this period or is a somewhat later insertion is open to some question.

The historical sequence was continued in Exodus 24:12 with the account of Moses' return to Sinai, and it may be that still another section of the Exodus scroll commenced with Exodus 25:1, when a complete roll of regulations concerning the Tabernacle was inserted. Apparently Moses received this material in oral form only at Mount Sinai, but such was its importance for the religious life of the nation that the details were preserved with meticulous care and inserted at the most appropriate point in the large narrative, which probably terminated with Exodus 31:11, 18. The brief section comprising Exodus 31:12-17, which dealt with certain sabbath enactments, may constitute a dislocation, and perhaps belonged originally in some manner to the fragment represented by Exodus 35:1-3.

A resumption of the historical sequences was undertaken with the narratives dealing with the golden calf (Exod. 32:1), and included the sequel to this act of apostasy, along with a further group of regulations

---

[11] For theories concerning the relation of Moses to the Decalogue see H. H. Rowley, *BJRL*, XXXIV (1952), pp. 81ff., reprinted in his *Men of God*, pp. 1ff.

given at Sinai. It would appear from the evidence presented by Exodus 34:27 that these enactments also existed in independent form at one period, and this document may have constituted the source upon which Moses drew in compiling this particular section of the Exodus scroll. If an additional break is made after Exodus 34:28, the rest of the book can be taken as a record of how the details prescribed on Mount Sinai were carried out. The entire roll concluded with a colophon dealing with the completed Tabernacle and the narrative of the guiding cloud (Exod. 40:36-38), a theme that was picked up again in Numbers 9:15-23.

Any conjecture as to how Exodus arrived at approximately its extant form ought to consider that post-Mosaic and non-Mosaic additions may be present in the text. This is not a matter of very great concern, however, since it is now well known that ancient Near Eastern scribes regularly revised ancient material in certain matters of style and content when making fresh copies, and saw no incompatibility between such activity and the attribution of pristine authorship to the material under revision. Post-Mosaic elements in Exodus have generally been thought to include Exodus 6:26f.; 16:33ff.; and 16:36. In connection with the first of these references, it has commonly been said that one would only write of individuals in such a manner if they were already dead, but as Young has pointed out, these two verses follow a genealogy, and in effect they comprise a colophon to the list, with the meaning of "this is the genealogy of Moses and Aaron to whom God spoke."[12] Thus when verse 26 is compared with verse 14 of the same chapter, it carries exactly the same force as verse 27 when it is compared with verse 13, thus raising some doubt as to whether or not it is actually post-Mosaic.

In Exodus 16:33-35, it is the phrase "before the testimony" that occasions the difficulty, as well as the reference to the Israelites eating manna for a forty-year period. The "testimony" comprised the Covenant tablets, which, according to the strict sequence of the narratives, had not yet been given to the nation. However, there is nothing in the reference that would necessarily preclude its insertion into the Exodus scroll within the lifetime of Moses. But if it is a genuine post-Mosaic scribal addition, it may be that Exodus 16:34-36 constituted an editorial comment designed to explain the significance of manna for the benefit of future generations of Israelites. The passage merely states that the pot of manna[13] was preserved near the tablets of the Covenant, and that manna had been the intermittent food of the Israelites throughout the generation of wandering in the Wilderness. Neither of these facts requires a particularly late date.

In Exodus 16:36, the gloss explaining the value of an omer has been thought to indicate a time of composition when such information was no

---

[12] *YIOT*, pp. 72f.
[13] On manna see K. A. Kitchen, *NBD*, p. 780.

longer current. Against this contention it merely needs to be observed that the word עמר is used throughout the chapter (vv. 16, 18, 22, 32, 33, 36) in a manner which would make its significance immediately evident to anyone who was at all acquainted with the phenomena of the wanderings. The word does not appear elsewhere in the Old Testament. The term was employed in a twofold sense of the measure itself (Exod. 16:18, 32f.) and the amount measured (Exod. 16:16, 22, 36) in such a way that, even if Exodus 16:36 is a part or the whole of an editorial gloss, the homogeneity of the narrative is preserved without apparent difficulty. In this as in other sections of Exodus it is important for the greatest caution to be exercised before pronouncements are made as to the post-Mosaic nature of specific passages, since given literary phenomena are not necessarily amenable to explanation in terms of one situation only.

With regard to the possibility of non-Mosaic interpolations, it is apparent that Exodus 11:3, which recorded that Moses was a person of high esteem in the land of Egypt, can hardly be ascribed to the great legislator without implications of pride and self-esteem, at least for the occidental mind. But here again there is very little difficulty in supposing that this is a characteristic redactional gloss, originating perhaps as a marginal comment and being subsequently incorporated into the text during the normal processes of scribal revision.

It is impossible to overestimate the importance of the first half of Exodus for the faith and history of the Hebrew nation. One weakness of the Graf-Wellhausen theory of Pentateuchal literary origins was that it contrived to diminish the majesty of the events which occurred at Yam Suph and Mount Sinai in favor of an emphasis upon alleged documentary sources whose nature and content were a matter of considerable dispute in those very critical circles from which they had emerged. In a reaction against the purely documentary approach, Pedersen declared his independence of the Wellhausenian theory by suggesting that Exodus 1–15 comprised the central core of the Pentateuch, and that it was derived ultimately from cultic ceremony.[14] For him the material comprised a cult-legend constituting a separate entity, and was not the result of a mechanical combination of independent parallel expositions. Inequalities in the text could not be explained satisfactorily simply by the assumption of separate "sources," for the narrative was not so much a straightforward history as a celebration of the divine victory by the worshipping people in the Passover festival. For Pedersen the story of the Exodus was intended primarily to describe those exploits in which God was glorified and a nation was made great.

While this view went far towards correcting the gross imbalance of the Wellhausen school, it raised certain important issues of its own. One of

---

[14] J. Pedersen, *Israel, Its Life and Culture,* III-IV (1940), pp. 726ff.

these was the question as to whether the cultus actually originated the Exodus material, or whether it simply used it in a variety of ways. Since liturgical forms in general tend to draw upon already existing material, the question of origins once again comes very much to the fore. Since Exodus speaks specifically of certain written sources, it is quite difficult to see precisely how the "legend" can have originated with the cultus as such. While liturgical movements and oral-traditionist circles may perhaps play a useful part in perpetuating certain historic events of profound spiritual significance, it is a very different matter to say they are responsible for creating either the tradition or the material underlying it. The principal point that Pedersen appears to be making over against the classical analytical theory is that since the material is, on his understanding, of a liturgical character, it is incorrect to assume that literary criticism can solve the basic problem regarding its form. Given this premise he is undoubtedly correct in his conclusion.

Much the same questions arise in connection with the liturgical interpretation of Exodus 20–24 as favored by von Rad.[15] For him the entire Sinai episode was a cultic legend, whose life-situation comprised a cultic festival embracing the themes of exhortation, recitation of the Decalogue and Covenant Code, the promise of blessing, and the conclusion of the Covenant. However valid this interpretation may be, it is, as Wright has pointed out, impossible to assume without question that the tradition, even in all of its written form, was created by the cultic ceremonies and their officiants.[16]

A nihilistic view of the origin of Hebrew tradition, based upon a fairly orthodox form of liberal criticism, was espoused by M. Noth, who has appropriated some of the results of the Uppsala school of Engnell to his own theories without, however, abandoning the documentary approach to Pentateuchal problems.[17] Noth maintained that the traditions of the Pentateuch were only to be understood against the background of a supposed amphictyonic society in Palestine during the Judges period. While the five major themes of the Exodus, the entrance into the Promised Land, the assurance to the patriarchs, the Wilderness wanderings, and the Sinai revelation can be isolated from the corpus of tradition, the whole sequence was held to be independent of the figure of Moses, who for Noth was only a minor tribal sheik.[18] Aside from his dependence upon a totally inadequate methodology (whose erroneous nature is by no means offset by the recognition that the alleged sources J and E both go back to a common original source or *Grundlage*),[19] Noth's

---

[15] G. von Rad, *Das formgeschichtliche Problem des Hexateuchs* (1938), reprinted in *Gesammelte Studien zum AT* (1958), pp. 9ff.

[16] G. E. Wright, *IDB*, II, p. 195.

[17] Noth, *Überlieferungsgeschichte des Pentateuch* (1948).

[18] *Ibid.*, pp. 190f.

[19] *Ibid.*, pp. 40ff.; cf. his *Exodus* (1962), p. 10 *passim*.

application of the *Überlieferungsgeschichtliche* method defeats its own purpose in making it clear that, for him, the *Überlieferung* has actually no real *Geschichte* at all.

C. THE MATERIAL OF EXODUS

1. Moses. The vagueness that characterized the attitude of the early critical scholars towards the personage of Moses still persists, unfortunately, in a good many quarters. No doubt these writers were eminently justified in protesting against the rabbinic concept of the great lawgiver as a quasi-divine being, an image that is in no way either encouraged or fostered in the Pentateuch itself. But in rejecting it they also contrived to dispense with the personality of the man who towered over all other Israelites in the second millennium B.C. His name, מֹשֶׁה, which is a play on the root *mšh*, "to draw out," was probably given to him by his mother, since the pun is Semitic in form.[20] The name does not appear to be the Amarna Age Egyptian word *ms(w)*, or "child," nor does it seem to correspond at all to the related grammatical form in a compound name such as *Har-mose*. It is possible that it constitutes an ellipsis for a longer form, or it may have been a strictly Semitic designation that was assimilated in some manner to the common word *ms(w)* by the Egyptian adoptive mother of Moses.

The vast increase within recent years of knowledge concerning the conditions of life in ancient Egypt has furnished an enriched background for an examination of the early life of Moses. In the New Kingdom period there were numerous royal residences and *harîms* in various parts of Egypt including the eastern Delta region, where ladies of noble blood resided along with royal concubines and other personnel.[21] The "daughter of pharaoh" who rescued the infant from the river would be the adolescent offspring of one of the pharaohs by a concubine or some lesser paramour, and not one of the chief princesses of full royal blood. Children of the *harîm*, especially male princes, were frequently educated under the supervision of the *harîm* overseer, and at a rather later stage the princes were placed in the care of tutors, who saw to it that their charges were educated by the priestly caste in reading and writing, the transcription of classical texts, civil administration, and in certain physical accomplishments.[22] On completing their course of instruction the royal princes could serve in a variety of capacities, either with the armed forces, the civil service, or in one of the numerous provincial strongholds of Egyptian religion.

[20] K. A. Kitchen, *NBD*, p. 843; on the problem of the name see A. H. Gardiner, *JAOS*, LVI (1936), pp. 192ff.; J. G. Griffiths, *JNES*, XII (1953), pp. 225ff.

[21] Cf. R. A. Caminos, *Literary Fragments in the Hieratic Script* (1956), pp. 19ff.

[22] Cf. F. L. Griffiths and P. E. Newberry, *El Bersheh* (1894), II, p. 40.

In the matter of writing ability, which earlier generations of liberal scholars refused to consider in relation to Moses, it has now been made abundantly clear by archaeological discoveries that a number of scripts were available for use by a literate person in the New Kingdom period. As a Semite, Moses would have experienced no difficulty whatever in using the simple linear proto-Canaanite alphabet for purposes of communication. The fact that such a script was freely utilized in Egyptian territory some two centuries before the time of Moses has been illustrated by the discovery of early fifteenth-century B.C. informal notations and dedications by Semitic captives from the Egyptian east Delta region who were being employed to work the Sinai turquoise mines.[23]

Even more eloquent testimony to the use of the "proto-Sinaitic" linear script by Semites in Egypt was furnished by an ostracon recovered from the Valley of the Queens at Thebes, some 350 miles south of Palestine and the eastern Delta region.[24] As Kitchen has stated, if mere workmen or their foremen at Theban tomb-sites and Sinai mines had no inhibitions about employing this script for mundane lists and religious memorials, it is both unwarranted and unrealistic to ascribe precisely those inhibitions to the eventual leader of an embryo nation, especially one conditioned in Egyptian attitudes to the written word, in favor of a theoretical oral tradition which is patently at variance with the usage of the ancient Near East.[25] In the light of the foregoing evidence, the suggestions of Nielsen that such a script ought to be considered as limited to specialist usage is particularly ludicrous.[26]

With regard to the topography of the early chapters of Exodus, it can be said that there was nothing especially unusual about the escape route that Moses chose when fleeing from Egypt (Exod. 2:15). In taking an easterly direction across the border he was following the time-honored route of Sinuhe, who himself also had left Egypt hurriedly some 600 years earlier,[27] and one which was commonly used by runaway slaves later on in the thirteenth century B.C.[28] If the reference in Exodus 1:11 to the building, or reconstruction, of Pithom and Rameses by Hebrew forced labor is to the period of rebuilding under Rameses II (ca. 1290-1224 B.C.), it alludes to one of the most active and brilliant eras in the whole spectrum of Egyptian history. During this time Rameses II moved his capital from Thebes to Avaris, and entered upon

[23] Albright, *BASOR*, No. 110 (1948), pp. 12f., 22.

[24] Cf. J. Leibovitch, *Annales du Service des Antiquités de L'Égypte*, XL (1940), p. 119, fig. 26, and pls. xvi, xix:50; Albright, *BASOR*, No. 110 (1948), p. 12 n. 33.

[25] K. A. Kitchen, *NBD*, p. 844.

[26] E. Nielsen, *Oral Tradition* (1954), pp. 24ff.

[27] *ANET*, p. 19.

[28] *ANET*, p. 259.

a program of reconstruction and expansion, the nature of which has become evident as a result of excavations at the site.[29]

That Moses should be able to gain ready access to the pharaoh, particularly since Tanis-Avaris was located in the northeast Delta region, is not at all surprising in view of the way in which people were able to present petitions freely to Rameses II, as recorded in Papyrus Anastasi III.[30] Work-journals belonging to the New Kingdom period have furnished, among other reasons for absenteeism, the offering of sacrifices by workmen to their gods,[31] and in view of the widespread nature of animal cult-worship in the eastern Delta region it is not in the least unrealistic to suppose that the Hebrews could request, and expect to receive (Exod. 8:26f.; 10:9, 25f.), a three-day absence from work in order to celebrate their own religious feast in the Wilderness without at the same time provoking Egyptian religious antagonism.[32]

2. *The ten plagues.* The early exponents of the literary-critical analysis of the Pentateuch professed to find evidence of duplicate accounts in the narratives dealing with the plagues of Egypt. According to Driver[33] this comprised the terms of the command addressed to Moses, the request made of Pharaoh, the description of the plague, and the formula that expressed the obstinacy of Pharaoh, all of which were supposed to agree frequently with corresponding differences in the sections of Exodus 3:1 –7:13, which the members of the critical school had assigned "on independent grounds" to P and JE. A careful examination of the text, however, shows that the close sequences of the narrative indicate the very opposite of underlying multiple sources. Thus, while the command in Exodus 7:15 was given to Moses, it was executed by Aaron (Exod. 7: 19f.) in strict accordance with the agreement in Exodus 7:1f., where God appointed Aaron as the spokesman-prophet for Moses. The theoretical basis of the chapter is thus a unity, a fact borne out by the development of the narrative. Although there are slight variations of phraseology in evidence, they are obviously merely stylistic considerations, and any attempt to employ them as indications of underlying duplicate material constitutes an improper use of the textual evidence.

Against the contention that in one record the description of the plagues is given at some length, whereas in the other it is very brief, it only needs to be remarked that here again there is stylistic variation evident without any essential difference in the narrative content. In the case of six of the first nine plagues, a formal demand was made of Pharaoh for the release of the people. In the account of the sixth and

---

[29] Cf. P. Montet, *Les nouvelles fouilles de Tanis* (1929-1933).
[30] P. Montet, *L'Égypte et la Bible*, p. 71; *ANET*, p. 471.
[31] A. Erman, *Life in Ancient Egypt* (1894), pp. 124f.
[32] P. Montet, *L'Égypte et la Bible*, pp. 99ff.
[33] *DILOT*, p. 25.

ninth plagues, the record of the preceding affliction terminated with the statement that Pharaoh refused to let the captive Israelites go free. Consistent with this pattern is the fact that the first six plagues were announced beforehand, and that in four instances they took effect as Moses stretched out his hand with his rod. This also occurred in connection with the third plague, which was not spoken of to Pharaoh. In the two remaining descriptions where the plague was not announced beforehand, mention was made either of the hands of Moses stretched towards the sky (the ninth plague), or of handfuls of ashes sprinkled skywards (the sixth plague). Stylistic diversity can certainly be granted in these descriptions, but there is clearly nothing to support the theory of an interwoven duplicate account of the plagues.[34]

A similar explanation can be given for the use of two different verbs, "to make heavy" (כבד) (Exod. 7:14; 8:15, 32; 9:7, 34; 10:1) and "to make strong" (חזק) (Exod. 7:22; 8:19; 9:12; 11:10), to describe the "hardening" of the will of Pharaoh. Quite obviously a process is involved in which a man whose will was slow to be affected gradually became first stubborn and then outrightly defiant, as a study of the incidence of these terms in the Hebrew text clearly indicates.

In conclusion it can be said that the critical presuppositions themselves are inconsistent, for the alleged distinguishing traits as related to the foregoing material do not always correspond with the theory. For example, the Hebrew of Exodus 8:5, which is supposed to restrict the divine command to Moses alone, actually mentions the name of Aaron explicitly as well, a fact which is also true for the Hebrew of Exodus 8:8, 12; 9:27; and 10:3, 8, 16. To eliminate the troublesome words "and Aaron" by the simple expedient of attributing them to a later editor, as was commonly undertaken by critical scholars in order to bolster the theory, is as unwarranted as it is unnecessary on a straightforward interpretation of the textual evidence. Such tiny literary fragments of the plague-accounts as would constitute a part of the hypothetical documentary sources and the schematic uniformity of features postulated for them correspond to no known ancient Near Eastern scribal or literary phenomena, making the unitary view of the plague narratives the only one that can be related logically and factually to observable physical and literary occurrences.

3. *The revelation of the Divine Name.* A great deal of discussion has surrounded the revelation of the Divine Name in Exodus 3:14 and 6:3.[35] The latter passage furnished the first "clue" to the distinguishing of the

[34] For the plague phenomena see G. Hort, ZAW, LXIX (1957), pp. 84ff., LXX (1958), pp. 48ff.

[35] For the literature see P. van Imschoot, *Théologie de l'Ancien Testament* (1954), p. 7; Th. C. Vriezen, *Theologie des AT in Grundzügen* (1956), pp. 164ff.

various alleged Pentateuchal documents.[36] In view of the common assumption that there are "different" names for God in the Pentateuch it should be noted that the Torah in particular and the Old Testament in general confine themselves to one *name* only, *YHWH*, and utilize all the others as titles or descriptions of deity. Ignoring this rather elementary fact, the members of the liberal school developed their theoretical approach on the basis that, while Exodus 6:3 stated that the name *YHWH* had not been known to the patriarchs, it appeared freely in the narratives concerning their lives. The inherent contradiction thus entertained was crystallized by Rowley as follows:

> Obviously it cannot be true that God was not known to Abraham by the name Yahweh [Exod. 6:3] and that He was known to him by that name [Gen. 15:2, 7]. To this extent there is a flat contradiction that cannot be resolved by any shift.[37]

Part of the problem lies in the fact that most English-speaking authors have taken the verses at their face value as they stand in the English versions of the Bible, and as far as Exodus 6:3 is concerned, this is an unfortunate situation, as will be shown presently.

With respect to the tetragrammaton *YHWH*, where considerations of sanctity demanded the substitution of Adonai in articulation, its pronunciation in the form "Yahweh" was arrived at from transliterations of the name into Greek in early Christian writings. Thus Clement of Alexandria preserved the form *iaoue*,[38] while Theodoret favored the rendering *iabe*.[39] There can be no question that the name is connected etymologically with the Hebrew word היה, "to be," or more preferably with an earlier variant form of the root הוה. However, it can no longer be regarded as an imperfect causative form of the root הוה, but must be considered instead as a regular substantive in which the root הוה is preceded by the preformative י.[40] As a proper noun it constitutes the name of a Person, in contrast with titles such as Elyon, El Elyon, and Elohim. The name emphasizes the being or existence of God in personal terms, and thus brings Him into relationship with other, human, personalities.

It may be noted in passing that the form "Jehovah" resulted from the transcribed vowels of Adonai being combined with the consonants of the

---

[36] Cf. J. Skinner, *The Divine Names in the Book of Genesis*, p. 171; A. H. McNeile, *The Book of Exodus*, pp. cxiii, 34.

[37] H. H. Rowley, *The Biblical Doctrine of Election* (1950), p. 25; cf. his *The Rediscovery of the OT* (1945), p. 60, *The Growth of the OT* (1950), pp. 20f., *The Unity of the Bible* (1953), p. 25, *The Faith of Israel* (1956), pp. 41f.

[38] *Stromat.*, V, 6, 34; cf. A. Deissmann, *Bibelstudien* (1895), p. 11; W. W. von Baudissin, *Kyrios*, II (1929), p. 216.

[39] *Quaestiones in Exodum*, I, p. 133.

[40] L. Köhler and W. Baumgartner, *Lexicon in Veteris Testamenti Libros* (1953), I, pp. 368f.; cf. L. Köhler, *Vom Hebräischen Lexikon* (1950), pp. 17f.

tetragrammaton *YHWH*, a form that is first attested from about A.D. 1100. Since the original pronunciation of *YHWH* is unknown, any modern vocalization must be regarded as tentative at the best.[41] While most contemporary scholars dislike the form "Jehovah," and prefer to use "Yahweh" or some similar transcription, it should be observed that the former is at least a genuine hybrid, and its long tradition of usage in English ought to insure it at least some place in modern literature dealing with the Old Testament.

The statement in Exodus 6:3 that God was the *Elohim* of the antecedents of Moses immediately suggests that the latter would be acquainted with the name of the family deity. The question of Moses in Exodus 3:13 should be interpreted as an attempt to investigate the character or meaning of the name, since it is introduced by means of the interrogative particle *māh*, "What?", and not by the particle *mî*, "Who?" which is the normal manner of inquiring as to the name of someone.[42] The following verse raises three possibilities of interpretation: first that the name of God is *Ehyeh*, secondly that it is *Ehyeh asher Ehyeh*, and finally that it is *YHWH*. Earlier generations of critical scholars supposed that there had been a conflation of several sources at this point, but there is absolutely no textual evidence that can be adduced to support this view. An alternative approach is to think of the three expressions as correl. .ive, and intended by the original author to explain each other.

In a comprehensive survey of the problems presented by this verse, Reisel accepted the traditional answer that *Ehyeh* is the clue to the entire situation, and held that it posits a relationship between itself and the recurring phrase, "I am the God of your father(s) . . . ," thus placing the Name directly in the context of the Covenant.[43] The root *hyh* has generally been understood in the static sense of existence, as in the Latin phrase *Ego sum qui sum*, but a more dynamic interpretation sees the expression as an example of *paronomasia*, where two verbs of related origin are used to emphasize the unity of action inherent in the basic verb-concept. On such an interpretation God would be actively engaged in revealing Himself as the God of creation and the Covenant.

Reisel favored a compromise between the static and dynamic approaches in order to relate satisfactorily the concepts of divine existence and readiness.[44] However, his suggestion as to "readiness" seems to interpret the play on words in Exodus 3:14 inadequately, since the emphasis appears to be on the fact that God was already at work on behalf of His people. Buber is nearer the true meaning in his translation,

[41] On this see M. Reisel, *The Mysterious Name of Y.H.W.H.* (1957), pp. 56ff.

[42] M. Buber, *Moses* (1946), p. 48; cf. J. A. Motyer, *The Revelation of the Divine Name* (1959), pp. 17ff.

[43] M. Reisel, *op. cit.*, pp. 6ff.

[44] *Ibid.*, pp. 18ff.

"I will be as I will be," and in his suggestion that the expression contains the assurance of continuing divine power and enduring presence with the Israelites in the process of their deliverance.[45]

The sequel in Exodus 6:2f. has been misconstrued by adherents of the documentary theory to the point where it has been regarded as a duplicate version of the account in chapter 3. Even a brief comparison will show that such is far from being the case, for there is no reference to a burning bush, no desert scene, and no parting from Jethro. The locale is Egypt, there is no reluctance expressed by Moses, and his partner in the enterprise is his brother Aaron, making the narrative a continuation of that found in chapter three, and not a "duplicate" of it. This passage contains the crux of the problem relating to the revelation of the Divine Name. As observed earlier, it not merely furnished the "clue" to the distinguishing of the imagined underlying documents, but also led to the commonly accepted critical opinion that the patriarchs did not know the name YHWH. A break with the latter tradition was made by Reisel, who based his arguments in part upon the assertion that yādha' means "to acknowledge" as well as "to know," and that nōdha'tî, which he retained in preference to the general critical emendation of hôdha'tî, does not mean "I have made known," but "I have manifested."[46] On such a textual foundation Reisel interpreted the verse in the sense that the promises made to the patriarchs were now being realized.

Clearly the problems presented by Exodus 6:3 are not as simple as the straightforward rendering of most English versions would appear to suggest. In the light of general Semitic usage it is possible to interpret the word "name" as expressive of "honor" or "character," so that when God revealed Himself as El Shaddai, it was with the intention of furnishing the patriarchs with the insight into the divine character which was appropriate to that title. A rather different approach has been suggested by Martin, who interpreted the text in terms of the presence of an elliptical interrogative, and rendered it, "for did I not let my name YHWH be known to them?"[47] If C. H. Gordon is correct in his belief that the Hebrew word lo' frequently approximates its English literal equivalent, the verse might well be rendered, "but by my name YHWH, behold, I was known to them."

In the light of the foregoing discussion the present writer would tend to follow Motyer, in rendering Exodus 6:3 as follows, "And God spoke to Moses, saying unto him: I am YHWH. And I manifested myself to Abraham, to Isaac and to Jacob in the character of El Shaddai, but in the character expressed by my name YHWH I did not make myself

---

[45] M. Buber, *Moses*, pp. 39ff.

[46] M. Reisel, *op. cit.*, pp. 27ff.

[47] W. J. Martin, *Stylistic Criteria and the Analysis of the Pentateuch*, pp. 17f., and in *NBD*, p. 405.

known to them,"[48] with the reservation that the elliptical interrogative rendering suggested by Martin may well be probable as an alternative. Such an approach does not deny to the patriarchs the knowledge of the name YHWH, though it may well preclude knowledge of the significance of that name in such circles.[49] It is in accordance with proper Near Eastern methodology, and it makes possible a theological synthesis of Genesis and Exodus that is in harmony with a truly Biblical form of progressive revelation. If Reisel is correct in his emphasis upon a background of covenantal theology, the revelation to Moses is not just that of a name per se, but of a Covenant-keeping Deity manifesting His character as one who is already fulfilling the promises given to the patriarchs. Thus the name YHWH, familiar from the pre-Mosaic period, would appear as the central idea inherent in the text, namely, that of the Covenant loyalty of the God of Israel, already revealed as one who keeps His promises.[50]

Such a revelation is, of course, of pre-eminent importance in the light of the mighty act of God in the deliverance achieved at the Exodus, and in the provision that was made for a more comprehensive Covenant relationship at Sinai. This interpretation also lends proper balance to the twofold principal themes of the Torah, and shows the importance of their interrelationship for the future history of the nation.

4. *The Book of the Covenant.* The Covenant association between God and Israel has been examined in the light of second-millennium B.C. international treaties[51] elsewhere in the present work, and will not be recapitulated at this particular point. Suffice it to say that of equal importance with the provision by the Covenant of a nucleus about which Israelite historical tradition and spiritual life could be fostered was the fact that the Hebrews were unique in the ancient world for their attempts to interpret the whole of national existence in terms of a solemn covenantal agreement with a single deity.

The Book of the Covenant, which was read by Moses at the ratification of the divine agreement with Israel at Sinai, was most probably in the first instance the record of the Decalogue (Exod. 20:2-17). However, it has become customary in scholarly circles to refer to Exodus 20:22–23:33 as the "Book of the Covenant," which in any case is the oldest extant codification of Hebrew law. It is an amalgam of civil and criminal

---

[48] J. A. Motyer, *The Revelation of the Divine Name,* p. 12. Cf. O. T. Allis, *The Five Books of Moses* (1943), p. 28.

[49] Cf. A. B. Davidson, *The Theology of the OT* (1904), p. 68.

[50] M. Reisel, *op. cit.,* pp. 28f.

[51] G. E. Mendenhall, *BA,* XVII, No. 3 (1954), pp. 50ff., reprinted as *Law and Covenant in Israel and the Ancient Near East* (1955), *IBD,* I, pp. 714ff.; cf. M. G. Kline, *Treaty of the Great King* (1963); J. A. Thompson, *The Ancient Near Eastern Treaties and the OT* (1964).

legislation, ritual rules, and humanitarian prescriptions, and the corpus is of such a nature that it could have been revised or supplemented to a limited extent in the immediate post-Mosaic age without any violence to its substantial Mosaicity. Thus Exodus 22:18, 19, 31; and 23:1 may be later additions, perhaps dating from the Judges period. But whether this was actually the case or not, it is incorrect to suppose, with Alt, that the origins of this code must be sought outside the nation of Israel,[52] or with Pfeiffer, that the Book of the Covenant resulted from successive enlarged editions whose final form was not much earlier than the post-exilic date assigned by the critical school to the ultimate edition of the Pentateuch.[53]

The Book of the Covenant includes "precedents" and "statutes," the former appearing as case-laws and the latter as categorical law, normally in the form of prohibitions. The casuistic or case-law type is the dominant form of law known from the ancient Near East, as observed previously, and in the Covenant Code it is expressed in conditional terms: "If a man does...he shall pay...." The "statutes" have been described as categorical or "apodictic" in nature, and comprise definite prohibitions that do not specify precisely how they are to be implemented. Yet another form of law that is quite similar to the apodictic variety commences in Hebrew with an active participle and closes with the strongly worded expression, "he shall surely be put to death." This type not infrequently replaced the casuistic class where the death penalty was prescribed.

In the light of the suggestion by critical scholars that the agricultural and community legislation presupposes a date for the Covenant Code not earlier than the time of Samuel, it should be remembered that the Israelites were originally intended to journey from Sinai directly to the Promised Land, within the space of a few years at the most. Due, however, to the events which occurred near Kadesh (Num. 13:1ff.), the situation was changed in order to punish the rebels by insuring that they died in the Wilderness. Furthermore, it is important to realize that the enactments concerning agricultural and other activities had as much bearing upon the past life of the Israelites in the Goshen region as upon the conditions of their future existence.

Too often it is forgotten that the Israelites at Sinai were in fact the heirs of four centuries of agricultural and pastoral experience in a rich and fertile region of the Nile delta, and that neither they nor their forefathers had ever been true desert nomads in the modern Bedouin sense.[54] It is quite possible that some of the legislative elements of the

---

[52] A. Alt, *Die Ursprünge des israelitischen Rechts* (1934), p. 24.

[53] R. H. Pfeiffer, *Harvard Theological Review*, XXIII (1931), pp. 99ff.; *PIOT*, p. 211.

[54] Cf. K. A. Kitchen, *The Tyndale House Bulletin*, Nos. 5-6 (1960), pp. 13f.

Covenant Code had been formulated during the period when the Hebrews were living in the land of Goshen, while others may have
emerged from the sojourn at Kadesh and even in Transjordan to represent the nucleus of material relating to social behavior that was thoroughly Mosaic in character and origin. What is clear is the fact that
there was certainly no need for the Israelites to be settled in Canaan
before such laws and regulations could be promulgated.

The contents of the Covenant Code in its extant form can be analyzed
as follows:

I. The General Form of Israelite Worship, 20:22-26
II. Civil Legislation, 21:1–23:13
    A. The rights of slaves, 21:2-6, 7-11
    B. The principle of *lex talionis*, 21:12-32
    C. Laws concerning property, 21:33-36
    D. Laws concerning theft, 22:1-4
    E. Laws concerning property damage, 22:5-6
    F. Laws concerning dishonesty, 22:7-15
    G. Laws concerning seduction, 22:16-17
    H. Laws involving social and religious obligations, 22:18-31
    I. Protection of rights, 23:1-13
III. Ceremonial Legislation Dealing with the Three Principal Feasts,
      23:14-19
IV. The Relation of the Covenant God to His People, 23:20-33

The principle upon which the laws in the Book of the Covenant were
arranged is not immediately apparent. The case-laws present affinities
with the codes of Ur-Nammu, Lipit-Ishtar, Hammurabi, and Eshunna, as
well as with certain aspects of Hittite legislation, although they also
reflect consistently a simpler way of life. It has been suggested also that
the Covenant Code can be divided up into sections, each of which falls
within the scope of one of the ten commandments to comprise a "running Midrash to the Decalogue,"[55] though to what extent this was the
intention of the compiler is uncertain at present.

5. *Sinai and the Wilderness wanderings.* Brief mention ought to be
made in passing of the problems associated with the location of Mount
Sinai, which have been a matter of considerable debate since the mountain itself has not been identified with absolute accuracy. Suggested
peaks have included Jebel Mūsa ("mount of Moses"), the neighboring
Ras eṣ-Ṣafṣafeh, Jebel Serbāl, or a volcanic mountain near al-Hrob. The
latter two are improbable on topographical grounds, while the tradition
associated with Jebel Mūsa only goes back to the pilgrimage of Silvia

[55] E. Robertson, *The OT Problem* (1950), p. 95. Cf. A. E. Guilding, *JTS*, XLIX
(1948), pp. 43ff.; H. Cazelles, *Études sur le Code de l'Alliance* (1946).

(*ca.* A.D. 388) and the time of Justinian (A.D. 527-565). The peaks of the mountain itself are somewhat smaller than those of neighboring ones to the west, south, and east. Against the claim of Ras eṣ-Ṣafṣafeh is the lack of tradition specifying it as a holy place, despite the presence at its foot of a large plain which could have accommodated the Israelite tribes. While Sinai was also called Horeb ("wilderness") in the Old Testament, this usage unfortunately throws no light upon the topographical problem. Many modern scholars follow ancient tradition in identifying Mount Sinai with Jebel Mūsa, which has its own small though elevated plain, and thus could have witnessed the events connected with the lawgiving.

The exact route followed by the Israelites in their journey from the Reed Sea to the edge of Moabite territory is still largely a matter for speculation, because few if any Israelite names of sites as recorded in the Pentateuchal narratives have survived in the late Arabic nomenclature of the Sinai peninsula. Despite this drawback, however, the traditional route is certainly feasible in entertaining the idea of a journey from the Yam Suph along the western coastal strip of the Sinai peninsula to Marah, generally identified with 'Ain Hawrah, and Elim, identified with the Wadi Gharandel.

That the subsequent camp was still in the area south of the Yam Suph (Num. 33:10) indicates clearly that the Israelites had not followed the northern or "Philistine" route, as earlier scholars suggested. Dophkah, situated outside the Wilderness of Sin, has been regarded as a "smeltery,"[56] and identified with Serabit el-Khadem, but in actual fact it could well be any copper-mining area of the metalliferous sandstone belt that extends across south-central Sinai, and which also favors a southerly route for the Exodus. There appears to be little doubt that Kadesh is to be identified with 'Ain Qudeirat, which is preferable on topographical grounds to the common association of Kadesh with 'Ain Qudeis, lying some five miles to the southeast. However, it is highly probable that during the thirty-eight-year stay of the Israelites at Kadesh, the facilities for water and vegetation afforded by 'Ain Qudeis and other oases in the region were utilized to the full.

While there are numerous problems of identification connected with the narratives of the Wilderness wanderings as preserved in Numbers 20:22ff. and 33:38ff.,[57] some of the incidents during that period furnish an accurate reflection of the natural phenomena of the region. Clearly the Israelites were familiar with the water-retaining capacities of Sinai limestone (Exod. 17:1ff.; Num. 20:2ff.), and the digging of wells indicates an awareness of the presence of water immediately below the

[56] *WBA*, p. 64; *WHAB*, p. 39.
[57] Cf. J. D. Davis and H. S. Gehman, *Westminster Dictionary of the Bible* (1944), pp. 638f.

surface of the ground in various areas of Sinai, the Negeb, and southern Transjordan (Num. 21:16ff.). The incidence of quail (Exod. 16:13 Num. 11:31ff.) furnishes some topographical hints as to the route of the Exodus, for since the birds were caught in the spring and during the evening, it is evident that they were returning in their normal migratory pattern to Europe across the upper limits of the Gulfs of Aqabah and Suez. This again supports, rather incidentally, a southerly direction for the Exodus.[58]

6. *The Tabernacle.* An important section of Exodus (chapters 25–31) deals with the instructions for the making and equipping of a portable shrine known as the Tabernacle, the place where the congregation of Israel could meet for worship and divine guidance. It contained, among other sacred objects, the richly ornamented acacia-wood Ark of the Covenant.[59] The evidence from Egypt for ancient prefabricated structures employed in cultic and other connections has been examined earlier in this book. All that need be said at this juncture is that such evidence antedates the very late and inexact parallels afforded by the pre-Islamic *qubbāh*, a miniature red leather tent with a dome-shaped top, which was utilized for carrying the idols and cultic objects of the tribe.[60] It also refutes decisively the charges of late fantasy or unrealism commonly held by the Wellhausen school, which are still entertained by some scholars.[61] The demonstrable antiquity of such prefabricated shrines is, in fact, a fundamental criticism of the Wellhausenian position and in the light of the available evidence it is captious to refuse the Tabernacle and the Ark of the Covenant a Mosaic date, particularly since, as Albright has remarked,[62] they were completely foreign to sedentary Canaanite practice, and in any event are known to have persisted for some time after the conquest of Palestine.

The instructions for the manufacture of the Tabernacle were in the nature of being general records rather than constituting a detailed plan and this makes for a certain lack of precision in the overall description. Thus the information furnished in Exodus makes it difficult to decide whether the Tabernacle proper had a flat, somewhat sagging drapery roof, or one which was tentlike in shape with a ridge-pole and a sloping roof.[63] Again, in the light of the general nature of the specifications

[58] Contrary to C. S. Jarvis, *Yesterday and Today in Sinai* (1931), pp. 169f.; Gray, *VT*, IV (1954), pp. 148ff.; *WBA*, p. 65; *BHI*, p. 114.

[59] Cf. A. R. S. Kennedy, *HDB*, IV, pp. 653ff.; F. M. Cross, *BA*, IX, No. 3 (1947) pp. 55, 60; D. W. Gooding, *The Account of the Tabernacle* (1959); K. A. Kitchen *The Tyndale House Bulletin*, Nos. 5-6 (1960), pp. 7ff., *NBD*, pp. 1231ff.

[60] Cf. J. Morgenstern, *HUCA*, XVII (1942), pp. 153ff., XVIII (1943-44), pp. 1ff.

[61] E.g. A. Bentzen, *Introduction to the OT*, II, p. 34.

[62] *FSAC*, p. 266.

[63] R. K. Harrison in the *Zondervan Pictorial Bible Dictionary* (1963), p. 822.

there is no valid ground for assuming that the text relating to the altar of incense and the laver (Exod. 30:1-10, 17-21) is dislocated, as some scholars of an earlier generation maintained. Instead, there is every reason to suppose that the present order is both original and deliberate.[64]

Some of the archaic technical terms associated with the Tabernacle merit a degree of consideration at this juncture. The designation אֹהֶל מוֹעֵד (Exod. 33:7) or "tent of meeting" was first applied to a structure that antedated the Tabernacle proper. It was pitched outside the camp, and Joshua was its sole attendant (Exod. 33:11) in the absence of a recognized and regularized priestly order. Apparently its function was that of a place of revelation, where the people met with God. The word מוֹעֵד has been discovered in an Egyptian document dated about 1100 B.C., referring to an assembly of the citizens of Byblos, and the term occurs again in Isaiah 14:13, where the reference is to the assembly of the gods in the remote northern regions, a popular theme in Canaanite pagan writings.

There seems no doubt, therefore, that the "tent of meeting" or the "tabernacle of the congregation" referred to in Exodus 33 was an interim structure, based upon the pattern of a simple desert shrine, and combining political and social functions with the religious revelation given by God to His covenanted assembly. The critical view that alleged that there was a discrepancy between the primitive "tent of meeting" of the older E source and the elaborate, unhistorical structure of the later P material was based upon the interpretation rather than the factual content of the Hebrew text, and in the light of the evidence for the Tabernacle as an historical structure it must be dismissed as pure fantasy.

The word מִשְׁכָּן, commonly used to designate the Tabernacle, is related to the ordinary Canaanite term for "dwelling-place" (mšknt), and meant originally "a tent," thus reflecting the nomadic background of the Tabernacle-worship generally. A related verb, שָׁכַן (A.V. "dwell") was employed to describe God as "tabernacled" with men (Exod. 25:8; 29:45),[65] a usage found in a number of ancient Semitic writings, which means "to encamp." The sense was that of God revealing Himself on earth in the midst of His chosen people, and as such was clearly distinguished from the use of the verb יָשַׁב, "to dwell," "inhabit," which was only employed in the Old Testament of God dwelling in heaven.

Exodus is a remarkable testimony to the saving acts of a God who has revealed Himself as the supreme Lord of nature and history alike. The central theme of this fundamentally important section of the Torah is the

[64] A. H. Finn, *JTS*, XVI (1915), pp. 449ff.; cf. his *The Unity of the Pentateuch* (1928 ed.), pp. 444f., 467.

[65] Cf. John 1:14, ἐσκήνωσεν ἐν ἡμῖν.

demonstration of power inherent in the divine deliverance of Israel from bondage in Egypt. However, the Exodus itself was no isolated act, for in conjunction with the Covenant relationship it furnished the emotional and spiritual basis for the conviction that the new nation was in fact the Chosen People of God.

The Hebrew text of Exodus is surprisingly free from transcriptional errors, although there has apparently been some confusion between similar letters in the ancient script, as in Exodus 23:25 and 34:19. The text of Exodus 1:16 is obscure, primarily because the meaning of the phrase וראיתן על-האבנים was lost at an early period, and there is also some uncertainty as to how Exodus 32:29 is to be translated in view of the divergences between the MT and some of the ancient versions.

Supplementary Literature

Allis, O. T. *God Spake by Moses.* 1951.
Finegan, Jack. *Let My People Go: A Journey Through Exodus.* 1963.
Gressmann, H. *Mose und seine Zeit.* 1913.
Jepsen, A. *Untersuchungen zum Bundesbuch.* 1927.
Kyle, M. G. *Moses and the Monuments.* 1920.
Lucas, A. *The Route of the Exodus of the Israelites from Egypt.* 1938.
Mowinckel, Sigmund. *Le Decalogue.* 1927.
Noth, M. *Die Gesetze im Pentateuch.* 1940.
von Rad, G. *Moses.* 1960.
Volter, D. *Mose und die aegyptische Mythologie.* 1912.
de Wit, C. *The Date and Route of the Exodus.* 1960.

IV. THE BOOK OF LEVITICUS

A. NAME AND OUTLINE

The third book of the Torah is referred to in Jewish usage as ויקרא, "and he called," the word with which it begins. In the Mishnah its contents were described by such terms as "priests' law," "priests' book," and "law of the offerings." In the LXX it bore the title *Leuitikon* or *Leueitikon,* an adjective qualifying the word *Biblion* ("book"), that is, the Levitical Book. This was rendered as *Leviticus* in the Vulgate; from this the English title is taken. The book itself is a collection of enactments intended to constitute the legal basis for the organized civil and religious life of the Chosen People. These laws were largely ritual, since it was naturally of considerable importance for the Israelites to be acquainted with the regulations concerning worship at the Tabernacle. At the same time it must be noted that the place Leviticus occupies in the Pentateuchal corpus exhibits the clear intention of the compiler to continue the narrative of the experiences at Sinai and to relate the legislation to the role of Israel as a witness to the power of God in human affairs. The name indicates that the legal corpus was the general responsibility of the cultus, and that the contents were the particular concern of the Levitical priesthood.

Leviticus can be subdivided into sections and analyzed as follows:

I. The Law of Sacrifice, ch. 1–7
  A. The burnt offering, 1:1-17
  B. The meal or cereal offering, 2:1-16
  C. The peace offering, 3:1-17
  D. The sin offering, 4:1–5:13
  E. The guilt offering, 5:14-19
  F. Conditions necessitating atonement, 6:1-7
  G. Burnt offerings, 6:8-13
  H. Cereal offerings, 6:14-23

I. Sin offerings, 6:24-30
J. Regulations concerning guilt offering, 7:1-10
K. Regulations for peace offering, 7:11-21
L. Prohibition of fat and blood, 7:22-27
M. Further regulations concerning peace offering, 7:28-38

II. The Consecration of Priests, ch. 8—10
   A. Preparation for anointing, 8:1-5
   B. The anointing ceremony, 8:6-13
   C. The consecration sacrifice, 8:14-36
   D. Instructions concerning sin offering, 9:1-7
   E. Entering of the Aaronides upon their office, 9:8-24
   F. The fate of Nadab and Abiram, 10:1-7
   G. Prohibitions concerning drunkenness of priests, 10:8-11
   H. Rules concerning the eating of consecrated food, 10:12-20

III. The Clean and Unclean, ch. 11—15
   A. Clean and unclean species, 11:1-47
   B. Purification after childbirth, 12:1-8
   C. Laws concerning leprosy, 13:1—14:57
   D. Purification after secretions, 15:1-33

IV. The Day of Atonement, ch. 16

V. Ritual Laws, ch. 17—25
   A. The blood of sacrifice, 17:1-16
   B. Religious and ethical laws and punishments, 18:1—20:27
   C. Canons of priestly holiness, 21:1—22:33
   D. Consecration of seasons, 23:1—24:23
   E. Sabbatical and jubilee years, 25:1-55

VI. Promises, Warning, and Appendix, ch. 26—27

As is apparent from the foregoing analysis, the contents of Leviticus fall within the purview of ritual law. This corpus, however, is a remarkably self-contained unit comprising two basic themes whose focal point is the chapter dealing with the Day of Atonement (Lev. 16). The first major emphasis occupies Leviticus 1—15, and can be said to be concerned with the removal of the defilement that separates men from God. The second broad consideration, taken up in the final eleven chapters of the book, is that of the means by which the disrupted fellowship between man and God can be restored. This general structure is not wholly dissimilar to the bifid nature of Isaiah and Daniel, for example, and it ought to be recognized as mechanical in the sense that the priestly material in Leviticus was arranged to conform to this kind of pattern.

Leviticus is composed of technical cultic material that was the prerogative of the priesthood, in contrast to Deuteronomy, which is a popular exposition of the more esoteric priestly writings and is related more specifically to the idea of the Covenant obligations. Furthermore, Leviticus contains certain unique prescriptions involving, for example, such widely different aspects of life as the Day of Atonement and the regulations concerning leprosy, which do not occur in any other ancient Near Eastern religious corpus.

B. DATE AND AUTHORSHIP

The priestly nature of the material in Leviticus affords important evidence for its probable date. In antiquity, all forms of education were under the supervision of the priesthood, a tradition that was established by the Sumerians.[1] Various branches of the priesthood were responsible for the different specialized areas of professional training, whether in the fields of law, the cultus, medicine, civil administration, the diplomatic service, and so on. In these major areas the procedural canons upon which the profession depended were generally committed to writing at a very early period, and following the conservatism of Sumeria they invariably remained almost completely unchanged. Of course, they were enriched over the centuries by means of additions to the basic corpus, and new material, faithfully modeled upon the old, appeared from time to time. However, the weight of Sumerian tradition was such that it formed alike the religious and secular basis for the whole of Mesopotamia and some of the lands beyond, so that, for example, the literary and liturgical forms of Akkad leaned heavily upon their Sumerian precursors, while the various types of law in the Near East reflected closely the traditions of the Sumerians. One of the principal reasons why the literature of that virile people has survived at all is that the pupils in the scribal schools copied out assiduously earlier literary sources instead of occupying themselves by and large with what would now be known as "creative writing."

Much the same can be said for ancient Egypt, where a great deal of the literature basic to the various professions came from a very early date. The so-called "Pyramid Texts" actually go back to the third millennium B.C., as does the Memphite theology, which magnified the deity Ptah as the First Cause. Early dating of professional sources and texts is also evident in Egyptian medicine, which attained to a definitely higher level than that of the Babylonians, particularly in the early days of the Old Kingdom period. While the four principal medical papyri are assigned roughly to the middle of the second millennium B.C.,[2] this only represents the date established on philological and other grounds for the particular papyrus manuscript under consideration, and does not refer to

---

[1] Cf. J. Kaster, *IDB*, II, pp. 27ff.
[2] The Edwin Smith surgical papyrus (*ca.* 1600 B.C.), the Ebers papyrus (*ca.* 1500), the Hearst papyrus (*ca.* 1500), and the Berlin papyrus 3038 (*ca.* 1290 B.C.).

the contents of the various documents in terms of provenance, which long antedated their written form. There seems little doubt that a good deal of traditional Egyptian medicine reaches back to the third millennium B.C., and that it was given stature by Imhotep (*ca.* 2650 B.C.), the chief minister, architect, and physician of Djoser, from whom a great many medical and other traditions descended.

The scribal practices of the ancient Near East point to a custom of preserving at an early stage those sources of information or procedure that were of importance to the particular profession. As regards cultic functionaries, the liturgies and rituals that they utilized were committed to writing and treasured in one form or another for many succeeding centuries. They were not transmitted down the ages in an oral form before emerging in their written state, as the modern oral-traditionists imagine. The primary purpose of oral usage was to afford the material in question widespread contemporary dissemination, and any other interpretation of the situation places a wrong emphasis upon the oral element in ancient Near Eastern usage. This contention is supported, as observed above, by the religious rituals and incantations from the third-millennium B.C. texts in the pyramids of Unis, Teti, and Pepi I (Fifth to Sixth Dynasties) at Saqqarah as well as by the third-millennium B.C. Sumerian religious texts, divine hymns, and mythological compositions from Ur, Nippur, and elsewhere. Equally important, whereas the Egyptian material, which was written on papyrus, was revised from time to time by various generations of scribes, the Sumerian literature has been handed down as it was actually written by the ancient copyists, unmodified and uncodified by later compilers and commentators.

Where specifically priestly traditions of an esoteric nature are concerned, and especially where they related to the cultus rather than to some other sphere of priestly activity such as government service or administration, the founding traditions of Mesopotamia and Egypt alike point to an early written recording of this kind of material. The fact that it may have been of a rather restricted character meant that it was generally only accessible to responsible persons who might or might not revise it, add to it, or compare with it other enactments, rituals, or similar prescriptions for particular usage. In general, however, it remains true that whereas Egyptian scribes undertook the revision of many ancient documents at specific times, their Mesopotamian counterparts preferred to transmit the material at hand much as they themselves had received it.

In the light of the available evidence it is therefore clear that one of the most egregious errors ever committed by the members of the Graf-Wellhausen school was to assign the Priestly Code, and particularly that portion of it which comprised Leviticus, to the post-exilic period, despite the assertions of Kuenen and a few other scholars that there might possibly be earlier material in the code as a whole. If the Graf-

Wellhausen school had been less obsessed with its determination to introduce law and order into the Pentateuchal compositional situation, whatever the cost, and had been prepared to be influenced by facts even as they were then known and available, the result would almost certainly have been to date the P material early rather than late, a conclusion that has finally been arrived at by one or two of the more perceptive liberal scholars.[3]

With regard to the questions relating to the authorship and compilation of Leviticus, the author is nowhere named in the composition as being responsible for a part or the whole of the work. This is quite different from the situation obtaining in Exodus, where Moses was named specifically as the author of certain sections of the work (cf. Exod. 17:14; 24:4; 34:27). Leviticus includes material from the revelation at Sinai (Lev. 7:37f.; 26:46; 27:34), but this, of course, does not answer the question of authorship. While it is possible that an editor or writer of a later generation arranged the Mosaic traditions in the order in which they are extant in Leviticus, there is also an equal possibility that the contents of the book were organized into something like their present order during the lifetime of Moses. If the priestly traditions of the ancient Near East mean anything at all, this would certainly have been the case for the prescriptions relating to the various offerings, the consecration of the priesthood, and the ceremonies involving the Day of Atonement, as well as for the unique specifications concerning hygiene.

The theories of the Graf-Wellhausen school concerning ancient Hebrew sacrifice were crystallized by Wellhausen, who laid down the principle that the sense of sin in Israelite sacrifice was a decidedly late development.[4] This view, modified somewhat as it was by later followers of Wellhausen, was effectively disproved by R. J. Thompson.[5] One of the most fundamental postulates in the Wellhausenian reconstruction of Israelite religion was swept away in this manner, and with it the necessity for ascribing the so-called P material to the post-exilic period. If it is legitimate to assume that the prescriptions concerning the sacrificial ritual and the ordering of the priesthood are as ancient as the traditions of the Hebrews would suggest, it is also permissible to think in analogous terms of other distinctive sections of Leviticus such as the laws governing hygiene. The distinction between clean and unclean animals (Lev. 11:1-47) has no parallel whatever in ancient life, particularly since the legislation in question is founded upon dietary principles unknown elsewhere in the Near East. If these precepts had emerged from the post-exilic period, as critical scholarship has long maintained, there would be

---

[3] E.g. Y. Kaufmann, ZAW, XLVIII (1930), pp. 22ff., VT, IV (1954), pp. 307ff., *The Religion of Israel* (tr. Greenberg, 1960), pp. 175ff. Cf. GBB, p. 293 n. 1.

[4] *Prolegomena to the History of Israel*, p. 81.

[5] *Penitence and Sacrifice in Early Israel Outside the Levitical Law* (1963).

clear indications in the text of the kind of situation that obtained in contemporary Babylonian medicine, where the empiricism of the code of Hammurabi had long succumbed to the influence of the magical practices inherent for many centuries in Mesopotamian therapeutics.

As it is, the dietary prescriptions are firmly grounded in attested procedures (Lev. 11:3f., 9f.), and it is to these, rather than to considerations of magic and sorcery, or the place that the proscribed species occupied in pagan religious practices, that the contents of the hygienic code must be related. Since highly organized medical material of various kinds was known both in Babylonia and Egypt from at least the second millennium B.C. onwards, there is no *a priori* reason why the hygienic code of Leviticus cannot be confidently credited to its attributive author Moses. In view of the tenacity with which this code was held in subsequent ages it is difficult to see how it could have emerged from a period subsequent to that of Moses without being recognized and dismissed as patently spurious and fraudulent. Nor is there valid ground for drawing a significant distinction in point of time between the antiquity of the tradition itself and the written form in which it has been preserved, for there is no specific element in the prescriptions that requires a date later than the end of the Amarna period.

The same may be said about the section containing the laws governing leprosy (Lev. 13:1–14:57), which are recorded in considerable detail. The passage is an obvious unity, and deals in a manner unprecedented in antiquity with one of the most urgent medical problems of the Near East. Precisely where leprosy originated is unknown, but it was certainly a familiar affliction in Mesopotamia and the countries of the Orient generally as far back as the third millennium B.C. Evidence for the existence of the ailment in Egypt is very scanty, and in any event needs critical appraisal before any conclusions can be drawn from it.

As with all medical functions in antiquity, it was the task of one particular branch of the priesthood to discharge the diagnostic and therapeutic procedures. The organization of the material in the section under discussion is similar to that of comparable ancient medical sources from the Near East, except that there is no hint whatever of the influence or authority of magic. The techniques are empirical in the best sense of that term: the symptoms are considered with a view to the possibility of differential diagnosis and the therapy enjoined is based upon the principle of prevention rather than attempts at radical cure, doubtful herbal therapy, or other similar procedures. Again, had the contents of this section originated in the post-exilic period, or even been edited at that time from ancient traditions, it is not easy to see how the material could possibly have escaped all traces of the demonism that had come to constitute the frame of reference alike for contemporary pathology and therapeutics. Yet this section, like other unique enactments in the book of Leviticus, reflects with complete fidelity the Sinai ideal of the one, supreme, all-powerful deity who repudiated the existence of pagan gods, denied the validity and authority of magical practices, and expressly prohibited their usage in any area of Hebrew life.

It is difficult to see how the regulations concerning leprosy could have arisen from any other than the Mosaic period without arousing the gravest of suspicions on the part of the priesthood, whose duty it was to safeguard and administer them. Since the section under discussion is a manifest unity, there seems to be no adequate reason for supposing that it did not represent for the ancient Hebrews what the early medical enactments of Egypt and Mesopotamia did for their particular cultures; and there is no cause to deny that it is genuine, original, and untroubled by subsequent scribal revision, since none would be necessary in the nature of the case.

Whereas the passages concerning dietary regulations and the diagnosis of leprosy could be related equally well to a semi-nomadic or an urban milieu, the narratives involving the Day of Atonement (Lev. 16:1-34) can only be envisaged against an original desert scene. The Tabernacle, with its furnishings and priesthood, dominated the religious situation; the people were described in terms of an encampment, and when the live goat had been made the recipient of national sins of inadvertence by symbolic imposition of hands, it was driven out into the wilderness. The origin of this event is too securely guarded by Hebrew tradition to be assigned to any other period than that of Moses, and the narrative description in which it is couched exhibits a freshness and vitality that could hardly be the work of one who composed it many centuries after its initial occurrence.

These observations should not be taken as contending that Leviticus was necessarily written on one occasion or within a very short interval of time, any more than might be the case with many other important pieces of legislation in antiquity. While the final unity of the composition makes it difficult to assess the manner of compilation, it may be possible as a result of close inspection to discern some of the stages by which the book reached its extant form. In the first instance it might well be that the introductory formula, "And the Lord spoke unto Moses (and Aaron) saying..." is a stereotyped way of introducing a fresh element in the revelation, which might have been recorded on a separate section of leather and joined with other similar sections after having been sorted and classified.[6]

[6] Cf. J. S. Wright, *EQ*, XXV (1953), p. 14. This would imply that some of the component sections of the book included Lev. 1:1–3:17; 4:1–5:13; 5:14-19; 5:20-26 (Heb.); 6:1-11 (Heb.); 6:12-16 (Heb.); 6:17–7:21 (Heb.); 7:22-38; 8:1–10:20; 11:1-47; 12:1-8; 13:1-59; 14:1-32; 14:33-57; 15:1-33; 16:1-34; 17:1-16; 18:1-30; 19:1-37; 20:1-27; 21:1-24; 22:1-16; 22:17-25; 22:26-33; 23:1-8; 23:9-22; 23:23-25; 23:26-32; 23:33-44; 24:1-23; 25:1–26:46; and 27:1-34. Such sections might have

Another example of the homogeneity of the work occurs in connection with the prohibitions concerning the eating of blood. This particular ban was first imposed in Leviticus 3:17, along with the prohibition of fat, and was renewed in Leviticus 7:26, where blood alone, whether that of animals or fowls, was specifically forbidden to be consumed. But in Leviticus 17:11 the rationale of the procedure previously enjoined without particular explanation was made plain in the stated relationship between the living flesh and its nutrient stream.

It is in the light of this pronouncement that the rituals associated with the shedding and sprinkling of sacrificial blood as contained in the first seven chapters of Leviticus have to be assessed theologically, thus making for a unity of thought in these sections. Once again, this is not to say that they were necessarily written on one and the same occasion, for it is probable that some interval of time elapsed before the various pronouncements were transcribed and assembled. On the other hand, it is important to recognize the originality and antiquity of the pronouncements, formulating as they did the basic attitudes of the ancient Hebrews towards sacrifice.

In precisely the same manner there are two links in the first seven chapters of Leviticus with the regulations concerning impurity, dealt with in some detail in chapters eleven to fifteen. In Leviticus 5:2 and 7:21, there is a pronouncement that deals with the ceremonial condition of impurity, acquired as the result of contact with an unclean thing or a prohibited rite, and with the status of the offender as a consequence. This situation was clarified in Leviticus 11:26f., a passage that contains the principles underlying the concepts of uncleanness and explains the extent to which the defilement is pervasive. This situation constitutes no mere literary accident, but it is rather a deliberate attempt to introduce homogeneity into the interpretation of the book as a whole.

---

comprised certain portions of the divine revelation given to Moses at various times during the period of Wilderness wanderings, and subsequently assembled according to suitability of topic, perhaps with some editorial changes in the interests of continuity. There is no guarantee that the foregoing suggested analysis into what appear to be component parts represents the actual facts of the compilatory situation, and it is only postulated on the assumption, which may be entirely gratuitous, that the introductory phrase in each case is a technical heading carried by the various units that were assembled to comprise the whole. Nor is there any means of knowing whether or not certain of these units were joined together in a subsection of the extant work and permitted to enjoy independent local circulation for some time. It may well be that the regulations concerning offerings (1:1–7:38) had once been in existence in priestly circles as a separate unit to constitute a manual of procedure. This appears to be indicated by the fact that Lev. 7:35-38 constitutes some kind of colophon which includes the titles of the various conjoined sections, attestation of ownership, and the date and place of the enactments. Yet whether this is actually the case or not, the section has been accommodated remarkably well to the overall pattern of the book of Leviticus.

From the standpoint of purely historical continuity, it might appear that chapters 11–15 constitute a block of material inserted haphazardly into a place where one portion of leather roll may have followed another, since Leviticus 10:20 concludes the incidents consequent upon the death of the sons of Aaron, and Leviticus 16:1 picks up the thread of the historical narrative once more at that precise point. However, it has already been noticed that the chronicler or historian has always to decide whether he is to follow the time-sequence dictated by the events themselves, to arrange his history in terms of topics or subjects, or to compromise between the two methods of approach. The latter procedure appears to have been adopted here, for while chapters 11–15 evidently constitute an insertion, they are by no means inimical to the organizational unity of Leviticus, being firmly integrated into the pattern of the whole by means of the antecedent references in Leviticus 5:2 and 7:21. This contention is further reinforced by the fact that the prescription in Leviticus 10:10 can be interpreted in the light of the detailed differentiation between clean and unclean species as contained in chapter 11. On such a basis there can be no serious doubt as to the suitability of chapters 11–15 for inclusion in the text of Leviticus in their present position, for when viewed in the light of the work as a whole the regulations dealing with purity and impurity demonstrate how necessary it was for the Israelites to impose a barrier between themselves and sin.

In a pattern of reversed parallelism that is not entirely unknown in bifid literary compositions,[7] there is a reference in Leviticus 20:25 to the regulations of chapter 11 which deal in detail with clean and unclean species. This verse thus serves to integrate the commandments of chapters 18 to 20 with those found in chapters 11 to 15, thus further preserving the coherence of the book. This principle of integration casts considerable doubt upon the supposedly separate existence of chapters 17 to 26, the so-called "Law of Holiness," as maintained by the members of the critical school. The designation of "Holiness Code" (H) was first applied to this material by A. Klostermann in 1877,[8] and it was subsequently taken over by Wellhausen[9] and his followers. Some of the latter detected instances of agreement with Ezekiel, another bifid composition, and promptly assigned the "Code" to a post-exilic date, evidently ignoring the possibility that Ezekiel was reflecting statements from the Torah in his utterances.

Be that as it may, there are clear traces of deliberate attempts to integrate chapters 17 to 26 into the narrative of Leviticus as a whole.

---

[7] Compare the tentative parallelisms of Isaiah as listed by W. H. Brownlee in *The Meaning of the Qumrân Scrolls for the Bible*, pp. 247ff.

[8] Cf. his later work, *Der Pentateuch: Beiträge zu seinem Verständnis und seiner Entstehungsgeschichte* (1893), pp. 368ff.

[9] *Die Composition des Hexateuchs* (1889), pp. 151ff.

Thus in Leviticus 21:1–22:16, expressions like those which occur in Leviticus 11:44f., 19:2 and 20:7 are repeated with reference to the ceremonial condition of the priests. Even if this section originally enjoyed independent existence for a time—a view that is by no means as assured as critical scholars have imagined in the past—it is rather doubtful if chapter 25 was ever part of such a combination of literary prescriptions. The reference in Leviticus 25:1 indicates that the following material relating to the sabbath of the land and the jubilee was revealed to Moses by God on Mount Sinai, just as was the case with the colophon in Leviticus 7:35ff., making it difficult to see how either of these two enactments could have been a post-exilic priestly invention, as was suggested by an earlier generation of critical scholarship. It seems well within the bounds of probability, therefore, that chapter 25 may have constituted an insertion into material which in other respects was concerned with canons of holiness, and as such it may not have comprised part of any original "Holiness Code" at all. This is not to imply, of course, that the prescriptions concerning the jubilee belong necessarily to any other period than that of Moses, a matter which in any event is scarcely an issue, since many modern liberal scholars, along with a few of their earlier counterparts, have conceded the ancient nature of the jubilee enactments.

A literary mosaic such as Leviticus is seldom easy to disentangle, particularly in view of the fact that the extant work has been compiled with consummate editorial skill into a literary and theological unity. Equally difficult is the task of resolving supposedly component elements into some sort of chronological sequence, even on the assumption that this would be necessary or desirable in an oriental composition. Whatever shades of critical opinion most writers espouse, all are agreed that Leviticus is essentially a priestly document. In the light of the evidence afforded by Near Eastern literary sources generally, it would seem prudent to assign the composition of the work to an earlier rather than a later date, and, if the Mosaic ascriptions and historical allusions found in the text are as genuine as they purport to be, to envisage the recording of the material, subject to possible minor revisions, within an interval of no more than a few years from the time when it was first promulgated in oral form.

C. THE MATERIAL OF LEVITICUS

1. The sacrificial system. From a great many standpoints Leviticus is fundamental to any understanding of the Biblical revelation to man. Not the least significant of these is the meaning of the work for the religious institutions of Israel in general, and for the sacrificial system in particular. While regulations governing sacrifice can be found scattered throughout the Pentateuch (e.g. Exod. 20:24ff.; 34:25ff.; Num. 15:1ff.; Deut. 12:6ff.), the sacrificial Torah as such comprises Leviticus 1–7. As observed above, the material offerings were required to conform to certain canons of cleanness, and were restricted to particular species of animals and birds.

The general principle undergirding the concept of an offering appears to have been that of property (2 Sam. 24:24), so that whereas it was legitimate to sacrifice domesticated animals and birds, which were in a sense the property of man through his own enterprise, it was not deemed permissible for wild animals to be sacrificed, since they were regarded as already belonging to God (cf. Ps. 50:10). The basic theme of property was even more evident in the case of vegetable and cereal offerings, which had been produced as a result of human labor. An extension of this principle related to property that had been acquired unlawfully; this also was unacceptable as a sacrifice to God (Deut. 23:18).

In accordance with the belief that only the very best of the species could constitute a legitimate offering, the male was generally preferred to the female; in any case matters of physical perfection and maturity were consistently emphasized. The economic state of individuals or families was considered sympathetically in the tariffs to the point where the poor were permitted to substitute a cheaper offering for a more expensive one. The earliest attestable public sacrifices were the feast of unleavened bread, with which the Passover had been linked by the time of the settlement period (Josh. 5:10ff.), the feast of weeks or firstfruits (Pentecost), and the feast of tabernacles (Exod. 23:14ff.; 34:18ff.; Deut. 16:1ff.). With the last of these there may have been associated certain rites connected with the renewal of the Covenant (cf. Deut. 31:10ff.; Josh. 24:1ff.). Additional public and private festal observances were also provided for in the Torah (cf. Num. 28:1ff.; 29:1ff.).

The major altar offerings described in Leviticus 1–5 followed a stereotyped ritual pattern of six acts, of which the worshipper executed three and the priest performed three.[10] In the individual rite the worshipper brought his sacrificial offering to the Tabernacle forecourt, laid his hand upon it in a manner implying that it represented the offerer himself, and then slaughtered the animal. On the occasion of a public communal sacrifice the animal was killed by a priest, the sacrificial blood was collected in a basin by the officiant and spattered against the four sides of the altar. In the case of small offerings such as birds, the diminished quantity of available blood was drained out beside the altar. Some portion of the sacrifice, including specified areas of fat, was then burned, and this procedure was even applied to cereal offerings. When a burnt offering was sacrificed, however, the entire animal was consumed by fire except for the hide, which became a priestly perquisite (Lev. 7:8). The remaining portions of the sacrifice were then eaten as a meal, either by

---

[10] R. J. Thompson, *NBD*, p. 1117.

the priests and worshippers together as with the peace offering, by the priests and their families, or by the priestly caste alone.

The different kinds of offerings can be described briefly as follows:

(a) burnt offering (עלה), apparently the typical Hebrew sacrifice, which became a regular sacrifice at an early period (1 Kgs. 9:25) and remained dominant throughout Old Testament history. The כליל (Deut. 33:10; 1 Sam. 7:9; Ps. 51:19) was basically the same as the עלה, but exhibited some variations.

(b) cereal or meal offering (מנחה), found in the Old Testament either as a present (e.g. Judg. 3:15), as a general reference to sacrifice (e.g. 1 Sam. 2:29; Mal. 2:13), or more specifically to the Levitical cereal offering. The term מנחה carried a propitiatory sense, and was not understood in the rituals generally as a mere "gift." It was frequently, though not invariably, an accompaniment to burnt and peace offerings.

(c) peace offering, generally described in Leviticus by the term זבח שלמים or זבחי שלמים, although זבח and שלמים were sometimes used interchangeably. By itself the שלמים may have constituted an expiatory offering, and when associated with זבח may have formed a rite of propitiation and reconciliation.

(d) guilt or trespass offering (אשם), usually involving ceremonial defilement and associated with such ceremonies as the cleansing of a leper (Lev. 14:1ff.) or the purification of a woman after childbirth (Lev. 12:1ff.).

(e) sin offering (חטאת), similar to the guilt offering in that it involved ceremonial defilement, but as exemplified in the Law it applied to deception or misappropriation (Lev. 6:1ff.) and seduction (Lev. 19:20ff.). The relationship between the two offerings is obscure, but the חטאת seems to have referred more to offenses against God and the אשם to violations of a general social nature.[11]

Since the pagan neighbors of Israel also indulged in sacrificial rites, it is natural to expect certain points of contact in ritual and intent. Excavations at Lachish (Tell ed-Duweir) uncovered the remains of three Canaanite shrines, built between the fifteenth and thirteenth centuries B.C., near to which large quantities of animal bones were found in a pile of debris. On examination most of them were found to have come from the right foreleg of the animal, which corresponds to the prescriptions for Hebrew sacrifice in Leviticus 7:32 and attests to the antiquity of that passage.

[11] On Hebrew sacrifice generally see W. P. Paterson, *HDB*, IV, pp. 329ff.; R. A. S. Macalister, *ERE*, XI, pp. 31ff.; J. J. Reeve, *ISBE*, IV, pp. 2638ff.; S. G. Gayford, *Sacrifice and Priesthood* (1924); W. O. E. Oesterley, *Sacrifices in Ancient Israel* (1937); H. H. Rowley, *The Meaning of Sacrifice* (1950); F. D. Kidner, *Sacrifice in the OT* (1952); R. de Vaux, *Studies in OT Sacrifice* (1964).

An offering analogous to the מנחה was mentioned in a sacrificial tariff from Ugarit;[12] a propitiatory peace offering appears to have been known there also.[13] Votive and tributary offerings were familiar to all the peoples of the ancient Near East,[14] as were schedules of sacrifices, especially in Babylonia.[15] Offerings of firstfruits have been attested from Mesopotamian, Hittite, south Arabic, and Aegean sources.[16] The same is true for the sacrifice of male children in honor of Hadad—recorded in north-Mesopotamian texts from the tenth to the seventh century B.C.— the offerings of children to Molech—described in texts from the Third Dynasty of Ur and in the eighteenth-century B.C. tablets from Mari— and the Aegean custom of passing children through flames in order to augment their strength. Human sacrifice was expressly prohibited among the Hebrews (Lev. 18:21; 2 Kgs. 23:10; Jer. 32:35), but whether the denunciation of the Ammonite deity Molech (Moloch) was a repudiation of genuine human sacrifice or a rejection of Aegean customs of invigoration or of attempting to acquire immortality has been a matter of some debate among scholars.[17]

While pagan and Hebrew sacrificial systems had certain common interests and objectives such as the desire for fellowship with the deity, the provision of atonement for ceremonial defilement, and the assurance of continued divine blessing, the Hebrew enactments were distinctive as the outcome of a unique covenantal relationship. The bond of union between God and Israel, which was forged at Sinai in order to give the nation its distinctive moral and spiritual undergirding and to furnish it with a sense of missionary destiny, was quite unlike anything else of a contractual nature in the ancient Near East.

The concept of divine holiness constituted the essence of the Sinai Covenant, and this factor was emphasized throughout the Pentateuchal legislation as a stated requirement in Israelite life. But whereas the demand that the Hebrews should be a holy nation was based upon the elevated moral and ethical content of the term "holy" (קדשׁ) as exhibited by the divine nature, the pagan neighbors of Israel in their own dealings with local or national deities knew nothing of such advanced religious concepts, and their use of the term generally had refer-

---

[12] *Corpus Inscriptionum Semiticarum*, I, 145.

[13] D. M. L. Urie, *EQ*, LXXXI (1949), pp. 75ff.

[14] Cf. T. H. Gaster, *IDB*, IV, pp. 148ff.

[15] *ANET*, pp. 343ff.

[16] *ARAB*, I, sect. 616f.; *Corpus Inscriptionum Semiticarum*, I, 166.3; *Keilschrifturkunden aus Boghazköi*, XII, 4, iv, 3f.; Isoc. *Panegyr.* 6ff.

[17] E.g. O. Eissfeldt, *Molk als Opferbegriff im Punischen und Hebräischen und das Ende des Gottes Moloch* (1935), opposed by W. Kornfeld, *Wiener Zeitschrift für die Kunde des Morgenlandes* (1952), pp. 287ff., and H. Dronkert, *De Molochdienst in het Oude Testament* (1953).

ence to a person dedicated to the service of a particular deity, as, for example, a cultic prostitute.

In connection with the implementing of covenantal provisions, the ceremonies associated with the annual Day of Atonement (Lev. 16:1-34) were of fundamental importance in Hebrew national life. On the tenth day of the seventh month (September-October) the Israelites observed their most solemn day of obligation. All work was forbidden, and the people were required to observe a strict fast. The High Priest, garbed in simple attire for the occasion, offered sacrifice for the entire priesthood and entered the Most Holy Place in an incense-burning ceremony. Subsequently a male goat was offered as a sacrifice for the people, and some of the blood was taken into the Most Holy Place, where it was sprinkled ceremonially about the Ark.

After purifying the Holy Place (Lev. 16:18f.), the High Priest took a second goat and confessed over it the sins of inadvertence committed by the nation as a whole. This animal was then driven into the desert, where it symbolically carried away the sins of the Israelites. Additional sacrificial rites concluded the ceremonies of the day, which had the effect of reminding Israel that the various sacrifices made at the altar of burnt offering were not of themselves sufficient to atone for sin. Alone of all other sacrificial occasions, the blood was brought into the Most Holy Place by the High Priest as the representative of the people on the solemn Day of Atonement.

The purpose of the sacrificial enactments, as defined in Leviticus, was to effect an "atonement" on behalf of the person offering the sacrifice. The Hebrew verb כפר, "to atone," has been related to the comparatively late Arabic word *kafara*, "to cover"; to the Akkadian term *kuppuru*, "to wipe away," and to the Hebrew noun *kōphēr*, "ransom." The latter best suits the specific purpose of Israelite sacrificial theory as elaborated in Leviticus 17:11, which identified the life with the blood and laid down the principle that the blood "makes atonement by reason of the life" (RSV). The animal victim thus constituted a substitute for the human sinner, and the offering up of its life in sacrifice effected a vicarious atonement for sin. The emphasis of this verse, which is crucial for the interpretation of Hebrew sacrifice, is opposed both to the theory that the death of the victim was only meant to release the life inherent in its blood so that the latter might constitute the atonement and to the view that the death of the animal was a quantitative penal satisfaction. The Hebrew sacrificial system must always be envisaged against a background of the Covenant principle of divine grace, and in this context the emphasis upon the categories of personal relationship is most properly expressed in the theory of substitution, where the chosen victim dies in the place of the human sinner.

It is far from easy to decide from the text if the sacrificial offering was meant to be a propitiation of divine anger as well as an expiation for human sin, for while there are undoubtedly some instances where the verb signifies "propitiation" (Exod. 32:30; Num. 16:41ff.), there are others where it simply means "to cleanse," as with the furnishings of the Tabernacle (Exod. 29:37; Ezek. 43:20). What is clear, however, is that man as a sinner incurs divine wrath, that God has provided the sacrificial system in order that human transgressors might return in penitence to fellowship with Him, and that God graciously permitted the death of a sacrificial victim as a substitute for the death of the sinner.

It should be noted in any study of the Hebrew sacrificial system that it was not by any means a complete and final scheme whereby all forms of sin could be removed. Much of the atonement procedure was concerned with sins of accident, inadvertence, or omission which individuals had committed, and there was no forgiveness for sins of sheer human obduracy (Num. 15:30), which by definition placed a man outside the range of Covenant mercies. Idolatry and apostasy also fell within this general area of self-exclusion from Covenant grace, and in the main it can be stated that for breaches of the Covenant agreement no form of sacrifice was of any avail. It is in the light of this latter consideration that the cultic denunciations of the prophets and their rejection of sacrifice need to be interpreted.

2. *Cleanliness and uncleanliness.* The classification of animal species into clean and unclean categories (Lev. 11:1-47) is significant because, being part of the Pentateuchal medical code, it constituted the basis of dietary regulations that are still adhered to by orthodox Jews and by those Gentiles who are concerned with maintaining good physical health. This categorizing is also important in view of the fact that it is unique in the annals of Near Eastern literature because its emphasis is not so much upon the avoidance of magical practices associated with certain animal species as upon the positive delineation of dietary principles intended to insure the physical well-being of the individual and the nation alike through a consistent prophylactic approach.

It is to be noted, of course, that the provisions of the Sinai revelation repudiated the very idea of magic as an influence in human life, and in this regard the Israelites were once again unique in the ancient world. As an additional safeguard against the taint of this all-pervasive factor in Near Eastern life, the practice of magic in any of its manifold forms was expressly prohibited by the Torah at all levels of Hebrew life. The system of therapeutics and preventive medicine enunciated in the Pentateuch, particularly in Leviticus, was grounded upon an empirical basis, in marked contrast to the approach of contemporary peoples, who were dominated by *a priori* magical considerations and as a result tended invariably to spiritualize pathological phenomena in terms of the activity of demons. The closeness of the relationship between the principles underlying the medical sections of Leviticus and those of the Covenant of Sinai, along with the fact that written medical traditions in the Near East tend invariably to be early rather than late, give strong support for crediting this material to Moses and the Wilderness period of Israelite history.

The Pentateuchal medical code recognized that healthy individual existence involved certain fundamental principles of hygiene that by nature required acceptance at both an intellectual and an emotional level. What was particularly distinctive about this situation was that the differentiation between clean and unclean, permissible and prohibited, was grounded in ethical considerations. The Mosaic law was a decided advance upon pagan concepts of cleanness and uncleanness, in that both these categories were made relative to the idea of holiness as associated with the God of Sinai. However, in the light of both the ceremonial and the therapeutic regulations it is important not to overestimate the nature of cleanness. In itself it could never be considered as the equivalent of holiness, but at best as a rather negative state whose existence implied that a positive holiness was attainable.

The medical code elaborated the principles of hygienic living in terms of seven basic enactments, five of which were contained in Leviticus and the remaining two elsewhere in the Torah. These were the sabbath for individuals (Lev. 23:3, et al.) and the land (Lev. 25:2ff.), dietary rules (Lev. 11:2ff.), circumcision (Gen. 17:11; Deut. 10:16), regulations concerning sexual relationships (Lev. 18:6ff.), provision for individual sexual hygiene (Lev. 15:2ff.), purification rituals (Lev. 1:9ff.; 14:2ff.; 15:2, et al.), and sanitary procedures (Deut. 23:12ff.; Num. 31:19ff.).

In view of the ethical concept of health that these regulations reflect, it should be remarked that they were not intended to exemplify some mysterious connection between morality and health so much as to emphasize that the observance of the precepts enshrined in the corpus of legislation would of itself insure a great measure of freedom from the diseases and scourges which afflicted neighboring peoples. Consequently, insofar as the Israelites followed the prescribed rules for sanitation, isolation, hygiene, and sexual behavior they were assured of the kind of immunity to disease that magic could never afford.

As regards the dietary regulations, the division of species into clean and unclean (Lev. 11:1ff.) is to be regarded not so much as a reaction against Egyptian totemism or the protest of a superior religion against contemporary pagan customs as the positive delineation of beneficial and noxious foods respectively. The specific concern of Leviticus 11:2 was with the kind of animal whose flesh could be ingested without any resultant harm to individual or communal health. Quadrupeds that were clovenfooted, parted the hoof, and chewed the cud were alone permitted for food. Such a designation of the ruminants proper excluded carnivorous and predatory species, and the list of possible animals was further restricted by the prohibition of swine, camels, hares, and coneys, which did not fulfill all the conditions necessary for "cleanness." It will be observed that the "clean" animals were exclusively vegetarian, and as such would be less likely to transmit infection than would the carnivorae, which fed on flesh that invariably decayed rapidly under conditions of a warm climate.[18]

The prohibition concerning the flesh of swine is interesting partly on hygienic grounds, and partly because of the place that the animal occupied in Egyptian cult-worship. According to Herodotus,[19] the pig was originally sacred to Osiris, and the cultic celebration of that deity involved the slaughter of a pig outside the houses of the participants. The violation of tabus regarding the pigs was remedied by means of a close and immediate contact with Osiris in the form of the Nile River. It does not seem likely, however, that the question of cult-worship was quite as important a consideration in the prohibition of swine for food as were purely dietary and hygienic reasons. Even under the most carefully supervised modern conditions of slaughtering and processing, the flesh of the pig is far more potentially dangerous as a source of infection than that of any of the other quadrupeds normally eaten for food. The pig is the intermediate host for several parasitic organisms producing afflictions of varying severity, and under warm climatic conditions the optimum opportunity is afforded for these organisms to develop when ingested.[20]

[18] The wild animals specified as suitable for food were the fallow-deer (probably *Dama vulgaris*), the gazelle (*Gazella dorcas, Gazella Leptoceras*), the roebuck (perhaps *Bubalis bucephalus*), the ibex (*Capra nubiana*), the addax (*Antilope addax*), the antelope (*Oryx beatrix*), and the mouflon (*Ovis tragelaphus*), Deut. 4:14; cf. F. S. Bodenheimer, *Animals and Man in Bible Lands* (1960), p. 41 *passim*. Of the prohibited quadrupeds the camel was already valuable as a source of milk in patriarchal times (Gen. 32:15), although great care had to be taken lest the milk sour before being ingested. The hare, which was also forbidden for food, existed in numerous varieties in Palestine, the most common being the *Lepus capensis aegyptius, Lepus europaeus connori*, and *Lepus europaeus syriacus*. The coney (*Procavia syriaca*) or rock-badger was also common: in general appearance it resembled a rabbit.

[19] *Hist.*, II, 47.

[20] One of the characteristic infections, trichiniasis, results from the parasitic *Trichinella spiralis* found in raw or partially cooked pork or pork products, and in the developing stages the invasion and migration of the organism are typified by symptoms of malaise, febrile states, vomiting, edema of the face and legs, muscular pains, and urticarial rash. Botulism and other food poisoning result from infection due to contaminated pork products, and in severe cases respiratory failure is a complication. At other times the ingestion of pork products issues in an allergic condition accompanied by malaise, some fever, and a rash. A more common infection is that of the *Taenia solium*, where the pig is the intermediate host and man the definitive host. The developed worm is about ten feet long with approximately one thousand segments, and is derived from the *Cysticercus cellulosae* parasite sometimes present in raw or improperly cooked pork. A rare degeneration of this condition is seen in somatic taeniasis, when nodules form in the muscles and the brain to produce

The medical code appears to have regarded as one class all the creatures that inhabited the waters, and in consequence merely divided them into clean and unclean categories, the latter embracing all those species without fins and scales. This distinction was also observed elsewhere in the ancient Near East, notably in Egypt. The exclusion from the Israelite diet of all edible crustaceae, many of which live on sewage and putrefying matter, would forestall the ravages of enteric or the paratyphoid fevers, or even of spirochaetal jaundice infection from the *Leptospira icterohaemorrhagiae*.

A similar principle applied to the legislation concerning the clean and unclean fowls. Leviticus 11:13 enumerated those which were unsafe for human consumption, but did not furnish any specific list of clean species. The rapacious, aquatic, and predatory kinds of birds were excluded, since their flesh, if eaten, might transmit infection from carrion. The pigeon, turtle-dove, goose, quail, domestic fowl, and partridge were numbered among the clean birds used by the Israelites. Four varieties of locusts were permitted for food (Lev. 11:21f.), a situation that reflected accurately the life of the desert nomad, who regularly included small insects such as grasshoppers or locusts in his diet. The species allowed were the locust (*Aedipoda migratoria*), the bald locust (*Acrydum peregrinum*), the cricket (*Aedipoda cristata*), and the grasshopper, probably the smallest of the locust tribe. These insects were eaten at all stages of their growth, and regarded from early antiquity as a palatable food. The Levitical code (Lev. 11:23) prohibited the eating of "all winged creeping things that have four feet," an expression that apparently

---

symptoms like epilepsy, or else become palpable subcutaneously. Yet another disease that can be contracted from ingesting improperly prepared pork has come to the notice of medical research in recent years. It is called "toxoplasmosis," and in its symptomatic form resembles pneumonia. While the method of its transmission still is imperfectly understood, it is widespread among animals, particularly pigs and rodents. The toxoplasma organism in pork is unaffected by the periods of pork storage prescribed by occidental food laws, and seems to be able to survive the usual cooking temperatures. It occurs in a cyst-like mass called a "pseudo-cyst," the structure of which is resistant to freezing or the action of gastric juices, but it tends to be broken down when subjected to prolonged cooking at above average temperatures. It should be observed in passing that the ruminants proper are not wholly free from parasites themselves, for the flesh of the ox is occasionally the intermediate host for the parasite *Taenia saginata*, and man, the definitive host, acquires the infection through eating improperly cooked flesh containing the organism *Cysticercus bovis*. The resultant tapeworm is about twenty feet long and has approximately two thousand segments. The parasitic organism known as *Diphyllobothrium latum* is a worm of about thirty feet with some three thousand segments. Man is the definitive host and fish the intermediate host, with infection occurring when caviar or imperfectly cooked fish are ingested. A pathological condition known as *tularemia*, marked by malaise, rigor, febrile states, and glandular swellings can also result in certain parts of the world, including North America, from eating poorly prepared fish or rabbits.

designated all swarming creatures of marine or terrestrial habitats, which in Leviticus 11:29 included vermin and reptiles. The latter were universally detested as loathsome and unclean, generally being associated with demonism.

Closely allied with the designation of suitable and unsuitable foods was the concern for protecting food and water from possible contamination by unclean objects. Levitical law (Lev. 11:31ff.) gave specific directions concerning vessels and foodstuffs that had been allowed to come into contact with any unclean thing. The principles underlying modern systematized public health are particularly prominent here, for the protection of foodstuffs would obviate the ravages of afflictions such as food-borne polioencephalitis, food-poisoning, the enteric fevers, and parasitic worms. Pollution of water was also avoided rigorously, for it too was recognized as a likely source of infection, disease, and death. An earthen vessel containing water defiled by anything unclean was itself deemed unsafe for use and had to be destroyed. But if an unclean animal or insect contaminated an article made of wood, or a garment of skin, or a sack (Lev. 11:32, RSV), it was considered sufficient to immerse it in water until the evening in order to cleanse it satisfactorily. Fountains, large pools, and streams were considered safe and clean. There is no doubt, once again, that the insistence upon maintaining a clean water supply was the means of preventing diseases and afflictions. Quite clearly a preventive approach to the problems of diet and hygiene was the only really satisfactory one, considering the necessary improvisations of nomadic existence in a desert milieu and the certainly primitive culinary standards of the time of the Wilderness wanderings and even later.

3. *Leprosy.* Another important aspect of the preventive approach to pathological problems involved the diagnosis and treatment of leprosy.[21] The Hebrew צרעת is a generic term derived from a root containing the idea of affliction with an eruptive cutaneous ailment. The Greek term *lepra* indicated a skin condition characterized by the appearance of rough, scaly patches, and was most probably a description of psoriasis. However, the term appears to have been rather indefinite, so that the LXX rendering could well have included leucodermia, favus infection, and psoriasis as well as true leprosy. For a skin disease that was much closer to the latter, the Greeks employed the term elephantiasis, which the Vulgate rendered as *lepra*, thereby adding to the terminological confusion. While leprosy was known in Mesopotamia as far back as the third millennium B.C., only one instance of true leprosy has been discovered to date in Egyptian mummies, giving some substance to the belief

---

[21] Cf. R. K. Harrison, *IDB*, III, pp. 111ff.; H. M. Spinka, *Journal of the American Scientific Affiliation*, XI (1959), pp. 17ff.; R. G. Cochrane, *Biblical Leprosy: A Suggested Interpretation* (1961), pp. 3ff.

that the individual concerned may have been an immigrant from Syria or Mesopotamia.

The organism causing leprosy was discovered by Hansen in 1871, who showed that the disease resulted from infection by the minute schizomycetous fungus *Mycobacterium leprae*. There are three commonly described varieties of clinical leprosy at present. The nodular type results in the formation of facial lumps and generalized thickening of the tissue. In addition, degenerative changes take place in the mucous membranes of the nose and throat. The second variety, the anesthetic, is less severe and is distributed in association with the cutaneous nerves. The thickening of the nerves causes discoloration and loss of feeling in certain areas of the skin, and after some time blisters form on these anesthetic patches. Perforating ulcers frequently occur on the feet, and portions of the upper extremities often become afflicted with necrosis and fall off, leaving a healed stump (*lepra mutilans*). This form of leprosy is chronic, sometimes lasting thirty years. A third or mixed variety exhibits a combination of all of the foregoing symptoms in varying degrees. Diagnosis of leprosy (or "Hansen's disease," as modern medical practitioners prefer to designate it) is established by demonstrating the presence of the bacillus *leprae* in the nodules or blisters.

The description of diagnostic techniques and quarantine regulations makes it quite evident that among other cutaneous conditions true clinical leprosy was being envisaged in the Levitical prescriptions. The Hebrew of chapter 13 is technical, suited to a professional textbook for the priest-physician. The language is like that of the Egyptian medical texts, and it is as obscure to the modern Biblical student as most advanced texts are to beginners in other fields of knowledge. For the average Bible reader the situation is further complicated by the obsolete English terminology occasionally used to translate the Hebrew. Such unfortunate renderings include "scall" (RSV "itch") and "tetter," the latter being virtually meaningless, but still perpetuated by the RSV (Lev. 13:39).

The affliction described could have occurred spontaneously (Lev. 13:2-17); it could have been consequent upon a furuncle (Lev. 13:18-23) or a burn on the skin (Lev. 13:24-28), or it might have arisen on the head or beard (Lev. 13:29-44). The first clinical indications included the presence of a swelling or subcutaneous nodule, a cuticular crust, and a whitish-red spot. If on examination these symptoms indicated subcuticular penetration resulting in depigmentation of the small hairs occurring in that area of the skin, the patient was tentatively pronounced unclean. If only one of these symptoms was present, he was quarantined for seven days and then re-examined. If no further degeneration was evident he was isolated for another week, after which he could be declared clean.

608

A chronic form of the disease was indicated by the presence of white hairs and red granular or ulcerated tissue in an elevated area of depigmented skin. Any person who exhibited these symptoms was pronounced unclean by the priests. If a patient manifested a white cutaneous condition covering his entire body he was considered clean (Lev. 13:13), and would probably have been the victim of what modern medicine would describe as acquired leucodermia (*vitiligo*). But if, on subsequent examination, he was found to be ulcerated, he was to be declared unclean (Lev. 13:14), although this drastic pronouncement could be revoked if the ulceration merely constituted the mild pustulation common to most cutaneous diseases.

Fundamental to the diagnosis of clinical leprosy was the extent to which cutaneous penetration had occurred. If the disease had affected the epidermis and had not produced morbid changes in the local hair, the affliction was not regarded as especially serious in nature. As such it might have been eczema, leucodermia, impetigo, psoriasis or some allied cutaneous disease. But if the condition under examination had infiltrated the dermis (*corium*), and had caused the local hairs to split or break off and lose their color, then leprosy was to be suspected.

In the matter of differential diagnosis, the presence of a white or inflamed spot on the site of an old boil or burn (Lev. 13:18-28) was of importance to the priest-physicians of Israel. If the dermis had not been penetrated, a seven-day quarantine period was imposed, after which the patient was again examined. If the swelling or pustule remained localized, the diagnosis of leprosy was excluded. The actual condition involved is obscure, and may have been a keloid or connective-tissue growth of the skin which usually arises in the scar of some previous injury or disease. The most probable diagnosis is that of diffuse symmetrical scleroderma (*sclerema adultorum*), in which uniform patches of the skin become hardened and thickened.

The foregoing diagnostic procedures were applied to the incidence of diseases affecting the scalp also (Lev. 13:29-37), and if quarantine showed that the disease was not progressing, one of several differential diagnoses was entertained. Where the presence of leprosy was definitely established, the afflicted person was banished from society, ordered to dress distinctively, and announce his uncleanness. Appropriate ritual ceremonies were prescribed for those occasions on which spontaneous healing occurred, and the leper was then declared clean (Lev. 14:1-32). Quite obviously the priest-physicians of the Mosaic and subsequent ages in Israel were able to distinguish between what modern physicians would describe as acute and chronic varieties of a number of skin diseases. That the term צרעת is not the same as modern clinical leprosy is immediately apparent from the fact that it was also used to describe, among other conditions, a "leprosy" of houses and clothing, neither of which is affected by the bacillus *leprae*. On the other hand, against the background of information provided in Leviticus, the Hebrew priest would be able to diagnose the genuine incidence of Hansen's disease without undue difficulty, even though he was approaching the clinical situation from an ancient oriental, rather than a modern occidental, diagnostic standpoint. This is substantiated by the manner in which present-day textbooks on leprosy refer to the remarkable passages relating to the diagnosis and prevention of leprosy in Leviticus.[22] This material is all the more significant because its technical nature attests to its antiquity, and also because it comprises the first formulation of the principles of quarantine and preventive medicine as applied to leprosy to be recovered from the culture of the ancient Near East.

The deteriorated condition of garments (Lev. 13:47-59) probably resulted from the incidence of dampness, mold, or fungus. Its occurrence was taken seriously, and the material thus affected was burned if the deterioration showed signs of spreading; otherwise washing was deemed sufficient to render the article clean. If discoloration of the walls of a house occurred (Lev. 14:34-47), the usual principle of quarantine was again applied. Affected masonry or woodwork had to be removed and replaced by new material, and it seems evident that the regulations enjoined in this connection were directed at halting the spread of dry rot in the woodwork and discouraging the growth of lichens, fungi, and mineral precipitates on the masonry of houses. Sterilization by washing was also prescribed for the incidence of various bodily secretions, whether of a benign nature such as a seminal emission (Lev. 15:16-18) and menstruation (Lev. 15:19-24), or of a more malignant character (Lev. 15:2), the latter perhaps including leukorrhea and gonorrhea.

4. Marital relations. That a strict attitude towards the marital union of those near of kin was typical of the Mosaic legal code is indicated by the enactments of Leviticus 18:1-30. These prohibitions have a distinct bearing upon the marital customs of the day and age. They contrast sharply with the customs among the Egyptians—who never had any specific formulation of marriage laws and where questions of consanguinity were ignored in favor of the dictates of the matriarchate—among the Canaanites—where fornication, adultery, bestiality, and incest were accredited functions of the sexual life as depicted in the Ras Shamra tablets[23]—and among the Hittites—where certain forms of bestiality were permitted (perhaps as the vestigial remains of an ancient animal cult), although incestuous relationships were prohibited.[24]

---

[22] R. P. Strong (ed.), *Stitt's Diagnosis, Prevention and Treatment of Tropical Diseases* (1944), I, p. 814.

[23] A. van Selms, *Marriage and Family Life in Ugaritic Literature* (1954), pp. 74ff.

[24] E. Neufeld, *The Hittite Laws* (1951), pp. 188ff.

The intention of the Levitical legislation was to represent sexual intimacy with those near of kin as a shameful act, and the list of prohibited degrees included a considerable number of relationships of affinity as well as consanguinity. While it would be unreasonable to expect in this delineation an exhaustive treatment of the problem, the resultant statements relating to consanguinity and affinity are remarkably comprehensive. The general principle was enunciated in Leviticus 18:6 in the form of a preamble, and successive verses illustrated the forbidden degrees of kinship in greater detail. These, however, constituted representative cases, and should not be thought of as indicating an exhaustive catalog or statement of possible incestuous combinations.

The prohibitions appear to reflect three fundamental concepts: first, that nearness of relationship in blood constitutes an impediment to union, and involves all ascendants and descendants but only the nearer cases of collaterals; secondly, that near relationship of affinity, or connection by marriage, is to be interpreted in the light of the contention that a man and his wife are "one flesh," that is, kin or blood relations; and finally, that relationship through the woman is exactly analogous to relationship through the man on the basis of the "one flesh."

Of the prohibited degrees, six were relationships of consanguinity and eight were of affinity. The enactment concerning the sister of a wife (Lev. 18:18), which is one of the closest relationships of affinity, has been a matter of dispute among scholars for many years. The prohibition was evidently designed in order to prevent a man from marrying the sister of a living wife, thus precluding further unions of the kind entered into by Jacob, who married Leah and Rachel (Gen. 29:23ff.).[25] At the same time it should be recognized that the marriage of a man with the sister of his deceased wife was not prohibited by the enactment, either expressly or by implication.

In any assessment of the rationale of these laws, it must be observed that the moral and social aspects appear to have predominated over any supposed biological or genetic considerations. Anthropologists have long been familiar with the dangers inherent in primitive and nomadic endogamous community life, where consistent patterns of marriage between close relatives would quickly result in an effective centralizing of influence, property, and wealth in the hands of a very few families. Such a restricted concept of social organization would thwart the development of an adequate social consciousness, and would be entirely out of harmony with the humanitarian concerns of the Covenant Code and other Pentateuchal legislation of a like order. It is perhaps not without significance that the occasions on which the Levitical prescriptions for marriage were flouted were set against a background of advanced social degeneration (Am. 2:7).

25 Cf. D. R. Mace, *Hebrew Marriage* (1953), pp. 152f.

The legislation does not appear to be either aware of, or amenable to, the concept that consanguineous union results in such conditions as familial idiocy or degeneration of the stock. It is now well known that, in the absence of clearly defined hereditary predispositions towards degeneration or disease in the stock itself, the consanguineous union of certain types of animals can be perpetrated over successive generations without any observable deterioration in mental or physical functions, provided always that bad recessive qualities are eliminated in the breeding process along with the more obvious dominant ones which may emerge. Much the same can be said also for human consanguineous unions, which are not as deleterious as some writers have imagined, despite the danger of a substantial increase in genes of the same origin. There does not appear to be any accredited physiological basis for the prohibitions concerning consanguineous union, as seems evident when the sequences are historically demonstrable. Thus Ruffer, in a study of Egyptian royalty from the Eighteenth Dynasty onwards, concluded that the issue was not obviously impaired by the marriage of those of near kinship, and showed that such pathological conditions as were demonstrable were hereditary in nature, with gout and obesity being the most notable.[26] These observations are all the more interesting in the light of the "control" that can be exercised over the study by the fact that the physical and mental attributes of the royalty of Egypt from the Eighteenth Dynasty onwards are attestable historically.

The average age of the Ptolemaic kings was sixty-four years, and according to extant records they were not subject to epilepsy, deafmutism, idiocy, infertility, insanity, or general deterioration of the familial stock, thus making it evident that a prolonged tradition of marriage within the prohibited degrees of marriage as enumerated in Leviticus had no discernibly detrimental effect upon them. It would appear, therefore, that other than purely biological or medical considerations were being contemplated when the laws concerning consanguinity were promulgated.

❀　　❀　　❀　　❀　　❀

Limitations of space preclude further discussion of the contents of Leviticus, important as it is for the entire fabric of Hebrew social, moral, and religious life. It should be observed, however, that the book is of great importance for the Christian student since it provides the necessary background for a theological understanding of the sacrifice and priesthood of Jesus Christ, both of which are expounded at some length in the Epistle to the Hebrews. Leviticus is rightly prized by the Jews as constituting the book which contains binding regulations with regard to sin and atonement, sanctification and physical health. The Christian

[26] M. A. Ruffer in *Studies in the Palaeopathology of Egypt* (ed. R. L. Moodie, 1921), pp. 325ff.

Church has traditionally based its table of prohibited degrees of marital relationship upon that found in Leviticus, and had it followed more rigorously the hygienic and dietary principles enshrined in that ancient legislation, it would have gained many more of the benefits contemplated in the Hebrew ideal for the health and well-being of the individual and the community alike.

The Hebrew text of Leviticus has been remarkably well preserved, which is hardly surprising in view of its priestly character. One or two slight improvements can be made upon the MT tradition by reference to such ancient versions as the Samaritan Pentateuch, the LXX, and the Peshitta, as in Leviticus 7:21; 25:47 and 26:39, but these are very minor. Fragments of Leviticus recovered from Qumran give support to the MT tradition, as do two fragments of the book found by Yigael Yadin at Masada during the 1964-65 season of excavating.

Supplementary Literature

Bonar, A. A. *Commentary on Leviticus.* 1861.
Cazelles, H. *Le Lévitique.* 1958.
Chapman, A. T. and A. W. Streane. *The Book of Leviticus.* 1914.
Dussaud, R. *Les origines cananéennes du sacrifice israélite.* 1921.
Gispen, W. H. *Het Boek Leviticus.* 1950.
Heinisch, P. *Das Buch Leviticus.* 1935.
Hicks, F. C. N. *The Fulness of Sacrifice.* 1946.
Hooke, S. H. *The Origins of Early Semitic Ritual.* 1938.
James, E. O. *The Origins of Sacrifice.* 1933.
Kornfeld, W. *Studien zum Heiligkeitsgesetz.* 1952.
Noth, M. *Leviticus.* 1964.

V. THE BOOK OF NUMBERS

A. NAME AND OUTLINE

The Jewish Synagogue named this book either וידבר ("and he spoke") or במדבר ("in the desert of"), after its first word or after one of the early words in the initial verse. An older name in Jewish circles was "The Fifth of the Musterings," a designation meant to indicate that particular portion of the five Mosaic writings describing the numberings of the Israelites.[1] The LXX translators gave the title 'Αριθμοί (Numbers) to the work, and this was followed by the Vulgate (*Numeri*) and English versions.

By contrast with Leviticus, which is almost entirely legislative, Numbers, like Exodus, combines history with legal enactments. The bulk of the work is concerned with the vicissitudes of the Israelites in their Wilderness wanderings subsequent to the Exodus until the time when, some thirty-eight years later, they were on the point of entering the Promised Land. The book can be analyzed in its extant form as follows:

I. Preparations for Leaving Sinai, ch. 1:1–10:10
    A. The census and marshalling of the tribes, 1:1–4:49
    B. Sundry legislation, 5:1–6:27
    C. Offerings at the dedication of the altar, 7:1-89
    D. The candlestick, the consecration of Levites, and rules concerning their service, 8:1-26
    E. The second passover, the cloud, and the use of silver trumpets 9:1–10:10

II. From Sinai to the Plains of Moab, ch. 10:11–21:35
    A. Preliminary movement from Sinai, 10:11-36
    B. Unrest among the tribes, 11:1-15
    C. The provision of quails, 11:16-35
    D. Miriam's leprosy, 12:1-16
    E. The twelve spies, 13:1–14:45
    F. Miscellaneous commands, 15:1-41

---

[1] J. H. Hertz, *The Pentateuch and Haftorahs*, p. 567.

B. COMPILATION OF NUMBERS

The composition of Numbers presents problems similar to those encountered in connection with Exodus and Leviticus. It can be assumed quite legitimately that the phrase "And the Lord spoke to Moses, saying . . ." represents the beginning of a new section of material, and that the introductory formula, when restricted to that specific expression, can be held to preface an agglomeration of material of a revelatory, instructional, didactic, legislative, or other character. When, however, this prefatory phrase is related to a particular locality, as for example in Numbers 1:1, where the Lord is said to have communed with Moses in the Wilderness of Sinai at a specific time, the implication is that the subsequent material must be regarded as historical and Mosaic in origin. This is not to say, of course, that certain modifications or revisions of material prefaced by the formula were not entertained at a later period, for as has been observed previously, such a procedure was an accredited scribal practice in parts of the ancient Near East. What it does imply, however, is that the component sections of Numbers must be contemplated against a desert milieu, and must be assessed consistently on such a basis. To regard certain possible scribal additions or recensions undertaken at a later period as evidence that the entire work was in fact of a comparatively late order, and needs to be projected back to an earlier age if it is to be credited to Moses in any sense at all, is an incorrect procedure methodologically and an improper use of the available evidence. Many modern scholars have now diverged from the Wellhausenian position in this regard to the extent that they acknowledge that the book contains material from very early times,[2] which may in fact be Mosaic in character and origin.

While there is an overall chronological pattern to Numbers, certain of the sections appear only loosely related to the particular period of the Wilderness wanderings with which they have been associated in process of compilation. Thus the promulgations made in connection with vows (Num. 30:1ff.) and the miscellaneous items relating to cultic and other observances (Num. 15:1ff.) could have emerged from any one of the years of sojourn in the Wilderness, and in consequence need not reflect any specific topographical or chronological situation. Numbers appears to be more fragmentary than its precursors in the Torah, and this is particularly evident in chapters 20 and 21, where the original form was probably in the nature of short topographical notes such as could be found in a travel diary.

This general difference in tone from that evident in Exodus and Leviticus has led many scholars to reject the Mosaic authorship of Numbers, and on the basis of an occidental scheme of documentary analysis to assign it to such avowedly hypothetical literary sources as J, E, P, and L. It is true, of course, that the scribal activity of Moses was mentioned only in Numbers 23 (cf. 5:23; 11:26), and that some sections of the book (e.g. 12:3; 15:22f.; 32:34) appear to have been composed by someone other than the great Hebrew legislator, or even abstracted from some such source as the "Book of the Wars of the Lord" (Num. 21:14).

In the light of what is known about processes of scribal revision in Egypt and certain other areas of the ancient Near East, there appears to be no difficulty whatever in assuming that the reference in Numbers 12:3 concerning the modesty of Moses constitutes an addition by a later hand, quite possibly either that of Joshua or Samuel. The objections raised in critical circles to the supposed non-Mosaic nature of Numbers 15:22 are much less assured, however, since the purpose of the reference was to stress the revealed origin of the sacrificial offering and its mediation to Israel through Moses. In such a case the allusion to Moses in terms of the third person would be entirely proper, although nonetheless emphatic.

A more accredited post-Mosaic insertion is evident in the reference in Numbers 21:14f., where there is a brief citation from a source designated "The Book of the Wars of the Lord." This is a genuine Pentateuchal source, unlike the hypothetical documents favored by the members of the Graf-Wellhausen school, albeit quoted in the briefest of forms. It was evidently a record of the mighty acts of God on behalf of Israel, and was most probably in its earlier stages of writing during the late Wilderness

---

[2] E.g. F. M. Cross, *BA*, X, No. 3 (1947), pp. 52ff.; J. Marsh, *IB*, II, p. 138; G. H. Davies, *IDB*, IV, p. 503.

period. Information concerning this matter is both scarce and uncertain, since the book has only survived in the fragment mentioned above. The events referred to in Numbers 21:15 can only have been written down subsequent to the time of Moses, but were quite probably in extant written, and certainly in oral, form by the time of Joshua when the ancient Book of Jashar, a national epic that commemorated the heroic course of Israelite history under God, was also taking substantial shape. Thus there are no reasonable grounds for supposing that the insertion, which probably commenced with the gloss in Numbers 21:13b, is any later than the time of Samuel, and it may well have arisen in the settlement period.

Similar considerations apply to the content of Numbers 32:33ff., which comprises an enumeration of Transjordanian cities built by the offspring of Gad, Reuben, and Machir, son of Manasseh. Quite clearly such constructional activity was only possible after the fulfilment of the promise made by those tribes to attend to their military responsibilities (Num. 32:17). Once again there appears little difficulty in regarding this section as a later scribal or editorial insertion to describe the outcome of the promises made earlier in the chapter to Moses. As such it completed the narrative in the form of a commentary upon subsequent events, and may even have been drawn up in this manner to redress any implied neglect of the Transjordanian Hebrews in the light of the prominence given to the Israelite victories during the conquest period. In connection with the constructional activities of these Transjordanian Hebrews, it should be noted that they were engaged in the hasty repair, rather than the actual founding, of such settlements as Aroer and Ataroth (cf. Num. 32:26f.), since Gilead was already long inhabited. It seems quite probable that Numbers 32:34-42 was a product of the settlement period, and may well have been introduced into the text of Numbers by the time of Samuel at the very latest. This is apparent from the fact that the names of certain of the sites were ancient Canaanite strongholds whose designation was to be altered, as noted in the gloss in Numbers 32:38, a situation that accords well with the late conquest period. Aside from these few possibilities of post-Mosaic addition, the internal evidence of Numbers consistently affirms that the regulations and laws it contains were revealed to Israel through the mediatorial offices of Moses and occasionally Aaron. Furthermore, it supports without equivocation the impression that these laws were promulgated against a desert milieu, and that they were implemented during the time spent in the Wilderness wanderings. Thus, apart from the foregoing passages that might conceivably constitute somewhat later additions, there is no single factor in the entire contents of Numbers that is in any respect incompatible with the conditions which are stated to have obtained during the period of desert sojourn.

Certain problems arise in any attempt to speculate as to the mechanics of compilation of Numbers, however. The first four chapters appear curiously situated, to say the least, since they do not particularly serve to integrate the book with the historical narrative as it terminated in Exodus. If the presence of the stereotyped formula in Numbers 1:1 and 2:1 indicates that these chapters were originally separate records that were placed side by side in the scroll, it then becomes difficult to account for the presence of what appears to be a genuine colophon in Numbers 3:1. If the latter as such refers to either or both preceding chapters, it is far from easy to see how they could have been Mosaic or Aaronic in any sense different from that of analogous material ascribed to Moses and Aaron.

But if Numbers 3:1 does not constitute the colophon of some preceding historical narrative, it becomes difficult to assess precisely what place the verse has in the early chapters of Numbers. The reference in Numbers 1:1, which speaks of the Wilderness of Sinai, can hardly be the title of a tablet whose colophon refers to a revelation upon Mount Sinai itself, so that if Numbers 3:1 is genuinely colophonic in form, it may be that only a fragment of the preceding material has been preserved, which in total amount may have exceeded the contents of the first two chapters or, on the other hand, may only have survived partially and without title in chapter two. Whatever the nature of their origin, the first four chapters of Numbers are a manifest unit in their final form, dealing as they do with the census and the regulations for the departure from the Sinai region.

The records of chapters 5 and 6 contain material relating to the rules governing the Nazirite order, uncleanness, and the jealousy ordeal, indicating that a group of specifically cultic promulgations was attached to the priestly records of the census and the regulations for the marshalling of the tribes. The general standpoint of the first four chapters reappears in chapter seven, which dealt with the offerings of the princes for the consecration of the Tabernacle. The same theme was continued in Numbers 8:1-4, and described the lamps in the Tabernacle, but it was interrupted in Numbers 8:5 by what may well have been the beginning of a fresh leather scroll or a new section of such material.

It is possible that Numbers 8:5-26, dealing with the separation of the Levites, was dislocated in the process of assembling the book, since as far as its contents are concerned it could easily have followed Numbers 4:49. An accredited historical section is represented by Numbers 9:1-14, which depicts events occurring prior to the first census and somewhat before the Tabernacle was erected, which again appears to be dislocated from the standpoint of a purely historical sequence. Quite possibly at least some of the priestly material in chapters five to eight antedated the first census-list, and if this is so the latter would have been added as prefatory material once the priestly enactments had been assembled, and not *vice versa*.

While the material arrangement of the early chapters in Numbers appears somewhat strange to the western mind, it is noteworthy that the finished form of the material sets the priestly enactments firmly against the records of the Sinai period of the Wilderness wanderings so as to authenticate them and demonstrate their originality in respect to the cultus. While the sections could possibly be interpreted as having been assembled rather haphazardly in contrast to occidental methods and standards, it remains true that they were collected in a fashion that was neither accidental nor inconvenient as far as the original compiler was concerned. This fact alone should serve as a warning against an injudicious approach to the problems of compilation of the book, and a reminder that the needs of an oriental people were the primary consideration of the editor or editors responsible for the finished product.

The gradually unfolding introduction of Numbers 9:15 seems to indicate quite clearly the commencement of another roll in the narrative, which carries the history of the Wilderness wanderings to the sojourn at Hazeroth without any discernible break (Num. 11:35). This was followed by the complaint of Miriam and Aaron against Moses (Num. 12:1ff.), which resulted in Miriam's being afflicted with a skin disease. From Hazeroth the Israelites moved to Paran, and the narrative described the succession of events which culminated in failure to enter the Promised Land (Num. 15:41).

The enactment relating to sacrifice (Num. 15:1-32) was probably inserted into the narrative at this juncture so as to provide legislative backing for the ritual procedures to be followed immediately upon entering Canaan. If this law was as mandatory and comprehensive in scope as the text appears to indicate, it obviously antedated the more elaborate sacrificial prescriptions of Leviticus, and evidently belonged to an early period of the sojourn to constitute an interim injunction for the remainder of the desert era.

Were this actually to be the case, it would indicate, as Wright has pointed out,[3] that Amos was correct in suggesting that the people as a whole did not offer animal sacrifices in the Wilderness (Am. 5:25). The sections dealing with sabbath violation (Num. 15:32-36) and the making of fringes for clothing (Num. 15:37-41) are obvious insertions of literary fragments of priestly interest that have a desert situation for their background, but which need not be in strict chronological order.

Much the same considerations apply to the contents of chapters 16, 18, and 19, where priestly concerns are obviously at the forefront. Chapter 17, dealing with the budding rod of Aaron, is obviously of Wilderness origin, although it is difficult to do more than assign it broadly to the

[3] J. S. Wright, *EQ*, XXV (1953), p. 15.

period prior to the encampment in the plains of Moab. Chapters 20 and 21 narrate incidents that took place in the same general phase of the wanderings, and depict with considerable fidelity the tensions of Israelite life at that time. The records are brief almost to the point of being fragmentary, so that important occasions, such as the situation attending the death of Aaron, were dealt with in a rather perfunctory manner. It is within the bounds of possibility that these chapters constituted part of an abbreviated travel diary, and that they were assembled by an editor somewhat after the death of Moses and supplemented by an itinerary of that particular phase of the wanderings and a triumphal paean (Num. 21:27-30), perhaps in fragmentary form, as well as by a snatch of a popular work-song (Num. 21:17b-18b).

The narratives describing the prophetic activities of Balaam (Num. 22:1–24:26) are of interest partly because they illustrate the role of the Mesopotamian seer in military affairs, and partly because of the problems associated with their composition and integrity. The name "Balaam" (בלעם) has been variously understood to mean "the clan brings forth," "glutton," or, as suggested by Albright, "the (divine) uncle brings forth," the last being based upon a comparison of בלעם with the thirteenth-century B.C. Amorite proper name *Yabil-'ammu*.[4]

Balaam was unusual in the Old Testament as a foreigner who was subject to the command of God, and whose career exhibited the tremendous potency attributed in the Old Testament and elsewhere in the ancient Near East to the spoken word.[5] He lived in Pethor on the River Euphrates, south of Carchemish, probably the *Pitru* of the Assyrian texts,[6] described as situated on the River Sagur near its junction with the Euphrates. Precisely how the narratives relating to his oracles came to be in written form is unknown. It seems difficult to imagine that they could have been recorded by an Israelite scribe, since no Hebrews were present when the incidents described took place. It may be that a disciple of the Mesopotamian seer was responsible for the survival of the narratives, although this cannot be regarded as being any more than purely conjectural. What is evident, however, is that the traditions concerning Balaam were well known in oral form by the time of Joshua (Josh. 13:22), and if the written narratives were not already extant by then, they could hardly have been delayed much beyond the period of the Judges.

In the view of the present writer they were in written form not later than the twelfth century B.C., and were inserted during the settlement phase into the historical sequence of Numbers. In any event they ought not to be regarded in any sense as dating in their extant form from a period later than the time of Samuel. Chapter 25:1-18 can be construed as

---

[4] W. F. Albright, *JBL*, LXIII (1944), p. 232.
[5] R. F. Johnson, *IDB*, I, p. 341.
[6] *ANET*, p. 278; cf. W. F. Albright, *BASOR*, No. 118 (1950), p. 15 n. 13.

forming an appendix to the Balaam oracles, and it is instructive in the light of the fact that the Mesopotamian seer subsequently associated himself with the Midianites and counselled them to entice Israel into the licentious cult-worship of Baal-peor (Num. 31:16). The chapter is thus placed into proper religious and historical context, and forms a fitting conclusion to material that is thoroughly Mesopotamian in character, as exemplified by discoveries at Mari and elsewhere that have demonstrated the role occupied by diviners in relationship to military affairs.

Numbers 26:1 apparently represents the commencement of another roll of priestly material that contained data relating to the second census, the record of the appointment of Joshua as the successor of Moses, and certain other details of interest to cultic and administrative circles in Israel. The insertion of such material at that particular juncture in the narrative raises some question as to the rationale of the arrangement, especially where the regulations concerning the feasts are involved. In contemplating the situation against a desert background it seems quite probable that the insertion actually reflected a chronological reminder to the Israelites to the effect that the rather casual practices with regard to celebrations and other cultic requirements (cf. Josh. 5:5) obtaining in the Wilderness were shortly to be replaced on entrance into the Promised Land by the more rigorous stipulations as set forth generally in the priestly enactments of Leviticus. On the other hand, as Wright has suggested, Numbers 28 and 29 may have existed as "festival offerings" independently of the somewhat more general regulations for the people as found in Leviticus 23, and may have been promulgated in their extant form as an act of cultic discipline.[7]

Presumably a further section of the assembled scroll of Numbers commenced with chapter 31, which dealt with the revenge taken upon the Midianites. This material comprised Numbers 31:1–32:32, and included a statement concerning the allotment of land on the east side of the Jordan to certain of the tribes. The remaining chapters of the book comprise a miscellany of material that included a general catalog of the places visited by the Israelites between the time of the Exodus and the entrance into Canaan, as well as regulations concerning the division of the land once it had been acquired, and various laws that envisaged a sedentary state in Canaan.

If the foregoing analysis corresponds in any respect to the manner in which Numbers was actually assembled from written sources, it will be seen that it was compiled by means of a far less elegant literary process than that underlying either Genesis, Exodus, or Leviticus. Quite possibly this very fact could be used as an argument for the early date of the composition, on the assumption that the combination of historical, cultic, and other material against a desert life-situation would tend to result in

---

[7] J. S. Wright, *EQ*, XXV (1953), p. 16.

a more haphazard literary arrangement than that obtaining for purely cultic regulations, as in Leviticus, for narratives of a primarily historical nature, as in Exodus, or for pre-existing literary, and perhaps oral material, as in Genesis.

The relationship between the various sections of Numbers is by no means clear to modern observers, and becomes even more obscure when contemplated against a background of classical European documentary analysis. Most probably the framework was of a chronological order, marked by specific links with the general narration of events, and amplified by means of various regulations and statistical data, especially where these had a bearing upon the desert life-situation of the Wilderness wanderings. It should be remembered that ancient scribes generally did not distinguish between cultic, judicial, social, and moral enactments as carefully as their modern counterparts, which probably goes far towards accounting for the fact that the connection between apparently unrelated sections of a book such as Numbers was more obvious to the people for whom the work was intended than for readers in a different day and age.

What may reasonably be assumed to be post-Mosaic segments of Numbers, along with the brief narrative form of portions such as chapters 20 and 21, might suggest that a good deal of responsibility for the final form of the scroll was exercised some time after the death of Moses by a compiler or editor, perhaps even Joshua, who drew upon Mosaic and other material so as to produce Numbers in something that approximated closely to its extant form. In the view of the present writer there is no single section of the work that requires a date later than the time of Samuel, and the bulk of the work is regarded as issuing from the Mosaic era itself.

C. The Material of Numbers

1. The encampment. The history narrated in Numbers covered a period of some thirty-eight years, and embraced the time between the second and fortieth years of the Exodus era (cf. Num. 1:1; 7:1; 9:1, 15; 10:11; 33:38; Exod. 40:2; Deut. 1:3). At Sinai a census was taken of the people one month after the erection of the Tabernacle (Exod. 40:17), and included those who could serve in a military capacity to arrive at a total of 603,550 individuals (Num. 1:46). The census in chapter 2 gave the tribes in their camps in the order in which they were related to the tent of meeting, and presupposes a condition in which the Israelites were not settled in the Promised Land.

The arrangement of the tribes by their standards in the form of a hollow rectangle around the Tabernacle (Num. 2:2ff.), long held by liberal critics to constitute an indication of the late date of the priestly material in the Pentateuch, is now known to have been a common deployment of encamped forces in the Amarna period. As Kitchen has remarked, it is significant in this connection to note that precisely the same strategic layout was utilized by Rameses II, the contemporary of Moses, in his Syrian campaign, when the large portable war-tent of the divine king was pitched in the center of a rectangular encampment of the army divisions.[8] It is especially noteworthy that this important Egyptian comparison should have emerged from the very century in which Moses lived, for later on, in the first millennium B.C., such military encampments changed their shape, as indicated by the round form of deployment on Assyrian reliefs.[9] Therefore it appears eminently probable that the arrangement depicted in Numbers indicates that Moses was utilizing earlier Egyptian training in the military arts for the welfare of the infant Israelite nation.

Another matter which has a decided bearing upon the antiquity of the sources in Numbers relates to the use of long silver trumpets for convening a civil assembly as well as for religious and military purposes (Num. 10:1ff.). Such trumpets were in common use in Egypt during the Amarna Age,[10] and some particularly elegant specimens that were interred with the pharaoh Tutankhamen (ca. 1350 B.C.) were recovered by Howard Carter in the twentieth century.

Equally ancient is the use of six wagons drawn by oxen for the service of the Tabernacle (Num. 7:3ff.). As Kuentz has shown,[11] ox-drawn wagons were employed regularly on campaigns in Syria by the pharaohs from the time of Tuthmosis III (ca. 1470 B.C.) onwards for several centuries.[12] It only remains to be observed that the wagons of Moses and the Israelites in Sinai,[13] which were drawn generally by two yoked oxen, compare favorably with the ten wagons (עגלה)[14] drawn by six spans of oxen that transported supplies for 8,000 quarrymen of Rameses IV (ca. 1160 B.C.) from the Nile valley into the desert areas of the Wadi Hammamat, between the Nile and the Red Sea, under conditions very similar to those obtaining in the Sinai peninsula.[15] In these, as in so many other respects, a proper use of the available evidence serves to dispose of uninformed subjective criticisms of the genuineness of the narratives.

2. *Legal enactments.* The rite which has become known to scholars as the "jealousy ordeal" (Num. 5:11-31), is of some interest because it was

---

[8] K. A. Kitchen, *The Tyndale House Bulletin*, Nos. 5-6 (1960), p. 11, *NBD*, p. 847; cf. Ch. Kuentz, *La Bataille de Qadech* (1928-34), pls. 34, 39, 42.

[9] Cf. G. Contenau, *Everyday Life in Babylonia and Assyria* (1954), pl. 17.

[10] Cf. H. Hickmann, *La Trompette dans l'Égypte Ancienne* (1946), p. 46.

[11] Ch. Kuentz, *La Bataille de Qadech*, pl. 39.

[12] Cf. *ANET*, p. 240.

[13] K. A. Kitchen, *NBD*, p. 847.

[14] Num. 7:3, 6f. The Egyptian word *'grt*, "wagon," was derived from the Hebrew.

[15] *ARE*, IV, sect. 467.

not entirely unknown among other peoples of antiquity.[16] In this enactment Numbers supplemented the prescriptions of Leviticus, for whereas the latter had pronounced the death penalty upon both participants in an adulterous act, the former outlined the procedure to be followed when a man suspected his wife of adultery that he was actually unable to prove. The dramatic ritual that the woman was required to undergo, all the more significant for its advanced degree of psychological suggestibility, is distinctly reminiscent of the forms of treatment prescribed by the Babylonian priest-physicians of the second millennium B.C.[17] From the standpoint of the history of therapeutic procedures in Israel, it is of some interest to note that the narrative under discussion is the only one in the entire Old Testament to mention the oral administration of potions or medicines.

Numbers 6 furnishes the regulations that governed an institution familiar to the Hebrews throughout their entire history. The charismatic body known as the Nazirites (AV "Nazarite") exemplified the concepts of consecration and holiness inherent in the Mosaic Torah, although the origin of certain Nazirite practices is obscure and most probably antedates Moses. Historically the Nazirite was a sacred person, who in the earlier stages of the institution became charismatic as a result of a divine endowment, which may or may not have been initiated from the human standpoint by a specific maternal vow.[18]

At a later stage of Israelite history the Nazirite acquired his special spiritual status as the result of a vow which he undertook of his own accord. In all periods, however, this particular concept of sanctity and consecration to God was marked outwardly by abstinence from wine and strong drink (the latter generally approximating to intoxicating liquor) and by permitting the hair of the head to remain uncut through the period covered by the vow of self-dedication. The pre-Mosaic origin of the latter appears in the fact that many primitive peoples, along with some Semites, frequently left the hair uncut during certain undertakings that necessitated more than purely human help, and subsequently consecrated the hair to the service of their particular deity (cf. Judg. 5:2). Echoes of this general procedure are not unknown at the present day among Semitic peoples, as Lods has shown with reference to modern Bedouin Arab tribes.[19]

The enactments in Numbers 6 fall conveniently into three groups, of which the first consisted of prohibitions.[20] One of the most important of these required the Nazirite to abstain from any form of alcoholic bever-

[16] Compare Code of Hammurabi, sect. 132 in *ANET*, p. 171; G. B. Gray, *A Critical and Exegetical Commentary on Numbers* (1903), p. 44.
[17] R. K. Harrison, *IDB*, III, p. 332.
[18] J. C. Rylaarsdam, *IDB*, III, p. 526.
[19] A. Lods, *Israel* (1932), p. 305.
[20] J. D. Douglas, *NBD*, pp. 871f.

age or from any of the ingredients from which such a drink might be made. This regulation may perhaps have been designed as a warning to individuals and society as a whole against the dangers inherent in alcoholism, a condition that was widely prevalent in ancient Near Eastern society and was not entirely unknown among the Hebrew priesthood (cf. Lev. 10:9). Abstinence from any form of alcohol would thus insure that the Nazirite was firmly in control of his faculties at all times in his special relationship of sanctity towards God and witness to the nation of Israel. This view seems preferable to the explanation offered by Kittel, who conjectured that abstinence in this area constituted a protest against Canaanite culture and pointed to the superiority of the nomadic ideal.[21] A second prohibition concerned the hair of the head, which was to be left in its natural condition during the entire period of consecration to God, perhaps in the belief that the hair was in some manner the seat of life and virility.[22] Finally, the Nazirite was not permitted to approach a dead body, even that of a relative, lest his state of ceremonial purity should be contaminated by contact with that which was deemed unclean.

The second section in the Nazirite enactments (Num. 6:7-12) concerned violation of the vow, whether through inadvertence or otherwise. Under such conditions the Nazirite was required to submit to detailed purificatory procedures, and to commence his period of dedication anew if he so desired. A final section of the regulations (Num. 6:13-21) was concerned with the sacrificial acts required of the Nazirite at the termination of his vow, which included the cutting and burning of the hair.

Despite the rather serious restrictions imposed upon an individual by the law of the Nazirites, it was not entirely impossible for normal domestic or social duties to be carried out, and there was nothing in the enactments which required a votary to live under something approaching a monastic regime. The distinctive feature of the status attached to the Nazirites was that of complete individual consecration alike of body and personality to the divine service. It extended to the ordinary members of Israelite society a form of holiness normally associated only with the priesthood, and afforded an individual the kind of status enjoyed by groups such as the Rechabites (Jer. 35:5).

Early Nazirites were lifelong devotees, as in the case of Samuel, who was not specifically named a Nazirite in the MT (1 Sam. 1:11), but who was described as such in a fragment of the book of Samuel recovered from 4Q, which terminated 1 Samuel 1:22 with the words, "he shall become a Nazirite for ever,"[23] thus confirming a Mishnaic tradition. Samson was evidently another permanent Nazirite, and although doubts

---

21 R. Kittel, *Geschichte des Volkes Israel* (1925), II, p. 250.
22 Cf. G. B. Gray, *JTS*, I (1900), p. 206.
23 F. M. Cross, *BASOR*, No. 132 (1953), pp. 15ff.

have been expressed as to his status,[24] he was certainly a charismatic figure in the normal sense of that term. It is difficult to tell from the stories concerning Samson whether he actually abstained from wine or not. However, the affinities between Samson and the Nazirites were sufficiently self-evident to allow him to have been thought of as a Nazirite, even though he may not have fulfilled all the technical prescriptions of Numbers 6.

In the time of Amos, the perversity of Israel was such that individuals deliberately attempted to undermine the institution by encouraging the Nazirites to adopt patterns of behavior that were completely at variance with their principles (Am. 2:11f.). From the exilic period onwards the Nazirites became increasingly related to a fixed interval of consecration, as opposed to the lifelong dedication of the individual evident in earlier days. Motives other than sanctification, obedience, and penitence were entertained,[25] and in the immediate pre-Christian period casuistry began to appear in connection with the enactments.[26]

3. *The Wilderness wanderings.* The narrative of Numbers 10:11 shows that, in the second year of their departure from Egypt, the Israelites left the Sinai region and journeyed to Kadesh-barnea, in the vicinity of the Promised Land. Kadesh was located on the borders of the Wilderness of Zin and the Wilderness of Paran (Num. 12:16; 13:26), and has frequently been identified with the spring of 'Ain Qudeis, some sixty-six miles southwest of the southern end of the Dead Sea. Modern explorers, however, have shown that the water supply at 'Ain Qudeis is very limited,[27] and that 'Ain Qudeirat, approximately five miles northwest of 'Ain Qudeis, is a much more suitable location for Kadesh.[28] However, there can be little doubt that the entire group of springs in that area was utilized at one time or another during the thirty-eight-year sojourn of the Israelites, with 'Ain Qudeirat being the principal source of water.

Not long after the second occurrence of the quail (Num. 11:31ff.), Moses was criticized by Aaron and Miriam for marrying a woman described as "Cushite." Presumably his first wife Zipporah had died subsequent to being returned by Jethro to Moses (Exod. 18:2), although this fact is nowhere stated in the text. The term "Cushite" is usually taken as the equivalent of "Ethiopian," and as such the woman concerned may have left Egypt among the Israelites and their followers. If, however, "Cushite" is to be derived from *Kushu* and the Hebrew "Cushan," associated with Midian (Hab. 3:7), the woman could con-

[24] Cf. G. B. Gray, *A Critical and Exegetical Commentary on Numbers,* p. 60.

[25] Cf. *BJ,* II, 15, 1.

[26] Cf. the Mishnaic *Tract Nazir.,* V, 5ff.

[27] C. L. Woolley and T. E. Lawrence, *PEF Annual,* III (1914-15), pp. 53ff. and pls. 10ff.; D. Baly, *Geography of the Bible* (1957), p. 266.

[28] Y. Aharoni, *The Holy Land: Antiquity and Survival* (1957), II, 2-3, pp. 295f. and figs. 1-3.

ceivably have come from a family stock related to that of Jethro and Zipporah. The cutaneous affliction that struck Miriam (Num. 12:10ff.) by way of punishment, and which was described in the text by the generic Hebrew term translated "leprosy," was evidently not equivalent to Hansen's disease. Precisely what its exact nature was is difficult to determine, and the most that can be said from the untechnical description of the phenomenon is that it may have constituted some such transient form of skin eruption as psoriasis.

The incident involving the dispatch of scouts to Canaan occupies a strategic position in the history of the Wilderness wanderings. The land of Canaan was fertile and pleasant, as the spies soon discovered, but its inhabitants were powerful and militant (Num. 13:17ff.). On hearing this report the perfidious Israelites rebelled against Moses and Aaron, and would have stoned them and returned to Egypt, had it not been for divine intervention at the peak of the crisis. Despite the magnanimity exhibited by Moses, the Israelites were sentenced to sojourn in the Wilderness areas until the rebellious generation had died out (Num. 14:20ff.). In connection with this episode it is important to remember that Israel was intended to have crossed from Egypt directly into the Promised Land via Sinai within the space of a very few years at the most, and that the enforced stay in Sinai was not part of the original plan for the infant nation.

As has been stated previously, this situation needs to be noted carefully in connection with the legislation contained in Exodus 22 and 23, which relates to a settled agricultural situation and looks back to a long tradition of Hebrew sedentary activity in this regard (cf. Deut. 11:10). There is absolutely no evidence to suggest that the ancient Hebrews were ever nomads in the sense of the modern desert Bedouin Arab. Studies in ancient Mesopotamian life have shown that a community such as Ur of the Chaldees, for example, was typically urban in nature, and based, as was the case with similar settlements in early Mesopotamia, upon a thoroughly agricultural and pastoral economy.[29] The patriarchal migration to Canaan was set against a similar background (Gen. 26:12, et al.), and the 430-year period of Israelite settlement in the eastern Delta region of the Nile was of a specifically sedentary and agricultural character. During their sojourn in Goshen, the Hebrews inhabited a region that was renowned for its lush pastures and cultivated crops and for its marshes teeming with game-birds, fish, and other forms of wild life.[30] Under such conditions it is simply unthinkable for anyone to suppose that the inhabitants of the Goshen region could not have augmented and sustained the agricultural and pastoral experience of their less sedentary precursors during a period of four centuries. Quite aside from the nature

[29] Cf. H. A. Frankfort, *The Birth of Civilization in the Near East* (1951), pp. 49ff.
[30] *ANET*, pp. 470f.

of the political and other conditions in Egyptian territory during the Hyksos period, there was ample opportunity for the dwellers in the east Delta region to become acquainted with the current situation in neighboring Canaan, since there was a constant crossing of the frontier by both Egyptians and Semites.[31]

Thus there is absolutely no reason why Moses, or anyone else in an analogous position, should not have been able to draw upon a prolonged tradition of agricultural and pastoral activity among the Hebrews in attempting to plan for a pattern of sedentary life in Canaan. Certainly there was absolutely no necessity whatever for the Israelites to occupy the territory before the appropriate legislation could be given, as was commonly imagined by an earlier generation of critical scholars. In fact, far from envisaging a purely future situation, a great many of the enactments in Exodus 22 and 23 actually look back to the four centuries of sedentary activity in the land of Goshen. It is well within the limits of possibility that some of the legislative material in these two chapters had its origin within that period of time, and that the lessons learned in connection with organized social life were subsequently incorporated, perhaps in a revised form to some extent, into the corpus of civil enactments promulgated under the direction of Moses, and that as such they could therefore be regarded as Mosaic in the best sense of the term.

It should be noted in passing that there were several distinct desolate areas located in the peninsula of Sinai, through which the Israelites passed in their journeyings. These included the *Wilderness of Shur* in the northwest part of the peninsula east of Goshen, the *Wilderness of Etham,* a zone controlled by Egyptian military forces situated between Lake Timsah and the Bitter Lakes, the *Wilderness of Sin,* located near Elim in the western part of Sinai and within striking distance of the oasis of Dophkah, the *Wilderness of Paran,* a desolate area in the east-central region of the Sinai peninsula bordering the Arabah and the Gulf of Aqabah, and the *Wilderness of Zin,* a rather ill-defined tract of territory including the extensive area between the Hebrew camp-site at Kadesh-barnea and the "*Scorpion Pass*" marking the later border of Judah (Josh. 15:3).

4. The rebellion of Korah, Dathan, and Abiram. Rebellion appears to have been a periodic feature of Israelite life during the Wilderness wanderings, of which the revolt of Korah, Dathan, and Abiram is illustrative. Critical scholars have long been accustomed to discern the presence of at least two, and possibly three, different narrative sources underlying the extant account. Thus it has been alleged that the rebellion of Dathan and Abiram (Num. 16:12ff.) was that of laymen against the

[31] *ANET,* pp. 258f.; K. A. Kitchen, *The Tyndale House Bulletin,* Nos. 5-6 (1960), p. 14.

civil authority of Moses, while that of Korah, against Moses and Aaron, was concerned primarily with religious matters. Traces of a third account have been supposed to subsist in the opposition of the tribe of Levi to the rights claimed by the Aaronites. In addition, it has also been maintained that the fate of the two different parties varied, with the first being swallowed by the earth and the second being devoured by means of heavenly fire.[32]

In view of these criticisms it should be noted initially that the narratives do not deal with two separate revolts, but with a joint or twin rebellion in which Korah protested against the ecclesiastical role of Moses and Aaron (Num. 16:3), while Dathan, Abiram, and On challenged the civil authority of the two Israelite leaders. The data of the text will not permit a legitimate division of the narrative into supposed underlying documents, for the true nature of the revolt is only seen most properly when the passage in question is regarded as unitary. On such a basis it will be evident that three grounds of discontent were being raised: the first was that Moses and Aaron had set themselves above the remainder of the people (Num. 16:3, 13); the second that Moses had failed to bring Israel to the Promised Land (Num. 16:14); and the third that Moses and Aaron had monopolized the functions of the priesthood (Num. 16:7-11).

To unite various grievances in a joint act of protest was as familiar a procedure in antiquity as it is at the present day. While the incident is depicted as a bifurcated attack upon authority, it is also manifested as united in nature, since Numbers 16:1-3 makes it explicit that Korah, Dathan, Abiram, and On, along with the two hundred and fifty princes, acted as a corporate unit. As regards the fate of the conspirators, the text does not say specifically that Dathan and Abiram were consumed by the earth, but only mentions Korah in this respect, although if he were regarded as the leader of the rebellion, his followers would naturally be subsumed under his designation, as Numbers 16:32f. indicates. However, the mention of Korah alone in this respect is not without significance for the critical analysis, since it was only the latter that posited such a fate for Dathan and Abiram. When fire is mentioned it should be noted that Korah was not included among those who were burned, since that fate was reserved for the two hundred and fifty princes (Num. 16:35). The incident is only amenable to a proper interpretation when the narrative is read as a unitary account, a situation made clear by a careful examination of the text.

Of the various explanations offered for the phenomenon of the earth's swallowing up the rebels, an attractive one has been proposed by Hort, who located the incident in the Arabah between the Dead Sea and the

32 *DILOT*, pp. 63ff.

Gulf of Aqabah.[33] In several parts of this region are to be found mud flats in various stages of development, the upper layers of which are formed of mud, clay, and salt. When dry such a structure can be crossed readily, but when wet it will not bear weight to any significant extent. Hort has supposed that the Israelites withdrew from the tents of the rebels just before a storm approached. The latter weakened the crust of the ground to the point where it collapsed, and during the storm the two hundred and fifty princes were struck by lightning. While in the nature of the case it is impossible to say precisely what happened on that occasion, the physical conditions that obtain in specific areas of the Sinai peninsula need not be regarded in any sense as incompatible with the tenor of the narrative.

5. *Balaam.* Archaeological discoveries in Mesopotamia have thrown a good deal of light upon the activities of such individuals as Balaam, as was observed previously. Texts recovered from Mari on the middle Euphrates have demonstrated the existence of different varieties of prognosticating priests who included the diviner (*bārûm*), the oracle-priest (*āpilum*), and the ecstatic seer (*maḫḫûm*), all of whom were well recognized in the eighteenth century B.C. and whose traditions were perpetuated in other areas of the ancient Near East to a large extent, including Ugarit. This latter fact is of interest in that the Balaam oracles (Num. 22–24) are full of Ugaritic parallels, and like the Song of Miriam (Exod. 15:1ff.) go back in their written form to between the thirteenth and twelfth centuries B.C.

An interesting seal bearing the legend "Manum, the *bārû*, the servant of Ea" was recovered from a thirteenth-century B.C. stratum at Bethshan, and was assigned to the early second millennium B.C., indicating the long tradition of Mesopotamian divinatory influence in Canaan. It would thus appear, as Daiches pointed out long ago, that Balaam was a typical Mesopotamian diviner (cf. Josh. 13:22), hired in accordance with the customs of the day for a specific purpose.[34] He was not primarily a prophet, even though, when subject to the will of God, he behaved in a manner very similar to that of the later Hebrew prophets. While the way in which the Balaam oracles came to be included in Numbers is unknown, as observed above, it is clear that the traditions concerning the Babylonian diviner were well established in the time of Joshua (Josh. 13:22), and it is quite possible that they may have come originally from Moabite sources. Linguistic and other considerations would suggest that the oracles were in written form by the twelfth century B.C., and that they were probably inserted into the text of Numbers in order to complement the history at some point either in the settlement period or even earlier, and in any event not later than the time of Samuel.

[33] G. Hort, *Australian Biblical Review*, VII (1959), pp. 19ff.
[34] S. Daiches, *Hilprecht Anniversary Volume* (1909), pp. 60ff.

In connection with the Balaam material it used to be asserted by an earlier generation of critics that Numbers 25 contained two underlying narratives.[35] The first of these was supposed to describe the way in which the Israelites were led into idolatry through immoral relations with Moabite women, while the second dealt with the suggestion of Balaam, who was then living in Midian, that the women should seduce the Israelites into idolatry and insure their destruction as the result of divine anger. This sort of speculation was typical of the conjectural atomizing of the Hebrew text undertaken by an earlier generation of literary critics, for even a casual reading of the material makes it clear that the counsel of Balaam was never mentioned in the text of chapter 25. The view that maintained that one account described the seduction of Israel into idolatry whereas the other merely referred to intermarriage is refuted by the fact that the *qubbāh* referred to in Numbers 25:8 was the sacred tent, before whose door the penitent Hebrews were weeping, and as such it has no connection whatever with a place reserved for prostitution, as the Vulgate rendering of *lupanar* or "brothel" would seem to indicate.

However, it remains true that fornication at the "door of the tabernacle of the congregation" was not unknown among both priests and laity in Israel during times of moral laxity, and was inevitably an occasion for the punishment of the nation (cf. 1 Sam. 2:22ff.). The conflict between Moabites and Midianites in the narrative is more apparent than real, for as was pointed out in connection with the Joseph narratives, there was a considerable amount of overlapping of Midianites, Ishmaelites, Medanites, and Moabites from the late patriarchal period onwards (cf. Gen. 25:2; 37:36; Judg. 8:24; 1 Chron. 1:32). There are thus no adequate textual or historical grounds for regarding the narrative as anything other than the unity which it purports to be.

6. *The census-lists.* The census-lists preserved in chapters 1 and 26 have occasioned considerable debate on the part of scholars generally. In certain particulars the problem here is that of other large numbers preserved in different parts of the Old Testament, especially in the earlier records of Hebrew history. As has been observed in a previous chapter, the situation is made appreciably more difficult by the presence of variant figures in the different texts and versions. In any event, numbers in antiquity were peculiarly liable to corruption in transmission, and there are several instances in the Old Testament narratives where a good deal of uncertainty exists regarding the correctness of the MT.

As far as the census in the first chapter of Numbers is concerned, some conservative scholars have accepted the text at face value, and have argued from Numbers 1:46 to the conclusion that the total of Israelite

---

[35] G. B. Gray, *A Critical and Exegetical Commentary on Numbers,* pp. 381ff.; *DILOT,* p. 67, *et al.*

warriors who attained their majority, along with other elements of the populace, amounted in all to a total of between two and three million Israelites in the Wilderness.[36] Despite protests that God would have been able to supply food for the needs of so great a multitude, a literal estimate of this kind raises a number of pressing problems, as critical scholars have pointed out.[37] An understanding of the contemporary situation with reference to the population of Canaan is instructive in this respect, for it is evident from sources such as the Tell el-Amarna tablets, as well as from the excavation of Canaanite cities of the thirteenth century B.C., that the overall population of the Promised Land was itself well below three million people.[38] If inferences from Exodus 23:29 and Deuteronomy 7:7, 17, 22 that the Israelites were fewer in number than the Canaanites are correct, it is clearly erroneous to take the census numbers at their face value.

Various expedients have been resorted to in an attempt to make the numbers conform to modern occidental concepts of "reality." One of these consists in the suggestion that the Hebrew word אלף, rendered as "thousands" in translations of the two census-lists, should actually be interpreted as "family" or "tent-group," as in Judges 6:15,[39] and this would give totals of between five and six thousand warriors. Substantially the same argument, presented against a background of more recent archaeological knowledge, was advanced by Mendenhall,[40] and followed, among others, by Bright.[41] The former argued that אלף should be taken as indicating a tribal sub-unit instead of being translated as "thousand," so as to bring the final computation to a more "realistic" level of population.

A similar attempt to reduce the large numbers found in Old Testament narratives generally, including those of Numbers, was made by Clark,[42] who suggested that the consonants of 'eleph should be revocalized so as to produce the word 'allûph, which with its Ugaritic cognate means "chief," "leader," or "captain." Thus in the census recorded in Numbers 1, it could have been possible for the word 'allûph to have been replaced by 'eleph during processes of transmission, which on a purely oral basis would be readily understandable. For Clark, then, the

---

[36] E.g. A. A. MacRae in F. Davidson, A. M. Stibbs, and E. F. Kevan (eds.), *The New Bible Commentary* (1953), p. 165; *YIOT*, p. 55.

[37] E.g. G. B. Gray, *A Critical and Exegetical Commentary on Numbers*, pp. 11ff.

[38] Cf. J. Garstang, *Joshua-Judges* (1931), pp. 120f.

[39] A. H. McNeile, *The Book of Numbers* (1911), p. 7; W. M. F. Petrie and C. T. Currelly, *Researches in Sinai* (1906), pp. 207ff.; W. M. F. Petrie, *Egypt and Israel* (1911), pp. 42ff.; J. Garstang, *Joshua-Judges*, p. 120.

[40] G. E. Mendenhall, *JBL*, LXXVII (1958), pp. 52ff.

[41] *BHI*, p. 144; cf. J. M. Wenham, *Tyndale Bulletin* (1967), No. 18, pp. 1ff.

[42] R. E. D. Clark, *Journal of the Transactions of the Victoria Institute*, LXXXVII (1955), pp. 82ff.

62,700 persons recorded for the tribe of Dan might well have read originally 60 captains and 2700 warriors.

None of these attempts to scale down the Old Testament numbers is able to account satisfactorily for all the data involved, and hence the suggestions made cannot be taken as uniformly valid for purposes of interpretation. If other evidence from Near Eastern sources concerning numbers generally is of any value in this connection, it would imply that the Old Testament numerical computations rest upon some basis of reality which was quite familiar to the ancients, but which is unknown to modern scholars. In the view of the author, the numbers in the census-lists and in such narratives as the Exodus from Egypt are used as symbols of relative power, triumph, importance, and the like, and are not meant to be understood either strictly literally or as extant in a corrupt textual form. By any standards the majesty and the miracle of the deliverance of Israel at the Yam Suph could only be expressed numerically in terms of enormous quantities, which taken on a purely literal basis are far in excess of what actually obtained at the time. Similarly, in the census-lists, the important and influential groups tended to be written up in terms of large numbers, while the more insignificant tribes were accorded much less prominence.

The long list of names which has preserved various stations in the Wilderness (Num. 33:19-35) along with the description of the route taken past Edom (Num. 20:22ff.; 21:4ff.; 33:38-44) presents numerous problems of identification. Most of the station-names fall within the thirty-eight-year period of sojourn at Kadesh-barnea, and cannot be located readily at the present. That the list is genuine seems apparent from the fact that the incidents associated with this period reflect accurately the natural phenomena of the area in which the stations are supposed to have been located. Thus the producing of water by means of a blow upon rock shows acquaintance with the water-retaining properties of Sinai limestone.[43] Similarly the excavating of shallow wells, as in Numbers 21:16ff., indicates the known incidence of sub-surface water in various parts of the Sinai peninsula and southern Transjordan.[44] G. E. Wright has suggested that the reason why the detailed list of stations between Mount Sinai and Kadesh as recorded in Numbers 33:16-36 was preserved so carefully was that pilgrimages of the kind undertaken at a subsequent period by Elijah (1 Kgs. 19:4ff.) may have been a frequent occurrence during the early days of Israelite national history.[45] While this may well be true, it is surely just as valid to argue that the pilgrimages could never have been carried out at all successfully had the list of stations not been preserved in some detail in the first place. The

---

[43] C. S. Jarvis, *Yesterday and Today in Sinai*, pp. 174f.
[44] N. Glueck, *Rivers in the Desert* (1959), p. 22.
[45] G. E. Wright, *IDB*, IV, p. 376.

form of the material under discussion suggests that it was in writing from a very early period, since it is simply an itinerary of the most compact and summary fashion, and unsuitable for serious transmission over subsequent generations in oral form in the manner so commonly suggested by liberal scholars.

❉ ❉ ❉ ❉ ❉

Numbers must never be regarded as merely comprising a catalog of the outstanding incidents which marked the Israelite sojourn in the Wilderness. Not only did the book record such events, but it interpreted them so as to demonstrate the Covenant love of God for His people in every emergency of distress and danger, as well as the stern and severe judgments of God against apostasy and rebellion. This revelation is uniformly evident throughout the book, and furnishes a theological emphasis that serves to integrate the literary selections into one harmonious corpus. The theme of divine holiness, so apparent in Leviticus, is also central to the theology of Numbers. While God dwells in the midst of His people, His innate sanctity demands that any who approach Him do so through carefully prescribed rules.

Because of the reciprocal nature of the Covenant agreement, it was of fundamental importance that Israel should reflect the holiness of her God in her subsequent dealings with the inhabitants of the Promised Land. This obligation was reinforced by the message of the Biblical narratives, which showed that God could engage a heathen diviner to serve His own purposes, a theme that was to be repeated with some variation in a later age of prophecy. Similarly, the fact that Israel was in Covenant relationship with the God of Sinai did not mean that any breach of that sacred agreement on her part would be tolerated by an indulgent deity. The consistency and justice of God as revealed to Israel were marked by a note of sternness, implying that any transgression of the Covenant would meet with an appropriate punishment. It was thus not without significance that Israel should experience the severity of God just prior to entering the Promised Land to fulfil her destiny.

The text of Numbers has not been as well preserved as that of Leviticus, although there is comparatively little in the way of actual corruption. In Numbers 21:14 something appears to have dropped out of the Hebrew, while in Numbers 21:18 Mattanah is probably not a place name, as in the RSV, but rather a noun derived from the root *nāthan*, and meaning "gift." Some difficulties of translation also exist in connection with Numbers 21:30 and 23:10.

Supplementary Literature

Binns, L. E. *The Book of Numbers*. 1927.
Eissfeldt, O. *Hexateuch-Synopse*. 1922.
Fish, S. *The Book of Numbers*. 1950.
Kennedy, A. R. S. *Leviticus and Numbers*. No date.

VI. THE BOOK OF DEUTERONOMY

A. NAME AND OUTLINE

The fifth book of the Torah was known in Jewish circles by the name אלה הדברים ("these are the words"), or simply דברים ("words"). It was also familiar to the Jews as משנה התורה, or sometimes merely משנה, from the words of Deuteronomy 17:18. Another title by which Deuteronomy was known in Jewish circles was *sēpher tôkhāhôth* or the "book of admonitions." The English designation was derived from the LXX τὸ δευτερονόμιον τοῦτο in Deuteronomy 17:18 (rendered by the Vulgate as *Deuteronomium*), which reflects an incorrect understanding of the words "copy of this law."

Deuteronomy comprises a collection of the last addresses given by Moses to the Israelites in the plains of Moab, and can be analyzed as follows:

I. The Acts of God, ch. 1:1–4:43
  A. Introduction; review of divine guidance, 1:1-46
  B. Events from Kadesh to the victories over Sihon, Og, 2:1–3:29
  C. Exhortation to obey the law, 4:1-43
II. The Law of God, ch. 4:44–26:19
  A. Introduction, 4:44-49
  B. Exposition of the Decalogue, 5:1–11:32
  C. Exposition of the principal laws of Israel, 12:1–26:19
    1. Centralization of worship, 12:1-32
    2. Punishment of idolatry, 13:1-18
    3. Dietary rules, 14:1-29
    4. The slaves and the poor, 15:1-23
    5. Three annual feasts, 16:1-17
    6. Appointment of judges, 16:18-20
    7. Prohibition of sacred trees and pillars, 16:21-22
    8. Punishment of idolatry, 17:1-7
    9. Court of appeal, 17:8-13
    10. Choosing a king, 17:14-20
    11. Priests, Levites, and prophets, 18:1-22
    12. Criminal laws, 19:1-21

13. Laws concerning future wars, 20:1-20
14. Laws concerning murder, captive women, rights of firstborn, and punishment of a refractory son, 21:1-23
15. Laws concerning social and moral behavior, 22:1-30
16. Rights of citizenship in the congregation, 23:1-25
17. Regulations concerning divorce; warnings against injustice to the poor; laws concerning gleaning, 24:1-22
18. Corporate punishment; levirate marriage; equitable dealings in society, 25:1-19
19. Thanksgiving and tithes, 26:1-19

III. The Covenant with God, ch. 27—30
   A. Ratification of the law, 27:1-26
   B. Blessings and curses, 28:1-68
   C. Exhortation to obedience, 29:1-29
   D. Conclusion of the renewed declaration of the Sinai Covenant, 30: 1-20

IV. Appendices, ch. 31—34
   A. Final injunctions of Moses, 31:1-21
   B. Commission of Joshua and address to elders, 31:22-30
   C. Song of Moses, 32:1-47
   D. Epilogue, 32:48-52
   E. Blessing of Moses, 33:1-29
   F. Death of Moses, 34:1-14

Deuteronomy perpetuates the tradition of Exodus that direct recording of events, statutes, and other material was the usual practice of Moses. Whereas nothing was said in this regard concerning the transcription of Leviticus and Numbers, Deuteronomy makes it clear that its contents were substantially the work of Moses (Deut. 31:9ff., 24ff.). Such a reference to "this law" is presumably to one section of Deuteronomy, and not to the Pentateuch as a whole. It is important to note that the work is actually what it purports to be, namely a collection of laws rather than a legal treatise drawn up for the ordering of the common life according to certain predetermined principles.[1]

While it is true that the spirituality implicit in the book is in essential harmony with that of other legalistic works in the Pentateuch, the contents of Deuteronomy comprise an assemblage of material issuing from various periods of the Wilderness wanderings, and should not be regarded technically as a "second law," as the English title might seem to imply. The work contains the essentials of Leviticus rewritten in such a manner as to make the more priestly and esoteric material amenable to the populace, and in this sense Deuteronomy can be said to comprise a popular version of the Levitical law, thereby approximating to something

[1] L. Köhler, *Hebrew Man* (1956), p. 141.

like an "Everyman's Torah." On the other hand, the relationship of Deuteronomy to the Book of the Covenant must not be forgotten, since for at least some of the Old Testament writers the Book of the Covenant appears to have been synonymous with Deuteronomy (2 Kgs. 23:2, 21; 2 Chron. 34:30).

B. AUTHORSHIP, COMPILATION, AND DATE OF DEUTERONOMY

Of the apparently post-Mosaic additions to Deuteronomy, the geographical descriptions in Deuteronomy 1:1f. are of particular interest. The book is rich in such data, which invariably view the land of Canaan from the outside.[2] In Deuteronomy 1:1 the expression "beyond the Jordan" (עבר הירדן) has been taken to imply the standpoint of one who was in Palestine,[3] and so to point to a post-Mosaic age for the verse in question. The phrase is found elsewhere in the Pentateuch (Gen. 50:10f.; Num. 22:1; 32:32; 35:14; Deut. 4:46), and although it is possible to assume that its incidence is non-Mosaic, since Moses never crossed the Jordan,[4] it is equally correct to assert that Moses could have known the geography of the situation without actually having visited the locations involved. The River Jordan figured prominently in Deuteronomy, being mentioned no fewer than twenty-six times. Of the occurrences, fifteen referred to the crossing of the river, one defined the boundaries of the territory of Reuben, and other occurrences were mentioned in the form of the expression "beyond the Jordan." That this phrase was rather indefinite is apparent from the fact that on twenty-four occasions it was accompanied by some modifying clause such as "towards the sea" or "towards the sunrising."[5] Indeed, the Hebrew phrase could well be rendered by an expression analogous to "by the banks of" or "at the ford of" the Jordan, or, if Gemser is correct, "in the region of the Jordan."[6] The necessity for clarity in the use of the phrase is apparent from Numbers 32:19, where it was employed to indicate both sides of the river by the children of Reuben and Gad. In each case an additional qualifying word was deemed necessary in order to make completely clear which side of the Jordan was intended to be signified. The words were used on six occasions in Deuteronomy (1:1, 5; 4:41, 46, 47, 49) of the eastern side—always in conjunction with some qualifying clause—and three times in speeches by Moses with reference to the western side (Deut. 3:20, 25; 11:30). In Deuteronomy 11:30 it was used of the western area with a defining clause, but in Deuteronomy 3:8, again with proper qualification, of the eastern side. The reference in Joshua 9:1,

---

[2] Cf. G. T. Manley, *EQ*, XXI (1949), pp. 81ff.
[3] *DILOT*, pp. 84f.
[4] So G. Ch. Aalders, *A Short Introduction to the Pentateuch*, p. 107.
[5] G. T. Manley, *The Book of the Law* (1957), p. 49.
[6] *VT*, II (1953), pp. 349ff.

however, was to the western bank, which presumably was the home of the narrator. The expression "beyond the Jordan," therefore, would appear to be as lacking in specific definition as the modern term "Transjordan," and the fact that the latter name can be employed intelligibly without requiring residence in the Near East would suggest that the use of the phrase cannot by itself indicate or determine the location of the writer.

While many of the places mentioned in Deuteronomy 1:1 were familiar to the narrator, and as such were recorded without explanation, they have proved difficult to identify in modern times. However, the explanatory gloss in Deuteronomy 1:2 is of some interest in the light of the customary identification of Mount Sinai with Jebel Mūsa. The tradition of an eleven-day period for the journey from Horeb via Mount Seir to Kadesh has been vindicated by Aharoni, who traced the route from the starting-point of Jebel Mūsa to Dahab on the east coast of Sinai, and continued northward and across the peninsula to 'Ain Qudeirat (Kadesh).[7] This identification would imply that the places mentioned in Deuteronomy 1:1 had a similar basis in fact, and it is possible that, if they are not actually Mosaic, they may have been preserved by one or more of the Levitical priests mentioned in Deuteronomy 31:9.

Perhaps a rather more assured post-Mosaic addition may be seen in Deuteronomy 3:14-17, which dealt with the assigning of lands, situated apparently on both sides of the Jordan, to the tribes of Israel. Whereas the delineation of Transjordanian territory is comparatively detailed, and suggests close acquaintance with the contemporary situation, the description of the allocation of supposedly Canaanite territory (Deut. 3:17) is of a very general nature. This latter would indeed be surprising had the passage in question emerged from a period even as late as that of the Judges, when the division of the land was known in detail. If the ערבה of Deuteronomy 3:17 refers to some area other than the familiar Arabah, a term applied in a general sense to the rift valley running from the Sea of Galilee to the Gulf of Aqabah, the standpoint of the author could well be that of one living in Transjordan.

The word ערבה really describes conditions of the soil, and has been transferred from such a restricted usage to the wider function of designating whole areas of "steppe" land. Although such regions were rather arid they afforded a certain amount of pasture, and Deuteronomy entertained the concept of steppe-land in connection with Moreh (Deut. 11:30) and the "plains of Moab" (Deut. 34:1, 8). Both these areas stood well above the Jordan valley, and made for excellent natural camp-sites. By contrast, the "way of the Arabah from Elath" (Deut. 2:7) described the low-lying terrain south of the Dead Sea, and in this it was in agreement with the modern description of the Arabah, which begins

[7] Y. Aharoni, *The Holy Land: Antiquity and Survival,* II, 2-3, pp. 289f., 293, fig. 7.

properly to the south of the Scorpion cliffs and terminates in the Gulf of Aqabah. In the light of the foregoing considerations it is far from certain that the section under examination is genuinely non-Mosaic. If it is, however, it can hardly be assigned to a period much later than the time of Joshua.

Another brief passage that has occasioned considerable discussion in relation to Mosaic authorship was the one which mentioned the death of Aaron at Moserah, and the subsequent journey of the Israelites from that place to Jotbath by way of Gudgod (Deut. 10:6f.). This has presented difficulty in view of the stated fact that the death of Aaron occurred long after the Sinai sojourn, and at Mount Hor (Num. 20:22ff.), making it difficult to see precisely why the incident was introduced at that point in the narrative. Furthermore, the order of the stations on the route was listed in Numbers 33:31ff. as Moseroth, Bene-jaakan, Hor-haggidgad and Jotbath, which is different from that of Deuteronomy 10:6f.

In this connection it should be noted that the various references to the death of Aaron (Num. 20:22ff.; 33:38f.; Deut. 10:6; 32:50f.) are supplementary rather than contradictory. While they are rather different in nature, they are by no means inconsistent in their presentation of fact. Although in the strictest sense Mount Hor was the physical scene of the death of Aaron, the name "Moserah" or "Moseroth" described the character of that event as "chastisement."[8] That this word was used as a common noun is indicated by the plural form in Numbers 33:30f. Like Massah, Meribah, and Taberah it denoted the nature of the event as well as the place where the incident occurred. Any analysis that ascribes Numbers 33 to a post-exilic source and then attempts to make Deuteronomy 32:48-52 conform to this pattern can be dismissed immediately, since the itinerary in Numbers is undoubtedly very ancient.

The geographical interest of the compiler is evident in the preservation of names such as those under immediate discussion. Bene-jaakan was prefixed in Deuteronomy 10:6 by the word "Beeroth" or "wells," indicating a concern for water. The site was obviously an oasis, and while it cannot be located with absolute certainty at present it was evidently in the vicinity of Ezion-geber. Jotbath is perhaps the modern 'Ain Ṭabah, about twenty-two miles north of Ezion-geber. The description in Deuteronomy 10:7 would imply that it was situated in a swampy depression that could rapidly become a shallow lake in the wintertime. Gudgod, another of the four places spoken of as having been visited on the way to Kadesh-barnea, was described in Numbers 33:33 as Hor-haggidgad or "the cave (?) of Gidgad." That there may perhaps have been some early textual confusion at this point seems apparent from the LXX version, which read *har* for *ḥōr*, and rendered it "the mountain of Gadgad." A location near the modern Wadi Ḥadaḥid may possibly be

---

[8] G. T. Manley, *EQ*, XXVII (1955), pp. 201ff.

implied by the reference, but this is uncertain at best. Other considerations apart, Deuteronomy 10:6f. bears the marks of being a textual
insertion, perhaps from a Levitical priestly source interested in perpetuating the traditions concerning Aaron and the tribe of Levi, recording the
fact that Eleazar succeeded to priestly office. This latter is in harmony
with subsequent statements regarding Phinehas as the officiating priest
in Israel during the early Judges period (cf. Josh. 24:33; Judg. 20:28).

The view that Deuteronomy was substantially Mosaic in origin was,
with a few exceptions, held by both Jews and Christians until the
nineteenth century. With the rise of liberal criticism the Mosaic authorship of the book was denied, and it was assigned tentatively to the
period of Josiah. Wellhausen gave classic expression to a view of the
authorship and date of Deuteronomy which soon gained widespread
scholarly acceptance by maintaining that the author of the composition,
which for him comprised chapters 12 to 26, was a prophet, who compiled the material about 622 B.C. The ostensible intention of this individual was to reform current religious practices and to abolish the pagan
"high places" in favor of centralizing worship in Jerusalem. To further
this laudable plan the author, Wellhausen alleged, concealed his work
in the Temple and permitted it to be "discovered" by Hilkiah the High
Priest during renovations to the fabric of the building. When its contents
were perused, they were found to be so relevant to the contemporary social and religious situation that the reforms described in 2 Kings 22 and
23 were the result.[9] This novel theory was an integral part of the evolutionary reconstruction of Hebrew religion which Wellhausen promulgated upon a basis of Hegelian philosophy. At first it was regarded as
heresy, but so pervasive was the influence doctrinaire Wellhausenism had
on the contemporary mind that it was soon accepted by a majority of
scholars, thereby becoming one of the more important tenets of the classical liberal criticism of the Pentateuch. The closely established relationship between the work of the "Deuteronomist" and the religious reforms
of King Josiah has always been integral to the orthodox Wellhausenian
theory of Israelite religious development. As H. H. Rowley, an adherent
of the Graf-Wellhausen approach to Old Testament studies, has commented, "the Code of Deuteronomy is . . . of vital importance in Pentateuchal criticism, since it is primarily by relation to it that the other
documents are dated."[10]

Although as early as 1805 De Wette had proposed a seventh-century
B.C. date for Deuteronomy in the belief that it was actually the law-book
used by Josiah in his religious reforms, other scholars accepted a quite
different view of the matter. Assuming that the legal code recovered

---

[9] J. Wellhausen, *Die Composition des Hexateuchs* (1889), p. 76 *passim, Prolegomena to the History of Israel* (1885), p. 9 *passim*.
[10] H. H. Rowley, *The Growth of the OT*, p. 29.

from the Temple was the "Holiness Code" (Lev. 17–26), Berry suggested that Deuteronomy was definitely of post-exilic origin,[11] while Kennett proposed a date in the time of Haggai and Zechariah, that is to say, about 520 B.C.[12] Hölscher adopted a similar view in placing the book at least one hundred years after the time of Josiah,[13] while Pedersen and other members of the Uppsala school supposed that the work reached its final form about 400 B.C., though recognizing that parts of it existed in writing at a much earlier period.[14]

Not all scholars agreed that Deuteronomy should be assigned to a later rather than an earlier date, however. Ewald placed the composition of the work in the time of Manasseh;[15] Westphal related it to the earlier period of the reign of Hezekiah.[16] Von Rad held that Deuteronomy may have arisen in circles of "country Levites," and have been in its completed form shortly after 701 B.C.[17] The pre-monarchic origin of the work was asserted by Robertson, who maintained that it may have been largely the work of Samuel.[18]

A similar position was adopted by Brinker, who in process of refuting the arguments for a Josianic date of Deuteronomy regarded the legislation as basically Mosaic, with supplements made by priests and judges from decisions given at different sanctuaries.[19] For Brinker the guiding principle of Deuteronomy was not that of the centralization of worship in Jerusalem, as maintained by the critical school, but the protection of the people from the threat of Canaanite idolatry.[20] W. F. Albright, although adhering to the broad pattern of liberal criticism, assigned the Song of Moses (Deut. 32:1-43) to the time of Samuel, following Eissfeldt,[21] and demonstrated its archaic nature in the light of the manuscript scraps recovered from 4Q.[22] It will be clear from the foregoing selection of scholarly views that there has been considerable doubt as to the actual date of the book even in liberal circles, and while most adherents of the Wellhausenian position would posit a seventh-century B.C. date for the origin of Deuteronomy, an increasing number

---

[11] *JTS*, XXVI (1925), p. 156.
[12] *Deuteronomy and the Decalogue* (1920), pp. 6ff.
[13] *ZAW*, XL (1922), pp. 161ff.
[14] *Israel*, III-IV, p. 96.
[15] *History of Israel* (1876), I, p. 127.
[16] *The Law and the Prophets* (1910), p. 304.
[17] *Studies in Deuteronomy* (1953), p. 66.
[18] *The OT Problem*, p. 42.
[19] *The Influence of Sanctuaries in Early Israel*, pp. 189ff.
[20] Cf. A. C. Welch, *The Code of Deuteronomy* (1924), p. 195.
[21] *BPAE*, p. 45.
[22] W. F. Albright, *VT*, IX (1959), pp. 339ff.; cf. P. W. Skehan, *BASOR*, No. 136 (1954), pp. 12ff., *JBL*, LXXVIII (1959), p. 22.

of scholars have finally become aware of the need for a more flexible position on the whole matter than was once the case.[23]

One of the important points at issue in the discussion of the provenance and date of Deuteronomy has been the question of the centralization of worship, which for many has been held to be the principal theme of the composition. Deuteronomy 12 prescribed that all sacrifices and offerings would be brought in the Promised Land ". . . unto the place which the LORD your God will choose" (Deut. 12:5, 11, 14, 18, 21, 26). This matter was interpreted along Hegelian lines by Wellhausen and his followers to the point where it was assumed, quite without proof, that Jerusalem was the place where the cult was intended to be centralized.[24]

Not all critical scholars were convinced by this sort of reasoning, however, for as Skinner pointed out, the book itself laid no stress whatever upon the peculiar claim of Jerusalem to be the sole place of worship.[25] Rowley also observed correctly that there was nothing in Deuteronomy to the effect that the central and solitary legitimate sanctuary was to be located in Jerusalem.[26] A. C. Welch maintained that apart from Deuteronomy 12:1-5, which he regarded as a later insertion, there was no prescription that stipulated that sacrifices could only be offered upon one altar.[27]

The regulations concerning sacrifice in Deuteronomy 12 represent an expansion of the provision recorded in Exodus 20:24, where the scene was set in Horeb.[28] But when the religious situation that would be encountered in Canaan once the tribes began to occupy the terrain was contemplated, the different conditions required a somewhat diverse approach from that of a desert milieu. Accordingly it is important to notice that Deuteronomy 12:14, which speaks of the place that the Lord will choose in the jurisdiction of one of the tribes, does not necessarily imply that there will be one, and only one, tribal territory where God may be worshipped.[29]

The real force of the contrast in Deuteronomy 12 is not between many altars of God and one, but between those of the Canaanites dedicated to alien deities and the place where the name of God is to be revered. As Manley has put it, the thing which is in question is not their

[23] Cf. C. R. North, *OTMS*, p. 82. For the literature on the date and composition of Deuteronomy see H. H. Rowley, *Studies in OT Prophecy Presented to T. H. Robinson* (1950), pp. 157f.

[24] *Prolegomena to the History of Israel*, p. 368.

[25] J. Skinner, *Prophecy and Religion: Studies in the Life of Jeremiah* (1922), p. 167.

[26] H. H. Rowley, *Studies in OT Prophecy Presented to T. H. Robinson*, p. 166.

[27] A. C. Welch, *The Code of Deuteronomy*, p. 31.

[28] *Ibid.*, p. 30.

[29] Cf. R. Brinker, *The Influence of Sanctuaries in Early Israel*, p. 199.

number but their character.[30] Whether the words be interpreted to mean one or more centers, however, it still remains true that they do not of themselves exclude the possibility that there were other duly authorized altars for Israelite worship. Although the building of one official altar on Mount Ebal was commanded in Deuteronomy 27:1ff., the rule enshrined in Deuteronomy 16:21f. entertained the existence of several such places in Canaan.

The assumption that Jerusalem was the place intended by Deuteronomy where the cultus was to be centralized is entirely subjective in nature, and has no textual warrant for it whatever. This theory has been criticized by von Rad as in fact resting upon a very slender basis.[31] In the German original of his *Studies in Deuteronomy* he maintained that the command in Deuteronomy 27:1-8 to build an altar upon Mount Ebal and to inscribe the Law upon stones raised a "barricade" against the centralization theory.[32] His observation is mild to say the least; in point of fact the command relating to Mount Ebal is absolutely fatal to the position of Wellhausen and his followers. It specifically prescribes that which the Law is supposed to prohibit, and even utilizes the words of Exodus 20:24, which, according to the critical viewpoint, the Deuteronomic law was intended to revoke. Furthermore, it was confirmed by the account in Joshua 8:30-35, which described the building of the altar by Joshua. A comparison of Deuteronomy 27:1-8 and Joshua 8:30-35 shows that while both passages are related, they are quite independent of each other in matters of detail. The Deuteronomic passage commands first of all the setting up of stones, which are then to be covered with a cement coating, after which an altar is to be erected. The account in Joshua commences with the altar of unhewn stones and then proceeds to the matter of the inscription, making no mention of the cement coating. In Deuteronomy nothing is said about judges and officers, or of the reading of the Law, while the account in Joshua contains no reference to the dividing of the tribes, and in any event cannot be considered at all "Deuteronomic" in terms of literary style.

That both passages appear to have a firm basis alike in Hebrew religious tradition and history appears evident from the fact that Shechem, situated in the uplands of Ephraim in the vicinity of Mount Gerizim, was one of the sites from which fragments of primitive writing belonging to the conquest period were recovered.[33] Since Deuteronomy 27:1-8 cannot

30 G. T. Manley, *The Book of the Law*, p. 132.
31 G. von Rad, *Studies in Deuteronomy*, p. 68.
32 G. von Rad, *Deuteronomium Studien* (1947), p. 47.
33 Cf. E. Nielsen, *Shechem, A Traditio-Historical Investigation* (1955), pp. 3ff.; G. E. Wright, *BASOR*, No. 144 (1956), pp. 9ff., *BA*, XX, No. 1 (1957), pp. 19ff., *BASOR*, No. 148 (1957), pp. 11ff.; B. W. Anderson, *BA*, XX, No. 1 (1957), pp. 10ff.; W. Harrelson, *BA*, XX, No. 1 (1957), pp. 2ff.; H. C. Kee and L. E. Toombs, *BA*, XX, No. 4 (1957), pp. 82ff.

be dismissed as a later insertion,[34] it clearly confirms the ordinary meaning of Deuteronomy 12 in that it forbids any association with Canaanite worship and looks forward to a national cultic center, but allows for the worship of God at any duly authorized altar elsewhere. Thus the centralization theory of Wellhausen—described frequently as the keystone in his system of chronology[35]—is evidently far from being firmly fixed. As with so many other postulates of classical liberalism, it can only be supported by a misreading of the history, and by contrived and artificial interpretations of the Hebrew text.

What seems to have transpired during the early conquest and settlement periods was that the tribes gathered at intervals around the Tabernacle, following the traditions and practices familiar from the Wilderness wanderings. Altars were erected and sacrifices offered at such places as Shechem, Ophrah, and Ramah, but Mount Gerizim was firmly fixed as the place appointed by Moses for whatever central observations of the cultus were deemed necessary. A relapse into Canaanite idolatry was followed by a religious revival when the Temple in Jerusalem was constructed, but further syncretism and religious degeneration ensued until the southern kingdom was taken into captivity in the sixth century B.C. by the Babylonians.

The Deuteronomic law fits admirably against such a background of history and cultic practice if it is placed at the close of the Mosaic period. The Canaanites were then in sole occupation of the Promised Land, apart from the area where the Philistine cities were located, and one prominent feature of the subsequent Israelite conquest of the territory was to be the destruction of pagan shrines so as to remove all temptation from the midst of Israel. The gifts and sacrifices of the Chosen People were to be brought only to an authorized altar, accompanied by the proper ritual safeguards. The altar of God was not to be defiled by the pagan fertility symbols common at that period (Deut. 16:21f.), nor was there to be any taint of admixture with Canaanite religious practices (Deut. 12:29ff.). After the Jordan had been crossed the Israelites were to erect an altar upon Mount Ebal and inscribe the Law of Moses on prepared stones (Deut. 27:1ff.). The primitive character of the enactment in Deuteronomy 27:1-8 is evident from the absence of such words as ba'al and bāmôth, and by the indefiniteness of the allusions to the "place" where God would allow His Name to be revered.

Of all possible claimants to this high honor, Jerusalem is clearly the least likely. In the time of Joshua it was a Jebusite fortress that had been bypassed during the second stage of the conquest. It was only brought within the orbit of Israelite life during the time of David, and at that

[34] S. R. Driver, *A Critical and Exegetical Commentary on Deuteronomy* (1895), p. 294.
[35] E.g. by G. W. Anderson, *OTMS*, p. 283.

from a standpoint of purely political expediency, since it was situated in neutral territory and therefore could claim the loyalty of northern and southern tribes alike without prejudice to either. Furthermore, it is important to notice that Jerusalem as a proper name does not occur in the Pentateuch, although it was spoken of in the fourteenth-century B.C. Tell el-Amarna tablets. It has been assumed that the designation "Salem" in Genesis 14:18 and Psalm 76:3 is a shortened form of "Jerusalem," but this view, which owed a great deal to Josephus, has never gone unquestioned in Christian circles since the time of Jerome and Eusebius. There seems little doubt that the name "Salem" cannot be considered to be either another name for Jerusalem or an abbreviated form of the designation of the city, the pre-Israelite origin of which is assured, but rather that in Genesis it referred to some quite distinct locality, and that in the Psalter it constituted a poetic and religious appellation. If it is correct to assume, with Eusebius in his *Onomasticon*, that the Salem of Genesis referred to a village of the Jordan valley south of Scythopolis, it might be possible to identify the site with the Salim of John 3:23, tentatively localized at Umm el-ʿAmdan. If the AV rendering of Genesis 33:18, "Shalem, a city of Shechem," which is based upon Greek, Latin, and Syriac textual traditions, is correct, Salem could well be identified with the village of Salim, some four or five miles east of Balaṭa-Shechem.

What is made clear in this general connection by the book of Deuteronomy is that Moses appointed a central place in Canaan, namely Mount Ebal, the more northerly of the two mountains that overshadow the modern town of Nablus, two miles northwest of ancient Shechem, as the locale for major cultic celebrations. There is no evidence that the prescription of Deuteronomy 27:1-8 commanded a centralizing of the cultus as such in the Ebal-Gerizim area; instead the site was to be regarded as focal to Israelite national and spiritual aspirations. It is not without significance, therefore, that the Samaritans have venerated Mount Gerizim as the place where God chose to put His Name (Deut. 12:5).[36] As C. H. Gordon has pointed out in this connection, the Samaritans are right in their claim that the text has been tampered with in order to suppress the priority of their Gerizim shrine and convey the impression, fostered in orthodox Judaeo-Christian circles, that Moses had Jerusalem in mind as the center of subsequent Hebrew national worship.[37] The Samaritans, who insist that the "place" of Deuteronomy 12:5 is Gerizim and not Jerusalem, have a better argument in that the altar erected "near" Gerizim was the only one built in accordance with the specific orders of Moses. Several Hebrew manuscripts and ancient versions show that the text has been altered at this point, since the altar was actually "on" Mount Gerizim. The Samaritan view

---

[36] Cf. E. Robertson, *The OT Problem*, pp. 157ff.
[37] *IOTT*, pp. 132f. Cf. J. Macdonald, *The Theology of the Samaritans*, p. 16.

is obviously correct, but the trend of history has been such as to make heretics of them and bestow orthodoxy upon Judaism.

If it was not the aim of the author of Deuteronomy to institute a centralization of worship in Jerusalem, what is to be said about the claim that his object was to reform current practices in religion and to abolish the במת or "high places"? That the latter consideration was not paramount in any attempted centralization of the cultus appears clear from the fact that the במת were not mentioned at all in Deuteronomy 12. Furthermore, the aim of the author was, as Pedersen has pointed out, to protect the Israelite community against Canaanite influence, and in sure that the Chosen People would obey the divinely revealed law of the Covenant relationship.[38] At the time contemplated by Deuteronomy, Israelite worship had not become sufficiently depraved to require the kind of thoroughgoing reformation characteristic of later periods in the history of the southern kingdom.

Part of the difficulty involved in this situation has resulted from the doctrinaire pronouncement of Wellhausen to the effect that the book was to be dated about 622 B.C., and ought to be credited with serving as the stimulus for the reforms of Josiah. To set the matter in correct perspective it needs only to be observed that the reformation of Josiah resulted in an abolition of idolatry, and not in the establishing of a centralized sanctuary, the latter having obtained since the days of Solomon. If the book was composed about 680 B.C. by a follower of Isaiah, as Rowley proposed in a modification of the views of Driver, it is significant that no mention occurred either of the במת or of Jerusalem in the centralization issue.[39] Furthermore, there are no traces in the extant work of the influence of the prophet Isaiah, whether of a literary or a doctrinal nature. Deuteronomy is written in flowing Hebrew prose of great elegance and beauty, and is essentially oratorical and hortatory, in accordance with its general purpose. By contrast, Isaiah was a poetic genius whose wealth of imagination and vividness of expression combined with a chaste and dignified literary style to perpetuate the majesty and dimension of his communion with God.

In Deuteronomy there is no doctrine of a "remnant," no occurrence of the prophetic formula "thus saith the Lord," and no use of the title "the Holy One of Israel." Finally, it is extremely difficult to conceive of the book of Deuteronomy as constituting anything approaching a program of religious reform purporting to come from a disciple of Isaiah in the early days of the reign of Manasseh. While the reforms of both Hezekiah and Josiah may have drawn in part for their inspiration upon the contents of Deuteronomy, the correspondence of the legal material in

---

[38] J. Pedersen, *Israel, I-II*, p. 27.
[39] H. H. Rowley, *The Growth of the OT*, p. 31. S. R. Driver, *A Critical and Exegetical Commentary on Deuteronomy*, p. lv.

the work with what transpired in the reigns of Hezekiah and Josiah is not sufficiently close to make evident an immediate dependence upon the provisions of Deuteronomy.

The nature and extent of the law-book discovered by Hilkiah in the Temple has been a matter of considerable discussion among scholars for many decades. From the time of De Wette it was considered axiomatic that it comprised the bulk of Deuteronomy, but this view has been contested increasingly by modern scholars.[40] The fact is that it is simply impossible to determine from the text (2 Kgs. 22:3ff.) either the length or the contents of the "book of the Torah." It may have included part of Deuteronomy, but it could equally have comprised the Book of the Covenant, either in its original or in an augmented form.

A much more serious problem has been presented by the view of De Wette and his followers that Deuteronomy was a "pious fraud." That such an assertion is entirely out of harmony with what is now known of literary practices among ancient Near Eastern scribes has been made plain by Albright, who has stated that it cannot be emphasized too strongly that there is hardly any evidence at all in the ancient Near East for documentary or literary fabrications.[41] A few such are known from Egypt, including the Bentresh *stele* and the decree of Djoser on a cliff near Elephantine, both of which purport to reach back to very ancient times. It is now known, however, that both these inscriptions belong properly to the Ptolemaic era, and emerge from a time when the ethos of the ancient Orient had already vanished.

Arguments that suggest the possibility of "pious fraud" are therefore based upon analogies from the Graeco-Roman period, and as such have no bearing upon the literary practices of the ancient Near East, where such fabrications simply did not occur. As C. H. Gordon has shown, the fact that neither Josiah nor his immediate precursors knew anything of the Law does not prove that the ספר recovered by Hilkiah was necessarily a forgery.[42] Throughout the ancient Near East law codes generally, whether they claimed divine origin, as did the Code of Hammurabi, or not, were regularly disregarded in actual life. Mesopotamian judges consistently omitted any reference to law codes in their court decisions, preferring instead to be guided by tradition, public feeling, and their own estimate of the situation confronting them. Processes of codification naturally took cognizance of custom and previous experience in the matter of legal precedents, but once they had been formulated such codes were only studied by research scholars, and in general had very

---

[40] For the literature on the subject see O. Eissfeldt, *Einleitung in das AT*, pp. 186ff. De Wette was anticipated in his conclusions by Athanasius, *PG*, XXVII, col. 44; Chrysostom, *PG*, LVII, col. 181, LXI, col. 58; Jerome, *PL*, XXIII, col. 227, XXV, col. 71; and Procopius, *PG*, LXXXVII, i, col. 915f.

[41] *FSAC*, p. 78.

[42] *IOTT*, p. 239.

647

little bearing upon current legal and social practice. Thus the rediscovery of lost Sumerian legal codes some centuries after their promulgation would have constituted as complete a surprise to the contemporary Babylonians generally as the finding of the "book of the Torah" did to Josiah. The significance of the latter event is that the trend of religious and social affairs in the kingdom of Judah was confronted anew by the prescriptions of a forgotten law-book whose inspiration guaranteed it success as an instrument of religious revival where other legal codes in the Near East had failed in their laudable aim of raising the moral, social, and religious tone of national life.

In view of the peculiar difficulties attaching to the liberal view of the authorship and date of Deuteronomy, it seems important to emphasize at this juncture that there is nothing in the work that can be proved conclusively to be incompatible with substantial Mosaic authorship. The legal content is primitive and authoritarian in nature, and is thoroughly permeated with the moral, ethical, and humanitarian concepts inherent in the Covenant relationship. Brinker, following Robertson, appears to be incorrect in his view that Deuteronomy was an expansion of the Mosaic "Book of the Covenant," and formulated by a council of priests under the supervision of Samuel.[43] The two books of Samuel do not contain the word "*tôrāh*" or "law," nor do they suggest the existence of a conclave of priests and scribes. Furthermore, the leader of Israel appointed by Samuel was a charismatic נגיד or "military commander," and not the מלך or "king" envisaged by Moses (Deut. 17:14ff.). The simplest and most probable account of the authorship and date of Deuteronomy is that Moses "wrote" the legislation himself, that is to say, chapters 12 to 26, and that the discourses and the concluding poems were added at a somewhat later time.

The structural unity and integrity of Deuteronomy have been emphasized by Kline, in the light of the rediscovery of treatises of major kings of Near Eastern antiquity.[44] While there is nothing either new or particularly unusual in a comparison of Hittite suzerainty treaties with the form of the Covenant agreement at Sinai, the application of this concept to Deuteronomy as a whole is an unusual departure in the field of literary criticism. Kline has shown that when Deuteronomy is viewed holistically or as an integer, it exhibits on a large scale the complete covenantal formulation of the ancient Near East; and he has made it clear that this phenomenon points to its fundamental structural unity.

[43] R. Brinker, *The Influence of Sanctuaries in Early Israel*, p. 223; E. Robertson, *The OT Problem*, pp. 60ff.

[44] M. G. Kline, *Treaty of the Great King* (1963), pp. 13ff.; cf. G. E. Mendenhall, *BA*, XVII, No. 3 (1954), pp. 50ff., republished as *Law and Covenant in Israel and the Ancient Near East* (1955), *IDB*, I, pp. 714ff.; K. Bultzer, *Das Bundesformular. Seine Ursprung und seine Verwendung im AT* (1960); D. J. Wiseman, *The Vassal-Treaties of Esarhaddon* (1958).

As such it can no longer be considered the product of a series of redactions of the document that produced the Josianic reformation. The so-called "two introductions" to the book (Deut. 1–4 and 5–11) need not be regarded now as the product of two editorial hands, since in the suzerainty treaties of the ancient Near East an historical prologue regularly follows the preamble and precedes the stipulations of the agreement. In the light of this situation Deuteronomy 1:5–4:49 qualifies admirably as just such an historical prologue.[45] Deuteronomy 5–11 must now be recognized as expounding the Covenant way of life in precisely the same manner as chapters 12 to 26, which together declare the demands of the suzerain. The differences between Deuteronomy 5 to 11 and 12 to 26 only represent for Kline variant treatments of this one theme, namely the stipulations of the suzerain in relation to his subjects. In the same manner it is possible to relate the appendix material (Deut. 31–34) to the treaty pattern discerned in earlier sections of the book, and to see in it a concern for succession rights which, according to Near Eastern parallels, were an important part of the legal deposition to which allegiance was required.

Kline is further interested in the date of Deuteronomy, since his marshalling of Covenant parallels down to the time of Esarhaddon (681-669 B.C) does not in itself require a Mosaic date for the book. Arguing from a difference in form between second- and first-millennium B.C. treaties, he has maintained that there is an "early" and a "late" structure for ancient Near Eastern covenants generally. For him, the most remarkable difference is that the historical prologue, the distinctive second section of the second-millennium B.C. treaties, is no longer found in the later texts.[46] Without any doubt, therefore, Deuteronomy belongs to the classic stage in this process of documentary evolution, and furnishes significant confirmation of the *prima facie* case for the Mosaic origin of the Deuteronomic treaty of the Great King.

While it is still uncertain at the time of writing as to precisely how far the language of covenant in the Old Testament has been shaped by wider concepts, this consideration has little bearing upon the important problems of literary criticism with regard to Deuteronomy. There can be no question that the study undertaken by Kline is of the greatest significance for any future discussion of the questions relating to the authorship and date of the composition, and that his work has the undeniable merit of being properly based upon an accredited Near Eastern methodology. As Kline himself has remarked:

> . . . Now that the form critical data compel the recognition of the antiquity not merely of this or that element within Deuteronomy but of the Deuteronomic treaty in its integrity, any persistent insistence on a final edition of the book

[45] Kline, *op. cit.*, p. 31; cf. J. A. Thompson, *The Ancient Near Eastern Treaties and the OT* (1964), pp. 13f.

[46] Kline, *op. cit.*, pp. 42f.

around the seventh century B.C. can be nothing more than a vestigial hypothesis, no longer performing a significant function in Old Testament criticism.[47]

Of the institutions included in Deuteronomy, that which has become known as the "levirate law" (Deut. 25:5ff.) is of interest in that it constitutes an expansion of the Levitical marriage promulgations, and affords regularized status to a custom found among people other than the Hebrews. The term "levirate" is derived from the Latin *levir* or "husband's brother," and the legislation thus characterized required that when a married man died without leaving children, his brother was to take his widow in marriage and raise a family on behalf of the deceased man. The purpose of the legislation was to prevent the marriage of an Israelite woman to an outsider; to provide for the purely material and emotional needs of the bereaved woman, and to continue the name of the dead man within the nation of Israel. The custom thus reinforced the importance for many Semitic peoples of endogamous marriage, and the production of offspring from such unions.

One form of this tradition was made evident in the story of Judah and Tamar (Gen. 38:8ff.), where Onan took the wife of his deceased brother Er, but refused to impregnate her at copulation on the ground that his own children would not have the primary inheritance. However, this instance is hardly typical of levirate marriage as such, and in any event it furnishes no ground for any concept of birth control in antiquity, as some scholars have maintained. The book of Ruth indicates that the custom occasionally extended beyond the brother of a husband, but again the general situation is rather different from that contemplated in Deuteronomy.[48] As in ancient Hittite law, the act of Boaz extended the levirate custom to other male relatives of the deceased in the event that no brothers survived.

The levirate law did not apply if daughters had been born, and regulations for the inheritance of such individuals constituted an early concern of codified Hebrew law (Num. 27:1ff.). Even though the provisions of Numbers 27:9-11 might appear to ignore or even contravene the general provisions of the levirate law, it seems evident that these regulations would be operative where there were daughters only; when a childless wife had died before her husband did, when the brother of the late husband refused to take the childless widow, or when the wife remained childless after being married to the brother.

Levitical law (Lev. 18:16; 20:21) prohibited a man from marrying his brother's wife, as has already been observed. Thus, if the document in which such legislation is as late and priestly as adherents of the Graf-Wellhausen theory have popularly supposed, it is curious that such an

[47] *Ibid.*, p. 44.
[48] O. J. Baab, *IDB*, III, p. 282.

authoritative pronouncement would ignore entirely, if not directly repudiate, the long-established Hebrew custom of the levirate and its variations. However, it would appear that the emphasis in Leviticus was upon sexual relations rather than marriage as such. The provision in Leviticus 20:21 is analogous to that in the preceding verse, and in neither case is it possible to decide from the text whether the uncle or the brother is already dead. At all events, the institution was designed to preserve the homogeneity of the family group, to perpetuate the name of its male members in Israel, and to provide in a characteristically humanitarian fashion for the welfare of the widow.

The influence of Deuteronomy upon the historical and prophetic writings is a matter of some concern in the light of the arguments adduced in the present work for its antiquity and substantial Mosaicity. It can be stated immediately as a general principle that Deuteronomy deals in a distinctive prophetic manner with the lessons to be learned from the trend of past events, having regard, of course, to the central fact of the Covenant relationship. In an historical composition such as 1 and 2 Kings, the compiler is also looking back to the Covenant ideal, and like the author of Deuteronomy expounds events against a theological background. The two books of Kings are directly concerned with the implications of the Covenant for the life of Israel, and judgment is pronounced both upon individuals and the nation as a whole in accordance with the degree to which they are thought to have strayed from the Covenant ideal.

The familiarity of the prophets with the Law generally is apparent from the books of Joshua and Kings (cf. Josh. 1:8; 8:34; 1 Kgs. 2:3f.); and the Deuteronomic law in the sense of "statutes and judgments" was by no means unknown to David (Ps. 18:22). The latter phrase occurred again in the pronouncement of the prophet Ahijah to Jeroboam (1 Kgs. 11:33f.), when he charged the people with forsaking the precepts that David himself had kept. In 2 Kings 14:6, the authority of the "book of the law of Moses" was appealed to, the reference being to Deuteronomy 24:16. Again, the "Book of the Covenant" mentioned in 2 Kings 23:2 was evidently intended to be synonymous with a part of Deuteronomy. Thus it appears that for some time before the historical books were written, the Israelites believed that a book of the law of Moses existed that had regulated the conduct and aspirations of such notable individuals as Joshua, David, and Amaziah.

In much the same manner the eighth-century B. C. prophets knew of the existence of a *tôrāh*, for the word was used by Hosea (4:6; 8:1, 12), Amos (2:4), Micah (4:2), Isaiah (1:10; 2:3; 5:24; 8:16, 20), and Zephaniah (3:4). While the term can refer to a body of "teaching," including the oracles of the prophets themselves, it is also apparent from the context that in certain definite instances it indicates the existence of a body of divine law that the priests had to teach (Hos. 4:6; Zeph. 3:4)

651

and the people had to observe (Isa. 5:23f.; Hos. 4:6; 8:1, 12). Besides these explicit references to a *tôrāh* there are indications that particular enactments contained in Deuteronomy were well known in Israel. These included the law of the landmark (Hos. 5:10 and Deut. 19:14), the need for a standard measure (Am. 8:5; Mic. 6:10f. and Deut. 25:13ff.), the triennial payment of the tithe (Am. 4:4 and Deut. 14:28), and the authority of the priest (Hos. 4:4ff.; Zeph. 3:4 and Deut. 17:12; 24:6).

All this does not prove, of course, that the eighth-century B.C. prophets were acquainted with Deuteronomy either in its developing or extant form, nor, for that matter, that they had the least knowledge of J or E. What it does indicate, however, is that the religious traditions enshrined in the Pentateuch had been perpetuated over successive generations albeit, perhaps, in limited circles. This is entirely consistent with the general situation in the ancient Near East, where individuals and communities alike pursued their lives in happy and untroubled indifference to extant written legal codes.

Regarding the influence of Deuteronomy upon the work of Jeremiah critical scholars have varied considerably in their estimates of the situation. Driver discerned traces of Deuteronomy on nearly every page of Jeremiah; [49] but J. N. Schofield, who assigned a comparatively late date to Deuteronomy, denied that Jeremiah ever knew the work, and regarded any similarities as being due to the influence of the prophet upon the compilers of Deuteronomy.[50] For the present it will be sufficient to note that indications of the influence of Deuteronomy that can be discerned in Jeremiah are similar to those found in earlier prophets. In some instances, however, there is a greater degree of precision (e.g. Jer 11:1-5), which may possibly owe something to the discovery of the law-book in the Temple. If Jeremiah was at all familiar with the content of the latter, he manifests no awareness that its supposed intent was to restrict the offering of sacrifices to Jerusalem. Indeed, the opposite is true to some degree in that Jeremiah preserved the tradition that there was once a legitimate altar of the God of Israel at Shiloh. For Jeremiah the moral law was predominant, as in the Pentateuchal legislation generally, and while he did not entirely reject the cultic ritual he insisted upon its purity and the superiority of the moral law.

In the prophetic writings from Amos to Jeremiah, there are certain observable trends corresponding to the national development as depicted in the historical books. But whereas in these works there is a gradual change as the religious fortunes of Israel decline, the outlook of

[49] S. R. Driver, *A Critical and Exegetical Commentary on Deuteronomy*, p xlvii.

[50] J. N. Schofield in *Studies in History and Religion Presented to H. W. Robinson* (ed. E. A. Payne, 1942), pp. 44ff.; a reply by H. H. Rowley is found in *Studies i OT Prophecy Presented to T. H. Robinson*, pp. 157ff.

Deuteronomy is consistently more optimistic and elevated, viewing the destiny of the individual and the nation in the light of a Covenant relationship that was vital and full of meaning for Israel. The virility of the Deuteronomic proclamation of salvation as a present reality, as contrasted with the forbidding eschatology of the eighth- and seventh-century B.C. prophets, speaks of an earlier age of religious fervor in which enthusiasm for the ideals of the Covenant was still running high. For von Rad this situation is problematical and paradoxical, deriving as it does from the setting of Horeb but addressed, as he supposes, to the Israel of the later regal period.[51] Accordingly it should be noted that there is neither problem nor paradox if the work is taken at its proper face value and assigned to the Mosaic period, instead of being distorted and manipulated so as to fit into some purely fictional scheme of supposed literary and historical development. What von Rad and so many other liberal writers have failed to take into proper consideration is the fact that the prophets derived their fundamental theological concepts from the Law, and that in their exposition of the various facets of the Covenant relationship and its implications for the life of the nation they adduced no single theological element that was not already present in some form in the Mosaic legislation.

C. THE MATERIAL OF DEUTERONOMY

The time and circumstances of the book can be held unquestionably to be that of the last days of Moses, and into this framework there has been inserted the collection of legal material that emerged for the most part from an earlier period of the Wilderness wanderings. The book commences with a lengthy discourse relating the nature of divine guidance from the Horeb period to the sojourn at Kadesh-barnea (Deut. 1:5–3:29). This served as an adequate introduction to one of the principal themes of the work, namely an exhortation to the Israelites to obey the revealed Law of God (Deut. 4:1-43). Such an arrangement appears to be normal and original, and there are no evident dislocations of the text, although there may perhaps be a few later additions present in the narrative.

The second address of Moses (Deut. 4:44–26:19) deals in a comprehensive sense with the Law of God, and commences with the foundation-principle of the theocracy, namely the Decalogue, in an extended form. This all-important canon of spirituality was rooted firmly in the history of the Wilderness period by means of a reminder of the phenomena that accompanied the initial revelation of the Law, so that no one could doubt either its supernatural origin or its fundamental historicity. The ethical and moral implications of the Covenant relationship (Deut.

---

[51] G. von Rad, *Studies in Deuteronomy*, pp. 72f.

6:4ff.) prefaced a series of enactments relating to situations envisaged as occurring once the Promised Land had been occupied.

Of great importance among other matters was the question of idolatry, which constituted an ever-present threat to the integrity of the Covenant relationship between Israel and her God. Since idolatry was inextricably intermingled with other alien threads in the pattern of Canaanite religious and social life, it was clear that the Israelites had no other choice than to exterminate the Canaanite inhabitants of the land. This section of material (Deut. 7:1-26) again follows in natural sequence, but it is interrupted by Deuteronomy 8:1-20, which comprises a reminder of the divine dealings with Israel in the past so that the nation would not forget God in the future. Although the section is rather independent, it is not out of harmony with the following important portion of the speech (Deut. 9:1–10:11), in which the past sins of Israel were recounted as a means of warning the nation against self-righteousness. The ethical precepts of the Covenant (Deut. 10:12-22) are again evident in the following section (Deut. 11:1-32), in which the ultimate choice of blessing or affliction was set deliberately before the people.

The first two Mosaic discourses are homogeneous, and relate the general ethical concepts underlying the Sinai revelation to the nationalistic aspirations, social responsibilities, and spiritual obligations of the Israelites in the Promised Land. As such they constitute the religious preamble to an exposition of the main regulations that would govern Israelite life. Deuteronomy 12:1–26:19 is the section concerned with this material, and consists of statutes and ordinances that repeat in part the legislation of Mount Sinai, but which also consider certain circumstances not covered by that stage of revelation. As observed above, the general intent of the legislation was to regulate the entire life of the nation as the holy people of God prior to the entrance into Canaan, and while the arrangement of the enactments was comprehensive, it was not specifically related to chronological sequences, and so was somewhat discursive in nature. This situation befits a collection of laws and statutes that have arisen during an interval of time, or which tend to envisage future situations on the basis of past experience. Deuteronomy 12:17-19 appears to have existed as a separate fragment, and its insertion into the text of chapter 12 tends to disrupt the pattern of the narrative. More properly it belongs to the section dealing with the tithes (Deut. 14:22-29), and could well have been placed after Deuteronomy 14:29.

The preceding chapter is evidently a unity, dealing as it does with diviners and idolatry. The essence of the Levitical laws concerning uncleanness and cleanness is recapitulated in Deuteronomy 14:3-21, as is the material relating to the sabbath of the land in Deuteronomy 15. Much the same is true of the enactments involving the Passover (cf. Exod. 12:1ff.), which follow the traditions concerning the three annual feasts (cf. Exod. 23:16; 34:22; Lev. 23:15ff.; Num. 28:26ff.; 29:12ff.).

The term "passover" apparently included all the sacrifices offered during the seven days of *mazzôth* as well as the paschal lamb itself (Deut. 16:2). An administrative fragment has evidently survived in Deuteronomy 16:18-20, while Deuteronomy 16:21–17:1 seems to comprise another independent section relating to idolatrous practices. Closely associated with the latter, however, is Deuteronomy 17:2-13, which deals with judicial procedures and questions of appeal. In this passage the tradition of Numbers 15:30 is continued in the verdict rendered against the man who behaves in an obdurate and self-willed fashion (Deut. 17:12).

A section of quite a different character (Deut. 17:14-20), which like certain others appears to have been inserted rather haphazardly into the framework of the book, has to do with the principles governing the choice of a king. The standpoint of the narrative is undeniably futuristic, and the life-situation is clearly that of the Wilderness rather than the settled conditions of a much later age that had been projected back into the earlier history of the nation so as to furnish some justification in the Torah for the existence of the Davidic monarchy. This passage is of interest also for the light it sheds upon the activity of Moses as a chronicler of events and enactments relating to the infant nation.

As Wright has remarked in this connection, a verse such as Deuteronomy 17:18, which commands the future king to "write for himself in a book a copy of this law, from that which is in charge of the Levitical priests" presupposes either that the people knew that Moses was recording the speeches day by day, or that he actually had the script in front of him as he was speaking.[52] The reference to "a copy of this law" is to the particular enactment concerning the king, and not to Deuteronomy as a whole. It was because this phrase was incorrectly understood by the LXX translators as referring to the whole of the fifth book of Moses that the name "Deuteronomy" or "second law" arose in the first place.

Another isolated fragment dealing with the rights of the priests and Levites (Deut. 18:1-8) follows the enactment concerning the appointment of a king. In connection with this and similar passages in Deuteronomy it has frequently been maintained by liberal scholars that the book knows of no distinction between the priests and the Levites. A careful examination of the Hebrew text, however, shows that this view is untenable, for the Levitical priests (Deut. 18:1) were distinguished from the Levites who were thought of as scattered throughout Israel (Deut. 18:6f.).

Furthermore, the fact that different portions were ascribed to priests in Deuteronomy 18:3ff. and to Levites in Deuteronomy 18:6ff. would

[52] J. S. Wright, *EQ*, XXV (1953), p. 6.

suggest that the distinction was maintained without difficulty.[53] Whereas Numbers characteristically described the priests as the "sons of Aaron," Deuteronomy frequently employed the expression "the priests the Levites," rendered "the Levitical priests" in the RSV. This appears to be quite legitimate, since in a book such as Numbers, which was intimately concerned with the consecration of the Levites (Num. 8:5ff.), it would be entirely proper for the priests to be designated as the sons of Aaron. By contrast, in Deuteronomy, which is a work of a more general and prophetic character, a generic form of description is appropriate. The phrase "the priests the Levites" (Deut. 17:9, 18; 18:1; 24:8; 27:9; cf. Josh. 3:3; 8:33) appears to mean "the priests of the tribe of Levi," to whom the Deuteronomic code assigned a variety of duties (cf. Deut. 17:8f., 18; 24:8; 27:9).

An independent fragment warning against participation in pagan magical rites can be seen in Deuteronomy 18:9-14, which is followed by another isolated section relating to the rise of a prophetic figure. The juxtaposition of these two passages was presumably intended to depict the relative natures of false and true prophecy. Once Israel had entered the Promised Land there would arise the necessity for further divine revelation that would be based upon, and be of a character with, the moral, ethical, and legislative enactments of Sinai. To meet this need the prophetical institution would be established, and would be quite distinct in nature from all contemporary pagan forms of prophetism. The prophet would be an Israelite, and, like Moses, would function as a mediator between God and the Chosen People (Deut. 18:14f.).

Certain laws governing criminal behavior were the concern of chapter 19, with the first three verses dealing with the cities for refugees, and like Numbers 35:9-34 constituting an elaboration of the law first given in Exodus 21:12ff. The content of Deuteronomy 19:14 seems to imply that the boundaries that earlier individuals had established should not be removed by later settlers, since such activity was equivalent to theft. A small independent section (Deut. 19:15-21) dealt with the laws involving witnesses, and established the legal principle of *lex talionis* or retribution in kind. The procedures to be adopted in the case of future wars reflected the humanitarian concerns of the Sinai legislation in that an attack upon an enemy town ought only to be made after an offer of peace had been spurned. Even when a siege was in progress, the fruit trees in the vicinity were to be spared.

A group of laws of diverse character can be found in chapters 21 to 25. Of some interest is the procedure for the expiation of a murder committed by an unknown person (Deut. 21:1-9), which reflected ancient Mesopotamian practices in this regard.[54] The legislation concern-

[53] D. A. Hubbard, *NBD*, p. 1029.
[54] Cf. *ANET*, p. 167.

ing marriage with a woman captured in war (Deut. 21:10-14), which inculcated thoughtfulness and forbearance on the part of victorious Hebrew males, stood in its humanitarian concerns in entire contradistinction to the brutal and callous attitudes of contemporary pagan nations in this regard. The same general emphasis is continued in Deuteronomy 22:1-12, which treated of correct social attitudes under particular circumstances, and also engendered respect for the animal species. Sexual relationships were the subject of the legislation in Deuteronomy 22:13-29.

The rights of citizenship in the congregation (Deut. 23:1-25) dealt with those who were to be excluded (Deut. 23:1-9), the purity of the camp in time of war (Deut. 23:10-15), the prohibition of religious prostitution (Deut. 23:17), and other rights of citizenship (Deut. 23:16, 18-25). The enactments concerning divorce were set out in summary form (Deut. 24:1-4), and a specific provision exempted the newly married man from service in war for an entire year (Deut. 24:5). Among other prohibitions assembled in chapter 24 were warnings against the oppression of the poor (Deut. 24:10-15), against injustice (Deut. 24:14-17), and a lack of charity towards underprivileged members of society.

A section that furnished additional evidence of the profoundly humanitarian concern of the Torah related, among other matters, to corporal punishment. Extreme severity in this matter was prohibited (Deut. 25:1-3), in contrast with some of the procedures followed in contemporary cultures, and the spirit of humanitarianism and toleration was extended quite naturally to the animal creation (Deut. 25:4). A brief section that seems to have no immediate logical connection with what precedes or follows dealt with the procedures attending levirate marriage (Deut. 25:5-10), which has already been discussed above.

The conclusion of this important body of legislation was marked by various enactments concerning equitable business dealings (Deut. 25:11-16), an order for the extermination of the Amalekites (Deut. 25:17-19), and the ritual for the thanksgivings at the presentation of the firstfruits and tithes. It is not without significance that the closing sections of the Book of the Covenant (Exod. 20:22–23:33) also contained the law of the firstfruits (Exod. 23:19), which would suggest that the Deuteronomic legislation drew for its inspiration upon much that the Covenant Code contained.

The legislative corpus of Deuteronomy 12:1–26:19 can be classified into three principal groups according to the specific terms employed in the text. The first of these classes is "judgments" (מִשְׁפָּטִים) , which describes a rule established by authority or formulated by ancient custom, and serving either as a precedent or as a guide to a judge under certain specified conditions. Typical of this sort of enactment is the content of Exodus 21. In this connection it is interesting that many of the judgments occurring in that chapter can be paralleled by the case-law represented in the Code of Hammurabi and in other Semitic collections of laws from the pre-Mosaic period. There is no reason to doubt that the Israelites were acquainted with at least some of this secular legislative material during the Goshen period, and if the Mosaic enactments contain laws that had their origin among the Israelites at that time, as has been suggested already in the present work, it is quite probable that non-Israelite legislation applicable to the sedentary situation in Goshen would also be incorporated into the legal structure as having, in some sense at least, an accredited background in Hebrew tradition.

The second term, "statutes" (חֹק), was derived from a root meaning "to engrave," "to inscribe," and as such designated a permanent rule of conduct. It differed from the "judgment" in that whereas in the latter the appeal was to the judge, in the former it was to conscience and to God.[55] The distinction was made clear in the case of Solomon (1 Kgs. 6:12), who was instructed to "walk" in the statutes of God, and to "execute" His judgments. The statutes were generally in the nature of moral precepts, and as such constituted a divine rule of life. They do not occur in this form in other Semitic legal codes, for fairly obvious reasons. While some dealt with religious institutions such as different kinds of offerings, others were concerned with the laws of justice, purity, clemency and the like.

The third category, or "commandments" (מצות), was more generally applicable. In Deuteronomy the word referred predominantly to commands that were not to be considered as binding or permanent obligations but could be fulfilled in one operative act. Such commandments included the destruction of pagan shrines, the appointment of officers and judges, and the establishing of cities for refugees.

Notice should again be taken of the fact that the foregoing body of legal material is essentially a collection of laws rather than a law-book in the strictest sense of that term. The difference between these concepts, as Köhler has pointed out, is that a collection of laws lacks the unified and thoroughgoing spirit that results when a lawgiver sets out his individual precepts with the specific intention of laying down the law.[56] This had already been done in essence in the Decalogue, the Covenant Code, and other supplementary legislation; and all that Deuteronomy did was to rewrite the relevant material in such a manner that the laws governing national life would be as available to the people as they were to the priesthood. Deuteronomy, of course, was not meant to preserve the technicalities of the Law in the same manner as Leviticus, but, like the Code of Hammurabi, was intended to be accessible to all who had as their concern the spiritual and ceremonial requirements of the Law. This

[55] G. T. Manley, *NBD*, p. 309.
[56] L. Köhler, *Hebrew Man,* p. 171 n. 1.

658

consideration is important in view of the fact that, whatever the specific oral or written promulgations of the law, ancient Near Eastern peoples generally tended to live either according to inclination or in deference to the traditions and customs of their forbears, secure in the knowledge that the law-books were stored in temple archives, should it ever become necessary for some priest-scholar to consult them for research purposes. Because of the essential nature of Deuteronomy as a collection of laws, it is as impossible to divide the work up into strata through the use of supposed literary criteria as it is to attempt to assign a specific date to any particular legislative item.

The renewal of the Covenant with God (Deut. 27:1—30:20) involved the ratification of the Law and the engraving of its precepts upon stones to be set in position upon Mount Ebal. Here also an altar was to be erected for the offering of burnt and slain sacrifices. The standpoint of the narrative is clearly futuristic, with the occupation of the land of Palestine represented as yet to occur (Deut. 27:2ff.). The method of engraving the Law upon cement-surfaced rocks was well known in antiquity. Apparently a stylus was to be used upon an already prepared surface, as was the custom in Egypt. The engraving of the law of the land upon stone monuments that were readily accessible to the public was also known to the peoples of the ancient Near East, as can be illustrated by reference to the celebrated Code of Hammurabi.

Verses nine and ten of chapter 27 furnish an important connecting link in the narrative, in that they unite its two sections by means of a divine injunction to Israel to obey the Law. Blessings were to be expressed at the top of Mount Gerizim, and curses from the twin peak of Mount Ebal (Deut. 27:12f.), the general theme being continued in chapter 28, in which the first fourteen verses set out the blessings consequent upon obedience, while the remainder of the chapter delineated the courses which would accompany disobedience. Deuteronomy 29:1—30:20 can be regarded as a renewed declaration of the Covenant established at Sinai, and as concluding the Covenant section proper.

The group of appendices (Deut. 31:1—34:12) contained among other items the appointment and commission of Joshua (Deut. 31:1-8, 14-23), and the specific reference to the activity of Moses as a compiler of the Law. There can be no question that the reference to a "book" is to anything other than a written source, since the term ספר was never employed in the ancient Near East of orally transmitted material. The obvious concern of Moses was that the essentials of the legislation which was to be the guide of the nation in its future pilgrimage should be readily available to the priesthood at the least (Deut. 31:26) before his own death, an attitude that was amply justified in the light of subsequent events. The reference in Deuteronomy 31:22 might be taken as implying that Moses wrote down the song that followed before he actually recited it to the people. There is no warrant on the basis of either internal or external evidence for the assumption that the Song of Moses (Deut. 32:1-43) is to be dated as late as the fifth century B.C.[57] or even in the time of Jeremiah or Ezekiel.[58]

The poem, like some other sections of Deuteronomy, comprises a prophetic anticipation of the future: the Exodus had occurred within the recent past, and ahead stretched the occupation of the land of Canaan. The general setting of the poem is rooted in the events of the patriarchal age, and the theology is that of uncovenanted grace. There is no single element of the poem incompatible with Mosaic authorship, nor are there any evident editorial glosses or insertions in the material. The concepts and vocabulary are compatible with the late Amarna period. Certain rare words occur only in the Pentateuchal writings, and other expressions have been found in the texts from Ras Shamra. Among the words found only in the Pentateuch are ישרון (Deut. 33:5, 26) and גדל (Deut. 3:24; 11:2; Num. 14:19).

Whereas the Song of Moses was possibly in written form before it was actually delivered to the Israelites orally, the blessing of Moses (Deut. 33:1-29) was originally extant orally. From Deuteronomy 33:1 it would appear that the one who recorded the blessing is to be distinguished from Moses himself, and this is in full accord with normal Mesopotamian practice. From the many examples of benedictions that have survived from Nuzu society,[59] it is evident that a pronouncement of this sort uttered by a man who was dying had an irrevocable and legally binding status accorded to it. Thus the Mosaic benediction stands firmly within the tradition of the patriarchs as recorded in Genesis (Gen. 27:27ff.; 49:3ff.) and can be viewed with complete confidence as being both genuine and original.

The fact that Simeon was not mentioned in the blessing need not be taken as an indication that the material reached its extant form long after Simeon had been absorbed into Judah, as earlier liberal scholars were wont to maintain, since the utterance, being prophetic, envisaged the situation mentioned in Genesis 49:7, where the identity of Simeon as a tribe was prophesied to disappear (cf. Josh. 19:2ff.). However, there seems no valid reason for denying that the Simeonites were included in the general blessing bestowed upon Israel (Deut. 33:29), even though they were not mentioned specifically by name. There is thus no warrant whatever for assigning the blessing to some date within the period of the divided monarchy, as Riehm, Stade, and other earlier critics did.[60]

[57] *PIOT*, p. 280.
[58] *DILOT*, pp. 96f.
[59] R. K. Harrison, *Archaeology of the OT*, pp. 28f.
[60] D. E. Riehm, *Einleitung in das AT* (1889), I, p. 313; B. Stade, *Geschichte des Volkes Israel* (1887), I, pp. 150ff.

The final chapter, which described the death and burial of Moses, is of some interest because of the attitude adopted in antiquity towards its composition. Josephus, among other Jewish authorities, believed that Moses wrote the account of his own death,[61] a view that was modified somewhat in rabbinic circles, where the words were assigned to Joshua.[62] *Baba Bathra* stated that Moses wrote his own book and the section concerning Balaam and Job. Joshua wrote his own book and eight verses of the Law (i.e. Deut. 34:5-12). Among later Jewish exegetes, Ibn Ezra taught that chapter 34 had been compiled by Joshua.[63]

Some early liberal critics set great store by the fact that, since Moses could not possibly have written the account of his own death, he could not be regarded in any serious sense as the attributive author of the Pentateuch, an opinion that is as illogical as it is fatuous. From the evidence presented by the text it would appear that once the "book of the law" had been placed near the Ark of the Covenant as a witness to Israel (Deut. 31:24ff.), the literary activity of Moses came to an end. Whatever the nature of the book that he compiled, it did not contain chapters 32 to 34 at the very least. However, the Mosaicity of this latter is not open to serious doubt in terms of general provenance, and there is every reason for thinking that it was added to Deuteronomy in order to complete the narrative content of the work not long after Moses died. Jewish tradition may well be correct in assuming that Joshua was the author of at least part of the final chapter of Deuteronomy, although the actual facts of the situation are, of course, unknown.

As a whole, then, the book of Deuteronomy may be regarded quite legitimately as a popular promulgation of the spiritual and moral issues inherent in the Covenant revelation at Sinai. While many of the enactments are compressed in an obviously artificial manner into a framework of discourse that is related chronologically to the last month of the forty years of Wilderness wanderings, there can be no denial of their validity for the continued moral health and material prosperity of the nation. The regulations are in strict accord with the more technical prescriptions of Leviticus, making the entire work, in the words of Keil, "a hortatory description, explanation, and enforcement of the most essential contents of the Covenant revelation and the Covenant laws, with emphatic prominence given to the spiritual principle of the law and its fulfilment, and with a further development of the ecclesiastical, judicial, political and civil organization which was intended as a permanent foundation for the life and well-being of the people in the land of Canaan."[64]

---

[61] *AJ*, IV, 8, 48.
[62] *Bab. Bath.*, 14b.
[63] J. H. Hertz, *The Pentateuch and Haftorahs*, p. 916.
[64] C. F. Keil and F. Delitzsch, *Biblical Commentary on the OT* (1949 ed.), III, p. 270.

The theology of Deuteronomy is comparatively simple and unsophisticated, and is in complete harmony with other aspects of religious thought attributed to overall Mosaic origin. Characteristic of the book is its monotheistic outlook, whether such be regarded as incipient[65] or genuine.[66] The concept of the Covenant relationship is predominant, and the future destiny of the nation as the People of God, obedient to the provision of the Sinai agreement, is consistently at the forefront of the theological outlook of the work. The power that underlay the mighty acts of God at the time of the Exodus from Egypt can constitute a continuing experience if the Covenant is honored, and this theme is emphasized repeatedly in Deuteronomy. For His part God will be with His people in prosperity and adversity alike, and will fight for them in battle wherever they are engaged by the enemy, just as He did when they were at the mercy of the Egyptians. The positive, futuristic outlook of the book can well be illustrated by references to the two most frequently occurring phrases in Deuteronomy: "go in and possess," which is found 35 times, and "the land which the LORD thy God giveth thee," which occurs 34 times. Optimism, faith, and divine power are the hallmarks of the prophetic outlook of the author.

While the Hebrew text of Deuteronomy has been well preserved, there are certain difficulties evident in translation that appear to have arisen in part through processes of transmission. Thus in Deuteronomy 4:33, which is parallel to Deuteronomy 5:26, the adjective "living" is omitted from the MT but occurs in two Hebrew manuscripts, as well as in the LXX. In Deuteronomy 11:24, the preposition "to" has evidently dropped out of the text immediately before the word "Lebanon." In Deuteronomy 20:19 the end of the verse is only intelligible if read as an interrogative sentence. Some doubt as to the proper vocalization of the MT exists in Deuteronomy 4:48; 5:10; 20:8; 28:22; 31:7; 33:26.

Supplementary Literature

Bertholet, A. *Deuteronomium.* 1899.
Horts, F. *Das Privilegrecht Jahves.* 1930.
McNeile, A. H. *Deuteronomy, Its Place in Revelation.* 1912.
Siebens, A. R. *L'Origine du code deutéronomique,* 1929.
Welch, A. C. *Deuteronomy: The Framework to the Code.* 1932.

[65] So H. H. Rowley, *The Rediscovery of the OT,* p. 88, *ET,* LXI (1949-50), pp. 333ff.

[66] Cf. *FSAC,* pp. 2, 257ff., Albright, *Samuel and the Beginnings of the Prophetic Movement,* p. 4; *KRI,* pp. 212ff.

Part Nine

THE FORMER PROPHETS

The second division of the Hebrew canon, the Prophets, falls into two sections, the Former Prophets—Joshua, Judges, Samuel, and Kings—and the Latter Prophets, which include the major literary prophets as well as the Twelve Minor Prophets. The Former Prophets are anonymous works recounting the history of the relationship between God and the Chosen People from the time of the entrance into the Promised Land to the dissolution of the southern kingdom at the time of the exile. This historical material is of great importance for supplying a proper background against which the activity of the Latter Prophets is to be understood.

The association of prophetic functions with the Former Prophets arose because prophets were thought to have compiled the various works.[1] The distinction between Former and Latter Prophets was not based on chronology as much as on the relative order the two sections followed in the second division of the canon. The Latter Prophets have also been known as the "Writing Prophets," since they composed in one way or another the literary productions that are prominent in this section of the canonical books.

[1] Cf. *Bab. Bath.* 14*b*.

I. THE BOOK OF JOSHUA

A. NAME AND OUTLINE

The book of Joshua was named after its principal character, Joshua, the son of Nun. His name had four forms in the Hebrew (יְהוֹשֻׁעַ in Deut. 3:21; הוֹשֵׁעַ in Deut. 32:44; יְהוֹשֻׁעַ in Josh. 1:1; יֵשׁוּעַ in Neh. 8:17), which the LXX rendered as Ἰησοῦς Ναῦς, and the Vulgate as *Iosue*. In most versions the book stands immediately after the Pentateuch, but in the Syriac version Job was placed between Deuteronomy and Joshua, on the theory that Moses had been the author of Job. Some canons in the Greek church regarded the books from Genesis to Ruth as an *Oktateuchos*, while certain Latin lists counted the books from Genesis to Judges as a *Heptateuchos*, a distinction mentioned by Ambrose.[2] Jewish authorities, however, invariably tended to differentiate clearly between the Torah and subsequent literature in the Hebrew canon, so that their tradition never subscribed to a theory of a Hexateuch, Heptateuch, or Octateuch (cf. Ecclus. 48:22ff.; Josephus, *Contra Apionem*, I, 7ff.).

The book can be analyzed as follows:

I. The Occupation of the Promised Land, ch. 1–12
   A. Preparations for crossing the Jordan, 1:1-18
   B. The spies at Jericho, 2:1-24
   C. The fording of the Jordan, 3:1–5:1
   D. The ceremonies at Gilgal, 5:2-12
   E. The conquest of Jericho, 5:13–6:27
   F. The campaign at Ai, 7:1–8:29
   G. The Covenant ceremony at Shechem, 8:30-35
   H. Campaigns in southern and central Canaan, 9:1–10:27
   I. Victory in southern Palestine, 10:28-43
   J. The northern campaign, 11:1-15
   K. Summary of the conquest, 11:16–12:24
II. The Settlement of the Promised Land, ch. 13–24
   A. Unfinished task, 13:1-7
   B. Disposition of land to the tribes, 13:8–19:51

---

[2] *PL*, XV, col. 1584.

   1. Reuben, Gad, and Manasseh, 13:8-33
   2. Judah, 14:1—15:63
   3. The clan of Joseph, 16:1—17:18
   4. The other tribes, 18:1—19:51
  C. Cities of refuge, 20:1-9
  D. Levitical cities, 21:1-45
  E. The return of the Transjordan tribes, 22:1-34
  F. The last days of Joshua, 23:1—24:28
  G. The death of Joshua, 24:29-31
  H. A note on two other burial traditions, 24:32-33

B. DATE AND AUTHORSHIP

Modern theories of the authorship of Joshua have rejected the literary activity ascribed to Joshua himself by the Talmud, discerning instead a multiplicity of authors. Among contemporary scholars Fernández, Steinmüller, Kaufmann, and Young are among the few who have found a major source of the book in the writings of Joshua.[3] Others have commonly argued that the Pentateuchal documents of the literary critics can be traced throughout the book, thus making for a Hexateuch rather than a Pentateuch.[4] With a few differences in matters of detail, such as the extent of the various Pentateuchal documents and their interrelationship in Joshua, virtually all liberal introductions and commentaries are agreed that, with the addition of editorial comments, glosses, and the like, the sources underlying the Pentateuch can be seen clearly in Joshua.

For liberal critics, therefore, the first twelve chapters consist primarily of JE and D material, with occasional post-exilic redactions. Attempts to separate J sources from E material have met with an indifferent reception, even among adherents of the analytical theory, primarily because the subjectivity connected with the operation of source-isolation produced widely divergent results.[5] In consequence the more cautious adherents of the liberal view were content to concede the presence of the combined sources without making any serious attempt to separate them.[6] The remainder of the book, dealing with the disposition of the

---

[3] A. A. Fernández, *Commentarius in Librum Josue* (1938), pp. 3ff. J. E. Steinmueller, *A Companion to Scripture Studies* (1942), II, p. 73. Y. Kaufmann, *BACP*, pp. 97f. *YIOT*, pp. 162f.

[4] *DILOT*, pp. 104ff.; *PIOT*, pp. 295ff.; *IBOT*, pp. 69ff.; *IB*, I, pp. 185ff.; *et al.*

[5] E.g. H. Holzinger, *Das Buch Josua* (1901), pp. vii ff.; J. E. Carpenter and E. Harford-Battersby, *The Composition of the Hexateuch* (1902), pp. 353ff.; O. Procksch, *Die Elohimquelle* (1906), pp. 239ff.; G. A. Cooke, *The Book of Joshua* (1918), pp. xiv ff.; J. Garstang, *Joshua-Judges* (1931), pp. 3ff.; O. Eissfeldt, *Einleitung in das AT* (1934), pp. 283ff.; C. A. Simpson, *The Early Traditions of Israel* (1948).

[6] Cf. *DILOT*, pp. 103ff.; H. W. Robinson, *Deuteronomy and Joshua* (1908), pp. 255ff.; G. A. Smith, *HDB*, II, p. 784; *OTFD*, pp. 144f.; E. M. Good, *IDB*, II, pp. 989f.

tribes and certain priestly matters, was assigned almost completely to the post-exilic P document, with the activity of the "Deuteronomic historian" being conceded for portions of chapters 23 and 24. On this basis the literary problems of Joshua were envisaged as merely constituting an extension of those of the Pentateuch, and the solution of the latter involved the former as a matter of course.

A reaction against this view occurred in the school of Albrecht Alt, notably in the writings of Noth, who explained the underlying material of the first twelve chapters in terms of aetiological and hero stories,[7] and regarded the Deuteronomic document alone as being present in Joshua. The tribal boundary- and city-lists were put into coherent form about the sixth century B.C., according to Noth, and the Deuteronomic editor rewrote them before adding them to his narrative of the conquest in chapters 2 to 11.[8]

In general Noth concluded that, whatever the true nature of the underlying sources, the predominantly Deuteronomic character of the final form pointed to the work of a single individual. While the conclusions of Noth regarding Pentateuchal sources are, as he himself has admitted,[9] in substantial accord with the result of the German critical school, his observations concerning the documents underlying Joshua and the relation of the work to the Deuteronomic corpus represent an interesting departure from traditional liberal criticism in this particular matter.

In spite of some variation in treatment, however, the general consensus of critical opinion has been that, from the standpoint of literary history and contents, Joshua belongs properly to the Pentateuchal corpus.[10] Nevertheless, it has been conceded that the component parts have been assembled by a method different from that used in the Pentateuch itself.[11] Thus the E strand is held to be basic to the first section of the book (Josh. 1–12), and to have been supplemented by means of a few additions from priestly sources (supposedly including Josh. 4:19; 5:10ff.; 9:17-21). The editing of this material by the "Deuteronomist" was thought to have been so thorough that virtually all traces of J were suppressed from the original JE source of the early chapters (leaving principally Josh. 5:13f.; 9:6f.; 10:12f.).

---

[7] Cf. A. Alt in P. Volz (ed.), *Werden und Wesen des AT* (1963), pp. 13ff., *Kleine Schriften zur Geschichte des Volkes Israel* (1953), I, pp. 176ff., reprinted from *BZAW*, LXVI (1936), pp. 13ff.; *GI*, pp. 63ff., Noth, *Das Buch Josua* (1938), pp. ix ff., *Überlieferungsgeschichtliche Studien I* (1943), pp. 40ff., *Die Welt des AT* (1940), pp. 50ff., 97ff.

[8] Cf. A. Alt, *Sellin Festschrift: Beiträge zur Religionsgeschichte und Archäologie Palästinas* (1927), pp. 13ff., M. Noth, *Zeitschrift des deutschen Palästina-Vereins*, LVIII (1935), pp. 185ff.; *GI*, pp. 45ff.

[9] M. Noth, *Überlieferungsgeschichte des Pentateuchs* (1948), p. 24.

[10] For an analysis into documentary sources see *IBOT*, pp. 69f.

[11] *OTFD*, p. 144.

The difference between the J and E sources has been held to consist in their variant conceptions of the conquest of Canaan; E seems to favor a united undertaking by the whole of the nation under Joshua, whereas J conveys the impression that conquest was by individual tribal groups on separate occasions and in different places without the benefit of Joshua's leadership. The second part of the book (Josh. 13–21) is held to be P material, which has developed the E tradition independently and also incorporated older material such as the lists in chapters 15 and 19. The farewell address in chapter 22 is commonly assigned to the "Deuteronomist," and his editorial activity has also been seen in chapter 24.

Even for those scholars who accept the Graf-Wellhausen analysis of Pentateuchal sources, the discovery of these documents in Joshua presents considerable embarrassment. First of all, it is extremely difficult to explain why Joshua is essentially "Deuteronomic" in character if the Pentateuch has a basic framework of priestly material. Secondly, it is far from easy to see why the so-called J source should have been suppressed in the manner alleged by the commentators if Joshua is homogeneous in character with the Pentateuch, where J sources are given their proper place.

Again, even Bright has been compelled to admit that the position of the priestly material in chapters 13 to 21 is somewhat peculiar.[12] Whereas the older narratives in the Pentateuch were held to be inserted into the framework of P, the so-called P material in Joshua has been inserted into the framework of the "Deuteronomist."[13] Consequently, by employing arguments suggested by Noth,[14] he is forced to the conclusion that there is no good reason for assigning chapters 13 to 19 to P, and that at most only a few Priestly glosses can be demonstrated. In view of the radically different conclusions at which those who attempt the analysis of Joshua along the lines of Pentateuchal documentary criticism have arrived, it seems safe to conclude with Good that it is extremely unlikely that the documentary sources associated in the liberal mind with the Pentateuch have survived into Joshua.[15]

A further argument against the basic homogeneity of Joshua and the Pentateuch consists in the fact that when the Samaritans adopted the latter, they did so independently of the book of Joshua. Had this composition been as closely allied with the Pentateuch as the liberal critics generally have claimed, it would have been difficult for the Samaritans to make the separation without depriving themselves at the same

[12] J. Bright, *IB*, II, p. 544.

[13] Cf. Josh. 13:1, 7; 21:43-45; H. Wheeler Robinson, *Deuteronomy and Joshua*, p. 259.

[14] M. Noth, *Überlieferungsgeschichtliche Studien I*, pp. 182ff., *Das Buch Josua*, pp. xi ff.

[15] E. M. Good, *IDB*, II, p. 990.

time of what they would have regarded as traditionally Mosaic material.

Joshua is clearly part of a larger historical corpus dealing with Hebrew life from the settlement period to the exile. As such it does not constitute the concluding element of a literary Hexateuch, even though it was written in an ancient linguistic style like that which characterized Deuteronomy. In order to explain this phenomenon, however, it is not necessary to assign Deuteronomy to the seventh century B.C. and then to postulate its influence over a post-exilic compiler of Joshua. The degree of consonance is not at all surprising if both works typified the outlook of the eastern Mediterranean Heroic Age culture.

Even though one may not adopt the Graf-Wellhausen view of Hexateuchal origins, the problems associated with the source material underlying the extant book are quite complicated. A clear use of genuine sources (as opposed to the spurious ones spawned by liberal criticism) is seen in Joshua 10:13, where the author refers to the Book of Jashar,[16] a pre-monarchic national epic that originated no later than the conquest period, and probably contained poetic material such as the training-poem on bowmanship mentioned in 2 Samuel 1:18.[17] Another source would seem to be that of the traditions associated with Gilgal (Josh. 4:20ff.), the permanent camp of the Israelites until the land was surveyed (Josh. 18:1) and the site of the Benjamite sanctuary. The traditions concerning the conquest of Jericho, Ai, the submission of Gibeon, and the list of the southern fortresses reduced by Joshua (Josh. 10:28-43), were no doubt preserved at this location. The brief record of a northern campaign (Josh. 11:1-15) may have constituted an extract from an ancient annal, and as such might represent an additional source separate from, though related to, the summary of conquest in the south. Further source material is to be seen in the border- and town-lists (Josh. 13–19), in the appointment of cities of refuge (Josh. 20:1-9; cf. Num. 35:9ff.), and in the institution of Levitical cities (Josh. 21:1-45; cf. Num. 35:1ff.).

Any estimate of the nature and provenance of the remaining source material must be regarded as purely conjectural. That Joshua is not entirely lacking in artistry in its compilation, however, can be seen in the fact that the extant work constitutes a literary bifid, a phenomenon that will be observed subsequently in connection with other works in the Old Testament canon. The book comprises two balanced halves. The first of these (Josh. 1:1–12:24), as observed above, deals with the occupation of the Promised Land, and the second (Josh. 13:1–24:33) treats of the manner in which the tribes settled in their newly acquired territory and

---

[16] I.e. "The Book of the Upright." If the LXX reading of 1 Kgs. 8:53a is followed, יׁשׁר could be emended to יׁשׁיר, furnishing the title "The Book of Song."
[17] Cf. *GBB*, p. 263.

brings the entire episode to a fitting end with the death of Joshua. While there is no balancing of literary and other themes in the book, as can be found, for example, in Isaiah, the composition is a genuine bifid, with the two halves being complementary to each other. Attempts to assign a date to the anonymous book of Joshua should be based upon the history of the individual units of tradition underlying the work rather than upon any hypothetical literary sources.

The Book of Jashar probably comprised an ancient national song-book that may have originated as early as the period of the Wilderness wanderings.[18] The view that it was an anthology in which poetic compositions by David (cf. 2 Sam. 1:19ff.) and Solomon (1 Kgs. 8:53 LXX) were included is based upon a mistaken interpretation of the gloss in 1 Samuel 1:18, which should read, "he instructed them to train the Judaeans in bowmanship, the training-poem for which is written in the Book of Jashar." That this rendering is actually what the glossator intended to be understood is now apparent from discoveries relating to military arts in the eastern Mediterranean Heroic Age (fifteenth to tenth centuries B.C.), which have shown clearly that music, poetry, and dancing were all part of military training. The Davidic material suggested by some scholars thus formed no part of the Book of Jashar, contrary to Pfeiffer and his followers,[19] and the LXX addition that inquires rhetorically whether the passage attributed to Solomon was not in the Book of Jashar is obviously secondary and finds no support in the Hebrew text. The Book of Jashar thus belongs to the Heroic Age, and as such is definitely pre-Davidic.

The tradition associated with Gilgal and the northern campaign may have been based in part upon annals that were contemporary or nearly so, and it is probable that a portion of them survived in oral form and were preserved by the Benjamites. The authenticity and antiquity of this material is attested by the fact that for a period of time Gilgal took a leading part in the military and religious life of the Israelite confederacy.

The historical importance of the lists in Joshua 13—19, once regarded by critical scholars as worthless and as such generally assigned to the post-exilic period, has been demonstrated by the valuable studies of Alt and Noth.[20] These scholars have made it clear that the border-lists of

---

[18] Cf. H. St. J. Thackeray, *JTS*, XI (1909), pp. 518ff.; S. Mowinckel, *ZAW*, LIII (1935), pp. 130ff.; J. A. Montgomery, *A Critical and Exegetical Commentary on the Book of Kings* (1951), pp. 189ff.; E. Nielsen, *Oral Tradition* (1954), pp. 39ff.; C. F. Kraft, *IDB*, II, p. 803.

[19] *PIOT*, p. 294.

[20] A. Alt, *PJB*, XXI (1925), pp. 100ff., *ZAW*, XLV (1927), pp. 59ff., *Kleine Schriften zur Geschichte des Volkes Israel*, I, pp. 193ff., reprinted from the *Sellin Festschrift* (1927), pp. 13ff.; M. Noth, *Zeitschrift des deutschen Palästina-Vereins*, LVIII (1935), pp. 185ff., *Das Buch Josua*, p. ix *passim; Überlieferungsgeschichtliche Studien I*, pp. 181ff.

the tribes are an authentic reflection of conditions in Canaan during the pre-monarchic period. Whereas Alt dated the city-lists of Joshua 15:21-62 in the period of Josiah, Cross and Wright have shown that it is more likely that the lists go back to the ninth century B.C., reflecting a still older system of social organization.[21] The list of Levitical cities (Josh. 21:1-42) originated at a time when the heads of Levite families, rather than judges or kings, were in a position to formulate, or at least to influence, the development of social organization, a situation that reflects the conditions of the Wilderness wanderings much more closely than those of the tenth century B.C., as Albright has supposed.[22]

The entire question of the partition of the land among the tribes, including the part played by the priestly classes, constituted the logical extension of the theory of land-tenure as enshrined in the Torah. Because God had delivered His people from bondage in Egypt and had furnished them with a country of their own, the Israelites were by definition tenants of that land on an indefinite basis, having regard to the provisions of the Covenant relationship. As such the conquering heroes of the settlement period received inalienable grants of territory in perpetuity, in return for which they acted as the ruling and administrative class in Canaan and served the nation in a military capacity in times of crisis. As Gordon has remarked, there is a basic parallel to this in Heroic Age Greek society, where the aristocracy had inalienable land tenure, and where the subject native population was reduced to servitude.[23] The situation described in Joshua is thus firmly placed against the traditions of the eastern Mediterranean in the latter part of the second millennium B.C.

The pre-exilic dates assigned by Alt and Noth to certain portions of Joshua which formerly were thought to be post-exilic in origin illustrate the extent to which earlier critical opinions regarding the date of the book have been reversed. At the other extreme, Kaufmann has suggested that Joshua was written at the beginning of the Judges period, and that it drew in part upon the living memory of the conquest.[24] Although this date appears to the present writer to be at least a century too early, it is not impossible for the author to have compiled his work on the basis of certain written sources, contrary to the general standpoint of Bright, who is clearly surprised by the suggestion.[25] Nor is it necessary to postulate a long period of oral transmission for certain portions of Joshua, as Albright

[21] A. Alt, *PJB*, XXI (1925), pp. 100ff. F. M. Cross and G. E. Wright, *JBL*, LXXV (1956), pp. 202ff. Albright, *ARI*, pp. 123f., held that the border-lists reflected pre-monarchical conditions, as against the views of Z. Kallai-Kleinmann, *VT*, III (1958), pp. 134ff.
[22] In *Louis Ginzberg Jubilee Volume* (1945), pp. 49ff.
[23] *GBB*, p. 295. Cf. *Iliad* I: 162, II:609; *Odyssey* XXIV: 207.
[24] Y. Kaufmann, *BACP*, pp. 97f.
[25] J. Bright, *Early Israel in Recent History Writing*, p. 72.

has done, following the usual liberal patterns, which invariably misinterpret the nature and the role of oral transmission in the ancient Near East.[26]

The most direct evidence for an early date for the book is the fact that the account in which the Sidonians were designated for expulsion does not mention the city of Tyre (Josh. 13:6). According to ancient tradition, Sidon was the first Phoenician city to be founded, and the absence of Tyre from the list of cities conquered by Tuthmosis III about 1485 B.C. has been taken by some scholars as an indication that it had not been founded at that time as a colony of Sidon. If the narrative in Joshua describes the situation at all correctly, it would point to a time when Tyre was still a comparatively minor Phoenician port, and not the formidable stronghold that it subsequently became (2 Sam. 24:7; cf. Josh. 19:29).

Another indication of pre-monarchic conditions in the narratives of Joshua is the mention of the inability of Israel to dispossess the Jebusites from Jerusalem. This objective was not accomplished until the days of David; and modern archaeological discoveries have shown both how well-organized and impregnable the Jebusite fortress was and how David and his men were probably able to gain access to the city.[27] Other indications of an early date for specific passages of the book are to be seen in the descriptions of Simeonite and Danite territory and the Levitical allocations, all of which may have originated at Shiloh. The evidence for a contemporary writing of the material is almost completely lacking, however, since the use of the pronoun "we" in Joshua 5:1 is rendered by some Hebrew manuscripts as "they."

Evidence for a somewhat later date has been adduced from the mention of Secacah as a settlement in the plain of Judah (Josh. 15:61), which is perhaps to be identified with the modern Khirbet es-Samrah. From the presence of typical Iron Age II remains of casemated walls and pottery, it has been suggested that the site was one of those fortified by Jehoshaphat (870-848 B.C.; 2 Chron. 17:12), although some construction may have taken place in the time of Uzziah (767-740/39 B.C.; 2 Chron. 26:10). It is quite possible that the site was inhabited prior to the tenth century B.C., and that it was subsequently made into a fortified town because of its strategic importance.[28]

---

[26] FSAC, p. 274.

[27] Cf. F. G. Kenyon, The Bible and Archaeology (1940), p. 176. These tunnels were similar to those found at Gezer and Megiddo. Cf. R. A. S. Macalister, The Excavation of Gezer (1912), I, pp. 256ff., The Megiddo Water System (1935). For the translation of צנור as "hook," see W. F. Albright in Alleman and Flack (eds.), OT Commentary, p. 149.

[28] On Secacah see F. M. Cross, BA, XIX, No. 1 (1956), pp. 12ff.; F. M. Cross and J. T. Milik, BASOR, No. 142 (1956), pp. 5ff.

Since there is nothing to require a specifically late date for Joshua, and furthermore much of the material commonly assigned to P and a consequent post-exilic period is now regarded by many liberal scholars as much older, there seems to be no significant reason why the book should not be dated at the beginning of the monarchy, perhaps about 1045 B.C., and thus within the lifetime of Samuel, who may actually have contributed in some manner to its compilation, particularly where traditions involving Shiloh were concerned.

C. The Material of Joshua

The problems connected with the archaeology and historicity of Joshua have been surveyed elsewhere in the present work, and accordingly will only be mentioned in passing at this juncture. The archaeological situation with regard to the Jericho of the thirteenth century B.C. is confused, and at the time of writing very little can be said with certainty about the city as it existed in the days of Joshua. The older critical view that the conquest was a gradual infiltration of the country by separate tribes and clans, based to a large extent upon alleged discrepancies between the accounts in Joshua and the summary of events in Judges 1 has now been shown to be completely wrong.

Although early excavations in Palestine seemed to support the critical contention that the conquest was neither rapid nor complete,[29] later work demonstrated that cities such as Bethel, Lachish, Kiriath-sepher, Hazor, and others were destroyed in the second half of the thirteenth century B.C., thus confirming the general picture of conquest as presented by Joshua.[30] These excavations have not only revealed a sharp break in the continuity of culture at thirteenth-century B.C. levels, but have also shown that subsequent buildings erected by the Hebrews were inferior in design and structure to their Canaanite precursors.[31] This technological inferiority was also evident in the pottery remains from all the Early Iron Age settlements of the Hebrews.[32] All this has resulted in new respect for the general picture of the conquest as narrated in Joshua.[33]

The historical reliability of the conquest stories in Joshua was assailed by scholars such as Noth and Möhlenbrink, and defended with equal

[29] E.g. H. Vincent, *Canaan d' après l'exploration récente* (1907), pp. 463ff.; S. R. Driver, *Modern Research as Illustrating the Bible* (1909), p. 87; C. F. Burney, *Israel's Settlement in Canaan* (1918), pp. 10ff.

[30] Cf. R. K. Harrison, *Archaeology of the OT* (1962), pp. 49ff.; K. Elliger, *PJB*, XXX (1934), pp. 47ff.; G. E. Wright, *JNES*, V (1946), pp. 105ff.

[31] Cf. W. F. Albright, *The Archaeology of Palestine and the Bible* (1935), pp. 101f.; G. E. Wright, *JBL*, LX (1941), pp. 27ff.

[32] *WMTS*, pp. 166ff.

[33] G. E. Wright in H. R. Willoughby (ed.), *The Study of the Bible Today and Tomorrow*, p. 83.

vigor by Albright.[34] The aetiological approach of Alt and Noth has come in for a good deal of criticism in many quarters, and not least because it has gone far beyond the point which was justified by the small amount of external evidence available.[35] From what is now known of the settlement period in Canaan there can be little doubt as to the correctness of Albright's assertion that the actual course of events in the days of Joshua was more probably closer to the Biblical tradition than any modern critical reconstructions. However, as he wisely remarked, some vital clues have eluded research workers to date.[36]

Certainly the conquest of Canaan could hardly have taken the form of a punitive assault, since as Gordon has pointed out, a well-fortified land such as Canaan would have had little difficulty in repelling a weak or badly organized attack.[37] Instead, as the narratives clearly indicate, the invasion was only launched after intelligence reports had been collected and evaluated, a familiar practice in the time of both Hammurabi and Homer. Other aspects of Joshua can also be paralleled from the eastern Mediterranean cultures, such as the standing still of the sun and moon in order to assure the victorious conclusion of the fight, since in antiquity battles normally ended at sunset each day, regardless of the outcome.[38]

Again, the ban or חרם, although ruthless and immoral by western standards, served a practical purpose in controlling looting and offering the enemy a chance to surrender without a struggle.[39] The devoting of an unsubmissive foe to destruction was well established in Homeric and Semitic traditions alike, and in the latter connection it is important to note that the ninth-century B.C. Mesha Stone described how a Moabite king massacred the Israelite population of Ataroth in order to satisfy the blood-lust of Chemosh, the national deity.[40]

Considering the diversity of source material upon which Joshua drew, it is significant that there are very few internal inconsistencies present in the narrative. Some alleged incompatibilities have been listed by Pfeiffer,[41] with his usual facility, following Möhlenbrink,[42] but they are

[34] M. Noth, *PJB*, XXXIV (1938), pp. 7ff.; *GI*, pp. 63ff. K. Möhlenbrink, *ZAW*, LVI (1938), pp. 238ff. W. F. Albright, *BASOR*, No. 74 (1939), pp. 11ff.; *FSAC*, pp. 274ff.

[35] Cf. *FSAC*, pp. 70f., 274ff., 381; J. Bright, *Early Israel in Recent History Writing*, pp. 91ff.

[36] *FSAC*, p. 274 n. 1.

[37] *GBB*, p. 294.

[38] Josh. 10:13f. Cf. *Iliad* XVIII:239ff. For attempts to explain this phenomenon see E. W. Maunder, *The Astronomy of the Bible* (1908), pp. 351ff.; R. D. Wilson, *PTR*, XVI (1918), pp. 46ff.; E. W. Maunder, *Journal of the Transactions of the Victoria Institute*, LIII (1921), pp. 120ff.

[39] H. H. Rowley, *The Rediscovery of the OT* (1946), p. 16.

[40] *FSAC*, pp. 279f.; *BPAE*, p. 31.

[41] *PIOT*, p. 295.

[42] K. Möhlenbrink, *ZAW*, LVI (1938), pp. 256ff.

generally more apparent than real, and rest to some extent upon ancient styles of factual reporting. Thus in Joshua 3:17, the people had crossed the Jordan, whereas in Joshua 4:4f., 10b, the narrative implies that they had not crossed. As Young has pointed out, however, the order of events in Joshua 3:17 summarized the crossing of the people, while the priests remained in the middle of the river.[43] Once the people had crossed, and while the priests were still at their station, Joshua gave directions concerning the building of a memorial cairn (Josh. 4:5-9). The situation was summarized in Joshua 4:10, and described in complete form by being connected with Joshua 4:11, which stated that the priests and the Ark crossed the river last of all.

Again, according to Joshua 4:9, the twelve stones were erected in the middle of Jordan, whereas according to Joshua 4:20 they were set up at Gilgal as a perpetual memorial cairn. A careful reading of the narrative will show that verses 3, 8, and 20 refer to one incident, culminating in the building of a cairn in Gilgal, whereas verse 9 relates to an entirely separate event with which Joshua alone was connected. It would have seemed a little strange to the Israelites to remove twelve stones from where the priests had stood firm in the Jordan mud (Josh. 4:3), and after being told to carry them to their encampment, to be required to replace them in the very spot from which they had been taken (Josh. 4:9). As a casual reading of the narrative shows, the cairn that Joshua erected was built quite independently of any such construction by the Israelites, whether at Gilgal or anywhere else.

The allegation that the book preserved two accounts of the fall of Jericho is yet another figment of literary-hypercritical imagination. According to Pfeiffer, one of these comprises Joshua 6:3b, 4, 6, while the other consists of Joshua 6:3a, 5, 7, 10, 16b, 17, both of which were obviously harmonized by means of glosses to produce a confused account in the MT.[44] A reading of the section in question shows that verse 3b clearly belongs to 3a, since the Hebrew כה refers there, as elsewhere (e.g. Gen. 15:5), to what immediately precedes. Again, verse 5 belongs properly to the narrative of the preceding verse, since the "they" of Joshua 6:5 clearly refers to "the priests" of Joshua 6:4, otherwise the sequence is completely meaningless. The instructions thus required the Israelites to march around the city once a day for six days, and on the seventh day to march around it a symbolic seven times, a procedure that constitutes an interesting example of psychological warfare in antiquity.

The list of Levitical cities in chapter 21:1ff. proves on examination to be at some variance with the earlier border-lists, so that Shechem was located in Ephraim rather than in Manasseh, Daberath was placed in Issachar rather than in Zebulun (cf. Josh. 19:13), Jokneam was assigned

[43] *YIOT*, p. 164.
[44] *PIOT*, p. 295.

to Zebulun rather than to Asher, and Heshbon was located in Gad instead of in Reuben (cf. Josh. 13:17). It seems fairly clear that tribal boundaries were somewhat fluid, and as in more recent times in the Orient were apt to be changed on occasions without particular notice of the fact being given. This circumstance can easily account for the variation with regard to Shechem, Daberath, and Jokneam, since the adjacent territories doubtless claimed them for their own at various times. Heshbon is in a rather different category, however, being east of the River Jordan, for it was originally a Moabite city which was taken subsequently by Sihon, king of the Amorites, and made into his capital city (cf. Num. 21: 26). When Sihon was defeated by the Israelites, Heshbon was given to Reuben (cf. Num. 32:37), but later it came under the control of Gad, whose territory bordered upon that of Reuben. Gad assigned the city to the Levites (Josh. 21:39). While, therefore, there are certain divergences of usage in this area of source material, their nature is quite readily amenable to proper explanation. It is of some interest to note that several of the towns in chapter 15 were designated by their ancient names, as in the case of Baalah, later Kiriath-jearim (Josh. 15:9), Kiriath-sannah, later Debir (Josh. 15:49), and Kiriath-arba, later Hebron (Josh. 15:54). The Canaanites were still in possession of Gezer at the time of the events referred to in Joshua 16:10, a state of affairs that existed until the Solomonic era (1 Kgs. 9:16). The references that associated the Jebusites with the territory of Jerusalem (Josh. 18:28) indicate that the city was not at that time the capital of the Israelites.

The historical perspective of the compiler of Joshua accounts for what has been described as the standardized picture of the conquests under Joshua,[45] in which the invasion was complete and final, whereas the initial narratives of Judges depicted attempts by individual clans to establish themselves at various points in the land. Joshua marked the beginning of an historical sequence that took its rise in a description of events occurring after the death of Moses and culminating in the exile of the southern kingdom. It is not, as Noth and many others have supposed, the second phase of a "Deuteronomic history" which commenced with Deuteronomy itself, for although it was written in the ancient style of that book, it was never, by the uniform witness of Hebrew tradition, a part of the Torah itself.

Joshua was compiled in order to show that the Hebrews ultimately occupied the Promised Land in accordance with the divine purpose. In this connection it is important to note that territorial occupation must be distinguished carefully from the subjugation of the native inhabitants. The narratives of Joshua make it abundantly evident that the principal aim of the tribes was to occupy the land to its greatest extent, and that while some enemy strongholds were destroyed, others were bypassed

---

[45] E.g. *BPAE*, p. 43.

and left for subsequent overthrowal, as with the Jebusite fortress of Jerusalem, against which a number of sorties were apparently made (Judg. 1:8) before it finally fell to David. Had the operation of the חרם or "ban" been more widespread than it was, there would not have been quite the degree of Canaanite resurgence in the land as depicted by the record of subsequent events. Despite this, however, the various accounts in Joshua make it abundantly clear that even when the great Israelite leader was at an advanced age, there still remained a good deal of territory to be won and consolidated (Josh. 13:1ff.; cf. 15:63; 16:10; 17:12f., 16ff.). If scholars had differentiated a little more closely in the past between occupation and subjugation, the picture of conquest as represented in Joshua would have emerged in far clearer focus than it did, and as a result there would have been no need to regard the initial narratives of Judges as historical at the expense of their counterparts in Joshua.[46]

It is true, of course, that archaeological discoveries at such sites as Jericho and Ai have contributed to the historical confusion instead of clarifying it, as they might have been expected to do. Yet as Albright has pointed out, the school of Alt is not justified in considering Joshua as only an insignificant local chieftain, nor yet in denying the historicity of Israelite traditions of the conquest simply because minor modifications may have to be made to the traditional picture.[47] Indeed, the evidence for the Biblical tradition is sufficiently strong to warrant only the most cautious changes until more conclusive discoveries relating to the period are forthcoming. If such new information should follow the usual pattern, it will support the Biblical narrative rather than discredit it.

Thus, contrary to the remark of Good that there is no archaeological evidence for the existence of Gibeon at the time of the Joshua campaign,[48] the excavations of Pritchard at the site, identified with El-Jib, have shown the existence of a culture that reaches back to the Late Bronze Age IIb period (1300-1200 B.C.).[49] The name of the place was inscribed in archaic Hebrew characters on the handles of large jars found among the debris removed during the excavation of a large rock pool inside the north wall of the city. This pool, which has been associated with that mentioned in 2 Samuel 2:12ff., seems to have been in use somewhat after 1200 B.C. Further excavations have revealed the presence of at least five cities, built on distinct occupational levels, and

---

[46] So G. F. Moore, *A Critical and Exegetical Commentary on Judges* (1895), pp. 7f.; *PIOT*, p. 301.

[47] *FSAC*, p. 276.

[48] E. M. Good, *IDB*, II, p. 993.

[49] J. B. Pritchard, *BA*, XIX, No. 4 (1956), pp. 66ff., *VT* suppl. vol. VII (1959), pp. 1ff.

dating from about 2800 B.C. to 100 B.C. In the light of this evidence there is no reason to appeal to the principle of aetiology in order to explain the doings of the Gibeonites, nor is there any reason to suppose that Gibeon was not in fact a settled site in the early days of the conquest, as Joshua indicates.

※　　※　　※　　※　　※

The theological standpoint of Joshua is covenantal, reflecting the religious tradition of Exodus and Deuteronomy. The Promised Land was regarded as the gift of God to His Covenant people according to the assurance given to Abraham (Gen. 17:8), and renewed on subsequent occasions. Joshua recorded the fidelity of God to the provisions of the Covenant (cf. Deut. 7:7f.) but at the same time it indicated clearly that the Israelites failed at a comparatively early period to carry out the divine plan for their destiny (Josh. 17:13; 18:3). While Hebrew morale was probably higher under Joshua than under Moses, the threat of a lapse into pagan nature-worship and polytheism was no less real (cf. Num. 25:2f.; Deut. 4:3, 23).

Joshua is not so much a tribute to such matters as military skill or human enthusiasm as it is to the mighty acts of God Himself. The injunctions of Deuteronomy (1:17ff.; 4:1ff.; 7:1ff.) set the alternatives of life and death before the Israelites, and furnished the moral energy for the initial conquests (Josh. 1:1ff.). While Joshua was rightly celebrated for his leadership and general powers of coordination, the narrative makes it clear that, in the light of the Covenant provisions, the true glory must be given to God alone (cf. Josh. 3:10; 4:23f.; 6:16, et al.). The secret of success in both the material and moral spheres was obedience, which was enjoined upon Israel as the highest form of divine service (Josh. 22:5). The privileges of the Covenant carried responsibilities with them, however, for the establishing of the divine kingdom was based upon the settlement of Israel in an already occupied land. The Hebrews were required to bear spiritual witness to the essentially moral and holy nature of their God, and it was fidelity to this cause that would determine the way in which the kingdom ideal would be realized. Though the Israelites failed in this high endeavor, as subsequent events proved, the concept of a divine kingdom became from that time an indelible element of the Hebrew spiritual consciousness.

The Hebrew text of the book of Joshua is in quite good condition, and seldom requires emendation. The LXX version indicates attempts to expand the Hebrew through the addition of words and phrases. Certain LXX manuscripts such as Codex Vaticanus (B) exhibit wide variations, and may possibly represent an independent textual tradition from that of the MT. The Lucianic recension of the LXX appears to have been corrected by reference to Palestinian Hebrew sources.

Supplementary Literature

Abel, F. M. *Le Livre de Josué.* 1950.

Cohen, A. *Joshua and Judges.* 1959.

Cooke, G. A. *The Book of Joshua.* 1918.

Eerdmans, B. D. *The Covenant at Mount Sinai Viewed in the Light of Antique Thought.* 1939.

Garstang, J. and J. B. E. *The Story of Jericho.* 1940.

Noth, M. *Das System der zwölf Stämme Israels.* 1930.

Rowley, H. H. *From Joseph to Joshua.* 1950.

II. THE BOOK OF JUDGES

A. Name and Outline

The book of Judges describes the history of the period between the death of Joshua and the rise of Samuel. It received its title from the "rulers" or "judges" (שפטים) who guided the fortunes of Israel at that period, and this designation, which occurred in the Talmud (*Baba Bathra* 14b; cf. Ecclus. 46:11), was followed by the LXX (Κρίται) and the Vulgate (*Judicum*).

The term "judge" carried a wider meaning in antiquity than does its English counterpart. In the book of Judges the noun was used once of God as the chief judge of the land, in a dispute between the Israelites and the Ammonites (Judg. 11:27), and on six occasions to describe the inspired deliverers of the nation (Judg. 2:16ff.). Eight individuals were said to have "judged" Israel in the sense of delivering the nation from an enemy by means of war—Othniel (3:10), Tola (10:2), Jair (10:3), Jephthah (12:7), Ibzan (12:8f.), Elon (12:11), Abdon (12:13f.), and Samson (15:20; 16:31). One woman, Deborah, was described in a manner that indicated her activity as a judicial arbitrator (Judg. 4:4f.). The vast majority of the Judges thus came into prominence either as local or national heroes raised up and endowed charismatically for the deliverance of the people of Israel,[1] and continued their rule after the end of the war. They established no dynasties, and only Jephthah was assured of a continual rule, provided that the Ammonites were expelled (Judg. 11:6, 11).

In this latter sense of "ruler" the Hebrew term שפטים corresponded to the *shuphetim* or regents of Phoenicia,[2] the Akkadian office of *shapitu*, and the *sufetes* or chief magistrates of Carthage, who were similar in status to the Roman consuls.[3] The concept of the "judge" in Judges can

---

[1] So M. Weber, *Gesammelte Aufsätze zur Religionssoziologie* (1921), III, pp. 92ff., and adopted by A. Alt, *Die Staatenbildung der Israeliten in Palästina* (1930), p. 9; O. Grether, ZAW, LVII (1939), pp. 110ff.; M. Noth in *Festschrift Alfred Bertholet* (1950), pp. 404ff.; FSAC, p. 283.

[2] Cf. Josephus, *Contra Apion.* I, 21.

[3] Cf. Z. S. Harris, *A Grammar of the Phoenician Language* (1936), p. 153; Livy, *Hist.*, XXX, 7, 5.

thus be seen to be related to similar offices in the ancient Near East and the Mediterranean regions on the one hand, and to the situation that existed in the days of Moses (cf. Exod. 18:21ff.; Deut. 1:9ff.) on the other. The more primitive judicial proceedings of the Wilderness wanderings were adapted to the requirements of the future settlement by the provision in Deuteronomy 16:18 for the appointment of Judges and officers to assist in dispensing justice in Israel. The duty of these latter was apparently to insure that proper records pertaining to national life were kept.[4]

The view of Weber, Alt, and others that the Judges were simply charismatic leaders should not be taken to emphasize the inspirational aspect of their status at the expense of the hereditary factor. When the Hebrews occupied Canaan and displaced the national population, they constituted the landed warriors and the administrative ruling class, as was also the case in the Aegean tradition. From them came the leadership of the people, whether through aristocratic wives or, as on certain other occasions, through concubines. Examples of Judges taking their rise from aristocratic fathers and servile mothers included Abimelech (Judg. 3:31) and Jephthah (Judg. 11:1), both of whose fathers were among the גברי חיל or landed aristocracy.

Thus while there was generally an inspirational element discernible in individual Judges, they normally came from the ruling classes, and were not raised from the mass of the people through inspiration alone. As Gordon has pointed out, the key to the institution of the Judges is to be found in Mycenaean kingship in the twelfth and eleventh centuries B.C. in the same eastern Mediterranean cultural continuum.[5] What was important about such a situation was not linear succession from father to son, though this was naturally a consideration, but the fact that the rulers emerged from the fighting and landed aristocracy in which ultimately the kingship was vested. So with the Hebrew Judges, the dominant concern was with descent from the גברי חיל, from whom alone membership in the ruling classes was acquired. The nature or size of the clan or tribe was of secondary importance, provided that this prime consideration for leadership had been met.

The book of Judges can be analyzed as follows:

I. Conditions in Canaan After the Death of Joshua, ch. 1:1–2:5
II. The Judges of Israel, ch. 2:6–16:31
    A. The religious characteristics of the period, 2:6–3:6
    B. Periods of oppression, 3:7–16:31
        1. Cushan-rishathaim vs. Othniel, 3:7-11
        2. Eglon vs. Ehud; the Philistines vs. Shamgar, 3:12-31
        3. Sisera and Jabin vs. Deborah and Barak, 4:1–5:31

---

[4] G. T. Manley, EQ, XXIX (1947), pp. 149ff.
[5] GBB, pp. 295ff., also in A. Altmann (ed.), Biblical and Other Studies, pp. 12f.

    4. Midianites and Amalekites *vs.* Gideon, 6:1–8:32
    5. Abimelech, Tola, and Jair, 8:33–10:5
    6. Ammonites and Philistines *vs.* Jephthah; Ibzan, Elon, and Abdon, 10:6–12:15
    7. Philistines *vs.* Samson, 13:1–16:31
III. Appendices, ch. 17–21
    A. The episode of Micah the Ephraimite, 17:1–18:31
    B. The crime at Gibeah and the Israelite crusade, 19:1–21:25

The purpose of the appendix appears to have been that of illustrating the extent to which the Hebrews had transgressed the provisions of the Decalogue and the Book of the Covenant. Thus the evils that resulted when every man did what was right in his own judgment included theft (Judg. 17:2), idolatry (Judg. 17:5), immorality (Judg. 19:2), homosexuality (Judg. 19:22), and mass abduction (Judg. 21:23).

B. THEORIES OF COMPILATION

Because many liberal critics have been accustomed to discover in Judges the same hypothetical documentary sources as those held to underlie Joshua and the Pentateuch, there has been a good deal of confusion in the delineation of sources in Judges. Many scholars have insisted upon a "Deuteronomic" core to the book,[6] and have regarded any alleged "pre-Deuteronomic" material as of a kin with the JE sources dated between 630 and 600 B.C.[7] This type of literature is thought to have been introduced by fragments of chapter two (Judg. 2:6, 8-10, 13, 20-21) and contained the stories of Ehud, Deborah, and Barak, sections of the Gideon narrative, the accounts of Abimelech, Jephthah, and Samson, as well as the references to the five minor Judges (Judg. 10:1ff.; 12:8ff.).

The editor of this material was alleged to have omitted Jehovistic material in chapter one, as well as the contents of chapters 17 to 21. The Song of Deborah in Judges 5 was omitted by the "Deuteronomic" editor, who also ignored the reference to the five minor Judges, the narrative dealing with Abimelech, and the last story in the Samson cycle (Judg. 16:1-31). A priestly editor in the third century B.C. was supposed to have restored to the literary corpus the early J material omitted for some reason by the JE editor.[8] Whether the "Deuteronomic" editor inserted material into the main body of the work is doubtful, although some have maintained that the passages mentioning the minor Judges constitute a

    [6] Judg. 2:6–16:31, but perhaps omitting 3:31, 10:1-5; 12:8-15, and possibly chapter 9. C. F. Burney, *The Book of Judges* (1918), p. xlvi, denied the presence of Deuteronomic elements in Judges.
    [7] *PIOT*, pp. 316f.
    [8] *PIOT*, pp. 317ff., following W. R. Arnold, *Ephod and Ark* (1917), pp. 100f.

late addition.[9] On the other hand, Eissfeldt held that these very traditions were part of the oldest sources of the book.[10]

Those scholars who still adhere to a literary background of Pentateuchal documents for the books of Joshua and Judges have differed as
to whether the pre-Deuteronomic Judges they envisage can be regarded
as a JE Judges. In the fourth chapter there are supposed to be two
stories interwoven, one recounting the defeat of Sisera by Barak, and the
other narrating the conflict between Zebulun and Naphtali against King
Jabin of Hazor. The first of these has commonly been assigned to the E
source except by Eissfeldt, who regarded it as an element of J^1, or what
he called the *Laienquelle*, the oldest strand of the Pentateuchal sources.
The second has commonly been held to be part of the J narratives,
although as Pfeiffer has remarked,[11] this need not imply that the author
of J in Judges can be identified with the compiler of the J source in the
Pentateuch, a circumstance that also applies to the alleged E sources of
both compositions. In fact, it may be that they are to be related more
closely to sources in Samuel than to the Pentateuch, a position Rowley
endorsed.[12]

More enthusiastic critics have traced the Pentateuchal J, E, D, and P
sources into 1 Kings,[13] while other scholars have been equally as insistent that these alleged sources do not go beyond the Pentateuch.[14]
Small wonder, then, that Eissfeldt could write in 1938 about the remarkably varied and contradictory picture exhibited with regard to source-
criticism of Judges.[15] Clearly the contents of the "pre-Deuteronomic"
edition of Judges, if, indeed, such a work ever existed, are extremely
difficult to determine, as is the question of whether or not such material
was continuous with the postulated J and E sources of the Pentateuch.

The influence of the aetiological approach associated with Alt and
Noth and the traditio-historical outlook of Engnell had been reflected in a
departure from the classical type of source-criticism in favor of an
emphasis upon hero-sagas and strata of tradition[16] as oral and literary
antecedents of a Deuteronomic recension. Thus specific units of tradition

---

[9] Cf. G. F. Moore, *A Critical and Exegetical Commentary on Judges*, pp. xxviii-xxix;
J. A. Bewer, *The Literature of the OT in Its Historical Development* (1922), p.
272.
[10] O. Eissfeldt, *Die Quellen des Richterbuches* (1925), pp. 67ff., 115f., cf. *ETOT*,
pp. 285f.
[11] *PIOT*, p. 315.
[12] H. H. Rowley, *The Growth of the OT*, p. 60.
[13] E.g. S. Mowinckel, *ZAW*, XLVIII (1930), pp. 233ff.; O. Eissfeldt, *Einleitung
in das AT* (1934), pp. 288ff.; *ETOT*, pp. 288f.
[14] L. Rost, *Die Überlieferung von der Thronnachfolge Davids* (1926), pp. 27ff.;
H. M. Wiener, *The Composition of Judges ii. 11 to I Kings ii. 46* (1929), p. 10
passim; E. Jacob, *La tradition historique en Israël* (1946), p. 62.
[15] In H. Wheeler Robinson (ed.), *Record and Revelation* (1938), p. 75.
[16] So A. Bentzen, *Introduction to the OT*, II, p. 90.

have been held by some scholars to have reached back to cycles of legends concerning such heroes as Gideon, Jephthah, and Samson, which may be attributed to earlier or later periods, depending upon the predilections of the particular scholar concerned. A composition such as the Song of Deborah, one of the more ancient Hebrew poems, has been shown by Albright to go back to the twelfth century B.C.[17]

These and other units of tradition cannot, according to the views of Pedersen, have belonged to the Pentateuchal sources, since they are entirely different in nature.[18] They comprise for him the survival of tribal legends and stories that narrated the deeds of national leaders and heroes during the settlement period and later, together with aetiological material and certain traditions concerning the establishing of religious sanctuaries. Following the usual critical tradition, Pedersen contemplated long periods of time during which the various units circulated in oral form, and maintained that they only attained to literary fixity during or after the exile.

The majority of liberal scholars, whether guided by literary-critical or form-critical considerations, would generally concede that Judges passed through a lengthy process of development, characterized by the following distinct stages: first, an oral period, when many of the stories were composed (twelfth to tenth centuries B.C.); second, the writing of these sources in prose form, possibly by the authors of the Pentateuchal sources (tenth to eighth centuries B.C.); third, the early redaction of Judges on the basis of JE sources (eighth to seventh centuries B.C.); fourth, the Deuteronomic recension comprising Judges 2:6–16:31 with some omissions (late seventh century B.C.); and fifth, the final edition of the book as in the MT (post-exilic period).[19]

In the light of the careful but confusing delineation of source material in Judges by many critical scholars, it is somewhat anticlimactic to assert, as the present writer does, that such painstaking effort is largely wasted because of an incorrect understanding of what is meant by source material. The completely fallacious nature of the documentary system alleged to underlie the Pentateuch has entirely misled literary critics in their examination of Judges. As form-critical method correctly indicates, the real sources are the traditions of the tribal or national heroes, which doubtless circulated in different localities in either prose or poetic form. These traditions may have been preserved at various sanctuaries, as with that concerning the migration of the Danites (17:1–18:31), which probably originated at their northern shrine. It is quite possible that

---

[17] W. F. Albright, *BASOR*, No. 62 (1936), pp. 26ff.; cf. *BASOR*, No. 78 (1940), pp. 7ff. For earlier studies see G. F. Moore, *A Critical and Exegetical Commentary on Judges*, pp. 127ff.; C. F. Burney, *The Book of Judges* (1930), pp. 94ff.

[18] J. Pedersen, *Israel: Its Life and Culture*, III-IV, p. 727.

[19] After J. E. Myers, *IB*, II, pp. 679f. So *IBOT*, pp. 78f.; *PIOT*, pp. 332ff.; C. F. Kraft, *IDB*, II, pp. 1019f.; *OTFD*, pp. 156f.

many of these traditions circulated independently at the beginning in oral form, as with the Song of Deborah and the Samson cycle. It is equally probable that many of them found their way into writing at an early period also, and were not transmitted primarily in oral form for many centuries, as commonly assumed by critical scholars.

The advanced degree of literacy in evidence during the Amarna-Mycenaean period, as attested by the Canaanite Ugaritic epics, furnishes strong support for the contention that there was an extensive amount of written material underlying the Hebrew literature of the Heroic Age. Indeed, C. H. Gordon has argued persuasively for a degree of popular literacy from the passage in Judges 8:14, in which a young man was captured by Gideon, and after interrogation furnished his captors with a written list of prominent officials in Succoth.[20]

It seems correct, therefore, to assume, with Gordon, that Judges constitutes an excellent example of what classical scholars styled as the work of the rhapsodists or "song-stitchers."[21] In ancient Greece the rhapsodist was a person who strung songs together, in particular one who recited epic poetry. The term was sometimes applied, as in the case of Homer, to an author who recited his own compositions,[22] but at a later time it was commonly used of a class of persons who derived their livelihood from reciting the works of Homer.[23] Whatever bearing the term may originally have had upon the processes of composition by an original author, it seems clear that Judges consists largely of different heroic cycles that have been "stitched together" for the purpose of describing in something approaching epic form the events that transpired during a particular period of early Hebrew history.

Some of these cycles were evidently more popular than others, and in consequence appeared in greater detail, as with the Samson cycle. This material has considerable affinity with the traditions of the eastern Mediterranean Heroic Age, one important factor being that of the concept of *mēnis* or wrath. In the Greek mind a *mēnis* was produced by an insult, and resulted in a chain of events whose consequences were completely disproportionate to the nature and extent of the original affront. Thus, when Agamemnon took away Briseis, the anger of Achilles was only appeased after Agamemnon had been punished and many brave Achaeans had been killed. Even Achilles finally conceded that this situation had its irrational elements.[24] The theme of *mēnis* was also found in the Gilgamesh Epic, where Enkidu insulted Ishtar, and in the Ras Shamra texts, where Anat was infuriated by the affronts of Aqhat. In

---

[20] *GBB*, pp. 282f. There is no evidence that נער referred in any sense to scribal functions or capacities.

[21] *GBB*, p. 283.

[22] Cf. Plato *Republic*, 600D.

[23] Herodotus *Hist.*, V, 67.

[24] Homer *Iliad*, XIX:56ff. Cf. the wrath of Meleager, *Iliad*, IX:529ff.

the same way the "wrath of Samson" (Judg. 15:1-8) depicted an angry man's completely irrational behavior because his wife had been given to someone else, and his refusal to be calmed until he had dissipated his rage by killing a number of Philistines, a situation that parallels the "wrath of Achilles" very closely.[25]

Indeed, it can be stated that the Samson cycle, unfolding as it does in a Philistine milieu, is one of the most important connecting links between the eastern Mediterranean cultures of antiquity and Judges.[26] The cycle could well have been a Hebrew version of an old Greek epic if only for the identity of social customs, but this, of course, is not the case. In addition to the parallel between the Greek *mēnis* and the "wrath of Samson," the stratagem of driving foxes bearing firebrands on their tails into the Philistine vineyards can be regarded as comparable to the act of Hannibal, who caused chaos by turning loose cows with burning torches attached to their bodies.[27] To whatever extent this particular aspect of the Samson story may have been subjected to folkloristic influences, the fact remains that it reflected an actual tactical usage current in eastern Mediterranean antiquity.

Another cycle in Judges, that of Deborah, was preserved in two versions, one in prose (Judg. 4:4-24) and the other in verse (Judg. 5:1-31), the latter having been reduced to writing first in the opinion of many critical scholars. Apparent discrepancies between the two accounts have been noted by various commentators, including the fact that in the prose section Sisera was the commander of the forces of Jabin, king of Hazor, whereas in the poem he was a leader of an alliance of Canaanite rulers. In the prose passage some ten thousand infantry from Zebulun and Naphtali were involved in the battle, whereas in the poem six tribes put forty thousand men into the field on the plain of Esdraelon. Again, the troops of Barak charged the enemy from Tabor, whereas the Song itself only mentioned Taanach, the waters of Megiddo, and the Kishon. These difficulties are more artificial than real, although in some respects a little more detailed information would help to make the situation entirely clear. Thus, if the references in Joshua 19:22, Judges 8:18, and 1 Chronicles 6:77 are to the same place, Tabor was situated on the Zebulun-Issachar border, presumably on or near Mount Tabor. This evidently served as the marshalling area for the troops of Barak, whose numbers

---

[25] *GBB*, p. 271.

[26] For other studies see G. F. Moore, *A Critical and Exegetical Commentary on Judges*, pp. 312ff.; P. Carus, *The Story of Samson and Its Place in the Religious Development of Mankind* (1907); A. S. Palmer, *The Samson-Saga and Its Place in Comparative Religion* (1913); P. Haupt, *JBL*, XXXIII (1914), pp. 296ff.; M. Noth, *Die israelitischen Personnenamen* (1928), pp. 38, 223; C. F. Burney, *The Book of Judges*, pp. 335ff.; A. van Selms, *JNES*, IX (1950), pp. 65ff.; *ARI*, pp. 111f.; *FSAC*, pp. 283ff.

[27] *GBB*, p. 298.

more probably approximated to those in the prose narrative, since the Song was clearly celebrating a notable triumph, and as such employed an exaggerated number as a symbol of great victory.

The destruction of Megiddo in the third quarter of the twelfth century B.C. has not merely illuminated the dating of the Song of Deborah, but has also furnished valuable information relating to the alleged topographical discrepancies in the cycle. References in the poem to the "waters of Megiddo" and the "river Kishon" (Judg. 5:19-21) denoted the stream that arose in neighboring springs and flowed around the site of Megiddo. The Israelite defeat of the resurgent Canaanite oppressors is not to be confused with the conquest of Hazor by Joshua, as some have imagined,[28] for in the former all the Israelite warriors participated, whereas in the latter Reuben, Dan, Gilead, and Asher took no part in the battle (Judg. 5:16f.).

While Sisera was the commander of the Hazor chariot division, he was also in charge of the military strategy of a local Canaanite confederation (Judg. 5:19) which included the petty kingdoms from Meerom south to the plain of Esdraelon. The Israelites joined battle with this powerful group at Taanach, some four miles to the southeast, and not at Megiddo itself, the most powerful fortress in the plain. The reason for this is that the Canaanites were conquered at a time when Megiddo lay in ruins, and Taanach was the nearest inhabited site with which the victory could be associated. This fact would indicate, among other things, that the Song of Deborah is to be dated about 1100 B.C., before Megiddo was rebuilt.[29] With regard to the relative dates of the two versions of the victory, it was observed in the preceding chapter that a study of Egyptian "control" material has shown that historic events of some importance were sometimes recorded simultaneously in prose and verse. If this tradition had any influence over the habits of Israelite scribes or traditionist circles, it may well be that the accounts in Judges 4 and 5 are roughly contemporaneous.

Other alleged discrepancies in the cycle include the assertion that only two tribes (Judg. 4:10) participated in the battle, not six (Judg. 5:14f., 18). This objection is trivial, since the earlier reference was to the initial marshalling of Israelite strength under Barak, and took no cognizance of subsequent reinforcements. Pfeiffer saw a contradiction between the account (Judg. 4:21) that described the death of Sisera while he was sleeping and that which related his demise (Judg. 5:25f.) while "drinking sour milk outside the tent."[30] As in some other instances, Pfeiffer has here deliberately misrepresented the content of the Hebrew, for nowhere in the Song of Deborah was Sisera spoken of as sitting outside a tent

---

[28] E.g. *PIOT*, p. 328; J. M. Myers, *IB*, II, p. 683.
[29] W. F. Albright, *BASOR*, No. 78 (1940), pp. 8f.; *BPAE*, pp. 39f.
[30] *PIOT*, pp. 328f.

drinking buttermilk when the fatal blow was struck, nor was his condition of relative awareness mentioned in the poetic section of Judges 5:26f. Quite obviously there is no contradiction of the kind alleged by this sort of hypercriticism.[31]

The cycle concerning Gideon and the Midianites (Judg. 6:1–8:35) appears to be yet another well-attested unit of tradition comprising one of the sources of Judges. Literary critics have been accustomed to find a mixture of J and E material in this cycle, which they have admitted to be very closely intertwined.[32] Such an analysis is based in part upon the familiar "name" criterion, by which Gideon was called "Jerubbaal" in the alleged E passages whereas in the supposed J sections both names were employed indiscriminately. This kind of conclusion is far from convincing, however, for the cycle is an obvious unit in matters of language and style, with little if anything that can be attributed realistically to an editor.

The importance of this cycle of tradition arose from the way in which a new threat to the delicately balanced Hebrew economy, that of sporadic raids at the harvest period and at other times by camel-riding nomads, was dealt with by Gideon, and a subsequent intertribal breach was healed. The narratives concerning Gideon stood in the best tradition of the conquest and settlement era, for the celebrated Israelite leader commenced his campaign against Midian with a dramatic assault upon Hebrew idolatrous practices (Judg. 6:25ff.). He then assembled the northern tribes of Asher and Naphtali as well as his own central tribe of Manasseh, and caused complete confusion among the Midianites and their ally the Amalekites in a surprise night attack upon their camp. The Ephraimites were offended by the resultant victory because they had not been invited to participate, but the threat to intertribal relations was averted when they were complimented upon their capture of the Midianite princes Oreb and Zeeb. Because Gideon refused to accept the idea of hereditary rule in his desire to maintain the theocratic concepts of the Torah (Judg. 8:32), he inadvertently provoked much of the dissension among his sons after his death, as described in the supplement (Judg. 9:1-57) to the Gideon cycle.

Of two other traditions underlying Judges, one involved the move of the Danites to the north (Judg. 17:1–18:31), and the transfer of the cult-objects associated with the household shrine of Micah to their own new sanctuary of Laish. The other furnished the background to the bitter war against the Benjamites (Judg. 19:1–21:25), which was provoked by the waywardness and immorality of that tribe. The near-extinction of the Benjamites was averted by allowing the surviving males

---

[31] Cf. B. L. Goddard, *Westminster Theological Journal,* III (1941), pp. 93ff.

[32] E.g. *PIOT*, pp. 317, 328f.; G. F. Moore, *The Literature of the OT* (1913), pp. 86f.; *IBOT*, p. 80.

to capture maidens from Jabesh-gilead and Shiloh, a procedure fully in accord with the traditions of the Heroic Age and later eras of Mediterranean civilization.

Yet another interesting cycle involved the exploits of Shamgar, son of Anath, who came to prominence at a critical time in the settlement period (Judg. 3:31). From a later allusion to this hero (Judg. 5:6) it appears that his doings were evidently of such repute that events in his day were dated by reference to him, a situation that must surely have constituted the supreme accolade in antiquity. Yet despite the fact that Shamgar became a legend in his own time, the traditions surrounding his name have been reduced to a minimum by the compiler of Judges, for reasons that are not readily apparent.

Clearly there was a good deal of material available upon which the editor of Judges was able to draw, as indicated by the cycles of tradition that make up the bulk of the book. The pursuit of mythical J and E sources into Judges is completely pointless, for the only sources which can be identified with certainty are the tradition-units represented in the various cycles themselves. Judges is no more the work of a compiler who pasted together various documents than is the Pentateuch itself, for as Gordon has remarked, it is more than the sum of what a redactor has excerpted.[33] Viewed holistically it furnishes a remarkably coherent picture of a specific age in Hebrew history, the general political, cultural, geographical, and religious aspects of which are consistent with what is now known of Palestine between 1200 and 1000 B.C.

Concerning the antiquity of the literary sources underlying the canonical book of Judges there can be little serious doubt in any quarter. Precisely when these materials were compiled and edited, however, is rather difficult to state. According to Talmudic tradition (Bab. Bath. 14b), Samuel was the author of the book, although this statement is naturally difficult to substantiate. However, there are clear indications of the early origin of some of the literary forms in the book, as may be illustrated by the reference in Judges 1:21, which indicated that the Jebusites were still in Jerusalem when the summary of the conquest was compiled. It seems highly improbable that an editor who was compiling the account in writing for the first time at a much later period would have allowed the text to stand had contemporary conditions been different, for he would almost certainly have furnished an explanatory gloss for the verse in question. Therefore it would appear that this particular section, and perhaps even the book as a whole, was in substantially its present form before David made the Jebusite stronghold his capital city (2 Sam. 5:6ff.).

In Judges 1:29, the Canaanites were still living in Gezer, so that this portion of the summary must also have been written before the time

---

[33] *GBB*, p. 283.

when the pharaoh of Egypt handed the city over as a gift to his daughter, who had married Solomon (1 Kgs. 9:16). Again, the narrative of Judges 3:3 indicates that Sidon, rather than Tyre, was the principal city of Phoenicia, and this fact would seem to point to a date about 1140 B.C. In this connection it should be noted that the historical perspective exhibited by this passage most probably suggests something that the compiler already knew as history. This is also the case with the references to the absence of a king in Israel, in later sections of the book (Judg. 17:6; 18:1; 21:25), which seem to point to a time in the early monarchy when its benefits and blessings were still very much to the forefront of the Hebrew consciousness. As far as the present writer has been able to determine, the various cycles of tradition that have been "stitched together" to form the extant book contain no specific elements which are demonstrably late. Therefore, in the light of the comparatively early nature of the written sources, and the complete absence of late editorial indications, it would seem proper to conclude that the work was compiled anonymously during the early monarchical period.

C. THE MATERIAL OF JUDGES

1. The organization of Israel. Judges shows the progressively chaotic state of the national life (Judg. 17:6, 18:1, 19:1, 21:25), and by implication points to the contrast in matters of political organization between Israel and her pagan neighbors.[34] The nascent Hebrew kingdom was organized in a comparatively simple manner in terms of a division into a number of clan-groups based on the descendants of Jacob, and known as "tribes." Religiously they were bound together by loyalty to the Covenant tradition of Sinai, and by the existence of a central shrine at Shiloh to which each tribe could send representatives (cf. Josh. 18:1; Judg. 21:12; 1 Sam. 1–4; Jer. 7:12). Authority could be discerned at two levels, the first being that of the primitive democracy of the Elders, as Kaufmann styled it.[35] This institution was secular rather than religious, and had its roots in the tribal council of Elders formulated in the days of Moses and Joshua.[36] The second level of authority comprised that of the Judges themselves insofar as they exercised an inspired function of leadership in the nation. It is important to notice, however, that the latter concept did not enshrine the religious essence of the period to quite the degree which Kaufmann assumed, for aside from any military or inspirational leadership furnished by the Judges, the religious traditions of the nation were being pursued to a greater or lesser extent at

---

[34] Cf. A. Alt, *Die Staatenbilding der Israeliten in Palästina,* pp. 31ff.

[35] *KRI,* p. 256.

[36] On the antiquity of the *nāsî* see M. Noth, *Das System der zwölf Stämme Israels* (1930), pp. 151ff.

certain well-established local sanctuaries such as those at Shiloh and Laish.

In contrast with the neighboring peoples, who were constituted as monarchies or city-states ruled over by local kings or princes, the nation of Israel was at best little more than a loose confederation of tribes, fond of their freedom, and yet bound together in a manner unique in the ancient world by a common loyalty to the Sinai Covenant. The political structure of this specific period of Hebrew history has been likened by the school of Alt to the amphictyonic organization of eastern Mediterranean cultures during the early centuries of the first millennium B.C.,[37] an observation that is of some significance in that it associated the book of Joshua with the traditions of the Heroic Age and with a subsequent political structure in the Mediterranean basin. Albright has pointed out that, like Greek and Italic amphictyonies of a rather later period, the Hebrew social structure of the Judges era consisted of a federation of distinct tribes grouped around a central sanctuary, which exercised a strong cohesive function by unifying the tribes in matters of religion and politics, as well as in other respects.[38]

In certain important areas, however, the Israelite confederation differed from Greek amphictyonies, and not least in the matter of authority. For the Greeks the latter was bound up with religious considerations, whereas in the book of Judges it was primarily a question of leadership by elements of the גברי חיל, whether under inspiration or not. Furthermore, none of the Greek or Italic amphictyonies ever possessed anything remotely comparable to the Abrahamic or Sinaitic Covenant between God and His people. While the Sinai Covenant was religious in character, a subsequent one between God and Israel, solemnized at Shechem by Joshua (Josh. 24:1ff.) and implementing the provisions of the Sinai agreement, had both religious and political overtones. Mendenhall has shown the closeness of the relationship between this covenant and the suzerainty treaties of the fourteenth- and thirteenth-century B.C. Hittite kings with the vassal rulers of Anatolia, Syria, and Mesopotamia.[39] These secular parallels attest to the antiquity of the covenant solemnized by Joshua, and help to set the conquest and settlement era still more firmly against a background of the Heroic Age. In this connection, however, the social configurations are Semitic rather than Greek, and

---

[37] Ibid.; cf. Noth, The History of Israel, pp. 85ff.; ARI, pp. 102ff. For criticisms of the amphictyonic concept see KRI, p. 256; H. M. Orlinsky, Ancient Israel (1954), pp. 58ff., and in M. Ben-Horin, B. D. Weinryb, and S. Zeitlin (eds.), Studies and Essays in Honor of Abraham A. Neuman (1962), pp. 375ff., reprinted in Oriens Antiquus, I (1962), pp. 11ff.

[38] BPAE, p. 36.

[39] G. E. Mendenhall, Law and Covenant in Israel and the Ancient Near East (1955), pp. 41f.

might well imply that the Greek and Italic amphictyonies were in fact based upon earlier Semitic models.

2. *Chronological problems.* The chronological problems associated with Judges have been discussed earlier in this book, and in consequence will receive only the briefest review here. If the archaeological evidence that points to a date of about 1240 B.C. for the beginning of the conquest is correct, it furnishes an extent of some two hundred thirty years for the period from the time of Joshua to the accession of David, the latter being dated at approximately 1010 B.C. If, however, the individual periods during which the various Judges ruled are added together, and reckoned in conjunction with the period of leadership exercised by Joshua, the Elders, Samuel, and Saul, the number of years is probably in excess of five hundred.

The problem appears to be largely one of the occidental approach to oriental methods of computation. In the first instance, the Hebrew text does not warrant the assumption that all the Judges exercised consecutive periods of leadership, whether or not the individuals concerned were local or national heroes. At least three principal groups appear to have been partly concurrent, so that the narratives involved would actually be describing as contemporary happenings those circumstances which later interpreters might understand to constitute consecutive events. Again, ancient Near Eastern scribal methods of computation and chronological assembly must also be taken into account here. Quite obviously the rhapsodists were merely concerned with certain phases or aspects of a particular period, and if these subsequently became joined together it was from a poetic rather than a strictly chronological standpoint. The actual historical sequence would naturally be sufficiently retained so that the order of the material would not be offensive to those who were familiar with the trend of the events being recounted, but at the same time certain principles of selection would be utilized. As a result, the total picture, while coherent artistically, might ultimately fail to meet the exacting specifications of the modern occidental chronologist or historian. When it is remembered that ancient scribes did not draw up synchronistic tables or lists like those common today, but utilized principles of selectivity whose nature is still largely obscure, it will be seen that there is sufficient ground for restraint in approaching the problems of chronology in Judges.

3. *The purpose of the book.* The purpose of the work was to show that a centralized hereditary kingship was necessary for the well-being of the Covenant theocracy. Because there was no single superior authority to whom continuous appeal could be made, a significant disintegration of political and social life began to put in an appearance among the Hebrew people. Consequently, in times of emergency and stress like those typified by the onslaughts of the marauding Ammonites, Moabites, and

Midianites, the nation as a whole was virtually paralyzed. In addition, the cultural superiority of the Canaanites soon made itself apparent, and contributed in a great degree to the dominance that the Philistines had managed to exercise over important areas of Hebrew social life.

While the inspired leadership of the Judges partly remedied this unfortunate situation, it appears to have proceeded largely on an *ad hoc* basis, and in consequence lacked the degree of permanence and continuity necessary for political and social stability in the nation. The rise of tribal misunderstandings (Josh. 22:10ff.; Judg. 8:1ff.; 20:12ff.), coupled with the seductive attractions of Canaanite religion, furnished powerful forces for disunity and disintegration in Israel, and prompted the demand for a regularized monarchy following contemporary pagan patterns.

Judges has an important place in the history of the Covenant people because it sustained the principle, established in the Torah, that obedience meant life and peace, whereas defiance or disobedience could only result in hardship, oppression, and death. Such a theory of primary causation constituted a powerful stimulus to the aspirations of the Chosen People, and at the same time served as a warning for future behavior. The dynamic concept of the Covenant deity was clearly indicated in the attitudes and exploits of many of the Hebrew Judges. Equally important was the awareness that God was always prepared to forgive His penitent people and redress their grievances.

Yet the concluding pronouncement of the book gives some indication of the way in which the Israelites had already departed from the advanced moral and ethical spirit of the Sinai Covenant, and were living as their pagan neighbors had done for centuries, that is to say, according to local tradition and personal inclination rather than by law. However near and supreme the God of Israel was avowed to be, He was evidently no substitute in the minds of many of the Hebrew people for an earthly, tangible symbol of material stability in the realm of politics and social organization.

* * * * *

The Hebrew text of Judges has been preserved and transmitted remarkably well, and aside from corruptions in the Song of Deborah it is among the best of the non-Pentateuchal writings as regards purity. Occasionally the LXX is of help in textual emendation, but the problem of the relationship between the LXX and the MT is complicated by what appears to be the presence of two Greek recensions of the Hebrew book of Judges. One of these was represented by Codex Alexandrinus, and followed by uncials and cursives from the fifth century of the Christian era. The other was found in Codex Vaticanus and a large number of cursives, as well as in the Sahidic version.[40] The printing

---

[40] Cf. F. G. Kenyon, *Our Bible and the Ancient Manuscripts* (1940), p. 68.

of the two recensions on opposite pages gives some indication as to the lack of unanimity on the question as to which text is actually superior.[41] Most probably, however, Oesterley and Robinson are correct in stating that Codex Vaticanus, which in other instances offers such an excellent text, must be regarded as being of secondary importance insofar as Judges is concerned.[42] Of the other versions, the Vulgate followed the LXX in most of the important areas, as was the case with the Syriac.

Supplementary Literature

Cohen, A. *Joshua and Judges.* 1959.
Hertzberg, H. W. *Josua, Richter, Ruth.* 1953.
Moore, G. F. *The Book of Judges: Critical Edition of the Hebrew Text.* 1900.
Simpson, C. A. *Composition of the Book of Judges.* 1957.
Thatcher, G. W. *Judges and Ruth.* 1904.

[41] Cf. C. F. Burney, *The Book of Judges,* p. cxxvii.
[42] *IBOT,* p. 82.

694

III. THE BOOKS OF SAMUEL

A. NAME AND OUTLINE

Like 1 and 2 Kings the two books of Samuel were originally one volume in the Hebrew,[1] as indicated by the fact that the Massoretic note, which appears at the end of each canonical work, occurs only at the end of 2 Samuel. The Massoretes thus treated the work as a unit, and designated it as "The Book of Samuel," giving the central verse as 1 Samuel 28:2f. The composition was named after Samuel because he was the principal character of the earlier narratives, and also because of the part he played in anointing the two other prominent personages in the book, namely Saul and David.

The division into two books occurred with the LXX version, because the Greek text, written as it was with vowels, required considerably more space than the unpointed Hebrew characters. The LXX translators called 1 and 2 Samuel the First and Second Books of Kingdoms (Βίβλοι Βασιλεῶν); the two books of Kings were then known as the Third and Fourth Books of Kingdoms. The change from "Kingdoms" to "Kings" is found in the Vulgate, and has been followed by most English versions. The first Hebrew text to divide Samuel into two sections was the first edition of Daniel Bomberg's Hebrew Bible (Venice, 1516-1517), and this division became the accepted fashion. The AV follows the division of Samuel, giving as an alternative title "Otherwise Called the First (Second) Book of the Kings."

The two books present a continuous account of the history of Israel from the end of the Judges period to the latter years of King David. The purpose of the work was to describe the way in which the monarchy was established, and the part played by the prophet Samuel in its institution. The books of Samuel can be analyzed as follows:

I. Samuel as Judge, 1 Sam. 1–7
  A. The childhood of Samuel, 1:1–3:31
  B. The end of the Shiloh priesthood, 4:1-22
  C. The Ark in the war against the Philistines, 5:1–6:21
  D. Rededication near Mizpah, 7:1-17

---

[1] *Bab. Bath.* 14b; Eusebius *Hist. Eccl.* VII, 25, 2.

II. Samuel and Saul, ch. 8—15
   A. Samuel's accession to the people's request for a king, 8:1-22
   B. The anointing of Saul, 9:1—10:27
   C. Victory over the Ammonites, 11:1-15
   D. Responsibilities of kingship in the Covenant, 12:1-25
   E. Saul's early reign: mental affliction and rejection, 13:1—15:35

III. Saul and David, 1 Sam. 16—2 Sam. 1
   A. The choice of David, 16:1-23
   B. The last days of Saul, 17:1—31:13
      1. David and Goliath, 17:1-58
      2. Saul's jealousy of David, 18:1-30
      3. Saul's attempt to kill David, 19:1-17
      4. David's flight, 19:18—30:31
      5. The death of Saul, 31:1-13
      6. David's avenging of Saul's death, 1:1-16
      7. David's lament over Saul, 1:17-27

IV. David as King of Judah and Israel, ch. 2—8
   A. The counterclaim of Ishbosheth and Abner, 2:1—4:12
   B. The capture of Jerusalem, 5:1-25
   C. The permanence of the Davidic dynasty, 6:1—7:29
   D. Summary of David's wars and list of officials, 8:1-18

V. Events at the Davidic Court, ch. 9—20
   A. The reinstatement of Mephibosheth, 9:1-13
   B. Ammonite and Syrian wars, 10:1—11:1
   C. David and Bathsheba, 11:2—12:24
      1. David's adultery and subsequent marriage, 11:2-27
      2. Nathan's denunciation of David and his repentance, 12:1-23
      3. The birth of Solomon, 12:24
   D. Amnon and Tamar; the flight of Absalom, 13:1-39
   E. Absalom's readmittance to the court, 14:1-33
   F. Absalom's revolt and death, 15:1—18:32
   G. David's lamentation, 18:33—19:7
   H. Joab's rebuke and David's attempt at reorganization, 19:8-43
   I. The revolt of the northern tribes, 20:1-26

VI. Appendices, ch. 21—24
   A. The burial of Saul's family, 21:1-22
   B. A psalm of David, 22:1-51
   C. Summary of the exploits of David's heroes, 23:1-39
   D. The census and its consequences, 24:1-25

B. THEORIES OF COMPILATION

Evidence for independent sources as strata of the work has been seen in parallel accounts, incongruities, and apparent discrepancies in the narrative as a whole. As listed by Pfeiffer, these include the announcement concerning the end of Eli and his house on two occasions (1 Sam. 2:31ff.; 3:11ff.); the secret anointing of Saul (9:26–10:1), followed later by two public ceremonies (10:21; 11:15); two occasions on which Samuel rejected Saul as king (13:14; 15:23); two introductions of David to Saul (16:21; 17:58); two escapes of David from the court of Saul (19:12; 20:42); two occasions on which David spared the life of Saul (24:3; 26:5); three different covenants between David and Jonathan (18:3; 20:16, 42; 23:18); two flights by David to Gath (21:10; 27:1), and the confused tradition regarding the killing of Goliath (1 Sam: 17:51; 2 Sam. 21:19).[2]

On the basis of the foregoing material, critical scholars attempted to solve the problems associated with the composition of the books of Samuel principally in terms of literary sources, of which as many as five have been suggested, or with a saga-cycle theory of origins. A two-source theory has seen comparatively early material in 1 Samuel 1, 2, 4–6, 18, and 20, supplemented by such fragments as 9:1–10:16; 11:1-11; 13:15-23, and in 2 Samuel by chapters 9 to 20, and additional sections comprising 1:17–6:23; 21:1-22; 23:8-39. A later source was held to include 1 Sam. 1–3, portions of chapters 4 to 6 and 20 to 23, with fragments of chapters 7, 8, 12, 17, 18, 19, 26 and 28, supplemented by a few verses from 2 Samuel 1.

These two sources were first identified with the Pentateuchal J and E documents by Budde, as continuations or portions of the same works.[3] The final composition of the book was attributed to a "Deuteronomic editor," who compiled and edited certain materials somewhat in advance of 586 B.C. Those scholars who favored the Graf-Wellhausen theory of Pentateuchal composition acclaimed the views of Budde, although there was considerable variation of opinion as to the extent to which the J and E sources of Samuel could be identified with the J and E Pentateuchal documents, despite the attempts of Klähn to prove that J and the early source of Samuel actually came from the same hand.[4] Some scholars experienced a good deal of difficulty in distinguishing between later segments of the E source and the supposed "Deuteronomic recension,"[5]

---

[2] *PIOT*, p. 340. For critical analyses of sources see *IBOT*, p. 88; H. H. Rowley, *The Growth of the OT*, pp. 64ff.; W. A. Irwin, *AJSL*, LVIII (1941), pp. 113ff.; L. Rost, *Die Überlieferung von der Thronnachfolge Davids* (1926), pp. 10ff.; M. Noth, *Überlieferungsgeschichtliche Studien I*, pp. 54ff.

[3] K. Budde, *Die Bücher Richter und Samuel, ihre Quellen und ihr Aufbau* (1890), pp. 167ff.

[4] Cf. T. Klähn, *Die sprachliche Verwandtschaft der Quelle J des Heptateuchs* (1914), p. 15 *passim*.

[5] C. F. Burney, *The Book of Judges*, p. xxxvii; C. R. North, *The OT Interpretation of History* (1940), p. 36.

while others were uncertain as to precisely how far the Pentateucha source-theory could be regarded as valid for Samuel.[6]

Lods maintained that the early source was composed of two conflict ing narratives, one associated with Jabesh, and the other a "seer source.[7] Eissfeldt equated the latter with his "L" source of the Pen tateuch, and assigned to it the Ark stories (1 Sam. 4–6; 2 Sam. 4) certain biographical details (1 Sam. 14:49ff.; 2 Sam. 8:16ff.), the lamen of David over Abner (2 Sam. 3:33f.), and details concerning the found ing of the monarchy (1 Sam. 10:21-27; 11:1-5).[8] Invoking his three source theory, Eissfeldt maintained that whereas in 1 Samuel they wer largely interwoven, in 2 Samuel they were written consecutively. Whil Oesterley and Robinson conceded that he might well be correct insofa as the narrative describing the founding of the monarchy was concerned they questioned whether the three-source analysis could be sustaine throughout.[9]

Pfeiffer, who in the main followed the analysis of Budde, was com pletely unable to accept the source-theory postulated by Eissfeldt.[10] Kennedy, for his part, found no fewer than five sources underlying th book of Samuel, and these comprised an infancy source, a history of th Ark, a positive and a negative chronicle of the monarchy, and a cour history of King David.[11] An even more varied background was sug gested by Weiser, who posited numerous separate traditions including the narrative that described the founding of the monarchy (1 Sam 9–10), the battles of Saul (1 Sam. 11, 13–14), certain Davidic annal and utterances (2 Sam. 1:17ff.; 3:33f.), the prophecy of Nathan (2 Sam 7), and the Ammonite war of David (2 Sam. 10–11).[12] These tradi tions were assembled with others in an attempt to write the history o Saul and David, and were subjected to processes of chronological ar rangement. At a later period the work fell into the hands of a "Deutero nomic editor," and before being issued in its final form was furthe amended and interpolated.

Midrashic additions to Samuel were posited by Pfeiffer, but wer entertained only in connection with two principal sections, namely l

---

[6] A. Bentzen, *Introduction to the OT*, II, p. 95; E. Jacob, *La tradition historique en Israël*, pp. 82ff.; J. Pedersen, *Israel: Its Life and Culture*, III-IV, p. 727.

[7] A. Lods, *Israël des origines au milieu du VIIIe siècle* (1930), pp. 408ff.; cf. I Hylander, *Der literarische Samuel-Saul Komplex (1 Sam. 1:15) traditionsgeschichtlich untersucht* (1932), pp. 13ff., 56ff.

[8] O. Eissfeldt, *Die Komposition der Samuelisbücher* (1931), *Einleitung in da AT*, pp. 302ff., *ETOT*, pp. 275ff.

[9] *IBOT*, p. 90.

[10] *PIOT*, p. 341.

[11] A. R. S. Kennedy, *I and II Samuel* (n.d.), pp. 13ff.

[12] A. Weiser, *ZAW*, XLIV (1936), pp. 1ff., *Einleitung in das AT* (1949 ed.) p. 130; cf. *OTFD*, pp. 160ff.

Samuel 2:27-36 and 2 Samuel 7:1-29.[13] These two portions of material concerned the destiny of the Zadokite priesthood and that of the Davidic dynasty, and had been attributed by Wellhausen to one author who lived in the time of Josiah.[14] Steuernagel was one of the few critics who dated the second of these passages in the time of David,[15] with the majority of authors favoring an exilic or a post-exilic date.[16] For Pfeiffer they constituted worthless additions to the narrative, and though ostensibly exegetical in nature they failed to contribute anything of value to the period of Saul and David. This extreme view has rightly been repudiated by the majority of scholars.

Attempts by the traditio-historical school to elucidate the literary problems of Samuel have generally resulted in the assumption that certain independent cycles of saga were rather loosely connected to make up the book. These cycles included, among other elements, the Ark narratives (1 Sam. 4–6; 2 Sam. 6), and the court history of David (2 Sam. 9–20), as well as other units of oral tradition. However, the saga-cycle theory is much more applicable to Judges than to Samuel, for the sagas are not at all clearly delineated in the latter. The Davidic court history is unquestionably of the greatest value as a source, being nearly contemporary with the events described, and as such constitutes a thoroughly authoritative document. But the traditions involving the earlier periods in the lives of Saul and David are complex, and do not lend themselves to facile analysis. There are certain differences in the form of the traditions, it is true, but even this fact does not permit a clear separation of source material of the kind postulated by certain liberal writers.

The authorship and date of the earlier source thought by many critics to underlie 1 and 2 Samuel was a matter of considerable speculation at the end of the nineteenth century. In preference to the claim of Seraiah the scribe (2 Sam. 8:17), Klostermann suggested that the real author was Ahimaaz, the son of Zadok, who may have had some knowledge of the events connected with the Ark.[17] On the other hand, Duhm proposed Abiathar as the likely candidate for authorship, owing to his close connections with David throughout his lifetime, a theory that was re-

---

[13] R. H. Pfeiffer in R. P. Casey (ed.), *Quantulacumque: Studies Presented to Kirsopp Lake* (1937), pp. 303ff.; *PIOT*, pp. 368ff.

[14] J. Wellhausen, *Die Composition des Hexateuchs und der historischen Bücher des AT* (1889), p. 257.

[15] C. Steuernagel, *Einleitung in das AT*, p. 325.

[16] Cf. B. Stade, *EB*, IV, col. 4278; H. P. Smith, *A Critical and Exegetical Commentary on the Books of Samuel* (1899), pp. 297f.; W. R. Arnold, *Ephod and Ark*, pp. 42f.; *PIOT*, p. 373.

[17] A. Klostermann, *Die Bücher Samuelis und der Könige* (1887), pp. xxxii-xxxiii. Cf. W. R. Arnold, *Ephod and Ark*, pp. 61f.

ceived with enthusiasm by Sellin.[18] Although it is doubtless entirely correct to think in terms of contemporary or near-contemporary authorship, the identity of the compiler or compilers must remain unknown.

In connection with the later source postulated by literary analysis, the expression of critical opinion was as varied regarding its date as it was in relation to its contents. This was partly due, no doubt, to the supposition that "Deuteronomic redaction" modified some of the earlier elements of the tradition, thus making precise dating difficult. Most scholars who adhered to this particular form of analysis for Samuel tended to assign the later source to the early seventh century B.C. On such a basis the "Deuteronomic edition" would be dated about the middle of the sixth century B.C.[19]

While the narratives involving the early relationships between Samuel, Saul, and David do not present quite as uniform a picture as those dealing with Joshua in the book of that name, it ought to be observed that facile critical assertions of discrepancies, incongruities, and the like have frequently been made on very inadequate grounds. Thus in connection with the election of Saul as leader of Israel, it has long been a common supposition that the text contains two, perhaps even three, divergent strands, one of which (1 Sam. 9:1–10:16; 13:3-15) tacitly favored the monarchy, and at least one other which manifested hostility to it (1 Sam. 8; 10:17-27; 12).[20] A subjective analysis of this kind is completely unnecessary, however, since it disintegrates the profile of Samuel that the compiler was endeavoring strenuously to project.

Any reconstruction of the sequence of events must commence with the warning note sounded by Samuel in chapter eight, which condemned alike the outright repudiation of the theocratic ideal of the Covenant by the nation of Israel, and the popular demand for an earthly king (מֶלֶךְ) of the Canaanite variety. This passage in fact constituted an accurate characterization of earlier and contemporary Canaanite kingship, as subsequent archaeological discoveries have made abundantly clear.[21] As such it can be dated with confidence in the lifetime of Samuel himself, and regarded as a genuine and ancient element of the early monarchy tradition.

It should then be noted that, when Samuel had finished delivering his warning to Israel, he was specifically empowered by God to appoint a leader (נָגִיד) for the people, regardless of his own feelings on the matter. Furthermore, at that point he was in complete ignorance of the real identity of the individual whom God had chosen to occupy that exalted office. The first event in the selection of Saul (1 Sam. 9:1–10:10) was

---

[18] B. Duhm, *Das Buch Jeremia* (1901), p. 3. E. Sellin, *Introduction to the OT,* p. 114.

[19] Cf. G. B. Caird, *IB,* II, p. 862.

[20] *BHI,* pp. 166f.

[21] Cf. I. Mendelsohn, *BASOR,* No. 143 (1956), pp. 17ff.

his encounter with Samuel on quite a different errand, at which time it was revealed to Samuel that this man was the future leader of Israel. Saul was thereupon elected as נגיד in private, and was informed as to the nature of the signs which would confirm his divine election.

It is incorrect to assume, as Bright does, that part of a second component narrative depicted Samuel yielding with angry protests to the popular desire for a king (1 Sam. 10:17-27).[22] The facts of the situation are that when the people were assembled at Mizpah they were reminded of the Covenant provisions, against which was set their urgent desire for a king (מלך). Whatever the prophet Samuel may have felt about the incompatibility of theocratic concepts with those of an earthly monarch as envisaged by the people, the text makes it quite evident that he spoke more in sorrow than in anger. If the traditions concerning Samuel are to be comprehended in depth, it has to be realized that his attitude as depicted in 1 Samuel 10:17-27 was in essential harmony with his expressed feelings in chapter eight, with the difference that on the second occasion he was acting under divine sanction. In this general connection it must be remembered that whereas the people were demanding a מלך (1 Sam. 8:5), Samuel was actually commissioned to anoint Saul, and subsequently David, as נגיד or military leader of the tribes, the significance of which will be discussed subsequently.

Saul was formally elected in a public ceremony after a warning regarding the nature of the obligations being assumed had been given, and the procedure was duly recorded (1 Sam. 10:25). Thus, under the supervision of Samuel, the leader of the people had been appointed by properly constituted means, namely selection by lot. The subsequent ceremony at Gilgal (1 Sam. 11:14f.), spoken of as "the renewal of the kingdom," was in fact the public institution of the duly elected נגיד into his office. No doubt the procedure would be tantamount in the popular mind to the enthronement ceremonies of the more ancient monarchies in the Near East, despite the fact that Saul was initially, in the words of Albright, little more than a rustic chieftain.[23] It is of some interest to note that the fundamental pattern of election and institution depicted in the narratives has been much favored since that time, and can be found operative at many levels of modern society, both in religious and non-religious circles.

The Gilgal ceremonies concluded with a further reaffirmation by Samuel of his own integrity, and this was followed by a powerful appeal to the Israelites to implement the popular kingship concept with the emotive spirituality of the Covenant. Such a reconstruction of events, pursued in complete independence of artificial literary sources, is not so much an attempt to harmonize supposedly divergent narrative stand-

---

[22] BHI, p. 167.
[23] FSAC, p. 292.

points as to view the election of Saul holistically, and to interpret the significance of the events described accordingly.

A duplicate account has been seen by some scholars to be indicated by the fact that Saul was twice rejected from the kingship (1 Sam. 13:14; 15:23ff.). In point of fact this is a superficial and incorrect observation, for a careful reading of the text shows that in 1 Samuel 13:14 it was stated, not that Saul was rejected from his high office, but that his dynasty would not continue, which is a rather different situation. In 1 Samuel 15:23ff. Saul was specifically rejected, and although he evidenced some signs of repentance (1 Sam. 15:30f.) he continued in office in the absence of divine support and prophetic encouragement (1 Sam. 15:35).

A further discrepancy is said to exist in a supposedly twofold introduction of David to Saul (1 Sam. 16:14ff.; 17:55ff.), raising the question as to why Saul should have inquired whose son David was after the killing of Goliath, if he had come to know him as well as chapter 16 would seem to indicate.[24] Attempts to elucidate this particular problem have included the suggestion that Saul pretended not to recognize David, or that his particular mental condition occasioned such non-recognition. In connection with the second of these theories it is true, of course, that mental imbalance can affect recollection and recognition, and this could be particularly true in the case of Saul, who was evidently suffering from a paranoid schizophrenia, and not the manic-depressive condition entertained by most scholars and commentators.

However, neither of these suppositions is necessary in order to resolve the apparent discrepancy. Whereas on the first occasion (1 Sam. 16:14ff.) Saul was made aware of David as an individual, on the second (1 Sam. 17:55ff.) the inquiry of the king concerned the lineage and social standing of David, presumably as a prerequisite to the admission of the hero to the royal company and court. Had Saul merely been interested in the name of the warrior and that of his father, the apparently lengthy conversation between Saul and David (1 Sam. 18:1) would have been quite unnecessary. It would thus appear that other things than the matter of parentage were discussed on that occasion.

A second double account involving the activities of David has been seen in the escape from the court of Saul (1 Sam. 19:12; 20:42), and in the fact that, although Saul knew of the first flight, he expressed surprise that David was not present at a subsequent meal (1 Sam. 20:25ff.). The difficulties inherent in this situation can be resolved quite satisfactorily when it is realized that the first flight from Saul occurred when the king

[24] For a characteristic emendation, based upon the LXX, see S. R. Driver, *Notes on the Hebrew Text and the Topography of the Books of Samuel* (1913), pp. 137ff. The charge of incompatibility was dismissed by W. J. Martin in C. F. H. Henry (ed.), *The Biblical Expositor: The Living Theme of the Great Book* (1960), I, pp. 282ff.

was in an irrational frame of mind (1 Sam. 19:9). David subsequently became aware that his presence would be missed in the royal household (1 Sam. 20:6), and made an anniversary celebration the official excuse for his absence from the court.

David then left Naioth, where Saul had come earlier and been compelled to prophesy (1 Sam. 19:23f.), and met with Jonathan. Precisely where the rendezvous was cannot be ascertained with certainty, but the mention of a "city" and a "field" would imply that it was somewhere in the vicinity of Gibeah. However, there is no evidence that David returned to the royal court, only to flee a second time. He was in fact hiding in the area of the rendezvous (1 Sam. 20:24), and not in the city itself, so that his action in departing after bidding farewell to Jonathan (1 Sam. 20:42) was in effect merely a continuation of his initial flight, and does not therefore represent a second distinctive escape from the royal court.

Another indication of composite authorship has been urged from an alleged duplicate account of the manner in which David spared the life of Saul (1 Sam. 24:3ff.; 26:5ff.). Once again a careful reading of the text clears up the apparent difficulties. In the first account Saul entered a cave (מערה) in order to relieve himself. Quite unknown to him, David and his men were already hidden in some passages leading off the cave. While Saul was partially disrobed and probably in some sort of seclusion, David made a token conquest by cutting off part of the robe that the king had removed. Realizing, however, that he had his enemy at a distinct disadvantage, David magnanimously permitted the opportunity to kill him to pass, doubtless being governed at the same time by a reluctance to slay the Lord's anointed one. The second narrative described how David came to the place where Saul had pitched his camp (1 Sam. 26:5), and discovered the king lying in a slit-trench (מעגל) in the middle of his army. Once again David resisted the temptation to kill a man who was disarmed and entirely unaware of danger, contenting himself, as previously, with a token victory (1 Sam. 26:12) of important psychological proportions. The two events are clearly quite different in nature and occasion, even though they involved a twofold sparing of the life of Saul in the same general inhospitable area of southeastern Canaan.

It must be remarked again that many of the alleged discrepancies in the Biblical narratives are the direct result of careless reading—or sometimes of deliberate misrepresentation—of the Hebrew text, and the foregoing constitute no exceptions to this general observation. The canonical Hebrew writings are replete with problems of one kind or another that perplex the western mind as the situation now stands, without needing to be augmented by artificially constructed difficulties which in fact only exist in the critical imagination. However much this sort of activity may help to justify the existence of the literary critic, it constitutes in fact an entirely unwarranted handling of the text.

A much more valid question has been raised in connection with the slaying of Goliath. In 1 Samuel 17 and elsewhere (cf. 19:5; 21:19; 22:10, 13) David was said to have killed Goliath, but 2 Samuel 21:19 credits Elhanan with the death of the Philistine warrior. A further complication of the situation resulted from the tradition in 1 Chronicles 20:5, where Elhanan was said to have killed Lahmi, the brother of Goliath. The principal problem here appears to be one of textual transmission rather than strict interpretation. On further examination a clear relationship can be seen between 2 Samuel 21:19 and 1 Chronicles 20:5, and it is evident that the former contains certain transcriptional errors. First of all, the name of Elhanan's father (יערי ארגים) should not contain the word ארגים, which is obviously a copyist's mistake resulting from the appearance of the word, meaning "beam" or "shuttle," at the end of the verse. The name יערי should be revised to agree with the textual variant of 1 Chronicles 20:5, יעור. Furthermore the accusative particle את in the Samuel account should read אחי ("the brother of") as in Chronicles. Finally, the word in Chronicles from which the name Lahmi is derived, את-לחמי, should be corrected to read בית הלחמי following 2 Samuel 21:19. The corrected text would read, "And Elhanan, the son of Jairi the Bethlehemite, slew the brother of Goliath," which removes the apparent difficulty.

With the possible exception of Edward Robertson and Kaufmann,[25] most historians of the liberal school have experienced considerable difficulty in reconstructing the historical background of the Samuel traditions.[26] By far the most realistic modern appraisal of the situation was Albright's.[27] He began by conceding the impossibility of analyzing satisfactorily the sources of the Samuel material as extant according to traditional literary-critical patterns, and instead treated the apparently discrepant traditions on an holistic basis. He upheld the relative antiquity of the Samuel traditions, and maintained that they constituted true reflections of different early Israelite attitudes towards this notable prophet-judge. He also suggested that such differences should no longer be interpreted as constituting hopeless contradictions, but rather should be regarded as essential contributions to the total historical picture of Samuel.

Albright maintained that the narratives were rather unusual to the extent that they furnished material for a wider historical perspective than was the case for any other comparable period of ancient Hebrew history. He isolated four kinds of real or superficial discrepancies, the first of which spoke of Samuel initially as an Ephraimite layman of the Zuphite clan (1 Sam. 1:1), but elsewhere referred to him as one of a

[25] E. Robertson, *The OT Problem: A Reinterpretation* (1950), pp. 105ff.; cf. *KRI*, pp. 263ff.

[26] E.g. M. Noth, *The History of Israel* (1960), pp. 168ff.; *BHI*, pp. 165ff.

[27] W. F. Albright, *Samuel and the Beginnings of the Prophetic Movement* (1961), pp. 10ff.; *BPAE*, pp. 42ff.

704

family of Levitic singers (1 Chron. 6:16ff.). According to rabbinic tradition Samuel was regarded as a *nāzîr* (Num. 6:1ff.), based on the content of the vow of Hannah in 1 Samuel 1:11. Although this was not affirmed expressly in either the Hebrew text or the LXX version, it appeared in an early recension of 1 Samuel recovered in fragmentary form from the fourth Qumran cave, [28] as well as in the Hebrew recension of Ecclesiasticus found in the Ezra Synagogue in Cairo in 1897.[29] In the manuscript published by Cross the phrase "he shall be a *nāzîr* for ever" had dropped out of the Hebrew at 1 Samuel 1:22 as the result of a form of scribal omission known as haplography. Several varieties of the text of 1 Samuel were recovered in fragmentary form from 4Q, and indicate a wide divergence between pre-Massoretic types of the text and its subsequent extant form in the Hebrew Bible.

Fuller knowledge of these archetypal texts would greatly enlarge the scholarly perspective regarding the traditions of Samuel, and would also show the fallacy of much critical reasoning based upon artificial literary sources. Be that as it may, once Samuel was considered a *nāzîr*, he would have been drawn almost automatically by the nature of his Levitical obligations into family attachment to the tribe of Levi. In the popular mind he was certainly associated with the Levites, and this impression may easily have been augmented by the well-attested use of instrumental music in his prophetic gatherings, and his consequent connection with Levite musicians. Albright has pointed out that the term *nāzîr* was a pre-Israelite word identical with the Ugaritic, Hebrew, and Aramaic root *ndr*, "to vow," and parallel in formation to *nābhî'* or "prophet."[30] The meaning of *nāzîr* was originally "one who is vowed," that is to say, to divine service, and in the case of Samuel etymology and way of life were fully coincident.

A second alleged discrepancy mentioned by Albright was that whereas Samuel was judge over all Israel and decreed his power to his sons on retirement (1 Sam. 7:5ff.; 8:1ff.), he appeared in the story of Saul as a little-known diviner (1 Sam. 9:6ff.). As the inspired leader of Israel he was automatically a *shōphēt* who arbitrated between the tribes and clans. But as a leader of the ecstatic prophets he was also a seer (*rō'eh*), and insofar as he was called directly by God to His service he was a prophet (*nābhî'*). Thus all the public roles ascribed by the traditions to Samuel were correct in their proper time and setting.

A further discordancy in the accounts of the life and work of Samuel was seen in the fact that he was alleged to have delivered the Israelites from Philistine oppression "all his days" (1 Sam. 7:13), whereas elsewhere Israel was said to have been under Philistine domination in the

---

[28] F. M. Cross, *BASOR*, No. 132 (1953), pp. 15ff.

[29] In Ecclus. 46:13, reading נזיר יהוה, i.e., "Nazirite of God."

[30] W. F. Albright, *Samuel and the Beginnings of the Prophetic Movement*, pp. 13f.

lifetime of Samuel (e.g. 1 Sam. 10:5; 13:3). Albright has seen no reason to dispute one or more Israelite victories under the leadership of Samuel of a sort which would be sufficient for the Hebrews to gain important concessions from their traditional enemies. At the same time Albright assumed that not all of the traditional accounts could be correct.

In any attempt to assess the nature of the Samuel tradition in this regard, it is important to locate the Philistines accurately in the contemporary economic and military picture. When the Hebrews left Egypt, the Philistines began to settle in strength along the coastal strip between Egypt and Gaza (Exod. 13:17), thereby augmenting previous migrations in the same general area from patriarchal times. While the Israelites did not encounter the Philistines in Canaan during the conquest period, the last days of Joshua saw the activity of a developed five-city Philistine alliance. In subsequent periods this group imposed considerable military and economic pressure upon the occupying Hebrews, and their interrelationships were such that the Israelites even adopted Philistine gods (Judg. 10:6f.).

While the Philistines constantly pressed inland from the coastal plain, the hill-country was never under Philistine control in the Judges period, since Samson was able to flee there (Judg. 15:8). By the time the sacred Ark fell into Philistine hands, the group probably controlled Esdraelon, the coastal plain, the Negeb, and some of the uplands of Judah. Because the Philistines had adopted the iron-fitted chariot as a weapon of war, their hold upon the hill-country was less secure than was the case elsewhere, since the chariot had limited tactical and military value in such terrain. Consequently the first major defeat at the hands of Saul and the Israelite warriors occurred in the hills of Judaea (1 Sam. 14:1ff.). This military situation. along with the economic restrictions that the Philistines applied, exerted an undoubted pressure upon the Israelites, and was certainly one of the reasons for the rise of the monarchy.

On the other hand, the Hebrews exercised control, although sometimes tenuous, over large sections of the country west and north of the Dead Sea. It is therefore incorrect to assume that the Israelites were entirely in bondage to the Philistines, although the serious degree of economic dependence by Israel upon them was a matter of great concern (cf. 1 Sam. 13:19ff.). While the Israelites were at best only able to eke out a scanty living, their very presence and military potential remained a firm obstacle to complete Philistine occupation of the land. The two peoples were thus a threat to the security and national aspirations of each other, with the balance of this state of tension favoring the Philistines because of their superiority in technology, weapons, and economic resources.

The Hebrew narratives do not lend substance to the belief that Samuel crushed Philistine oppression during his lifetime, as Albright and some others have tended to assume. Instead, they merely show that, with divine assistance, Samuel was able to keep the Philistine forces at bay, and prevent additional encroachments onto the already restricted Israelite territorial holdings. This seems further indicated by the fact that the initial activity in the direction of reducing the Philistine hold upon the land consisted of the subjugation of individual Philistine military strongpoints in the uplands of Judah, a tactical move that could hardly have been assured of success if the Philistines had been able to fight at will without fear of recrimination. That the Philistines had managed to achieve a large-scale penetration of the land, however, is immediately evident from the narratives. But that they had effectively subjugated the Israelites in the process is not, for had this been the case the Hebrews would never have been able to elect a king in order to crush the Philistines. The Biblical traditions, therefore, appear to be an accurate reflection of what actually transpired in the days before a resolute onslaught was made against Philistine territorial aspirations.

The final real or apparent discrepancy mentioned by Albright involved the opposition of Samuel to the monarchy at one period (1 Sam. 8:6ff., *et al.*), and his approval at another time (1 Sam. 9:16ff., *et al.*).[31] Attempts to harmonize the divergent accounts by supposing that Samuel subsequently changed his mind about the idea of monarchy do not represent the traditions adequately. The latter make it clear that Samuel was unalterably opposed to the idea of kingship in Israel, presumably for the very good reason that it conflicted with his concept of the theocratic ideal. The discrepancy can fortunately be explained quite readily by noting that in two passages referring to Saul (1 Sam. 9:16; 10:1), the Hebrew text spoke of Samuel anointing Saul as a נגיד not as a מלך over Israel. Similarly, David was on several occasions referred to in exactly the same capacity (cf. 1 Sam. 13:14; 25:30; 2 Sam. 5:2; 6:21; 7:8 *et al.*), although in other contexts the term מלך was applied both to David and Saul. The title of נגיד was also conferred upon Solomon (1 Kgs. 1:35) in association with that of מלך, as well as upon Jeroboam I (1 Kgs. 14:7), Baasha (1 Kgs. 16:2), and Hezekiah (2 Kgs. 20:5). From the nature of the post-Solomonic references it would appear that the designation of נגיד rapidly became obsolete, being replaced by the popular title מלך.

As Albright has pointed out, it is certain in view of the great significance attached to titles in the ancient Orient that the preference for נגיד rather than מלך in the formula of installation was quite deliberate. In short, Saul and David were not intended either by Samuel or the tribal heads to be enthroned as kings, but only to be anointed as military leaders of the tribal confederation. The נגיד was thus at best a charismatic figure, and was never intended to be understood as an hereditary monarch. Although the term נגיד soon lost its basic charismatic meaning and became equated with מלך when hereditary succession was established in Judah, the concept of elective leadership was never com-

[31] *Ibid.,* pp. 14ff.

pletely obliterated either in Israel or Judah, as the references to Jeroboam, Baasha, and Hezekiah indicate.[32] In practice, however, a distinction between the two words rapidly became impossible to maintain, a circumstance that was already apparent even in the later days of Saul (cf. 1 Sam. 15:1, 17; 2 Sam. 5:2), and this was particularly the case in the light of the fact that every Canaanite princeling was known as מלך.

The meaning of the term נגיד, rendered by "captain" in the AV and "prince" or "leader" in most other English versions, following the later Aramaic terms neghîdha' and naghîdha', can be traced at least as far back as the middle of the eighth century, where it occurred in plural form in reference to important state offices in the Sefireh treaties, ca. 750 B.C.[33] In this document the term clearly meant "military commanders," and as such demonstrates that the office to which Saul and David were appointed was intended by Samuel to constitute military leadership over the tribal confederation, stabilized by means of a formal election and supported by religious sanction. Whether Samuel entertained this as a temporary or a permanent situation is, of course, unknown. What is evident, however, was his unrelenting insistence upon opposition to the kingship ideal of the popular mind.

The elimination of apparent discrepancies in the Samuel tradition removes some of the basis upon which the theories of literary analysis were established. Further damage to the procedures of critical source-identification in Samuel has been done by the discovery that there are several different textual types of Samuel represented in the findings from 4Q. These latter occurred in fragmentary form, and as Albright has pointed out, ranged from a variety akin to the MT to one which stands between that and the LXX recension, and to yet another one that comes close to an archetypal recension from which both the Hebrew Bible and the LXX version were clearly derived.[34]

As the result of these discoveries it is now evident that the text of Samuel that circulated before the present extant recension was considerably longer than either the latter or the LXX version, and that it differed in some important respects from both of them. Indications of this state of affairs were already apparent from the fact that the translators of the LXX had before them a Hebrew manuscript which in many instances represented a purer form of the text than that adopted by the Massoretes. It contained passages that had fallen out of the MT, but at the same time it omitted material which was preserved in the traditional Hebrew (as in 1 Sam. 17:12-31, 41, 48b, 50, 55–18:5). Quite obviously the text of Samuel never achieved the precise degree of literary fixity accorded to

---

[32] Cf. Ecclus. 46:13. It appeared in the Hebrew recension of Psalm 151 of the Greek Bible from 11Q. Cf. J. A. Sanders, *BASOR*, No. 165 (1962), p. 15.

[33] Cf. J. Fitzmyer, *CBQ*, XX (1958), pp. 444ff.

[34] W. F. Albright, *Samuel and the Beginnings of the Prophetic Movement*, p. 11.

many of the other canonical writings, and in view of the fluid condition of the Hebrew text it seems impossible to attempt an analysis into literary sources with any expectation of success.

There can now be no doubt that the indications are decidedly against a complex three-source theory such as that postulated by Eissfeldt, which seems in any event to have received little critical support.[35] Equally improbable is the two-strand hypothesis, since the sources which have been alleged to be present are clearly artificial, both from the evidence presented by the text itself and also in the light of the findings at Qumran. The fact is that there is insufficient data available for the literary analysis of the Samuel tradition along classical hypothetical lines. The most that can be said concerning the sources of 1 and 2 Samuel is that the compiler or compilers made use of a so-called "Throne Succession" source (2 Sam. 9–20), along with certain stories concerning the Ark (1 Sam. 4:1–7:2), and elements of tradition involving Saul and David. In the light of the preceding discussion it will be seen that apparent discrepancies cannot be used any longer as the foundation for some sort of literary analysis of the early Samuel tradition. Whoever was responsible for the compilation must have had access to sources that defy isolation and identification by conventional literary-critical methods.

The author or authors of the work received no mention in the text, although it is explicitly stated that Samuel made written records (1 Sam. 10:25). The compiler of the books of Chronicles also referred to the fact that events in the life of King David were included in the writings of Nathan the prophet and Gad the prophet-seer (1 Chron. 29:29), and these compositions may possibly have furnished some source material for the author or authors of Samuel. As with other chronicles of a similar character, it is impossible to state what the precise contents of these written documents comprised. The date of general compilation is also uncertain, but it may be that the anonymous author or authors wrote Samuel with the aid of certain literary sources and cycles of tradition somewhat after the founding of the northern kingdom, perhaps about 920 or 900 B.C. The general perspective of the work seems to favor Judah rather than Israel as the home of the compiler or compilers, though this fact again cannot be established with any degree of certainty.

C. THE MATERIAL OF SAMUEL

1. Religious revival. First and Second Samuel are of immense importance as an accredited historical source for the early period of the monarchy. They marked the transition from the chaos of the Judges era to the more settled conditions of the kingdom, and showed the part that Samuel played in establishing the social and political foundations of an

---

[35] It was followed, however, by S. Szikszai, *IDB*, IV, pp. 205f.

institution that, in the time of Solomon, was without equal in the ancient Near East. But while Samuel was of importance as the dominant religious figure in the transition from tribal confederation to centralized monarchy, he was of equal significance for the way in which he replaced the priestly hierarchy of Shiloh with an ecstatic prophetism. To what extent this substitution was complete is unknown, but it is certainly significant that the Hebrew text nowhere referred to the Tabernacle, the Ark of the Covenant, or the priesthood of Eli's line after his death and the ravaging of Shiloh by the Philistines (Ps. 78:60ff.; the "ark" of 1 Sam. 14:18 should be translated "ephod," following the LXX).

Little imagination is needed to understand the reasons why Samuel rejected the priestly traditions of Eli at Shiloh. As Albright has suggested, Samuel may have been subjected as a boy to persecution and abuse from the resident Levite families there,[36] but in any event the text makes it clear that he found the corrupt and immoral behavior of Eli's line completely alien to the traditions of the Sinai Covenant and its priesthood. Samuel was presented in the book bearing his name as the first great religious reformer after the time of Moses, and as one who scaled down radically the spiritual role of the priests and Levites by employing the ecstatic prophets and local sanctuaries in preference to the central cultic shrine at Shiloh. This kind of reformation marked the beginning of conflict between prophetic and priestly elements in the culture, and has been continued periodically throughout Judeo-Christian history in the partial or complete replacement of the established ecclesiastical hierarchy by new spiritual leadership from the ranks of the laity.[37] Albright has observed in this connection that it is because of this ever-renewed tension between hierarchy and charism that the Judeo-Christian continuum has always been capable of periodic self-criticism, a process to which western conscience owes it persistent revivals of sensitivity.[38]

Intimately connected with his efforts at religious revival was the attitude of Samuel towards sacrifice. On several occasions he himself offered sacrifice, apparently as a normal procedure, in the absence of a specific cultic background. As regards the ritual procedures of the cultus, Samuel appears to have maintained that the efficacy of the sacrifice was dependent upon considerations other than those of purely ritual performance. His views thus approximated closely to those of the eighth- and seventh-century B.C. prophets (1 Sam. 15:22) who emphasized motive rather than priestcraft. As Albright has shown, his attitude towards sacrificial ritual extended to the entire institutionalized system, so that he was completely in accord with the replacing of the official central

[36] *Samuel and the Beginnings of the Prophetic Movement*, p. 18.
[37] *BPAE*, p. 44.
[38] *Samuel and the Beginnings of the Prophetic Movement*, p. 19.

sanctuary by local high places.[39] These בּמֹת, which were the sites of objectionable licentious behavior in later times, should be interpreted in their origins against the background of the traditions current in the Heroic Age. Albright has pointed out that most probably the בּמֹת served an original memorial purpose quite close to that of the hero-shrines of Greek culture.[40] While some of the high places may perhaps have contained certain pagan religious symbols originally, there can be little doubt that the reforming fervor of Samuel and the prophetic guilds would have been more than adequate to deal with such circumstances.

The nature of the ecstatic prophetism that appeared suddenly on the scene in the days of Samuel has been a matter for considerable discussion by scholars, based to no small extent upon the meaning of the expression בּני הנביאים or "sons of the prophets," that is to say, the members of the prophetic guild. The word נביא is used consistently in the Old Testament of individuals who stood in a special relationship to God, a situation that was in general accord with ancient Near Eastern religious traditions. As Albright has made clear,[41] the term, related as it is to the Akkadian word nabā'um, should be interpreted as "the one who is called" or "the one who has a vocation," and not as "speaker" or "announcer."[42] The basic sense of vocation enshrined in the Hebrew term has been reinforced by lists of northwest Semitic names from eighteenth-century B.C. Mari archives, in which there appeared several names formed with the same verb and carrying the same meaning.

The נביא was thus an individual who had been favored with a special call from God, and the term designated a charismatic religious figure, a person without hereditary right or political appointment, who was authorized to speak or act on behalf of God.[43] Although there is considerable evidence for the activity of ecstatic prophets from Mari and elsewhere in Mesopotamia, there is nothing that would indicate that the prophetic guilds directed by Samuel received their impetus from extra-Israelite sources. Like other manifestations of the divine spirit they appeared spontaneously, and the ecstatic functions for which they were notable constituted but one aspect of their basic spirituality.[44]

The guild members were individuals who had passed through what in modern evangelical terms would be known as a "conversion experience," and their sense of divine favor and vocation was doubtless enhanced by the ecstatic performances which were a manifestation of their emotional

---

[39] Ibid., p. 17.

[40] W. F. Albright, VT, supp. vol. IV (1957), pp. 242ff.

[41] FSAC, pp. 17, 303ff.

[42] As in E. König, Hebräisches und aramäisches Wörterbuch zum AT (1936), p. 206 b; A. Guillaume, Prophecy and Divination (1938), pp. 112f.

[43] W. F. Albright, Samuel and the Beginnings of the Prophetic Movement, p. 6.

[44] On these guilds see M. A. van den Oudenrijn, Biblica, VI (1925), pp. 165ff.; H. Junker, Prophet und Seher in Israel (1927), pp. 30ff.; KRI, pp. 100f., 275f., 354.

and spiritual reorientation, as is also the case in some modern cults and sects. An emotionally unstable person such as Saul could well be expected to find satisfying expression for the divinely transformed patterns of behavior (1 Sam. 10:9) in such an environment, and the description of his encounter with the ecstatic prophets and its outcome appears to be entirely representative of the situation. In fairness to more modern religious associations in which ecstatic performances constitute one aspect of the group-experience, one should hasten to add that individual membership in such cults or sects is by no means necessarily correlative with emotional instability.

2. *The age of Saul.* The record of 1 Samuel 13:1 stating that Saul began to reign at the age of one year, which has caused difficulties for students of the text and perplexity for commentators, is actually an interesting reflection of the Heroic Age. The Hebrew of the verse reads בֶּן-שָׁנָה שָׁאוּל בְּמָלְכוֹ וּשְׁתֵּי שָׁנִים מָלַךְ עַל-יִשְׂרָאֵל. The AV handles the difficulty by translating the verse as "Saul reigned one year; and when he had reigned two years. . . ." The American Standard Version offers "Saul was *[forty]* years old when he began to reign; and when he had reigned two years . . . ," explaining in a marginal note that the number represented by *"forty"* is lacking in the Hebrew text. The RSV, using the same marginal note, renders the text "Saul was . . . years old when he began to reign; and he reigned . . . and two years over Israel." Such a textual emendation has been justified on the ground that the Biblical writer, as Noth put it, had omitted the number because he had no evidence at hand.[45]

A similar passage, however, is found in Homer's *Odyssey* (XIX:179), which asserts that King Minos ruled over Knossos when only nine years old. Neither the Biblical nor the Homeric tradition appears particularly strange when viewed against the epic background of the Mediterranean Heroic Age. As Cyrus Gordon has made plain, ancient kings were viewed as having to deal directly with the gods; and although this naturally called for some degree of maturity, King Minos was an exception.[46] In epic tradition he was no less than the son of Zeus himself, and it was from him that Minos received the law. The remarkable status of Minos was further enhanced by the fact that at the age of nine he was able to fulfil his role as divine king. The apparent precocity of Saul at the time when he became ruler of Israel as exemplified by 1 Samuel 13:1 is thus yet another illustration of the character of this epic tradition. This man, a member of the גִּבּוֹרֵי חַיִל, was the first of a long line of regal personages in Hebrew tradition, but his appointment as נָגִיד was more than the popular election of a secular מֶלֶךְ. He represented a material extension of the theocratic Covenant ideal, for he was the earthly head to whom the twelve tribes could look for leadership and command. But his anointing

---

[45] M. Noth, *The History of Israel,* p. 177 n. 1.
[46] *GBB,* pp. 228f.

by a theocratic prophet placed him, at least ideally, in a special relationship with the God of the Covenant, whose laws he was bound to keep. The particular nature of his position and his connection with Jehovah were correctly reflected by the Hebrew text, following as it did the ancient eastern Mediterranean tradition in assigning precocity to Saul. In this sense the text is perfectly correct, and needs no emendation once it is realized that Greek epic tradition is being followed at this point. By strict comparison with the more factual data in other sections of the narrative concerning Saul's rule, the epic tradition is obviously out of keeping. However, this need raise no difficulty, for once the point regarding the special character of Saul the נגיד had been established in epic terms, which alone were adequate for the exalted occasion, it was no longer necessary to continue in that vein, as subsequent verses indicate.

From the factual standpoint of the western mind, there is a certain degree of obscurity regarding the actual length of the reign of Saul. He succeeded to office as a young adult (בחור), as recorded by 1 Samuel 9:2, but soon after his death his fourth son, Ishbosheth, was murdered (2 Sam. 4:6ff.) at about 42 years of age (2:10). This would require a minimum of about thirty-five years for Saul's reign—perhaps forty. If Jonathan, Saul's eldest son, died about the age of forty, his father would probably have been about sixty at the time of his death. Therefore, at the period of his own anointing, Saul would probably have been between twenty and thirty, and if a median figure of twenty-five is adopted for his age at accession for purposes of convenience, the purely biological situation is compatible with a minimum reign of thirty-five years, which is in general accord with the tradition in Acts 13:21. The date of his accession would then most probably have occurred between 1050 and 1045 B.C.

It should be noted in passing that three successive reigns of some forty years each, as occurred in the case of Saul (1050/45-1011/10 B.C.), David (1011/10-971/70 B.C.), and Solomon (971/70-931/30 B.C.), need not necessarily be construed in epic terms, or, alternatively, be dismissed as an improbability. David was not, of course, a member of the house of Saul, while Solomon, who was born comparatively late in the reign of David, was also young at accession. In other Near Eastern countries reigns of forty years were by no means uncommon, as for example in Egypt, where out of eight monarchs in the Twelfth Dynasty, five enjoyed reigns of between thirty and fifty years in length.

3. *The brutality of war.* The brutality of war as depicted in the epic poetry dealing with events in the Mycenaean age is also reflected in the narratives of the early monarchy. The ruthless destruction of the enemy in warfare (cf. Josh. 6:17ff.; 8:2ff.) was naturally the prime objective, but the actual nature of the atrocities perpetrated tended to differ in matter of detail with various cultures and ages. The compulsory slaying

713

of captured enemy heroes depicted in 1 Samuel 15:18ff. can be paralleled in the *Iliad* (VI:55ff.) by the advice given to Menelaus to kill his captive rather than hold him for ransom, and insure that no male Trojan fetus survived. The latter atrocity, that of disembowelling pregnant women, was practiced by the Assyrians and the west-Semitic peoples generally (cf. 2 Kgs. 8:12; 15:16; Am. 1:13; Hos 13:16).

The custom known as the חרם, a term which is sometimes rendered "ban" or "devotion," involved the slaughter of a captured people and their flocks, and the incident in 1 Samuel 15:3ff. was a common feature of warfare in the Heroic Age, as noted earlier. Snaith's explanation that the word חרם was the opposite of קדש or "holiness," so that what was קדש to Jehovah was חרם to Chemosh,[47] is entirely fanciful, and finds no support whatever in the literature of eastern Mediterranean cultures.

4. Medical matters. There are several situations described in the books of Samuel that are of interest to the historian of medicine. The first is concerned with the description of an outbreak of bubonic plague (1 Sam. 5:6ff.), and constitutes one of the most important and authentic records of its kind to emerge from the ancient world.[48] The heavy mortality of the plague was preceded by the incidence of inguinal buboes in the sufferers (1 Sam. 5:12), after which the disease spread rapidly along lines of human communication. An important concomitant to the situation was noted in the presence of many rodents which also had succumbed to the effects of the plague (1 Sam. 6:5).

This description, remarkably objective as it is, furnishes abundant evidence symptomatically for a diagnosis of bubonic plague, the dreaded scourge of antiquity, which is conveyed to man by the rat flea (*pulex cheopis*), and spread by droplet infection with a short incubation period. Sudden illness supervenes, accompanied by malaise, petechial patches, diarrhea, pains in the limbs, rigor, and vomiting. After about twenty-four hours the characteristic buboes appear in the inguinal lymph glands, and it is these swellings which have given the disease its standard medical designation.

Somewhat different forms of bubonic plague may furnish symptoms of a pulmonary, intestinal, cerebral or septicemic nature, but in any event the mortality rate is generally in excess of eighty per cent of those afflicted with the disease. The interest of the narrative to the medical historian lies not least in the fact that the Philistine diviners quite correctly associated the incidence of rodent and human mortality in a time of epidemic sickness, a feature peculiar to bubonic plague, and also in the transmission of the disease along the principal lines of travel. It appears highly probable that the curtains of the Ark had become infested with the rat fleas that occasioned the original outbreak of the

[47] N. H. Snaith, *The Distinctive Ideals of the OT* (1946), p. 40.
[48] Cf. R. K. Harrison, *IDB*, III, pp. 821f.

plague, so that the moving of the Ark from place to place helped facilitate the spread of the disease, quite apart from its dissemination by means of infected rats. This is most likely illustrated by reference to the men of Beth-shemesh (1 Sam. 6:19).

A second medical phenomenon recorded in the book involved the mental affliction that overtook Saul. In conformity with the uniform witness of ancient Near Eastern tradition, which held mental disease in consistent terror and abhorrence, the Old Testament contained very few references to insanity. Madmen were regarded as standing in a peculiar relationship to a possessing deity or demon, and in consequence they were left strictly alone by the rest of the population. The remarkable objectivity of the Hebrew record, which was a dominant characteristic of Hebrew historiography and which gave the Israelite scribes an ultimate pride of place in the company of Near Eastern historiographers, furnished early indications of weakness in the personality of Saul in describing the dramatic emotional response evoked by a chance contact with a guild of ecstatic prophets. It is true, of course, that this form of activity was based upon an experience of genuine spiritual conversion, with a consequent alteration in behavioral patterns and mental attitudes that are wholly compatible with a deepening of the individual spiritual life. But whereas the majority of such experiences in modern times constitute powerful factors in the integration of the individual personality, in the case of Saul it was followed by a progressively deteriorating mental condition (1 Sam. 16:14) which was probably precipitated to some extent by the emotional stresses resulting from the break with Samuel (1 Sam. 15:35). Whether the latter is true or not, the narrative points quite clearly to a latent mental pathology that became active as Saul grew older.

The picture of psychological degeneration exhibited in the case of Saul has commonly been interpreted by commentators in terms of typical manic-depressive insanity.[49] In actual fact Saul appears to have been suffering from the much more malignant psychotic reaction of paranoid schizophrenia. This disease, which like all paranoid conditions demonstrates the patient in divorce from reality, is frequently characterized by delusions of grandeur and also of persecution, which may be further complicated by fluctuations in the general level of mental deterioration. The patient is frequently moody and suspicious by disposition, and his attempts to compensate for personality weaknesses are generally operative against a background of delusions and hallucinations.[50]

As the disease progresses, the sufferer may try to commit an act of violence, particularly against someone who is suspected of being an

[49] Cf. A. Macalister, HDB, III, p. 327; J. C. Schroeder, IB, II, p. 969; J. M. Myers, IDB, IV, p. 232.

[50] R. K. Harrison, IDB, III, p. 220. Cf. ibid., I, pp. 850f.

actual or even a potential enemy. At this stage the patient is a danger to those around him, since they are liable at any time to feel the weight of his suspicions. The condition frequently terminates in complete intellectual and emotional deterioration, although death sometimes supervenes from purely physical causes. From the foregoing it will be apparent that the record of mental pathology exhibited in the case of Saul (cf. 1 Sam. 18:11; 20:30ff.; 28:20; 31:5) was one of serious proportions, and significant because of the accuracy and objectivity with which it preserved in untechnical language the nature and development of the pathological sequences.

Another individual of clinical interest was Goliath of Gath, who by uniform tradition was a physical giant. Since there is no information about his family (if "Lahmi" is removed from 1 Chron. 20:5 by emendation, as proposed above, p. 704), it is impossible to state whether or not his gigantism was in fact hyperostosis, occasioned as the result of deterioration of the familial stock. In the absence of specific indications to the contrary, it seems probable that he was afflicted with a tumor of the anterior lobe of the pituitary body. The anterior lobe is concerned with general growth and with sexual development, and in young subjects hypertrophy of this lobe results in gigantism as the bones of the body increase in length.

The existence in Canaan of a number of men who were remarkable for their gigantic stature was indicated in the account of the exploits undertaken by the warriors of David (2 Sam. 21:16ff.). These giants appear to have constituted the remnants of a prehistoric group that inhabited areas of the Promised Land (Num. 13:33), and may have been connected with the Nephilim of Genesis 6:4. Their size and disposition by families would seem to indicate that as a species they were on the point of extinction, and were doubtless tolerated by the Philistines as much for their value as curiosities as for their prowess in battle. Numbered also among the inhabitants of Gath was another giant afflicted with a congenital abnormality consisting of an extra digit on the hands and feet (2 Sam. 21:20; 1 Chron. 20:6). That such a deformity was more common than one might expect from a casual reading of the Old Testament can be seen in the fact that individuals thus afflicted were excluded from service in the Temple (Lev. 21:18).

5. *Evidences of a matriarchate.* No survey of the contents of Samuel would be complete without some mention of the place that the matriarchate may have occupied in the social and political structure of the period.[51] Although the system of inheritance through the female of the line rather than through the male was characteristically Egyptian, there seem to be indications of its influence in Canaan during the period of

---

[51] Cf. R. K. Harrison, *A History of OT Times* (1957), pp. 87, 143f., 150f., 154.

the early monarchy. This possibility in itself need occasion no particular surprise, since southern Palestine was an Egyptian dependency from the beginning of the Amarna Age, if not indeed somewhat earlier.

If the matriarchal system claimed any validity for the particular period of Hebrew history under discussion, it would go far towards explaining the concern of David when Merab married Adriel instead of becoming his own wife, since the husband of Merab would then be in direct line of succession to the throne. By marrying Maachah daughter of Talmai, king of Geshur (2 Sam. 3:3), David would have become heir to that small kingdom also, if the matriarchal pattern was valid to any extent in Canaan, and it is perhaps of some interest in this connection to observe that it was to this place that Absalom fled after murdering his brother Amnon (2 Sam. 13:37f.). The actions of the latter, concluding with a sexual assault on his half-sister, could certainly be interpreted on the basis of the matriarchate as a calculated plan to possess the heiress and thus insure his own succession to the throne.

If it can be established that Ahinoam, wife of David (1 Sam. 25:43), was the same person as Ahinoam, daughter of Ahimaaz and wife of Saul, it could be argued without undue difficulty that the importance of the matriarchal system had led David to lure the wife of the reigning king into a marital alliance, thereby affording him clear title to the throne of Israel. Such circumstances would then furnish Saul with pressing reasons for the immediate eradication of David, if possession of the heiress to the throne carried with it the right of succession by marriage. Again, if the matriarchate was at all operative in Israelite popular thought at this period, it would assist in explaining the pathetic attachment of Phaltiel to Michal (2 Sam. 3:16), the former wife of David, since by remaining married to her he would be in direct line of succession to the throne. While there are obvious difficulties attaching to the theory of a partially or wholly functioning matriarchate in the early kingdom period, not the least of which involves the true identity of Ahinoam and Maachah, there seem to be some grounds for thinking that factors other than those of temperamental imbalance or lustful speculation underlay the political and social configurations of the early monarchy.

❖   ❖   ❖   ❖   ❖

In the light of earlier observations about the text of the book of Samuel, it will be apparent that the extant work is corrupt in a great many places. Occasionally, however, it is possible for the text to be reconstructed satisfactorily by recourse to parallel accounts in Chronicles and also in the ancient versions. The LXX is of particular value in this connection, since it appears to have been based upon a purer and considerably different form of Hebrew text than the MT. The discovery of manuscript fragments at Qumran has pointed to a remarkable fluidity of the text in early times, and has indicated the existence of non-Massoretic forms of the Hebrew.

This situation would also support the view that the periodic divergences of the LXX from the MT cannot be explained wholly in terms of liberties taken by the translators during the course of their work, but instead must be related to the content of one or more different textual types upon which the LXX may have drawn. While certain omissions in the Hebrew can be supplied by reference to the LXX, the reverse is also true, for sections omitted in the LXX have been preserved in the MT, the most notable instances occurring in 1 Samuel 17–18. While the Hebrew text cannot be studied properly without constant reference to the LXX, the latter is itself evidently far from reliable as a guide, and accordingly should be used with considerable caution.

Supplementary Literature

Douglas, G. C. M. *Samuel and His Age: A Study in the Constitutional History of Israel.* 1901.

Eissfeldt, O. *Geschichtsschreibung im Alten Testament.* 1948.

Rehm, M. *Text-Kritische Untersuchungen zu den Parallelstellen der Samuel-Königsbücher und der Chronik.* 1937.

Truyols, A. F. *1 Samuel 1-15 Critica Textuae.* 1917.

Wellhausen, J. *Der Text der Bücher Samuelis untersucht.* 1872.

IV. THE BOOKS OF KINGS

A. NAME AND OUTLINE

The Hebrew title of this work is simply מלכים or "Kings," and like the two books of Samuel it was originally a unity in Hebrew. The division into two books was first introduced in the LXX version, doubtless because the vocalized Greek text occupied considerably more space than the unpointed Hebrew. The division of the Hebrew text into two sections first appeared in a mid-fifteenth-century manuscript, and as with Samuel the printed form of the MT was first divided into two parts with the edition of Daniel Bomberg (1516-17), a practice that became current thereafter.

In the LXX 1 and 2 Kings were entitled the "Third and Fourth Book of Kingdoms," while in the Vulgate they were given the title *Liber Regum tertius et quartus.* The English title "Kings" followed Jerome rather than the LXX rendering. In both Greek and Latin Bibles Samuel and Kings were regarded as one continuous history, divided for convenience into four sections. Some Greek texts varied the point at which Samuel divided from Kings, furnishing evidence for a break at 1 Kings 2:11, when the reign of David terminated, or at 1 Kings 2:46a, which marked the point at which Solomon succeeded to the throne. In any event the arbitrariness of the division is evident from the character of the break in the narrative at the end of 2 Samuel, which can only have been entertained as a means of insuring the continuity between Samuel and Kings. Even more artificial is the division between 1 and 2 Kings, where the account of the reign of Ahaziah, king of Israel, with which 1 Kings concluded, was continued in the first chapter of 2 Kings. The same is true of the last days of Elijah, whose translation was recorded in 2 Kings, whereas his previous ministry had been narrated in detail in 1 Kings. Again, the desire to demonstrate the essential unity of 1 and 2 Kings can alone have determined the point at which the original unit was divided.

In *Baba Bathra* 15a, the authorship of Kings was attributed to Jeremiah, along with the prophecy bearing his name and Lamentations. This ascription reflected the dogmatic approach of the Talmudic authori-

719

ties, who supposed that all the Old Testament books were somehow written by prophets. At first sight this theory is somewhat attractive, for 2 Kings 24:18–25:30 is repeated in Jeremiah 52; and in other respects there is much in Kings that is in harmony with the outlook of Jeremiah. However, the Kings account of the deportation and imprisonment of Jehoiachin was evidently composed in Babylon, whereas Jeremiah was in Egypt at that time. Verbal differences between the parallel sections in 2 Kings and Jeremiah may indicate that both passages are abstracts from a more comprehensive source, written by someone other than Jeremiah. As will appear subsequently, 2 Kings seems to have been compiled by an anonymous author or authors in the exilic period, and would thus be almost certainly later than the time of Jeremiah in any event.

Kings recorded the history of the kingdoms of Israel and Judah from the last days of David to the fall of Jerusalem in 597 B.C. It can be broadly analyzed as follows:

I. The Reign of Solomon, ch. 1–11
    A. The death of David and choice of Solomon, 1:1–2:11
    B. The establishment of Solomon's kingship, 2:12–3:28
        1. Elimination of enemies, 2:12-46
        2. Solomon's marriage, 3:1-2
        3. Solomon's prayer, 3:3-15
        4. Solomon's judicial decision, 3:16-28
    C. The organization of the kingdom, 4:1-34
    D. The building of the Temple, 5:1–7:51
    E. The dedication of the Temple, 8:1-66
    F. Activities during the Solomonic period, 9:1–11:43
        1. The divine Covenant with Solomon, 9:1-9
        2. Miscellaneous details, 9:10-28
        3. The visit of the Queen of Sheba, 10:1-13
        4. The wealth of Solomon, 10:14-29
        5. Solomon's apostasy and final years, 11:1-43
II. The Divided Monarchy, 1 Kgs. 12–2 Kgs. 17
    A. The division of the kingdom, 12:1–14:20
        1. The obstinacy of Rehoboam, 12:1-19
        2. The establishment of Jeroboam, 12:20-33
        3. Prophecies against Jeroboam, 13:1–14:20
            a. A "man of God" against calf-worship, 13:1-34
            b. Ahijah's prediction of destruction of the dynasty, 14:1-20
    B. Various kings, 1 Kgs. 14:21–2 Kgs. 10:36
        1. Rehoboam in Judah, 14:21-31
        2. Abijam and Asa in Judah, 15:1-24
        3. Nadab in Israel, 15:25-32
        4. Baasha in Israel, 15:33–16:7
        5. Elah in Israel, 16:8-14

B. THE COMPILATION OF KINGS

From the foregoing analysis it is apparent that, as far as pure history is concerned, Kings presents an uneven picture. For example, Omri, one of the most important rulers of the northern kingdom, who made Samaria his capital city and fortified it heavily against the Syrians, and in addition renewed trade affiliations with Phoenicia as a means of thwarting Syrian commercial ambitions, has his achievements dismissed in six scant verses (1 Kgs. 16:23-28). Again, three whole chapters are devoted to the exploits of Hezekiah (2 Kgs. 18–20), whereas the rule of Jeroboam II of Israel, which for a great many in the north recalled the Golden Age of David and Solomon, was recounted in only seven verses (2 Kgs. 14:23-29). On the other hand, the comparatively short period of the ministries of Elijah and Elisha is described in great detail, occupying nearly one-third of the entire book. This imbalance is obviously deliberate. The constant reference to sources of additional information shows that the purpose of the book is not to furnish the reader with an exhaustive account of Israelite history, but, while continuing the story of the theocracy until its termination at the time of the exile, to present the divine view of Israelite history.[1] Against a background of implicit monotheism the compiler(s) endeavored to show the principles underlying the dealings of God with the theocratic nation,[2] thus demonstrating that the primary concern was not with the problems of secular historiography *per se*. Everything was subordinated to the basic objective of narrating the history of divine relationships with the Chosen People from the standpoint of God Himself, and so fundamental was this postulate that not even the inculcating of great lessons to be learned from history was permitted to interfere with the overall purpose of the compilation. Only those elements of the historical process that were deemed to have a bearing upon the developing divine plan were considered important to the author or authors, and anything that did not assist in demonstrating the principles by which God dealt with His people was either ignored or else accorded only the barest treatment.

1. *General patterns of compilation.* The books of Kings are frequently spoken of in terms of "Deuteronomic" redactional activity by critical writers, and an impressive case can be made for such a supposition by the device of drawing up lists of phrases and expressions common to Deuteronomy and the books of Kings.[3] Because of this tendency it is important to realize that there is a fundamental difference of emphasis exhibited in the two works. Although both are based strictly upon the precepts of the Covenant relationship at Sinai, Deuteronomy deals with the lessons to be gleaned from history, whereas 1 and 2 Kings are concerned directly with the Covenant ideal, and the extent to which men and nations strayed from it. Whereas in Deuteronomy the blessings of God accrued to those who kept the provisions of the Covenant agreement, in the books of Kings both men and nations alike were evaluated morally and spiritually according to whether or not they had deviated from the Covenant. While it is too much to say that the issue was one

---

[1] J. C. J. Waite, *NBD*, p. 697; J. Gray, *I and II Kings: A Commentary* (1963), p. 12.

[2] S. Szikszai, *IDB*, III, p. 35.

[3] *DILOT*, pp. 200ff.

between an historical and a theological approach, it nevertheless remains true that the compiler of Kings expounded the significance of the Covenant in theocentric terms, and adduced facets of the historical situation in order to substantiate his case. In setting up the Sinai Covenant as the pivotal standard by which the actions of men and peoples were to be judged, the author of Kings was introducing no innovation. He merely stood firm in the tradition of the eighth- and seventh-century B.C. prophets, who themselves uniformly looked back to the Torah for their inspiration. Although each of them expounded characteristic features of the Mosaic corpus in his own distinctive manner, it is nevertheless a fact that there was no single element of prophetic teaching that was not already present in the Torah, albeit, perhaps, in embryonic form. Therefore, what the prophets and the compiler of Kings did in effect was to make explicit that which was already implicit in the Law.

The books of Kings exhibit clear indications of compilation based upon several sources, some of which are more obvious than others. These different sources were probably edited by more than one author, and presented as a unified composition by the use of certain formulae. Unlike most modern histories, the result can hardly be said to constitute an original composition, for the individual or persons responsible for the compilation of Kings constructed an historical narrative by recourse to a careful selection of extracts from written sources and from cycles of tradition. The finished anthology was considerably in excess of the sum of its parts, however, for it was intended to present the overall religious aim of the author or authors, as noted above, and as such was the result of careful and discriminating planning.

In the nature of the case it is impossible to pronounce with any certainty upon the unity or diversity of authorship, and in subsequent discussion only the singular will be employed in reference to editors and authors. The compiler exhibited particular literary skill in the way in which the narratives dealing with the period of the divided monarchy were treated, for he placed the histories of the two kingdoms in parallel form and dealt alternately with each against a framework of introductory and concluding formulae. The author began with an account of the reign of Jeroboam I of Israel, tracing the events occurring during his rule before turning his attention to contemporary happenings in Judah. Then the narrative was focused upon the southern kingdom until the death of Asa, after which the pattern was alternated.

The framework itself was constructed in a regularized manner, and permitted a differentiation between the two kingdoms that was thoroughly consistent with the theological emphasis of the author. The introductory formula normally synchronized the year of accession for the one king with the reign of the monarch in the other kingdom. Thus, in 1 Kings 15:1 the beginning of the reign of Abijam was correlated with the eighteenth year of Jeroboam I of Israel, while in 1 Kings 15:25 the accession of Nadab, the son of Jeroboam I, was related to the second year of Asa, king of Judah. In the case of Nadab (1 Kgs. 15:28) and Elah (1 Kgs. 16:10), the synchronized date of decease was also furnished.

Having established the identity of the particular ruler, the author then furnished, in the case of the southern kingdom, the age of the king at his accession, a procedure which was omitted for Abijam and Asa. Then the length of the reign was given and the mother of the ruler was identified, the latter being omitted in the case of Jehoram (2 Kgs. 8:17) and Ahaz (2 Kgs. 16:2). Finally the compiler furnished his estimate of the particular reign, based upon his special theological approach.

For the northern kingdom the length of rule of the individual king under discussion was stated, as well as the site of the royal residence. While the place where Jeroboam I and Nadab lived was not given, it can be assumed that it was Tirzah, a Canaanite town noted for its beauty, which became the Israelite capital in the days of Baasha (1 Kgs. 15:21, 33; 16:6) and remained as such until Omri moved the government to Samaria after six years of rule. Having established the reign under consideration, the compiler formally condemned each monarch with the exception of Shallum, whose conspiracy nevertheless did not entirely escape notice. In general it was the father rather than the mother of the king who was named, although this did not obtain in the case of Zimri (1 Kgs. 16:11) and Omri (1 Kgs. 16:23). No stereotyped introduction was employed in the case of Jehu (2 Kgs. 9:6ff.).

A concluding formula followed much the same pattern for both the northern and the southern kingdoms. It generally referred to some such chronicle sources as those of the kings of Judah and Israel, and contained a statement of death to the effect that the particular king "slept with his fathers." If the king died a violent death, however, the phrase "and he slept" was omitted, as with Joash (2 Kgs. 12:21). While the place of burial was usually mentioned, as with Jerusalem for Rehoboam (1 Kgs. 14:31), in the case of Hezekiah (2 Kgs. 20:21) and Jehoiachin, mention of the burial place was omitted. Unless the king was followed by a usurper, as happened in the northern kingdom, the narrative stated that his son reigned in his stead.

Although the reasons for the condemnation of individual kings varied somewhat, they were consistent with the theocentric and covenantal standpoint of the compiler. Rehoboam was castigated for general evil behavior and for encouraging the spread of Canaanite high places in the land. References to the northern pilgrim shrines in Bethel and Dan were equally derogatory in depicting them as the "way of Jeroboam" or the "sin which he committed in making Israel to sin" (cf. 1 Kgs. 15:26, 34; 16:9). The Israelite kings were condemned as a group by the comprehensive observation that they did evil in the sight of the LORD, although

724

in the case of Jehu (2 Kgs. 10:29-31), Jehoram (2 Kgs. 3:2), and Hoshea (2 Kgs. 17:2), the criticism was modified somewhat.

Denunciation of some rulers occurred because of their veneration of foreign deities, and this fault was generally described as the "way of the kings of Israel" (2 Kgs. 16:3) or the "way of the house of Ahab" (2 Kgs. 8:27). Included in those rulers who fell under this condemnation were Ahab (1 Kgs. 16:31-33), Ahaziah of Israel (1 Kgs. 22:53), Jehoram (2 Kgs. 8:18), Ahaziah of Judah (2 Kgs. 8:27), Ahaz (2 Kgs. 16:2-4), Manasseh (2 Kgs. 21:2-9), and Amon (2 Kgs. 21:20-22). Only Hezekiah (2 Kgs. 18:3-7) and Josiah (2 Kgs. 22:2) received unreserved commendation for their suppression of the high places and for the general reform of the cultus. Those rulers whose activities met with qualified approval included Asa (1 Kgs. 15:11-14), Jehoshaphat (1 Kgs. 22:43), Jehoash (2 Kgs. 12:2f.), Azariah (2 Kgs. 15:3f.), and Jotham (2 Kgs. 15:34f.), the principal cause of complaint being that they had not removed the high places at which the people were accustomed to sacrifice and burn incense.[4]

2. *Three named sources.* There are three sources actually mentioned by name in Kings, the first of which is the "Book of the Acts of Solomon" (1 Kgs. 11:41). While it is naturally impossible from the rather general nature of the reference to be certain as to its contents, it appears fairly obvious that it comprised contemporary annals, biographical material, and extracts from records in the Temple archives. A reconstruction of the source would suggest that it recounted the marriage of Solomon with the Egyptian princess (1 Kgs. 3:1), the dream of Solomon in Gibeon (1 Kgs. 3:4-15) and his wise judgment (1 Kgs. 3:16-28), as well as a series of lists, probably from the court archives, including a catalog of court officials (1 Kgs. 4:1-6) and provincial administrators (1 Kgs. 4:7-19, 27f.). It is very doubtful if these lists actually came from the biography of Solomon, as Oesterley and Robinson suggested,[5] since they are primarily administrative in nature.[6]

Three other important sections probably comprised the treaty with Hiram of Tyre and preparations for building the Temple (1 Kgs. 5:1-18; 5:15-32 Heb.), the construction of the Temple and the royal palace (1 Kgs. 6:1—7:51), and the dedication of the Temple (1 Kgs. 8:1-66). This material may well have been derived from the Temple archives, and probably had no immediate connection with any supposed biography of Solomon. The source doubtless included in addition the further dealings between Solomon and Hiram (1 Kgs. 9:11-14), the construction of the Millo (1 Kgs. 9:23-25),[7] the wisdom of Solomon and the visit of the

---

4 Cf. *YIOT*, p. 194f.; N. H. Snaith, *IB*, III, pp. 9f.; S. Szikszai, *IDB*, III, p. 30.
5 *IBOT*, p. 94.
6 Cf. W. F. Albright, *JPOS*, V (1925), pp. 17ff.; *WBA*, p. 130.
7 Cf. *LAP*, p. 150.

Queen of Sheba[8] (1 Kgs. 9:26–10:29), and possibly an account of two enemies of Solomon (1 Kgs. 11:14-25). The source unquestionably contained some historical material of great value, and while the description of the Solomonic wisdom had already acquired a legendary tone, the "Book of the Acts of Solomon" was certainly based upon reliable ancient archival tradition.

The second source named was that of the "Book of the Chronicles of the Kings of Israel" (1 Kgs. 14:19–2 Kgs. 15:31), covering events from the reign of Jeroboam I to that of Pekah, and being referred to on seventeen different occasions. The term "The Book of the Chronicles" means literally "the record of current events," and was a technical designation for official records of significant political happenings that were kept for safety in the state archives. Such references as those to the "acts of Jeroboam" (1 Kgs. 14:19), the conspiracy of Zimri (1 Kgs. 16:20), the building activity of Ahab (1 Kgs. 22:39), and the conflict between Joash and Amaziah of Judah (2 Kgs. 13:12) point to the annalistic nature of the source, which probably contained all that was memorable in the reign of each king, in accordance with the general pattern of contemporary ancient Near Eastern society.

The third source which was cited in Kings was designated "The Book of the Chronicles of the Kings of Judah" (1 Kgs. 14:29–2 Kgs. 24:5), dealing with events from the time of Rehoboam to the reign of Jehoiakim, and being cited some fifteen times in all. From this source it was possible to derive additional information relating to all the kings of Judah except Ahaziah, Jehoahaz, Jehoiachin, and Zedekiah. It contained no reference to Athaliah, who usurped the throne of Judah and held it for seven years (2 Kgs. 11:1ff.). The omission of a reference to the source in the cases of three of the last four kings of Judah may have been due to the fact that in none of these cases were the death and burial recorded. References to the constructional activities of Asa (1 Kgs. 15:23), the wars of Jehoshaphat (1 Kgs. 22:45), and the conduit of Hezekiah (2 Kgs. 20:20), make clear the annalistic character of this source also, and indicate that it comprised court records which were deposited in the royal archives of Jerusalem.

3. *Possible other sources.* Apart from these three written sources there may well have been others upon which the compiler drew for information. The court memoirs of David were concluded in the first two chapters of Kings, and this material is of great historical value, as has been observed previously, coming as it does from a period no later than the second half of the tenth century B.C. It may perhaps be possible to posit the existence of three cycles of tradition involving Elijah, Elisha,

---

[8] Cf. J. A. Montgomery, *Arabia and the Bible* (1934), p. 180; S. Perowne, *PEF Quarterly Statement* (1939), pp. 199ff.; E. Ullendorf, *BJRL*, XLV, No. 2 (1963), pp. 486ff.

and Ahab, which would furnish a good deal of information for that particular period. In this connection it is interesting to note that the Elijah stories (1 Kgs. 17–19, 21; 2 Kgs. 1), which were interrupted by the account of the war of Ahab against the Syrians, were firmly rooted in the history of the northern kingdom, and the work of the prophet was described in great detail. Of the moral and theological issues dealt with by Elijah, the most important were the question of monotheism (1 Kgs. 18:21ff.),[9] the revelation of God (1 Kgs. 19:9ff.), the responsibilities of the prophetic office (1 Kgs. 19:14-17), and the ethical issues involved in the Naboth incident (1 Kgs. 21:1ff.). The cycle was completed by the account of the translation of Elijah, a feat that was most probably accomplished by means of a tornado.

A cycle of tradition which, though emerging from the same general environment, appears to have been independent of that concerning Elijah,[10] can be associated with Elisha (2 Kgs. 2–13). Whereas the ministry of Elijah had important political overtones, that of Elisha was extended into an even wider area to take cognizance of the needs of religious groups and individuals alike. Elisha emerged as a seer who stood in the general tradition of Samuel, and who, like his distinguished forbear, came to the assistance of both king and peasant without specific discrimination. He exercised a ministry as the head of the prophetic guilds of his day, and was involved in miracles and wonderful acts at the individual and the national level. In military matters the cycle dealt with the narratives of the wars against Mesha, king of Moab (2 Kgs. 3:4-27), and the conflict with Syria (2 Kgs. 6:8–7:20). These sections reveal a close affinity in their relationship to the actual trend of historical events, a fact that is also evident in the narratives concerning the accession of Hazael (2 Kgs. 8:7-15), the Jehu revolution (2 Kgs. 9:1–10:36), and the death of Elisha (2 Kgs. 13:14-19).

The treatment accorded the group of stories dealing with Elisha is of particular interest because of the way in which the author interwove the majority of them (2 Kgs. 3:1–9:28) with the account of the reign of Jehoram, second son of Ahab, king of Israel. The Elisha stories have not been kept in precise chronological order, and since the author of Kings deliberately suppressed the name of the Israelite ruler in the Elisha cycle, it is uncertain as to exactly how many of them actually belong to the reign of Jehoram. The suppression of the name of this man has been taken by many scholars as signifying that in the mind of Elisha the nation itself had already been rejected by God because of its failure to implement the supreme demonstration of monotheism by Elijah on Mount Carmel. If this was actually the case, it would appear that the task of Elisha

---

[9] Cf. H. H. Rowley, *BJRL*, XLIII (1961), pp. 190ff., *Men of God* (1963), pp. 37ff.
[10] Cf. *OTFD*, p. 176.

was to build up the righteous remnant which, according to the divine promise to Elijah (1 Kgs. 19:18), would be left in Israel.

The episodes that record the life and ministry of Elisha are as follows: (1) his call (1 Kgs. 19:19-21); (2) his adoption of the role of Elijah (2 Kgs. 2:1-18); (3) a miraculous act of beneficence (2 Kgs. 2:19-22; cf. Exod. 15:22-25); (4) judgment on mockers (2 Kgs. 2:23-25); (5) campaign against Moabite kings (2 Kgs. 3:1-27); (6) a miracle wrought for a widow (2 Kgs. 4:1-7; cf. 1 Kgs. 17:8-16); (7) Elisha and the Shunammite (2 Kgs. 4:8-37; cf. 1 Kgs. 17:8-24); (8) two incidents at Gilgal (2 Kgs. 4:38-41, 42-44); (9) healing of Naaman (2 Kgs. 5:1-27); (10) the iron axe-head (2 Kgs. 6:1-7); (11) Elisha as counselor of kings (2 Kgs. 6:8-23); (12) Elisha as deliverer of the nation (2 Kgs. 6:24–7: 20); (13) continuation of the Shunammite narrative (2 Kgs. 8:1-6; this may belong before 2 Kgs. 5:1-27); (14) three narratives showing Elisha dealing with affairs of state (2 Kgs. 8:7-15; 9:1-13; 13:14-19); and (15) death of Elisha and a post-mortem miracle (2 Kgs. 13:20-21).

To what extent it is possible that there was an Ahab source (1 Kgs. 20; 22:1-38) independent of the Elijah cycle is difficult to say. It is true that these passages differ from the Elijah narratives considerably in their portrayal of Ahab, although this can be explained at least in part by observing that their primary interest was in the Syrian wars rather than in the theological issues of contemporary prophetism. The material concerning Ahab interrupted the continuity of the Elijah narratives, but was nevertheless closely interwoven with the prophetic traditions of the northern kingdom, which contained an account of the dispute between Ahab and an anonymous prophet (1 Kgs. 20:35-43) and the controversy with Micaiah the son of Imlah (1 Kgs. 22:5-28). One outstanding feature of the Ahab narratives is their attitude of avowed enmity towards the Syrians (1 Kgs. 20:42).

While it may be possible to regard the narratives dealing with Elijah, Elisha, and Ahab as having originally constituted separate sources, it must also be recognized that they may have been merely constituent elements of one prophetic source in which narratives concerning the activities of certain prophets were collected. Further evidence for this view may be adduced from the presence in Kings of what might be described in terms of an "Isaiah source." The structure of this material comprised an introductory formula (2 Kgs. 18:1-12), the main content of the source itself (2 Kgs. 18:13–20:19), and a short conclusion (2 Kgs. 20:20f.). The central section appeared almost word for word in Isaiah 36–39, hence its suggested designation. Whether this material was written by Isaiah himself, or was derived from a collection of extant narratives describing events in the eighth century B.C., cannot, of course, be known for certain. If the latter was actually the case, it would furnish yet another written source for the compiler of Kings to use as the basis of his historical composition. The reference in 2 Chronicles 32:32 might well indicate that there were two separate sources dealing with the same general period, though perhaps from somewhat divergent standpoints. The inference seems to be that the secular sources depended for their information upon one "vision" of Isaiah.

To what extent the narratives of independent prophetic activity constitute a separate source, as alleged by Szikszai[11] and others, is a matter of dispute. Following the example of the Chronicler, who was apparently familiar with as many as sixteen such prophetic sources for the history of the kings,[12] the term *midrash* was adopted by Montgomery and Gehman for the remaining prophetical stories of the northern kingdom.[13] These included the prophecies of Ahijah the Shilonite (1 Kgs. 11:29-39; 14:1-8) and their fulfilment (1 Kgs. 12:15; 15:29), the utterances of Shemaiah (1 Kgs. 12:21-24), and the condemnation of the Bethel altar by an anonymous prophet (1 Kgs. 12:32–13:34) who foretold the birth of Josiah (1 Kgs. 13:2) some 330 years in advance of the event. Another anonymous prophecy connected with the southern kingdom was highly critical of Manasseh, and was acquainted with the fall of Jerusalem (2 Kgs. 21:7-15).

Montgomery and Gehman have adopted a rather low view of the historicity of such narratives, and have tended to think of the entire prophetic material in Kings in terms of the political history of the northern kingdom.[14] While the existence of cycles for Elijah and Elisha is recognized, the corpus is regarded as a continuous series of prophetical documents, interrupted only by certain annalistic items, and extending from 1 Kings 17 to 2 Kings 10.

Fortunately, it is possible to have a reasonably clear view of the date of most of the sources suggested above. The court annals of David would probably be in written form no later than the second half of the tenth century B.C., while the Solomonic source would doubtless have been crystallized in the early ninth century B.C. A date of about 724 B.C. for the chronicles of the kings of Israel would place their compilation just prior to the fall of Samaria, while the corresponding material for the southern kingdom would most probably be compiled about 590 B.C. If a separate Ahab source can be postulated successfully, it might well have arisen in the late ninth century B.C., and the one involving the times of Isaiah not later than half a century after the events described. Precisely when the prophetic material crystallized is difficult to say, but there seems little reason for separating at least the historical narratives any great distance from the period of the events described.

---

[11] S. Szikszai, *IDB*, III, pp. 33f.

[12] E. L. Curtis and A. A. Madsen, *A Critical and Exegetical Commentary on the Books of Chronicles* (1910), p. 21.

[13] J. A. Montgomery and H. S. Gehman, *A Critical and Exegetical Commentary on the Books of Kings* (1951), pp. 41f.

[14] *Ibid.*, p. 41.

C. CRITICAL VIEWS OF KINGS

Modern liberal scholars have been in virtual agreement that there were two "Deuteronomic" editions of Kings, one about 600 B.C. shortly after the death of King Josiah,[15] followed by a more thoroughgoing revision about 550 B.C., which has been held to have been part of a larger form of editorial activity which was brought to bear upon the material in Genesis to Kings. Gustav Hölscher held that there was a pre-Deuteronomic book of Kings, just as was the case for Samuel,[16] and following the pattern of Pentateuchal criticism he maintained that J and E sources could be found in the work. This extreme view was also upheld by Benzinger,[17] and even though Eissfeldt observed that there was no clue for unravelling the possible threads continuing the critical sources of the Pentateuch,[18] he himself held to a pre-Deuteronomic edition of Kings of which the constituent elements comprised his L, J, and E sources.[19] Smend pursued an equally independent line of analysis in which he saw his own J^1 and J^2 sources in the earliest edition of Kings.[20] H. H. Rowley was much more cautious, however, and contented himself with thinking of an original Kings written before the fall of Jerusalem in 587 B.C.[21]

There are certain problems associated with this view, however, one of which concerns whether or not the author wrote before or after the death of Josiah in 609 B.C. at Megiddo. Pfeiffer held that the writer knew of this event but that he deliberately ignored it,[22] and if this was actually the case it would, as Snaith has pointed out, destroy the entire thesis of the author that those who obey the Deuteronomic laws live long and prosper.[23] To offset this difficulty it was proposed by Bentzen that the original book had ended at 2 Kings 23:28 but did not include the last part of verse 25 nor verses 26 and 27 of that chapter.[24] But surely if such an original work is to be postulated, it would be far more satisfactory to suppose that the author compiled his material before Josiah died, that is to say, about 610 B.C. A second editor is thought to have interpolated a series of northern tales into the original book, and these consisted predominantly of the prophetic cycles. This individual presumably carried out his activities after 581 B.C., since he knew of the exaltation of the

---

[15] Cf. *PIOT*, pp. 377f.

[16] G. Hölscher in H. Schneidt (ed.), *Eucharisterion für H. Gunkel* (1923), I, pp. 158ff.

[17] I. Benzinger, *Jahwist und Elohist in den Königsbüchern* (1921).

[18] O. Eissfeldt, *Einleitung in das AT*, p. 150; *ETOT*, pp. 287ff.

[19] O. Eissfeldt, *Einleitung in das AT*, pp. 335ff.

[20] R. Smend, *ZAW*, XXXIX (1921), pp. 181ff.

[21] H. H. Rowley, *The Growth of the OT*, p. 73; cf. J. Gray, *I and II Kings*, pp. 13ff.

[22] *PIOT*, p. 378.

[23] N. H. Snaith, *IB*, III, p. 11; *OTMS*, p. 103.

[24] A. Bentzen, *Introduction to the OT*, II, p. 100.

exiled Jehoiachin (2 Kgs. 25:27-30), and before the capture of Babylon by Cyrus in 539 B.C. Whereas the earlier author was supposed to have been concerned chiefly with the worship at the high places, the later one, reflecting the concerns of the exiled Jews, was much more involved in the questions relating to idolatry.[25] Passages in Kings attributed to this late editorial activity are thought to include 1 Kings 4:20-26, 11:14-40, 12:1-24, 2 Kings 13:22-25, 14:25-27, 17:7-20, and 21:13f. Some glosses that were thought to have emerged from a period as late as the second century B.C. have been alleged by Pfeiffer.[26]

The extent of the disagreement among those who accept the postulate of two Deuteronomic editors is an indication of the basic weakness of the theory. Another grave deficiency consists in the underlying assumption that it is possible to trace the fictitious Pentateuchal sources J and E, along with their variants, into Kings, and thereby presume to relate the compilation of the work to the developing corpus of J, E, and D. The book supplies its own sources, of course, both explicit and implicit, and much of the confusion in critical circles has arisen because this simple fact was not recognized. Further difficulties have been furnished by the supposition that one or more editors were needed to shape the work into something that represented the Deuteronomic standpoint. This again has been a source of considerable error, since Kings represents a significantly different point of view, as shown above.[27]

Most probably the opinions of Noth regarding the compilation and date of Kings come closest to what actually transpired.[28] For him one author only was responsible for the work, which was part of a corpus extending from the beginning of Deuteronomy to the end of Kings. He drew upon official annals for his material, as well as incorporating a number of stories collected in the north and south of Palestine, and compiled his work about 550 B.C. If this conclusion is substantially correct, as appears to the present author, there seems to be no room for the view, commonly advanced by liberal scholars, that the section dealing with the release of Jehoiachin from prison was added in the fashion of a postscript, and that the original book was completed at a considerably earlier date. Similarly, on the assumption that the entire work was written about 550 B.C., when the author would have had ample opportunity for reflection on the causes for the disruption of the monarchy, there is no need whatever to postulate the existence of two

---

[25] N. H. Snaith, *IB*, III, p. 11.

[26] *PIOT*, p. 412.

[27] As against J. A. Montgomery and H. S. Gehman, *A Critical and Exegetical Commentary on the Books of Kings*, p. 44, *et al.*

[28] M. Noth, *Überlieferungsgeschichtliche Studien I*, pp. 66ff.

"Deuteronomic" recensions, or to suppose that the second of these editors was faced with the task of resolving the theological crux posed by the untimely death of Josiah.

In this general connection it is important for the reader to be clear as to the proper significance of the term "Deuteronomic." As used by liberal scholars it relates to one who was associated in some manner with the national reform group which, according to the critical theorists, was responsible for producing Deuteronomy in the seventh century B.C. Thus, on the basis of a dual recension of Kings, the first editor was doubtless among those who unified the disparate J, E, and D sources, and who participated in the editing of books such as Joshua, Judges, and Samuel. The second "Deuteronomic" editor wrote in the reforming spirit of his precursor, but was more concerned with the idolatries of the nation, as befitted one who was suffering from their consequences, than with the cultic ceremonies at the high places or the reasons for the break between the northern and southern kingdoms.

As employed in this sense the term "Deuteronomic" begs the entire critical question of the authorship of Kings, for it assumes that someone intimately associated with the compilation of Deuteronomy was responsible for the production of Kings. Since it has never been proved beyond doubt that Deuteronomy was first composed in the time of King Josiah, such a use of the term "Deuteronomist" involves an essentially artificial approach to the history of the nation and of the Hebrew canon alike, and obscures the development of the Joshua-Kings literary corpus by imposing upon it the false values of a Wellhausenian monolinear evolutionary theory.

The term "Deuteronomic" can only be applied unexceptionably to Kings in the sense that the author recognized, with Moses (Deut. 28:1ff.), that obedience to God brought blessing, while disobedience resulted in calamity. However, this observation constituted but one facet of the Covenant relationship that the author of Kings employed as his standard of evaluation. His overriding concern was to demonstrate that the basis by which God judged human activity in the continuing historical process was absolute. Any consideration of the lessons to be learned from history was subordinated to the exaltation of the Covenant ideal as an inviolable and final standard, in the light of which the doings of both men and nations could be assessed. This is not to say, of course, that there is any basic contradiction between the approach of Deuteronomy and that of the books of Kings. There is, however, a significant difference of emphasis in the two works, and this fact alone should be sufficient to deter the casual ascription of the epithet "Deuteronomic" to the work of the author of Kings.

D. THE MATERIAL OF KINGS—CHRONOLOGICAL PROBLEMS

The chronology of the divided monarchy has until recently presented a great many difficulties for students of this period of Hebrew history.[29] From a comparison of king-lists, historical texts, and the Assyrian *limmu* or eponym lists,[30] it was possible to establish certain fixed points in Hebrew chronology, such as 853 B.C. for the date of the battle of Qarqar, and the accession of Ahaziah to the throne of Israel consequent upon the death of Ahab in that same year. However, certain chronological difficulties still persisted, and it was only in 1951, when Thiele published his standard work on the subject,[31] that almost all the problematical issues, with the possible exception of the reign of Pekah of Israel, were resolved satisfactorily.

Thiele's approach was superior to that of his many predecessors in the field in that it was grounded firmly in the computational methods of the ancient Near Eastern scribes. He was able to show that different types of reckoning had been entertained at various periods in the history of the northern and southern kingdoms, which naturally had an important bearing upon the compilation of the various lists. Thus at the time of the schism, Israel followed a nonaccession-year method of computation and continued in this manner until the end of the ninth century B.C., when a change was made to the accession-year system of Mesopotamia, this method being retained throughout the history of the northern kingdom. Judah, on the other hand, employed the accession-year reckoning to the middle of the ninth century B.C., changing over after that time to the nonaccession-year system.

[29] For representative earlier studies see E. Krey, *Zeitschrift für wissenschaftliche Theologie*, XX (1877), pp. 404ff.; A. Kamphausen, *Die Chronologie der hebräischen Könige* (1883); F. Rühl, *Deutsche Zeitschrift für Geschichtswissenschaft*, XII (1895), pp. 44ff.; E. König, ZDMG, LX (1906), pp. 606ff.; E. Mahler, *Handbuch der jüdischen Chronologie* (1916); M. Thilo, *Die Chronologie des AT* (1917); A. M. Kleber, *Biblica*, II (1921), pp. 3ff., 170ff.; J. Morgenstern, HUCA, I (1924), pp. 3ff., X (1935), pp. 1ff., JBL, LIX (1940), pp. 385ff.; W. J. Chapman, HUCA, II (1925), pp. 57ff., VIII-IX (1931-32), pp. 151ff.; T. H. Robinson, *The Decline and Fall of the Hebrew Kingdoms* (1926), pp. 228ff.; J. Begrich, *Die Chronologie der Könige von Israel und Juda, und die Quellen des Rahmen der Königsbücher* (1929); S. Mowinckel, *Acta Orientalia*, X (1932), pp. 161ff.; W. F. Albright, JBL, LI (1932), pp. 77ff., BASOR, No. 87 (1942), pp. 23ff., No. 88 (1942), pp. 28ff., No. 100 (1945), pp. 16ff., BPAE, pp. 116f.; R. de Vaux, RB, XLV (1934), pp. 512ff.; S. Smith, *Alalakh and Chronology* (1940); R. A. Parker and W. H. Dubberstein, *Babylonian Chronology 626 B.C.–A.D. 45* (1942); E. R. Thiele, JNES, III (1944), pp. 137ff.; M. Vogelstein, *Biblical Chronology I. The Chronology of Hezekiah and His Successors* (1944), *Jeroboam II—The Rise and Fall of His Empire* (1945).

[30] Cf. A. Ungnad in E. Ebeling and B. Meissner (eds.), *Reallexikon der Assyriologie* (1938), II, pp. 412ff.

[31] E. R. Thiele, *The Mysterious Numbers of the Hebrew Kings* (1951, revised in 1965).

Reigns from Jehoram (848-841 B.C.) to Joash (835-796 B.C.) were reckoned according to the latter pattern, but with the reign of Amaziah (796-767 B.C.) the chronology reverted to the accession-year method of computation, and continued in this fashion to the time of the exile.[32] In brief, the divided monarchy began with Israel using the nonaccession-year system of reckoning, while Judah employed the accession-year patterns of Mesopotamia. From the end of the ninth century B.C. to the fall of Samaria, Israel adopted the accession-year method of computation, whereas Judah departed from this procedure about 850 B.C. in utilizing the nonaccession-year system for half a century before finally reverting to the accession-year type of reckoning.

The great merit of this approach resides in the fact that Thiele permitted the ancient canonical narratives to testify from their own standpoint, and not from the *a priori* position of the nineteenth-century liberal critics, who almost to a man maintained the complete worthlessness of the material for constructing any sound scheme of chronology, and whose attempts in this direction proved pitifully inadequate.[33] However, far from confirming this extreme position, the work of Thiele has shown that the passages commonly regarded as obvious disclosures of carelessness, if not of sheer ignorance, on the part of the ancient Hebrew historians, are in fact astonishingly reliable in content. As W. A. Irwin remarked in an introduction to *The Mysterious Numbers of the Hebrew Kings,* it is a matter of first-rate importance to learn that the books of Kings are reliable in precisely those features that formerly excited only derision.[34]

As suggested by Kitchen and Mitchell, only slight modifications of the position established by Thiele need be entertained.[35] Thus the synchronisms of 2 Kings 17:1, where the twelfth year of Ahaz was equated with the accession of Hoshea of Israel; 2 Kings 18:1, where the third year of Hoshea marked the accession of Hezekiah of Judah; and 2 Kings 18:9f., where the fourth and sixth years of Hezekiah were synchronized with the seventh and ninth years of Hoshea, are not to be interpreted in terms of years of sole rule, as Thiele supposed, but instead as a continuation of the co-regency system which found expression first of all in the brief joint rule of Solomon with his father David (1 Kgs. 1:33ff.).

[32] *MNHK*, p. 38.

[33] Cf. J. Wellhausen, *Jahrbücher für deutsche Theologie,* XX (1875), pp. 607ff.; B. Stade, *Geschichte des Volkes Israel* (1889), I, pp. 88ff., 558ff.; W. R. Smith, *Journal of Philology,* X (1882), pp. 209ff.; F. Bleek, *Einleitung in das AT* (1878 ed.), pp. 263f. Some system in the narratives was recognized by A. Kamphausen, *Die Chronologie der hebräischen Könige* (1883), pp. 5ff.; F. Rühl, *Deutsche Zeitschrift für Geschichtswissenschaft* (1895), pp. 44ff., *DILOT,* p. 189; *PIOT,* pp. 393ff.; E. L. Curtis, *HDB,* I, pp. 400ff.

[34] *MNHK*, p. xxiii.

[35] K. A. Kitchen and T. C. Mitchell, *NBD,* pp. 217ff.

Thus Ahaz was co-regent with Jotham for a period of twelve years, and Hezekiah with Ahaz for some thirteen years. The period from the time of Hezekiah to the reign of Jehoiachin can be estimated accurately, ending in the capture of Jerusalem on the second of Adar, 597 B.C. But from that point there exists some uncertainty as to the exact way in which the Hebrew civil year was computed, as well as the regnal years of Nebuchadnezzar and Zedekiah in 2 Kings 24:18ff. and Jeremiah 52:1ff. Thus whereas Thiele preferred a date of 586 B.C. for the fall of Jerusalem,[36] Albright placed that event in 587 B.C.[37]

The chronology of the divided monarchy, following Kitchen and Mitchell, is given in the accompanying table.

Israel	Judah
Jeroboam I 931/30-910/09	Rehoboam 931/30-913
Nadab 910/09-909/08	Abijam 913-911/10
Baasha 909/08-886/85	Asa 911/10-870/69
Elah 886/85-885/84	
Zimri 885/84	
Tibni 885/84-880	
Omri 885/84-874/73	
Ahab 874/73-853	Jehoshaphat 870/69-848 (Co-regent from 873/72)
Ahaziah 853-852	
Joram 852-841	Jehoram 848-841 (Co-regent from 853)
Jehu 841-814/13	Athaliah 841-835
Jehoahaz 814/13-798	Joash 835-796
Jehoash 798-782/81	Amaziah 796-767

[36] *MNHK*, pp. 169ff.; cf. *BASOR*, No. 143 (1956), pp. 22ff.; *Zondervan Pictorial Bible Dictionary* (1963), p. 169.

[37] W. F. Albright, *BASOR*, No. 100 (1945), p. 22, No. 143 (1956), pp. 283ff.; *BPAE*, pp. 84, 116f.; cf. H. Tadmor, *JNES*, XV (1956), pp. 226ff.

Jeroboam II
782/81-753
(Co-regent from 793/92)

Zachariah
753-752

Shallum
752

Menahem
752-742/41

Pekahiah
742/41-740/39

Pekah
740/39-732/31
(Counted his years
from 752)

Hoshea
732/31-723/22

Fall of Samaria
722

Azariah (Uzziah)
767-740/39
(Co-regent from 791/90)

Jotham
740/39-732/31
(Co-regent from 750)

Ahaz
732/31-716/15
(Co-regent from 744/43;
senior partner from 735)

Hezekiah
716/15-687/86
(Co-regent from 729)

Manasseh
687/86-642/41
(Co-regent from 696/95)

Amon
642/41-640/39

Josiah
640/39-609

Jehoahaz
609

Jehoiakim
609-597

Jehoiachin
597

Zedekiah
597-587

Tibni is enclosed in brackets in the chronology to indicate that he (originally perhaps named Tabni) was one of three ninth-century B.C. army commanders who struggled to gain control of the throne of Israel after the fall of the short-lived dynasty of Baasha. Following the defeat of Zimri, the victorious Omri engaged in civil war with Tibni for about four years, and when this period ended with the death of Tibni, Omri ascended the throne of the northern kingdom in 885/84 B.C.

The Hebrew text of Kings contains numerous corruptions, and for purposes of reconstruction the LXX version is an invaluable aid, since although it is shorter than the MT, it preserves more reliable variants and in general can be said to have been based upon a purer form of the Hebrew than that which is now extant. Fragments of the books of Kings were recovered from the caves at Qumran, and seem to support the view that there once existed a Hebrew text that was closer for the most part to that underlying the LXX than that underlying the MT, and which in certain instances was superior to both. What appears to be a second account of the disruption of the kingdom was interpolated after 1 Kings 12:24 of the LXX version. It narrated events connected with the death of Solomon and the reign of Rehoboam, and furnished an account of the revolt of Jeroboam with some repetition of material from 1 Kings 11 and 12. Swete held that this interpolation constituted a second and distinct recension of the disruption story, resting equally with the first on a Hebrew original.[38] Whatever the value of this particular account may be, there is no doubt whatever that the LXX, and occasionally the Lucianic recension of it, are indispensable for textual studies in the books of Kings.

Supplementary Literature

Burkitt, F. C. *Fragments of the Books of Kings According to the Translation of Aquila.* 1897.
Church, B. P. *The Israel Saga.* 1932.
Honor, L. A. *Sennacherib's Invasion of Palestine.* 1926.
Jepsen, A. *Die Quellen des Königsbuches.* 1956.
Klamroth, E. *Lade und Tempel.* 1932.
Mahler, E. *Biblische Chronologie und Zeitrechnung der Hebräer.* 1887.
Milligan, W. *Elijah: His Life and Times.* No date.
Slotki, I. W. *Kings I and II.* 1950.
Wallace, R. S. *Elijah and Elisha.* 1957.

[38] H. B. Swete, *Introduction to the OT in Greek* (1900), p. 248; J. Gray, *I and II Kings*, p. 45.

Part Ten

THE LATTER PROPHETS (I)
THE MAJOR PROPHETS

I. PROPHETS IN THE OLD TESTAMENT

The second division of the Prophets in the Hebrew canon is also known by the name "Writing Prophets," since in antiquity they were generally acknowledged as the authors of the works attributed to them. The anonymous four Former Prophets of the canon narrated and, to a certain extent, interpreted the history of the divine dealings with the theocracy from the conquest and settlement periods to the time of the exile. They showed the way in which the life and law of the nation was founded upon the Covenant with God at Sinai, and in some instances they assessed the behavior of the nation in the light of this inviolable standard. Such a treatment of the historical sequences was not only of great value for the moral insights it possessed, but also for the temporal background it furnished, against which the activities of the Latter Prophets could be understood.

A. Nābhî', Ro'eh, and Ḥozeh

Although the first person to be designated a *nābhî'* (נביא) in the Old Testament was Abraham (Gen. 20:7), prophetism as such among the Hebrews can legitimately be said to have begun with the historical Moses, who later became a standard of comparison for all subsequent prophetic personages (Deut. 18:15ff.; 34:10). This may actually have been nothing more than an elementary safeguard, for the Old Testament term *nābhî'* was applied to a wide range of personalities with many functions, varying from the comparatively primitive to the highly sophisticated, and including both the advanced visionary and the concretely ethical individual.

The derivation of the term *nābhî'* has long been a matter of debate, with some scholars associating the verbal root with uncontrolled behavior[1] as though the *nābhî'* was an ecstatic individual.[2] Others have followed Gesenius in connecting the lost primary stem of the verbal root

---

[1] F. Häussermann, *Wortempfang und Symbol in den Alttestamentlichen Propheten* (1932), pp. 10f.

[2] Compare the exaggerated picture by T. H. Robinson, *Prophecy and the Prophets in Ancient Israel* (1923), p. 50.

with the Hebrew נבא, "to bubble forth," as though under inspiration.[3] More realistic philologically was the attempt to relate the lost root to some Akkadian form such as *nabû*, "to call," "to announce." König regarded *nābhî'* as an active derivation in the sense of "an announcer,"[4] whereas Guillaume understood a passive connotation, envisaging the prophet as one who was in the state of proclaiming a message that had been communicated to him.[5]

The original meaning of the Hebrew word *nābhî'* may now be considered settled, due principally to the work of Albright.[6] He showed that the usual interpretation of "speaker" was incorrect, since the *nābhî'* was invariably a special favorite of God. By relating the word to the Akkadian verb *nabû*, "to call," and to the incidence of *nabā'um* in northwest Semitic personal names from the eighteenth-century Mari tablets, he established the basic meaning of "call" for the Hebrew root. That the word *nābhî'* should be interpreted in a passive sense, as one who is called of God, rather than in an active form, as one who calls to men in the Divine Name, is clearly evident from Akkadian usage, where the king was repeatedly styled as "the one called (*nibît*) by the great gods." In the Code of Hammurabi the verbal adjective *nabi'* means "called," while the Old Babylonian term *nabā'um* was invariably used with respect to some person designated by the gods to occupy an important function in human society. The Hebrew *nābhî'* was thus someone who had experienced a vocation or divine call, and who was fundamentally an independent religious and charismatic figure. He had no hereditary claim to the office, nor could he appropriate the title of *nābhî'* by virtue of political appointment.

Two other terms were also applied to the Hebrew prophets, namely (*rō'eh*) ראה and (*hōzeh*) חזה. The first of these is the active participial form of the verb "to see," and is generally translated "seer." The second is an active participle of another verb meaning "to see," but since it has no specific equivalent in English it is commonly rendered "prophet." In the contexts in which these terms occur they suggest some parallel to prophetic functions, for example, 2 Samuel 24:11, where the prophet Gad was the court seer, or 2 Kings 17:13, where the prophet and the seer were

---

[3] *Thesaurus Linguae Hebraeae et Chaldaeae Veteris Testamenti* (1840), II, 2, p. 838; cf. H. Hackmann, *Nieuw Theologisch Tijdschrift*, XXIII (1934), p. 42; S. Mowinckel, *Psalmenstudien*, I, p. 16. This etymology was rightly rejected by W. Robertson Smith, *The Prophets of Israel* (1912), p. 391; A. R. Johnson, *The Cultic Prophets in Ancient Israel* (1944), p. 24n.

[4] E. König, *Hebräisches und aramäisches Wörterbuch zum AT* (1936 ed.), p. 260.

[5] A. Guillaume, *Prophecy and Divination* (1938), pp. 112f.; cf. R. B. Y. Scott, *The Relevance of the Prophets* (1944), pp. 11f.

[6] Cf. FSAC, pp. 17, 303ff., *Samuel and the Beginnings of the Prophetic Movement*, pp. 5f.; this etymology was first suggested by H. Torczyner, ZDMG, LXXXV (1931), p. 322.

equally responsible for warning the two kingdoms. Again, in Isaiah 30:9f., both terms were employed in parallel form in the general sense of prophetic function. What appears to be a notation as to some sort of chronological relationship between the office of the seer and that of the prophet is found in 1 Samuel 9:9, where "he who is now called a *nābhî'* was previously called a *rō'eh.*" Most literary criticism has ascribed the verse to the early source of Samuel, without, however, being very clear as to its precise significance.[7] What appeared to some scholars to be a more preferable reading was that adopted by the LXX, which rendered the verse to the effect that "the people used to call a prophet a seer."[8] In consequence, as Rowley pointed out, all that this then meant was that "seer" was a popular name for *nābhî'*, so that the text could not be used to establish the argument that originally the seer and the *nābhî'* were two distinct types, one of which preceded the other.[9] Indeed, Aalders adhered to the synonymity of the two terms, and repudiated any suggestion that separate classes had even been envisaged in this matter in early Hebrew history.[10]

That Aalders was probably incorrect seems indicated by the fact that, whereas a *nābhî'* was specifically called by God for some purpose, a *rō'eh* or *hōzeh* was merely a diviner of a rather unexalted order, who perceived that which was invisible to the ordinary individual by some form of divination or clairvoyance, and functioned without any specific vocation from God. The wide variety of divinatory and oracular activity undertaken by various branches of the priesthood in antiquity has been abundantly illustrated by means of tablets discovered throughout Mesopotamia, which speak of the *ashipu*-priest, frequently connected with exorcism and healing, the *bāru*-priest, or diviner, the oracle-priest or *āpilu*, the ecstatic or *mahhum*, the *qôsem* or master-diviner, and others who functioned in pagan antiquity without being in a peculiar relationship of divine call.[11]

Despite the careful delineation of functions in Babylonia, and the apparent discrimination with which such terms as *rō'eh, hōzeh* and

---

[7] J. Morgenstern, *HUCA*, XI (1936), p. 51n. and *Amos Studies* (1941), I, p. 35n., dated this gloss in the eighth century B.C.

[8] This reading was preferred by E. König, *ERE*, X, p. 385; W. Caspari, *Die Samuelbücher* (1926), p. 106; and I. Hylander, *Die Literarische Samuel-Saul-Komplex*, p. 140n.

[9] *RSL*, p. 99.

[10] G. Ch. Aalders, *De Profeten des Ouden Verbonds* (1918), p. 11; cf. E. Dhorme, *Revue de l'Histoire des Religions*, CVIII (1933), p. 123; H. Junker, *Prophet und Seher in Israel* (1927), p. 82.

[11] For prophetism at Mari see A. Lods in *Studies in Old Testament Prophecy Presented to Professor T. H. Robinson* (1950), pp. 103ff.; G. Dossin, *RA*, XLII (1948), pp. 125ff.; M. Noth, *BJRL*, XXXII (1950), pp. 194ff.; F. M. Th. de L. Böhl, *Nederlands Theologisch Tijdschrift*, IV (1950), pp. 82ff.; W. von Soden, *Die Welt des Orients* (1950), pp. 397ff.; H. B. Huffmon, *BA*, XXXI, No. 4 (1968), pp. 101ff.

nābhî' were used in the Old Testament (cf. 1 Chron. 29:29), it is disappointing to discover that the canonical Hebrew writings did not in fact preserve the precise shade of meaning that terms relating to prophecy and divination generally claimed in antiquity. Before the time of Samuel the divine messenger was described as a "man of God" in general preference to *nābhî'*, and during the early monarchy the two expressions appear to have been synonymous. The reference in 1 Samuel 9:9 would seem to point to a time when *rō'eh* and *nābhî'* meant different things, and to another period, coinciding with the work of Samuel, when the functions of a *rō'eh* were subsumed under those of the *nābhî'*, whatever meaning the latter term might have had at an earlier phase in its history.

Throughout subsequent Old Testament usage every shade of meaning inherent in the verb from which *hōzeh* was derived can be paralleled in its counterpart underlying *rō'eh*. Both were used in connection with divination (Zech. 10:2; Ezek. 21:21), the perception of the significance of events (Ps. 46:8; Isa. 5:12), the assessment of character (1 Sam. 16:1; Ps. 11:4, 7), the vision of God (Ps. 27:4; Isa. 6:5), prophetic activity generally (Isa. 1:1; Ezek. 13:3), and the executing of vengeance (Ps. 58:10; 54:7). In Isaiah 29:10, *nābhî'* and *rō'eh* were used in a parallel sense, as were *rō'eh* and *hōzeh* in Isaiah 30:10. Whereas 2 Chronicles 16:7 described Hanani as a *rō'eh*, a subsequent reference in chapter 19:2 spoke of "Jehu the son of Hanani the *hōzeh*." At a later period, therefore, it seems that little distinction was made between the two terms;[12] and that, further, there were some instances of the same individual's being designated as a *nābhî'* and a *hōzeh*.[13] Again, Amaziah addressed Amos as a *hōzeh* and urged him to prophesy (*tinnābhē'*) in Judah (Am. 7:12f.), to which Amos replied that he was not a *nābhî'* nor the offspring of one.[14] Whatever may have been the difference between the terms at an earlier period, it is clear that it was not sustained in the Old Testament narratives, and that they were employed synonymously during the monarchy, even though there continued to be in Israel religious persons of the kind formerly designated *rō'îm*, as in Isaiah 30:10.

Individuals with prophetic or divinatory gifts were encountered under a wide variety of circumstances in ancient Israel. Seers were sometimes associated with shrines, as was Samuel at Ramah (1 Sam. 9:6ff.), or possibly Ahijah at Shiloh (1 Kgs. 14:1),[15] although in the case of the

---

[12] Cf. M. A. van den Oudenrijn, *Biblica*, VI (1925), pp. 294ff., 406ff.; G. R. Driver, *Problems of the Hebrew Verbal System* (1936), p. 99.

[13] Cf. 1 Sam. 22:5; 2 Sam. 24:11; 1 Chron. 21:9; 29:29; 2 Chron. 29:25 (concerning Gad); 9:29; 12:15; 13:22 (concerning Iddo).

[14] Cf. J. D. W. Watts, *Vision and Prophecy in Amos* (1958), pp. 5ff.

[15] For the archaeology of Shiloh see H. Kjaer, *PEF Quarterly Statement* (1927), pp. 202ff., (1931), pp. 71ff.; A. Mallon, *Biblica*, X (1929), pp. 369ff.; WBA, p. 88—showing that it fell about 1050 B.C.

latter the sanctuary had long been destroyed and it is probable that Ahijah merely had his family residence in that locality. The seer Gad was attached to the royal court (2 Sam. 24:11), where he was available for consultation when important matters arose which involved the welfare of the nation (cf. 2 Kgs. 3:11). The *nābhî'* was occasionally to be found alone by the wayside, as in 1 Kings 20:38, or in company with others (1 Sam. 10:5; 19:18; 2 Kgs. 2:3; 4:38). Groups of prophets sometimes constituted part of the royal retinue, as was the case with those maintained by Jezebel (1 Kgs. 18:19; cf. 22:6), or else were associated with the Temple (Jer. 23:11; 26:7; Lam. 2:20). Oracular utterances were occasionally given after consultation (as with the early seers) or as the result of a dream (Num. 12:6; Jer. 23:28), intoxication (cf. Isa. 28:7; Mic. 2:11), or musical stimulation (2 Kgs. 3:15; cf. 1 Sam. 10:5).

B. OLD TESTAMENT PROPHECY AND THE CULTIC SETTING

That prophecy was an integral part of the cultic setting in ancient Canaanite religion can now be attested from Ugaritic discoveries. Indeed, on one occasion of crisis in the history of Israel, there occurred a notable instance of prophecy within a cultic setting (2 Chron. 20:14),[16] in which, after Jehoshaphat had been present in the Temple court on a day of national prayer, a Levite prophesied victory for the armies of Judah. On the basis of this and other considerations it was suggested by Hölscher that there were probably cultic prophets in existence in Israel who were associated with the priests in the worship at the shrines.[17] Such prophets, it was suggested, were of the popular rather than of the reform or writing variety, and rather than being exponents of a kind of religion different from or opposite to that practiced by the priests, they were actually fellow-members of the same cultic staff. Mowinckel developed this theory by asserting that many of the reform prophets belonged to the cultic staffs of local sanctuaries, and in this belief he was followed by a number of European and British scholars.[18] Advocates of

---

[16] Cf. J. A. Motyer, *NBD*, p. 1042.

[17] G. Hölscher, *Die Profeten* (1914), p. 143.

[18] S. Mowinckel, *Psalmenstudien, III: Die Kultprophetie und prophetische Psalmen* (1923), pp. 16ff. Cf. A. Causse, *RHPR*, VI (1926), pp. 1ff.; J. W. Povah, *The OT and Modern Problems in Psychology* (1926), pp. 67ff.; H. Junker, *Prophet und Seher in Israel*, pp. 32ff.; I. Hylander, *Le monde oriental*, XXV (1931), pp. 53ff.; G. von Rad, *ZAW*, LI (1933), pp. 109ff.; O. Eissfeldt, *Einleitung in das AT*, pp. 115ff.; *OTMS*, pp. 119f.; A. Jepsen, *Nabi: soziologische Studien zur alttestamentlichen Literatur und Religionsgeschichte* (1934), pp. 143ff., 191ff.; A. R. Johnson, *ET*, XLVII (1935-36), pp. 312ff.; J. Pedersen, *Israel: Its Life and Culture*, III-IV, pp. 115ff.; P. Humbert, *Problèmes du livre d'Habacuc* (1944), pp. 296ff.; A. Haldar, *Associations of Cult Prophets Among the Ancient Semites* (1945), pp. 90ff.; I. Engnell, *Religion och Bibel*, VIII (1949), pp. 10ff.; T. J. Meek, *Hebrew Origins* (1960 ed.), pp. 172ff.

this view adduced as evidence for their position the fact that Samuel, who was an official at Shiloh (1 Sam. 3:19ff.), presided over a cultic meal at Ramah (1 Sam. 9:12ff.); that the prophet-seer Gad commanded David to erect the altar on the threshing-floor of Araunah (2 Sam. 24:1ff.) and revealed the divine will concerning the guilds of Temple singers (2 Chron. 29:25); that Nathan the prophet was consulted about the building of the Temple (2 Sam. 7:1ff.); that Elijah enacted a ritual performance at an ancient shrine (1 Kgs. 18:30ff.); that it was customary for the Israelites to visit the prophet on cultic occasions (2 Kgs. 4:23); that the Old Testament contained numerous references (e.g. 2 Kgs. 23:2; Isa. 28:7; Jer. 2:26; 8:10; 13:13) relating to friendly associations between prophets and priests in Jerusalem or Judah,[19] and that there were quarters for prophets within the Temple building itself (Jer. 35:4). In certain of the Psalms (e.g. 60:6ff.; 75:4ff.; 82:3ff.; 110:2ff.) the section in the first person singular was thought to represent the oracular response of the prophet who was concerned to bring the contemporary reply of God to the offerings of His worshipping people.[20] Again, the guilds of Levitical singers which were prominent in the post-exilic period were held to be survivals of groups of cultic prophets attached to the various pre-exilic shrines.

Adherents of this theory claimed that if it was true that such prophetic assemblages did exist in Israel, it would go far towards explaining the frequent Old Testament references that linked prophet and priest in a single phrase, and would help to account, at least in part, for the presence of cultic and ritual concepts in the writings of the canonical prophets. Accordingly, the approach outlined above would interpret the ostensibly anti-cultic oracles of the Old Testament as revealing only hostility to the wrong or foreign cult, as in the book of Amos; to the cult regarded as an end in itself, as in Isaiah and Jeremiah; and to the cult insofar as its activities were offered in the wrong spirit, as in Hosea and Micah. Such an interpretation, it was claimed, would prevent prophetic concepts from being severed so sharply from their roots in the life of the Hebrew people, and would enable the basic unity of the Old Testament to be entertained once again at yet another level.

Not all scholars were enthusiastic about the theory of cultic prophets, however. B. D. Eerdmans flatly denied that they had ever existed in the entire history of Israel.[21] Rowley urged scholars to beware of outrunning the evidence, or of supposing that the theory of cultic prophets was anything more than a theory.[22] Such cautions are timely, for the evi-

---

[19] A. Jepsen, *Nabi: soziologische Studien zur alttestamentlichen Literatur und Religionsgeschichte*, p. 161.

[20] S. Mowinckel, *Psalmenstudien*, III, p. 3.

[21] B. D. Eerdmans, *The Religion of Israel* (1947), p. 141.

[22] *RSL*, p. 105; cf. his *The Changing Pattern of OT Studies* (1959), pp. 23, 27.

dence adduced to date in support of the existence of a cultic prophet is unfortunately inferential for the most part. The fact that Samuel could leave Ramah, where he had presided at a sacrifice (1 Sam. 9:1ff.) and journey to Gilgal in order to offer sacrifice there (1 Sam. 10:8) indicates not merely that Samuel could function equally well as priest or prophet, but also that he was peripatetic, and was not "attached" to any one shrine.

Since the prophets were men who, by definition, stood in a special relationship with God, it could hardly be considered unusual for them to be found periodically at those places where worship was a mode of behavior. This fact in itself, however, did not necessarily make them "staff-members" of the particular shrine, and this can be illustrated by reference to the prophet Amos, who, although prophesying at the Bethel shrine, was clearly not attached to it in the capacity of a cultic prophet. The commands of Gad concerning the building of an altar on the threshing-floor of Araunah and his revelations concerning the guild of Temple singers actually have little bearing upon the theory of cultic prophets, since his communications involved his essentially prophetic activity, and as far as the rituals were concerned assigned priestly functions to King David (2 Sam. 24:25).

Although there might appear to be a strong connection between priest and prophet in the pre-exilic period at first sight as a result of the allotment of quarters to the prophets in the Temple, the reference in Jeremiah 35:4 immediately vitiates such an idea by stating that similar chambers were allocated to the princes, who, of course, were not cultic personnel. Other questions have been raised in connection with the group of prophets residing at Jericho (2 Kgs. 2:5). The site had been inhabited only intermittently from the time that it had been destroyed by the Israelites under Joshua, and the walls had evidently been reconstructed just a little prior to the activity of the prophetic guild there (1 Kgs. 16:34). Clearly Jericho had not been occupied to any significant extent for a prolonged period, and it is a little farfetched to suppose that it already boasted a flourishing and well-staffed shrine. In view of the foregoing objections it seems best to conclude, with Motyer, that the theory of the cultic prophet must remain nothing more than a hypothesis.[23]

If it were possible to demonstrate conclusively by some means the existence of the cultic prophet in Israel, another problem would arise, namely, the extent to which the literary prophets were to be thought of as members of the association of cultic prophets. Haldar was emphatic in asserting that scribal prophets belonged to such cultic groups, and that they were not to be differentiated from any of their prophetic prede-

[23] J. A. Motyer, *NBD*, p. 1043.

cessors in that respect.[24] From Babylonian and Assyrian sources he argued to the conclusion that the Hebrew prophets represented a cultic phenomenon current throughout the ancient Near East; and in particular he endeavored to demonstrate that the *bāru* and *maḥḥû* guilds of Mesopotamia were actually organizations of cultic prophets headed by the king. Haldar maintained that both David and Ahab were leaders of this kind, and that in consequence the prophets who functioned in their day were actually cultic personnel, an arrangement that he extended to the times of Isaiah and Jeremiah.[25] Unfortunately, his attempts to force certain of the prophetic utterances into cultic situations are decidedly artificial, and there is no more real evidence for the position which he adopted than there is for the existence of an annual New Year festival in Israel like the Babylonian *'akîtu* festival (as has been mentioned in a previous section).

Adherents of this latter view, such as Mowinckel, frequently included both Isaiah and Jeremiah in the Temple personnel,[26] while Lindhagen held that several of the scribal prophets, including Isaiah, Nahum, Joel, Habakkuk, Haggai, and Zechariah, had been closely connected with the cultus.[27] On the other hand, Johnson, who drew much of the inspiration for his work on the cultic prophets in ancient Israel from Mowinckel, avoided the question as to the extent to which the literary prophets could be considered as members of a cult-prophet association, and had virtually nothing to say about the phenomenon of cult-prophetism in the ancient Near East. This was a very different approach from that of another Scandinavian, Ivan Engnell, who argued from the conceptions of kingship arrived at in his *Studies in Divine Kingship in the Ancient Near East* to the correspondence between the Hebrew literary prophets and the cultic prophets of other nations. In a later work he examined the call of Isaiah against a background of pagan enthronement rituals and ideas of sacral kingship, concluding that the call-vision of Isaiah (Isa. 6:1ff.) manifested certain specifically "royal" characteristics and received a peculiar intensity owing to the coincidence of the enthronement and New Year festivals.[28]

Even the most convincing attempt to invoke the Mesopotamian concepts of myth and ritual does not establish the relationship of the literary prophets to the cultus generally. Appeal has commonly been made to a small number of references (Am. 5:21-25; Hos. 6:6; Isa. 1:11-15; 43:22-24; Mic. 6:6-8; Jer. 7:21-23) in order to show that the prophets

[24] A. Haldar, *Associations of Cult Prophets Among the Ancient Semites*, pp. 79ff.
[25] *Ibid.*, pp. 104ff., 143, 157ff.
[26] S. Mowinckel, *Acta Orientalia*, XIII (1935), p. 267, *JBL*, LIII (1934), pp. 210ff.; cf. I. Hylander, *Le monde oriental*, XXV (1931), pp. 64f.; N. W. Porteous in H. Wheeler Robinson (ed.), *Record and Revelation*, p. 233.
[27] C. Lindhagen, *The Servant Motif in the OT* (1950), p. 117.
[28] A. Haldar, *The Call of Isaiah* (1949), pp. 33ff.

roundly condemned cultic worship and repudiated the suggestion that it was even the will of God. As a matter of fact there are other circumstances relating to the eighth-century prophets that point rather clearly to the contrary. When Isaiah experienced his vision-call, there can be no question that the event occurred within a cultic setting, as the text makes plain. The prophet Hosea employed a phrase that spoke strictly of sacrificial cultic activity (Hos. 8:13), and this would have been strange if the prophet was actually repudiating the manifold aspects of cultic worship.

The testimony of Jeremiah in this regard is of some significance, since he did not condemn the inhabitants of Judah because they engaged in cultic worship in defiance of the wishes of God (Jer. 7:9f.), but because they had profaned divine worship through their sin and moral transgression. Jeremiah made a point of designating the Temple as the house of God (Jer. 7:11), and used the example of Shiloh to show that the shrine was not destroyed to manifest divine rejection of cultic worship, but because of the gross iniquity of the worshippers. Clearly in the mind of Jeremiah the wrath of the prophets in this respect was directed not so much against the worship of the cultus as against the pagan and immoral abuses that had come to characterize so much of that worship.

Perhaps the crux of the problem is to be seen in Amos 5:25, where the prophet asks a rhetorical question that would expect a negative answer if Amos had been an avowed opponent of cultic sacrifice. What Amos was in fact condemning was an *ex opere operato* interpretation of sacrificial ritual, in the realization that sacrifice had indeed been part of the religion of the patriarchs and also of Moses. The concern of the prophet was not that God had rejected sacrifice, but that He had repudiated the current debased cultic practices (Am. 5:21-23), primarily because the essential moral and ethical elements were missing. In offering this criticism Amos made it clear that one of the basic requirements of their divinely revealed religion was precisely that of sacrifice, based upon true confession and obedience to the divine Law. Because this overall pattern had not been followed, the Israelites were to be punished by means of exile (Am. 5:27). It seems quite evident that the Hebrew prophets adopted an holistic view of their religious situation, which required that the manifold aspects of the moral and ceremonial law should be met conjointly. In any question of priorities the prophets stood unswervingly behind the classic dictum of Samuel: "To obey is better than sacrifice; to listen than the fat of young rams" (1 Sam. 15:22).

Careful interpretation of Isaiah 1:11-15 is needed if the passage is to reflect adequately the thought of the prophet. If it is understood as a comprehensive attack upon sacrifice (Isa. 1:11f.), such a condemnation must be extended also to the sabbath (Isa. 1:13) and prayer (Isa. 1:15). In point of fact, however, the prophet is simply stating that no amount of religious activity is valid if the life of the participant is defiled by persistent sin. As Motyer has observed, this interpretation is correct because of the incidence of the initial verbs in chapter 1:16, the first of which was uniformly employed in the book of Leviticus for ceremonial purification, while the second was invariably used in the context of moral cleansing and renewal.[29] Had Isaiah considered ceremonial purification as practiced in the cultus to be contrary to the will of God, he would hardly have employed technical priestly designations of this character in any denunciation of contemporary attitudes. The fact that the intentions of God concerning the place of sacrifice in the spiritual regime of the nation had been abused was again made evident in Isaiah 43:22-24, where the prophet clearly implied that it was not the divine purpose that the cultus should be transformed to the point where the sacrificial offerings became an onerous and compulsory religious ritual.

Against this background it is of interest to note the criticisms made by Dobbie[30] of the general views of H. H. Rowley concerning the attitude of the eighth- and seventh-century B.C. prophets towards sacrifice.[31] Dobbie maintained that the pre-exilic prophets denounced sacrifices in principle because their theological presuppositions were at variance with the prophetic faith. But as Rowley pointed out in a rejoinder, if Isaiah did in fact utter an absolute denunciation of sacrifice in chapter one of his prophecy, then his condemnation of prayer must be taken as equally absolute, since it was included in the same utterance.[32] Such a procedure would clearly be out of harmony with the general position of the pre-exilic prophets on the matter of cultic sacrifices, which was to criticize the aberrations and wrong emphases which were typical of such worship rather than to declare that sacrifice was alien to the will of God. Nevertheless, the position maintained by Dobbie is extremely valuable in that it serves as a warning against too facile an acceptance of the idea of cultic prophetism, and constitutes a reminder that in all its stages the prophetic movement subjected the cultus to persistent critical scrutiny.

There would therefore seem to be no fundamental dichotomy between the functions and objectives of the prophets and the priests in Hebrew religion of the kind asserted by the members of the Graf-Wellhausen school. Israelite faith assumed its characteristic form under the prophet-priest Moses, and continued in this manner as a joint prophetic-priestly

[29] J. A. Motyer, *NBD*, p. 1043.

[30] R. Dobbie, *ET*, LXX (1958-59), pp. 297ff.

[31] As, for example, in *BJRL*, XXIX (1946), pp. 351ff., *ET*, LVIII (1946-47), pp. 69ff. In this connection see J. Jocz, *The Spiritual History of Israel* (1961), p. 71n., and the rejoinder by Rowley, *Men of God*, p. 162n. See also H. H. Rowley, *BJRL*, XXXIII (1951), pp. 91ff., *The Unity of the Bible* (1953), pp. 43ff.

[32] H. H. Rowley, *ET*, LXX (1958-59), pp. 341f.

activity (Exod. 24:4-8).[33] Insofar as the priests incurred censure from prophetic figures (cf. Jer. 5:31; 32:32; Ezek. 22:26), they did so because they had condoned the pagan license of Canaanite religion, and had encouraged the Hebrews to think that attendance at important religious festivals and the punctilious payment of prescribed offerings constituted an acceptable substitute for true spiritual motivation in worship.

That members of the prophetic group were themselves not above censure for deluding the people and extending false values to them is apparent from the denunciations of Ezekiel (13:9f., 16; 22:25) and others (cf. Jer. 2:8; 14:14; 23:26; Mic. 3:11; Zeph. 3:4). The ideal of cultic worship was exemplified by Ezekiel, who demanded absolute ritual propriety as a safeguard against the recrudescence of idolatry, but who nowhere made this a substitute for the correct moral attitudes of the worshipping individual or community. In effect his concept represented a return to the Mosaic principles, which saw prophetic and priestly activities in proper balance as essential to the well-being of the theocratic community.

C. THE NATURE OF PROPHETIC INSPIRATION

The nature of prophetic inspiration has long been a matter of debate among scholars of differing standpoints. While visions, dreams, symbolic acts, clairvoyance, and the like have often been seen to have played a part in shaping the particular utterance recorded in the text, it needs to be observed that the prophet invariably prefaced his message by the assertion that it constituted the expression of a direct personal experience of divine revelation (cf. Exod. 4:15f.; 7:1f.; Jer. 1:9; 23:22; Hos. 1:1, et al.). Although this recognition is extremely important, it is rather unsatisfactory as a means of shedding light upon the mechanics of prophetic inspiration, since it does little more than relate the phenomenon to some specific functioning of the spiritual life. On numerous occasions the activity of the spirit of God was associated with prophetic functions (e.g. Num. 11:29; 1 Sam. 10:6ff.; 1 Chron. 12:18; 2 Chron. 24:20; Neh. 9:20; Ezek. 11:5; Hos. 9:7; Joel 2:28f.), but without any apparent consistency, since the eighth-century prophets seldom alluded to the working of the divine spirit in connection with the utterances. Jeremiah, in fact, never once mentioned the spirit of God in this respect. This is particularly interesting since, as Rowley has remarked, he of all the prophets was most conscious of the compelling character of his vocation; and, despite the attempts that he made to avoid his prophetic responsibilities, he came to the realization that it constituted an inner constraint that he was powerless to control.[34]

---

[33] Cf. O. T. Allis, *The Five Books of Moses,* p. 172.
[34] *RSL,* p. 116.

The fact that passages in some of the prophets (e.g. Hos. 9:7; Mic. 2:11; Jer. 5:13; Zech. 13:3) could be understood as appearing to depreciate the work of the divine spirit as the instrument of revelation led Mowinckel to maintain that the major pre-exilic prophets did not claim to be activated by the spirit of God, but rather to be possessors of the divine Word.[35] The ostensible purpose of this distinction, so it was suggested, was to enable the major prophets to dissociate themselves from the group-inspiration and ecstasy of the prophetic guilds. Such a differentiation between the "spirit" and the "word" as activating media seems largely artificial, however, and, as Rowley has commented, it is doubtful if any of the great prophets would have directly repudiated the divine spirit as the medium of their inspiration.[36] Even Mowinckel was compelled to acknowledge that Ezekiel recognized the function of the spirit in revelation (Ezek. 11:5), while a similar attitude was evident in Isaiah (11:2; 28:6; 32:15; 48:16; 61:1) and elsewhere (Joel 3:1–Heb.). As regards Isaiah, however, it must be remembered that Mowinckel assigned many of the passages in Isaiah to a comparatively late date on grounds that cannot be considered as being other than purely subjective in nature.[37] The conclusions of Mowinckel and others regarding the differentiation between the "word" and the "spirit" appear to be both unnecessary and improbable. None of the literary prophets would have espoused such a distinction, since for them the very presence of the word presupposed the activating divine spirit. Both true and false prophets mediated what they claimed to be the word of the Lord, and if false prophecies could be considered to be the product of a lying spirit (cf. 1 Kgs. 22:22ff.) there seems little doubt that true ones could be regarded quite legitimately as the end-result of activity by the divine spirit.

In this same connection Mowinckel distinguished between true and false prophets by asserting that the latter were ecstatic whereas the former were not, a position that was also adopted by Obbink and Jepsen.[38] That ecstasy had long been considered to be an element of prophecy is evident from the attitude of certain early Church Fathers[39]

[35] *JBL*, LIII (1934), pp. 199ff., *RHPR*, XXII (1942), pp. 79ff. Cf. A. Jepsen, *Nabi: soziologische Studien zur alttestamentlichen Literatur und Religionsgeschichte*, pp. 189f.; R. B. Y. Scott, *The Relevance of the Prophets*, pp. 85f.; I. P. Seierstad, *Die Offenbarungserlebnisse der Propheten* (1946), pp. 156ff.; L. Köhler, *Theologie des AT* (1953 ed.), pp. 98ff.; E. Jacob, *Theology of the OT* (1958), pp. 243ff.; Th. C. Vriezen, *An Outline of OT Theology* (1958), pp. 237f., 250ff.

[36] *RSL*, p. 111; cf. H. Knight, *The Hebrew Prophetic Consciousness* (1947), p. 73.

[37] S. Mowinckel, *JBL*, LIII (1934), p. 201n.

[38] Mowinckel, *JBL*, LIII (1934), pp. 214f.; cf. *JBL*, LVI (1937), pp. 261ff. H. Th. Obbink, *HUCA*, XIV (1939), pp. 23ff. A. Jepsen, *Nabi: soziologische Studien zur alttestamentlichen Literatur und Religionsgeschichte*, pp. 45ff.

[39] Cf. A. Lods, *Revue de l'Histoire des Religions*, CIV (1931), pp. 279f.

752

as well as from the writings of some nineteenth-century literary critics.[40] The view that ecstasy constituted the essence of prophetism was given prominence by Hölscher, and in this he was followed to a greater or lesser degree by Gunkel, T. H. Robinson, Lindblom, Lods, Jacobi, Knight, and others.[41]

Unfortunately the term "ecstasy" was treated in a very loose manner in many of the discussions, a fact that did not escape the attention of some scholars.[42] Hölscher distinguished between an earlier type of prophetic ecstasy characterized by only partly intelligible sounds, and a later variety exemplified by the literary prophetic movement in which divine truths were clearly enunciated.[43] The distinction between an elevated state of spiritual rapture and an inferior condition of emotional frenzy had already been made as early as 1837 by Knobel, who employed the term "ecstasy" to describe a degree of spiritual upliftment experienced by the prophets of Israel.[44] A very different condition, allied to catalepsy or catatonia, was believed by T. H. Robinson to be characteristic of prophetic ecstasy,[45] but this view did not commend itself to most scholars,[46] who preferred to think that, while something which could be

[40] F. Giesebrecht, *Die Berufsbegabung der alttestamentlichen Propheten* (1897), pp. 38ff.; B. Stade, *Biblische Theologie des AT* (1905), I, pp. 131f.

[41] G. Hölscher, *Die Profeten*, pp. 129ff. H. Gunkel, *The Expositor* (1924), 9th ser., I, pp. 356ff., 427ff.; *ib'd.*, II, pp. 23ff.; *Die Propheten* (1917). T. H. Robinson, *The Expositor* (1921), 8th ser., XXI, pp. 217ff.; *ZAW*, XLV (1927), pp. 4ff., XLIX (1931), pp. 75ff. J. Lindblom, *Die literarische Gattung der prophetischen Literatur* (1924), p. 43, *Profetismen i Israel* (1934), pp. 121ff., also in *Festschrift Alfred Bertholet* (1950), pp. 325ff., *Prophecy in Ancient Israel* (1962), p. 4 *passim*. A. Lods, *Revue de l'Histoire des Religions*, CIV (1931), pp. 279ff., *Les prophètes d'Israël et les débuts du Judaïsme* (1935), pp. 55ff. W. Jacobi, *Die Ekstase der alttestamentlichen Propheten* (1920), pp. 4ff. H. Knight, *The Hebrew Prophetic Consciousness*, pp. 53ff.

[42] So N. Micklem, *Prophecy and Eschatology* (1926), p. 50; S. Mowinckel, *Acta Orientalia*, XIII (1935), p. 273n.; N. W. Porteous in H. Wheeler Robinson (ed.), *Record and Revelation* (1938), p. 288, *et al.*

[43] *Die Profeten*, p. 197; he was followed by, among others, W. Jacobi, *Die Ekstase der alttestamentlichen Propheten*, p. 14; A. Lods, *Les prophètes d'Israël et les débuts du Judaïsme*, pp. 63f.; J. Skinner, *Prophecy and Religion: Studies in the Life of Jeremiah* (1922), pp. 220f.

[44] A. W. Knobel, *Der Prophetismus der Hebräer* (1837), I, pp. 155f.

[45] T. H. Robinson, *Prophecy and the Prophets in Ancient Israel*, p. 50.

[46] E.g. W. Robertson Smith, *The OT in the Jewish Church* (1907 ed.), p. 289; H. Wheeler Robinson, *The Relig'ous Ideas of the OT* (1913), p. 115; G. Ch. Aalders, *De Profeten des Ouden Verbonds* (1918), pp. 49ff.; E. König, *ERE*, X, p. 391; A. Causse, *RHPR*, II (1922), pp. 349ff.; W. F. Lofthouse, *AJSL*, XL (1924), pp. 231ff.; N. Micklem, *Prophecy and Eschatology*, pp. 10ff.; S. Mowinckel, *Acta Orientalia*, XIII (1935), pp. 264ff., *RHPR*, XXII (1942), pp. 69ff.; A. Heschel, *Die Prophetie* (1936), pp. 31f.; N. W. Porteous in *Record and Revelation*, pp. 216ff.; I. P. Seierstad, *ZAW*, LII (1934), pp. 22ff.; S. A. Cook, *The OT: A Reinterpretation* (1936), pp. 168f.; H. Knight, *The Hebrew Prophetic Consciousness*, pp. 53ff.; *FSAC*, pp. 304f.; E. Jacob, *Theology of the OT* (1958), pp. 241ff.

described as "ecstasy" did play a part in the prophetic consciousness, the utterances of the prophets themselves were the product of self-control in the light of divine revelation.[47]

There can be little doubt that the psychology of prophetism presents features which are unusual and difficult to comprehend for the present age, but which were by no means uncommon in different areas of the ancient Near East. However much the latter may have been the case, it nevertheless remains true that the frenzied activities characteristic of the members of the prophetic guilds earned for certain individuals the taunt that in "playing the prophet" they were nothing more than madmen (cf. 1 Sam. 19:24; 1 Kgs. 18:28f.; 2 Kgs. 9:11; Jer. 29:26; Hos. 9:7). The prophets were frequently depicted as profoundly introspective persons, who on occasions could exhibit a remarkable degree of prescience (cf. 1 Kgs. 13:2; 2 Kgs. 5:26). Sometimes they received their inspiration by means of dreams and visions, the significance of which could be perverted through indulgence in wine and liquor (cf. Isa. 28:7). Under certain conditions there was clearly some sort of mystic element present in their self-projection, although insofar as there was a clairvoyant aspect in evidence it seems incorrect to regard it as pathological rather than mystical, as Albright does.[48]

That the prophetic personality was somewhat removed from the common run of Israelite mentality can hardly be disputed.[49] What is far from certain, however, is the extent to which "ecstasy" can be predicated as a norm for this kind of situation, even in the case of avowed visionaries such as Ezekiel.[50] While, as Hyatt has remarked, the major prophets may have occasionally experienced mild forms of ecstasy, there is no ground for assuming that ecstasy was normal in, or even significantly characteristic of, their emotional experiences, as Wheeler Robinson observed.[51] To attempt to reduce all forms of Old Testament prophetism to a single causative function is to do less than justice to a phenomenon which is highly complex in nature and obscure in provenance. Modern methods of psychological interpretation should only be used with the greatest of care,[52] since as Porteous has pointed out, it is fallacious to

---

[47] K. Weidel, *Zeitschrift für Religionspsychologie*, II (1908), pp. 190ff.; A. J. Heschel, *Die Prophetie*, pp. 170ff., *The Prophets* (1962), pp. 324ff., 351; J. Mauchline, *ET*, XLIX (1937-38), pp. 295ff.

[48] *FSAC*, p. 302.

[49] S. A. Cook, *The OT: A Reinterpretation*, pp. 168f.; H. Wheeler Robinson, *ZAW*, XLI (1923), p. 5, *Redemption and Revelation*, pp. 143f.

[50] Cf. S. Mowinckel, *Acta Orientalia*, XIII (1935), p. 277; N. W. Porteous in *Record and Revelation*, p. 230.

[51] J. P. Hyatt, *Prophetic Religion* (1947), p. 17. H. Wheeler Robinson in A. S. Peake (ed.), *The People and the Book* (1925), p. 373.

[52] Cf. A. Causse, *RHPR*, II (1922), p. 351.

assume *a priori* that the experience of the major prophets is directly amenable to such an approach.[53]

Appeals to the phenomenon of hypnosis or of hallucination can throw very little light upon the prophetic consciousness, and the use of such terms as the "sublimation of a real perception" and the "sublimation of sentiments" predicates psychological situations which are extremely difficult to demonstrate.[54] Interpretations of this kind are unfortunately far too subjective, and are therefore largely uncharacteristic of the experience that belonged to each prophetic utterance. Whatever may have been the emotional structure of those large uncharted areas of the human spirit from which prophetism took its rise, it is evident that the spoken word was much more than a subjective conviction concerning the divine will. As Rowley has pointed out, the vital issue involved the relation of the prophet and his word to God.[55] The true prophet was a person who knew God in the immediacy of experience, who was inescapably constrained to utter the word revealed to him by inspiration, who discerned the life of men in the light of his divine vision, and who brought the spiritual issues of existence into focus by challenging his hearers to respond to the divine standards of spirituality through acts of cleansing and renewal of life.[56]

Despite the urgings of Mowinckel and his followers, therefore, it appears very unlikely that false prophets as such could be distinguished by their ecstatic behavior, for if the orders denounced by the canonical prophets were characterized by ecstatic activity, the fact would certainly have been much more clearly indicated.[57] It is false to the historical situation to separate the prophetic guilds and the canonical prophets to the extent proposed by Jepsen,[58] for as Lods commented, the major prophets regarded any differences between themselves and their predecessors or contemporaries as being very slight indeed.[59]

As far as external considerations were involved, therefore, there would appear to have been virtually no means of differentiating the true from the false prophet.[60] This is made especially clear in the conflict between Jeremiah and the false prophet Hananiah in the Temple (Jer. 28:1ff.). Jeremiah was wearing a wooden yoke, symbolic of captivity, and was

---

[53] N. W. Porteous in *Record and Revelation*, p. 227.

[54] E. Jacob, *Theology of the OT*, pp. 241f.

[55] H. H. Rowley, *Harvard Theological Review*, XXXVIII (1945), pp. 37f.; *RSL*, p. 128.

[56] Cf. *FSAC*, p. 303.

[57] On false prophets see E. Auerbach, *Die Prophetie* (1920), pp. 17ff.; K. Harms, *Die falschen Propheten* (1947), pp. 9ff.; G. Quell, *Wahre und falsche Propheten* (1952), p. 218.

[58] Cf. G. Widengren, *Literary and Psychological Aspects of the Hebrew Prophets* (1948), p. 121.

[59] A. Lods, *Les prophètes d'Israël et les débuts du Judaïsme*, p. 64.

[60] J. Skinner, *Prophecy and Religion: Studies in the Life of Jeremiah*, p. 188.

challenged by Hananiah the prophet, who broke the yoke of Jeremiah and confidently predicted deliverance from Babylonian oppression within a two-year period. The episode was obviously an encounter between two men who claimed the status of prophet, and who assured their hearers of their ability to forecast correctly the trend of future events.[61]

While the popular view current in the seventh century B.C. distinguished a true prophet from a false one on the basis of whether their predictions were fulfilled or not, this attitude merely constituted an inversion of the situation as it ultimately emerged, and not an absolute criterion of truth or falsity as such. As Albright has pointed out, the fulfilment of prophecies was only one important element in the validation of a genuine prophet, and in some instances was not even considered to be an essential ingredient, as illustrated by the apparent failure of the utterances of Haggai (2:21f.) against the Persian empire.[62] Of vastly greater importance was the moral and religious content of the prophetic utterance, and its ability to recall to the minds of the hearers the obligations of the Covenant relationship. The truth belonged, as Rowley remarked, to the content, where alone it could be tested and shown to be the veritable word of God.[63]

Whatever the historical circumstances by which it was conditioned, the divine word seems to have been expressed by the prophets in a primarily spoken rather than written form, although there can be little doubt that the oracles and other utterances were quickly reduced to writing. Although the prophet was completely constrained by the power of God, he left the imprint of his own personality upon the divine word.[64] While the prophetic oracles constituted the words given by God to a human agent, they were nonetheless delivered under distinctive circumstances at a particular time in the human situation, and thus given consonance with other aspects of the divine revelation. Modern liberal scholars have been accustomed to argue from this fact to the conclusion that the divine word became to some degree fallible through its association with mortal man, thereby requiring a differentiation between human "words" and the divine "word." Whatever grounds modern writers may employ as the basis for such a contention, it is clear that they would have been repudiated by the Hebrew prophets, who never entertained the notion that the divine message might be invalidated to some degree

---

[61] For the view that "woe" constituted the essence of genuine prophecy see B. Baentsch, *Zeitschrift für wissenschaftliche Theologie*, I (1908), p. 464; H. Gressmann, *Der Messias* (1929), p. 77; H. Gunkel, *Die Religion in Geschichte und Gegenwart*, IV, col. 1543f.; S. Mowinckel, *JBL*, LIII (1934), p. 219.

[62] *FSAC*, p. 18.

[63] *RSL*, p. 111; cf. S. Mowinckel, *Acta Orientalia*, XIII (1935), pp. 279f.

[64] Cf. L. H. Brockington in E. A. Payne (ed.), *Studies in History and Revelation* (1942), p. 35; E. Jacob, *Theology of the OT*, p. 243; *RSL*, p. 126.

simply because it was communicated through a human medium. To a man the prophets spoke with singular conviction and certainty, conscious alike of their inspiration and of the responsibilities that accrued to their office.

For them the word of God was no less authoritative because they themselves functioned as the agents in its propagation. Indeed, they recognized that it had an absolute and objective quality that consistently transcended the limits of the individual prophetic personality, even though the particular utterances were known to have originated in the close spiritual fellowship that existed between the prophet and his God. Any imperfection in the ultimate written form of the oracle was certainly not the deliberate intent of the original speaker, who delivered his utterances in the conscious belief that he was recounting the true revealed word of God to the absolute limit of his capabilities.

D. PROPHECY AND PREDICTION

The prophet was a man of the divine word, even when he illustrated its significance by symbolic actions or objects.[65] Against a background of Covenant theology the Hebrew prophets addressed themselves to the local, national, and international situation by means of warnings about the future consequences of present sin, and by issuing exhortations to that type of spiritual dedication that would insure divine blessing instead of destruction. Permeating their utterances invariably was some distinctly predictive element, which was based in part upon the spiritual awareness that the individual prophet had of the future consequences of past and present iniquity and the consistent rejection of the Covenant ideal. This was reinforced by the fact that the prophets delivered their utterances in the name of the Ruler of History, within whose power lay the destiny of individuals and peoples, and who guided the processes of history according to the immutable principles that characterized His nature.

Again, the predictive function was normative for many individual prophets, who were clearly depicted to be the possessors of distinctive psychic gifts. Thus Elisha had the ability to discern the content of plans made in secrecy at some distance (2 Kgs. 6:12), while an unnamed prophet, with remarkable prescience, foretold the birth of Josiah some 330 years prior to the event (1 Kgs. 13:2). Since there is no question of textual corruption in either of these two instances, the only logical explanation must be that of predictive insight. This type of individual shared in the capacity for intuitive grasp of wide fields of perception that, as Albright has remarked, has also characterized certain figures of

---

[65] On prophetic symbolism see A. Regnier, *RB*, XXXII (1923), pp. 383ff.; H. Wheeler Robinson, *OT Essays* (1927), pp. 1ff., *JTS*, XLIII (1942), pp. 129ff.; W. F. Lofthouse, *AJSL*, XL (1924), pp. 239ff.; G. Fohrer, *Die symbolischen Handlungen der Propheten* (1953); J. Lindblom, *Prophecy in Ancient Israel*, pp. 165ff.

the last two hundred and fifty years (he mentions Jules Verne and Heinrich Heine), at least in sporadic moments of exaltation, and which is conspicuously absent in the personalities of those trained in accordance with modern scientific method.[66]

That prophecy was typified by *forth*telling rather than by *fore*-telling was a commonplace assertion of the Graf-Wellhausen school, although there were notable individuals of that persuasion who repudiated this dictum.[67] A differentiation of this kind rests upon a fundamental misunderstanding of the oriental mind, for as Rowley has put it, the modern antithesis between forthtelling and foretelling would have had little meaning in ancient Israel.[68] The prophets continually predicted the future, on the perfectly logical basis that, as Augustine and others have expressed it, what is to happen is already inherent in the present situation. They experienced little immediate difficulty in surveying both the nearer and the more distant historical scene, and uttered remarkably accurate predictions with regard to some events which had no immediate causal relationship to the happenings of their own day. Indeed, it was no less a person than Isaiah who appealed to the idea of fulfilled prediction as the vindication of prophetic activity (45:21; 46:9f.).

There can be no doubt that predictive abilities were regarded as an important part of prophetic endowment in the ancient world. In Greece, inspired persons were credited with the power to foretell future events, and according to the *Phaedrus* of Plato—which dealt in part with the phenomena of ecstasy and inspiration—those who were possessed by the gods could utter important statements without any recourse to human reason, since they were merely acting as the agents of the deities.[69] In the Heroic Age of Canaan, the story of the visit by Wen-Amon to Phoenicia (*ca.* 1100 B.C.) contained an episode attesting to the existence of prophetic phenomena in ancient Phoenicia, the nature of which is familiar from Ugaritic discoveries.[70] Equally well known is the prophetism of Mesopotamia, with its wide varieties of functionaries including the oracular personages of the eighteenth-century Mari tablets.

Perhaps a little less familiar is the fact that prediction of the future was regarded as a valid concept by the ancient Egyptians from the twenty-second to at least the thirteenth century B.C., embracing the

[66] *FSAC*, p. 19; cf. J. Lindblom, *Prophecy in Ancient Israel*, pp. 12ff.

[67] Cf. H. C. Ackerman, *Anglican Theological Review*, IV (1922), p. 116; H. Gunkel, *The Expositor*, 9th ser., I (1924), p. 433; A. Guillaume, *Prophecy and Divination*, p. 111; *FSAC*, p. 17; A. G. Hebert, *The Authority of the OT*, pp. 255f.

[68] *RSL*, pp. 125f.

[69] Cf. E. Fascher, ΠΡΟΦΗΤΗΣ, *Eine Sprach- und religionsgeschichtliche Untersuchung* (1927), pp. 66ff.

[70] *ANET*, pp. 25ff.

patriarchal period and the time of Moses.[71] Evidence for this attitude consists of allusions in literary works and also in written sources which were pseudo-prophetical in nature. Thus the *Admonitions of Ipuwer* (*ca.* 2300-2050 B.C.), which described the social and economic chaos in Egypt after the Pyramid Age, referred to "that which the ancestors had predicted."[72] The *Instruction for King Meri-ka-Re,* dated about the end of the twenty-second century B.C.,[73] contained a warning against dealing in an evil way with the southern region, "for thou knowest the prophecy of the Residence City concerning it."[74] The pseudo-prophecy of Nefer-rohu,[75] dating from about 1990 B.C., but set some seven hundred years earlier in the reign of King Snefru of the Fourth Dynasty, purported to show how a prophet foretold the downfall of the Old Kingdom and the re-establishment of order by Amenemhet I, the first ruler of the Twelfth Dynasty.[76] That such pseudo-predictions should have been deliberately produced in the first place is a powerful argument for the validity of prediction in the minds of contemporary Egyptians. In a New Kingdom work from about the thirteenth century B.C. the writer praised the wisdom of Egyptian antiquity, and on two occasions spoke of the sages as having predicted the future.[77]

E. LITERARY CRITICISM OF THE PROPHETS

Although a number of the prophetic writings contain clear indications of editorial activity, there is no need to suppose that the individuals credited with authorship of prophetic material did not play some part in the compilation of their works. That many of the prophets wrote down at least certain of their oracles appears most probable from internal evidence (cf. Isa. 30:8; Jer. 29:1; 36:2ff.; 2 Chron. 21:12). Some prophecies, in fact, may never have been delivered orally, but may have constituted purely literary products, as is perhaps the case with sections of Jeremiah, Isaiah, and other prophets. A man such as Isaiah was associated with a group of disciples (cf. Isa. 8:16), who may have been the recipients of the prophetic teaching as a whole and guardians of the written oracles. In the case of a work such as Isaiah, therefore, the

[71] K. A. Kitchen, *The Tyndale House Bulletin,* 5-6 (1960), pp. 6f.

[72] *ANET,* pp. 441ff.; G. Posener, *Littérature et Politique dans l'Égypte de la XIIe Dynastie* (1956), p. 28; cf. A. Erman and A. M. Blackman, *The Literature of the Ancient Egyptians* (1927), p. 94; J. H. Breasted, *The Dawn of Conscience* (1933), pp. 193ff.

[73] Erman and Blackman, *The Literature of the Ancient Egyptians,* p. 79.

[74] *ANET,* p. 416.

[75] For the translation of this name as *Neferti* see G. Posener, *Revue d'Égyptologie,* VIII (1951), pp. 171ff.

[76] A. Erman and A. M. Blackman, *The Literature of the Ancient Egyptians,* pp. 110ff.; *ANET,* pp. 444ff.

[77] Cf. A. H. Gardiner, *Hieratic Papyri in the British Museum* (1935), 3rd ser., I, pp. 38f.; II, pls. 18-19.

followers of the prophet may have been ultimately responsible for collect
ing and editing selected utterances of the master in the form of an
anthology. It is even possible that the reference to the "book of the
LORD" in Isaiah 34:16 is to a scroll on which some of the oracles o
pronouncements of the prophet had been written down.

On any basis of literary criticism it seems fairly certain that the
majority of the prophetic books contain in their extant form less than the
sum total of utterances given by the particular prophet during his
lifetime. Precisely how the principle of selectivity operated is as uncer
tain for the ancient anthologist as for his more modern counterpart
although it is clear that certain important theological considerations, such
as fidelity to the provisions of the Covenant, played an important part in
the process. Some prophets, Jeremiah for example, had the advantage of
secretarial assistance (Jer. 36:4ff.), and the manner in which such scriba
activity was described makes it plain that it was by no means unusual.

The extent to which the prophetic guilds were responsible for the
preservation and transmission of prophetic oracles must always remain a
matter of some debate. Elijah appears to have had only rather casual
contact with such groups, but Elisha was much more involved in their
activities, and availed himself of their services from time to time (2 Kgs.
4:38; 5:1ff.; 9:1). Members of these guilds manifested certain gifts of
prophetism (2 Kgs. 2:3ff.), but whether they were specifically called as
disciples of a prophet, or were attracted to such an individual by his
teaching, is difficult to say. The major prophets do not appear to have
taken their rise from the prophetic guilds, and Amos disclaimed any
connection with them (7:14), without, however, necessarily repudiating
their activity—if, indeed, they were functioning as late as the eighth
century.

Modern criticism has been accustomed to think of a continuous development of the prophetic writings in terms of three easily definable
stages.[78] First were the oral utterances of the prophet dealing mostly
with contemporary happenings, which were handed on orally by the
hearers and subsequently written down, often after the death of the
prophet. At this time unauthentic accretions that were in the general
spirit of the master were added to the small collection of earlier oracles.
The second phase saw the editorial arrangement of this material, sometimes according to subject-matter, as with collections of oracles or woes
against foreign nations, or the grouping of material in some mnemonic
form. The third stage saw the various collections worked up, perhaps by
numerous hands and over many years, into the full-scale extant books
ascribed to the various authors by tradition, and not infrequently marked
by the addition of other unauthentic matter.

[78] Cf. T. H. Robinson, *Prophecy and the Prophets in Ancient Israel* (1923), pp.
50ff., ZAW, XLV (1927), pp. 3ff., *Theologische Rundschau*, n.f. III (1931), pp. 75ff.

This view, overlooking the possibility that some prophecies may well have been first issued in written form, follows general critical procedures in giving pride of place to oral over written transmission. It also neglects clear elements of internal testimony that speak of prophetic material being written down in the lifetime of the prophet himself, as was the case with Jeremiah. It further assumes—quite gratuitously—that each prophet was surrounded by followers who constituted some sort of "school," whereas in point of fact there is no evidence that, apart from Isaiah, any of the scribal prophets claimed a following of disciples as such. Again, if Jeremiah is excepted, there is no direct indication that a prophet had scribal assistance during his lifetime, although this may have been the case with Isaiah, and possibly one or two others.

Not all the prophecies need to have been compiled after the death of the attributive author, and there is little evidence for the supposition that others added sections of unauthentic material to collections of prophetic utterances. Indeed, the reverse is most probably the case if, as seems likely, the various anthologies of prophetic oracles comprised less than the total of pronouncements made by the individual concerned during his lifetime. Finally, such a view of the evolution of the prophetic writings is based upon the fallacious assumption that nineteenth-century literary-critical techniques can effectively isolate different strata in what are actually anthologies. It should also be noted in passing that the hypothesis that the books of the prophets are the result of editing and re-editing in many different periods and by many scribes who added passages and changed the text at will here and there is as unacceptable to some liberal scholars as it is to conservative writers generally.

The reluctance to ascribe literary activity to individual prophets as over against oral function was reflected in the work of Nyberg, who had very great doubt that the *ipsissima verba* of the Old Testament prophets would ever be regained, since in his view only the traditions of their sayings had survived.[79] Similar sentiments were voiced by Birkeland, who found himself unable for the most part to distinguish between what had come from the prophet himself and what had originated in the tradition.[80] Since the latter is deemed to be the dominant form of transmission, the literary-critical approach to the prophetic writings is clearly inferior in the minds of Scandinavian scholars generally to the more favored traditio-historical method. Unfortunately, in its more extreme form this approach has virtually eliminated the possibility of discerning a clear prophetic personality behind the tradition.[81] Such a

[79] H. S. Nyberg, *Studien zum Hoseabuche: zugleich ein Beitrag zur Klärung des Problems des alttestamentlichen Textkritik* (1935), pp. 8ff.

[80] H. Birkeland, *Zum hebraischen Traditionswesen: die Komposition der prophetischen Bücher des AT* (1938), pp. 20ff.

[81] Cf. I. Engnell, *Svensk Exegetisk Årsbok*, XII (1947), pp. 94ff., *The Call of Isaiah* (1949), pp. 54ff.; S. Mowinckel, *Prophecy and Tradition* (1946), pp. 61ff.

761

contingency has been partly offset by the work of Widengren, who ha
argued from internal evidence to show that not only Isaiah, Jeremiah
and Ezekiel, but even Amos and Hosea, wrote down or dictated at leas
part of their prophetic messages, and that in no instance is it possible t
speak of a purely oral transmission of their utterances.[82]

In this connection it must again be noted that the function of ora
transmission is still largely misunderstood by modern scholars. Its prima
ry purpose was that of disseminating material over territorial areas in a
contemporary situation, and not for the preservation of traditions within
the stream of time. Undoubtedly, of course, it came to have the latte
effect in certain specific areas as a secondary manifestation of its origina
function. In the ancient Near East, anything of any importance wa
committed to writing, either within the contemporary situation or shortly
thereafter, and was not left either to the chance recollections of wander
ing rhapsodists or the purveyors of folk-tales. Part of the current scholar
ly misunderstanding may have arisen from a consideration of the role of
oral tradition in cultures such as that of the ancient Greeks. Here
however, it has to be remembered that an astonishingly high proportion
of the Greek population was illiterate, and this situation contrasts un
favorably with what obtained in Canaan, Egypt, and Babylonia, where
the degree of literacy was very much greater.

As far as the Hebrew prophets are concerned, one means of perpetuat
ing their messages may possibly have been the "schools." Yet for all this
there are certain difficulties to be faced in such considerations, as indicated above, and it is particularly important to be quite clear as to what
would have been most probably involved with regard to the number
distribution, and activity of prophetic disciples or followers, so as to
avoid a false estimate of the situation. Although holy men in the east
have frequently been known to attract around them others who wished
to participate more fully in their outlook and way of life, it is unwarranted to assume from this fact that the Hebrew prophets, whether major
or minor, had anything of a serious following among the populace, or
that, with the possible exception of Isaiah and Jeremiah, such disciples
as there were played any significant role in the literary formulation of
the extant works. Indeed, it seems much more probable that scribal
groups associated with the Temple or the royal court of pre-exilic times
exercised a far greater influence over the Hebrew Scriptures generally
than did any of the supposed prophetic "schools."

Whatever the processes by which the Latter Prophets were compiled,
the tendency of rabbinic scholars was to attribute each composition in
the second division of the Hebrew canon to prophetic authorship. The
early Church Fathers normally accepted the traditional ascriptions of

[82] G. Widengren, *Literary and Psychological Aspects of the Hebrew Prophets*
(1948), p. 77.

the prophecies, although there were occasional dissident voices to be heard on the matter. Thus Isaianic authorship of the entire prophecy was challenged as early as A.D. 110 by Moses ben Samuel Ibn Gekatilla, whose views survived in the numerous references to his commentaries in the writings of Ibn Ezra (d. A.D. 1167). It is interesting to note that the theories of Ibn Gekatilla apparently influenced the thought of Ibn Ezra to the point where he himself came to reject the Isaianic authorship of chapters 40–66.[83]

The efforts of European literary criticism were by no means confined initially to the Pentateuch, for some of the problems involving the authorship of Isaiah were examined in 1775 by Döderlein, whose commentary laid the foundation for all subsequent divisive theories of authorship.[84] An examination of Jeremiah by Duhm repudiated its claims to integrity of composition and authorship;[85] and a similar conclusion resulted from the study of Ezekiel by Hölscher and Torrey.[86] The prodigious output of literature dealing with the scribal prophets has been such that opportunity has been afforded for the expression of every shade of opinion upon matters of provenance, literary strata, authorship, date, and the like, as they affect both the Major and the Minor Prophets.

In the Hebrew Bible the Latter Prophets constitute four "rolls," three for the Major Prophets and one for the Minor Prophets. The latter followed the same order in the Hebrew canon as in the English versions; the LXX, however, placed the Minor Prophets before Isaiah. The general intention seems to have been to arrange the books in something like chronological order, but Talmudic tradition had the rabbis teaching that the order of the prophets was Joshua, Judges, Samuel, Kings, Jeremiah, Ezekiel, Isaiah, and the Twelve.[87]

This arrangement was based on stylistic considerations, however, for *Baba Bathra* goes on to explain:

> But was not Isaiah before Jeremiah and Ezekiel? Then Isaiah should be placed at the head! The reason . . . is that Kings ends with desolation, and Jeremiah is all of it desolation, while Ezekiel opens with desolation and closes with consolation, and Isaiah is all of it consolation; accordingly, we join desolation to desolation and consolation to consolation.[88]

---

[83] Cf. J. Fürst, *Der Kanon des AT* (1868), p. 16.

[84] J. C. Döderlein, *Esaias* (1775).

[85] B. Duhm, *Jeremia* (1901).

[86] G. Hölscher, *Hesekiel: der Dichter und das Buch* (1924); C. C. Torrey, *Pseudo-Ezekiel and the Original Prophecy* (1930).

[87] *Bab. Bath.* 14b.

[88] Quoted by H. E. Ryle, *The Canon of the OT* (1904), p. 285.

II. THE BOOK OF ISAIAH

A. NAME AND OUTLINE

First among the Latter Prophets in the Hebrew canon was the book of Isaiah. It was named after the prophet himself: the form ישעיה occurs in the title, probably as the result of Talmudic influence (this form also occurs in 1 Chron. 3:21; Ez. 8:17, 19; Neh. 11:7), but the text of the prophecy itself has the variant spelling ישעיהו. The LXX adopted the form Ἠσαίας, and the Latin versions rendered it *Esaias* or *Isaias*.

As it now stands, the book can be analyzed briefly as follows:

I. The First Half, ch. 1–33
  A. Prophecies about the ruin and restoration of Judah, 1–5
  B. The call of Isaiah; biographical material, 6–8
  C. Present world empires and their roles, 9–12
  D. Prophecies regarding foreign nations, 13–23
  E. Universal judgment and the deliverance of Israel, 24–27
  F. The moral indictment of the Chosen People, 28–31
  G. The restoration of the Davidic regime, 32–33

II. The Second Half, ch. 34–66
  A. Judgment upon Edom and the restoration of the ransomed, 34–35
  B. Biographical material from the time of Hezekiah, 36–39
  C. Prophetic assurances, 40–45
    1. Comfort, 40
    2. Deliverance, 41–44
    3. Divine judgment, 45
  D. Pronouncements against Babylon, 46–48
  E. Redemption through the work of the Servant, 49–55
  F. Ethical pronouncements, 56–59
  G. Life in the restored Zion, 60–66

B. AUTHORSHIP

Questions about the authorship of this book form one of the most widely discussed issues in the entire field of modern Old Testament scholarship. In order to appreciate the significance of this situation it is

764

necessary to survey briefly the history of the literary criticism of this particular composition, commencing with the Talmudic traditions. *Baba Bathra* 15*a* stated that "Hezekiah and his company wrote Isaiah, Proverbs, the Song of Songs and Ecclesiastes," the verb "wrote" being employed in the sense of "edited" or "compiled." The reference to the "company" of Hezekiah in this task was evidently to his eighth-century contemporaries, who were responsible, under his direction, for certain compilatory and editorial activities (cf. Prov. 25:1). The testimony of the Talmud regarding the authorship of Isaiah clearly credited the prophet with the composition of the various oracles attributed to him, and the men of Hezekiah with their arrangement in extant form.

The general tendency of the Early Church, influenced to a large extent by the numerous references to the person and utterances of Isaiah in the writings of the New Testament, was to adhere to the Isaianic authorship of the prophecy.[1] However, as has been noted above, a Jewish author of the twelfth century after Christ, Moses ben Samuel Ibn Gekatilla, wrote a commentary on Isaiah in which he held that the prophecies in the earlier chapters were the work of Isaiah himself, but attributed the subsequent sections of the book to the period of the Second Temple. His observations were preserved by the medieval Jewish commentator Ibn Ezra (1092-1167), who shared his view that chapters 40–66 were the work of someone other than the eighth-century B.C. prophet.

1. History of criticism. The period of modern criticism of Isaiah can be said to have begun with Döderlein, who based his commentary on the book upon the supposition that the book comprised two distinct works.[2] About 1780, J. B. Koppe suggested in the German edition of the commentary by Lowth that chapter 50 might have been the work of an exilic writer, possibly Ezekiel.[3] Eichhorn adopted much the same position, but extended very considerably the amount of the material assigned to the exilic period, regarding chapters 40–66 as the work of someone other than Isaiah.[4] With Gesenius came the assertion that, while chapters 40–66 were non-Isaianic in nature, they were an essential unity, a view which commanded the assent of numerous scholars.[5]

[1] For a list of these NT references see *YIOT*, p. 206; cf. G. B. Gray, *A Critical and Exegetical Commentary on the Book of Isaiah* (1911), I, pp. xxxiv-xxxv; G. W. Wade, *The Book of the Prophet Isaiah* (1911).

[2] J. C. Döderlein, *Esaias* (1775), p. xii.

[3] R. Lowth, *Isaiah: A New Translation with Preliminary Dissertation and Notes* (2 vols., 1778), German ed. (1779-81), 4 parts.

[4] J. G. Eichhorn, *Einleitung in das AT* (1780-83), III, p. 76.

[5] W. Gesenius, *Philologisch-kritischer und historischer Commentar über den Jesaia* (2 vols., 1821); cf. his *Der Prophet Jesaia übersetzt* (1820). Following him were L. Seinecke, *Der Evangelist des AT* (1870), pp. 20ff.; A. Knobel, *Der Prophet Jesaja erklärt* (1872 ed.), p. 331; G. A. Smith, *The Book of Isaiah* (1888), I; (1890), II; E. König, *Das Buch Jesaja eingekeitet, übersetzt und erklärt* (1926); C. C. Torrey, *The Second Isaiah* (1928), p. 53; W. F. Albright, *The Archaeology*

However, not all critics were convinced that chapters 40–66 were the work of one individual—an unknown prophet of the exile, who had become known to scholars as Deutero- or Second Isaiah. While Bleek cautiously suggested that the last four chapters, or even the last eight, might have issued from a later date than chapters 40–58, though still being written by the same author,[6] Stade roundly denied that the last five chapters of the book in their final form could have been written by the Second Isaiah at all.[7] Budde enlarged this number to include chapters 56–59 and possibly 61, paving the way for Duhm and Marti to present the theory that the Second Isaiah composed chapters 40–55 in Babylon somewhat prior to 538 B.C., while a third or Trito-Isaiah was credited with the authorship of chapters 56–66, which were thought to have been written in Palestine after 538 B.C.,[8]

This view was given wide circulation, and was quickly adopted in scholarly society as the standard explanation of the composition of the book of Isaiah. It was not without its critics in liberal circles, however, many of whom attacked the postulated unity of chapters 40–55. One of the earliest of these protagonists was Rückert, who on the basis of the dictum, "there is no peace, saith the Lord, unto the wicked" in Isaiah 48:22 (occurring in a similar form in 57:21; 66:24), divided chapters 40–55 into two subsections comprising chapters 40–48 and 49–55.[9] Kuenen held that much of chapters 50–55 had been written after 536 B. C., though possibly in part by the Second Isaiah, but Kosters denied that any portion of chapters 40–55 had come from the hand of the Second Isaiah.[10] This view was adopted by Cheyne in the *Polychrome Bible*, published in 1898.[11] The pervasive influence of Duhm was reflected in the writings of Skinner, who, with A. B. Davidson and G. A. Smith, was principally responsible for propagating German critical views regarding the composition of Isaiah among English-speaking peoples.[12]

---

of *Palestine and the Bible* (1932), p. 218; L. Glahn and L. Köhler, *Der Prophet der Heimkehr, I* (1934); G. A. Barton in E. Grant (ed.), *The Haverford Symposium on Archaeology and the Bible* (1938), pp. 61, 73; F. James, *Personalities of the OT* (1939), p. 363, *et al.*

[6] F. Bleek, *Einleitung in das AT* (1878 ed.), pp. 345f.

[7] B. Stade, *Geschichte des Volkes Israel* (1888), II, pp. 70n., 80ff.

[8] K. Budde, *ZAW*, XI (1891), p. 242; B. Duhm, *Das Buch Jesaia* (1892), p. 8ff.; for a careful criticism of his position see E. J. Young, *Studies in Isaiah* (1955), pp. 39ff.; K. Marti, *Der Prophet Sacharja* (1892), p. 40 and *Das Buch Jesaja* (1900).

[9] R. Rückert, *Hebräische Propheten* (1831).

[10] A. Kuenen, *Historisch-critisch Onderzoek* (1889 ed.), II, pp. 137ff. W. H. A. Kosters, *Theologisch Tijdschrift*, XXX (1896), pp. 577ff.

[11] T. K. Cheyne, *The Book of the Prophet Isaiah* in P. Haupt (ed.), *The Sacred Books of the Old and New Testaments* (1898).

[12] J. Skinner, *Isaiah* in *The Cambridge Bible for Schools and Colleges* (1896-98), 2 vols.

On the basis of the *Gattungsforschung* or type-critical procedures established by Gunkel, some European scholars thought of chapters 40–55 as an anthology of detached poems composed by the Second Isaiah, and assembled without particular regard to logical order.[13] Such a criticism of the division of Isaiah 40–55 into two sections, both supposedly issuing from the hand of the Second Isaiah, was made, among others, by Gressmann, Mowinckel, Eissfeldt, and Volz.[14]

When Bernard Duhm in 1892 separated chapters 56–66 from the Second Isaiah and assigned them to another prophet of the period of Ezra and Nehemiah who had become known as Trito-Isaiah, he opened the way for a further fragmentation of Isaianic authorship of the prophecy. Apart from making some alteration in the dating that Duhm assigned to those chapters, many scholars gave solid support to his theory that a Third or Trito-Isaiah wrote this portion of the prophecy.[15] However, it ought to be noted at this point in the discussion that such a designation can only be regarded as legitimate under two conditions: first, that chapters 56–66 can be isolated successfully in terms of authorship from chapters 40–55, and secondly, that they do in fact purport to comprise a literary unit that can be ascribed with confidence to a single author. Some of the scholars who supported the general concept of a Trito-Isaiah entertained distinct reservations with regard to the second of the above considerations, and preferred to attribute various portions of chapters 56–66 to the work of individual writers, thus carrying the process of fragmentation to all kinds of subjective extremes.[16]

The extent and provenance of the Servant poems of Isaiah also constituted matters of considerable debate among critical scholars, and pro-

---

[13] For an exposition of these principles relating to Isaiah see S. Smith, *Isaiah Chapters XL–LV: Literary Criticism and History* (1944), pp. 6ff.

[14] H. Gressmann, *ZAW*, XXXIV (1914), pp. 254ff. S. Mowinckel, *ZAW*, XLIX (1931), pp. 87ff., 242ff., *Acta Orientalia*, I (1937), pp. 1ff. O. Eissfeldt, *Einleitung in das AT*, pp. 377ff.; *ETOT*, pp. 332ff. P. Volz, *Jesaja Übersetzt und Erklärt*, II (1932).

[15] Cf. W. H. A. Kosters, *Theologisch Tijdschrift*, XXX (1896), pp. 577ff.; H. Gressmann, *Über die Jes. 56-66 vorausgesetzten zeitgeschichtlichen Verhältnisse* (1898); E. Littmann, *Über die Abfassungszeit des Tritojesaja* (1899); *DILOT*, pp. 231ff.; K. Cramer, *Der Geschichtliche Hintergrund der Kap. 56-66 im Buch Jesaja* (1905); A. A. Zillesen, *ZAW*, XXVI (1906), pp. 231ff.; G. E. Box, *The Book of Isaiah* (1908); R. Abramowski, *Theologische Studien und Kritiken*, XCVII (1925), pp. 90ff.; K. Elliger, *ZAW*, XLIX (1931), pp. 112ff., *Deuterojesaja und sein Verhältnis zu Tritojesaja* (1933); E. Sellin, *Neue Kirchliche Zeitschrift* (1930), pp. 73ff., 145ff.; H. Odeberg, *Trito-Isaiah* (1931); L. Glahn and L. Köhler, *Der Prophet der Heimkehr* (1934).

[16] T. K. Cheyne, *Introduction to Isaiah: Jewish Religious Life After the Exile* (1901), p. xvi; K. Budde, *Geschichte der althebräischen Literatur* (1909), p. 177; M. Buttenwieser, *JBL*, XXXVIII (1919), pp. 94ff.; J. Marty, *Les Chapitres 56-66 du livre d'Esaïe* (1924); R. Levy, *Deutero-Isaiah* (1925), pp. 30ff.; A. Lods, *Les prophètes d'Israël* (1935), pp. 309f., *et al.*

duced a wide variety of opinion in consequence. Some of the implications of this material have been discussed previously in the present work (part seven, section IV, B), and accordingly it is sufficient at this point merely to mention the proposed relationship of the oracles (Isa. 42:1-4, or 1-9; 49:1-6, or 1-9; 50:4-9, or 1-11; 52:13–53:12) to the work of the Second Isaiah.[17] According to some scholars the poems were composed by this supposed author as part of his book,[18] while in the view of others they were written at a considerably later period by the Second Isaiah and subsequently incorporated into the extant prophecy.[19]

Another opinion, differing somewhat from those above, had it that the Servant oracles had been composed by the Second Isaiah after the prophecy had been written, and that he interpolated them into the Hebrew text.[20] Wellhausen suggested an independent theory to the effect that the oracles had been composed by an earlier author and taken over by the Second Isaiah, who then incorporated them into his own writings.[21] A further hypothesis supposed that the poetic sections in question were the work of someone who wrote at a later period than the Second Isaiah, and whose compositions were subsequently added to the prophecy by an unknown editor.[22] Other critics such as Sellin and Volz attributed the final Servant oracle to a different author on the grounds of variation in style and content.[23]

The imaginative powers that Duhm brought to his task of dissecting the prophecy of Isaiah, coupled with the nineteenth-century evolutionary *Zeitgeist*, were sufficient to provoke a surge of what can only be described as rank emotionalism in this area of Old Testament study. The

[17] For comprehensive surveys of the literature see C. R. North, *The Suffering Servant in Deutero-Isaiah: An Historical and Critical Study* (1948), pp. 28ff.; *RSL*, pp. 3ff.

[18] E.g. by O. Fullkrug, *Der Gottesknecht des Deuterojesaja* (1899), pp. 68f.; J. Ley, *Theologische Studien und Kritiken* (1901), pp. 659ff.; S. H. Blank, *HUCA*, XV (1939-40), p. 20, *et al.*

[19] E.g. A. Condamin, *RB*, XVII (1908), pp. 162ff.; E. Sellin, *Einleitung in das AT*, p. 77; R. Levy, *Deutero-Isaiah* (1925), pp. 138ff.

[20] So M. G. Glazebrook, *Studies in the Book of Isaiah* (1910), pp. 15ff.; J. Fischer, *Isaias 40-55 und die Perikopen vom Gottesknecht* (1916), p. 240; W. Rudolph, *ZAW*, XLIII (1925), pp. 90ff.; J. Hempel, *Zeitschrift für Systematische Theologie*, VII (1930), pp. 631ff.

[21] *Israelitische und jüdische Geschichte* (1914), p. 152 n. 1; cf. W. Staerk, *Die Ebed-Jahwe Lieder in Jesaja 40ff. Ein Beitrag zur Deuterojesajakritik* (1913), p. 138.

[22] B. Duhm, *Das Buch Jesaia übersetzt und erklärt* (1892), pp. xv, 14f.; M. Schiau, *Die Ebed-Jahwe-Lieder in Jes. 40-66. Ein litterarkritischer Versuch* (1895), pp. 13f., 59; R. Kittel, *Zur Theologie des AT* (1899), p. 22f.; L. Laue, *Theologische Studien und Kritiken* (1904), pp. 319ff.; R. H. Kennett, *The Composition of the Book of Isaiah in the Light of History and Archaeology* (1910), p. 72, *The Servant of the Lord* (1911), p. 121.

[23] E. Sellin, *Neue Kirchliche Zeitschrift*, XLI (1930), pp. 73ff., 145ff., *ZAW*, LV (1937), p. 207. P. Volz, *Jesaia II übersetzt und erklärt*, pp. 149ff.

divisive theories of Duhm virtually swept the field. Not even the moderating tendencies of S. R. Driver[24] were sufficient to place this critical emotionalism in proper perspective, and by the end of the nineteenth century it was considered academically bizarre and unrespectable to begin to suggest views that could be interpreted as maintaining the unity of the prophecy. In Europe, as in England, the appointment to University chairs in Old Testament depended to no small extent upon the amount of enthusiasm with which the prospective candidate adhered to the "assured findings" of the critical school in both Pentateuchal and Isaianic studies, a situation prevalent to a considerable degree also in North America. This emotionalism was naturally not by any means unilateral, for those who held conservative views regarding the authorship and composition of Isaiah were certainly not slow in making their sentiments known. It needs hardly to be observed that such conditions of conflict can evoke the best as well as the worst in Biblical study, and the finest literary products of both the liberal and conservative schools in this particular area of endeavor stand as permanent monuments to the erudition of late nineteenth- and early twentieth-century Old Testament scholarship.

One of the outstanding conservative contributions to the study of Isaiah, and one which anticipated many subsequent critical objections to the integrity of the book, was made in 1846 by J. A. Alexander.[25] A brilliant linguist and learned Biblical scholar,[26] Alexander rejected what he regarded as the critical excesses of Koppe, Eichhorn, and Bertholdt, and while he preferred the more moderate positions adopted by De Wette and Gesenius, he was not slow to point out the basic fallacies which underlay their critical procedures.

In upholding the Isaianic authorship of chapters 40–66, he declared that it would be unparalleled in literary history for an author of brilliance and erudition to produce a series of prophecies of such far-reaching importance for the Babylonian exiles, and then to disappear without leaving any trace of his own personality upon them.[27] Furthermore, he raised the question as to how such anonymous writings could become attached to the work of Isaiah ben Amoz when, on the critical view, they had scarcely anything in common. Alexander also pointed out how comparatively few references there were in chapters 40–66 to Babylon and the exile, a matter that C. C. Torrey was to press still further many years later. The work of Alexander was marked by brilliant

---

[24] *DILOT*, pp. 230ff.
[25] J. A. Alexander, *The Earlier Prophecies of Isaiah* (1846); *The Later Prophecies of Isaiah* (1847).
[26] E. J. Young, *Studies in Isaiah*, p. 10; T. K. Cheyne, *The Prophecies of Isaiah, A New Translation with Commentary and Appendices* (1884 ed.), I, p. 225 n. 2.
[27] J. A. Alexander, *The Later Prophecies of Isaiah*, p. xxv.

exegetical insights, and stands as one of the finest literary products to emerge from the hands of any nineteenth-century Biblical scholar.

Of a similarly high standard was *Der Prophet Jesaja, Übersetzt und Erklärt*, begun by Drechsler in 1845 and completed by Delitzsch and Hahn in 1857. Hahn wrote the commentary on chapters 40–66, in which he maintained their unity and attributed their composition to Isaiah ben Amoz. In an appendix to the commentary, Delitzsch made some observations on the general nature of the source material of chapters 40–66, whose standpoint, he maintained, was that of the Babylonian exile, and not the period of Hezekiah. This, however, did not militate against Isaianic authorship, and Delitzsch emphasized that insufficient stress had been placed by critical scholars upon the weight of tradition, which, over the centuries, had recognized Isaiah as the author of the prophecies. He regarded chapters 36–39 as a link between the Assyrian and Babylonian periods, and maintained that chapters 1–39 served as a preparation for chapters 40–66.

Another voluminous commentary from the same period, which also adopted a conservative attitude towards the authorship of chapters 40–66, was that by Rudolf Stier.[28] According to this author, the second half of the prophecy was written by the author of the first thirty-nine chapters, namely Isaiah ben Amoz. Although Stier was not as brilliant a philologist as Delitzsch, he had a firm grasp of the principles of prophetic interpretation, and his commentary constituted a masterpiece of devotional exposition. Five years after Stier published his work an important Jewish commentary on Isaiah was issued by Luzzatto.[29] It was written predominantly in Hebrew, since it was intended largely for a Jewish audience, but it was also furnished with an Italian translation of the verses. The commentary was of disproportionate size in that Isaiah 1–39 occupied more than two-thirds of the completed volume. As regards the authorship of the last twenty-seven chapters, Luzzatto held that they were from Isaiah ben Amoz, and constituted prophecies concerning the future. He noted the existence of divergent views on this matter, but made no attempt to examine or refute them.[30]

In 1866 the first German edition appeared of the celebrated *Biblical Commentary on the Prophecies of Isaiah* by Franz Delitzsch.[31] The fourth edition of this work (1889) was translated into English and furnished with an introduction by S. R. Driver in 1890. The commentary constituted a rare combination of philological acumen and devotional insight, and is rightly regarded as one of the outstanding works on Isaiah. According to Driver's introduction, the fourth edition was accom-

[28] R. Stier, *Jesaias, nicht Pseudo-Jesaias* (1850).

[29] S. D. Luzzatto, ספר ישעיה (1855); its Italian title was *Il Profeta Isaia volgarizzato e commentato ad uso degl'Israeliti*.

[30] *Ibid.*, p. 446.

[31] F. Delitzsch, *Biblische Kommentar über den Propheten Jesaja* (1866).

modated throughout to the views of the origin and structure of the prophecy as accepted by the bulk of contemporary liberal scholars.[32] In point of fact, however, Delitzsch never fully surrendered to the critical theory of multiple authorship of Isaiah, for he preferred to think of chapters 40–66 as "testamentary discourses of the one Isaiah, and the entire prophetic collection as the progressive development of his incomparable charism."[33] However, there appears to be a sense in which Delitzsch bowed to the contemporary surge of literary criticism on the subject, for he spoke of the author of chapters 40–66 as "in any case a prophet of the Isaianic type, but of an Isaianic type peculiarly developed," and of the material itself as being the outcome of impulses springing from Isaiah if he were not, in fact, the immediate author.[34] Clearly such an ambivalence needs to be estimated in the light of the orthodox interpretation that characterized his commentary as a whole. Delitzsch always maintained that Isaiah might have written the entire prophecy attributed to him, and never gave unqualified approval to a theory of a Deutero-Isaiah, despite the suggestions of some writers to the contrary.

While the foregoing represented the most outstanding conservative contributions to the debate during the nineteenth century, they were by no means the only ones. Other defenses of the unity of authorship of the book of Isaiah were furnished by Caspari, Rutgers, and Jeffreys, while in the twentieth century the traditional position was upheld by such scholars as Margoliouth, G. L. Robinson, Lias, Ridderbos, and Kaminka.[35]

The unity of Isaiah was maintained from a rather novel standpoint by Wordsworth, who in 1939 published an analysis of the prophecy based upon the contention that the theme of the book involving Immanuel and the Servant was in fact the traditional messianic proclamation of the Christian Church.[36] Wordsworth regarded Isaiah ben Amoz as the author of the material attributed to him, and assigned tentative dates within his lifetime to most of the oracles. His emphasis upon the word-plays and rhythms of the original led him to cast the various chapters into poetic form, whether or not the Hebrew actually required it. The oracles were

---

[32] I, p. xv.

[33] *Ibid.*, II, pp. 125f.; cf. O. T. Allis, *The Unity of Isaiah* (1950), p. 83 n. 5.

[34] F. Delitzsch, *op. cit.*, II, pp. 129, 133; cf. W. T. Dawson, *ET*, II (1890-91), pp. 16f.

[35] C. P. Caspari, *Beiträge zur Einleitung in das Buch Jesaja* (1848). A. Rutgers, *De echtheit van het tweede gedeelte van Jesaja* (1866). L. D. Jeffreys, *The Unity of the Book of Isaiah: Linguistic and Other Evidence of the Undivided Authorship* (1899). D. S. Margoliouth, *Lines of Defence of the Biblical Revelation* (1903), pp. 72ff. G. L. Robinson, *The Book of Isaiah: In Fifteen Studies* (1910). J. J. Lias, *Bibliotheca Sacra*, LXXII (1915), pp. 560ff., LXXV (1918), pp. 267ff. J. Ridderbos, *De Profeet Jesaja* (1922). A. Kaminka, *Revue et Études Juives*, LXXX (1925), pp. 42ff., 131ff., LXXI (1925), pp. 27ff.

[36] W. A. Wordsworth, *En Roeh* (1939).

interpreted by means of historical observations, and were annotated with considerable skill. The book as a whole constituted a serious attempt to treat the prophecy as an anthology, and despite a certain amount of awkwardness in sections of the translation the work represented an important contribution to the study of Isaiah.

A valuable and erudite commentary on Isaiah written by the Roman Catholic scholar E. J. Kissane was published in two volumes at the beginning of World War II.[37] The author was an individual who possessed considerable philological ability, and who had as his objective the refutation of the divisive theories of Duhm. He argued forcibly for the unity of the prophecy, and successfully exposed the weaknesses of the position adopted by Duhm. Some of the exegetical conclusions at which Kissane arrived left certain things to be desired, and in some other respects he exhibited traces of the influence of critical thought, particularly in his view that an unknown Babylonian prophet had appended chapters 36—39 to the first thirty-five chapters of Isaiah. Nevertheless, his treatment of the Hebrew text was noteworthy, and his commentary was of value in calling attention to the fundamental weaknesses of divisive theories of authorship.

The unity of Isaiah was also upheld subsequently by O. T. Allis and E. J. Young, both of whom have laid considerable stress upon the strictly predictive element of prophecy,[38] in opposition to the naturalistic views of A. B. Davidson,[39] and many others. Young in particular has brought a great deal of erudition to bear upon his writings, and his observations have to be reckoned with in any discussion of the authorship and integrity of Isaiah. Another commentary with a traditional bent was published in the *Soncino* series by I. W. Slotki.[40] While the author recognized the existence of critical views regarding the authorship of Isaiah, he was clearly far from impressed with their validity, and did not pronounce in favor of the liberal school.

Despite solid opposition from conservative quarters, the vast majority of scholars continued to espouse the divisive theories of Duhm, and regarded the critical issues relating to the book as settled to all intents and purposes. Nevertheless it seemed improbable that the surface of this monolithic theoretical structure could remain unscarred indefinitely, and by about 1940 unmistakable cracks in the facade began to be discernible. The most obvious of these emerged from a series of lectures given

[37] *The Book of Isaiah: Translated from a Critically Revised Hebrew Text with Commentary*, I (1941); II (1943).

[38] O. T. Allis, *The Unity of Isaiah* (1950). E. J. Young, *YIOT*, pp. 202ff., *Studies in Isaiah* (1955), *The Book of Isaiah*, I (1965).

[39] A. B. Davidson, *HDB*, IV, p. 118, *OT Prophecy*, p. 11.

[40] *Isaiah* (1959).

by Sidney Smith, in which he drew attention to the historical material that he thought to be illustrative of Isaiah 40–55.[41]

Smith outlined the principles of *Gattungsforschung* or type-analysis, as proposed by Gunkel and Gressmann, and related them to the section under study, which according to the exponents of form-criticism could be divided into some fifty units comprising hymns, oracles, denunciations, and the like. Smith rejected this kind of classification in a thoroughgoing critique of the vagaries of the *Gattungsforschung* approach, and instead related the historical events of 547-538 B.C to chapters 40 to 55 of the prophecy.[42] Having established as far as possible the extent to which the various sections of Isaiah 40–55 were composed during this decade of Hebrew history, he set them out in the form of speeches composed by the prophet, and then, presumably, delivered in the form of pamphlets, numbering about twenty-two in all. For Smith these included the first three so-called Servant oracles,[43] as well as the section consisting of Isaiah 52:13–53:12, which he associated with the death of the prophet.

The book met with a storm of criticism, and it must be said in all honesty that some of the objections raised were quite valid. The initial lecture failed to do justice to much of the literature in existence up to that time which dealt with the problems posed by Isaiah. Some of the alleged references to historical events between 547 and 538 B.C. could only be maintained on the flimsiest of grounds, and the treatment by Smith of the Servant passages, and particularly of Isaiah 52:13–53:12, left much to be desired. Nevertheless, the very fact that Smith attempted to postulate a definite link between chapters 40–55 and the period of 547-538 B.C. constituted an important advance in the study of Isaiah, and it is difficult to resist the impression that critical objections to his conclusions were prompted less by his findings than by their implications for the entire liberal position with regard to the criticism of Isaiah.

Further evidence of fissures in the facade of liberal scholarship regarding the pre- and post-exilic sections of the book emerged in 1962 with the publication of a commentary on the first thirty-nine chapters of Isaiah by Mauchline.[44] He adopted a distinctly conservative attitude towards many passages that had been commonly regarded by earlier writers as constituting interpolations by later hands, and this enabled him to see Isaiah as the substantial author of chapters 13–27, a section in which many liberal scholars had detected the activity of numerous composers. What was of particular interest, however, was his recognition that some passages which critical scholars had all too easily assigned to a

---

[41] S. Smith, *Isaiah Chapters XL-LV: Literary Criticism and History* (1944).

[42] *Ibid.*, pp. 6ff.

[43] 42:1-4; 49:1-6; 50:4-9. For other suggested Servant poems see W. H. Brownlee, *The Meaning of the Qumrân Scrolls for the Bible* (1964), pp. 193ff.

[44] J. Mauchline, *Isaiah 1-39. Introduction and Commentary* (1962).

post-exilic period may well belong in fact to the time of Isaiah himself.[45]

Mauchline supported his contentions in part by arguing from the analogy of Hosea, who came to have hope for his people, to the prospect that Isaiah also passed ultimately through the very same experience. Despite this important recognition, Mauchline was beset by certain inconsistencies. Thus he saw no incompatibility, as some other critics had done, between the Babylonian references in chapter 39 and Isaianic authorship of that section, and yet at the same time he used the mention of the Medes and Babylon in Isaiah 13:17ff. as a reason for postulating an exilic date for the passage. In point of fact there is no inconsistency of the kind implied by Mauchline, for his fault lies in his inability to allow room for a genuine predictive element in the narrative, a deficiency shared by many liberal writers.

2. *Arguments for division of authorship.* In summary it can be remarked that, while there is evidence of some dissatisfaction in liberal circles with the general position of Duhm and his followers regarding the authorship and composition of the book of Isaiah, the vast majority of scholars still continue to cling to the positions established by an earlier generation of European critics. Consequently, some notice should be taken at this juncture of the arguments adduced over the years for the critical division of the prophecy. As recorded by Driver, these fell into three categories.[46] First, on the basis of internal evidence the section points to a period towards the close of the Babylonian captivity as the time of the composition of chapters 40—66. According to this argument the exile was presupposed rather than predicted, and those who were addressed were thought to be experiencing suffering in Babylonia and looking forward to a return to the homeland. Critical postulates held that it was impossible for Isaiah to maintain such a prolonged futuristic standpoint and converse with generations over a century distant.

The second argument for the separation of chapters 40—66 was based upon stylistic considerations, in which it was maintained that new images and phrases replaced to some extent at least the ideas and terms of the first thirty-nine chapters,[47] with phenomena such as duplication of words being more prominent in chapters 40—66. The style of Isaiah ben Amoz was held to be terse and compact, exhibiting a measured movement alike of thought and rhetoric. The alleged author of chapters 40—66, however, was frequently given to impassioned lyricism, and drew for his imagery upon the sphere of human emotion. He personified cities and nature alike, and heightened such representations by his peculiar dramatic abilities.

[45] *Ibid.*, pp. 9f.
[46] *DILOT*, pp. 236ff.
[47] Cf. T. K. Cheyne, *Introduction to the Book of Isaiah* (1894), pp. 255ff.

The third principal criticism envisaged by critical scholars concerned the theological concepts of chapters 40—66. Whereas the earlier sections of the prophecy spoke of the divine majesty, later chapters described His uniqueness and eternity. As contrasted with the emphasis found in the first thirty-nine chapters, where Jehovah was exalted above all other gods, the remaining chapters of the prophecy denied their very existence, and instead discussed the concept of God as the sole deity. In the first portion of Isaiah, the remnant was held to constitute the faithful left behind in Jerusalem, whereas in the latter part of the work it was thought of as the faithful exilic group about to be brought back to Palestine. Finally, the messianic king of chapters 1—39 was held to have been replaced by the concept of the Servant in chapters 40—66.

While many conservative writers recognized that there were differences in the perspective of time represented in the prophecy, they were not slow to insist that the standpoint of chapters 40—66 was an ideal rather than a real one. In particular they urged that, if critics such as Driver could concede that there were instances in the earlier sections of Isaiah (cf. 5:13ff.; 9:1ff.; 23:1, 14) when the speaker projected himself into the future and from that standpoint described events anterior to the situation as though they had already actually happened,[48] why could it not be possible for so great a prophet as the author of chapters 40—66 to have maintained this ideal standpoint for some length of time also. It was further pointed out that in a very real sense the exile was not an event that was still future to Isaiah, but a process that had been initiated before his time, and whose culmination was a commonplace of prophetic observation. Thus it was unnecessary for Isaiah to repeat the warning of exile in later chapters of the book, since he had already given prominence to the imminence of this event previously (5:5f.; 10:20ff.; 32:13-18).

Against the objection—made as a result of the critics' minimizing of the purely predictive element in prophecy—that it would be without precedent for the name of Cyrus to be mentioned more than a century and a half in advance, it was pointed out that other prophetic utterances also applied to events far off in the future. Conservative scholars cited the prophecy which foretold the name of Josiah more than three centuries prior to his birth (1 Kgs. 13:1f.), the mention of Bethlehem by Micah (Mic. 5:2 = Matt. 2:6), the contemporary of Isaiah, as the birthplace of the Messiah, and the subjugation of Tyre by the Babylonians as promised by Ezekiel (26:2ff.) and Zechariah (9:1ff.). The first of these prophecies was particularly embarrassing to critical scholars, since there was no possiblility of textual corruption *in loco*. However, on the basis of their insistence that there was no predictive element in prophecy, they

---

[48] *DILOT*, p. 237.

tried to dismiss the problem, or more commonly, to avert the critical gaze from it.

When pressed, the liberal school found it impossible to adduce convincing evidence for their contention that chapters 40–66 were written elsewhere than in Palestine. Following Duhm, various scholars indulged in a wide range of assumptions, but actual proof was never forthcoming. Indeed, C. C. Torrey, who was one of the more extreme Old Testament critics, roundly asserted that the few references to Babylon and Cyrus in chapters 40–66 were bungling and tendentious insertions, and that almost the whole of the material could in consequence be assigned to a Palestinian writer, whom he dated about a century after the restoration.[49] While some scholars purported to see a Babylonian background in the description of religion, buildings, and scenery, others frankly conceded that nothing in the geographical, topographical, or cultural background suggested any land other than Palestine as the country of origin of the prophecy. Notice was also taken of the fact that in chapters 40–66 no places other than Judah and Jerusalem were mentioned as the actual home of the inhabitants of the southern kingdom.

Arguments from literary style were greatly in vogue at the end of the nineteenth century, but in the light of a much wider knowledge of ancient Near Eastern languages they have now assumed a far less important position. The very subjectivity of stylistic considerations had a great appeal for the adherents of the Graf-Wellhausen theory of literary analysis, who saw no inconsistency whatever in perusing material ascribed to a Biblical author, and then denying parts of that very corpus to him because the literary form and vocabulary of each chapter did not happen to be identical. Apparently it did not occur to those early investigators that it was only possible to derive some concept of the style of an ancient author as the result of careful study of all the material ascribed to him, and that subsequent rejection of part or all of that corpus could only be validated on the basis of some rigorous external control.

Perhaps the most serious fault of the Graf-Wellhausen school in this general regard, as mentioned above, was the fact that they remained serenely confident and unmoved by that anomaly of reasoning that would purport to determine knowledge of style of various portions of a book on the presumption that the author wrote it, and then proceed to deny his authorship of certain sections of that composition on the ground that their style varied somewhat from the other sections. That the kind of fundamental divergence imagined by many nineteenth-century critics does not obtain for Isaiah, even on the basis of divisive theories of authorship, is indicated by the closeness of the verbal agreements between chapters 1–39 and 40–66, as well as by distinct resemblances in

---

[49] C. C. Torrey, *The Second Isaiah: A New Interpretation* (1928), p. viii.

thought and literary figure.[50] Even the mechanics of construction of the book exhibit unexpected parallels, as will be seen subsequently.

Conservative scholars generally met the arguments relating to differences in theological standpoint by demonstrating that the ideas in later chapters of the prophecy were broader and more extended than their counterparts in chapters 1–39. Thus the Messiah, who had appeared in earlier passages as a king of the Davidic lineage, was subsequently described in terms of the divine Servant. Yet the fact that David was referred to in Isaiah 55:3 makes it clear that the earlier concept had not been abandoned in favor of the later one. Indeed, a careful reading of the text shows that there is a great deal to be said for the close correspondence of the theology contained in chapters 40–66 with that found in the prophecy of Micah, a contemporary of Isaiah.

W. F. Albright has pointed out that competent scholars are increasingly cognizant of the fact that most of the prophetic books may more correctly be styled "anthologies of oracles and sermons," since their contents are seldom in correct order.[51] Had this observation been applied seriously to the study of Isaiah by scholars from the time of Duhm down to that of Albright himself, the bulk of critical effort would have unquestionably been expended along far different and more constructive lines. One of the gravest weaknesses of critical methodology, here as in Pentateuchal studies, lay in the wholesale begging of the question by liberal scholars. For all the imaginative analyses fostered by Duhm, the unfortunate fact remains that divisive theories of the composition of Isaiah are strictly matters of assumption rather than of factual proof. Because of the subjective extremes to which some followers of Duhm went, the "assured results" of the literary criticism of Isaiah were in fact far less securely established than their proponents fondly imagined to be the case. The wide diversity of opinion in this matter has already been indicated in the outline of literary criticism of the prophecy, and the consequent fragmentation of the book at the hands of liberal scholars resulted in a grave weakening both of the literary artistry and the essential spiritual message of the composition, a situation that some critics noted to their embarrassment.

For all their persuasiveness, liberal writers have not been as careful in the study of the text as they have liked to imagine, or as the situation clearly warrants. It is one thing to become caught up in a movement of thought that assigns chapters 40–66 with complete assurance to an exilic or post-exilic date, but it is quite another to take these chapters *seriatim* and make an honest effort to relate them to the sequences of a more carefully delineated segment of Hebrew history. Upon making such an attempt one immediately recognizes that certain sections in chapters

[50] J. H. Raven, *OT Introduction* (1910), pp. 190ff.
[51] *FSAC*, p. 275.

40–66 cannot be relegated to the exilic period at all. Thus, in Isaiah 40:9, the stronghold of Zion and the cities of Judah are still in existence, a situation that hardly accords with the known conditions of the exile. Again, in Isaiah 62:6, the walls of Jerusalem were explicitly mentioned in a context of prosperity, and this represents a state of affairs that was by no means characteristic of the exilic or early post-exilic period. On the other hand, the prophet regarded the captivity as an already accomplished fact in Isaiah 1:7-9; 5:13; and 14:1-4. The supposedly divergent historical standpoints of the two main sections of the prophecy as isolated by critical study are certainly by no means as different as had been imagined.

Various parts of the Isaianic anthology represent contrasting standpoints of time, as has been recognized by both liberal and conservative scholars. But whereas the latter have given credence to the possibility of a specifically predictive element in prophecy, the former, with a few exceptions, have denied it, and in the process have left themselves open to a degree of inconsistency. This can be illustrated from the work of North, who stated that the fourth Servant oracle (Isa. 52:13–53:12) could be understood as a projection of sufferings viewed from a futuristic standpoint.[52] If a Deutero- or a Trito-Isaiah was able to indulge in such a projection, assuming for the moment that it would even be necessary from their standpoint of composition, why should it be deemed impossible for a Proto-Isaiah to have had precisely the same experience with regard to the exile and restoration of Israel? If pronouncements from a futuristic standpoint are denied to one, they ought to be denied to all. But if the existence of such phenomena is in fact conceded, all *a priori* objections to a Proto-Isaiah's occasionally adopting an ideal standpoint are immediately removed. The critical case is clearly rather precariously established at this important point.

While criteria of literary style are less in vogue as arguments in connection with authorship than was the case in an earlier generation, it may be advantageous to make a few observations on this matter at the present juncture. A careful reading of the Hebrew text will show that there are remarkable similarities between chapters 1–39 and 40–66 in questions of both language and style, as illustrated by the substantial verbal agreements between 40:5, 58:14 and 1:20; 43:13 and 14:27; 60:21 and 29:23; 51:11 and 35:10; 56:8 and 11:12; 61:2, 63:4 and 34:8; 65:25 and 11:6ff. Duplication of words such as in Isaiah 40:1 and 57:19, held to be characteristic of the style of Second Isaiah, also occur in 21:11, 24:16, 28:10, and 29:1.

Somewhat less precise are the similarities of thought or literary figures, as the following list will indicate: 40:3-4, 49:11 and 35:8-10; 41:17-18, 43:19 and 35:6-7; 42:1, 61:1 and 11:2; 42:13 and 31:4; 42:18-20,

[52] C. R. North, *IDB*, IV, p. 293.

43:8 and 6:9; 43:13 and 14:27; 42:24 and 1:14; 45:9, 64:8 and 29:16; 45:15 and 8:17; 47:3 and 3:17, 20:4; 47:10 and 29:15, 30:1; 49:2 and 11:4; 49:26 and 9:20; 51:4 and 2:3; 51:9 and 27:1; 53:2 and 11:1, 10; 54:7-8 and 26:20; 55:12 and 14:8; 32:15, 35:1-2 and 51:3; 56:7 and 2:2; 56:8 and 11:12; 56:12 and 22:13; 59:3 and 1:15; 59:11 and 38:14; 60:13 and 35:2; 60:18 and 26:1; 60:21 and 11:1; 61:8 and 1:11, 13; 62:10 and 11:12; 63:17 and 6:10; 65:3, 66:17 and 1:29; 65:19 and 35:10; 66:16 and 27:1.

In the later chapters of the prophecy there is a far greater consonance with the religious and moral conditions obtaining in the eighth century B.C. and with the utterances of contemporary prophets than the majority of literary critics have been prepared to recognize. Such reflections are to be seen in 44:23f.; 45:8; 50:1; 55:12f.; 56:1; 57:1; 59:3; 61:8; 63:3ff. Particularly striking are the resemblances between the doctrines of Isaiah 40—66 and the teachings of Micah, as illustrated by the following comparisons: Isaiah 41:15f. and Micah 4:13; Isaiah 47:2f. and Micah 1:11; Isaiah 48:2 and Micah 3:11; Isaiah 49:23 and Micah 7:17; Isaiah 52:12 and Micah 2:13; Isaiah 56:10f. and Micah 3:5; Isaiah 58:1 and Micah 3:8. Obviously the same glorious expectation of the future under divine providence, the same broad conception of the nations of the Near East, and the confident expectation that a renewed Israel would return from exile, were characteristic of both prophets.

One of the most impressive pieces of internal evidence for the close literary association between Proto- and Deutero-Isaiah consists in the references to idolatry, particularly as they occur in chapters 40—66. It has apparently passed unnoticed by critical scholars that, with the exception of the description of Babylonian idolatry in Isaiah 47:13, all other references to such practices in chapters 40—66 are specifically to the pre-exilic Canaanite variety mentioned in Isaiah 1:13, 29; 2:8ff.; 8:19; and elsewhere.[53] Such allusions in the later chapters include 40:19; 41:7, 29; 42:17; 44:9ff., 25; 45:15ff.; 46:6f.; 48:5; 57:5; 63:3ff.; 66:3, 17. Of these, Isaiah 44:9ff., 25, and 57:5 cannot possibly be interpreted as anything other than Canaanite idolatry. If this section was written in Babylon by an unknown prophet of the exile, as liberal scholars have so commonly assumed, it is curious that the author should have been so actively preoccupied with something which had long since become a dead issue. The social and religious background of this material is clearly that of the pre-exilic period, as Kissane so ably demonstrated.[54] Quite obviously the arguments for a divisive authorship of Isaiah as

---

[53] Cf. D. S. Margoliouth, *Lines of Defence of the Biblical Revelation*, pp. 75ff.

[54] E. J. Kissane, *The Book of Isaiah* (1943), II, pp. xlvi ff., against H. Gressmann, *Der Ursprung der israelitisch-jüdischen Eschatologie* (1905), pp. 250ff., 305ff., and E. Meinhold, *Einführung in das AT* (1932), pp. 250ff.

based upon considerations of language and style are very much weaker than their critical proponents have supposed in the past.

3. *The book as an anthology.* The present writer holds to the view that Isaiah, like the majority of the other extant prophetic writings, represents an anthology of utterances given at various times, and as such the work merits no different treatment from that accorded the other major Old Testament prophecies. In this connection it is important to note that arguments based upon differences of style or literary expression are immediately vitiated by this approach, since an anthology may be taken quite fairly as representing the total style of the author over the different periods of his creative activity. Justification for describing the work as an anthology in the best sense of that term is furnished by the opening verse of the prophecy, which constitutes a heading for the work, and speaks specifically of the revelatory material that Isaiah the son of Amoz received in visions concerning Judah and Jerusalem in days of Uzziah, Jotham, Ahaz, and Hezekiah. As with all anthologies it is fairly evident that the book contained only a selection of the available prophetic oracles and sermons, and it is highly probable that Isaiah produced considerably more material than has survived in his book. The nature of the prophecy as an anthology is further indicated by the presence of superscriptions in Isaiah 2:1 and 13:1, which may have represented, or pointed to the presence of, earlier collections of prophetic utterances.

Although it constitutes a work of this special kind, the prophecy must not be regarded as a rather arbitrary selection of discourses put together in a disconnected form. That a particular device of literary mechanics familiar in antiquity was employed in the construction of the book will be made plain subsequently. For the present, however, it should be noted that there was a certain chronological arrangement apparent in the material as extant, for in the first thirty-nine chapters the prophecies in chapters 2–5 appear to have come from the earliest period of the ministry of Isaiah, while Isaiah 7:1–9:7 probably originated during the Syro-Ephraimite conflict, about 734 B.C. Chapters 18–20 may have been the product of activity between 715 and 711 B.C., though this fact cannot be established with any degree of certainty.

The historical section comprising chapters 36–39, which exhibits only minor variations from 2 Kings 18:13–20:19, has been held to be later than Isaiah, since it mentions the death of Sennacherib (681 B.C.) (Isa. 37:38), which would be later than the time of Isaiah, unless the prophet survived into the reign of Manasseh (687/86-642/41 B.C.), as Jewish tradition has maintained. It may be, of course, that this historical material was assembled by the disciples of Isaiah rather than by the prophet himself, although this is naturally unknown. What does seem more difficult to maintain, however, is the view that chapters 36–39, in which Isaiah played a prominent part, were actually extraneous and specifically non-Isaianic in origin.

In this latter connection it should be observed that, although there seems little doubt that the chapters in Isaiah were written not later than half a century after the events described, there is some question as to which of the two narratives was the original. According to Driver the version in Kings antedated that found in Isaiah, and was used with certain modifications by the compiler of the prophecy.[55] However, there are some grounds for thinking that this material constituted an "Isaiah source" upon which the compiler of Kings drew. By comparing 2 Kings 16:5 and Isaiah 7:1, it seems probable that the author of Kings had the Isaiah material before him, from which he abstracted the particular information needed for his work. The existence of a separate Isaianic source, in which events from the life of Hezekiah were recorded, seems indicated from the evidence furnished by 2 Chronicles 32:32, which speaks as though the excerpt in the Book of the Kings of Israel and Judah might have been taken from the חזון or "vision" of Isaiah. Furthermore, the fact that the song of Hezekiah (Isa. 38:9-20) appeared in the prophecy but was omitted by the compiler of Kings seems to indicate that the latter considered the material unsuitable for his purposes.

Attempts to assign dates to other portions of the prophecy, as Smith and Wordsworth have done,[56] appear to be unwise, partly because of the ideal standpoint of some chapters, which makes such a procedure extremely speculative, and also because the general character of the references, such as those concerning Canaanite idolatry, make it impossible to do much more than entertain the possibility of a pre-exilic date for the material. That strict chronological sequences were not of overriding importance to the compiler is evident from the fact that Isaiah 9:8-21 may well constitute the earliest utterance of Isaiah. Again, the prophecy dealing with Damascus (Isa. 17:1-14) may be dated shortly before 735 B.C., a period that appears to be close to the events narrated in chapter seven.

While most of the prophecies that presuppose the exile occur in chapters 40–55, an exilic standpoint is clearly evident also in Isaiah 1:7ff., 5:13; 14:1ff.; and 35:1ff. Evidence of some sort of chronological arrangement can be seen in chapters 40–55, however, which predict the return from exile and the period of restoration. These include sections in which the work of Cyrus was given some attention (41–45), the utterances concerning the downfall of Babylon (46–47), and the promises concerning the glories of the new Jerusalem (49–54). Note should also be taken of the suggestion that the compiler or compilers arranged the contents of chapters 56–66 in such a manner as to present in alternate sequence prophetic utterances whose standpoints were pre-exilic (Isa.

[55] *DILOT*, p. 226.

[56] S. Smith, *Isaiah Chapters XL-LV. Literary Criticism and History*, pp. 49ff. W. A. Wordsworth, *En Roeh*, pp. 35ff.

56:1–57:12; 59:1–60:22; 62:1–63:19; 65:1-25) and exilic (Isa. 58:1-14; 61:1-11; 64:1-12; 66:1-14) respectively, with Isaiah 57:14-21 and 66:15-24 perhaps constituting fragments of oracles. However, this view needs to be assessed in the light of other considerations affecting the process of compilation, as will become evident shortly.

The somewhat inexact chronological arrangement of the book has been thought to be paralleled to some extent by a similar procedure in the matter of compilation, whereby the contents were arranged according to subject matter. Thus the work has been seen to open with a series of utterances relating to the contemporary situation of the prophet (Isa. 1–35), followed by a section of historical material (Isa. 36–39). The fragment comprising Isaiah 38:9-20 has been thought to constitute a psalm of thanksgiving composed by King Hezekiah, which may quite possibly have been incorporated from the court annals into the prophecy by Isaiah himself. A subsequent group of utterances presupposed the Babylonian exile (Isa. 40–55), as some earlier references had done, while the remainder of the prophecy (Isa. 56–66) constituted a collection of rather diverse oracles that paralleled concepts already expressed in earlier sections of the book.

However, even this arrangement was by no means mechanical, for whereas chapters 13–23 consisted principally of prophecies concerning foreign nations, chapter 22 dealt with the desolation of Jerusalem by alien forces. Again, the prophecy contained three superscriptions (Isa. 1:1; 2:1; 13:1), which may originally have constituted the headings of separate written compilations by the prophet himself, and preserved material upon which the compiler or compilers drew. A theory of this sort is chiefly notable for the recognition of parallelism between specific areas of the book, but is deficient as an attempt to explain the mechanics of compilation. Despite certain differences in matters of detail, it is evident that there is a distinct consonance in structure between the earlier and later chapters of the book, the significance of which will be outlined in the following pages.

From the preceding observations it will have become clear that the questions concerning the compilation of the book are much more involved than is assumed by many critical and conservative estimates that are based on an occidental approach to oriental literature. It seems eminently reasonable to suppose that the present book was compiled on the basis of shorter collections of prophetic utterances and historical sources, but as Ridderbos has pointed out, the actual history of its composition can no longer be reconstructed.[57] It may be possible to think of separate collections as represented by chapters 1–12, 13–23, 24–27, 28–35, and 40–55, but estimates of this kind are extremely subjective, and cannot be demonstrated in terms of fact.

[57] N. H. Ridderbos, *NBD*, p. 572.

Attempts to analyze the prophecy into its component parts are made difficult by the chapter divisions in the Hebrew and English texts, which do not always follow the logical sequences of thought or utterance. While any analysis must therefore be regarded as highly speculative—including those of the *Gattungsforschung* variety—it would seem to the present writer that separate prose and poetic utterances might include the following passages: Isa. 1:1-31; 2:4—3:8; 3:16—4:6; 5:8-30; 6:1-13; 7:1-9, 10-25; 8:9—9:7; 10:1-19, 20-34; 11:1—12:6; 24:1-23; 25:1-12; 26:1—27:13; 28:1-29; 29:1-24; 30:1-33; 31:1-9; 32:1-20; 33:1-24; 34:1—35:10; 36:1—39:8; 40:1—41:29; 42:1—45:25; 46:1-13; 47:1-15; 48:1-15; 49:1-26; 50:1-11; 51:1-8, 9-16, 17-23; 52:1-10, 11-15; 53:1-12; 54:1-17; 55:6-13; 56:1-8; 57:1-12; 58:1-14; 59:1-21; 60:1-22; 61:1-6; 62:1-12; 63:7-19; 64:1-12; 65:1-25; 66:1-14. Sections to be regarded specifically as oracles would probably include 13:1—14:27; 14:28-32; 15:1—16:14; 17:1-14; 18:1-7; 19:1-25; 21:1-10, 11-12, 13-17; 22:1-25; and 23:1-18. Chapters 46:1—48:22 constitute a group of anti-Babylonian utterances. Purely historical material is found in Isaiah 6:1-13; 7:1-9; 20:1-6; and 36:1—39:8. Passages such as chapters 2:1-4; 3:9-15, 5:1-7; 8:1-4, 5-10; 9:8-12, 13-21; 48:16-22; 55:1-5; 56:9-12; 57:13-21; 61:7-11; 63:1-6; and 66:15-24 might comprise a variety of utterances that were originally either independent in character or of a fragmentary nature. However, it must be emphasized again that an analysis like the foregoing is extremely speculative, and may have no real relationship at all to the actual components from which the prophecy was compiled.

In crediting the anthology of utterances and oracles to a general origin with Isaiah ben Amoz, the present writer is seeing the activity of the prophet in the light of the superscription in chapter 1:1, which speaks of his receiving revelatory material in visions during the reigns of Uzziah, Jotham, Ahaz, and Hezekiah. Although Isaiah was active in court circles, there is no evidence for the Jewish tradition which regarded him as being of royal blood. His call to prophetic office dated from 740/39 B.C., although it is uncertain whether or not he actually prophesied under Uzziah. His last public appearance about which anything can really be known was at the time of the invasion of Sennacherib in 701 B.C. If, as some scholars have maintained, Sennacherib undertook a second unsuccessful campaign against Jerusalem, this date could be extended to 688 B.C. It should be remarked, however, that the evidence for such a campaign is extremely meager. It is entirely gratuitous to assume that 2 Kings 19:37 implies that Sennacherib met his death shortly after his return to Nineveh, instead of in 681 B.C. Furthermore, there is no mention of any second and unsuccessful campaign against Jerusalem either in the extant Assyrian annals or the Babylonian Chronicles, so that the attack against Jerusalem in 701 B.C. would appear to be the only one of its kind undertaken by Sennacherib. While the lack of mention of such a defeat on either one or two occasions would not be the least surprising as far as the cuneiform sources are concerned, it would be rather strange if a second Assyrian attack upon Jerusalem was unrecorded when a previous one had been chronicled by Hebrew scribes.

While the actual date of death of Isaiah is unknown, there may be some ground for the Jewish tradition that maintained that the prophet was sawed asunder during the reign of Manasseh.[58] Whether this actually occurred or not, it is quite possible for Isaiah to have survived into the time of Manasseh (687/86-642/41 B.C.), and if this was so, the absence of this king from the superscription in chapter 1:1 need only indicate that the prophet played no public role after Manasseh ascended the throne of Judah.

As opposed to all liberal scholars, the present writer takes the view that there is almost no extraneous material at all in the prophecy of Isaiah. There are certain problems connected with chapters 36–39, as has been indicated earlier, but the grounds on which this section of material is attributed to a period later than that of Isaiah ben Amoz appear very unconvincing. It seems certain that, in common with other similar individuals, Isaiah claimed a following of disciples (Isa. 8:16; 28:9f.), who derived counsel and instruction from his utterances. Consequently it needs to be observed that in antiquity it was not unknown for disciples to reshape and sometimes augment the words of the revered master, or even to associate with his prophecies work that was not actually original with him. But in this same connection it must also be remembered that the tenacity of the Semitic memory was such that verbal utterances could be remembered in great detail over prolonged periods of time if need so required, and also that written and oral versions of the same events or prophecies probably co-existed in a great many instances. It is therefore possible to envisage circumstances under which disciples of a prophet might have intruded non-original work into a prophetic anthology. It has to be recognized as coming within the bounds of these circumstances that the disciples of Isaiah, or even some of his later admirers, could have done this sort of thing. But exactly the same group of conditions makes it eminently possible for anyone who was acquainted with the verbal pronouncements of the prophet to detect immediately the presence of extraneous matter, and this is particularly true of those individuals whose concern it was to preserve the traditions and pronouncements of Isaiah. While therefore it is theoretically possible to assume that non-Isaianic material was added at a later date to the prophecy in a rudimentary form, as liberal critics have uniformly done, it is quite another matter to demonstrate in practice that this procedure actually occurred in connection with the book of Isaiah.

There appear to be good grounds for thinking that the final portion of the prophecy of Jeremiah contains material that was not original with

---

[58] *Martyrdom of Isaiah*, V.

the author, and which was doubtless added at a somewhat later date than the remainder of the prophecy. Unfortunately, however, these same conditions do not apply to the commonly alleged non-Isaianic material in Isaiah, for although certain sections have been generally assumed to be extraneous since the time of Duhm, these passages have never been susceptible to rigorous proof of such an assumption. Indeed, the kind of critical appeal to ignorance contained in the postulate of "an unknown prophet of the exile" can never be amenable to anything approaching proof in any sense of the term.

In the opinion of the present writer, the extant prophecy of Isaiah was compiled as an anthology of the utterances and proclamations of Isaiah ben Amoz by the disciples of the prophet, and produced in bifid form to comprise a manual of instruction. This composition was most probably in its extant form, or in something approximating closely thereto, within half a century after the death of Isaiah, and thus may be assigned with reasonable confidence to a date about 630 B.C. That the disciples rather than the master prophet himself appear responsible for the final form of the bifid anthology seems indicated by the supposition that, had Isaiah played a major part in the compilation of his utterances, they might have survived in a more chronological order, and not in the bifid form in which they are now extant. On the other hand, the complexity of the arrangement of material in the prophecy, as indicated previously, combined with the literary artistry of the bifid structure, might well point to the activity of an individual with more than ordinary ingenuity and aesthetic tastes, such as Isaiah himself appeared to be.

4. *Postulates of the critical school.* Further attention must be devoted at this point to an examination of some of the tenaciously held postulates of the critical school with regard to the composition of Isaiah before further remarks are made about the bifid form of construction. It seems abundantly clear that, as a result of the discoveries at Qumran, the prophecy of Isaiah is one of the areas of Old Testament study in which the bulk of nineteenth-century research will have to be undertaken anew.

a. *The date of the prophecy.* One of the theories that can now be laid to rest is the view that certain portions of the prophecy can be assigned confidently to the Maccabean period.[59] There is now no doubt that the Qumran sect was itself Maccabean in origin. Since the numerous books of Scripture that were found in the collection amassed by the sectaries were all copies, it is obvious that none of the books in the Old Testament canon originated during the Maccabean period, since there would have been an insufficient interval of time elapsing between the original autograph and the general acceptance of the particular work as

---

[59] Cf. G. B. Gray, *A Critical and Exegetical Commentary on the Book of Isaiah I-XXXIX* (1912), I, pp. lvi, 332ff., 397ff.; C. F. Kent, *The Sermons, Epistles and Apocalypses of Israel's Prophets* (1910), pp. 497ff.

Scripture, and as therefore suitable for accredited scribal transmission. This fact is as important for the criticism of Daniel and certain of the Psalms as it is for the prophecy of Isaiah, as will be shown in a subsequent part of the present work.

If, then, the Old Testament Scriptures found in the possession of the Qumran brotherhood are copies, it is obviously necessary to advance the date of the original autograph by several centuries. One of the criteria of ultimate canonicity of the second and third divisions of the Hebrew canon was the fact that the individual compositions were subjected to evaluation as to their acceptability and spiritual quality by comparison with the Mosaic Torah, and it was partly on this basis that they were accepted or rejected. As observed above, this procedure involved, among other elements, a certain lapse of time between the compilation of the original work and the period of final acceptance.

If Millar Burrows and others are correct in dating the large Isaiah scroll (1QIsa^a) about 100 B.C.,[60] it is evident that Isaiah was in its final form not later than the beginning of the second century B.C. Allowing for the lapse of time necessary to insure knowledge of the work as a whole by responsible scribal authorities, and acceptance of it as a genuine component of the prophetic section of the Hebrew canon by general approval, it would seem necessary to advance the date of the original autograph to the middle of the Persian period at the very latest, as has also been done in connection with certain Psalms that were formerly assigned to the Maccabean period. Burrows comments with respect to 1QIsa^a and the date of the prophecy itself: "The Book of Isaiah certainly comes from a time several centuries before the earliest date to which this manuscript can be assigned on any grounds."[61]

These observations unequivocally repudiated the views of critical scholars such as Volz, who maintained that chapters 65—66 were written after 331 B.C.,[62] and Eissfeldt, who assigned chapter 65 to a period between 400 and 200 B.C.[63] Equally erroneous is the view that the suffering-servant concept owed its beginnings to the persecution of the pious Jewish martyrs under Antiochus IV Epiphanes,[64] or that the so-called "Isaiah apocalypse" (chapters 24—27) should properly belong to the reign of John Hyrcanus (135-104 B.C.).[65]

 b. The "identity" of Deutero-Isaiah. Although the theory of a Trito-Isaiah of comparatively late date appears somewhat incongruous in the light of the Qumran discoveries, the view that there existed an unknown

---

[60] M. Burrows, *The Dead Sea Scrolls* (1955), p. 118.

[61] *Ibid.*, p. 109; cf. R. K. Harrison, *OT Archaeology*, p. 156 n. 99.

[62] P. Volz, *Jesaja*, II, p. 200.

[63] O. Eissfeldt, *Einleitung in das AT*, p. 387.

[64] R. H. Kennett, *The Composition of the Book of Isaiah* (1909), p. 85, *OT Essays* (1928), p. 146.

[65] B. Duhm, *Das Buch Jesaia*, pp. 9f.

prophet of the exile, otherwise designated Deutero-Isaiah, must be criticized on rather different grounds. When the existence of an ancient Isaiah scroll from Qumran was announced, it was hoped that the manuscript might help to settle the long-debated question as to the number of "Isaiahs" who were responsible for the production of the prophecy in its extant form. When the manuscript was published in a photographic edition, it became immediately evident that there was no space left between the end of chapter 39 and the beginning of chapter 40, as is the case in some modern translations of the prophecy. Since chapter 40 commenced on the bottom line of a column, it would have been very easy for the copyist to have observed a division in the Hebrew text had such actually been present in the manuscript or manuscripts before him as he worked.

It was noticed, however, that a break in the text occurred at the end of chapter 33, where a space of three lines intervened before the beginning of chapter 34. While such considerations might at first sight only appear to refute the idea of a change of authorship at the end of chapter 39, and assign it instead to a position some six chapters earlier in the prophecy, as at least one nineteenth-century scholar had suggested,[66] they actually achieve a much more important objective by furnishing considerable information as to the mechanics involved in the production of the prophecy in its extant form. In antiquity it was not uncommon for books to be produced in two parts, a practice which H. St. John Thackeray attributes to the need for convenience in handling the scrolls.[67] There is also good evidence for the contention that literary works of high caliber were frequently so planned as to yield a natural division in the material about the middle of the work. That this procedure applied to certain of the Hebrew literary prophets was recognized by Josephus, who spoke of Ezekiel, Daniel, and Isaiah as having left their writings behind in "books."[68] The plural form would describe adequately the scrolls corresponding to the two halves of the complete prophecy.

In modern Bibles such a division would embrace two sections of thirty-three chapters each, and it is interesting to note in this connection that the mid-point of Isaiah according to the computation of the Massoretes was at 33:20. It is therefore possible to regard the gap occurring between chapters 33 and 34 in 1QIsaᵃ as actually constituting an indication of the ancient practice of bisecting a literary work. The orthographic and other peculiarities of the scroll were accounted for by Brownlee on the supposition that the scribe of 1QIsaᵃ began to copy from a manuscript containing only the first thirty-three chapters of the prophecy, and

[66] W. Robertson Smith, *The Prophets of Israel* (1895), p. 355.
[67] H. St. J. Thackeray, *The Septuagint and Jewish Worship* (1923), pp. 130ff.
[68] *AJ*, X, 5, 1; X, 11, 7; X, 2, 2.

concluded his work from another manuscript which was badly worn at the margin, resulting in certain lacunae in the text of the Qumran scroll.[69] Later Brownlee became convinced that the manuscript containing Isaiah 1–39 used by the scribe of 1QIsa* was to be regarded as the first volume of the prophecy, which had become separated in some way from the second volume.[70]

Paul Kahle was the first to comment on the textual gap between chapters 33 and 34 of the scroll, claiming that it vindicated the conclusions of C. C. Torrey that chapters 34–35 were to be credited, along with chapters 40–66, to Deutero-Isaiah.[71] This suggestion was not so plausible as it appeared at first, for it failed to explain why chapters 36–39 came to be included in the scroll of this Second Isaiah. Much more acceptable is the suggestion made by Brownlee that the extant prophecy was the work of an Isaianic school whose major activity was the publication of a two-volume edition of Isaianic material.[72] Brownlee analyzed the structure and outline of the prophecy to show that chapters 1–33 were remarkably parallel to chapters 34–66, and showed the way in which each half contained corresponding sections, as follows:

Ruin and restoration (1–5, paralleled by 34–35)
Biographical material (6–8, paralleled by 36–40)
Agents of divine blessing and judgment (9–12, paralleled by 41–45)
Oracles against foreign powers (13–23, paralleled by 46–48)
Universal redemption and the deliverance of Israel (24–27, paralleled by 49–55)
Ethical sermons (28–31, paralleled by 56–59)
The restoration of the nation (32–33, paralleled by 60–66)

This arrangement, as Brownlee pointed out, constitutes less an analysis of the literary units comprising the book than a way of viewing the completed work from the standpoint of the ancient editors, who had no concern for literary origins, but were interested primarily in the parallelistic and balanced structure of the prophecy. He maintained that chapters 36–39 were most probably borrowed independently from the same stream of Isaianic material as that from which the compiler of Kings derived his information, and that it was inserted in order to furnish a parallel to the biographical sections in chapters seven and eight.

In the view of the present writer such an analysis represents a distinct advance upon the fragmentary theories with which earlier criticism of Isaiah was beset, and constitutes by far the best attempt to date to account for the remarkable consonance between earlier and later chap-

[69] W. H. Brownlee, *BASOR*, No. 127 (1952), pp. 16ff.
[70] W. H. Brownlee, *The Meaning of the Qumrân Scrolls for the Bible*, p. 253, cautiously accepted by E. J. Young, *Westminster Theological Journal*, XXVII (1965), pp. 94ff.
[71] P. E. Kahle, *Die Hebräischen Handschriften aus der Höhle* (1951), pp. 72f.
[72] W. H. Brownlee, *The Meaning of the Qumrân Scrolls for the Bible*, pp. 247ff.

ters of the prophecy in its extant form. It possesses the undoubted advantage of viewing the work holistically, and seeing it not so much from the standpoint of the modern occidental literary-critical concepts as from the point of view of the ancient editors, who neither knew nor cared anything about such concepts. However, while Brownlee recognized the anthological nature of the prophecy and regarded it quite correctly as a complete product of the Isaianic school, he made an unfortunate concession to liberal criticism by the curious assumption that the "Exilic prophet, commonly called Deutero-Isaiah, arose within this school,"[73] and somewhat doubtfully attributed chapters 40–55 to his activity.

Taken at face value this assertion would imply that there were still members of an Isaianic school in existence up to one hundred and fifty years after the death of the master, despite the influential career of Jeremiah, the catastrophe of the exile for the inhabitants of the southern kingdom, the tribulation of the early stages of captivity in Babylonia, and the fundamentally important ministry of Ezekiel. Furthermore, it would endeavor to assert that the Palestinian Isaianic tradition received a new burst of life in Babylonia during the period of the exile with the labors of an "unknown prophet" who added to the prophetic corpus in the spirit of the long-deceased master in language seldom paralleled for its beauty and majesty of expression, but whose theology bore little relationship to the crucial issues of the day as exemplified in the thought and teaching of Ezekiel.

The mention of this alleged exilic "Second Isaiah" is the only weak point in Brownlee's theory, which in other respects accords with what is known of ancient Near Eastern scribal methodology in this regard. Brownlee, unfortunately, fell into the common critical error of treating the Isaianic prophetic anthology in a different manner from that of other literary prophets, and did not appear to realize that, at least on *prima facie* grounds, it would also be possible to posit Deutero-Jeremiahs, Deutero-Ezekiels, and the like.

Furthermore, he failed to observe that the traditions enshrined in chapters 40–55 reflect a Palestinian rather than a Babylonian background of life and religion. Had the author of this material been living in the exilic period, he could hardly have failed to express himself concretely and specifically concerning the social, moral, and religious conditions of that era. In point of fact, the nature of the prophetic standpoint is such that anything more than the most general of allusions to the exile is virtually precluded. Whatever inkling Isaiah may have had of the occurrence of the exile itself, there is no evidence whatever in the prophecy that details of the conditions under which the exiles would live and serve were revealed to him. A careful reading of chapters 40–55

[73] *Ibid.*, p. 253.

will show that the prophet possessed no special information about such conditions that could not already have been the common property of his day and age.

On the other hand, however, the work of a truly exilic prophet whose identity is clearly known, namely Ezekiel, gives every indication of immediate and continuing contact with the exilic situation, ranging from the typically composite Babylonian beasts of the first vision (Ezek. 1:5 ff.) to the use of building terminology describing the foundation and summit of Babylonian staged towers or *ziggurats* (Ezek. 43:14f.). Of particular interest in this connection is that the theological position of Ezekiel has little in common either with the eighth-century prophets or with the so-called Second Isaiah. Instead, Ezekiel reflected the thought of Jeremiah, by whom, apparently, he had been greatly influenced. In consequence he was able to introduce the vastly important theological concept of the New Covenant about which Jeremiah had taught (Jer. 31:31ff.), thus making a break with the older corporate ideas of sin and forgiveness.

By contrast, the so-called "unknown prophet of the exile" has no knowledge of the New Covenant and its implications. In two instances in Isaiah where the concept of Covenant was mentioned (Isa. 42:6; 49:8), it was spoken of in connection with the work of the Servant as a "covenant of the people." In Isaiah 54:10 it was merely referred to in a general way as "my peaceful covenant," which was undergirded by ideas of divine compassion. While critical scholars have invariably tended to evade the issue, it still remains a fact that the relationship of the work of Deutero-Isaiah to the accredited ministry and writings of Ezekiel constitutes one of the greatest difficulties in the way of the Second Isaiah theory, and it is of such magnitude that it has never been resolved to the satisfaction of all concerned by any liberal scholar.

Any attempt in this direction would have to take cognizance of Ezekiel 2:5, which suggests that there was no other prophet in the community who was issuing the same warnings as Ezekiel. Again, in Ezekiel 22:30 God was represented as stating to the prophet that He had sought for a man to stand in the breach, but had discovered nobody. This would be distinctly surprising if the "unknown prophet of the exile" was actually living in the community at that time, and inspiring his hearers to new heights of spiritual endeavor by means of his lucid and stimulating utterances, as credited to him by the activities of critical scholars. Surely under such circumstances he would have been ideally suited for whatever tasks God had for him to perform on behalf of the dispirited exiles. The evidence furnished by Ezekiel, however, points to quite a different situation.

It has long been a commonplace conservative objection to liberal claims about Deutero-Isaiah that if this unknown individual had actually been all that was claimed for him by Duhm and others, and is to be regarded as one of the greatest, if not the most notable of the Hebrew prophets, it would indeed be most surprising if every trace of this eminent and talented man had been so completely erased from Hebrew tradition that not even his name had managed to survive. This objection has been raised many times since the days of J. A. Alexander, and over the generations it has gained rather than lost in its cogency. In fact, it is so telling that to date no convincing rebuttal has been forthcoming from critical circles, and in the nature of the case it appears highly improbable that one ever will emerge.

Other difficulties encountered in connection with this "unknown prophet of the exile" made themselves felt with regard to his specific literary abilities and also to his actual domicile. Both liberal and conservative scholars were unanimous in their view that chapters 40–66 were the most exalted and remarkable literary achievements of any of the Hebrew prophets. Quite aside from the fact that it would be without parallel for the name of such an incomparable individual to pass from human memory, it would also be inconceivable for his work to become the mere appendix to that of an inferior Palestinian prophet, however much the latter may have been admired by the former, and that for two thousand years his writings should have been uniformly regarded by Jewish tradition as being the work of this inferior prophet.

As Raven pointed out, it is even more improbable that sections of material emerging from a later period should have been intermingled with the writings of Isaiah by an incompetent editor to the point where it has become extremely difficult to extricate the true work of the prophet and arrange it in something like chronological order.[74] Furthermore, it is incredible that the Jews, with their almost superstitious veneration of sacred records, would have permitted them to be mutilated in such a way.

Although critics were unable to arrive at reasonably firm conclusions regarding the identity of the "unknown prophet of the exile," they made strenuous attempts to locate him geographically. While the majority of the earlier liberal scholars regarded Babylonia as his home, Causse, following Duhm, held that he lived in the general Lebanon region.[75] Ewald, Marti, and Hölscher regarded Egypt as his residence;[76] Cobb, Maynard, Buttenwieser, Torrey, Mowinckel, Finkelstein, Blank, and others rather prudently located him in Judaea.[77] The latter group

[74] J. H. Raven, OT Introduction, p. 195.

[75] A. Causse, Les dispersés d'Israel (1929), p. 35.

[76] H. Ewald, A History of Israel (1874), V, p. 42. K. Marti, Jesaja (1900), p. xv. G. Hölscher, Die Profeten, pp. 321f., 373.

[77] W. H. Cobb, JBL, XXVII (1908), pp. 48ff. J. A. Maynard, JBL, XXXVI (1917), pp. 213ff., The Birth of Judaism (1928), pp. 25ff. M. Buttenwieser, JBL, XXXVIII (1919), pp. 94ff. C. C. Torrey, The Second Isaiah: A New Interpretation, p. 53. S. Mowinckel, ZAW, XLIX (1931), p. 244. L. Finkelstein (ed.), The Pharisees (1938), II, p. 629. S. H. Blank, HUCA, XV (1940), p. 29 n. 55.

tacitly recognized that the author of chapters 40–55 did not manifest that degree of familiarity with the land or religion of Babylonia that could normally be expected of one who was supposed to be living among the Hebrew exiles. What they did not concede, however, was the fact that such ignorance of detail regarding Babylonian life indicated that the standpoint of the prophet in relationship to the exiles was essentially ideal rather than real.

If this unknown exilic individual were to be regarded as anything more than a sheer figment of the critical imagination, it would be necessary to establish his place in the history of Hebrew thought and religious institutions. Despite his alleged exalted abilities he was evidently completely unknown to Ezekiel and Daniel, and neither his name nor his theological contributions played any noticeable part in the representations of the post-exilic period by Haggai and Zechariah on the one hand, or by Ezra and Nehemiah on the other. The facts of the situation are that it was the thought of Ezekiel that influenced the nature of both Temple and synagogue worship in post-exilic Judaea, and the enthusiastic application of the Mosaic Torah by Ezra that gave Judaism its characteristic stamp of legalism.

The preoccupations of Deutero-Isaiah with the kind of idolatry current in pre-exilic Canaan would obviously be anachronistic in such a political structure as the post-exilic theocracy, for above everything else the experience of the exile had made Baalism a completely dead issue. Certainly his contemporaries were evidently so little aware of his existence that from the very beginning they ascribed to Isaiah the work usually credited by critical writers to Deutero-Isaiah. Again, it can only be concluded that if this unknown exilic prophet was as outstanding as commonly claimed, it seems both unlikely and unreasonable to imagine that his name would be lost to history at the time when the exiles were placing great value upon their religious traditions, and that his magnificent literary productions would be subsumed under the work of an earlier, and presumably less notable, individual.

The fact that there was never any tradition of the Deutero-Isaiah, either among the Jews of the exilic period in Babylonia, or among the returned community of Judaea, makes the hypothesis highly suspect. Isaiah has always been venerated in Jewish tradition as the work of the eighth-century prophet Isaiah ben Amoz. One of the earliest references to this is to be found in Ecclesiasticus 48:24f. where Ben Sira recorded that Isaiah confronted those who mourned in Zion, showing the things that should be to the end of time before they even occurred. Ben Sira makes it clear that in his day—about 200 B.C.—Isaiah was considered to be the author of the entire prophecy.

Further evidence of the Jewish tradition is to be found in the New Testament, where some twenty-one sections of prophecy are specifically referred to the activity of Isaiah, again without any hint of the existence of a "Deutero-Isaiah." Although the present writer is not among those who imagine that the New Testament association of a passage of Scripture with some prominent Old Testament personage is an immediate and final guarantee that the individual concerned wrote all that has been attributed to him, it is nevertheless abundantly clear from the New Testament citations that the tradition of single authorship for the prophecy of Isaiah was firmly established by the first century A.D.

Enough has been said to indicate that the commonly accepted theory of a Deutero-Isaiah exhibits disconcerting weaknesses when subjected to critical investigation. What is particularly unfortunate about the situation is that, as with certain aspects of Pentateuchal studies, something that has always been at best a hypothetical matter has come, over the process of time, to be accepted uncritically in some circles as sober fact. On the basis of a purely scientific and objective investigation there are some who, in the light of the foregoing evidence, would reject the Deutero-Isaiah hypothesis out of hand, and stigmatize it as entirely unworthy of serious consideration. But because of the prolonged time that this theory has flourished, the present writer will content himself with a more moderate, though nonetheless firm position, and will simply return the old Scottish verdict of "not proven."

c. Cyrus. One of the reasons scholars have given for attributing an actual exilic background to chapters 40–55 is the mention by name of the Persian king Cyrus (539-530 B.C.). While some of the passages that have been thought to refer to him are highly debatable, there can be no questioning the fact that his name (כּוֹרֶשׁ) appears in the Hebrew text of Isaiah 44:28 and 45:1. The problem has been met in three principal ways, the first of which, as has already been mentioned, is to treat the material as having been written in the exilic period. This view has been taken by many scholars of conservative persuasion as being based partly upon the lack of regard for a genuinely predictive element of Old Testament prophecy, and a disregard for the fact that both references are obviously to future events, which would certainly preclude anything later than an early exilic date.

The second approach, which is favored by modern conservative scholars such as Allis and Young,[78] considers the references to be prophetic previsions of the work of Cyrus, which in point of fact occurred over a century and a half later. The centrality of Cyrus and his mission as depicted in chapters 40–48 received considerable emphasis, being thought of in past, present, and future contexts. Against this it has to be remembered that he remained a foreign conqueror, and to all intents and purposes a political polytheist, as the Cyrus Cylinder indicates.[79]

[78] O. T. Allis, The Unity of Isaiah, pp. 51ff. YIOT, pp. 237f.
[79] Cf. LAP, p. 191. For a linguistic comparison of the Cyrus Cylinder and the Isaiah Cyrus prophecies see R. Kittel, ZAW, XVIII (1898), pp. 149ff.

While this notable monarch was a divine servant, he was clearly not *the* Servant. Allis in particular accepted rather uncritically the view of Josephus (*AJ*, XI, 1, 1) that Cyrus had actually read Jewish copies of Isaiah that described his destiny as the restorer of Israel, and that he had responded to this by making a serious endeavor to fulfil all that had been written of him.[80] In general, it can be said that the orthodox interpretation depends upon the fact of a proper predictive element in Old Testament prophecy, and on these grounds it is usually repudiated by the majority of liberal scholars, who instead would employ the mention of Cyrus as evidence for an exilic date for the section concerned.

A third approach to the problem, and one which is favored by the present writer, is to regard the references to Cyrus in Isaiah 44:28 and 45:1 as constituting explanatory glosses imposed upon the original text by a post-exilic copyist. It is of some significance that these two occurrences are the only instances in Isaiah where Cyrus is actually mentioned by name, and since they are found in such close proximity it seems most probable that they comprise scribal additions inserted in order to explain what was thought to be the real significance of the prophecy. C. C. Torrey, in reaction against the Trito-Isaiah theory, maintained that if the five or so references to Babylon and Cyrus could be eliminated as later insertions, almost all of chapters 40–66 could then be assigned to a Palestinian milieu.[81] In adopting this position he was the first important scholar to recognize the possibility that the specific references to Cyrus could in fact constitute later glosses.

From a rather different standpoint the same general conclusions were reached by Wordsworth, who saw in the incidence of the title one of the principal reasons for the division of authorship of Isaiah.[82] He maintained that it was incredible for any prophet to denounce idolatry on the one hand, and yet on the other to assign to a worshipper of Marduk the exalted title "my shepherd and anointed." Wordsworth interpreted *lekhôresh* as "the crushed," on the supposition that the original text had read *lekhā rēsh*, and referred it to Hezekiah, then sick unto death for the second time. The "anointed" of Isaiah 45:1 would thus refer to Jerusalem, as represented by its head Hezekiah, the monarch of Davidic line. By this means Wordsworth maintained that it was possible to read the whole of chapters 40–66 against the background of events occurring between 700 and 690 B.C., that is to say, the last years of Hezekiah, subsequent to the invasion of Sennacherib and the beginning of the reign of Manasseh.

[80] Allis, *op. cit.*, p. 57.
[81] C. C. Torrey, *The Second Isaiah: A New Interpretation*, pp. vii-viii.
[82] W. A. Wordsworth, *En Roeh*, pp. 327ff.

Wordsworth subsequently modified his treatment of Isaiah 44:28 on the ground that the LXX reading of *phronein* for *rō'î* presupposed the presence of *yādha'* in the Hebrew manuscript from which the translation was made, a reading that does not occur in the family represented by 1QIsaᵃ. He suggested that both readings resulted from the confusion in the mind of a scribe about 540 B.C, who thought that Isaiah ought to have written *lᵉkhôresh rō'î* instead of a probable *lākh wᵉrāsh dᵉ'î rō'î* addressed to Jerusalem. The passage would then read, "who saith to thee, '(and) the Crushed One acknowledge as my shepherd, and all my delight he shall fulfil'; even saying to Jerusalem, 'she shall be builded; and a palace-Temple she shall be founded.' Thus saith *Yeabe* [Wordsworth's form for יהוה] to his Anointed: to thee and to the Crushed One whom I have held by his right hand . . . !" Thus the word "thee" refers to Jerusalem, while the "crushed" or "impoverished" one was her king, whom the uninitiated would take to be Hezekiah whereas the disciples of Isaiah would interpret it as a reference to the Second Immanuel, the true head and heir.

While the foregoing suggestions rest to a certain extent upon secondary sources, they have considerable merit in their bringing smoothness to what is admittedly an awkward and problematical passage in the Hebrew text. At the same time they eliminate the reference to Cyrus, which, in the view of the present writer, is a rather obvious gloss upon the text. In addition, the emendation focuses attention upon Jerusalem, and gives rich promise of restoration in the future, in harmony with other portions of chapters 40–66. Although the references to the ailing Hezekiah as the "crushed one" are attractive, they raise certain questions as to precisely how nations would be subdued before him in his lifetime. However, the allusion to holding his right hand to subdue nations might well refer to the support which God had given to Hezekiah at an earlier period of his life. Whether the suggestions of Wordsworth are followed or not in any detail, they serve to indicate the possibilities raised by the recognition that the name of Cyrus in Isaiah 44:28 and 45:1 may well constitute a textual gloss.

C. THE MATERIAL OF ISAIAH

Even those scholars who subscribe to divisive theories of authorship can hardly fail to be impressed by the remarkable degree of theological agreement that exists between the earlier chapters (using that term in a juxtapositional rather than a chronological sense) of the prophecy and the work of the alleged Deutero-Isaiah. Thus North finds it permissible to speak of the theology of the latter in terms of emphasis upon God as the sole creator of the universe, the Lord of History, the Saviour of Israel, and, indeed, of all men.[83] Yet according to Oesterley and Robinson, each

[83] C. R. North, *IDB*, II, p. 741.

of these constituted an important element in the doctrinal corpus of the eighth-century prophets, with Amos as a particularly significant example of these tendencies of thought.[84] Again, North concedes that the most obvious link with the earlier chapters of Isaiah is in the concept of God as the "Holy One of Israel," which appears in chapters 1–39 on thirteen occasions, in chapters 40–55 in eleven places, and in chapters 56–66 twice, as contrasted with the remainder of the Old Testament writings, where the expression is only employed in five passages.

Literary resemblances between sections of Isaiah and the thought of the prophet Micah have already been noted, and as such will not be recapitulated. It is of some interest also to observe that there are distinct relationships in form and subject-matter between Isaiah and Jeremiah, particularly where the question of pre-exilic idolatry was concerned (compare Isa. 44:12-15; 46:7 and Jer. 10:1-16; Isa. 48:6 and Jer. 33:3; Isa. 53:7 and Jer. 11:19; Isa. 66:15 and Jer. 4:13). Needless to say, such parallels are embarrassing for the critical view of the origin of Isaiah 40–66, and a number of devious explanations have been offered, none of which is convincing. Similar points of contact are evident in the prophecy of Zephaniah (compare Isa. 47:8-10 and Zeph. 2:15; Isa. 17:1, 7; 66:20 and Zeph. 3:10), which is generally assigned by scholars to the period of Josiah (640-609 B.C.). These matters are of considerable importance in any consideration of the affinity between chapters 1–39 and 40–66 of the prophecy of Isaiah.

Even a casual reading of the text will be sufficient to convey the impression that the author or compilers of Isaiah adhered to a lofty conception of God, and matched it by equally elevated religious phraseology. More than any other Old Testament work the book emphasizes the holiness of the deity (Isa. 1:4; 5:16; 8:14; 10:17; 17:17; 30:11; 37:23; 43:15; 45:11; 48:17 et al.) and the fact that God has associated Himself in a special way with the Hebrew people (Isa. 5:1ff.; 8:13, 18; 11:1, 9; 55:3). This relationship imposed certain requirements upon Israel, prominent among them the sanctification of the Divine Name (Isa. 8:13). In the light of the Covenant relationship, any act of sin on the part of Israel was nothing less than apostasy. Against this high view of sin the prophet denounced the contemporary emphasis upon the peripheral issues of worship (Isa. 1:10; 29:13, et al.), and was especially severe in his condemnation of indulgence in pagan rituals (Isa. 17:7; 31:7; 44:9ff., et al.).

In applying the idea of divine holiness to political affairs, Isaiah sought to prevent the nation from succumbing to the taint of heathendom by discouraging foreign alliances. He appears to have exercised a considerable influence in the royal court, particularly in his earlier years, a fact

---

[84] W. O. E. Oesterley and T. H. Robinson, *Hebrew Religion: Its Origin and Development* (1930), pp. 225ff.

that may have been connected with the (unproved) Jewish tradition that he was of royal blood. He was adamant about the question of a coalition with Egypt (Isa. 14:28ff.; 30:1ff.; 31:1ff., *et al.*), and while his warnings may have been heeded somewhat on occasions, it is quite evident that his contemporaries disagreed with him on fundamental issues (cf. Isa. 7:12; 29:15; 30:1ff.; 36:4ff.).

The message of Isaiah concerning divine judgment involved the Chosen People and their pagan neighbors alike. While Assyria would be the rod of divine anger to be wielded over Israel, when her task was accomplished she too would be punished by destruction (Isa. 10:5-19). In the same way the pride of Babylon would be humbled (Isa. 46—47) after she had served as the instrument of divine wrath upon Judah (Isa. 39:6ff.). While the prophet made it clear that such judgments upon the Chosen People were conditional, and that they could be averted by repentance and complete trust in God, there was little hope from the beginning that the obdurate behavior of the Israelites would undergo a substantial transformation. Yet He who was the Lord of History had a place for His people, even though it involved the drastic discipline of the exile and the rebirth of spirituality in an alien land.

The eschatological vision of the prophet involved a definite concept of salvation in which the faithful remnant would be forgiven (Isa. 40:2; 43:25; 51:2, *et al.*) and restored to a re-created Zion (Isa. 44:28; 45:13). This act of salvation would commence with the liberation of the captives from exile, a mighty act that would be even more significant than the release of the enslaved Hebrews from Egypt (Isa. 43:16ff.; 48:21; 51:9f., *et al.*). Integral to these events was the assurance of the prophet that the power of the universal creator was more than equal to such an enormous task, the end-result of which would be that all nations would do homage to God (Isa. 45:23).

Little will be said about the theology of the Messiah and the Servant at this juncture, except to observe that the former is by no means neglected in the later chapters of the prophecy. The first thirty-nine chapters are not restricted to considerations of the glory of the Messiah (cf. Isa. 11:1 and 53:2), any more than chapters 40—66 are preoccupied almost exclusively with the sufferings of the Servant (cf. 42:1-7; 53:11-12). The present writer is of the opinion that the Servant oracles have received a disproportionate amount of attention in the theological evaluation of chapters 40—55. Doubtless as a consequence of divisive theories of authorship, scholars have overlooked the presence of another servant oracle in the prophecy, occurring in Isaiah 22:20-25. This passage was written in prose, but despite this factor it is nevertheless genuinely oracular in nature, and described the function of the divine servant, whose name was given as Eliakim, the son of Hilkiah. This servant would be endowed with the appurtenances of divine commission, and be given complete authority over the inhabitants of Jerusalem and the house of

Judah. Though standing firmly in the Davidic tradition, the time would come when he would be removed from his high office, and his regime would be seen to collapse about him. This utterance is of some significance because of the discovery at Tell Beit Mirsim and Beth-shemesh of three sixth-century scarab-type seals bearing the inscription "belonging to Eliakim, intendant of Joiachin." The office of steward had existed since the time of Solomon in both the northern and southern kingdoms (cf. 1 Kgs. 4:6; 16:9; 18:3; 2 Kgs. 10:5). The narratives in Kings make it clear that Eliakim was the state official who held conversations with the Assyrian staff-officer who was threatening Jerusalem with destruction (2 Kgs. 18:18ff.; Isa. 36:3ff.). Subsequently Eliakim was sent in mourning by Hezekiah to inform Isaiah of the trend of events (2 Kgs. 19:2; Isa. 37:2). Eliakim evidently failed in his high vocation as the servant of God, and the reference to the "burden" in Isaiah 22:25 might imply that considerations of nepotism occasioned his downfall.

The final ten chapters of the prophecy deal with the ethical prerequisites for the redemption of Israel, and the glories that would be experienced in the day of regeneration and renewal in Zion. God was represented in these utterances as a living being who is terrible in anger (Isa. 59:16ff.; 63:1ff.), but who loves to show mercy to His people and delights in the glories of Zion. Even under these comparatively favorable conditions the prophet felt compelled to draw a sharp distinction between those of the Chosen People who reciprocated the acts of divine love and those who repudiated the deity and disobeyed His revealed will (Isa. 57:1; 65:13ff.; 66:5). In view of this he urged humility upon the Israelites (Isa. 66:2), and indicated that the practicing of righteousness involved much more than a purely formal attitude towards the requirements of the Law (Isa. 58:2ff.).

❀   ❀   ❀   ❀   ❀

The Hebrew text of Isaiah has, on the whole, been very well preserved, despite the presence of certain obscurities and corruptions. While the LXX version is often useful in elucidating certain difficulties, it is itself somewhat free in its renderings, and appears to depend in many instances upon a rather different type of text from that used by the Massoretes.[85] The Qumran scrolls included two Isaiah manuscripts, one of which (1QIsa[a]) was complete, and presented many readings which were different from those of the MT. On examination, however, the variations were found to be mostly occasioned by considerations of orthography,[86] although some, as for example 1QIsa[a] 65:3, may be

---

[85] Cf. R. R. Ottley, *Isaiah According to the Septuagint* (1904), I; (1906), II; A. Zillessen, *ZAW*, XXII (1902), pp. 238ff., XXIII (1903), pp. 49ff.; S. Mowinckel, *ZAW*, XLIX (1931), pp. 87ff., 242ff.

[86] Cf. M. Burrows, *BASOR*, No. 111 (1948), pp. 16ff., No. 113 (1949), pp. 24ff.; *JBL*, LXVIII (1949), pp. 195ff.

nearer than the MT to the original tradition in reflecting contemporary pagan practices.

The other Isaiah scroll (1QIsa[b]), which was fragmentary, preserved the Massoretic tradition in an almost identical form. In 1QIsa[a] there is evidence of a number of characteristic scribal errors; fortunately they are not serious as such.[87] Its orthography exhibited certain phonetic peculiarities that were less prominent in the MT and in 1QIsa[b], and point to some deviation from the tradition of the early pre-Christian period. This scroll apparently furnished a contemporary phonetic spelling that was designed to facilitate reading without actually altering the traditional pronunciation. By contrast, the fragmentary scroll 1QIsa[b] followed the older form of spelling used in the post-exilic period. Quite apart from their great importance in reflecting the transitional phases of Hebrew orthography,[88] these manuscripts are of immense value because they indicate the way in which Hebrew was pronounced just prior to the Christian era.

Several readings from 1QIsa[a] were incorporated into the RSV rendering of Isaiah by the revision committee.[89] While some of these represent very little improvement upon the traditional MT, there can be no doubt that the reading preserved in 1QIsa[a] 21:8 was far superior to that of the Massoretes. As rendered by the AV, this text spoke of a watchman awaiting the arrival of a messenger from the east, and then without warning it suddenly introduced the irrelevant figure of a wild beast:

> And he cried, A lion: My lord, I stand continually upon the watchtower. . . .

which when corrected by reference to 1QIsa[a] read:

> Then the seer cried: Upon a watchtower I stand. . . .[90]

Another reading preserved by both Isaiah scrolls, but which was ignored by the RSV, is worthy of mention. Isaiah 53:11 (MT), as rendered by the AV and RV reads:

> He shall see of the travail of his soul and shall be satisfied. . . .

The LXX version inserted the word "light" before the second verb in the sentence, and this change was confirmed independently by the Qumran scrolls. Thus the passage should read:

> After the travail of his soul he will see light, he will be satisfied. . . .

---

[87] Cf. W. H. Brownlee, *The Meaning of the Qumrân Scrolls for the Bible,* pp. 156ff.

[88] Cf. M. Burrows, *The Dead Sea Scrolls,* pp. 109ff.

[89] These were Isa. 3:24; 7:1; 14:4, 30; 15:9; 21:8; 23:2; 33:8; 45:2, 8; 49:17, 24; 51:19; 56:12; 60:19; cf. M. Burrows, *The Dead Sea Scrolls,* p. 305.

[90] "Seer" (הראה) is employed as synonymous with "watchman" (21:6), the latter probably being Isaiah himself.

Unlike Orlinsky, who regarded the large Isaiah scroll as worthless for the study of the pre-Massoretic Hebrew textual tradition,[91] the majority of scholars have been impressed by the manner in which it has preserved certain superior readings, while at the same time lending firm support to the Massoretic tradition. Even the inferior variations in the large Isaiah scroll testify indirectly by their very nature to the immense worth of the MT. While the rather interpretative character of certain variants in the scroll will in itself act as a precaution against their wholesale adoption, the importance of the divergent readings is such that it will commend them for serious study on the part of any who expect to publish translations of the text of Isaiah.[92]

Supplementary Literature

Blank, S. H. *Prophetic Faith in Isaiah.* 1958.

Boutflower, C. *The Book of Isaiah (Chapters I-XXXIX) in the Light of the Assyrian Monuments.* 1930.

Gordon, A. R. *The Faith of Isaiah.* 1919.

Kennett, R. H. *The Composition of the Book of Isaiah in the Light of History and Archaeology.* 1910.

Margalioth, R. *The Indivisible Isaiah.* 1964.

North, C. R. *Isaiah 40-55: Introduction and Commentary.* 1952.

————. *The Second Isaiah.* 1964.

van der Ploeg, J. S. *Les Chants du Serviteur de Jahvé dans la Seconde Partie du Livre d'Isaïe.* 1936.

Schelhaas, J. *De Lijdende Knecht des Heeren.* 1933.

Steinmann, J. *Le Prophète Isaïe.* 1950.

---

[91] H. M. Orlinsky, *JQR*, XLIII (1952-53), p. 33.

[92] For a study of certain readings see W. H. Brownlee, *The Meaning of the Qumrân Scrolls for the Bible,* pp. 170ff.

III. THE BOOK OF JEREMIAH

A. NAME AND OUTLINE

The book of Jeremiah was named after the celebrated seventh-century prophet. In the Hebrew Bible it preceded Ezekiel, although there was a rabbinic tradition that maintained that Jeremiah should stand at the head of the Latter Prophets.[1] In the LXX version Jeremiah occupied the place in which it is normally found in English Bibles, but in the Peshitta the book appeared immediately after the twelve Minor Prophets. The LXX form of the Hebrew name ירמיה or ירמיהו was ʼΙερεμίας, rendered in the Latin versions by *Jeremias*.

The book may be analyzed briefly as follows:

I. Prophecies Against Judah and Jerusalem, ch. 1–25
    A. Inaugural prophetic visions, 1:1-19
    B. Oracles of the early ministry, 2:1–6:30
    C. Criticism of cultic worship, 7:1–8:3
    D. Utterances concerning the coming destruction of Judah, 8:4–10:25
    E. Incidents in the life of the prophet, 11:1–12:6
    F. The lament over Israel, 12:7-17
    G. Parables, warnings, and laments, 13:1–15:21
    H. Further threats and miscellaneous utterances, 16:1–17:27
    I. The parable of the potter, 18:1-17
    J. A plot against Jeremiah, 18:18-23
    K. Symbolic acts and imprisonment, 19:1–20:18
    L. Oracles concerning Judah, 21:1–23:8
    M. Utterances concerning the prophets, 23:9-40
    N. Warnings to Judah, 24:1–25:38

II. Biographical Material Connected with Jeremiah, ch. 26–45
    A. Conflicts with religious personages, 26:1–29:32
    B. Pronouncements concerning consolation, 30:1–31:40
    C. The purchase of a field, 32:1-44
    D. Promises of restoration, 33:1-26

---

[1] Cf. H. E. Ryle, *The Canon of the OT* (1895), pp. 237ff.

E. Warnings, 34:1-22
F. The example of the Rechabites, 35:1-19
G. The scrolls of the prophecies, 36:1-32
H. The siege and fall of Jerusalem, 37:1–40:6
I. The regime of Gedaliah, 40:7–41:18
J. The flight to Egypt, 42:1–43:7
K. The prophet in Egypt, 43:8–44:30
L. The oracle to Baruch, 45:1-5
III. Various Oracles Against Foreign Nations, ch. 46–51
IV. Historical Appendix, ch. 52

B. THE BACKGROUND OF JEREMIAH'S PROPHECY

1. Judah among the nations. The work of Jeremiah took place during one of the most critical eras in the history of the Hebrew people. The prophet was born about 640 B.C. in Anathoth, a village some two miles northeast of Jerusalem. Of priestly stock, his father was Hilkiah, who may have been a descendant of Abiathar and possibly the discoverer of the law scroll (cf. 1 Kgs. 2:26).[2] Little is known of the earlier years of the prophet, but he was most probably reared in the tradition of the Torah, as indicated by his earliest poems, in which Jeremiah shows an understanding of the election and Covenant concepts of the Mosaic age. He was also profoundly influenced by the utterances of the eighth-century prophets, and equally revolted by the pagan religious syncretisms prominent in the time of Manasseh.

His call came in 626 B.C.,[3] in the thirteenth year of the reign of Josiah, perhaps the year of the death of Ashurbanipal, the last of the great

[2] For the relationship between Jeremiah and the priestly family of Abiathar see G. Duhm, *Das Buch Jeremia*, pp. 2f.; G. Hölscher, *Die Profeten*, p. 268n.; J. Skinner, *Prophecy and Religion: Studies in the Life of Jeremiah*, p. 19; E. Bruston in *Dictionnaire encyclopédique de la Bible* (1932), I, p. 603; A. Condamin, *Le Livre de Jérémie*, p. v; A. Lods, *Histoire de la littérature hebräique et juive* (1950), p. 405; E. A. Leslie, *Jeremiah, Chronologically Arranged, Translated, and Interpreted* (1954), p. 20; B. W. Anderson, *Understanding the OT* (1957), p. 300. Those who have supposed that Hilkiah was the High Priest who found the "book of the law" in the Temple included Clement of Alexandria, *PG*, VIII, col. 849; J. W. Colenso, *The Pentateuch and the Book of Joshua Critically Examined* (1879), VII, p. 259; F. C. Jean, *Jérémie, sa théologie, sa politique* (1913), p. 5. Doubts about this view were expressed by C. W. E. Nägelsbach, *Jeremia* (1868), p. x; T. K. Cheyne, *Jeremiah, His Life and Times* (1904), p. 19n.; P. Volz, *Der Prophet Jeremia* (1928), pp. x-xi. For the theory that Jeremiah was not of priestly stock see T. J. Meek, *The Expositor*, 8th ser., XXV (1923), pp. 215ff., followed by J. P. Hyatt, *JBL*, LIX (1940), p. 511, *IB*, III, p. 795. With this contrast A. Haldar, *Associations of Cult Prophets Among the Ancient Semites*, pp. 112, 121.

[3] For a date about 614-612 B.C. see J. P. Hyatt, *JBL*, LIX (1940), p. 512, *JNES*, I (1942), pp. 156ff., *IB*, V, pp. 779f., arrived at by rejecting Jer. 1:2. Cf. the reply of H. H. Rowley, *Studies in OT Prophecy Presented to T. H. Robinson*, p. 158 and in his *Men of God*, pp. 136ff.

Assyrian rulers.[4] During the four decades in which Jeremiah prophesied, momentous events took place in the ancient Near East, beginning the very year that the prophet received his call. The death of Ashurbanipal was the signal for Babylon to assert her independence under Nabopolassar (626-605 B.C.), and this, along with the resurgence of vitality in Egypt under Psammetichus (664-610 B.C.), was to have an important bearing upon the course of life in the southern kingdom of Judah.

It was for this time of upheaval and crisis that Jeremiah was called as the servant of God to rebuke, warn, console, and exhort his countrymen, thereby preparing them to some extent for the tribulations of the future. He evidently felt his personal inadequacies quite keenly, and although the picture presented by Oesterley and Robinson[5] seems to be a little overdrawn in this respect, there can be no doubt that his description of himself as an infant (Jer. 1:6) was meant to convey his sense of personal spiritual and social immaturity.

During the period between the time of his call and the religious reformation of 621 B.C. Jeremiah was primarily concerned with denouncing contemporary religious corruption and proclaiming imminent invasion from the north. Considerable discussion has been provoked by attempts to identify the invaders whose impending activities claimed the attention of the prophet. Following Herodotus, many scholars associated them with the Scythians who lived beyond the Caucasus, but this view was contested by Wilke, who argued that the invading host from the north of which Jeremiah spoke (cf. Zeph. 1:2ff.; Joel 2:20) constituted the armies of Nebuchadnezzar, and not the Scythian hordes.[6]

---

[4] This date is approximate. For discussions see A. Poebel, *JNES*, II (1943), pp. 88f.; W. H. Dubberstein, *JNES*, III (1944), pp. 38ff.; F. M. Cross and D. N. Freedman, *JNES* XII (1953), pp. 56ff. K. A. Kitchen and T. C. Mitchell, *NBD*, p. 220, dated it 627 B.C., following Albright, *BPAE*, p. 79.

[5] *IBOT*, pp. 309f.

[6] Herodotus, *Historiae*, I, 103ff. Following the Scythian interpretation are H. Venema, *Commentarius ad librum Jeremiae* (1765), I, pp. 142f.; C. F. Cramer, *Skythische Denkmähler in Palästina* (1777), pp. 22f.; J. G. Eichhorn, *Die hebräischen Propheten* (1819), II, p. 9; F. Hitzig, *Jeremia* (1841), p. 33; S. Davidson, *Introduction to the OT* (1863), III, p. 92; B. Stade, *Geschichte des Volkes Israel* (1889 ed.), I, pp. 643ff.; R. Smend, *Lehrbuch der alttestamentlichen Religionsgeschichte* (1899), p. 244; B. Duhm, *Das Buch Jeremia* (1905), pp. 82ff.; S. R. Driver, *The Book of the Prophet Jeremiah* (1908), p. 21; A. S. Peake, *Jeremiah* (1908), pp. 20f.; C. Steuernagel, *Lehrbuch der Einleitung in das AT* (1912), pp. 544f.; H. P. Smith, *The Religion of Israel* (1914), pp. 163ff.; J. A. Bewer, *The Literature of the OT* (1922), p. 143, *The Prophets* (1955), p. 185; J. M. Powis Smith, *The Prophets and Their Times* (1925), pp. 106ff.; D. G. Hogarth, *Cambridge Ancient History* (1925), III, pp. 145f.; C. F. Kent, *The Growth and Contents of the OT* (1926), p. 117; T. H. Robinson, *A History of Israel* (1932), I, pp. 412ff.; *PIOT*, pp. 482, 488, but compare Pfeiffer in *Dictionnaire encyclopédique de la Bible* (1932), II, p. 648; B. D. Eerdmans, *The*

On the basis of a late date for the first ten chapters of the prophecy, C. C. Torrey identified the northern foe with Alexander the Great,[7] but Hyatt adopted a more conservative position in regarding the enemy as the Chaldeans and Medes who destroyed Nineveh in 612 B.C.[8] In the absence of compelling evidence to the contrary it appears unwise to reject entirely the tradition of a Scythian invasion of Palestine as preserved by Herodotus, or to suppose that none of the early poems was the result of such an emotional stimulus. Whether the relevant material in chapters 4–6 and 8–10, which may have referred originally to the Scythians, was later rewritten by Jeremiah and made to apply to the subsequent Babylonian invasion, as maintained by Pfeiffer, Muilenburg, and others,[9] is quite uncertain, since as Hyatt has pointed out, such a supposition hardly does justice to the poems themselves or to the methods of the prophet.[10]

In 621 B.C., during the eighteenth year of his reign, Josiah initiated a systematic reformation of religion and morals in the southern kingdom (2 Kgs. 23:3ff.).[11] This was provoked by the discovery of a law-book

Religion of Israel (1947), p. 190; I. G. Matthews, *The Religious Pilgrimage of Israel* (1947), p. 146; F. James, *Personalities of the OT* (1947), p. 307; J. Paterson, *The Goodly Fellowship of the Prophets* (1948), p. 99; O. Eissfeldt, *Einleitung in das AT* (1956 ed.), pp. 421, 521; *ETOT*, p. 358; B. W. Anderson, *Understanding the OT*, pp. 301ff. Wilke, who rejected the view, *Alttestamentliche Studien R. Kittel dargebracht* (1913), pp. 222ff., was supported by E. F. C. Rosenmüller, *Scholia in Vetus Testamentum*, VIII (1826), p. 137; C. F. Keil, *Jeremia und Klagelieder* (1872), pp. 77ff.; R. P. Smith, *Speaker's Bible* (1875), V, p. 314; F. Bleek–J. Wellhausen, *Einleitung in das AT* (1878 ed.), p. 359; C. von Orelli, *Jesaja und Jeremia* (1891), pp. 222f.; A. Condamin, *Le Livre de Jérémie* (1920), pp. 61ff.; P. Volz, *Das Buch Jeremia* (1921), pp. 57f.; J. Meinhold, *Einführung in das AT* (1932 ed.), p. 231; F. Nötscher, *Das Buch Jeremias* (1934); J. P. Hyatt, *JBL*, LIX (1940), pp. 499ff.; J. Bright, *JBL*, LXX (1951), p. 28n., *Interpretation*, IX (1955), p. 275, *BHI*, p. 293; J. Steinmann, *Le Prophète Jérémie* (1952), pp. 58f.; F. Horst, *Die Zwölf Kleinen Propheten* (1954 ed.), p. 195. Those who were doubtful about the Scythian interpretation included A. Bentzen, *Introduction to the OT*, II, pp. 121f.; A. S. Kapelrud, *Svenskt Bibliskt Uppslagsverk*, II (1952), col. 1190; K. Elliger, *Die Zwölf Kleinen Propheten* (1956), II, p. 56; C. Kuhl, *The OT: Its Origins and Composition* (1961), p. 185.

[7] C. C. Torrey, *JBL*, LVI (1937), pp. 208f., *Vom AT, Marti Festschrift* (1925), pp. 281ff.

[8] J. P. Hyatt, *JBL*, LIX (1940), pp. 499ff.; cf. H. G. May, *JBL*, LXI (1942), p. 146n.; *YIOT*, p. 232.

[9] *PIOT*, pp. 494f.; J. Muilenburg, *IDB*, II, p. 826.

[10] J. P. Hyatt, *IB*, V, p. 779.

[11] For the view that in Jer. 11:1ff. the prophet was advocating the Josianic reform see F. Giesebrecht, *Das Buch Jeremia* (1907), pp. 65ff.; W. W. von Baudissin, *HDB*, IV, p. 91; S. R. Driver, *The Book of the Prophet Jeremiah*, p. 65; C. Steuernagel, *Einleitung in das AT*, p. 546; E. Bruston, *Dictionnaire encyclopédique de la Bible*, I, p. 605; *PIOT*, pp. 493ff.; R. Augé, *Jeremias* (1950), pp. 17, 117; H. Cazelles, *Recherches de Science Religieuse*, XXXIX (1951), pp. 5ff.; B. W. Anderson, *Understanding the OT*, p. 318.

during the course of renovations to the Temple fabric. Although Jeremiah was still not a public figure at the time apparently, since it was Huldah the prophetess (2 Kgs. 22:14) who was consulted regarding the validity of the discovery, it was not long afterwards that Jeremiah was commanded by God to proclaim the contents of this covenant in Jerusalem (Jer. 11:1ff.).

Precisely what the law-scroll contained has been a matter of debate for many decades. Adherents of the Graf-Wellhausen approach to Old Testament study have commonly imagined it to have constituted the book of Deuteronomy, which had supposedly been written twenty years or so earlier, and was being foisted upon the populace for the first time. Jewish tradition, on the other hand, held that it comprised the entire Pentateuch,[12] although this seems unlikely in view of the fact that 2 Chronicles 34:30 speaks of the work as the "Book of the Covenant," and it could apparently be read within a reasonably short time. Other considerations regarding the nature and content of this work have been discussed in another chapter, and accordingly will not be recapitulated here. There can be little doubt, however, that the scroll was recognized at once as being both ancient and authoritative, and venerated as a lost and forgotten sacred book which had been miraculously recovered.

Apart from the possible indications of prophetic enthusiasm for the reforms of Josiah (Jer. 11:1-8), Jeremiah contains no further references to the last decade or so of the reign of Josiah. Eight years prior to the king's death, the Babylonians under Nabopolassar allied with the Medes against Assyria and commenced a systematic reduction of strongpoints throughout the empire. The capital city Ashur fell in 614 B.C., and after two further years of bitter fighting came the collapse of mighty Nineveh. All other military resistance was crushed in 610 B.C. with the conquest of Harran, which had been occupied by the remnant of the Assyrian army.

With the fall of Assyria the pharaoh Necho (610-594 B.C.), successor of Psammetichus, asserted the military might of Egypt and marched into the Palestinian coastal plain. From the Babylonian Chronicle it is clear that Necho was advancing to the aid of the beleaguered Assyrians in Harran. However, Josiah did not want Necho to assist the hereditary enemies of Judah, so he attempted to stop him at Megiddo. When he was assassinated in 609 B.C. Jehoahaz II, the son of Josiah, was made king by popular demand, but after three months he was deposed by Necho (who continued to interfere in the internal affairs of Judah) and was replaced on the throne by his elder brother Jehoiakim. Necho then

---

[12] The traditional Jewish view has been largely supported by C. H. Gordon, *GBB*, p. 293. For the modern theory that it contained part or all of Deuteronomy see H. H. Rowley, *Studies in OT Prophecy Presented to T. H. Robinson*, pp. 157ff., *Men of God*, p. 161.

imposed heavy tribute on Judah, requiring the southern kingdom to pay one hundred talents of silver and one talent of gold (2 Kgs. 23:31ff.).

During the reign of King Jehoiakim (609-597 B.C.) the fortunes of the prophet Jeremiah were at a low ebb. This situation was precipitated by the so-called "temple address" (Jer. 7:1–8:12), delivered about 609 B.C., in which Jeremiah castigated the people of Judah for their superstitious trust in the Temple at Jerusalem as a source of deliverance in time of crisis. When he prophesied that God would destroy the Temple as He had previously obliterated the shrine at Shiloh, and cast the people of Judah out of His sight, he provoked an angry uprising that almost cost him his life. His earlier experience at Anathoth (Jer. 11:18-23) was thus repeated, and might well have daunted one who was less conscious of his inspiration and mission.

From the nature of his prophetic utterances it is clear that Jeremiah perceived the dangers inherent in the position that Judah occupied in the contemporary international struggle for power. The Assyrian empire had disintegrated, and its place in Mesopotamian affairs had been taken by a powerful Babylonian regime. Egypt had once more asserted its claim to a voice in the political doings of the Near East after more than a century of decline, and appeared certain to challenge Babylonian military might sooner or later. If Judah was to become an ally of Egypt she would naturally suffer severe consequences if an Egyptian defeat took place, or if the Babylonians decided to invade southern Palestine and use it as a base for future operations against Egypt. Painfully aware of what the future held, Jeremiah foretold that Judah would be engulfed by the might of Babylon under Nebuchadnezzar (Jer. 25:9), and in consequence of this foresight he made dramatic, if unavailing, attempts to influence the foreign policy of his country so that Judah might become a vassal of Babylon, and thus be spared the horrors and agonies of destruction (Jer. 27:6ff.).

The military situation came to a head in 605 B.C., when Necho marched to the Euphrates, and Nabopolassar sent his son Nebuchadnezzar II with an army to fight against him. A decisive battle took place at Carchemish, in which the Egyptians were routed and the balance of power in the Near East fell firmly into Babylonian hands. Since all routes to the Egyptian border were now under Babylonian control, it was merely a question of time before the victory at Carchemish was implemented by a further advance against Egypt. It was this consideration that prompted Jeremiah to urge submission to Babylonian suzerainty, and when Ashkelon fell to Nebuchadnezzar in 604 B.C., the situation became more acute than ever (cf. Jer. 47:5ff.; Zeph. 2:4ff.).

King Jehoiakim had little time either for the prophet or his message (Jer. 26:20ff.; 9:26), for his religious inclinations were idolatrous, and this, combined with his selfishness and personal vanity, contributed to the misfortunes of the southern kingdom.[13] He was essentially a political opportunist, as his vacillating policies with regard to Egypt and Babylon clearly indicate. Having been a Babylonian tributary (2 Kgs. 24:1) for some three years, Jehoiakim rebelled in a desperate bid for independence, despite the warnings of Jeremiah (Jer. 22:18) as to the outcome of such a policy. Babylonian retribution occurred with the invasion of Judah by Chaldean forces in 597 B.C. and the initial attack upon Jerusalem. Jehoiakim died just prior to the capture of the city, perhaps as the result of a court uprising, and was succeeded by his son Jehoiachin, who capitulated to the Babylonians and was taken captive to Babylon along with other exiles.

Valuable information has been furnished with regard to this crucial period of Hebrew history by the cuneiform material containing the Chronicles of the Chaldean kings, which was published in 1956 by D. J. Wiseman of the British Museum. Since the significance of this material has been discussed previously, it will merely be recorded at this juncture as being of the greatest importance for supplementing what is already known from Biblical sources about the events of this particular era.

After the attack of 597 B.C., Nebuchadnezzar established Zedekiah (Mattaniah), the uncle of Jehoiachin (2 Kgs. 24:17), as a puppet ruler in Judah. He thereby inadvertently sealed the doom of the southern kingdom, for Zedekiah was essentially a weak and vacillating person. Despite an oath of allegiance to Babylon he was unable to prevent intrigue with Egypt, particularly among the members of the new ruling class in Judah. The latter were continually urging him to ally with the Egyptians, and the accession of the pharaoh Hophra in 589 B.C., who himself had political ambitions in Palestine, added impetus to this movement, despite the most solemn warnings from Jeremiah (cf. Jer. 37:6ff.; 38:14ff.).

When Zedekiah ultimately decided to rely upon Egyptian support and revolted against Babylon, the Chaldean armies again swept down upon southern Palestine in 587 B.C. The small Syrian states collapsed before the onslaught of Babylonian might, as Jeremiah had foretold (Jer. 25:9), and Nebuchadnezzar besieged Lachish and Azekah. Vivid illustration of the conditions of the time as reflected in Jeremiah has been provided by the discovery of the Lachish ostraca in 1935 and 1938. These documents clearly indicate the state of crisis that had overtaken Jerusalem, and show the extent to which the morale of the populace had been weakened both by internal dissension and by the threat of invasion.

When Jerusalem finally felt the weight of Babylonian might in 587 B.C., Jeremiah advised Zedekiah to surrender, as, indeed, he had urged him previously (cf. Jer. 21:1ff.; 34:1ff.; 37:3ff.; 38:14ff.). When this counsel was rejected the prophet attempted to leave the city, but was accused of deserting to the enemy and was thrown into prison. Although

---

[13] J.G.S.S. Thomson, NBD, p. 606; J. Bright, Jeremiah (1965), p. xlviif.

Zedekiah subsequently sought his advice (Jer. 38:14ff.), the doom of Judah was sealed, and in 587 B.C. the second captivity took place, during which the Temple was pillaged and the land of Judah was ravaged. Nebuchadnezzar treated the prophet Jeremiah with great deference, and when Gedaliah was appointed governor of Judah, Jeremiah joined him at Mizpah (Jer. 40:1). When the governor was murdered, the remnant at Mizpah fled to Egypt, taking Jeremiah along with them (Jer. 42:1ff.). He passed his final days with Baruch his secretary at Tahpanhes in Egypt, where he prophesied the conquest of Egypt by Nebuchadnezzar (Jer. 43:8ff.).

2. *The personality of Jeremiah.* The personality of Jeremiah is one of the most clearly marked of all the Old Testament prophetic figures. Of his tender and emotional temperament[14] there can be little doubt, as indicated by his deep love for his people (Jer. 8:18ff.), his intercession for them in a time of great dearth (Jer. 14:1ff.), and his lamentation over their doom (Jer. 9:1; 13:17; 14:17). While a great many of his oracles throw light upon his emotional state, those which are sometimes incorrectly styled "confessional"[15] are particularly revealing. They show that the life of the prophet was characterized by pronounced tension, occasioned by the pressure of his natural desires and inclinations on the one hand, and by his compelling sense of divine vocation on the other. The latter was so overwhelming as to compensate more than adequately for the natural reticence, sensitivity, and introspection that were such marked features of his nature. It was this kind of inner conflict that furnished his life with a tragic content, and depicted him as a man perpetually caught up in emotional turmoil. He was empowered by God in his struggle to overcome his lower self and resist the determined demands of his personality to forsake his divine vocation; yet in all this he was well aware from the start of his complete inability to evade his prophetic function (cf. Jer. 5:14; 15:16; 20:9; 23:29).

Since his message was invariably one of warning, violence, and destruction, the hatred and persecution that he engendered compelled him to find in his God the solace and refuge necessary to sustain him in his prophetic mission. While Jeremiah was occasionally despondent (cf. Jer. 15:10; 20:14ff.; 20:7), he was also caught up in periods of spiritual exaltation (cf. Jer. 2:13; 15:16; 20:11). The nature of his office precluded

---

[14] J. Skinner, *Prophecy and Religion: Studies in the Life of Jeremiah*, p. 21.

[15] Jer. 10:23; 11:18ff.; 15:10ff.; 17:9ff.; 18:18ff.; 20:7ff.; cf. 1:4ff.; 6:27ff.; 8:18ff.; 16:1ff.; *et al.* On these passages see W. Baumgartner, *Die Klagegedichte des Jeremia* (1917); J. A. Skinner, *Prophecy and Religion: Studies in the Life of Jeremiah*, pp. 201ff.; G. A. Smith, *Jeremiah* (1923), pp. 317ff.; E. A. Leslie, *The Intimate Papers of Jeremiah* (1953), *Jeremiah, Chronologically Arranged, Translated and Interpreted*, pp. 137ff.; G. M. Behler, *Les Confessions de Jérémie* (1959); B. Gemser, *VT*, suppl. vol. III (1955), p. 134; H. H. Rowley, *Men of God*, pp. 155ff.; *et al.*

participation in the more normal activities of human society, including marriage (Jer. 16:1ff.), leading him to the conclusion that his life must be pursued apart from his fellow men under the guiding hand of God (Jer. 15:17). In the event this was by no means an unmixed blessing, for in the day-to-day existence of Jeremiah the Old Testament ideal of spiritual communion with God reached its finest stage of development. It was this which not merely enabled the prophet to withstand the corrosive effects of loneliness, despair, failure, and futility, but made of him a symbol of courage in the pursuit of his vocation. Through periods of persecution and imprisonment alike he maintained his spiritual integrity, and never once stooped to an act of compromise in the face of danger.

While there were times when Jeremiah was obviously thoroughly irritated by the obdurate attitude of his fellow-countrymen (Jer. 11:20; 12:13; 15:15; 17:18; 18:21), there were also occasions when he interceded eloquently with God on their behalf (Jer. 11:14; 14:11; 17:16; 18:20). In the last analysis, however, Jeremiah was signally successful in that one area of spiritual responsibility that alone is determinative in the sight of God. As Hyatt has expressed it, "he was not called to perfection of character, but to faithfulness: Jeremiah did not fail in his response to that call."[16]

C. THE COMPILATION OF JEREMIAH

1. History of criticism. As with many other literary prophets the material that comprises the extant book of Jeremiah actually represents an anthology of prophetic utterances. In its poetry and prose it exhibits a wide range of literary forms and types, from lyric war poems to the bathos of outpoured grief, from vivid biographical material to the drama of the acted parable. The comparative consistency of literary style in various parts of the book has led scholars to identify the presence of what they deemed to be underlying strata in the work. The modern phase of literary criticism of Jeremiah was initiated in 1901 with the writings of Duhm.[17] While this scholar showed an appreciation of the literary style of the prophet, his views concerning the composition of the book were extreme, in that they limited the authentic oracles of the prophet to those poetic sections written in 3:2 rhythm, and regarded his only prose composition as the letter to the exiles in chapter 29. The study of the book was carried a stage further in 1914 by Mowinckel, who based his observations upon the fact that conflicting indications of order and confusion within the body of the prophecy bespoke the prolonged process of editorial compilation and redaction.[18] He paid particular attention to the prose speeches of Jeremiah, and saw them in their recast

---

[16] J. P. Hyatt, *IB*, V, p. 783; cf. A. B. Davidson, *HDB*, II, p. 576.
[17] B. Duhm, *Das Buch Jeremia* (1901).
[18] S. Mowinckel, *Zur Komposition des Buches Jeremia* (1914).

extant form as being imbued with the teaching and philosophy characteristic of Deuteronomy.[19]

Mowinckel's total analysis recognized three major collections of material, the first of which comprised a composition of authentic prophetic oracles recorded without either prefatory or concluding formulas, and distributed throughout chapters 1–25, with the exception of chapters 7, 19, and possibly 24. The second major group consisted of personal and historical material attributed to the author of the book as a whole, and included sections in chapters 19, 20, 26, 28, 29, 36, 37, 38, and 40–44. Mowinckel did not credit Baruch with the authorship of this work, but assigned it to an Egyptian background in the period 580-480 B.C. after the death of Jeremiah. However, his imaginative theory failed to explain how anyone other than either Jeremiah or Baruch could have been responsible for such material in Egypt; and in view of the animosity that Jeremiah inevitably stirred up among the Jews in Egypt by his condemnation of their way of life (Jer. 44:1ff.), it is not particularly easy to see precisely who else would have been sufficiently sympathetic towards the prophet to have recorded certain rather important phases of his ministry. The third prominent section of material, which proved of particular interest to Mowinckel, comprised a special group of pronouncements of marked Deuteronomic style introduced by the formula, "The word which came to Jeremiah from the LORD." Such utterances occurred in chapters 7, 8, 11, 18, 21, 25, 32, 34, 35, and 44, and all of them were rejected by Mowinckel on the ground that they were unauthentic. While his general analysis of the prophecy was characteristically original, it came in for considerable criticism among scholars because of the position which he had adopted with regard to the second and third collections of source material.

The rather radical view that denied the authenticity of all sections in the prophecy that appeared to be dependent upon or otherwise related to Deuteronomy was supported, among other scholars, by Hölscher and Horst.[20] Some authorities who adhered to the same opinion concerning the date of Deuteronomy as that held by Hölscher took a very different view of the relationship between Deuteronomy and the writings of Jeremiah. Thus Kennett claimed that Deuteronomy was influenced by Jeremiah, and in this he was followed by Schofield.[21] Others, in suggesting that Deuteronomy constituted the basis of the religious reforms in

---

[19] *Ibid.*, pp. 31ff.

[20] G. Hölscher, ZAW, XL (1922), pp. 233ff. F. Horst, ZAW, XLI (1923), pp. 94ff., ZDMG, LXXVII (1923), pp. 220ff.

[21] R. H. Kennett, *JTS*, VI (1905), pp. 182f., VII (1906), pp. 481ff., *The Church of Israel* (1933), pp. 73ff. J. N. Schofield in E. A. Payne (ed.), *Studies in History and Religion* (1942), pp. 49ff.; cf. G. R. Berry, *JBL*, XXXIX (1920), p. 46.

the time of Hezekiah, made it antecedent to Jeremiah by about a century.[22]

Despite differences of opinion regarding relative dating and the question of authenticity of particular sections, the general analysis of the literary sources into sayings and poems, narratives involving Jeremiah, and prophetic speeches with apparent or actual Deuteronomic overtones, was accepted in a commentary on Jeremiah by Rudolph, with certain modifications in matters of detail.[23] A year before Rudolph published his work, Mowinckel himself altered his views to some extent, reflecting the emphases of the Scandinavian school in maintaining that the prose speeches were not to be construed as a separate literary source so much as an intrinsic circle of tradition that perpetuated the sayings of Jeremiah in a Deuteronomistic style to produce an independent parallel transmission of memories about the sayings of the prophet.[24]

While a great many scholars were prepared to follow Mowinckel to a greater or lesser degree in his enumeration of three major classes of material underlying the prophecy, H. G. May adhered to a different view of the composition of Jeremiah.[25] In his opinion Baruch was not the biographer of Jeremiah, but his amanuensis. The extant prophecy was the work of an anonymous biographer who lived no earlier than the first half of the fifth century B.C. He was interested in the return of both Israel and Judah from exile, and had as his primary concern the restoration of the Davidic monarchy. In spite of being influenced by the editor of Deuteronomy and such outstanding figures as the "unknown prophet of the exile," the biographer manifested his own ideological concepts in the course of assembling his material. His biography, according to May, comprised sayings and recollections of Jeremiah, to which he had added speeches and certain other materials of his own composition.

The weakness of this view lies in the fact that it credits far too little of the written material to Jeremiah himself. While the extent of such compositions cannot, of course, be ascertained with any degree of certainty, the prophecy makes it clear that a significant amount of the underlying sources was available in written form in the lifetime of Jeremiah. Again, as Leslie has pointed out,[26] May's view ignores the

---

[22] Cf. C. Steuernagel, *Lehrbuch der Einleitung in das AT* (1912), pp. 191ff.; E. König, *Das Deuteronomium* (1917), pp. 48ff.; G. A. Smith, *The Book of Deuteronomy* (1918), p. cii; E. Sellin, *Introduction to the OT* (1923), pp. 73ff. For a study of the relationship between Deuteronomy and Jeremiah see Rowley, *Studies in OT Prophecy Presented to T. H. Robinson*, pp. 157ff., and his *Men of God*, pp. 160ff.

[23] W. Rudolph, *Jeremia* (1947), pp. xiv ff.

[24] S. Mowinckel, *Prophecy and Tradition* (1946), pp. 62f.

[25] H. G. May, *JBL*, LXI (1942), pp. 139ff.

[26] E. A. Leslie, *Jeremiah, Chronologically Arranged, Translated and Interpreted*, p. 18 n. 4.

significance of Baruch's reputation (Jer. 43:3), and fails to deal adequately with the complexity and diversity of the literary types in the extant prophecy. Whereas May concluded that the biographical narratives could not have come from a contemporary of Jeremiah,[27] Bright took the view that the material in question was essentially trustworthy, and was in fact the work of a contemporary author.[28]

Despite the broad acceptance of Mowinckel's analysis of the material of the book, there are significant divergences in scholarly opinion regarding the whole problem of the composition of Jeremiah. Thus, critics such as Skinner and Volz maintained that the oracles against foreign nations in chapters 46–51 were no part of the work of Jeremiah.[29] On the other hand, Bardtke claimed that the prophet prepared a collection of foreign oracles in which much of this material occurred.[30]

The attempt to reconstruct the scroll dictated to Baruch has constituted yet another approach to the elucidation of the problems concerning the composition of the prophecy. Chapter 36 describes the manner in which Jeremiah dictated his utterances against Judah from the time of Josiah to his secretary Baruch, and the way in which the finished document was destroyed after being read in December 605 B.C. on a fast day. The contents were subsequently dictated anew with additions, and this second scroll apparently constituted the first edition of the extant prophecy.

It must be conceded immediately that the various attempts to determine the contents of the original document have not been impressive in their degree of unanimity. One of the procedures followed was to try to assemble all the oracles that appear to have been delivered prior to 605 B.C., but as Oesterley and Robinson noted, this left room for subjectivity in determining the dates of the various passages.[31] In theory, at all events, three considerations would need to be met, the first of these being that relating to the period extending from 626 to 605 B.C., during which the original material was uttered. The second would involve the nature of the proclamations characteristic of this particular time, and would seem to point to pronouncements of warning and judgment. The final consideration would concern the actual length of the scroll, whose contents were such that it could be read three times in one d⸗

Mowinckel, who was followed to a large extent by Rudolph, favored a reconstruction of the original roll in terms of some of the sayings and poems that he had isolated as Class A of his underlying material. This view was rejected by Robinson and Eissfeldt, who preferred to think

---

[27] H. G. May, *JBL*, LXI (1942), p. 152.

[28] J. Bright, *JBL*, LXX (1951), pp. 15ff.

[29] J. Skinner, *Prophecy and Religion: Studies in the Life of Jeremiah*, p. 239 n. 3. P. Volz, *Der Prophet Jeremia*, pp. 379ff.

[30] H. Bardtke, *ZAW*, LIII (1935), pp. 209ff., LIV (1936), pp. 240ff.

[31] *IBOT*, p. 306.

that the original scroll had contained the speeches which Mowinckel had described as Class C of his collection.[32] Hyatt conjectured that the Baruch scroll contained parts of chapters 1–6 and possibly 8, concluding with 9:1.[33] Eissfeldt also suggested another set of passages, including the Temple address (Jer. 7:1ff.), threats against the nation (Jer. 13:1ff.) and Jerusalem (Jer. 11:6ff.), and the denunciation of sabbath profanation (Jer. 17:19ff.).[34] Muilenburg cautiously noted that certainty on the matter is excluded, but that the original writing was probably contained within the compass of Jeremiah 1:4–25:13.[35] In the light of the diversity of scholarly opinion and the essential subjectivity of the approach, it seems only reasonable to concede that the contents of the original Baruch scroll will never be recovered.

According to Pfeiffer the prophecy can be analyzed into three groups of writings, the first being the words which were dictated or written by Jeremiah himself, the second comprising a biography of Jeremiah, presumably written by Baruch, while the third consisted of miscellaneous contributions from the hands of editors and later authors.[36] On the assumption that Baruch did not produce the words of Jeremiah *verbatim*, Pfeiffer supposed that the scribe compiled his own edition of the prophecy, after the death of Jeremiah, and working over many of the speeches in his own Deuteronomistic style. Even this recension was subjected to later revision, during which long prose and poetic sections were interpolated. This view overlooks the fact that, apart from Jeremiah 52:1ff., there is almost no possibility of the presence of extraneous matter in the prophetic anthology. Furthermore, it is entirely gratuitous to assume that Baruch exercised a "Deuteronomistic style," since the literary style of the amanuensis cannot be recovered from the extant prophecy and is therefore unknown. Again, such a view attaches much too wide a range to the functions of Baruch, who is consistently depicted in the prophecy as the scribe of Jeremiah, and not the editor of his compositions.

In the opinion of Oesterley and Robinson, the compiler of the prophecy, who could probably be assigned to the fourth century B.C., employed three principal types of material in his work, comprising small collections of oracular utterances in poetic form, descriptive prose in the third person, and oracles worked over into rhetorical prose in the first person.[37] The prose passages not infrequently bore some kind of head-

---

[32] T. H. Robinson, ZAW, XLII (1924), pp. 209ff. O. Eissfeldt, *Einleitung in das AT*, pp. 393ff.; cf. *ETOT*, pp. 350ff.

[33] J. P. Hyatt, *IB*, V, p. 787.

[34] O. Eissfeldt, *Einleitung in das AT*, p. 425.

[35] J. Muilenburg, *IDB*, II, p. 833.

[36] *PIOT*, pp. 500ff.

[37] *IBOT*, pp. 290ff. For those scholars who adhere to a post-exilic date for the book see H. H. Rowley, *From Moses to Qumran*, p. 188 n. 3.

ing to furnish the date or some other type of information relating to comparable circumstances, and this situation almost invariably occurred where a prose passage preceded a group of oracles. In formulating the prophecy the compiler would take each section of oracular utterances and preface it by means of an appropriate selection from one or other of the two prose groups. He appeared to prefer passages of autobiographical prose, and did not utilize any material from the group of biographical prose until chapter 19, by which time he had almost exhausted the resources of the first person prose section. Oesterley and Robinson purported to distinguish no less than fourteen of the groups of oracular poetry, and maintained that the Deuteronomistic style of some of those passages merely constituted the form that Hebrew rhetorical prose took in the late seventh and early sixth centuries. They held that only a part of the poetic oracles could be dated in the time of Jeremiah, since some of them were evidently the product of the late fifth or early fourth century. On the other hand, the biographical material was in the main roughly contemporaneous and might perhaps have come from the hand of Baruch. The work of the prophet himself was seen in the autobiographical prose sections, though several of these were assigned by Oesterley and Robinson to the exilic period.

J. P. Hyatt used the Baruch scroll as the basis for his estimate of the compilation of Jeremiah, to which was added a second collection from chapter 9:2 to chapter 23.[38] The latter was probably the work of Baruch, and may have included the "confessions" of Jeremiah (10:23f.; 11:18–12:6; 15:10-21; 17:9, 10, 14-18; 18:18-23; 20:7-12, 14-18) along with oracles of condemnation or warning, laments over national or personal sorrow, and parabolic materials. To this was appended a series of biographical passages written in prose, and occupying an important position in the second half of the prophecy. These memoirs were the work of Baruch, and may have occurred to some extent both in the original scroll and the subsequent collection of material that is generally attributed to him. A Deuteronomistic edition of the prophecy was made about 550 B.C., according to Hyatt, perhaps by some individual or group in Egypt. This edition sometimes preserved the *ipsissima verba* of the prophecies, but on other occasions gave an interpretative or expanded form of the oracles.[39]

Hyatt's analysis was considerably less elaborate than those suggested by European scholars such as Cornill and Giesebrecht,[40] and his assessment of alleged Deuteronomic elements was very much closer to the thought of Mowinckel than that of Hölscher.[41] However, he weakened

---

[38] J. P. Hyatt, *IB*, V, pp. 787ff.

[39] J. P. Hyatt in *Vanderbilt Studies in the Humanities*, I (1951), pp. 71ff.

[40] C. H. Cornill, *Das Buch Jeremia erklärt* (1905), pp. xxxix ff. F. Giesebrecht, *Das Buch Jeremia* (1907), pp. xx ff.

[41] G. Hölscher, *Die Profeten*, p. 382 n. 2.

his case by positing the presence of numerous late additions in the book, including certain eschatological sections and the so-called "Book of Comfort" in chapters 30 and 31. The relegation of the latter to a period as late as the time of Nehemiah seems hardly appropriate to the general context, and is even more surprising in view of the fact that Pfeiffer regarded the oracles in question as authentic, and, indeed, extended the collection to include chapter 33.[42] The broad position adopted by Hyatt is typical evolutionary liberalism. It is deficient in attributing to Baruch a more advanced function than the evidence actually warrants, and denying to Jeremiah passages that appear to be genuine products of the seventh century B.C.

Despite the prolonged history of criticism of Jeremiah, it is evident that scholars are far from being in agreement as to the nature of the process by which the prophecy acquired its extant form. As with Isaiah and other similar compositions, it is almost certain that the process of transmission of the oracles from the lips of the prophet to the ultimate form of the prophecy itself was considerably less complex than has been assumed by the majority of liberal writers on the subject. One thing is sure, namely, that the history of its composition and growth is not to be explained entirely on a purely literary basis.

A great deal has been made in some circles of the fact that the contents of Jeremiah do not occur in strict chronological sequence. On the other hand, even a cursory examination of the prophecy makes it apparent that there is some kind of underlying plan to the work as a whole. Chapters 1–25 constitute a distinct unit, to which the LXX lends support in inserting groups of poems about the nations (ch. 46–51 and 25:15-38 of the MT) after Jeremiah 25:14, perhaps reflecting an arrangement followed by a different Hebrew textual tradition. Another separate group is represented by chapters 26–45, which deal with the personal life of the prophet. Some authorities such as Weiser divide it into two sections consisting of chapters 26 to 36 and 37 to 45, even when attributing the material substantially to Baruch.[43] Since the group as a whole is marked by narratives in the third person singular, there seems little real ground for dividing it into two parts. The prophecies against foreign nations occurring in chapters 46–51 constitute a clearly defined group, while the historical appendix, chapter 52, is also an obvious unit of the composition.

Despite the underlying unity of the extant book, it is a little difficult to see why certain passages should occur in their present position. It may be that their particular incidence reflects the form of the components, such as the Baruch scroll or its later counterpart. On the other hand, the overall arrangement made it possible for the basic theme of national

[42] *PIOT*, pp. 501f.
[43] *OTFD*, pp. 213ff.

sinfulness and judgment to be stressed repeatedly. While any chronological rearrangement of the prophecy is apt to be speculative in at least some areas, it may perhaps be possible to entertain a broad distribution of the work against its historical background as follows:

(a) Under Josiah: 1:1-19; 2:1–3:5; 3:6–6:30; 7:1–10:25; 18:1–20:18.
(b) Under Jehoahaz: nothing.
(c) Under Jehoiakim: 11:1–13:14; 14:1–15:21; 16:1–17:2; 22:1-30; 23:1-8, 9-40; 25:1-14; 15:38; 26:1-24; 35:1-19; 36:1-32; 45:1-5; 46:1-12, 13-28; 47:1-7; 48:1-47.
(d) Under Jehoiachin: 31:15-27.
(e) Under Zedekiah: 21:1–22:30; 24:1-10; 27:1-22; 28:1-17; 29:1-32; 30:1–31:40; 32:1-44; 33:1-26; 34:1-7, 8-11, 12-22; 37:1-21; 38:1-28; 39:1-18; 49:1-22, 23-33, 34-39; 50:1–51:64.
(f) Under Gedaliah: 40:1–42:22; 43:1–44:30.
(g) Historical Appendix: 52:1-34.

Some of the above passages are difficult to date, and others require a certain amount of comment. The account of the arrest of Jeremiah under Pashhur (Jer. 19:14–20:3) probably does not refer to the period of Zedekiah, since the Pashhur whom he sent to Jeremiah (Jer. 21:1) was the son of Melchiah, whereas the Pashhur of chapter 20:1-3 was the son of Immer. A scribal error appears to have credited Jehoiakim (Jer. 27:1) with events that, as the context shows, clearly happened in the reign of Zedekiah. No specific date was attached to chapters 30 and 31, but it would appear from the tenor of the narrative that the deportation to Babylonia had already taken place.

Certain difficulties arise in connection with chapters 50 and 51, in which it would appear (Jer. 50:28; 51:11, 51) that the Temple had been destroyed, an event that had not taken place in the fourth year of Zedekiah. Either this material dates from a later period and reflects the activity of the prophet in Egypt, or else it depicts Jeremiah contemplating the certainty of future desolation for the Temple. The former view seems more attractive in the light of such references as Jeremiah 50:4, 17 and 51:34, 45, which indicate that the exile was an accomplished fact.

Chapter 52 presents a different kind of difficulty, since it is practically identical with 2 Kings 24–25. In the view of the present writer this chapter constitutes the only extraneous material of any significance in the prophecy. It is purely historical in character, and was most probably abstracted from a larger source, of which the prophet Jeremiah was not the author and which was also utilized by the compiler of Kings. There is little doubt that it was added to the prophecy within seventy years after the events which it narrated had occurred.

The account of the numbers of captives mentioned in Jeremiah 52:28ff. has sometimes been questioned in the light of larger estimates of those taken to Babylonia. However, there seems to be no adequate reason for rejecting the authenticity of the compilation, since such estimates were not at all uncommon in the ancient Near East. Thus the archives of a Hurrite family *ca.* 1400 B.C. preserved a similar document describing the fall of a small state and furnished details of the deportation and the numbers of the people involved.[44]

The prophecy of Jeremiah obviously took initial shape when the oracles were first committed to writing in the fourth year of Jehoiakim. This material covered a period beginning about 626 B.C., and presumably ended with certain events which occurred in 605/4 B.C. The augmented version (Jer. 36:32) of these oracles marked the next major stage in the compilation of the prophecy, and the result constituted the nucleus of the extant work. In this connection it is very easy to overstate the role of Baruch, as has been mentioned previously. The necessity for the kind of revision which would give the work a "Deuteronomic" flavor seems obviated by two considerations: first, that Jeremiah was probably familiar with Deuteronomy, whatever the content of the scroll discovered in the time of Josiah; and second, that, as Oesterley and Robinson have pointed out, the so-called "Deuteronomic" style of some of the oracles was in any event nothing more than the form of Hebrew rhetorical prose during the late seventh and early sixth centuries B.C.[45] Consequently the numerous "Deuteronomic" redactional elements that many critics have detected in the prophetic anthology are probably contemporary literary forms, based, no doubt, upon ancient models as exemplified in the Torah.

While it is almost impossible to conjecture the manner in which the prophecy was given its final form, the irregular nature of the oracles seems to imply that they were assembled at a time of stress and turmoil, probably while the prophet and his secretary were concluding their days in Egypt. The presence of the final chapter with its concomitant considerations of dating might suggest that Jeremiah was in substantially its extant form not later than 520 B.C.

2. *Divergences between the LXX and MT.* There are few books in the Old Testament canon that show such striking divergences between the MT and the LXX. A surprising amount of the Hebrew text was omitted in the Greek version, representing, according to the computation of Giesebrecht, about 2700 words or between six and seven chapters.[46] In addition, the LXX contained approximately one hundred words not found in the MT, though as Pfeiffer has noted, these are unimportant.[47] As with the additions, the omissions characteristic of the LXX are rather minor, due among other considerations to the intentional omission of

---

[44] E. Chiera and E. A. Speiser, *JAOS*, XX (1927), pp. 57ff.

[45] *IBOT*, p. 298.

[46] F. Giesebrecht, *Das Buch Jeremia* (1894 ed.), p. xix; cf. W. Rudolph, *ZAW*, XLVIII (1930), pp. 272ff.

[47] *PIOT*, p. 487.

doublets in the Hebrew text (Jer. 8:10-12; 30:10f.; 48:10f.) or to what is probably a condensed form of the Hebrew, as in chapters 27 and 28. By far the most prominent divergence, however, is to be seen in the respective arrangement of the oracles against foreign nations, which appeared in the LXX after Jeremiah 25:13. Verse 14 of the Hebrew text was omitted, and after the oracles had been inserted, the LXX continued from chapter 25:15. This situation contrasted with that of the MT, where the material was grouped at the end of the prophecy, occupying chapters 46–51. The differences can be demonstrated in tabular form as follows:

Hebrew text	LXX version
Egypt (46:1-28)	Elam
Philistia (47:1-7)	Egypt
Moab (48:1-47)	Babylon
Ammon (49:1-6)	Philistia
Edom (49:7-22)	Edom
Damascus (49:23-27)	Ammon
Kedar (49:28-33)	Kedar
Elam (49:34-39)	Damascus
Babylon (50:1–51:58)	Moab

Quite evidently there can be no means of ascertaining the original order of the oracles in the prophecy, and there is nothing in the sequence of the Hebrew text to suggest any particular organizational scheme on the part of the compiler. Perhaps the LXX translators placed Elam first in deference to Mesopotamian military and cultural influence, but this cannot be determined with certainty. It is possible also that the LXX followed an independent Hebrew textual tradition which has not yet come to light, but this again is a matter for conjecture, and cannot be proved. While the shorter text of the LXX occasionally furnishes a rhythmical regularity which the Hebrew lacks, it must not necessarily be assumed that the LXX is uniformly superior to the Hebrew text. Generalizations of this kind are dangerous, and most commentators have wisely followed the course of considering each instance of textual variation independently on its own intrinsic merits.

D. The Message of Jeremiah

To speak of the theology of Jeremiah as such is to encounter some difficulty, since the prophet was less concerned with a systematic or formally articulated theological presentation than with the burning necessity for acting as the spokesman of God to the people of his own day. The vitality of his religious experience and his sense of intimate communion with God virtually preclude logical formulations. Consequently, a better approach is the consideration of specific emphases in the prophetic outlook of Jeremiah. His concept of God had much in common with that entertained by the eighth-century prophets, in that he acknowledged the Deity as the creator and sovereign overlord of the universe (Jer. 23:23; 27:5; 31:35) as well as the ruler of history, who could commission individuals such as Nebuchadnezzar to do his bidding (Jer. 27:6). The God whom Jeremiah worshipped knew the inner hearts of all men (Jer. 17:5ff.), and was an ever-invigorating "fountain of living waters" (Jer. 2:13) for those who trusted in Him. While He showed tender love towards Israel, He demanded their implicit obedience (Jer. 2:2; 7:1ff.; 31:1ff.) and abhorred both sacrifices to pagan deities (Jer. 7:30f.; 19:5) and oblations offered to Him by a disobedient nation (Jer. 6:20; 7:21f.; 14:12).

In the thought of Jeremiah there is a marked departure from the concept of a national corporate personality such as that enshrined in the Mosaic tradition. Indeed, it is not too much to say that the later ideas concerning personal religion had their roots in Jeremiah's life and teaching. While he believed firmly that the nation was the elect of God and as such stood in Covenant relationship with Him (Jer. 2:3, 21; 11:15; 12:7ff.; 13:17, et al.), he was also aware of the long history of faithlessness and apostasy which had characterized the religious life of Israel. For this the nation had been rebuked many times by God through the prophets, and had sustained various forms of affliction (Jer. 2:30; 5:3; 7:28), but all to no purpose. For such repeated acts of rebellion the Israelites were to endure the chastisement of exile, but even in this experience of calamity the faithful would be sustained by the promise of a New Covenant (Jer. 31:31) to be established with the house of Israel and the house of Judah.

Jeremiah was particularly forceful in his condemnation of immoral behavior, which in his day—as in earlier periods—was a concomitant of idolatry (cf. Jer. 5:1ff.; 23:10ff.). In denouncing these violations of the Covenant ideal he was quick to point out that the priests and prophets were oblivious to the moral demands of their calling (cf. Jer. 5:30f.; 6:13ff.; 14:14), and that their delinquency was in fact hastening the doom of the nation. At a time when the popular view of religion gave esteem only to the ritual performances demanded by cultic tradition, Jeremiah consistently emphasized that true obedience to God could be engendered entirely independently of either Temple or cultus. On such a basis the hallmark of his concept of personal religion was the elevation of the moral law over the ceremonial, a principle that he applied resolutely to such matters as reverence for the Ark of the Covenant (Jer. 3:16), the tables of the Law (Jer. 31:31), the sign of circumcision (Jer. 4:14; 6:10; 9:26), the sacrificial system (Jer. 6:20; 11:15; 14:12), and other material adjuncts of Israelite religion.

For Jeremiah the sole remedy for the sin of the nation lay in sincere repentance and following a life of obedience to the divine will (Jer. 9:23f.). He viewed sin as a perversion of the Hebrew spiritual genius, a pursuit of that which has no ultimate value and which results in the repudiation of the bond linking Israel to her God. The nature of sin was as compelling as the biological forces evident in wild animals (Jer. 2:24), and its stain penetrated so deeply that it could not be cleansed with lye (Jer. 2:22). The consequence of sin was judgment, and the longer the prophet lived the more certain he became that such an eventuality would overtake the nation in the end.

Although he preached this fate in stern, unwavering tones, Jeremiah nevertheless entertained considerable hope for his countrymen. The tribulations of captivity would ultimately come to an end (Jer. 25:11; 29:10), and even Babylon herself would be overthrown (Jer. 50:1ff.; 51:1ff.). Such a message of hope was present in the early utterances of the prophet (Jer. 3:14ff.; 12:14ff.), and it is noteworthy that as the spiritual fortunes of the nation deteriorated progressively, the confidence of the prophet in the power of God to preserve and restore became increasingly evident (cf. Jer. 23:1ff.; 30:3ff.), culminating in his singular act of faith at a time of great crisis (Jer. 32:1ff.). But because the temporal accidents of Hebrew religion were soon to be destroyed for the most part, the vital necessity for the implementation of this hope of survival was the engraving of the divine Law in the human heart and will, rather than on tablets of stone.

As with other prophets, Jeremiah contemplated a glorious future for the exiles. Jerusalem would reflect the ethical holiness of the deity (Jer. 31:23ff.; 33:16), and its inhabitants would exemplify that degree of penitence and obedience (Jer. 3:22ff.; 31:18ff.) that would insure their forgiveness (Jer. 31:34). Even Samaria would have a part to play in the ideal future life of the restored community (Jer. 3:18; 31:4ff.), and the Gentile nations would also be permitted to participate in the blessings accruing to the restored nation (Jer. 3:17; 16:19; 30:9). The messianic prince, a righteous branch of the house of David (Jer. 23:5; 30:9; 33:15f.), would insure that justice and equity were prevailing features of life in the land. Jeremiah had nothing to say about a restored Temple and cultus, for his predominant concern was with a future that would be characterized by spiritual regeneration and moral purification in the lives of the Chosen People.

Supplementary Literature

Blank, S. H. *Jeremiah, Man and Prophet.* 1961.
Calkins, R. *Jeremiah the Prophet, A Study in Personal Religion.* 1930.
Cash, W. *Jeremiah, A Prophet to the Nations.* 1945.
Elliot-Binns, L. E. *Jeremiah, A Prophet for a Time of War.* 1941.

Hyatt, J. P. *Jeremiah, Prophet of Courage and Hope.* 1958.
Lofthouse, W. F. *Jeremiah and the New Covenant.* 1925.
Overholt, T. W. *The Threat of Falsehood.* 1970.
Robinson, D. W. B. *Josiah's Reform and the Book of the Law.* 1951.
Von Orelli, C. *The Prophecies of Jeremiah.* 1905.
Welch, A. C. *Jeremiah, His Time and His Work.* 1951.
Whitley, C. F. *The Prophetic Achievement.* 1963.

IV. THE BOOK OF EZEKIEL

A. NAME AND OUTLINE

Like its immediate predecessor in the Hebrew canon, the book of Ezekiel was named after its principal prophetic figure. His cognomen יחזקאל probably means "may God make strong." It is rendered 'Ιεζεκιήλ in the LXX and *Ezechiel* in the Vulgate. Apart from its two occurrences in the prophecy, the name of Ezekiel does not occur elsewhere in the Old Testament.

The book itself is in bifid form. Its two principal divisions can be analyzed as follows:

I. The Approaching Destruction and Dissolution of the Nation, ch. 1–24
   A. Introduction and call, 1:1–3:3
   B. Instructions to Ezekiel, 3:4-21
   C. Prophecies and visions of judgment, 3:22–7:27
   D. Visions relating to abominations in Judah and the destruction of the state, 8:1–11:25
   E. Oracles predicting the captivity of Jerusalem, 12:1–19:14
   F. Final warnings prior to the fall of the city, 20:1–24:27
II. Oracles Against Foreign Nations; the Restoration of the Religious Community, ch. 25–48
   A. Prophecies against foreign nations, 25:1–32:32
      1. Ammon, 25:1-7
      2. Moab, 25:8-11
      3. Edom, 25:12-14
      4. Philistia, 25:15-17
      5. Tyre, 26:1–28:19
      6. Sidon, 28:20-26
      7. Egypt, 29:1–32:32
   B. Prophecies of hope after the fall of Jerusalem, 33:1–48:35
      1. The New Covenant, 33:1-22
      2. Spiritual revival, 34:1-31
      3. The devastation of Edom, 35:1-15
      4. The restoration of Israel, 36:1–37:28

822

   5. Gog and Magog, 38:1–39:29
   6. The ideal Temple, 40:1–46:24
   7. The restored City of God, 47:1–48:35

B. AUTHORSHIP

According to the traditions preserved in rabbinic circles, the men of the Great Synagogue wrote Ezekiel and the Twelve,[1] a statement that probably means that they edited or copied out the book. There was some dispute between leading rabbinic scholars concerning its genuineness, however. The school of Shammai repudiated the prophecy, holding it to be apocryphal on the ground that the first ten chapters appeared to be theosophical in character, and that the book conflicted at certain important points with the Torah, which for them was the norm of canonical Scripture. In this connection the school of Shammai pointed out that, whereas the Torah required two bullocks, seven lambs, and one ram as the new moon offering (Num. 28:11), Ezekiel prescribed only one unblemished bullock, six lambs, and one ram (Ezek. 46:6).

According to Talmudic tradition Hananiah ben Hezekiah, head of the school of Shammai, burned the midnight oil to the extent of three hundred jars before he was able to justify the admission of the exilic work to the Scriptural canon.[2] That his attempts at harmonizing may not have been an unqualified success seems indicated in the Talmud, where it was stated that when Elijah came (cf. Mal. 4:5), the discrepancies between Ezekiel and the Pentateuch would be explained.[3]

1. History of criticism. The first serious challenge to the traditional authorship of the prophecy of Ezekiel came from Spinoza (1632-1677),[4] and was taken up nearly a century later by G. L. Oeder, whose work was published posthumously in 1771.[5] He was of the opinion that the prophecy proper concluded with chapter 39, and maintained that chapters 40–48 constituted a spurious addition to the genuine work. In 1798 an anonymous contributor to a British periodical adopted a similar attitude towards the first twenty-four chapters of the prophecy, which he found to be quite incompatible in terms of literary and moral standards with the rest of the work, which he attributed to Daniel.[6]

In the nineteenth century, further attacks were made upon the authorship of the prophecy by Leopold Zunz, who thought that Ezekiel was a product of the early Persian period,[7] an opinion which he subsequently modified to the point of assigning the work to a date between 440 and

---

[1] *Bab. Bath.* 15a.
[2] Cf. *Shabb.* 14b; *Menahoth* 45a; *Hagigah* 13a.
[3] *Menah.* 45a.
[4] *Tractatus Theologico-Politicus,* p. 207.
[5] *Freie Untersuchung über einige Bücher des AT.*
[6] *Monthly Magazine and British Register,* V (1798), pp. 189f.
[7] *Die gottesdienstliche Vortäge der Juden* (1832), pp. 157ff.

400 B.C.[8] A. Geiger appears to have followed Zunz in his general conclusions,[9] while a more radical view was adopted by Seinecke, who regarded the entire composition as a pseudepigraph which had been compiled during the Maccabean period.[10]

Despite allegations of this nature, the majority of the nineteenth-century Old Testament scholars were greatly impressed with the marks of unity and authenticity that the book exhibited. As late as 1913 it was possible for G. B. Gray to sum up the consensus of critical opinion by stating that no other Old Testament book was distinguished by such decisive indications of unity of authorship and integrity, a view in which he was followed by Driver.[11] However, it was not long before this unusual scene of critical unanimity and harmony was abruptly disturbed. From the pen of Gustav Hölscher in 1924 came one of the most radical treatments to which the prophecy of Ezekiel has ever been subjected,[12] marking a distinct departure from the views of unity of authorship which Hölscher himself had maintained a decade earlier.[13]

Hölscher complained that Ezekiel had for too long escaped the "critical knife," and that the only methodological analysis to date had been that of Herrmann, who had attempted to explain duplicates in the book by supposing that the prophecy had been compiled by Ezekiel on the basis of small prophecies or summaries of oracular utterances which he had collected at various times, and which had been subjected to revision by later hands.[14] Starting from the premise that Ezekiel was a poet and therefore would probably not have been responsible for the indifferent prose found in much of the prophecy, Hölscher ascribed to Ezekiel some sixteen passages of high poetic quality, and five short sections in prose. The remainder of the book, and particularly those areas in which there was thought to be a literary relationship to Leviticus and Jeremiah, was credited to the activity of a later editor of Levitical tendencies who functioned between 500 and 450 B.C. Out of the extant 1273 verses of the prophecy, Hölscher credited the historic Ezekiel with no more than 170 verses in all.

[8] In *ZDMG*, XXVII (1873), pp. 676ff.

[9] A. Geiger, *Urschrift und Uebersetzungen der Bibel* (1857), p. 23.

[10] L. Seinecke, *Geschichte des Volkes Israel* (1884), II, pp. 1ff. On this period see S. Spiegel, *Harvard Theological Review*, XXIV (1931), pp. 245ff.; W. A. Irwin, *The Problem of Ezekiel* (1943), pp. 5ff.; C. G. Howie, *The Date and Composition of Ezekiel* (1950), pp. 1ff.; G. Fohrer, *Die Hauptprobleme des Buches Ezechiel* (1952), pp. 5ff.

[11] G. B. Gray, *A Critical Introduction to the OT* (1913), p. 198. *DILOT*, p. 279. Cf. R. Smend, *Der Prophet Ezechiel* (1880), p. xxi; A. B. Davidson, *The Book of the Prophet Ezekiel* (1892), p. ix; H. A. Redpath, *The Book of the Prophet Ezekiel* (1907), p. xiv.

[12] G. Hölscher, *Hesekiel, der Dichter und das Buch* (1924).

[13] In *Die Profeten*, pp. 298ff.

[14] J. Herrmann, *Ezechielstudien* (1908), and *Ezechiel* (1924).

The subjective extremes to which Hölscher had gone were based in part upon the methods of literary analysis laid down by Duhm in his study of the book of Jeremiah. That his postulates regarding Ezekiel as a poet who could consequently have had little or no connection with the prose sections of the prophecy were not merely weak in substance but basically unacceptable was maintained by Kessler, who pointed out the close connection between the prose and poetic sections of the prophecy.[15]

The stimulus that Hölscher had given to the critical dissection of Ezekiel found a response in 1930, when C. C. Torrey advanced the view that, while the work was a substantial unity, it had originally been formulated against a Palestinian rather than a Mesopotamian religious and cultural milieu.[16] Torrey held that the original work purported to have been written in Jerusalem by a prophet of the seventh century B.C. who functioned in the time of Manasseh, but that actually it was composed in the Greek period, perhaps towards the end of the third century B.C. A later editor then gave the work its extant prophetic cast and set it against a Babylonian exilic background. According to Torrey, this editor could be regarded as a representative of a literary movement that had as its objective the vindication of the religious tradition of Jerusalem.[17]

Disregarding the precise and full chronological data furnished by the book, he held that the author must have drawn upon a collection of oracles denouncing paganism in the time of Manasseh (2 Kgs. 21:10ff.; 24:2), the first of which was assigned to the thirtieth year of the reign of Manasseh, and the others extending, according to his revised chronology, to the thirty-fifth year.[18] To add further support to his arguments Torrey invoked the presence of Aramaisms in the prophecy as evidence for a later rather than an earlier date for the work as a whole. This assertion is somewhat surprising, to say the least, since in the light of the prolonged history of usage enjoyed by Aramaic, it would be quite proper to expect the presence of Aramaisms in Semitic literature composed about the time in which Ezekiel is traditionally believed to have lived.

[15] W. Kessler, *Die innere Einheitlichkeit des Buches Ezechiel* (1926). Further criticisms of Hölscher's methods and conclusions were made by, among others, G. A. Cooke, *JTS*, XXVII (1926), pp. 201ff., *A Critical and Exegetical Commentary on the Book of Ezekiel* (1936), p. xxi; W. F. Lofthouse, *Israel After the Exile* (1928), p. 68; R. Kittel, *Geschichte des Volkes Israel* (1927), III, pp. 158ff.; V. Herntrich, *Ezechielprobleme* (1932), pp. 12ff.; C. C. Torrey, *JBL*, LIII (1934), p. 299; J. Battersby Harford, *Studies in the Book of Ezekiel* (1935), pp. 13ff.

[16] C. C. Torrey, *Pseudo-Ezekiel and the Original Prophecy* (1930), *Transactions of the Connecticut Academy*, XV (1909), p. 248, *Ezra Studies* (1910), p. 288 n. 8, and in *Vom AT, Marti Festschrift*, p. 284.

[17] *Pseudo-Ezekiel and the Original Prophecy*, p. 102.

[18] *Ibid.*, p. 113.

The conclusions of Torrey were strongly assailed by many liberal scholars,[19] and although Torrey attempted to refute some of their arguments, his efforts met with little success.[20] Only two scholars followed Torrey in his dating of Ezekiel, one of whom was his doctoral student, Millar Burrows. After examining the literary relations of the prophecy, Burrows concluded that it was probably written at a later period than Isaiah 56–66 and the Aramaic part of Daniel, and quite certainly before Ecclesiasticus, so that in his opinion the date suggested by Torrey was substantially correct.[21] The only other scholar to accept this chronology was G. Dahl.[22]

Working from an independent point of view, another writer, James Smith, reached conclusions that had elements in common with those of Torrey.[23] Smith maintained that the prophecies did in fact appear to belong to the age of Manasseh, and were addressed in their original form to Palestinians. But whereas Torrey had asserted that the prophecy was pseudepigraphic in nature from the very beginning and not the work of Ezekiel at all, Smith upheld the traditional author as a real person who worked in northern Israel during the time of Manasseh, but whose writings were subsequently revised and assigned, with his ministry, to a later age.

For Smith, Ezekiel hailed from northern Palestine and was deported in 734 B.C., but returned to Palestine in 691 B.C., perhaps in order to instruct the new settlers in the religious traditions of the local deity.[24] Like Torrey, Smith acknowledged the fundamental unity of the book and its historical background in the time of Manasseh, and also recognized the activity of a later editor who had effected a radical transformation of the original prophetic material. Unlike Torrey, however, he refused to consider the work as pseudepigraphic.

In 1932 Volkmar Herntrich attempted to combine the traditional dating of Ezekiel with the idea of a Palestinian setting for the ministry of

---

[19] E.g. S. Spiegel, *Harvard Theological Review*, XXIV (1931), pp. 245ff.; K. Budde, *JBL*, L (1931), pp. 20ff., C. Kuhl, *Theologische Literaturzeitung*, LVII (1932), cols. 27ff.; W. F. Albright, *JBL*, LI (1932), pp. 97ff., *Religion in Life*, XXI, No. 4 (1952), p. 546; W. E. Barnes, *JTS*, XXXV (1934), pp. 163ff.; J. Battersby Harford, *ET*, XLIII (1931-32), pp. 20ff., *Studies in the Book of Ezekiel* (1935), pp. 38ff.; O. Eissfeldt, *PJB*, XXVII (1931), pp. 58ff.; W. O. E. Oesterley, *Church Quarterly Review*, CVI (1933), p. 194; L. Dennefield, *Introduction à l'Ancien Testament* (1935), p. 172.

[20] In reply to S. Spiegel, *JBL*, LIII (1934), pp. 291ff.; cf. the rejoinder of Spiegel, *JBL*, LIV (1935), pp. 144ff. In reply to Albright see *JBL*, LI (1932), pp. 179ff.

[21] M. Burrows, *The Literary Relations of Ezekiel* (1925), pp. 102ff.

[22] G. Dahl in *Quantulacumque, Studies Presented to Kirsopp Lake* (1937), pp. 265ff.

[23] J. Smith, *The Book of the Prophet Ezekiel: A New Introduction* (1931).

[24] *Ibid.*, pp. 95f. This concept of return was criticized by C. Kuhl, *The OT: Its Origins and Composition*, p. 195.

the prophet as entertained by Torrey and Smith.[25] In so doing he was one of very few scholars who paid significant attention to the position that Smith had endeavored to establish.[26] Herntrich maintained that the oracles addressed to Jerusalem were actually delivered there, and suggested that the Babylonian framework was the result of editorial activity during the exilic period. While he conceded that Ezekiel might have joined the exiles in Babylonia at some period subsequent to 586 B.C., he viewed with complete disfavor the tradition that the prophet had exercised a ministry there.[27]

Herntrich followed Holscher in rejecting chapters 40–48 as a part of the original work,[28] and in general he exceeded both Torrey and Smith in his estimate of the amount of editorial activity discernible in the prophecy. The views of Herntrich were followed principally by Battersby Harford and I. G. Matthews. The former differed from Smith in stating that the phrase "house of Israel" was a description of the population of Judah and Jerusalem,[29] and both of them agreed with Torrey in regarding the original oracles as exclusively Palestinian in provenance. Matthews maintained that the prophet might have been a northern Israelite, but that he lived in Jerusalem.[30] It was thought possible that he had visited Babylonia at some time, although he could well have been numbered among the exiles of 581 B.C. The work of this Palestinian mystic was edited in the exile by a Babylonian priest, whose activity, Matthews felt, was supplemented in later times by the addition of apocalyptic matter and oracles against foreign nations.[31] Matthews was not as adept at the expertise of literary criticism as Torrey and others, with the unfortunate result that, as May has pointed out, he occasionally assigned material of an analogous literary and theological standpoint to rather diverse sources, as illustrated by his analysis of chapter 36 of the prophecy.[32]

Herntrich also exercised considerable influence over the views of Oesterley and Robinson, who maintained that Ezekiel was active in Jerusalem between 602 and 597 B.C., placing his call to the prophetic

25 V. Herntrich, *Ezechielprobleme* (1932); cf. J. E. McFadyen, *ET*, XLIV (1932-33), pp. 471ff.

26 This view was favored somewhat by W. A. L. Elmslie in *Essays and Studies Presented to S. A. Cook* (1950), p. 17.

27 *Op. cit.*, p. 126.

28 As did N. H. Snaith in T. W. Manson (ed.), *A Companion to the Bible* (1939), pp. 423f.

29 *Studies in the Book of Ezekiel*, pp. 77ff.

30 I. G. Matthews, *Ezekiel* (1939); cf. his *The Religious Pilgrimage of Israel* (1947), p. 166.

31 *Ezekiel*, p. xxix f.

32 H. G. May, *IB*, VI, p. 44.

office about 600 B.C.[33] They anticipated the opinions of some later scholars by postulating a twofold ministry for Ezekiel, the second portion of which took place among the exiles in Babylonia after 597 B.C.[34]

The theory that Ezekiel exercised his office both in Palestine and Babylonia proved attractive to Bertholet, who published a second commentary on Ezekiel in 1936 in which the influence of Herntrich was again apparent.[35] His earlier work[36] was modified to the point where Bertholet placed the call of Ezekiel (Ezek. 2:3–3:9) in 593 B.C., which was somewhat later than the date assigned by Oesterley and Robinson to that event.[37] From that time he prophesied in Palestine until 587 B.C., when he was carried captive with the second group of exiles. In Babylonia he received a second call (Ezek. 1:4–2:2) in the thirteenth year of the captivity of Jehoiachin, that is to say, in 585 B.C. To sustain his theory Bertholet found it necessary to emend the "thirtieth" of Ezekiel 1:1 to "thirteenth," against the background of a dual recension theory of the text.[38]

In this he reflected the views of Kraetzschmar, who argued from the Talmudic tradition that Ezekiel was placed between Jeremiah and Isaiah and edited by the men of the Great Synagogue to the position that the prophecy had been compiled by a redactor from two recensions of the text, evidences of which were detected in the parallel passages and doublets such as chapters 3:16b-21 and 33:7-9; 10:8-17 and 1:16-21; 18:21-25 and 33:10-20.[39] Bertholet held that the prophet left his material unfinished, and, aside from recognizing secondary additions, felt able to divide the text into two broad sections, one of which came from the Judaean period (Ezek. 2:3–3:9; 12:3, 17-20; 14:12-20; 15:1-8; 24:1-14; 33:21-29; and most of ch. 25–32) and the other from the years of exile in Babylonia (Ezek. 1:1, 4–2:2; 3:10-16; 11:14-21; 14:4-23; 17:22-24; 20:33-44; 34:1-22; 35:1-6; and most of ch. 40–48).

Part of the difficulty of the two-recension theory as envisaged by Kraetzschmar and developed by Bertholet consisted in the fact that, as Cooke remarked, so many of the alleged parallels when scrutinized turn

---

[33] *IBOT*, pp. 318ff.; cf. T. H. Robinson, *Prophecy and the Prophets in Ancient Israel* (1923), p. 145.

[34] Following R. Kittel, *Geschichte des Volkes Israel*, III, pp. 144ff.

[35] A. Bertholet and K. Galling, *Hesekiel* (1936). Galling contributed introductory material and studies relating to 40:1–42:20; 43:10-17.

[36] A. Bertholet, *Das Buch Hesekiel* (1897). For a comparison of the two works see S. Spiegel, *JBL*, LVI (1937), pp. 403ff. Bertholet was followed by P. Auvray, *RB*, LV (1948), pp. 503ff., and *Ezechiel* (1949), pp. 13ff.

[37] *IBOT*, p. 328.

[38] On this passage see K. Budde, *JBL*, L (1931), pp. 20ff.; W. F. Albright, *JBL*, LI (1932), p. 97; C. G. Howie, *The Date and Composition of Ezekiel*, pp. 91f.

[39] R. Kraetzschmar, *Ezechiel* (1900).

out to be not actually parallel at all.[40] As a result, critical confusion is compounded when a theory which already rests on unstable foundations is pushed too far. The work of Cooke reflected the more traditional views of authorship and date of the prophecy, for he maintained the substantial unity of the book and the sole location of the prophetic ministry in Babylonia. In his view the final chapters contained a number of secondary additions,[41] while the visions and other unusual phenomena of the book were to be explained in the light of modern psychological discoveries.

A much more radical examination of Ezekiel, following the general critical tradition of Hölscher, was made by Irwin in 1943.[42] He endeavored to discover the original poetic oracles of the book, which, he maintained, had been overlaid by spurious commentary. Most of this poetic material had been composed in Jerusalem by the prophet before he went to Babylon in the second deportation of captives. In an attempt to recover the genuine poetic oracles, which he maintained were buried deep in prose chapters, Irwin isolated the verses that purported to interpret the oracles as being unauthentic, and not the work of the prophet himself. Thus in chapters 4 and 5 he claimed to have recovered an original poem of six tristichs in 4:1-2, 9, 11 and 5:1-3, with the rest of the material in that section constituting later commentary—perhaps issuing from several hands—upon the oracle. By distinguishing in this manner between what was deemed authentic and what was not, Irwin succeeded in improving upon the efforts of Hölscher to the extent of allowing Ezekiel only some 251 verses of the entire prophecy.[43] Yet despite his careful attempts at analysis it is not always easy to be certain that what he purported to isolate as poetry was in fact the genuine poetic form that he claimed to have recognized. Furthermore, Irwin failed to appreciate what Torrey had called the "overwhelming impression of an individuality which is the same throughout the book,"[44] or the extensive homogeneity of the work, as made evident by Muilenburg and other scholars.[45]

The twofold view of the ministry of Ezekiel as developed by Bertholet attracted a few adherents, including Wheeler Robinson,[46] who towards the end of his life abandoned his earlier and more traditional opinions

---

[40] G. A. Cooke, A Critical and Exegetical Commentary on the Book of Ezekiel, p. xx.

[41] Ibid., pp. 426ff.

[42] W. A. Irwin, The Problem of Ezekiel (1943); for criticisms of his method see H. H. Rowley, Men of God, pp. 193f.

[43] W. A. Irwin, op. cit., p. 283.

[44] C. C. Torrey, JBL, LVIII (1939), p. 77.

[45] J. Muilenburg in M. Black and H. H. Rowley (eds.), Peake's Commentary on the Bible (1962), p. 568.

[46] H. Wheeler Robinson, Two Hebrew Prophets (1948), pp. 65ff.

concerning the work of the prophet.[47] Delorme, van den Born, and Augé also accepted the theory of Bertholet with some modifications.[48] For van den Born, Ezekiel was active in Jerusalem until 586 B.C., after which he continued his ministry in Babylonia. While a certain amount of the book could, in his view, have come from Ezekiel himself, it was difficult to deny that it possessed a certain pseudepigraphic character. The call-vision of chapter 1 was transferred so as to follow chapter 32, since it obviously was intended originally to commence the Babylonian period of the prophetic ministry.

Some attention to the theories of Herntrich, whose views, as noted above, influenced Oesterley and Robinson, Bertholet, and others, was given in 1945 by Messel.[49] As against the opinion that the recipients of the original speeches lived in Palestine, and that the present form of the work was due to a Babylonian editor who was attempting to demonstrate the superiority and unity of the Hebrew God over against the Babylonian pantheon, Messel objected that in such an event the Babylonian exiles would already have been familiar with the work of the prophet, and would have repudiated immediately the kind of situation entertained by Herntrich. For Messel the gôlāh comprised those in Palestine who had returned from exile, among whom Ezekiel worked towards the end of the fifth century B.C. Of the prophecy itself chapters 1–24 and 40–48 constituted the genuine sayings of Ezekiel, while chapters 25–32 were the work of a redactor who edited and augmented the oracles, perhaps about 350 B.C.

A view that placed the activity of the prophet Ezekiel even later than the period contemplated by Messel was espoused by Browne, who set his ministry in the time of Alexander the Great.[50] He suggested that Ezekiel had been deported from Jerusalem to Hyrcania in 344 B.C., and that it was from such an exile that most of the dates in the chronology were computed. The three exceptions to this general principle (Ezek. 1:1; 29:17; 40:1) were reckoned from the accession of Artaxerxes III (359/8-338/7 B.C.). Browne rearranged the contents of the prophecy to a considerable extent, but did not question the substantial unity of the work. Such a view is entirely out of harmony with what is known of Hebrew chronology, however, and makes the prophecy itself unnecessarily late.

[47] H. Wheeler Robinson, The OT, Its Making and Meaning (1937), pp. 104ff.

[48] Delorme in Mémorial J. Chaine (1950), pp. 115ff. A. van den Born, De historische Situatie van Ezechiels Prophetie (1947), Studia Catholica, XXVIII (1953), pp. 94ff., Dictionnaire encyclopédique de la Bible (1960), cols. 635f. R. Augé, Ezequiel (1955), pp. 26f.

[49] N. Messel, Ezechielfragen (1945).

[50] L. E. Browne, Ezekiel and Alexander (1952), and in Peake's Commentary on the Bible, p. 131.

While it is certainly incorrect to say with Fisch that there never was a period when the unity of Ezekiel was questioned,[51] it is undoubtedly true that in the time of Smend and later there were few who raised objections to the authorship and authenticity of the book.[52] That the prophecy constituted a composition that did not admit of literary analysis and distribution among several hands was a view held by liberal and conservative scholars alike, showing an unusual degree of unanimity concerning an Old Testament book. Even when this scholarly harmony was disrupted by Hölscher and others, there were still a great many writers who adhered to traditional opinions concerning the substantial unity of the book,[53] while at the same time frequently recognizing the possibility of secondary additions in the prophecy.

One of the most penetrating studies of the origin of Ezekiel was published in 1950 by C. G. Howie.[54] This stood in marked contrast to the speculative analyses of Hölscher, Torrey, and Irwin. Howie took the view that the basic unit of the prophecy comprised chapters 1–24, which were recorded by a scribe while Ezekiel spoke in his thirtieth year; chapters 25–32, dealing with the oracles against foreign nations, were added as an appendix to the original prophetic material; chapters 34–39 consisted of oracles which were either written down from memory or collected from already extant sources, and were linked with chapters 25–32 by means of chapter 33. Chapters 40–48, dealing with the visions of the ideal Temple, existed independently and were committed to writing subsequent to the ecstatic experience. Howie thus supported the substantial accuracy of the traditional view regarding the composition and date of Ezekiel, and adduced linguistic and other evidence to

---

[51] S. Fisch, *Ezekiel* (1950), p. xiv.

[52] R. Smend, *Der Prophet Ezechiel* (1880), p. xxi.

[53] E.g. P. Heinisch, *Das Buch Ezechiel* (1923), p. 227; R. Kittel, *Geschichte des Volkes Israel*, III, pp. 144ff.; W. L. Wardle in F. C. Eiselen, G. Lewis, and D. G. Downey (eds.), *The Abingdon Bible Commentary* (1929), pp. 714ff.; J. Meinhold. *Einführung in das AT* (1932 ed.), pp. 269ff.; E. Sellin, *Einleitung in das AT* (1935 ed.), p. 100; O. Eissfeldt, *JPOS*, XVI (1936), pp. 286ff.; G. A. Cooke, *A Critical and Exegetical Commentary on the Book of Ezekiel*, pp. xx ff.; L. Hudal and J. Ziegler, *Précis d'Introduction à l'Ancien Testament* (1938), pp. 217f.; J. E. Steinmueller, *A Companion to Scripture Studies* (1942), II, p. 265; M. Schumpp, *Das Buch Ezechiel* (1942), pp. 1f.; B. Balscheit, *Der Gottesbund* (1943), pp. 189ff.; E. Bruston, *La Bible du Centenaire* (1947), II, p. xxvi; J. Paterson, *The Goodly Fellowship of the Prophets*, pp. 161f.; Th. C. Vriezen, *Oudisraëlitische Geschriften* (1948), pp. 174ff.; M. A. Schmidt, *Prophet und Tempel: eine Studie zum Problem der Gottesnähe im AT* (1948), pp. 109ff., *Theologische Literaturzeitung*, VI (1950), pp. 81ff.; *YIOT*, pp. 257ff.; A. Lods, *Histoire de la littérature hébraïque et juive* (1950), pp. 443ff.; G. Fohrer, *Die Hauptprobleme des Buches Ezechiel*, pp. 5ff.; E. Power in *A Catholic Commentary on Holy Scripture* (1953), pp. 601ff.; H. G. May, *IB*, VI, pp. 51f.; J. Muilenburg in *Peake's Commentary on the Bible*, pp. 568ff.; *FSAC*, pp. 247f.; H. H. Rowley, *Men of God*, p. 209.

[54] *The Date and Composition of Ezekiel.*

show that neither the diction nor the contents of the prophecy suited any place outside Babylonia, nor any period other than that of the early sixth century B.C.

Similar conclusions were reached independently by Weir, who maintained that, while certain secondary elements could most probably be detected in the prophecy, the book in the main was the work of one who exercised his ministry wholly in Babylonia during the period of time covered by the extant text.[55] His view went far towards correcting the traditional liberal misinterpretation of the oracles of Ezekiel prior to 586 B.C. as being addressed to doomed Jerusalem.

From the foregoing discussion it is evident that, since the time of Hölscher, a wide range of critical opinion concerning the prophecy of Ezekiel has arisen. In the view of the writer, subsequent studies quite failed to attain the goal set for them by Kuhl, who looked to critical scholarship to remove the book from the crisis of divergent opinion to a clear understanding of its nature and origin.[56] Instead, it seems more accurate to conclude with Ellison that the intensive critical studies of thirty-five years have largely cancelled themselves out, and while they contributed to the understanding of much of the book, they have left the general position much as it was prior to 1924.[57] This opinion has also been espoused in the writings of Muilenburg, Rowley, and other scholars.[58]

2. *The historical background of the book.* Any attempt at evaluation of the prophecy should consider first of all the historical background against which it purports to have been compiled. There can be little doubt that the bulk of the work is concerned strictly with the exilic period, although isolated portions such as chapter 27 have occasionally been relegated to the fifth[59] or fourth[60] centuries B.C. The identity of Buzi, father of Ezekiel (Ezek. 1:3), is obscure, but it seems likely that he was a member of a well-known Zadokite priestly family and had come into prominence during the Josianic reformation of 621 B.C. He probably continued his ministry after the death of Josiah at Megiddo in 609 B.C., even though the religious reforms were no longer emphasized. It may be that Ezekiel himself became a Temple priest during the regime of Jehoiakim, or was at least in training for the priesthood at that time.

[55] C. J. M. Weir, *VT*, II (1952), pp. 97ff.

[56] C. Kuhl, *Theologische Rundschau*, V (1933), p. 115.

[57] H. L. Ellison, *NBD*, p. 407. For a survey of research between 1943 and 1952 see W. A. Irwin, *VT*, III (1953), pp. 54ff.

[58] J. Muilenburg in *Peake's Commentary on the Bible*, p. 569. H. H. Rowley, *Men of God*, pp. 209f.

[59] J. Morgenstern, *HUCA*, XVI (1941), pp. 10ff.

[60] Cf. L. Zunz, *ZDMG*, XXVII (1873), p. 678; C. C. Torrey in *Vom AT, Marti Festschrift*, pp. 284f.; L. E. Browne, *Ezekiel and Alexander*, pp. 4f.

According to Ezekiel 1:1; 33:21; 40:1, the prophet was deported to Babylon in 597 B.C. with a group of Judaean nobles, and lived in Tel-Abib on the Kabar canal (*nâru kabari*) near Nippur (Ezek. 1:1)[61] in his own house (Ezek. 3:24; 8:1). According to the opening verse of the book, his call occurred in 592 B.C., in the thirtieth year, in the fourth month, and the fifth day of the month, although the reference does not specify the point from which the reckoning began. The next verse, however, synchronizes this dating with the fifth year of the exile of Jehoiachin. The extent of Ezekiel's ministry, based upon the latest date in the remainder of the book (Ezek. 29:17), was at least twenty years.

His wife appears to have died about the time that Jerusalem was desolated (Ezek. 24:1, 15ff.), but it is uncertain whether Ezekiel himself lived to see the release from prison of Jehoiachin, under Amel-Marduk (2 Kgs. 25:27ff.; Jer. 52:31). Traditionally he spent the whole of his ministry in Babylonia, there enjoying special esteem as a prophet (Ezek. 8:1; 14:1). The first major division of his book (chapters 1–24) depicted him as the prophet of inexorable destruction, interpreting to the exiles the significance of the tragic events that were to overtake the inhabitants of Jerusalem. The second section (chapters 33–39) comprised his attempts to restore morale and rebuild the remnant into a virile spiritual community.

One of the more widely accepted critical hypotheses concerning Ezekiel was that suggested by Torrey and Smith to the effect that the bulk, if not all, of the ministry of Ezekiel was pursued against a Palestinian setting. This was prompted largely by the fact that most of the contents of chapters 1–24 appeared directed to the inhabitants of the doomed city of Jerusalem, and seemed to have little relevance as far as content was concerned for the exiled community in Babylonia.[62] Furthermore, it seemed to scholars who held to a Palestinian locale for the prophetic ministry that Ezekiel possessed such an intimate knowledge of people and events in Jerusalem as to make a Babylonian setting seem improbable. Whatever else may be said about this standpoint, it is worth noting that it claimed a respectable history, since a rabbinic tradition held that Ezekiel had commenced his prophetic activity in Palestine.[63]

Unfortunately the best support that could be mustered for the view that, whether or not Ezekiel went into captivity in 597 B.C., he was still prophesying in the vicinity of Jerusalem as late as 586 B.C., rested upon a complete misinterpretation of the early oracles. It was assumed that

---

[61] Cf. A. T. Olmstead, *History of the Persian Empire* (1948), pp. 299, 356ff.

[62] C. C. Torrey, *Pseudo-Ezekiel and the Original Prophecy*, pp. 24ff.; cf. *PIOT*, pp. 538ff.; G. R. Berry, *JBL*, XLIX (1930), p. 83, LVIII (1939), pp. 163ff.

[63] *Mekhilta Bo, 1b;* Targ. Ezek. 1:3. Cf. S. Spiegel, *JBL*, LIV (1935), pp. 169f.; P. Auvray, *RB*, LV (1948), p. 514. The tradition of a twofold ministry in the Targum of Jonathan on Ezek. 1:2f. was criticized by H. M. Orlinsky, *BASOR*, No. 122 (1951), p. 35n.

the utterances referring to events prior to 586 B.C. were addressed to doomed Jerusalem, whereas in actual fact the prophet Ezekiel was expounding the significance of coming events to the exiled group in Babylonia. The fact that his oracles were addressed to the inhabitants of Jerusalem is no proof that they were actually delivered there. By analogy, there is no reason to suppose, as Rowley has pointed out, that Amos travelled to the surrounding peoples in order to deliver against them the appropriate oracles in his book, or that all the denunciations against foreign peoples which occur in various prophetic books were delivered to other ears than those of the Israelites.[64] Thus there would seem to be no *a priori* reason for assuming that the prophecies of the period prior to 586 B.C. could not have been spoken to the exiles in the form of an address to the inhabitants of Judah.[65] If it was possible for a communication from Jeremiah to reach the exiles in Babylonia (Jer. 29:1ff.), it should in theory be at least equally possible for some of the utterances of Ezekiel to have come to the ears of those living in Judah and Jerusalem.

If the ministry of Ezekiel actually commenced in Palestine, as many scholars have suggested, it is far from easy, as Orlinsky has shown, to see precisely what an editor could have hoped to gain by transferring the prophetic ministry to Babylonia, against all known facts.[66] While it is possible to adduce from the early chapters some evidence for a Palestinian locale, it is very much more difficult to excise from the text the many other references that clearly point to a Mesopotamian setting for the ministry of the prophet. The very imagery of the inaugural vision, for example, clearly presupposes a background of Babylonian metallurgy, images of mythological beasts, semi-precious stones and the like,[67] which presents grave difficulties for an initial Palestinian call, whatever date might be suggested for the occasion.

In an attempt to meet objections of this nature it was suggested by O. R. Fischer that, while Ezekiel had gone to Babylon with the 597 B.C. deportation, he had returned to Jerusalem upon receiving his call.[68] This theory fails to account for the strictly Babylonian coloring of the early utterances against Judah and Jerusalem, and also raises the acute question as to whether it was at all possible for one of the exiles to return at will to his native land. It is true, of course, that Jeremiah was given free choice by the Babylonian captain of the guard to go to Mesopotamia or to remain in Judaea as he desired (Jer. 40:1ff.). However, there is no

[64] H. H. Rowley, *Men of God*, p. 194.
[65] G. A. Cooke, *A Critical and Exegetical Commentary on the Book of Ezekiel*, p. xxiv.
[66] H. M. Orlinsky, *BASOR*, No. 122 (1951), p. 35.
[67] G. R. Driver, *VT*, I (1951), pp. 60ff.
[68] *The Unity of the Book of Ezekiel* (unpublished dissertation, 1939), cited in *PIOT*, p. 531.

evidence that, while certain Judaean captives in Babylonia may have ultimately been released from prison (2 Kgs. 25:27), there was ever permission given, officially or otherwise, for any of the Babylonian exiles to return independently to Judaea during the period of captivity.[69]

An even less likely attempt to place Ezekiel in Judah for a certain period of time was made by Bentzen, who suggested that the prophet was actually some sort of secret agent in the service of the Babylonians, and as such was permitted to return to Jerusalem a few years before the fall of that city.[70] This improbability is made even more unlikely by referring to the experiences of Jeremiah, who came close to death when he was suspected by the nobility of such activity before 587 B.C. Had Ezekiel been prophesying the destruction of the city in Jerusalem itself or in Judaea at the same time as Jeremiah—a supposition for which there is not the slightest evidence—he could have expected to share a similar fate, particularly if his political integrity had become suspect in the process.

Although Kuhl cited certain references (Ezek. 2:3, 5f.; 3:7, 9, 24f.) in an attempt to prove that Ezekiel did endure some form of suffering,[71] there is nothing in the passages mentioned which would indicate that judicial or state authorities were imposing punishment upon the prophet, as was the case with Jeremiah. Instead, such privation as Ezekiel endured was completely compatible with a local Babylonian situation, and of a character that would suggest that his fellow-exiles were in fact principally responsible for it.

The weakness in Herntrich's view that an exilic disciple transferred the prophecies of Ezekiel from a Palestinian to a Babylonian framework was clearly shown by Messel, who suggested that the exiles would in any event have known the facts concerning the life of Ezekiel, and would in consequence have repudiated it, had the situation been as Herntrich had proposed.[72] As far as Smith's emphasis upon the significance of the phrase "house of Israel" in this connection is concerned, it merely needs to be noted that it has been nullified by the work of Battersby Harford, who showed that the expression was also used in connection with the inhabitants of Judah and Jerusalem, quite aside from any possibility of the kind of northern ministry contemplated by Smith.[73] A further blow to this view was provided by Danell, who adduced evidence to prove that the term "house of Israel" was used of the exiles also.[74] Quite clearly the expression cannot therefore be used

[69] Cf. C. J. M. Weir, VT, II (1952), p. 101.
[70] A. Bentzen, Introduction to the OT, II, p. 128.
[71] C. Kuhl, Theologische Literaturzeitung, VIII (1952), pp. 410ff.
[72] N. Messel, Ezechielfragen, pp. 12f.
[73] J. Battersby Harford, Studies in the Book of Ezekiel, pp. 93ff.
[74] G. A. Danell, Studies in the Name of Israel in the OT (1946), pp. 237ff.

as a demand for the recognition of a Palestinian ministry, in part or in whole, by Ezekiel.

In the light of the foregoing discussion it would appear that there are serious difficulties confronting those who have objected to the traditional locale of Ezekiel in his prophetic role. It needs to be remembered, as May has stated, that in itself there is no insuperable difficulty inherent in a prophet's uttering oracles or performing dramatic scenes in Babylonia primarily for the benefit of people in Palestine.[75] It would be quite possible for his words to be carried there, as must have happened at other times under different conditions, when prophets in Palestine pronounced oracles of judgment against foreign nations. On balance it seems best to conclude with Howie that Ezekiel, as tradition maintains, was a prophet among the exiles in Babylonia, where he was called to be a spokesman of God, both to his immediate company and also to the Judaeans who remained in the land of Palestine.[76]

The problems connected with the chronology of chapter 1:1f. and the call of Ezekiel have come in for considerable discussion, particularly in the light of Bertholet's suggestion that chapters 1:4–2:2 and 2:3–3:9 contained two separate calls to prophetic office, the second indicating the commencement of the Palestinian ministry and the first marking the beginning of activity in Babylon. It should be remarked that the general dating sequences in Ezekiel are quite precise, and that no oracle in the work is dated earlier than the one contained in the first chapter. Furthermore, there is no evidence that any other utterance ought to be dated previous to this particular vision. Thus there seems to be no valid reason for transferring the date in Ezekiel 1:1f. to the vision of Ezekiel 2:3ff. and then placing the vision of chapter one later in point of time than that occurring in chapter two, as Bertholet did. Moreover, Rowley has made it clear that on such a procedure the vision of chapter one becomes purposeless, since it contains neither a call nor a commission. Again, the call of Ezekiel 2:3–3:9 is made to commence with the commission to the prophet, but without any indication of the identity of the person who commissioned him, or the occasion respecting which such activity was entertained.[77]

The reference to the "thirtieth year" in Ezekiel 1:1 has been of interest to scholars, partly for the reason that there is no indication in the text of the point from which the dating commenced. Begrich held that the reference to the same month in Ezekiel 1:1 and 1:2 indicated that the thirtieth year was to be identified with the fifth year of Jehoiachin as captive.[78] As such it would indicate the date when Ezekiel received his

[75] H. G. May, *IB*, VI, pp. 51f.

[76] C. G. Howie, *IDB*, II, p. 206.

[77] H. H. Rowley, *Men of God*, p. 197.

[78] J. Begrich, *Die Chronologie der Könige von Israel und Juda* (1926), p. 206; cf. D. Kidner, *Ezekiel* (1969), pp. 36ff.

prophetic call, but since Ezekiel 1:1 constituted one of the latest dates in the prophecy when reckoned in terms of the captivity of Jehoiachin,[79] it would seem to be distinct from the other chronological notations in the book. Bertholet was so convinced that the reference to "thirtieth" should in fact be related to Jehoiachin that he quite arbitrarily changed the text so as to read "thirteenth," and then reckoned it in terms of the captivity of Jehoiachin.[80] This was no more satisfactory than the view of Herntrich, who maintained that the original text had spoken of a "third" year, which he interpreted in terms of the reign of Zedekiah.[81] Snaith, however, suggested that the computation was made in relation to the entire length of the life of King Jehoiachin, which would place the call of Ezekiel about 576 B.C., following 2 Chronicles 36:9, or about 586 B.C., following 2 Kings 24:8.[82]

Torrey held that the reckoning was in terms of the rule of Manasseh,[83] while Browne dated it according to the regnal years of Artaxerxes III.[84] Cooke, on the other hand, followed the suggestion of Begrich that the meanings of "thirtieth" in Ezekiel 1:1 and "fifth" in Ezekiel 1:2 were identical, the difference being accounted for by varying systems of chronological computation.[85] Some scholars followed the tradition in the *Targum of Jonathan* in interpreting the date as the thirtieth year after the Josianic reforms,[86] while others, adopting the view of Rosenmüller, held that the text referred to the thirtieth year after the founding of the Neo-Babylonian empire.[87] Yet another interpretation of some antiquity, and one to which the present writer is favorably disposed, is that the "thirtieth year" was that of the prophet himself.[88] This view is reinforced by the tradition that Levites, and doubtless priests also, were about thirty years of age when they commenced their official duties

---

[79] As computed by S. Spiegel, *Harvard Theological Review*, XXIV (1931), p. 289, *JBL*, LVI (1937), p. 407; G. R. Berry, *JBL*, LI (1932), p. 55; W. F. Albright, *JBL*, LI (1932), p. 90; B. D. Eerdmans, *The Religion of Israel*, pp. 196f.; C. G. Howie, *The Date and Composition of Ezekiel*, p. 41.

[80] A. Bertholet and K. Galling, *Hesekiel*, p. 3.

[81] V. Herntrich, *Ezechielprobleme*, p. 74.

[82] N. H. Snaith, *ET*, LIX (1947-48), pp. 315f.

[83] C. C. Torrey, *Pseudo-Ezekiel and the Original Prophecy*, pp. 63f.

[84] L. E. Browne, *Ezekiel and Alexander*, p. 10.

[85] G. A. Cooke, *A Critical and Exegetical Commentary on the Book of Ezekiel*, pp. 3f. J. Begrich, *Die Chronologie der Könige von Israel und Juda*, pp. 206f.

[86] So Jerome, *PL*, XXV, col. 17; J. Herrmann, *Ezechiel*, p. 10; L. Finkelstein, *The Pharisees*, II, pp. 632ff.

[87] E. F. C. Rosenmüller, *Scholia in Vetus Testamentum*, VI (1808), p. 15; S. Davidson, *An Introduction to the OT* (1863), III, p. 141; R. Smend, *Der Prophet Ezechiel* (1880), p. 5.

[88] So Origen, *PG*, XIII, cols. 672, 675; R. Kraetzschmar, *Das Buch Ezechiel* (1900), p. 4; C. Steuernagel, *Lehrbuch der Einleitung in das AT* (1912), p. 127; O. Eissfeldt, *PJB*, XXVII (1931), p. 66n.; K. Budde, *JBL*, L (1931), p. 29; J. A. Bewer, *AJSL*, L (1934), pp. 96ff.; *YIOT*, p. 244, *et al.*

(Num. 4:3ff.; cf. Lk. 3:23). Accordingly the birth of the prophet occurred about 622 B.C., a date that corresponds closely to the outside limit set by Pfeiffer from a study of the historical allusions in the prophecy itself.[89]

While no explanation of the comparative chronology of Ezekiel 1:1 and 1:2 is entirely without difficulty, the best approach seems to be that of regarding the reference to the "thirtieth year" in 1:1 as standing apart from the other notations in the prophecy. The latter are seen to be based consistently upon the captive years of Jehoiachin, a fact that Albright considered as furnishing striking confirmation of the genuineness of the prophecy.[90] While it was obviously discreet to adopt this procedure, it was also realistic in the sense that, apart from a period of a few months' rule (2 Kgs. 24:8), the regnal years of Jehoiachin, as far as his people were concerned, were also the years of his exile.

The discoveries of Koldewey relating to the ration allotments for the Hebrew royal house have shown by implication that the Babylonians recognized Jehoiachin as the legitimate ruler of Judah, and have given substance to the custom of the exiles in dating events by his reign rather than by that of Zedekiah.[91] If the "thirtieth year" of Ezekiel 1:1 is taken as referring to the prophet himself, the chronology of the prophecy remains undisturbed. On such a basis it is possible to assume that the prophet died somewhat after 571 B.C., and this would give him a life-span of a little over fifty years. While it is true that such a means of drawing attention to the age of the prophet is rather unusual, it can be said in reply that Ezekiel himself was far from an ordinary individual; also the verse in question presents certain unique characteristics on any interpretation.

C. The Compilation of the Book

Any attempt to discuss the provenance and composition of Ezekiel must begin by noting a theme that has occurred consistently in critical study of the prophecy, namely, that, despite the possible presence of secondary elements in the composition, the work as a whole bears the decided imprint of a single personality.[92] While this in itself does not automatically guarantee the integrity of the prophecy in its extant form, it is certainly a powerful argument in its favor. However, a number of those who have sought to recover the "original oracles" of Ezekiel from the substance of the prophecy have attributed this homogeneity to the

---

[89] *PIOT*, pp. 534f.

[90] W. F. Albright, *JBL*, LI (1932), p. 93, *BA*, V, No. 4 (1942), p. 54.

[91] R. Koldewey, *Das Wieder Erstehende Babylon* (1925), pp. 90ff.; E. F. Weidner, *Mélanges syriens offerts à Monsieur R. Dussaud*, II (1939), pp. 923ff.; *ANET*, p. 308; *ANE*, p. 205; *DOTT*, pp. 84ff.

[92] So J. Skinner, *HDB*, I, p. 817; *DILOT*, p. 279; C. C. Torrey, *JBL*, LVIII (1939), p. 77; H. H. Rowley, *Men of God*, p. 187, *et al.*

thorough manner in which the book was edited.[93] Even so, some of those who adhere to this position have not lost sight of the fact that the principal editor of the composition may well have been one and the same person, rather than a variety of hands.

Like the majority of the prophetic writings, Ezekiel comprises an anthology of material associated with the exilic ministry of that great prophet. In some respects it is quite similar in structure to Isaiah and Jeremiah—for example, in the manner in which oracles against foreign nations were grouped together. Unlike any other prophecy, however, Ezekiel ascribes specific dates to several of its sections (Ezek. 1:2; 8:1; 20:1; 24:1; 26:1; 29:1, 17; 30:20; 31:1; 32:1, 17; 33:21; 40:1). There seems to be no reason for doubting that Albright and others are correct in accepting the validity of these dates as they stand, and reckoning them in terms of the captivity of Jehoiachin, which, as noted above, would correspond to the years of his reign. Despite the substantial correctness of the dates, not all the sections prefixed in this manner are in chronological order, nor is it necessarily the case that all the material associated with a particular date was written or uttered entirely on that specific occasion, as may perhaps be illustrated by the oracles against Tyre (Ezek. 26:1–28:26).[94]

Critical estimates of the literary abilities of Ezekiel have varied considerably. Whereas Lowth equated his poetic achievements with those of Aeschylus,[95] Driver regarded him as the most uniformly prosaic of the earlier Hebrew prophets,[96] and Bewer maintained that he was prosaic even when writing poetry.[97] Regardless of individual assessments of the literary abilities of Ezekiel, it is of great importance to avoid undertaking an analysis of the work on the naive assumption that the author was essentially a poet, as Hölscher and Irwin did. To what extent the book as a whole was written down in the time of Ezekiel cannot be ascertained with absolute certainty, although Widengren has adduced evidence to show that portions of the prophecy indicate that the prophet wrote down at least some of his utterances during his lifetime.[98] This opinion stood in contrast to the view of Hempel, who maintained that the oracles of Ezekiel were transmitted orally, and that several subsequent collections were made prior to the ultimate compilation of the extant book.[99]

---

[93] E.g. H. G. May, *IB*, VI, p. 45.

[94] Cf. O. Eissfeldt, *Einleitung in das AT*, pp. 417ff.

[95] R. Lowth, *Lectures on the Sacred Poetry of the Hebrews* (1835), pp. 231f.

[96] *DILOT*, p. 296.

[97] J. A. Bewer, *The Literature of the OT with Historical Development* (1922), p. 183; cf. *PIOT*, pp. 564f.

[98] G. Widengren, *Literary and Psychological Aspects of the Hebrew Prophets*, pp. 74ff.

[99] J. Hempel, *Die althebräische Litteratur* (1930), pp. 167ff.

It is at least possible that Ezekiel, like Jeremiah, prepared a collection of his own oracles which served as the basis for the extant prophecy, if, in fact, they did not actually constitute the bulk of it. Reflecting the general methodology of the literary analytical school, Kraetzschmar suggested that the book was constructed out of two sources, one written in the first person and the other in the third. Although this means of accounting for the doublets and parallel texts was accepted with some reserve by Budde,[100] it failed to win scholarly approval, particularly when Sellin pointed out that the third person was employed on one occasion only of Ezekiel.[101] A two-source theory of the kind envisaged by Kraetzschmar, therefore, quite obviously goes far beyond the available evidence. Furthermore, as has been noted previously, on examination some of the alleged doublets prove to be rather different from what Kraetzschmar had imagined, thus making for a further weakening of his theory.

A somewhat better explanation of the duplicate sections in Ezekiel was furnished in the commentary by Herrmann, who maintained that Ezekiel himself compiled the book on the basis of notes of his prophetic oracles that he had accumulated over a period of time, and that he subsequently edited and augmented the first edition of his work.[102] The view that such doublets were the work of copyists is weak in that it tends to disrupt the acknowledged unity of character exhibited by the book, and confuses the activity of the copyist with that of an editor.[103]

Much of the critical analysis of the book has turned upon the amount of "genuine" oracular material it contains, a theoretical postulate that invites a further question as to how far it is possible to establish canons of genuineness, and what in fact constitutes an oracle thus defined. Is an oracle to be regarded as valid only when it has the appearance of a *verbatim* record, or is it equally authentic when it preserves the substance of an earlier prophetic utterance, perhaps with some omissions or additions? Such considerations lead in turn to the ultimate question as to whether it is possible in the last analysis to know precisely what constituted the detailed form of the original utterance. In this last respect the scholar is dependent upon the witness and integrity of the ancient author to a greater extent than has been realized by many critical analysts, particularly in a case such as that presented by Ezekiel, where there is a remarkable degree of uniformity in the finished product. To regard such homogeneity as due principally to editorial activity at a subsequent period is to overlook the fact that had this uniformity not been characteristic of the original work, the diversity between author

---

[100] K. Budde, *Geschichte der althebräischen Litteratur*, p. 156.
[101] E. Sellin, *An Introduction to the OT* (1923), p. 155.
[102] J. Herrmann, *Ezechiel*, pp. v ff.
[103] Cf. M. L. Dumeste, *RB*, XLVI (1937), p. 431.

and editor would have been clearly apparent at a later stage in the history of the book.

Efforts to recover the "original book" of Ezekiel have frequently commenced with an estimate of the authenticity of the throne-chariot vision in the first two chapters. For Hölscher only the vision of the storm in Ezekiel 1:4, 28 was original, while the remainder was deemed to be secondary material.[104] Herntrich rejected the originality of the vision in chapter one, as did Irwin,[105] while Messel held that it had been misplaced textually, having in his view originally occurred before chapter 45.[106] Matthews concluded that fragments of a poem were embedded in the throne-chariot vision, and that the first two chapters were essentially composite.[107]

H. G. May, on the other hand, argued strongly for the originality of the material, stating that the vision of the storm, the throne, and the chariot comprised an ideological unit which did not admit of unnatural and artificial separation.[108] May reinforced his argument by an appeal to the concept of divine glory reflected in Psalm 29, which he regarded as being most probably considerably earlier than the time of Ezekiel. He adduced a further presupposition for the originality of the throne-chariot vision from the myth-and-ritual pattern connected with the enthronement of the deity and the rites of Tammuz.[109] However, there are some fairly obvious difficulties in any interpretation of this material in terms of divine enthronement, as May himself has conceded. There is neither evidence nor proof for the existence in Israel during the pre-exilic period of an annual enthronement ceremony similar to that found in Babylonia, so that any interpretation along these lines must necessarily be regarded as being highly speculative. Secondly, the vision in chapter one makes it clear that Ezekiel was not witnessing an enthronement ritual. Thirdly, there is no hint from the exilic literature that the Tammuz rites were practiced by the Hebrews in exile, and no indication from chapters one and two that the prophet was remotely concerned with either the departure or the death of Tammuz. The throne-chariot vision is a unity, as May noted, and was ultimately connected with the call of the prophet. So forceful was its impact that it was reflected with remarkable similarity of diction in utterances occurring many years later, as recorded in chapters 40 to 48. As such it may quite legitimately be regarded as

[104] G. Hölscher, *Hezekiel, der Dichter und das Buch*, pp. 45ff.

[105] V. Herntrich, *Ezechielprobleme*, p. 77. W. A. Irwin, *The Problem of Ezekiel*, pp. 223ff.

[106] N. Messel, *Ezechielfragen*, pp. 39ff.

[107] I. G. Matthews, *Ezekiel*, pp. 3ff.

[108] H. G. May, *IB*, VI, pp. 46f.

[109] J. Morgenstern, *HUCA*, V (1928), pp. 45ff., VI (1929), pp. 1ff.; cf. F. J. Hollis in S. H. Hooke (ed.), *Myth and Ritual* (1933), pp. 87ff.; H. G. May, *JBL*, LVI (1937), pp. 309ff.; T. H. Gaster, *JBL*, LX (1941), pp. 289ff.

being integral to the spiritual experience of the prophet, and therefore authentic.

Attempts have been made to analyze chapter 27 into prose and poetic elements, and to assign them to different hands. Morgenstern held that the chapter referred to the events of 480 B.C.;[110] an even later date in the period of Alexander the Great was proposed by Browne and supported in general by Torrey.[111] On the other hand, Sidney Smith has shown in a detailed examination of the chapter that it contains nothing incompatible with the sixth-century B.C. siege of Tyre by Nebuchadnezzar, and that the entire chapter must be interpreted as a unity if the background as a whole is to be understood properly.[112]

Other extraneous material has been held to include the sections dealing with Gog and Magog (Ezek. 38:1–39:29), which described the attack of Gog, from the northern land of Magog, against the house of Israel living in Palestine. The identification of Gog has been disputed for many years, with Delitzsch identifying him with Gyges of Lydia[113] and Weber linking him with the city of Carchemish by means of the Amarna term *Gaga*.[114] The latter view was rejected forcibly by Albright, who preferred to think in terms of Gašga, a name occurring in Hittite tablets and describing a wild location on the borders of Armenia and Cappadocia.[115] Because of the apocalyptic elements involved it was suggested that the word Gog was actually derived from the Sumerian term *gug*, meaning "darkness," and that therefore Gog was the personification of darkness and evil.[116]

Yet another view suggested that Gog was a deliberately coined secondary form of Magog. By reversing the letters of Magog (מגג) and reading it in the ancient cipher in which the following letter of the alphabet was employed for the one intended, the real recipient of the prophecy, Babylon (בבל), was meant to be conveyed to the hearers.[117] Returning to a consideration of historical personages it is interesting to note that at the turn of the twentieth century Winckler suggested that Gog was a

---

[110] J. Morgenstern, *HUCA*, XVI (1941), pp. 10ff.

[111] L. E. Browne, *Ezekiel and Alexander*, pp. 4f. C. C. Torrey in *Vom AT, Marti Festschrift*, pp. 248f.

[112] S. Smith, *PEQ*, LXXXV (1953), pp. 97ff. Cf. S. Spiegel, *Harvard Theological Review*, XXIV (1931), pp. 292f.

[113] F. Delitzsch, *Wo lag das Paradies?* (1881), pp. 246f. On the general problem see J. L. Myers, *PEF Quarterly Statement* (1932), pp. 213ff.

[114] O. Weber in J. A. Knudtzon (ed.), *Die El-Amarna Tafeln* (1915), II, p. 1015; cf. *YIOT*, pp. 246ff.

[115] W. F. Albright, *JBL*, XLIII (1924), pp. 381f.

[116] A. van Hoonacker, *ZA*, XXVIII (1914), p. 336; cf. Rev. 20:8, where Gog and Magog appear to be persons.

[117] J. Boehmer, *Zeitschrift für wissenschaftliche Theologie*, XL (1897), pp. 347f. L. Finkelstein, *The Pharisees*, I, p. 338, envisaged a cipher using the preceding Hebrew letter to produce *Babel*.

pseudonym for Alexander the Great,[118] while Seinecke identified him with Antiochus IV Epiphanes.[119] Berry thought that Gog was Antiochus V Eupator (163-162 B.C.),[120] and Schmidt placed him even later, identifying him with Mithridates VI, king of Pontus from 120 to 64 B.C.[121]

While the problems associated with the personage of Gog will probably never be resolved, it seems proper to observe that the Hebrew form of the name is the equivalent of *Gûgu*, the Assyrian rendering of Gyges, the cognomen of a Lydian king about 670-652 B.C. If an identification with some purely historical personage were to be required, this would seem to be one of the most reasonable suggestions. However, an apocalyptic interpretation of the passage in question should not be dismissed out of hand, since the oracle depicts happenings at the end of a prolonged period of time (Ezek. 38:8, 16). Furthermore, the association of Gog and Magog with peoples at the extremities of the then-known world (Ezek. 38:5f.) might suggest an eschatological motif rather than an historically identifiable individual or group. In connection with the latter concept it is of some interest to note that the LXX understood "Magog" as a people rather than as a country, and while this is no doubt correct, the advance in comprehension is not a particularly significant one. If an eschatological interpretation is valid, it constitutes a strong argument for originality of authorship of this section, coming as it does immediately after the vision concerning the resurrected bones of Israel (Ezek. 37:1-14) and the renewal of the nation (Ezek. 37:15-28), a sequence that can hardly have been accidental.

Questions have also been raised by literary critics concerning the date of portions of chapter 36. Irwin maintained that Ezekiel 36:7-12 reflected conditions in Judaea just before the work of Nehemiah commenced, that is to say, about 445 B.C.[122] Similarly, Matthews related the reference to the "nations" in Ezekiel 36:5 to the racial groups that were causing unrest at the time of Nehemiah.[123] According to May, the presumed viewpoint of the author was the Diaspora, as indicated by Ezekiel 36:17-20, so that the entire chapter could be relegated accordingly to a post-Ezekiel date in the fifth century B.C.[124] While these views appear plausible at first sight, they tend to outrun the evidence furnished by the text. Ezekiel 36:7-12 comprises pure prophecy about the future of the restored Israel, in which the revitalized nation is to constitute the blessing that the Gentiles will seek with great earnestness (Ezek. 36:12), a

[118] H. Winckler, *Altorientalische Forschungen,* II (1901), pp. 160ff.

[119] L. Seinecke, *Geschichte des Volkes Israel,* II (1884), pp. 13f.

[120] G. R. Berry, *JBL,* XLI (1922), pp. 224ff.

[121] N. Schmidt, *EB,* IV, cols. 4332f.

[122] W. A. Irwin, *The Problem of Ezekiel,* pp. 59f.

[123] I. G. Matthews, *Ezekiel,* p. 136.

[124] H. G. May, *IB,* VI, p. 48.

theme not unknown to other prophetic writers. Furthermore, the ideal nature of the conditions reflected in chapter 36:8-11 ill accords with the facts of the political and social situation just prior to the time of Nehemiah, as recorded in that book.

As against the contention of Matthews, the reference is in fact to the Edomites and their allies, who took advantage of the fall of Jerusalem in 587 B.C. to migrate into the heart of southern Judah, south of Hebron. For this as well as for traitorous acts against the captives generally, the Edomites were rebuked by several of the prophets (Jer. 49:7ff.; Lam. 4:21f.; Obad. 10ff.), including Ezekiel (25:12ff.; 35:3). That May is clearly wrong in his supposition of a post-Ezekiel date for Ezekiel 36:17-20 is indicated by the fact that the prophet was reminding the exiles of the idolatrous wrongdoings in which they indulged before Jerusalem was overthrown, and the punishment and shame that had resulted. The entire action is depicted as being in the past, and concluded with a note of pity on the part of God, which promised some hope of future restoration. While the Jews in exile were certainly far removed from their native land, it was by forcible action and not by the kind of voluntary dispersion of Israel that is commonly understood by the term "Diaspora." The locale of the prophecy in chapter 36 was undoubtedly Babylonia, and the standpoint that of an exilic prophet.

Despite the attempts of Hölscher and Irwin to assign the bulk of the prophecy of Ezekiel to secondary sources, the fact remains that the homogeneity of the composition demands little if any source material that does not go back for its origin to Ezekiel himself. The visions and oracles are unquestionably the experiences of the attributive author, since it is impossible to posit them of any other known contemporary writer. To relegate passages that might at first sight appear unauthentic to the activities of an editor is a questionable undertaking in view of the manner in which the prophecy reflects the stamp of a single personality, unless, of course, such an editor is identified with the prophet himself.

While it is possible to list a number of expressions held to be characteristic of an editor, as May has done,[125] such an attempt to isolate phrases from the prophecy can only be achieved at the expense of destroying the homogeneity of the work and disrupting the ideological interrelationship of the various parts. Even May conceded defeat in admitting that such activity made it improbable objectively to presume a multiplicity of authors. In sum, as Rowley has stated, there appears to be little that has been incorporated into the prophecy which does not go back at all to the work of Ezekiel.[126]

The major oracles of Ezekiel can probably be determined somewhat as follows: 1:1–3:27; 4:1-19; 5:1-17; 6:1-14; 7:1-22; 8:1–10:22; 11:1-25;

---

[125] *Ibid.*, pp. 50f.
[126] H. H. Rowley, *Men of God*, p. 190.

13:1-23; 14:1-11, 12-23; 15:1-8; 16:1-63; 17:1-21; 18:1-32; 19:1-14; 20:1-44; 21:1-7, 8-32; 22:1-16; 23:1-49; 24:1-14, 15-27; 25:1-17; 26:1–28:26; 29:1-16; 30:1-26; 31:1-18; 32:1-32; 33:1-29; 34:1-31; 35:1-15; 36:1-15, 16-38; 37:1-14, 15-28; 38:1–39:16; 39:17-29; 40:1-49; 41:1-26; 42:1-20; 43:1-17, 18-29; 44:1-8, 9-31; 45:1–46:24; 47:1-23; 48:1-35. Subsidiary oracles or fragments might perhaps include 7:23-27; 12:1-16, 17-20, 21-25, 26-28; 17:22-24; 20:45-49; 22:17-22, 23-31; 29:17-21; and 33:30-33.

While there are difficulties in determining the chronology of the oracles on the basis of the dates furnished in the text, an attempt has been made to relate them to existing calendars. Parker and Dubberstein have furnished tables based on autumnal and spring calendars which compute the dates of the oracles as follows (parenthetical dates correspond to the spring calendar): Ezek. 1:2, July 1, 592 B.C. (July 1, 592 B.C.); 8:1, Sept. 7, 591 B.C. (Sept. 17, 592 B.C.); 20:1, Sept. 1, 590 B.C. (Aug. 13, 591 B.C.); 24:1, Jan. 15, 588 B.C. (Jan. 15, 588 B.C.); 29:1, Jan. 6, 587 B.C. (Jan. 6, 587 B.C.); 29:17, Apr. 16, 570 B.C. (Apr. 26, 571 B.C.); 30:20, Apr. 19, 586 B.C. (Apr. 29, 587 B.C.); 31:1, June 11, 586 B.C. (June 21, 587 B.C.); 32:1, Mar. 3, 585 B.C. (Mar. 3, 585 B.C.); 32:17, Apr. 16, 585 B.C. (Apr. 27, 586 B.C.); 33:21, Jan. 8, 585 B.C. (Jan. 8, 585 B.C.); 40:1, Apr. 17, 572 B.C. (Apr. 28, 573 B.C.).[127]

Of uncertain date was the oracle in Ezekiel 26:1ff., since some manuscripts of the LXX version read "twelfth" rather than "eleventh." It is probably to be dated just before 587 B.C. when, according to Josephus, Nebuchadnezzar besieged Tyre.[128] If it was originally dated in the twelfth year, the oracle could be assigned to February 3, 585 B.C., but as it stands the Hebrew text is nearer to the probable date of the utterance.

Aside from Ezekiel 26:1, two other verses (29:17; 33:21) contain dates out of strict chronological order, a fact that has been interpreted in favor of their authenticity, since a later schematic arrangement would presumably have corrected this imbalance. Albright and Howie in particular have followed a variant reading for the date given in Ezekiel 33:21, as furnished by some eight LXX manuscripts and the Syriac, which substituted "eleventh" for "twelfth"[129] making the fugitive arrive in Babylonia six months after the fall of Jerusalem, which occurred in the fourth month of the eleventh year.

On the basis of the autumnal reckoning, the tenth month of the twelfth year would be less than six months after the fourth month of the

[127] R. A. Parker and W. H. Dubberstein, *Babylonian Chronology 626 B.C.–A.D. 45* (1942), pp. 25f.
[128] *Contra Apion.*, I, 21. Cf. W. F. Albright, *JBL*, LI (1932), pp. 94f.; O. Eissfeldt, *Forschungen und Fortschritte*, X (1934), p. 165; M. Vogelstein, *HUCA*, XXIII (1950), pp. 197ff.; C. G. Howie, *The Date and Composition of Ezekiel*, pp. 42f.
[129] Cf. J. A. Bewer, *ZAW*, LIV (1936), pp. 114f.

eleventh year, and would seem to indicate that the date of January 8, 585 B.C., as represented by the Hebrew text, is quite reasonable. As against the views of literary analysts such as Hölscher, Torrey, Irwin, Fohrer, and others that the dates constitute later editorial addenda,[130] it merely needs to be observed that the contents of the oracles are consistent with the dates ascribed to them, and the latter should therefore be accepted as authentic unless there are pressing textual and contextual reasons to the contrary. As Finegan has shown, given an historical basis for deduction such as that furnished by cuneiform sources that supplied dates from the tenth to the thirty-fifth years of Nebuchadnezzar II, that is to say, from 594 to 569 B.C., Ezekiel is both understandable and historical when related to Jehoiachin as the legitimate though exiled ruler of Judah.[131]

Attempts by adherents of form-criticism to envisage the process by which the prophecy assumed its extant form have generally included the reconstruction of prose and poetical complexes. Those who have regarded Ezekiel as being primarily a poet, following Hölscher, have seen the poetic sections as constituting the *ipsissima verba* of the prophet, transmitted orally in the first instance, and subsequently fixed in writing. The prose sections, on the other hand, have frequently been interpreted as only generally reflecting the words of the master, and being the object of revision by disciples or redactors to the point where they were ultimately joined to the group of poems already in existence. This view suffers from the assumption, frequently implicit rather than explicit, that Ezekiel was only capable of writing poetry, a supposition for which the text furnishes no evidence whatever. Both poetic and prose sections exhibit a uniformity of diction and ideology that mark them out as the work of a single mind; and any attempt to isolate poetic passages in the arbitrary manner employed by Hölscher, Irwin, and others is an entirely unwarranted disruption of the form in which the material was transmitted. Instead of drawing what is essentially an artificial distinction between poetry and prose, it is surely much more realistic to group the constituent materials in terms of visions, oracles, fragments, and the like. Because of the special nature of these sources, it seems probable that much of it was in written form within a comparatively short period after the events described had occurred. This is almost certainly true of chapters 40—48, in which the ideal Temple and the priesthood are described.

---

[130] G. Hölscher, *Hezekiel, der Dichter und das Buch*, pp. 108, 125, 147. C. C. Torrey, *Pseudo-Ezekiel and the Original Prophecy*, pp. 58ff., *JBL*, LVIII (1939), pp. 73ff. W. A. Irwin, *The Problem of Ezekiel*, p. 265. G. Fohrer, *Die Hauptprobleme des Buches Ezechiel*, p. 29.

[131] J. Finegan, *JBL*, LXIX (1950), pp. 61ff.; cf. C. G. Howie, *The Date and Composition of Ezekiel*, pp. 34ff.

Some scholars have questioned the originality of those sections dealing with the allotment of the land (Ezek. 45:1-9; 47:13—48:35) and the regulations concerning measures (Ezek. 45:10—46:18). However, since matters of this kind were a firm and continuous concern of the priestly tradition from the time of Moses onwards, there seems no reason why a Zadokite priest should not have had some interest in these things also. Chapters 40—48 may well have existed independently for some time before being joined to other written parts of the prophecy. That the vision of the Temple in Ezekiel 40:5ff. was a subconscious reflection of a real structure is indicated by the fact that the east gate, on reconstruction, proves to be of the same general type as that excavated from the Solomonic period of Megiddo by Nelson Glueck. Such a memory must have arisen, as Howie has observed, from one who was acquainted with the Solomonic Temple in some detail, since gates constructed after the general pattern described in Ezekiel were not found after the early ninth century B.C.[132]

Some scholars have held that a comparatively late date for the extant prophecy is required by the presence of Aramaisms in the text. However, the much wider knowledge of the west-Semitic group of languages now available has shown this argument to be invalid, since Aramaisms can be expected to occur in any writings from the late Amarna Age onwards. In any event, Aramaic constituted the *lingua franca* of the Assyrian empire from the middle of the eighth century B.C. on, and therefore the presence of Aramaic forms cannot constitute valid evidence for a fourth-century date of composition in final form, as some scholars formerly argued.

Howie has shown that critical assertions that Ezekiel was saturated with Aramaisms were accepted quite uncritically for the most part by those who followed the arguments of the liberal school. In point of fact, only nine definite Aramaic roots occur, two of which were drawn from earlier Aramaic sources. Regarding questions of syntax, the influence of Aramaic is negligible, and it is only in the area of morphology that alterations in pronominal forms, noun-endings, and verbs reveal occasional Aramaisms.[133] Clearly the amount of Aramaic influence upon the syntax and vocabulary of the book has been grossly exaggerated, and on the basis of all available evidence there would seem to be nothing in the linguistic structure of the oracles and visions that is incompatible with a date in the early sixth century B.C.

Among those scholars who regard the prophecy as substantially authentic and original with Ezekiel, some have taken the "thirtieth year" of Ezekiel 1:1 as the date when the prophet completed the draft of his

[132] C. G. Howie, *IDB*, II, pp. 206f.
[133] C. G. Howie, *The Date and Composition of Ezekiel*, pp. 47ff.

847

work.[134] For those critics who assigned a conspicuous role to editors in the preparation of the final recension of the work, the date had very little to do with the completion of the prophecy.

Some light has been shed on one tradition concerning the formulation of Ezekiel by the manuscript discoveries at Qumran. According to Josephus, Ezekiel "left behind him in writing two books."[135] This statement has generally been interpreted to mean that the first twenty-four chapters of the prophecy, consisting of oracles of doom for Judah, comprised one-half of a bisected work, while the remaining twenty-four chapters, which included oracles against foreign nations as well as promises of restoration for Judah, constituted the other half. The evidence from 1QIsa[a], which indicates that Isaiah was itself originally a bifid, can be applied with equal success to the book of Ezekiel.

Brownlee has pointed out the antithetical and parallelistic features that arise when the book is viewed as a two-volume work.[136] The call of the prophet is recorded in 3:16-21 and also in 33:1-9; whereas in the former his commission was followed by dumbness (3:25-27), in the latter passage it resulted in release from that affliction (33:21f.). The first half of the bifid anthology closed with a prophecy concerning the destruction of the Temple (24:15-27), whereas the second half concluded with the restoration of the Temple and cultus (40:1ff.). The divine glory that forsook the sacred edifice in chapters 8 to 11 returned in the final vision of chapter 43:1-5 to sanctify the entire land.

Brownlee suggested what might be an even better arrangement whereby the second volume of the bifid would commence at Ezekiel 24:1 or 24:15, thereby dealing with Jerusalem as a beginning rather than with foreign nations. According to this pattern the antithesis between the destroyed and restored Temple would be embraced by the beginning and the end of the second scroll. It would have the further merit of placing the second and final mention of the name of Ezekiel (Ezek. 24:24) at the commencement of the second portion of the work, and as such would be analogous in pattern to the renewed claim to authorship made by Thucydides in his *History* (V, 26) at the probable beginning of the second roll of his work.[137]

Quite aside from the fact that this theory explains the manner in which the prophecy most probably arrived at its final form, that is, that it was consciously constructed as a literary bifid following certain customs

---

[134] Holding to this view were W. F. Albright, *JBL*, LI (1932), p. 96; S. Spiegel, *Harvard Theological Review*, XXIV (1931), p. 289 and *JBL*, LVI (1937), p. 407; G. R. Berry, *JBL*, LI (1932), p. 55; B. D. Eerdmans, *The Religion of Israel*, pp. 196ff.; and C. G. Howie, *The Date and Composition of Ezekiel*, p. 41.

[135] *AJ*, X, 5, 1.

[136] W. H. Brownlee, *The Meaning of the Qumrân Scrolls for the Bible*, pp. 250f.

[137] H. St. J. Thackeray, *The Septuagint and Jewish Worship*, p. 132.

in antiquity, it helps to account in a much more satisfactory manner for some of the doublets and repetitions that perplexed earlier writers. The literary structure and plan of the bifid anthology furnishes the reason for the repetition of the prophetic commission to be a watchman. Again, the experience of mutism is no longer seen to have been a concomitant of much of the prophetic ministry, but merely to have been characteristic of the period just prior to the destruction of the Temple. While it is neither possible nor desirable to explain all the phenomena of the book in terms of a bifid composition exhibiting minute contrasts or parallels, such a theory is of considerable assistance in explaining the structure of the extant work.

It is also superior to the tripartite division envisaged by Cooke,[138] or the analysis of Howie who, while recognizing the unity of chapters 1–24, divided up the remainder into an appendix (25–32), a collection of oracles (34–39), an independent visionary corpus (40–48), and a connecting link by which chapters 25–32 were united with chapters 34–39.[139] In the view of the present writer the prophecy was compiled as a bifid anthology of the utterances and visions of Ezekiel, and can be dated without question in the early sixth century B.C. against a Babylonian background of composition. The work exhibits such homogeneity that serious questions must be raised about any theory of editorial activity by someone other than the prophet himself, in which respect the book is rather unusual.

D. EZEKIEL THE MAN

That the personality of the attributive author was also quite distinctive is evident from even a casual reading of the prophecy. Albright has described him as "one of the greatest spiritual figures of all time, in spite of his tendency to psychic abnormality—a tendency which he shares with many other spiritual leaders of mankind."[140] Some early critics followed Klostermann in regarding Ezekiel as a victim of catalepsy, a pathological condition allied to autohypnosis, in which the afflicted person manifests a tonic rigidity of the limbs to the point where they can be placed and maintained in various positions for periods of differing lengths.[141]

---

[138] G. A. Cooke, *A Critical and Exegetical Commentary on the Book of Ezekiel*, pp. xviii ff.

[139] C. G. Howie, *The Date and Composition of Ezekiel*, pp. 95ff.

[140] *FSAC*, p. 325.

[141] A. Klostermann, *Theologische Studien und Kritiken*, L (1877), pp. 391ff. So A. Bertholet, *Das Buch Hesekiel*, pp. 18ff.; R. Kraetzschmar, *Das Buch Ezechiel*, p. vi; J. Meinhold, *Einführung in das AT*, p. 260; A. Lods, *Histoire de la littérature hébraïque et juive*, pp. 435f.

This view was rejected on various grounds by other scholars,[142] and was replaced by Buttenwieser by the less morbid condition of ecstasy.[143] Freudian concepts of eroticism were invoked by Broome in an attempt to explain the psychological condition of the prophet, and his ultimate diagnosis of catatonic or paranoid schizophrenia was properly refuted by Howie.[144] Kittel argued from a double residence of the prophet to the curious diagnosis of "two souls within one man,"[145] while Knight found traces of schizophrenia, and employed these alleged antithetic aspects of personality as the basis of a theory of dual or plural authorship of the extant prophecy.[146] A much more realistic psychological appraisal was that offered by Widengren, who argued that Ezekiel was probably participating in periodic acts of levitation.[147]

Attempts at psychiatric or psychological profundity by amateurs are serious enough in their import when foisted upon their contemporaries, but when they are urged in all earnestness in connection with long-dead individuals of another culture and a different age they become merely amusing. As Howie has commented, it is absurd for the non-professional student of psychiatry to claim success in psychoanalyzing a person who has been dead for 2500 years.[148] Psychiatric concepts in this connection were deemed unnecessary by Wheeler Robinson, who felt that the difficulties could be resolved most satisfactorily by placing Ezekiel in Jerusalem up to 586 B.C. and in Babylonia from that time onwards.[149] Unfortunately such a proposal does nothing to account for the mystical elements in the personality of Ezekiel, and tends, as Eissfeldt observed, to come into definite conflict with established factors of the tradition.[150]

It is true, of course, that the incident leading to the death of Pelatiah (Ezek. 11:13) is considerably easier to explain on the supposition that Ezekiel was actually in Jerusalem instead of merely projecting himself in some visionary form to that city. On the other hand, the mention of the

---

[142] E.g. J. Herrmann, *Ezechielstudien*, pp. 75ff.; J. Touzard, *RB*, XIV (1917), pp. 91f.; P. Heinisch, *Das Buch Ezechiel* (1923), pp. 14ff.; W. L. Wardle in *The Abingdon Bible Commentary*, p. 714; E. Power in *A Catholic Commentary on Holy Scripture*, p. 603; C. L. Feinberg, *The Prophecy of Ezekiel* (1969), pp. 11f. ·

[143] M. Buttenwieser, *HUCA*, VI (1929), pp. 3f.

[144] E. C. Broome, *JBL*, LXV (1946), pp. 277ff. C. G. Howie, *The Date and Composition of Ezekiel*, pp. 69ff.

[145] R. Kittel, *Geschichte des Volkes Israel*, III, p. 146.

[146] H. Knight, *ET*, LIX (1947-48), pp. 115ff.; cf. his *The Hebrew Prophetic Consciousness*, pp. 80ff.

[147] G. Widengren, *Literary and Psychological Aspects of the Hebrew Prophets*, p. 110.

[148] Quoted by A. T. Pearson in C. F. Pfeiffer and E. F. Harrison (eds.), *Wycliffe Bible Commentary* (1962), p. 704.

[149] H. Wheeler Robinson, *Two Hebrew Prophets*, p. 78.

[150] O. Eissfeldt, *OTMS*, p. 157.

cherubim indicates that the experience of Ezekiel was strictly visionary, not objective.

Howie made two attempts to explain this incident, the first of which presumed that Ezekiel 11:13 was a later addition made by Ezekiel himself when he wrote down the oracle in the thirtieth year, by which time he knew that Pelatiah had died.[151] This explanation is weak in its failure to show exactly how Ezekiel could have known that the death of Pelatiah was coincident with his prophecy. The second interpretation held that it was possible for Pelatiah, though seen in a vision by the east gate of the Temple, to have actually been in residence at Tel-Abib with the Judaean exiles, and to have been offering the kind of false hope which was so roundly condemned by Jeremiah in his letter to the captives (Jer. 28:1ff.).[152] Accordingly, on hearing the prediction of Ezekiel that Jerusalem would collapse, Pelatiah himself expired. The latter explanation raises even greater difficulties than the first, in view of the fact that the tradition consistently located Pelatiah in Palestine, not Babylonia, and regarded Ezekiel alone as the one who was transported. Furthermore, as Weir has pointed out, the text does not state that Pelatiah died as the direct result of the prophetic utterance.[153] The significance of the incident appears to be that Ezekiel was transported in a vision to Jerusalem and was so conscious of what was taking place there that he uttered a prophecy against those who were giving evil counsel to the people. Having completed his denunciation, he became aware that Pelatiah had fallen down dead.[154]

It is important to note that those who were being denounced gave no indication whatever that they were aware of the presence of Ezekiel, which would certainly have been a matter of notice had he actually been physically present in their midst. Insofar as there can be a satisfactory explanation of the phenomenon, it rests in the understanding of the phrase "the spirit lifted me up and brought me. . . ." Whatever else this obscure expression might imply, it shows clearly the impact of extraneous spiritual forces upon a receptive personality, and gives no ground for views that would resort to innate pathology alone for an explanation of what actually transpired.

The most that can be said safely about the personality of Ezekiel is that the prophet was a highly developed mystic who was able to utilize channels of communication not normally available to others.[155] This would help to account for the way in which Ezekiel was immediately aware of the siege of Jerusalem (Ezek. 24:2), a matter that has caused concern to many commentators. As in other descriptive areas of the Old

151 C. G. Howie, The Date and Composition of Ezekiel, pp. 82f.
152 C. G. Howie, IDB, II, p. 206.
153 C. J. M. Weir, VT, II (1952), p. 104.
154 H. H. Rowley, Men of God, p. 208.
155 C. G. Howie, The Date and Composition of Ezekiel, p. 84.

Testament, it is quite probable, as Cooke observed, that the modern reporter would express the situation in quite different and more comprehensible language.[156] This is not to say, however, that modern technical terms, which so frequently have little fundamental meaning, are in any way significantly superior in their descriptive abilities to their counterparts in the ancient world, particularly those within the field of medicine.

E. The Message of Ezekiel

Like all the prophetic writings, Ezekiel was not so much a manual of theology as the expression of the divine word spoken to men. In this case it was communicated in a variety of ways to a demoralized and unhappy remnant in exile, and it is only against such a background that the distinctive contribution of Ezekiel can be appreciated. Whereas Jeremiah had emphasized the concept of divine immanence, Ezekiel appeared from the time of his first vision to exemplify the idea of divine transcendence. God had recoiled from the sin of His people, and in bringing down upon them the long-promised judgment had vindicated the holiness of His person and the expectations of His prophetic servants. Because of Israel's stubbornness, the generation of which Ezekiel was a member had to bear the brunt of divine anger.

Ezekiel had experienced the presence of God both in Judah and Babylonia, and was thus aware that the deity could not be localized. It may well be that the emphasis upon divine transcendence served to clarify the fact that the omnipotence of God could not be restricted by such contingencies as the failure of His people to implement the provisions of the Covenant relationship forged on Mount Sinai. Nevertheless, the requirements of God remained the same, and Ezekiel insisted that the exiles must manifest implicit obedience to the divine will. In a scathing review of Israelite history and religion (cf. Ezek. 2:1ff.; 8:7ff.; 13:1ff.; 17:1ff.; 20:1ff.) the prophet exposed the depravity of a moral situation in which no attempt whatever had been made to meet the requirements of God. That the consequent destruction was in fact self-imposed was made clear by the prophet, who stated that God did not desire the death of the sinner, but rather that he should repent and live (Ezek. 18:32; 33:11ff.).

One of the most important themes to be developed in the book is that of the moral responsibility of the individual. In this concept Ezekiel embodied in part his own experience, while at the same time expanding a truth proclaimed by Jeremiah.[157] In the recent calamity that had overtaken Jerusalem, righteous persons claimed bitterly that they had

[156] G. A. Cooke, *A Critical and Exegetical Commentary on the Book of Ezekiel*, pp. xxiii, xxvii, xxviii.
[157] R. L. Ottley, *The Religion of Israel* (1926), p. 116.

been wrongly involved, and the common cry was that they were suffering for the sins of their ancestors. Jeremiah had predicted that the time would come when every individual would have access to his God (Jer. 31:34), consequent upon the removal of sin. Ezekiel, however, went somewhat further, and boldly declared that each individual was responsible for his own sin (Ezek. 18:4, 20). Henceforward, if a man suffers for the evil which he has committed, he cannot absolve himself from moral responsibility by an appeal to the behavior of his forbears.

The great contribution of the prophet Ezekiel to the doctrine of man lies in his emphasis upon personal responsibility. The New Covenant (Jer. 31:31ff.; cf. Ezek. 36:26ff.) would not exhibit a corporate character in the strictly Mosaic sense, but would be made with a redeemed society formulated on the basis of individuals who responded to the free expression of divine love. Because everything in the future was to be based upon divine grace, the relationship of the individual to God was not dependent upon considerations of heredity and environment, any more than it was on past religious and historical influences (Ezek. 18:1ff.; 33:10ff.).

Earlier prophets had proclaimed that the very concept of divine holiness demanded the rejection of rebellious Israel, if only for a short period. Ezekiel, however, argued conversely that this same holiness rendered the ultimate restoration of the nation inevitable, since divine honor was bound up with the destiny of Israel. The promise of restoration itself constituted an act of divine grace which would lead to repentance on the part of the faithful minority among the exiles (Ezek. 36:16ff.). With an act of cleansing and the creation of a new spiritual attitude of mind, the process of regeneration would commence in earnest. Only then could the dry bones of Israel (Ezek. 37:1ff.), horribly and helplessly abandoned heretofore, become clothed with flesh through the action of the divine spirit and live, quickened to a regenerate life.

Some scholars have seen in chapters 40–48 a picture of Ezekiel as a priestly ritualist whose only concern was with the minutiae of liturgy and worship. In view of such a criticism it needs to be recognized that the prophet was contemplating the future of the theocratic community, in which divine holiness would be the regulatory feature. As a reaction against the idolatry that had brought about the collapse of the nation, Ezekiel emphasized that the new community must necessarily follow a rigid pattern of worship, with continual emphasis upon the concept of the sanctifying presence of God in the midst. While he may have appeared to present the discipline of a correct ritual as a means of maintaining holiness and guarding against the recrudescence of idolatry, it is plain from the prophecy as a whole that Ezekiel nowhere substituted ritual rectitude for the true obedience of the heart and mind.

The triumph of restoration which Ezekiel contemplated was summed up in the two final words of his prophecy, "Jehovah is there." God had formerly forsaken His land and Temple, thereby permitting the Chaldeans to do their worst. Now He was to return and bring the blessings of His presence to Jerusalem in the midst of a revitalized community. By this proclamation of hope for the future the prophet showed that man is dead until quickened by the divine spirit, and that society cannot flourish in the truest sense unless sustained by the presence of God.

*   *   *   *   *

The text of Ezekiel has been poorly preserved, due partly to the fact that obscurities in the language, as well as technical expressions and *hapax legomena*, have led copyists into frequent error. The LXX is often very valuable in attempts to correct the Hebrew,[158] but nevertheless it must be used with great care. Quite frequently the translator was entirely ignorant of what unfamiliar words meant, and in consequence he resorted to a transliteration of the Hebrew. On other occasions he furnished a literal rendering of the Hebrew that naturally made for almost incomprehensible Greek. In addition, he indulged in free translations at certain points, and provided additions to the text in order to make the language of the translation flow more smoothly. Textual studies of Ezekiel have been enriched by papyrus Codex 967, which originally contained the LXX text of Ezekiel, Daniel, and Esther. This document formed part of the celebrated Chester Beatty papyri, in which sections of Ezekiel 11:25–17:21 occurred,[159] and also figured in the John H. Scheide collection of Biblical papyri, which contained portions of Ezekiel 19:12–39:29.[160] Codex 967 has been dated in the late second century or early third century of the Christian era, and with other important codices of the LXX such as Vaticanus, Alexandrinus, and Marchalianus (sixth century after Christ) has furnished an assured basis for detailed textual studies.[161] Two fragments of the Hebrew text of Ezekiel 4:16–5:1 were recovered from the first Qumran cave.[162] They were dated tentatively in the first century B.C., and had affinities with the traditional Hebrew text.

As well as furnishing additions in the interests of narrative smoothness, the LXX translator frequently omitted repetitious words and phrases so as to make for a simpler form of the text. There may have been occasions on which this was done accidentally, however, as argued

[158] C. H. Cornill, *Das Buch des Propheten Ezechiel* (1886), pp. 96ff. Cf. G. A. Cooke, *A Critical and Exegetical Commentary on the Book of Ezekiel*, pp. xl ff.

[159] F. G. Kenyon, *The Chester Beatty Biblical Papyri* (1933-37), fasc. I, VII.

[160] A. C. Johnson, H. S. Gehman, and E. H. Case (eds.), *The John H. Scheide Biblical Papyri: Ezekiel* (1938).

[161] Cf. H. S. Gehman, *JBL*, LVII (1938), pp. 281ff., *JAOS*, LVIII (1938), pp. 92ff.; J. B. Payne, *JBL*, LXVIII (1949), pp. 251ff.; J. W. Wevers, *JBL*, LXX (1951), pp. 211ff.

[162] Cf. D. Barthélemy and J. T. Milik, *Qumran Cave I* (1955), pp. 68f. and pl. XII.

THE BOOK OF EZEKIEL

by Filson in the case of two omissions (Ezek. 12:26-28; 36:23b-38) in Codex 967.[163] Whatever else may be said in favor of the LXX version of Ezekiel, the known fluidity of the Hebrew text prior to A.D. 70 makes it impossible to regard the LXX as either a faithful translation or a reliable witness to the state of the Hebrew which was familiar in Alexandria in the third century B.C.[164]

Supplementary Literature

Duerr, L. *Die Stellung des Propheten Ezechiel in der israelitisch-jüdischen Apokalyptik.* 1923.
Eichrodt, W. *Ezekiel.* 1970.
Ellison, H. L. *Ezekiel, the Man and His Message.* 1951.
Jahn, G. *Das Buch Ezechiel auf Grund der Septuaginta hergestellt.* 1905.
Toy, C. H. *The Book of Ezekiel.* 1899.
Wevers, J. W. *Ezekiel.* 1969.

[163] F. V. Filson, *JBL*, LXII (1943), pp. 27ff.
[164] Contrary to *IBOT*, p. 329.

855

Part Eleven

THE LATTER PROPHETS (II)
THE MINOR PROPHETS

In the Hebrew canon the Major Prophets are followed by a collection of smaller works that, following the tradition of the Vulgate, are commonly designated as the Twelve Minor Prophets. This grouping was known in the time of Ben Sira (Ecclus. 49:12), and was also familiar to Josephus.[1] Rabbinic tradition held that the men of the Great Synagogue edited the Twelve Minor Prophets,[2] and the writings were known in this form to the patristic authors. LXX manuscripts departed from the sequence of the Hebrew in placing Hosea first, probably because of its size, followed by Amos, Micah, Joel, Obadiah, and Jonah, while in Codices Alexandrinus and Vaticanus the Twelve were placed before the Major Prophets. From the Talmud it would appear that chronological considerations governed the arrangement in the Hebrew canon to a certain extent,[3] but the real reasons for the order of the books in its present form are unknown.

[1] *Contra Apion.* I, 8, 3.
[2] *Bab. Bath.* 15a.
[3] *Bab. Bath.* 14b.

I. THE BOOK OF HOSEA

A. NAME AND OUTLINE

The prophecy was named after its attributive author הושע, whose name in the Latin and Greek versions appeared as *Osee* ('Ωσηέ). One of the four great Hebrew prophets of the eighth century B.C., he was called to his ministry in the reign of Jeroboam II (782/81-753 B.C.). Although details of his personal life are rather scanty, it appears that his father was named Beeri (not the Reubenite prince of 1 Chron. 5:6). Hosea was unique among the literary prophets in that his childhood home was in the northern kingdom. His actual birthplace remains unknown, however, as does his occupation in life, though from the reference in Hosea 7:4ff. it has been assumed that he worked as a baker.[4] From the various agricultural allusions in the book it could be maintained with equal seriousness that Hosea was a farmer. However, a peasant origin seems improbable in the light of his knowledge of history, his grasp of political affairs, and the elegant, well-chosen imagery with which his style abounds. His wife Gomer was described as the daughter of Diblaim, who is otherwise unknown, and was the mother of three children. Some scholars have seen in the expression בת דבלים a reference to her place of birth, and have located it in Gilead, but this is rather doubtful for lack of topographical evidence.

The prophecy of Hosea may be analyzed as follows:

I. The Relations of Israel with God, Portrayed Against the Background of Hosea's Marital Experience, ch. 1–3
II. Denunciations of Pride, Idolatry, and Corruption, ch. 4–8
III. The Certainty of Approaching Punishment for the Northern Kingdom, ch. 9–10
IV. A Parenthetical Utterance Dealing with the Triumph of Divine Love and Mercy, ch. 11:1-11
V. Destruction as the Result of Israel's Infidelity and Rebellion, ch. 11:12–13:16
VI. Future Mercies for a Penitent People, ch. 14

---

[4] E.g. by G. A. F. Knight, *Hosea* (1960), p. 13.

B. THE DATE OF HOSEA'S MINISTRY

The work of Hosea is to be placed in the last generation of the history of the northern kingdom, which had been enjoying a revival of material prosperity under Jeroboam II. It is not easy to say precisely when the ministry of Hosea commenced, and as a consequence scholarly estimates of its length have varied considerably. The superscription in Hosea 1:1 furnished a twofold indication of date, one of which placed Hosea against a Judaean background of chronology in the reigns of Uzziah (767-740/39 B.C.), Jotham (740/39-732/31 B.C.), Ahaz (732/31-716/15 B.C.), and Hezekiah (716/15-687/86 B.C.), while the other related him to the period of Jeroboam II (782/81-753 B.C.).[5] The verse in part or in its entirety may, of course, constitute an editorial addition originating in Judah, since the mention of Judaean kings takes precedence over that of the king who ruled in the area where the prophecies were actually given. On the other hand, such an arrangement may merely indicate that Hosea regarded the Davidic line alone as legitimate, and in that event the form of the superscription that gave Uzziah priority could well have originated with the prophet himself.

The reference in Hosea 1:4 to the house of Jehu points to a date before the death of Jeroboam II in 753 B.C., and if the allusion to Assyria in Hosea 8:9 is to the tribute paid by Menahem to Tiglathpileser III about 739 B.C. (cf. Hos. 5:13; 7:11f.; 10:5f.; 12:2), this would indicate a date of about 743 B.C. for the continuation of the prophetic ministry. If the reference in Hosea 5:8—6:6 is to the Syrian-Ephraimite war of 735-734 B.C., it would imply that the ministry of Hosea continued well beyond the death of Jeroboam II, while the mention of relations with Egypt in Hosea 7:11, 9:6 and 12:2 would seem to indicate the activity of Hoshea, the last king of Israel. The ministry of Hosea thus extended from about 753 B.C. to a time just before the fall of Samaria in 722 B.C. Precisely what transpired in the life of the prophet at that point is unknown, but the fact that the superscription in Hosea 1:1 mentioned Judaean kings as contemporaries might indicate that the message of the prophet, if not actually the personage of the man himself, was by no means unknown in the southern kingdom after the fall of Samaria. It is not outside the bounds of possibility that Hosea spent his latter days in Judah in retirement, though certainty on this particular point is lacking.[6]

[5] For the chronology see W. F. Albright, *BASOR*, No. 100 (1945), pp. 21f.; E. R. Thiele, *JNES*, III (1944), pp. 176f.; K. A. Kitchen and T. C. Mitchell, *NBD*, pp. 217ff.

[6] Cf. H. Ewald, *Commentary on the Prophets of the OT* (1875), I, pp. 221ff. G. Hölscher, *Die Profeten*, pp. 205f., made him a Benjamite, while I. Engnell, *Svenskt Bibliskt Uppslagsverk* (1948), I, cols. 874f., regarded him as a native Judaean.

C. HOSEA AND GOMER

The circumstances attending the marriage of Hosea and its implications for the meaning of the prophecy have been matters of perennial discussion among scholars.[7] The primary sources are chapters 1 and 3, the first containing a third-person account of the marital relations of Hosea, and the second comprising a short selection of similar material written in the first person. In Hosea 1:2, the prophet was commanded to "take a woman of whoredom and children of whoredom," as a result of which he married Gomer, who subsequently bore three children. Each was given a symbolic name, the first of which, *Jezreel* (Hos. 1:4), implied that God would punish the house of Jehu for the bloodshed of Jezreel. The second name, *Lo-ruhamah* or Unpitied (Hos. 1:6), signified a lack of divine compassion for the house of Israel, and the third, *Lo-ammi* or Not-my-people (Hos. 1:9), was an assurance of divine rejection. In the second of the primary sources (Hos. 3:1ff.), the prophet stated that God had commanded him to love a woman who was cherished by her paramour, and went on to relate how he purchased this adulteress and kept her under discipline for some time (Hos. 3:1-3), an act that was also given a symbolic meaning.

These two sources constitute a single unit, comprising biographical and autobiographical material linked by a sermon to Israel in the second chapter. This unity is characterized by the fact that chapters 1 to 3 employ the marriage-relationship to describe the bond between God and Israel and the reaction of the Chosen People to this situation in terms of the adultery of the wife. Because of the moral difficulties inherent in the marriage of a prophet of God with a prostitute, a number of views on the matter have commanded the attention of commentators. Medieval Jewish interpreters insisted that the entire story was symbolical, and had no relationship whatever to historical fact. Other expositors took the first chapter as historical but the third as allegorical, while a different view insisted that both were literal, and suggested that Gomer became a slave after her third child was born, being ultimately bought back by Hosea. Some scholars claimed that chapter three actually preserved a more intimate account of the marriage of Hosea and Gomer than chapter one, attributing the latter to the personal reminiscences of Hosea himself. Still other scholars raised the whole question as to the premarital sexual activity of Gomer. Regarding the type of material in chapters 1 to 3, it seems sufficient to recognize it as comprising biography, sermonic material, and autobiography, without invoking the three categories of

---

[7] For a survey of the problems see H. H. Rowley, *BJRL*, XXXIX (1956-7), pp. 200ff., reprinted in *Men of God*, pp. 66ff.

material that Mowinckel entertained in the compilation of some of the prophetic books.[8]

In Hosea 1:2, Gomer was described by the term אֵשֶׁת זְנוּנִים or "woman of harlotries" instead of by the more common term for prostitute, and this difference was taken by Ehrlich as implying that Gomer was merely inclined towards harlotry.[9] Yet in Hosea 3:1, the woman is referred to as an adulteress who was beloved of her paramour,[10] and whom the prophet was commanded to love also. Some problems arise concerning the syntax of the Hebrew word עוֹד, "again," with Ehrlich and Pfeiffer maintaining that it should be construed with the words immediately preceding, that is, "The LORD said to me again, Go . . . ,"[11] while other scholars have been influenced by the Massoretic minor accentuations of "to me" and "woman," which in effect joins up 'ôdh with the subsequent words.

Even if the latter interpretation is adopted, as it is by most scholars, the word "again" could imply continuance of a process and be rendered, "Go on loving a woman . . . ," in which case Gomer is clearly indicated. It could also denote repetition of an earlier action, that is, "Go again, love a woman . . . ," which might or might not apply to Gomer. If Ehrlich and Pfeiffer are correct, the woman referred to could also be someone other than Gomer. For Pfeiffer the instructions were to be understood symbolically, with Gomer being regarded as a model of conjugal fidelity and the adultery of Hosea 1:2 typifying spiritual unfaithfulness to God.

The view that the rendering, "Go again, love a woman..." involved another woman can hardly be substantiated, since the comparison is only concerned with the love of God for Israel, not for any other nation. The LXX rendered the phrase in Hosea 3:1 as "loving evils and adultery," the active form of the participle being supported by the Syriac version. Ibn Ezra adopted the active form of the verb in his rendering of "loving another man," whereas Rashi followed the passive pointing of the Massoretes, and interpreted the word rēa' to mean "husband," as in the RV

---

[8] S. Mowinckel, *Zur Komposition des Buches Jeremia* (1914), pp. 17ff.; cf. *IBOT*, pp. 224ff.; T. H. Robinson, *Prophecy and the Prophets in Ancient Israel*, pp. 50ff.

[9] A. B. Ehrlich, *Randglossen zur Hebräischen Bibel* (1912), V, pp. 163f., followed by T. O. Hall, *Review and Expositor*, LIV (1957), pp. 503ff.

[10] For a cultic interpretation of this phrase see A. D. Tushingham, *JNES*, XII (1953), pp. 150ff.

[11] A. B. Ehrlich, *Randglossen zur Hebräischen Bibel*, V, pp. 170f. *PIOT*, p. 567. So also R. Gordis, *HUCA*, XXV (1952), pp. 29f. This view had been rejected earlier by K. Budde, *Theologische Studien und Kritiken*, XCVI (1925), p. 57. The deletion of "again" was suggested by C. Steuernagel, *Lehrbuch der Einleitung in das AT*, p. 605; L. Gautier, *Introduction à l'Ancien Testament* (1939), I, p. 465n.; O. Eissfeldt, *Einleitung in das AT*, p. 432; cf. *ETOT*, pp. 387f.; J. Lindblom, *Hosea literarisch untersucht* (1928), p. 17.

margin.[12] The most probable meaning of Hosea 3:1 is that of the RSV, which reads, "Go again, love a woman who is beloved of a paramour and is an adulteress."

The reasons why Hosea had to "buy back" his wife are also unclear. Although the form in Hosea 3:2 is rather unusual, the meaning of the verb elsewhere (e.g. Deut. 2:6; Job 6:27) is that of "buy." The LXX rendered it by a verbal form that commonly denoted "hiring," but this is also the meaning of the Arabic root cognate with the Hebrew.[13] Arguing from Amarna Age texts, Gordon proposed to derive the Hebrew verb from a word referring to payment upon remarriage.[14] Why part of the price was paid in money and the remainder in grain is unknown, but the amount was most probably handed over to the paramour in compensation for the loss of her services, or to her master if she had become a slave.

Some scholars have maintained that the account of the marriage in chapter 3 constituted a parallel though variant description of the manner in which Hosea married Gomer, and that historically it antedates what was described in the first chapter.[15] If this is so it is difficult to account for the absence of mention of the children, who played so prominent a part in the narrative, even if it is borne in mind that the third chapter may have been subjected to rigorous editorial revision. Again, the isolation in Hosea 3:3, indicating, as Wellhausen noted, that the prophet would abstain from sexual contact with her,[16] would seem to contradict the evidence of Hosea 1:3, which suggests that the first child was born within a year of the marriage. In view of the foregoing objections it seems more logical to integrate the material of the third chapter with the events of the first two chapters, the second of which could only have been written after the birth of the third child.

Among those scholars who have adopted a literalistic view of the marriage narratives, some have suggested that chapter three referred to events which occurred prior to the union, while chapter one furnished a record of the marriage and its outcome.[17] This theory attempts to show

12 Cf. R. Gordis, *HUCA*, XXV (1952), p. 24n. In Jer. 3:1, *rēa'* is used of a paramour.

13 Cf. H. S. Nyberg, *Studien zum Hoseabuche* (1935), p. 23.

14 C. H. Gordon, *JBL*, LVII (1938), p. 409, a view he abandoned later (*Ugaritic Handbook*, p. 251; *UL*, pp. 69ff.) and subsequently readopted. Cf. J. Gray, *The Krt Text in the Literature of Ras Shamra* (1955), p. 37.

15 So R. Kittel, *Geschichte des Volkes Israel* (1925 ed.), II, p. 348n.; J. M. P. Smith, *The Prophets and Their Times*, p. 59; O. Eissfeldt, *Einleitung in das AT*, pp. 431f.; J. Paterson, *The Goodly Fellowship of the Prophets*, p. 43; P. R. Ackroyd in M. Black and H. H. Rowley (eds.), *Peake's Commentary on the Bible*, p. 603.

16 J. Wellhausen, *Die kleinen Propheten übersetzt und erklärt* (1898 ed.), p. 105.

17 Cf. W. R. Harper, *A Critical and Exegetical Commentary on Amos and Hosea* (1910), p. 208.

that the infidelity from which Hosea redeemed his wife was not actually misbehavior towards the prophet himself. Even if chapter three is held to precede chapter one, which, as has been pointed out, is very unlikely, such a view is confronted by the fact that Gomer was unfaithful after her marriage to Hosea. This is clear from Hosea 2:2, and may also be suggested by absence of a direct claim to paternity regarding the second and third children.

Such infidelity has been accounted for by the suggestion that Gomer was a temple prostitute before she married the prophet.[18] Although there are numerous references to ritual prostitution in the Old Testament narratives,[19] and considerable information available about the status and functions of female prostitutes in Babylonia,[20] not very much is known about the women who participated as hierodules in the Baal fertility cults. Certainly there is insufficient evidence either for the postulate that they were respected as a class in Israel,[21] or that Gomer had functioned as some sort of local saint at a shrine.[22] There is, however, abundant ground for the assertion that the orthodox spirituality of Israel roundly condemned such behavior.

Varying slightly from the above theory were the views of Wheeler Robinson, who maintained that Gomer had become a temple prostitute by the time she was reclaimed in Hosea 3:2,[23] and Tushingham, who differentiated between Gomer and the harlot of chapter three, holding the latter to be a cultic prostitute.[24] Intriguing as these suggestions may be, they fail to meet the requirements of a straightforward reading of the text, which clearly shows that Gomer indulged in harlotry both before and after her marriage to Hosea. In the same way the view that, while both chapters one and three can be regarded as historical, the woman of chapter three must be regarded as someone other than Gomer,[25] becomes equally untenable. On such a basis it would be difficult to assume

[18] H. Schmidt, ZAW, XLII (1924), pp. 245ff.; O. R. Sellers, AJSL, XLI (1925), p. 245; H. G. May, JBL, LV (1936), p. 287; E. A. Leslie, OT Religion (1936), p. 173; T. H. Robinson and F. Horst, Die zwölf kleinen Propheten Hosea bis Micha (1936), pp. 16f.; IBOT, p. 350; R. B. Y. Scott, The Relevance of the Prophets, p. 75; G. Fohrer, Die symbolischen Handlungen der Propheten (1953), p. 21. This view was rejected by J. P. Hyatt, Prophetic Religion (1947), p. 41, and questioned by J. A. Bewer, The Book of the Twelve Prophets (1949), I, p. 37.

[19] Cf. H. G. May, AJSL, XLVIII (1932), pp. 89ff.

[20] Cf. B. Meissner, Babylonien und Assyrien, II, pp. 70f.

[21] Cf. H. Schmidt, ZAW, XLII (1924), p. 254n.

[22] So L. Waterman, JBL, XXXVII (1918), pp. 199ff.

[23] H. Wheeler Robinson, Two Hebrew Prophets, p. 14.

[24] A. D. Tushingham, JNES, XII (1953), pp. 150ff.

[25] E.g. S. Davidson, An Introduction to the OT, III, p. 237; C. von Orelli, The Twelve Minor Prophets (1893), p. 19; G. Hölscher, Die Profeten, p. 427; P. Humbert, Revue de l'Histoire des Religions, LXXVII (1918), p. 170; PIOT, pp. 568f.; B. D. Eerdmans, The Religion of Israel, pp. 152f.; A. D. Tushingham, JNES, XII (1953), p. 156.

that, after Israel had rejected her espoused deity, He went in search of another bride. If the prophetic analogy concerning Israel is to have its true force, the wife of one chapter must surely be identified with the wife of the other.[26]

Some writers reconstructed the trend of events to the point where they felt able to repudiate the assertion of the text to the effect that Gomer was an immoral person.[27] Others, following medieval Jewish interpreters, have found it hard to believe that a moral deity would deliberately command His servant to marry a woman of loose character,[28] and have suggested that the opprobrium of immorality was related to Gomer as an inhabitant of debauched Israel, and not to her personal character.[29] Perhaps a more satisfactory explanation, and one commonly adopted by scholars of widely varying standpoints, is that the term "harlot" was used proleptically in Hosea 1:2.[30] According to this view Gomer was either pure or thought to be pure when Hosea married her, and the infidelity described in the prophecy manifested itself subsequently. As such it was attributed by Hosea not so much to a fall from grace as to the expression of a basically corrupt nature.

It is true that a parallel exists between a situation in which Hosea might have married a woman, only to discover after a time that she was being unfaithful and needed to be disciplined after a short period of separation, and that in which Israel, espoused to her God, had shortly thereafter forsaken Him for the pursuit of the Baal deities. However, the term "wife of whoredoms" seems to imply that Gomer was unchaste prior to her marriage with the prophet, and for those who place chapter three before chapter one, this is confirmed by the description of her as an adulteress, which cannot possibly be proleptic. Even if the usual order of the chapters is maintained the difficulty is still present, for as Rowley has pointed out, it was as reprehensible among the ancient Hebrews for a man to take back an adulterous wife as it was for him to marry an unchaste woman.[31] For Hosea, who abhorred immorality, to marry

[26] H. H. Rowley, *Men of God*, pp. 84f.
[27] Cf. G. Hölscher, *Die Profeten*, pp. 424f.; W. R. Arnold, *Ephod and Ark*, p. 126n.; D. Buzy, *RB*, XIV (1917), pp. 376ff.; J. Fueck, *ZAW*, XXXIX (1921), pp. 283ff.; L. W. Batten, *JBL*, XLVIII (1929), pp. 257ff.; *PIOT*, pp. 567f.
[28] A. B. Davidson, *HDB*, II, p. 421; E. Day, *AJSL*, XXVI (1910), pp. 105ff.
[29] Cf. *PIOT*, p. 569, rejected by W. R. Harper, *A Critical and Exegetical Commentary on Amos and Hosea*, p. 207.
[30] So A. B. Davidson, *HDB*, II, p. 421; K. Marti, *EB*, II, col. 2123; W. R. Harper, *A Critical and Exegetical Commentary on Amos and Hosea*, p. 207; C. F. Kent, *The Growth and Contents of the OT* (1926), p. 111; G. A. Smith, *The Book of the Twelve Prophets*, p. 248; H. Wheeler Robinson, *Two Hebrew Prophets*, p. 13; J. P. Hyatt, *Prophetic Religion* (1947), p. 42; J. A. Bewer, *The Book of the Twelve Prophets*, I, p. 41; E. S. P. Heavenor, *NBD*, pp. 539ff.
[31] H. H. Rowley, *Men of God*, p. 76. Cf. L. M. Epstein, *Sex Laws and Customs in Judaism* (1948), p. 199.

a known prostitute, whether a cultic functionary or not, constituted an act of self-abnegation explicable only in terms of a divine directive. Psychological analyses of the kind suggested by Oesterley and Robinson to the effect that Hosea suffered from a sex-obsession that drove him into the thing he feared most do not seem to be borne out by the character of the prophet as revealed in other portions of the book,[32] and in view of the lengthy time-lapse must necessarily be deemed rather futile.[33]

The character of Gomer is perhaps rather less discreditable when related to a third method of interpretation, which was the initial approach listed in previous pages. This view, the allegorical, was favored by many ancient and medieval interpreters as the proper approach to the understanding of the prophecy. In modern times it has been propounded by Van Hoonacker, and supported by such eminent scholars as Calès, Gressmann, Gunkel, and Young.[34] A "theatrical" variation of this interpretation has been entertained by Kaufmann, who along with some others has separated the first three chapters from the remainder of the book.[35]

Even a visionary interpretation has been alleged by a few modern scholars, reviving an older view.[36] Such approaches to the problems of the first three chapters of Hosea are rendered highly improbable by certain details, particularly, as Oesterley and Robinson have pointed out,[37] that of the name Gomer. There can be little doubt that the name was real, not symbolical, as Hoonacker proposed,[38] since unlike other names in the narrative it was not interpreted symbolically. Whatever the meaning of the name Gomer, it could not lend reality to the story unless it actually designated the wife of the prophet.[39] There certainly appears to be very little of an allegorical nature about the divine command to the

---

[32] *IBOT*, pp. 350ff. Cf. A. Allwohn, *Die Ehe des Propheten Hosea in psychoanalytischer Beleuchtung* (1926), pp. 54ff.; O. R. Sellers, *AJSL*, XLI (1945), pp. 243ff.; A. Lods, *The Prophets and the Rise of Judaism*, pp. 91f.

[33] A. J. Heschel, *The Prophets*, p. 397.

[34] A. van Hoonacker, *Les douze petits prophètes* (1908), pp. 38f. A. Calès in *The Catholic Encyclopedia* (1911), XI, p. 337. H. Gressmann, *Die Schriften des AT in Auswahl* (1921), II, pp. 369f. H. Gunkel, *Die Religion in Geschichte und Gegenwart* (1928), II, col. 2022. *YIOT*, p. 253.

[35] *KRI*, pp. 370f. Cf. C. H. Toy, *JBL*, XXXII (1913), p. 77; P. Humbert, *Revue de l'Histoire des Religions*, LXXVIII (1918), pp. 163f. This procedure was rejected by R. Gordis, *HUCA*, XXV (1953-54), p. 9n.

[36] Cf. J. Pedersen, *Israel, III-IV*, p. 112; J. Ridderbos, *De Kleine Profeten* (1952), I, pp. 22f.

[37] *IBOT*, p. 350; cf. K. Marti, *EB*, II, col. 2123.

[38] A. van Hoonacker, *Les douze petits prophètes*, p. 15.

[39] For different interpretations of the name see E. Nestle, *ZAW*, XXIII (1903), p. 346, XXIX (1909), pp. 233f.; W. Baumgartner, *ZAW*, XXXIII (1913), p. 78; P. Haupt, *JBL*, XXXIV (1915), p. 44; J. M. Powis Smith, *The Prophets and Their Times* (1925), p. 58; H. Hirschfeld, *JAOS*, XLVIII (1928), pp. 276f.; E. Sellin, *Das Zwölfprophetenbuch* (1929), p. 27.

prophet to marry a harlot, and had the narrative been of the dramatic kind contemplated by Kaufmann there would clearly have been some other indication of this fact in the text. Again, Gomer could hardly represent Israel even symbolically, since the Chosen People had not been unfaithful to God before their espousal, for fairly obvious reasons. Even if chapter three is held to be allegorical while chapter one is regarded as historical,[40] it is difficult to conclude either that Gomer was not a real person or that she was not immoral. Furthermore, the details connected with the purchase price, which were treated in a strictly literal manner in the text, argue strongly against a purely allegorical interpretation.[41]

Probably the most satisfactory explanation of the section relating to the marriage of Hosea is the view that chapters one and three are historical, that they occur in proper chronological order, are descriptive of one and the same woman, and are supplementary rather than either repetitive or variant.[42] It is not necessary to maintain with Budde that the first three chapters originally constituted a single consecutive narrative written in the first person and that the third person sections were the result of editorial alteration, since there is no factual evidence for such a position.[43] The second chapter is closely related in subject-matter and style to chapters one and three, and constitutes a grouping of divine oracles. Together these chapters depict Israel as the divine spouse who has broken faith with her husband. The punishment of separation from her lovers which God meted out constituted an act of discipline which was intended to reawaken her former love.

It is not to be expected, of course, that the life-experience of Hosea should be matched with absolute precision by the history of idolatrous Israel, but in any event the parallels are surprisingly close.[44] What is important to observe, however, is the fact that Hosea knew the waywardness of his wife from the very beginning of their marriage, just as God was aware of the infidelity of Israel from the time of the Wilderness period. There would thus seem to be no ground for the plausible exegesis

---

[40] Cf. P. Volz, *Zeitschrift für wissenschaftliche Theologie*, XLI (1898), pp. 321ff.; P. Humbert, *Revue de l'Histoire des Religions*, LXXVII (1918), p. 170; L. W. Batten, *JBL*, XLVIII (1929), pp. 271ff.

[41] Cf. W. R. Harper, *A Critical and Exegetical Commentary on Amos and Hosea*, p. 219; J. A. Bewer, *AJSL*, XXII (1906), p. 124n.; H. S. Nyberg, *Studien zum Hoseabuche* (1935), p. 23; R. Gordis, *HUCA*, XXV (1952), p. 26n.

[42] So J. Wellhausen, *Die kleinen Propheten übersetzt und erklärt*, p. 104; W. Robertson Smith, *The Prophets of Israel* (1912), p. 178; G. A. Smith, *The Book of the Twelve Prophets*, I, pp. 241ff.; E. Sellin, *Das Zwölfprophetenbuch*, p. 46; H. Wheeler Robinson, *Two Hebrew Prophets*, pp. 16f.; A. Weiser, *Das Buch der zwölf kleinen Propheten* (1949), I, p. 24; *OTFD*, pp. 234f.

[43] K. Budde, *Theologische Studien und Kritiken*, XCVII (1925), pp. 7f.; cf. E. Sellin, *Einleitung in das AT* (1935 ed.), p. 103.

[44] Cf. H. H. Rowley, *Men of God*, p. 92.

of George Adam Smith, who followed Ewald and Wellhausen in suggesting that Gomer was pure, or thought to be so, prior to her marriage. Equally dubious is the assertion that the prophetic call of Hosea arose out of his unhappy marital situation,[45] for as Volz showed long ago, it was through the divine command that Hosea was led to marry Gomer, and therefore his prophetic call preceded his marriage.[46]

D. THE COMPILATION OF THE BOOK

Considerations relating to the compilation and date of the prophecy have been affected partly by the view that chapters 4 to 14 may have circulated separately from chapters 1 to 3 for at least some time, and partly by the view that the passages of hope for Israel (Hos. 1:10–2:1; 2:14-23; 3:5; 11:8-11) belong to the exilic period, since they seem inconsistent with the teaching of Hosea.[47] While it is true that much of chapters 4 to 14 is concerned with the depravity of the Baal cults and the deficiencies of the monarchy, it is not easy to see how the characteristic message of Hosea could have been proclaimed except on the basis of chapters 1 to 3. Certainly by the time the oracles of chapters 4 to 14 were in writing, a knowledge of the contents of chapters 1 to 3 was necessary to an understanding of the unique prophetic emphasis of Hosea. It seems highly probable, therefore, that even if chapters 4 to 14 circulated independently for some time, it could only have been for a comparatively short period, and certainly fell within the lifetime of the prophet himself, since there is no tradition of the book as anything but a unity.

Against the view that a bright future for Israel was inconsistent with the prophetic standpoint it must be remarked that there is no evidence for the dogmatic assertion that passages of hope were not the work of Hosea himself. Indeed it is more probable, as Mauchline has pointed out, that when challenged on this score Hosea would have made specific reference to his own experience of divine mercy in which love triumphed over judgment, and would have extended a similar prospect for the nation.[48]

Another consideration affecting the dating of the prophecy is the theory of the alleged Judaistic revision of the work, which in an extreme

[45] Cf. W. Nowack, *Die Kleinen Propheten* (1897), pp. 9f.; A. B. Davidson, *HDB*, II, pp. 421f.; C. H. Cornill, *Introduction to the Canonical Books of the OT*, p. 321; H. P. Smith, *The Religion of Israel*, p. 140; C. F. Kent, *The Growth and Contents of the OT*, p. 112; *IBOT*, p. 352; J. P. Hyatt, *Prophetic Religion*, p. 43; J. Mauchline, *IB*, VI, p. 562.

[46] P. Volz, *Zeitschrift für wissenschaftliche Theologie*, XLI (1898), p. 322. So H. H. Rowley, *Men of God*, p. 96.

[47] W. R. Harper, *A Critical and Exegetical Commentary on Amos and Hosea*, pp. clix-clx.

[48] J. Mauchline, *IB*, VI, p. 563.

form attributed all references to the southern kingdom to later editing.[49] It is possible, of course, to entertain the notion that southern scribes modified the text of the prophecy, which admittedly exhibits definite corruptions, to contrast their own fidelity with the unfaithfulness of the northern kingdom. However, it is not easy to see precisely how this could have been done within the lifetime of the attributive author, and it is a little difficult to say why it should have been deemed necessary after 722 B.C. in any event, since the apostasy of the northern kingdom, and by contrast the implied virtue of the southern kingdom, was no longer of pressing concern. Certainly by the time of the prophet Jeremiah in the seventh century there would be very few Judaean scribes sympathetic to the tradition of Hosea who could flaunt the virtue of their own nation.

In this connection it should be noted that only about four references to Judah are in any way commendatory (Hos. 1:7, 11; 3:5; 4:15; 11:2). The remainder, which constitute a considerable majority, have a distinctly critical tone, and could hardly be the work of Judaean redactors desirous of glorifying their country. Thus the references in Hosea 6:11, 8:14, and 12:2 were sufficient to show that Judah was also to be caught up in the coming judgment. It is of some interest to note that Hosea 8:14 recalls the style of Amos, and may perhaps constitute a fragmentary quotation of that prophet.

In connection with the reference in Hosea 12:2, it has been asserted by some scholars that the name "Judah" has been substituted for "Ephraim" or "Israel." If this was actually the case, and was the result of activity on the part of a later editor in the southern kingdom, it is difficult to see why he should have introduced such an adverse note when others of his fellows, according to critical authors, were seeking to glorify Judah at the expense of Israel. That the name "Judah" does not constitute a secondary substitution, however, is clear from the sense of Hosea 12:2ff., the significance of which is beyond question. The prophecy as a whole shows that Hosea was not merely concerned with the nation of Israel, but with the House of Israel (Hos. 3:5). This consideration, as well as the fact that the prophet regarded the northern kingdom as a usurpation (Hos. 8:4), might account for the dating of the composition with respect to southern as well as northern rulers, as indicated in the superscription. Against Oesterley and Robinson it must be said that there is nothing in the passages concerning Judah to require an exilic or post-exilic date,[50] nor is there any ground for the view of Kaufmann that chapters 1 to 3 came from a prophet living between 853 and 842 B.C. who was quite unrelated to the Hosea of the remaining chapters, to which alone the superscription in chapter 1:1 referred.[51] Although the prophecy may

---

[49] Cf. R. E. Wolfe, ZAW, LIII (1935), pp. 90ff.
[50] IBOT, p. 349. Cf. E. Day, AJSL, XXVI (1910), pp. 109ff.
[51] KRI, p. 309.

well have come down through Judaean agencies, who were possibly responsible for certain minor redactions, including the extension of the prophetic tradition to the days of Hezekiah, there is no assured reason for denying the bulk of the extant work to the lifetime of Hosea himself. Arguments for a later date generally appeal to the corrupt state of the text as evidence for the existence of a prolonged interval between the occurrence of the spoken word and the written compilation. Perhaps an even better explanation might be that the written prophecy was not only well known as such during the later years of the prophet Hosea, but that it was also well used in subsequent days of political and religious crisis.

Hosea shared with Jeremiah a remarkable sensitivity and depth of feeling. He was a warm humanitarian whose patriotism was made evident in the fact that, unlike his contemporary Amos, he never referred to foreign peoples except insofar as they were related politically in some manner to Israel. Mention of a series of historical events (Hos. 5:1; 6:9), the nature of which cannot always be determined, pointed to his love for the historical traditions of his own nation. His devotion to his wife constitutes a particularly expressive indication of the depths of his spirituality, and however long prior to his marriage he may have received his call to prophetic office, there can be no doubt that he learned obedience to the will of God through the things which he suffered.

The basic message of Hosea needs to be set firmly against the historical and social circumstances under which it was proclaimed. The prosperity that characterized the reign of Jeroboam II in Israel rested in point of fact upon insecure foundations, and when the shadow of Assyria fell upon the land with the usurpation of Tiglathpileser III in 745 B.C., it marked the final days of political confusion under Zechariah, Shallum, and Menahem. In a desperate bid for time the latter attempted to placate Assyria, whereas two of his successors, Pekah and Hoshea, resorted to resistance, perhaps in the hope that Egypt would come to their aid, but to no ultimate avail.

In the matter of religious activity the nation had been corrupt since the days of Jeroboam I, whose calf-worship, accompanied by the sensuous rituals of the Baals, had constituted the procedural norm in the cultus. The religious festivals were times of license and gross abandon in which the moral claims of the Covenant God had long since ceased to have either meaning or validity. It is possible that Hosea may have uttered certain of his oracles in connection with some of these festive occasions, when crowds of people would be assembled to hear his words. This was suggested as likely by Wellhausen in connection with Hosea 9:1-6,[52] and the same may be true of other portions of the prophecy. However, there is always the danger of reading into the narrative more than is war-

---

[52] J. Wellhausen, *Die kleinen Propheten übersetzt und erklärt*, p. 122.

ranted by the facts of the case. Thus it is unnecessary to suppose with May or Leslie that the figure of marriage and adultery in the prophecy is actually an allusion to the Adonis myth.[53]

Nor is it correct to assume with Mauchline that the Feast of Ingathering or Tabernacles marking the close of the agricultural year (Exod. 23:14ff.; 34:23; Deut. 16:16) was celebrated in association with the supposed New Year festival.[54] Whereas the Feast of Tabernacles took place in the seventh month (September-October), the pre-exilic New Year commenced with the vernal equinox (Exod. 12:2, 18) in March-April. Furthermore, there is no evidence whatever that during the monarchy there was even a New Year festival in Israel, whether of the Babylonian type or not,[55] and this, along with the alleged concomitant kingship and fertility rites, is to be rejected emphatically.[56] While the suggestion of Wellhausen noted above might have some merit, it is not necessary to invoke festive occasions as in themselves the most suitable opportunities for the prophet to disseminate the divine message. Although crowds were certainly in attendance at the principal shrines during the festivals, their preoccupations were such as to make them less favorably disposed towards the oracles of God than at other times under different conditions.

Whereas his contemporary Amos denounced social inequalities and the exploitation of the lower classes, Hosea was concerned primarily with moral, religious, and political abominations in the nation. Against the background of the marriage relationship, now viewed metaphorically, he regarded the aforementioned offenses as a repudiation of the loving father (Hos. 11:1ff.) and the betrayal of a faithful husband (Hos. 2:2ff.). The particular characterization of the intimate relationship existing between God and the worshipper employed by Hosea comprised his distinctive contribution to religious thought. Whereas in the cultic observances of his day it was merely the part of the worshipper to respond dutifully in slavish and unquestioning obedience, Hosea showed that God required of His followers a reciprocal participation at the emotional and spiritual level, the nature of which was summed up in the comprehensive term ḥeṣedh.

For Amos iniquity consisted in the failure of Israel to meet the divine demand for righteousness. For Hosea sinfulness was envisaged in terms of the breaking of a covenant or agreement that needed by definition to be honored by both the participants.[57] The prophet taught that the relationship between Israel and God was characterized by ḥeṣedh, which for

---

[53] H. G. May, *AJSL*, XLVIII (1932), pp. 73ff. E. A. Leslie, *The OT Religion* (1936), p. 184.

[54] J. Mauchline, *IB*, VI, p. 557.

[55] Cf. M. Noth, *Gesammelte Studien zum AT* (1957), pp. 188ff.

[56] *BHI*, p. 205.

[57] Cf. W. F. Lofthouse, *ZAW*, LI (1933), pp. 29ff.

him constituted the essence of the Covenant. The term is difficult to render by means of a single word, and attempts to equate it with "zeal"[58] or "piety" tend to substitute only a part for the whole. Ḥeṣedh embodies the concept of true love in the light of some specific relationship, and is marked by a profound emotional and spiritual content. Oesterley and Robinson approach the facts of the situation in defining ḥeṣedh as "a fundamental quality of soul which serves as a spring and motive for all right action in personal relationships."[59]

Hosea saw that the iniquity of Israel could only result in punishment by exile, a standpoint given symbolic expression in the names of his children. This fate was made the more certain by the continued inconstancy of the nation, whose repentance was as ephemeral as the morning cloud (Hos. 6:4). Restoration was certainly possible, but only on the basis of genuine contrition and a firm resolve to repudiate the idolatry and immorality that was such a formidable part of contemporary life. An impediment to true repentance was the lack of understanding displayed by Israel in connection with the ethical nature of her God. Although the prophet Hosea realized that present grace alone afforded hope for the doomed nation, he was also aware of the fact that Israel was hopelessly deficient in precisely those moral and spiritual qualities that would insure her return to a loving and forgiving God (Hos. 5:4; 11:7). Despite this gloomy picture, however, there was some hope that God would be more successful in His dealings with Israel than Hosea himself had been in his relationships with Gomer.[60] Any future restoration, however, would constitute a deliberate act of divine grace rather than a purely human achievement.[61]

* * * * *

The Hebrew text of Hosea is probably more corrupt than that of any other Old Testament book, although many of the alterations appear to be accidental. These include transpositions of consonants (Hos. 1:6; 5:2, 11; 10:13; 13:10, 14), different division of the letters making up words (Hos. 5:2; 6:3, 5; 11:2), and the occasional confusion of similar consonants (Hos. 2:14; 4:18; 5:8, 11; 7:14; 12:2, 12; 13:5, et al.). Wide variations in translation frequently result where scholars have resorted to conjectural emendation on occasions when the versions have proved inadequate for a reconstruction of the text. The LXX and Syriac versions were apparently made from a Hebrew text that had close affinities with the MT. The greatest assistance in the task of restoring the text is furnished by the LXX, which has occasionally preserved superior readings (e.g. Hos.

[58] Cf. N. H. Snaith, The Distinctive Ideas of the OT, pp. 122f.
[59] IBOT, p. 353.
[60] N. H. Snaith, Mercy and Sacrifice (1953), pp. 45ff.; C. Östborn, Yahweh and Baal: Studies in the Book of Hosea (1956), p. 84.
[61] G. Farr, ZAW, LXX (1958), pp. 98ff.

2:20; 5:15; 8:10; 10:10) as well as additional phrases (e.g. Hos. 2:14; 8:13; 13:13). From evident differences in the vocalization of the Hebrew it would appear that the manuscript employed by the LXX translators did not contain certain vowel-letters or *matres lectionis* ("mothers of reading"), notably *waw* and *yodh*. The complexity of the textual problem regarding Hosea may be one reason why there has been such a diversity of approach to passages such as Hosea 11:1ff.

Supplementary Literature

Cheyne, T. K. *Hosea with Notes and Introduction.* 1884.
Scott, M. *The Message of Hosea.* 1921.
Snaith, N. H. *Amos, Hosea and Micah.* 1956.

II. THE BOOK OF JOEL

A. NAME AND OUTLINE

Nothing is known of the history or personal circumstances of the attributive author of this prophecy, apart from his name יוֹאֵל בֶּן פְּתוּאֵל which occurs in the title of the book. As is the case with the prophet himself, nothing is known about his father. The LXX renders his name "Bethuel," a variant possibly following a transcriptional error in the Hebrew. The name Joel was widely used in Israel,[1] and at least a dozen individuals are so designated in the canonical writings. The attributive author made it clear that he was not to be regarded as a member of the priesthood in that he referred to it objectively (Joel 1:13; 2:17). Because of this attitude he has been styled a "temple-prophet" by Kapelrud.[2] Although the superscription of the book gives no indication as to the locale of the prophet, the nature of the oracles points to Jerusalem, or certainly Judah, as their place of origin.

The composition falls into two distinct sections, and can be analyzed as follows:

I. The Plague of Locusts, ch. 1:1–2:27
   A. The devastating plague, 1:1-12
   B. A call to repentance, 1:13-20
   C. The approaching day of divine wrath, 2:1-17
   D. Promises of restoration, 2:18-27
II. The Vision of the Outpoured Spirit of God, ch. 2:28–3:21 (3:1–4:21 Heb.)
   A. The outpouring of the divine spirit, 2:28-32
   B. The judgment of nations and renewal of Judah, 3:1-21

It would appear that the prophecies were prompted by the unusual severity of the locust plague, which suggested to all the imminence of the Day of the LORD.

B. THE UNITY OF THE BOOK

The chief problem of the book of Joel has to do with its integrity, a problem that is raised by the juxtaposition of historical and apocalyptic

---

[1] M. Noth, *Die israelitischen Personennamen* (1928), pp. 16, 70ff., 107, 140.
[2] A. S. Kapelrud, *Joel Studies* (1948), pp. 176ff.

literary sections in the extant work. Thus it has been argued that if the narrative section is to be understood literally, which is the most natural interpretation, it becomes a little difficult to see how an author can then intermingle such a diverse theme as an apocalyptic prophecy and still present what certainly purports to be a unified composition. In an elaborate history of interpretation of the book from the period of the LXX translators to the time of Calvin, Merx argued for the unity of the prophecy, regarding the first section of the book as equally predictive as the second, holding that the locusts constituted a figure for the enemies of Jerusalem.[3] Duhm maintained that the apocalyptic sections, including such insertions in Joel 2:1-11, which otherwise was assigned to the narrative passages, were added to the original oracle concerning the locust plague.[4] On this basis he argued for a duality of authorship, and was followed in his conclusions by Marti, Bewer, and Oesterley and Robinson, among other scholars.[5]

Any interpretation that would regard chapters 3 and 4 as a Hebrew apocalypse added at a later time to an account of a devastating locust plague must assume that the eschatological applications of this calamity to the Day of the LORD in chapters 1 and 2 (1:15; 2:1f., 10f.) must be interpolations by the hand of one or more later apocalyptists.[6] But as Weiser has pointed out, these passages show no indications of having been inserted afterwards, since they fit smoothly into the whole composition with respect to both style and subject-matter, thus pointing to the unity of the literary materials in question.[7] If both sections of the book were written about the same time, as Pfeiffer maintained,[8] there would be no need to suppose, with Oesterley and Robinson,[9] that the narrative portion was written by a prophet and was subsequently utilized by an apocalyptist for the purpose of reinforcing his teaching concerning the coming Day of the LORD.

In point of fact there seems to be no ground for presuming otherwise than that Joel saw in the devastation wrought by the locusts a symbol of the awesome crisis to come, in which God would preside in judgment over men and nations. The very presence of apocalyptic elements in the first two chapters is sufficient warrant for the apocalyptic expositions of the remainder of the prophecy, which constituted an elaboration of the futuristic theme implicit in the first section. In view of the fact that many prophetic passages interwove the contemporary with the eschato-

---

[3] A. Merx, *Die Prophetie des Joel und ihre Ausleger* (1879), p. 63.

[4] B. Duhm, *ZAW*, XXXI (1911), pp. 184ff.

[5] K. Marti in *Die Heilige Schrift des AT* (1923), II, p. 23. J. A. Bewer, *A Critical and Exegetical Commentary on Joel* (1911), pp. 49ff. *IBOT*, pp. 357ff.

[6] Cf. L. Dennefeld, *Revue des Sciences Religieuses*, V (1925), pp. 591ff.

[7] *OTFD*, p. 239.

[8] *PIOT*, p. 575.

[9] *IBOT*, p. 357.

logical, critical arguments for divisive authorship of the book lose much of their force.

Further indications of the essential unity of the prophecy can be seen, as Thompson has shown,[10] in the elaborate correspondences between the section dealing with the locusts and that concerning the pagan enemies, which serve to knit the book together into a symmetrical whole. Again, several distinctive stylistic features occur in both principal divisions, particularly the borrowings from other prophets and the repetition of important phrases.[11] The association of a concern for the present with an apocalyptic hope for the future must not be regarded as uniquely characteristic of Joel, for as Pfeiffer showed, prophets such as Isaiah (13:9ff.), Obadiah (3ff.), and Zephaniah (1:2ff.) envisaged in a present or imminent national catastrophe a sample of the future world judgment.[12] A final indication of unity of authorship may be seen in the uniform historical background exhibited throughout the book.

C. THE DATE OF THE BOOK

Though the vast majority of scholars have seen Joel as the product of one hand, there have been widely divergent views expressed as to the date of the composition, ranging in extent over half a millennium. In the absence of specific historical details that would serve to give some indication as to the probable period of authorship, it is necessary to consider a possible date on the basis of internal evidence alone. This procedure would include an evaluation of any historical allusions appearing in the work, together with the implied religious and social conditions existing in the nation; parallels to its distinctive ideas in prophecies that can be dated with reasonable assurance, literary relationships between the prophecy and other analogous compositions, and questions of style and diction.

While the occurrence of a plague of locusts such as Joel described was undoubtedly calamitous and productive of rigorous famine conditions, it was an incident that occurred far too frequently in the ancient Near East to afford any evidence for purposes of dating. Even the allusions to places and peoples such as Tyre, Sidon, Philistia, the Greeks, and so on are so vague as to be equally indecisive in matters of a date of composition. Favoring an early period is the tradition that placed Joel between the eighth-century B.C. writers Hosea and Amos, or, with the LXX, in fourth place after Micah. Again, the enemies of Judah that were mentioned were not those of the exilic age, such as the Assyrians, Babyloni-

---

[10] J. A. Thompson, *IB*, VI, p. 733.

[11] Cf. G. B. Gray, *The Expositor*, 8th ser. (1893), pp. 208ff.; *DILOT*, pp. 312f.; G. W. Wade, *The Books of the Prophets Micah, Obadiah, Joel and Jonah* (1925), pp. lxix-lxx; S. R. Driver, *The Books of Joel and Amos* (1934), pp. 19ff.; J. A. Thompson, *IB*, VI, pp. 731f.

[12] *PIOT*, p. 575.

ans, and Chaldeans, but rather the Philistines, Egypt, Phoenicia, and Edom, most of whom opposed Judah in some way in pre-exilic times.

Tyre was denounced by Amos (Am. 1:9f.) in the eighth century B.C., apparently for selling slaves to Edom, and again in the sixth century B.C. by Ezekiel (Ezek. 27:13) for purchasing persons in exchange for its own goods, a factor that might point to a date not later than the exilic period. The reference to the captivity of Judah and Jerusalem (Joel 3:1; 4:1 Heb.), which God would "bring again," envisages a future period, and cannot be used decisively as an argument for either an exilic or a post-exilic date. On the other hand, the conditions relating to the Temple (Joel 1:9ff.) have distinct affinities with the days of Haggai and Zechariah in 520 B.C. The threat of desolation in Egypt and Edom for the violence that they did to Judah in murdering innocent people in the land (Joel 3:19; 4:19 Heb.) suggests an exilic period at the earliest, as does the reference to the Greeks (Joel 3:6; 4:6 Heb.). However, with regard to the latter it should be noted that the Ionians appeared in Assyrian literary sources as early as the eighth century B.C., so that this allusion cannot be used as an assured basis for a later rather than an earlier date for the prophecy.

Certain questions are also in evidence concerning the relationship between the theological concepts of Joel and those present in other datable prophets. The idea that God would assemble all nations to Jerusalem to battle and ultimate destruction was found also in Isaiah (66:18), Ezekiel (ch. 38–39), and Zechariah (12:1ff.; 14:1ff.). The motif of the fountain issuing from the Temple that would nourish the neighborhood also occurred in Ezekiel (47:1ff.) and Zechariah (14:8ff.). Whatever may be said in favor of a late date for the references in Isaiah and Zechariah, it appears evident that Ezekiel wrote in the sixth century B.C., raising the question as to whether these concepts were current from that time onwards or whether they went back to an even earlier period to form aspects of a common eschatological motif. The idea that a day was coming when God would arise in judgment was expressed forcibly by Amos (5:18ff.), and repeated in essence by Joel (2:2f.), which suggests that Joel was thoroughly familiar with such eschatology. If he was not actually contemporary with it, as some have thought, he was certainly repeating a well-established prophetic theme of the eighth century B.C.

The parallels in phraseology between Joel and other prophecies are substantial, and as Gray commented indicate either that the prophet was greatly influenced by earlier authors or that he lived early and his prophecy exerted a remarkable influence over a large number of other writers.[13] These points of correspondence include emphasis upon the Day of the LORD (cf. Isa. 13:6; Am. 5:18; Zeph. 1:15), the sole existence

[13] G. B. Gray, A Critical Introduction to the OT, p. 209.

of God (Isa. 45:5), the outpouring of the divine spirit (Ezek. 39:29), and the restoration of the nation (Isa. 2:4; Mic. 4:3; Am. 9:13).[14]

After a careful study of the parallel passages, Gray concluded that Joel was quoting from other sources, and not *vice versa*, an opinion that has been shared by the majority of scholars.[15] Citations from Ezekiel would point to a sixth-century B.C. date for the composition of the book at the earliest, if it can be proved that the quotations are genuine, and not expressions derived from a common prophetic theology reaching back to the pre-exilic period. Whatever may have been the case, it remains true that there is no single element of the thought of Joel that is incompatible with a pre-exilic date for the prophecy.

The literary style of the author also makes the question of dating very difficult. The syntax and diction of the prophecy mark it out as a literary masterpiece, composed in stirring rhythms and littered with acutely descriptive figures of speech. Hexameter and pentameter stress-systems served to provide a powerful vehicle for conveying a graphic description of the locust plague, the coming judgments of God, and the blessings of restoration. Characteristic of the author are frequent changes in the persons of verbs and pronouns (Joel 1:5, 13f., 19; 2:2f.; 3:9ff.), the use of repetition to heighten degrees of contrast or succession (Joel 1:4ff.; 2:19ff.; 3:4ff.), the drawing of parallels between corresponding situations (Joel 1:6 and 3:9ff., 1:4–2:11 and 3:2ff.; 1:13 and 2:32; 2:19ff. and 3:18), the deployment of metaphors and similes in descriptive passages (Joel 1:6; 2:2, 5; 2:7; 2:13; 3:13), and the use of contrast (Joel 1:4ff.; 2:19ff.).

Certain post-exilic terms, including some Aramaisms, have been seen in the work,[16] such as the short form of the personal pronoun and the title of the priests or "ministers," which might indicate that, although the author was thoroughly familiar with earlier Hebrew literature, his own work was composed in the post-exilic period. Even these supposed evidences of lateness are not as assured as might be imagined, and have been contested, among others, by Kapelrud.[17]

From the foregoing discussion it will be evident that there is no easy solution to the problem of the dating of Joel, a matter that is complicated still further by the timelessness of the prophecy itself. Arguments from the international political situation thought to be reflected by the composition are at best inconclusive, as are opinions based upon the ideological concepts of Joel. Supposed reflections of such post-exilic

[14] Cf. *DILOT*, p. 312; G. W. Wade, *The Books of the Prophets Micah, Obadiah, Joel and Jonah*, pp. lxix-lxx.

[15] G. B. Gray, *The Expositor*, 8th ser. (1893), pp. 211ff.; cf. J. A. Thompson, *NBD*, p. 903; *IB*, VI, pp. 858f.

[16] Cf. A. Holzinger, *ZAW*, IX (1889), pp. 89ff.; G. R. Driver, *JTS*, XXXIX (1938), pp. 400ff.

[17] A. S. Kapelrud, *Joel Studies*, pp. 67, 86f., 111f.

prophets as Malachi (compare Joel 2:11, 31 and Mal. 3:2; 4:5) are also indecisive as evidence for dating, making for still more complexity. As a result, scholarly estimates of the period of Joel[18] have ranged from the ninth century B.C. to the Maccabean period, with Engnell, Kapelrud, and Young maintaining a pre-exilic date,[19] and the majority of liberal scholars suggesting a date about 400 B.C.[20] or later.[21] Oesterley and Robinson regarded the apocalyptic sections as datable not earlier than about 200 B.C., making the extant prophecy roughly Maccabean in date.[22] While there is a great deal to be said for both a pre-exilic and a post-exilic date for the prophecy, the present writer tends on balance to favor the latter, and envisages a date of composition somewhat in advance of 400 B.C.

D. The Message of Joel

Scholarly views regarding the compilation of the book have been affected by studies in the history of its form. Thus Engnell rejected the literary-critical view that frequently postulated a divisive authorship of Joel on the ground that it was untrue to the *Sitz im Leben des Volkes* and the genetic history of the prophetic works. He maintained that Joel 1:1–2:27 comprised a "prophetic liturgy" forming part of the New Year festival ritual, to which apocalyptic fragments had been added later. By employing a traditional series of ideas, these apocalyptic portions made it possible for the prophecy to be utilized later on in cultic worship.[23]

This traditio-historical standpoint rested to some extent upon the findings of Gunkel and Mowinckel, who had previously purported to discover liturgical elements in Joel.[24] Kapelrud, however, was more cautious in maintaining that the problems of the book must be solved by an interpretation that combined both cultic and historical aspects.[25] Such prudence is commendable, since any conjecture as to its composition that is based upon the ritual patterns of the ancient Near Eastern

[18] Cf. J. H. Kritzinger, *Die Profesie van Joël* (1935), pp. iii ff.

[19] Cf. A. S. Kapelrud, *Joel Studies*, pp. 191ff.; *YIOT*, pp. 255f.

[20] So K. Budde, *Das prophetische Schrifttum* (1906), p. 59; J. A. Bewer, *A Critical and Exegetical Commentary on the Book of Joel*, pp. 61f.; E. Sellin, *Einleitung in das AT* (1935 ed.), pp. 106f.; *BHI*, p. 417.

[21] B. Duhm, *Theologie der Propheten* (1875), pp. 275ff., ZAW, XXXI (1911), pp. 184ff., *Israels Propheten* (1916), pp. 398f.; K. Marti, *Das Dodeka-propheton* (1904), pp. 112ff.; *PIOT*, p. 575; J. Morgenstern, *Amos Studies* (1941), I, p. 120.

[22] *IBOT*, p. 362.

[23] Cf. I. Engnell, *Studies in Divine Kingship*, p. 159, *Svenskt Bibliskt Uppslagsverk*, II, cols. 727ff.

[24] H. Gunkel, *Die Religion in Geschichte und Gegenwart*, IV, col. 1614; S. Mowinckel, *Psalmenstudien*, III, p. 29.

[25] A. S. Kapelrud, *Joel Studies*, p. 14.

fertility cults goes far beyond the available evidence.[26] By contrast, there is no compelling reason for abandoning the traditional view that both major sections of the book were written by one author at approximately the same time.

Brief mention ought to be made at this juncture of the numerous attempts over the centuries to interpret the significance of the locust-plague. The insects described in chapters one and two have been taken as literal species by both ancient and modern expositors in terms of the *Pachytylus migratorius* and *Acridium peregrinum,* both of which were common in ancient Palestine. This view has been endorsed by a modern biologist, who regarded the description of a locust invasion in Joel as being unsurpassed for its dramatic picturesqueness and amazing accuracy of detail.[27] An interpretation that combined the allegorical and historical approaches was also favored in antiquity by the rabbinic and patristic writers, who thought of the locust-plague as an allegory of human historical invasions. A variation of this view commended itself to Calvin, who combined a literal interpretation of the first chapter of Joel with an allegorical understanding of the second chapter.[28]

Against this kind of opinion is the objection that both the destruction and the restoration are confined to vegetable matter, and also that the locusts are made to symbolize a human army, instead of actually constituting such a force. The apocalyptic interpretation of Merx and others, who regarded the locusts of chapter one as supernatural apocalyptic creatures symbolic of the invading armies of the last days depicted in chapter two, fails to comprehend the immediacy of the situation (Joel 1:16), and the fact that the prophet was utilizing an historical event for purposes of spiritual instruction. There seems little reason to doubt that the locusts of chapter one were literal, and that they were likened with some vividness to an invading army.[29]

Using this natural calamity as a starting-point, Joel interpreted it as a warning of imminent divine judgment (Joel 1:15), and urged all his hearers to heed the presage of doom so clearly portended. The only escape from the coming visitation was seen in genuine repentance for past evil, as a result of which men would again become receptive to divine mercy. In the hope that this ideal would be realized and that prosperity would once again descend upon the land, Joel issued two calls to repentance (1:13f. and 2:12-17), the second more detailed than the first. The expectations of revival (Joel 2:18-27) might imply that the

[26] Cf. W. Neil, *IDB,* II, p. 927.

[27] B. P. Uvarov, *Annual Report of the Board of Regents of the Smithsonian Institution* (1944), p. 33; cf. his *Locusts and Grasshoppers* (1928), pp. 250ff.; O. R. Sellers, *AJSL,* LII (1936), p. 82.

[28] R. H. Pfeiffer (*PIOT,* p. 574) held a similar view, replacing the allegorical with apocalyptic elements.

[29] Cf. J. A. Thompson, *JNES,* XIV (1955), pp. 52ff.

prophetic utterance met with immediate acquiescence on the part of the people to whom it was addressed, and that after predicting a prospect of material sufficiency, Joel spoke of the more important spiritual blessings to follow. God would pour out His spirit in such a manner that all would be possessed in that day of prophetic insight into the divine nature and purpose (Joel 2:28f.), needing no one to interpret for them as in former times. In consequence, the true worshippers of God would experience no fear when the Day of the LORD approached,[30] for their situation would be established on the basis of grace, through faith (cf. Rom. 10:13). Heathen nations would be called to account for the evils they had inflicted upon the Chosen People, and elements of the House of Israel which were scattered abroad would be returned to their ancestral home in triumph, to dominate their former enemies. Joel reflects the particularism by which Israel was thought to be the sole beneficiary of divine favor, a view that occurred far more commonly in priestly than in prophetic circles. The attitude of the prophet is understandable, however, in view of his intensely nationalistic feelings and his concern that the Chosen People should be legitimate participants in divine blessing. But even his particularism fell under critical examination, for he emphasized that only the remnant of Israel that was faithful to God would be saved, not the House of Israel in its entirety (Joel 2:32). Again, pagan nations were not to be punished by God because they did not happen to be Israelite in character, but because of the grave and inhuman offenses that they had perpetrated against their fellow men (cf. Matt. 25:31-46).

In the final conflict the heathen would be cut down in the Valley of Judgment in the midst of a cosmic cataclysm, while the elect of God would remain secure in divine keeping until Judah and Jerusalem were restored. Apart from the concepts of a messianic figure and the resurrection, Joel presents a remarkable eschatological interpretation of divine purpose in relation to human history, and it is not surprising that the Apostles in the primitive Christian Church were able to see in the wonderful happenings of Pentecost the literal fulfilment of some of the dramatic utterances of Joel (Acts 2:16ff.).

* * * * *

Apart from a few minor corruptions (Joel 1:7, 17f.; 2:11; 3:11), the Hebrew text of Joel has been transmitted in a very satisfactory manner. The LXX, Peshitta, and Vulgate versions diverge only slightly from the MT and from each other. A few minor additions are found in the LXX (Joel 1:5, 8, 18; 2:12; 3:11), but it is doubtful if these actually represent a better Hebrew text. The chapter divisions adopted by the Massoretes[31]

---

[30] Cf. W. W. Cannon, *Church Quarterly Review,* CIII (1926), pp. 32ff.
[31] Cf. E. Nestle, ZAW, XXIV (1904), pp. 122ff.

resulted in the prophecy falling into two sections, Joel 1:1–2:27 and 2:28–3:21. Since the sixteenth century most Hebrew Bibles have followed a four-chapter division comprising Joel 1:1-20; 2:1-27; 3:1-5; 4:1-21.

Supplementary Literature

Bič, M. *Das Buch Joel.* 1960.
Calkins, R. *The Modern Message of the Minor Prophets.* 1947.
Rinaldi, G. M. *Il libro di Joele.* 1938.
Wolff, H. W. *Dodekapropheton: Joel.* 1963.

III. THE BOOK OF AMOS

A. NAME AND OUTLINE

The book of Amos, which was named after the prophet עָמוֹס, was placed third in the order of the Twelve in the Hebrew Bible. The LXX, however, placed it second before Joel, but this tradition was not adopted by the Peshitta nor the Vulgate, which followed the order of the Hebrew. The attributive author of the prophecy lived in Tekoa, an uplands village in the wilderness of Judah some five miles southeast of Bethlehem. Apart from his writings, nothing is known of Amos, who appears to have eked out a meager livelihood as a sheep raiser (Am. 1:1; 7:14f.). The region in which he lived was particularly suited to the rearing of sheep and goats (cf. 1 Sam. 25:2ff.), although small amounts of grain, grapes, and figs were coaxed from the land (cf. 1 Sam. 25:18). Perhaps for at least part of the year Amos went to the western area of Judah where sycamores grew (cf. 1 Kgs. 10:27), and where he worked as a dresser of these trees.[1]

The reference in Amos 7:14 has been incorrectly translated by both the AV and the Douay version, the former describing the prophet as a "gatherer of sycamore fruit" and the latter as "a herdsman plucking wild figs." "Herdsman" should be translated "shepherd," with the LXX and targums. Goodspeed and Moffatt furnished translations that were more accurate botanically, speaking of the prophet as "dressing" or "tending" sycamore trees. Cultivators of this fig found it necessary to perform an incision on the fruit when it was about an inch in length, some three or four days before it was harvested. Accordingly, a small area at the center

---

[1] The tree referred to is the familiar *Ficus sycomorus L.*, sometimes called the "fig-mulberry" and referred to by some writers under the designations *Ficus sycomora, Ficus sycomorus,* and *Sycomorus antiquorum.* The tree was a robust evergreen that reached a maximum height of forty feet (H. N. and A. L. Moldenke, *Plants of the Bible,* 1952, p. 107; W. Walker, *All the Plants of the Bible,* 1958, p. 206; E. W. Heaton, *Everyday Life in OT Times,* 1956, p. 111; *WBA,* p. 183) and produced fruit abundantly in clusters on all parts of the tree. The *Ficus sycomorus* is very similar to the common fig, *Ficus carica L.,* but is smaller in size and inferior in quality. Because of its sweet taste it proved an attractive item of food to the inhabitants of ancient Palestine and Egypt, and was used extensively by the poorer classes.

point was pared or pierced with a sharp-pointed instrument, so that the fruit could ripen quickly. If this procedure was not followed the fig would not mature properly, and on being plucked would contain a quantity of watery juice. Apparently the task of Amos was to make such incisions in each fig just prior to the time of harvest. Although this occupation may have been tedious, it was certainly a most responsible one. So great was the value of the sycamore-fig in antiquity that King David appointed a special overseer for it, as for the olive (1 Chron. 27:28). When the sycamores of Egypt were destroyed by frost (Ps. 78:47), it was regarded as one of the most serious calamities ever to befall the nation.

From the fact that the sycamore-fig did not actually grow in Tekoa itself, Budde and a few other scholars inferred that Amos was not a native Tekoan, but rather a northern Israelite who had gone into exile in Judah.[2] Against this view it need only be said that in Amos 7:12 Amaziah clearly regarded Amos as a native Judaean, and bade him return home with all speed. The significance of the information concerning his occupation appears to lie in the fact that Amos had not been brought up in the social class from which prophets such as Isaiah or Hosea had come, nor had he been trained for office in any way by the prophetic schools or guilds, with which Amos expressly denied any connection (Am. 7:14f.)[3]

The book of Amos can be analyzed as follows:

  I. Utterances Against the Nations, ch. 1–2
      A. Prophecies against neighboring peoples, 1:3–2:3
      B. Prophecies against Judah and Israel, 2:4-16
 II. Judgment Against Israel, ch. 3–6
III. Five Visions of Judgment, ch. 7:1–9:10
 IV. Promise of Restoration and Blessing, ch. 9:11-15

B. BACKGROUND OF THE PROPHECY

From the superscription to the prophecy (Am. 1:1) it is evident that Amos lived during the reigns of Uzziah, king of Judah (767-740/39 B.C.), and Jeroboam II of Israel (782/81-753 B.C.). Since the leprosy which afflicted Uzziah necessitated a co-regency towards the end of his reign (2 Kgs. 15:1ff.), the ministry of Amos should perhaps be placed about 750 B.C. Morgenstern dated the Bethel address in chapter seven

---

[2] K. Budde, *JBL*, XLIV (1925), p. 81.

[3] On Amos as *nābhî* see H. H. Rowley in *Festschrift Otto Eissfeldt* (1947), pp. 191ff.; I. Engnell, *Svenskt Bibliskt Uppslagsverk*, I, cols. 59ff.; M. Buber, *The Prophetic Faith* (1949), p. 110; E. Würthwein, ZAW, LXII (1950), pp. 10ff.; W. S. McCullough, *JBL*, LXXII (1953), p. 251; G. R. Driver, *ET*, LXVII (1955-56), pp. 91f.; P. R. Ackroyd, *ET*, LXVIII (1956-57), p. 94; K. Roubos, *Profetie en Cultus in Israel* (1956), pp. 116, 121; J. D. W. Watts, *Vision and Prophecy in Amos* (1958), pp. 5ff.; A. S. Kapelrud, *Central Ideas in Amos* (1956), pp. 5ff.

in the autumn of 751 B.C., while Watts placed it in 752 B.C.[4] Albright held that Amos began his prophetic career about 752 B.C., while Carlier placed his initial activities some two years earlier.[5] One of the latest dates entertained by scholars was the one assigned by Snaith, who suggested that Amos commenced his ministry in 744 B.C.[6]

The prophecy is of very great value in that it forms the chief source of information relating to the internal conditions in the northern kingdom during the reign of Jeroboam II. By any standards this period was the most brilliant in the entire history of the Samaritan regime. The traditional rivalry between Israel and Damascus was in suspension owing to the resurgence of military power in Assyria. This fact compelled the Damascenes to look to the protection of their eastern flank, a move that relieved Israel of considerable military pressure to the point where Jeroboam II was even able to recover for Israel certain territories east of Jordan. Internal weakness prevented Egypt from interfering in the schemes of Jeroboam II, and with a resurgent Judah to act as a buffer in the eventuality of military activity on the part of the Egyptians, the northern kingdom experienced a sense of security unknown since the Golden Age of David and Solomon.

Trade and commerce flourished, and there was a pronounced drift of labor from the land to the city. A generation from whom the ever-present threat of military attack had been removed began to concentrate upon more material things, and this quickly resulted in a demand for luxury items that had previously been the prerogative of only the highest levels of Israelite society. Such preoccupation with materialistic goals went hand in hand with moral and religious depravity, and struck hard at the traditional concepts of social justice inherent in the Torah. Bribery of officialdom was frequently employed by unscrupulous individuals who wished to amass lands and wealth in a comparatively short time. This trend was carried to its extreme in the corruption of the judiciary, with the result that one who was illegally deprived of his property or other holdings could seldom if ever expect to receive justice in the courts of the land.

Self-interest of this kind soon created a powerful aristocracy of wealth, and this was accompanied by the virtual disappearance of the middle class in Israelite society. Since there was then no social level that could maintain the tensions necessary for a healthy communal climate, the gap between rich and poor became ominously wide. Within a few short years the poor had been reduced to the level of servitude, and when condi-

---

[4] J. Morgenstern, *HUCA*, XIII (1938), p. 46. J. D. W. Watts, *Vision and Prophecy in Amos*, p. 35.

[5] *BPAE*, p. 71. A. Carlier, *La Chronologie des Rois de Juda et d'Israël* (1953), p. 40f.

[6] N. H. Snaith, *Mercy and Sacrifice*, p. 12.

tions made it necessary they were sold into bondage by their masters, often for trivial considerations (Am. 2:6).

In the area of religion the depravity of worship in the northern kingdom had reached its fullest point of development. Self-interest in social affairs made for self-indulgence in matters of religion. The northern sanctuaries were crowded with worshippers who, in the main, were rejoicing in the prosperity of the times, and found an expression for their desires in the erotic religious rites that were the concomitant of a pagan Canaanite Baal worship. Prophets and priests associated with the sanctuaries profited from the lavish gifts of the worshippers, and naturally condoned these exercises in the name of religion, appearing completely oblivious to the conditions of rapid decay which lay immediately underneath the surface of social life.

C. The Message of Amos

It was to this scene of degenerate political, moral, and religious behavior that Amos addressed himself. His oracular utterances clearly reflect the life of the poor shepherd, but they also show that the prophet was acutely aware of the oppression, injustice, and immorality that marked the trend of life in urban areas. The general vitality and rhetorical force of the prophetic oracles in Amos need occasion no particular surprise, coming as they did from a shepherd and dresser of figs, since, as Smart has pointed out, rudeness of occupation does not necessarily indicate rudeness of thought and speech.[7] Many of the great leaders of Israel came from a pastoral setting, and it would appear from Amos that it was in the homes of the peasant class that the traditions of the true Hebrew faith were preserved from one generation to another.

Nor is it necessary to regard the wide knowledge and understanding that Amos had of urban life and political conditions in Israel as being inconsistent with the life and work of a shepherd. As Oesterley and Robinson have shown, Amos was familiar with the great cities and famous sanctuaries of the north, while the detachment of his home life, far removed from the turmoil and intrigue of Bethel and Samaria, furnished him with a certain sense of austerity and isolation from the evils that he so clearly saw inherent in northern society.[8] This perception was based upon his conviction that a holy and just God could only be served properly by a nation that itself reflected such exalted moral properties in its way of life.

Because he came from the outside Amos was in a particularly suitable position to castigate the falsity of worship, the profligacy of professional religion as expounded by priests and cultic prophets alike, and the crass dishonesty of contemporary commercialism. His vigorous poetry exposed

[7] J. D. Smart, *IDB*, I, p. 117.
[8] *IBOT*, pp. 366f.

the inhumanity of the upper classes for neglecting and even denying the legitimate demands of human individuality in their shameful treatment of the lower classes of Israelite society. All these factors, compounded by the complete failure of the professional prophets to speak critically to the needs of the day and generation, led Amos to forsake his native wilderness, and in the calling of a prophet of God to preach divine judgment at the very center of corruption in the northern kingdom.

His remedy for national and social evils alike was simple. If men desired to live they must abandon their immoral way of life, and in seeking God must reflect in their characters those qualities of justice, righteousness, and holiness that were typical of the divine nature as revealed in the Torah. Formal recognition of the implications of the Mosaic Covenant was not sufficient to restore the vitality of Israelite national life. Instead, the spiritual essence of the Covenant had to become the dominating concern of all, lest divine retribution overtake them for their wickedness. So exacting were the demands of a righteous God that no consideration whatever must prevent the establishment and continuance of an advanced moral and ethical way of life, if a secure and blessed future was to be assured. This would not conform to the general idea of the Day of the LORD, which played an important role in popular eschatology, for the expectations of the nation were based upon false foundations. By contrast, the coming visitation of God would be a day of darkness rather than light, one of punishment and sorrow rather than reward and gladness. On that solemn day God would reassert the claims of His moral character upon those who had repudiated them previously, and would not vindicate Israel indiscriminately merely because of the ancient Covenant relationship. Small wonder, then, that the prophetic denunciation of the contemporary modes of behavior and the passionate plea of Amos for social justice and righteousness met with so little approval from the highest officials in the land, for his message constituted a categorical rejection of all the values that the upper-class Israelites held dear.

The prophecy itself falls into three important divisions, comprising Amos 1:1–2:16, which consists of several brief oracles against foreign peoples and one against Israel; 3:1–6:14, a collection of short addresses pronouncing judgment against Israel; and 7:1–9:15, comprising a series of visions into which biographical material concerning Amos was interpolated (Am. 7:10-17), along with an oracle denouncing wealthy merchants (Am. 8:4-7). The form of the superscription with which the first division begins is interesting in that Uzziah was placed before Jeroboam II in the dating-sequences. This may be due to the fact that, as a Judaean, Amos dated events primarily in terms of his own reigning monarch, but more particularly because in all probability Amos regarded the Davidic line alone as legitimate, a consideration that may also have influenced Hosea (Hos. 1:1).

887

The mention of the earthquake may possibly constitute an editorial addition that associated the work of the prophet Amos with the incidence of a severe seismic disturbance in the southern kingdom.[9] However, such a situation throws no light upon the dating of the prophecy itself, since earthquakes occurred frequently in Palestine, and there is unfortunately no means of correlating the one mentioned in Amos with other known events of the eighth century B.C. The earthquake in question evidently occurred two years after Amos had prophesied, but before his utterances were committed to writing.

The prophetic mission of Amos appears to have been of comparatively short duration, and to have taken place in the reign of Jeroboam II of Israel. Driver, following some earlier writers, placed the ministry of Amos about 760 B.C.,[10] but the majority of scholars have favored a date some ten years later. Cripps and Snaith have argued for a date about 745 B.C. for the original utterances, on the ground that Amos could hardly have envisaged Assyria as the means by which Israel would be overthrown until the rise of Tiglathpileser III in 745 B.C.[11] This argument seems inadequate for the very good reason that Amos alone was able to interpret the signs of the times, whereas after 745 B.C. any reasonably astute Israelite would have been able to read the handwriting on the wall. By contrast, as Skinner so admirably put it, the mind of the prophet was the seismograph of providence, vibrating to the first faint tremors that heralded the coming earthquake.[12]

The oracles against foreign nations in the first division of the prophecy dealt with Damascus (1:3-5), Gaza (1:6-8), Tyre (1:9f.), Edom (1:11f.), Ammon (1:13-15), and Moab (2:1-3). It should be noted that the last three were blood-relatives of Israel, whereas the first three were not. By a climactic use of numbers and the incorporation of surrounding peoples, including Judah, into his prophecy, Amos approached in a relentlessly progressive manner his massive denunciation of the nation of Israel. All the utterances appear to be quite genuine, and it is incorrect to argue, as Pfeiffer did, that the oracle against Edom was spurious since it reflected the aftermath of the destruction of Jerusalem in 586 B.C. [sic].[13] In this connection it merely needs to be recalled that the Edomites allied with Ammon and Moab in the time of Jehoshaphat (870/69-848 B.C.) in an attack upon Judah (2 Chron. 20:1, 22f.); that they subsequently rebelled against Jehoram (848-841 B.C.),

---

[9] Equated by J. Morgenstern, *HUCA*, XI (1936), p. 140 with the events of 2 Chron. 26:16-21; cf. Zech. 14:5 for analogous dating.

[10] S. R. Driver, *The Books of Joel and Amos*, p. 100; cf. *DILOT*, p. 314.

[11] R. S. Cripps, *A Critical and Exegetical Commentary on the Book of Amos* (1929), pp. 35ff.; N. H. Snaith, *Amos, Part III: Study Notes on Bible Books* (1946), pp. 8f.

[12] J. Skinner, *Prophecy and Religion*, p. 38.

[13] *PIOT*, p. 579.

who was unable to subjugate them (2 Kgs. 8:20ff.; 2 Chron. 25:11f.), and that only after forty years were they conquered by Amaziah (796-767 B.C.).

The second main division, comprising denunciations of Israel, has three addresses commencing with "Hear this word" (Am. 3:1; 4:1; 5:1; cf. 8:4), and two others beginning, "Woe unto you that. . ." (5:18; 6:1). Here the people were warned that, far from making Israel secure, her election under the terms of the Sinai Covenant demanded her punishment. The luxurious living of the capital city, achieved by improper accumulation of wealth, would come under judgment (Am. 3:9ff.). Although premonitory events such as famine and pestilence had occurred, the people of Israel had not taken due warning. This situation resulted in a *qînāh* lament by the prophet from a futuristic standpoint (Am. 5:1ff.), as though the nation were already obliterated. The coming Day of the LORD would achieve this end, and would bring with it both desolation (Am. 6:7ff.) and plague conditions (Am. 6:9f.) consequent upon the siege.

The third portion of the prophecy consists of a number of visions (Am. 7:1–9:15), which expounded the theme of the coming judgment. The first four of these (Am. 7:1-3, 4-6, 7-9; 8:1-14)[14] were introduced by the phrase, "Thus hath the LORD showed me," and the fifth vision by the words, "I saw" (Am. 9:1-10). To this material was added the historical section in Amos 7:10-17, dealing with the instructions given by Amaziah to Amos to leave the locality forthwith. This particular group of visions concluded with an apocalyptic passage (Am. 9:11-15) promising restoration to the nation, and constitutes a feature which was common to other prophetic authors also.

There seems no good reason for assuming, as Weiser does, that since the prophet was originally commissioned to proclaim his message orally, the purpose that required that the utterances should be committed to writing must have been very different from the motives for their oral delivery.[15] The iterative character and poetic form of the various oracles would enable them to be remembered easily, while their written form would lend a degree of permanence and emphasis to their message that an oral tradition could hardly sustain to the same extent. As far as form and content are concerned, it is possible to recognize the presence of two

---

[14] Cf. G. Hölscher, *Die Profeten*, p. 198; J. Hänel, *Das Erkennen Gottes bei den Schriftpropheten* (1923), pp. 98, 105ff.; F. Häussermann, *Wortempfang und Symbol in den alttestamentlichen Propheten* (1923), pp. 34, 69, 80; R. S. Cripps, *A Critical and Exegetical Commentary on the Book of Amos*, pp. 91ff., 100ff.; W. Rudolph, *Imago Dei, Gustav Krüger Festschrift* (1932), p. 24.

[15] *OTFD*, p. 243.

groups, the visions in the first person singular (Am. 7:1-9; 8:1-3; 9:1-4), and the oracles in chapters 1 to 6.

That the visions make up a literary as well as a spiritual homogeneous unit is evident from their construction, which rises rhetorically to a climax, and also by the general consonance of their form and subject-matter. They doubtless constituted a unified group from the time that they were proclaimed orally, and the fact that the first person singular was employed for the visions is a clear indication that Amos himself was the author. There is no ground for supposing that some of the visions took place after Amos had been requested to leave Israel, since the interpolation of the biographical section (Am. 7:10-17) is designed to show that the visions were an integral part of his mission in the northern kingdom. The material in Amos 8:4-14 belongs in nature to earlier oracular utterances of the prophet, although it may have been placed in its present position in order to supplement the account of the visions.

The collection of oracles in chapters 1 to 6 exhibits certain stereotyped features including the climactic use of numbers. The careful arrange-ment of denunciations, first against pagan races, then against blood-relatives of Israel, followed by a castigation of Judah and culminating in a powerful oracle against Israel itself, constitutes an arresting dramatic device that appears to be original with Amos, though somewhat analo-gous examples have been noted in Egyptian literature. It is unlikely that the biographical section concluded this group of material, as some scholars have supposed, since its presence in the visionary materials was necessary to indicate that they constituted an essential part of the northern ministry.

D. THE COMPOSITION OF THE BOOK

The extent to which Amos himself left behind written documents containing his oracles and visions cannot, of course, be determined with any certainty. Adherents of the Scandinavian traditio-historical theories maintain that the oracles of Amos, like those of all other prophets, were transmitted orally over a prolonged period of time. However, as Smart has pointed out, the remarkably sound condition of the Hebrew text lends support to the view that either Amos or an amanuensis set down the oracles in writing.[16] It may be that the account of the visions and the collection of oracles may have enjoyed independent existence for a comparatively short time. Thus Weiser has suggested that the visions belonged to a period preceding the mission to Israel and were compiled as a separate document at the time of the earthquake, which served to emphasize their message of doom, and to which Amos 8:4-14 was added

---

[16] J. D. Smart, *IDB*, I, p. 118.

subsequently.[17] The oracles in chapters 1 to 6 were collected at the close of the northern ministry, and concluded originally with the biographical section. According to this view, both documents were subsequently united in exilic or post-exilic days to form the extant work, along with some editorial additions. The theory was based in part upon the presence of parallel verses in Amos 1:1, which for Weiser pointed to the presence of two collections, namely "The Words of Amos" and "The Visions of Amos which he saw." These two had been combined in the extant title by a redactor in order to give proper unity to the ultimate composition.

This theory of the composition of Amos in terms of two distinct books being subsequently integrated was supported, with some modifications, by Gressmann, Hempel, Morgenstern, Fosbrooke, and Watts, among others.[18] Gordis maintained that, aside from minor additions, the book was the authentic work of Amos, but he envisaged a twofold division, the first portion of which, comprising Amos 1:2–7:9, recorded the speeches and events prior to the Bethel encounter. The second section, consisting of Amos 8:1–9:15, contained subsequent speeches and visions of the prophet. The process of union between these divisions was entertained in terms of the liberal view of the unification of Isaiah, with Amos 7:10-17 being added to the first division of Amos just prior to the unification of the prophecy.[19]

Any theory that makes something approaching a hard and fast division between oracles and visions in Amos rests necessarily upon extremely fragile foundations, since there is no evidence that such a division, if indeed it ever existed, did not originate with the prophet himself, and that in any event it was meant to indicate anything approaching the nature of a bifid structure such as is evident in some other Old Testament prophecies. Again, it appears unlikely that the visions can be dated in relationship to the oracles as being early, as Weiser imagined, since there is an obviously close connection between the vision in Amos 7:7ff., in which Amos foresaw the overthrow of the royal house, and the consecutive narrative passage which recounted his expulsion from Israel for pronouncing against the regime of Jeroboam II. That the visions must be integrated with the oracular utterances in the ministry of Amos is evident from the fact that in the first vision (Am. 7:1-3) the prophet was already exercising characteristic intercessory functions in begging God to

---

[17] A. Weiser, *Die Profetie des Amos* (1929), pp. 249ff., *Einleitung in das AT* (1949 ed.), pp. 181f., *Das Buch der Zwölf Kleinen Propheten* (1949), I, pp. 110ff.; *OTFD*, pp. 243f.

[18] H. Gressmann, *Der Messias* (1929), p. 69. J. Hempel, *Die Althebräische Literatur und ihr Hellenistisch-Jüdisches Nachleben* (1930), p. 129. J. Morgenstern, *HUCA*, XI (1936), pp. 19ff. H. E. W. Fosbrooke, *IB*, VI, p. 773. J. D. W. Watts, *ET*, LXVI (1954-55), pp. 109ff., *Vision and Prophecy in Amos*, pp. 27ff.

[19] R. Gordis, *Harvard Theological Review*, XXXIII (1940), pp. 239ff.

be merciful in His dealings with Israel. Again, it is doubtful whether the kind of dichotomy that Weiser contemplated can actually be supported to any real extent in view of the fact that when the contents of the visions and oracles are compared, there is no fundamental difference of emphasis or nature.

Annotations to the prophecy by various hands have been detected by some scholars, but attempts to distinguish individual editors are pointless in virtue of a complete lack of supporting evidence.[20] The vast majority of scholars accept the authenticity of the work of Amos,[21] although many are prepared to accept the theory of minor insertions, principally in connection with material relating to Judah and the messages of hope (Am. 9:11-15). On the basis of the available evidence there seems little doubt that Amos, with or without scribal help, was responsible for recording the oracles and visions attributed to him.

The degree to which Amos may have attracted disciples depends to some extent upon whether or not he followed the advice of Amaziah as recorded in Amos 7:12, and subsequently exercised a ministry in the southern kingdom.[22] For this, however, there is no evidence, and all indications point to the fact that the public ministry of Amos was of comparatively short duration, extending, perhaps, over no longer a period than a few months. While his prophecy may have been subjected to minor redactional processes in Judah, it is difficult to determine either the nature or the scope of such activity in the prophecy, which exhibits a remarkable uniformity of standpoint.

The words of Amos, as Hempel observed, were formulated with a freshness and originality that demanded the attention of his hearers and gave authenticity to his pronouncements.[23] The lyrical and dramatic heights to which Amos rose compare favorably with the finest efforts of Hosea or Isaiah, and far exceeded those of Jeremiah and Ezekiel. Indeed, his poetry may be classed with the very best in Hebrew literature, and as Pfeiffer has noted, none of the prophets apart from Isaiah managed to equal the purity of his language and the classical simplicity of his style.[24]

---

[20] R. E. Wolfe, ZAW, LIII (1935), pp. 90ff., Meet Amos and Hosea (1945), p. xvii.

[21] Cf. W. S. McCullough, JBL, LXXII (1953), p. 247.

[22] As suggested by T. K. Cheyne, EB, I, col. 154; W. S. McCullough, JBL, LXXII (1953), p. 250. For the view that the prophecy applied to both kingdoms see E. A. Edgehill and G. A. Cooke, Amos (1913), p. 92; M. Buttenwieser, The Prophets of Israel (1914), pp. 232ff.; R. S. Cripps, A Critical and Exegetical Commentary on the Book of Amos, p. 13.

[23] J. Hempel, Die Althebräische Literatur und ihr Hellenistisch-Jüdisches Nachleben, p. 128.

[24] PIOT, p. 583.

He employed rhetorical devices in the proclamation of his oracles, and heightened the effectiveness of his words by the use of aural imagery. Particularly effective for his purposes were the dirge-like *qînāh* rhythms, which he employed skillfully to build up an ominous sense of expectation in relationship to the coming doom of the nation. Yet for all the stylistic devices he utilized, the basic simplicity of the man himself was firmly embedded at the core of his utterances. He could employ a play on words (Am. 8:2—"summer fruit," קִיץ and "end," קֵץ) with devastating eschatological force, and at the same time could promise in lyric language the restoration of the nation (Am. 9:13ff.).

Whether Amos incorporated citations from an earlier hymn into his prophecy, as some scholars have maintained,[25] is rather doubtful. There seem good reasons for thinking that the three fragments considered to be such (Am. 4:13; 5:8; 9:5-6) are so closely integrated with their context that they cannot be isolated without a basic disruption of the text.[26] They appear to be genuine words of the prophet Amos that proclaimed a belief in God as the creator of the world and the guiding spirit in all of life. This doctrine was firmly rooted in the Mosaic Torah,[27] and was merely being recapitulated by Amos in a form designed to meet particular circumstances. It is very doubtful whether the eschatology of Amos 4:13 ever occurred in the form of a hymn that could have been perpetuated either by Judaean peasantry or cultic prophets. Notes of doom seem generally to have been entirely foreign to the expectation of the common people, as Amos himself clearly showed in his repudiation of popular eschatology, and only those prophets such as Elijah and Elisha, who stood firmly in the Mosaic tradition, were given to uttering pronouncements concerning national calamity. Those cultic prophets who functioned in the northern kingdom were notorious for their indifference to true morality and religion, and it is doubtful if they could have fostered the kind of eschatology that the verses in question enshrined. Finally, the serious difficulties that earlier scholars encountered in their attempts to reconstruct the "hymn" and the lack of unanimity in their conclusions would seem to indicate that the alleged fragments are in fact integral to the text of the prophecy and that they originated with Amos himself.

---

[25] Cf. H. Schmidt, *Der Prophet Amos* (1917), p. 23 n. 1; K. Budde, *JBL*, XLIV (1925), p. 106; F. Horst, *ZAW*, XLVII (1929), pp. 45ff.; T. H. Gaster, *Journal of the Manchester Egyptian and Oriental Society*, XIX (1935), pp. 23ff.; E. Hammershaimb, *Amos* (1946), pp. 72, 79; A. Weiser, *Das Buch der zwölf Kleinen Propheten*, I, p. 135; V. Maag, *Text, Wortschatz und Begriffswelt des Buches Amos* (1951), pp. 24, 56ff.; J. D. W. Watts, *Vision and Prophecy in Amos*, pp. 51ff.

[26] So A. K. Cramer, *Amos* (1930), p. 90; W. S. McCullough, *JBL*, LXXII (1953), p. 248.

[27] For references to events narrated in the Torah cf. Am. 1:11; 2:9; 3:1; 3:13; 4:11; 5:6; 5:25; 7:16. For references to the Law compare Am. 2:4 with Deut. 17:19; Am. 2:8 with Exod. 22:26; Am. 8:5 with Lev. 19:35f.

Consequently it does not appear necessary to assume with Watts and others[28] that prophets such as Amos occasionally picked up some phrase or motif from the cult-liturgy and expanded it to furnish the particular emphasis needed for that hour. Surely it is evident from the corpus of prophetic writings that, whatever the relationship of the individual prophet to the cultus may have been, the prophets themselves were not liturgical commentators as much as men who were under compulsion to declare the oracles of God. The fact that in the process they denounced much of that which was dear to the mind of the ritualist, insisting instead upon the primacy of correct moral and spiritual attitudes, ought to dispel even further any notion that the prophets received inspiration for their utterances from within the exercise of cultic ritualism. More often than not they were profoundly provoked by what they saw, and this furnished an emotional tone to their denunciations that might otherwise have been lacking. Emotional reaction, however, is only one aspect of inspiration, and a contingent one at that.

E. THE THEOLOGY OF AMOS

The concept of God that Amos espoused is fundamental to any understanding of his prophetic message. He maintained that the LORD was the creator and sustainer of the cosmos (Am. 4:13), and as such determined the incidence of famine (Am. 4:6ff.) or plenty (Am. 9:13). In common with other prophets of his generation Amos maintained that God controlled the destinies of nations, establishing one (Am. 6:14) and putting down another (Am. 2:9).[29] Not only did God exercise restraint over them, but acted as their judge (Am. 1:3–2:3) when they offended against His moral precepts.[30]

As far as Israel was concerned, Amos proclaimed that the Creator had entered into a Covenant relationship with her (Am. 3:2), a privileged position that at the same time involved great responsibilities. Failure to recognize this situation could only bring a more devastating judgment upon Israel than that which would be incurred by pagan nations. Since Israel had avowedly broken the divine laws and neglected the Covenant obligations, she could only expect retribution at the hands of Him who was the Lord of History.

It was a matter of prime concern to Amos, as indeed it was to many of the other prophets, to stress that violations of the moral law could not be remedied by means of festive rites, offerings, or liturgical indulgence on the part of the sinner. In point of fact, God was already standing beside the altar (Am. 9:1ff.), poised and ready to shatter it. No ritual,

---

[28] J. D. W. Watts, *Vision and Prophecy in Amos*, p. 66.

[29] Cf. W. O. E. Oesterley and T. H. Robinson, *Hebrew Religion: Its Origin and Development*, pp. 224ff.

[30] J. G. S. S. Thomson, *NBD*, p. 33.

however elaborate and symbolic in nature, could possibly substitute for the sincere worship of the human spirit, grounded in the high moral and ethical principles of God as revealed in the Torah. From the fact that Amos nowhere directly condemned the calf-worship of the northern kingdom it has been assumed that he was favorable to the cultus to some extent. However, there is no evidence from the book itself that Amos appeared regularly at the sanctuaries, despite some scholarly assertions to the contrary. The fact that he mentioned Gilgal, Carmel, and other locations by name need not imply that he had participated in festivals there,[31] but merely that he was aware of the existence of cultic rites in such places, and the abuses (Am. 2:7, 8, 12; 5:26; 7:9; 8:14) that characterized them.[32]

Although the cultic prophet in Israel was closely connected with the Jehovistic traditions of the people and helped to preserve the right relations necessary for the Covenant to survive, as Davies and Pedersen have pointed out,[33] Amos appeared to be independent of group life, much as Elijah was.[34] There is no evidence from his book that he participated in cultic divination, nor do his utterances indicate that he ever furnished an oracular reply to a questioner. He was depicted in his prophecy as an isolated figure whose prophetic motivation stemmed from God alone, and led him to serve in a particular place at a specified time. The tenor of his utterances shows clearly that, far from condoning the use of idols, Amos actually repudiated completely the cultic practices of the northern kingdom. As Smart has pointed out, the removal of idols from the sanctuaries could not by itself have placated Amos, since for him the evil of the nation lay not so much in the material idols as in the delusion they fostered that God could be kept favorably inclined towards the nation by means of sacrificial offerings or the ritual procedures of the cultus.[35]

If Hosea stressed true love as a characteristic feature of the divine dealings with man, it fell to Amos to emphasize divine righteousness, which for him comprised the most important moral attribute of the divine nature. A righteous God was unable to tolerate successive violations of the moral law, and could only meet such behavior with stern reprisals. This standpoint constituted the spiritual basis for the message of judgment that Amos proclaimed in the ears of Israel, during which he roundly repudiated the popular concept that the Day of the LORD would be one of blessing and prosperity.

[31] So A. Alt, *Kleine Schriften zur Geschichte des Volkes Israel* (1953), I, pp. 79ff.
[32] Cf. M. Lehay, *Irish Theological Quarterly*, XXII (1955), pp. 68ff.
[33] G. H. Davies in H. H. Rowley (ed.), *Studies in OT Prophecy Presented to T. H. Robinson*, pp. 37ff.; J. Pedersen, *Israel*, III-IV, p. 125.
[34] Cf. W. S. McCullough, *JBL*, LXXII (1953), p. 251.
[35] J. D. Smart, *IDB*, I, p. 121.

A good deal of discussion has taken place regarding the possibility of the existence of such eschatological ideas in the eighth century B.C.[36] While part of the problem is semantic, it seems clear from the nature of the rival systems depicted in Amos that both were in fact distinct realities. Precisely what the actual form of the Day of the Lord was has also been a matter for scholarly consideration, and has resulted in a wide diversity of opinion.[37] The popular eschatology may have been related to some sort of cultic celebration at the sanctuaries,[38] since the latter would constitute the most likely situation under which such an idea would be propagated. Aside from the difficulties involved in reconstructing the Canaanite New Year ritual and then imposing it upon a nonexistent Israelite New Year festival, it appears evident from Amos that a popular and a prophetic eschatology, both of which employed the same title, existed side by side in the eighth century. It was the supreme task of Amos to demonstrate which of the two ideologies was the valid one, and in this respect he was following the tradition of Elijah (1 Kgs. 18: 21ff.).

His final word was one of hope and restoration, consistent with his view that repentance and righteous dealing would insure divine forgiveness and blessing. However, the ultimate fate of the northern kingdom makes it evident that even if his words struck an anxious note in the minds of his Israelite hearers, it was soon obliterated in the welter of license and indulgence. The prophecy of Amos constitutes a dramatic affirmation of the existence and activity of a sovereign Being, motivated by high moral and ethical considerations, who manifests Himself in His world and overrules the various phases of human history. It is a salutary warning as to the characteristics that such a deity demands of His followers, and a stern admonition to any who would think that the God of heaven and earth can be identified uniformly with the fortunes of any particular national or ecclesiastical group.

*　*　*　*　*

The text of the prophecy is in very good condition, as has been remarked above, although some scholars have seen the need for emenda-

---

[36] Cf. A. S. Peake, *The Servant of Yahweh* (1931), pp. 95f.; S. Smith, *Isaiah XL-LV: Literary Criticism and History*, p. 18; R. S. Cripps, *A Critical and Exegetical Commentary on the Book of Amos*, pp. 55ff.; E. Jacob, *Théologie de l'Ancien Testament* (1955), pp. 255ff.

[37] Cf. R. H. Charles, *EB*, II, cols. 1348ff.; W. Robertson Smith, *The Prophets of Israel*, p. 398; G. Hölscher, *Die Ursprünge der jüdischen Eschatologie* (1925), p. 13; A. von Gall, *Basileia tou Theou* (1926), pp. 26f.; J. Pedersen, *Israel, I-II*, p. 545 n. 1; H. Wheeler Robinson, *Inspiration and Revelation in the OT*, pp. 135ff.; B. D. Eerdmans, *The Religion of Israel*, p. 150; N. H. Snaith, *The Jewish New Year Festival*, p. 69 n. 17.

[38] Cf. A. von Gall, *Basileia tou Theou*, pp. 24ff.; A. Weiser, *Das Buch der zwölf Kleinen Propheten*, I, p. 111; A. Bentzen, *Oudtestamentische Studien* (1950), III, p. 92; A. S. Kapelrud, *Central Ideas in Amos*, p. 69.

tion in passages such as Amos 2:7; 3:12; 5:6, 26; 7:2; and 8:1, to mention the more important verses. The LXX and other versions appear to have been made from a text akin to that of the MT; as a result they present no important variations from the Hebrew.

Supplementary Literature

Honeycutt, R. L. *Amos and His Message.* 1963.
McFadyen, J. E. *A Cry for Justice.* 1912.
Mitchell, H. G. *Amos, an Essay in Exegesis.* 1900.
Neher, A. *Amos.* 1950.
Von Orelli, C. *The Twelve Minor Prophets.* 1893.

IV. THE BOOK OF OBADIAH

A. NAME AND OUTLINE

The brief prophecy of Obadiah occupied fourth place among the Twelve Minor Prophets in the Hebrew Bible, between Amos and Jonah. This position was adopted by some of the versions, including the Peshitta, the Vulgate, and the most modern Hebrew Bibles. In the LXX, however, the book of Obadiah was placed fifth, following Joel and preceding Jonah.

The name of the author, עבדיה, which appeared in the LXX as Ὀβδίου and in the Vulgate as *Abdias,* was common in the canonical period, with about a dozen individuals so named in the Old Testament narratives.[1] The home of the prophet Obadiah was presumably in Judaea, although the Old Testament furnishes no direct information concerning his life or circumstances. The Babylonian Talmud identified him with the steward of King Ahab,[2] while Pseudo-Epiphanius, in his *Lives of the Prophets,* thought that he was a high military official in the forces of King Ahaziah (2 Kgs. 1:12ff.). In view of the fact that the prophet almost certainly did not live before the exile, it seems inadvisable to follow such traditions regarding him.

The prophecy was set against a background of inveterate hatred on the part of the Israelites for the people of Edom. This tension had its roots in the differences between Jacob (Israel) and Esau (Edom), as portrayed in Genesis (25:23; 27:39f.). By the time of the united monarchy it was a firm policy of the Hebrew rulers to maintain as much control as possible over Edomite territory. The inhabitants of Edom naturally resented such impositions, particularly when they were unable to impose taxes on the lucrative trade that passed from Ezion-geber, the port on the Gulf of Aqabah, through Edomite territory into Palestine proper.

Although the Edomites were kept in subjection to Israel and Judah during the period of the divided monarchy, it was not without some cost to the overlords, as the accounts of battles fought in the pre-exilic period show clearly (cf. 2 Sam. 8:13f.; 1 Kgs. 11:14ff.; 2 Kgs. 14:22; 16:5f.; 2

---

[1] J. A. Thompson, *NBD,* p. 902.
[2] *Sanhed.* 39*b.*

898

Chron. 20:1ff.; 21:8ff.). Edom was also subjected from an early period to repeated raids by the surrounding Arab tribes (cf. Judg. 6:1ff.; 2 Chron. 21:16f.), whose activities in areas to the west of the northern Arabian desert were recorded in the seventh-century B.C. annals of Ashur-banipal.[3] When Jerusalem fell in 587 B.C., the Edomites capitalized on the plight of Judah, rejoicing in its calamity (Lam. 4:21) and generally behaving in a vengeful manner towards the stricken nation (Ezek. 25:12). They aided the Babylonians in the destruction of Jerusalem, and occupied the area of the Negeb (Ezek. 35:10; 1 Esdr. 4:50) later known as Idumaea. But even at this time the Edomites were under pressure from the surrounding Arab tribes. Inscriptions recovered from Tell el-Kheleifeh, the Biblical Ezion-geber, make it evident that the governor of the city about 600 B.C. was still an Edomite, whereas a century later Arab names were coming into increasing prominence there.[4] The account in Diodorus Siculus of the campaign waged in 312 B.C. by the armies of Antigonus Cyclops against Petra show clearly that the Nabataean Arabs had long been established in this former Edomite center.[5] Thus it would appear that the Edomites were expelled from their ancestral territory in the late sixth or early fifth century B.C., and it may be to this event that verse seven of the prophecy alluded.

The book may be analyzed as follows:

I. The Warning Concerning Edomites, 1-14
   A. Warning of the fall of Edom, 1-4
   B. Destruction and humiliation of the Edomites, 5-9
   C. Reasons for divine judgment on Edom, 10-14
II. The Universal Judgment, 15-16
III. The Restoration of Israel, 17-21

B. THE COMPOSITION OF THE BOOK

Various views have been advanced in scholarly circles with regard to the composition of the prophecy. The first serious questions raised in connection with the integrity of the work seem to have appeared in the writings of Eichhorn, who in the fourth edition of his *Einleitung* regarded verses 17-21 as an appendix compiled in the time of Alexander Jannaeus (103-76 B.C.).[6] Wellhausen held that verses 15a and 16 constituted a further part of such an appendix, which for him had been added to expand the fate of Edom into an eschatological picture of divine

---

[3] *ANET*, pp. 297ff.

[4] W. F. Albright in Alleman and Flack (eds.), *OT Commentary*, p. 167.

[5] Diodorus Siculus, *Bibliotheca*, XIX, 94ff.; cf. II, 48; F.-M. Abel, *RB*, XLVI (1937), pp. 373ff.; J. Starcky, *BA*, XVIII, No. 4 (1955), pp. 84ff.

[6] *Einleitung in das AT* (1824), IV, pp. 320ff.

judgment upon the heathen generally,[7] a view that was adopted by many other scholars.

More recent analyses have divided the prophecy into two or more oracles, as did Rudolph, who envisaged two sections, verses 1-14, 15b and 16-18, both of which he attributed to Obadiah.[8] Robinson held that the prophecy comprised a collection of different oracles, originally anonymous and directed against Edom.[9] Bewer thought that verses 15a, 16-21 were written by a different author, in view of the sudden change of address in verse 16.[10] Oesterley and Robinson questioned the existence of a prophet named Obadiah, and suggested that the name could have been applied quite easily to a collection of anonymous prophecies.[11] They thought of the composition of the work in terms of the assembling of seven fragmentary oracles.

Pfeiffer maintained that the original oracle had come down in two recensions, namely verses 1-9 and Jeremiah 49:7-22.[12] For him Obadiah 10-14 and 15b had never enjoyed independent existence apart from verses 1-9, and he assigned verses 1-15b to a date around 460 B.C. The remainder of the prophecy, verses 15a, 16-21 came from a period about 400 B.C. Weiser adhered to the substantial integrity of the book, regarding 1-14, 15b as a homogeneous oracle from the period after 587 B.C.[13] Verses 15a, 16-21 could not have arisen out of the same situation as 1-1 ' but despite this assertion Weiser saw no compelling reason for denying the authorship of Obadiah completely.

Earlier critical scholarship had established the position that two internal questions were important in any consideration of the composition and date of the work, namely the relationship of Obadiah to the prophecy of Jeremiah, specifically Jeremiah 49:7-22, and the historical problems raised by the mention of the fall of Jerusalem in verses 10-14. The incidence of numerous identical phrases in verses 1-9 and Jeremiah 49:7-22 clearly indicates a close literary relationship between the two passages. Caspari undertook a detailed study of the situation, and showed that the sequence in Obadiah was better than that in Jeremiah; that the language of Obadiah was more compact and forceful than its counterpart in Jeremiah, where there were evident expansions; and that in the parts of Jeremiah that had no parallels in Obadiah there were marked affinities with the normal style of Jeremiah.[14]

---

[7] J. Wellhausen, *Die Kleinen Propheten übersetzt und erklärt* (1898 ed.), pp. 213f.

[8] W. Rudolph, *ZAW*, XLIX (1931), pp. 222ff.

[9] T. H. Robinson, *JTS*, XVII (1916), pp. 402ff.

[10] J. A. Bewer, *A Critical and Exegetical Commentary on the Book of Obadiah* (1911), pp. 3ff.

[11] *IBOT*, pp. 370f.

[12] *PIOT*, pp. 585ff.

[13] *OTFD*, pp. 248f.

[14] C. P. Caspari, *Der Prophet Obadjah ausgelegt* (1842), pp. 7ff.

This situation indicated to Caspari that Jeremiah had taken materials from an older prophecy against Edom and had embellished it with his own work, a hypothesis that was accepted as conclusive by Graf, Driver, and others.[15] Consequently Ewald suggested that the resemblances between the two prophecies ought to be explained by the supposition that the common elements were derived from an earlier prophecy that Obadiah accepted with little alteration, whereas Jeremiah treated it with considerably greater liberty.[16] This older prophecy would thus consist of at least the first nine verses of the book of Obadiah, which contained no specific allusion to the events of 587 B.C.

A further argument for the view that both prophets were quoting an earlier oracle against Edom was seen in the fact that the order of the phrases in the two prophecies was different. However, the material in Jeremiah appears to have been written down somewhat prior to its counterpart in Obadiah, since for Jeremiah the judgment reserved for the city of Jerusalem (Jer. 49:12) was still in the future, whereas for Obadiah (verse 11) the city had already been captured and plundered.[17]

Scholars such as Keil, who adhered to the priority of Obadiah over Jeremiah, suggested that the historical background of Obadiah consisted in the attack of the Arabians and Philistines upon Judah in the reign of Jehoram, early in the ninth century B.C. (2 Kgs. 8:20ff.; 2 Chron. 21:16f.), or with the Edomite attack upon Judah in the reign of Ahaz (2 Chron. 28:17).[18] Others who adhered to the priority of Jeremiah interpreted the calamity in Obadiah 11-14 in terms of the fall of Jerusalem in 587 B.C. at the hands of the Chaldeans. It is important to note in this connection that the attack of 587 B.C. was the only capture of Jerusalem concerning which it was recorded that the Edomites had participated at all (Ps. 137:7; 1 Esdr. 4:45).

As against this indication of an exilic date for the prophecy, some scholars have seen indications in the Hebrew text of a reference to the post-exilic period. Thus verse 7 stated that the Edomites had been expelled from their ancestral homeland (cf. Mal. 1:3f.), which might point to a date of composition around 450 B.C. Again, verses 8-10 foretold the obliteration of the Edomites as a nation, and this prediction must have been fulfilled before the Maccabean period when, according to Josephus, that event took place.[19] Verses 19-20 have been taken as

[15] K. H. Graf, Der Prophet Jeremia erklärt (1862), pp. 559ff.; DILOT, p. 319.

[16] H. Ewald, Prophets of the OT (1868), II, pp. 277ff. So K. H. Graf, Der Prophet Jeremia erklärt, pp. 560f.; C. A. Briggs, Messianic Prophecy (1902), pp. 315f.; DILOT, pp. 319f.

[17] J. A. Thompson, IB, VI, p. 858.

[18] So J. H. Raven, OT Introduction, p. 222; YIOT, p. 261; A. B. Fowler, The Zondervan Pictorial Bible Dictionary, p. 592.

[19] AJ, XIII, 9, 1.

reflecting the period of Nehemiah, since the territory in the vicinity of Jerusalem which was promised to the Jews corresponded to that described in Nehemiah 11:25ff.

Aside from its connection with Jeremiah, Obadiah has literary affinities with other prophecies, and these are important also in any consideration of the date of the work. There are several phrases common to Obadiah and Joel (cf. Obad. 10 and Joel 3:19; 11 and Joel 3:3; 15 and Joel 1:15; 2:1; 3:4, 7, 14; 18 and Joel 3:8), while the use by Joel (2:32) of the words, "as the LORD hath said" indicates that he was quoting directly from Obadiah, which would indicate that the latter preceded Joel. It should also be noted that other prophets denounced Edom in terms similar to the ones occurring in Obadiah, including Isaiah (34:5ff.; 63:1ff.), Jeremiah (49:7ff.; cf. Lam. 4:21f.), Ezekiel (26:12ff.; 35:13ff.), and Amos (1:11f.). Such indications might suggest that as a literary composition Obadiah belonged at the latest to the exilic period. G. A. Smith inclined to such a date, since for him the reference to the sufferings caused by the fall of Jerusalem were so vivid as to suggest a composition that was contemporary or nearly so.[20] Since the Edomites were no longer a cause for concern to the Jews by the fifth century B.C., there would be little need for anyone to utter such vigorous denunciations of them after that period.

If it can be maintained, as appears probable, that Obadiah and Jeremiah employed an earlier oracle against Edom, and that the form in Jeremiah was in writing prior to its counterpart in Obadiah, it would place the latter in the exilic period at the earliest. Verses 17-21 imply a pre-Maccabean post-exilic situation that has much in common with the conditions obtaining in the mid-fifth century B.C.[21] Since Joel 2:32 seems to cite Obadiah 17, it is evident that the latter preceded the former in point of time, with the prophecy of Joel being dated, in the view of the present author, somewhat before 400 B.C.

It seems most probable that the literary and historical situations exhibited by Obadiah are most compatible with a date of authorship around 450 B.C. Although the prophecy embodies an earlier oracle, it shows clear indications of progression of thought and literary unity, making fragmentary theories of authorship untenable. The literary style is terse, with 3:2 and 3:3 rhythmic stresses being dominant. The vividness of the prophecy can be seen from the use in verse 2 of prophetic perfects to describe as an accomplished fact something still in progress. The catalog of crimes in verses 10-14 builds up to a climax, and the descriptive power of the prophecy as a whole is heightened by the use of metaphors and striking comparisons. The work progresses from the par-

---

[20] G. A. Smith, *The Book of the Twelve Prophets*, II, pp. 171f.
[21] Cf. C. C. Torrey, *AJSL*, XXXIV (1918), pp. 185ff.

ticular to the general;[22] from the judgment of Edom to universal judgment, and from the restoration of Israel to the coming of the divine kingdom. The identity of historical background in verses 10-21 is a further indication of the literary unity of the prophecy.

Against a background of divine inspiration (vv. 1, 4, 8, 18) the prophet proclaimed a message of divine moral judgment of nations throughout history. Edom was held up as an example of such judgment, primarily because of her intolerable lack of humanity towards Judah, a blood relative. In view of the fact that the prophet Obadiah has been condemned for narrow nationalism as the result of such an attitude, it should be noted that he had accepted the captivity of his own nation as one aspect of this universal judgment, and that he was looking for the extension of this kind of retribution in the Day of the LORD.

That Obadiah had a wider hope of restoration than one that merely involved the reconstitution of his own people is evident from his vision of the divine kingdom. While the nation of Israel will be dominant at that time, those whose lands they possess will benefit from the renewed moral nature of the sovereignty that will be exercised. Holiness will be the outstanding ethical characteristic of the kingdom, which will constitute an association of free individuals under divine protection.

* * * * *

The text of this short prophecy has been well preserved on the whole. The LXX is decidedly inferior, but on occasions can be useful in restoring the text. In verse 9, the final words, "by slaughter" were placed by the LXX at the beginning of the next verse to read, "For the slaughter and violence . . . ," which is probably a preferable reading. Another variant that has been favored by some scholars occurs in the LXX and Syriac of verse 21, which instead of "saviors" reads "those who have been saved."

Supplementary Literature

Peters, N. *Die Prophetie Obadjas.* 1892.

---

[22] J. A. Thompson, *IB,* VI, p. 858, *NBD,* p. 903.

V. THE BOOK OF JONAH

A. THE IDENTITY OF THE PROPHET

This book derived its name from its principal character יוֹנָה, rendered Ἰωνᾶς in the LXX and *Jonas* in the Vulgate. It stood fifth in the list of the Twelve Minor Prophets, but differed from them in that it did not contain a collection of prophetic oracles, but instead comprised a story about a prophetic figure.

The book commenced by recording the divine instructions given to Jonah the son of Amittai, who was described in 2 Kings 14:25 as a prophet from Gath-hepher near Nazareth. He was notable for his prophecy that Jeroboam II would recover from Syria vast expanses of terrain previously held by that nation. Having perceived the tenor of the communication from God (Jon. 1:1f.), Jonah sought to escape his responsibilities by fleeing to Tarshish (1:3), but en route the ship in which he was travelling was overtaken by a great storm (1:4f.). The reason for this gale was ultimately divined by the superstitious sailors (1:6-10), who were finally persuaded with difficulty by Jonah to cast him overboard so as to placate the elements (1:11-16).

In the meantime, God had prepared a great fish that swallowed the recalcitrant prophet (1:17), and he remained imprisoned there for three days, during which he prayed to God in repentance (2:1-9). Thereupon he was regurgitated (2:10) and bidden a second time to go to Nineveh and demand the repentance of that great city (3:1f.). His only recorded oracle spoke of speedy destruction (3:3), but its delivery was immediately followed by profound repentance (3:5-9), resulting in divine forgiveness (3:10), much to the chagrin of the prophet (4:1). Jonah prayed for his own death rather than witness the spectacle of Gentiles being admitted to divine favor (4:2f.), and when reproached by God for his petulance (4:4) he moved outside the city to await the trend of events (4:5). When a large shady plant grew up beside his temporary shelter, Jonah was glad, but when the growth was destroyed senselessly he became angry once more (4:6-9). From this, however, came his lesson (4:10f.), for God made it clear that pity for a decaying plant was less important than compassion for all men, whether Gentiles or not.

904

Early critics of the modern school such as Winckler and Cheyne denied that the Jonah of the prophecy was the same individual as the one mentioned in 2 Kings 14:25.[1] Such a circumstance, however, is extremely improbable in view of the tenacity of the ancient traditions with respect to Jonah as a prophet.[2] Jewish interpreters held that he prophesied in the reign of Jeroboam II, and fostered exaggerated traditions regarding his person and adventures. According to Rabbi Eliezer his mother was the Zarephath widow who entertained Elijah (1 Kgs. 17:9ff.),[3] while he himself was said to have attained extreme old age,[4] and even to have become immortal.[5] Rabbi Eliezer taught that the fish that swallowed Jonah had been created from the beginning of the world for this very purpose,[6] while other rabbinic traditions recounted the incredible experiences of the prophet when he was imprisoned inside the great fish.[7]

B. THE INTERPRETATION OF THE PROPHECY

From the vast corpus of literature, both ancient and modern, dealing with Jonah, there have emerged three distinct approaches to its interpretation.

1. Historical. The traditional explanation among Jews and Christians alike for many centuries regarded the book as an historical narrative. Accordingly Jonah was held to have prophesied in the reign of Jeroboam II, and to have engaged in a mission to Assyria during his ministry. This activity constituted the counterpart of the missions to Sidon and Syria that had been undertaken by his immediate predecessors Elijah and Elisha (cf. 1 Kgs. 17:9ff.; 2 Kgs. 5:1ff.), and was characterized by the same kind of miraculous features evident in their own ministries. The historical view also commended itself to its adherents because the book was written as though it was an historical composition.[8] For Christian scholars the emphasis that Jesus Christ placed upon the incident as a prefiguring of His own period of death after the crucifixion (cf. Matt. 12:39ff.; Lk. 11:29f.) lent credibility to the historicity of the entire prophecy, not least because Christ regarded the repentance of the

---

[1] H. Winckler, *Altorientalische Forschungen* (1906), II, pp. 260ff., a view that he retracted three years later in *Allgemeine Evangelisch-Lutheranische Kirchenzeitung* (1909), p. 1224. T. K. Cheyne, *EB,* II, col. 2570.

[2] Cf. K. Budde, *JE,* VII, p. 226. The identification was positively affirmed by K. Marti, *Das Dodekapropheton,* p. 241.

[3] *Pirke Rab. Eliezer,* XXXIII.

[4] 120 years or more in *Seder 'Olam;* 130 years in *Sepher Yuhasin.*

[5] *Yerush. Sukkah V,* 1, 55a.

[6] *Pirke Rab. Eliezer,* X.

[7] *Yalkut Jonah* 550.

[8] J. Raven, *OT Introduction,* p. 227.

Ninevites as an historical fact (Matt. 12:41).[9] A final argument for the traditional literal interpretation was that only within recent times had it been challenged, and at that in an attempt to placate incredulous scientists who found difficulty in accepting the ingestion of a man by a great fish.[10]

This interpretation has been questioned on additional grounds, however. Many scholars have attributed comparatively little significance to the words of Christ regarding Jonah, holding that Jesus merely used the details of a well-known story in order to drive His teaching home in the minds of His hearers.[11] This criticism, which would place the story of Jonah in the parabolic category of the Prodigal Son (Lk. 15:11ff.), overlooks the fact that Christ clearly regarded Jonah as an historical personage, that He gave no evidence whatever of supporting exaggerated Jewish traditions respecting the prophet, and that He considered the repentance of the people of Nineveh to have been accomplished by the mission of Jonah. Whatever else Christ may have thought about Jonah, He certainly did not view it as a parable, but as something that was firmly rooted in history.[12] Even on the unlikely supposition that the Matthean reference is an apostolic interpolation intended to show the way in which Scripture was being fulfilled, an assertion, incidentally, for which there is absolutely no textual authority in the Gospel narrative, it is no less valid than the reference to the Queen of Sheba, who was without doubt an historical personage.

The miracle of the great fish has been one of the most widely debated objections to the historical interpretation of the prophecy. Nineteenth-century scholars regarded this as a mythical theme occurring among widely divergent peoples, and included in the Greek sagas of Hercules and Perseus.[13] E. B. Tylor held that the dragon-myth lay at the root of the narrative,[14] while Cheyne saw clear indications of Babylonian mythology dealing with the dragon of the subterranean ocean.[15] Arguing from an ancient Assyrian religious tradition that the beginnings of Assyrian culture were formulated under the direction of Dagan, a creature who was part fish and part man, Trumbull suggested that Jonah appeared to the superstitious people of Nineveh as one of the incarnations

[9] Cf. F. V. Filson, St. Matthew (1960), p. 153.

[10] W. Neil, IDB, II, p. 965.

[11] J. D. Smart, IB, VI, p. 872.

[12] E. König, HDB, II, p. 749. Cf. R. A. Ward, Royal Theology (1964), pp. 51ff. and especially p. 54 n. 1.

[13] Cf. Homer, Iliad, XX:145ff.; XXI:44ff.; Horace, Odes, III:26ff.; W. Robertson Smith, The Religion of the Semites (1894 ed.), p. 159; WJ, III, 9, 3; E. Hardy, ZDMG, L (1896), p. 153; M. Kalisch, Bible Studies (1878), II, pp. 162f.; H. Schmidt, Jona, eine Untersuchung zur Vergleichenden Religionsgeschichte (1907).

[14] E. B. Tylor, Primitive Culture (1871), I, p. 306; cf. his Researches into the Early History of Mankind (1865), pp. 336f.

[15] T. K. Cheyne, EB, II, cols. 2568f.

of Dagan.[16] While rejecting this theory as improbable, König postulated some connection between the mention of the "great fish" and the fact that the Assyrian pseudologographic form for Nineveh, comprising an enclosure, perhaps the uterus of the goddess Nina (Ishtar) with a fish inside, signified a "fish-dwelling."[17] Whatever may have been the reason for the latter, it is quite evident from the prophecy that Jonah was not, nor could have been, represented as a fish-god to the inhabitants of Nineveh.

As regards the credibility of the event described, it has frequently been remarked that the true whale has such a narrow gullet that it could only swallow comparatively small fish, and certainly nothing approaching the size of a man. In this general connection, however, it is important to observe that the Hebrew spoke of a "great fish" (Jon. 1:17), that is to say, some kind of sea denizen, and that the interpretation "whale" is the result of translations into English.[18] Furthermore, while the true whale, whose habitat is the Arctic Ocean rather than the Mediterranean Sea, cannot swallow a man, the sperm whale or *cachalot* most probably can. Despite this constitutional obstacle it was shown as long ago as 1915 that even a true whale could save a man from drowning if he managed to negotiate the air-supply tract of the mammal and reach the great laryngeal pouch.[19] From time to time there have appeared in various publications accounts of incidents that purport to be similar to that in which Jonah was apparently involved. Thus Eichhorn recorded that a "*Seehund*" began to swallow a sailor, but immediately released him almost unharmed from its jaw.[20] On another occasion a whale-hunter was reportedly swallowed in 1891, but was recovered the following day in unconscious condition from the inside of the mammal.[21] Again, a seaman was said to have been swallowed by a large sperm whale in the vicinity of the Falkland Islands, and after three days was recovered unconscious but alive, though with some damage to his skin.[22] There have been other reports of similar happenings that unfortunately have been accepted uncritically and circulated, sometimes with embellishments, by avid listeners. Without doubt some of these alleged incidents are as false as tales dealing with mermaids, and on occasions have actually been repudiated by certain of the supposed participants. On the other hand, not all of these ought to be dismissed as ridiculous, and since it has been shown that certain large marine species are capable of

---

[16] H. C. Trumbull, *Jonah in Nineveh* (1892), pp. 9f.

[17] E. König, *HDB*, II, p. 747.

[18] Matt. 12:40 has κῆτος, meaning "sea-monster."

[19] G. Macloskie, *Bibliotheca Sacra*, LXXII (1915), pp. 336f.

[20] J. G. Eichhorn, *Einleitung in das AT*, IV, pp. 340f.

[21] *Neue Lutheranische Kirchenzeitung* (1895), p. 303.

[22] A. J. Wilson, *PTR*, XXV (1927), p. 636.

swallowing large objects there is at least no *a priori* reason for rejecting the possibility in the case of Jonah and some other individuals.

One serious difficulty in the Jonah narrative as against similar reported occurrences from more recent times is that whereas modern sailors who were allegedly swallowed by large marine animals were recovered unconscious, and sometimes dead, the ancient prophet was represented as being very much alive throughout his incarceration. He was fully conscious and coherent, both mentally and emotionally, being able to compose a penitential psalm and worship his god before being regurgitated by the great fish. This is a vastly different experience from that of any modern counterpart of Jonah, and in itself raises a major obstacle to the acceptance of a literal interpretation of the prophecy. Wellhausen, in fact, suggested that the mention of weeds in Jonah 2:5 precluded the suggestion that the prophet was in the belly of the fish, since weeds did not grow there.[23] The Hebrew text, of course, says nothing about the growth of weeds, but merely refers to the prophet as though he were submerged in a locality where seaweed existed.

To some scholars, an even more incredulous occurrence than the incident involving the great fish was the dramatic conversion of the pagan Ninevites to monotheism as depicted in Jonah.[24] While for obvious reasons the cuneiform records of Assyria would make no reference to such an occurrence, some scholars have seen a possible allusion to it in the religious reforms instituted about 800 B.C. by Adad-nirari III (805-782 B.C.). Hugo Winckler compared this movement with the monotheistic tendencies of Amenhotep IV of Egypt,[25] and interpreted it as part of an Assyrian trend towards monotheism.[26] While this is true in the sense that it tended to concentrate the cult-worship of the Assyrians upon the deity Nebo,[27] its importance should not be overestimated. Whatever may have been the actual facts of the case, it is difficult to believe that the Assyrians would have perpetuated a religious reformation in their own country in the name of a foreign deity. While these reforms may possibly have been connected with the mission of Jonah, such repentance towards God as was engendered was evidently of short duration. In any event, it is by no means impossible for the kind of contrition described in Jonah to have taken place,[28] particularly if the

[23] J. Wellhausen, *Die Kleinen Propheten übersetzt und erklärt*, p. 221.

[24] E.g. A. Feuillet, *RB*, LIV (1947), p. 161.

[25] H. Winckler, *A History of Babylonia and Assyria*, p. 232.

[26] H. Winckler, *Keilinschriftliches Textbuch zum AT* (1909), p. 28. Cf. A. Jeremias, *Monotheistische Strömungen Innerhalb der Babylonischen Religion* (1904), pp. 28f.

[27] Cf. R. W. Rogers, *Cuneiform Parallels to the OT* (1912), pp. 307f.

[28] For an account of Persian animals being involved in mourning rites see Herodotus, *Hist.* IX, 24. Cf. Judith 4:10.

superstitious Assyrians had any inkling of the adventures that had befallen Jonah prior to his arrival as depicted in the prophecy.

Questions have also been raised concerning the size of Nineveh at the time and the identification of the king mentioned in the narrative. The use of the past tense in Jonah 3:3 might suggest that at the time of writing the city was no longer in existence, but on the other hand the narrative itself was written in the past tense, and a present verb in such a situation would certainly appear incongruous. In any event, there seems no good reason why the tense should not be interpreted as synchronistic, indicating the nature or extent of the city as Jonah found it (for a NT parallel see Lk. 24:13). Archaeological excavations at Nineveh have shown that the city was approximately eight miles in circumference and could have housed at least 175,000 people.

The figure of 120,000 given in Jonah 4:11 is in accord with the evidence available from Nimrud, a city of less than half the size, which in 879 B.C. was able to accommodate 69,574 persons. The reference to the "three days' journey" is not to the breadth of the city itself, as is commonly understood, but to the entire administrative district of Nineveh, which was between thirty and sixty miles across. The first day referred to in Jonah 3:4 might allude to the distance from the southern suburbs to the north of the city, since as Wiseman has pointed out, the Hebrew text, by employing נינוה in each instance did not distinguish between the metropolis proper [(al) ninua] and the district [ninua (ki)].[29] In any event it need not imply that the prophet journeyed as far as it was possible to walk in one day, but merely that he entered the city and began to preach his message in various areas.

No exception need be taken to the designation of the Assyrian monarch as "king of Nineveh," since the writer merely intended a passing reference to the ruler as such. This practice was not uncommon in Hebrew writings, as indicated by the reference to the king of Edom (2 Kgs. 3:9, 12) and the king of Damascus (2 Chron. 24:23). Under ordinary circumstances the Israelites spoke of the ruler as king of Assyria, but the usage in Jonah is similar to that which described Ahab of Israel as "king of Samaria" (1 Kgs. 21:1) and Benhadad of Syria as "king of Damascus" (2 Chron. 24:23).

An additional objection to the literalistic interpretation of the book has been seen in the miraculous growth of the gourd that arose overnight to protect the prophet from the heat (Jon. 4:10). The verse has been understood to mean that the plant grew at an unnaturally rapid rate, since it was described as the "son of a night," and this appears, *prima facie*, to be the meaning of the reference. The קיקיון itself, rendered κολόκυνθα in the LXX, has been the subject of considerable argument among scholars. A marginal note in the RV furnished as an alternative to

---

[29] D. J. Wiseman, *NBD*, p. 889.

"gourd" the translation "palm-christ," a rendering that had been supported at one time by Jerome and by some other patristic writers. The "Palma-Christi" is the ordinary castor-bean, *Ricinus communis L.*,[30] a shrub that grows in excess of twelve feet in height and bears huge leaves that are excellently adapted for producing shade in the proximity of a bower. In hot climates it exhibits a tree-like appearance, and is remarkable for the rapidity of its growth, according to some naturalists. The plant also grew in ancient Egypt and from it was extracted the oil, which was known locally as "kiki oil," suggesting some etymological connection with the Hebrew form occurring in Jonah.

Augustine was one of several patristic writers to dispute this identification, and held that the plant was a true gourd species that grew even more quickly in the orient than the castor-bean, while affording an equally dense shade. The species *Cucurbita pepo* var. *ovifera L.* has been suggested by modern botanists as a suitable variety, but this choice is unfortunate in that it and its varieties are indigenous to tropical America, and were unknown in Mesopotamia in Biblical times. Insofar as it is possible to suggest a suitable species for the gourd of Jonah, the castor-oil plant, *Ricinus communis L.* would appear to be the most adequate, considering all the factors involved. In tropical locations it can grow at least a foot a day, and if the reference in Jonah 4:10 is not intended to be strictly literal, it can at least be regarded as hyperbole to characterize the unusually rapid growth of the plant.

From the foregoing considerations it will be readily apparent that while none of the objections brought against the literal interpretation of the book is absolutely insuperable, some of them raise serious questions that the present status of the evidence makes it impossible to answer convincingly. Most prominent among these is the matter of the great fish. It seems unlikely that this particular topic constituted a motif which had been incorporated into the story from popular folklorist sources, since it cannot be shown that the prophet was ever remotely familiar with such tales, and particularly, as Feuillet has pointed out, that he was guilty of borrowing from sources of this kind.[31]

In any evaluation of the traditional interpretation it is of great importance not to overstate arguments based upon the historical form of the narrative. As Aalders has shown, all the parables of Jesus resemble a record of historical events,[32] and as such it is impossible to argue from the literary form of Jonah to the conclusion that it must have been meant as a record of actual happenings. This is particularly significant in view of the fact that the prophecy constitutes an independent piece of literature, and is not an element of a larger historical corpus, as with events in

[30] H. N. and A. L. Moldenke, *Plants of the Bible,* pp. 94f.

[31] A. Feuillet, *RB,* LIV (1947), pp. 162ff.

[32] G. Ch. Aalders, *The Problem of the Book of Jonah* (1948), pp. 11f.

the lives of Elijah and Elisha (cf. 1 Kgs. 17–21; 2 Kgs. 1–7; 13:14-21). Had the story of Jonah appeared as part of the record of the books of Kings, there could have been little reason for doubting that it implied an account of historical events. Considering that it is an isolated prophetic composition, however, and that it occupies a unique place among the Minor Prophets, it is hardly justifiable to draw any firm conclusion as to historicity from its form and style alone.

2. *Allegorical.* If the traditional historical interpretation appears to be beset with difficulties, the same can also be said for another approach, which purports to see in Jonah a complete allegory in which each feature represents an element in the historical and religious experience of the Israelites. This interpretation may have arisen from the fact that the name "Jonah" meant "dove" in Hebrew, and that this species had for long been a symbol of Israel (cf. Ps. 74:19; Hos. 11:11).[33] On such a basis the experiences of the prophet represented the mission and failure of Israel to be the true people of God.[34] The flight of Jonah to Tarshish symbolized Israel's default in respect to its spiritual mission before the exile; the fish represented Babylon, which swallowed up the Hebrew people during the time of exile and subsequently disgorged them during the restoration period, and the deliverance from the chastening experience of being engulfed furnished both Jonah and the returned remnant with the opportunity for presenting anew the faith to the surrounding pagans.[35]

Before considering this approach further it is of some value to survey the general characteristics of such allegories as are found in the Old Testament narratives. Familiar examples of Semitic allegories can be seen in the description of senility and death in Ecclesiastes (12:3ff.), the vintage-cup from which all nations would drink (Jer. 25:15ff.), the eagles and the vine (Ezek. 27:3ff.), the lioness and her cubs (Ezek. 19:2ff.), the boiling pot (Ezek. 24:3ff.), and the shepherd and his two staffs (Zech. 11:4ff.). Not only are these allegories rather brief, unlike Jonah, but as Aalders has indicated, they contain unmistakable indications of their allegorical nature.[36] Thus the meaning of the Ecclesiastes allegory is given in Ecclesiastes 12:5, where the man has died and the mourners are present in the streets. The vintage-cup of Jeremiah is clearly figurative, being described as "the wine-cup of this fury." Similarly the branch of the cedar which the eagle broke off was said to be

---

[33] J. A. Bewer, *The Literature of the OT*, p. 403; Aalders, *The Problem of the Book of Jonah*, pp. 24f.

[34] W. Neil, *IDB*, II, p. 967.

[35] So C. H. H. Wright, *Biblical Essays* (1886), pp. 34ff.; J. C. Ball, *Proceedings of the Society of Biblical Archaeology*, XX (1898), pp. 9ff.; T. K. Cheyne, *EB*, II, col. 2568, *Theological Review*, XIV (1877), pp. 291ff.; G. A. Smith, *The Book of the Twelve Prophets*, II, pp. 498ff.; A. D. Martin, *Holborn Review*, XII (1921), pp. 510ff.; *IBOT*, pp. 377f.

[36] *The Problem of the Book of Jonah*, p. 16.

carried into a "land of traffick" and set up "in a city of merchants" (Ezek. 17:4, AV). In Ezekiel 19:2ff., the princes of Israel were addressed, and the lioness was spoken of as their mother. One of her cubs was said to be brought with chains to the land of Egypt, while another, who "laid waste their cities," was beset on every side by the surrounding peoples and was brought in captivity to the king of Babylon. The pot of Ezekiel 24:6 was identified specifically with the "bloody city," and in Zechariah 11:7 the symbolic nature of the unusual names given to the two staffs is evident when they were cut in pieces, for this action represented the breaking of the Covenant made by God with the people of Israel at Sinai, as well as the shattering of the brotherhood between Judah and Israel.

An allegory may be defined as a story consisting of a series of incidents that is analogous to another series of happenings that it is meant to illustrate. In the foregoing examples of Old Testament allegories this tendency is amply illustrated, whether the allegories themselves are short or more lengthy. In Jonah, however, such indications are entirely lacking in the Hebrew text. The narrative has a direct story form, and exhibits neither implicit nor explicit allegorical tendencies. Such an interpretation, therefore, must be regarded as being highly questionable in nature, even though its rather complex and frequently exaggerated approach has been favored by many writers from rabbinic and patristic times onwards. That it has been virtually abandoned by most responsible scholars may be taken as yet another indication of its unsuitability as an interpretative approach to Jonah.

3. *Parabolic.* A third and simpler system, which, like the allegorical, is based upon resemblance, is the parabolic, and this has gained considerable approval among modern scholars as a method of interpreting the prophecy of Jonah. Those who lend support to this position claim that the book is nothing more than a moral story with a didactic aim in view, and that it is therefore similar to New Testament parables such as that of the Good Samaritan (Lk. 10:29ff.).[37] This view presupposes such literary antecedents in the Old Testament as the story of the ewe-lamb as told to King David by the prophet Nathan (2 Sam. 12:1ff.), that of the avengers of blood narrated by the widow of Tekoa (2 Sam. 14:6f.), the parable of Jotham to the Shechemites (Judg. 9:8ff.), and that of Jehoash to King Amaziah of Judah (2 Kgs. 14:9). Of a similar nature is the story involving a missing captive as narrated to King Ahab (1 Kgs. 20:39f.), and since this body of evidence would indicate that there is obviously an established tradition of parable in the Old Testament, it is necessary to examine the basic characteristics of such material. In each

---

[37] So J. A. Bewer, *A Critical and Exegetical Commentary on the Book of Jonah* (1912), p. 4, *The Literature of the OT*, pp. 403ff.; *DILOT*, p. 323; *IBOT*, pp. 375f.; *PIOT*, p. 387; *OTFD*, p. 250.

case the parables are based upon resemblance, but whereas the allegory can frequently appear at some length in narrative form, the parables are invariably short and pithy. They are essentially simple, and are always accompanied by some specific explanation of their inner meaning.

By contrast the book of Jonah is a much more lengthy and complex literary unit. The prophecy combines two distinct themes, namely that of the flight of Jonah and the incident of the great fish, with the preaching mission to Nineveh and the matter of the growth and death of the gourd. Whereas in the instances of Old Testament parables mentioned above the story is immediately followed by an explanation, in the case of Jonah this is entirely lacking. It may be, of course, that the writer thought his message to be so self-evident as to require no further comment. If, however, the prophecy is to be interpreted according to the parabolic method, the absence of an explanation is certainly most unusual, and might imply on the basis of such an understanding that the prophecy was at best only a potential or implied parable.

The two most important objections to such an approach, thus, are the unparalleled complexity and length of the story and the fact that the moral was not made immediately and abundantly clear. One result of this situation has been the disparity of views regarding the true aim of the book among those who adhere to the fictitious character of the narrative.[38] The most common interpretation is that Jonah protests against narrow-minded nationalism, and emphasizes the universalistic concerns of God.[39] If this is in fact the true emphasis of the parable, it fails to account for the incident of the great fish, since it is difficult to explain how narrow nationalism could be combated by the introduction of an irrelevant folkloristic motif, however well it may have been understood under other circumstances.

It is recognized, of course, that the parabolic interpretation avoids the subjective excesses of the allegorical approach, and as such it must be regarded as an improvement methodologically. Yet such an understanding leaves the central figure of the drama untouched, since it depicts the man who was sent to convert the heathen to belief in the one universal God as himself unconvinced and unchanged by the beliefs which he was expounding. As William Neil has put it, if Jonah is intended to be no more specific a character than the "certain man" of the parables of Jesus, there still remains unmistakably a portrait of the narrow and intolerant Hebrew of the Ezra period, or for that matter, the narrow and intolerant Christian of the present day, who refuses to face the universalistic

---

38 *DILOT*, pp. 323f.; E. König, *HDB*, II, p. 752.

39 So E. Renan, *Histoire du peuple d'Israel*, III, p. 512; G. A. Smith, *The Book of the Twelve Prophets*, II, p. 501; G. A. Cooke in C. Gore, H. L. Goudge, and A. Guillaume (eds.), *A New Commentary on Holy Scripture*, p. 580; H. Wheeler Robinson, *Record and Revelation*, pp. 34f.; *PIOT*, p. 588; B. Balscheit, *Der Gottesbund: Einführung in das AT* (1943), p. 218; J. D. Smart, *IB*, VI, p. 872.

implications of the divine revelation and its concomitant call to world mission.[40] A final criticism of the parabolic interpretation is the complete failure on the part of scholars to discover why the author chose the historical prophet Jonah ben Amittai as the hero of a fictitious story, and why in particular he made him the proclaimer of its moral teaching if he had no real connection with the events described.

It seems clear that any interpretation of the book will need to reckon with the fact that, since Jonah was a well-known historical patriot of the northern kingdom, it is difficult to see precisely how the bizarre story associated with him could have arisen in the first place, and subsequently have been so widely accepted, if there had not been some sort of foundation in reality for it. That it may possibly have been embellished somewhat at a later time is rather beside the point in this regard, since most modern interpreters of the "great fish" have themselves embellished the ancient Hebrew tradition in certain particulars.

Again, it needs to be observed that, as far as the tribes that comprised the northern kingdom were concerned, a parabolic or allegorical interpretation of the prophetic experience with regard to the great fish could have no meaning or significance. Their captivity was final and irrevocable, with absolutely no prospect of a return and restoration for the exiles, whatever their state of repentance. For them the events associated with Jonah could be accepted at face value, or, failing that, be relegated to the corpus of tradition concerning the prophet. But of hope for the future or of an outpouring of divine mercy and forgiveness there could be no assurance for the northern tribes. Whether the people of Judah were sufficiently impressed by the circumstances under which the prophecy arose to take some heart with respect to their own destiny is unknown.

It will be clear from the foregoing discussion that any view of the interpretation of the book of Jonah is beset with certain difficulties. The subjectivity of the allegorical approach has unfortunately worked to its disadvantage, and it is not now favored by modern scholars. There are no insuperable difficulties connected with the parabolic interpretation, which some Christian expositors regard as the most natural, in contrast with others who favor the traditional historical connotation. The choice, therefore, would seem to lie between the latter two.

C. THE COMPOSITION OF THE BOOK

The integrity of the composition has been challenged by Böhme, who purported to distinguish four separate strata in the prophecy as the result of utilizing the literary-analytical methods of the Graf-Wellhausen

[40] W. Neil, *IDB*, II, p. 967.

school,[41] a conclusion which was rejected by König and others.[42] On the basis of the alternation between YHWH and Elohim as the name for God in the prophecy, Schmidt attempted to divide the work up into two distinct sources, but with little success.[43]

More recently questions have been raised by scholars with regard to the psalm (Jon. 2:2-9), which is reminiscent of similar compositions (Pss. 5:7; 18:6; 31:22; 42:7; 120:1; 142:3; 143:4),[44] and in the view of some writers appears to be unsuited to its present position.[45] It should be noted that numerous psalms speak of mortal peril without being so similar in character as to imply that they influenced the author of the prayer, as Feuillet has pointed out.[46] While it is true that verses 3-9 make no reference to the belly of the fish, it should be noted that they follow on logically from verse 2, which speaks metaphorically of the "belly of hell." Furthermore, if, as Knobel and others have suggested,[47] this composition was supplemented by a later writer who missed the contents of the prayer alluded to in Jonah 2:2, he would most certainly have made his additions correspond more precisely to the circumstances of incarceration. The absence of such references should therefore be taken as an indication of the authenticity and integrity of the psalm.

If it is to be placed more appropriately after Jonah 2:10 than 2:1, as some critics have suggested, the homogeneity of the narrative would be completely disrupted as a result. While the psalm is of a different character from the remainder of the prophecy, there is insufficient evidence to show that it has actually been interpolated by a later hand. Even if the psalm does contain a note of thanksgiving, it is surely not inappropriate to the situation, since the prophet was represented in the narrative as being confident of deliverance from his predicament so that he would again see both the celestial (Jon. 2:4), and the earthly (Jon. 2:7) temples. Under such circumstances a simple petition for rescue was hardly necessary. Until more favorable evidence presents itself, it seems unwise to the present author to disrupt the obvious homogeneity of the work by attempting to transpose the psalm, or to regard it as being a later addition by an unknown hand.

[41] W. Böhme, ZAW, VII (1887), pp. 224ff.

[42] E. König, Einleitung in das AT (1893 ed.), pp. 378f.

[43] H. Schmidt, ZAW, XXV (1905), pp. 285ff.; cf. Schmidt's work in Theologische Studien und Kritiken, LXXIX (1906), pp. 180ff.

[44] Cf. YIOT, pp. 264f.

[45] So K. Budde, ZAW, XII (1892), p. 42; DILOT, p. 325; J. A. Bewer, A Critical and Exegetical Commentary on the Book of Jonah, pp. 21ff.; IBOT, pp. 379f.; S. A. Cook, The OT: A Reinterpretation, p. 53; J. A. Bewer, The Literature of the OT, p. 405; for the interpretation of this passage as a "cultic phantasy" see A. R. Johnson in Studies in OT Prophecy Presented to T. H. Robinson, pp. 82ff.

[46] A. Feuillet, RB, LIV (1947), pp. 181ff.

[47] A. Knobel, Der Prophetismus der Hebräer, II, p. 377.

Questions of authorship and date are dependent to a large extent upon the interpretation of the work. If the prophecy is dependent upon Jonah ben Amittai for its extant form, it could have well been written in the eighth century B.C. Internal evidence is somewhat inconclusive, since the book furnishes no indication as to who the author was. Although Jonah may possibly have had a hand in compiling it, the prophecy nowhere uses the first person singular, as contrasted with works by other eighth-century prophets such as Hosea (3:1). If the reference in Jonah 3:3 is interpreted to imply that Nineveh was no longer in existence, as is claimed by some scholars, the book could hardly have been written before 612 B.C.

On an historical interpretation, however, the date ought to fall within the period between the reign of Jeroboam II and a time shortly after the fall of Nineveh. The author of the entire work need not have been the prophet himself, but a person who could have obtained certain information that may have been unknown to Jonah himself, such as that relating to the action of the sailors in Jonah 1:5, 16, from sources that went back to the original situation. On the other hand it is by no means impossible for Jonah to have become aware of such details at a subsequent period, perhaps on his return to his native land.

If the story is interpreted as an allegory or a parable, the question of authorship and date becomes even more involved. If Jonah is no longer to be credited with writing a part or the whole of the composition, it becomes impossible to say precisely who wrote it, or at what specific period of Hebrew history it was composed. In consequence, those scholars who hold the work to be fictitious have been compelled to posit anonymous authors, and assign the finished product to periods which include the fifth century,[48] the fourth century,[49] or later.[50] On the assumption that the psalm (Jon. 2:2-9) is not an integral part of the work but constitutes a later addition, the completed work could be as late as 200 B.C. in the view of some scholars.[51]

It has sometimes been maintained that the prophecy shows clear literary dependence upon earlier compositions. Feuillet purported to show that the book of Jonah relied upon information from Kings as well as some of the prophetic writings, notably those of Jeremiah and Ezekiel,[52] but his arguments rested upon extremely slender evidence and were refuted without difficulty by Aalders.[53] While the author appears to have been familiar with Joel (compare Jon. 3:9 with Joel 2:14; Jon.

[48] E.g. DILOT, p. 322.
[49] E.g. IBOT, p. 374; PIOT, p. 589; W. Neil, IDB, II, p. 967.
[50] J. A. Bewer, The Literature of the OT, p. 403; J. D. Smart, IB, VI, p. 873.
[51] E.g. E. Sellin, Das Zwölfprophetenbuch, p. 241; PIOT, p. 589.
[52] A. Feuillet, RB, LIV (1947), pp. 167ff.; cf. K. Budde, ZAW, XII (1892), p. 41; DILOT, p. 322n.
[53] The Problem of the Book of Jonah, pp. 17ff.

4:2 with Joel 2:13), it is important not to lay too much emphasis upon such apparent correspondences, as Oesterley and Robinson have rightly warned.[54] In works such as Joel, whose dating presents a problem, it is almost impossible to say which author was the borrower in instances of alleged dependence. Nor is it possible to be certain that either or both of them did not borrow from yet another source which is no longer extant.[55]

Arguments for a later rather than an earlier date have been drawn from Aramaisms and expressions unfamiliar to Classical Hebrew.[56] On examination these suggestions prove to be rather inconclusive,[57] and none can properly be taken as proof of a post-exilic date for the book. Again, the universalistic emphasis of the work has been held to constitute a criticism of the ultra-nationalistic spirit of the Jews after the period of Ezra and Nehemiah. Thus it would comprise a call for tolerance towards the heathen, and a recognition of the rightful place they occupied in the divine economy. In this connection, however, it should be observed that universalistic emphases were by no means confined to the post-exilic period, for they occurred as early as the eighth century B.C. (Isa. 2:2ff.), so that the universalistic approach does not in itself guarantee a post-exilic date.

Since the Twelve Minor Prophets were known and venerated by the end of the third century B.C. (cf. Ecclus. 49:10) it would appear that the latest date that can possibly be assigned to the work would be in the early or middle portions of the third century B.C. It is not impossible for the book to have been a product of the late eighth or early seventh century but the available evidence seems to indicate that it assumed its extant form no earlier than the sixth century B.C.

As has been observed above, there is a surprising diversity of opinion among scholars, both ancient and modern, with regard to the interpretation of the book of Jonah. Some of those who adhere to the literalistic view maintain that the primary purpose of the book is not to be found in its missionary concepts or universalistic teaching, but rather in the way in which it illustrated the death and resurrection of the Messiah and furnished certain didactic values for the pre-exilic Israelites.[58] Those who support the view that the work is basically unhistorical in nature have frequently discerned a universalistic theme to the story, although not exclusively so. Thus Balscheit has made certain doctrinal concepts the principal theme of the book, balancing the thought of divine

---

[54] *IBOT*, p. 372.
[55] R. D. Wilson, *PTR*, XVI (1918), p. 443.
[56] Cf. *DILOT*, p. 322; *IBOT*, pp. 372ff.
[57] Aalders, *The Problem of the Book of Jonah*, pp. 9f.; J. A. Raven, *OT Introduction*, pp. 224f.; R. D. Wilson, *PTR*, XVI (1918), p. 289.
[58] *YIOT*, p. 263.

provision and mercy against the inexorable demands of a moral and ethical deity.[59]

In assigning an early date to the prophecy, Kaufmann held that the work bore the stamp of that early universalism characteristic of pre-Classical prophecy.[60] For him, therefore, the book contained no national-historical element, and had nothing to do with the quarrel between Israel and the Gentile world. Instead, the issue was wholly moral in nature, dealing with the questions of sin, punishment, repentance, and forgiveness.

A careful reading of this prophecy would seem to make clear that it was meant in the main to impress upon the Israelites the fact that the mercy and salvation of God extended far beyond the Chosen Race to embrace the whole of humanity. A perceptive Hebrew might also see in the dealings of God with Jonah a rebuke to Israel for its failure to implement the missionary concepts inherent in the Sinai Covenant. Again, the ready response in repentance and faith to the message of the prophet by the people of Nineveh constituted a salutary lesson to the Jews, who were notorious for their inveterate stubbornness and lack of faith, a point that was emphasized by Jesus Christ (Matt. 12:41).

❊   ❊   ❊   ❊   ❊

Apart from the possibility of an occasional gloss, the Hebrew text of Jonah has been preserved in good condition, and there are no real grounds for postulating dislocations. The LXX is of little consequence as far as this prophecy is concerned, but it is of some interest to note that, as Swete has pointed out, some Greek uncial manuscripts and numerous cursives contain a collection of liturgical songs after the book of Psalms, and among these canticles is the psalm in chapter two of the prophecy.[61]

Supplementary Literature

Hart-Davies, D. E. *Jonah: Prophet and Patriot.* 1925.
Kennedy, J. *On the Book of Jonah.* 1895.
Martin, H. *The Prophet Jonah.* 1891.

---

[59] B. Balscheit, *Der Gottesbund: Einführung in das AT,* p. 218.
[60] *KRI,* pp. 282ff.
[61] H. B. Swete, *Introduction to the OT in Greek,* p. 253.

VI. THE BOOK OF MICAH

A. NAME AND OUTLINE

The prophecy of Micah was named after a Judaean contemporary of Isaiah. The name מיכה appears in a longer form as מיכיהו in Judges 17:1, 4. The LXX rendered the name after the longer form as Μιχαίας while in the Vulgate it appeared as *Michaeas*. In the Hebrew canon, the Peshitta, and the Vulgate, the prophecy of Micah stood sixth among the Twelve Minor Prophets, following Jonah and preceding Nahum. In the LXX it stood third after Amos, probably being placed in that position on account of its length.

The prophecy may be outlined as follows:

  I. The Coming Judgment Upon the House of Israel, ch. 1
 II. The Punishment and Restoration of Israel, ch. 2
III. Princes and Prophets Condemned, ch. 3
 IV. The Future Glory of the Kingdom, ch. 4–5
  V. Contrast of Prophetic and Popular Religion, ch. 6
 VI. Reproof of Social Corruption; Promise of Divine Blessing, ch. 7

B. THE MESSAGE OF MICAH

According to the superscription the prophet came from a town named Moresheth, which is usually identified with Moresheth-gath in the Shephelah or lowlands of Judah.[1] A chronological reference noted that he prophesied during the reigns of Jotham (740/39-732/31 B.C.), Ahaz (732/31-716/15 B.C.), and Hezekiah of Judah (716/15-687/86 B.C.). On this basis his prophecies began at least a decade before the fall of Samaria, and were concurrent with those of Isaiah. The fact that Micah lived halfway between Jerusalem and Gaza near the Judaean fortress of Lachish and close to the Philistine cities goes far towards explaining both his love for the countryside and its inhabitants, and also his

---

[1] The modern Tell el-Judeideh, about 20 miles southwest of Jerusalem. Cf. J. Jeremias, *PJB*, XXIX (1933), pp. 42ff.; K. Elliger, *Zeitschrift des deutschen Palästina-Vereins*, LVII (1934), pp. 119ff.

acquaintance with international affairs, living as he did on the route taken in previous days by invading enemy forces.[2]

As Leslie has pointed out, the birthplace of Amos was less than twenty miles from the home of Micah, and this would help to account for the influence of the former upon the thought of the latter (compare Mic. 2:6 and Am. 2:12; 5:11; 7:10f.).[3] It is almost certain that the countryman Micah was familiar with the plea for justice that Amos uttered, and since his oracles give the impression that they were proclaimed in Jerusalem,[4] it is natural to assume that he both knew Isaiah and was influenced to some extent by his utterances also (compare Mic. 1:10-16 and Isa. 10:27ff., Mic. 2:1-5 and Isa. 5:8ff.; Mic. 5:9-14 and Isa. 2:6ff.). According to Jeremiah 26:18f. the prophet Micah had preached his message of doom for Zion so effectively that his words were remembered in Jerusalem a century later, and this happy circumstance actually saved the life of Jeremiah on one notable occasion.

Perhaps inspired by the example of Amos, Micah turned early in his ministry to Samaria, which to that point had managed to survive the military ambitions of Assyria. Micah saw clearly that the capital of the northern kingdom could not withstand serious attack by the Assyrians, and in his utterances he sought to awaken the Israelites to the fact of imminent destruction. Turning his attention to the southern kingdom the prophet urged the inhabitants to take warning from the catastrophe that was to overtake Samaria. Unlike Isaiah, who was much more concerned with political issues, Micah had at heart the interests of the lonely peasant in the Judaean countryside. Life as he had experienced it was very much like that which Amos had seen in the northern kingdom, for in the south the rich were also oppressing the poor and reducing the peasant classes to the most impoverished of living conditions (Mic. 2:1f.).

But there was corruption evident in other than the purely social field, and accordingly Micah not merely condemned the rich landowners for their unjust behavior, but also castigated the religious leaders of his day for condoning and even encouraging such immoral and depraved activity (Mic. 2:11). He was especially scathing in his denunciation of those who, while allegedly devoted to the upholding of the law, permitted gross miscarriages of justice to take place unchecked in the land (Mic. 3:10). The fact that all this activity was carried on in an atmosphere of false religiosity proved for Micah to be the crowning insult.

[2] R. E. Wolfe, *IB*, VI, p. 897.
[3] E. A. Leslie, *IDB*, III, pp. 369f.
[4] *OTFD*, p. 252.

Like his contemporaries Amos, Hosea, and Isaiah, the prophet Micah emphasized the essential righteousness and morality of the divine nature. He was particularly concerned to point out that these qualities had immediate ethical implications for the life of the individual and the community alike. If the people of Israel and Judah were to take their Covenant obligations at all seriously, the justice and morality that were so characteristic of the divine nature would necessarily be reflected correspondingly in the life and affairs of the people of God.

Whereas Amos and Hosea had a good deal to say about the idolatry and immorality that were rampant in the kingdom as a result of the influence of pagan Canaanite religion, Micah confined his prophetic interests to the problems arising from the social injustices perpetrated upon the small landowners, farmers, and peasants. He uttered stern warnings to those who wrongfully deprived others of their possessions, indicating that God was devising a drastic punishment for them. His denunciation of the ruling classes in Israel (Mic. 3:1-4) and the false prophets (Mic. 3:5-8) contemplated the ultimate destruction of Jerusalem, since the state of corruption which they represented had permeated to the very core of national life.

Suggestions to the effect that Micah was a cultic prophet or a member of some prophetic guild seem contraindicated by chapter 3:8, where the prophet contrasted himself forcibly with such religious functionaries. Like Jeremiah he found the task of prophesying difficult, yet at the same time he was fortified in his proclamation of their sins to the disobedient Israelites by an acknowledgment of his divine call and inspiration. In this prophetic capacity he discerned that the underlying cause of social disintegration was the false sense of religious security, based upon the erroneous supposition that the presence of God in the midst of the land was itself sufficient guarantee of protection from misfortune and calamity (Mic. 3:11f.). Consequently he proclaimed boldly that the absence of the characteristic ethical attributes of the deity in the life of the nation would bring its own severe punishment.

Micah was in general accord with Amos, Hosea, and Isaiah in his belief that God would utilize a pagan nation to chastise His own guilty people. As a result he foretold clearly the depredations of Shalmaneser V in the northern kingdom, and the ultimate destruction of Samaria, capital of Israel (Mic. 1:6-9). However, he did not view the collapse of the northern kingdom in quite the same broad terms as did Isaiah. For Micah it brought the threat of invasion to the very doors of "this family" (Mic. 2:3), thus making the Assyrian invader Sennacherib the dread herald of a larger doom (Mic. 5:5f.). The unity of his thought in this connection is evident from the striking resemblance between the prophecies of destruction proclaimed for Samaria (Mic. 1:6) and for Jerusalem (Mic. 3:12). In the mind of the prophet there could be absolutely no question as to the ultimate fate either of Samaria or the house of Judah.

C. LITERARY CRITICISM OF THE BOOK

From a literary standpoint the prophecy itself exhibits certain indications of internal order and arrangement. Chapters one to three, with the exception of 2:12f., contain warnings of doom exclusively; chapters four and five carry promises of divine blessing; chapters 6:1–7:6 again are filled with threats of impending ruin, while Micah 7:7-20 enshrines a promise of hope for the future. This stylized alternation between doom and hope has distinct artistic as well as spiritual merit, and while it may be too much to suppose that the prophetic oracles themselves were uttered in precisely this order, there can be no doubt that the extant form of the prophecy adds to the attractiveness of the work considerably, and reinforces the general impression of prophetic vitality and sensitivity.

The oracles contained in the first three chapters are usually regarded as genuine. Since Samaria was threatened in Micah 1:6, the date of the first oracle (Mic. 1:2-7) must be in advance of 722 B.C. Elliger has suggested that Micah 1:8-16, with its tone of lament for the destruction of the Judaean homeland, arose from the personal experience of Micah in connection with the Assyrian military expedition to Jerusalem in 701 B.C.,[5] but this, of course, cannot be shown with certainty. Aside from these it appears impossible to fix exactly the date of the other oracles in chapters 1 to 3. It hardly seems necessary to regard Micah 2:12f. as a later addition, since although it presupposes the dispersion of Israel in exile it is in harmony with the thought of other eighth-century prophets—Isaiah, for example—in this particular regard. The literary criticism of chapters four and five has had a lengthy career. Oort made the first serious attack upon the integrity of this material with the suggestion that Micah 4:1-7, 11-13 constituted an insertion by a later author who regarded Micah as a false prophet and was at pains to correct his errors.[6] This contention was challenged by Kuenen, who acknowledged that Micah 4:11-13 was somewhat incongruous in a passage describing future conditions, but nevertheless defended the traditional authorship of both passages.[7] The first major objection to this came from Stade in 1881, who roundly denied that Micah wrote chapters 4 and 5, and extended his

---

[5] K. Elliger, *Zeitschrift des deutschen Palästina-Vereins*, LVII (1934), pp. 81ff.
[6] H. Oort, *Theologisch Tijdschrift*, V (1871), pp. 501ff.
[7] A. Kuenen, *Theologisch Tijdschrift*, VI (1872), pp. 45ff.

views to include chapters 6 and 7.[8] While his opinions were contested by Nowack,[9] they were supported by Cornill, Kosters, Cheyne, Budde, and others.[10] Volz modified the conclusions of Stade somewhat,[11] while Driver refused to commit himself to any definite opinion on the matter.[12]

The critical division of chapters 6 and 7 was also commenced in the nineteenth century, with Wellhausen following the arguments of Ewald in assigning Micah 6:1–7:6 to the period of Manasseh, and relegating 7:7-20 to the exilic era.[13] This view, with some modifications, was adopted by Stade, Kuenen, Cornill, König, Driver, and others.[14] The authenticity of these chapters was urged by Cornill and Kirkpatrick, principally on the ground that everything which could be brought forward to support their origin in the time of Manasseh applied equally well to the period of Ahaz.[15] An even more radical step was taken by Stade in 1887, when he assigned chapter 6 to the post-exilic period,[16] a process that was completed in 1903 when he regarded chapter 7 as being of late date also.[17] In these conclusions he was followed with slight modification by Giesebrecht, Kosters, Driver, Cheyne, and other scholars.[18]

Representatives of the conservative position included Wildeboer, who maintained that there was no single element in the prophecy that was not consistent with authorship by Micah in the eighth century B.C.[19] He noted that the principal argument for the position arrived at by critical authors included a lack of logical unity in chapters 6 and 7, which for them could be divided into a number of detached oracles of various dates. While it was possible for Micah to have written Micah 6:9-16 and 7:1-6, he could not have composed the remainder, since it appeared to reflect the thought and conditions of the post-exilic period.

---

[8] B. Stade, ZAW, I (1881), pp. 161ff., III (1883), pp. 1ff.

[9] W. Nowack, ZAW, IV (1884), pp. 277ff.

[10] C. H. Cornill, ZAW, IV (1884), p. 89. W. H. Kosters, Theologisch Tijdschrift, XXVII (1893), pp. 249ff. T. K. Cheyne, EB, III, col. 3068. K. Budde, Geschichte der althebräischen Litteratur (1906), p. 89.

[11] P. Volz, Die vorexilische Jahmeprophetie und der Messias (1897), pp. 63ff.

[12] DILOT, p. 330.

[13] J. Wellhausen in F. Bleek, Einleitung in das AT (1878), pp. 425f.

[14] B. Stade, ZAW, I (1881), pp. 161f., IV (1884), pp. 291ff., VI (1886), pp. 122f. A. Kuenen, Einleitung in das AT, II, pp. 363f. C. H. Cornill, Einleitung in die kanonischen Bücher des AT (1891), pp. 183ff. E. König, Einleitung in das AT (1893), pp. 329f. DILOT, pp. 333f.

[15] C. H. Cornill, ZAW, IV (1884), pp. 89f. A. F. Kirkpatrick, The Doctrine of the Prophets (1892), pp. 229f.

[16] B. Stade, Geschichte des Volkes Israel, I, p. 634.

[17] B. Stade, ZAW, XXIII (1903), pp. 164ff.

[18] F. Giesebrecht, Beiträge zur Jesaiakritik (1887), pp. 216f. W. H. Kosters, Theologisch Tijdschrift, XXVII (1893), pp. 249ff. DILOT, pp. 330ff. T. K. Cheyne, EB, III, cols. 3070ff.

[19] G. Wildeboer, De Profeet Micha (1884), p. 57.

A great many modern scholars have followed the nineteenth-century critics in their estimate of chapters four to seven.[20] Part of the difficulty lies in the oracles of messianic expectation, and in the promises of restoration in Micah 4:6f. and 5:6ff. The poem dealing with universal peace in Micah 4:1-4 is also found in Isaiah (2:2-4), and would seem to present no difficulty with regard to an eighth-century date. On the same grounds it is difficult to see precisely how this passage contains post-exilic eschatological concepts. Micah 4:6-13 is a prophecy concerning the captivity in Babylonia, where the term "Babylon" was employed by metonymy for Mesopotamia, and as such need not be regarded as a later interpolation. This is in general consonance with the reference to the Assyrian in 5:5, an attitude that was also exhibited by Isaiah, indicating that the peril was to come from the east, and the resulting captivity would be in Mesopotamia. Against a poetic background of the kind employed by Micah, both "Assyrian" and "Babylon" would be perfectly acceptable surrogates. The material in Micah 5:9-14 is reminiscent of Isaiah 2:6-8, and does not require any other than an eighth-century date with its mention of horses, chariots, strongholds, witchcraft, and Canaan-ite idolatry.

The powerful indictment of Micah 6:1-8, the threat of 6:9-16, and the lament of 7:1-7 are all perfectly compatible with authorship by Micah in the eighth century B.C., particularly if, as Lindblom has suggested, the reference in 6:14-16 was to Samaria before the destruction of 722 B.C.[21] There is in fact no convincing proof that can be adduced against the authenticity of the oracular material in chapters 4 to 7. Even the pro-phetic liturgy of Micah 7:8-20 is not inconsistent with the time of Micah, since it contains distinct elements that are completely in accord with the thought of Amos, Hosea, and Isaiah. Further consonance with eighth-century prophetic concepts is seen in the affinity between Micah and Isaiah regarding the Messiah (Isa. 9:1ff.; 11:1ff. and Mic. 5:2ff.), as well as in the dramatic poetic imagery describing the eschatological assault of the heathen upon Zion and their subsequent defeat (Isa. 10:24ff.; 17:12ff.; 29:1; 31:4f.; cf. Ps. 46:5ff.).

In view of these demonstrable correspondences it appears improbable that anything more than the most modest of redactional additions can be postulated for Micah. The prophet was a man of considerable artistic ability, whose poetic formulations, while falling short of the heights achieved by Amos or Isaiah, are nevertheless superior to those of Ezek-

[20] E.g. K. Budde, ZDMG, LXXXI (1927), pp. 52ff.; S. Mowinckel, Norsk Teolo-gisk Tidsschrift, XXIX (1928), pp. 13ff.; G. W. Anderson, Scottish Journal of Theology, IV (1951), pp. 191ff.; L. P. Smith, Interpretation, VI (1952), pp. 210ff.; J. P. Hyatt, Anglican Theological Review, XXXIV (1952), pp. 232ff.; OTFD, pp. 254f.

[21] J. Lindblom, Micha literarisch untersucht (1929), pp. 116ff.

iel.[22] Critical scholarship has clearly been deficient in its estimate of the literary capabilities of this forceful and distinguished prophet. While it cannot be ascertained for sure that Micah himself wrote down each of his oracles, the double alternation of denunciation and promise which the final form of the prophecy exhibits would seem to suggest that the material was collected during his lifetime and arranged in an artistic manner comparable to that of Isaiah and later works. As against most modern scholars there appears to the present writer to be no insuperable difficulty inherent in the view that, apart from possible minor redactions, the prophecy of Micah was a genuine product of the eighth century B.C.

* * * * *

The Hebrew text of Micah is in a good state of preservation, and is in probably the best condition of any of the eighth-century B.C. prophecies. A midrash on the text of Micah, recovered in a fragmentary condition from Qumran, lends support to the traditional Hebrew text.[23] The LXX and other versions are of little value for the textual transmission of the prophecy, since few such problems exist.

Supplementary Literature

Marsh, J. *Amos and Micah.* 1954
Snaith, N. H. *Amos, Hosea and Micah.* 1956.
Tait, A. J. *The Prophecy of Micah.* 1917.

[22] Cf. J. M. P. Smith in R. F. Harper *et al.* (eds.), *OT and Semitic Studies in Memory of W. R. Harper* (1908), II, pp. 415ff.
[23] J. T. Milik, *RB*, LIX (1952), pp. 412ff.

VII. THE BOOK OF NAHUM

A. The Prophet and his Historical Background

In all the canonical lists of the Twelve Minor Prophets the book of Nahum stands seventh, following Micah in the Hebrew Bible, Peshitta, Vulgate, and modern versions, and following Jonah in the LXX. The book was named נחום after its author, who was known in the LXX as Ναουμ and in the Vulgate as *Nahum.*

Little is known about the prophet, whose name means "comfort" or "compassion" (cf. Isa. 57:18), except that he was said to be an Elkoshite. Precisely where Elkosh was located is unknown, but several traditions have survived concerning the supposed site.[1] Eastern medieval tradition located both the birthplace and the tomb of Nahum at Al-Qush, some fifty miles north of modern Mosul, which itself is situated on the River Tigris opposite the mounds of ancient Nineveh. However, this tradition does not go back beyond the sixteenth century of the Christian era, and the internal evidence furnished by the book itself makes such a suggestion improbable. Pseudo-Epiphanius placed it with considerably more accuracy in southern Judaea, making specific reference to the vicinity of Begabar,[2] the modern Beit Jibrin. This tradition seems to be more in keeping with the chronological and circumstantial setting of the prophecy, since the reference in Nahum 1:15 appears to imply that Nahum came from Judah. In the prologue to his *Commentary on Nahum,* Jerome identified Elkosh with the village of Hilkesi in Galilee, perhaps the modern El-Kauzeh. A late Galilean tradition centered upon Capernaum as implying the "village of Nahum," but any such location seems contraindicated in view of the fact that the northern kingdom had fallen almost a century before the prophecy was uttered.

It is rather difficult to date the book precisely, although limits can be set to the period in which the threats against Nineveh, the subject of the prophecy, actually originated, since they refer to accredited historical

---

[1] Cf. R. H. Pfeiffer, *Harvard Theological Review,* XXVII (1932), p. 282; E. G. Kraeling, *Bible Atlas* (1956), p. 310; W. A. Maier, *The Book of Nahum* (1959), pp. 20ff.

[2] *De Vitis Prophetarum,* XVII.

926

events. From internal evidence the *terminus a quo* is the capture of Thebes (No-Amun) in Upper Egypt by the Assyrians under Ashurbanipal in the years 664 and 663 B.C., which was mentioned in Nahum 3:8f. as a memorable occurrence in the fairly recent past. On the other hand, the *terminus ad quem* would appear to be about 612 B.C., the year in which Nineveh was destroyed, since the prophetic denunciations in chapters two and three antedated that event.

The immediate historical background of the prophecy involved events consequent upon the death, about 627 B.C., of Ashurbanipal, the last great Assyrian ruler. Almost at once the empire began to crumble, with Babylon asserting her independence in 626 B.C. under the vigorous Chaldean dynasty headed by Nabopolassar. A decade later the Babylonians allied with the Medes in an attack upon Assyria, with the intention of systematically reducing every military stronghold in the empire. The capital city Ashur fell in 614 B.C., and after a further two years of bitter fighting the same fate overtook proud Nineveh. There is important extra-Biblical material from Babylon relating to this period, which as events transpired had profound implications for the history of the southern kingdom.[3]

B. THE PROPHECY OF NAHUM

The prophecy of Nahum commenced with an introductory psalm (Nah. 1:1-14), in which the prophet magnified his God, declaimed vengeance upon the foes of the deity, and declared the goodness of God to those who trusted in Him. Part of this prefatory hymn (Nah. 1:2-10) has a form vaguely reminiscent of an alphabetic acrostic, although this arrangement can only be discerned from א to ס, and that only by placing verse 2b after verse 9 and rearranging the content of verse 9. Although various attempts have been made to reconstruct the entire chapter so as to bring the complete Hebrew alphabet into proper acrostic form, they have been unconvincing and unsuccessful to date.[4]

The description of the siege and sack of Nineveh began in the Hebrew text with Nahum 2:2, and continued to verse 14. Chapter three outlined the iniquitous character of Nineveh, and drew a comparison with the situation at No-Amun. In predicting the collapse of Nineveh there was no better example for Nahum to adduce (Nah. 3:8-10) than the fate which had overtaken Thebes, which fell as spoil to the conquering Assyri-

---

[3] Cf. C. J. Gadd, *The Fall of Nineveh: The Newly Discovered Babylonian Chronicle* (1923); D. J. Wiseman, *Chronicles of Chaldean Kings (626-556 B.C.) in the British Museum* (1956); W. F. Albright, *BASOR*, No. 143 (1956), pp. 28ff.; H. Tadmor, *JNES*, XV (1956), p. 226; J. P. Hyatt, *JBL*, LXXV (1956), pp. 227ff.; E. Vogt, *VT*, suppl. vol. III (1957), pp. 67ff.

[4] Cf. G. Bickell, *ZDMG*, XXXIV (1880), pp. 559ff.; H. Gunkel, *ZAW*, XIII (1893), pp. 223ff.; W. R. Arnold, *ZAW*, XXI (1901), pp. 225ff.; P. Haupt, *ZDMG*, LXI (1907), pp. 275ff.; *PIOT*, p. 595.

ans in 663 B.C. amid scenes of fire and slaughter. The prophecy concluded with an ironic comment upon the decadence that had led to its fall, and the rejoicing that this event would produce among neighboring peoples.

C. LITERARY CRITICISM OF THE BOOK

The prophecy has a combined title, referring first to the "burden" of Nineveh, a term generally employed of an oracular threat, and second to the "book of the vision of Nahum." On this basis scholars have frequently made a distinction between the actual material of Nahum, generally thought to have been Nahum 2:4–3:19 in the Hebrew text, and prefatory redactional elements added by a different author. Thus Pfeiffer, following Arnold, assigned to Nahum a "triumphal ode" on the fall of Nineveh (Nah. 2:3–3:19; 2:4–3:19 Heb.), and regarded the intervening material in Nahum 1:11–2:2 (2:3 Heb.) as partly editorial and partly an original section of the ode itself. The psalm of Nahum 1:2-10 was held to have been written about 300 B.C. by a redactor who attempted to record an acrostic composition from a somewhat faulty memory.[5]

While it is true that the alphabetic section does not exhibit the same passion as the material which contained the denunciation of Nineveh, its contents cannot be said to be at serious variance with the general standpoint of the remainder of the prophecy, and in consequence its implicit claim to authenticity must be taken at something resembling face value. The grave difficulty that the view of Pfeiffer encounters is that it is entirely subjective and incapable of demonstration. The homogeneity of the material is indicated by the skill with which the author combined a message of promise for Judah (Nah. 1:1-13, 2:1, 3) with the beginnings of a threat against Nineveh (1:10f., 2:2). The promise concerned the destruction of the oppressive Assyrians and the consequent recovery of Israel, which are treated as related themes, and as such do not warrant the view held by some scholars that an oracle of salvation for Judah had somehow become confused with a threat against Nineveh.

There seems little doubt that the prophecy was written by Nahum in the second half of the seventh century B.C., and that it is a genuine prediction of events.[6] The presence of a compound title might suggest that the alphabetic hymn was composed at a different time from the

---

[5] *PIOT*, pp. 594f.

[6] So J. M. P. Smith, *A Critical and Exegetical Commentary on the Book of Nahum* (1912), pp. 280ff.; S. Mowinckel, *Jesaja-disiplene* (1926), pp. 56, 144f.; W. C. Graham, *AJSL*, XLIV (1928), pp. 57ff.; H. Birkeland, *Zum hebräischen Traditionswesen* (1938), p. 78; *YIOT*, p. 270, *et al.* W. A. Wordsworth, *En Roeh*, pp. 494ff., made Ethiopia the conqueror referred to in 3:8, and assigned dates between 721 and 703 B.C. for the entire work.

oracles denouncing Nineveh, perhaps even after the city had fallen, but this cannot be substantiated from the contents of the poem itself. On the basis of Nahum 2:1 (Heb.) it has been supposed that the completed prophecy was recited on a festal occasion, perhaps the one commemorating the fall of Nineveh.

The concept of the prophecy as a liturgy was first seriously entertained by Haupt, who, however, arrived at the impossible conclusion that the work comprised four liturgical poems, the first two of which originated in the Maccabean period.[7] The idea of a prophetic liturgy was taken up again by Humbert,[8] and accepted substantially by Sellin.[9] According to this view the prophecy was not composed as a whole until after the fall of Assyria, and it was used for the first time in a liturgical setting that celebrated the overthrow of Nineveh at the New Year festival in 612 B.C. Quite aside from the gratuitous nature of the assumptions relating to the New Year festival, this theory breaks down because the denunciations of Nineveh in Nahum 2:4–3:17 look forward in a genuine fashion to future events, and do not recall what has already happened.

In addition to noting the liturgical forms in the text of Nahum, Mowinckel detected the presence of a cult-motif and related the victory of God over Assyria to the myth and ritual enactments of the enthronement festival.[10] On such a basis the prophet appears to have taken certain elements of the Babylonian creation myth and endowed them with historical form. A similar emphasis upon the way in which cultic tradition was thought to have shaped the transmission of the prophecy was made by Haldar, who argued from the history of oriental religions to an explanation of the struggle with the Assyrians against the mythological and cultic background of the primeval battle between cosmic adversaries depicted in the Babylonian New Year festival.[11]

The evidence of the prophecy, however, lends little support to the theory that Nahum was a cultic functionary. He was certainly a poet, as indeed were most of the other prophets, but he was also an ardent patriot who in his prophetic capacity called down the wrath of God upon a decadent oppressor. While Judah was warned to "keep her solemn feasts," there is nothing specifically cultic about this composition,

[7] P. Haupt, ZDMG, LXI (1907), pp. 275ff., JBL, XXVI (1907), pp. 1ff.

[8] P. Humbert, ZAW, XLIV (1926), pp. 266ff., Archiv für Orientforschung, V (1929), pp. 14ff., RHPR, XII (1932), pp. 1ff. It was rejected by O. Eissfeldt, Einleitung in das AT, p. 462.

[9] E. Sellin, Das Zwölfprophetenbuch, II, pp. 355f. So also A. Lods, RHPR, XI (1931), p. 213.

[10] S. Mowinckel, Jesaja-disiplene, p. 58. Cf. his Psalmenstudien, II, pp. 8ff., 57ff., 107ff.

[11] A. Haldar, Studies in the Book of Nahum (1947), pp. 88ff.

and no grounds exist for assuming that it was compiled under the auspices of the cultus.

Any interpretation of the prophecy that sees Nahum as a narrow-minded patriot obsessed by fanatical nationalistic tendencies fails to observe that the prophet was seriously concerned with the concept of the power and justice of God in history in the same way as the eighth-century prophets. As Taylor has pointed out, the prophecy constitutes a classic rebuke of militarism, for it demonstrates clearly that the kind of ruthless tyranny that characterized the Assyrian empire carried within itself the seeds of its own destruction.[12] In this small prophecy of doom the author demonstrated in vigorous and memorable language that the God of the nation whom the Assyrians had despised was in fact the artificer and controller of all human destiny. To His justice even the greatest world power must submit in humility and shame.

* * * * *

The text of the prophecy is reasonably well preserved, apart from a few possible instances of corruption in the acrostic poem. The Greek and Syriac versions are of limited assistance in elucidating textual problems, since in general they follow the Hebrew form. The prophecy of Nahum was popular with the Qumran sectaries, who wrote a commentary upon it.[13] The Qumran composition, however, had reference to Alexander Jannaeus (103-76 B.C.) and the atrocities he perpetrated in Judaea.

Supplementary Literature

Deane, W. J. *Nahum.* 1913.
Pilcher, C. V. *Three Hebrew Prophets and the Passing of Empires.* 1931.
Stonehouse, G. G. *Nahum.* 1929.

---

[12] C. L. Taylor, *IB*, VI, p. 954.
[13] J. M. Allegro, *The Dead Sea Scrolls* (1956), pp. 96, 99f.; *JBL*, LXXV (1956), pp. 89ff.; H. H. Rowley, *JBL*, LXXV (1956), pp. 188ff.; D. Leibel, *Tarbiz*, XXVII (1958), pp. 12ff.

VIII. THE BOOK OF HABAKKUK

A. THE IDENTITY OF THE PROPHET

The prophecy of Habakkuk was named after its attributive author חבקוק (Hab. 1:1), and invariably occupied eighth place among the Twelve Minor Prophets, between Nahum and Zephaniah. So little is known of the life or external circumstances of Habakkuk that anything said about him must be largely conjectural. Even his name has been transmitted in a somewhat variant form, being read Ἀμβακούμ by the LXX compared to *Habacuc* in the Vulgate. Reiser associated his name with the garden plant known in Assyrian herbals as *hambakuku*, and argued from the linguistic character of Habakkuk 2:2 that the prophet received his education at Nineveh, but this is pure speculation.[1]

The suggestions that he was the son of the Shunammite woman (2 Kgs. 4:16), or the watchman of Isaiah (Isa. 21:6), have as little evidence in their favor as the tradition found in the LXX version of *Bel and the Dragon*, whose title described the prophet as "Habakkuk, son of Jesus of the Tribe of Levi," and which subsequently associated him with Daniel in the den of lions (Bel 33ff.). He may perhaps have been a cultic prophet who lived in Judah during the last days of Josiah (640/39-609 B.C.) and the earlier part of the regime of Jehoiakim (609-597 B.C.). This conjecture is based upon the reference to the Chaldeans in Habakkuk 1:6, who were in power from about 720 B.C. to 538 B.C. Since a threat appears to be implied by the reference rather than actual enslavement to the Chaldeans, the prophecy is generally dated at the close of the seventh century B.C., shortly after the battle of Carchemish (605 B.C.) when the Chaldeans first posed a serious threat to the existence of the southern kingdom.

[1] F. Reiser, *Mitteilungen der vorderasiatischen Gesellschaft*, VIII (1904), pp. 5ff.; cf. B. Duhm, *Das Buch Habakuk* (1906), pp. 6, 11; M. Noth, *Die israelitischen Personennamen*, p. 231.

B. THE DATE OF THE PROPHECY

This traditional dating of the book has been accepted by many liberal as well as conservative scholars.[2] However, it has been contested on the ground that the prophecy may not in fact constitute the literary unity it purports to be, but may instead be an agglomeration of material, some of which might even have originated in the Maccabean period. The first two chapters are generally conceded to comprise five short prophetic utterances, somewhat in the form of a dialogue between God and the prophet, consisting of Habakkuk 1:2-4, a complaint to God concerning unpunished lawlessness; 1:5-11, a divine oracle concerning the Chaldeans, who will conquer nations and kingdoms; 1:12-17, a renewed appeal by Habakkuk, who questioned the propriety of a holy and just God's permitting the wicked to consume the righteous; 2:1-5, the divine answer, to the effect that the wicked will be punished while the righteous will be saved through his faithfulness; and 2:6-20, a taunt-song comprising five "woes" predicting dire consequences upon the rapacious Chaldeans for their acts of inhumanity. The third chapter (Hab. 3:1-19) was held to be an independent poetic composition, perhaps with liturgical associations, which was incorporated into the prophecy of Habakkuk and may be original or else the work of a later hand.

On the ground that in Habakkuk 1:13-16, 2:8, 10, 17, the prophet described Chaldean depredations as though he were perfectly familiar with them, whereas in 1:5-6 the growth of Chaldean might appears to lie in the future, Wellhausen and Giesebrecht in particular argued that 1:5-11 was an older independent prophecy composed before the other material in Habakkuk, and in a displaced position in the extant prophecy, since for them Habakkuk 1:12 was the proper sequel of 1:4.[3] They dated this material about 605 B.C., separating it from the remainder of the prophecy, which was assigned to the exilic or post-exilic period. Budde agreed that Habakkuk 1:4 and 1:12 should be brought together, but maintained that 1:5-11 was not in fact an independent earlier prophecy.[4] Instead, it was to be regarded as an integral part of the same work that had been removed from its original place and referred, not to Chaldea, but to Assyria.

---

[2] Cf. *DILOT*, pp. 339f.; W. W. Cannon, *ZAW*, XLIII (1925), pp. 62ff.; M. J. Gruenthauer, *Biblica*, VIII (1927), pp. 129ff., 257ff.; K. Budde, *ZDMG*, LXXXIV (1930), pp. 139ff.; *IBOT*, p. 392; *PIOT*, p. 599; W. F. Albright in H. H. Rowley (ed.), *Studies in OT Prophecy Presented to T. H. Robinson*, p. 2.

[3] J. Wellhausen, *Die Kleinen Propheten übersetzt und erklärt*, pp. 162ff. F. Giesebrecht, *Beiträge zur Jesaiakritik* (1890), pp. 197f.

[4] K. Budde, *Theologische Studien und Kritiken*, LXVI (1893), pp. 383ff. Cf. Budde in *The Expositor*, 5th ser., I (1895), pp. 372ff., *EB*, II, cols. 1922ff., *ZDMG*, LXXXIV (1930), pp. 139ff. His substitution of Assyria for Chaldea was followed, among others, by G. A. Smith, *The Book of the Twelve Prophets*, II, pp. 117ff. Cf. O. Eissfeldt, *Einleitung in das AT*, pp. 471ff.

Stade suggested that much of Habakkuk 2:9-20 was inapplicable to the Chaldeans, and that 2:6-8 constituted the original end of the prophecy,[5] a view that was refuted by Wellhausen and Davidson.[6] Kirkpatrick suggested that while Habakkuk 1:5-11 might have been written down by Habakkuk at an earlier date, the work as a whole embodied profound religious reflection which had been arrived at only after a lengthy spiritual struggle.[7] Davidson sought to harmonize the passage with its context by treating it as less of a prediction and more of an explanation in dramatic form of the appearance of the Chaldeans, a view that even he admittedly regarded as deficient.[8] Driver questioned whether the objections raised to the integrity of chapter one were serious enough to justify the conclusions based on them, a position that accorded closely with the views of Cannon on the subject.[9] Lods held that Habakkuk 1:5-10 and possibly 1:14-17 in an earlier form had comprised a prophecy composed about 603 B.C., when it was thought that the Chaldeans might be expected to be instrumental in restoring divine law and order in Judah.[10] The author of the prophecy, however, lived and wrote half a century later, about 555 B.C., just prior to the rise of Cyrus, when there was still hope of a successful revolt against Chaldea. In consequence he adapted the earlier prophetic oracle to contemporary needs and used it as the basis of his reflections upon powerful aggressors. Such a view assumes the necessary existence of an earlier prophetic oracle in chapter one, a position for which there is no positive proof. It is further deficient in its failure to realize that the internal conditions depicted by the prophecy are more suited to the period shortly after the battle of Carchemish (605 B.C.) than to the days immediately prior to the rise of Cyrus.

Duhm was followed by Torrey in a radically different conception of the prophecy.[11] On this view the mention of the Chaldeans was the result of a textual corruption, since it was really the victorious Greeks under Alexander the Great whom the prophet Habakkuk had in mind. Therefore the *Kasdîm* of Habakkuk 1:6 should be corrected to *Kittîm*, a term used properly of the Cypriots but also employed as a general

[5] B. Stade, *ZAW*, IV (1884), pp. 154ff.; cf. A. Kuenen, *Einleitung in das AT*, II, pp. 371ff.

[6] J. Wellhausen, *Die Kleinen Propheten übersetzt und erklärt*, pp. 163ff. A. B. Davidson, *The Books of Nahum, Habakkuk and Zephaniah* (1896), pp. 55ff.

[7] A. F. Kirkpatrick, *The Doctrine of the Prophets*, p. 268.

[8] A. B. Davidson, *op. cit.*, pp. 48-50, 55.

[9] *DILOT*, p. 338. W. W. Cannon, *ZAW*, XLIII (1925), pp. 62ff.

[10] A. Lods, *The Prophets and the Rise of Judaism* (1937), p. 165.

[11] B. Duhm, *Das Buch Habakuk* (1906), pp. 20ff.; C. C. Torrey in K. Budde (ed.), *Karl Marti zum siebsigsten Geburtstage* (1925), pp. 281ff., *Jewish Studies in Memory of George A. Kohut* (1935), pp. 565ff. The late dating of Duhm was rejected by K. Budde, *ZDMG*, LXXXIV (1930), pp. 129ff., and O. Eissfeldt, *Einleitung in das AT*, p. 471.

designation of the Greeks (cf. 1 Macc. 1:1). This proposal is of some interest in the light of the Qumran commentary on the book of Habakkuk, in which the Kittîm were specifically mentioned, and about which a little more will be said subsequently. In addition, Duhm proposed that the word for "wine" in Habakkuk 2:5 should be rendered "Greek," since the two words in Hebrew are very similar. As a result, Duhm and Torrey felt able to date the book in 331 B.C., between the battles of Issus and of Arbela.

In criticism of this theory it must be admitted readily that the textual changes are comparatively easy to make, particularly in the light of the evidence from Qumran, and that, as Oesterley and Robinson have pointed out, no objection would be raised to them if the theory could be justified on other grounds.[12] The issue turns on the word "Chaldeans" in Habakkuk 1:6,[13] for if it is original, the first two chapters of the book belong to the period 615-600 B.C. If it is not, the book may well reflect the conquests of Alexander the Great, since 1:9 would better suit the Greek invasion from the west and a fourth-century B.C. date than the incursions of Nebuchadnezzar from the north or east at an earlier period. The grave weakness associated with the view supported by Duhm and Torrey is that there is absolutely no textual evidence for the reading Kittîm in Habakkuk 1:6, even though the Qumran sectaries interpreted the word Kasdîm in this manner.

· A Maccabean date for the prophecy is clearly precluded by the reference of Ben Sira to the Book of the Twelve Minor Prophets, as well as by the existence of the Qumran Commentary on Habakkuk. While a date within the Greek period for the first two chapters has certain external conditions to commend it, such a date can only be arrived at finally by an entirely unjustified textual emendation of Habakkuk 1:6. Furthermore, the description of the invaders on horseback could be applied just as well to the Chaldeans as to the Greeks, while the interpretation of Habakkuk 1:5-11 as the victorious march of Alexander, which on such a view had already occurred, is decidedly forced.[14]

Arguments for a date in the late Persian or early Greek period, based upon the circle of ideas entertained by the prophet, appear to have little if any compelling force. Even granted the possibility that some of the oracles were modified before the book arrived at its extant form, a position that could take some support from the Qumran Commentary, the book itself is remarkably reminiscent of the time of Jeremiah. This is true even of the problem of theodicy raised in Habakkuk 1:12-17, which was also raised in a similar way by Jeremiah (12:1ff.). The description

12 *IBOT*, pp. 394f.
13 *PIOT*, p. 599.
14 For an eschatological interpretation of this section see W. Staerk, ZAW, LI (1933), pp. 1f.

of the Chaldeans in Habakkuk is distinctly reminiscent of the foe whom Jeremiah contemplated (Jer. 4:13; 5:6), while the condemnation of the tyrant in Habakkuk 2:9, 12 recalls the judgment pronounced upon Jehoiakim in Jeremiah 22:13ff. Because this last reference suited a domestic rather than a foreign tyrant, Rothstein postulated the existence of a conflict inside Israel between the wicked and the righteous at the time of Jehoiakim.[15] This view is unlikely, however, since the prophet was thinking quite obviously about the advent of a great foreign power, and not the political excesses of a domestic tyrant. The prophecy contains other indications of a period not later than the time of Jeremiah, such as echoes of Isaiah (compare 2:14 with Isa. 11:9), Micah (compare 2:12 with Mic. 3:10), and Jeremiah (compare 2:13 with Jer. 51:58). In view of the foregoing evidence it appears preferable to the present writer to adhere to the traditional dating (605-600 B.C.) for at least the first two chapters of the prophecy.

The third chapter, which consists of a magnificent lyric poem, has for long been held to be independent of the first two chapters. The title in Habakkuk 3:1 and the dedication in 3:19, along with the musical notations in verses 3, 9, 13, 19, resemble closely those in the Psalter, and in consequence it was suggested by Wellhausen, Cheyne, and others that this poem was excerpted from one of the collections of psalms used in the worship of the Temple.[16] This psalm may have been appropriated by the editors of the prophetic canon before the Psalter emerged in its final form, though there can naturally be no proof of this point.

Stade was the first to claim from internal evidence that authorship of the material by Habakkuk was an impossibility, and in this contention he was followed by Wellhausen and others.[17] Duhm, on the other hand, regarded it as the very apogee of the prophecy, and apart from verses 17-19 attributed it to the prophet himself. If the poem has any connection with the theme elaborated in chapters one and two, it could be interpreted as describing the revelation of God coming in majesty, bringing judgment upon the pagans and joy and salvation to the Chosen People. Although there is nothing specific in the psalm that would preclude a pre-exilic date, the combination of theophany and historical retrospect would accord rather better with the exilic or even the immediate post-exilic period. Whatever the date of the final chapter, the book was certainly known as a unity by the beginning of the fifth century B.C.

The fact that the Commentary on Habakkuk from the Qumran caves made no reference to the psalm can be explained quite readily by noting

---

[15] J. W. Rothstein, *Theologische Studien und Kritiken*, LXVII (1894), pp. 51ff.

[16] J. Wellhausen, *Die Kleinen Propheten übersetzt und erklärt*, pp. 167ff. T. K. Cheyne, *The Origin of the Psalter*, pp. 156f.

[17] B. Stade, ZAW, IV (1884), pp. 157f. J. Wellhausen, *Die Kleinen Propheten übersetzt und erklärt*, pp. 168ff.

that it contained nothing suitable for their particular exegetical purposes, and was therefore ignored. It was certainly associated with the prophecy long before the Maccabean period, as the mention of the Twelve Minor Prophets in Ben Sira indicates, and it could only have been regarded as unsuitable for their requirements by the Qumran sectaries, who in other respects were notable for the high esteem in which they held the Scriptural writings.

Some scholars have viewed the entire prophecy as a "prophetic liturgy," perhaps designed for a specific penitential occasion.[18] If the Temple prophets in the cultus of Judah found it necessary to attend to the position of the Temple singers,[19] and if Habakkuk was, as tradition appears to indicate, a prophet and a musician who flourished during the last years of the First Temple, he would be very familiar with cultic compositions. While it is possible that chapter three was connected in some manner with the cultus, it is difficult to see how the first two chapters could have been employed as a liturgy. Although they are poetic in form, as, indeed, many prophetic oracles were, their specifically predictive content makes it improbable that they were used in liturgical form in the manner suggested by Mowinckel and others, since such liturgies normally commemorated events that had already passed. The apocalyptic elements in the psalm have been held to reflect the myth of conflict between God and the primordial dragon of the sea,[20] although it seems probable that in actual fact the reference is to the great saving act of the Exodus and its associated phenomena rather than to Babylonian or even Canaanite mythology.

Albright is probably correct in his view that the prophecy is a substantial unity, to be dated between 605 and 598 B.C.[21] Certainly Habakkuk stands close to Nahum both in time and also in subject-matter. For Nahum, the God who controlled the destinies of men and peoples was Himself governed by discernible principles of morality and righteousness. In the thought of Habakkuk, the concept of the justice of God formed the central issue in any attempt to comprehend history from a religious point of view. If the first two chapters are interpreted as a form of dialogue between the prophet and God, it may well be that Habakkuk derived his warrant for such an approach from this specific standpoint.

[18] So E. Balla, Die Religion in Geschichte und Gegenwart, II, cols. 1556f.; S. Mowinckel, Theologische Zeitschrift, IX (1953), pp. 1ff.

[19] Cf. A. R. Johnson, The Cultic Prophet in Ancient Israel (1944), pp. 59ff.

[20] E.g. F. J. Stephens, JBL, XLIII (1924), pp. 290ff.; T. H. Gaster, Iraq, IV (1937), pp. 21ff.; U. Cassuto, Annuario di Studi Ebraici 1935-37 (1938), pp. 7ff.; W. A. Irwin, JNES, I (1942), pp. 10ff.; cf. F. C. Burkitt, JTS, XVI (1915), pp. 62ff.; H. Bévenot, RB, XLII (1933), pp. 499ff.; M. Delcor, Miscellanea biblica B. Ubach (1953), pp. 287ff.; P. Leguerie, Études sur les Prophètes d'Israël (1954), pp. 53ff.

[21] W. F. Albright in Studies in OT Prophecy Presented to T. H. Robinson, pp. 2, 9.

Looking back upon the old cultic tradition of a theophany at Sinai (Hab. 3:3-15), the prophet expected the almighty power of God to manifest itself and sweep away all opposition to the advance of the divine kingdom.

C. THE MESSAGE OF HABAKKUK

There still remained a moral problem, however, namely, that which resulted from God's allowing an iniquitous enemy nation to punish a people more righteous than itself (Hab. 1:13). The answer to this was given in Habakkuk 2:4, which showed that human arrogance carries within itself the seeds of its own ruin, whereas the man of faith is assured of an existence pursued in the light of divine favor. Such a contrast not merely separated the Chaldeans from the elect of Israel, but reflected a situation basic to the spiritual aspirations of mankind as a whole. While it is obviously incorrect to assume that the Pauline meaning of faith cannot be found in Habakkuk 2:4, it can be stated that the LXX, by employing *pistis* for "faith," furnished a legitimate development of the prophetic thought in this manner, and that the *logion* itself did not receive its fullest meaning until it was incorporated into the gospel of the New Testament (Rom. 1:17; Gal. 3:11; Heb. 10:3ff.).[22] Other important emphases made by this short prophecy include the assertion that spiritual rectitude is an absolute necessity for both individuals and nations: that wealth is at best a treacherous foundation for a secure life; that evil is bound to fail ultimately even though it may experience temporary triumphs at the expense of good, and that trust in the power of God is the only sure basis of strength, both individual and communal, whatever the external circumstances may be.

The recovery of a Commentary on Habakkuk from the Dead Sea caves furnished an important stimulus to fresh study of the prophecy. The Commentary was found on examination to have interpreted Habakkuk 1:4–2:20 only in the light of the history of the Qumran brotherhood.[23] The peculiar exegetical method employed unfortunately threw no light upon either the meaning or the origin of the prophecy itself, but instead interpreted the *Kasdîm* of Habakkuk 1:6 to mean "*the Kittim*," which in other instances were thought of as comprising two distinct branches, the

---

22 Cf. A. G. Hebert, *The Authority of the OT*, p. 85.

23 Cf. W. H. Brownlee, *BASOR*, No. 112 (1948), pp. 8ff., No. 114 (1949), pp. 9f., No. 126 (1952), pp. 10ff.; M. Delcor, *Les manuscrits de la Mer Morte: essai sur le Midrasch d'Habacuc* (1951), *Revue de l'Histoire des Religions*, CXLII (1952), pp. 129ff.; H. E. Del Medico, *Deux manuscrits hébreux de la Mer Morte* (1951); H. H. Rowley, *The Zadokite Fragments and the Dead Sea Scrolls* (1952); K. Elliger, *Studien zum Habakuk-Kommentar vom Toten Meer* (1953); C. Detaye, *Le cadre historique du Midrash d'Habacuc* (1954); F. F. Bruce, *The Teacher of Righteousness in the Qumran Texts* (1956).

Kittim of Assyria and the Kittim of Egypt.[24] Precisely what the Qumran sectaries themselves understood by the use of the term *"Kittim"* has been a matter of considerable debate in scholarly circles, as Rowley has shown,[25] and the matter is still by no means settled at the time of writing.

While the text of the prophecy appears to have been in a fairly fluid state even when the Commentary was made, there is no evidence that the original *Kasdîm* of Habakkuk 1:6 was ever in need of emendation. Notable readings in 1QpHab included 1:11, which was rendered, "then the wind changed and was removed, and he made his strength his god"; 1:17, which had the interrogative form removed to read, "he shall therefore draw his sword, and not to spare . . ."; and 2:15, which was rendered, "Woe unto him who causes his neighbors to drink of the mixture of his fury unto drunkenness, that he may look on their feasts. Thou art sated with shame instead of glory. Drink also, and stagger drunkenly. . . ."

✦   ✦   ✦   ✦   ✦

The text of the prophecy has not been particularly well preserved, and contains some obscurities, a fact that is also true of the Qumran text. While the LXX may perhaps contain better readings as far as Habakkuk 1:6 and 3:10 are concerned, it is of little value in the elucidation of textual difficulties, and this is also true of the other versions.

Supplementary Literature

Humbert, P. *Problèmes du livre d'Habacuc.* 1944.
Leslie, E. A. *The Prophets Tell Their Own Story.* 1939.
Lloyd-Jones, D. M. *From Fear to Faith: Studies in the Book of Habakkuk.* 1953.
Vischer, W. *Der Prophet Habakuk.* 1958.

---

[24] Cf. E. L. Sukenik, *Megilloth Genuzoth* (1948), I, p. 18n.
[25] H. H. Rowley, *The Zadokite Fragments and the Dead Sea Scrolls*, pp. 43ff.

IX. THE BOOK OF ZEPHANIAH

A. NAME AND OUTLINE

The book of Zephaniah occupies ninth place in any listing of the Twelve Minor Prophets, following Habakkuk and preceding Haggai. The work was named after the Judaean prophet צפניה—a cognomen borne by three other individuals in the Old Testament (1 Chron. 6:36ff.; Jer. 21:1; Zech. 6:10).[1] In the LXX the name appeared as Σοφονίας, a form that was followed by the Vulgate *Sophonias*.

Contrary to the usual custom, the title of the book contains the lineage of the prophet, which is carried back to an ancestor of the fourth generation named Hezekiah. On this basis Zephaniah was the great-great-grandson of Hezekiah, king of Judah (716/15-687/86 B.C.). While the individual spoken of as Hezekiah was not actually described as "king," there seems little doubt that he was in fact intended to be understood by the reader, since otherwise the person who was responsible for the title to the prophecy, whether Zephaniah or not, would scarcely have troubled to furnish the ancestry of the prophet. There appears to be little ground for the supposition of Bentzen that Cushi his father was actually an Ethiopian, and that Zephaniah was a Negro slave in the service of the Temple.[2] In any event the reference in the title to the fact that the prophet was active in the period of King Josiah (640/39-609 B.C.) appears undoubtedly correct.

The book consists of a single collection of short oracles that fall into three principal divisions. It may be analyzed briefly as follows:

I. The Day of the LORD, ch. 1:1–2:3
    A. Threat of desolation against Baal worshippers, 1:2-6
    B. The implications of the Day of the LORD, 1:7-13
    C. The ensuing judgment, 1:14-18
    D. Means of avoiding judgment, 2:1-3

---

[1] M. Noth, *Die israelitischen Personennamen*, p. 178; O. Eissfeldt, *Baal Zaphon* (1932), pp. 2ff.

[2] A. Bentzen, *Introduction to the OT*, II, p. 153.

II. Judgments Against Foreign Nations, ch. 2:4-15
   A. Philistia, 2:4-7
   B. Moab and Ammon, 2:8-11
   C. Egypt, 2:12
   D. Assyria, 2:13-15
III. Woe and Blessing, ch. 3
   A. Threat of punishment for Jerusalem, 3:1-8
   B. Assurance of blessing for a faithful remnant, 3:9-20

B. THE PROPHECY OF ZEPHANIAH

Although nothing is known about the prophet beyond what can be ascertained from the superscription to his work, it can be inferred from his allusions to the state of morality and religion in Judah (Zeph. 1:4ff., 8, 9, 12; 3:1-3, 7) that his activities took place before the great reformation of 621 B.C. The fact that in Zephaniah 1:8 only the royal princes, and not the king himself, were mentioned might imply a period in the minority of Josiah, though this contention cannot be proved. If Zephaniah was of royal ancestry, he may have been trained by the same teachers as Josiah himself,[3] but whether this is the case or not, Zephaniah showed much greater familiarity with the court and the princely circles than with the common people, so beloved of the prophet Micah. Thus, at some period before 621 B.C., this cousin of Josiah could have been instructed in the traditional Hebrew faith out of the recorded words of Isaiah and Amos, as his preaching appears to indicate, and under the threat of the Scythian invasions he could have uttered his prophecies

The Scythian question has been a matter of considerable debate in scholarly circles, as has been noted earlier,[4] and in the view of the present writer these nomadic hordes have some substance in history. They apparently attacked Assyria in 632 B.C.,[5] making it possible for Josiah to carry out his reforms without fear of Assyrian intervention, though whether Herodotus was correct in his statement that the Scythians marched through Palestine to invade Egypt before being bought off by Psammetichus[6] is difficult to say

Partly in the light of these considerations, the dating of Zephaniah in terms of the Scythian raids, with which Jeremiah also was apparently concerned, has been held to be without objective support by some

---

[3] C. L. Taylor, *IB*, VI, p. 1009.

[4] For a survey of scholarly opinion see H. H. Rowley, *Men of God*, pp. 141ff.

[5] Cf. J. Lewy, *Mitteilungen der vorderasiatischen Gesellschaft*, XXIX (1925), pp. 1ff.; E. H. Minns, *Cambridge Ancient History* (1925), III, pp. 188f.

[6] *Hist.*, I, 105f. It has been challenged by F. Wilke, *Alttestamentliche Studien R. Kittel dargebracht* (1913), pp. 222ff.; J. P. Hyatt, *JBL*, LIX (1950), p. 501.

scholars.[7] On the other hand, the majority of commentators have seen in the Scythian peril the background of his prediction of woe.[8] In view of the eschatological standpoint of the prophet it is probably true to assert that, while the immediate threat to internal security in Judah may have been the Scythians, the real foe was Assyria, which would usher in the great day of reckoning. This fearsome nation was the ultimate concern of Zephaniah, as it was also for Isaiah, Nahum, and Habakkuk. While the Scythian incursions may have furnished a foretaste of the end for Zephaniah, they were without doubt of minor importance compared with the dreaded Assyrians, whose destruction he foretold in Zephaniah 2:13ff.

Discussions concerning the integrity of the prophecy have invariably allowed chapter one as the genuine work of Zephaniah, although even here traces of editorial activity have been detected, as for example in 1:13b. The authenticity of sections of the remaining two chapters was questioned by Stade, who disallowed to Zephaniah verses 1-3 and 11 of the second chapter as well as the bulk of chapter three.[9] Schwally ascribed to the prophet only chapter 1, chapter 2:13-15, and possibly 2:1-4, assigning 2:5-12 to the exile—owing to the mention of the "remnant" (2:7ff.)—and the whole of chapter three to the post-exilic period.[10] Budde rearranged portions of chapters 2 and 3 (2:1-3, 3:1-5, 7, 8, 6 in that order, following chapter 1) to secure a date for them in the pre-exilic era, but assigned 3:9-20 to a post-exilic setting.[11] A. B. Davidson defended the general integrity of chapter 2, and only expressed minor doubts about verses 10 and 14-20 of the third chapter.[12] Baudissin held a similar view of the integrity of chapters 2 and 3, denying only 2:7a, 8-11 and 3:14-20 to the prophet.[13] Driver, following critical trends with his customary caution, thought that possibly Zephaniah

---

[7] E.g. E. König, Einleitung in das AT (1893), pp. 352ff.; G. Gerleman, Zephanja textkritisch und literarisch untersucht (1942), p. 126; J. P. Hyatt, JNES, VII (1948), pp. 25ff.; F. Horst, Die Zwölf Kleinen Propheten (1954), II, p. 195.

[8] So W. Nowack, Die Kleinen Propheten, p. 278; J. A. Selbie, HDB, IV, p. 975; K. Marti, Dodekapropheton, pp. 395f.; J. M. P. Smith, A Critical and Exegetical Commentary on the Book of Zephaniah (1912), pp. 162f.; C. Steuernagel, Einleitung in das AT, p. 636; H. C. O. Lanchester, Nahum, Habakkuk and Zephaniah (1920), pp. 105f.; E. Sellin, Das Zwölfprophetenbuch, p. 415; G. G. V. Stonehouse, Zephaniah (1929), pp. 3, 8f.; O. Eissfeldt, Einleitung in das AT, pp. 520f.; ETOT, p. 424; IBOT, p. 400; C. L. Taylor, IB, VI, p. 1009; E. A. Leslie, IDB, IV, p. 951.

[9] B. Stade, Geschichte des Volkes Israel, p. 644n.

[10] F. Schwally, ZAW, X (1890), pp. 218ff., 238ff.

[11] K. Budde, Theologische Studien und Kritiken, LXVI (1893), pp. 393ff.

[12] A. B. Davidson, Zephaniah (1896), pp. 99ff.

[13] W. W. von Baudissin, Einleitung in das AT (1901), pp. 553ff.

2:7b, 11 and 3:9-10, 18-20 were somewhat later additions,[14] and many subsequent writers have postulated the presence of spurious material in the second and third chapters.[15]

The problem of originality or otherwise thus appears to turn upon the hopeful outlook of the latter part of the prophecy, which according to some scholars ill accords with the *dies irae, dies illa* of Zephaniah 1:14-18 and similar passages. However, it should be noted that there are no *a priori* reasons why Zephaniah could not have prophesied concerning the final salvation of the remnant (Zeph. 3:8-13), purified from sin in the coming judgment, since this was a theme familiar to the eighth-century prophets, notably Isaiah, in whose teachings Zephaniah was almost certainly instructed, if the points of theological contact which he had with the former are any indication.

While the ending of the book is rather stereotyped, there is no valid reason for denying it to Zephaniah, nor can there be said to be any incongruity between it and the remainder of the work, since other prophecies of woe commonly concluded with an expectation of restoration and final felicity, such as are found in Amos, Micah, Nahum, and Habakkuk. It must therefore be concluded that literary analyses that would deny to the author various portions of the prophecy are based upon entirely subjective considerations, and that there is no sufficient reason for attributing to anyone other than Zephaniah himself any particular section of the prophecy.

The purpose of the work, which commenced on a note of gloom, was to warn the southern kingdom of approaching devastation. The prophet denounced the idolatry that he witnessed in Jerusalem, where there had been no spiritual revival since the time of his ancestor Hezekiah. Zephaniah adopted ideas from older prophetic sources, and in particular employed the concept of the Day of the LORD as found in Amos (5:18f.) and Isaiah (2:7ff.) to describe the nature of the divine judgment. Again, the thought that underlay the emergence of the religious community from the faithful remnant was one that went back to Isaiah, while in his concept relating to the purifying nature of the divine judgment the prophet combined the emphasis of Amos on eradication with that of Hosea upon rehabilitation. His own contribution may well be seen in terms of his recognition of the corruption involved in magical practices, and his declaration that they had absolutely no place whatever in the religion of the Chosen People. Like his precursors and his contemporary Jeremiah, he pointed out the deceitful and iniquitous character of human nature, and emphasized that spiritual and social security could only result from the divine renewing of the individual personality.

---

[14] *DILOT*, pp. 343f.
[15] E.g. *IBOT*, p. 401; *PIOT*, pp. 600f.; L. P. Smith and E. R. Lacheman, *JNES*, IX (1950), pp. 137ff.; C. L. Taylor, *IB*, VI, p. 1001; *OTFD*, p. 266.

The Hebrew text of the prophecy has been quite well preserved, and it is only on fairly rare occasions, as for example in Zephaniah 2:2, 14; 3:7 that the LXX version is able to throw some light on the text.

Supplementary Literature

Kuhner, H. O. *Zephanjah*. 1943.
Pilcher, C. V. *Three Hebrew Prophets and the Passing of Empires*. 1928.

X. THE BOOK OF HAGGAI

A. NAME AND OUTLINE

The title of this book was derived from its attributive author, the prophet Haggai (חַגַּי), whose name appeared in the LXX as Ἀγγαῖος and in the Vulgate as *Aggaeus*. The designation "Haggai" appears to have been derived from the word for "festival,"[1] which might suggest that the prophet had been born on some feast-day. A name of a similar character was Shabbethai (Ez. 10:15), meaning "born on the sabbath," and there are other similar commemorations in the Old Testament such as Haggiah (1 Chron. 6:30) and Haggith (2 Sam. 3:4).

Nothing is known about the family or the social circumstances from which Haggai emerged, and not even the name of his father has survived. Jerome's commentary on Haggai (I, 13) maintained that Haggai was of priestly descent, and this may underlie the references in the LXX, Syriac, and Vulgate versions that attributed the authorship of certain canonical psalms to him.[2] Although it might be inferred from chapter 2:11 and elsewhere that Haggai was familiar with cultic interests and priestly techniques, Jewish tradition associated him firmly with Zechariah, his contemporary in the prophetic office.[3]

The historical activity of Haggai is corroborated by references in Ezra (5:1; 6:14). Along with the prophecy of Zechariah the book is of great importance as a source of information concerning the period between the return to Palestine and the work of Ezra and Nehemiah. Following upon the decree of Cyrus in 538 B.C., which permitted exiled national groups in Babylonia to return to their native land, some of the Jewish captives commenced the long and hazardous journey back to Judaea under the leadership of Sheshbazzar and Zerubbabel. In 537 B.C., the first year of the return, the altar of burnt offering was reconstructed, some of the ancient rites were restored to public worship, and the foundation of the Second Temple was laid (Ez. 3:8ff.).

---

[1] M. Noth, *Die israelitischen Personennamen*, pp. 222, 242; J. Wellhausen in F. Bleek, *Einleitung in das AT* (1878), p. 434.

[2] Cf. B. Jacob, *ZAW*, XVI (1896), p. 290; C. H. H. Wright, *Zechariah and His Prophecies* (1879), pp. xix-xx.

[3] *Megill. 3a.*

Since neither Haggai nor Zechariah was mentioned until 520 B.C. (Ez. 5:1f.), it has been suggested that they had returned from Babylonia with a fresh group of exiles about that time. Although it is possible that the picture of a mass exodus of Jews from Babylonia, as painted by the Chronicler, is somewhat exaggerated in the interests of his special tendencies, there is no ground for the view that Haggai and Zechariah had arrived as adults in Judaea just prior to the start of their prophetic ministry. Nor is there the slightest evidence that Haggai was at the time of his ministry an aged man who had known the splendor of the Solomonic Temple and had participated in the exile, however picturesque such a view might happen to be, a position that Weiser finally conceded.[4] In point of fact, neither prophet gives the slightest hint that the above situations had obtained, and it is probable that both men were children when their parents returned to Judaea in 537 B.C. In that event Haggai and Zechariah would have witnessed the steadily deteriorating morale of the people prior to receiving their prophetic commission, and in the case of Haggai at least this factor may well have played an important role in shaping his message.

The book of Haggai comprises four short oracles given by the prophet himself, written in the third person singular and connected with the restoration of the Temple in 520 B.C. These addresses were delivered on the first day of the sixth month (1:1), the twenty-first day of the seventh month (2:1), and the twenty-fourth day of the ninth month (2:10ff.; 2:20ff.) respectively. It is of some interest that they were related in such a precise manner to the reign of Darius I (522-486 B.C.).

The book can be summarized as follows:

I. The First Address and Response, ch. 1:1-15
II. The Second Message of Encouragement, ch. 2:1-9
III. An Argument from the Ritual Law, ch. 2-10-19
IV. A Special Promise Made to Zerubbabel, ch. 2:20-23

B. THE CONTENTS OF THE BOOK

In the first utterance the prophet summoned the governor Zerubbabel[5] and the High Priest Joshua to rebuild the Temple. He accused the populace as a whole of regarding their own material comforts, slight as they were, as having priority, instead of exerting themselves to rebuild the House of God immediately upon their return from exile. The neglect of the past sixteen years had been observed by God, who had punished them by means of natural disasters in order to remind them that they were not attending to the most important concerns of the time. An interlude of twenty-four days (Hag. 1:12-15) gave some opportunity for the people to respond to these accusations.

---

[4] *OTFD*, p. 267.
[5] Cf. Noth, *Die israelitischen Personennamen*, p. 63.

The second oracle constituted words of encouragement to those who thought that the foundations of the new building looked impoverished, perhaps deceptively so, in comparison with the majestic and splendid edifice constructed in the time of King Solomon. Haggai restored popular confidence in the project by stating that the future Temple would be the recipient of far greater glory than that which had been visited upon the Solomonic structure. In Haggai 2:7 the "desirable things" constituted gifts from Gentile peoples that would assist in beautifying and adorning the Temple, a promise which was partially fulfilled shortly afterwards under Ezra (Ez. 6:8f.) and later on under the Herodian dynasty.

The third oracle dealt with spiritual issues, and drew for its inspiration upon an aspect of ritual law. Haggai pointed out that if a man is carrying part of the sacrificial flesh and his clothes come into contact with some object, the latter is not consequently rendered holy. But if a man is ceremonially unclean, his clothes defile whatever they touch. The Temple ruins were unclean and defiled the nation precisely because they were ruins, but the laying of a fresh foundation and the prosecution of the work to completion would be attended by divine blessing.

It may well be, as Stafford Wright has suggested, that the revival of enthusiasm had been marked by a fresh foundation ceremony (Hag. 2:18; cf. Ez. 3:10), since it was by no means unusual to have more than one foundation ritual for dwelling-houses and temples alike.[6] The date given in Haggai 2:18 may perhaps be a scribal error that has confused the twenty-fourth day of the sixth month (Hag. 1:15) with the twenty-fourth day of the ninth month, when the prophecy was uttered (Hag. 2:10).

The final pronouncement was that of a promise to Zerubbabel that, despite disturbances in the Persian empire, he himself would be kept safe, since he was to be the signet-ring of God.[7] This was reminiscent of the fate that had overtaken Jehoiachin, the grandfather of Zerubbabel, subsequent to the pronouncements of Jeremiah (22:24ff.). As the vice-regent of God upon earth (cf. Zech. 3:8; 6:12f.), Zerubbabel was to bear the stamp of divine authority, and it was as a "signet upon the right hand" that he was remembered by Ben Sira (Ecclus. 49:11).

Some scholars have argued from the fact that the extant addresses appear as résumés to the contention that the book as it stands cannot have come from the hand of Haggai.[8] Consequently it has been suggested that the prophecy was the work of a disciple or circle of disciples.[9] However, as Eissfeldt has pointed out, the possibility that the prophet himself was the author and that he furnished his story in a

---

[6] J. Stafford Wright, *The Building of the Second Temple* (1958), p. 17, in *NBD*, p. 498.

[7] Cf. A. Poebel, *AJSL*, LV (1938), pp. 142ff., 285ff.

[8] *IBOT*, p. 407.

[9] A. Bentzen, *Introduction to the OT*, II, p. 156.

strictly objective form must not by any means be dismissed out of hand.[10] Weiser has remarked that the book gives the impression of being close to the events and of going back to reliable sources.[11] There may be some possibility of textual dislocation,[12] as in Haggai 2:15-19, which may have arisen from the confusion of dates in Haggai 1:15 and 2:18. There is no factual evidence for the supposition that the work is a compilation of two different literary forms, namely narrative material and a small collection of oracles.

While some commentators assume the presence of numerous glosses on the text, it is more probable in the view of the present writer that stylistic clumsiness is predominantly responsible for awkward passages in the Hebrew text. Although the prophecy is generally considered to have been written in prose, Driver and others are correct in stating that the thoughts of Haggai not infrequently fall into the kind of parallelistic form characteristic of Hebrew poetry.[13]

The book of Haggai is historical rather than religious in character, but despite this it has an important bearing both upon the growth of the post-exilic cultus in Judaea and also upon specifically spiritual matters. Haggai was following the ideals of Ezekiel with regard to the development of a priestly commonwealth, as indicated by the way he related the prophetic eschatology of salvation to the building of the Temple. In this respect he, along which his contemporary Zechariah, is of great importance in any assessment of the nature of early Judaism.

As against the view of T. H. Robinson and others that Haggai possessed little that could be called a spiritual message, it should be observed that in his third oracle he furnished the most concise statement to be found anywhere in the Old Testament of the fact that evil is far more penetrating and diffusive than goodness.[14] This realization needs to be brought to bear upon what has been described as his "superficial view"[15] that material prosperity was assured provided that the mechanics of worship were guaranteed. As in the case of Ezekiel, who also gave punctilious attention to details of worship and ritual, the emphasis of Haggai was upon correct motivation, so that his concern was ultimately with the most profound aspects of human nature.

---

[10] O. Eissfeldt, *Einleitung in das AT,* p. 478.

[11] *OTFD,* p. 268.

[12] Cf. K. Budde, ZAW, XXVI (1906), pp. 1ff.; C. R. North, ZAW, LXVIII (1956), pp. 25ff.

[13] *DILOT,* p. 344. Cf. H. G. Mitchell, *A Critical and Exegetical Commentary on the Book of Haggai* (1912), pp. 37f.; P. F. Bloomhardt, *HUCA,* V (1928), pp. 153ff.; A. Bentzen, *Introduction to the OT,* II, p. 156 n. 3.

[14] T. H. Robinson, *Prophecy and the Prophets in Ancient Israel* (1923), p. 177; *IBOT,* pp. 408f.

[15] W. Neil, *IDB,* II, p. 511.

The Hebrew text of the prophecy has been well preserved in the main, although there are certain corruptions, as in Haggai 1:2, 10; 2:17 as well as the possibility of textual dislocation. The LXX appears to represent a superior text in most instances, but in 2:9 it contains an addition that does not occur in the Hebrew. Whether or not it stood there originally is a matter of some doubt. Another significant addition in the LXX occurred at the end of Haggai 2:14. All things considered it seems improbable that these two additions formed part of the original text.[16]

Supplementary Literature

Barnes, W. E. *Haggai and Zechariah*. 1917.
Browne, L. E. *Early Judaism*. 1920.

[16] D. W. Thomas, *IB*, VI, p. 1038.

XI. THE BOOK OF ZECHARIAH

A. NAME AND OUTLINE

The title given to this work was derived from the cognomen of the prophet זכריה, the contemporary of Haggai, who appeared in the LXX and the Vulgate under the designation Ζαχαρίας. The name "Zechariah" was, with slight variations, very common among the Hebrews, with over twenty-five individuals being thus styled in the Old Testament alone.[1] According to Zechariah 1:1 the prophet was the son of Berechiah and the grandson of Iddo. In Ezra 5:1 and 6:14 (cf. Neh. 12:16), however, he was mentioned as being the son of Iddo, and nothing was said about the existence of Berechiah. This discrepancy has been accounted for by supposing that a copyist confused "Zechariah ben Jeberechiah" mentioned in Isaiah 8:2 with the man who was the contemporary of Haggai, and that the words "the son of Berechiah" in Zechariah 1:1 constitute an interpolation.[2] A much more plausible explanation, however, is that which regards the Hebrew word בֶּן in בֶּן עִדּוֹ as equivalent to "grandson," for which there is, of course, ample evidence in the Old Testament. On such a basis of practice the alleged discrepancy is cleared up.

Iddo, the ancestor of Zechariah, was included among the heads of priestly families that returned from the exile in Babylonia to Judaea (Neh. 12:4, 16). If this is correct, it would follow that Zechariah was a priest (Neh. 12:16), and may even have officiated as a cultic prophet. He is generally assumed to have been a young man, like Haggai, when he entered upon his prophetic ministry two months after his worthy contemporary concluded his final oracle. His utterances extended over a longer period of time than those of Haggai, however, and from the dates given in Zechariah 1:1 and 7:1 it would appear that the prophetic oracles of Zechariah were pronounced over a two-year period.

The fourteen chapters of the extant work fall naturally into two principal sections, and can be analyzed as follows:

[1] Cf. T. M. Mauch, *IDB*, IV, pp. 941ff.
[2] E.g. *PIOT*, p. 604 n. 27; D. W. Thomas, *IB*, VI, p. 1053.

I. Dated Prophecies, ch. 1–8
  A. Introduction and call to repentance, 1:1-6
  B. Eight visions, 1:7–6:8
    1. Four horsemen; the promise of divine restoration, 1:7-17
    2. Four destroying horns and four smiths, 1:18-21 (2:1-4 Heb.)
    3. The immeasurable greatness of Jerusalem, 2:1-13 (2:5-17 Heb.)
    4. The cleansing of Joshua; an oracle to him, 3:1-10
    5. The seven-branched lampstand, 4:1-14
    6. The large, flying scroll, 5:1-4
    7. The woman in an ephah removed to Babylon, 5:5-11
    8. Four horse-drawn chariots traversing the earth, 6:1-8
  C. Historical section: Joshua symbolic of the Messiah, 6:9-15
  D. An inquiry of Zechariah concerning fasting, 7:1–8:23
II. Undated Prophecies, ch. 9–14
  A. Judgment of national enemies; the coming of the peaceful prince, 9:1-17
  B. Gathering in of the chosen flock by the Divine Leader, 10:1-12
  C. Good and foolish shepherds; the suffering of the flock, 11:1-17
  D. Eschatological oracles, 12:1–13:6
  E. The purifying judgment of Israel and the blessings of the divine kingdom, 13:7–14:21

The visions in the first section of the prophecy appear to exhibit some definite arrangement. The first and the last are independent, but the remainder seem to have been grouped in pairs intentionally. It is not entirely clear as to why this pattern was followed, unless it was intended to be a variation of form in one half of a bifid composition; in any event, the material furnishes the impression of being a self-contained and homogeneous literary unit. Throughout the first eight chapters Zechariah is named as the author. Specific dates are given; the period in question is that of Ezra 5:1–6:22.

B. THE PROBLEM OF AUTHORSHIP

Almost all scholars have accepted the authenticity of chapters 1 to 8, although occasional attempts have been made to distinguish the Zechariah of the prophecies from the subject of the visions.[3] Probably the only legitimate question that can be raised in this regard, however, is whether the visions were real experiences or merely a literary form, as in later apocalyptic writings.

The problems associated with chapters 9 to 14 are more complex, but again critical scholars are virtually unanimous in their opinions, namely that the chapters are not the work of the prophet Zechariah, and may not even constitute a unity in themselves. It is possible to argue from the

[3] S. B. Frost, *OT Apocalyptic* (1952), p. 96.

Matthean reference (27:9), which ascribed Zechariah 11:12f. to Jeremiah, that there was some uncertainty regarding the authorship of Zechariah for these chapters at an early period.[4] This phenomenon, however, may imply nothing more than faulty recollection of the Greek Bible on the part of Matthew, or an incorrect citation of material from his collection of messianic *testimonia*.

Be that as it may, it was evidently the starting-point for literary criticism of the prophecy, the first traces of which appeared in the writings of Joseph Mede in 1653. As a result of his studies this author felt compelled to relegate chapters 9 to 11 to a pre-exilic period, and to credit their authorship to the prophet Jeremiah.[5] He was followed in 1700 by Richard Kidder, who supported the views of Mede to a great extent but went even further in declaring that chapters 12 to 14 were also the work of Jeremiah.[6] William Whiston, a Cambridge professor, was in agreement with the opinions of Mede as modified by the studies of Bishop Kidder.[7]

A new phase in the criticism of Zechariah began with the treatise of Archbishop William Newcome, entitled *An Attempt Towards an Improved Version, Metrical Arrangement and an Explanation of the Twelve Minor Prophets,* which was published in 1785. In this work he declared that chapters 9 to 11 were composed before the downfall of Samaria, perhaps about the time of Hosea, but that chapters 12 to 14 were of later date, perhaps originating between the death of Josiah and the fall of Jerusalem. The pre-exilic hypothesis attracted the attention of a number of scholars including Hitzig, Knobel, Ewald, Bleek, Von Orelli, and Schultz.[8]

The first serious challenge to this view originated in the work of Corrodi, who maintained that chapters 9 to 14 were written long after the time of Zechariah, and in this he was followed by Paulus.[9] In the fourth edition of his *Einleitung,* Eichhorn suggested a late date for those

[4] So A. Bentzen, *Introduction to the OT*, II, p. 158.

[5] J. Mede, *Dissertationum ecclesiasticarum triginta quibus accedunt fragmenta sacra* (1653).

[6] R. Kidder, *Demonstration of the Messias in Which the Truth of the Christian Religion Is Defended, Especially Against the Jews* (1726 ed.), pp. 76ff.

[7] W. Whiston, *Essay Towards Restoring the True Text of the Old Testament and for Vindicating the Citations Made Thence in the New Testament* (1722), pp. 93ff.

[8] F. Hitzig, *Theologische Studien und Kritiken*, III (1830), pp. 25ff. A. Knobel, *Der Prophetismus der Hebräer* (1837), II, pp. 166ff., 280ff. H. Ewald, *Die Propheten des Alten Bundes* (1840), I, pp. 308ff., 398ff. F. Bleek, *Theologische Studien und Kritiken*, XXV (1852), pp. 247ff., XXX (1857), pp. 316ff. C. von Orelli, *Die älteste Weissagung von der Vollendung des Gottesreiches* (1882), pp. 272ff. H. Schultz, *Alttestamentliche Theologie* (1889), pp. 64f.

[9] H. Corrodi, *Versuch einer Beleuchtung der Geschichte des jüdischen und christlichen Bibelkanons* (1792), I, p. 107. H. E. G. Paulus, *Exegetisches Handbuch über die drei ersten Evangelien* (1805), pp. 117ff.

chapters, maintaining that Zechariah 9:1–10:12 contained a description of the invasion of Alexander the Great, while Zechariah 13:7–14:21 comprised a song commemorating the death of Judas Maccabaeus in 161 B.C.[10]

Whereas De Wette had adhered to a pre-exilic date for chapters 9 to 14 up to 1829, he changed his views about that time, and in the fifth edition of his *Lehrbuch* he advocated a post-exilic origin of Zechariah 9 to 14.[11] Other scholars who supported this position included Stade, who placed the material in late Hellenistic times, Cornill, Wellhausen, Eckardt, Cheyne, Kirkpatrick, Driver, Kraeling, Heller, and other scholars.[12] As a result of these critical tendencies the pre-exilic hypothesis, once touted as being among the surest results of Biblical criticism, has now been abandoned, and the question of date turns upon either the integrity of the prophecy or the possibility that chapters 9 to 14 originated about the third century B.C.

The main arguments against authorship by Zechariah include the pronounced difference of atmosphere between the first and second sections of the book, the absence of any reference to a recent reconstruction of the Temple, a mention in Zechariah 9:13 of Greece as the dominant power rather than Persia,[13] as in the days of Zechariah, and the apocalyptic pictures in chapter 14, which are commonly held to be indications of a late date.[14] Eissfeldt has maintained that, while some of the chapters depend upon earlier material, they show evidences of a late period and cannot be considered as the work of one author.[15] Thus Zechariah 10:3–11:3, although it contains certain archaisms, should on this view be assigned to the Greek period, as should also Zechariah 11:4-17 and 13:7-9, which do not contain any archaic features. The eschatological outlook of Zechariah 12:1–13:6 would also furnish yet another reason for assigning it to a late date.

The objections which have been raised with regard to the mention of the "sons of Javan" are actually not quite as weighty as many critics have supposed. Greek influence in the Near East was felt as early as the seventh century B.C., and Javan was named by Isaiah (66:19) and

[10] J. G. Eichhorn, *Einleitung in das AT* (1824), pp. 444ff.

[11] W. L. M. de Wette, *Lehrbuch der historisch-kritische Einleitung in das AT* (1840), I, pp. 343ff.

[12] B. Stade, *ZAW*, I (1881), pp. 1ff., II (1882), pp. 151ff., 275ff. C. H. Cornill, *Einleitung in die Kanonischen Bücher des AT* (1891), pp. 196ff. J. Wellhausen, *Prolegomena zur Geschichte Israels* (1886), pp. 438ff. R. Eckardt, *ZAW*, XIII (1893), pp. 76ff. T. K. Cheyne, *JQR*, I (1888-89), p. 82. A. F. Kirkpatrick, *The Doctrine of the Prophets*, pp. 449ff. *DILOT*, pp. 348ff. E. G. Kraeling, *AJSL*, XLI (1925), pp. 24ff. B. Heller, *ZAW*, XLV (1927), pp. 151ff.

[13] O. Eissfeldt, *Einleitung in das AT*, pp. 491ff.

[14] Cf. H. H. Rowley, *The Relevance of Apocalyptic*, p. 24.

[15] O. Eissfeldt, *Einleitung in das AT*, pp. 429f.; *ETOT*, p. 438. Cf. B. Otzen, *Studien über Deuterosacharja* (1964), pp. 38ff.

Ezekiel (27:13, 19) as being one of the places where Israelite mission-
aries would go in order to witness to the divine glory. There is little
doubt that Zechariah could have seen in Greece the coming menace to
the Persian regime, since Greek mercenary troops had long constituted
the bulk of the Persian armed forces, and were only precluded from
united action against their commanders by the fact that they perpetuated feuds and sharp differences of native tradition among themselves.

Impetus to such a viewpoint could well have been furnished for the
prophet by the sporadic raids made by the Greeks upon the Palestinian
coastline, which appear to have begun about 500 B.C. with the great
Ionian revolt. It should also be noted that the prophecy against Javan is
one of defeat, not victory, and this is an important consideration in view
of the actual interpretation of Javan as the dominant world power
threatening Zion. Since chapter 9 deals with other mighty peoples also, it
appears unwarranted to promote the claims of Greece at the expense of
those of Tyre, Ashkelon, Gaza, Damascus, and the like. Accordingly it
would seem to the present writer inadvisable to place undue emphasis
upon the nation of Greece as a means of supporting a late date for the
section under consideration.

Considerable discussion has centered upon Zechariah 11:4-17, in an
attempt to interpret it symbolically in terms of Maccabean history.
Onias III has been suggested as the historical figure implied by the
image of the "good shepherd" (cf. 2 Macc. 4:1ff.), while the three
shepherds who were cut off have been identified with Simon, Lysimachus, and Menelaus, the sons of Tobias. The complexity of the problem can be seen from the fact that Kremer listed no fewer than thirty
proposed identifications of the three shepherds.[16] Aware of the subjectivity involved in such a procedure, Elliger suggested that the basis of
the narrative in Zechariah 11:4-16 was intended to be symbolic, but was
distorted at a later period because of allegorical interpretations.[17] It
represented for him the beginnings of the schism between the Jewish
and Samaritan communities towards the end of the fourth century B.C.
On any basis of understanding, whether symbolic or not, the principal
difficulty encountered in this passage is that of giving a satisfactory
explanation of the references to the shepherds. To date, critical scholarship has been notably deficient in interpreting this extremely important
passage.

From a more positive standpoint there are certain areas of contact
between the first and second sections of Zechariah. These include the
necessity for repentance and cleansing (1:4; 3:3, 4, 9; 5:1ff.; 7:5ff.; 9:7;

16 J. Kremer, *Die Hirtenallegorie im Buch Zacharias* (1930), pp. 83ff.
17 K. Elliger, *ZAW*, LXII (1950), pp. 63ff.

12:10; 13:1, 9), the return of the nation (2:6, 10; 8:7f.; 9:12; 10:6ff.), the exaltation of Jerusalem (1:16f.; 2:11f.; 12:6; 14:9f.), and the subjection and conversion of the enemies of Israel (1:21; 12:3ff.; 14:10ff.). In both portions of the book there is an absence of allusion to a king in Israel, coupled with an acknowledgment that the true ruler of Israel is the Messiah (6:12f.; 9:9), whose personage and work were presented from a uniform standpoint.

Similarities of style in both portions of the work include the use of "two" as a favorite number (4:3; 5:9; 6:1; 11:7; 13:8), the persistent vocative form of address (2:7, 10; 3:2, 8; 4:7; 9:9, 13; 11:1f.; 13:7), the presence of the phrase "go to and fro" (7:14; 9:8), which occurs nowhere else in the Hebrew Scriptures, and the recurrent phrase "saith the LORD," which is found in some sixteen places throughout the book. Again, the Qal or "light" form of the Hebrew verb "to dwell" is used in a passive sense in four instances in Zechariah (2:8; 7:7; 12:6; 14:10), and only rarely thus outside that prophecy. If these phenomena do not actually constitute evidence for the close literary affinity of the two sections, they certainly indicate that the author of the second portion was careful to model his style and expression upon that which obtained in the first part, a fact that would hardly be surprising if the book is to be considered as a literary bifid.

It has frequently been pointed out by scholars that chapters 9 to 14 of the prophecy are intimately connected with Malachi, which follows it immediately in the canon, by the superscriptions of Zechariah 9:1, 12:1 and Malachi 1:1, in which the Hebrew term for "oracle" occurs. Consequently it has frequently been assumed that the three sections introduced in this manner originally belonged together, but that Malachi in its extant form was separated in order to complete the number of the Twelve Prophets.[18] This theory is immediately confronted by the weighty objection that other prophets, notably Isaiah, used the term in exactly the same sense as that found in Zechariah in passages that cannot properly be denied to their authorship. Furthermore, if Malachi was separated in the manner suggested above, it is curious that such material should be attributed, albeit pseudonymously, to an individual. While it was not unknown in antiquity for extraneous material to become attached to the work of a reputable author, it is far from easy to understand by what warrant the supposed separation from the extant Malachi was made in the first instance.

The postulating of diverse authorship of the book of Zechariah on the ground of the apocalyptic content of chapters 9 to 14 rests upon rather circular arguments. Liberal scholarship has succeeded, to its own satis-

---

18 E.g. A. Bentzen, *Introduction to the OT*, II, p. 158.

faction at all events, in relegating apocalyptic works, such as Daniel, to the Maccabean period, and then utilizing this as a basis for dating other writings that exhibit apocalyptic themes. Such a procedure is quite arbitrary, to say the least, and leads to an incorrect understanding of the nature of apocalyptic such as that espoused by Pfeiffer, who assumed that apocalyptic could only appear when prophetic expectations had decayed irreparably.[19] While it is true that there is much apocalyptic material that can be dated in the intertestamental period, the presence of such passages in the canonical writings must not be taken as evidence of a late date for that particular section, lest some rather ludicrous conclusions result.

That there can be a legitimate prophetic-apocalyptic is evident from the dualistic element in the eschatology of Isaiah.[20] In common with many other prophets he placed the scene of the final redemption in this world. But while the new kingdom would be continuous with the present historical order, it would be different in the moral and spiritual sphere in that evil, suffering, and wrongdoing would no longer exist (Isa. 11:6ff.). This new era would be introduced by means of a specific divine visitation, and not by forces operating immanently within the sphere of nature or history (Isa. 24:1ff.; 26:21). On this basis it was possible to envisage through the medium of revelation a messianic personage who would establish the promised kingdom by ushering in the new age of grace. The final state, and one which was contemplated by many of the prophets, consisted of the cleansing of Jerusalem from sin and the restoration of the community under conditions of continuing peace and prosperity.

Such a prophetic apocalyptic is of great significance for the later chapters of Zechariah. To attempt the task of discovering the presence of contemporary figures in Zechariah 9:8, 15ff. and 12:10 is not merely an exercise in subjectivity, but an admission of failure to comprehend the messianic nature of these and other sections in chapters 9 to 14. The general picture presented by chapters nine, ten, and eleven is that of God visiting the nations in judgment and His people in mercy. The peaceful prince will come and will confound the evil shepherds, that is, rulers, but he will be rejected by the flock, which in turn will again experience suffering.

In chapters 12 to 14, the three apocalyptic pictures presented to the reader depict the siege of Jerusalem and its termination by divine intervention, the salvation of the remnant of Judah, and the manner in which the nations will share in the blessings to be showered upon Israel.

---

[19] *PIOT*, p. 611.
[20] Cf. G. E. Ladd, *JBL*, LXXVI (1957), pp. 192ff., *NBD*, p. 44.

This pattern has much in common with the highest aspirations of prophets such as Isaiah, who contemplated similar sequences in the future existence of his nation. It was precisely because the members of the primitive Christian Church were looking for the "consolation of Israel" that they found a ready messianic interpretation for passages such as Zechariah 9:9; 11:12f.; 12:10; and 13:7.

From the foregoing discussion it will be clear that there are strong arguments both for and against the unity of Zechariah. Whereas most liberal writers have thought in terms of Zechariah and "Deutero-Zechariah," the unity of the work has been maintained by scholars such as Robinson, Van Hoonacker, Young, and Barabas.[21] While it is not possible to prove the unity of the book, as Stafford Wright has pointed out,[22] some caution should be exercised in any discussion of its integrity, since there are equally cogent reasons which can be adduced both for and against unity of authorship by Zechariah.

If it is maintained, with some scholars, that the Minor Prophets concluded with three anonymous prophecies, two of which (Zech. 9–11; 12–14) became attached to Zechariah while the third was designated as Malachi, the date of the additions to Zechariah would probably be no later than 350 B.C. As Pfeiffer has stated, a date later than about 200 B.C. would be precluded in any event by the fact that Ben Sira (Ecclus. 49:10) knew the Twelve Minor Prophets in substantially their extant canonical form.[23] Quite apart from this consideration, however, there would seem to be a disparity between the dating for the material accruing to Zechariah and that which comprises the book of Malachi, which adds a further dimension to the problem.

* * * * *

The text of the prophecy has suffered in the course of transmission, although the corruptions are not major and may possibly indicate the interpolating activity of a scribe or scribes. Wellhausen suggested that in Zechariah 6:11 the name of Joshua was substituted for that of Zerubbabel by a later editor after the messianic predictions concerning the latter failed to materialize, but there is no proof of this contention.[24] Interpolations of a minor nature can probably be seen in the Hebrew of Zechariah 2:2; 7:1; and 8:13, while in 11:6 and 14:2 there may perhaps be textual glosses. There are numerous places where the LXX points to a better form

---

[21] G. L. Robinson, *The Prophecies of Zechariah* (1896), pp. 10ff., and *ISBE*, V, pp. 3136ff. A. van Hoonacker, *RB*, XI (1902), pp. 61ff. *YIOT*, pp. 278ff. S. Barabas, *The Zondervan Pictorial Bible Dictionary*, p. 910.

[22] J. Stafford Wright, *NBD*, p. 1356.

[23] *PIOT*, p. 612.

[24] J. Wellhausen, *Israelitische und jüdische Geschichte* (1907), pp. 148ff.

of the text, as in the Hebrew of 2:7, 10; 3:4f.; 8:9; 9:15ff.; 11:7f.; 14:5f. and elsewhere. Despite the importance of the LXX generally, however, it does not have quite the same value for the text of Zechariah as it does for some other Old Testament writings.

Supplementary Literature

Baron, D. *Visions and Prophecies of Zechariah.* 1918.

Ellison, H. L. *Men Spake From God.* 1952.

Rignell, L. G. *Die Nachtgesichte des Sacharja.* 1950.

Unger, M. F. *Zechariah.* 1963.

Wright, C. H. H. *Zechariah and His Prophecies.* 1879.

XII. THE BOOK OF MALACHI

A. The Problem of the Prophet's Identity

Unlike the Hebrew, the LXX took the word "Malachi" not as a proper name but as a common noun, rendering מלאכי as "my messenger," which is in fact the meaning of the Hebrew. Many scholars have been influenced by the LXX to the point of regarding this prophecy as an anonymous composition. Unless this work was one of three independent prophetic oracles which terminated the Twelve Minor Prophets, as some scholars have thought, it might seem better, on the analogy of the other prophetic writings, to regard the term as a proper name, since the compositions of the literary prophets are not anonymous works. That there was some question as to the whole matter, however, seems evident from the targum of Jonathan ben Uzziel, which added to Malachi 1:1 the explanatory phrase, "whose name is called Ezra the Scribe." Although this tradition was accepted by Jerome, it is actually no more valuable than similar ones associated with Nehemiah and Zerubbabel. While the historical period and the general interest of the composition might suggest any one of these individuals as the author, there appears to be some legitimacy for the view that regards the work as an anonymous composition. For convenience, however, the author is generally referred to as Malachi by scholars, and will be so regarded in the present work.

B. The Oracles of Malachi

The prophecy consists of six sections or oracles that can be distinguished quite clearly. After the superscription (Mal. 1:1) the first oracle (1:2-5) reaffirmed the proclamation of divine love for Israel as stated, for example, by Hosea. This was demonstrated by the fact that Edom was devastated because of her wickedness, while by contrast Israel would soon learn that God would be magnified in her. Whereas Edom would never recover her ancestral home, the elect nation would inhabit Mount Zion in glory.

The second oracle (1:6—2:9) denounced in dialogue form the priestly class for its failure to supply the requisite moral and spiritual leadership in the community. Against each accusation of God a challenge was

958

raised, the upshot of which was to demonstrate priestly indifference to the divine requirements. Contrary to the stipulations of the Torah (Lev. 22:20ff.; Deut. 15:21; 17:1), which laid down that nothing less than the best was to be offered in sacrifice to God, the priests in the period of Malachi had been sacrificing animals of inferior quality. Such laxity was even reproached by the witness of the Gentiles, who offered to God far purer and more reverential service than the Levitical priesthood. If repentance was not forthcoming, a curse would fall upon the priests. In Malachi 2:5-7, the responsibilities of the latter were made quite clear, implying a considerable degree of contrast between the ideal and that which actually obtained during the time of Malachi.

The third oracle (2:10-16) was concerned with the question of mixed marriages and divorce. Disregarding their common father and their own sense of brotherhood within the provisions of the Covenant, the Jews had gone outside the family of Israel for purposes of marriage and had found themselves pagan wives who in turn brought with them religious beliefs and traditions that were alien to the Torah. Both mixed marriages and divorce were abhorrent to God, who made it clear that the resultant sufferings were the sole responsibility of the participants.

The fourth oracle (2:17–3:5) prophesied the coming of God in judgment. Having grown weary of individuals' rationalizing their sinful ways, or else complaining that there is no justice in life, God would shortly manifest Himself in judgment upon the nation. While both priests and people would feel the weight of divine chastisement, the faithful remnant would not be consumed completely. As the result of this refining work the offering of Judah and Jerusalem would once again become pleasing to God.

The fifth oracle (3:6-12) traced the current social and economic distress to an attitude of indifference towards the payment of tithes. It made clear to the people the fact that a change of divine favor was the result of failure on their part to keep the Law. Once the obligations imposed by the Torah were fulfilled, the displeasure of God would be removed and would be replaced by blessing.

The sixth oracle (3:13–4:3; 3:13-21 Heb.) turned once more to the problem of the moral ordering of life. The pious doubters had raised a question as to what benefit was ultimately to be derived as the result of complete obedience to God, prompted by the observation that the arrogant and ostentatious unbeliever seemed both to prosper and to avoid punishment for his misdeeds. To this the prophet replied that in the great assessment of human values, the good works of the faithful would be remembered while the wicked would be destroyed for their sin.

A brief conclusion (4:4-6; 3:22-24 Heb.), which may be an integral part of the sixth oracle, warned the nation to be obedient to the Law of

Moses, and promised that a messenger, under the figure of Elijah, would herald the dread Day of the LORD.

C. THE DATE OF THE PROPHECY

Taken superficially, the book of Malachi is most closely related to the concluding chapters of Zechariah (9–14), and notice has already been taken of the view that it could have comprised the third part of a collection of anonymous prophecies (Zech. 9–11; 12–14; Mal. 1–3) added to the Twelve Minor Prophets so as to complete their number. According to some scholars two of the above sections had been added to the work of the sixth-century prophet Zechariah, and the third section had been given a separate existence under the name "Malachi."

This view gained currency partly because each of the three sections carried as a superscription the word משׁא or "oracle" (Zech. 9:1; 12:1; Mal. 1:1). The isolation of the material under the designation of "Malachi" has been held to constitute an editorial device designed to secure the historically significant number of twelve for the total of the Minor Prophets. Such a theory, however, breaks down when it is realized that, whether Malachi is anonymous or not, the basic justification for its existence as an independent composition lies in the complete difference that it exhibits respecting both historical background and theological content from the material in Zechariah 9–14. The only real resemblance between the latter and Malachi lies in the apparently anonymous nature of the oracles, and as far as Zechariah is concerned it still remains to be demonstrated conclusively that chapters 9–14 are not the work of the sixth-century prophet. By contrast Malachi bears all the marks of a single author, and reflects an accredited historical background to the point where it can be dated with considerable assurance. The series of questions and answers in the book have quite clearly been arranged in such a manner as to convey a total message concerning divine judgment and blessing, although the identity of the individual who formulated them in this manner, whether the original author or a subsequent editor or editors, is completely unknown.

Despite this total lack of information concerning the author of the composition, there is sufficient internal evidence relating to the period of his prophetic activity to enable a reasonably accurate date to be given to the work itself. From Malachi 1:7-10 and 3:8 it appears that sacrifices were being offered in the Temple, implying that this structure had been standing for some time. That the building involved was the Second Temple is indicated in Malachi 1:8 by the reference to the *peḥāh* or Persian Governor (cf. Neh. 5:14; Hag. 1:1), thus pointing to the post-exilic period. The prophecy shows that cultic rituals had been flourishing for some time, even to the point where the priests had grown weary of them (Mal. 1:13). Malachi inveighed against mixed marriages (Mal. 2: 10-16), but lack of appeal or reference to any specific legislation against

960

them would seem to indicate a date prior to the religious reforms of Nehemiah in 444 B.C. (Neh. 13:23ff.). Furthermore, the prophecy as a whole described abuses that Nehemiah sought to correct, and this would point to a date for the composition about 450 B.C., with which the majority of scholars are in general agreement.

The only serious challenge to the integrity of the work has been entertained in relation to the concluding words of the prophecy (Mal. 4:4-6; 3:22-24 Heb.). The reference to Elijah has been taken by many commentators as a later addition by the editor of the Minor Prophets, who apparently believed that prophecy had come to an end and was urging his readers to observe the Torah as a preliminary to the coming of the divine herald. Although this theory may have certain points in its favor, it cannot be demonstrated objectively.

Despite the fact that Malachi evidently lived in a day when classical prophetism was at a discount, he himself shared the insights that were the property of more notable individuals such as Amos, Hosea, Isaiah, and Jeremiah. Although he did not attain to the rhetorical and poetic eminences of his spiritual ancestors, his work bears the stamp of an original personality, as exhibited by the unusual literary form in which his book is cast. While he was careful, like Ezekiel, to emphasize the importance of proper ritual performance in the divine service and to cherish the ideal of a pure and holy nation, he was not slow to recognize the fundamental necessity of holiness and righteousness as ingredients of the national and individual life. The initial step to be taken in formulating a right relationship with God was moral rather than ceremonial, consisting of confession and true repentance. Honesty, mercy, and justice had to constitute the hallmarks of a life consecrated to God, and the sinner could rest assured that his iniquities would ultimately receive their deserved punishment.

His eschatology drew heavily upon that of prophets such as Amos and Zephaniah (cf. Am. 5:8ff.; Zeph. 1:7ff.), but he introduced the new concept of a book of remembrance in which the names of the righteous were recorded, which is of considerable significance for the later development of belief in a future life. Of equal importance was the idea of the forerunner who would prepare the way for a specific divine appearance among men. Jesus Christ interpreted this statement in terms of the work of John the Baptist (Mk. 9:11ff.), while the primitive Church was convinced that this oracle was fulfilled by the work of the Baptist in relationship to the messianic kingdom inaugurated by Jesus Christ (Mk. 1:2; Lk. 1:17).

❖ ❖ ❖ ❖ ❖

The Hebrew text of the book of Malachi has been transmitted in good condition, with only a few minor corruptions being at all noticeable. The

LXX is frequently helpful in attempts to restore the text, and contains an occasional extra word which may have fallen out of the original Hebrew, as in Malachi 1:6; 2:2f.; and 3:5. One notable LXX omission is the Hebrew of Malachi 3:21, although not all the LXX manuscripts omitted it.

Supplementary Literature

Von Bulmerincq, A. *Einleitung in das Buch des Propheten Maleachi* (2 vols.). 1926-1932.

Part Twelve

THE SACRED WRITINGS (I)
THE BOOK OF TRUTH

The third division of the Hebrew canon of Scripture—the Sacred Writings or Hagiographa—contains writings of quite a diverse character. While many critics have raised questions concerning the inclusion in the Hagiographa of such compositions as the Song of Solomon, it seems fairly certain that incorporation into this section of the canon was an indication of the fact that the books concerned reflected a tradition of "holy writ," whether as native compositions or because of their dependence upon earlier authentic religious or historical sources.

I. HEBREW POETRY

Of these Sacred Writings, the books of Psalms, Proverbs, and Job were regarded by the Jews as specifically poetical in nature, and were described by a mnemonic title, "The Book of Truth."[1] Although there are elements of epic, dramatic, and lyrical poetry in these three compositions, they are outstanding for the vitality and beauty of their didactic passages, in which profound spiritual truths are enshrined for the edification of humanity. This constitutes a decided development in thought from that which obtained in connection with some of the very early fragments of Hebrew poetry such as occurred in the Pentateuch (e.g. Exod. 15:20; Num. 10:35), where the mighty acts of God were commemorated, or in the earlier historical writings (Num. 21:14; Josh. 10:13; 2 Sam. 1:17ff.), which contained references to two books or anthologies compiled from material which may have been in written—and certainly oral—form by the time of Joshua. The *Book of the Wars of the Lord* in particular narrated the victories of the God of Israel over His enemies and His deliverance of the Covenant People, while the *Book of Jashar*, including as it did the charge of Joshua to the sun and moon (Josh. 10:13), again testified to the fact of divine intervention on behalf of Israel.

As in other areas of Old Testament study it is true that, in the matter of Hebrew poetic compositions, there are fundamental differences between what the orientals understood by poetry and that which is commonly denoted by the use of the term in the western world. In the first instance there is nothing that can be recognized as rhyme in Hebrew poetic compositions. The nearest approach to rhyme occurs when the same pronoun suffix appears at the end of two or more *stichoi* (Isa. 41:11f.), but it is difficult to believe that this is anything more than purely accidental. Second, while it is possible to speak about meter in Hebrew poetry, it is more accurate to think in terms of periodic accentuation and the balance of component clauses. Third, the forms in which the Hebrew poems were transmitted are radically different from their

---

[1] The word "truth" (אמת) was composed of the initial letters of each book— א (איוב, Job), מ (משלי, Proverbs), and ת (תהלים, Praises or Psalms).

965

counterparts in occidental writings. Whereas in western poetry, which in general has followed the patterns that were established by the Classical authors, the units of speech were based upon sounds, in Hebrew, as in some other oriental poetry, the units were formulated in terms of concepts or ideas.[2]

Hebrew has been regarded as by far the most suitable of all human languages for the expression of noble poetic sentiments, due in part to the manner in which words were accented.[3] Since accentuation is found in both prose and poetry, there must clearly be some attestable means of distinguishing between the two forms of literary expression. Probably the first definite hint of such a difference was furnished in connection with poetic structure, and occurred in the writings of Josephus,[4] who stated explicitly that Hebrew poetry consisted of trimeters, pentameters, and hexameters. With this general opinion Philo concurred,[5] while among ancient patristic writers Josephus was followed by Origen,[6] Eusebius,[7] and Jerome.[8] According to Ley, Origen distinguished between Greek and Hebrew methods of writing pentameter and hexameter poetry.[9]

A. PARALLELISM

Seventeenth- and eighteenth-century Christian scholars generally attempted to measure Hebrew syllabic forms in terms of Classical poetry,[10] an approach that was repudiated by the pioneer work of Bishop Robert Lowth in 1753. He subjected to critical scrutiny a phenomenon that had long been observed, namely the parallelism in Hebrew poetry. In his treatise on the subject, *De Sacra Poesi Hebraeorum*, he maintained that Hebrew poetry consisted of measured lines, and that the individual verses contained two or more components, the thought of which exhibited an internal parallel relationship (*parallelismus membrorum*). Lowth distinguished between three varieties of parallelism as follows:

> (a) *Synonymous,* in which the second line of a poetic verse repeated the thought expressed in the first line (e.g. Ps. 83:14; Isa. 1:3).
>
> (b) *Antithetic,* in which two portions or *stichoi* of the verse were involved in contrast (e.g. Prov. 1:29); the same idea was sometimes expressed positively first, then negatively (Ps. 90:6).
>
> (c) *Synthetic,* in which the sense carried on continuously (e.g. Ps. 1:1f., 2:3). This form is hardly parallelism in the strictest sense, as subsequent critics came to recognize.

[2] T. H. Robinson, *The Poetry of the OT* (1947), p. 20.
[3] *IBOT*, p. 139.
[4] *AJ*, II, 16, 4; IV, 8, 44; VII, 12, 30.
[5] *Vita Mosis*, I, 5.
[6] On Ps. 118.
[7] *Praep. Evang.* XI, 5.
[8] Preface to the book of Job.
[9] J. Ley, ZAW, XII (1892), p. 212.
[10] E.g. F. Gomarus, *Davidis Lyra* (1637); F. Hare, *Psalmorum libri in versiculos metrice divisus* (1736).

Starting from this discovery other later writers began to apply the rhythmic or metrical principles of different varieties of Semitic poetry to Hebrew, but this procedure involved a consideration of syllabics rather than accentuation.[11] Some scholars, following Anton, Meier, and Ley, made the accent the determining principle of poetic measurement in Hebrew,[12] and this approach gained increasing approval among English-speaking scholars,[13] although there were some who disapproved of the textual emendations in which most German scholars indulged.[14]

The strophic arrangement of Hebrew poetry was emphasized by Köster, who built upon the foundations established by Lowth to distinguish different varieties of strophes.[15] Although a number of commentaries were published in which the poetical material of the Hagiographa was dealt with in various ways, the gains were comparatively modest.[16] Briggs cited three additional varieties of parallelism that scholars had come to recognize as a result of studying Hebrew poetry:[17]

(a) *Emblematic*, in which one *stichos* represented a literal statement while the other suggested a metaphor (Ps. 42:1).

(b) *Stairlike*, where only a part of the first *stichos* was repeated, and made the point of departure for a new development (Ps. 29:1f.).

(c) *Introverted*, involving four *stichoi* so arranged that the first corresponded to the fourth and the second to the third (Ps. 30:8ff.).

The first significant advance upon the work of Lowth was made by Gray, who distinguished two broad categories of parallelism, as follows:[18]

---

[11] Cf. W. Jones, *Poeseos Asiaticae commentariorum* (1776); H. G. Bickell, *Metrices Biblicae* (1879); G. Gietmann, *De Re Metrica Hebraeorum* (1880).

[12] C. G. Anton, *Conjectura de metro Hebraeorum* (1770). E. Meier, *Die Form der Hebräischen Poesie* (1853). J. Ley, *Die Metrischen Formen der Hebräischen Poesie* (1866).

[13] Cf. C. A. Briggs, *Homiletic Quarterly* (1881), pp. 398ff., 555f., *General Introduction to the Study of Holy Scripture* (1899), pp. 370ff.; T. K. Cheyne, *The Book of Psalms* (1888); C. H. Toy, *A Critical and Exegetical Commentary on the Book of Proverbs* (1899); W. R. Harper, *A Critical and Exegetical Commentary on the Books of Amos and Hosea* (1905).

[14] E.g. *DILOT*, p. 362n.

[15] F. B. Köster, *Theologische Studien und Kritiken*, IV (1831), pp. 40ff., *Die Psalmen nach ihrer strophischen Anordnung* (1837).

[16] E.g. J. Olshausen in *Kurzgefasstes Exegetisches Handbuch zum AT* (1853); H. Hupfeld, *Die Psalmen* (1855-62); F. Hitzig, *Die Psalmen* (1863); J. J. S. Perowne, *The Book of Psalms* (1864-68); T. K. Cheyne, *Aids to the Devout Study of Criticism* (1892); B. Duhm in K. Marti (ed.), *Kurzer Hand-Commentar zum AT* (1899).

[17] C. A. Briggs, *A Critical and Exegetical Commentary on the Book of Psalms*, I, pp. xxxvi ff. Cf. T. Witton Davies, *ISBE*, IV, p. 2411; W. O. E. Oesterley, *The Psalms* (1939), I, p. 21.

[18] G. B. Gray, *The Forms of Hebrew Poetry* (1915).

(a) *Complete,* in which every word in one *stichos* was balanced by a corresponding word in the other *stichos* (Isa. 1:3; Ps. 83:14).

(b) *Incomplete,* which had two subsidiary forms, (i) in which a part of the second *stichos* was parallel to the first (Ps. 59:16), and (ii) in which a term was inserted that had no counterpart in the first *stichos* (Pss. 23:4, 75:6).

Subsequent examinations of the forms of Hebrew poetry have, in the main, followed Gray, who was the first to suggest that the term *synthetic parallelism* could more properly be replaced by *formal parallelism.* Other descriptions coined by scholars to designate Hebrew poetic forms have included *external parallelism,*[19] involving two or more entire consecutive lines, either repeating the general sense without too specific a correspondence of words (Ps. 27:1) or involving an internal parallelism (Ps. 59:1f.).

The fact that the phenomenon of parallelism is so consistent an element in Hebrew poetry will be sufficient to indicate the importance to the ancient Semites of the balance of thought or logical rhythms as distinct from the concept of meter in many modern languages, which involves a balance of sound or phonic rhythm. Every other stylistic or rhetorical feature of Hebrew poetry, such as acrostic forms (Pss. 9, 34, 37, 119; Prov. 31:10ff.; Lam. 1–4), assonance (Gen. 49:17; Exod. 14:14; Ezek. 27:27), and alliteration (Pss. 6:8; 27:7; 122:6; Isa. 1:18ff.), must now be regarded as being consistently subordinate to the parallel expression of thought-forms.[20] Such a reiterative structure is a remarkable adjunct to didactic poetry, for it enables the mind to absorb the content of the composition through insistent emphasis upon the basic concepts enshrined in the work. At the same time the repetition is so amenable to skillful literary variation that the underlying theme never becomes commonplace or boring.

B. METRICAL DIVISION

Regarding metrical division, it should be remarked immediately that there is no tradition of meter in the classical Hebrew compositions, and even the Talmud had nothing to say about this particular topic. While Josephus applied the occidental concepts of Classical poetic meter to the writings of the Hebrew in stating that the songs of Moses (Exod. 15:1ff.; Deut. 32:1ff.) were written in hexameters, he did this only to show his Gentile readers that a specific poetic form underlay certain portions of the Hebrew Scriptures.[21] However, Classical analogies are unfortunately misleading here, since any discernible meter in Hebrew poetry can only be determined by relationship to the forms of other ancient poetry in

[19] *IBOT,* pp. 141f.
[20] Cf. E. König, *Stilistik, Rhetorik, Poetik* (1900); J. Muilenburg, *VT,* suppl. vol. I (1953), pp. 97ff. On alliteration see O. S. Rankin, *JTS,* XXXI (1930), pp. 28ff.
[21] *AJ,* II, 16, 4; IV, 8, 44.

which the essential basis of the structure was a balance of thought, and by implication from the parallel lines themselves.[22]

Several grounds may be adduced for the contention that some of the Hebrew poetic compositions exhibited concepts of meter. In the first place, several of the psalms were apparently meant to be sung to the accompaniment of a variety of musical instruments. Furthermore, the fact that the poetry of the ancient Near East and of Egypt pointed to the presence of meter might also support this idea. On the basis of a comparative study of the Syriac language, Bickell repudiated the idea that Classical Greek and Latin concepts of poetry could be related to an oriental language, and sought to transpose the poems of the Old Testament into metrical forms similar to those employed by Ephraem and other Syrian poets.[23] These writers commonly composed verses that consisted of feet of two syllables, one long and one short, occurring in alternation. In effect this was the Classical trochee (- ◡) or iambus (◡ -). Unfortunately the transcriptions of Bickell involved considerable textual emendation, which some other scholars opposed on principle.[24]

Much closer to the basic principles underlying Hebrew poetry were the studies of Ley, who emphasized that the character of the particular verse could only be determined by reference to the number of accented or stressed syllables.[25] The minimal metric unit was the foot, following Classical and other usage, which was frequently found in the form of an anapest (◡ ◡ -). But Ley also noticed that a verse quite often consisted of a three-stress *stichos*[26] separated by a caesura from a parallel two-stress *stichos*, and this 3:2 characteristic he regarded as an elegiac pentameter. Budde gave careful consideration to this phenomenon, and noticed that it also occurred in Lamentations.[27] In consequence he gave it the name of *Qinah* or "dirge-meter," although the structure occurred in other types of poetry as well.

Further investigations in the general field were undertaken by Sievers, who built upon the tonic principle established by Ley, but felt that the unaccented syllables were also important.[28] As a result he postulated the theory that one accented syllable was actually the equal of two unaccented ones, and that therefore each foot should include unaccented as

---

[22] Cf. N. K. Gottwald, *IDB*, III, p. 834.

[23] G. Bickell, *Metrices Biblicae* (1879); he was followed in many of his conclusions by G. Hölscher, *BZAW*, XXXIV (1920), pp. 93ff.

[24] Cf. W. H. Cobb, *A Criticism of Systems of Hebrew Metre* (1905).

[25] J. Ley, *Die Metrischen Formen der Hebräischen Poesie* (1866), *Grundzüge es Rhythmus des Vers- und Strophenbaues in der Hebräischen Poesie* (1875), *Leitfaden der Hebräischen Metrik* (1887).

[26] In the present work this term (στίχος) denotes each of the two parts that normally constitute a line of Hebrew poetry. For comments on nomenclature see N. K. Gottwald, *IDB*, III, p. 831.

[27] K. Budde, *ZAW*, II (1882), pp. 1ff., *HDB*, IV, pp. 3ff.

[28] E. Sievers, *Metrisch Studien I-III* (1901-1907).

well as accented syllables, thus comprising four *ictus* or stresses. Although this concept ultimately proved to be incorrect, his view that the *stichoi* might consist of *ictus* combinations such as 2:2, 3:3, 4:4, 4:3 or 3:4, 3:2 or 2:3, was actually quite close to the facts of the matter.

The recognition of stress-patterns in Hebrew poetry is thus based upon the assumption that it is legitimate to accord an *ictus* to each of the major words in a distich or a tristich. This principle may be established on the analogy of Near Eastern Semitic compositions, particularly when a comparison is made between the Babylonian penitential psalms and the laments of the Hebrews on the one hand,[29] and between Hebrew and Ugaritic poetic compositions on the other.[30]

It should be emphasized, however, that whatever metrical schemes could be discovered were essentially fluid. Consequently, while in Babylonian poetry the commonest line comprised two parallel *stichoi* containing two stresses each (2:2), it frequently happened that in one or other of the *stichoi* a third stress was inserted (2:3 or 3:2). On such a basis the comparative simplicity of the Hebrew diction might suggest a 2:2 line as the primary form, and although this structure occurs quite frequently in Hebrew poems, 3:2 "pentameter" is far more common. By far the most widely used scheme in Hebrew poetry, however, is the 3:3, occurring in the poetic sections of Job, in many prophetic oracles, in Proverbs, and in the bulk of the psalms. While Babylonian poetry often has a predominantly 2:2 meter, individual compositions are generally interspersed with lines that can only be read in terms of a sevenfold *ictus*, making for a 2:2:3 combination. A six-stress line often seems to require a scanning in terms of 2:2:2.

The Ugaritic poetic compositions reveal a popular 3:3 pattern,[31] but this was by no means the only one to be employed, and of the many variations from this pattern the most noticeable is the tristich arrangement of 3:3:3 or 2:2:2. From this it would seem quite probable that the Hebrew poets occasionally made an entirely deliberate use of a tristich form in their compositions (e.g. Ps. 77:16-19). Yet the very fact that these Canaanite discoveries from the Amarna period exhibit such metrical inexactitude ought in itself to constitute sufficient warning against attempts to demonstrate meter as such in Hebrew poetry.[32] While it is

[29] Cf. G. Widengren, *The Accadian and Hebrew Psalms of Lamentation as Religious Documents* (1937); W. O. E. Oesterley, *The Psalms*, I, pp. 37ff.

[30] Cf. J. H. Patton, *Canaanite Parallels in the Book of Psalms* (1944); *ARI*, pp. 128f.; F. M. Cross, *BASOR*, No. 117 (1950), pp. 19ff.

[31] C. H. Gordon, *Ugaritic Handbook* (1947), pp. 102ff. Cf. R. Dussaud, *Les Découvertes de Ras Shamra et l'Ancien Testament* (1937), pp. 66f.; C. F. A. Schaeffer, *The Cuneiform Texts of Ras Shamra-Ugarit* (1939), p. 58.

[32] Cf. G. D. Young, *JNES*, IX (1950), pp. 124ff.

true that the 3:2 scheme was widely favored by the psalmists and others, it is equally noticeable that the authors seldom adhered to one particular meter, and that on occasions they may even have mixed them, whether by design or by sheer accident. On this basis there is obviously no warrant for resorting to processes of textual emendation in order to force the Hebrew to conform to a particular metrical scheme. Even in the light of present knowledge it is still far from certain that there are anything approaching definite metrical systems in Hebrew poetry. If such do actually exist in the Old Testament, it is because they constitute the rhythmical counterparts of parallel thought-forms, with the former invariably being subordinated to the latter.

It must always be borne in mind that there is no intrinsic evidence for meter in the Hebrew of the Old Testament, a fact that was conceded by scholars of the caliber of Duhm,[33] and it can only be postulated inferentially on the basis of literary and conceptual parallelisms and by reference to the Massoretic system of accentuation. This system was formulated upon the principle that each word received only one *ictus*, regardless of length, except for words connected by a *maqqeph*, the Hebrew hyphen, in which case only the final word of the group was accentuated. Thus, in a line of poetry, the separate ideas are summed up by an accented word or group of words. If there are two important items of thought in one *stichos*, balanced by two others in the corresponding *stichos*, the particular line can be recognized as falling within a 2:2 scheme, and can be classified accordingly. However important or significant the word, it is rare for it to carry more than one *ictus*, and this circumstance is never the case in a simple two-stress *stichos*, for fairly obvious reasons.

Although there is a certain degree of subjectivity attached to this method of metrical determination, it is possible to recognize certain basic patterns in Old Testament poetry as a result of employing it. A development of the 2:2 pattern appears in those instances where an extra *ictus* is added to one or other of the *stichoi* to make 3:2 and 2:3 respectively, or where both *stichoi* exhibit such an addition, as in 3:3. This latter, as has been remarked above, is by far the commonest stress-pattern in Hebrew poetry. It is unusual for 2:2 or 3:2 to occur alone in a poetic composition, although the 3:2 pattern is particularly noticeable in the first four chapters of Lamentations. The designation *Qinah*, which Budde applied, is not entirely satisfactory, since there appear to be various kinds of 3:2 rhythms. While it may be asserted that the 3:2 balance (or more rarely, 2:3) is admirably suited to an emotional expression, it should be noted that such an emotion can just as readily constitute joy and gladness as

---

[33] B. Duhm, *EB*, IV, cols. 3194f.; cf. R. C. Culley in J. W. Wevers and D. B. Redford (eds.), *Essays on the Ancient Semitic World* (1970), pp. 12ff.

lamentation, a fact illustrated by some of the compositions in which the *Qinah* pattern is the dominant form (e.g. Ps. 65).[34]

Again it should be emphasized that there has never been any rigid metrical scheme in existence to which ancient Hebrew poetry was required to conform. Thus many Old Testament poetic compositions contain lines of mixed metric length, and of such an uncertain nature that it is virtually impossible to assign them with any certainty to a basic pattern. There are occasions on which the scholar can arrive at a reasonably regular text in terms of stress-rhythms by resorting to the readings of the LXX or other ancient versions, but a good deal of caution needs to be exercised generally with regard to considerations of textual emendation, as the discoveries at Ras Shamra have clearly shown. In some cases there may be hints as to the presence of textual disorder, but on examination it will become apparent that the situation is incapable of resolution. On other occasions the scholar has no choice but to accept the hybrid rhythms when they occur as constituting part of the normal Hebrew poetic tradition.

Insofar as it is possible to speak of meter in connection with Hebrew poetry, the parallel thought-forms would seem to reflect three basic tendencies in the balancing of parts, in which precise accentual values may never even have been measured in antiquity. These are:

(a) *Qinah* or dirge-meter—3:2 (Ps. 27:1), or sometimes 2:3 (Pss. 42:4; 79:13), varied by 2:2 (Ps. 23:4ff.).

(b) *Hexameter*—3:3 (Jer. 12:2), 2:2:2 (Ps. 59:6), 3:3:3 (Ps. 77:16ff.).

(c) *Heptameter*—4:3 or 2:2:3 (Jer. 4:23ff.).

C. STROPHIC ARRANGEMENT

Within the last century a good deal of discussion has centered upon the question as to whether the lines of Hebrew poetry could be grouped in order to form stanzas or strophes. In general it can be said that the majority of the older critics held to the view that the psalms were arranged in regular strophic organization, the nature of which had been obscured to some extent by later liturgical glosses. More recent studies have shown that while such an arrangement is possible, as indicated by the presence of acrostic poetry in the Old Testament, the grouping of distichs or tristichs into larger formal units cannot be demonstrated.[35]

---

[34] Mowinckel, following Hölscher, maintained that the *qinah* should be construed in terms of 4:4 meter. Cf. S. Mowinckel, *Festschrift Alfred Bertholet* (1950), pp 379ff., *VT*, V (1955), pp. 13ff. In *The Psalms in Israel's Worship* (1962), II, p 165, he described it as *asymmetrical mashal* (4:3) or *shortened (brachycatalectic) mashal bicolon*.

[35] For discussions of the strophe see F. Perles, *Zur althebräischen Strophik* (1898); C. A. Briggs, *A Critical and Exegetical Commentary on the Book of Psalms*, I, pp xlv ff.; F. Brown, *JBL*, IX (1890), pp. 71ff.; K. Fullerton, *JBL*, XLVIII (1929) pp. 274ff.; H. Möller, *ZAW*, L (1932), pp. 240ff.; A. Condamin, *Poémes de le*

The fact that strophic arrangement in Hebrew poetry was never allowed to interfere with the real sequence of thought would imply that the stanza was never basic to the structure of such compositions. This is in contradistinction to modern poetic usage, in which the stanza comprises a group consisting of a specific number of lines marked by a particular rhyming pattern. Even where there might appear to be some kind of strophic division in Hebrew poetry, it seems clear that the stanzas followed the logical divisions associated with the thought-forms rather than the rhyming-patterns of modern poetic usage. There would thus seem to be no evidence for the kind of rigid, metrically constructed strophes entertained by earlier Old Testament scholars.

If, however, a strophe can be defined in a more fluid fashion as an informal arrangement of lines characterized by certain external indications, it may perhaps be possible to speak of strophes. Thus, the close of a stanza may be indicated by the presence of a recurring refrain (cf. Pss. 42:5-11; 43:5; 46:7-11), and, as Köster pointed out, by the inclusion of *selah* at the end of a line. There has been some doubt expressed as to the validity of *selah* as a criterion for strophic delineation, since the meaning of the term itself is obscure. Generally the word stands outside the balanced arrangement of the thought-form, and its association with many psalms headed by a supposed musical title has led some scholars to the conclusion that it called for the raising of the voice in praise.[36]

The LXX appears to have had some sort of liturgical usage in view when the term was rendered by *diapsalma*, with the implication being that stringed instruments were used to accompany the rendering of the psalm concerned. The Hebrew verb could thus mean either the "lifting up" of voices in music or religious recitation, or the cessation of the voices and the crescendo of musical instruments. That the latter seems more probable is indicated by the fact that *selah* normally occurred at the end of a division of thought, where the voice would presumably pause in any event.[37] In the absence of the foregoing, the only other reasonable indication of some form of strophic arrangement may be seen in the symmetrical organization of the thought-forms. Thus the Song of the Vineyard in Isaiah 5:1-8 can be subdivided into four sections of two verses each, comprising four distichs each, except for the third, which contains four distichs and one tristich.

Bible avec une introduction sur la strophique hébraïque (1933); C. F. Kraft, *The Strophic Structure of Hebrew Poetry* (1938), and in E. C. Hobbs (ed.), *A Stubborn Faith* (1956), pp. 62ff.; S. Mowinckel, *The Psalms in Israel's Worship*, II, pp. 170ff.

[36] So C. A. Briggs, *A Critical and Exegetical Commentary on the Book of Psalms*, I, p. lxxv.

[37] *IBOT*, p. 185.

Before the discovery of the Ugaritic material it was frequently assumed by scholars that the regular strophic order that they had postulated had been disturbed by glosses or dislocations of the text. This furnished a warrant for wholesale rearrangement of lines, textual emendations, and the like, sometimes being undertaken with reference to the LXX and later versions, but on other occasions being indulged in on a basis of purely subjective speculation. Aside from any other considerations that might preclude such activity, it should now be fairly apparent to all scholars as a result of the discoveries at Ras Shamra that the text of the Hebrew Psalter is by no means as faulty or corrupt as was supposed by a great many nineteenth-century critics. Furthermore, the wide degree of freedom that the literary compositions of Ugarit enjoyed with respect to form and fluidity of meter indicates that considerations of meter *per se* are not by any means adequate as criteria for textual criticism, and that in fact wholesale reorganization of the text of the kind indulged in by Duhm and others is specifically contraindicated by the epic texts from Ras Shamra.

As a concluding comment on the matter of strophic arrangement, some mention should be made of a device known to scholars as *anacrusis*. This consists generally of a single word such as an exclamation or an interrogative particle that stands outside the normal rhythmical pattern of the verse to which it is prefixed. Thus, in Lamentations 1:1, the word "how," employed as an exclamation, can be isolated from the text without disturbing the 3:2, 2:2, 2:2 rhythmic pattern of the verse. Again, in Jeremiah 12:1b-2, the word "wherefore" can be separated in an analogous manner, leaving the passage to conform to the 3:3 pattern, which is by far the most frequently found in Hebrew poetry. The early poetic forms of the Hebrews appear mostly to have reflected the activities of the nation as a whole, whether in the Song of Miriam, in the shouts uttered in connection with the movement of the Ark (Num. 10:35f.), or in such dynamic compositions as the Ode of Deborah and Barak (Judg. 5:1ff.). However, there were other poetic sections in which the main theme was more personal, including the patriarchal benedictions of the Pentateuch (Gen. 27:27ff.; 49:1ff.), which followed second-millennium B.C. Mesopotamian practices; the priestly blessings of the early historical period (Gen. 14:19f.; 48:15f.; Num. 6:24ff.), and such individualistic compositions as the lament of David over Saul and Jonathan (2 Sam. 1:19ff.). Whatever the specific genre of the early poetic sections, however, they were ultimately capable of a religious interpretation, and involved the deity in a more or less direct fashion, a feature that was also characteristic of Mesopotamian epic and other poetic compositions.

Quite aside from the use of poetry in prophetic denunciations, oracles, songs, and the like, there was a specific variety that seemed peculiarly appropriate for the worship of the deity, whether in private meditation or in public celebration. Such poems may have originated from some profound spiritual experience in individual life, or they may have constituted a recital of one or more "saving acts" of God. Despite an obviously wide range in nature and provenance, these compositions appear to have commended themselves over several centuries of Israelite life as particularly suitable vehicles for divine worship, and it may be that some were preserved from a fairly early period in the form of a psalter so that they would be amenable to this lofty purpose.

II. THE BOOK OF PSALMS

A. The Name of the Book

Possibly it was in view of the considerations outlined above that the Psalter used to be styled by critics such as Cornill, Wellhausen, Robertson Smith, and others as the "hymnbook of the Second Temple."[1] While this is no doubt true in certain respects, it should not be understood as implying that all the psalms were composed in the exilic or post-exilic period, or that there was no place for music or psalmody generally in the First Temple. In the light of the ancient traditions associated with Hebrew poetry, there seems little valid reason for denying that the Psalter was representative of a particular literary form that the Hebrews utilized from the period of the Exodus up to the time of the Second Temple and somewhat beyond as a vehicle for devotion. The importance of the Psalter may be inferred from its position at the head of the third division of the Hebrew canon, the Sacred Writings, and the acknowledgment of its pre-eminence by Jesus Christ (cf. Lk. 24:44), following Jewish tradition.

The Hebrew Psalter was by no means an isolated literary phenomenon, since the pagan cultures of the ancient Near East, being themselves polytheistic, were intensely religious and reflected their attitudes in a wide variety of extant literature, which included epic poetry, hymns, penitential psalms, prayers, incantations, thanksgivings, and petitions addressed to the deities.[2] Nevertheless, the Psalms of the Hebrews must be considered *sui generis*, since they constituted the supreme example of religious devotion and served as effective vehicles for the propagation of truths unfolded in the processes of divine revelation.

The Hebrew title of the entire collection was "The Book of Praises" or "Praises" (ספר תהלים or simply תהלים), the former corresponding to the

---

[1] For a criticism of this concept see B. Duhm, *Die Psalmen* (1899), p. xxiv; *PIOT*, pp. 619f.

[2] Cf. *ANET*, pp. 365ff.; H. Zimmern, *Babylonische Hymnen und Gebete* (1905-1911); M. Jastrow, *Die Religion Babyloniens und Assyriens* (1905); A. Erman, *Die Literatur der Ägypter* (1923); H. Gressmann, *Altorientalische Texte zum AT* (1926); J. Jeremias, *Handbuch des altorientalischen Geisteskultur* (1929).

New Testament designation βίβλος ψαλμῶν, "The Book of Psalms" (Lk. 20:42; Acts 1:20). Many Greek manuscripts entitled the literature ψαλμοί, although in Codex Alexandrinus of the LXX it was designated ψαλτήριον, an apparent allusion to a musical instrument used in the accompaniment of singers (Heb. מזמור—"to pluck"). The Vulgate title *Liber Psalmorum* followed the LXX, and from this the English term was derived. The designation "Praises" was felt to be hardly appropriate to the book as a whole, since, although praise is a constant theme in a great many of the compositions, only Psalm 145 has the word תהלה or "praise" in its title.

Whereas the Hebrew designation of the Psalter broadly expresses the contents of the book as praises, the Greek and English ascriptions point to the nature of the work as comprising hymns to be sung to musical accompaniment. That this need not be a uniform connotation, however, is indicated by a note at the end of Psalm 72, which might imply that some if not all of the preceding compositions had been regarded as "prayers" or תפלות. Here again a general title of this sort would have been inappropriate, since only Psalm 17 was designated in this manner by title.

B. THE TITLES OF THE PSALMS

The presence of superscriptions for all except thirty-four psalms (Pss. 1–2, 10, 33, 43, 71, 91, 93–97, 99, 104–107, 111–119, 135–137, and 146–150) poses certain difficulties of historicity and interpretation. Some of the allusions purporting to relate to King David, for example, follow a tradition that is at variance with Samuel. Thus, in Psalm 34, the king before whom David simulated madness was named Abimelech, whereas in 1 Samuel 21:10ff.[3] he was named Achish. Again, the title of Psalm 56 seems to imply that David was captured by the Philistines and brought to Gath, whereas in 1 Samuel 21:10 David is indicated to have fled there on his own initiative.

It seems probable that in at least some instances the titles were the result of editorial activity that may well have been intended to preserve some historical tradition with respect to specific compositions, or to perpetuate a certain familiar usage, whether in connection with the origin, character, music, or liturgical function of the psalm. There appears to be little doubt that the vast majority of the titles were later than the psalms to which they were attached, although this may not be entirely true of certain of the psalms ascribed to David. From the evidence furnished by the LXX version it is apparent that the titles were well-known long before the Christian period, and they should therefore be regarded as preserving certain Jewish traditions about the psalms and probably about the manner in which the Psalter was compiled.[4]

[3] Cf. *YIOT*, pp. 300f.
[4] W. S. McCullough, *IB*, IV, p. 8.

977

The superscriptions of thirteen psalms purport to preserve the historical traditions relating to the life of David, in terms of which the particular psalms were composed:

(a) Ps. 3. Cf. 2 Sam. 15:1–18:33.

(b) Ps. 7. Cush of Benjamin is nowhere mentioned in the Old Testament accounts of the life of David.

(c) Ps. 18. Cf. 1 Sam. 19:1ff., 24:1ff., 26:1ff., 2 Sam. 5:17ff., 8:1ff., 10:1ff., 15:1–18:33, 21:15ff.

(d) Ps. 34. Cf. 1 Sam. 21:10ff., but perhaps this psalm refers to another occasion of simulated madness than that which occurred in the presence of Achish, and which is not recorded in the Old Testament.

(e) Ps. 51. Cf. 2 Sam. 11:1ff.

(f) Ps. 52. Cf. 1 Sam. 22:6ff.

(g) Ps. 54. Cf. 1 Sam. 23:14ff.

(h) Ps. 56. This may preserve a different tradition from that in 1 Sam. 21:10ff.; 22:1; 27:1ff., regarding the reasons why David went to Gath.

(i) Ps. 57. Cf. 1 Sam. 22:1f., 24:1ff.

(j) Ps. 59. Cf. 1 Sam. 19:8ff.

(k) Ps. 60. Cf. 2 Sam. 8:3ff., 10:15ff.

(l) Ps. 63. Cf. 1 Sam. 24:1ff.; 2 Sam. 15:1ff.

(m) Ps. 142. Cf. 1 Sam. 22:1f., 24:1ff.

It may well be that in at least some of the foregoing instances the titles were added by an editor who was aware of the circumstances under which the particular compositions arose, and if so, the title would aid in the understanding of the psalm in question. That some of them may also reflect a genuine historical tradition that is different in important areas from the contents of Samuel is worthy of some consideration, since, for example, Psalm 60 contains details that do not occur in the Samuel narratives.

Of the titles that do not relate specifically to historical occasions, many appear to involve tunes or musical directions. The word "Alamoth" (עֲלָמוֹת) is rare, occurring only in Psalm 46, 1 Chronicles 15:20, and as the final word of Psalm 48.[5] Its association with the Hebrew noun עַלְמָה might indicate that it was meant to designate a tune for female voices. Names of melodies appear to be reflected by several titles: "Do Not Destroy"—AV "Al-taschith" (אַל תַּשְׁחֵת, Pss. 57–59, 75; cf. Isa. 65:8); "The Dove on Far-off Terebinths"—AV "Jonath-elem-rechokim" (יוֹנַת אֵילִים רְחֹקִים,[6] Ps. 56); "The Hind of the Dawn"—AV "Aijeleth Shahar" (הַשַּׁחַר אַיֶּלֶת, Ps. 22); "Lilies"—AV "Shoshannim" (שׁוֹשַׁנִּים, Pss. 45, 69, 80);[7] and "The Lily of the Testimony"—AV "Shushan-eduth" (שׁוּשַׁן עֵדוּת, Ps. 60). Uncertain in this regard are "Gittith" (גִּתִּית, Pss. 8, 81, 84), which may be (following the LXX) a vintage-tune associated with the word גַּת, meaning "Winepress" (cf. Joel 4:13), or may refer to a Philistine (Gath)

---

[5] Cf. R. D. Wilson, PTR, XXIV (1926), pp. 1ff., 353ff.

[6] Reading אֵילִים ("terebinths") for the meaningless אֵלֶם ("silence"?).

[7] The OT: An American Translation (1927) has "hyacinths" in Cant. 2:2, 16.

musical instrument; "Mahalath" (מחלת, Pss. 53, 88), which may have been a tune named after a woman (cf. Gen. 28:9; 2 Chron. 11:18); and "Mahalath Leannoth" (מחלת לענות, Ps. 88), which also may have been dedicated to some female, although לענות may mean "for affliction" or "for singing." An obscure expression "Muth-labben" (מות לבן, "die for the son"?) in the title of Psalm 9 may perhaps be a corruption of עלמות, or alternatively, the name of a tune.

Musical instruments may be referred to under the names Nehiloth (Ps. 5), which occurs only here in the Old Testament and is consequently obscure in meaning, and Sheminith (Pss. 6, 12), but the latter seems to refer to an "octave," and in its only other occurrence (1 Chron. 15:21) it is of doubtful meaning. Stringed instruments as such are mentioned in the titles of Psalms 4, 6, 54, 55, 67, and 76. Four of these also contain the word "mizmor," pointing clearly to instrumental accompaniment of singers.

The term "choirmaster" (Vulgate "*in finem*"; AV "To the chief musician") appears to be reasonably assured in the light of the evidence furnished by 1 Chronicles 15:21,[8] and it may be that the psalms to which this designation was attached had been taken from a collection belonging to an unknown precentor, or perhaps from one dedicated to him. Although there seems to be no idea of propitiation connected with the term, as Mowinckel had suggested, it must be admitted that its meaning is not absolutely certain. Jeduthun, the name of a Levitical choir-leader in the Solomonic period (2 Chron. 5:12; cf. 2 Chron. 35:15 as the name of a seer in Josiah's time), and also the cognomen of a Levite in the time of Nehemiah (Neh. 11:17), appeared in the titles of three psalms (39, 62, 77), and may have had some significance in connection with choral work, but this also is uncertain.

Individuals or guilds of singers appeared under various designations, one of the more common being Asaph (Pss. 50, 78–83). A prominent court-musician in the time of David bore this name (1 Chron. 6:39; 15:17), and it may well be that the "sons of Asaph" in the period of Nehemiah (Neh. 7:44) were members of a musical guild that went back to the days of David and the monarchy.[9] Ugaritic sources have testified amply to the existence of a class of Temple personnel known as *sarim,* who were analogous to the Hebrew singers of the monarchy and later times.[10] As far as the Psalter was concerned, Asaph could refer either to the guild, to some member of it, or to their collection of religious poetry. The mention of Ethan the Ezrahite (Ps. 89; cf. 1 Chron. 6:44; in 1 Kgs.

---

[8] The verb seems to imply the rendering of music, and not "smoothing the countenance of Yahweh," as Mowinckel understands it, *The Psalms in Israel's Worship,* II, p. 212; cf. his *Psalmenstudien IV, Die technischen Termini in den Psalmenüberschriften* (1923), pp. 17ff. למנצח also occurs in Hab. 3:19.

[9] Cf. *ARI,* pp. 125ff.

[10] Cf. C. H. Gordon, *Ugaritic Handbook,* p. 272, No. 1934; cf. No. 1991.

4:31 Ethan is a Hebrew sage) and Heman the Ezrahite (Ps. 88; cf. I Chron. 6:33) enshrined the native Canaanite tradition of music and psalmody, since as Albright has shown,[11] the term *'ezrāh* means "aboriginal." Mention of the sons of Korah (Pss. 42, 44–49, 84–85, 87–88) may imply the existence of another musical guild whose traditional origins probably reached back to Korah, the great-grandson of Levi (Num. 16:1ff.; 1 Chron. 6:31ff.; 2 Chron. 20:19).

Allusions to authorship most frequently embrace the seventy-three compositions attributed to David (the RSV, inadvertently omitting the ascription in Ps. 133, has seventy-two). Solomon was mentioned in two titles (Pss. 72 and 127), and one psalm was attributed to Moses (Ps. 90). Mention of literary types within the psalm titles includes the common description "song" (*shîr*), occurring in some thirty instances, and frequently associated with *mizmor*, which is found in fifty-seven titles. Other varieties included a psalm for the sabbath (Ps. 92), one used at the dedication of the Temple (Ps. 30), a wedding song (Ps. 45), an instructional composition (Ps. 60), a psalm of "testimony" (Ps. 80),[12] a psalm of praise (Ps. 145), two memorial psalms (Pss. 38, 70; cf. Lev. 2:2, 9), five prayers (Pss. 17, 86, 90, 102, 142), and one composition specifically written for a thank offering (Ps. 100; cf. Lev. 7:11ff.).

The title "song of praise" appeared once only (Ps. 145), despite the fact that the plural of that word is the Jewish designation of the Psalter. A group known as the "songs of ascents" presents an interesting problem in interpretation. Comprising some fifteen psalms (Pss. 120–134) this corpus was thought of by older exegetes such as Theodoret and Kimchi as the one used by the exiles on their return from Babylon.[13] From considerations of internal evidence certain of these compositions appear to indicate a settled Palestinian milieu (Pss. 125–9, 131, 133), while others (Pss. 122, 132, 134) point to Jerusalem as the focal point of long-established Israelite worship. The Mishnah (*Midd.* II, 5) ascribed the title to the tradition that the psalms in question were chanted by the Levites on the fifteen steps separating the courts of the men and women in the Second Temple, but such an explanation is highly improbable. Other conjectures as to the meaning of the title were related to an alleged internal climactic parallelism in the compositions themselves. Unfortunately this is pure speculation, since such a structural form does not characterize all the psalms that occur in this group, and in addition it is found in others which are not designated by this particular title. It may be that Psalms 120–134 were used during the post-exilic period by the pilgrims who went up to Jerusalem in order to celebrate the three

---

[11] *ARI*, p. 210 n. 95.

[12] Perhaps owing to textual corruption the title should be "Shushan Eduth," as in Psalm 60.

[13] D. Kimchi (d. 1235), *Commentary on Psalms*. In Ez. 7:9 מעלה means "to go up," and was thought to be related to the title שׁיר המעלות.

annual feasts (cf. Deut. 12:5ff.; Ps. 122:1ff.), but it is impossible to be certain about this.

Of doubtful meaning are the titles *maskîl, mikhtām* and *shiggāyôn*. The first, which occurred in thirteen titles (Pss. 32, 42, 44, 45, 52–55, 74, 78, 88–89, 142), has been interpreted to mean a "didactic" or "meditative" psalm. The root idea of the verb appears to be that of "prudence" or "insight" (cf. Am. 5:13), and since *maskîl* is causative in force it might imply the conveying of insight. In 2 Chronicles 30:22, however, the causative form was employed in connection with the Levites, and as such might apply to their musical talents or their skill as instructors. The general nature of the *maskîl* psalms would seem to point to the former explanation as the more plausible.

The true meaning of *mikhtām* has been a matter of debate for a good many years in scholarly circles. The word occurs in six psalm titles only (Pss. 16, 56–60), and whatever its original meaning it was almost certainly not "golden," as in the AV (derived from כתם, "gold"). Arguing from the Assyrian term *ka-ta-mu*, "to cover," Mowinckel suggested that *mikhtām* pointed to the atoning or expiatory functions or associations of the psalms concerned,[14] but there is no evidence for this speculation.

The final designation in this category, *shiggāyôn*, is found on one occasion only (Ps. 7; cf. Hab. 3:1), and though it may be related to the Akkadian *shegu* or "lamentation psalm" its actual meaning is unknown. It is very doubtful if the term designates any kind of gathering accompanied by ceremonial acts, in which king and people stood together in readiness to meet the heathen and ask for divine judgment upon them, as Mowinckel suggested.[15]

There are thirty-four psalms in the Psalter that bear no title of any kind, a circumstance for which there is no immediate explanation. This—and other considerations, such as ascribing Mosaic, Davidic, or Solomonic authorship to compositions that older critics were accustomed to regard as Maccabean in origin—has led many scholars to depreciate the value of the psalm titles.[16] In the view of the present writer the absence of precise information regarding many of the technical terms employed therein makes them an area for undesirable speculation, and it it not particularly easy to see what value they have other than constituting possible hints of some antiquity as to the manner in which the Psalter was compiled.[17]

---

[14] *Psalmenstudien*, IV, pp. 4f., *The Psalms in Israel's Worship*, II, p. 209. For the suggestion that the title referred to a "psalm for military training," see *GBB*, p. 264 n. 1.

[15] *The Psalms in Israel's Worship*, II, p. 209.

[16] E.g. Gunkel and Begrich, *Einleitung in die Psalmen* (1933), II, pp. 455ff.

[17] The writer has dispensed with them in his translation of the Psalms into current English in O. M. Norlie and R. K. Harrison, *Norlie's Simplified NT with the Psalms for Today* (1961), pp. viii *passim*.

Mowinckel was followed by Leslie in the view that the titles of the psalms could be divided into four categories:[18]

(a) Titles that comprise technical designations of psalms, including *mizmôr, mikhtām, maskîl, t^ephillāh,* and *shîr hamma'^alôth.*
(b) Titles pointing to the purpose of the psalm, such as thanksgiving, *hazkîr, y^edhûthûn,* and *l^{e'}annôth.*
(c) Titles of cultic origin—which for Mowinckel included the bulk of the psalms—such as the "choirmaster" collection, those titles mentioning melodies, and perhaps the obscure *mûth labbēn* (Ps. 9).
(d) Titles containing specific musical references such as *n^eghînôth, selāh, higgāyôn, n^ehîlôth.*

Rabbinic sources ascribed the authorship of the psalms to a number of hands, the classic statement of the position being that of *Baba Bathra:*

David wrote the book of Psalms with the help of ten elders; with the help of Adam, the first, and Melchizedek, and Abraham, and Moses, and Heman, and Jeduthun, and Asaph and the three sons of Korah.[19]

Clearly while this view seeks to assert the antiquity of the book, it must be rejected as unhistorical. On the other hand, there was a uniform Jewish tradition which, in the words of Josephus, held that "David composed songs and hymns to God in varied meters,"[20] and this became part of the heritage of the early Christian era (cf. Acts. 4:25; 13:36; Rom. 4:6ff.; Heb. 4:7).

On archaeological grounds there is no basis for questioning the validity of the tradition that included music and poetry in the activities of David, and this would also seem to underlie certain of the references to the "sweet singer of Israel" (Am. 6:5; Ez. 3:10; Neh. 12:24; 1 Chron. 6:31; 16:7). Whether, however, it is possible to regard all the psalms attributed to David as in fact his own compositions is another matter. The reference may mean that the authorship was credited to David though in reality the work of someone other than the great king, that David was actually the writer of the composition under consideration, that the particular piece of poetry had been modeled upon those written by David, that it was inspired by such poetry, or that it was dedicated to the celebrated ruler of Israel. In the nature of the case it is impossible to say precisely which of the seventy-three psalms associated with David are in fact the product of his own hand. There is little doubt from the historical narratives of Samuel that King David was a person who possessed considerable gifts of feeling and imagination, both at the aesthetic and religious levels, and it is difficult to believe that these

[18] E. A. Leslie, *The Abingdon Bible Commentary* (1929), pp. 509ff. Cf. J. G. S. S. Thomson, *NBD*, pp. 1054f.
[19] *Bab. Bath.* 14*b.* In *Sanhed.* 38*b,* Adam was regarded as the author of Ps. 139.
[20] *AJ*, VII, 12, 3. Cf. *Pirqe Ab.* VI, 9.

capacities did not find expression in permanent form during the monarchy.

Most probably David gave firm definition to the concept of poetry in Israel, as Moses had done for the Law, and it may be that his poetic compositions, along with any which may have been attributed to him in part or in whole, formed the nucleus of the Hebrew Psalter. On such grounds a notable religious corpus of this kind could be called Davidic in the best sense, since it owed its very existence to the inspiration and example of the versatile Israelite monarch. Only on the basis of this assumption is it possible to account at all adequately for the later Davidic tradition regarding Hebrew psalmody.

The evaluation of other ascriptions of authorship encounters much the same problem as that of David. Nevertheless, they appear to point to a strong tradition of origin within priestly circles, beginning during the period of the monarchy and continuing into the post-exilic era. Early critics such as Duhm and Gunkel virtually denied any possibility of Davidic authorship, and placed the majority of the psalms in the Maccabean period.[21] In this extreme opinion they were followed by Pfeiffer and Kennett among others,[22] though such a standpoint was viewed with disfavor by Bentzen, Buttenwieser, and Böhl and Gemser.[23] These and other scholars denied the existence of Maccabean psalms and assigned a considerable number of the Hebrew poetic compositions, including the "royal psalms," to the pre-exilic period.

C. Problems of Dating and Compilation

Among the earlier critics it was a well-established principle that the presence of Aramaisms denoted a composition of comparatively late origin.[24] While the Elephantine papyri have shown that Aramaic was coming into widespread common usage among the Jews in the Persian and Greek periods, it is clear from 2 Kings 18:26 that it was by no means unknown to certain circles in Jerusalem in the eighth century B.C. Thus to cite the presence of Aramaisms in certain psalms as an indication of late date is an extremely precarious procedure, as will be made evident subsequently. The discovery of the Ras Shamra texts has pointed clearly to the close interrelationship between Ugaritic and Hebrew poetry in terms of language, poetic form, and syntax, revealing quite incidentally

[21] B. Duhm, *Die Psalmen* (1899). H. Gunkel and J. Begrich, *Einleitung in die Psalmen* (1928-1933), 2 vols.

[22] *PIOT*, p. 629. R. H. Kennett, *OT Essays* (1928), pp. 119ff.

[23] A. Bentzen, *Forelaesninger over Indledning til de gammeltestamentlige Salmer* (1932), *Fortolkning til de gammeltestamentlige Salmer* (1939). M. Buttenwieser, *The Psalms: Chronologically Treated with a New Translation* (1938). F. M. Th. Böhl and B. Gemser, *Die Psalmen,* I (1946); II (1947); III (1949).

[24] Cf. H. Hupfeld, *Die Psalmen* (1888 ed.), I, p. xlii.

the presence of certain Aramaic elements in Ugaritic.[25] These and other considerations make it evident that there is no *a priori* reason why some psalms at least should not have been composed during the monarchy.

Archaeological discoveries at Qumran have also thrown some light on the validity of earlier discussions regarding the *terminus ad quem* of Hebrew psalmody. Whatever the precise nature of the Qumran brotherhood, it was evidently Maccabean in origin, and since all the manuscripts of the Psalter found at the site were attestable copies of earlier scrolls, the final compilation of the book must be placed at a considerably earlier date than the Maccabean period. This conclusion had already been anticipated by Böhl, Bentzen, and Buttenwieser, and in the light of the evidence from Qumran it can now be considered assured.[26] More specifically, a second-century B.C. copy of the canonical Psalter, coming from the fourth Qumran cave (4QPsaᵃ), although fragmentary, indicates clearly that the collection of canonical psalms was fixed in pre-Maccabean times, and this discovery bears out the current tendency that would date the latest canonical psalms in the Persian period.

Any question of dating involves both the psalms as individual compositions and the Psalter as a whole. Following the lead of many nineteenth-century scholars, writers such as König, Barnes, Eerdmans, Calès, and Buttenwieser adopted the procedure of dealing with the psalms on an individual basis in the matter of dating by reference to actual or implied historical incidents in the subject-matter, or with respect to their suitability for some particular occasion or festival.[27] This approach involved a significant degree of subjectivity, and as a result it did less than justice to the religious faith and spiritual values contained in the Psalter as a whole. Aside from such psalms as those which refer specifically to the kingdom period, the very timelessness of most of the compositions is such that it is extremely difficult to assign a date to individual psalms with any degree of confidence.

Under such conditions it is probably the best procedure to attempt to relate specific compositions to one of three broad classes. The first, the pre-exilic, includes those poems which have affinity with Ugaritic material of a similar sort in matters of language and syntax, as well as the

[25] Cf. *ARI*, pp. 128f.

[26] Cf. W. F. Albright, *OTMS*, p. 25; W. Baumgartner, *Schweizer Theologische Umschau*, XXIV (1954), p. 51; A. Weiser, *The Psalms* (1962), p. 92. On a Persian period dating for the latest psalms see F. M. Cross, *BA*, XVII, No. 1 (1954), p. 3, *The Ancient Library of Qumran* (1961), p. 165; J. P. Hyatt, *JBL*, LXXVI (1957), p. 5.

[27] E. König, *Die Psalmen* (1927). W. E. Barnes, *The Psalms* (1931). B. D. Eerdmans, *The Hebrew Book of Psalms* (1947). J. Calès, *Le Livre des psaumes* (1936). M. Buttenwieser, *The Psalms: Chronologically Treated with a New Translation* (1938).

so-called "royal" psalms and those which mention the existence of the northern kingdom. References to the dispersion would normally place a psalm within the second broad category, namely the exilic period, which would also include some dirge psalms and possibly those mentioning the betrayal of Judah by her enemies, notably the Edomites. A final post-exilic group might well include the compositions dealing in one manner or another with the problem of the righteous sufferer, the way in which the Torah should be observed, the nature and significance of wisdom, and the concern for atheism.

When considering the Psalter as a unit it is probably the best procedure to argue from a general *terminus ad quem* in the Persian period to a *terminus a quo* in the monarchy, allowing for the distinct possibility that at least some psalms may be pre-Davidic in date, as Böhl and others have suggested. In connection with the psalms attributed to David it should be remarked that the use of the second (Ps. 110) or third (Ps. 21:7) person in reference to the king does not of itself preclude Davidic authorship. Furthermore, some verses that have been interpreted as allusions to the Temple, and assigned in consequence to a post-Davidic period, may quite possibly refer to the Tabernacle at Shiloh, which was variously known as the "holy place" (Exod. 28:43; 29:30), "the house of the LORD" (Josh. 6:24; 1 Sam. 1:7ff.; 3:3; cf. 2 Sam. 12:20), and the "house of God" (Judg. 8:31). In Psalm 27, the structure designated "the house of the LORD" and "his temple" (v. 4) was also described synonymously by the terms *hêkhāl* and *ṣukkāh* (v. 5) which were never employed in connection with the Solomonic structure.

Closely connected with the questions pertaining to the authorship and date of the Psalter are the considerations underlying its compilation. It seems fairly certain that the psalmist was originally a lone composer who in some instances probably did not write with a view to forming a collection, or even having his meditations included as part of a collection of religious poetry. While it may well be that the authors of some psalms were Temple personnel, it is also true, as Weiser has made clear, in opposition to the cultic views of Mowinckel, that the composing of Hebrew psalmody was never the prerogative of the priestly caste.[28] While some collections may have been made during the lifetimes of the authors, others were doubtless the product of activity in subsequent centuries.

That there were earlier collections of psalms underlying the form of the extant Psalter seems to be indicated by the fact that there is a wide variety in the kinds of psalms, in the divergent religious experiences of the authors themselves, and in the historical situations from which the particular compositions arose. Furthermore, there is a degree of duplica-

---

[28] A. Weiser, *The Psalms*, p. 95; cf. Mowinckel, *The Psalms in Israel's Worship*, II, pp. 90ff.

tion within the Psalter itself (Pss. 14 and 53; 40:13ff. and 70; 57:7ff. 60:5ff., and 108), which might point to the existence of separate collec tions of poetic compositions, while the reference to the "prayers of David the son of Jesse" (Ps. 72:20) would indicate the presence of an independ ent body of material designated by the title "prayers." Other hints as to the existence of earlier collections consist in the ascription of groups of psalms to persons such as Asaph and Korah, the categorizing of certain psalms such as the "songs of ascents," and the fact that twenty-eight out of the thirty-four untitled psalms occur in a body at the end of the Psalter.

The first formally collected group probably originated during or short ly after the reign of David, and may possibly have included considerably more than the number of psalms attributed to David in the Hebrew Psalter. From this corpus a selection was doubtless made, to which was attached the note in Psalm 72:20. To what extent this group contained the Davidic compositions so designated in the first seventy-two psalms and precisely which psalms were actually composed by David, is, of course, uncertain. Although David instituted the liturgical use of some psalms (cf. 1 Chron. 6:31; 16:4ff.; Ez. 3:10ff.), there is no evidence that he employed all of his compositions in that manner. According to 2 Chroni cles 29:30 there were collections of the compositions of David and Asaph extant in the time of Hezekiah, and this might well account for the compilation of the first eighty-nine psalms.[29] At a still later date another editor, perhaps even Ezra himself, added the remainder of the Psalter to the earlier collection as other groups of poetic material became available for the purpose.

While nothing is known for certain, of course, about the processes of compilation, the completed Psalter gives evidence of having been con structed carefully. The various sources upon which the compilers drew were arranged in five sections or books, as follows:

Book I	Pss. 1–41.
Book II	Pss. 42–72.
Book III	Pss. 73–89.
Book IV	Pss. 90–106.
Book V	Pss. 107–150.

Each of these books closed with a doxology, while Psalm 150 constituted in itself an appropriate doxology to the Psalter as a whole. This pattern is somewhat artificial, and most probably drew for its inspiration upon the division of the Torah into five books, particularly if Ezra the scribe was responsible for casting the Psalter into substantially its extant form.

[29] R. Kittel, *Die Psalmen* (1929), p. xxi, dated Asaph and Korah collections during the Greek period, but this appears late unless it refers to the very last stage of editing.

Of some interest also is the fact that the Psalter can be divided into three principal sections based upon the predominant incidence of the particular name of God. The first of these, comprising Psalms 1–41, used the tetragrammaton 273 times and *Elohim* only fifteen. The second, embracing Psalms 42–89, used the tetragrammaton 74 times and *Elohim* 207. The final division, comprising Books IV and V, utilized the tetragrammaton on 339 occasions, whereas the name *Elohim* was found only 7 times. While Psalm 53 repeated the substance of Psalm 14, the name *Elohim* was substituted for the tetragrammaton. Precisely why the divine names were used in this manner is unknown, but it would seem to be connected with editorial preferences rather than with either historical or theological considerations.

The earliest Hebrew manuscripts did not divide the Psalter into one hundred and fifty psalms, and the divergence of tradition in this regard was reflected in rabbinic writings. Thus the Jerusalem Talmud (*Shabb.* 16) spoke of one hundred and forty-seven psalms, to correspond to the extent of the life of Jacob, while *Berachoth* (9b) regarded Psalms 1 and 2 as a unity. The LXX also reflected this lack of unanimity in that it regarded Psalms 9 and 10 and Psalms 114 and 115 as one psalm each. On the other hand it divided Psalms 116 and 147 into two psalms each. Finally it added an extra seven-verse composition to the corpus, which bore a note in its title to the effect that it stood outside the usual number of psalms in the Hebrew Psalter.[30] It seems most probable, however, that this composition, which also occurred in some Psalter manuscripts recovered from Qumran and was originally written in Greek, is in fact apocryphal.

While the psalms are not arranged in anything approaching chronological order, it is noticeable that related psalms tend to occur in groups, such as Psalms 3–4, 9–10, 42–43, as well as larger groupings including Psalms 95–100 and 146–150. Other categories have been classified in terms of attributed authorship, as for example Psalms 42, 44–49 (*Korahite*) and Psalms 73–83 (*Asaph*), while others were grouped according to similarity of superscriptions such as Psalms 50–60 (*Mikhtam*) and Psalms 120–134 (*Songs of Ascents*).

D. MUSIC IN THE ANCIENT NEAR EAST

The many references to music in the Psalter naturally raise questions as to the character of music generally in the ancient Near East. While the identity of the Jubal to whom the beginnings of ancient Hebrew music were traditionally ascribed (Gen. 4:21) is obscure, there can be no doubt from archaeological discoveries that musical activity in the

---

30 Οὗτος ὁ ψαλμὸς ἰδιόγραφος εἰς Δαυεὶδ καὶ ἔξωθεν τοῦ ἀριθμοῦ, ὅτε ἐμονομάχησεν τῷ Γολιάδ. On this psalm see H. B. Swete, *Introduction to the OT in Greek* (1900), p. 253; M. Noth, *ZAW*, XLVIII (1930), pp. 1ff.

Near East was one of the earliest and most characteristic of cultural manifestations.[31] Among the ancient musical instruments that were uncovered during processes of archaeological excavation in Mesopotamia was the *sistrum*, which was found in Sumerian levels at Ur and Kish.[32] This instrument made its way from Palestine to Egypt, where it was frequently depicted in connection with the worship of Hathor.[33] It was included among the instruments on which David played, and was described by the term מְנַעַנְעִים (2 Sam. 6:5, from the verb נוע, "to shake"), incorrectly rendered "cornets" by the AV, but accurately by the Vulgate as *sistra*. A *sistrum* was unearthed at Bethel in 1934, and was dated by Albright in the pre-Israelite period.[34]

A very popular instrument throughout the ancient world was the *shôphār*, a term derived from the Akkadian *shapparu* or "wild ibex." It was by far the most frequently named musical instrument in the Hebrew Scriptures, since it was the basic means by which signals were communicated (Lev. 25:9; 1 Kgs. 1:34; Jer. 4:5, 19; Ezek. 33:3; Joel. 2:1, 15). The earliest kind was made from the horns of rams (Josh. 6:4ff.), but in the Second Temple era the horns of the ibex and antelope were used for the purpose.

The antiquity of pipes is attested by the presence in Akkadian tablets of the term *ḥalḥallatu* or "double clarinet" long before the mention of the clarinet (הָלִיל, LXX αὐλός) in 1 Samuel 10:5. This instrument was popular in the ancient Near East for purposes of celebrating secular occasions of joy or sorrow, and most probably did not have any liturgical function. By the time of the monarchy the double clarinet was a familiar instrument, and was normally equipped with a reed mouthpiece.[35] The more primitive pipe, often associated with pastoral occupations (cf. Judg. 5:16; Dan. 3:5ff.), was frequently made of reeds or wood, although an elegant silver flute was recovered from Ur. This instrument was popular during the Old and Middle Kingdom periods of ancient Egypt, and was employed exclusively for secular purposes.

Another commonly used instrument was the *tōph*, mentioned seventeen times in the Old Testament, and played by both men (1 Sam. 10:5) and women (Exod. 15:20). This membranophone, translated by the AV as "timbrel" and "tabret," was not permitted in the Temple, although it was mentioned in the Psalter and in religious hymns (Ps. 150:4; Jer. 31:4). Ancient Mesopotamian forms of this instrument would suggest that it was shaped like a tambourine and had two membranes,

---

[31] Cf. E. Werner, *IDB*, III, p. 470.

[32] On this general subject see F. W. Galpin, *Music of the Sumerians* (1937).

[33] Pictured in C. Sachs, *Reallexikon der Musikinstrumente, Der Alte Orient* (1920), XXI, 3-4, p. 17.

[34] Cf. *BA*, IV, No. 3 (1941), pl. 12b.

[35] Cf. J. Wellhausen, "The Book of Psalms" in *Holy Bible, Polychrome Edition* (1898), p. 219.

with pieces of bronze inserted around the rim so that it would rattle when shaken.

The antiquity of stringed instruments that could be classified under the general category of chordophones has been well attested by archaeological excavations in the Near East. The *kinnôr* or lyre, mistakenly translated "harp" in many renderings in English of the Old Testament, was popular on sacred and secular occasions alike. It was used by David and the Levites, and corresponded to the *cithara* of the Greeks and Romans. Of prehistoric origin, the lyre had between three and twelve strings made of animal tissue, and some Mesopotamian reliefs that depicted it showed an interesting degree of affinity with Cretan and Minoan instruments. An early type of lyre, probably containing seven strings, was unearthed at Ur.[36] The earliest Semitic representation of the *kinnôr* occurred in the Beni-Hasan tableau. Such later varieties as were depicted on frescoes and murals constituted variations or modifications of the basic lyre structure (compare the קיתרס–LXX *κίθαρα*–and שַׂבְּכָא–LXX *σαμβυκή*–of Dan. 3:5, 7, 10, 15).

One of the most popular instruments throughout the entire ancient Near East was the harp,[37] and it is probably the one referred to in the Hebrew Bible as נבל.[38] In the time of Josephus it had twelve strings,[39] and this number seems to have been current on Egyptian harps at the beginning of the New Kingdom period, although instruments with as many as twenty strings existed in Egypt long before the time of Josephus. The harp was characteristically an instrument played by men, and as such it was a regular component of the Levitical orchestras. Collective terms such as "stringed instruments" (Pss. 45:8; 150:4) and "instruments of music" (Am. 6:5; 1 Chron. 16:42; 2 Chron. 5:13) indicated without actual specification the predominant place of stringed instruments in Biblical musical activity in contrast to others such as cymbals or trumpets, which were also used by the priests.[40]

While it is far from easy to determine the exact role of music in connection with the Temple rituals of the pre-exilic period, it is known from Amos 5:22f. (cf. 8:3) that songs and the music of the harp accompanied the offering of the sacrifices in the sanctuary. The eighth- and seventh-century B.C. prophets furnished similar evidence of music in connection with Temple rituals (Isa. 30:29; 64:11; Jer. 33:11), while

---

[36] Cf. V. Christian, *Altertumskunde des Zweistromlandes* (1940), I, tab. 247.

[37] Cf. *UC*, pl. 5*a*.

[38] LXX *ψαλτήριον*, *νάβλα*, *ὄργανον*; Vulgate, *psalterium, nablium, lyra, cithara,* and *vas psalmi*.

[39] *AJ*, VII, 12, 3.

[40] On this general subject see H. Gressmann, *Musik und Musikinstrumente im AT* (1903); S. B. Finesinger, *HUCA*, III (1926), pp. 21ff.; C. Sachs, *Geiste und Werden der Musikinstrumente* (1929), *The History of Musical Instruments* (1940); and P. Gradenwitz, *The Music of Israel* (1949).

according to Ezra 3:10f. the laying of the foundation of the Second Temple was accompanied by songs of praise and the music of cymbals and trumpets. In the light of these traditions it is clearly important to give due weight to the testimony of Chronicles concerning the arrangements for music in the sanctuary rituals, and although the fully developed form would certainly be post-exilic, it seems apparent that it was the historical outcome of practices that began in the early monarchy.

E. TYPES OF PSALMS

The relationship between music, psalmody, and the Temple cultus may perhaps throw some light upon the purpose of the writing of at least some of the psalms. One such composition was related specifically to a notable occasion in the history of the Temple (1 Kgs. 8:31ff.), and it may be that some of the psalms had either a liturgical[41] or a cultic beginning.[42] It is important not to make these considerations the criteria of origin for all the psalms, however, since otherwise a completely artificial picture will result. The fact is that a good many psalms are devoid either of liturgical character or of specific ritual directions, and cannot in any sense be directly related to the cultus. Indeed, there are numerous occasions on which the psalm is clearly within the realm of devotional poetry, particularly in those psalms that employ the first person pronoun. Some have a more didactic character than others (e.g. Pss. 1, 112, 127), while a further type, which may have been related to community usage independently of Temple worship (Pss. 11, 16, 23, 27, 62, 131) is in harmony with some of the great poetical expressions of faith and trust found elsewhere in the Old Testament narratives (Gen. 49:2ff.; Exod. 15:1ff.; Deut. 32:1ff.; 1 Sam. 2:1ff.; Jer. 11:18ff.; 12:1ff.; Hab. 3:1).

From a very early period commentators on the Psalter had detected the presence of several different types of psalms in the literary corpus. Thus it was customary to classify them in terms of such concepts as praise, lamentation, petition, meditation, and other categories of like kind. While this was valuable in itself, it soon became apparent in the light of the expanding field of ancient Near Eastern studies that such was an insufficient basis for type-classification. The pioneer in the latter area was Hermann Gunkel, who emphasized the importance of considering the general *Sitz im Leben des Volkes* from which the various compositions were thought to have arisen, as well as the several categories or *Gattungen* with which they could be associated. On the basis of his investigations into the history of Hebrew religious literature Gunkel sought to relate the Biblical corpus of psalms to analogous compositions

---

[41] Cf. J. P. Peters, *The Psalms as Liturgies* (1922).
[42] S. Mowinckel, *Psalmenstudien I-IV* (1921-1924).

from the early cultures of Mesopotamia and Egypt.[43] His conclusions,[44] while not carrying equal weight in every quarter, have nevertheless made a great contribution to the study of the Hebrew psalms, and many scholars subsequently based their own investigations of the problems connected with the Psalter on the methodological approach which he had followed.

An analysis of the elaborate scheme of classification of psalm-types that Gunkel established indicates the existence of five principal categories:

(a) Hymns (*Hymnus*) meant for the praise of God, to be sung as solos or in chorus. So Pss. 8, 19, 29, 33, *et al.*

(b) Community laments (*Klagelieder des Volkes*), which on the basis of some national disaster presented the calamity before God and appealed for divine intervention. So Pss. 44, 74, 79, 80, *et al.*

(c) Royal psalms (*Königspsalmen*), relating to outstanding events in the lives of reigning Hebrew kings. Since the Hasmonean rulers had "laid waste" the Davidic throne and not "established" it, [45] Gunkel related these compositions to native Israelite monarchs of the pre-exilic era. Such psalms included Pss. 2, 18, 20, 45, 72, 101, 110, and 132.

(d) Individual laments (*Klagelied des Einzelnen*), the counterpart of communal dirges. Gunkel regarded the first person utterances in the normal sense, and not, as with the earlier critics,[46] in terms of a personification of the nation. So Pss. 3, 7, 13, 25, 51 *et al.*

(e) Individual thanksgivings (*Danklieder des Einzelnen*), said or sung in connection with ceremonies in the Temple to enable the worshipper to participate more significantly in divine grace. So Pss. 30, 32, 34, *et al.*

Within these principal categories Gunkel recognized the existence of other subsidiary classes. Thus, in the first division he included the "songs of Zion" (*Zionslieder*) (Pss. 46, 48, 76, and 78), as well as certain compositions of an eschatological character commemorating the enthronement of the deity as ruler of the universe. These latter (including Pss. 47, 93, 97, 99 and one or two others from the principal group) were designated as "enthronement psalms" (*Thronbesteigungslieder*). The fourth category was held to include a subsidiary type designated the "psalm of confidence" (*Vertrauenspsalmen*) (exemplified by Pss. 4, 11, 16, 23, and a few others).

Additional varieties included the "vow" (*Gelübde*), which generally occurred as part of a larger composition (as in Pss. 7:17ff.; 13:5f.; 31:7f.); a small group styled "pilgrimage songs" (*Wallfahrtslieder*) comprising

---

[43] Cf. H. Gunkel in P. Hinneberg (ed.), *Die Kultur der Gegenwart* (1906), I, 7, pp. 51ff.; *Deutsche Literaturzeitung*, XXVII (1906), cols. 1797ff., 1861ff., translated in *What Remains of the OT? and Other Essays* (1928), pp. 57ff.

[44] H. Gunkel, *Ausgewählte Psalmen* (1904), in *Die Religion in Geschichte und Gegenwart*, IV (1913), cols. 1927ff., *Die Psalmen* (1926). See also the list of studies in H. Gunkel and J. Begrich, *Einleitung in die Psalmen*, I, pp. 20f.

[45] Cf. E. Sellin, *Introduction to the OT* (1923), p. 200.

[46] Cf. R. Smend, *ZAW*, VIII (1888), pp. 49ff.

Psalms 84 and 122; "community thanksgivings" (*Danklieder des Volkes*), which consisted of Psalms 76 and 124; "wisdom poems" (*Weisheitsdichtung*) such as Psalms 1, 37, 49, and others that reflected the wisdom-concepts of ancient Near Eastern literature, and a type of composition styled "liturgies" (*Liturgien*), whether of the cultic order (Pss. 8, 42, 43, 46, and others), the prophetic variety (Pss. 12, 75, and elsewhere), or the Torah-liturgies (Pss. 15, 24, and perhaps 134). Since the contents of the Psalter were still not covered by the foregoing main and subsidiary classifications, Gunkel proposed a final category of "mixed poems" (*Mischungen*), in which Psalms 9, 10, 40, 78, and others occurred as representatives of mixed varieties of psalm types.

While an assessment of the cultural background is a matter of very great importance in any estimate of the Hebrew Scriptures, the dictum of Gunkel that it was axiomatic that nothing could be understood apart from its cultural milieu (*Zusammenhang*) seems to be particularly rigid in its application to the material of the Psalter. The very timelessness of some of the Hebrew psalms indicates that they could well have emerged from different cultural situations over a vast range of centuries, if for no other reason than that they are precisely the expression of facets of the human spirit, which in basic character has remained unchanged to all intents and purposes throughout recorded history.

Furthermore, as with any comprehensive scheme of classification, there is bound to be a considerable degree of subjectivity exercised in the assigning of the various poetic compositions in part or in whole to the different groups and subdivisions proposed, as A. R. Johnson has made clear.[47] More serious is the criticism that Gunkel, in his attempts to envisage a development from simple to complex forms in the poetry itself, and in endeavoring to trace the emergence of monotheism in terms of a monolinear pattern, actually stands firmly within the traditions of the Graf-Wellhausen school of thought, whose reconstruction of Hebrew history and religion is no longer tenable. This, allied with massive emendations and reconstructions of the text of the Psalter, has made other more notable aspects of his work the object of suspicion in some quarters.

The tremendous stimulus that the penetrating insights of Gunkel provided for the study of the Hebrew Psalter can be seen in the work of subsequent European scholars such as Hempel, Eissfeldt, Weiser, Engnell, and Lods.[48] Among English writers the methodological principles enunciated by Gunkel were appropriated to a greater or lesser

---

[47] *OTMS*, pp. 180f.

[48] J. Hempel in O. Walzel (ed.), *Handbuch der Literaturwissenschaft* (1930), pp. 30ff. O. Eissfeldt, *Einleitung in das AT* (1934 ed.), pp. 114ff. A. Weiser, *Einleitung in das AT* (1939), pp. 22f., *The Psalms* (1962), pp. 23ff.; cf. his *Die Psalmen* (1935), pp. 20ff. I. Engnell, *Gamla Testamentet*, I, pp. 52ff. A. Lods, *Histoire de la littérature hébraïque et juive* (1950), pp. 725ff.

degree by Oesterley and Robinson, Welch, James, Paterson, Leslie, and others.[49] While R. H. Pfeiffer was governed to some extent by the approach of Gunkel, he viewed with outright disfavor the manner in which Gunkel had assigned many psalms to the pre-exilic period.[50] As mentioned previously, some other scholars did not follow the procedures laid down by Gunkel, preferring instead to consider each composition on its own merits in terms of subject-matter, provenance, date, and the like.[51]

By far the most outstanding example of the influence of Gunkel can be seen in the work of the Scandinavian scholar Mowinckel, who in his studies freely acknowledged his debt to Hermann Gunkel. While the latter regarded the various psalm-types as exhibiting almost complete independence from their cultic origins and thus constituting more broadly based spiritual compositions, Mowinckel went to the other extreme of maintaining that almost all the psalms (except perhaps for Pss. 1, 112, and 127) originated in the work of cultic priests or prophets who were closely associated with the Temple and its rituals.[52]

His most important contribution to the study of the Psalter, and one which has been seriously criticized by many scholars, was his suggestion that some forty-three psalms belonged originally to a class styled "enthronement psalms" (*Thronbesteigungspsalmen*). He argued that, on the analogy of the accession of an earthly king, there was in Israel an annual celebration at the New Year festival that commemorated the enthronement of God as the universal king. His theory was based in part upon the cultic rites of Babylonia in which Marduk was ceremonially enthroned at the annual New Year ceremonies, and also upon influences from rabbinic traditions concerning the festive occasions of post-exilic Judaism. He reinforced this by an appeal to certain passages in the Psalms (e.g. 93:1; 96:10; 97:1) in which the expression יהוה מלך occurred, and which, he alleged, ought to be interpreted as "יהוה has become king."

Following the Babylonian theme of the conflict of Apsu and Tiamat, Mowinckel entertained the idea of an enthronement festival as marking the annual assertion of the divine triumph over primeval chaos in a

---

[49] *IBOT*, pp. 191ff. A. C. Welch, *The Psalter in Life, Worship and History* (1926). F. James, *Thirty Psalmists: A Study in the Personalities of the Psalter* (1938). J. Paterson, *The Praises of Israel: Studies Literary and Religious in the Psalms* (1950). E. A. Leslie, *The Psalms: Translated and Interpreted in the Light of Hebrew Life and Worship* (1949).

[50] *PIOT*, pp. 630ff.

[51] Cf. E. König, *Die Psalmen* (1927); W. E. Barnes, *The Psalms* (1931); H. Herkenne, *Das Buch der Psalmen* (1936); M. Buttenwieser, *The Psalms: Chronologically Treated with a New Translation* (1938); B. D. Eerdmans, *The Hebrew Book of Psalms* (1947).

[52] Cf. S. Mowinckel, *Psalmenstudien*, I, pp. 140ff.; II, pp. 94ff.; III, pp. 30ff.; V, pp. 35ff., 82ff.; VI, p. 20 *passim*. Cf. G. Quell, *Das kultische Problem der Psalmen* (1926), pp. 150ff. Quell is generally far less emphatic on this matter.

ritual which saw the Israelite Ark of the Covenant carried ceremonially into the sanctuary. In addition, he related the origin of the eschatological "Day of the LORD" to the annual cultic enthronement, and held that the eighth-century prophets projected it into the future and contemplated a time when the deity would indeed return to earth with kingly power as supreme ruler of the world.

Although Mowinckel had been anticipated in his conclusions, at least in part, by the work of Volz,[53] his theory gained considerable acceptance in certain circles, and was reflected in works published by Böhl, Bentzen, Leslie, and others,[54] while in a modified form it was accepted by Schmidt, Keet, and Weiser.[55] Those who either saw inadequacies in the general theory, or else opposed it outright, included Eissfeldt, who pointed out that Mowinckel and his followers should have associated the divine kingship with the Semitic religious concept of God as king, and not with the ritual of the Babylonian New Year festival.[56] Oesterley stated pointedly that there was never any such occasion in Israel as the "festival of the enthronement of Yahweh," and that alleged references in the Psalter were to a larger feast, of which the enthronement was the initial ceremony.[57] However, he accepted the postulate that the so-called "enthronement psalms" were of genuine cultic origin and related to a New Year festival, but at the same time he adhered to the older eschatological interpretation of these compositions in terms of the future ideal historical monarch. But he was unable to integrate these two concepts successfully, and his resulting idea of the kingship of God proved to be extremely vague and unsatisfying.

The manner in which Mowinckel utilized the Biblical evidence came in for criticism by Pap, who stated flatly that the material adduced as evidence actually had nothing to do with an alleged New Year festival, and that it was completely inadequate for the purpose of demonstrating the existence of the kind of occurrence suggested by Mowinckel.[58] Buttenwieser also was particularly emphatic in his denunciation of the theory advanced by Mowinckel, maintaining that the designation of God

53 P. Volz, *Das Neujahrfest Jahwes* (1912).

54 F. M. Th. Böhl, *Nieuwjaarsfeest en Koningsdag in Babylon en in Israël* (1927). Cf. A. Bentzen, *Introduction to the OT*, I, pp. 147ff. E. A. Leslie, *The Psalms: Translated and Interpreted in the Light of Hebrew Life and Worship* (1949).

55 H. Schmidt, *Die Thronfahrt Jahves am Fest der Jahreswende im Alten Israel* (1927), pp. 36ff. C. C. Keet, *A Liturgical Study of the Psalter* (1927), pp. 81ff. Cf. A. Weiser, *The Psalms*, pp. 62ff.

56 O. Eissfeldt, *ZAW*, XLVI (1928), pp. 81ff. Cf. Mowinckel's attempt at refutation in *The Psalms in Israel's Worship*, II, pp. 223f. On the place of the monarchy in Old Testament life and religion see C. R. North, *AJSL*, XLVIII (1931), pp. 1ff., *ZAW*, L (1932), pp. 8ff.

57 W. O. E. Oesterley, *The Psalms*, I, p. 44.

58 L. I. Pap, *Das israelitische Neujahrsfest* (1933).

as king did not originate either in the cultus or from a mythological background, but rather that the term served a hymnal purpose or had a social content.[59] Criticism of the theory on the basis of Mowinckel's use of rabbinic sources was made by Snaith, who took the view that the enthronement psalms were post-exilic in origin, and unconnected with the New Year festival.[60]

While the theory adduced by Mowinckel is unquestionably the product of a virile and imaginative mind, it is beclouded by certain important subjective considerations. In the first instance it is completely improper and incorrect to render the phrase, מלך יהוה as "Adonai has become king," with Mowinckel, Gunkel, and Schmidt, for as Eissfeldt pointed out quite rightly, the phrase should be rendered "the Lord is king" or "the Lord reigns." Any allegation to the contrary must therefore be considered to be purely speculative, and as such is an inadequate basis for a developed theory. Again, analogies from Babylonian ritual practices have not been as validly based as some exponents of the theory have liked to imagine. Thus there is no concrete evidence for the view that Marduk was treated as dying and rising again in the New Year festival, as Von Soden has shown.[61]

Parallels that have sometimes been taken from other cultures have frequently been misunderstood also, as is the case in connection with references to the Hittites, whose religious festivals included a spring rite for re-invigoration of the earth, and a ceremony held at the vernal equinox in which the king generally took part.[62] The latter may well have been a New Year festival, but although much of the ritual involved the royal personage, including a procession to the temple, the king did not "hold the hand" of the deity as in the Babylonian rites. The fact of the procession of the Hittite god need have no relationship whatever to the Babylonian ceremonies, partly because there are certain significant differences between the two rituals, and partly because such processions were a common feature of ancient Near Eastern religious traditions. If, therefore, there is any connection at all between the Hittite royal festival and the Babylonian New Year ceremonies, it is at best rather incidental and tenuous.

The fact is that almost nothing is known about any celebrations that were associated with the advent of the New Year in Old Testament

[59] M. Buttenwieser, *The Psalms: Chronologically Treated with a New Translation*, pp. 321ff. For a denial that kings were ever a divine institution in Israel see H. Frankfort, *Kingship and the Gods* (1948), p. 339.
[60] Cf. N. H. Snaith, *The Jewish New Year Festival: Its Origins and Development* (1947), pp. 195ff. For criticisms of his position see A. R. Johnson, *OTMS*, pp. 194f.
[61] W. von Soden, *ZA*, LI (1955), pp. 161ff.
[62] *TH*, pp. 152ff.

times, and the theory that it was marked by ritual performances of the kind found in Babylonia is highly speculative at best.[63] There is no ground whatever in the Old Testament Scriptures for the view that the Hebrew deity could in any sense be enthroned annually, since such a concept ran counter to all that is known of pre-exilic prophetic theology. It must therefore be concluded that the speculations of Mowinckel suffer from one grave deficiency: they cannot be supported by any objective evidence.

While it is obviously very important for any interpreter to be aware of the cultural and historical background from which particular psalms may have emerged, the *Sitz im Leben des Volkes* approach, here as elsewhere, is by itself an inadequate principle upon which to proceed. The nature of many of the psalms is such that it is often completely impossible to determine with anything approaching certainty either its date or the historical circumstances under which it was written. In order to avoid the gross subjectivism which must inevitably follow if the *Sitz im Leben des Volkes* approach is being employed exclusively, some other form of classification into types has been entertained by scholars. Thus, on the basis of Temple usage the psalms have been divided into two principal groups, the first of which included public and private categories of thanksgiving psalms, hymns of praise, petitions, and laments, and the second consisting of compositions describing spiritual relationships, or psalms in praise of wisdom.

A classification according to subject-matter might be somewhat as follows: (a) psalms of praise and adoration; (b) royal psalms; (c) psalms concerning the divine kingdom; (d) meditations; (e) psalms of thanksgiving and worship; (f) psalms describing divine control over history; (g) penitential poems; (h) psalms of lamentation; (i) compositions extolling wisdom and the Law.

Probably the most reliable scheme of classification is one that employs as a criterion the basic character of the religious concepts contained in the particular psalm under study. It is all too readily forgotten by scholars that the Hebrew psalms were not primarily cultural expressions, but rather that they comprised means of devotion, beginning most probably with the individual psalmist's expressing his needs to God on the basis of private worship, and only at a subsequent time involving situations which depicted the nation as a religious culture. These latter, it may be remarked, did not include an annual enthronement festival in Israel, since as has been observed above, there is absolutely no evidence whatever that such a religious feast was held among the Hebrews.

---

[63] So W. S. McCullough, *IB*, IV, p. 7, as against the exegetical comments of W. R. Taylor, *IB*, IV, pp. 245f., 502f.

If the religious concepts are taken as one means of classifying the various kinds of psalms, a broad pattern might emerge as follows:

(a) *Prayers*, whether for divine protection, deliverance, intervention, or blessing
(b) *Praises*, both general and specific
(c) *Penitential* psalms, including acts of confession
(d) *Intercessions*, for the king, the nation, Jerusalem, and other nations
(e) *Confessions of faith*, in God as king, ruler, moral judge, and governor of the universe
(f) *Homiletical*, dealing with wisdom, divine power, the true service of God, and the place of the Torah in national and individual life
(g) *Imprecatory*, constituting a reply to the national enemies, and calling upon God to exercise retribution
(h) *Problems of the moral order*, involving the suffering of the righteous, the prosperity of the wicked, and the hope of immortality

Classifications of this kind encounter periodic difficulty when a particular psalm can be assigned to more than one category. This fact, however, need not vitiate the classification as such, since the ancient writers generally did not observe rigid lines of type-demarcation when composing their psalms. Where a multiplicity of religious ideas is apparent there is no reason why the poems concerned should not be assigned to more than one category, since in the last resort any attempt at classification along occidental lines must necessarily be somewhat artificial.

F. THE ARCHAEOLOGICAL BACKGROUND

The emphasis that Gunkel placed upon the Hebrew psalms as part of the corpus of ancient Near Eastern literary expression was reinforced by the study of the cultic poems recovered by nineteenth- and early twentieth-century archaeological activity.[64] Because of the fact that many of the hymns and prayers involved exhibited a number of stylistic patterns, rhythmic structures, and developments of thought that were very similar in nature to those evident in the Hebrew psalms, many scholars naturally concluded that the latter must have depended for their origin upon the cultures of Mesopotamia or Egypt, either directly or through the mediate influence of Canaan. Thus Gressmann was convinced that the Psalter furnished direct parallels in language and thought-forms to analogous Babylonian compositions,[65] while Blackman cited a number of parallels

[64] E.g. M. Jastrow, *Die Religion Babyloniens und Assyriens* (1905); A. Bertholet, *Religionsgeschichtliches Lesebuch* (1908); H. Zimmern, *Babylonische Hymnen und Gebete in der Alte Orient* (1905-11); H. Winckler, *Keilinschriftliches Textbuch zum AT* (1909); F. Stummer, *Sumerisch-akkadisch Parallelen zum Aufbau alttestamentlicher Psalmen* (1922); H. Gressmann, *Altorientalische Texte zum AT* (1926); A. Erman, *Die Religion der Ägypter* (1934); G. Widengren, *The Akkadian and Hebrew Psalms of Lamentation as Religious Documents* (1937); E. R. Dalglish, *Psalm Fifty-One in the Light of Ancient Near Eastern Patternism* (1962).

[65] H. Gressmann in D. C. Simpson (ed.), *The Psalmists* (1926), pp. 1ff.

from Egyptian sources that seemed to imply some Semitic dependence upon Egyptian culture, though by no means of an exclusive nature, in the second millennium B.C.[66] However, some doubts about the supposed direct dependence of Hebrew writers upon their Babylonian or Egyptian counterparts were voiced by Driver, who maintained that correspondences could have been quite spontaneous in nature, and that if dependence upon Babylonian literature was to be posited, it was most probably mediated through Canaanite culture.[67]

The general correctness of this latter estimate was subsequently confirmed by the discoveries at Ras Shamra, which demonstrated the close literary affinity between the Ugaritic and Hebrew poetic compositions,[68] and showed that the dependence upon Babylonian and Egyptian sources was by no means as evident as had been imagined formerly.[69] It is now apparent that the earliest poetry of the Bible is replete, not with Babylonian or Egyptian forms, but with rhythmical patterns that are thoroughly characteristic of the Canaanite poems of Ugarit. Far-reaching parallels in grammar and syntax, as well as literary style, have served to emphasize the closeness of the relationship between Ugaritic and Hebrew poetry, and to minimize the connection with other areas of the ancient Near East.

The discoveries at Ras Shamra have thrown a good deal of light upon the text of the Psalter itself, which in the light of the above observations is hardly surprising. Older critics had commonly maintained that the Hebrew text was highly corrupt, having passed, as was said, through the hands of a multitude of copyists who made a wide range of alterations over the various generations in order to render the psalms in a manner that would be more suitable for congregational usage.[70] This postulate led to that wholesale variety of textual emendation adopted by Rudolf Kittel in his *Biblia Hebraica* (1905-07) and a general depreciation of the estimate in which the text of the psalms was held. From the nature of the Ugaritic compositions it is now evident that the religious poetry of the Hebrews has preserved many ancient literary and idiomatic expressions that were the common property of the inhabitants of the land during the late Amarna period.[71] This literary interdependence has shown that what Kittel and others regarded as textual anomalies in the Psalter are really not true corruptions of the Hebrew text at all.

[66] A. M. Blackman in *ibid.*, pp. 177ff.
[67] G. R. Driver in *ibid.*, pp. 109ff.
[68] Cf. J. H. Patton, *Canaanite Parallels in the Book of Psalms* (1944), p. 2 *passim*.
[69] As shown by R. G. Castellino, *Le lamentazioni individuali e gle inni in Babilonia e in Israele* (1939).
[70] So C. A. Briggs, *A Critical and Exegetical Commentary on the Book of Psalms*, I, p. xxxiii, *et al.*
[71] Cf. H. L. Ginzberg, *BA*, VIII, No. 2 (1945), pp. 55ff.; W. F. Albright, *Religion in Life*, XXI, No. 4 (1952), pp. 542ff.; M. Dahood, *Psalms I* (1966), pp. xviiiff.

In point of fact, the vast majority of such instances, as Patton and others have shown, constitute instead accurate reflections of peculiarities in Canaanite grammar and forms of speech whose significance, once Ugaritic culture had gone into decline, gradually lapsed with the passing of the generations. Now that the true nature and provenance of these archaic forms have been recognized, it is evident that the precipitate textual emendations of scholars such as Kittel will need to be revised drastically in the light of the study of Ugaritic sources, and that a second and much more cautious look will be necessitated in connection with the Massoretic tradition, the reliability of which has been greatly enhanced both by the discoveries at Ras Shamra and Qumran.

G. TEXTUAL CORRUPTIONS

That the text of the Psalter contains certain irregularities is evident from a comparison of the differences in duplicate versions of specific poems (compare Pss. 14 and 53; Ps. 18 and 2 Sam. 22), or by reference to the acrostic arrangement of Psalms 9 and 10. There may well be theological reasons for many of these changes, however, as for example in the invocation of God as *Elohim* instead of *YHWH* in certain psalms. Nevertheless, despite such textual emendations and the occasional involuntary scribal error during processes of transmission, the MT is incomparably superior to that of the LXX, which preserved some curious readings,[72] and to any of the secondary versions. There can be little doubt that Hempel is correct in attributing the comparative infrequency of textual error in the Hebrew Psalter to the living tradition of liturgy and prayer in the Temple and synagogue alike.[73] The LXX version may well have been based upon a rather different form of the Hebrew text than that in the possession of the Massoretes, but even this possibility would hardly account for the transcriptional errors and meaningless renderings that occur in most LXX manuscripts. Of the three oldest of these, only Codex Sinaiticus contained all the psalms, with Codex Vaticanus being deficient in the Hebrew text of Psalm 106:27 to 138:6, and Codex Alexandrinus in Psalm 50:20 to 80:11.[74]

Of the Latin versions, the *Psalterium Romanum* comprised a rather hasty revision by Jerome of the Old Latin with reference to the LXX text, while his *Psalterium Gallicanum*, made after A.D. 386 in Palestine, constituted a more careful product which, while being based upon extant manuscripts of the LXX, probably also depended to some extent at least upon the *Hexapla* of Origen. This revision furnished the text of the

---

[72] Cf. H. B. Swete, *Introduction to the OT in Greek,* p. 315.

[73] J. Hempel, *IDB,* III, p. 944.

[74] The text given in H. B. Swete, *The OT in Greek* (1891), II, is that of Vaticanus, with the lacunae supplied by Sinaiticus. Cf. Rahlfs, *Septuaginta-Studien* (1907), II.

psalms in much later editions of the Vulgate.[75] Although the *Psalterium iuxta Hebraeos* was made by Jerome about A.D. 392 from Hebrew manuscripts current in Palestine,[76] it never gained official recognition for use in the public worship of the Church.

H. THE MESSAGE OF THE PSALTER

Because the psalms emerged from a wide variety of circumstances over a prolonged period of Hebrew history, the religious standpoint that they present can hardly be regarded as carefully systematized. Indeed, very few of the compositions can be said to have been written with such a purpose in view, for while the psalmists frequently had a didactic aim, they did not set out to treat schematically the abiding truths of the Hebrew faith. The psalms can therefore be said in general to comprise the divine word spoken *in* rather than *to* men, and it is this factor that has done much to perpetuate the Psalter as a vehicle of abiding devotional value, and to furnish many of the individual psalms with a sense of timelessness.

However, it is possible to recognize certain fundamental themes that occur throughout these compositions, one of the most prominent being that of ethical monotheism. Allusions to "gods" generally referred to the misguided conceptions of pagan peoples, and there was no doubt in the minds of the various psalmists that God reigned supreme and alone, whether in heaven (Pss. 33:13, 53:2, *et al.*) or on Mount Zion (Ps. 132:13f.). His government was based upon the principles of justice and righteousness, fidelity, and mercy (Pss. 89:14, 97:2, *et al.*), and these qualities were directed supremely towards His covenant people Israel. This special position of privilege appears to account for the moral inequity of the imprecatory utterances in the Psalter, which were prompted not by personal considerations of vindictiveness so much as by zeal for the Holy One of Israel, who because of His nature must insure that judgment, as well as grace, operated in the moral world-order.

Consequently, while the psalmists occasionally drew attention to the beauties of nature, their concern with the world around them was primarily with the sphere of moral activity. Since they enjoyed no assurance of a future life, the question of retribution for wickedness was entertained in terms of the contemporary or immediate future situation, and undergirded by the traditional Hebrew belief in the divine moral governance of the world.

Although there are some psalms that depict Israel in a narrow, particularistic spirit as being completely dominant in a physical sense as well as a moral one over the whole Gentile world (Pss. 2:8, 18:43ff., 45:5, *et al.*), others saw God in a different sense as being the ruler over all the

---

[75] E.g. M. Hetzenauer (ed.), *Biblia Sacra* (1906).

[76] J. M. Harden (ed.), *Psalterium iuxta Hebraeos Hieronymi* (1922).

nations of the earth (Ps. 47:8) and as such the legitimate object of praise
from mankind (Pss. 2:11, 22:27ff., 68:32, et al.). For some psalmists this
situation was evidently ideal, and the manner in which it was to be
made actual, including the part to be played in this enterprise by Israel,
was never clearly enunciated in the Psalter, although there may well be
grounds for thinking of this concept along eschatological lines (Pss. 9:8,
67:4, et al.). However, aside from the pious expectation of a time when
disease, evil, and misfortune would be banished from the earth (Ps.
27:13), there is little that can be called eschatology in the Psalter in the
strictest sense of that term.

In general the psalmists were concerned predominantly with the more
immediate problems of life, and apart from such instances as Psalms
49:15 and 73:24, they believed that the death of the body meant that
the individual was virtually isolated from God in Sheol, so that any
concentration of thought upon an existence other than that which obtained in the physical world was virtually precluded by definition.
Despite the general focussing of attention upon this world and this life,
however, there were some psalmists who expected to encounter the
divine presence even in the shadowy realms of Sheol (Ps. 138:9); and
while there can obviously be no theology of a future life implicit in the
Psalter, there was certainly a distinct feeling that all individual spiritual
values were by no means obliterated in the decease of the body. Indeed,
the very fact that certain authors entertained the concept of some kind
of vague existence in Sheol at least suggested the possibility of a future
reawakening.

The older view that the Psalter looked forward to the time when God
would restore His people (Pss. 14:7, 53:6, et al.) through the agency of
an anointed personage or Messiah has been generally abandoned by
most liberal scholars, on the ground that the "anointed one" of the
Psalter (e.g. Pss. 2:2, 18:50, 20:6, et al.) referred to a reigning Hebrew
king. This position unfortunately takes inadequate cognizance of the
scope that the mission of the anointed personage was to reflect and
embrace. Not merely was he to be of the Davidic line, but he was to be
the supreme ruler of the coming messianic age (Ps. 72:1ff.), in which
the kingdom would be universal in extent (Ps. 2:8) and governed by the
Messiah in association with God.

The universality of the messianic rule was again emphasized in Psalm
72. The Messiah himself was depicted as conqueror, king, and priest,
reigning in glory on the right hand of God (Ps. 110:1ff.). Even in their
most exalted flights of poetic fancy the psalmists could hardly have
attributed such advanced qualities and functions to David, Solomon, or
any individual ruler of Israel or Judah, if they were to remain faithful to
the known historical situation. Quite obviously the idea of earthly kingship was used as a basis for fostering the messianic hope, and the
psalmists proved their value as agents for communicating and perpetuat-

ing this great spiritual expectation. Certainly the breadth of vision that the psalmists enjoyed in this respect cannot be completely accounted for by reference to the recorded internal happenings of the Hebrew monarchy, and failure to recognize this factor constitutes a grave weakness in the liberal position with regard to the messianic outlook of the Psalter.

Judging from the frequency of references to ceremonial practices, it appears that the Temple rituals were a well-established part of Israelite religious life throughout the bulk of the period in which the psalms were composed. However, it should be noted that such ceremonies were generally rather incidental to the larger purpose of the various authors, although there were some who depreciated the value of certain ritual emphases, as, for example, those of the sacrifice (Pss. 40:6, 50:13, 69:30f., *et al.*). It is of some interest to note that the priesthood received comparatively little mention (Pss. 115:10, 118:3), despite the various references to sacrifice (Pss. 4:5, 20:3, 27:6, *et al.*), the several types of offerings (Pss. 20:3, 50:8, 56:12, *et al.*), and the payment of vows (Pss. 22:25, 50:4, 56:1, *et al.*).

The concept of man exhibited by the psalmists was very different from that of the ancient Sumerians, who regarded the species *homo sapiens* as constituting little more than an appendix to the vaster processes of divine creativity. For the Hebrews, man was the overlord of the animal world, but although he was pre-eminent in creation he was still mortal. He had an allotted life-span (Ps. 90:10) like other elements of the natural world, and his final destiny was repose in Sheol, where there was neither remembrance nor praise of the Lord (Ps. 6:5, 30, *et al.*). Though the psalmists occasionally manifested amazement that man should have been so exalted by God (Ps. 144:3), the general view of man as a sinner in the sight of God served to keep the situation within proper bounds, and demonstrated the essential dependence of man upon his Creator.

The revelation of God as a supremely holy and moral being established by implication certain requirements on the part of those in ·Covenant relationship with Him. Failure to meet these standards, or direct rebellion against them, constituted an act of sin, the atonement for which followed the normal prescriptions of the Torah. Sacrificial worship was by no means as prominent in the Psalter as in some other books of the Old Testament, and while certain psalmists assumed that individuals adopted the usual course of participation in sacrificial rituals (Pss. 20:3, 50:8, *et al.*), others tended to minimize the sacrificial element in favor of the spiritual form of religion envisaged by Jeremiah and other prophets. Aside from the ingredients of confession and contrition, a notable feature of the Hebrew psalms was the confidence with which individuals approached God in expectation of an immediate response to their petitions. However, not all the psalmists were concerned with the granting of requests, for some of them were content to rest in the assurance that the entire course of human history was under divine control. For others, one of the greatest benefits of life consisted in the fact of fellowship with God, whether in the Temple or in private worship, and in the realization that the divine presence overshadowed the everyday affairs of existence.

The deeply personal religion of the psalmists and the intensely spiritual and devotional nature of their compositions furnished abiding qualities that enabled the Hebrew Psalter to transcend all barriers of time, culture, and nationality. The very fact that the psalms enshrined a living expression of the deepest human needs in relationship to God has guaranteed them a place in all true spiritual worship among Jews and Christians alike. It has also made this great body of literature a favored subject over the centuries for Biblical commentators who have discovered, as the ancient composers did, that in this approach to the material and spiritual problems of life there can be found something of that inner peace that is the property of all those who find the highest expression of their personalities in the performance of the divine will.

Supplementary Literature

Budde, K. *Die Schönsten Psalmen.* 1915.
Cheyne, T. K. *The Christian Use of the Psalms.* 1899.
Cohen, A. *The Psalms.* 1945.
Cumming, G. C. *The Assyrian and Hebrew Hymns of Praise.* 1934.
Davison, W. T. *The Praises of Israel.* 1893.
Gemser, B., et al. *Studies on Psalms.* 1963.
Gevirtz, S. *Patterns in the Early Poetry of Israel.* 1963.
Hitzig, F. *Die Psalmen.* 1863.
Lamb, J. A. *The Psalms in Christian Worship.* 1962.
Löhr, M. *Psalmenstudien.* 1922.
Olshausen, J. *Die Psalmen.* 1853.
Smith, J. M. P. *The Religion of the Psalms.* 1922.
Snaith, N. H. *Studies in the Psalter.* 1934.
Spurgeon, C. H. *The Treasury of David.* 1870-1875.
Tsevat, M. A. *A Study of the Language of the Biblical Psalms.* 1955.
Wutz, F. *Die Psalmen textkritisch untersucht.* 1925.

III. HEBREW WISDOM LITERATURE

One of the more notable products of the ancient Hebrew religious culture consisted of that group of compositions known as the Wisdom Literature. In the canonical writings it included the books of Proverbs, Job, Ecclesiastes, and certain of the psalms, particularly those dealing with the topic of wisdom. In the extra-canonical literature it was represented by such works as Ecclesiasticus, the Wisdom of Solomon, Tobit, 4 Maccabees, *Pirke Aboth*, and portions of other apocryphal or pseudepigraphal compositions. These writings preserved in one form or another the maxims and observations of generations of sages, and in so doing fostered among the Hebrews a didactic tradition that had its roots in Near Eastern antiquity.

In Mesopotamia, the concept of wisdom may originally have been applied equally to the dexterity of the magician, the manual skills of the craftsman in metal, and the organizing abilities of the *ensi* priest. While the basic usage was most probably utilitarian, it appears to have been uniformly connected with specific abilities, and doubtless as the result of priestly interests it became associated with religious activities at a comparatively early period.

It should be noted that the kind of wisdom (*nēmequ*) that was commonly understood by the Babylonians of antiquity was only infrequently associated with moral considerations, being used principally in reference to magical lore and cultic rites.[1] The wise man was thus the one who was initiated into such skills, and since this function was normally the prerogative of the priestly classes, the association of wisdom with priestly functions and personages would be a comparatively easy matter.

Such wisdom took its rise from the gods, among whom Marduk was its pre-eminent exponent, as indicated by the Babylonian composition *Ludlul bēl nēmeqi*. This masterly paean, named after its opening lines, "I will praise the Lord of Wisdom," spoke of the power of Marduk, patron

---

[1] Cf. the "Counsels of Wisdom" in W. G. Lambert, *Babylonian Wisdom Literature* (1960), pp. 96ff.; S. H. Langdon, *Proceedings of the Society of Biblical Archaeology*, XXXVIII (1916), pp. 105ff., 131ff.; R. W. Rogers, *Cuneiform Parallels to the OT* (1913), pp. 175ff.

deity of Babylon, and described his wisdom in terms of skill in the rituals of exorcism. In the developed Babylonian cosmogony, which was patterned upon earlier Sumerian forms, Wisdom was held to have inhabited the depths of the sea with the primeval deity Apsu, who was known variously as "the Deep" and "the House of Wisdom."[2] In the cosmogonic texts the wisdom of Ea (earlier "Enki"), the powerful water-deity, was represented as emerging from the abode of Apsu, and for this reason Ea was frequently styled "the Lord of Wisdom." In later incantation rituals Ea was normally associated with Marduk in attempts by the exorcists and priest-physicians to dispossess demons, cure illnesses, banish misfortunes, and the like.[3]

To speak, therefore, of Babylonian "wisdom" literature as a corpus in the Hebraic sense is incorrect, since no such group of writings existed in ancient Mesopotamia. In the strictest sense, the idea of Wisdom as a category in Babylonian literary compositions cannot be related to anything more than a number of scattered texts that happen to deal in a somewhat diverse manner with the same general topic. Thus certain texts treat of the practical issues of everyday life, such as the *Counsels of Wisdom*,[4] *Counsels of a Pessimist*,[5] and the *Instructions of Shuruppak*,[6] while others attempted to grapple with the moral problems of existence (as did *Ludlul bēl nēmeqi*) or to furnish groups of sayings, proverbs, or fables as a general guide to proper behavior.[7] Insofar as cosmological problems were concerned, many of the Babylonian epics could be included quite readily in this sort of grouping of "wisdom" compositions.

While the later Babylonian texts, which frequently represented an adaptation of earlier Sumerian originals, are considerably more prominent than their Sumerian counterparts, the scope of the latter has been enlarged considerably by archaeological discoveries in Mesopotamia,[8] particularly by those at Nippur, where tablets containing didactic and proverbial material going back to the third millennium B.C. were recovered.[9] By comparison, the *Story of Ahikar*, which survived in a fifth-century B.C. Aramaic version and indicated an Assyro-Babylonian origin, is a distinct latecomer in this general area of literature.[10]

The assumptions of Gunkel and others that there were points of contact between Egyptian and Hebrew gnomic concepts were borne out

---

[2] On Sumerian cosmogony see S. N. Kramer, *Sumerian Mythology*, pp. 28, 73.

[3] For these rituals see R. C. Thompson, *The Devils and Evil Spirits of Babylonia* (1904), II, pp. 90ff.

[4] Cf. S. H. Langdon, *Babylonian Wisdom* (1923), pp. 88ff.

[5] W. G. Lambert, *Babylonian Wisdom Literature*, pp. 107ff.

[6] H. Zimmern, ZA, XXX (1916), pp. 185ff.; W. F. Albright, *JAOS*, XXXVIII (1918), pp. 60ff.

[7] Cf. W. G. Lambert, *Babylonian Wisdom Literature*, pp. 151ff.

[8] Cf. J. J. A. van Dijk, *La sagesse suméro-accadienne* (1953); ANET, pp. 405ff.

[9] Cf. E. I. Gordon, *JAOS*, LXXIV (1954), pp. 82ff.

[10] Cf. B. Meissner, *Babylonien und Assyrien* (1920), II, p. 430; ANET, pp. 427ff.

by the dicovery of Erman that there was a close relationship between Proverbs 22:17–23:11 and the Egyptian *Wisdom of Amenophis*.[11] The latter was secured for the British Museum in 1888 by Sir E. A. W. Budge, but it was only in 1922 that he published extracts from the text, to be followed in 1923 by the complete work in the *Second Series of Facsimiles of Egyptian Hieratic Papyri in the British Museum*. Other Egyptian sapiental literature included the *Instruction for King Meri-ka-re*,[12] the *Instruction for the Vizier Ptah-hotep*,[13] the *Instruction of King Amen-em-Het*,[14] and the *Instruction of Ani*,[15] as well as didactic tales such as the celebrated *Dispute over Suicide*[16] and the *Protests of the Eloquent Peasant*.[17] On this basis scholars such as Humbert were able to postulate a considerable degree of Hebrew dependence upon Egyptian gnomic sources in books such as Proverbs, Ecclesiastes, and some of the psalms that treated of wisdom.[18] In the Egyptian literature, as in Babylonian compositions, wisdom was attributed to the inspiration and activities of the gods. For the ancient Egyptians the deity Thoth was the accredited fount of Wisdom, and to him was ascribed the "leadership of mankind."[19]

That Hebrew Wisdom Literature was part of a larger corpus which included Canaanite-Phoenician didactic material has become abundantly clear from Ugaritic discoveries.[20] Story has shown that the metrical style of Proverbs is in close agreement in many areas with that found in the Ugaritic epics,[21] while Albright has traced the presence of numerous Canaanite expressions and reminiscences in the same canonical book as well as in Job and Ecclesiastes.[22] It would seem clear, therefore, that not merely was Hebrew wisdom far from being an isolated literary or didactic phenomenon, but that in fact it was part of a large cultural heritage common to the whole of the ancient world. Scholars have not always realized that the closeness of association resulting from geographical lo-

---

[11] A. Erman, *Sitzungsberichte der preussischen Akademie der Wissenschaften* (1924), pp. 86ff.; cf. H. Gressmann, *ZAW*, XLII (1924), pp. 272ff. Cf. *ANET*, pp. 421f.; *DOTT*, pp. 172ff.

[12] *ANET*, pp. 414ff.; *DOTT*, pp. 155ff.; A. Erman, *The Literature of the Ancient Egyptians* (1927), pp. 75ff.

[13] *ANET*, pp. 412ff.

[14] *ANET*, pp. 418f.

[15] *ANET*, pp. 420f.

[16] A. Erman, *The Literature of the Ancient Egyptians*, pp. 86ff.; *ANET*, pp. 405ff.

[17] A. H. Gardiner, *JEA*, IX (1923), pp. 5ff.; *ANET*, pp. 407ff.

[18] P. Humbert, *Recherches sur les sources Égyptiennes de la littérature sapientale d'Israël* (1929). Cf. L. Dürr, *Die Wertung des Lebens im AT* (1926), pp. 7f.; W. O. E. Oesterley, *The Book of Proverbs* (1929), pp. xlvi ff.

[19] Cf. A. Erman, *Die Literatur der Aegypter* (1923), p. 186.

[20] For the equating of Canaanite and Phoenician see B. Maisler, *BASOR*, No. 102 (1946), pp. 7ff.; *BANE*, p. 351 n. 1.

[21] C. I. K. Story, *JBL*, LXIV (1945), pp. 319ff.

[22] W. F. Albright, *VT* suppl. vol. III (1955), pp. 6ff.; cf. *FSAC*, pp. 283f.

cation and commercial activities in antiquity might also be reflected in the reciprocal interdependence of literary categories such as the gnomic compositions.

In consequence it is not merely sufficient to suppose that the Hebrew writers depended entirely upon other ancient Near Eastern wisdom sources for their inspiration, for now a question must be raised about the extent to which Phoenician and Hebrew cultural expressions contributed to the gnomic corpus of Egypt and Mesopotamia. A tentative step in opposition to the commonly accepted view that sections of Proverbs were dependent upon the Egyptian *Wisdom of Amen-em-ope* was accordingly taken by Drioton, who argued from the irregular grammatical and syntactical forms of the Egyptian to the conclusion that it was most probably a translation of a Semitic work, perhaps identical with or similar to the one used in the compilation of the canonical book of Proverbs.[23]

In line with the common tradition of the ancient Near East, the concept of wisdom among the Hebrews was essentially practical. The Hebrew term חכמה, "wisdom," and its cognate חכם, "wise," the counterparts of the Akkadian *ha-kamu* and the Ugaritic *hkm*, might be said to describe the art of being successful.[24] As was most probably the case in ancient Mesopotamia, it was applied among the Hebrews to those possessing technical skills (Exod. 31:3; Isa. 40:20) and to those individuals whose insight (בינה, Job 39:26; תבונה, Ps. 136:5) made them of value as advisers to kings,[25] the latter being particularly in need of wisdom.[26] This is not surprising in view of the fact that, in cultures other than that of Israel, the idea of wisdom was also closely associated with the personage of a counsellor, whose functions were to maintain the conditions of existence and formulate decisions for future conduct and well-being.[27] It may be that by the time of Jeremiah an official caste had come into being to fulfill this counselling activity (cf. Jer. 18:18; 22:1; 2 Chron. 25:16f.), and if this was so, such a group would constitute the Hebrew counterpart of the astrologers, magicians, diviners, and sorcerers of the heathen courts (cf. Gen. 41:8; Exod. 7:11; Dan. 1:20; 2:2), functioning, of course, in independence of magical techniques.

As in other cultures, wisdom in its fullest sense was attributable to God alone (Job 12:13ff.; Isa. 31:2), who manifested His wisdom alike in the creation of the world (Prov. 3:19f.; 8:22ff.) and mankind (Job 10:8ff.; Ps. 104:24). This wisdom included an infallible means of discrimination between good and evil, and as such it constituted the basis for

---

[23] E. Drioton, *Mélanges Bibliques, André Robert* (1957), pp. 254ff., *Sacra Pagina*, I (1959), pp. 229ff.

[24] So D. A. Hubbard, *NBD*, p. 1333.

[25] For the wise man at court see S. H. Blank, *IDB*, IV, pp. 853f.

[26] N. W. Porteous, *VT* suppl. vol. III (1955), pp. 247ff.

[27] Cf. P. A. H. de Boer, *VT* suppl. vol. III (1955), pp. 42ff.

the rewards of the righteous and the just punishment of the wicked (Prov. 10:3; 11:4; Ps. 37:1ff.). Since all wisdom was derived from God, there must ultimately be a religious element in what the Hebrews envisaged as wisdom. For them there was no dichotomy between the intellectual and practical, the religious and the secular, for while they recognized that the knowledge and fear of the Lord constituted the highest form of wisdom, they were also aware that worldly wisdom, though less elevated in nature, was different only in degree and not in kind from divine wisdom. The whole of life was thus connoted in terms of religious experience, and wisdom was held to be relevant at all points of existence. The inscrutable nature of divine wisdom was such that man needed a revelation of divine grace if he was to grasp it at all (Job 28:23, 28), but given this it was possible for the insights of wisdom to be applied to all walks of life.

The problem of the hypostatizing or personification of wisdom has been widely discussed for a number of years with differing results, varying from theories of a mythological origin of wisdom to the interpretation of the concept as a literary or artistic device.[28] The theory of an underlying mythology seems contraindicated by the suddenness with which the personification of wisdom arrived on the Biblical scene. It can perhaps be said to be anticipated by Job (28:12ff.), which presented wisdom as something inscrutable to man but clear to God. In Proverbs (1:20ff.; cf. 3:15ff.), wisdom was likened to a woman urging men to find security in her, and reached a climax of personification (Prov. 8:22ff.; cf. 3:19) in claiming to be the first act of divine creation and an assistant in subsequent work.

It may be, as Wheeler Robinson indicated, that the characteristic resistance of the Hebrew mind to philosophical or metaphysical speculation and abstraction often compelled the poets of Israel to deal with inanimate objects or concepts as though they were endowed with some degree of personality.[29] Such may well have been the case in Proverbs, where the personification of wisdom was effected in order to incite men to pay to her the proper degree of respect (cf. 8:32ff.). Whatever the specific motives of the various Hebrew writers were in relationship to the topic of wisdom, there can be no doubt that when they indulged in personification they were following a literary and religious tradition of

[28] Cf. W. Schencke, *Die Chokma (Sophia) in der jüdischen Hypostasenspekulation* (1913); P. Heinisch, *Personifikationen und Hypostasen im AT* (1921); *Die persönliche Weisheit des AT* (1926); O. S. Rankin, *Israel's Wisdom Literature*, pp. 222ff.; J. Arvedson, *Das Mysterium Christi* (1937), pp. 158ff.; H. Ringgren, *Word and Wisdom: Studies in the Hypostatization of Divine Qualities and Functions in the Ancient Near East* (1947); K. A. Kitchen, *Tyndale House Bulletin*, No. 5-6 (1960), pp. 4ff.

[29] H. Wheeler Robinson, *Inspiration and Revelation in the OT*, p. 260.

great antiquity, the nature and extent of which will be examined subsequently.

That such a tendency was followed in later Hebrew gnomic literature is no indication whatever of a progressive development in the concept of wisdom in Hebrew thought, as has been commonly supposed by liberal scholars. Following ancient Near Eastern customs of advanced age, personifications of wisdom occur in both early and late compositions, and in this regard it is significant to note that in a work such as Ecclesiasticus, which was written in the second century B.C., the concept of wisdom was identified with that of the Torah to the point where there were remarkably few personifications of wisdom. Another matter of historical and religious importance in this question of hypostatizing is that the personification of wisdom formed an important link between the Palestinian and Hellenic forms of Judaism. From the standpoint of Christian theology it set the pattern for the incorporation of certain pagan elements of thought, such as the *Logos*,[30] into the larger body of Christian doctrine, a tendency that saw its climax in the Aristotelianism of the *Summa Theologica* of Thomas Aquinas.

[30] W. Fairweather, *The Background of the Gospels* (1908), p. 84.

IV. THE BOOK OF PROVERBS

A. NAME AND OUTLINE

This work bears the longest title of any book in the canonical Hebrew Scriptures, and in many ways it is similar to the title-page of a modern published composition. It contains the descriptive heading of the subject-matter, the name and status of the attributive author, and a subtitle explaining the wider purposes of the book and beginning, "that men may know wisdom." In this manner the first six verses described the nature and scope of the work, which under normal conditions is generally styled The Proverbs of Solomon (משלי שלמה) or, simply, Proverbs. The LXX bore the title, Παροιμίαι Σαλομῶντος ("proverbs" or "parables" of Solomon), while the Vulgate edition was captioned *Liber Proverbiorum*.

In rabbinic tradition (*Bab. Bath.* 14*b*, 15*a*) Proverbs followed the Psalms and Job, and the order of these three books in the English versions may perhaps have arisen from some chronological scheme based upon the rabbinic tradition, which assigned Job to Moses, the Psalter to David, and Proverbs to Hezekiah. The LXX regrouped its canonical sources in order to bring together the three books of Proverbs, Ecclesiastes, and Canticles, which by tradition were attributed to Solomon.

In common with other races of antiquity, as has been observed above, the Hebrews possessed a number of wisdom-utterances that probably circulated at least partly in oral form prior to being collected and preserved in writing. These sayings enshrined certain truths gleaned from the experiences of life, and while they were intended to serve as practical guides for successful living, they ultimately reached back for their inspiration and vitality to the distinctive features of the Israelite faith. In this sense, therefore, they can never be regarded as purely secular in the sense in which the proverb is sometimes understood. Indeed, the idea of a proverb in Hebrew thought seems capable of a distinct range of understanding. The Hebrew term משל came from a verb meaning "to be like," "to resemble" (cf. Akkadian *mashālu*, "be resembling"), and seems to have been closely related to the Akkadian *mishlu* or

1010

"half," indicating two portions of similar character.[1] The basic sense, as Johnson pointed out, would thus appear to be that of similarity or congruity, and the most primitive type of proverb in the Hebrew Scriptures would probably conform to this basic pattern (Ezek. 16:44; cf. 1 Sam. 24:13; Jer. 31:29). In the more developed sense the proverb was employed as an art-form, and this is commonly found in the Wisdom Literature, whether as a single balanced line consisting of two parallel *stichoi,* or as a didactic poem. These two categories generally exhibit one or other of the rhythmic structural forms found in Hebrew poetry, principally those of synonymous (e.g. Prov. 16:31), antithetic (e.g. Prov. 28:1), or synthetic (e.g. Prov. 26:11) parallelism. A further type not found in the Psalter, Lamentations, or Job, occurred in the book of Proverbs and is known as a *parabolic distich,* in which one or more factual elements are related to a moral concept (e.g. Prov. 26:3).

The first eleven chapters of Proverbs contain addresses or exhortations of varying length that in fact constitute didactic poems in their own right, and as such represent a development of the simple *māshāl.* These discourses are well represented by warnings against highway robbery (1:10ff.), the appeal of wisdom to those who would neglect her (1:20ff.), the warnings relating to the adulteress (7:1ff.), and the acrostic poem in praise of the prudent wife (31:10f.). As the equivalent of the English "byword," the term *māshāl* occurred in certain poetic compositions (cf. Pss. 44:13f.; 69:11f.), while elsewhere it was used in the context of scorn or mocking (cf. Deut. 28:37; Isa. 14:4ff.; Hab. 2:6).

Proverbs consists largely of short, incisive statements that could be employed with the greatest effect in the communication of behavioral, moral, and spiritual truths. Commencing from humble beginnings (cf. Gen. 10:9)[2] they were developed over many generations into a variety of forms with the overall aim of inculcating certain behavioral principles by means of associating and contrasting certain facets of everyday experience. As with other elements of the wisdom corpus, the purpose of the book was to furnish instruction for a particular class of young men. In ancient Israel it was customary for young children to be instructed within the family circle, and in adolescence the girls normally followed the pattern of domestic duties while the boys came increasingly under paternal tutelage. In the upper-class families the young men were given more specific schooling aimed at the development of character and the furthering of success in life, this program of education being based upon

---

[1] For representative studies of מָשָׁל see O. Eissfeldt, *BZAW,* XXIV (1913); A. H. Godbey, *AJSL,* XXXIX (1923), pp. 89ff.; M. Hermaniuk, *La Parabole Évangelique* (1947), pp. 62ff.; A. S. Herbert, *Scottish Journal of Theology* (1954), pp. 180ff.; A. R. Johnson, *VT* suppl. vol. III (1955), pp. 162ff.; C. T. Fritsch, *IB,* IV, pp. 771ff.; O. Eissfeldt, *Einleitung in das AT* (1956 ed.), pp. 73ff., 94ff., 106ff.; S. H. Blank, *IDB,* III, pp. 934ff.

[2] Cf. L. Köhler, *Hebrew Man* (1956), p. 104.

the principles inherent in Proverbs and similar books. That such instruction was intended for a rather restricted section of the adolescent male population seems evident from the contents of Proverbs. The teachings of the book were not intended for the edification of young women, and certainly not for young children if the caution against the adulterous woman is any criterion. The concern of the book is predominantly with the youths of the upper classes, since they alone would be most likely to be able to afford the kind of excesses described in Proverbs and similar gnomic literature.[3]

According to Jeremiah 18:18 the cultural life of the Hebrews was molded by the prophets, the priests, and the wise men. Though the latter were never as prominent in national life as the specifically religious personages, they nevertheless exerted considerable influence as teachers of folk-wisdom. Their origins are obscure, but it may be that during the period of the later monarchy they gained prominence through association with the scribes who were employed in government service. Jeremiah 8:8f. equated the scribes and the wise men, and it may be that the reference in Isaiah 29:14 pointed to their existence as a group before the middle of the eighth century B.C. However, they do not appear to have been rigidly organized at any time during the period covered by the canonical Hebrew books, and the picture presented by some liberal scholars of the existence between the fifth and third centuries B.C. of "schools of wisdom" similar in character to the contemporary Greek Sophistic schools has been correctly relegated by Albright to the realm of myth.[4]

In the early period the wisdom of the sages was pronounced at the city-gates (cf. Job 29:7ff.), for the benefit of any who desired to listen to it, while at a later time such instruction was given by the individual sage either out-of-doors or in some suitable building. In the post-exilic era the *bēth hammidhrāsh* or "house of instruction" arose, perhaps at first in connection with synagogue functions, though subsequently it appears to have existed independently. After the Maccabean period the wise men declined in influence, and their teachings were taken over by the scribes of later Judaism.

The problems of authorship and date of Proverbs are intimately bound up with the composite nature of the book, which can be divided into several sections, as follows:

I. Title of the Work and Motto, ch. 1:1-7
II. Various Discourses, ch. 1:8—9:18
III. First Collection of the Proverbs of Solomon, ch. 10:1—22:16

---

[3] Cf. R. Gordis, *HUCA*, XVIII (1943-44), pp. 77ff., as against C. T. Fritsch, *IB*, IV, p. 776, who denied that the instruction in Proverbs was intended for any specific class.

[4] W. F. Albright, *VT* suppl. vol. III (1955), pp. 4f.

Of these sections, three have no titles, two are ascribed to Solomon, and the remainder to individuals or anonymous groups. In view of the general tendency of Hebrew antiquity, which ascribed anything involving wisdom to Solomon, the traditions concerning him in 1 Kings 4:32 have been called into question, and more radical critics have gone as far as to deny that he had any responsibility at all for the literary material attributed to him in Proverbs. Representative of the latter group was Pfeiffer, who repudiated any suggestion of Solomonic authorship.[5] In assigning a late date to the book generally he stressed the Edomite and north-Arabic sources of important areas of Hebrew wisdom, a position which was challenged by Albright.[6] Scott, who also disliked the tradition of Solomonic authorship, recorded that most historians accepted the Hebrew accounts of the Solomonic talents at face value, citing in particular the opinions of Eissfeldt and Baumgartner.[7] Most scholars who have studied the problem intensively have favored the historical nature of the Solomonic tradition to a greater or lesser degree,[8] though some have been far from certain about it,[9] and others have entertained the presence of legendary accretions.[10]

B. SOURCES OF THE PROVERBS

Despite a certain degree of skepticism concerning extant Solomonic material in Proverbs, Albright agreed with Baumgartner in his suggestion that wisdom had become associated with Solomon owing to the well-known connections of the king with Egypt, where wisdom literature had

---

[5] *PIOT*, p. 645; C. H. Toy, *A Critical and Exegetical Commentary on the Book of Proverbs*, pp. xix-xx.

[6] R. H. Pfeiffer, ZAW, XLIV (1926), pp. 13ff. *ARI*, pp. 127f.

[7] R. B. Y. Scott, *VT* suppl. vol. III (1955), pp. 262f. O. Eissfeldt, *Einleitung in das AT*, p. 527. W. Baumgartner, *OTMS*, p. 213.

[8] Cf. E. Sellin, *Geschichte des israelitisch-jüdischen Volkes*, I, p. 197, II, p. 179; A. T. Olmstead, *History of Palestine and Syria* (1931), p. 341; J. Skinner, *I and II Kings*, p. 97; O. S. Rankin, *Israel's Wisdom Literature*, p. 6; W. A. Irwin, *IB*, I, p. 179.

[9] H. R. Hall, *Ancient History of the Near East* (1927 ed.), p. 433; *GI*, pp. 200f.; A. Alt, *Theologisch Literaturzeitung* (1951), LVI, pp. 139ff.

[10] H. Wheeler Robinson, *History of Israel*, pp. 69f.; J. Skinner, *I and II Kings*, p. 97; *FSAC*, p. 224.

flourished from at least the Middle Kingdom period,[11] and his favorable attitude towards the Egyptian monarchy.[12] Gemser went even further, and postulated the establishing of an official corps in Jerusalem under Solomon along the lines in existence at the Egyptian court.[13] This was in direct opposition to the views of Oesterley, who had held it improbable that at that period the Hebrews were sufficiently receptive to such influences from Egypt.[14]

Albright, having demonstrated the important place that Canaanite thought and literature had in relationship to Proverbs,[15] and having repudiated the late date assigned by Pfeiffer to the work,[16] held to the probability of a Solomonic nucleus for Proverbs, maintaining that the role of the great king as a patron of didactic literature must have been of considerable proportions in order for the book to have been dedicated to him. As with the question of Davidic authorship of certain psalms, there must always be some uncertainty as to the exact amount of the proverbial literature that may be said to be strictly Solomonic.

However, there seems to be no adequate reason for denying the substantial validity of the tradition that ascribed the uttering of wise sayings to Solomon. There appears to be little doubt that, even on the lowest estimate, he was an individual of considerable gifts of mind and personality, and it is very probable that his reputation as a sage and an intellectual was enhanced rather inadvertently by the simple fact that contemporary monarchs in the Near East were not themselves particularly outstanding persons. If the composing of proverbs constituted a court activity or pastime in the Solomonic era, it may be that the three thousand proverbs attributed to the king were actually the product of the court as a whole, in which Solomon himself no doubt took a leading part.

The first collection of the "Sayings of the Wise" (Prov. 22:17–23:14) has, since the days of Erman, been regarded as dependent upon the *Wisdom of Amen-em-ope* (Amenophis).[17] In view of the fact that the *Wisdom of Amenophis* contained thirty chapters or "houses," Erman, Gressmann, and Eissfeldt have amended the corrupt reading שִׁלְשׁוֹם in Proverbs 22:20 to שָׁלִישִׁים, "thirty," with a view to indicating the intention

---

[11] Cf. *ANET*, pp. 412ff. A. Erman, *Die Literatur der Aegypter*, pp. 86ff., 294ff., placed the beginnings of Egyptian gnomic literature in the third millennium B.C.

[12] W. Baumgartner, *Theologische Rundschau*, V (1933), p. 270.

[13] B. Gemser, *Sprüche Salomos* (1937), p. 2.

[14] W. O. E. Oesterley, ZAW, XLV (1927), pp. 16f.

[15] W. F. Albright, *VT* suppl. vol. III (1955), pp. 6ff.

[16] *JBL*, LXI (1942), p. 123.

[17] Cf. W. O. E. Oesterley, *The Wisdom of Egypt and the OT in the Light of the Newly Discovered 'Teaching of Amen-em-ope'* (1927), *The Book of Proverbs* (1929), pp. xlvi ff.; J. Fichtner, *Die altorientalische Weisheit in ihrer israelitisch-jüdischen Ausprägung* (1933), pp. 3f.; D. Kidner, *Proverbs* (1964), pp. 23f.

of the author to present thirty proverbs. This, however, must be regarded at best as tentative, since only about one-third of the section corresponds at all closely to the *Wisdom of Amenophis*, and the remainder is either Israelite in origin or derived from other sources, as for example in the case of Proverbs 23:13, which is borrowed from the oriental *Sayings of Ahikar*. Probably the most satisfactory explanation attaching to the proposed emendation is not to render שלשום as though it meant "thirty," but to regard it as an elliptical form of אתמול שלשום, "formerly," "already." Thus the clause would be translated, "Have I not written for thee already, with counsels of knowledge?"

That there is a general connection between this portion of Proverbs and the *Wisdom of Amenophis* is scarcely in dispute. What is not so clear, however, is the question of their interrelationship. Baumgartner affirmed that scholars in general had accepted the theory that Amenophis furnished the original for Proverbs 22:17—23:11,[18] but while this has been the prevailing view it has not by any means gone unchallenged. R. O. Kevin was among the first to suggest that Amenophis was dependent upon the Hebrew book and other sections of the Old Testament Wisdom Literature, a position that was subsequently adopted and enlarged by the distinguished French Egyptologist E. Drioton.[19] He maintained that certain peculiarities in grammatical and syntactical forms indicated that the Egyptian composition was a rather literal translation of a Semitic original. This latter may have been entitled "The Words of the Wise," and may have either actually constituted, or at least closely resembled, the collection used by Solomon (Prov. 22:17; cf. 10:1), so that in effect both Proverbs and Amenophis may well have borrowed independently from some already extant Semitic source. The thesis propounded by Drioton was examined and rejected by R. J. Williams, who argued that the *Wisdom of Amenophis* was not dependent upon Proverbs.[20] At the time of writing the situation is such that rash conclusions concerning the dependence of the relevant section of Proverbs upon the *Wisdom of Amenophis* should be avoided. It can be observed, however, that all portions of Proverbs contain vocabulary, idiomatic expressions, and gnomic concepts of great antiquity; and in view of the important place that Canaanite wisdom is now known to have occupied in the Near Eastern gnomic corpus, it might not be amiss to devote more careful study than has been the case hitherto to the theory that both Amenophis and Proverbs depend to some extent upon earlier Semitic originals, perhaps of Mesopotamian provenance.[21]

---

[18] *OTMS*, p. 212.
[19] R. O. Kevin, *Journal of the Society of Oriental Research*, XIV (1930), pp. 115ff. E. Drioton, *Mélanges Bibliques, André Robert*, pp. 254ff., *Sacra Pagina*, I (1959), pp. 229ff.
[20] R. J. Williams, *JEA*, XLVII (1961), pp. 100ff.
[21] Cf. M. Dahood, *Proverbs and Northwest Semitic Philology* (1963).

As regards the authorship and date of specific collections in Proverbs the first group (Prov. 1:8–9:18) has been taken to be anonymous, and has generally been assigned to a late date.[22] While the final editing may have occurred around 600 B.C., there is actually not a single piece of factual evidence that would establish the post-exilic date for this section of the book. Indeed, the contrary is the case, for as Albright has shown, the number of parallels in thought, structure, and phraseology with Ugaritic literature make it entirely possible that specific aphorisms and even longer sections go back into the Bronze Age in substantially their extant form.[23] Earlier critics were accustomed to date this general section at a late period on another basis, namely, that the personification of wisdom depended for its inspiration upon Greek influences emerging from the time of the Sophists. Such a view blatantly disregards the antiquity of personification of concepts and qualities in the Near Eastern cultures generally, as can be demonstrated from extant literary sources. Thus in the third millennium B.C., *Hike* or Magic was personified as a god in human form in reliefs and texts,[24] while in the second millennium B.C. there were abundant examples of this tendency in Egypt.[25] A double personification, that of "Sight and Hearing," came from the Middle Kingdom period, reflecting a parallel phenomenon in Ugaritic literature.[26] At least as early as the second millennium B.C. in Mesopotamia, the wife of the deity Enki (Ea) was believed to be served by two attendants personifying "Hearing" and "Intelligence" respectively, and this form of personification became widespread, being applied to the Underworld, Justice, Law, and so on.

The Hittites and Hurrians followed Babylonian practices in personifying ethical concepts.[27] Texts at Ras Shamra have also yielded a number of important personifications.[28] As Kitchen has shown, arguments for a late date of passages in Proverbs upon the basis that wisdom is personified therein must clearly be abandoned in the light of such evidence.[29] Furthermore, following the pattern of Ptahhotep and Amenophis in Egypt, it would be quite proper for a ruler such as Solomon to preface his own proverbs with an introductory discourse. In the light of the evidence from Near Eastern antiquity there would seem to be no good

[22] E.g. *IBOT*, p. 207; *PIOT*, pp. 657f.; *OTFD*, pp. 296f.

[23] W. F. Albright, *VT* suppl. vol. III (1955), pp. 7ff.

[24] A. H. Gardiner, *Proceedings of the Society of Biblical Archaeology*, XXXVII (1915), pp. 253ff., XXXIX (1917), pp. 134ff.

[25] Gardiner, *ibid.*, XXXVIII (1916), pp. 43ff., 83ff., XXXIX (1917), pp. 138f.

[26] R. A. Caminos, *Literary Fragments in the Hieratic Script* (1956), p. 35; K. A. Kitchen, *JEA*, XLIV (1958), p. 128.

[27] E. Dhorme, *Les Religions de Babylonie et d'Assyrie* (1949), pp. 73ff.

[28] C. H. Gordon, *Ugaritic Manual*, p. 282; Glossary No. 989.

[29] K. A. Kitchen, *Tyndale House Bulletin*, No. 5-6 (1960), pp. 4ff.

reason why Solomon and others should not have personified wisdom in an endeavor to communicate the nature of divine truths.

The first principal group of material attributed directly to King Solomon (Prov. 10:1–22:16) appears to be of considerable antiquity, and consists of about three hundred and seventy-five proverbs. No system of grouping is evident, and the majority of the proverbs are unrelated. While some of them appear to conform to the type of reflective, academic moralizations entertained by Toy,[30] others are quite obviously folk-sayings.[31] Although they were grounded in the traditional religious concepts of Israelite faith, the bulk of them were concerned with secular and practical issues that pointed to the material and moral benefits to be gained by the pursuit of wisdom, and there is nothing in their contents at all inconsistent with a date in the Solomonic period.

The first collection of "Sayings of the Wise" (Prov. 22:17–23:14) depends for its dating upon its relationship to the *Wisdom of Amenophis*, which has been dated by some scholars as low as the sixth century B.C., but which, according to Albright, is to be dated in or about the twelfth century B.C. on archaeological and other grounds.[32] In the light of the evidence at hand, the position adopted by Albright appears to interpret the situation more realistically by far than any other current attempt, and, whatever the nature of the relationship between Amenophis and Proverbs, or their dependence to any extent upon an earlier Semitic source, it would imply an early date for this collection of "Wise Sayings" and also for a subsidiary one (Prov. 24:23-34), which is of a similar character. Neither is apparently Solomonic in origin, but both belong to the lore of the Hebrew sages who collected and preserved such maxims.

The second collection of material attributed to Solomon (Prov. 25:1–29:27) preserved the tradition that Hezekiah and his company played a part in formulating and editing collections of proverbs amassed in Hebrew gnomic circles. The interest that Hezekiah had in Hebrew literature was indicated by the reference in 2 Chronicles 29:25ff., and it may be that these proverbs had been preserved, as Bentzen suggested, in oral form until the time of Hezekiah, when they were copied out.[33] Driver listed a number of proverbs that in his view indicated a certain restiveness concerning the monarchy,[34] and it is possible that these reflect the disturbed conditions of the eighth century B.C.

The "Words of Agur" (Prov. 30:1-33) refer initially to individuals of obscure identity. The first four verses are introduced as an oracle to

---

[30] C. H. Toy, *A Critical and Exegetical Commentary on the Book of Proverbs*, p. xi.

[31] W. O. E. Oesterley, *The Book of Proverbs*, p. lxxv.

[32] W. F. Albright, *VT* suppl. vol. III (1955), pp. 6, 13.

[33] A. Bentzen, *Introduction to the OT*, II, p. 173.

[34] *DILOT*, p. 401.

demonstrate how the skeptic concludes that it is impossible to know God. Subsequent verses refute the position thus set out by an appeal to the divine revelation, and verses 10-33 consist of nine groups of "numerical" proverbs. Several exhibit a rhythmical pattern that is to be found in certain eighth-century prophets (cf. Am. 1:2; Mic. 5:5), and that is also of common occurrence in the Ugaritic texts.[35] This section is unquestionably pre-exilic in provenance. The "Words of Lemuel" (Prov. 31:1-9) constitute a short section in which the influence of Aramaic is noteworthy. Lemuel as an individual is unknown, and the tenor of the advice harmonizes well with a pre-exilic date for the material. The stylized form of the acrostic poem dealing with the prudent wife (Prov. 31:10-31) indicates that it is probably the latest section of the book, and it may have been added during the exilic period.

The final form of the book could hardly have appeared before the time of Hezekiah (716/15-687/86 B.C.), though it was probably not very much later, apart from the poem concerning the prudent wife, since there is no positive evidence whatever for postulating a post-exilic date for the extant work. Albright has shown that the contents of Proverbs must, on literary grounds, be dated before the seventh-century B.C. Aramaic *Sayings of Aḥikar*, and there is no reason to suppose that the work could not have been completed at any period from 700 B.C. onwards.

C. THE TEXT OF PROVERBS

Despite certain corruptions and other difficulties that have arisen in the process of transmission, the Hebrew text of Proverbs has survived in remarkably good condition. There are about twenty-five readings that present particular difficulty for the translator,[36] and emendations at this point must be regarded as purely conjectural in nature. Proverbs also contains some ancient words whose meaning had become lost over the centuries, and whose nature is still obscure.[37] Other phrases have had remarkable light shed upon them as the result of Ugaritic discoveries, which have served to show the nature of the *Sitz im Leben des Volkes* from which many of the practical sayings emerged.[38]

While the LXX is the most valuable ancient version for purposes of studying the text of Proverbs, it must be utilized with caution, since the Greek text itself has suffered considerably from corruptions and other

[35] C. H. Gordon, *Ugaritic Handbook,* pp. 34, 201.

[36] These include 6:26; 7:22; 12:12; 13:23; 14:9; 17:14; 18:19; 19:7; 19:22; 21:12; 22:21; 25:11, 20; 26:8, 10; 27:9, 16; 28:17; 30:1, 31. Cf. A. R. Hulst, *OT Translation Problems* (1960), pp. 114ff.

[37] E.g. אמֹון, 8:30, perhaps an error for אמֻן as read by Aquila and the AV; יתר 12:26; חֵבֶל, 23:34; מִנּוֹן, 29:21; עֲלוּקָה, 30:15; אלקום, 30:31, זרזיר.

[38] W. F. Albright, *VT* suppl. vol. III (1955), pp. 7ff.

peculiarities during its transmission.[39] The LXX contains certain material that the Hebrew lacks, and a study of these supplementary verses
indicates that at least some of them go back to an original Hebrew
collection no longer extant, such as the couplets after Proverbs 9:12,
while others that do not read like a translation from the Hebrew may
well constitute insertions from a Greek collection. Some of the textual
divergences may be due to the fact that certain proverbs were known in
a somewhat different form in the post-exilic era, and the compilers of the
LXX may have drawn upon these variants in preference to the MT or
some other similar Hebrew tradition.

The LXX also exhibited a less-than-sacrosanct attitude towards the
Hebrew text by rearranging the order of the collections of sayings. The
Greek followed the pattern established by the Hebrew up to Proverbs
24:22, after which it inserted a short section (30:1-10) from the "Words
of Agur," followed by 24:23-34. After this brief passage came another
insertion from the "Words of Agur" (30:11-33), then the section entitled
the "Words of Lemuel" (Prov. 31:1-9), followed by the four chapters
of Solomonic material collected by the men of Hezekiah. The LXX,
like the Hebrew, concluded with the acrostic poem lauding the prudent
wife. This variation of order probably indicates that the collection of
sayings originally circulated in separate form, and that there may well
have been more than one Hebrew textual tradition regarding the order of
the collections.

The nature of the teaching enshrined in Proverbs viewed humanity in
terms of two classes: those who possessed the moral qualities to which
wisdom could make a successful appeal, and who as a result would
themselves ultimately become wise, and those who by native disposition
were deficient in such qualities, and were thus regarded as *hᵃşar-lēbh*.
This designated lack of understanding functioned for the Hebrew sages
as much at the moral, emotional, and spiritual level as it did in the area
of intellectual inquiry, since the repudiation of wisdom was ultimately a
moral issue. While such an undergirding for an educational system has
the undeniable merit of associating religion almost inextricably with the
issues of daily life, it has one unfortunate weakness. Like other forms of
humanistic dogma it fails to appreciate the nature of the connection
between character and motive, so that, for example, a man of reputedly
high character could, on occasions, indulge in anti-social or anti-gnomic
behavior from entirely unworthy and incorrect motives without any
guidance for such a contingency from the ancient Hebrew sages. This
deficiency is all the more surprising because of the association of Prov-

---

[39] Cf. the early studies by P. de Lagarde, *Anmerkungen zur Griechischen
Übersetzung der Proverbien* (1863) and A. J. Baumgärtner, *Étude critique sur l'état
du texte du Livre des Proverbes* (1890). Cf. K. G. Kuhn, *Beiträge zur Erklärung
des Salomonischen Spruchbuches* (1931).

erbs with Solomon, who proved to be an outstanding example of this unfortunate tendency, if the historical sources that narrate his doings are to be given any credence at all.

This practical handbook of prudent living contained some remarkable insights into the relationship between the individual personality and physico-mental states. It has been the common practice among scholars generally to relate such speculations in Proverbs to the ancient Egyptian system of humoral pathology, in which health was determined by the internal balance of four specific fluids. This is by no means the case, however, for the Hebrew sages were in fact engaged in making accurate empirical observations upon the relationship between emotional states and bodily changes, which have been recognized as valid by modern psychosomatic medical research.[40] It was the task of wisdom to emphasize constantly the connection between positive affectivity and physical health, and in this respect the Hebrew sages were far ahead of their day in the matter of theories concerning the origin of health and disease.[41]

There can be no question as to the high ethical teaching of Proverbs, concerned as it was with the relating of individual virtue to the will of God. The wisdom that it enshrined was not that of prophet or priest, but of human experience in its manifold aspects. It was particularly noteworthy for the manner in which it showed that even the smallest and apparently least significant aspects of life are in fact an important religious experience when lived in the light of divine wisdom. The book contained no references to the events of Hebrew history, and very few allusions either to sacrifice or the worship of the cultus. Concepts of sin were related to questions of prudence or success rather than to metaphysics, and in the absence of a doctrine of immortality the concept of retribution was thought of in terms of the present existence, with the wicked being cut off suddenly in the prime of life.

The fact that events did not always accord with this pattern must have raised serious questions in the minds of the sages as to the validity of their theories, and it may have been as a result of this that Proverbs presented a slightly more developed eschatology than that occurring in the Psalter. In Proverbs, the abysmal abode of the departed, named Sheol and Abaddon (Prov. 15:11), was not irretrievably dissociated from God, but was represented in such a manner as to indicate that God was concerned to some extent with the region and its populace. Although there seems to be a distinct moral connotation associated with the idea of Sheol, it represents no more than a vague foreshadowing of later concepts of paradise and hell.

[40] Cf. R. K. Harrison, *IDB*, I, p. 848.
[41] Cf. D. I. Macht, *Bulletin of the History of Medicine*, XVIII (1945), pp. 301ff.; F. Dunbar, *Emotions and Bodily Changes* (1954), pp. 651, 659.

While Proverbs constitutes a rich legacy of human experience, it is important to note, as C. T. Fritsch has shown, that the very presence of the book in the Old Testament canon indicates that wisdom constitutes the revelation of the divine orderly plan in the universe and in human life, and not just the mere accumulation of intelligent observations concerning life through the ages.[42] The fact that Jesus Christ associated Himself with it (cf. Lk. 11:31) brings it into proper perspective in the redemptive purposes of God.

Supplementary Literature

Boström, G. *Proverbiastudien*. 1935.

Cheyne, T. K. *Job and Solomon, or the Wisdom of the Old Testament*. 1887.

Cohen, A. *Proverbs*. 1946.

Greenstone, J. H. *Proverbs with Commentary*. 1950.

Kidner, F. D. *Proverbs: An Introduction and Commentary*. 1964.

Macdonald, D. B. *The Hebrew Philosophical Genius: A Vindication*. 1936.

Perowne, T. T. *The Proverbs*. 1916.

Plaut, W. G. *Book of Proverbs*. 1961.

Pollock, S. *Stubborn Soil*. No date.

Power, A. D. (ed.). *The Proverbs of Solomon*. 1949.

Ranston, H. *The Old Testament Wisdom Books and Their Teaching*. 1930.

Rylaarsdam, J. C. *Revelation in Jewish Wisdom Literature*. 1946.

Whybray, R. N. *Wisdom in Proverbs*. 1965.

---

[42] C. T. Fritsch, *IB*, IV, p. 778. Cf. Fritsch in *Theology Today*, VII (1950), pp. 169ff.

V. THE BOOK OF JOB

A. NAME AND BACKGROUND

Whereas this book was placed by the Jews in the third division of the Hebrew canon on the basis of anonymity of authorship (*Bab. Bath.* 15a; cf. its attribution to Moses, 14b), other traditions assigned it a rather different position in the list of canonical books. The LXX placed all the poetical books after the historical writings but before the prophets, with the result that Psalms, Proverbs, Ecclesiastes, and Canticles preceded Job. This order was altered somewhat in Codex Alexandrinus, which placed Job between Psalms and Proverbs, while some of the early Fathers, including Cyril of Jerusalem, Epiphanius, and Jerome, knew of a canon in which Job preceded the Psalter and Proverbs. On the theory that the book was the work of Moses the Peshitta placed it immediately after Deuteronomy, while the Vulgate located it at the head of the great poetic trilogy. This order was fixed by the Council of Trent, and most modern versions, including the English, adhere to this pattern.

The book derived its title from the Hebrew name of its principal character אִיּוֹב, and by any standard of comparison it ranks among the most significant pieces of world literature. Certainly it is unmatched in the writings of the Old Testament for its artistic character, its grandeur of language, depth of feeling, and the sensitivity with which the meaning of human suffering is explored. Over the centuries Job has received the consistent approbation of men of letters, sometimes in exaggerated terms,[1] but despite the latter there can be no doubt as to the influence that it has exerted in the field of literature, especially upon such compositions as the *Divina Commedia*,[2] *Paradise Lost*,[3] *Faust*,[4] and other literary masterpieces.

---

[1] For references see S. Terrien, *IB*, III, p. 877n. For a full review of literature on the book of Job up to 1953 see C. Kuhl, *Theologische Rundschau*, XXII (1953), pp. 163ff., 257ff.

[2] Cf. G. Baur, *Theologische Studien und Kritiken*, XXIX (1856), pp. 583ff.

[3] Cf. T. K. Cheyne, *Job and Solomon or the Wisdom of the OT* (1887), p. 112.

[4] O. Vilmar, *Zum Verständnis Goethes* (1860), p. 33.

1022

Pfeiffer held the book to be one of the most original works in the entire corpus of human poetry, and of such a kind as to defy classification in terms of lyric, epic, poetic, reflective, or didactic categories.[5] However accurate this observation may be, Pfeiffer can hardly be correct in asserting that the influence of oriental writing upon the literary art of the author was negligible, even though he quite rightly repudiated the dependence of Job upon Greek compositions.[6] In point of fact the format of the book followed rather closely certain clearly defined rules of composition in the ancient Near East by enclosing the main body of the work within language of a different style, a matter that will be mentioned subsequently.

Since the wisdom literature generally appears to display a distinctly international character, it is legitimate to inquire as to possible parallels with elements of the Near Eastern gnomic literature of antiquity in order to assess the extent to which they may be related to Job. Because of the Edomite setting of the work, the use of the divine name *Eloah*, and the general connection that the characters appear to have had with Edom, some scholars have concluded that Job represented a specimen of the renowned wisdom of the Edomites.[7] Unfortunately for this theory, very little has survived either of the language or literature of ancient Edom, thus making it difficult to estimate the nature of Edomite influence upon Job.

Any literary association or dependence would seem, at least on *prima facie* grounds, to posit northwest Semitic sources rather than any corpus of north-Arabic gnomic writings, since although it is true that certain rare words can be explained by reference to Arabic and Aramaic roots, they also go back to Akkadian sources. The character of the poetic section of Job is such as to manifest aspects in common with northwest Semitic literature no longer extant, although some compositions of this kind, such as the *Poem of the Righteous Sufferer*, are gradually coming to light.[8] Job is evidently dependent upon Phoenician sources of the late Amarna period and early Iron Age for a good deal of its imagery. However, the book has few points of contact with the literary style or syntax of the Ugaritic epics, as seems evident from the work of Feinberg.[9] Nevertheless, Albright is probably correct in stating that many of

---

[5] *PIOT*, pp. 683f.

[6] As suggested, for example, by H. M. Kallen, *The Book of Job as a Greek Tragedy Restored* (1916); K. Fries, *Das philosophische Gespräch von Hiob bis Plato* (1904); B. Stade, *Geschichte des Volkes Israel* (1888), II, p. 351; J. Neyrand, *Études*, LIX (1922-24), pp. 129ff. Cf. M. H. Pope, *IDB*, II, pp. 916f. Theodore of Mopsuestia first suggested the dependence upon Greek dramas, a view that the Council of Constantinople repudiated; cf. *PG*, LXVI, cols. 697f.

[7] Cf. E. ben Yehudah, *JPOS*, I (1921), pp. 113ff.; R. H. Pfeiffer, *ZAW*, XLIV (1926), pp. 13ff.; *PIOT*, pp. 683f.; P. Dhorme, *Le livre de Job* (1926), p. lxxxix n. 7.

[8] Cf. W. G. Lambert and O. R. Gurney, *Anatolian Studies*, IV (1954), pp. 65ff.

[9] C. L. Feinberg, *Bibliotheca Sacra*, CIII (1946), pp. 283ff.

the lexicographical difficulties in Job will ultimately be resolved by reference to Canaanite-Phoenician literary sources.[10]

By far the closest relationship to extant Near Eastern gnomic literature is seen with respect to certain Babylonian sources. Until 1952, the only material from Babylon dealing with the concept of theodicy and the related problem of the suffering of the innocent was contained in two texts assigned, for want of more certain criteria, to the period between 1200 and 800 B.C.[11] The first of these was the poem of the "Babylonian Job," entitled, "I will praise the Lord of Wisdom,"[12] and consisted of a monologue extending to four tablets. The central figure of the lamentation section was a man, originally wealthy and influential, but subsequently deprived of his position in life and afflicted with a repulsive ailment of obscure aetiology for which neither magic nor priestcraft availed. Supplication to the gods appeared vain and past piety seemed of no value at all for the existing circumstances, thus leading the sufferer to conclude that the divine will was inscrutable and that divine justice fell considerably short of its human counterpart. The third tablet narrated the unexpected intervention of Marduk when all appeared lost, and in the course of three dreams he restored the sufferer to health, an act that amazed the contemporaries of this unfortunate man. The thanksgiving section of the text described the joyful offerings that the restored individual made to Marduk out of gratitude for his deliverance.

The second text, the Acrostic Dialogue or "Babylonian Theodicy," was originally published by Craig in 1895,[13] followed by an edition in 1926 by Ebeling,[14] and studies by Landsberger and others.[15] This composition, an acrostic poem of twenty-seven strophes containing eleven lines each, represented two participants as speaking to one another in alternate stanzas. The first of these men had experienced unrelieved calamity in life, and on this basis he rejected unequivocally the existence of divine justice. The second was a pious individual who believed in complete submission to the will of the gods and in punctilious attention to the requirements of the cultus. After prolonged effort the pious believer converted the skeptic by showing how mistaken his view of life actually was.

---

[10] W. F. Albright, *VT* suppl. vol. III (1955), p. 14.

[11] W. von Soden, *ZDMG*, LXXXIX (1935), pp. 164ff., had argued that such questioning of religious ideas resulted from the overthrow of the Old Babylonian dynasty by the Kassites, *ca*. 1550 B.C.

[12] Cf. S. H. Langdon, *Babyloniaca*, VII (1923), pp. 131ff.; R. J. Williams, *JCS*, VI (1952), pp. 4ff.; *ANET*, pp. 434ff.

[13] J. A. Craig, *Assyrian and Babylonian Religious Texts* (1895), I, pp. 44ff.

[14] E. Ebeling in H. Gressmann (ed.), *Altorientalische Texte zum AT* (1926), pp. 287ff.

[15] B. Landsberger, *ZA*, XLIII (1936), pp. 32ff. For the literature see W. G. Lambert, *Babylonian Wisdom Literature*, p. 68.

These two compositions were enriched by the publication in 1952 of a tablet that had been placed in the Louvre in 1906.[16] This source was of importance in that, while it dealt with the same general material as the others, it antedated them by a considerable period, and confirmed the views of Von Soden and others who had maintained that the dominance of the Kassites in Babylonia had occasioned the questioning of traditional religious concepts. The tablets may thus be dated in the reign of Ammiditana (ca. 1619-1583 B.C.), the third successor of Hammurabi, and in all probability it was part of a larger series. Although incompletely preserved, the text described the intercessions of a friend on behalf of the sufferer, whose afflictions had presumably been narrated in a preceding tablet. The torments of this pious man were described in some detail by his friend, and upon hearing this account the god was so moved that he acceded to the pleas uttered on behalf of the distraught man, set about healing the various ailments that had overtaken him, and redressed the general imbalance of calamity in his favor.

By contrast with Babylonia, the problem of theodicy and the suffering of the righteous received only scant attention in Egyptian literature, probably because the general outlook of the people envisaged the situation against an entirely different frame of reference. Long before the second millennium B.C. the Egyptians had come to recognize justice as right rather than as despotic favor, so that questions of injustice were related to human perversions of ma'at, the divinely established order, and not to deficiencies of an internal nature within the order itself.[17] Thus while the *Admonitions of Ipuwer*[18] and the *Dispute over Suicide*,[19] which date from the First Intermediate Period, reflected the troubles of the time and indicated that they caused men to reassess the traditional religious beliefs and ethical principles, they contained no sense of disillusionment with the celestial deities, but instead showed the way in which men had perverted the social order.

The same theme was also dealt with in another contemporaneous production, the *Tale of the Eloquent Peasant*, in which the duty of social justice was emphasized by the successive processes involved in a man insisting upon his rights.[20] Rather closer to the general problem of theodicy was *The Teaching of Amenemhet*, composed for Senwosret I

[16] J. Nougayrol, *RB*, LIX (1952), pp. 239ff. Cf. R. J. Williams, *Canadian Journal of Theology*, II (1956), pp. 14f.

[17] *IAAM*, p. 208.

[18] Cf. A. H. Gardiner, *The Admonitions of an Egyptian Sage* (1909); A. Erman, *The Literature of the Ancient Egyptians*, pp. 92ff.; *ANET*, pp. 441ff.

[19] A. Erman, *The Literature of the Ancient Egyptians*, pp. 86ff.; R. Faulkner, *JEA*, XLII (1956), pp. 21ff.; *ANET*, pp. 405ff.; *DOTT*, pp. 162ff.

[20] Cf. A. H. Gardiner, *JEA*, IX (1923), pp. 5ff.; A. Erman, *The Literature of the Ancient Egyptians*, pp. 116ff.; T. E. Peet, *A Comparative Study of the Literatures of Egypt, Palestine and Mesopotamia* (1931), pp. 112ff.; *ANET*, pp. 407ff.

after his father Amenemhet I, founder of the Twelfth Dynasty, had been assassinated.[21] In this document, the words placed in the mouth of the departed pharaoh could be interpreted as a vigorous protest against the injustice of a righteous man's having to endure suffering, but once again the responsibility for the situation was placed squarely upon the shoulders of humanity, not the gods.

There is therefore very little relationship between Egyptian material of this kind, which is concerned primarily with the prevalence of unsettled or corrupt conditions of society, and Job, which had as its chief interest the incidence of personal calamity and its propriety in view of the spiritual status of the sufferer.[22] Considerably closer is the connection between Job and the Babylonian literature mentioned above, both of which deal with the same basic theme and reach superficially similar conclusions. Albright has suggested that the Babylonian writings may have been known to the author of Job in some Aramaic form in much the same manner as certain Akkadian texts became enshrined in the Aramaic *Sayings of Aḥikar,*[23] but this cannot be demonstrated as yet.

Despite obvious similarities in content, there are equally significant differences between the Babylonian material and the book of Job. Thus Lambert has pointed out that there is no direct connection between the Babylonian Theodicy and the content of Job.[24] The fact that only a small part of the text of *Ludlul bēl nēmeqi* deals with the suffering of the righteous, and the remainder with the restorative activity of Marduk, would demand a title such as "The Babylonian *Pilgrim's Progress*" rather than the popular designation, "The Babylonian Job."[25] Quite apart from this, the literary form of Job far exceeds that of any similar Babylonian compositions, while the conclusions at which Job arrived are very much more profound than those of the unknown Babylonian authors.

A degree of dependence by Job upon Iranian and Indian folklore has been detected by some scholars in reference to a righteous man's being tested by rival deities against a dualistic background. Thus the Indian story of Harisiandra, which appeared in many variant forms, recorded the trying of a righteous man by the consent of the divine assembly and his subsequent restoration when his integrity and perfection had been demonstrated to the satisfaction of the gods.[26] It seems probable, how-

---

[21] A. Erman, *The Literature of the Ancient Egyptians,* pp. 72ff.; *ANET,* pp. 418f.

[22] Cf. T. W. Thacker, *DOTT,* p. 163.

[23] *FSAC,* p. 331.

[24] *DOTT,* p. 97.

[25] W. G. Lambert, *Babylonian Wisdom Literature,* p. 27.

[26] Cf. P. Volz, *Hiob und Weisheit* (1921), pp. 8f.; P. Bertie, *Le poème de Job* (1929), p. 54; E. G. Kraeling, *The Book of the Ways of God* (1939), pp. 187f. Cf. A. Lods, *Histoire de la littérature hébraïque et juive,* pp. 691f.

ever, that these traditions are comparatively late corruptions of much earlier Mesopotamian material, and it is highly improbable that they influenced the composition of Job to any significant extent, whether on grounds of date or theological content. With regard to the latter, as Terrien has indicated, the Biblical author ignored the matter of the value of merits among celestial beings, since his purpose was to establish the thesis that Job had been serving God to no constructive end.[27]

B. THE MATERIAL OF THE BOOK

Apart from the fact that the book bears his name, and that there are isolated references elsewhere in the Bible to him (Ezek. 14:14, 20; Jas. 5:11), there is no reliable information about Job himself. The name first appeared in the form *'ybm* in the Egyptian Execration Texts, *ca.* 2000 B.C., in which certain Palestinian chieftains were listed, and once in an Amarna letter as *Ay(y)âb*,[28] as well as in second-millennium B.C. texts from Mari and Alalakh. It was thus an ordinary designation of west Semites in the second millennium B.C., though its derivation and meaning are still uncertain.[29] Perhaps the frequency with which the name was employed in antiquity made it desirable as a symbol of Everyman in his struggle against adversity in life, although a comprehensive view of this kind is by no means assured. On the contrary, it may well be that some ancient hero of this name passed through experiences similar to those described in the book, and subsequently became the model of the righteous sufferer.

As obscure as the meaning of the name Job was the land of Uz, where the story was set. It is nowhere described specifically, and has been placed as far apart as northern Mesopotamia and Edom. The two most favored locations are at Hauran, south of Damascus, and in the region between Edom and northern Arabia. The former was supposed by Josephus to have been the most likely,[30] and it was also supported both by Christian and Moslem traditions. A great many modern scholars, however, favor the latter area, since the friends of Job came from the vicinity of Edom. The location of the story was apparently accessible to both Sabean Bedouins from Arabia and Assyrian marauders from Mesopotamia.

In Jeremiah 25:20, Uz was mentioned in conjunction with Philistia, Edom, Ammon, and Moab, thus indicating a more southerly territory, while in Lamentations 4:21 the Edomites were spoken of as occupying

---

[27] S. Terrien, *IB*, III, p. 879.

[28] *FSAC*, p. 331. Cf. W. F. Albright, *JPOS*, VIII (1928), p. 239, *JAOS*, LXXIV (1954), pp. 227ff.; *BHI*, pp. 70f.

[29] M. H. Pope, *IDB*, II, p. 911. For the view that the author lived in a sixth-century B.C. Hebrew settlement in Arabia see A. Guillaume in F. F. Bruce (ed.), *Promise and Fulfillment* (1963), pp. 106ff.

[30] *AJ*, I, 6, 4.

the land of Uz. Since, however, the LXX omitted Uz in both references, it is impossible to associate such territory with the land in which Job lived with any degree of assurance. Perhaps the fact that Job was included among the people of the east (Job. 1:3; cf. Judg. 6:3, 33; Isa. 11:14; Ezek. 25:4, 10) indicates an Edomite location. On the other hand the scene of the drama may be purposely vague, since the description of Uz showed it both as essentially a part of the desert areas east of Palestine and yet comprising extensive farmlands and towns of considerable size (cf. Job 1:3, 15, 17, 19; 29:7).

The book falls quite readily into five divisions, consisting of a prose prologue (Job 1–2), the dialogue (Job 3–31), the speeches of Elihu (Job 32–37), the theophany and divine speeches (Job 38:1–42:6), and a prose epilogue (Job 42:7-17). The introductory words of the prologue indicate that the narrative deals with something other than Hebrew history, and sets the scene for subsequent events. Job, the central figure of the drama, was depicted as a patriarchal figure and as one who offered the burnt offering, factors that tend to give the narrative great antiquity. The description of a scene depicting God and the adversary in dispute established the thesis that nothing could take place on earth without first having been decreed by God. Upon the suggestion of the adversary that the piety, rectitude, and spiritual integrity of Job were ..ot in fact matters of pure disinterest, there came upon Job a series of calamities that stripped him of property and personal belongings, leaving him only a nagging wife and a particularly loathsome disease.[31] Hearing of his misfortunes three friends came along in order to console him, and showed respect for his sufferings by maintaining a prolonged silence (Job 2:11-13).

This led Job to precipitate the dialogue by formulating a bitter outburst, in which he regretted being born (Job 3:3-10), wished that he had been stillborn (Job 3:11-19), and wondered why he should continue to live under such conditions (Job 3:20-26). With this tirade commenced the dialogue proper, consisting of three cycles of six speeches in which Job replied separately to discourses by each of his three friends. The first speech of Eliphaz (Job 4:1–5:27) began in the usual courteous oriental manner, but soon implied that Job was suffering because of some guilt, despite his protestations of complete innocence and rectitude. He urged Job to turn in repentance to God, who after a suitable chastening would restore his fortunes.

In reply Job appealed to the intensity of his sufferings as ground for his utterances (Job 6:1-7), and taxed his friends with having to supply

---

[31] On the latter see R. K. Harrison, *IDB*, I, p. 850. For earlier observations cf. G. N. Munch, *Die Zaraath (Lepra) der hebräischen Bibel* (1893), p. 143; A. Macalister, *HDB*, III, pp. 329ff.; E. W. G. Masterman, *PEF Quarterly Statement* (1918), I, p. 168; C. J. Ball, *The Book of Job* (1922), p. 114; S. Terrien, *IB*, III, p. 920.

him with much-needed moral support. Still asserting his innocence, he challenged his companions to prove that he had deserved such calamities (Job 6:24-30), and from this position he expostulated upon the miseries of life, begging God to leave him alone (Job 7:1-21). The first speech of Bildad (Job 8:1-22) emphasized in a more blunt form the basic premise of Eliphaz, namely that the very fact that Job was experiencing suffering implied previous sin. Bildad held that the death of the children of Job was a divine judgment (Job 8:4), thus perpetuating the popular punitive interpretation of such events, and urged Job to undertake acts of repentance.

By way of answer (Job 9:1–10:22) Job admitted that on the basis of power rather than justice it is impossible for man to be just before God (Job 9:1-21). Then he launched into a bitter tirade against God, accusing Him of an irresponsible exercise of power (Job 9:22-35), and criticized God for having brought him into being. The first speech of Zophar (Job 11:1-20) followed the general pattern established by Eliphaz and Bildad, but showed a more superficial understanding of the position in which Job found himself (Job 11:1-7).

He stressed the inscrutability of the divine wisdom, and urged Job to repent of his sin. To this the latter replied (Job 12:1–14:22) that the wisdom of Zophar was pretentious, and that in fact God was acting unjustly in his case (Job 12:7-25). At this point there is a development in the thought of Job, for having previously accepted the view that in this life good is rewarded and evil punished, he began to raise questions about it. In desiring to discuss the matter with God, Job in reality recognized His essential justice (Job 13:10f.), and the fact that God was his superior who would listen to his complaints. He professed his resignation to the thought of death, and lamented greatly over the weakness of mankind (Job 14:1-22).

The second cycle of discourses (Job 15:1–21:34) commenced with a speech by Eliphaz (Job 15:1-35), in which he characterized the utterances of Job as being so much empty and impious talk, appealing for support to the sages and authorities of antiquity (Job 15:17-35). Job replied that if he was fortunate enough to be in the situation occupied by his friends, he too would be able to confuse with meaningless and vain remarks. However, he had come under divine judgment (Job 16:6-17), and overwhelmed by this thought he relapsed into a hostile attitude towards God (Job 16:18–17:16).

In his second speech (Job 18:1-21), Bildad reproached Job again, and continued his counsel by painting a somber picture of the woes that overtake the wicked (Job 18:5-21). This naturally provoked Job to utter a stinging reply (Job 19:1-29), in which he charged his friends angrily for their unsympathetic assessment of his position, expressed his innocency of behavior once again, and asserted his belief in ultimate vindication before his *gō'ēl*, who would defend his good name (Job 19:13-27). In return, Zophar furnished a forceful description (Job 20:1-29) of the punishment that would overtake the wicked, and ignored the appeal of Job to a final judgment in the flesh in favor of declaring that the wicked have been judged already.

The sixth reply of Job (Job 21:1-34) revealed a further deepening of his understanding, and an increasing dissatisfaction with the view that he had held originally. The simple fact was that many wicked people prospered in life, while death came ultimately to all, irrespective of the kind of life which they had led. Job criticized the attitude of his friends by stating that they were speaking quite disparagingly of the inscrutable ways of God, and with this assertion the second cycle of discourses concluded.

The third cycle of speeches (Job 22:1–31:40), which appears to be somewhat incomplete since Zophar had nothing further to contribute to the debate, commenced with a statement from Eliphaz (Job 22:1-30), who opined that God derived no benefit from human virtue, since He exhibited neither interest in nor concern for human suffering, save insofar as they vindicated His own justice. He again urged Job to repent and turn to God, who would subsequently restore his fortunes. In his seventh reply (Job 23:1–24:25), Job showed his perplexity at his inability to find God, but his attitude lacked the bitterness of earlier speeches. Though the ways of God were hidden, Job had confidence in His ability to render justice. The third speech of Bildad (Job 25:1-6) is short and lacking in coherence, which is probably due to faulty textual transmission, a circumstance that has been adduced as a warrant in some scholarly circles for rearranging the last section of this cycle of speeches.

Following the order of the MT, however, Job furnished another reply to Bildad (Job 26:1-14), in which he repudiated the value of the arguments brought forward, and expressed his own consciousness of divine power in the world of men, and this he interpreted in terms of divine transcendence. His final speech in the dialogue (Job 27:1–31:40) set forth his position once more. He appears to quote here from the arguments of Zophar (cf. Job 27:13 and 20:29) as a preparation for discoursing upon the source of true wisdom. This he sees, not in the practicalia of everyday life, but in the knowledge of the divine way (Job 28:28). After a summary of his life he listed a series of social and moral offenses to which he attached self-imprecations if he had ever been guilty of them (Job 31:1-40). Having done this he rested his defense, and challenged God to a reply (Job 31:35-37).

A change of content is indicated by the presence of a short prose introduction (Job 32:1-5), which is accented as though it were poetry. In this passage the three friends of Job ceased to argue with him because they thought that he was self-righteous, and also for the more practical reason that they had no further answers to the problem at hand. Thereupon a young man, Elihu, who had been listening deferentially to the arguments of his elders and had come to realize the deficiencies of their approach, took it upon himself to speak. Referring to the innocence of Job he declared that suffering had a disciplinary value, not necessarily a punitive one, and hence Job ought at least to consider that God may not have been acting unfairly in his case after all. In a second phase of his address (Job 34:1-37) he charged Job with blasphemy for questioning the divine justice and conceding that piety was actually of little avail. Furthermore, in denying that God was just in the manner in which He awarded blessings and punishments, Job had, in the view of Elihu, added rebellion to his other offenses. Addressing himself to the subject once more (Job 35:1-16), Elihu established the principle that God, being transcendent, could not be affected by individual actions, but that the individual himself reacted for good or ill. God only ignored appeals when they proceeded from human insincerity, and this was evidently the case with Job. In a final speech (Job 36:1-37:24) he again came to the defense of divine justice, and showed that, in the inscrutable ways of God, affliction could well be the means of deliverance.

In the theophany that followed (Job 38:1-42:6) the Creator argued from the phenomena of creation and the incomprehensible nature of the universe to His own transcendence. Job was challenged to reply, but was unable to do so (Job 40:1-6), and after a subsequent demonstration of human inadequacy (Job 40:7-41:34) he acknowledged the divine omnipotence and his own inadequacy, repenting with true humility.

The prose epilogue (Job 42:7-17) represented God as rebuking the three friends of Job for their rashness in not speaking rightly of Him, as Job had done. They were commanded to offer sacrifices and secure the intercessory offices of Job in order to avoid divine punishment. His innocence now established beyond any question, the fortunes of Job were reversed and he himself lived in prosperity and security to an advanced age.

C. CRITICAL PROBLEMS CONNECTED WITH JOB

Although Job bears the mark of the wisdom literature in general, it is by no means easy to classify. This fact became apparent in Talmudic tradition, where the composition was assigned to various periods, and the suggestion that Job was only a typical, and therefore unhistorical, figure was repudiated by Rabbi Samuel ben Nachmani.[32] The view that the work constituted a parable of the righteous nation in affliction seems adequately disproved by the complete absence of national issues or involvements in the composition. Furthermore, as Pope has pointed out, it is hardly probable that a descendant of Esau would have been chosen

---

[32] Cf. V. E. Reichert, *The Book of Job* (1946), p. xx.

to represent the offspring of Jacob, assuming, of course, an Edomite origin for the work.[33]

Comparisons with the epic poetry of Greece reveal few if any significant points of contact, while, as observed previously, the religious insights of the book far surpass the conclusions of those Mesopotamians who grappled with the problem of theodicy. Nor can Job be regarded as a dialogue in the stricter sense of that term, since the bulk of the work consists of lengthy poetic speeches arranged in a distinct order which is not that of the dialogue pattern. While it possesses narrative, didactic, lyric, and epic features, this great work defies classification in the rigid terms to which modern occidental scholarship is accustomed.[34]

While the book cannot be regarded as history in the ordinary sense, there seems little reason to doubt the existence of an historical personage behind the narrative who passed through some sort of experience involving suffering, which resulted in a questioning of accepted theological beliefs. On any other basis it would be simply impossible to explain the virility of the traditions concerning Job in Hebrew life and culture, or the lofty, if somewhat immoderate, estimate of the book which caused it to be attributed to Moses.

According to W. B. Stevenson, there are in excess of one hundred words in Job that do not occur elsewhere,[35] which will perhaps furnish some indication of the difficult nature of the poetic form. This was evidently as true for the ancient scribe as the modern scholar, with the result that the versions generally are of little practical use in assessing readings in the Hebrew text. In particular, the LXX has to be employed with great caution, since in its earlier form nearly four hundred *stichoi*, which now appear in the MT and more recent LXX texts, were omitted from the translation. Furthermore, the renderings are frequently free and periphrastic, indicating to some extent the difficulties that the ancient scribes experienced in translating the obscure Hebrew expressions. To make the problem even more complex, there are some grounds for assuming that the extant Hebrew book contains certain dislocations of the text, particularly in chapters 24 to 27 and in the Hymn to Wisdom in chapter 28.

The third speech-cycle differs from its precursors in three particulars: first, Job appears on occasions to espouse the cause urged by his friends (cf. Job 24:18-24; 26:5-14; 27:13-23); secondly, the discourse of Bildad (Job 25:1-6) seems unusually short and out of character with his previous utterances, and finally, the discourse of Zophar, which would normally complete the balance of the three cycles, is absent.

[33] M. H. Pope, *IDB*, II, p. 920.
[34] S. Terrien, *IB*, III, pp. 878, 892.
[35] *The Poem of Job* (1947), p. 71.

Apart from a few earlier scholars such as Budde, who regarded the MT as genuine,[36] the majority of commentators have indulged in a greater or lesser rearrangement of the Hebrew text, mostly with the intention of recovering the "lost" speech of Zophar.[37] In 1780 Kennicott set the pattern by assigning Job 27:13-23 to Zophar, and this was followed with slight variations by Stuhlmann and Reuss.[38] Among those who added verses 7 to 11 of the same chapter to comprise the "lost" speech were Bickell, Duhm, and Barton.[39] Hoffmann and Laue, among others, included sections of chapter 28 in the reconstructed speech of Zophar,[40] while Dhorme and Buttenwieser assigned portions of chapter 24 to Zophar.[41] Included in the list of critics who omitted a part or the whole of chapters 24 to 27 were Grill, Studer, Cheyne, Baumgärtel, and Kraeling.[42]

While it is theoretically possible to construct a third speech for Zophar consisting principally of Job 24:18-24 (his description of the wicked) and 27:14ff. (the fate awaiting the offspring of oppressors) with a pivot (27:13) between them, such a procedure involves a more serious re-arrangement of the text than the circumstances warrant. The general pattern of the poetic speeches exhibits a progressive shortening, so that the absence of a third speech by Zophar need not be particularly surprising. Indeed, in his second speech (Job 20:1-29), it was becoming evident that he had already encountered the law of diminishing returns in his argument, and this simple fact may constitute the sole reason why he was not credited with a third speech. The primary reason for rearranging the text has invariably been the incongruity of certain statements placed in the mouth of Job with the general position adopted by him in earlier chapters of the book. While these may in fact be due to sheer textual disorder, it may also be that Job was merely quoting verbatim from the arguments of his friends, and placing in the process, as is evident, a rather different emphasis upon the words (cf. Job 20:29 and 27:13).

[36] K. Budde, *Beiträge zur Kritik des Buches Hiob* (1876), pp. 132f.
[37] For detailed lists see G. A. Barton, *JBL*, XXX (1911), pp. 66ff.; A. Regnier, *RB*, XXXIII (1924), pp. 186f.
[38] B. Kennicott, *Vetus Testamentum Hebraicum* (1780), II; *Dissertatio General-is*, p. 155; *Remarks on Select Passages in the Old Testament* (1787), pp. 169ff. M. H. Stuhlmann, *Das Buch Hiob* (1804). E. Reuss, *Job*, in *La Sainte Bible* (1878), VI; *Vortrag über das Buch Hiob* (1888).
[39] G. Bickell, *Das Buch Hiob* (1894). B. Duhm, *Das Buch Hiob* (1897). G. A. Barton, *JBL*, XXX (1911), pp. 66ff.
[40] G. Hoffmann, *Hiob* (1891). L. Laue, *Die Komposition des Buches Hiob* (1895).
[41] P. Dhorme, *Le livre de Job* (1926); M. Buttenwieser, *The Book of Job* (1922).
[42] J. Grill, *Zur Kritik der Komposition des Buches Hiob* (1890). G. L. Studer, *Das Buch Hiob* (1881). T. K. Cheyne, *EB*, II, col. 2476. F. Baumgärtel, *Der Hiobdialog* (1933). E. G. Kraeling, *The Book of the Ways of God* (1939).

Many of the suggested textual reconstructions have been extremely subjective, and the omissions appear to have been prompted by little more than arbitrary judgments. Typical were the opinions of many authors in considering that the superb hymn on divine wisdom in chapter 28 was an editorial addition that had formed no part of the original principal work,[43] although according to some it could have been an independent composition of the author.[44] While the poem unquestionably interrupts the soliloquy of Job,[45] and appears to contain concepts of wisdom that are foreign to the previous discourses, there seem to be valid exegetical reasons for assuming its logical connections with the surrounding passages. Indirectly the hymn adumbrates the thesis unfolded in the divine speeches (chapters 38–41), as well as indicating that neither Job nor his friends really knew anything about how God deals with men. Furthermore, there are clear points of contact between the hymn and the divine speeches.[46] There is an Egyptian flavor evident in both sections: in Job 28:1-11 the reference may be to the mineral deposits of Serabit el-Khadem, and in the divine discourses there are descriptions of characteristically Egyptian animal species such as the crocodile and the hippopotamus (chapters 40–41). Again, the relationship between the "deep" and the "sea" in Job 28:14 reappears in 38:16. Peculiar expressions connected with celestial phenomena in Job 28:26b and 28:24 occur again in 38:25b and 41:11 (41:3 Heb.) respectively.[47] The passage in Job 28:25ff. describing divine control over the elements has its counterpart in Job 38:7ff. It seems at least probable, therefore, that the author of the Hymn to Wisdom is also the composer of the divine discourses, and by implication, of the work as a whole.

There appears to be a genuine case for suggesting the rearrangement of the text at the end of the final speech of Job (Job 27:1–31:40) in the dialogue section. The passage where Job concludes his argument (Job 31:35-37) is better read after Job 31:38-40a, leaving the phrase, "the words of Job are ended" as a concluding declaration. More serious are the questions raised concerning the genuineness of the Elihu speeches, for since the time of Stuhlmann they have frequently been regarded as supplementary and unauthentic material.[48] The most outstanding defense of their integrity was in the work by Budde,[49] but comparatively

---

[43] B. Duhm, *Das Buch Hiob*, p. 134; C. Steuernagel, *Einleitung in das AT*, p. 698; S. R. Driver and G. B. Gray, *A Critical and Exegetical Commentary on the Book of Job* (1921), I, p. xxxviii; O. Eissfeldt, *Einleitung in das AT*, p. 508; A. Lods, *Histoire de la littérature hébraïque*, p. 680; *OTFD*, p. 290.

[44] R. H. Pfeiffer, *Le problème du livre de Job* (1915), p. 14; *PIOT*, p. 672; S. Terrien, *IB*, III, p. 888.

[45] P. Dhorme, *Le livre de Job*, p. lxxvi.

[46] P. Scherer, *IB*, III, p. 1100.

[47] תחת כל-השמים (28:24); ודרך לחזיז קלות (28:26b).

[48] Cf. W. A. Irwin, *Journal of Religion*, XVII (1937), pp. 37ff.

[49] K. Budde, *Beiträge zur Kritik des Buches Hiob*, pp. 65ff.

few scholars followed his lead.[50] Arguments that have commonly been adduced against their genuineness have included their lack of connection with other sections of the book, the language and literary style of the passages in question,[51] their teaching, and the fact that whereas Elihu quoted Job verbatim, this phenomenon did not occur elsewhere in the book.

In this connection it should be observed that the presence of Aramaisms in one section of a poetic composition that abounds in difficult and obscure expressions need be no indication at all that the particular passage is spurious. As Young has pointed out, such a phenomenon could well be due to the individuality of the speaker,[52] and this is particularly the case since he was represented largely in the role of an intruder, and as such was unmentioned in the epilogue. It has been observed above that quite probably Job quoted his friends on occasions, and in consequence there need be no inherent difficulty with regard to Elihu's doing the same thing (compare Job 33:8-11 and 13:24, 27; 34:5-9 and 27:3; 35: 3 and 7:20).

As Terrien has demonstrated, considerable loss can be sustained by underestimating the value of the Elihu discourses.[53] While they may not attain to the same heights as those achieved by earlier speeches, they show considerable insight into the educational purpose of suffering (Job 36:7-11) as well as advancing the concept of an angel-mediator (Job 33:23ff.) and making more explicit the earlier hints at a doctrine of salvation by faith (Job 33:26ff.). Accordingly it does not seem necessary to posit, as Pfeiffer did, a later recension of Job in which the speeches of Elihu had been added by an incensed redactor in order to defend Jewish orthodoxy and refute much of the teaching of the original recension.[54]

Comparatively little objection has been raised in scholarly circles to the divine discourses (Job 38:1–42:6), although some critics have rejected them in part or in whole, based principally upon the purely gratuitous assumption that the original recension of Job was restricted to a discussion of the misfortunes of the sufferer, and that the work arrived

[50] Cf. J. H. Raven, *OT Introduction* (1906), p. 278; C. H. Cornill, *Introduction to the Canonical Books of the OT* (1907), pp. 425ff.; M. Thilo, *Das Buch Hiob* (1925), pp. 135ff.; P. Szczygiel, *Das Buch Hiob* (1931), p. 22; L. Dennefield, *RB*, XLVIII (1939), pp. 163ff.; *YIOT*, pp. 329f. R. H. Pfeiffer, *Le problème du livre de Job*, pp. 13f., supported the position of Budde and Cornill in 1915, but abandoned it subsequently on theological grounds. Cf. R. H. Pfeiffer, *ZAW*, XLIV (1926), pp. 23f.; *PIOT*, p. 673.

[51] Cf. S. R. Driver and G. B. Gray, *A Critical and Exegetical Commentary on the Book of Job*, I, pp. xlii ff.

[52] *YIOT*, pp. 329f.

[53] S. Terrien, *IB*, III, p. 891.

[54] *PIOT*, p. 673.

at its extant form as the result of interpolations in successive editions.[55] Pfeiffer criticized this by remarking that on such a theory the supplementers of the original work must have composed some of the most profound and beautiful portions of the extant book. With rare insight he pointed out the dangers of imposing categories of Aristotelian logic and consistency upon an ancient oriental poet of great imagination and perception in the expectation that his work should fall into some such category as the purely lyric, epic, dramatic, or didactic. He concluded by reminding his readers that the book that left the hands of the original author is not necessarily in harmony with the literary standards demanded of it by modern critics, a sober observation that could be applied with considerable profit to other portions of the Hebrew Scriptures.[56] As some critics have recognized, these speeches constitute the apogee of poetic expression in the book.[57] Rather than contradicting the main burden of the dialogue, they give it a new perspective by raising the whole question under discussion from the finite to the infinite level in their communication of divine truth. As has been observed previously, there are close affinities in language and style with the dialogue, and these even extend to such passages as that describing the ostrich (Job 39:13-18), which is deficient in the LXX and which has been regarded as a later interpolation by some scholars. There may be grounds for assuming the presence of textual corruptions in the reply of Job to God, where verses 3a and 4 in chapter 42 appear to have been copied in error from Job 38:2, 3b and 40:7b, but this is a minor consideration. It can be stated by way of a general affirmation that there are definite grounds for asserting that the text of Job is of uneven quality, and not least in those areas which involve the discourses of Elihu. While this fact may be due entirely to transmissional corruptions, it could well have resulted also from the inability of the author to maintain firm control over his material, which in view of the complicated nature of the various speeches would hardly be surprising.

Any consideration of the contents of Job is bound to raise questions as to the unity and integrity of the work, particularly since the prologue (Job 1:1–2:13) and epilogue (Job 42:7-17) appear to form a literary unit of a homogeneous character written in prose, as contrasted with the remainder of the book. However, even here some scholars have consid-

---

[55] Cf. G. L. Studer, *Das Buch Hiob*, pp. 137ff.; T. K. Cheyne, *EB*, II, cols. 2480f., *Job and Solomon* (1887), pp. 66ff.; P. Volz, *Hiob und Weisheit*, pp. 84ff.; P. Bertie, *Le poème de Job* (1929), pp. 48ff.; F. Baumgärtel, *Der Hiobdialog*, p. 1; L. Finkelstein, *The Pharisees*, I, p. 234; E. G. Kraeling, *The Book of the Ways of God*, pp. 143ff.

[56] *PIOT*, p. 674.

[57] Cf. P. Dhorme, *Le livre de Job*, pp. lxxi ff.; A. Lods, *Histoire de la littérature hébraïque et juive*, pp. 677ff.; *OTFD*, pp. 290f.; S. Terrien, *IB*, III, pp. 891f. For the relationship between Job 38 and ancient Egyptian wisdom see G. von Rad, *VT* suppl. vol. III (1955), pp. 293ff.

ered these as constituting separate works of different dates,[58] while others have maintained that the prologue and epilogue comprised an independent *Volksbuch* antedating the author of the poetic section[59] and employed by him as a frame of reference for his own composition.[60] Another group of scholars adhered to the view that the poet also wrote the prose story in the prologue and epilogue under the inspiration of ancient traditions, possibly of Edomite origin,[61] while some exegetes suggested that the prose narratives were added to the poem at a comparatively late date by an editor.[62] Quite clearly all possibilities have been exhausted by such speculations, and some scholars have come to regard as purely academic the question as to whether or not the poet wrote the prose story, on the theory that the prose section constituted a folk-tale narrated orally long before it achieved literary fixity.[63]

If it is maintained that the prose sections are older than the poetic passages, and that the poet transformed an ancient and familiar story into luminous poetry, there seems to be no crucial issue at stake in the matter of integrity. However, not all those scholars who separate the prose prologue and epilogue from the rest of the book are aware that there is no objective evidence whatever for the suggestion that the prose sections were added at a later period to the poems by an anonymous redactor. Alleged evidences of discrepancy between prose and poetic passages are often quite unconvincing. Thus the argument that the Divine Name in the prose material is the tetragrammaton, whereas in the poetic passages the names *El, Eloah, Elohim* and *Shaddai* occur, but never the tetragrammaton, loses much of its validity when it is observed

[58] Cf. K. Fullerton, ZAW, XLII (1924), pp. 116ff.; E. König, *Das Buch Hiob* (1929), pp. 3ff.; L. Finkelstein, *The Pharisees*, I, p. 235; S. Spiegel, *Louis Ginzberg Jubilee Volume* (1945), pp. 323ff.

[59] Cf. J. Wellhausen, *Jahrbücher für deutsche Theologie*, XVI (1871), pp. 555ff.; K. Budde, *Beiträge zur Kritik des Buches Hiob*, pp. 29ff., *Das Buch Hiob*, pp. xiii ff.; T. K. Cheyne, *Job and Solomon*, pp. 66ff.; M. Vernes, *Revue de l'Histoire des Religions*, I (1880), pp. 232ff.; B. Duhm, *Das Buch Hiob*, pp. vii ff.; D. B. Macdonald, *JBL*, XIV (1895), pp. 63ff., *AJSL*, XIV (1898), pp. 137ff.; P. Volz, *Hiob und Weisheit*, p. 16; *IBOT*, pp. 171ff.; J. Lindblom, *La composition du livre de Job* (1945), pp. 30ff.; A. Weiser, *Einleitung in das AT*, p. 214, *Das Buch Hiob* (1951), p. 7.

[60] Cf. L. Gautier, *Introduction à l'Ancien Testament* (1914), II, pp. 98f.; K. Kautzsch, *Das sogennante Volksbuch von Hiob* (1900), pp. 3ff.

[61] T. K. Cheyne, *EB*, II, col. 2469; J. Meinhold, *Einführung in das AT* (n.d.), pp. 277ff.; C. Steuernagel, *Lehrbuch der Einleitung in das AT* (1912), p. 694; P. Dhorme, *Le livre de Job*, pp. lvii ff.; J. E. McFadyen, *An Introduction to the OT*, pp. 274ff.; *ETOT*, pp. 456f.; G. Hölscher, *Das Buch Hiob* (1952 ed.), pp. 1ff.; M. Buttenwieser, *The Book of Job*, pp. 24ff.

[62] Following R. Simon (1685) and A. Schultens (1737). Cf. B. D. Eerdmans, *Studies in Job* (1939), pp. 17ff.; W. B. Stevenson, *The Poem of Job*, pp. 73ff.; and with considerable hesitation, E. G. Kraeling, *The Book of the Ways of God*, pp. 179ff.

[63] *PIOT*, p. 669.

that the name *Elohim* occurred in the prologue in connection with the trials of Job (Job 1:5, 9; 2:9f.).

Inconsistencies between the picture of the hero in the prose portions as an owner of vast herds (Job 1:2) and in the poetic sections as an agriculturalist (Job 31:8ff.) and a city-dweller (Job 19:15; 29:7) seem to be resolved by archaeological evidence from Mesopotamia, which has shown the Biblical patriarchs to have been crop-growers and semi-sedentary inhabitants of the land.[64] Quite obviously Job was depicted, as Terrien has suggested, as a semi-nomad who lived in a walled city during the winter and migrated with his flocks throughout the remainder of the year.[65]

Arguments for composite authorship based upon the fact that in the prologue Job was a model of moral innocence, whereas in the poetic passages he was depicted as proud, rebellious, and questioning, are equally lacking in validity. The one shows a deeply religious figure in harmony with his surroundings and at peace with God and man, whereas the other depicts his mental distraction after his cherished beliefs and ideals had been rudely shaken by the realization that God had not acted according to current theories of divine behavior. The nature of the traumatic experience was such as to reveal the true humanity of Job, and it was obviously this from which he had to repent. The book in fact constitutes a graphic illustration of the manner in which the divine and human elements in man cohere and interact.

Linguistic arguments for diversity of authorship are also far from convincing, since as Kautzsch and Dhorme have shown, there are a remarkable number of affinities between the prose and poetic sections of the book.[66] The fact that the prose happens to have been written in good Hebrew whereas the poetic material contains a remarkable assortment of words originating in Aramaic, Akkadian, Egyptian, and Phoenician[67] may only indicate that the poetic author knew of the traditions associated with Job, and based his composition upon this foundation. By presenting the reader with an elegant prologue and epilogue in the classical style the author heightened the effect of literary contrast in the poetic passages of the book.

The problems of unity and integrity must now be related to the composing styles found in ancient Near Eastern literature. As Gordon has remarked, the book, for all its difficulties, is infinitely greater than the sum of its parts after it has yielded to scholarly dissection.[68] Certainly the kind of criticism that separates the prose passages from the poetic

[64] Cf. K. A. Kitchen, *Tyndale House Bulletin*, No. 5-6 (1960), pp. 13f.
[65] S. Terrien, *IB*, III, p. 886.
[66] K. Kautzsch, *Das sogennante Volksbuch von Hiob*, pp. 24ff., 40ff. P. Dhorme, *Le livre de Job*, pp. lxv ff.
[67] Cf. F. Delitzsch, *Das Buch Hiob* (1902), pp. 13, 72, 125ff.
[68] C. H. Gordon, *Christianity Today*, IV, No. 4 (1959), p. 132.

sections on the ground that poetry and prose are incompatible ingredients in the same composition, is operating in gross ignorance of ancient Mesopotamian literary practices.

The scribes of antiquity commonly set prose and poetical material in conscious juxtaposition in the same composition, and this procedure often had the effect of enclosing the main portion of the literary work in language of a contrasting style. The celebrated Code of Hammurabi is an excellent illustration of this principle, for in this composition the prose legal enactments which constituted the bulk of the work were set within the framework of a poetic prologue and epilogue. In Job the situation was reversed: the principal part of the composition was poetic, and the prologue and epilogue were in prose. Against the background of a great many examples of this kind of structure from the ancient Near East it is now abundantly clear that the extant book of Job was a consciously constructed integer, deliberately composed as one whole unit, in accordance with traditional Mesopotamian scribal patterns.[69] In the light of all the evidence, therefore, it seems safe to conclude, with Pope, that apart from the Elihu speeches Job manifests an overall unity, and that even these discourses, whether interpolated or not, do not disturb the basic integrity of the book to any significant extent.[70]

Questions of authorship and date present other difficulties, however, particularly in view of the fact that the book is *sui generis* in the corpus of the canonical Hebrew Scriptures, and partly because of critical analyses which would posit an astonishing variety of dates for the composition of the work. The anonymity of the book, coupled with its avowed intention of setting out to narrate certain familiar traditions about a celebrated personage, adds to the dimensions of the problem. Concerning the hero himself, or the period in which he lived, there is no reliable information to the present, and such legends as have been preserved about him in Jewish circles and in Moslem sources can be dismissed immediately as unauthentic.

Even the location of the home of Job may be no more than a reasonable deduction from the narratives, although one modern author has discovered an Edomite settlement of antiquity known as Khirbet el 'Is, which could possibly be identified with ancient Uz with some charity.[71] If one is able, as the author believes, to identify the "Daniel" mentioned in Ezekiel 14:14 not with the distinguished personage of the exile, but with the *Dan'el* who occurred in the Ugaritic epic texts,[72] it is also possible to assign with considerable confidence the three individuals mentioned by Ezekiel to a very early date. If such an identification is

[69] Cf. *IOTT*, pp. 72f.
[70] M. H. Pope, *IDB*, II, p. 922.
[71] A. Musil, *Arabia Petraea* (1908), II, pp. 337ff.
[72] *UL*, pp. 84ff.; cf. pp. 66ff.

not accepted, however, there is no other hint in the Old Testament narratives as to the period when Job lived.

Because of the great variation in the views of individual critics, the dates assigned to the extant composition exhibit wide divergence. On the basis of quite authentic patriarchal details of background such as the primitive nature of the religion, the absence of a priesthood and a central shrine, the representation of the Sabeans and Chaldeans as marauding nomads, the monetary unit in Job 42:11 (קְשִׂיטָה), which occurs only in Genesis 33:19 and Joshua 24:32, and the exceptional longevity of Job (42:17), some scholars have followed one aspect of Talmudic tradition and have assigned the composition to Moses, dating it about 2100 B.C.[73] From an apocryphal addition to the LXX version Job was identified with Jobab, king of Edom (Gen. 36:33), and this led some Church Fathers, Eusebius, for example (*Praep. Evang.* IX, 25), and a few modern authors, to assign a pre-Mosaic date for the lifetime of the hero,[74] a suggestion that, in the light of Ugaritic discoveries, may not be as absurd as Pfeiffer supposed.[75] In the view of the present writer a date of

[73] E.g. J. D. Michaelis, *Einleitung in das AT* (1787), I, sect. xii; G. W. Hazelton, *Bibliotheca Sacra,* LXXI (1914), pp. 573ff.; F. A. Lambert, *Das Buch Hiob* (1919), p. 22.

[74] Cf. J. G. Eichhorn, *Einleitung in das AT* (1824 ed.), pp. 375f. For the view that Moses and Job were contemporaries see H. Torczyner (N. H. Tur-Sinai) in M. Soluweiczik (ed.), *Vom Buch das tausend Jahre wuchs* (1932), pp. 148ff., reprinted from *Monattschrift für Geschichte und Wissenschaft des Judentums,* LX (1925), pp. 236ff. Cf. N. H. Tur-Sinai (H. Torczyner), *The Book of Job: A New Commentary* (1957), pp. lxviii-lxix.

[75] *PIOT,* p. 676. Gregory of Nazianzus postulated a date in the Solomonic Age; in the modern period this was followed by H. A. C. Hävernick, *Handbuch der historisch-kritischen Einleitung in AT* (1849), III; C. F. Keil, *Lehrbuch der historisch-kritischen Einleitung in die kanonischen Schriften des AT* (1853); K. Schlottmann, *Das Buch Hiob* (1851); F. Delitzsch, *Das Buch Hiob* (1864); E. J. Young, *An Introduction to the OT* (1949). Hengstenberg, *Das Buch Hiob* (1870), I, p. 62; and Prat, *Dictionnaire de la Bible* (1903), III, col. 1567, advanced a date prior to the eighth century. Many nineteenth-century critics supported a period of composition at some point within the seventh century B.C., e.g. J. G. Stickel, *Das Buch Hiob* (1842); Th. Nöldeke, *Die Alttestamentliche Literatur* (1868); E. Riehm, *Einleitung in das AT* (1890), III; W. W. von Baudissin, *Einleitung in das AT* (1901); R. H. Pfeiffer, *Le problème du livre de Job* (1915); N. Schlogl, *Das Buch Hiob* (1916). Stickel, *Das Buch Hiob* (1842), p. 261; S. Davidson, *Introduction to the OT* (1863), II, pp. 195f.; and F. Bleek, *Introduction to the OT* (1894), II, p. 286, dated it in the seventh century. König, *Das Buch Hiob* (1929), pp. 495f.; Gunkel, *Die Religion in Geschichte und Gegenwart* (1912), III, cols. 47f.; and J. E. Steinmueller, *A Companion to Scripture Studies* (1944), II, p. 165, placed the book more specifically within the period of Jeremiah. Pfeiffer (*PIOT,* pp. 675ff.) dated the prologue and epilogue not earlier than the sixth century B.C., and the poetic sections between 700 and 200 B.C. The work was placed in the late monarchy or early exile by E. C. S. Gibson, *The Book of Job* (1899), p. xxii and N. H. Tur-Sinai, *The Book of Job: A New Commentary,* pp. xxxvi-xxxvii. A. B. Davidson, *The Book of Job* (1884), p. lxvii; and T. K. Cheyne, *Job and Solomon,*

composition not later than the end of the fifth century B.C. would seem to account for most of the peculiar features of the book, despite the inconclusive nature of much of the evidence.

The original language in which the work was composed has occasioned considerable discussion for many years. On the basis of the Edomite connections of the characters in the story and the general setting of the drama it was assumed by some writers that the poet was himself of Edomite extraction,[76] and that he wrote in Arabic, of which the extant book is a translation.[77] While, as Delitzsch pointed out, numerous rare words in the poem can be explained by reference to the Arabic,[78] this phenomenon need only imply that the author was acquainted with Arabic ways, and perhaps even with an Arabic dialect. In any event, as Terrien has stated, it is rather fanciful to assume that a Jewish poet would have translated an Arabic poem during the early part of the post-exilic period, and at that prior to the insertion of the Elihu discourses, which Terrien regarded as an addition.[79]

---

p. 74, placed the extant composition in the exilic era proper, although Cheyne reduced the date to the Persian period, *EB*, II, cols. 2385ff. Gautier, *Introduction à l'Ancien Testament* (1914), II, p. 120; Naish, *The Expositor*, III (1925), pp. 34ff., 94ff.; and Driver (*DILOT*, p. 431) assigned the book either to the late captivity or early post-exilic period. In general it can be said that a post-exilic date was favored by many scholars, e.g. H. Holtzmann in B. Stade's *Geschichte des Volkes Israel* (1888), II, pp. 351f.; K. Budde, *Das Buch Hiob*, p. liii; B. Duhm, *Das Buch Hiob* (1897), p. ix; C. Steuernagel, *Einleitung in das AT* (1912), p. 710; R. H. Strahan, *The Book of Job* (1913), pp. 18f.; G. F. Moore, *The Literature of the OT* (1913), p. 248; J. A. Bewer, *The Literature of the OT* (1922), p. 317; P. Dhorme, *Le livre de Job*, p. cxxxv; C. F. Kent, *The Growth and Contents of the OT* (1926), p. 291; H. Creelman, *Introduction to the OT* (1927), p. 239; J. E. McFadyen, *Introduction to the OT* (1932 ed.), p. 319; G. Hölscher, *Das Buch Hiob* (1937), p. 7; L. Finkelstein, *The Pharisees*, I, p. 231; L. Bigot in *Dictionnaire de Théologie Catholique* (ed. A. Vacant, 1947), VIII, 1483; A. Lods, *La Bible du Centenaire* (1947), III, p. xiii, and *Histoire de la littérature hébraïque et juive*, pp. 688f.; H. Junker, *Das Buch Hiob* (1951), p. 7; A. Weiser, *Das Buch Job* (1956 ed.), p. 13, and *Einleitung in das AT* (1957 ed.), p. 236. These dates varied from a fifth-century date to the second-century B.C. date suggested by C. Siegfried, *JE*, VII, p. 197, on the basis that Job 15:20ff. possibly alluded to Alexander Jannaeus. The wide range in the estimate of dating indicates the difficulties inherent in the problem, particularly when the book is divided into fragments of differing provenance. Albright, *FSAC*, p. 331 and in *JBL*, LXI (1942), pp. 123f., has assigned the composition of the book to the sixth or fifth century B.C., although he regarded the date of the hero himself as belonging to the first half of the second millennium B.C., *VT* suppl. vol. III (1955), p. 13 n. 3.

[76] J. G. von Herder, *Vom Geist der Ebräischen Poesie* (1782-83), I, pp. 101ff.; F. M. A. Voltaire, *Dictionnaire philosophique* (1816), IX, 299; E. Renan, *Le livre de Job* (1865), p. xxvii; *PIOT*, pp. 678ff.

[77] Cf. F. H. Foster, *AJSL*, XLIX (1932), pp. 21ff.

[78] F. Delitzsch, *Das Buch Hiob*, pp. 125ff.; cf. P. Dhorme, *Le livre de Job*, pp. cxl ff.

[79] S. Terrien, *IB*, III, p. 892.

Thus, despite the suggestion first made by Ibn Ezra that Job was a translation from the Arabic, linguistic affinities of the canonical work with this tongue are insufficient to warrant acceptance of such a theory. A striking feature of the language of the book is its pronounced Aramaic coloring, which exceeds that of any other composition in the canon of the Old Testament. However, caution should be urged in any attempt to argue on this basis for a post-exilic date of the book, as Pfeiffer has shown, since the mutual influences of the two languages go back to very early times.[80] Tur-Sinai maintained that the original Aramaic of Job was Babylonian, and not later than the sixth century B.C.[81] The author was apparently a Jew who composed the poem in the early exile on the basis of an ancient legend, and several generations afterwards a Palestinian "translator" rendered it into its Hebrew form. Such a theory seems rather elaborate in view of the fact that the language of the work is genuinely Hebrew, and as such does not presuppose either an Arabic or an Aramaic original.

D. CORRUPTIONS IN THE TEXT

The text of the book has suffered greatly from attempts of varying ingenuity at emendation. While the MT is corrupt in many instances and in need of alteration, the straightforwardness of other passages might well imply that much of the difficulty in this regard is due to sheer ignorance of the language and phraseology employed by the author. Accordingly it would appear unwise to engage in more than the minimum of textual emendation, since further discoveries and studies in languages such as Ugaritic may throw unexpected light upon the Hebrew text as it now stands.

Reliance upon the LXX as a corrective is ill advised, for, while it is helpful in a few instances, it is known that the original LXX omitted between three hundred fifty and four hundred *stichoi*. This fact is evident from the recension of Origen, who supplied the missing lines from Theodotion and marked them by means of asterisks. The view that this shorter Greek form represented the earliest recension of Job, and that the MT constituted a later expansion, is less likely than the simpler explanation of the omissions in Greek, namely that the translator regarded any attempt to render the less intelligible passages into Greek as an exercise in futility. In certain cases the LXX is a paraphrase of the Hebrew text, while in others it is evident that a certain manipulation of the sense has occurred. There are some places in which the Peshitta exhibits a certain independence of approach, and since this version was made from the Hebrew it assists in clarifying some of the obscure passages. According to Jerome, the Vulgate was translated directly from

[80] *PIOT*, pp. 686f.
[81] N. H. Tur-Sinai, *The Book of Job: A New Commentary*, pp. xxx ff.

an ancient text of the fourth century after Christ, but even here the translator conceded that he had experienced the kind of difficulties which confront all who endeavor to render the text of Job into another language. There are a great many problematical philological and textual issues in the book, and it is not too much to hope that they will be resolved to an increasing extent by future discoveries.

E. THE MESSAGE OF JOB

Because of its vast poetic sweep Job has managed to reflect a great many aspects of human experience, including some of the more profound moral issues that confront humanity. On this account it has been held to supply an answer to the problem of evil, and particularly to the mystery of unmerited suffering. If this was the real aim of the work, it is clearly a conspicuous failure, as Rowley has indicated.[82] Indeed, the dialogue section shows that Job was considerably more concerned with the treatment that he received from his friends and former associates than with his affliction, although this, of course, formed part of his pattern of suffering.[83]

There is a good deal of truth in the observation that one important aim of the book was to challenge the popular view that human suffering was self-entailed, and that justice was to be expected uniformly to occur in this life.[84] There can be no doubt that on the basis of empirical observation the Hebrews were justified in entertaining the operation of cause and effect, since it is a simple fact that the bulk of human suffering, using that term in its widest possible sense, is strictly a product of the relationship between man and his environment. On the other hand, this did not constitute an elevation of the cause-effect sequence to the status of an official doctrine in Israel, since the monism of the Hebrews ultimately related the incidence of all phenomena to God alone. While it was often assumed that righteous conduct was the precursor of divine blessing in the form of moral and material benefits, it was recognized that the nature of life in society was such that occasionally the innocent might be involved in the fate of the guilty, and that periodically wickedness might flourish unchecked (cf. Pss. 37:1ff.; 49:5ff.; 73:3ff.; Jer. 12:1f.; 31:29f.; Hab. 1:13f.).

The general expectation that justice would triumph in this life was based first upon the conviction that the world was upheld by a divine moral order, and second, that in the absence of a doctrine of immortality, if such justice was to be a reality it had to occur in this life. In the latter regard, however, it should be noted that the Old Testament

---

[82] H. H. Rowley, *The Book of Job and Its Meaning* (1958), pp. 194f.
[83] Cf. W. B. Stevenson, *The Poem of Job,* pp. 34ff., who attributed the sufferings of Job to persecution (pp. 31ff.).
[84] *DILÔT,* pp. 409f.

nowhere presented a rigidly deterministic doctrine of retribution. All that a man could do in the face of rampant, unchecked evil was to trust in divine mercy, and hope to see the power of God triumph over wickedness.

The popular view of theological issues is almost always apt to be somewhat different in important areas from that contained in the authoritative sources, however, and in this instance it happened that men argued from the fact that, because sin was followed by suffering, therefore the latter was necessarily the result of antecedent sin, a position that was espoused by the friends of Job. While it is true that by divine standards Job was a sinner, the prologue endeavors to make clear the disinterested righteousness of the hero from the very beginning. By placing the popular view in the mouths of the friends, the author permitted Job to criticize it with comparative impunity, since the facts of the case as known to the reader clearly showed that it was somewhat deficient. In this same connection it may be that other cherished ideals were also being subjected to criticism. One of these was the prevailing concept of wisdom, which, if the teachings of the Hebrew sages have been interpreted correctly, assured the upright and prudent of prosperity in life. If such a man, having attained to success, was suddenly deprived of his blessings while still continuing to live righteously, it could be inferred that perhaps there was some radical deficiency in the concept of wisdom as commonly interpreted. Possibly it was with this in view that the author, in his Hymn to Wisdom in chapter 28, related the idea of wisdom to metaphysical issues, rather than to the practicalia of everyday life.

Another important criticism of ancient Hebrew life and thought as furnished by Job seems to the present writer to be related to the ancient patriarchal organizational concepts. This social structure dominated the ancient world, and still survives in many countries in various modified forms. Job followed the usual courtesies in permitting the elders to speak first on the issues before them, but thereupon departed completely from tradition by allowing a young man, who in any event ought to have had no particular opinions of his own, or who ought to have echoed those of his betters, to express views that, by the very nature of their language, have been suspected by scholars of being interpolations from a later hand.

Budde was quite correct in arguing for the originality of these addresses, for they constitute a direct challenge both to the views of the friends of Job and to the social structure that permitted the aged to believe that they understood the deep mysteries of existence.[85] In pointing out this deficiency, and in repudiating the generally accepted connection between human greatness and wisdom, the author of Job

[85] K. Budde, *Das Buch Hiob*, pp. xlv ff.

furnished the first direct and explicit criticism of the patriarchal system in the Old Testament. While the arguments of Elihu were rejected by God (Job 42:7), it was because they were far too restricted in standpoint, and not because they were simply untrue. This situation accounts for the apparently unsatisfactory "solution" of the problem of righteous suffering, for it is only when Job has confronted God that his doubts vanish. His appreciation of the vastness of divine power as a result of this encounter was accompanied by the realization that no answer to his problem was really needed. In any event he was reminded that there are many mysteries beyond human penetration, and that even if an answer had been forthcoming its nature would most probably have transcended mortal comprehension.

While Job repudiated the views of his friends, he appears to have felt that their general outlook ought somehow to have been right, and this accounts for much of the inner conflict that Job obviously experienced. Modern psychosomatic medical research has shown the tremendously damaging effect which subconscious mental conflict can have upon body and mind alike, and it is perhaps in this connection that some of the physical symptoms of the sufferer should be evaluated.[86] The book of Job is not so much a theodicy, a justification of the divine ways with humanity, as an examination of the intrinsic nature of man himself. It reveals something startlingly modern in its implications, namely that there is practically no suffering that can be called exclusively physical, and indeed very little that is specifically mental or spiritual.

Suffering involves the entire personality in a manner that was never appreciated by the enthusiastic advocates of Cartesian dualism, and Job shows clearly that man is a personality, rather than a mere physical extension with certain rather ill-defined spiritual aspects associated with it. The symptomatic characteristics of the sufferer point to a distinct disturbance within his personality, and an evident lack of integration that needed what Barton called "a first-hand experience of God" as a specific remedy.[87]

In view of the fact that there is so much suffering among human beings, a great deal of which is entirely needless, and because it is so often under these conditions that the real personality of the individual emerges, the pastoral and evangelistic implications of such a situation are readily obvious. From the religious experience through which Job passed came the supreme benefit of a matured personality, and one of the great merits of the book is its insistence that the experience of suffering, in one form or another, is necessary for spiritual maturity. In the last resort it is only when a man experiences a conscious deepening of his relationship

[86] Cf. R. K. Harrison, *EQ,* XXV (1953), pp. 18ff.
[87] G. A. Barton, *JBL,* XXX (1911), p. 67.

with God that the therapeutic powers of the divine Being can start to operate effectively within his personality.

Job does not set out to answer the problem of suffering, but instead shows that even a righteous man can utilize such an experience as that through which the hero passed to attain to new heights of emotional and spiritual maturity. Quite obviously nobody can be exempt from suffering, for where there are men there will always be emotional and mental conflicts, with corresponding adverse effects. The supreme exemplar of the righteous sufferer was Jesus Christ, who neither explained nor dismissed suffering, but instead absorbed it into His own spiritual experience, and through His fellowship with God achieved what Rowley has happily styled "the wresting of profit from the suffering," which has been of incalculable value to subsequent humanity.[88]

Supplementary Literature

Ellison, H. L. *From Tragedy to Triumph.* 1958.
Green, W. H. *The Argument of the Book of Job Unfolded.* 1881.
Jung, C. G. *Antwort auf Hiob.* 1952.
Larcher, C. *Le livre de Job.* 1950.
Möller, H. *Sinn und Aufbau des Buches Hiob.* 1955.
Patterson, C. H. *The Philosophy of the Old Testament.* 1953.
Robinson, H. Wheeler. *The Cross of Job.* 1955.
Robinson, T. H. *Job and His Friends.* 1954.
Snaith, N. H. *The Book of Job.* 1945.
Stewart, J. *The Message of Job.* 1960.
Sutcliffe, E. F. *Providence and Suffering in the Old and New Testaments.* 1955.
Watson, R. A. *The Book of Job.* 1899.

[88] H. H. Rowley, *BJRL,* XLI (1958), p. 207.

Part Thirteen

THE SACRED WRITINGS (II)
THE MEGILLOTH

I. CANTICLES OR THE SONG OF SOLOMON

A. PROBLEMS OF AUTHORSHIP AND DATE

The Song of Solomon is the first of the five Megilloth, the five scrolls read by the Jews at various feasts: Canticles (Passover), Ruth (Pentecost), Ecclesiastes (Tabernacles), Esther (Purim), and Lamentations (anniversary of the destruction of Jerusalem). Normally Canticles is placed after Job in the Hebrew Bible. Its title in Hebrew, שִׁיר הַשִּׁירִים, "The Song of Songs," is a superlative expression denoting the best, or most excellent of songs. The LXX rendered the title Ἀσμα Ἀσμάτων, and placed it after Ecclesiastes, a position that both Protestant and Roman Catholic editions of the Bible have adopted. The Vulgate entitled it *Canticum Canticorum,* hence the alternative English title Canticles.

The only evidence for attributing the work to Solomon occurs in the title, where, as in other instances, the attributive particle can mean "to," "for," "concerning" and "in the manner of," as well as denoting direct authorship, so that the evidence is quite ambiguous. The name Solomon appeared six times in the composition (1:5; 3:7, 9, 11; 8:11, 12), of which the first and last two alluded to the great wealth of the monarch, while those in the third chapter probably referred to the historical Solomon. Three additional occurrences involving the king (Cant. 1:4, 12; 7:6) probably implied Solomon also, and although he was the chief figure in much of the poetry he was not actually credited with any utterances. The attribution to Solomon may also be based upon his prowess as a composer of lyrics (1 Kgs. 4:32), of which Canticles may be the supreme example.

Talmudic opinion (*Bab. Bath.* 15a) assigned its composition to Hezekiah and his company, reflecting the activities of this group with regard to other Solomonic material also (cf. Prov. 25:1). In favor of a time of composition either during or shortly after the Solomonic era is the fact that the work speaks of various places throughout Palestine as though they belonged to one and the same kingdom, such as Jerusalem, Carmel, Sharon, Lebanon, Engedi, and the like. This diversity could be accounted for, however, by supposing, as do Pfeiffer and others, that the book was based upon the rustic songs of shepherds and peasants heard

1049

at wedding-feasts.[1] The songs exhibit a close knowledge of animals and exotic plants, over twenty species of the latter being mentioned. In view of the fact that Solomon introduced horses from Egypt (1 Kgs. 10:28), the reference in Canticles 1:9 that compared the bridegroom with a horse harnessed in the chariots of pharaoh may actually be to the king himself.

Most modern authors have repudiated the tradition of Solomonic composition, partly on grounds of language, but also through considerations of locale. There are a number of Aramaic forms in the book, including the uniform use of the particle שׁ for אֲשֶׁר as the relative pronoun,[2] as well as what appear to have been originally Greek and Persian terms.[3] These loan-words may point to the Persian period for the date of composition, or they may merely indicate editorial activity on the part of a scribe at a subsequent period.

The names of the various exotic substances and plants need not militate against composition in the late Solomonic or early post-Solomonic period, since trading-caravans had been visiting both Egypt and Palestine from northern India for many centuries previously, and trade in the Near East during the early monarchy was virtually controlled by Solomon himself.[4] These trading contacts appear in the Sanskrit parallels for some of the substances mentioned in Canticles, as for example with nard (Sanskrit *naladu*) and purple dyed ware (Sanskrit *ragaman*). Even the supposed Grecism in 3:9 ("palanquin") may well have come directly from the Sanskrit *paryanka*, a possibility that Driver did not exclude completely.[5] The presence of Aramaic forms can throw no light upon questions of authorship, however, since they occur in numerous Old Testament compositions of differing origin and date. Again, the influence of Aramaic may be as much a matter of regional dialect as anything else if, as some scholars have assumed, part of the work originated as separate songs in northern Israel, where Aramaic seems to have constituted an important linguistic factor.

As far as locale is concerned, various places in the north and south are considered as likely possibilities. Northern sites have included Damascus, Sharon, Carmel, Lebanon, and Hermon, while in Transjordan it is possible to identify Heshbon and Gilead with certainty, and in the south to recognize Jerusalem and Engedi as being mentioned by name. Certain allusions to "Sharon" and "Zion" (cf. Cant. 2:1, 7; 3:5, 10f.; 5:8, 16) are quite probably literary or idiomatic, and not specifically geographic. While some sections of the work presuppose a rural, and perhaps a

---

[1] *PIOT*, p. 711.

[2] *DILOT*, pp. 448f.

[3] אַפִּרְיוֹן (Cant. 3:9), from the Greek φορεῖον ("chariot" AV, "palanquin" RSV); פַּרְדֵּס (Cant. 4:13), from the Persian ("orchard").

[4] Cf. N. K. Gottwald, *IDB*, IV, p. 421.

[5] *DILOT*, p. 449n.

northern, background, at least one appears to be set in some such urban locale as Jerusalem (Cant. 3:6ff.).

The mention of Tirzah in Canticles 6:4 as parallel to Jerusalem seems to indicate that the particular section was composed at a period prior to the time of Omri (885/84-874/73 B.C.), who built Samaria as his capital city to replace Tirzah, which was the chief city of the northern kingdom in the early ninth century B.C. Such a reference might perhaps allude to the "charm" of Tirzah, or alternatively the northern capital of earlier times could have been mentioned in an attempt to avoid the use of the name Samaria by later Jews. If this was in fact adopted as an editorial device it would add to the obscurity of the situation by employing an archaic historic name whose significance would probably have lapsed with the passing of time, so that the particular reference, as well as the general context, would appear to point to the capital of the northern kingdom as a parallel to Jerusalem in the south. Assuming that the book is to be regarded as a unity in its extant form, it must thus be granted that Solomon pursued his bride into the northern part of the land, which is, of course, by no means impossible. If the book is to be regarded as an anthology of poetry, the passage concerned may well have originated in or near Samaria.

Although Solomon was reputedly well acquainted with the flora and fauna of his land, there is some question as to whether he would have composed lyrics that in the end exhibited such an extensive theme. Again, the sentiments expressed in the poems are relatively simple, and as such may appear to be out of harmony with the character of Solomon as a licentious and capricious oriental despot. In the last analysis it was possibly only the attribution to Solomon that secured Canticles a place in the canon of the supposed Council of Jamnia, when, according to tradition, Rabbi Aqiba uttered his famous dictum after some dispute: "For in all the world there is nothing to equal the day on which the Song of Songs was given to Israel, for all the Writings are holy, but the Song of Songs is the Holy of Holies."[6] The fact that such a statement should have survived indicates that in the days of Rabbi Aqiba there were distinct questions about the provenance and propriety of the composition.

While the present work appears to be based upon a collection of love poems of rather uncertain origin, it has distinct indications of literary unity. As Rowley has observed, the repetitions in the book point to the activities of a single hand, while in addition there is a greater unity of style and theme than would be the case in a diverse collection of lyrics from several authors in widely separated ages.[7] In consequence it would

---

[6] *Mish. Yadaim*, III, 5; cf. *Toseph. Sanhed.* XII, 10.
[7] *RSL*, pp. 212f. This chapter incorporates material by the same author in *JTS*, XXXVIII (1937), pp. 337ff., and *JRAS* (1938), pp. 251ff.

appear that attempts by scholars such as Oesterley to divide the book up into something under thirty different poems are hardly in keeping with the character of the extant product.[8]

Some of the material may be genuinely Solomonic, though sections that refer to a northern locale for the narrative may not. If the work as a whole was not actually composed in the Solomonic period, a date that few modern authorities would accept,[9] the final redaction of the book may well have occurred in the immediate pre-exilic period. In view of the available evidence for cultural and commercial intercourse between India, Canaan, Ionia, and Egypt in the Solomonic era, there seems to be no valid reason for postulating a date of composition as late as 300 B.C.

B. Interpretations of the Book

Few books of the Old Testament have experienced as wide a variety of interpretation as the Song of Songs. The absence of specifically religious themes has combined with the erotic lyrics and the vagueness of any plot for the work to furnish for scholars an almost limitless ground for speculation. Aside from the purely erotic interpretation, four or five principal approaches have been adopted by scholars over the centuries in an attempt to furnish a reasonable account of the composition.

1. Allegorical. The rabbis and Church Fathers solved the difficulties attaching to the acceptance of a group of love-poems into the canon of Scripture by interpreting the book allegorically, an attitude that still finds some favor among Orthodox Jewish and Roman Catholic scholars. Traces of this method occur in the Mishnah[10] and the Talmud,[11] while the targum of Canticles interpreted it in terms of the gracious love of God towards His people as manifested in Hebrew history.[12] This view has been revived within modern times by some European scholars, but it has not gained any extended following.[13]

Christian allegorists, following New Testament tradition (cf. John 3:29; Eph. 5:22ff.; Rev. 18:23ff.), altered the Jewish pattern to the point where the bride became the Church, a trend represented in the chapter-

---

[8] W. O. E. Oesterley, *The Song of Songs* (1936), p. 66.

[9] A Solomonic date is maintained by Young (*YIOT*, pp. 332f.). For a fifth- to fourth-century B.C. date see W. F. Albright in D. W. Thomas and W. D. McHardy (eds.), *Hebrew and Semitic Studies Presented to G. R. Driver* (1963), p. 1.

[10] *Ta'anith*, IV, 8.

[11] Cf. P. Vulliaud, *Le Cantique des Cantiques d'après la tradition juive* (1925), pp. 53ff.

[12] Cf. R. H. Melamed, *JQR*, XII (1921-1922), pp. 57ff.

[13] Cf. E. A. Fraisse, *La clé du Cantique des Cantiques* (n.d.); P. Joüon, *Le Cantique des Cantiques* (1909); R. Breuer, *Lied der Lieder* (1923); G. Ricciotti, *Il Cantico dei Cantici* (1928).

headings of the AV, and one that has also been favored occasionally in modern times.[14] Few patristic writers matched the virtuosity of Origen as an allegorical interpreter of Canticles, and he was followed by Jerome, Athanasius, Augustine, and others in his speculations. Some medievalists saw in the work a few references to the Virgin Mary,[15] while the anti-papal writer Cocceius interpreted it in terms of a prophetic history of the Church culminating in the Reformation.[16]

As with all allegorical interpretations, the essential subjectivity of the method is its greatest drawback. Perhaps the most acceptable would be the view that the book entertains a *double entendre,* in which the theme of human love is interpenetrated with a mystical concept of a far deeper order,[17] an understanding that is very different from the allegorism of early Jewish and Christian interpreters. A fundamental objection to allegorical method, based upon other Old Testament Scriptures (cf. Ezek. 16:3ff.; 23:2ff.; Hos. 1–3), is that when the male-female relationship is employed allegorically it is clearly indicated as such, whereas in Canticles there is no hint of an allegorical approach. Again, while some oriental erotic poetry is said to have an esoteric meaning, this can hardly be the case for Canticles, since the composition furnishes no ground for postulating such an esoteric interpretation.

2. *Dramatic.* The second approach to the understanding of the work, the dramatic, came into prominence when the allegorical view began to decline about 1800, although there was one occasion on which Origen himself described Canticles in this sense.[18] The dramatic interpretation took two major forms, the first being advanced by Delitzsch, who suggested that there were two characters, Solomon and a Shulammite shepherdess, in the drama.[19] Falling in love with her, the king took her from her homeland to marry her in Zion, and as a result was lifted from the levels of physical attraction to pure love. This theory was rightly criticized on the ground that Solomon would be out of character in the capacity of a shepherd (Cant. 1:7), and that the closing scene of the drama would hardly have taken place in the home village of the bride. Furthermore, in Canticles 6:8f., the bridegroom appeared to set the bride in favorable contrast to the royal *harîm,* which ill accords with the traditions associated with Solomon.[20]

---

[14] Cf. E. Tobac, *Les cinq livres de Salomon* (1926), pp. 110f.

[15] *PL,* XVI, cols. 326f.; LXVII, col. 978; CXCVI, col. 482.

[16] *Cogitationes de Cantico Canticorum Solomonis* (1665).

[17] So A. Miller, *Das Hohe Lied* (1927), pp. 7ff.

[18] *PG,* XIII, col. 61.

[19] F. Delitzsch, *Biblischer Commentar über die poetischen Bücher des AT* (1875), IV, pp. 9f.

[20] *DILOT,* p. 444.

A variation of this approach was popularized in the work of Ewald, and became known as the so-called "shepherd" hypothesis.[21] Ewald postulated the existence of three figures, namely Solomon, the Shulammite maiden, and her shepherd-lover, in the drama. He suggested that the king had carried off the maiden by force to his *harîm,* but that when she resisted his advances he permitted her to return to the locale of her rustic lover. This theory was accepted by Driver, Junès, and others, while some writers developed the dramatic aspect by stressing the presence of a chorus somewhat along classical Greek lines.[22] While such a theory avoids some of the difficulties which Delitzsch encountered by indicating why the lover was depicted in a pastoral role, and why the poem terminates in a northern setting, it nevertheless has certain grave weaknesses of its own. Whereas the theory of Delitzsch portrayed the joys of conjugal union as exemplified in the hero Solomon, the view of Ewald and his followers presented a picture of attempted seduction by the king, who thus became the villain of the piece.

The scheme suggested by Ewald was modified by a great many interpreters to the point where some of the reconstructions appeared to preclude others entirely. It must be observed that to assume that the maiden mentioned in the poems was Abishag the Shunammite (1 Kgs. 1:1ff., 15; 2:17ff.), as some interpreters did, is entirely gratuitous, and the identification of the "daughters of Jerusalem" with either the Solomonic *harîm* on the one hand, or with some kind of professional chorus on the other, is equally conjectural. The literary character of Canticles is such that it prohibits analysis into speeches and mimes, scenes, acts, and the like, save on the most subjective of bases, while the dramatic nature of the work is so little in evidence that it is impossible to trace any convincing development of the plot. Whatever dramatic interpretation is adduced faces the insuperable difficulty mentioned by Oesterley, namely that among the Semites generally, and the Hebrews in particular, drama as such was unknown.[23]

3. Literal. The erotic-literary view has seen in Canticles a collection of love-songs or an erotic poem to be understood in its plain and literal sense. This approach was commonly entertained in the first century of the Christian era, and had apparently gone to such lengths that Rabbi Aqiba is said to have uttered a curse upon those who sang portions of Canticles at festive occasions or banquets: "He who trills his voice in the chanting of Song of Songs and treats it as a secular song, has no share in

[21] H. Ewald, *Das Hohelied Salomos übersetzt mit Einleitung, Anmerkungen und einem Anhang* (1826).
[22] *DILOT,* pp. 436ff. E. Junès, *Le Cantique des Cantiques de Salomon* (1932), pp. 8f. The Greek chorus suggestion was made by E. Renan, *Le Cantique des Cantiques* (1860), pp. 72ff., 179ff.; cf. *PIOT,* p. 715.
[23] W. O. E. Oesterley, *The Song of Songs,* p. 10a. For further criticism see R. Gordis, *The Song of Songs* (1954), pp. 11ff.

1054

the world to come."[24] There seems little doubt that the literal interpretation of the book prompted some of the doubts expressed in the Mishnah as to its canonicity.[25]

Although the work was understood in the main in allegorical terms by the rabbis, the literal view, as Gordis has pointed out, won a measure of unconscious acceptance in rabbinic circles.[26] Among Christian interpreters, Theodore of Mopsuestia adhered to this view, which was rejected as heresy by the Second Council of Constantinople in A.D. 553. While the broader concept of canonicity in Judaism did not require such steps to be taken, at least one Jewish commentator in twelfth-century France thought it prudent to present his literal interpretation anonymously.[27] Grotius inclined to a literal view of Canticles, although he also assigned a mystical meaning to the poem.[28] Herder thought that Canticles was a collection of separate compositions extolling human love,[29] while Reuss held the work to be profane, and unworthy of inclusion in the canon of Scripture,[30] a view also favored by others.

4. Collection of wedding songs. The concept of Canticles as an amalgam of nuptial songs received its impetus from the observations of Renan, who noted that there was a certain degree of correspondence between Canticles and Syrian wedding-poetry.[31] Shortly afterwards a study of Syrian nuptial customs was published by Wetzstein, in which he called attention to the *waṣfs* or poems sung in honor of the bride and bridegroom.[32] The theory was given its classic form in 1894 by Budde, and was adopted subsequently by Eissfeldt, Sellin, and Lods.[33]

Important objections to this view include the criticism that the collection is insufficient to last for the seven-day period of Syrian marriage-festivals, unless, of course, the poems preserved in Canticles represent but a small portion of available material. Equally telling is the doubt cast by Granqvist on the whole situation, inquiring whether the customs

---

[24] *Toseph. Sanhed.* XII, 10.

[25] *M. 'Eduy.,* V, 3; *Toseph. Yad.,* II, 14.

[26] R. Gordis, *The Song of Songs,* pp. 3 n. 11, 9.

[27] Edited by H. J. Matthews, *Festschrift zum 80en Geburtstag Moritz Steinschneiders* (1896), pp. 164ff., 238ff.

[28] *Opera omnia theologica* (1732), I, p. 276a.

[29] J. G. von Herder, *Lieder der Liebe* (1778), pp. 89ff.

[30] E. Reuss, *Le Cantique des Cantiques* (1879), p. 3.

[31] E. Renan, *Le Cantique des Cantiques,* p. 86.

[32] J. G. Wetzstein, *Zeitschrift für Ethnologie,* V (1873), pp. 270ff., and in F. Delitzsch, *Biblischer Commentar* (1875), pp. 162ff. Cf. St. H. Stephan, *JPOS,* II (1922), pp. 199ff.

[33] K. Budde, *The New World,* III (1894), pp. 56ff., *Preussische Jahrbücher,* LXXVIII (1894), pp. 92ff. O. Eissfeldt, *Einleitung in das AT* (1934 ed.), pp. 531f.; *ETOT,* pp. 487f. E. Sellin, *Einleitung in das AT* (1935 ed.), p. 146. A. Lods, *Histoire de la littérature hébraïque et juive,* pp. 748ff.

described by Wetzstein ever existed in Palestine.[34] Since according to Dalman there are certain pre-nuptial *waṣfs* in evidence among the Arabs, it is impossible to be sure that, even if Canticles contained material akin to *waṣfs*, such compositions were meant specifically for the marriage occasion.[35] Finally, as Rothstein pointed out, the Shulammite is not designated "queen" anywhere in Canticles, which is out of harmony with Syrian marriage customs.[36] In consequence, critics such as Reuss, Wheeler Robinson, Weiser, Pfeiffer, Bentzen, and others have returned in large measure to the view of Herder, that Canticles contains a group of love-lyrics rather than nuptial songs as such,[37] a standpoint accepted with some reserve by Rowley.[38]

5. *Liturgical.* Another interpretation that has gained considerable attention was published in 1922 by Meek.[39] He suggested that Canticles had been derived from the liturgical rites of the Adonis-Tammuz cult, the existence of which in Israel was apparent from certain references in the prophets (e.g. Isa. 17:10f.; Ezek. 8:14; Zech. 12:11). Babylonian cuneiform texts of the Tammuz cult, which had been published earlier,[40] appeared to Meek to support his theory, and in the general tenor of his opinions he was followed by many scholars including M. L. Margolis, McFadyen, Waterman, Wittekindt, Snaith, Oesterley, Dornseiff, and Widengren.[41] Certain of these scholars presented a picture of the situation that varied somewhat from that of Meek; Snaith, for example, thought he detected the presence of two alternating cycles in Canticles relating to specific aspects of Hebrew history; Wittekindt envisaged the composition in terms of a Jerusalem liturgy celebrating the union of Ishtar and Tammuz at the spring lunar festival.

[34] H. Granqvist, *Marriage Customs in a Palestinian Village* (1935), II, p. 137n.
[35] G. Dalman, *Palästinischer Diwan* (1901), pp. xi ff.
[36] J. W. Rothstein, *HDB*, IV, p. 593.
[37] E. Reuss, *Die Geschichte der Heiligen Schriften AT* (1881), p. 223. H. Wheeler Robinson, *The Old Testament: Its Making and Meaning* (1937), p. 161. A. Weiser, *Einleitung in das AT* (1939 ed.), p. 250. *PIOT*, p. 711. A. Bentzen, *Introduction to the OT*, II, p. 182.
[38] *RSL*, pp. 212f.
[39] T. J. Meek, *AJSL*, XXXIX (1922), pp. 1ff., and in W. H. Schoff (ed.), *The Song of Songs: A Symposium* (1924), pp. 48ff., and *JBL*, XLIII (1924), pp. 245ff.
[40] Cf. W. W. von Baudissin, *Adonis and Esmun* (1911); S. H. Langdon, *Tammuz and Ishtar* (1914); E. Ebeling, *Keilschrifttexte aus Assur religiösen Inhalts* (1919), I, 4, No. 158.
[41] M. L. Margolis, *The Song of Songs: A Symposium*, p. 16. J. E. McFadyen in A. S. Peake (ed.), *The People and the Book* (1925), p. 214. L. Waterman, *JBL*, XLIV (1925), pp. 171ff. W. Wittekindt, *Das Hohe Lied und seine Bezeihungen zum Istarkult* (1926), pp. 176ff. N. H. Snaith, *AJSL*, L (1934), pp. 199ff., *The Jewish New Year Festival* (1947), pp. 54ff. W. O. E. Oesterley, *The Song of Songs*, pp. 11ff. F. Dornseiff, *ZDMG*, XC (1936), pp. 589ff. G. Widengren, *Religion och Bibel*, VII (1948), pp. 17ff. For criticisms of the general theory see N. Schmidt, *JAOS*, XLVI (1926), pp. 154ff.; H. H. Rowley, *JRAS* (1938), pp. 251ff.

While it is generally recognized that there are certain indistinct ritual survivals in the Old Testament narratives, it seems more likely that these should be interpreted in terms of Phoenician, rather than Egyptian[42] or Babylonian ritual practices. As far as the extant Song of Solomon is concerned, it is extremely improbable that a pagan liturgy of a generally immoral character would ever be incorporated into the canon of Hebrew Scripture without a radical revision of its theological presuppositions, and there are no indications in Canticles that such a redaction took place at any time.

Of those who supported Meek originally, at least one scholar, Waterman, modified his views and returned to an historical basis for Canticles.[43] He alleged that after the death of David, and subsequent to the tragic request of Adonijah for the hand of Abishag, the young Shunammite maiden (1 Kgs. 1:3), the latter refused the advances of Solomon and remained faithful to her rustic lover.[44] Unfortunately much of this is an appeal to ignorance, since there is no evidence whatever for the contention that the Shunammite girl had a lover in her home village, and an equal lack of foundation for the basic assumption that the words "Shunammite" and "Shulammite" can be equated.[45]

6. *Didactic-moral.* The didactic-moral interpretation of the book maintains that Canticles presents the purity and wonder of true love. Exponents of this position have generally regarded the work as historical, and as far as some Christian interpreters are concerned it is alleged that the love portrayed therein directs the reader to the greater love of Christ.[46] Basically, however, the composition teaches the beauty and holiness of the marriage-love relationship that God has ordained for humanity, and it is on such a basis that Rowley would support the inclusion of Canticles in the Hebrew canon.[47]

With regard to the teaching of the book, the last word can conveniently rest with E. J. Young:

> The Song does celebrate the dignity and purity of human love. This is a fact which has not always been sufficiently stressed. The Song, therefore, is didactic and moral in its purpose. It comes to us in this world of sin, where lust and passion are on every hand, where fierce temptations assail us and try to turn us aside from the God-given standard of marriage. And it reminds us, in particularly beautiful fashion, how pure and noble true love is. This, however,

[42] Cf. O. N. de Jasny, *Le Cantique des Cantiques et le Mythe d'Osiris-Hetep* (1914), pp. 16ff.

[43] L. Waterman, *The Song of Songs Translated and Interpreted as a Dramatic Poem* (1948), pp. 2ff.

[44] For a criticism of this view see T. J. Meek, *JBL*, LXVIII (1949), pp. 177ff.

[45] Cf. H. H. Rowley, *AJSL*, LVI (1939), pp. 84ff.

[46] Cf. *YIOT*, p. 336.

[47] *RSL*, p. 234.

does not exhaust the purpose of the book. Not only does it speak of the purity of human love; but, by its very inclusion in the Canon, it reminds us of a love that is purer than our own.[48]

C. Analysis of the Book

The literary form of the Song of Solomon is extremely difficult to analyze objectively. There are dialogue passages (2:9ff.) and soliloquies (2:8–3:5), but apart from the lovers it is not easy to identify other conversationalists. The appeal of such material as Canticles to the oriental mind lies in the intensity of the love and devotion expressed in the phraseology, and in the voluptuous descriptions of secondary sexual characteristics, neither of which would seem particularly out of place in rustic love-songs. Canticles supplies almost no information about Hebrew marriage institutions, but appears to be based upon an underlying ethos of monogamy. In common with other aspects of Hebrew literature there is no evident self-consciousness connected with the male-female relationship, unlike the Greek lyricists and some more modern authors. Despite the frankness with which the whole question of love and gratification is discussed, the work is never lewd or obscene.

Broadly the book can be analyzed as follows:

I. The Longing of the Bride for the Bridegroom, ch. 1:1–2:7
II. Increasing Love; the Praises of the Maiden, ch. 2:8–3:5
III. Praises of King Solomon; the Espousal; Praise of the Bride, ch. 3:6–5:1
IV. The Bride's Longing for the Bridegroom, ch. 5:2–6:9
V. Descriptive Passages on the Beauty of the Bride, ch. 6:10–8:4
VI. Concluding Section: The Durability of True Love, ch. 8:5–14

✻ ✻ ✻ ✻ ✻

While the Hebrew text is sometimes obscure, this may be due rather to the presence of an unusual number of rare words than to transmissional corruption as such. But the LXX and the Peshitta followed the MT tradition fairly closely, and so are of rather limited value in elucidating the more difficult sections of the Hebrew.

Supplementary Literature

Buzy, D. *Le Cantique des Cantiques*. 1949.
Feuillet, A. *Le Cantique des Cantiques*. 1953.
Graham, W. C. and H. G. May. *Culture and Conscience*. 1936.
Jastrow, M. *The Song of Songs*. 1921.
Schonfield, H. J. *The Song of Songs*. 1959.

[48] *YIOT*, p. 336. Cf. S. M. Lehrman, *The Five Megilloth* (1946), pp. xii-xiii.

II. THE BOOK OF RUTH

A. The Story of Ruth

This charming tale of human devotion and kindness is one of the most beautiful in the entire Old Testament, constituting a model of the art of story-telling. The story told the way in which a Bethlehemite family had sought to escape from a famine in southern Canaan by going to Moab, and how the two sons had married Moabite women named Orphah and Ruth. When death left all the women in the family widows, the mother offered her Moabite daughters-in-law the opportunity of returning to their own people. Only Orphah did so, however, and Ruth declared her undying loyalty to her mother-in-law Naomi.

These two returned to Bethlehem at the beginning of the barley harvest (Ru. 1:6ff.), and Ruth went to glean after the reapers on the land of a relative of Elimelech, her deceased father-in-law (Ru. 2:1-3). Boaz, the kinsman, treated Ruth with great kindness, and at the end of the harvest Naomi persuaded Ruth to appeal to the protection of Boaz, who stayed all night in the harvest field (Ru. 3:1-7). By appealing to his chivalry Ruth received an assurance that Boaz would act as kinsman-redeemer in accordance with the prescription of the Torah (cf. Lev. 25:25, 47f.), provided that her near-kinsman did not wish to exercise the privilege of levirate marriage (Ru. 3:8-18). When the near-kinsman renounced his right to purchase the field of Naomi and marry Ruth because of his poverty, he removed his shoes in ratification of his decision (Deut. 25:5ff.). Boaz then married Ruth, who bore him a son named Obed, grandfather of King David (Ru. 4:1-17). The book concluded with a genealogy of David reaching to Perez, the son of Judah and Tamar (Ru. 4:18-22).

B. Problems of Dating and Authorship

Like Job this composition presents great difficulties for estimating its authorship and date, since it furnishes no assured indication of either. The book received its name from its principal character, and the historical setting was that of the Judges period (Ru. 1:1). The fact that the extant work belongs to a later date is indicated by the presence of explanatory glosses (Ru. 4:1-12) intended to throw light upon ancient practices.

According to Talmudic tradition[1] Samuel was the author of Judges and Ruth, and while this is possible, it appears unlikely, in that the concluding genealogy implied that David was well known at the time. In rejecting this tradition modern critical scholars have entertained varying periods of composition for the work. Thus Keil ascribed the book to the time of the early monarchy,[2] while Wright thought that it was not later than David in its extant form,[3] a date that he subsequently modified to include the possibility of later pre-exilic composition.[4] Other scholars to adhere to a Davidic date included Steinmueller and Young.[5]

A period of writing between the early monarchy and the exile was suggested by Oettli and Driver,[6] while the period of Hezekiah was advanced as the probable time of composition by Davidson and Reuss.[7] A number of scholars assigned the work to the exilic age, including Ewald, König, and Jepsen.[8] The majority of scholars, however, followed the lead of Wellhausen in placing the book firmly in the post-exilic period, including Bertholet, Nowack, Steuernagel, Gautier, Sellin, Meinhold, Oesterley and Robinson, Eissfeldt, Pfeiffer, and Weiser.[9]

The later dating of the work is based in part upon the antiquarian interests of the author, as shown in such matters as explanatory glosses, and also on the supposed connection with the reforms of Ezra and Nehemiah, when an attempt was being made to eliminate Moabite links altogether from the theocratic nation. It has been argued that the genealogy at the end of the book is similar to those of the post-exilic period in

[1] *Bab. Bath.* 14b, followed by R. Cornely, *Introductio in Veteris Testamenti libros sacros* (1897), II, i, pp. 223f.

[2] C. F. Keil, *Lehrbuch der historisch-kritischen Einleitung in die Schriften des AT* (1873 ed.), p. 437.

[3] C. H. H. Wright, *The Book of Ruth in Hebrew* (1864), p. xliv.

[4] C. H. H. Wright, *Introduction to the OT* (1890), p. 126.

[5] J. E. Steinmueller, *Companion to Scripture Studies* (1942), II, p. 82. YIOT, p. 339.

[6] S. Oettli in *Die geschichtlichen Hagiographen und das Buch Daniel* (1889), pp. 215f. *DILOT*, pp. 454f.

[7] S. Davidson, *Introduction to the OT* (1862), I, pp. 482ff. E. Reuss, *Littérature politique et polémique* (1879), pp. 26f.

[8] H. Ewald, *Geschichte des Volkes Israel* (1864 ed.), p. 225. E. König, *Einleitung in das AT* (1893), p. 287. A. Jepsen, *Theologische Studien und Kritiken*, CVIII (1938), p. 424.

[9] J. Wellhausen in F. Bleek, *Einleitung in das AT* (1878 ed.), pp. 204f. A. Bertholet in *Die fünf Megilloth* (1898), pp. 49ff. W. Nowack, *Richter, Ruth und Bücher Samuelis* (1902), pp. 180f. C. Steuernagel, *Lehrbuch der Einleitung in das AT*, pp. 430f. L. Gautier, *Introduction à l'Ancien Testament* (1939 ed.), II, p. 150. E. Sellin, *Einleitung in das AT* (1935 ed.), p. 147; cf. his *Introduction to the OT* (1923), p. 226, for a date in the first years after the return. J. Meinhold, *Einführung in das AT* (1932), pp. 336f. IBOT, p. 84. O. Eissfeldt, *Einleitung in das AT* (1934 ed.), pp. 542f.; ETOT, p. 483. PIOT, pp. 717ff. OTFD, p. 304.

language and content (cf. Ru. 4:18ff.; 1 Chron. 2:4ff.), particularly in the use of the verb "to beget," although it has to be remembered that such technical terms could conceivably be the work of a later editor. Other verbal forms thought to be Aramaic and comparatively late in nature included *nāsā'*, "take a wife" (Ru. 1:4), *lāhēn*, "therefore" (Ru. 1:13), and *mārā'*, "bitter" (Ru. 1:20). As elsewhere it should be noted that the presence of Aramaisms is no necessary indication of a late date, since they were prevalent in Palestine from at least the Amarna Age on. There is, in any event, some doubt as to whether *lāhēn* ever occurs in Aramaic in the sense of "therefore"[10] and the reading in Ruth 1:13 is probably a corruption of *lāhem*, "to them," which some versions adopted.

As far as the genealogy in Ruth is concerned, its shortness argues for an earlier rather than a later date of composition, since otherwise the name of Solomon would almost certainly have been included in the list of the offspring of Boaz. The direct character of the narrative seems to imply that David had not yet become a legendary personage in Israel, since had this been the case, the traditions of the "Golden Age" would have once again required the presence of Solomon in the genealogy.

Against the view that the book can most suitably be assigned to the post-exilic period because the narrative shows how a foreign woman became a member of the most respected family in Israel[11] and that this incident was particularly apt for the period of Ezra and Nehemiah, it needs only to be said that such a story would have served precisely the opposite aims that the reformers had in view. Ezra in particular was concerned with the task of purifying the blood-stock of the Jews, and not with finding reasons why it could be diluted with impunity through marriage with women of foreign extraction, however pious they were. If one of the sons of Joiada son of Eliashib the High Priest, had been able to appeal to Ruth as a recently written "tract for the times," the Samaritan situation at that particular period would probably not have taken the course which it did subsequently. Although in the view of the present writer the book was composed at a considerably earlier date, the fact that it was not fully canonical in the days of Ezra would prevent it from being utilized as a ground of appeal, however widely known the story itself was.

Other arguments for an early date have been adduced from the use of ancient Hebrew prose idioms and classical syntactical forms, although it is by no means impossible for a much later writer to have imitated such literary characteristics.[12] The setting of the book reflects in a uniform manner the period of the Judges, and however skilled the author, it has

---

[10] The word in Dan. 2:6, 9; 4:24 (Aramaic) can equally be translated "wherefore."

[11] D. Harvey, *IDB*, IV, p. 132.

[12] *PIOT*, p. 718.

to be admitted that such an atmosphere would be very difficult indeed to recapture in the post-exilic era. In addition, the attitude of the Torah towards foreign marriages (cf. Deut. 23:3), in which a Moabite was forbidden to enter the congregation, seems to point to an early rather than a late date for composition, even for critics who assign Deuteronomy to the period of Josiah.

Again, as Rowley has pointed out, it is significant that the book refers to the only Old Testament passages that were concerned with levirate marriage (Gen. 38:1ff.; Deut. 25:5ff.), thus harmonizing the matrimonial situation involving Ruth with the practices and customs of antiquity, the significance of which was explained by the author of the book.[13] Obviously the custom of removing the shoe as a symbol whereby claims were renounced was no longer current when the book was written, but it did obtain during the Judges period in which the narrative was set.[14] Despite some variation in the interpretation of the traditional levirate marriage law,[15] the book is in essential harmony with that ancient custom, and may, as Driver and Miles have suggested, represent an extension of levirate marriage from the brother-in-law to more remote kinsmen.[16]

In narratives such as this it is obviously very difficult to assign the work to a specific period with any confidence, since as shown above, the contents can be employed variously to demonstrate an early or a much later date. To the writer the former would appear more preferable, and it may be that the work was in existence at the close of the ninth century B.C., or the early part of the following century.

Although most scholars have assigned genuine historical value to the book, some, including Gunkel and Pfeiffer, have adhered to the position that the book has no historical worth at all.[17] Pfeiffer held it to be an idealizing romance which eliminated all unpleasant traits from ancient life, and presented as an important theme the strong religious faith of the participants. Its fictional character was further indicated for him by the symbolic names of some of the characters mentioned, as well as by the exemplary behavior of Ruth. However, it should be noted that the

[13] RSL, pp. 166ff.
[14] For the antiquity of levirate marriage see C. Westermarck, History of Human Marriage (1921 ed.), III, pp. 208ff.; E. Neufeld, The Hittite Laws (1951), p. 192. For a review of theories as to its origin see L. M. Epstein, Marriage Laws in the Bible and the Talmud (1942), pp. 77ff.; E. Neufeld, Ancient Hebrew Marriage Laws (1944), pp. 23ff. For parallels from Nuzu see E. R. Lacheman, JBL, LVI (1937), pp. 53ff.; E. A. Speiser, BASOR, No. 77 (1940), pp. 15ff.
[15] Cf. M. Burrows, JBL, LIX (1940), pp. 445ff.; RSL, pp. 171ff.
[16] G. R. Driver and J. C. Miles, The Assyrian Laws (1935), pp. 244f. Cf. J. Morgenstern, HUCA, VII (1930), pp. 175f.
[17] H. Gunkel, Die Religion in Geschichte und Gegenwart, IV, col. 2181. PIOT, p. 718.

story opens in the form of an historical narrative that reflects accurately the customs of the period depicted, as, for example, the fact that in the early days of the monarchy there were friendly relations existing between Israel and Moab (cf. 1 Sam. 22:3f.). As Young has said, it is hardly likely that a writer of fiction would set out to trace the line of the great King David to a Moabite ancestress, but this is in fact precisely what the book does.[18]

Many suggestions as to the purpose of composition of the work have been made by scholars, and perhaps the most obvious is the endeavor to trace the ancestry of King David, since his family tree was omitted from the books of Samuel. Incidental to this purpose was the inculcation of filial piety and unselfish devotion, as well as the recording of a pointed reminder to Israel that a foreigner who exemplified the qualities of piety and fidelity, in conjunction with a sincere trust in the providence of God, was certainly worthy to be reckoned among the Chosen People. In this sense the composition not only presented a case for racial tolerance, but also demonstrated convincingly that true religon transcended the bounds of nationality. Whether any of these themes other than the genealogical consideration were uppermost in the mind of the author, or merely incidental to the composition of the work, is very difficult to say. The absence of polemic or invective makes improbable the view that it was an anti-separatist tract written to counteract the stringent measures of Ezra and Nehemiah. Equally unlikely is the theory advanced by Staples that the book was composed as a midrash on a Bethlehem fertility-cult myth, in which Elimelech represented the dying god, Naomi the mother-goddess, and Ruth her devotee.[19] The place of the book in the Hebrew canon as the work to be read at the Feast of Weeks, when the close of the grain harvest was celebrated, indicates the importance that Jewish tradition assigned to this delightful narrative. In the Hebrew Bible the book occupied a position in the *K^ethubhim*, as noted earlier; and the Talmud placed it at the head of this great division of Scripture, before the Psalter.[20] More recent Jewish tradition incorporated it into the Megilloth. The LXX placed Ruth after Judges, presumably because of the identity of historical background, and this tradition, which was also followed by the Vulgate, has been maintained in most modern versions of the Old Testament. Josephus also joined Ruth with Judges.[21]

*   *   *   *   *

The Hebrew text of the composition has been well preserved, and there are very few passages indeed where there can be any doubt as to

[18] *YIOT*, p. 340.
[19] W. E. Staples, *AJSL*, LIII (1937), pp. 145ff.
[20] *Bab. Bath.* 14*b*.
[21] *Contra Apionem*, I, 8.

the reading intended. The most important of these are Ruth 1:21, 2:7, and 4:4, where there is a certain amount of obscurity. Since the versions follow the MT tradition to a great extent they are of limited value when textual problems arise.

Supplementary Literature

Bettan, I. *The Five Scrolls.* 1950.
Cooke, G. A. *The Book of Ruth.* 1919.
Gerleman, G. *Ruth.* 1960.
Kennedy, A. R. S. *The Book of Ruth.* 1928.
Lattey, C. *The Book of Ruth.* 1935.
Slotki, J. J. *The Five Megilloth.* 1946.

III. THE BOOK OF LAMENTATIONS

A. The Contents of the Book

In the Hebrew Bible Lamentations was placed third among the five Megilloth, and was read on the ninth day of Ab, the day of mourning over the destruction of the Temple. The composition originally bore no title, but the first word איכה, the characteristic lament "Ah, how!" (Lam. 1:1; 2:1; 4:1) of three of the elegies, served as a superscription. The LXX entitled it Θρῆνοι or "Dirges," and placed it after the book of Jeremiah. This position was also adopted by the Vulgate, which furnished the subtitle *"Id est lamentationes Jeremiae prophetae."* The English versions followed the tradition of associating the book with Jeremiah, and enlarged the LXX title and its Vulgate counterpart *Threni* to read "The Lamentations of Jeremiah." The work was very similar to those that the ancient Sumerians wrote to commemorate the fall of some of their great cities, particularly Ur, to marauding enemy forces,[1] and from this it is evident that the author stood in a long and venerated literary tradition.

The book comprises five poems, each forming one chapter of Lamentations, of which four are acrostic in form. The construction of this portion is highly elaborate, for the twenty-two consonants of the Hebrew alphabet occur in succession throughout each of the four poems at the beginning of each strophe or stanza. The first poem followed the normal order of the consonants in the Hebrew alphabet, but in the second, third, and fourth the letter פ preceded ע to make for a slight irregularity. The first three chapters contained three lines to each strophe, except for two instances of a four-line stanza (Lam. 1:7; 2:19), which are probably accidental.

A more elaborate form of the acrostic pattern occurred in chapter three, where each of the three verses of the stanza commenced with the same letter. The fourth poem was written in such a manner as to have two lines only to each strophe. The fifth poem was not actually acrostic in form, but was alphabetic in the sense that it comprised twenty-two lines, and was similar in nature and content to certain psalms of corpo-

[1] Cf. *ANET*, pp. 455ff.

rate lament (cf. Pss. 44:9ff.; 80:4ff.). The dominant rhythmical or stress pattern is 3:2 or *qînāh*, with an admixture of 2:2, 2:3, and 3:3 forms.

Despite a superficial resemblance between them, each of the chapters manifests its own special character. The first poem is arranged in three-line strophes in the *qînāh* parallelism, a form that was first recognized in Lamentations by Budde, and from which it received its name "dirge meter."[2] The acrostic form follows the usual order of the Hebrew alphabet, and the elegy comprises a lament in which Jerusalem, weeping bitterly like a bereft widow, remembers her past glories and bewails her destitute condition. Out of sorrow for the destruction of Jerusalem comes an appeal to all for pity (Lam. 1:12), and a cry to God for vengeance upon the enemies who had brought such devastation and desolation in their train (Lam. 1:22).

The second elegy closely resembles the first in character, save that the positions of ס and ע in the alphabet were reversed, as noted above. In this lament the author bewailed the ruin that had resulted from an outpouring of divine anger (Lam. 2:1-12), and saw one cause of the disaster in the negligence of the prophets, who had not been diligent in warning the people of impending doom (Lam. 2:14). Henceforward the only hope would lie in contrition and earnest supplication to God (Lam. 2:13-22).

Chapter three of Lamentations is significantly different from the remainder of the composition in that it was made up of single lines grouped together in threes and commencing with the same letter of the Hebrew alphabet. In this lament the personified nation bewailed the tragedy that had overtaken it (Lam. 3:1-20), but found some consolation in the assurance of divine favor and mercy for those who seek it (Lam. 3:21-39). Thus the nation was urged to examine its way of life critically, and turn in repentance to God (Lam. 3:40-54). After becoming aware that God had heard its pathetic cry, the nation appealed for vengeance upon its enemies (Lam. 3:55-66).

Early critics suggested that this chapter had originally comprised two psalms, which according to Löhr had constituted verses 1 to 24 and 52 to 66, into which the compiler had inserted an address to the people, using Jeremiah as a mouthpiece.[3] He maintained that the intervening section, consisting of verses 25-51, was the composition of the compiler himself, who had shaped the whole into an acrostic poem. This scheme was extended by others, including Oesterley and Robinson, who postulated the existence of four original psalms in the chapter, three of which were individual units like certain of the Psalms, and comprising verses 1 to 24, 25 to 39, and 52 to 66 respectively.[4] The remaining fragment, verses

[2] K. Budde, *ZAW*, II (1882), pp. 1ff.
[3] M. Löhr, *ZAW*, XXIV (1904), pp. 1ff.
[4] *IBOT*, p. 315.

40-51, was uttered in the name of the people. Such analyses appear to be rather unnecessary in view of the fact that the personification of the nation, with which the chapter commenced, makes in itself for a unified theme which exhibits but slight variation (Lam. 3:40-54). It seems highly improbable that the author would need to draw for his inspiration upon several already existing fragments in order to depict the nation in deep mourning, particularly if he was also responsible for any of the other laments in the book.

The fourth chapter resembles the second closely, except that each strophe contains two lines instead of three. The horrors of the siege were depicted (Lam. 4:1-10), and the priests were included with the prophets as the principal culprits. The nation as a whole, however, had sinned, and the chastisement of God had involved the captivity of Israel. With this the iniquity of the people had been expiated (Lam. 4:21-22), and the triumph of Edom would soon be reversed.

The fifth chapter constituted a prayer for the lamenting community to be delivered from its misery (Lam. 5:2-18), and to be restored to something approximating to its former state (Lam. 5:19-22). This passage is not in acrostic form, nor does it exhibit the *qînāh* rhythms or stresses, since each verse has the 3:3 form of parallelism. As has been observed earlier, the short, throbbing structure of *qînāh* is admirably suited for the task of conveying emotional reactions, particularly that of grief. It was typical of Hebrew elegiac poetry (cf. 2 Sam. 1:19ff.; Am. 5:2), and was attractive because its didactic emphasis enshrined, among other aspects, the device of dramatic contrast, which served to drive home the implications of the immediate situation by comparing it with what had obtained formerly.

B. THE ANALYSIS OF THE BOOK

1. The purpose of Lamentations. Against the background of the Gunkel type-analysis or *Gattungsforschung*, Gottwald characterized the primary nature of the elegies in Lamentations as national or communal laments.[5] Because of its distinctive character, the third lament has been the object of considerable dispute as to its correct type-classification, opinion being divided as to whether it constituted an individual lament or the sorrowful expression of the nation construed as a separate personality. Löhr followed such scholars as Stade and Budde in adopting the individualistic interpretation,[6] but in the light of studies in the corporate

---

[5] N. K. Gottwald, *Studies in the Book of Lamentations* (1954), pp. 34, 42. Cf. H. Gunkel, *Die Religion in Geschichte und Gegenwart*, III, cols. 1058f.; H. Jahnow, *Das hebräische Leichenlied im Rahmen der Völkerdichtung* (1923), pp. 168ff.

[6] M. Löhr, *ZAW*, XXIV (1904), pp. 2ff.

personality concept of the Hebrews,[7] it seems probable that the collective interpretation as advanced by Smend[8] constitutes the more likely explanation.

The acrostic form that characterizes much of the book has also come in for examination at the hands of some scholars. Precisely why the author should have employed so mechanical a device to convey such a passionate and dramatic outpouring of grief remains unknown. While it is known that the Hebrew consonants were accorded sanctity from an early period,[9] it is difficult to believe that the author of the poems was concerned with anything remotely resembling the mystical preoccupations of the medieval Cabbala, so that magical considerations, at any rate, would seem to be ruled out immediately.

Acrostics have also been regarded as devices by which Egyptian schoolboys were taught the alphabet, and while there are examples of this custom from Egyptian sources, it seems unwise to assume, with Munch, that Lamentations constituted an exercise for practicing the style of the funeral dirge.[10] The dramatic outpouring of emotion on the part of the poet speaks of the deepest realities of chastisement, sin, confession, and trust in divine mercy, making it inconceivable that the work was merely compiled as an exercise in literary style.

The mnemonic function of the acrostic has also been invoked as an explanation of the peculiar mechanical structure of much of Lamentations.[11] While such a device might conceivably be of some value in assisting a person to commit to memory an isolated section of literature, it would tend to confuse rather than help the mind when related to several contiguous passages, even if the poems were written separately. More probable is the suggestion made by De Wette, Keil, and others that the acrostic structure furnished a form of exhaustive completeness to the lamentation, as though to express the full range of human sufferings.[12] The cathartic role of the acrostic has been stressed by Gottwald as a means of achieving a complete cleansing of the conscience through a total confession of sin.[13] For a people such as the Hebrews who were

[7] H. Wheeler Robinson in P. Volz (ed.), Werden und Wesen des AT (1936), pp 47ff.; A. R. Johnson, The One and the Many in the Israelite Conception of God (1942), p. 10 passim.

[8] R. Smend, ZAW, VIII (1888), pp. 49ff.

[9] Cf. A. Jeremias, Das AT im Lichte des Alten Orients (1930 ed.), p. 665.

[10] P. A. Munch, ZDMG, XC (1936), p. 710. Cf. W. Rudolph, Die Klagelieder (1939), p. 3.

[11] Cf. R. Lowth, Lectures on the Sacred Poetry of the Hebrews (1829), pp. 39, 318; S. Oettli, Die Klagelieder (1889), p. 199; A. W. Streane, Jeremiah and Lamentations (1913), p. 355 et al.

[12] W. M. de Wette, A Critical and Historical Introduction to the Canonical Scriptures of the OT (1858), II, p. 532. C. F. Keil, The Lamentations of Jeremiah (1874), p. 337.

[13] N. K. Gottwald, Studies in the Book of Lamentations, p. 30.

readily given to emotional expression of a kind seldom seen in occidental society, the structure of the acrostic lent an important degree of control and restraint to what could otherwise have degenerated into an incoherent display of grief.

2. *Authorship of the book.* Although an anonymous composition, Lamentations was traditionally ascribed to the prophet Jeremiah by Jewish tradition, and this was followed by the LXX and the Vulgate.[14] The LXX began with the statement, "And it came to pass, after Israel was led into captivity and Jerusalem laid waste, that Jeremiah sat weeping and lamented with this lamentation over Jerusalem, and said . . . ," to which the Vulgate added the qualification ". . .with a bitter spirit sighing and wailing. . . ." This tradition may well have arisen from a misreading of the passage in 2 Chronicles (35:25), which stated that Jeremiah composed lamentations over Josiah, and that these were written in the lamentations. Josephus stated that the dirge over Josiah was extant in his day, and he appeared to think of it as the fourth chapter of Lamentations.[15] This is very improbable, however, since the elegy concerned is an outpouring of grief over the city of Jerusalem, and not over a deceased king or other individual. The Jewish tradition of authorship was also followed by the Talmud, the targum at Jeremiah 1:1, the Old Latin and Syriac versions, and by a great many Church Fathers.

Quite aside from the fact that the author of Lamentations is unknown, there are certain reasons for doubting the validity of the traditional ascription. Although there are striking similarities to Jeremiah in matters of literary style and phraseology,[16] there are also a number of significant variations that suggest that Lamentations has closer affinities with certain of the psalms, Ezekiel, and the latter part of Isaiah.[17] Again, the standpoint of Lamentations seems to have been different from that of Jeremiah in the matter of regarding the Chaldeans as the means of divine punishment of the Chosen People (cf. Lam. 1:21; 3:59ff.).

However, this objection is more hypothetical than real, since it assumes that the agent of divine anger is *ipso facto* beyond punishment, which is manifestly untrue. The suggestion that the remark in Lamentations 2:9 concerning the cessation of the prophetic oracle is out of harmony with the attitude of Jeremiah rests on a similar basis of misunderstanding, since in reality the author is merely stating that in the light of the recent calamity the old order has been changed completely, a situation to which the false prophets (cf. Jer. 14:14; 23:16) had contributed materially.

[14] *Bab. Bath.* 15a.

[15] *AJ*, X, 5, 1.

[16] Cf. *DILOT*, p. 462.

[17] Cf. M. Löhr, *ZAW*, XIV (1894), pp. 31ff., XXIV (1904), pp. 1ff., XXV (1905), pp. 173ff.

In favor of the authorship of Lamentations by Jeremiah is the fact that the poems seem to contain the remarks and observations of an eyewitness, and that the calamities mentioned were traced to the same causes in both Lamentations and Jeremiah. Similar representations and figures occur in both books, such as the virgin daughter of Zion as being irreparably breached, the appeal to the righteous Judge for vengeance, and the expectation that the nations who rejoiced over the fall of Jerusalem would themselves suffer desolations subsequently. Again, as Driver has remarked, the same sensitive temper, profoundly sympathetic in national sorrow, and ready to pour forth its emotions unrestrainedly, manifests itself both in Lamentations and Jeremiah.[18]

Clearly there is much to be adduced both for and against Jeremianic authorship of Lamentations, and all arguments appear to be inconclusive. Those who have abandoned the traditional position regarding the composition of the work have frequently assumed that Lamentations was the product of two or possibly more poets. While there are certain differences in imagery and literary construction between the various poems, there is little doubt that, as Gottwald has pointed out, a single mood pervades the entire collection, so that probably the first four poems, and possibly even all five, came from the same hand.[19] They appear to be the work of an eyewitness of the tragedy that overtook Jerusalem in 587 B.C., although it is possible that chapter 5 may date from a somewhat later period. In any event there appears to be no convincing reason for placing the book, in part or in whole, after 550 B.C. While the authorship must remain unknown, it seems less desirable to posit the activity of an unfamiliar contemporary of the prophet Jeremiah, as Driver did,[20] than to suppose that Jeremiah himself was moved to elegiac expression by the fall of Jerusalem.

3. *The theology of Lamentations.* Although the book is one of the most tragic in the Old Testament, it is by no means devoid of theological meaning. If Job relates suffering to personal considerations, Lamentations deals with it in terms of national and historic crisis. The elegiac poems sought to discover the real meaning of the catastrophes that had overtaken the southern kingdom in the days of Jeremiah, and interpreted the situation as a tragic reversal of the former glory. The theology of Lamentations has been seen by Gottwald against a background of doom and hope, the former constituting the logical outcome of the kind

[18] *DILOT*, p. 462.
[19] N. K. Gottwald, *IB*, III, p. 62.
[20] *DILOT*, p. 464. Cf. H. Wiesmann, *Biblische Zeitschrift*, XXIII (1935), pp. 20ff. For the views of this Roman Catholic author on the general problems of the Book see *Biblica*, VII (1926), pp. 141ff., 412ff., VIII (1927), pp. 339ff.; *Biblische Zeitschrift*, XVIII (1928), pp. 38ff.; *Zeitschrift für Aszese und Mystik*, IV (1929), pp. 97ff., *Theologische Quartalschrift*, CX (1929), pp. 381ff., *Biblische Zeitschrift*, XXII (1934), pp. 20ff., *Biblica*, XVII (1936), pp. 71ff.

of divine activity characterized by righteousness.[21] The destruction of
Jerusalem thus resulted from a defiance of the ordinances of God, and
the tragic nature of the situation was heightened by the realization that
it could have been avoided. Amidst all this it was to the fidelity of God
that the poet could look for future hope, for although Jerusalem undoubtedly deserved her fate, the deity who had brought this destruction
upon her was still the Covenant God, who required the unswerving trust
and loyalty of His people as a necessary prerequisite to blessing (Lam.
3:19ff.).

It may be that these five poems had some place in the memorial
rituals that the exiles employed in Babylonia as a means of commemorating the fall of Jerusalem (cf. Jer. 41:4f.; Zech. 7:3). There is little
doubt that they would constitute by far the most suitable vehicle for
conveying the deep sorrow and chastened spirit of the faithful remnant.
If prophecy and ritual can be said to meet in Lamentations, they can
also be regarded as being enriched by the emphasis upon wisdom, in
which the problem of suffering was contemplated in national and historic dimensions.

❊   ❊   ❊   ❊   ❊

The Hebrew text is well preserved, and has very few corruptions.
Variations in the LXX seem to be due predominantly to the fact that the
Greek text itself suffered during processes of transmission, and in all they
do not furnish sufficient evidence to show that the LXX translators
employed a Hebrew text different from that which was familiar to the
Massoretes.[22]

Supplementary Literature

Albrektson, B. Studies in the Text and Theology of the Book of Lamen-
      tations. 1963.
Haller, M. Die fünf Megilloth. 1940.
Löhr, M. Die Klagelieder des Jeremia. 1906.
Nagelsbach, E. The Lamentations of Jeremiah. 1871.
Peake, A. S. Jeremiah and Lamentations. 1912.
Rudolph, W. Die Klagelieder. 1923.
Streane, A. W. Jeremiah and Lamentations. 1913.

[21] N. K. Gottwald, Studies in the Book of Lamentations, pp. 63ff.
[22] Cf. W. Rudolph, ZAW, LVI (1938), pp. 101ff.

IV. THE BOOK OF ECCLESIASTES

A. Problems of Authorship and Date

The English title "Ecclesiastes" was adopted from the Vulgate and originally from the LXX Ἐκκλησιαστής. In Hebrew the title read "The Words of Qoheleth, the son of David, king in Jerusalem," or simply "Qoheleth" (קהלת, Eccles. 1:1; cf. v. 12). The term Qoheleth is rare, occurring only seven times in Ecclesiastes and nowhere else in the canonical Hebrew writings. It is possible that it is the feminine singular Qal active participle of the verb קהל, which perhaps carries the basic meaning of "assembling." The relationship to the masculine noun קהל, "assembly," appears to have influenced the LXX designation, which means "one who participates in a popular assembly." Jerome interpreted this in Latin by the use of the term *concionator*, or "speaker before an assembly," and it was from this that the English concept of "Preacher" was derived. This, however, is not the best of translations, since Qoheleth appears to be philosophizing rather than preaching.

The obscurity of the term Qoheleth is not at all resolved by the fact that, although it is feminine in form, it was regularly construed with masculine verbs (1:2; 12:8ff.; the feminine of 7:27 may be an error); and interpreted as a male function. The reason for the incidence of the feminine form may well lie in the fact that the word denoted an office, on the basis of analogous terms occurring among the "servants of Solomon." [The English versions, for example, render the ספרת ("scribe"?) of Ezra 2:55 and Nehemiah 7:57, and פכרת ("gazelle"—"tender"?) of Ezra 2:57 as proper names (Hassophereth, Pochereth-hazzebaim).] If this reasoning is correct, Qoheleth could perhaps designate the "Officer of the Kahal" or "Master of Ceremonies (Speaker?) of the Assembly," and if there is any intensive force in the term it could signify one who fulfilled the requirements of the situation completely. Qoheleth was employed by the author as a proper noun, perhaps by metonymy for the office rather than the person who occupied it. In this sense Albright may well be correct in maintaining that the Hebrew מלך should be repointed to mean "counsellor" rather than "king," indicating that Qoheleth occupied a position in Jerusalem comparable to that of the wise men in royal courts throughout the ancient Near East.[1]

Since no immediate son of David except Solomon was king in Jerusalem, the term Qoheleth would appear to be a substitute for Solomon, on the assumption, of course, that מלך should be rendered "king." If, on the other hand, it is to be translated as "counsellor," the word Qoheleth would designate the author, who still remained anonymous and did not impersonate Solomon, but presented an excursus upon the futility of existence, a theme that may well have occupied the mind of the historic Solomon towards the close of his life.

Assuming that it is legitimate to regard Ecclesiastes as the product of a Semitic sage rather than the direct composition of the renowned king of Israel, it is possible to place the work firmly within the didactic categories of ancient Hebrew wisdom, since on such a basis it would not be autobiographical, but would comprise instead a manual of instruction for successful living based upon certain philosophical presuppositions. Thus the Solomon of the book can, as Rankin has observed,[2] be regarded not so much as a preacher but as the ideal, authoritative exponent of wisdom, a situation that is not entirely out of harmony with certain traditions connected with the historical Solomon.

Ecclesiastes was grouped with Proverbs and Canticles in the LXX version, and placed after the Psalter on the theory that, granted Solomonic authorship of the former, the work of the son ought to follow that of the father. The AV, RV, and RSV adhered to this order, but the English version of the Jewish Publication Society included Ecclesiastes with the remainder of the five scrolls or *Megilloth,* which in the Hebrew canon were placed after the longest poetical works in the Hagiographa.

Baba Bathra (14b-15a) grouped Proverbs, Canticles, and Ecclesiastes as in the LXX on the ground that they had been preserved by Hezekiah and his school, although elsewhere Solomon was expressly stated to be the author of Ecclesiastes.[3] Another rabbinic source claimed that Solomon wrote Canticles, with its stress on love, in his youth; Proverbs, with its emphasis upon practical problems, in mid-life, and Ecclesiastes, with its characteristic pessimism, in old age.[4] It should be noted, however, that even in that midrashic section there was a decided difference of opinion among the authorities about the time of composition relative to the life of Solomon. No doubt the traditional attribution of authorship secured entry into the Hebrew canon for Ecclesiastes, for although the School of Shammai found the work obnoxious, the more liberal view of

---

[1] W. F. Albright, *VT* suppl. vol. III (1955), p. 15 n. 2, as opposed to the "property-holder" interpretation of H. L. Ginsberg, *Studies in Koheleth* (1950), pp. 12ff., and *VT* suppl. vol. III (1955), p. 149.

[2] O. S. Rankin, *IB,* V, p. 4.

[3] Cf. *Megill.* 7 a; *Shabb.* 30.

[4] Midrash *Shir hashirim Rabbah,* I, 1, sect. 10.

the Hillelites ultimately prevailed, though not until about the end of the first century of the Christian era.[5]

While the oldest source for Solomonic authorship is contained in the work itself, it should be noted that the name "Solomon" does not occur in Ecclesiastes, nor does the work make explicit claim to Solomonic authorship. It seems highly probable, as Gordis has pointed out, that had the author intended to represent his book as the work of Solomon, he would not have employed the enigmatic designation Qoheleth, but would instead have used the name of Solomon directly, as was the case with later pseudepigraphic literature.[6] The reference in the superscription of the book (Eccles. 1:1) to the author as the "son of David" was most probably not intended to indicate that the composition was truly Solomonic, but rather to show that wisdom as presented in the work was characteristic of those definite utterances in this regard which were attributed to Solomon.

The author thus introduced the figure of the renowned king in an ideal manner to lend backing to his contention that even the highest levels of wisdom and material luxury to which mortal man can attain have no absolute value or significance. It is difficult to see how this thesis could have been sustained at all consistently without an appeal to the life of Solomon, who embraced each of these goals of human endeavor, since any lesser personage could well have been regarded as incompetent to pronounce upon such matters. Further indications of a non-Solomonic authorship appear in Ecclesiastes 1:12, where, interpreting מֶלֶךְ as "king," the writer indicates that he was no longer in his former regal position, a situation that did not apply to Solomon at any time. Again, the economic and social background of the book hardly accords with the Solomonic era, for Ecclesiastes reflects a time of misery (Eccles. 1:2-11) and decline for Israel (Eccles. 3:1-15), when injustice and violence were rampant (Eccles. 4:1-3), and normal incentives for living appeared absent (Eccles. 7:1).[7]

Despite these and other indications to the contrary, there are still some scholars who have adhered to the tradition of Solomonic authorship, and these included Möller, Dean Milman, and Cohen,[8] although Protestant scholarship, following the lead of Martin Luther, generally repudiated it. Those who maintained that the author of Ecclesiastes lived at a later period than Solomon have tended to assign the work to a post-exilic setting, though with considerable difference of opinion as to matters of exact date. The divergence has rested in part upon the views held in connection with the language and style of the book. From the

[5] For the controversy see Mishn. 'Eduy., V, 3; Toseph. Yadayim, II, 14; III, 5.
[6] R. Gordis, Koheleth —The Man and His World (1951), p. 40.
[7] Cf. DILOT, pp. 471f.
[8] H. Möller, Einleitung in das AT, pp. 210ff. H. H. Milman, History of the Jews (1881), I, p. 325. A. Cohen, The Five Megilloth, p. 106.

presence of Aramaisms, Delitzsch argued that if Qoheleth were of old Solomonic origin there was no history of the Hebrew language.[9] On the other hand, it must be noted again that the presence of Aramaisms is no necessary indication of late date, as is now known from evidence that was not available to the same extent when Delitzsch wrote. As Albright has pointed out, there are distinct traces in Ecclesiastes of Phoenician influence, demonstrable in the areas of morphology, syntax, spelling, and vocabulary, and this alone is sufficient to account for many of the linguistic peculiarities that had caused some scholars to assign the work to a comparatively late period.[10]

Nineteenth-century writers commonly referred to the presence of Grecisms in the work as indications of a date of composition within the Greek period, but these were radically reduced in number by the researches of McNeile and Barton,[11] although Eissfeldt maintained the existence of a few definite examples.[12] Similar attempts were also made by many commentators during the nineteenth century to establish the position that the book was influenced by Greek philosophical thought in process of attaining its final form. Thus Pfleiderer maintained that the "catalog of seasons" (Eccles. 3:1-9) was dependent upon Heracleitan speculation, a position that was criticized by Menzel.[13]

More serious than the attempts to demonstrate the influence of Aristotelian philosophy over the author of Ecclesiastes[14] were those of Tyler, Plumptre, Haupt, and others who set out to show the extent to which Stoic and Epicurean philosophical tenets had impinged upon the mind of the author and had penetrated the extant composition.[15] Although Barton, among others, refuted this position conclusively by an appeal to treatises such as Zeller's *Stoics, Epicureans and Sceptics* (1892),[16] it was again taken up by Ranston, who sought to show that Qoheleth was less

[9] F. Delitzsch, *Commentary on the Song of Songs and Ecclesiastes* (1877), p. 190. For a rebuttal of this viewpoint see R. D. Wilson, *A Scientific Investigation of the OT* (1959 ed.), pp. 87f.

[10] W. F. Albright, *VT* suppl. vol. III (1955), p. 15.

[11] A. H. McNeile, *An Introduction to Ecclesiastes* (1904), pp. 30ff. G. A. Barton, *A Critical and Exegetical Commentary on the Book of Ecclesiastes* (1908), pp. 32f.

[12] O. Eissfeldt, *Einleitung in das AT* (1934 ed.), p. 557, *ETOT*, p. 498, found such in Eccles. 2:14; 3:12, 19; 9:2f. The first was rejected by K. Galling, *Theologische Rundschau*, VI (1934), p. 362.

[13] O. Pfleiderer, *Die Philosophie des Heraklit* (1886), pp. 255ff. P. Menzel, *Der Griechische Einfluss auf Prediger und Weisheit Salomos* (1889), pp. 1ff.

[14] A. Palm, *Qoheleth und die nach-Aristotelische Philosophie* (1885); M. Friedländer, *Griechische Philosophie im AT* (1904).

[15] T. Tyler, *Ecclesiastes—A Contribution to Its Interpretation* (1874), pp. 11ff. F. H. Plumptre, *Commentary on Ecclesiastes* (1881), pp. 44ff. P. Haupt, *The Book of Ecclesiastes* (1905), p. 6.

[16] G. A. Barton, *A Critical and Exegetical Commentary on the Book of Ecclesiastes*, pp. 34ff.

dependent upon the major Greek philosophers than upon popular aphoristic writers such as Theognis (*ca.* 520 B.C.).[17] Hertzberg supported this position to the extent of stating that Qoheleth had indirect knowledge of the work of Theognis.[18] Parallels between Ecclesiastes and the writings of Theognis were subjected to careful scrutiny by Galling, who showed that the aphorisms were in no instance very closely parallel in nature, and that their setting was quite different in any case.[19] At the same time Galling maintained that Qoheleth lived on the boundary between two periods of history, as McNeile had shown earlier.[20]

Barton showed convincingly that the resemblances between Stoicism and the concepts of Ecclesiastes were merely superficial, and that in reality the two works exhibited differences of a fundamental nature.[21] Again, he made it plain that the indeterminism of Epicurean philosophical speculation was entirely out of accord with the rigid, deterministic thought of Qoheleth. In particular he indicated that all that had been considered Epicurean in Qoheleth—eating and drinking, the delight in pleasure, the general enjoyment of life as the *summum bonum*, the sense that death terminated all existential values—had long been anticipated in Babylonian thought in the Gilgamesh Epic, which furnished a particularly close parallel to Ecclesiastes 9:7ff.[22]

That such in fact seemed to have constituted a generally accepted part of ancient thought appears borne out by the Egyptian "Song of the Harpist," which urged the hearer to an enjoyment of the present age in the face of inevitable death.[23] Paul Humbert adduced further parallels between Egyptian thought on questions of life and death and that which was contained in Ecclesiastes,[24] and although he may perhaps have overstated his case somewhat, he has at least made it clear that resemblances between Egyptian gnomic literature and Ecclesiastes show that it is unnecessary to postulate the dependence of the latter upon Greek philosophical influences. Qoheleth constructed his *Weltanschauung* upon accredited Biblical thought, however, and did not seek to harmonize his Hebrew heritage with any aspect of contemporary pagan speculation,

[17] H. Ranston, *Ecclesiastes and the Early Greek Wisdom Literature* (1925).

[18] H. W. Hertzberg, *Der Prediger* (1932), p. 51.

[19] K. Galling, *Theologische Rundschau*, VI (1934), p. 365.

[20] A. H. McNeile, *An Introduction to Ecclesiastes*, pp. 45f.

[21] G. A. Barton, *A Critical and Exegetical Commentary on the Book of Ecclesiastes*, pp. 34ff.

[22] G. A. Barton, *ibid.*, pp. 39f. The text was published by B. Meissner, *Mitteilungen der Vorderasiatischen Gesellschaft* (1902), I, p. 8. Cf. H. Grimme, *Orientalische Literaturzeitung*, VIII (1905), cols. 432ff.

[23] Cf. A. Erman, *The Literature of the Ancient Egyptians*, pp. 132ff.; M. Lichtheim, *JNES*, IV (1945), pp. 178ff.; *ANET*, p. 467.

[24] Cf. P. Humbert, *Die Religion in Geschichte und Gegenwart*, V, col. 1808, *Recherches sur les sources égyptiennes de la littérature sapientale d'Israël*, pp. 107ff.; A. Causse, *RHPR*, IX (1929), pp. 149ff.; K. Galling, *ZAW*, L (1932), pp. 276ff.

and least of all, as Bertholet maintained,[25] with such Greek concepts as may have been current in his day. Barton was correct in observing that Qoheleth represented an original development of Hebrew thought, which was thoroughly Semitic in its standpoint, and quite independent of Greek influences.[26]

These considerations have an important bearing upon any question of the dating in relationship to the book of Ecclesiastes. It can be said immediately that a Maccabean, or even later, date of composition for the work, as favored by certain scholars,[27] is entirely out of the question. First of all, Ecclesiastes appears to have been well known to the author of Ecclesiasticus,[28] who compiled his work prior to the Maccabean period proper. Secondly, the publication by James Muilenburg of several manuscript fragments of Qoheleth, found in 4Q and dated in the late second century B.C.,[29] makes a period of composition later than the third century B.C. extremely unlikely.

The vast majority of modern scholars have assigned the work to a date between 280 and 200 B.C., but a more realistic position was the one adopted by some of the older commentators such as Wright, who assigned Ecclesiastes to the period between 444 B.C. and 328 B.C.[30] Albright maintained that the author was an influential Jew who lived about 300 B.C., probably in southern Phoenicia, and whose orally transmitted aphorisms were collected after his death and put into written form in Phoenicia.[31] To the present author there is no need whatever to appeal either to a late date or to a prolonged period of oral transmission. Young is probably correct in stating that the book can be dated quite satisfactorily about the time of Malachi.[32]

The language and style of the work have met with varying estimates on the part of scholars. McNeile saw in the composition an originality that lifted it far above contemporary literary levels,[33] while Renan regarded it as the only pleasant literature that had been composed by a Jew.[34] Hertzberg also adhered to a high view of the literary excellence of

---

[25] A. Bertholet, *Kulturgeschichte Israels* (1919), p. 223.

[26] G. A. Barton, *A Critical and Exegetical Commentary on the Book of Ecclesiastes*, p. 43. Cf. H. L. Ginsberg in A. Altmann (ed.), *Biblical and Other Studies*, pp. 47ff.

[27] E.g. E. Renan, *L'Ecclésiaste traduit de l'Hebreu* (1882), ca. 125 B.C.; H. Graetz, *Kohelet oder der Salomonische Prediger übersetzt und kritisch erläutert* (1871), ca. 8 B.C.; T. Tyler, *Ecclesiastes—A Contribution to Its Interpretation* (1874), ca. 132 B.C.; cf. C. H. Toy, *EB*, II, col. 1172.

[28] Cf. Th. Nöldeke, *ZAW*, XX (1900), pp. 91ff.

[29] Cf. *BASOR*, No. 135 (1954), pp. 20ff.

[30] C. H. H. Wright, *Ecclesiastes in Relation to Modern Criticism and Pessimism* (1883), p. 136.

[31] W. F. Albright, *VT* suppl. vol. III (1955), p. 15.

[32] *YIOT*, p. 349.

[33] A. H. McNeile, *An Introduction to Ecclesiastes*, p. 32.

[34] E. Renan, *L'Antichrist* (1873), p. 101.

Ecclesiastes, stressing the originality of style and the consummate skill with which the author had constructed the extant product.[35] On the other hand, Schlatter declared that the heaviness of the language indicated that the author could not speak Hebrew, but could only read and write it.[36] Burkitt criticized the book in much the same manner, and suggested that it was a translation from the Aramaic, a theory that was subsequently taken up with some enthusiasm by Zimmermann, Torrey, and Ginsberg.[37]

There is no doubt, as Gordis has indicated, that the linguistic features of Ecclesiastes point to a period when Aramaic was exerting an influence upon spoken Hebrew.[38] Some of the forms in the book became much more familiar in Mishnaic literature, though occurring also in earlier Hebrew, and this fact would appear to point to a transitional stage in the development of the language of Qoheleth.[39] The presence of two Persian words (פרדס, 2:5; and פתגם, 8:11) is a further indication of this tendency. Be this as it may, there is insufficient evidence to support the view that Ecclesiastes was originally written in Aramaic and subsequently rendered into Hebrew. Gordis has demonstrated most convincingly that such a hypothesis creates more difficulties than it resolves, and that in actual fact Ecclesiastes was written in Hebrew by an author who, like his contemporaries, was familiar with Aramaic and doubtless used it freely in everyday life.[40]

B. THE MATERIAL OF ECCLESIASTES

The book itself commenced with a prologue (1:1-11), which included the superscription, and established the basic theme that everything is futility and frustration. Nature was a closed system, and history nothing more than a succession of events. The first main section (1:12–6:12) demonstrated the vanity and pointlessness of all things. The search for wisdom was discouraging (1:12-18) and the pursuit of pleasure constituted a vain objective (2:1-11). Although wisdom was to be preferred above all else, even this great quality meets its match in death, which contrives to defeat the wise and foolish alike (2:12-23). The best that man can do under such circumstances is to enjoy himself during his brief

[35] H. W. Hertzberg, *Der Prediger*, p. 10.

[36] A. Schlatter in P. Zeller (ed.), *Calwer Bibellexikon* (1924 ed.), pp. 585f.

[37] F. C. Burkitt, *JTS*, XXIII (1922), pp. 22ff. F. Zimmermann, *JQR*, XXXVI (1945-46), pp. 17ff. C. C. Torrey, *JQR*, XXXIX (1948-49), pp. 151f. H. L. Ginsberg, *Studies in Koheleth*, pp. 16ff.

[38] R. Gordis, *Koheleth—The Man and His World*, pp. 59f. Cf. C. H. H. Wright, *Ecclesiastes in Relation to Modern Criticism and Pessimism*, pp. 488ff.

[39] Cf. S. H. Blank, *IDB*, II, p. 8.

[40] R. Gordis, *JQR*, XXXVIII (1946-47), pp. 67ff., XL (1949-50), pp. 103ff., *Koheleth—The Man and His World*, pp. 59ff.; cf. M. Dahood, *Biblica*, XXXIII (1952), pp. 213ff.

existence (2:24-26), since while all activities have their appointed time (3:1-8), God has hidden the future from human sight (3:9-11). Man cannot appeal to a future life for the redress of injustices, and should therefore make the best of his present existence (3:16-22) in the face of injustice, oppression, deception, and the like (3:22—4:16). Reflecting upon the futility of wealth, the author maintained that man should be satisfied with his lot in life (5:10—6:9), for fate is his master (6:10-12).

The second main section (Eccles. 7:1—12:7) comprised miscellaneous maxims on the general theme of prudent behavior. Practical advice for a well-organized life (7:1-14) was followed by the admonition that all men are sinners, but that the wise person will derive strength from wisdom (7:15-22). Admitting his own failure to find wisdom, the writer pronounced on the general sinfulness of mankind (7:23-29). Other maxims on practical wisdom (8:1-8) were followed by observations on the problems associated with death, which overtakes good and bad alike (8:9—9:3). The only solution appeared to be that of utilizing individual powers vigorously, while they still remained (9:4-9). Sundry observations on wisdom and folly (9:11—10:3) were followed by additional advice for successful living (10:4-20). The author sagely observed that, since the future is inscrutable, man must cooperate as rationally as he can with the known laws of his natural environment (11:1-8). In particular, conscious veneration of God during the time of youth is of great importance, for senility weakens the faculties of an individual (11:9—12:7). The book concluded with an epilogue (12:8-14), which urged men to revere God and to keep His commandments, since all human actions will ultimately come under divine judgment.

C. CRITICAL TREATMENT OF ECCLESIASTES

Those studies which have dealt with the unity and composition of Ecclesiastes have revealed a wide degree of divergence among critical scholars. The objection raised in rabbinic circles—that the book contained internal contradictions[41]—was reflected in a commentary by Wildeboer, *Die fünf Megilloth*, written in 1898. He maintained that Ecclesiastes was a literary unity that had been subjected to minor editorial revision, although he did not subscribe to the view that the epilogue was the work of someone other than Qoheleth. Hertzberg disagreed with Wildeboer on the question of the epilogue, but apart from this he held that Ecclesiastes 1:2—12:8 was a literary unit in terms of language, structure, and style.[42]

Less certain as to the unity and integrity of Ecclesiastes was Volz, who held that certain theological interpolations (3:15b; 5:6b, 18, 19; 7:18b,

---

[41] Cf. *Tract. Shabb.* 30b.
[42] H. W. Hertzberg, *Der Prediger*, p. 14.

29; 8:5, 6, 12, 13; 9:7b; 11:9b; 12:1a, 13, 14) had been made in the original by a later editor to support the doctrine of divine retribution, and to inculcate reverence for God on the part of the reader.[43] Volz thought that these additions might have been the work of a pious scribe who contributed the admonition of Ecclesiastes 12:13f. to the epilogue. Aside from these interpolations, however, he adhered to the substantial unity of the book.

A more radical view of the composition was advanced in 1884 by Bickell, who declared that the extant work was unintelligible as it stood, and maintained that this factor was due to the fact that sheets of the work, which he alleged had been written in codex form, had become misplaced during transmission.[44] In refutation of this theory, which never gained wide acceptance at any time, it merely needs to be said that the discovery of the scrolls at Qumran militates firmly against any theory of transmission of the work in codex form.

One of the most ruthless treatments of Ecclesiastes was that undertaken in the commentary by Siegfried in 1898, in the series edited by Nowack.[45] The author divided the book into nine different sources, maintaining that the basic document had been written by a philosopher under the influence of Greek thought, and that a later Sadducean Epicurean supplemented this material by the addition of certain sections concerning the enjoyment of life. Of the other hands, the two most important were those of the wisdom editor or ḥākhām, who stressed the merits of wisdom as a way of life, and a pious orthodox Jew or ḥāsîdh, who interpolated the sections on divine judgment. Siegfried postulated the presence of at least three hands in the epilogue alone, which indicates the complexity of the provenance that he entertained for the composition.[46] The idea that such a small work as Ecclesiastes could be the result of so many contributors did not commend itself to scholars generally, and even Siegfried himself conceded that the uniformity of style pervading the book constituted a fundamental criticism of his view.

Equally radical was the treatment of Ecclesiastes by Haupt, who maintained with Zapletal that the composition had been written in metrical form, and that the original work had been overlaid with a great many textual glosses.[47] He regarded barely more than one-half of the

[43] P. Volz, *Weisheit* (1911), pp. 232f., 257.

[44] G. Bickell, *Der Prediger über den Wert des Daseins* (1884); *Koheleth's Untersuchung über den Wert des Daseins* (1886). For details of the theory see G. A. Barton, *A Critical and Exegetical Commentary on the Book of Ecclesiastes*, pp. 25f.

[45] D. C. Siegfried, *Prediger und Hoheslied* (1898).

[46] G. A. Barton, *A Critical and Exegetical Commentary on the Book of Ecclesiastes*, p. 28.

[47] P. Haupt, *Koheleth* (1905); *The Book of Ecclesiastes* (1905). V. Zapletal, *Die Metrik des Buches Kohelet* (1904); cf. his *Das Buch Kohelet* (1905).

book as genuine, and even here he detected the presence of an occasional gloss. To support his contentions Haupt was virtually compelled to rewrite Ecclesiastes so as to make the text conform to his metrical scheme and to represent the original genuine content of the book. Barton correctly judged that this particular attempt contributed little to the real understanding of Qoheleth, and that in almost every feature it rested upon assumptions that were incapable of proof and highly unlikely.[48]

In his *Introduction to Ecclesiastes* A. H. McNeile repudiated the extremes to which the analysis of Siegfried had gone, but nevertheless agreed with him in assuming the activity of *hākhām* and *hāṣîdh* interpolators. This modified view was also adopted by Barton in his commentary published in the *ICC* series. The same general approach was also followed by Podechard, who entertained glosses by the *hākhām* and *hāṣîdh* editors on the original material, and in addition suggested that the interpolation in the epilogue (Eccles. 12:9-12) came from a disciple of Qoheleth, who was also responsible for other third-person insertions (1:2; 7:27; 12:8).[49] Podechard thus summed up the general critical opinion of the first decade of the twentieth century that Ecclesiastes consisted of an original nucleus of heterodox material upon which orthodox glosses had been imposed. As Gordis has commented, however, none of these scholars attempted to explain why the book merited such strenuous efforts to legitimatize it when it could just as easily have been suppressed.[50] In addition, the critical view was based upon theories of transmission which considerations of chronology alone make extremely improbable.

A somewhat different estimate of the unity and composition of Ecclesiastes was contemplated by Galling, who advanced the theory that the work consisted of thirty-seven independent aphoristic units of between two and fifteen lines in length, compiled by Qoheleth the poet.[51] These were subsequently assembled by Qoheleth the editor and issued with minor redactions to comprise the final form of the composition. Galling held to the identity of the poet and the editor, but maintained that their functions must be distinguished sharply.[52]

This theory of construction had been anticipated to some extent by the views of Schmidt, who thought that Ecclesiastes had originally comprised a rough draft of material that was subsequently corrected and revised;[53] by the opinions of Condamin, who held it to have been an

---

[48] G. A. Barton, *A Critical and Exegetical Commentary on the Book of Ecclesiastes*, p. 30.

[49] E. Podechard, *RB*, IX (1912), pp. 161ff., *L'Ecclésiaste* (1912), pp. 142ff.

[50] R. Gordis, *Koheleth—The Man and His World*, p. 71.

[51] K. Galling, *ZAW*, L (1932), pp. 276ff., *Theologische Rundschau*, VI (1934), pp. 355ff.; cf. M. Haller and K. Galling, *Die fünf Megilloth* (1940), p. 49.

[52] Cf. K. Galling, *Theologische Rundschau*, VI (1934), p. 18.

[53] C. Schmidt, *Salomos Prediger* (1792), p. 82.

amalgam of impressions jotted down at intervals of time;[54] and by the studies of Zapletal, who attributed the contradictions in the work to the fact that individuals not infrequently appreciated the same things in varying ways under differing circumstances.[55]

The approach of Galling reflected a greater interest in arguing for the unity of the book than nineteenth-century scholars had, when the only prominent critic to advocate such a position had been Cornill. From a variety of standpoints came arguments for the substantial unity of Ecclesiastes from Levy, Hertzberg, and MacDonald, as well as Galling and Gordis, although in the main these and other scholars regarded the title (Eccles. 1:1) and the epilogue (12:9-14) as the result of editorial addition.[56]

Following a hint by Gunkel, who claimed that the general lack of symmetry in Ecclesiastes should not be resolved by means of literary-critical analysis,[57] Bleiffert published a book in 1938 in which he proposed to solve the literary problem along theological lines.[58] The internal contradictions reflected for him the outlook of the author, who was struggling to hold in balance the traditional concepts of the Hebrew faith along with an enlightened outlook upon the secular world. The latter was represented by the purely humanistic sections of Ecclesiastes, to which the addition of the former served as a necessary corrective; and on this basis the work could be regarded as a unity.

If proper recognition is made of the wide social and spiritual background against which the author lived and wrote, there seems to the present writer to be little need for invoking the kind of schizophrenia envisaged by writers such as Galling and Bleiffert. If Qoheleth was a teacher of traditional Semitic wisdom, there is no reason to think that he himself did not compose original proverbs also, in addition to propagating maxims with which he was already familiar and which may have had a long history of transmission. If the reference in Ecclesiastes 12:9 was in fact the work of someone other than Qoheleth, it would appear to be important testimony to the fact that Qoheleth himself contributed to the corpus of gnomic literature in his own special manner. As Gordis has pointed out, the intermingling of conventional and non-conventional wisdom in one literary unit, with traditional proverbs being embedded in original material, is not only completely comprehensible in terms of the personality of the author, but is also amply attested in the gnomic

[54] A. Condamin, *RB*, VIII (1899), p. 508.

[55] V. Zapletal, *Das Buch Koheleth* (1905), p. 32.

[56] L. Levy, *Das Buch Qoheleth* (1912), pp. 60ff. H. W. Hertzberg, *Der Prediger*, pp. 18f. D. B. MacDonald, *The Hebrew Literary Genius* (1933), pp. 197ff., *The Hebrew Philosophical Genius* (1936), pp. 68ff. Cf. K. Galling, *Theologische Rundschau*, VI (1934), p. 360; R. Gordis, *Koheleth—The Man and His World*, pp. 73f.

[57] H. Gunkel, *Die Religion in Geschichte und Gegenwart*, IV, cols. 1405ff.

[58] H. J. Bleiffert, *Weltanschauung und Gottesglaube im Buch Koheleth* (1938).

literature of Babylonia and Egypt.[59] It would seem safe to assume with this author, therefore, that the diverse *ḥākhām* glossators and *ḥāṣîdh* interpolations are figments of the scholarly imagination. While the *Weltanschauung* of Qoheleth was distinctive in that it contained strong overtones of skepticism, it still remains true that his metaphysics was strictly traditional.

As distinct from the prophets, with their characteristic emphases of faith, penitence, election, obedience, and the like, the author of Ecclesiastes stood firmly in the age-old pattern of the Hebrew sages in recounting for his readers the results of his observations regarding life in general, and the nature of the behavioral patterns that were to be followed for a successful existence. If he adopted a rather mechanistic view of the situation, it was because his innate skepticism saw it in terms of ultimate futility. Even his concept of opposites (Eccles. 3:1-8) had as its end the inquiry as to whether, from such given circumstances, an individual could ever derive any significant values for life.

This "catalog of seasons," as it has been styled by some authors, appears to have had far less in common with Greek thought than many older scholars realized. Instead, it is much nearer to the ancient Sumerian concept known as *merismus*, which is reflected on occasions in the narratives of the Old Testament and which designates the polar opposites of a situation in a relationship which is intended to depict a unified whole. As such the catalog rests firmly upon Sumerian and Egyptian foundations, and the presence of this delineation in Greek philosophical speculation may well be the result of derivation from Semitic originals.

The reliance of the author of Ecclesiastes upon traditional religious beliefs was evident in connection with the affirmation that God made mankind upright, but that the intervention of devices of human fashioning had led to the declension of mankind from pristine grace (Eccles. 7:29). Of a similar character was the belief regarding Sheol (Eccles. 3:20), where all men went at death, and although the following verse has been taken as indicative of some sort of belief in a future existence, it was in any event rejected as a doctrine by the author of Ecclesiastes. Although his work has been variously interpreted in terms of Epicurean or Stoic canons of thought and behavior, it is important to note that Qoheleth based his patterns of life firmly upon reverence for God and observance of the divine precepts. His basic proposition of wisdom, therefore, is that life in its manifold aspects is entirely devoid of meaning without God. Consequently this exposition of ways and means for achieving the greatest degree of success in mortal life can hardly be said to be pessimistic, either Buddhist or modern existentialist pessimism. Qoheleth was merely presenting a sober—indeed critical—appraisal of life, and against the background of traditional Hebrew faith he pro-

---

[59] R. Gordis, *Koheleth—The Man and His World,* pp. 73f.

nounced upon the ultimate validity of varying facets of human existence in the light of experience.

While his approach was intensely realistic, it proceeded from the premise that God, rather than man, was the ultimate standard by which all motives and forms of behavior in human society must be interpreted. This laudable standpoint is clearly significant for ages other than that in which the author himself lived, for it points to the true nature of the *summum bonum.* If God is the source and end of all values, the world and its phenomena can only be regarded as His creation, and a life lived under God will seek to use and enjoy the manifold aspects of human existence to the greater glory of the Creator. In such an approach alone resides true wisdom, since it is not given to man to know the metaphysical subtleties of the divine mind.

❀   ❀   ❀   ❀   ❀

The Hebrew text, which has a predominantly rhythmical character, has survived in good condition and has few corruptions or variations (e.g. Eccles. 2:12b; 3:11; 4:1, 17; 5:17). The LXX version was quite literal, and consequently is of small assistance in elucidating such corrupt passages as occur in the Hebrew text. Secondary versions made from the LXX include the Coptic and the Old Latin.

Supplementary Literature

Euringer, S. *Der Masorah-Text des Koheleth.* 1890.
Gordis, R. *The Wisdom of Ecclesiastes.* 1945.
Jastrow, M. *A Gentle Cynic, Being a Translation of the Book of Koheleth.* 1916.
Odeberg, H. *Qohaelaeth, A Commentary on the Book of Ecclesiastes.* 1929.
Williams, A. L. *Ecclesiastes.* 1922.

V. THE BOOK OF ESTHER

A. THE STORY OF ESTHER

The book of Esther, which narrates certain incidents in the court of the Persian monarch Ahasuerus relating to the deliverance of the Jews from persecution, furnishes the reason for the institution of the feast of Purim. This fascinating story is one of the most dramatic in the Old Testament, reflecting as it does the passions, luxury, intrigue, and the political and social organization of the Persian regime, in addition to demonstrating something of the vitality that characterized the Jewish colonists of the Persian period (539-333 B.C.).

The book opened with an account of a sumptuous banquet given by King Ahasuerus for all the dignitaries of the Persian empire. When the queen disobeyed the royal command to appear before the guests and display her beauty, she was deposed for insubordination. A decree was subsequently promulgated throughout the empire enforcing the submission of wives to their husbands, which followed ancient Semitic tradition. As a replacement for Vashti, the deposed queen, the king married the winner of what at the present day would be designated as a "beauty contest." The successful lady, named Esther when given her official Persian title as queen, or Hadassah, the Hebrew "myrtle," had been brought up in Susa by her cousin Mordecai, a Benjamite descendant of Kish, the father of King Saul. Mordecai had come from a family that had left Palestine during the first captivity in 597 B.C. under Nebuchadnezzar, and according to the story had adopted Hadassah on the death of her parents. In contrast to Daniel (Dan. 1:8) Esther concealed her Jewish religion and nationality (Est. 2:10), and in the tenth month of the seventh year, some four years after the deposition of Vashti, she became queen (Est. 2:15ff.), an occasion that was celebrated by means of a great banquet (Est. 2:18).

Subsequently Mordecai uncovered a conspiracy on the part of two chamberlains to assassinate the king (Est. 2:19-23), and when these tidings were conveyed through Esther to Ahasuerus, the traitors were unmasked and hanged. At some period after the seventh year of Ahasuerus, Haman, a descendant of the Amalekite King Agag who had been defeated by Saul (1 Sam. 15:8ff.) became Grand Vizier (Est. 3:1).

Mordecai incurred his immediate wrath by refusing to bow down before him, and as an act of revenge Haman determined to massacre all the Jews living in Persia (Est. 3:5f.), the specific time for which was chosen by the casting of a lot (*pur*). He obtained royal consent for this act, and a decree was drafted and sent out to all parts of the empire (Est. 3:12-15).

Esther was unaware of all this, being in comparative seclusion, but when she was informed by Mordecai of the seriousness of the situation (Est. 4:4-9), she determined to go into the inner court unannounced and visit the king, even though the penalty for this breach of prerogative was death (Est. 4:15-17). Three days later Esther put on her royal robes and presented herself with great misgivings to the king, who to her surprise received her graciously (Est. 5:1-3). She invited the king and Haman to a banquet (Est. 5:3-5), and at the end of that feast to yet another on the following day. Haman was irritated by the presence of Mordecai (Est. 5:9), but controlled his impulses, and on returning home acquainted all his relatives and friends with the good fortune that had overtaken him in being invited to dine with the queen (Est. 5:10-12). His wife and friends advised him to erect gallows some eighty feet in height, on which to hang Mordecai the next day.

Unable to sleep that night, the king ordered the royal chronicles to be read to him. When the account of the way that Mordecai had unmasked the conspiracy against the king was narrated, it was discovered that no reward had been given this man. Early in the morning Haman visited the king to ask permission for Mordecai to be hanged, but through a mis-understanding he prescribed great honor for his intended victim, a procedure that he, as Grand Vizier, was obliged to carry out (Est. 6:10f.). Returning to the banquet with considerable misgivings, Haman heard the petition of Esther that she and her people should not be extirpated. When the king on inquiry learned who was the author of this dastardly plan, he rushed outside onto the terrace (Est. 7:7). Returning almost immediately, he saw Haman crouched at the feet of Esther, and thinking that he was trying to assault her he ordered Haman to be executed on the very gallows that had been prepared for Mordecai (Est. 7:9f.).

Shortly thereafter Mordecai replaced Haman as Grand Vizier (Est. 8:1-2), and the queen, in a burst of patriotism, pleaded with the king to reverse the edict of Haman. Bound by the laws of the Medes and Persians (Est. 1:19), which made it impossible for the enactment to be revoked, the king nevertheless authorized another edict to be promul-gated, rendering the first harmless for the Jews (Est. 8:7f.). Instead, the Jews were given royal permission to massacre any who attacked them on the thirteenth day of Adar, the time chosen by the *pur* of Haman. This announcement was followed by public rejoicing on the part of Jews throughout the empire, and many heathen, anxious to escape any harm that might result from this turn of events, themselves became Jewish proselytes. On the fateful day the Jews killed some five hundred men (Est. 9:6) in addition to the son of Haman, and on the next day three hundred more were killed, following a request of Esther to Ahasuerus to continue the massacre. Outside the capital the Jews had put to death some seventy-five thousand people (fifteen thousand according to the LXX) on the thirteenth of Adar, and went on to celebrate their triumph on the fourteenth. In the capital city of Susa, however, after two days of killing, the Jews celebrated on the fifteenth of Adar (Est. 9:19) what was thereafter to become known as the feast of Purim. This occasion was celebrated annually with rejoicing and the distribution of gifts to the poor.

In an epilogue, Ahasuerus is recorded to have imposed tribute on his subjects, and, in the manner of the book of Kings, the reader is referred to other source material for the life of this notable monarch, notably that contained in the Chronicles of the Kings of Media and Persia (Est. 10:2). As Grand Vizier, Mordecai continued to show kindness to his people scattered throughout the Persian empire.

B. PROBLEMS OF DATING AND AUTHORSHIP

According to *Baba Bathra* (15a), the authorship of the book was attributed to the men of the Great Synagogue. Josephus held that Mordecai himself was the author, a view that was also prevalent in some rabbinic circles.[1] However, the mention of Mordecai and his benevolence in the epilogue (Est. 10:3) would seem to indicate that he was not responsible for compiling the work. The fact is that the identity of the writer is completely unknown, although it is obvious that he was a native of Persia rather than Palestine. His sources included some of the writings of Mordecai (Est. 9:20), the Books of the Chronicles of the Median and Persian kings (Est. 2:23; 6:1; 10:2), and most probably certain familiar oral traditions, but none of the foregoing furnishes any clue as to his identity.

In much the same manner the determination of the date of composition of the book is attended with certain difficulties. Internal evidence indicates that Ahasuerus had died before the book was written, and that the compilation of his official state history had preceded the writing of Esther. Even these allusions are ambiguous, however, for among other issues they raise the question as to the identity of the Persian ruler himself. He is commonly associated with Xerxes I (486-465/64 B.C.), the Hebrew name being the equivalent of the Persian *Khshayarsha*. The consonants appeared in the Elephantine papyri as *kshy'rsh*, which is reasonably close to the Greek form *Xerxes*. In the LXX the name Ahasu-

---

[1] *AJ*, XI, 6, 1, perhaps on the basis of references in Est. 9:20 and 32. Ibn Ezra (1092-1167) concurred in this view.

erus was read throughout as Artaxerxes,[2] which might imply an identification with Artaxerxes II (404-359 B.C.), though traditionally the reference was taken as indicative of Xerxes I.

However, some scholars have held that the events mentioned in the book transpired during the reign of Artaxerxes II,[3] and it seems at least possible that they may have been prompted in this not only by the LXX tradition but also by certain considerations of historicity, to be mentioned subsequently. If the association of Ahasuerus with Xerxes I is correct, the book could not have been written before 465 B.C., the generally accepted date of his assassination. The chronologically difficult reference in Esther 2:6 might well indicate that the author was writing some considerable time after the events mentioned, and the fact that the Dispersion was regarded as long-attested might also support this contention.

On the most conservative view the author may possibly have lived during the latter half of the fifth century B.C.,[4] or towards the close of the Persian period (539-333 B.C.). On the other hand, a Maccabean date has been suggested by more radical critics, such as Pfeiffer, on the basis of certain internal allusions.[5] The first reference to the feast of Purim, Pfeiffer maintained, was in 2 Maccabees 15:36, according to which the "Day of Nicanor," celebrating the defeat of that commander near Beth-horon in 161 B.C., preceded by one day the "Day of Mordecai" in the month of Adar. Purim was apparently unknown to, or unrecognized by, Judas Maccabaeus, since 1 Maccabees 7:49, which Pfeiffer assigned to about 100 B.C., mentioned the "Day of Nicanor" without referring to Purim. Following Spinoza, he maintained that the real historical background of the book was the ardent patriotism of the Maccabean revolt, and that Haman was none other than Antiochus Epiphanes, who tried, like Haman, to eradicate all those elements which resisted assimilation into his cultural patterns. The description of the Jews in Esther 3:8 suggested for Pfeiffer the Dispersion of the Greek period, which was further borne out by the references to mass conversions to Judaism (Est. 8:17; 9:27), reminiscent of the time when the Jews reversed the policies of Antiochus and compelled the heathen to become proselytes under penalty of death. Accordingly Pfeiffer dated Esther within the reign of John Hyrcanus (135-104 B.C.), perhaps about 125 B.C.[6]

2 So Josephus, *loc. cit.*

3 E.g. J. Hoschander, *The Book of Esther in the Light of History* (1923), p. 20 *passim;* A. T. Olmstead, *History of Palestine and Syria to the Macedonian Conquest* (1931), pp. 612ff.

4 *YIOT*, pp. 354f.; cf. Gunkel, *Esther* (1916), pp. 19f., and in *Theologische Literaturzeitung,* XLIV (1919), p. 214.

5 *PIOT*, pp. 740ff.

6 *PIOT*, p. 742.

A rather earlier date was suggested by A. E. Morris, who thought that the book reflected the earlier years of Antiochus Epiphanes, and maintained that the author advocated a policy of cooperation with the conqueror in order to secure benefits that might be lost if active resistance to his demands were to be entertained.[7] H. H. Rowley felt that the book reflected conditions obtaining prior to the time when Antiochus deliberately set about endeavoring to destroy Jewish religious life, and suggested a date of composition a few decades after 180 B.C.[8]

While these arguments may have certain points in their favor, there are, as Anderson has pointed out, some important facts that make a dogmatic pronouncement regarding a late date undesirable.[9] In the first instance it is not difficult to conceive of Jews exercising bitter hatred towards Gentiles before the period of 168-165 B.C., as Pfeiffer had supposed, since the Elephantine papyri furnish clear indications of the beginnings of anti-Semitism in the wanton destruction of the Jewish temple at Yeb by hostile Egyptian elements. If the happenings narrated in Esther do in fact relate to the fifth century B.C., they would show that at opposite ends of the Persian domain (Est. 1:1) there were contemporary outbursts of anti-Semitic feeling taking place. Against the opinion of Pfeiffer that the writer had curtailed the two centuries of the Persian period to one or two generations, it merely needs to be remarked that the author was establishing his chronology on the basis of the New Empire period (Est. 2:6), and nowhere stated it as his intention to describe the era as a whole (cf. Est. 1:1).

Again, in Esther the Jews are not portrayed as fighting for their religion, as in the Maccabean era, but for their very existence. The locale of the narrative is clearly Persia, and there is no reference whatever to any part of Palestine, nor to any religious or social conditions obtaining at any time during the Greek period. Furthermore, the Jews in Esther were not concerned with forming a tightly knit religious society that would serve as a lone island of true faith in the midst of a vast ocean of paganism. Instead, their prime interest was in securing for themselves and their religion the same degree of tolerance that had been given to foreign religions by the Persian rulers prior to Xerxes I.

Equally important for an earlier rather than a later date for the composition of Esther is the manner in which the work reflected the background of the Jewish dispersion. Evidence of this is to be found in the intimate knowledge the author had of the customs of Persia and the topography both of Susa and the Persian royal palaces. Details of the latter could hardly have survived in the west with such clarity until the Maccabean period or later unless they had been committed to writing

---

[7] *ET*, XLII (1930-31), pp. 124ff.
[8] *The Growth of the OT* (1950), p. 155.
[9] B. W. Anderson, *IB*, III, p. 828.

previously, which the narrative of Esther scarcely demands. Again, there are numerous Persian names and loan-words scattered throughout the book, which by nature would militate against its provenance in the late Greek period,[10] since in that case they would almost certainly have occurred in a modified form.

The fact that Ben Sira was apparently ignorant of Esther and the feast of Purim need only point to an origin for both in the eastern Diaspora,[11] and imply that they only became familiar to Palestinian Jews in the second century B.C. On any ground, and not least that provided by the manuscript discoveries in the Qumran caves, a Maccabean date seems out of the question, and it would appear preferable to the present writer to assign the composition to the efforts of a Persian Jew who compiled the work in the middle of the fourth century B.C., and to think in terms of a date not later than 350 B.C. until more concrete evidence is forthcoming.

C. THE HISTORICITY OF ESTHER

The historicity of the book has long been a subject of debate. Among the Jews it was highly esteemed, and as one of the five Megilloth it was read annually at the feast of Purim.[12] But even in rabbinic circles there were dissident voices, and as late as the second century after Christ the distinguished Rabbi Samuel declared that the book of Esther was apocryphal (*Megill. 7a*), though in the event with little practical result. Despite the fact that some modern scholars have defended the historicity of the composition,[13] the majority have deemed it to be without historical foundation. However, not all have been quite as radical as Pfeiffer, who regarded the work as entirely fictitious,[14] for such scholars as Streane, Driver, and Rowley have pointed out that the author had access to accurate information regarding the Persian regime, and that his work may well rest upon an historical basis.[15]

As Harvey has observed, the literary form of the book supports the claim to historicity, since the work commenced with the usual formula

[10] L. B. Paton, *A Critical and Exegetical Commentary on the Book of Esther* (1908), pp. 65ff.

[11] Cf. A. Bentzen, *Introduction to the OT*, II, p. 193.

[12] A. Cohen, *The Five Megilloth*, p. 93.

[13] A. H. Sayce, *Introduction to Ezra, Nehemiah and Esther* (1885), pp. 98ff., subsequently withdrawn in his *The Higher Criticism, and the Verdict of the Monuments* (1893), pp. 469ff. Cf. W. S. Watson, *PTR*, I (1903), pp. 62ff.; J. H. Raven, *OT Introduction* (1906), pp. 75ff.; M. Wolff, *Nieuw Theologisch Tijdschrift*, I (1916), pp. 75ff.; J. Hoschander, *The Book of Esther in the Light of History* (1923).

[14] *PIOT*, p. 737; cf. C. H. Cornill, *Introduction to the Canonical Books of the OT*, p. 257.

[15] A. W. Streane, *The Book of Esther* (1907), p. xiv. *DILOT*, p. 483. H. H. Rowley, *The Growth of the OT*, p. 155.

for the beginning of an historical account, and concluded with the typical reference to the complete chronicle (Est. 10:2; cf. 1 Kgs. 14:19, 29; 15:23).[16] The accuracy of the information with regard to the Persian royal residences and customs has also commended the historical character of the work.[17] On the other hand, critical scholars have adduced certain objections to the general historicity of the composition. One of the most serious is to be seen in connection with the reference in Esther 2:5ff., which has been interpreted as meaning that Mordecai was taken captive in 597 B.C., and that some 124 years later he was represented as the foster-father of a young and beautiful girl.[18] On this basis critics have supposed that the author was completely ignorant of Persian history, since he imagined that Xerxes I (486-465/64 B.C.) reigned shortly after the time of Nebuchadnezzar II (605-562 B.C.). A careful reading of the Hebrew text is sufficient to dispose of this objection, however, for on examination it becomes apparent that the relative pronoun "who" in verse 6 obviously refers to Kish, the great-grandfather of Mordecai, and not to Mordecai himself.

Another more serious historical difficulty has been urged in connection with the wife of Xerxes I, on the basis of an identification of this king with Ahasuerus. According to Herodotus, the wife of Xerxes I was Amestris, the daughter of a Persian general, and a woman who was renowned for her cruelty.[19] Though the name resembles that of Esther superficially, the two cannot be identified phonetically, and this, combined with the differences of character exhibited by the two women and the fact that no other wife of Xerxes was mentioned by Herodotus, makes the occurrence of Vashti and Esther just another fictitious element in the book as far as most critical scholars are concerned.

It is known that in the second year of his reign Xerxes attacked Egypt and subjugated it, while in the following year he called together an assembly to consider the possibility of an expedition against Greece.[20] If Xerxes I and Ahasuerus are to be identified, as most scholars think they should, the curious gap between the third year of Ahasuerus in Esther 1:3 and the seventh year of Esther 2:16 can be explained satisfactorily, since during this time, from 483 to 480 B.C., he was pursuing his ill-fated invasion of Greece. It should be noted also that Xerxes and Amestris had been married for a sufficient length of time to enable two of their sons to accompany Xerxes when waging war against Greece.

---

[16] D. Harvey, *IDB*, II, p. 151.

[17] Cf. M. Dieulafoy, *Bibliotheca Sacra*, LXVI (1889), pp. 626ff., *L'Acropole de la Suse* (1890); H. Gunkel, *Theologische Literaturzeitung*, XLIV (1919), pp. 2ff.; L. B. Paton, *A Critical and Exegetical Commentary on the Book of Esther*, p. 65.

[18] Cf. *PIOT*, p. 732; L. B. Paton, *A Critical and Exegetical Commentary on the Book of Esther*, p. 73.

[19] Herodotus, *Hist.*, VII, 114; IX, 108f.

[20] *Ibid.*, VII, 8.

According to Herodotus, the unhappy king consoled himself with the members of his *harîm* on his return to Persia, and it was at the beginning of this period that Esther presumably became queen (Est. 2:16ff.).[21] The character of Xerxes as a capricious, despotic, passionate man agrees with the estimate of him as made by secular historians,[22] and although the Persian king was, according to Herodotus, required to choose his wife from one of the seven noble families of the land (cf. Est. 1:14),[23] a regulation of this kind could easily be broken.

Aside from the rather obvious fact that Xerxes could have monopolized a large *harîm*, it is clear from the writings of Herodotus that the monarch was not averse to contracting improper sexual relationships even when he was tottering on the brink of defeat in Greece, so that he would have no compunction about choosing any woman who took his fancy if his circumstances at any given time dictated such a procedure.[24] Consequently there is no *a priori* reason why Esther should not have been promoted from the ranks of the *harîm*, and although secular history says nothing about the identity of Vashti or the fate of Amestris, this silence should not necessarily be interpreted as constituting a repudiation of the events narrated in Esther. Until more is known about the life of Amestris it seems unwise to conclude that she remained the only wife and the sole queen of Xerxes, even though she was a cruel and calculating woman of whom the king himself stood in some dread.

The objection to the king's sending out decrees in various languages (Est. 1:22; 3:12; 8:9) is very superficial, since the Persian empire contained numerous foreign elements that it had assimilated by one means or another, and that preserved their national identity to a certain extent. The Persians were tolerant towards such groups, and therefore there would be every reason for the communications to be addressed to the various peoples in their native tongues. Yet another criticism of the historicity of Esther has subsisted in the nature of the pogrom in chapter 9, and the number of the victims involved. As in so many other instances in the Old Testament, the Hebrew numbers were undoubtedly symbols of signal triumph for the faith, a fact which the translators of the LXX appeared to recognize when they scaled the 75,000 of the Hebrew to a mere 15,000. Whatever may be the actual facts of the case, massacres of large proportions have been by no means unknown in the history of the ancient Near East. Objections to the correctness of the statement in Esther 1:1 that Ahasuerus ruled over 127 provinces are not by any means as cogent as their proponents imagine. Under Darius I the realm was divided into

[21] *Ibid.*, IX, 108.
[22] E.g. Aeschylus, *Pers.* 467ff.; Juvenal, *Sat.*, X, 174ff.; Herodotus, *Hist.*, VII, 3ff., IX, 108ff.
[23] Herodotus, *Hist.*, III, 84.
[24] Cf. Herodotus, *Hist.*, IX, 108ff.

twenty satrapies, each of which was subdivided for purposes of administration into a number of provinces, thus making perfectly plausible the
tradition preserved in the book of Esther.

The origin of the feast of Purim as described in the book has been the
subject of considerable debate, since the word *pur* was not thought to
mean "lot," in accordance with the explanation offered by the book of
Esther.[25] On the basis of this assumption Meier and Hitzig postulated a
theory of the Persian origin of Purim, while Zunz also maintained
that it was an adaptation of a Persian spring festival.[26] One interesting
variant of this approach was the opinion of Von Hammer that Purim was
the Persian festival *Farwardigan,* which was celebrated in memory of
the dead on the last ten days of the year.[27] This theory was accepted by
Paul de Lagarde, Schwally, Haupt, and others, and more recently was
revived in part by Lewy, who held that the Jews explained the term *pur*
in the light of two Akkadian words, *purruru,* "to destroy," and *purum,*
"lot."[28]

Many early critics supposed that the feast was primarily of Babylonian
rather than Persian origin, and that the story of Esther was the particular
legend that was associated with the feast. This view was maintained by
Nowack, Meissner, Winckler, Frazer, and Toy, among others.[29] Zimmern
and Jensen, in particular, postulated a mythological origin for the feast
of Purim.[30] According to this theory Mordecai represented Marduk, the
patron deity of Babylon; Esther was identified with Ishtar,[31] the principal Babylonian goddess, Haman was Humman, the chief deity of the
Elamites, and Vashti was none other than Mashti, an Elamite goddess.
This theory belonged to the more vigorous days of the pan-Babylonian
school, when it was accepted procedure to seek the prototypes of all
important Jewish institutions in Babylonian social and religious customs.

Such a view fails to explain the renunciation of idolatry by the faithful
remnant among the exiles, as well as the fact that during the period of

---

[25] For an account of earlier theories see L. B. Paton, *A Critical and Exegetical
Commentary on the Book of Esther,* pp. 77ff.

[26] E. Meier, *Geschichte der poetischen National-Literatur der Hebräer* (1856),
p. 506. F. Hitzig, *Geschichte des Volkes Israels* (1869), p. 280. L. Zunz, *ZDMG,*
XXVII (1873), p. 686.

[27] J. von Hammer, *Wiener Jahrbücher für Literatur,* XXXVIII (1872), p. 49.

[28] P. de Lagarde, *Purim, ein Beitrag zur Geschichte der Religion* (1887). F.
Schwally, *Das Leben nach dem Tode* (1892), pp. 42ff. P. Haupt, *Purim* (1906),
p. 20. J. Lewy, *HUCA,* XIV (1938-39), pp. 127ff.

[29] W. Nowack, *Archäologie,* II (1894), pp. 194ff. B. Meissner, *ZDMG,* L (1896),
pp. 296ff. H. Winckler, *Altorientalische Forschungen,* II (1898), pp. 91ff., 182,
354ff., III (1902), pp. 1ff. J. G. Frazer, *The Golden Bough* (1903 ed.), pp. 138ff.
C. H. Toy, *EB,* III, col. 3980.

[30] H. Zimmern, *ZAW* (1891), XI, pp. 157ff. P. Jensen, *Wiener Zeitschrift für
die Kunde des Morgenlandes,* VI (1892), pp. 47ff., 209, *ZDMG,* LV (1901), p. 228.

[31] Cf. P. Haupt, *AJSL,* XXVIII (1907), pp. 112ff.

the return such idolatry was never again a serious problem for the theocracy. On this basis it is difficult to believe that the Jews would employ a polytheistic cult-ceremony for a new Jewish festival, particularly one that commemorated the survival of the Jews and their religion in the pagan environment of the Persian empire. Even if Purim represented an adaptation of a Babylonian folk-tale it is extremely unlikely that the Jews would have rewritten or reshaped it and at the same time retained the old names of the pagan deities. This is all the more improbable since Esther was used as a name for the heroine of the book after she had been given her official title as Persian queen, and as such it more probably derives from the Persian *stara*, "star," than from the designation of the Babylonian goddess Ishtar.

The incorrectness of the view that would imply a mythological association between Mordecai and Marduk appears indicated further by the fact that another Mordecai was mentioned in Ezra (2:2; cf. Neh. 7:7; 1 Esdr. 5:8), and this man was a leader of the exiles who returned to Judaea with Zerubbabel. If, however, a Babylonian original is to be posited for the name Mordecai, it is more likely to be found in the personal appellation *Mardukaia*, a derived and expanded form of the name Marduk, than in the actual designation of one of the chief Babylonian deities.[32] While this question is being considered it should be recognized that there were other instances of Jews being given names that may have contained fragments of a divine designation (cf. Dan. 1:7), but this need no more imply mythological associations than the modern custom of giving a child a name in which portions of divine appellations occur.

Even less satisfactory as theories of the origin of the Purim festival were those that supposed that it was nothing more than the Greek *pithoigia* or "cask-opening," a season marked by drinking and the giving of gifts, and comparable to the Roman *vinalia*. This view was maintained principally by Grätz, who thought that the word *purim* constituted an otherwise unknown plural of *pura* or "winepress."[33] He did not explain how winepresses came to be associated with the opening of wine-casks, and apparently ignored the fact that among orthodox Jews of the Greek period there was an intense resistance to anything savoring of Greek culture or religion, which would make the adoption of Greek ceremonies as a Jewish religious rite a highly improbable affair. Finally, this theory failed to account for the way in which the story of Esther, which is Mesopotamian in origin, came to be associated with a Greek or Roman feast.

[32] T. K. Cheyne, *EB*, III, col. 3983, denied the connection between the two names.

[33] H. Grätz, *Magazin für die Geschichte und Wissenschaft des Judenthums*, XXXV (1886), pp. 425ff., 473ff., 521ff.

Equally unrealistic as an explanation of origins was the theory of Pfeiffer that both the festival itself and its name constituted a hoax foisted upon an impressionable and gullible Jewish community during the Maccabean period to reinforce and serve as a vehicle for the expression of patriotic emotions during that turbulent era.[34] This view was in full accord with Pfeiffer's low opinions of other important sections of the Old Testament such as Deuteronomy, the "Priestly Code," and Daniel, which he held to be technically fraudulent, although their authors were considered to have been sincere and guileless men who were inspired by noble religious ideals. Such an approach to the problems of difficult Old Testament sources was unworthy of an erudite and deeply spiritual man such as Pfeiffer, and ought not to be entertained at all seriously.

Each of the foregoing views relating to the origin of the feast of Purim needs to be re-evaluated critically in the light of archaeological discoveries at Susa. Dieulafoy's work on the site of ancient Shushan has shed light upon the method employed by Haman for establishing a date upon which the Jews would be destroyed with the recovery of quadrangular dice on which were engraved the numbers one, two, five, and six.[35] The contemporary term for this prism was *pur*, and was derived from an Assyrian word *puru*, meaning a "die" or "lot." Thus the glosses in Esther 3:7 and 9:24 indicated that the Persian method of throwing dice was equivalent to the Jewish practice of "casting lots." That the usage of the word *pur* in this precise connection was one of great antiquity was shown by Albright, who made it clear from cuneiform sources that as early as the nineteenth century B.C. the word *puru'um* occurred in Assyrian texts in the sense of a "lot" or "die."[36] This, along with the later form of the same term, *puru*, was found in tablets of differing periods in association with a verb meaning "to throw" or "to cause to fall."

This evidence would seem to substantiate the claim of the book of Esther regarding the origin and nature of the feast of Purim. From the beginning it was observed among the Jews as a convivial and festive occasion for which there was no prescription in the Torah and no tradition of Palestinian origin. Subsequent additions to the festival maintained the character of Purim as a non-religious holiday.[37] As Anderson has observed, the present popularity of the feast of Purim among Jewish people can be accounted for in part by the fact that it

[34] *PIOT*, pp. 745f.

[35] M. Dieulafoy, *L'Acropole de la Suse* (1890), cf. *Bibliotheca Sacra*, LXVI (1889), pp. 626ff.

[36] W. F. Albright, *BASOR*, No. 67 (1937), p. 37. Cf. J. Lewy, *Revue Hittite et Asianique*, V (1939), pp. 117ff.; E. F. Weidner, *Archiv für Orientforschung*, XIII (1941), p. 308.

[37] Cf. H. Malter, *JE*, X, pp. 274ff.; H. Schauss, *The Jewish Festivals* (1938), pp. 237ff.

constitutes the only worldly holiday in the Jewish calendar for the expression of the light-hearted side of life.[38]

Certain other objections that have been levelled against the historicity of Esther are largely subjective. There seems to be no adequate reason for denying the validity of the attempt made by Haman to massacre the Jewish population of the empire, even though the very idea would be repugnant to the majority of people. The atmosphere of the book is typically oriental, and, as has been shown by compositions such as *The Arabian Nights*, oriental monarchs were easily swayed by their favorite courtiers. This would be particularly the case with Ahasuerus, since Haman had taken pains to represent the Jews as traitors to the empire. Again, the characteristic superstition of the Mesopotamians was reflected in the action of Haman when he cast lots in order to arrive at an auspicious day for his planned enterprise. As for the large bribe that Haman offered to Ahasuerus (Est. 3:9), the real significance of this gesture was that a substantial portion of the Jewish estates made available in consequence of the planned pogrom would find its way into the royal treasury, a procedure that is not unknown in more recent times.

When all is said and done, however, it must be recognized that there are certain difficulties connected with the view that Esther constitutes an historical composition. As has been noted earlier, questions of chronology led Hoschander and Olmstead to follow the LXX tradition in identifying Ahasuerus with Artaxerxes II, but this view is itself attended with grave difficulties if for no other reason than that the LXX reading is of doubtful accuracy. The principal problem concerns the identity of Vashti, her relationship to Amestris, and the place of both these women in the chronology of Xerxes I.

On the basis of the information supplied by Esther, Vashti was deposed before the four-year interval in the recorded reign of Ahasuerus. If the identification of the latter with Xerxes I is correct, this would imply that she was dismissed prior to the unfortunate campaign in Greece, on which, according to Herodotus, Xerxes I was accompanied by Amestris as queen. Since Amestris had sons serving in the Persian forces in the campaign, it would appear that she had been queen for a considerable period. On the other hand it should be noted that Herodotus spoke of Amestris as "wife of Xerxes,"[39] and not as "queen of Persia," and it may be that she was in fact a favorite concubine or even chief of the *harîm*, who had been appointed by Xerxes to accompany him on his campaign. Whatever the nature of the situation, her behavior on that occasion furnished sufficient grounds for the monarch to consign her to obscurity on their return to Persia. Until more is known about the identity of

[38] B. W. Anderson, *IB*, III, p. 825.
[39] Cf. Herodotus, *Hist.*, VII, 114; IX, 108f.

Vashti and Amestris, this particular difficulty for the historicity of the composition must remain.

Important evidence for the refutation of the mythological and fictional interpretations of Esther was supplied several years ago by the surprising announcement that an undated cuneiform text had been discovered in which there was a reference to a certain Mordecai (*Mardukâ*), who had lived during the Persian period.[40] This man apparently was a high official in the royal court at Susa during the reign of Xerxes I, and he possibly functioned in this capacity even prior to the third year of the rule of that king. There is also the additional possibility that this individual may even have served in some capacity under Darius I (522-486 B.C.), the predecessor of Xerxes I. This text goes far towards establishing the historicity of the book of Esther, and gives ground for the expectation that further discoveries may yet throw light upon the identity of Vashti and Amestris.

Even those who would dismiss the composition as being nothing more than an historical novel, assuming, of course, that historical novels as such were being written in the Persian or early Greek periods, have been compelled to concede that the author manifested an intimate knowledge of the royal palace of Shushan (Susa). Excavations at the site from 1852 uncovered the hall and throne-room of the palace on the north side of the mound. A trilingual inscription, reflecting the racial admixture of the Persian empire, was written on the pedestals of four columns in the palace, and furnished a brief account of the manner in which Artaxerxes II had restored the building:

> Says Artaxerxes, the great king, the king of kings. . .the son of king Darius, the son of king Darius Hystaspes: My ancestor Darius built the *apadana* [throne-room] in former times. In the time of Artaxerxes, my grandfather, it was burnt by fire. I have restored it. . . .[41]

Additional excavations under Marcel Dieulafoy from 1884 revealed that the ruined city had originally covered an area of almost five thousand acres in extent. At that time it was divided into four distinct districts that comprised respectively the citadel-mound, the royal city or "Shushan the palace," the business and residential area or "Shushan the city," and the district on the plain to the west of the river. The royal palace included three courts of different sizes surrounded by halls and apartments. It had been decorated in the Babylonian manner with beautifully colored glazed bricks on which figures of griffins, bulls, and spearmen were executed in relief. The bulk of this type of decoration was found to have come from the period of Artaxerxes II.[42] Clearly the author of Esther had more than a passing acquaintance with the topog-

---

[40] A. Ungnad, ZAW, LVIII (1940-41), pp. 240ff., LIX (1942-43), p. 219.
[41] I. Price, *The Monuments and the OT* (1925), p. 403.
[42] A. U. Pope (ed.), *A Survey of Persian Art* (1938), I, p. 351.

raphy of Susa as one of the three royal cities of the Achaemenid regime.

From the foregoing discussion it will be evident that there are good reasons for crediting the book with a substantial historical nucleus. It is well within the bounds of probability that the author idealized his heroine, and that in order to bring his account to a fitting climax he employed certain literary devices and embellishments such as would be appropriate to any writer of imagination and literary skill. But as Streane has remarked, there is no difficulty in supposing that, during the reign of Xerxes, one who occupied the position of a secondary wife was made the means of averting some calamity that threatened at least some of her compatriots, and that the extant narrative of the book was formed upon this foundation.[43] As against those who would dismiss the work as a tissue of improbabilities[44] the remarks of Anderson are timely:

> Historians and archaeologists have already confirmed the fact that the author possessed an amazingly accurate knowledge of Persian palaces and manners. Further light on this dark period of Jewish history may reveal that the author's claim for the historicity of his story is not totally erroneous.[45]

D. THE PURPOSE OF THE BOOK

In discussing the purpose of the work, many commentators have pointed out the fact that the name of God does not occur in Esther, nor is there any reference to prayer, praise, or the direct worship of God. Yet it is a palpable mistake to regard the composition as being purely secular in character. The ordinance of fasting (Est. 5:16; 9:31) certainly carried a religious connotation, while an awareness of the divine purpose in securing the survival of the Jews in Persia appears to underlie the conviction of Mordecai (Est. 4:14) that even if Esther did not intervene on their behalf, the Jews would be delivered nonetheless. Such a view appears to be based firmly upon the concept of an overriding providence. Young endeavored to account for the absence of the mention of God by supposing that the name of the Covenant Deity was no longer associated with those Jews who had remained in Mesopotamia when their fellows had returned to begin a new life in the theocratic community of post-exilic Judaea.[46] There is, however, no simple answer to this curious phenomenon, particularly in view of the fact that Esther is unique among the Old Testament Scriptures in the way in which it deals with religious and moral issues. The writer certainly seems to have stressed the value of political intrigue and human intellectual acumen,

---

[43] A. W. Streane, *The Book of Esther*, p. xiv.
[44] Th. Nöldeke, *EB*, II, cols. 1400ff.
[45] B. W. Anderson, *IB*, III, p. 827.
[46] *YIOT*, p. 358.

and to underplay, if not actually to disregard, the possibility of divine intervention. At the same time, the literary skill of the author leaves the reader in little doubt that he is observing the operation of divine providence as the narrative proceeds, and that the indestructible nature of the Covenant People will ultimately be made evident.

One important purpose of the composition was to furnish the historical background to the institution of a feast that was not prescribed in the Torah, but which, in a real sense, had emerged from the *Sitz im Leben des Volkes*. The feast of Purim, as has been remarked earlier, was one of secular merriment and festivity from its inception, since this was deemed the most appropriate means of celebrating the deliverance of the Jews from their pagan enemies.[47] Yet it is incorrect to suppose on this account that the omission of the Divine Name was deliberate in a work intended to be read at a festival of noise and conviviality,[48] since the reading of the Esther scroll was a later traditional accretion to the festive ceremonies, and was not prescribed as part of the original celebrations.

C. H. Gordon has drawn attention to the way in which the book of Esther has furnished the earliest evidence of a distinctively Iranian institution which has survived into modern times.[49] This is the doctrine of *kitmân* or *taqiyya*, which he rendered by the term "dissimulation." According to this procedure an individual is permitted to deny his religion and pose as a member of some other faith if confronted with acute personal danger. Gordon illustrated this situation from modern Iranian life by stating that the Shiites of Iran are permitted to pose with impunity as Sunnites when they undertake the pilgrimage to Mecca, which is in the hands of Arab Sunnites, who have been known to display violent hostility towards Shiites on occasions. Again, in Iran itself, religious minorities frequently pose as Shiites when their existence is threatened, and this procedure is part of the accepted social mores. Such a general pattern of behavior was manifested by Esther herself (Est. 2:10), who concealed her Jewish ancestry and faith without any apparent qualms of conscience. When the plans of Haman were frustrated and the pagan majority suddenly became mortally afraid of the Jews (Est. 8:17), they too adopted the practice of "dissimulation" and pretended that they were Jews.

Although the dominant theme of the triumph of Judaism over her enemies won an immediate and lasting degree of popularity for the work, there were sporadic protests about the inclusion of Esther in the canon of Scripture, and these continued long after the Council of

---

[47] Cf. J. C. Rylaarsdam, *IDB*, III, p. 649. For the celebration of Purim in antiquity see G. F. Moore, *Judaism* (1927), II, pp. 51ff.

[48] So D. Harvey, *IDB*, II, p. 150.

[49] *IOTT*, pp. 278f.

Jamnia supposedly pronounced upon its canonicity. Its popularity led to attempts at embellishment, as in the two targums on Esther, and at a later period it assumed somewhat of a dramatic character when read in the synagogues, with the members of the congregation partaking symbolically as the narrative was read. By about A.D. 120 the position of Esther in the canon was secured, and the Christian Church accepted it as such, albeit with some misgivings in certain quarters.

The integrity of the composition was first challenged by J. D. Michaelis in 1783, who maintained that the peculiarities of Esther 9:20–10:3 indicated that this section had been derived from a separate source.[50] Since that time many critics have regarded the passage in question either as partially or entirely spurious, a conclusion based to some extent upon linguistic and stylistic differences, and also upon considerations of internal inconsistency. With regard to the latter it was maintained that because the distinction between urban and rural Jews was ignored (Est. 9:19), both days of Purim were made binding upon the Jewish populace as a whole. Furthermore, it was alleged, the details of the recapitulation in Esther 9:24f. were out of harmony with what was contained in earlier sections of the narrative.

With reference to the question of the initial divergence in the celebration by city and country Jews of the victory over their enemies, it appears to have been one purpose of the book to legalize these "two days" (Est. 9:27), the nature of whose origin had already been explained, and to reconcile the divergent traditions which had arisen spontaneously. According to Josephus, the two days of official observance of Purim were accepted by the Jews,[51] and by the time of the Mishnah (ca. A.D. 200) had become legalized in the Jewish calendar. While modern celebrations of Purim are mostly confined to the fourteenth of Adar (February-March), there are some walled cities in Europe and the east where both days are observed.[52]

Quite aside from the explanatory nature of the section in question, a careful study of the syntax and literary style indicates, as Striedl has shown, that the characteristic style of the writer recurs throughout the book.[53] Such differences as Michaelis and those who followed him have observed are clearly due to the change in subject-matter. The fact that the basis of the subsequent designation of Purim was introduced in Esther 3:7 requires the retention of the concluding section if the story is to move towards its proper climax and be intelligible as an explanation of the significance of *pur*, whose etymology is correct as it stands,

---

[50] L. B. Paton, *A Critical and Exegetical Commentary on the Book of Esther*, p. 57.

[51] *AJ*, XI, 6, 13.

[52] B. W. Anderson, *IB*, III, p. 825.

[53] H. Striedl, *ZAW*, LV (1937), pp. 73ff.

contrary to the views of many earlier scholars. As Anderson has observed, the structure of the book, in which the end is anticipated at the beginning, indicates its fundamental unity,[54] a proposition to which the LXX lends some support by retaining almost all of the section 9:20–10:3.

       ❋   ❋   ❋   ❋   ❋

Scholarly opinion is virtually unanimous as to the fact that the Hebrew text of Esther has been well preserved, despite a few corruptions (1:22; 2:19; 7:4), and that it has survived in as pure a form as any of the Old Testament books. The only unusual feature of the work is that in Esther 9:10-17 the names of the sons of Haman were written in the MT in a perpendicular column, because, according to an ancient legend, they were hanged one over the other. For purposes of comparative study, the LXX is of comparatively little value in relation to the Hebrew text, but in other respects it is of some significance because it testifies to the existence of two recensions of the Greek text. While most manuscripts contain the normal LXX material, some have preserved the Lucianic recension of the LXX text. In addition, both types of the Greek have been supplemented to a considerable extent, so that whereas the MT contains 163 verses, the Greek has 270 verses, the balance of which most probably never at any time constituted part of the original Hebrew.[55]

It seems clear that these additions were not related to any Hebrew text during the first half of the third century after Christ, as Origen pointed out,[56] but were certainly included in the LXX in the first century of the Christian era, when Josephus paraphrased four of them.[57] The longer additions in the LXX, based on the Vulgate verse-order, are (a) The Dream of Mordecai (Est. 11:2–12:6, before 1:1 in the LXX); (b) The Edict of Artaxerxes (13:1-7, following LXX 3:13); (c) The Prayer of Mordecai (13:8–14:19, following LXX 4:17); (d) The Prayer of Esther (15:4-19, placed immediately after the preceding addition to the LXX); (e) The Edict of Artaxerxes favoring the Jews (16:1-24, following LXX 8:12); (f) Interpretation of the dream of Mordecai explaining the Feast (10:4–11:1, at the end of the book in the LXX).

The last verse of (f) constituted a footnote to the effect that a translation of Esther, presumably into Greek, prepared by Lysimachus son of Ptolemy a Jerusalemite, had been made in the fourth year of Ptolemy and Cleopatra. Since only the eighth Egyptian ruler who bore the name Ptolemy happened to be married to a Cleopatra in his fourth year of rule, the Greek translation could thus be dated in 113 B.C.[58] A

---

[54] B. W. Anderson, *IB*, III, p. 824.
[55] H. B. Swete, *Introduction to the OT in Greek*, p. 257.
[56] *Ad Afric.* 3.
[57] *AJ*, XI, 6, 5ff.
[58] Cf. B. Jakob, *ZAW*, X (1890), pp. 274ff.; E. Schürer, *Geschichte des jüdischen Volkes* (1909), III, p. 450.

somewhat later period was suggested by Willrich, in identifying these royal personages with Ptolemy XII and Cleopatra VII, who ruled jointly from 51 to 47 B.C.[59] To what extent the colophon is a genuine testimony to the existence of a Greek version of Esther before the end of the second century B.C. is, unfortunately, far from certain, despite its acceptance at face value by Swete.[60] The third addition, the Prayer of Mordecai (13:8—14:19), has been preserved as a separate entity in the English Apocrypha under the general title of "The Additions to the Book of Esther."

Supplementary Literature

Bettan, I. *The Five Scrolls.* 1950.
Gunkel, H. *Esther.* 1916.
Jampel, S. *Das Buch Ester auf seine Geschichtlichkeit untersucht.* 1907.
Siegfried, C. *Ezra, Nehemia und Ester.* 1901.

[59] H. Willrich, *Judaica* (1900), pp. 1ff.
[60] H. B. Swete, *Introduction to the OT in Greek,* p. 25; cf. *APOT,* I, p. 665.

Part Fourteen

THE SACRED WRITINGS (III)
DANIEL, EZRA-NEHEMIAH, AND CHRONICLES

I. THE BOOK OF DANIEL

A. The Story of Daniel

Daniel appears in English versions as the fourth major work in the prophetic literature, whereas it was assigned to the *Kethubhim* or Writings in the Hebrew canon. Apart from what is narrated in the work itself, nothing is known about the life and career of Daniel. An Israelite of royal descent,[1] he was carried captive to Babylonia by Nebuchadnezzar in the third year of Jehoiakim. Having been trained for the royal service (Dan. 1:1-6), he was given the Babylonian name "Belteshazzar," probably the Hebrew transliteration of *Balaṭsu-uṣur* or "protect his life," omitting the name of the particular deity invoked. If the deity is included (cf. Dan. 4:18), the form may have been *Belti-shar-uṣur*, or "Belti, protect the king."

True to his Jewish ancestry, Daniel, along with his three friends Shadrach, Meshach, and Abednego, refused to transgress Jewish dietary laws, and at the end of a period of three years all four had become renowned for their wisdom (Dan. 1:18-21).

This faculty was shortly thereafter put to the test, for according to the second chapter of Daniel, King Nebuchadnezzar had a dream in the second year of his reign, and, having forgotten it upon waking, he challenged his Babylonian wise men to demonstrate their skills by narrating the dream and interpreting its significance to him. When they failed they were all ordered to be executed, including Daniel and his friends (Dan. 2:12f.), but upon appealing to the king, Daniel was given the opportunity of fulfilling the royal command. After prayer to God, the nature and meaning of the dream were disclosed and were subsequently communicated to Nebuchadnezzar with an interpretation (Dan. 2:37-45). The king acknowledged the supremacy of the God of Israel, and promoted Daniel to a position of prominence in the kingdom (Dan. 2:47f.).

[1] Cf. *AJ*, X, 10, 1. The *Dānǐʾēl* of Ezek. 14:14 should properly be identified with the *Danʾel* of the Ugaritic texts, as against E. J. Young, *The Prophecy of Daniel* (1949), pp. 274f.

The third chapter dealt with the erection of a vast golden statue in the Plain of Dura, to which all were commanded to make obeisance. When the companions refused they were questioned as to the meaning of their defiance by the king, and later on were thrown into a hot furnace (Dan. 3:19-23). When they were miraculously delivered, Nebuchadnezzar again conceded the superiority of the God of Israel, and promoted them to a high position in the administration of the kingdom (Dan. 3:26-30).

Chapter four contained a record of another dream which was interpreted by Daniel, this one dealing with the impending insanity of Nebuchadnezzar and his subsequent religious conversion (Dan. 4:1-37; 3:31—4:34 Heb.). The fifth chapter described the feast of Belshazzar (Dan. 5:1-31; 5:1—6:1 Heb.), at which the king and his guests profaned the sacred vessels from the Temple at Jerusalem by drinking from them. A cryptic message was communicated by a mysterious hand, and Daniel was asked to interpret it. The event culminated in the death of Belshazzar and the rise of Darius the Mede. The familiar narrative of Daniel in the den of lions is recounted in chapter 6 (Dan. 6:1-28; 6:2-29 Heb.), an incident that, like so many previous ones mentioned in the book, was marked by pagan recognition of the superior might of Jehovah.

Whereas the first six chapters contain material which purports to be largely historical, the remainder of the book deals with visions that emphasized the destiny of the Hebrews in relationship to Gentile kingdoms. The first of these, dated in the first year of Belshazzar, dealt with four beasts and a personage likened to human offspring (Dan. 7:1-28); the second, in the third year of Belshazzar, described the ram and the goat (Dan. 8:1-27); the third (Dan. 9:1-27), dating from the first year of Darius, dealt with the significance of the seventy-year desolation of Jerusalem as predicted by Jeremiah (Jer. 25:11; 29:10), while the final vision (Dan. 10:1-21), dated in the third year of Cyrus, contained a revelation concerning the period preceding the messianic age. This general theme was continued in chapters 11 and 12, in which the events to occur in subsequent ages of Hebrew life were outlined. The esoteric nature of the communications was made evident by the command to "seal the book" (Dan. 12:4), and with a final eschatological comment the prophecy concluded.

B. THE NATURE AND UNITY OF THE BOOK

The assigning of this work to the third division of the Hebrew canon appears to have been the common practice in Judaism long before the supposed Council of Jamnia, and seems to have been based upon the conviction that Daniel could not be regarded as a prophet in the same sense as Isaiah, Jeremiah, or Ezekiel. The Talmud (*Baba Bathra* 15a) indicates clearly that Daniel was never placed among such prophets,[2] though it is evident that Daniel was widely accepted as Scripture from the second century B.C. onwards. If the pseudepigraphic material designated 1 Enoch borrowed from Daniel (compare 1 Enoch 14:18-22 with Dan. 7:9, 10), the section involved, which was probably written prior to 150 B.C.,[3] would testify to the use of Daniel as authoritative Scripture at that time.

Manuscript discoveries at Qumran have demonstrated the popularity of Daniel,[4] with two manuscripts of the Hebrew text being recovered from 11Q in 1956 to supplement portions of the work found in the other Qumran caves and the *florilegium* found in 4Q, which referred, like Matthew 24:15, to "Daniel the prophet." Since the community was itself Maccabean in origin, it testifies to the way in which Daniel was revered and cited as Scripture in the second century B.C. While Jewish authorities generally displayed little enthusiasm for the book, partly because of its eschatological and apocalyptic emphases, the Christian Church recognized the prophetic nature and value of the composition from the very beginning, basing its estimate in part upon the eschatological utterances of Jesus Christ (Matt. 24:4ff.; Mark 13:5ff.; Lk. 21:8ff.). In the LXX version Daniel was placed among the prophetic writings, following Ezekiel but preceding the Twelve, a position that it has retained in the English versions and in Christian translations generally.

The book lends itself readily to a division into two sections: chapters 1 to 6, consisting of narratives set against an historical background, and chapters 7 to 12, comprising the visions of Daniel. Similarity of subject-matter appears to have been the predominant consideration for such a grouping, and while in the first division a general chronological order was observed, in the second the visions were related to one another in terms of theme and content rather than the actual time when they were supposed to have been experienced. Elementary as this bifid division is, it has led a great many scholars to conclude that Daniel was a composite work. Spinoza and Sir Isaac Newton were among early exponents of this view, which was subsequently espoused by Eichhorn.[5] A variety of contributing authors had already been suggested by Michaelis,[6] and this idea was taken up avidly by Bertholdt, who detected the presence of no

---

[2] Cf. R. D. Wilson, *PTR*, XIII (1915), pp. 352ff.

[3] *APOT*, II, p. 170.

[4] F. F. Bruce, *Second Thoughts on the Dead Sea Scrolls* (1961), p. 57.

[5] B. Spinoza, *Tractatus Theologico-politicus* (1670), p. 130; I. Newton, *Observations Upon the Prophecies of Daniel and the Apocalypse of St. John* (1773), p. 10; J. G. Eichhorn, *Einleitung in das AT* (1803 ed.), III, p. 421.

[6] J. D. Michaelis, *Orientalische und exegetische Bibliothek* (1771), I, p. 190.

fewer than nine different hands in the book, placing them all in a comparatively late period.[7]

For the next half-century scholars generally followed Bleek in adhering to the unity of the book,[8] but with the work of Lenormant came an emphasis upon divisive theories once more, and this trend was continued in the writings of Meinhold and Strack.[9] An important defense of the substantial unity of Daniel was made by Von Gall, and this standpoint was accepted by Pusey, Cornill, and others.[10] But the theory of multiple authorship returned in an article by Barton, which was followed by the work of Dalman and Preiswerk.[11] C. C. Torrey was influenced to some extent by Dalman in suggesting that the first section of Daniel had been compiled in the third century B.C., while the remainder was composed during the Maccabean period, a view that was adopted by Kent, Montgomery, Eissfeldt, and Vriezen.[12]

Hölscher assigned the first six chapters of Daniel to the third century B.C., and the seventh to a slightly later period, with the remainder being of Maccabean origin,[13] an opinion that he appears to have modified subsequently by lowering the date of the early chapters considerably.[14] This view was followed in the main by Meinhold, Gressmann, Kuhl, and, to some extent, by Albright and Nyberg.[15] A development of the theory of Hölscher whereby the first seven chapters were regarded as constituting a unit, with the remainder coming from a considerably later

[7] L. Bertholdt, *Daniel neu übersetzt und erklärt* (1806), I, pp. 49ff., 83ff.

[8] F. Bleek, *Theologische Zeitschrift*, III (1822), pp. 171ff.

[9] F. Lenormant, *La Divination et la science des présages chez les Chaldéens* (1875), pp. 169ff. J. Meinhold, *Die Composition des Buches Daniel* (1884), p. 38, *Beiträge zur Erklärung des Buches Daniel* (1888), pp. 68ff., *Das Buch Daniel* (1889), p. 262. H. L. Strack in *Realencyclopädie für protestantische Theologie und Kirche* (1880 ed.), VII, p. 419, and in O. Zöckler, *Handbuch der theologischen Wissenschaften* (1883), I, p. 165. He modified his views somewhat in his *Einleitung in das AT* (1898 ed.), p. 150.

[10] A. F. von Gall, *Die Einheitlichkeit des Buches Daniel* (1895), p. 15 *passim*. E. B. Pusey, *Daniel the Prophet* (1891 ed.), pp. 80f. C. H. Cornill, *Einleitung in die kanonischen Bücher des AT* (1905), p. 243.

[11] G. A. Barton, *JBL*, XVII (1898), pp. 62ff. G. Dalman, *Die Worte Jesu* (1898), p. 11. H. Preiswerk, *Der Sprachenwechsel im Buche Daniel* (1902), pp. 115ff.

[12] C. C. Torrey, *Transactions of the Connecticut Academy of Arts and Sciences*, XV (1909), pp. 241ff. C. F. Kent, *The Growth and Contents of the OT* (1926), pp. 130f. J. A. Montgomery, *A Critical and Exegetical Commentary on the Book of Daniel* (1927), p. 90. O. Eissfeldt, *Einleitung in das AT* (1934 ed.), pp. 574ff.; cf. *ETOT*, pp. 520f. Th. C. Vriezen, *Oud-israelietische Geschriften* (1948), pp. 230f.

[13] G. Hölscher, *Theologische Studien und Kritiken*, XCII (1919), pp. 113ff.

[14] G. Hölscher, *RHPR*, IX (1929), p. 108.

[15] J. Meinhold, *Einführung in das AT* (1932 ed.), p. 355. H. Gressmann, *Der Messias* (1929), p. 346. C. Kuhl, *Die drei Männer im Feuer* (1930), pp. 77ff. W. F. Albright, *JBL*, XL (1921), pp. 116f. H. S. Nyberg, *Svenskt Bibliskt Uppslagsverk*, I (1948), col. 345.

period, was postulated by Welch, Eerdmans, and Weiser.[16] Haller maintained that chapter 7 was the oldest in the book, dating from the fourth century B.C., and in this opinion he was supported by Noth, who assigned chapter two to this period also.[17] A return to the theory of multiple authorship occurred in the writings of Ginsberg, who claimed to detect indications of no fewer than six separate authors in the book.[18]

In the meantime, however, there were staunch defenders of the unity of Daniel among both critical and conservative scholars, including Driver, Bewer, Charles, Möller, Wilson, Rowley, Pfeiffer, Hackman, and Young.[19] Although the majority of Roman Catholic scholars have defended the unity of authorship and the traditional sixth-century B.C. date of composition, a few including Lagrange, Bigot, Bayer, and Junker assigned the writing of the book as a whole to the Maccabean period.[20]

The foregoing selection will be sufficient to indicate the great divergence of opinion regarding the questions of integrity and authorship, and, by implication, the date of the book or its supposed parts. This very situation is unfortunately self-defeating, for as Rowley has pointed out, if there is so little consensus of opinion as to which were the earlier parts, it is difficult to have much confidence in the method whereby these varying results were reached.[21]

Arguments for diversity of authorship on the ground that the book contains two languages can no longer be sustained in the light of current information regarding the literary patternism of the ancient Near East.[22] As has already been mentioned in connection with Job, the

---

[16] A. C. Welch, *Visions of the End* (1922), p. 54. B. D. Eerdmans, *De Godsdienst van Israël* (1930), II, pp. 49ff., *The Religion of Israel* (1947), pp. 222, 249. A. Weiser, *Einleitung in das AT* (1949 ed.), p. 234; cf. *OTFD*, p. 313.

[17] M. Haller, *Theologische Studien und Kritiken*, XCIII (1920), pp. 83ff. M. Noth, *Theologische Studien und Kritiken*, XCVIII (1926), pp. 143ff.

[18] H. L. Ginsberg, *Studies in Daniel* (1948), pp. 5ff., 27ff.; cf. his *Studies in Koheleth* (1950), p. 42.

[19] *DILOT*, pp. 497ff. J. A. Bewer, *The Literature of the OT*, pp. 418f. R. H. Charles, *Critical and Exegetical Commentary on the Book of Daniel* (1929), pp. xxx ff. W. Möller, *Der Prophet Daniel* (1934), pp. 4ff. R. D. Wilson, *Studies in the Book of Daniel*, I (1917), II (1938). H. H. Rowley, *Darius the Mede and the Four World Empires in the Book of Daniel* (1935), pp. 176ff.; *RSL*, pp. 248ff. *PIOT*, pp. 760ff. G. G. Hackman in H. C. Alleman and E. E. Flack (eds.), *OT Commentary* (1948), p. 779. E. J. Young, *The Prophecy of Daniel* (1948), pp. 19f.; *YIOT*, pp. 360ff.

[20] M. J. Lagrange, *RB*, I (1904), pp. 494ff. L. Bigot in *Dictionnaire de Théologie Catholique* (1911), IV, cols. 63ff. E. Bayer, *Danielstudien* (1912), pp. 1ff. H. Junker, *Untersuchungen über literarische und exegetische Probleme des Buches Daniel* (1932), pp. 101ff.

[21] *RSL*, p. 248.

[22] For early attempts to explain this phenomenon see J. A. Montgomery, *A Critical and Exegetical Commentary on the Book of Daniel*, pp. 96ff.

device of enclosing the main body of a composition within the linguistic form of a contrasting style so as to heighten the effect of the work was commonly employed in the construction of single, integrated writings in the corpus of Mesopotamian literature. On the basis of this evidence, therefore, Daniel ought to be understood to form a unified and consciously formulated literary integer, involving Aramaic and Hebrew components.[23]

C. THE DATING OF THE BOOK

1. History of criticism. Although *Baba Bathra* 15*a* indicated that the "Men of the Great Synagogue" had had a part to play in the editing of Daniel, the uniform view of Hebrew and Christian tradition was that Daniel was an historic person who composed his book in the sixth century B.C. One of the first to question this outlook was the Neoplatonic philosopher Porphyry, who lived in the third century after Christ.[24] During a period of residence in Sicily he wrote a fifteen-volume work entitled *Against the Christians*, in which he endeavored to refute the leading tenets of Christianity. His opus was ordered suppressed by Constantine, but nevertheless it survived to the point where Theodosius II commanded it to be destroyed in A.D. 448. The composition is no longer extant, but portions of the twelfth book, in which Porphyry inveighed against Daniel, were preserved in the commentary on Daniel by Jerome.

On the ground that the later chapters depicted the events of the Maccabean age so accurately, Porphyry denied a sixth-century B.C. date for the book, and instead assigned it to the time of Antiochus Epiphanes. Unfortunately Porphyry commenced his reasoning from the *a priori* assumption that there could be no predictive element in prophecy (*si quid autem ultra opinatus sit, quia futura nescient, esse mentitum*), so that the work could only be historical in nature, and therefore of a late date. This formidable heathen antagonist of the Christian faith maintained that the author of Daniel had lied in order to revive the hopes of contemporary Jews in the midst of their adversities. Apparently Porphyry believed that Daniel had been written in Greek originally, since he employed the version of Theodotion for his diatribe, and sought to demonstrate a date of composition for the book within the Greek period by relating it etymologically to the *Story of Susanna*.

[23] For earlier studies in the Aramaic of Daniel see R. D. Wilson, *Biblical and Theological Studies by Members of the Faculty of Princeton Theological Seminary* (1912), pp. 261ff.; G. R. Driver, *JBL*, XLV (1926), pp. 110ff., 323ff.; W. Baumgartner, *ZAW*, XLV (1927), pp. 81ff.; H. H. Rowley, *The Aramaic of the OT* (1929).

[24] For an account of his criticism of Daniel see E. J. Young, *The Prophecy of Daniel* (1953), pp. 317ff.

In the medieval era a Jewish rationalist named Uriel Acosta (1590-1647) claimed that Daniel had been forged in order to support the doctrine of a bodily resurrection. A century later the book received some attention at the hands of an English deist named Anthony Collins, who, in an appendix to his work, *The Scheme of Literal Prophecy Considered* (1727), sought to dispute the integrity of the extant composition. This theme was taken up with considerable imagination by Bertholdt in 1806, as has been noted previously,[25] and from that time onwards any rejection of the literary integrity of Daniel involved the dating of the later chapters in terms of the Maccabean revolt.

The German literary-critical movement seized avidly upon the supposition that the prophecy could contain no predictive element, and repudiated the Jewish and Christian tradition of a sixth-century B.C. date of composition for the book, despite the arguments of some conservative scholars.[26] Objections to the historicity of Daniel were copied uncritically from book to book, and by the second decade of the twentieth century no scholar of general liberal background who wished to preserve his academic reputation either dared or desired to challenge the current critical trend. Since this position was obviously of great importance to those who maintained it, some appraisal of its principles and contents may well be desirable.

At the outset it has to be stated that there can be no question whatever as to the influence that the views of Porphyry exercised over the minds of those scholars who denied a predictive element to Hebrew prophecy. For them, prophecy consisted in forthtelling rather than foretelling, so that any aspect of the latter could have no place in true prophecy. Although this view was widely proclaimed in critical circles it was never by any means a unanimous opinion, and was challenged by such responsible authorities as Ackerman, Gunkel, and Guillaume.[27] Its basic shallowness is apparent upon even the slightest consideration of the extant literary prophets, who not merely spoke of contemporary events and circumstances, but pronounced upon happenings in the more distant future, and even uttered occasional prophecies concerning things that had no immediate or causal relationship to the events of their own

---

[25] L. Bertholdt, *Daniel neu übersetzt und erklärt* (1806), I, pp. 49ff.

[26] E.g. E. B. Pusey, *Daniel the Prophet* (1885); J. E. H. Thompson, *Daniel* (1897); C. H. H. Wright, *Daniel and His Prophecies* (1906), *Daniel and His Critics* (1906); J. D. Wilson in S. M. Jackson (ed.), *The New Schaff-Herzog Encyclopedia* (1909), III, pp. 347ff.; R. D. Wilson, *Studies in the Book of Daniel*, I (1907); A. C. Welch, *Visions of the End* (1922); G. Stokmann, *Die Erlebnisse und Gesichte des Propheten Daniel* (1922); C. Boutflower, *In and Around the Book of Daniel* (1923), *Dadda-'Idri, or the Aramaic of the Book of Daniel* (1931).

[27] H. C. Ackerman, *Anglican Theological Review*, IV (1921), p. 116. H. Gunkel, *The Expositor*, I (1924), p. 433. A. Guillaume, *Prophecy and Divination*, p. 111.

time. As Rowley has pointedly remarked in this connection, the common modern antithesis between foretelling and forthtelling would have had little meaning for the ancient Israelites, since the prophets were commonly engaged in predicting the future, frequently as it arose from contemporary happenings, though by no means exclusively so.[28]

2. *Internal objections to the traditional viewpoint.* If it can thus be conceded that prophecy may on occasions contain a distinctive element of prediction, it may be possible to examine a further objection to the traditional authorship as raised in critical circles. This consists of the allegation that Daniel is replete with historical inaccuracies or errors, and that these are of a kind that a responsible author in the sixth century B.C. would not have committed or tolerated.

a. Daniel 1:1. Characteristic of this approach is the allegation that the reference in Daniel 1:1 can only be regarded as an anachronism, since the verse implies the capture of Jerusalem and conflicts with the testimony of Jeremiah (Jer. 25:1, 9; 46:2), who spoke in the following year as though the Chaldeans had not yet conquered Jerusalem. This alleged error actually rests upon a scholarly misunderstanding of methods of chronological reckoning in antiquity. Superficially Daniel 1:1 refers to the arrival of Nebuchadnezzar to besiege Jerusalem in the third year of Jehoiakim, whereas Jeremiah 25:1 implies that this event took place in the fourth year of Jehoiakim, which was equated with the first year of King Nebuchadnezzar of Babylon.

This difference of one year can be accounted for by the fact that in Babylonia the year in which the king ascended the throne was designated specifically as "the year of the accession to the kingdom," and this was followed by the first, second, and subsequent years of rule. In Palestine, on the other hand, there was no accession year as such, so that the length of rule was computed differently with the year of accession being regarded as the first year of the particular reign. Daniel thus reckoned according to the Babylonian system of chronology, while Jeremiah followed the normal Palestinian pattern. Consequently, the third year of the Daniel-system of computation would be identical with the fourth year in that employed by Jeremiah, an explanation that removes the alleged difficulty.

It should be noted also that the reference in Daniel does not state that Jerusalem was captured in the third year of Jehoiakim (605 B.C.), but merely indicates that Nebuchadnezzar took with him to Babylonia certain Judaean hostages as evidence of good faith on the part of Jehoiakim, whom Nebuchadnezzar rightly suspected of being a political opportunist. This accords with the general situation depicted in Jeremiah 25:1, where the actual fall of Jerusalem had not yet taken place. Had

[28] *RSL,* pp. 125f.

the author of Daniel been an unknown Jew of the second century B.C., as critical scholars have been wont to insist, it is unlikely that he would have followed the obsolete Babylonian chronological system of computation in preference to his own Palestinian method, which had the sanction of so important a personage as the prophet Jeremiah.

b. "Chaldean." A second objection has been raised in connection with the fact that in Daniel the term "Chaldean" was employed in an ethnic sense and also in a restricted context to denote a group of wise men, a usage that occurs nowhere else in the Old Testament and is not found on inscriptions. This, it has been commonly assumed, is an inaccuracy, and is characteristic of a period considerably later than the sixth century B.C. A difficulty of this sort can be resolved quite readily by reference to the work of Herodotus (*ca.* 450 B.C.), who in his *Persian Wars* consistently spoke of the Chaldeans in ethnic terms, recognized their priestly office, and accepted the fact that certain of their religious procedures went back to at least the time of Cyrus.[29]

It is important to note in this connection that, in point of fact, the Old Testament did use the term "Chaldean" in an ethnic sense, along with secular cuneiform sources. As early as the tenth century B.C. the Assyrian annals employed the designation *kaldu* to designate the "Sea-land" of earlier cuneiform inscriptions. Ashurnasirpal II (883-859 B.C.) distinguished the peoples of this area from those of the more northerly reaches of Babylonia, while Adad-Nirari III (811-783 B.C.) recorded at the beginning of his reign the names of several Chaldean chiefs who were prominent among his vassals. When Merodach-Baladan (Marduk-apla-iddina II), chief of the Chaldean district of Bat-Yakin, sought his independence from Assyria after the death of Sargon in 705 B.C. and sent an embassy to Hezekiah of Judah, the prophet Isaiah warned of the dangers inherent in supporting the Chaldean rebels (Isa. 23:13) and foretold their defeat (43:14). The accession of Nabopolassar to the Babylonian throne in 626 B.C. saw the commencement of a regime during which he, as a native Chaldean, made the designation "Chaldean" an extremely reputable one, a tradition that was continued by such eminent successors as Nebuchadnezzar, Amel-Marduk (Evil-Merodach), Nabonidus, and Belshazzar, the latter being designated "king of the Chaldeans" in Daniel 5:30.

As Wiseman has pointed out, the prominence of the classes of priests who at Babylon and other centers maintained the ancient traditions of astrology and philosophy in the classical Babylonian languages led to the application of the designation "Chaldean" both to priests (Dan. 3:8), astrologers, and educated persons (Dan. 2:10; 4:7; 5:7, 11),[30] which is in general accord with the testimony of Herodotus. Against the objection

---

[29] Cf. Herodotus, *Hist.,* I, 181ff.
[30] D. J. Wiseman, *NBD,* p. 204.

that Daniel, as a pious Jew, would not have allowed himself to become initiated into such a class of "wise men," it needs only to be said that the narrative makes no such claim, merely remarking that Daniel was given political authority over all the wise men of Babylon (Dan. 2:48f.), and that it was because of his God-given ability as a seer (Dan. 1:17), not as the result of professional Babylonian training in the magical arts.

c. *Nebuchadnezzar's disease.* Another objection commonly urged against the historical accuracy of Daniel subsists in the statement that "history knows nothing of the madness of Nebuchadnezzar reported in Daniel."[31] In order to assess the accuracy of this statement it is necessary to examine the attitude of the Mesopotamian peoples towards mental illness, and also to observe the extent to which later traditions and other evidence either substantiate or repudiate it. The inhabitants of the ancient Near East were always highly superstitious, and while every form of disease was regarded as the malign work of the underworld deities who entered into the apertures of the head and began to create disturbances within the body itself, the incidence of mental affliction was regarded as possession *par excellence* by demonic powers. In consequence the mentally infirm were accorded a degree of fear and superstitious veneration that was never bestowed upon individuals who were the victims of other kinds of pathology, and this fact accounts for the general attitude adopted in the Old Testament narratives towards madmen.[32] This unholy dread of the mentally ill has persisted in the Orient to the present day, where there are far fewer facilities for the hospital treatment of mental conditions than for other kinds of illnesses. It can also be observed that a similar attitude of superstition is by no means unknown in the modern western world, where traditional medieval approaches to the problems of insanity die very hard. In antiquity, therefore, the most that could be done with a mentally disabled person was to banish him from society (cf. Mark 5:3), and to let subsequent events take their normal course.

History is, however, by no means silent as to the madness of Nebuchadnezzar, despite the understandable reluctance of contemporary writers to record or discuss the matter. It was only some three centuries after the death of Nebuchadnezzar that a Babylonian priest named Berossus preserved a tradition stating that Nebuchadnezzar was taken ill suddenly towards the end of his reign. As recorded in the writings of Josephus,[33] Berossus stated that, after a reign of forty-three years, Nebuchadnezzar became sick within a very short time of commencing the construction of a certain wall, and subsequently died. Since sickness prior to death was so common, then as now, there would seem to have

---

[31] S. A. Cartledge, *A Conservative Introduction to the OT* (1943), p. 221.
[32] Cf. R. K. Harrison, *IDB*, III, p. 220.
[33] *Contr. Apion.*, I, 20.

been no point in recording the matter had it not actually comprised a discreet way of referring to some embarrassing ailment that polite persons refrained from mentioning.

A different tradition, as preserved by Eusebius, went back to Abydenus (second century B.C.), and this recorded that in the last days of Nebuchadnezzar the king was "possessed by some god or other,"[34] and going up to the roof of his palace he announced the coming of a "Persian mule" (Cyrus) who would bring the people of the land into slavery. Having uttered this startling prediction he then disappeared from the city. This tradition seems to be a somewhat garbled reflection of the narrative in Daniel 4:31, but on the other hand it may have been preserved in such a form deliberately so as to conceal the presence of mental derangement and thus avoid an offense against propriety.

Of considerably greater importance was the recovery by Sir Henry Rawlinson of a damaged Babylonian inscription from the period of Nebuchadnezzar II. When translated it read as follows:

> For four years the seat of my kingdom in my city...did not rejoice my heart. In all my dominions I did not build a high place of power, the precious treasures of my kingdom I did not lay out. In the worship of Merodach my lord, the joy of my heart in Babylon, the city of my sovereignty, I did not sing his praises and I did not furnish his altars, nor did I clear out the canals.[35]

This notice in itself is all the more remarkable because of the magnificent and extensive building projects that were undertaken during the reign of Nebuchadnezzar, and equally because of the comparative scarcity of inscriptions from his later years.

In the light of the foregoing information it may be instructive to make a closer examination of the tradition preserved in Daniel 4. In modern psychiatric terminology Nebuchadnezzar would be described as suffering from paranoia, a mental disorder characterized by a lack of integrated relationship with environmental reality, which is generally complicated by the presence of systematized delusions. The entire mental situation is usually independent of other symptoms of mental imbalance, so that to the untrained eye paranoia, which is quite common in its incidence, might not present too unusual an appearance, and might even be interpreted in terms of a fluctuation of mood by someone who did not know the difference between neuroses and psychoses.

The illness described in Daniel, however, constitutes a rare form of *monomania*, a condition of mental imbalance in which the sufferer is deranged in one significant area only. The particular variety of monomania described is known as *boanthropy*, another rare condition in which Nebuchadnezzar imagined himself to be a cow or a bull, and

---

[34] *Praep. Evang.*, IX, 41.
[35] Cf. H. Rawlinson, *Historical Evidences of the Truth of the Scriptural Records* (1859), pp. 185, 440 n. 29; R. K. Harrison, *IDB*, I, p. 851.

acted accordingly. The European "werewolf" legends are based upon another infrequently encountered form of monomania known as *lycanthropy*. Rendle Short described yet another variety, *avianthropy*, in which the patient was convinced that he was a cock-pheasant, and roosted in a tree each night instead of sleeping in a bed.[36]

A great many doctors spend an entire, busy professional career without once encountering an instance of the kind of monomania described in the book of Daniel. The present writer, therefore, considers himself particularly fortunate to have actually observed a clinical case of boanthropy in a British mental institution in 1946. The patient was a man in his early twenties, who reportedly had been hospitalized for about five years. His symptoms were well-developed on admission, and diagnosis was immediate and conclusive. He was of average height and weight with good physique, and was in excellent bodily health. His mental symptoms included pronounced anti-social tendencies, and because of this he spent the entire day from dawn to dusk outdoors, in the grounds of the institution. He was only able to exercise a rather nominal degree of responsibility for his physical needs, and consequently was washed and shaved daily by an attendant. During the winter of 1946-47, when the writer observed him, he wore only light underclothing and a two-piece suit, with or without a sweater, during his daily peregrinations. The attendant reported to the writer that the man never wore any kind of raincoat or overcoat, and that he had never sustained such ill effects as coryza, influenza or pneumonia.

His daily routine consisted of wandering around the magnificent lawns with which the otherwise dingy hospital situation was graced, and it was his custom to pluck up and eat handfuls of the grass as he went along. On observation he was seen to discriminate carefully between grass and weeds, and on inquiry from the attendant the writer was told that the diet of this patient consisted exclusively of grass from the hospital lawns. He never ate institutional food with the other inmates, and his only drink was water, which was served to him in a clean container so as to make it unnecessary for him to drink from muddy puddles. The writer was able to examine him cursorily, and the only physical abnormality noted consisted of a lengthening of the hair and a coarse, thickened condition of the finger-nails.

Without institutional care the patient would have manifested precisely the same physical conditions as those mentioned in Daniel 4:33. After having passed through a difficult and debilitating period occasioned by the Second World War and its aftermath, the writer was soberly impressed by the superb physical condition of the patient. His skin exhibited all the clinical indications of a healthy body; his muscles were firm and well-developed, his eyes were bright and clear, and he ap-

[36] A. R. Short, *The Bible and Modern Medicine* (1953), p. 65.

peared to manifest a total immunity to all forms of physical disease. According to the attendant he was quiet in his behavior, reasonably co-operative for one so far divorced from reality, and never damaged institutional property.[37]

From the foregoing it seems evident that the author of the fourth chapter of Daniel was describing quite accurately an attestable, if rather rare, mental affliction. The Biblical source contains none of the legendary accretions detectable in the accounts of Berossus and Abydenus, and for this and other reasons the present writer regards it as an accredited historical record preserved by one who, because of his nationality, was under no particular obligation to conceal or distort the facts of the case so as to spare the royal family and the court officials any embarrassment. Despite this, however, the narrative presented the clinical facts with discrimination and good taste, and bears all the marks of a genuine contemporary or near-contemporary record.

d. Nabonidus and the book of Daniel. The discovery of a manuscript fragment in the fourth Qumran cave containing the "Prayer of Nabonidus"[38] has given rise to speculation that the mental affliction described in Daniel 4 was wrongly attributed to Nebuchadnezzar, and should have been associated instead with Nabonidus.[39] The fragment purported to preserve the prayer which Nabonidus, king of Assyria and Babylon, "the great king, prayed when he was smitten with a serious inflammation by the command of the Most High God in the city of Teima." According to this portion of manuscript, Nabonidus confessed his sin, a Jewish priest was sent from the Babylonian exiles to him, and he furnished a partial interpretation of the significance of the ailment.

According to Freedman, who with the majority of modern scholars assumed the Maccabean origin of Daniel, the Qumran manuscript appeared to have preserved the "older" tradition in regarding Nabonidus, rather than Nebuchadnezzar, as the victim of the illness, and this indicated to him that the Qumran community included Babylonian Jews who had migrated to Palestine long after the sixth-century B.C. return. Freedman followed Milik in supposing that the substitution of Nebuchadnezzar for Nabonidus occurred after the story had been brought to Palestine, where recollections of Nabonidus were dim. This theory is based upon the supposition that the book of Daniel in its extant form was the work of a Palestinian author who lived about 165 B.C. Now, assuming that the Qumran sect was in fact of Maccabean origin, as the majority of scholars maintain, it would follow on the dating of Freedman

---

[37] The foregoing is an extract from personal files, summarized in parentheses in *IDB*, I, p. 851.

[38] J. T. Milik, *RB*, LXIII (1956), pp. 407ff.

[39] D. N. Freedman, *BASOR*, No. 145 (1947), pp. 31f., following S. Smith, *Babylonian Historical Texts Relating to the Capture and Downfall of Babylon* (1924), pp. 36ff.

that if the Qumran community did not actually compile the work, it had access to the earliest completed form of Daniel. That this prophecy was unquestionably popular with the sectaries is evident from the number of fragments and copies of the book found in the Qumran caves. But since all these manuscripts are copies, and not the original composition, the date of the autograph of Daniel must of necessity be advanced by half a century at the very least, so as to allow the absolute minimum of time for the book to circulate and be accepted as Scripture.

Further evidence from 1Q seems to refute the dating assigned by Freedman and others to Daniel, for of three fragments of the book recovered from that cave,[40] two proved to be related palaeographically to the large Isaiah scroll, while the other was very similar in form to the Habakkuk script. The text was substantially the same as that of the Massoretes, the principal differences being in the matter of orthography. If this relationship is as genuine as scholars think, it will demand a significant upward adjustment of the Maccabean dating of Daniel so popular in critical circles, since as Burrows has pointed out, Isaiah certainly comes from a time several centuries before the earliest date to which the large Isaiah scroll can be assigned on any grounds.[41] While, at the time of writing, the Daniel manuscripts from Qumran have yet to be published and evaluated, it appears presumptuous, even in the light of present knowledge, for scholars to abandon the Maccabean dating of certain allegedly late Psalms and yet maintain it with undiminished fervor in the case of Daniel when the grounds for such modifications are the same.

Precisely why, as Milik alleges, the author of Daniel should have employed the "Prayer of Nabonidus" as the basis for his narrative in the fourth chapter of the book, but altered the names and the locale, is far from easy to determine. Burrows suggested that a modification of the original story had occurred in process of transmission rather than the kind of deliberate literary transformation entertained by Milik and Freedman.[42] This theory, however, ignores the fact that there was already a strong historical tradition associating Nabonidus with Teima, and that, among Semitic peoples, popular tradition was likely to remain virtually unchanged for many generations. When he suggests that the western habit of relating obscure and perhaps apocryphal incidents about well-known personalities underlies the transformation of the Daniel tradition as exhibited by the "Prayer of Nabonidus," he commits the serious methodological error of attempting to interpret the functioning of the oriental mind in terms of its occidental counterpart.

[40] G. E. Wright, BA, XII, No. 2 (1949), p. 33.
[41] M. Burrows, The Dead Sea Scrolls, p. 109.
[42] M. Burrows, More Light on the Dead Sea Scrolls (1958), p. 174.

So far from actually solving the problems relating to the provenance and date of Daniel 4, this theory goes far towards complicating the issue. Although there is much about the life of Nabonidus that is still unknown,[43] there is no tradition extant which specifically described him as a madman, even though some of his acts, such as absenting himself for long periods from the Babylonian *akîtu* festival, were unconventional by the standards of those days. Furthermore, while Milik is correct in his assertion that the Qumran "Prayer of Nabonidus" contains pathological elements that are "unknown to medicine," the same cannot in any sense be maintained for the account in Daniel, which, as has been shown above, falls into a recognized clinical category of psychotic states. The ailment mentioned in the "Prayer of Nabonidus" had to do with inflammation of the tissues, a condition that even the least adept of laymen can differentiate from mental affliction.

In their comparisons, Milik and Freedman have not paid adequate attention to the differences between the two sources, for it is quite clear that entirely separate traditions are involved here. Fragmentary though the Qumran "Prayer of Nabonidus" is, there can be no doubt that it belongs properly to the realm of folk-lore and popular tradition, and that in all probability it preserved an account of some illness, whether of a staphylococcal or other variety, that overtook Nabonidus during his period of residence in Arabia. It is unnecessary to suppose that he was virtually unknown in Palestine, since the extent of his activities in the neighborhood of Teima would almost certainly be familiar to the residents of Jerusalem and its environs.

To the present writer the Qumran "Prayer of Nabonidus" must be assigned to the area of legend, and in consequence is most probably haggadic in nature. The apocryphal additions to the book of Daniel, to judge by their popularity and persistence, show that the Biblical tradition of Daniel attracted a good deal of legendary material, and it may well be that the Qumran "Prayer of Nabonidus" is to be related to the type of pietism that produced the stories of Bel and the Dragon and of Susanna. On the other hand, it may perhaps constitute a near-contemporary of the apocryphal composition entitled The Prayer of Manasseh, to which it is closely related both in form and content.

The fact that the "Prayer of Nabonidus" was first found at Qumran might indicate that it was itself written in the Maccabean period, and it is not beyond the bounds of possibility that it originated with the Qumran sectaries. There is certainly nothing in its content which requires a date much in advance of the early Maccabean period, and it may perhaps be as late as about 100 B.C. While the present writer would agree with Freedman that there is no connection between the "Prayer of Nabonidus" and Daniel 4, he fails to see how, in the light of the

[43] Cf. A. L. Oppenheim, *IDB*, III, pp. 493ff.

arguments adduced above, the Qumran fragment can be said to underlie the tradition of Daniel in any sense, as Milik and others have assumed.

e. Belshazzar and Nabonidus. Yet another objection to the historicity of Daniel has involved the relationship between Belshazzar and Nabonidus. According to Daniel the former was king, whereas in cuneiform records it was Nabonidus, father of Belshazzar, who was actually the ruler of the Neo-Babylonian empire before it fell to Cyrus in 539 B.C. This difficulty has been resolved by archaeological discoveries that have shown that, for much of the reign of Nabonidus, his eldest son Belshazzar acted as co-regent. When Nabonidus took up residence in Teima, Belshazzar exercised sole rule in Babylonia, and for this reason was represented as the last king of Babylon in Daniel (Dan. 5:30).[44] The reference in Daniel 5:18 to Belshazzar as a son of Nebuchadnezzar is also correct according to Semitic usage, where the term "son" could also mean "grandson," for which there was no separate word, or simply "descendant," "offspring." As far as ancient royalty was concerned, the interest was predominantly in the succession itself rather than in the actual lineal relationship of individuals. In any event, according to Dougherty, Nitocris, the mother of Belshazzar, was apparently the daughter of Nebuchadnezzar, which would make for lineal descent as represented in Daniel.[45]

It seems clear from a straightforward reading of the narratives in the work that the author possessed a more accurate knowledge of Neo-Babylonian and early Achaemenid Persian history than any other known historian since the sixth century B.C. Even Pfeiffer, who was one of the more radical critics of Daniel, was compelled to concede that it will presumably never be known how the author learned that the new Babylon was the creation of Nebuchadnezzar, as the excavations have proved, and that Belshazzar, mentioned only in Babylonian records, in Daniel, and in Baruch (1:1), which is based upon Daniel, was functioning as king when Cyrus took Babylon in 539 B.C.[46]

This need not remain a mystery, however, if it is supposed that the author of the composition wrote considerably nearer to the time of the events themselves than the majority of modern critics have been prepared to allow. Quite evidently the writer knew enough about the customs of the sixth century B.C. to depict Nebuchadnezzar as able to enact and modify Babylonian laws with absolute sovereignty (Dan. 2:12f., 46), while representing Darius the Mede as being completely powerless to change the laws of the Medes and Persians (Dan. 6:8f.; cf. Est. 1:9; 8:8). Again, he was quite accurate in recording the change from

---

[44] Cf. R. P. Dougherty, *Nabonidus and Belshazzar* (1929), pp. 105ff.; *LAP*, pp. 189ff.

[45] R. P. Dougherty, *Nabonidus and Belshazzar*, pp. 59ff., 194.

[46] *PIOT*, pp. 758f.

punishment by fire under the Babylonians (Dan. 3:11) to punishment by being thrown to lions under the Persian regime (Dan. 6:7), since fire was sacred to the Zoroastrians of Persia.[47] In connection with the tradition of the "fiery furnace," it has been customary for many centuries to associate the ground fires at Baba Gurgur, near Kirkuk in Iraq, which are caused by gases seeping through cracks in the oil-rich ground, with the scene of the punishment meted out to Daniel and his companions, but this identification is at best uncertain.

In precisely the same way the author of Daniel was acquainted with the reasons for the setting up of the image of Nebuchadnezzar in the Plain of Dura, and the injunction compelling the populace to worship before it. Archaeological discoveries have shown that the ambitious building projects of Nebuchadnezzar extended to some of the ancient Sumerian cities, as, for example, to Ur of the Chaldees. Here he restored the huge complex of the temple dedicated to the moon-deity Nannar, and in the process he remodeled the building and raised the entire level of the outer court. This work appears to have been undertaken in the spirit of religious reformation, for when Woolley conducted excavations at the site he discovered that the rooms that the sacred hierodules and priestesses had occupied near the sanctuary had been removed completely during the work of renovation. A space had been cleared in front of the sanctuary, and an altar had been set up in full view of the worshippers, so that they could observe the priest as he performed his rituals and made his offerings in public on the altar.

This was a distinct departure from earlier procedures, since the ritual acts of the ministrant constituted secrets known only to the priesthood. It seems clear, therefore, that Nebuchadnezzar had initiated a program of religious reform that sought to modify the sensuous rituals of antiquity and permit the worshipping public to participate as a group in the sacrificial offerings. This reform of ritual is reflected in Daniel 3, which records the decree ordering the people to worship an image of the king that had been set up by royal command in the Plain of Dura in such a manner that all would have ready access to it. As Woolley commented on this situation:

> What was there new in the king's act? Not the setting up of a statue, because each king in turn had done the same; the novelty was the command for general worship by the public: for a ritual performed by priests the king is substituting a form of congregational worship which all his subjects are obliged to attend.[48]

f. Darius the Mede. A final argument against the historicity of Daniel is to be found in the long dispute about the identity of Darius the Mede. As this matter has already been discussed in an earlier section of the

[47] Cf. A. T. Olmstead, *History of the Persian Empire* (1948), p. 473.
[48] *UC,* pp. 151f.

present work, it will be sufficient at this point to observe that by far the most satisfactory solution to the problem has been provided by the researches of Whitcomb.[49] He has shown from cuneiform sources that two persons, Ugbaru and Gubaru, were mentioned in the Nabonidus Chronicle, and that Ugbaru, governor of Gutium, was associated with the fall of Babylon in 539 B.C., dying shortly afterwards, perhaps of wounds sustained in the battle. Upon this, the other individual, Gubaru, who was mentioned in numerous cuneiform texts, was appointed by Cyrus as the "Governor of Babylon and the Region beyond the River," and it is he who is now regarded as the most suitable individual for the designation of Darius the Mede.[50]

This personage is not mentioned as such by name outside the book of Daniel, and contemporary cuneiform inscriptions do not leave room for any king of Babylon between Nabonidus, Belshazzar, and the accession of Cyrus of Persia. On this and other grounds Rowley sought to show that the Old Testament records of the reign of Darius the Mede were actually a conflation of confused traditions.[51] Unfortunately Rowley's attempt to introduce clarity into a hitherto obscure situation was vitiated by the fact that his entire position was based upon arguments from inadequate and misleading secondary sources that failed to draw a distinction between Ugbaru and Gubaru. Thus his conclusions must be regarded at best as highly subjective and historically unreliable.

Any suggestion to the effect that the writer placed Darius I before Cyrus and made Xerxes the father of Darius I (cf. Dan. 6:28; 7:1) ignores the fact that Daniel was referring to Darius the Mede.[52] It is difficult to see how an intelligent second-century B.C. Jewish author could possibly have made such blunders as the critical scholars have ascribed to the compiler of Daniel, particularly if he had access to the writings of Ezra. Had the work contained as many frank errors as are usually credited to it, it is certain that the book would never have gained acceptance into the canon of Scripture, since it would have emerged very poorly by comparison with the writings of secular historians such as Herodotus, Ctesias, Menander, and others whose compositions are no longer extant.

It can only be concluded that the critical case against the historicity of Daniel has survived to the present because its adherents have failed to take a second and more critical look at the arguments that have been propounded so unimaginatively and with such tedious repetition in recent times. By contrast, when Dougherty had compared the statements

[49] J. C. Whitcomb, *Darius the Mede* (1959).
[50] Cf. W. F. Albright, *JBL*, XL (1921), pp. 112f.
[51] H. H. Rowley, *Darius the Mede and the Four World Empires in the Book of Daniel* (1935).
[52] So *PIOT*, p. 757.

of Daniel 5 with the cuneiform evidence that was available to him at that time, he came to the firm conclusion that the view that the chapter originated in the Maccabean period was thoroughly discreditable.[53] If, as many critics claim, the book is the work of one author, the remarks of Dougherty would thus apply to other sections of Daniel as well.

3. *External objections to the traditional viewpoint.* The fact is that critical scholars have made out an extremely poor case for a Maccabean dating (for example, the summary by S. B. Frost, *IDB*, I, p. 765), and the weaknesses of their position have become even more evident since the discovery of the Qumran manuscripts. Although an almost desperate appeal has been made to the fact that Daniel occurs in the third section of the Hebrew canon rather than among the prophets in the second section as an indication of late date, this circumstance merely testifies that Daniel was not regarded as having occupied the prophetic office as such. He was not a prophet in the classic sense associated with Amos, Isaiah, Jeremiah, and others of the literary coterie for the simple reason that he did not function as a spiritual mediator between God and a theocratic community, despite the fact that he was endowed with certain conspicuous prophetic gifts. Like Joseph of old, he was a Hebrew statesman in a heathen court,[54] and not a "writing prophet" or spiritual mediator in the commonly understood sense.

External evidence for a Maccabean date has been adduced by liberal scholars from the absence of the name of Daniel in the catalog of famous Israelites in Ecclesiasticus 44:1ff. Since this source was in extant form by about 180 B.C., it implies that the author knew nothing either of Daniel or his book. However, it seems difficult to conceive of such a traditional figure as Daniel being unknown to a second-century B.C. Hebrew sage, particularly in view of the fact that, according to critical theories, the sagas of Daniel were about to be written and received with enthusiasm by the populace. The shallowness and erroneous nature of such a position has been amply demonstrated by the Qumran discoveries, which make it impossible to deny the popularity of Daniel at that period, if the numbers of copies and fragments of the composition may be taken as furnishing any indication at all of the situation.

A proper assessment of the evidence provided by Ecclesiasticus should include recognition of the possibility that Ben Sira deliberately excluded Daniel from his list of notables for unknown reasons, as he did also with Job and all the Judges except Samuel, as well as Kings Asa and Jehoshaphat, Mordecai, and even Ezra himself. Ecclesiasticus is clearly limited in its usefulness as a ground of appeal for establishing the historicity of certain well-known Hebrew personages, if, indeed, it should ever be employed at all in this manner. It can be remarked, however,

---

[53] R. P. Dougherty, *Nabonidus and Belshazzar*, p. 200.
[54] E. J. Young, *The Prophecy of Daniel*, p. 20.

that there are allusions to Daniel and his book in Maccabees (1 Macc. 2:59ff.), Baruch (1:15–3:3), and the *Sibylline Oracles* (III, 397ff.), all of which are at least second-century B.C. compositions, and these works attest to the familiarity of the Daniel tradition at that time.

The linguistic evidence that critical scholars once advanced with such enthusiasm as proof of a Maccabean date for Daniel has undergone sobering modification of late as a result of archaeological discoveries in the Near East. In 1891 S. R. Driver could write quite confidently that the Persian words in Daniel presupposed a period of composition after the Persian empire had been well established; the Greek words demanded, the Hebrew supported, and the Aramaic permitted a date subsequent to the conquest of Palestine by Alexander the Great in 332 B.C.[55] This aphorism was widely quoted by English writers in succeeding decades, and as far as the Aramaic sections were concerned, H. H. Rowley sought to substantiate the assertions of Driver by means of several publications and articles.[56] However, subsequent discoveries and studies have shown the dangers inherent in appealing to the presence of Aramaic elements as incontrovertible evidence for a late date of composition. The term "Aramaic" is actually of a rather general order, and is employed to describe a group of Semitic dialects closely related to Hebrew and even more closely related to one another. Of the four groups established by linguistic research, namely Old Aramaic, Official Aramaic, Levantine Aramaic, and Eastern Aramaic, the first constituted the language of north-Syrian inscriptions dating from the tenth to the eighth century B.C., where Official Aramaic also took its roots. This latter was already being employed in governmental offices during the Assyrian period (*ca.* 1100-605 B.C.), and in the succeeding Persian period it was clearly the *lingua franca* of diplomacy and other areas of human activity, even though the Persian monarchs employed a system of cuneiform signs in which to carve royal inscriptions in their own Old Persian language. Aramaic "dockets" were already becoming attached to cuneiform tablets in Assyrian times, the purpose being to furnish a brief indication of names and dates connected with the tablet, as well as a summary of its contents. Official Aramaic was still in use on "dockets" throughout the Hellenistic period (330-30 B.C.), as well as on coins, on papyri and ostraca from Egypt, on Mesopotamian and Egyptian inscriptions, and in some bilingual inscriptions from Asia Minor. Levantine Aramaic appears to have arisen with the early Aramean nomads who penetrated Syria and Palestine, and despite the widespread use of Greek during the Hellenistic period Levantine Aramaic was still the popularly spoken language in New Testament times. Eastern Aramaic originated with the

---

[55] *DILOT*, p. 508.
[56] H. H. Rowley, *The Aramaic of the OT* (1929), pp. 23ff.; cf. his articles in ZAW, L (1932), pp. 256ff., and in *JRAS* (1933), pp. 777ff.

nomadic Arameans who invaded the Tigris-Euphrates region, and some of the dialects survived until Muslim times. As far as the Biblical record is concerned, the antiquity of Aramaic as a spoken language in dialect form can be seen in the use by Laban in Genesis 31:47 of the Aramaic designation Jegar-sahadutha of the cairn that Jacob described by the Hebrew form Galeed or "witness-heap." Again, as Young has pointed out, certain Aramaisms that were commonly regarded as late in form have been demonstrated in the Ras Shamra texts of the Amarna Age, and have been seen to include specific ones occurring in Daniel.[57]

The studies of Rosenthal[58] have shown that the kind of Aramaic employed in Daniel was that which grew up in the courts and chancelleries from the seventh century B.C. on and subsequently became widespread in the Near East. Thus it cannot be employed as evidence for a late date of the book, and in fact it constitutes a strong argument for a sixth-century B.C. period of composition. The Aramaic sections of Daniel (2:4b–7:28) are by nature closely akin to the language of the fifth-century B.C. Elephantine papyri and that of Ezra (4:7–6:18; 7:12-26),[59] while the Hebrew resembles that of Ezekiel, Haggai, Ezra, and Chronicles, and not the later Hebrew of Ecclesiasticus, as some writers have maintained, arguing from Hebrew fragments preserved in rabbinic quotations and also from the Syriac of the Peshitta version. More recent studies in Biblical Aramaic have cast grave doubts upon the advisability of distinguishing sharply between eastern and western branches of the linguistic group, as older scholars were wont to do,[60] thus seriously weakening the force of the assertion by Driver.

It is now known that Persian loan-words in Daniel[61] are consistent with an earlier rather than a later date for the composition of the book. In this connection scholars have now become aware that the term "satrap," which was once thought to have been Greek in origin, was actually derived from the Old Persian form *kshathrapān*, which also occurred in cuneiform inscriptions as *shatarpānu*, giving rise to the Greek term "satrap."[62] That Persian words should be used of Babylonian institutions prior to the conquests of Cyrus need not be as surprising as Driver supposed,[63] since the work was written in the Persian rather than

[57] E. J. Young, *The Prophecy of Daniel*, pp. 23, 274; YIOT, p. 371.

[58] F. Rosenthal, *Die Aramaistische Forschung* (1939), pp. 66ff.; cf. H. L. Ginsberg, *JAOS*, LXIi (1942), pp. 229ff. Cf. W. Baumgartner, ZAW, XLV (1927), pp. 123f.; H. H. Schaeder, *Iranische Beiträge* (1930), I, p. 253. For a careful treatment of the Aramaic of Daniel see K. A. Kitchen, *Notes on Some Problems in the Book of Daniel* (1965), pp. 31ff.

[59] Cf. K. A. Kitchen, *NBD*, p. 59.

[60] E.g. Th. Nöldeke, *EB*, I, col. 282; *DILOT*, pp. 502f.

[61] *DILOT*, p. 501; cf. K. A. Kitchen, *Notes on Some Problems in the Book of Daniel*, pp. 35ff.

[62] Cf. L. della Vida, *BASOR*, No. 87 (1942), pp. 29ff.

[63] *DILOT*, p. 501.

the Neo-Babylonian period. In the interests of objectivity it should be noted in passing that the Persian terms found in Daniel are specifically Old Persian words, that is to say, occurring within the history of the language to about 300 B.C. This would indicate that the Aramaic of Daniel in this respect at least is pre-Hellenistic, and that it did not draw upon any Persian expressions or terminology that might have become current after the fall of that empire.

The presence of three Greek names for musical instruments translated as "harp" (קיתרס, Dan. 3:5, 7, 10, 15; RSV "lyre"), "sackbut" (סבכא, 3:5, 7, 10, 15; RSV "trigon"), and "psaltery" (פסנתרין, 3:5, 7, 10, 15; RSV "harp") was also adduced by earlier critics as pointing to a Maccabean rather than an earlier period of composition.[64] This argument no longer constitutes a serious problem in the criticism of the book, because as Albright has shown, it is now well recognized that Greek culture had penetrated the Near East long before the Neo-Babylonian period.[65] The early nature and extent of Greek influence in the entire area can be judged from the presence of Greek colonies in mid-seventh-century B.C. Egypt at Naucratis and Tahpanhes, as well as by the fact that Greek mercenary troops served in both the Egyptian and Babylonian armies at the Battle of Carchemish in 605 B.C.

Furthermore, while the names of the instruments mentioned may appear to be Greek in nature, the instruments themselves are of Mesopotamian origin. The "harp" can probably be identified, according to Werner, with one of the many Asiatic precursors of the classical Greek *kithara*,[66] and being a strictly secular instrument it fitted quite well into the picture of the banquet of Nebuchadnezzar. The antiquity of the lyre in the Near East has been amply demonstrated by the work of Woolley at Ur, precluding the necessity of positing a Greek original for this type of instrument. The "sackbut" or *trigon* was another variety of chordophone, which may have been similar to, or derived from, the *sabitu* or seven-stringed lyre of the Akkadians. Among the Greeks the *sambuke* was of ill repute as the instrument played by vulgar musicians and prostitutes,[67] and of such general character as to earn its rejection from Plato's ideal Republic (III, 399d). The "psaltery," also translated "harp," was the old dulcimer, the Persian-Arabic *santir*, and its occurrence both on Assyrian reliefs and in eastern Mediterranean culture in the first millennium B.C. generally is amply attested.

In the light of the foregoing evidence, therefore, the arguments for the Maccabean dating of Daniel can hardly be said to be convincing. Such a

---

[64] On these instruments see T. C. Mitchell and R. Joyce, *Notes on Some Problems in the Book of Daniel*, pp. 19ff.

[65] *FSAC*, p. 337.

[66] Z. Werner, *IDB*, III, p. 475.

[67] Macrobius, *Satir.* III, 1417.

period of composition is in any event absolutely precluded by the evidence from Qumran,[68] partly because there are no indications whatever that the sectaries compiled any of the Biblical manuscripts recovered from the site, and partly because there would, in the latter event, have been insufficient time for Maccabean compositions to be circulated, venerated, and accepted as canonical Scripture by a Maccabean sect.

As Pfeiffer has indicated, the book has no real antecedents in Hebrew literature,[69] and suggestions to the effect that the work may have been based upon earlier Babylonian[70] or Egyptian[71] models are entirely without foundation. Folk-tales or legends cannot be posited successfully as the sources for the first six chapters of the work, and the same holds true for the remainder of the composition, despite attempts to discover a background of Babylonian mythology for chapter seven[72] and astrology for chapter eight,[73] or to think in terms of written, though not necessarily non-Jewish, material as underlying the eleventh chapter.[74]

D. THE APOCALYPTIC SECTION

The first six chapters of the book consist of selected incidents from the life of Daniel, which because of their narrative form and content doubtless commended themselves to the exiles from a comparatively early period and made for easy memorization. The remainder of the book comprised an anthology of visions that Daniel had at various periods, and the entire composition was arranged in simple bifid form. While the narratives and visions are set in general chronological order, the visions commence before the stories come to an end. This general arrangement would suggest that if the work was not actually written by Daniel himself in the sixth century B.C., it was compiled shortly thereafter, and in the view of the present writer it was extant not later than the middle of the fifth century B.C.

The apocalyptic sections of Daniel have for many years occasioned considerable discussion in scholarly circles. Part of the difficulty has arisen because of the general critical interpretation of the four temporal kingdoms in the second chapter in terms of Babylon, Media, Persia, and Greece respectively. This view was based upon the concept that the

---

[68] Cf. W. S. LaSor, *The Amazing Dead Sea Scrolls* (1956), pp. 42ff.

[69] *PIOT*, p. 766.

[70] J. A. Montgomery, *A Critical and Exegetical Commentary on the Book of Daniel*, pp. 77f.; G. H. Dix, *JTS*, XXVI (1925), pp. 241ff.

[71] C. C. McCown, *Harvard Theological Review*, XVIII (1925), pp. 357ff.

[72] Cf. H. Gunkel, *Schöpfung und Chaos* (1895), pp. 323ff.; J. A. Montgomery, *A Critical and Exegetical Commentary on the Book of Daniel*, pp. 321ff.; O. Eissfeldt, *Baal Zephon* (1932), pp. 25ff.; E. G. Kraeling, *Oriental Studies in Honor of D. S. C. E. Pavry* (1934), pp. 238ff.

[73] F. Cumont, *Klio*, IX (1909), pp. 263ff.

[74] G. A. Barton, *JBL*, XVII (1898), p. 76.

book implied the existence of an independent Median kingdom between the fall of Babylon and the rule of Cyrus.[75] However, the history of the Median kingdom allows no room for such an eventuality,[76] and a careful reading of the text of Daniel also fails to support such a view. The final word of the mystic message in Daniel 5:28 implied that the Neo-Babylonian kingdom was to succumb to a dual monarchy, with the Persians (*Paras*) rather than the Medes as the dominant power.[77] When Darius the Mede established his administration he was immediately subject to the "law of the Medes and Persians" (Dan. 6:8, 12, 15), which would not have been the case if Media had been an independent kingdom at that time.

As Whitcomb has pointed out, the mention of the Medes before the Persians is evidence of the early date of the narrative, since in later times the Persians usually took precedence in this respect (e.g. Est. 1:3, 14, 18f., but not 10:2; cf. 1 Macc. 6:56).[78] Finally, Daniel nowhere states that Darius was the king of the Medes or the king of Media, but simply notes that he was a Mede. On this basis, therefore, it seems correct to suppose the second kingdom of the four to have been Medo-Persia, and the third kingdom Greece.

According to many critical scholars the author of Daniel followed the erroneous precedent of Isaiah (13:17; 21:2) and Jeremiah (51:11, 28), according to which the Medes were the sole conquerors of Babylon in 539 B.C., as they had been of Nineveh in 612 B.C.[79] How this theory could ever have arisen is somewhat of a mystery, since one of the Isaiah references (21:2) speaks explicitly of Elam and Media as the joint-conquerors of Babylon, a point that was conceded by Rowley.[80] Be that as it may, archaeological discoveries have shown that it was quite

---

[75] As held by J. G. Eichhorn, *Einleitung in das AT* (1823 ed.), IV, pp. 483ff.; J. Bade, *Christologie des AT* (1850), III, 2, p. 79; F. Bleek, *Jahrbuch für deutsche Theologie*, V (1860), pp. 65f.; S. Davidson, *Introduction to the OT* (1862), III, p. 207; A. Kamphausen in *Völlstandiges Bibelwerk für die Gemeinde* (1867), III, pp. 640ff., *EB*, I, col. 1006; K. H. Graf in D. Schenkel (ed.), *Bibel-lexikon* (1869), I, p. 567; W. Vatke in H. G. S. Preiss (ed.), *Historisch-kritische Einleitung in das AT* (1886), p. 653; E. Reuss, *Die Geschichte der Heiligen Schriften des AT* (1890), p. 601; E. Schürer, *Geschichte des jüdischen Volkes im Zeitalter Jesu Christi* (1901-11 ed.), III, p. 265; K. Marti, *Das Buch Daniel erklärt* (1901), pp. 15f., 48; C. Steuernagel, *Lehrbuch der Einleitung in das AT* (1912), p. 654; W. Baumgartner, *Das Buch Daniel* (1926), pp. 16ff.; R. H. Charles, *A Critical and Exegetical Commentary on the Book of Daniel*, pp. 167ff.; O. Eissfeldt, *Einleitung in das AT* (1934).

[76] Cf. J. C. Whitcomb, *Darius the Mede*, pp. 68ff.

[77] E. J. Young, *The Prophecy of Daniel*, p. 127.

[78] J. C. Whitcomb, *Darius the Mede*, p. 55.

[79] So *PIOT*, p. 757.

[80] H. H. Rowley, *Darius the Mede and the Four World Empires in the Book of Daniel*, p. 58.

legitimate for Isaiah and Jeremiah to refer to the Medes as the conquerors of Babylon.

One aspect of the critical case against the historicity of Darius the Mede consisted of the allegation that the term "Mede" was wrongly used after 550 B.C., but on the basis of cuneiform evidence furnished by the Harran *stele* this argument is seen to be no longer valid. D. J. Wiseman has shown that this monument, in which Nabonidus described the events of his reign including his self-imposed exile to southern Arabia for ten years, spoke explicitly of the "king of the Medes" in the year 546 B.C., which was four years subsequent to the absorption of Media by Cyrus.[81] While the Medes were prominent in the capture of Babylon, they functioned as one part of the military forces under the command of Cyrus, and not as an independent entity. It would appear, then, that neither Isaiah, Jeremiah, nor Daniel was confused about the chronology of the Median empire, unlike a good many of their later critics.

The identity of the fourth kingdom has an important bearing upon the apocalyptic visions in the later chapters of Daniel. Thus in Daniel 7:6, the third beast represents the Greek empire rather than the Persian, as postulated by liberal critics, while the fourth beast (Dan. 7:7) is the Roman empire, which produced ten horns. This fourth beast differs radically in description from the he-goat of Daniel 8:5 symbolizing Greece, and thus can hardly be identified with the Greek empire, as critics have maintained.

Again, the "little horn" of Daniel 8:9, representing Antiochus Epiphanes, is quite different in character and function from the "little one" of Daniel 7:8, and so the latter cannot readily stand for Antiochus Epiphanes, as in the view of critical scholars. From this it would appear that they must represent two quite different concepts.[82] Since the beast of Daniel 7:4 is the last in the visionary series, it must depict an imperial power that followed Greece, namely, Rome. In Daniel 7:21 the "little horn" that emerged from the fourth beast was represented as engaging in conflict with the saints of God, prior to the time when they possessed the kingdom at the intervention of divine power.

In their attempts to interpret this enigmatic situation, some modern conservative commentators have seen the prophecies of the image, the four beasts, and the seventy weeks as culminating in the Incarnation of Christ and the fulfilment of the divine promises to the Jews.[83] Others, however, have thought of the apocalyptic passages in terms of references to the second coming of Jesus Christ. On the basis of the latter supposi-

---

[81] D. J. Wiseman, *Christianity Today*, II, No. 4 (1957), p. 10. Wiseman argued from this material for an identification of Cyrus with Darius the Mede, which was questioned by J. C. Whitcomb, *Darius the Mede*, p. 47.

[82] E. J. Young, *The Prophecy of Daniel*, p. 288.

[83] Cf. E. J. Young, *The Prophecy of Daniel*, pp. 17, 158ff., 220ff., *YIOT*, pp. 374ff.

tion, the horn that was to arise out of the final kingdom and subdue the three rulers (Dan. 7:24) constitutes the antichrist, who would persecute the saints of God for "a time, two times, and half a time" (Dan. 7:25, RSV). This phrase has been interpreted as an extent of three-and-a-half years when related to certain references in the New Testament book of Revelation (cf. 12:14, 16; 13:5) and envisaged in terms of the great tribulation, a supposition that was rejected by Young.[84] Exponents of this form of interpretation entertain the idea that the destruction of the antichrist will fall within the work of one "like unto a son of man" (Dan. 7:13), who comes "with the clouds of heaven" (cf. Matt. 26:64; Rev. 19:11ff.).[85]

The wars between the Ptolemies of Egypt and the Seleucids of Syria as depicted in the final two chapters of the book were introduced by means of a revelation to Daniel in chapter 10. These accounts have been commonly held by critics of orthodoxy as being too precise in their prediction of events to belong to the area of prophecy in the sense of foretelling. On closer examination, however, the visions with their accompanying interpretations are neither more nor less predictive and detailed than their counterparts in the earlier portions of the book, and if the visionary material in the later chapters of Daniel is to be rejected as fraudulent and spurious, the same considerations must be applied to that found in the beginning of the prophecy. As has been observed previously, Daniel was, like Joseph, a statesman in a heathen court, and in much the same manner Daniel possessed psychic gifts that enabled him to see and interpret visions. A comparison of the appropriate narratives will be sufficient to show that there was no fundamental difference between the activities of these two individuals in this regard.

The fact that the last two chapters of Daniel deal with historical rather than topical matters merely serves to give the visions added perspective. If it is granted that there is a predictive element in prophecy, this factor, combined with the psychic powers of a visionary, would be more than sufficient to produce the rather general descriptions recorded in Daniel 11 and 12. While these two sections are couched in the kind of mystical language appropriate to such a revelation, their contents evidence nothing that would be outside the powers of a gifted seer such as Daniel was reputed to be. Indeed, from such a person one might have expected considerably more clarification of certain elements in his vision, and less obscurity concerning such matters as the "little horn" of Daniel 7:8, which in any event is problematical, since it cannot be

[84] E. J. Young, *The Prophecy of Daniel*, pp. 195ff.
[85] For this view see A. C. Gaebelein, *The Prophet Daniel* (1911); H. A. Ironside, *Lectures on Daniel the Prophet* (1911); A. J. McClain, *Daniel's Prophecy of the Seventy Weeks* (1940); J. C. Whitcomb, *NBD*, p. 292; J. F. Walvoord, *Israel in Prophecy* (1962). For a study of the dispensational system see O. T. Allis, *Prophecy and the Church* (1945), pp. 16ff.

identified with Antiochus Epiphanes, as in Daniel 8:9. Had the book been written in the Maccabean period, as the majority of modern critics have claimed, such an obscure allusion would almost certainly never have arisen in the first place. Until more is known about the psychic factors that are involved in foresight and foretelling it would appear unwise to dismiss out of hand the claim of the author to have experienced the visionary material recorded in his work.

The theological standpoint of Daniel reflects that of Ezekiel in numerous respects. The doctrine of God as espoused by the former emphasized the transcendence of God as distinct from the approach of Jeremiah and the psalmists generally. While there appears to be a certain element of determinism in the mind of the author to the extent that he was able to think of all things as working out according to a predetermined plan, there is actually very little difference in this respect from the teachings of the eighth-century prophets, who maintained with conviction that God was firmly in control of the trend of events. Like them also the author of Daniel thought in terms of a unified approach to history, in which the coming of the Messiah was the culmination of a series of world empires, and the winding-up of the age a matter for divine rather than human decision.

The doctrine of resurrection contained in the book represents an advance upon the eschatology of the earlier prophets, although the coming kingdom was still thought of in a largely material manner. Whereas Hosea (6:1f.) and Ezekiel (37:11ff.) expected all Israel to be resurrected as a righteous nation, and Isaiah (24:1ff.; 27:1ff.) held that only the righteous individuals in the nation would experience resurrection, Daniel taught that wicked and righteous alike would be raised (12:2). Despite this, however, the thought of the book does not appear as advanced as that of the New Testament, which proclaimed a general resurrection of all mankind at the end of the age, prior to final judgment.

The angelology of Daniel is very similar to that found in Ezekiel, the concepts of which constituted an advance upon earlier ideas of rather impersonal divine messengers. The circumstances under which some of these angelic beings were described reflect at least a subconscious awareness by both Ezekiel and Daniel of the ponderous Babylonian statuary, although it is equally clear that in the minds of both authors the mythological elements associated with the Babylonian figures were completely lacking. While Daniel is somewhat vague on occasions in describing angelic beings (8:15; 10:18), the book recognizes that such entities possessed personalities, and even records the names attributed to two of them (8:16; 9:21; 10:13, 21; 12:1). Despite this, Daniel does not exhibit as elaborate an angelology as that found in later Jewish apocalyptic works like 1 Enoch, nor does it depict the position and activity of Gabriel in the manner found in the New Testament (cf. Lk. 1:11ff.). The angelic beings of Daniel were evidently a subordinate group, and only derived their authority and sense of mission from God. Although they seemed to possess a degree of freedom and independence, they were not represented as being able to act contrary to the divine will, as Jeffery asserted.[86]

The visionary material of Daniel has frequently been described in terms of "apocalypticism," which is popularly understood to have originated in Zoroastrianism, the religion of ancient Persia, and to comprise a dualistic, cosmic, and eschatological belief in two opposing cosmic powers, God and the evil one, and in two distinct ages, the present one, which is held to be under the power of evil, and the future eternal age in which God will overthrow the power of evil and reign supreme with His elect under conditions of eternal righteousness. While this approach has elements in common with the thought of certain Old Testament writers, it is important for a distinction to be drawn between Biblical and non-Biblical apocalyptic, and to avoid reading into the canonical Scriptures thought that either occurred in Jewish apocryphal and pseudepigraphal literature of a subsequent period, or that was foreign to the thought of Judaism altogether. In this connection it should be noted that the prophets of Israel placed the final redemption of the elect in this world. While the new order to be established by the coming of the divine kingdom would be continuous with the present world sequences, it would be different in that suffering, violence, and evil would be absent from the scene (Isa. 11:6ff.). This new era would be instituted by a divine visitation, and not by forces working immanently in history (Isa. 26:21). The course that events would take might be revealed as part of a vision, as in Daniel and Revelation. In fact, it is from the Greek word meaning disclosure that the term "apocalypse" has been derived. While developed apocalyptic writings generally contain the distinctive characteristics of dualism, determinism, pessimism about the conditions of the present age, and an ethical passivity on the part of the authors that precluded them from announcing divine judgments upon the people as did the prophets, caution should be urged in any approach to Biblical apocalyptic lest it be assumed that the visionary material in a book such as Daniel, or the non-visionary apocalyptic passage in Isaiah 24–27, is characteristic of oriental apocalypticism.

E. THE ORIGINAL LANGUAGE OF DANIEL

The question whether Daniel was originally written in Hebrew or Aramaic was a popular subject of discussion among critical scholars of an earlier period. The Hebrew sections of Daniel comprise 1:1 to 2:4a and chapters 8 to 12, while the Aramaic portion consists of 2:4b to 7:28. Dalman, Torrey, and Montgomery, among others, supposed that the first

---

[86] A. Jeffery, *IB*, VI, p. 351; H. H. Rowley, *The Relevance of Apocalyptic*, pp. 53f.

section was translated from an original Aramaic form into Hebrew, and that the visions were written subsequently in Hebrew, the first one of which had been rendered into Aramaic by a redactor.[87] Hölscher and Eissfeldt, however, maintained that chapter 7 was originally written in Aramaic, and so for them there merely remained the postulate that the introductory section of the book was a translation.[88]

A rather different view, proposed by Bevan, Von Gall, Prince, and others, following a theory advanced by Lenormant, maintained that the original language of the book was Hebrew, but that chapters 2 to 7 were lost subsequently, the lacunae being made up from an Aramaic translation.[89] R. H. Charles suggested that the entire work had originally been written in Aramaic, and that the first and the last four chapters were translated into Hebrew so as to secure ready acceptance of the composition into the Hebrew canon of Scripture.[90] This opinion was dismissed by Rowley, who held that chapters 2 to 7 were issued in Aramaic by a Maccabean author in order to encourage his fellows in their struggle for independence.[91] The eschatological visions were written in Hebrew, on the ground that they were less suitable for popular circulation; and as far as the introductory material was concerned the point of transition was determined by the amount that the author decided to rewrite, with the first chapter being translated into Hebrew when the entire collection was on the point of being issued. Such a theory of composition was quite properly rejected by Oesterley and Robinson as being unnecessarily complicated.[92] In view of the concrete evidence presented by other forms of ancient Near Eastern literature, there is now no reason whatever to regard Daniel as anything other than a consciously composed literary unit based upon such traditional patterns of structure as those reflected by the Code of Hammurabi and the book of Job.

❊ ❊ ❊ ❊ ❊

Since there is no targum of Daniel, all interpretations of the book must ultimately be based upon the MT. Broadly speaking, this is in good condition, a conclusion reinforced by the evidence of the LXX and other versions, which do not suggest the presence of significant textual corrup-

[87] G. Dalman, *Die Worte Jesu* (1898), p. 11. C. C. Torrey, *Transactions of the Connecticut Academy of Arts and Sciences*, XV (1909), p. 249. J. A. Montgomery, *A Critical and Exegetical Commentary on the Book of Daniel*, pp. 90ff.

[88] G. Hölscher, *Theologische Studien und Kritiken*, XCII (1919), pp. 113ff. O. Eissfeldt, *Einleitung in das AT* (1934 ed.), pp. 580f.

[89] A. A. Bevan, *A Short Commentary on the Book of Daniel* (1892), p. 27. A. von Gall, *Die Einheitlichkeit des Buches Daniel* (1895), p. 122. J. D. Prince, *A Critical Commentary on the Book of Daniel* (1899), p. 13.

[90] R. H. Charles, *A Critical and Exegetical Commentary on the Book of Daniel*, p. xlix; cf. K. Marti in E. Kautzsch and A. Bertholet, *Die Heilige Schrift des AT* (1923 ed.), II, p. 460.

[91] H. H. Rowley, ZAW, L (1932), pp. 256ff.

[92] *IBOT*, p. 341 n. 1.

tions. The LXX has survived in only one manuscript, Codex Chisianus, transcribed about the tenth century, and this document has revealed that the LXX was periphrastic in nature and marked by the presence of textual expansions. At an early period it was displaced in the Christian Church by the more literal version of Theodotion, which was used principally by the Church Fathers. But because there are characteristically "Theodotion" readings from Daniel in the works of authors who lived before his time, it would appear that Theodotion drew upon a version which long antedated him, and which he revised.[93]

The LXX and those versions that followed it in this regard inserted a lengthy passage after Daniel 3:23, known as the *Song of the Three Young Men*, found in English versions of the Apocrypha. In the LXX, the Syro-Hexaplar version, and the Vulgate, the apocryphal *Story of Susanna* appeared as a thirteenth chapter, while in the version of Theodotion Daniel opened with this narrative, which had presumably been placed in this position because it involved an alleged incident in the earlier life of Daniel. In the Greek versions and the Vulgate, a fourteenth chapter consisted of the twin narratives of *Bel* and *The Dragon*, being entitled in the LXX "From the prophecy of Habakkuk, son of Joshua, of the tribe of Levi."[94] The Latin versions represented the tradition of the Massoretic text, as did the Peshitta.

The manuscripts discovered at Qumran support the Hebrew-Aramaic text of Daniel in important areas, such as the transition to Hebrew at Daniel 7:28. Cross has remarked that the text of fragments from 4Q, while corresponding closely to the MT, also exhibits some rare variants that agree with the Alexandrian Greek against both the MT and Theodotion.[95]

Supplementary Literature

Bosanquet, J. W. *Messiah the Prince, or the Inspiration of the Prophecies of Daniel.* 1866.

Driver, S. R. *The Book of Daniel, with Introduction and Notes.* 1900.

Horner, J. *Daniel, Darius the Median, Cyrus the Great: A Chronologico-Historical Study.* 1901.

Keil, C. F. *Biblischer Commentar über den Propheten Daniel.* 1869.

Porteous, N. W. *Das Danielbuch.* 1962.

Riessler, P. *Das Buch Daniel erklärt.* 1902.

Wilson, J. D. *Did Daniel Write Daniel?* 1906.

Wright, C. H. H. *Daniel and Its Critics.* 1906.

Wyngaarden, M. J. *The Syriac Version of the Book of Daniel.* 1923.

---

[93] On this topic see J. A. Montgomery, *A Critical and Exegetical Commentary on the Book of Daniel,* pp. 43f.; B. J. Roberts, *The OT Text and Versions* (1951), p. 123.

[94] Cf. J. Linder, *Commentarius in Librum Daniel* (1939), pp. 521ff.

[95] F. M. Cross, *BA,* XIX, No. 4 (1956), p. 86.

II. THE BOOKS OF EZRA AND NEHEMIAH

A. NAME AND CONTENTS

The rabbinic authorities (cf. *Bab. Bath.* 15a) regarded the two books of Ezra and Nehemiah as a single composition attributed to Ezra. A similar opinion was also expressed by Josephus[1] and Melito of Sardis.[2] It was in the time of Origen (A.D. 185-253) that the mention of division into two works as being in accord with current Jewish usage first occurred. Jerome in his *Prologus Galeatus* considered Ezra and Nehemiah to be a unity, but in the Vulgate he recognized the existence of two separate works, designating Nehemiah as *liber secundus Esdrae,* and thereby established the precedent that grew into normal Christian practice.

From uncial manuscripts of the LXX it is evident that the two books were still joined together when the Greek recension was made, but by the time of Origen they had become separated in Greek versions, a procedure that had also extended to the Latin Bible when Jerome compiled the Vulgate. A Hebrew manuscript of 1448 introduced the division into two books, and this was sustained in the Bomberg edition of the Hebrew Bible in 1525.

Some confusion exists regarding the name Ezra or Esdras, since not merely was it the designation of the canonical works, but of a recension of the canonical writings commonly called the "Greek Ezra," and also of an apocalyptic composition in the Apocrypha. The canonical Ezra is designated Esdras B in most LXX manuscripts, and is the 1 Esdras of the Vulgate. The book of Nehemiah is the Esdras Γ of the LXX and 2 Esdras in the Vulgate. The "Greek Ezra" is designated 1 Esdras in many LXX manuscripts, but styled 2 Esdras in the Lucianic recension and 3 Esdras in the Vulgate. This work is printed in editions of the Apocrypha as 1 Esdras, and in the LXX it was entitled Esdras A in order to distinguish it from the canonical work. The pseudepigraphical apocalypse known as 2 Esdras was described as Esdras Δ in LXX manu-

---

[1] *Contr. Apion.* I, 8.
[2] In Eusebius, *Hist. Eccl.,* IV, 26.

scripts and 4 Esdras in the Vulgate. It is commonly styled 4 Ezra or the "Ezra Apocalypse."

Evidence for the close relationship of Ezra and Nehemiah in the Hebrew Bible is supplied by the fact that the Massoretic notes and comments, which normally occurred after each book of the Bible, were omitted after Ezra 10:44 and placed instead at the end of Nehemiah, thus marking the termination of the entire work. The Massoretic indication of the midpoint of the work occurred at Nehemiah 3:32, which is the middle of the combined books rather than of Nehemiah as a single composition. Yet despite the very common critical assertion that Ezra and Nehemiah were originally one, the fact that the second chapter of Ezra is repeated in Nehemiah 7:6-70 seems to point to the contrary. Had the work been a unified composition, there would have been absolutely no need whatever to repeat a lengthy list of Hebrew names. Nevertheless it is a fact that from a very early period the two books were recognized as one, and this may have occurred because Nehemiah continued the narrative history of Ezra, or alternatively, as Young has suggested, because of a desire to make the total number of canonical books agree with the number of letters in the Hebrew alphabet.[3]

Ezra and Nehemiah were placed in the third division of the Hebrew canon, and may have been regarded as canonical prior to 1 and 2 Chronicles, since the former recorded historical information that was not available from other sources, unlike 1 and 2 Chronicles, which related the narratives of Samuel and Kings with some alterations and additions. This might be one acceptable explanation of the order of these works in the Hebrew Bible, in which 1 and 2 Chronicles stand last. On the other hand, as Gordon has indicated, the chronological displacement might have been undertaken deliberately so as to conclude the Hebrew Bible on an optimistic note such as that which was supplied by the edict of Cyrus.[4]

The canon of the Syriac Church, of Theodore of Mopsuestia (d. *ca.* A.D. 428), of the Nestorians, and of many Monophysite groups omitted all of these works. The Babylonian Talmud placed Ezra and Chronicles after Esther, while some Palestinian manuscripts commenced the third section of the canon with Chronicles and ended it with Ezra, which they placed after Esther and Daniel. Some Old Latin manuscripts included Ezra and Nehemiah between Judith and the books of Maccabees, but Augustine put them between Maccabees and the Psalms. The order adopted in the English versions was based upon Alexandrian practice.

The books of Ezra and Nehemiah received their names from the principal characters of the narratives. The first composition opened with the proclamation of Cyrus (Ez. 1:1-4) permitting the Jewish exiles to

[3] *YIOT*, p. 378.
[4] *IOTT*, pp. 296f.

return to their native land under Sheshbazzar (Ez. 1:5-11). A register of those who returned was furnished (Ez. 2:1-70), and the task of restoring the traditional worship of God was undertaken. The altar was set up and the foundations of the Temple were laid (Ez. 3:1-13), the latter causing misgivings among those who remembered something of the majesty of the Solomonic structure.

The enemies of Judah and Benjamin sought to oppose the rebuilding of the Temple (Ez. 4:1-5), and the work was finally halted as the result of a letter sent to Artaxerxes (Ez. 4:6-24). A fresh beginning took place consequent upon the prophecies of Haggai and Zechariah, and despite protests to Darius the work continued (Ez. 5:1-17). Darius made inquiries concerning the decree of Cyrus, and as a result ordered the rebuilding of the Temple to continue (Ez. 6:1-12). On the third day of Adar in the sixth year of the rule of Darius, that is, in 515 B.C., the Temple was completed, and when the structure was dedicated the populace observed the Passover and the Feast of Unleavened Bread (Ez. 6:17-22).

After a considerable interval of time the events associated with Ezra himself took place. His lineage was furnished, and his commission from Artaxerxes described (Ez. 7:1-28). A list of those who accompanied him to Jerusalem in the seventh year of Artaxerxes was given (Ez. 8:1-14), followed by a description of events at the river by Ahava (Ez. 8:15-36). The mixed-marriage situation in Judaea caused Ezra much concern (Ez. 9:1-15), and reforms were undertaken (Ez. 10:1-17). The book terminated with a list of those among the priestly classes who had married foreign women.

The book of Nehemiah commenced with an introduction written in the first person, and stating the circumstances under which Nehemiah came to restore the city walls of Jerusalem. On hearing of the desolation of Judaea, he obtained permission to go to Jerusalem in an attempt to remedy the existing conditions (Neh. 1:1—2:20). The most pressing need was for a city wall, and accordingly Nehemiah mustered all available personnel for the task, beginning by erecting the Sheep Gate (Neh. 3:1-32). Samaritan opposition led by Sanballat and Tobiah threatened to halt the construction of the wall (Neh. 4:1-12), but as the result of resolute leadership by Nehemiah the work proceeded (Neh. 4:13-23).

Social abuses that were lowering the morale of the populace were corrected (Neh. 5:1-19), and further attempts by the Samaritan opposition to delay the rebuilding of the walls were frustrated (Neh. 6:1-19), the task being ultimately brought to fruition in fifty-two days. The register of Ezra 2 was repeated in Nehemiah 7:6-70, and the narrative continued with the renewal of the Covenant, in which Ezra played a prominent part (Neh. 8:1-18). Confession of sin was followed by a ratification of the Covenant provisions (Neh. 9:1-38) and the promise to obey (Neh. 10:1-39). A register of the inhabitants of Jerusalem and its environs (Neh. 11:1-36) was completed by means of a list of priests and Levites (Neh. 12:1-26). A description of the dedication of the walls (Neh. 12:27-47) and the existing abuses with their appropriate reforms (Neh. 13:1-31) concluded the work.

Traditionally Ezra was regarded as the work of the celebrated scribe, but this view has been rejected by many liberal scholars who regard Ezra and Nehemiah as having been shaped and transmitted by the anonymous author of 1 and 2 Chronicles.[5] The more extreme view of Torrey regarded this Chronicler as a person of considerable inventive skill, but one who was not averse to forging documents and distorting facts to suit his apologetic purposes.[6] He wrote many years after the events described, and may even have compiled his work as late as 250 B.C.[7] This theory was modified somewhat by less radically minded scholars to the point where it was thought that the Chronicler wrote Ezra and Nehemiah, as well as his own composition, but at a date much nearer that of the events themselves, and that he employed numerous historical sources as the basis of his narrative.[8]

B. The Criticism of the Book of Ezra

A number of arguments have been brought to bear upon the traditional view that Ezra was written in the fifth century B.C. One of the principal ones is that the title "king of Persia" was incorrect and superfluous, since the Persians were supreme rulers in the Near East and therefore did not need specific differentiation in relationship to other kingdoms. Furthermore, it was alleged, the title did not follow the customary designations of the day, such as "the king" (cf. Hag. 1:1, 15), "the great king" (as on the Cyrus Cylinder and other cuneiform sources), and "king of kings" or "king of the lands" (as in a Darius inscription).[9] R. D. Wilson long ago disposed of this particular objection when he pointed out that, in sources then available, eighteen different authors in nineteen different documents from the Persian period employed the designation "king of Persia" on thirty-eight different occasions with reference to at least six individual Persian monarchs.[10] As though this evidence were insufficient, Olmstead recorded one inscription that was dated about 600 B.C. and spoke of Ariyaramna, son of Teispes and brother of Cyrus I, as "the great king, king of kings, king of Parsa,"

[5] Cf. *PIOT*, p. 813; C. C. Torrey, *The Composition and Historical Value of Ezra-Nehemiah* (1896), pp. 57ff., *Ezra Studies* (1910), p. 211; *DILOT*, p. 544; *OTFD*, p. 319; R. A. Bowman, *IB*, III, p. 552.

[6] C. C. Torrey, *Ezra Studies*, pp. 250f.; cf. R. H. Pfeiffer, *IDB*, II, p. 217.

[7] *PIOT*, p. 811.

[8] W. Rudolph, *Esra und Nehemia* (1949), p. xxiii. Cf. L. S. Batten, *A Critical and Exegetical Commentary on the Books of Ezra and Nehemiah* (1913), p. 24.

[9] Cf. R. W. Rogers, *A History of Ancient Persia* (1929), p. 103.

[10] R. D. Wilson, *A Scientific Investigation of the OT* (1959 ed.), pp. 157f.

which should be sufficient in itself to dispose of all critical objections to the use of the title "king of Persia" by Ezra.[11]

A further criticism levelled against traditional theories of authorship has concerned the manner in which the author handled the chronology of the period mentioned in Ezra and Nehemiah.[12] More specifically it has been urged that Ezra 4:7-24 is misplaced chronologically, since it refers to the period of Xerxes I (486-465/4 B.C.) and Artaxerxes I (464-423 B.C.), and causes confusion by introducing events in improper relationship to the time of Darius I (522-486 B.C.).[13] This difficulty has been resolved by Young, who has shown that the avowed purpose of Ezra was to trace the entire history of opposition to the rebuilding of the Temple.[14] Such opposition appeared throughout the reigns of Cyrus (Ez. 4:1-5) and Darius (Ez. 4:24; 5:1-17), and was found even in the days of Xerxes I (Ez. 4:6), culminating in the reign of Artaxerxes I (Ez. 4:7-23) when a letter of complaint was dispatched to the king, resulting in the cessation of constructional activity. Having sketched the history of the controversy, the writer then reverted to the period of Cyrus and stated that the work ceased until the second year of Darius (Ez. 4:24), after which the topic was resumed in chapter five. Quite clearly chronological sequences were sacrificed in the interests of outlining the history of opposition to the task of rebuilding the Temple as a separate and self-contained subject.

Critics such as Pfeiffer have accused the Chronicler of a complete disregard for facts in stating that the people offered the daily sacrifices upon the altar before the Temple was built (Ez. 3:3),[15] apparently unaware that Haggai (Hag. 2:14) presupposed precisely this same sort of activity. An equally incautious criticism subsisted in the assertion that in Ezra 3:8 it was stated that the Levites commenced their religious service at the age of twenty, whereas in the Torah (Num 4:3; 8:24) they were required to be twenty-five or thirty before commencing such duties. This objection overlooks the fact that the Pentateuchal references were to service in the Tabernacle, whereas in Ezra (3:8) and 1 Chronicles (23:24; 31:17) it was the Temple that was being considered.

Confused thinking on the part of Pfeiffer led to the statement that Ezra entertained contradictions as to the time when the building of the Second Temple actually began.[16] According to Ezra 4:24 and 5:1ff., work commenced in the second year of Darius, whereas in Ezra 3:8ff.

---

[11] A. T. Olmstead, *History of the Persian Empire* (1959 ed.), p. 29; cf. R. D. Wilson, *PTR*, II (1904), pp. 257ff., 465ff., 618ff., III (1905), pp. 55ff., 238ff., 422ff., 558ff., XV (1917), pp. 90ff.

[12] E.g., *PIOT*, p. 822.

[13] *PIOT*, p. 829; *BCIA*, p. 13.

[14] *YIOT*, pp. 381f.

[15] *PIOT*, p. 822.

[16] *Ibid.*, p. 823.

and 5:16 it is said to have occurred in the reign of Cyrus. This objection rests entirely upon a misunderstanding of the text. The rebuilding of the Temple did in fact commence in the days of Cyrus (Ez. 3:8ff.; 5:16), but when opposition to the project arose (Ez. 4:1ff.), the work was delayed, and in the end it ceased until the time of Darius (Ez. 4:24), the interval thus occasioned being the principal cause why Haggai and Zechariah were sent to stimulate the people into activity (Ez. 5:1ff.). Haggai clearly implies that some preliminary work had been done at the site (Hag. 1:4, 9, 14), while for his part Ezra (Ez. 5:16) does not state that the task had been pursued smoothly and without interruption since its inception.

Another mistake on the part of Pfeiffer lay in his assumption that the "worthless concoction" of the Chronicler made Zadok a son of Ahitub and Ezra a son of Seraiah, since the latter is said to have died when Jerusalem fell (2 Kgs. 25:18ff.), thus making Ezra at least 127 years old when he went to Jerusalem in 458 B.C. While it is true that Ezra (7:1ff.) and 1 Chronicles (6:3ff., 50ff.) described Zadok as a son of Ahitub, the same statement occurs also in 2 Samuel 8:17. As far as the descent of Ezra is concerned, the writer is clearly using the term "son" as the equivalent of "descendant" when relating Ezra to Seraiah, as was commonly the case among Semitic peoples.

Archaeological discoveries have vindicated the authenticity of the official documents in Ezra in a signal manner. The decree of Cyrus by which the exiles were allowed to return to Judaea, and which appeared in two forms in Ezra (1:2ff.; 6:3ff.), is a matter of particular importance in this respect.[17] Older scholars frequently argued either that there was no evidence that Cyrus ever made a decree of this kind,[18] or that both versions of the decree were Jewish forgeries.[19] It is now apparent from the contents of the Cyrus Cylinder and the Nabonidus Chronicle that Cyrus was bent upon exploiting every opportunity for personal advancement, and one means of securing the good will of the various enslaved peoples in his empire lay in restoring the status of their dethroned deities and proclaiming a general amnesty for political prisoners in Babylonia.

Against such a background of polytheism it would be perfectly natural for Cyrus to treat the God of Israel as being of equal status with Marduk and the various deities of the captive national groups. Since Cyrus had employed the name of Marduk, god of Babylon, in proclaiming religious freedom within the empire,[20] there was every ground for following the same practice with respect to the Hebrew captives. Consequently there

[17] Cf. R. de Vaux, *RB*, XLVI (1937), pp. 21ff.
[18] E.g. C. C. Torrey, *Ezra Studies*, pp. 143ff.; W. O. E. Oesterley and T. H. Robinson, *A History of Israel* (1932), II, pp. 75, 81; *PIOT*, p. 821.
[19] Cf. R. H. Pfeiffer, *IDB*, II, p. 217.
[20] R. P. Dougherty, *Nabonidus and Belshazzar*, pp. 175ff.

can be no valid objection to the incidence of the name of the Israelite deity in the decree, regardless of whether or not Cyrus had been influenced by the prophecies of Isaiah, as has been maintained occasionally.[21]

When both decrees are compared with other royal proclamations in Mesopotamia and particularly with those of the Persian period, it becomes apparent that they are substantially accurate and authentic.[22] The first was designed for verbal utterance in the language of the particular national group to which it was addressed, while the second constituted a memorandum restricted to the official whose duty it was to implement the decisions contained therein.

The genuineness of the Aramaic correspondence occurring in the fourth chapter of Ezra has been strikingly vindicated by the discovery of the celebrated Elephantine papyri in 1903,[23] mention of which was made in an earlier part of this book. These documents indicate, among other things, that the rulers of the Persian empire took a genuine interest in the religious and social welfare of their subjects.[24] As far as Ezra is concerned, they are of great value because they indicate that the Aramaic used in the canonical book was the Imperial Aramaic characteristic of the age in which the book purported to be written, and consonant with it in matters of language and style.[25] There is some variation in the Biblical spelling of royal names from that current after the fifth century B.C., and it may be that the forms in Ezra were derived from Old Persian designations that were modified subsequently in Jewish orthography.[26]

Despite his name, Sanballat (Babylonian *Sin-uballit*) was almost certainly not Babylonian by birth, and with Tobiah was probably regarded by some of his contemporaries as being at least as devout a Jew as Ezra or Nehemiah. The names of Deliah and Shelemiah, which were given to

---

[21] Cf. W. Möller, *ZAW*, XVIII (1898), pp. 149ff.

[22] E. J. Bickermann, *JBL*, LXV (1946), pp. 254ff.; W. F. Albright, *Alexander Marx Jubilee Volume* (1950), pp. 61ff.

[23] Cf. *ANET*, pp. 222f., 491ff.; *ANE*, pp. 278ff.; *DOTT*, pp. 256ff.; A. Ungnad, *Aramäische Papyrus aus Elephantine* (1911); A. Cowley, *Aramaic Papyri of the Fifth Century B.C.* (1923); E. G. Kraeling, *The Brooklyn Museum Aramaic Papyri* (1953); cf. Kraeling, *BA*, XV, No. 3 (1952), pp. 50ff.

[24] *LAP*, pp. 201f.

[25] W. F. Albright in H. C. Alleman and E. E. Flack (eds.), *OT Commentary*, p. 154.

[26] H. H. Rowley, *BJRL*, XXXVII (1955), p. 536, maintained that the sources in question were not the original form of any sixth- or fifth-century B.C. Aramaic documents. Cf. W. Baumgartner, *ZAW*, XLV (1927), pp. 118, 122f., who assigned the Aramaic sections of Ezra to *ca.* 300 B.C., as against the period of 400-350 B.C. suggested by Albright, *JBL*, XL (1921), p. 119; cf. K. A. Kitchen, *NBD*, p. 59.

the sons of Sanballat, occurred in contemporary inscriptions from the Egyptian city of Elephantine,[27] and are unquestionably Hebrew rather than Egyptian in form.

Of two extra-Biblical sources testifying to the position of Geshem at this time, one consisted of a collection of silver vessels found at Succoth (Tell el-Maskhutah) in Egypt. Three of the bowls bore Aramaic inscriptions containing north-Arabic names, one of which read, "Qainu, son of Geshem (Gusham), king of Qedar,"[28] and was dated to the end of the fifth century B.C. The other inscription bearing the name of Geshem was recovered from Hegra in Arabia.[29] Taken together, these sources indicate that Geshem ruled over a powerful Arab kingdom that included Sinai, part of the Nile Delta, Edom, northern Arabia, and perhaps the southern part of Judah, where small altars similar to those from southern Arabia have been discovered.[30] This extensive Arab kingdom was under Persian control, with the local ruler functioning as a tributary.[31]

The family of Tobiah can be traced to the early second century B.C., as evidenced by the ruined family home at 'Araq el-Emir, north of the Jabbok River in Transjordan, which had been erected in the grand Hellenistic style between 200 and 175 B.C. by the last governor in the family. The name Tobiah is carved in Aramaic characters of the third century B.C. on the rock face near to the ancestral tombs.[32] Whether the name is that of the Tobiah who was a contemporary of Nehemiah, or else a descendant of the same name, is uncertain at the present. The Zeno papyri, discovered at Geraza in the Egyptian Fayyum, contained a letter from "Tobias the governor of Ammon" addressed to Zeno, an official in the government of Ptolemy II Philadelphus (285-246 B.C.), stating that Tobias was dispatching a shipment of animals. The author of this letter was unquestionably a descendant of the individual who opposed Nehemiah.[33]

Objections are sometimes raised to the number of exiles said to have returned to Judaea shortly after the decree of Cyrus. Accordingly it is urged that the 4600 men taken captive as mentioned in the records of Jeremiah 52:28ff. could hardly have increased over half a century to something in excess of 42,000 individuals who returned from captivity (Ezra 2:64), to say nothing of those Jews who had remained in Baby-

---

[27] *ANET*, p. 492; *ANE*, p. 281; *DOTT*, p. 264.

[28] I. Rabinowitz, *JNES*, XV (1956), pp. 1ff. Geshem was known as "Gashmu" in Neh. 6:6.

[29] Cf. F. V. Winnett, *A Study of the Lihyanite and Thamudic Inscriptions* (1937), pp. 14ff., 50f.; A. T. Olmstead, *History of the Persian Empire*, p. 295.

[30] *AP*, pp. 143f.

[31] Cf. F. M. Cross, *BA*, XVIII, No. 2 (1955), pp. 46f.

[32] *WMTS*, pp. 83, 133; *AP*, p. 149.

[33] *WMTS*, p. 111.

Ionia.[34] This difficulty is far more apparent than real, since it follows the pattern of the Exodus and similar traditions, where the large numbers were employed as symbols of the magnitude of the occasion with respect to the activity of God, and in this particular instance indicating the triumphant deliverance that God had achieved for His captive people.

Even a casual perusal of Ezra is sufficient to show that the narrative description is far from smooth, and this fact has been taken as having a bearing upon his sources, since gaps are found where material relating to a particular period, such as that of Cambyses (530-522 B.C.), was not available or was deemed irrelevant for the purposes of the narrative. The sources that have been detected in the work by scholars include the decree of Cyrus (Ez. 1:1-14), census and other lists (2:1-62; 8:1-14; 10:18-43), official documents and letters in Aramaic (4:7b–6:18; 7:12-26), and the Ezra Memoirs (principally 7:27f.; 8:1-34).

The first of these sources has already been examined and found to be accurate and historical. The list in chapter 2 appears to be a genuine compilation by Ezra (cf. Neh. 7:5)[35] and there seems to be no valid reason for dating it substantially later than 450 B.C. It comprised a catalog of the original returning exiles, and it is possible that it was subjected to a certain amount of correction or else supplemented by means of a few additional entries. Accordingly it is necessary to reject the radical views of Torrey and Pfeiffer that the list was in fact a concoction of the Chronicler,[36] and instead to uphold the historicity, not merely of the list itself, but also of Ezra.[37] Similarly there is no assured ground for rejecting the validity of the lists in Ezra 8:1-14 and 10:18-43, since both purport to relate to activity directly undertaken by Ezra himself, and were certainly within the scope of his knowledge and jurisdiction.

The Aramaic documents included some official pronouncements, but also contained certain narrative sections, as in Ezra 5:1-5, dealing with the prophecies of Haggai and Zechariah. The correspondence with Artaxerxes concerning the building of the wall was included in Ezra 4:8-23, while Ezra 5:6–6:12 contained the letter sent to Darius and a copy of his decree citing the edict of Cyrus concerning the building of the Temple. A promulgation by Artaxerxes that gave permission to Ezra and his company to journey to Jerusalem was preserved in Ezra 7:12-26. The historical validity of the Aramaic sections has been a matter of consider-

---

[34] R. H. Pfeiffer, *IDB*, II, p. 217.

[35] Cf. also H. L. Allrik, *BASOR*, No. 136 (1954), pp. 21ff.; K. Galling, *JBL*, LXX (1951), pp. 149ff.; J. O. Boyd, *PTR*, XI (1900), pp. 414ff.

[36] C. C. Torrey, *Ezra Studies*, p. 141 n. 5. *PIOT*, p. 822.

[37] As against M. Vernes, *Précis d'Histoire juive* (1889), pp. 579ff.; C. C. Torrey, *Ezra Studies*, pp. 238ff.; A. Loisy, *La Religion d'Israël* (1933 ed.), pp. 228f.

able debate, with older scholars regarding them as outright forgeries[38] and Pfeiffer concluding that they were written by the Chronicler some two centuries or so after the time of Darius.[39] On the other hand, the authenticity of the Aramaic letters was defended energetically by Meyer; and even Kosters, who rejected most of the Aramaic material as unhistorical, recognized that some of it was genuine.[40] Despite all critical attempts to prove the Aramaic sections in Ezra to be either forged, spurious, or late, archaeological discoveries relative to the Persian period have shown that they are in substantial agreement with what is known of the language and customs of the day.[41] As Wright has commented, the Aramaic of Ezra is precisely that of its age, while the government documents are of the general type commonly associated with the Persian regime.[42]

A further matter of discussion has been the scope of the "Ezra Memoirs," and this topic has attracted the attention even of those scholars who commonly regarded the material as unhistorical in nature.[43] The sections written in the first person are Ezra 7:27f., 8:1-34, and perhaps 9:3-15, which may have constituted verbatim extracts from written records. Material from the same or a similar source may be represented by passages speaking of Ezra in the third person, namely Ezra 7:1-10 and 9:1-10:44.

Some scholars have accepted the whole of Ezra 7 as constituting part of the "Memoirs," and these included Bleek, Schaeder, and Bewer.[44] Torrey restricted it to Ezra 7:1-10, 27f.,[45] while Cornill, Driver, and Sellin held that the Ezra narrative consisted of verses 12 to 28 of chapter seven.[46] Most modern scholars assign chapter eight to the "Memoirs" also, although Kosters and Oesterley and Robinson held that the original material concluded at verse 34,[47] while Batten restricted it to verses

---

[38] E.g. J. Wellhausen, *Nachrichten von der Königliche Gesellschaft der Wissenschaften zu Göttingen* (1895), pp. 109, 175f.; Th. Nöldeke, *Die Semitischen Sprachen* (1899 ed.), p. 35 n. 1; C. C. Torrey, *The Composition and Historical Value of Ezra-Nehemiah*, pp. 51ff., *Ezra Studies*, pp. 142ff.; H. H. Graetz, *Geschichte der Juden* (1911), II, 2, pp. 87n., 100n., 128n.; L. E. Browne, *Early Judaism* (1920), pp. 36ff., 44f.

[39] *PIOT*, p. 824.

[40] E. Meyer, *Die Entstehung des Judenthums* (1896), pp. 8ff. W. H. Kosters, *Die Wiederherstellung Israels in der persischen Periode* (1895), pp. 24f., 54ff.

[41] A. Lods, *Histoire de la littérature hébraïque et juive*, pp. 540ff.

[42] *WBA*, p. 208.

[43] See the bibliography in *PIOT*, pp. 830f.

[44] F. Bleek, *Einleitung in das AT* (1878 ed.), p. 282. H. H. Schaeder, *Esra der Schreiber* (1930), p. 9. J. A. Bewer, *The Literature of the OT*, p. 282.

[45] C. C. Torrey, *Ezra Studies*, p. 157.

[46] C. H. Cornill, *Introduction to the Canonical Books of the OT*, p. 244. *DILOT*, p. 550. E. Sellin, *Einleitung in das AT* (1950 ed.), p. 178.

[47] W. H. Kosters, *EB*, II, col. 1479. *IBOT*, p. 125.

15-19, 21-25, 28f., and 31f.[48] Chapter nine is generally conceded to the "Memoirs" also, though Eissfeldt regarded the first five verses only as genuine.[49] The tenth chapter is generally included in the corpus as well, although Kosters and Steuernagel maintained that the material was only based upon the original memoirs, and did not actually constitute part of them.[50]

C. THE CRITICISM OF THE BOOK OF NEHEMIAH

The book of Nehemiah, named after its principal character, recorded the mission of that eminent man to Jerusalem and the reforms that he subsequently instituted as part of his larger reconstructional activities. What Albright has described as his *apologia pro vita sua*[51] has been accepted as generally authentic in nature by the majority of scholars, although portions other than the memoirs of Nehemiah have been credited to the activity of the anonymous Chronicler.

The usual extent of the memoirs, including those portions that have been allegedly revised by the Chronicler, comprise Nehemiah 1:1– 7:72a; 11:1-2; 12:27-43, and 13:4-31. Nehemiah 13:1-3 is also thought to have been based upon the same source. Torrey regarded chapter three as the work of the Chronicler, but Batten denied this, and Rudolph suggested that Nehemiah had incorporated it into his own work.[52] Eissfeldt held that Nehemiah 12:27-43 was genuine, but Steuernagel restricted the authentic sections to verses 31f. and 37-40.[53] Torrey rejected chapter 13 entirely as in any case being the work of the Chronicler.[54] In general scholars have held that the memoirs were composed shortly after 432 B.C., with relatively little reworking,[55] and have seen a decided similarity between them and the memorial inscriptions commonly found in the ancient Near East.[56] It is also agreed that they comprise one of the most important and reliable historical sources for the post-exilic period in Judaea, and for the fifth century B.C. in particular.

[48] L. S. Batten, *A Critical and Exegetical Commentary on the Books of Ezra and Nehemiah*, pp. 16, 320ff.

[49] O. Eissfeldt, *Einleitung in das AT*, p. 586.

[50] W. H. Kosters, *EB*, II, col. 1479. C. Steuernagel, *Lehrbuch der Einleitung in das AT*, p. 421. Cf. L. S. Batten, *A Critical and Exegetical Commentary on the Books of Ezra and Nehemiah*, p. 17.

[51] *BPAE*, p. 90.

[52] C. C. Torrey, *The Composition and Historical Value of Ezra-Nehemiah*, pp. 37f. L. S. Batten, *A Critical and Exegetical Commentary on the Books of Ezra and Nehemiah*, p. 207. W. Rudolph, *Esra und Nehemia*, p. 211.

[53] O. Eissfeldt, *Einleitung in das AT*, pp. 588f.; *ETOT*, pp. 547ff. C. Steuernagel, *Lehrbuch der Einleitung in das AT*, p. 426.

[54] C. C. Torrey, *The Composition and Historical Value of Ezra-Nehemiah*, pp. 42ff.

[55] W. Rudolph, *Esra und Nehemia*, pp. 211f.

[56] Cf. N. H. Snaith, *OTMS*, pp. 112f.

Objections to the conservative view that Nehemiah was the author of his entire book have turned principally upon the reference in Nehemiah 12:11, 22, where mention was made of Jaddua, who was High Priest from 351-331 B.C. when Alexander the Great entered the city of Jerusalem. In this connection it should be noted that these references are found in a list of the priests and Levites, and it has been suggested by certain scholars that this may comprise a secondary addition to the text.[57] On the basis of such a hypothesis it would appear to be unwise to place too much reliance upon this section as a means of establishing a *terminus ad quem* for the composition of Nehemiah.

Some scholars have rejected the authenticity of Nehemiah 12:26, 47, where the phrase "in the days of Nehemiah" was used as though that period had already passed. This is not a serious objection, however, for the phrase was being employed to designate specific eras or periods such as those of Jehoiakim or Zerubbabel. Consistency suggests that the same usage would extend quite naturally to Nehemiah also, since it might have appeared somewhat strange had he employed a different style of reference to the period of his own activity. It should also be noted in passing that these verses are completely irrelevant as far as chronological considerations are concerned, since Nehemiah in his capacity as *tirshatha* or royal commissioner would certainly take priority over others in his own memoirs. In considering Nehemiah as a whole, there seem to be only highly subjective reasons for not regarding this work as the autobiography of the renowned civil governor of Judaea.

The chronological relationship between Ezra and Nehemiah and the question of the date when Ezra arrived in Jerusalem in order to begin his work have been subjects of heated debate for a prolonged period of time. The questions involved have been surveyed in an earlier chapter, and accordingly only a brief review will be undertaken here. While the majority of scholars regard Artaxerxes I Longimanus (464-423 B.C.) as the king under whom Nehemiah served, some writers have held that the king in question was Artaxerxes II Mnemon (404-359 B.C.).[58] Unfortunately this argument is based upon unreliable evidence from Josephus, and cannot be sustained historically.

More plausible was the suggestion that, whereas Nehemiah should be dated under Artaxerxes I, the work of Ezra more probably occurred during the reign of Artaxerxes II. This theory was first set out by Vernes,

[57] So H. Crosby, *The Book of Nehemiah* (1877), p. 2; M. Noth, *Überlieferungsgeschichtliche Studien I* (1943), p. 120 n. 1; W. Rudolph, *Esra und Nehemia*, p. xxiv.

[58] So J. Marquart, *Fundamente israelitischer und jüdischer Geschichte* (1897), p. 31; H. P. Smith, *OT History* (1906), pp. 382ff.; C. C. Torrey, *The Composition and Historical Value of Ezra-Nehemiah*, p. 65, *JBL*, XLVII (1928), pp. 380ff.; *The Second Isaiah* (1928), pp. 456ff.; in *Ezra Studies*, pp. 140, 355, Torrey tended to identify the king with Artaxerxes I.

and was developed by Van Hoonacker.[59] Despite criticisms from Kuenen, Kosters, and Kugler,[60] his opinions on the matter gradually attracted attention among both European and English-speaking scholars, who on the whole inclined favorably towards it.[61] Although it has received some modification in matters of detail over the years, and has won acceptance in some circles, it is of some interest to note that German scholars, with the possible exception of Hölscher,[62] have remained consistently unattracted to it. With all the support it has received it should be recorded, with Rowley,[63] that there has always been eminent opposition to it by both liberal and conservative writers, who have preferred instead to adhere to the traditional view. Albright regarded Ezra, Nehemiah, and Chronicles as the work of one author, whom he identified with Ezra, and thought that he had compiled Ezra-Nehemiah by affixing the memoirs of Nehemiah to his own version of his ministry in Jerusalem.[64]

The great variety of views expressed on the chronological relationship between Ezra and Nehemiah makes for a good deal of confusion in a situation in which, as Rowley has remarked, the evidence is insufficient for any demonstration, and nothing more than probability can be claimed for whatever solution is ultimately adopted.[65] Despite the opinions of certain modern scholars, there can be no doubt that, as Pfeiffer pointed out, the author obviously considered Artaxerxes to be the same king throughout the narratives of Ezra and Nehemiah.[66]

It can now be regarded as certain that Nehemiah belonged to the time of Artaxerxes I, on the basis of the evidence furnished by the Elephantine papyri.[67] These documents (ca. 408 B.C.) mentioned the High Priest Johanan and Sanballat, the governor of Samaria, the latter probably being quite advanced in age at the time. The Johanan of the papyri was

---

[59] M. Vernes, *Précis d'Histoire juive,* p. 582n. A. van Hoonacker, *Le Muséon,* IX (1890), pp. 151ff., 317ff., 389ff., *RB,* IV (1895), pp. 186ff., X (1901), pp. 5ff., 175ff., *Une communauté Judéo-Araméenne à Éléphantine en Égypte, aux VIe et Ve siècles avant J.-C.* (1915), pp. 19ff., *RB,* XXXII (1923), pp. 481ff., XXXIII (1924), pp. 33ff.

[60] A. Kuenen, *Gesammelte Abhandlungen zur Biblischen Wissenschaft* (1894), pp. 212ff. W. H. Kosters, *Die Wiederherstellung Israels in der persischen Periode,* p. 20 *passim.* F. X. Kugler, *Von Moses bis Paulus* (1922), pp. 215ff.

[61] For a bibliography see *RSL,* pp. 133f. This view was given some support by F. F. Bruce, *Israel and the Nations* (1963), pp. 106ff.

[62] In the 1910 edition of *Die Bücher Esra und Nehemia,* II, pp. 451f., he followed Van Hoonacker, but in the 1923 edition (*op. cit.,* II, pp. 491ff., 500f.), he abandoned it.

[63] *RSL,* pp. 134f.

[64] Cf. W. F. Albright, *JBL,* XL (1921), pp. 119f., *BA,* IX, No. 1 (1946), p. 15; cf. *BPAE,* p. 93.

[65] H. H. Rowley, *BJRL,* XXXVII (1955), p. 531.

[66] *PIOT,* pp. 818f.

[67] H. H. Rowley, *BJRL,* XXXVII (1955), pp. 552f.

a grandson of the Eliashib mentioned in Nehemiah 3:1, 20, and since Nehemiah was a contemporary of Eliashib, the Artaxerxes under whom he functioned can only have been Artaxerxes I. Hence Nehemiah can be assigned with confidence to the middle of the fifth century B.C. Since the author of Ezra placed the initial activity of the celebrated scribe before the arrival of Nehemiah in Jerusalem in terms of chronological sequence, against the better judgment of many modern scholars, it seems clear that he, at all events, dated the ministry of Ezra in the reign of Artaxerxes I also.

Certain misconceptions have attended some of the criticisms levelled against the traditional view. Thus it is commonly assumed that after Ezra arrived in Jerusalem in 458 B.C. in the seventh year of Artaxerxes I, his enthusiasm for promulgating the Law was such as to antagonize the populace, making for failure of his mission.[68] But as Stafford Wright has shown, the primary aim of Ezra on his first mission was to regulate the religious life of the theocracy on the basis of extant law, and not to promulgate a new lawbook with all the zeal of a religious reformer.[69] If there was any failure, it was surely on the side of the Jewish community for their inability to meet the requirements of the Torah.

As far as Ezra himself was concerned, his departure from the Judaean scene could readily be construed either as the result of an official recall due to the conspiracy of his enemies in Jerusalem, or to a voluntary desire to return and report to the Persian authorities as to the conditions which existed in Jerusalem. Since, as Schaeder has shown, Ezra held an official appointment in the empire corresponding to some such office as Secretary of State for Jewish Affairs,[70] he could hardly be expected to spend the entire period of his office in some distant corner of the imperial domain, but rather to be associated principally with the central administration in Susa and Babylon.

On this basis there is absolutely no reason why Ezra should not have returned to his normal duties in Mesopotamia of his own free will after a two-year tour of duty in the distant province of Judaea, whatever the outcome of his mission may have been. It is certain that an initial lack of success in achieving the intended reforms was not the principal reason for his return, any more than the ultimate accomplishing of his primary objective would have required him to stay for a prolonged period. Although the narratives are far from smooth chronologically, as has been observed above, they make it clear that abuses reappeared after the departure of Ezra, and that attempts to rebuild the city wall without proper authority (Ez. 4:7-16) were ultimately halted when the enemies

---

[68] Cf. *BHI*, pp. 377f.
[69] J. Stafford Wright, *The Date of Ezra's Coming to Jerusalem* (1958), p. 26.
[70] H. H. Schaeder, *Esra der Schreiber*, pp. 39ff., *Iranische Beiträge*, I, pp. 13ff.

of the Jews obtained a royal decree (Ez. 4:17-23; Neh. 1:3) about 446 B.C.

It was at this point that Nehemiah visited Jerusalem as Royal Commissioner, accompanied by Ezra as Secretary of State for Jewish Affairs. In his capacity as *tirshatha* Nehemiah saw to it that the walls were rebuilt and that recurrent economic problems were resolved. After this, Ezra was given an opportunity for reaffirming the Law and completing that which he had commenced previously, the result of which was that a covenant was sealed. The reforms of Nehemiah in 433 B.C. supplemented his previous enactments and presupposed the law that gave them validity.

It seems quite evident from the narrative that Ezra was not by any means promulgating an entirely new and unfamiliar law code, but instead was reimposing the regulations of the Mosaic Torah. Accordingly there would appear to be no ground for the supposition, first introduced by Wellhausen and subsequently maintained by a long line of scholars, including Albright, that it was Ezra who introduced the completely canonical Pentateuch into normative Jewish usage.[71]

Since there is no mention of Ezra following the dedication of the city walls in 445/4 B.C., it is possible that he had again returned to the central administration in Mesopotamia at that time. Alternatively, he may have died in Judaea at some period after the dedication ceremony, although there is no evidence whatever for this supposition. While no solution of the chronological problem is entirely satisfactory to date, it seems clear that, on the basis of the available evidence, there is no warrant at all for dispensing arbitrarily with the traditional order of Ezra and Nehemiah in favor of a chronological sequence that is even less certain.

D. AUTHORSHIP

In view of the complete contrast in approach between the anonymity of the Chronicler and the outright claims of both Ezra and Nehemiah to substantial authorship of the canonical material traditionally attributed to them, it seems to the present writer to be unwise to regard the Chronicler as the one who compiled and transmitted Ezra and Nehemiah along with his own writings and formulated them into a unified corpus. That these works together comprised a series that dealt in one way or another with significant aspects of Hebrew history is, of course, self-evident. What is not so clear is the common assumption that the Chronicler was the author of all three compositions, even though they date from the same general period as far as linguistic considerations are concerned. The literary style and historical standpoint diverge widely from what obtains in these respects in the books attributed to Ezra and

71 J. Wellhausen, *Geschichte Israels*, I (1878), p. 421. *BPAE*, p. 95.

Nehemiah, and this is equally true of the theological presuppositions that governed each of the authors. As mentioned earlier, it is probable that Ezra and Nehemiah were accorded canonicity before the writings of the Chronicler, since they dealt with recent history and were very important as the sole sources for their particular period.

Furthermore, as Rowley has pointed out,[72] there are serious difficulties attaching to a view such as that of Albright, who identified the Chronicler with Ezra himself.[73] In the first place it is difficult to assign the Chronicler to a period as early as that of Ezra, since certain portions of Chronicles, notably the lists, appear to bring the narrative down to the closing years of the fifth century B.C., if not somewhat beyond. Be that as it may, a second important consideration is the fact that Albright and his followers placed Ezra later than Nehemiah, whereas the Chronicler held that he came before Nehemiah chronologically. If the Chronicler was in fact none other than Ezra, it is strange that he should have been so confused about the trend of contemporary events in which he played such an important part. Furthermore, the suggestion that a later redactor introduced a certain deliberate disarrangement of the text raises the question as to why this would have been undertaken in the first instance, and what could have been expected to be gained from such a procedure. It has been shown above that the textual arrangement of Ezra and Nehemiah is not quite in the state of extraordinary confusion that Albright and others imagined to be so.[74] Had the Chronicler found the Ezra-Nehemiah narratives in such a condition, there is no reason why he could not have rearranged them to correspond to the correct chronological sequence of events, particularly since the books of Chronicles themselves do not exhibit notable instances of chronological disarray. While the relationship between Ezra-Nehemiah and the work of the Chronicler is still obscure, the least degree of difficulty is encountered when it is supposed that Ezra and Nehemiah were primarily responsible for the writings attributed to them: that they were contemporaries, with Ezra arriving in Jerusalem initially several years before Nehemiah; that their writings were in substantially their present form by about 440 and 430 B.C. respectively, and that the Chronicler compiled his work independently about 400 B.C. or slightly later.

E. The Particularism of the Work

The particularistic emphasis that the priestly interests of Ezra introduced into the post-exilic theocracy set the religious tone for later Judaism. His activities were of very great importance insofar as they stabilized the theocratic structure and insured its rigidity for a succeed-

[72] H. H. Rowley, *BJRL*, XXXVII (1955), p. 534 n. 4.
[73] W. F. Albright, *JBL*, XL (1921), pp. 119f., *BA*, LX, No. 1 (1946), p. 15.
[74] *BPAE*, p. 90.

ing time of stress and trial. It was abundantly clear to Ezra that the prophets had been correct in their view that foreign, and therefore pagan, influences upon life and religion in Israel could only bring disaster in their train. If Israel was to survive in the form of the theocracy, its watchword must be "holy to the LORD" (Zech. 14:20).

Hence a choice must be made between the blandishments of pagan cultures, with their inevitable religious depravities, and an unwavering adherence to the ideals of the ancient Covenant religion of Israel. Although the choice of the latter may have occasioned some minor losses in the area of cultural influences, its great merit was that it furnished the Jewish community with a degree of moral strength and spiritual resilience that enabled it to survive the engulfing tides of Hellenic culture under Alexander the Great. This same particularism has guaranteed that the ancient people of God will continue to survive for all time, despite the worst pressures of alien cultural or political influences.

Supplementary Literature

Bayer, E. *Das dritte Buch Esdras und sein Verhältnis zu den Büchern Esra-Nehemia.* 1911.

Fernández, A. *Comentario a los libros des Esdras y Nehemias.* 1950.

Gelin, A. *Esdras-Néhémie.* 1953.

Kapelrud, A. S. *The Question of Authorship in the Ezra Narrative.* 1944.

Kegel, M. *Die Kultusreformation des Ezra.* 1921.

Mowinckel, S. *Statholderen Nehemia.* 1916.

Welch, A. C. *Post-Exilic Judaism.* 1935.

III. THE BOOKS OF CHRONICLES

A. Name and Outline

The two books of Chronicles comprised a single volume in the Hebrew Bible, under the title דברי הימים, "the words of the days" or "events of past time," used in the sense of "annals" (cf. 1 Chron. 27:24). In the LXX the book was divided into two parts and given the title of Παραλειπομένων or "things omitted," a reference to the events added to the corresponding narratives in the books of Samuel and Kings. Jerome in the *Prologus Galeatus* suggested that a more representative title of the *verba dierum* would be *Chronicon totius divinae historiae* or "a chronicle of the whole of sacred history," although he acknowledged that, following the LXX, the works were commonly referred to as *Paralipomenon primus et secundus*.[1] Modern versions in English and other languages have adopted the title "Chronicles" that Jerome proposed. In the Hebrew canon the book concluded the list of works in the third division (Hagiographa), but in the LXX it was placed between Kings and Ezra-Nehemiah, presumably because of the historical nature of its contents. The two books of Chronicles comprise a history of the Hebrew people from Adam to the time of Cyrus, paralleling the writings from Genesis to Kings, with Ezra-Nehemiah as a conclusion.

The two books of Chronicles may be analyzed as follows:

I. Genealogical Material, 1 Chron. 1–9
    A. The patriarchs, ch. 1
    B. The twelve sons of Israel, ch. 2–3
    C. The family of Judah, 4:1-23
    D. The sons of Simeon, 4:24-43
    E. Reuben, Gad, and Manasseh, 5:1-25
    F. Levi and his families, 5:27–6:66
    G. Issachar, Benjamin, Naphtali, Ephraim, and Asher, ch. 8–9
II. The Rule of David, 1 Chron. 10–29
    A. The death of Saul, ch. 10
    B. The capture of Jerusalem, ch. 11–12

---

[1] *PL*, XXVIII, col. 554.

B. DATE OF THE COMPOSITION

The author of this anonymous composition, according to the rabbinic authorities, was Ezra the scribe, who "wrote the genealogy of Chronicles unto himself" (*Bab. Bath.* 15*a*). The concluding words of this ascription presumably mean that Ezra carried the narratives down to his own time. Whatever may be the truth or falsity of this proposition, it is evident from 2 Chronicles 36:22f. that the work could not have been compiled very much before the time of Ezra. Furthermore, 1 Chronicles 3:19-24 furnishes a list that purports to record the descendants of Zerubbabel to the sixth generation, which the LXX extended to the eleventh generation. If Zerubbabel can be dated about 520 B.C., this would require a date of about 400 B.C. for the last descendant, allowing a minimum of twenty years for each generation, and thus would suggest that the book was compiled about 400 B.C. or slightly later. Such a date could be reasonably compatible with authorship by Ezra, unless the latter flourished in the reign of Artaxerxes II (404-359 B.C.), as suggested by de Saulcy, Elhorst, Marquart, Torrey, and others, a view that is no longer tenable in the light of the evidence furnished by the Elephantine papyri.[2]

Furthermore, the literary and linguistic features[3] of both Ezra-Nehemiah and Chronicles are in harmony with a date of composition within the second half of the fifth century B.C., which again could be adduced in order to support the idea of a unity of authorship. On these and other grounds Albright took the view that Ezra was himself the

---

[2] F. de Saulcy, *Étude chronologique des livres d'Esdras et de Néhémie* (1868), pp. 41ff. H. J. Elhorst, *Theologisch Tijdschrift,* XXIX (1895), pp. 93ff. J. Marquart, *Fundamente israelitischer und jüdischer Geschichte,* pp. 31ff. C. C. Torrey, *The Second Isaiah,* pp. 456ff., *JBL,* XLVII (1928), pp. 380ff.

[3] Cf. F. Brown, *HDB,* I, pp. 389ff.; *DILOT,* pp. 535ff.; E. L. Curtis and A. A. Madsen, *A Critical and Exegetical Commentary on the Books of Chronicles* (1910), pp. 27ff.

Chronicler, as noted earlier.[4] A rather different opinion regarding the authorship of the composition respected the anonymity characteristic of the book, and on the basis of his concern for the Temple assumed that he was a minister, and perhaps even a Levite. Since he displayed considerable interest in the musicians who constituted one of the minor Temple guilds, it was thought that the Chronicler may have been numbered among the singers in the guild of Asaph,[5] and that he compiled his work about 250 B.C., or possibly a little earlier.

A date of composition between 350 and 250 B.C. has been urged by those who regard the writings of Ezra and Nehemiah as having been shaped and transmitted by the anonymous author of Chronicles. Arguing from the genealogy in 1 Chronicles 3:15-24, which is thought to extend the descendants of David to six generations beyond the time of Zerubbabel, a date not earlier than about 350 B.C. has been obtained by reckoning thirty years to a generation.[6] Additional support for such a date has been sought in the priestly list of Nehemiah 12:10-22, which included Jaddua, who was High Priest in the time of Alexander the Great, about 332 B.C.[7] A date between 300 and 240 B.C., based upon subjective considerations of style and vocabulary, has been suggested,[8] while Lods went so far as to place the composition about 180 B.C.[9]

Any warrant for sustaining a late view of authorship and date has been weakened seriously by the argument that a later hand has corrupted the text of 1 Chronicles 3:21, and that originally there were only four generations subsequent to Zerubbabel, not six.[10] If on this basis a generation is to be computed at twenty rather than thirty years,[11] a figure which in the view of the present author appears rather low, four such generations would bring the date of the Chronicler to about 440 B.C.

On the basis of the traditional view this would make the Chronicler a contemporary of Ezra, and argue for the kind of identification envisaged by Albright. But if, against such a background of computation, the text

[4] W. F. Albright, *JBL*, XL (1921), pp. 119f., *BA*, IX, No. 1 (1946), p. 15.

[5] C. C. Torrey, *Ezra Studies*, p. 211; *PIOT*, p. 797; *IDB*, I, p. 576.

[6] So Curtis and Madsen, *A Critical and Exegetical Commentary on the Books of Chronicles*, p. 5.

[7] So *DILOT*, p. 518; *IBOT*, pp. 111f., *et al.*

[8] H. Wheeler Robinson, *The OT: Its Making and Meaning*, p. 77; *PIOT*, p. 811.

[9] A. Lods, *The Prophets and the Rise of Judaism* (1937), p. 299.

[10] Curtis and Madsen, *A Critical and Exegetical Commentary on the Books of Chronicles*, pp. 6, 102; J. W. Rothstein and J. Hänel, *Kommentar zum ersten Buch der Chronik* (1927), pp. 43, 46f.; A. Bentzen, *Introduction to the OT*, II, pp. 215f.; W. Rudolph, *Esra und Nehemia*, p. xxiv.

[11] So R. Kittel, *Die Bücher der Chronik* (1902), p. 26; W. F. Albright in L. Finkelstein (ed.), *The Jews, Their History, Culture and Religion* (1949), I, p. 165 n. 139, allowed 27½ years for each generation.

of 1 Chronicles 3:21 is not corrupt, the six generations mentioned would bring the period of the Chronicler down to about 400 B.C. If, however, as some scholars have maintained,[12] the first nine chapters were not part of the original work of the Chronicler, any argument for dating-sequences based upon 1 Chronicles 3:21 is completely eliminated.

Unfortunately many scholarly arguments concerning this passage have suffered from the handicap of reading into the text something that is not in actuality present. When the section is examined carefully it will be seen that the genealogy of Zerubbabel was carried on for only two, not four or six or eleven, generations after his time. As Young has shown, the genealogy was recorded as far as Pelatiah and Jesaiah, grandsons of Zerubbabel, and in verse 21b it was followed by the mention of four Davidide families that were apparently contemporary with Pelatiah and Jesaiah.[13] It is of great importance in this connection, however, to note that these four families did not extend the line of Zerubbabel for four generations, as so many scholars have mistakenly imagined. On the basis of an accurate genealogy, and allowing thirty years to a generation, the Chronicler could have compiled his work somewhat before 455 B.C., which by any standard of computation or comparison appears rather early.

The passage containing the lists of priests and Levites in Nehemiah 12:10-22 has also been the object of considerable discussion as to its historicity and the possibility of textual corruption in it. At face value the section carried the narrative down to the time of Jaddua, who was High Priest from 351-331 B.C., and met Alexander the Great when he entered Jerusalem, as has been observed previously. Against this it is sometimes argued that the reference may have been to Jaddua as a young boy, and not to him in his subsequent capacity as High Priest, since in at least one verse (Neh. 12:11) he was not spoken of specifically in terms of that office.[14] On such a basis, it is urged, there is every probability that Nehemiah lived to see Jaddua, the great grandson of Eliashib, as a youth. This has been thought all the more probable since Nehemiah recorded that a grandson of Eliashib was married to a daughter of Sanballat (Neh. 13:28). While it is true that the reference in Nehemiah 12:11 could apply to the early days of Jaddua, there seems little doubt that Nehemiah 12:22, which associated him with other High Priests, thought of him in terms of adult life. Again, if the reference to Darius the Persian (Neh. 12:22) was to an individual who reigned when Jaddua was still a boy, the identification with Darius II Nothus (423-404 B.C.)

---

[12] Cf. A. C. Welch, *Post-Exilic Judaism* (1935), pp. 185f., *The Work of the Chronicler* (1939), pp. 1, 12 n. 1; C. R. North, *The OT Interpretation of History* (1946), p. 116; M. Noth, *Überlieferungsgeschichtliche Studien*, I, pp. 110ff., 120 n. 1, 130ff.; W. Rudolph, *Esra und Nehemia*, p. xxiv, *Chronikbücher* (1955), pp. 28ff.

[13] *YIOT*, p. 391.

[14] E.g. *YIOT*, pp. 386f.

would be reasonably assured. But since the verse under discussion appears to allude to Jaddua as an adult, and does not lend itself to a proleptic interpretation, the ruler would more probably be Darius III Codomannus (336/5-331 B.C.), as some scholars have argued. Once more, doubt has been cast upon the integrity of the text by the suggestion that the section constitutes a secondary scribal addition, perhaps incorporated from a marginal annotation designed to bring the list up to date.[15]

A careful examination of the verse in question shows that the presence of Jaddua makes for internal inconsistency in the material contained in verses 22 and 23. According to the first of these, Jaddua was apparently represented as the last High Priest, but the second repudiated this by making the list terminate in the High Priesthood before Jaddua, that is to say, in the time of Johanan the son of Eliashib. These two contiguous verses would only be consistent with themselves and with the history of Nehemiah as a whole if the name of Jaddua were to be omitted. On this basis there would seem to be ground for the contention, long entertained in critical circles, that the name of Jaddua constitutes a later addition to the text.

Since this may well have taken place in the manner suggested, that is to say, from the inclusion in the narrative of a marginal addition, it removes the second principal historical reference from the area of certainty, leaving linguistic considerations as the only other point of debate, and for those who regard Ezra and Nehemiah as the work of the Chronicler, a final criterion for dating that consists of the period to be assigned to the work of Ezra.

On this latter view, which assumes quite gratuitously that the Chronicler, in ignorance of the true state of affairs, erroneously placed Ezra before Nehemiah, a date of about 400 B.C. has been suggested for the composition of the work. Rudolph in particular would not countenance any more than a decade of latitude in either direction, since on the basis of a four-generation descent the secondary additions to Chronicles and Nehemiah reached only to about 400 B.C.[16] This date was preferred by Albright and also by Noth in an earlier book.[17] Those scholars who have placed the work of Ezra within the reign of Artaxerxes II have encountered difficulty in assigning the composition of the books of Chronicles to

---

[15] Cf. E. B. Pusey, *Daniel the Prophet*, p. 305 n. 5; H. Crosby, *The Book of Nehemiah*, p. 2; M. Noth, *Überlieferungsgeschichtliche Studien*, I, p. 120 n. 1; W. Rudolph, *Esra und Nehemia*, p. xxiv.

[16] W. Rudolph, *Esra und Nehemia*, pp. xxiv-xxv; cf. J. W. Rothstein and J. Hanel, *Kommentar zum ersten Buch der Chronik*, pp. lxvii-lxviii.

[17] W. F. Albright, *JBL*, XL (1921), pp. 104ff., LXI (1942), p. 125; cf. *Alexander Marx Jubilee Volume* (1950), pp. 61ff. M. Noth, *Die Gesetze im Pentateuch* (1940), p. 67 n. 2, but reversed in *Überlieferungsgeschichtliche Studien*, I, pp. 150ff.; cf. *Gesammelte Studien* (1957), p. 107. In *The History of Israel* (1960), p. 356, Noth lowered his earlier date to *ca.* 300 B.C.

a date much in advance of 350 B.C. The present writer maintains with Gordon, Morgenstern, and others[18] the traditional order of Ezra and Nehemiah in the reign of Artaxerxes I, and on different grounds from those of Albright would assign the composition of Chronicles to an anonymous writer in the closing decades of the fifth century B.C. or slightly later. Attempts to identify the Chronicler with Ezra appear inadvisable because of significant differences in style, historical and theological perspective, the treatment of source material, and the basic metaphysic of history as exhibited in the two compositions.

A final objection against an earlier rather than a later date of writing was based on the mention of the daric (AV "drams") in 1 Chronicles 29:7. This argument was popular at a time when the coin in question was identified by scholars with the Greek daric, but it began to wane when that identification was abandoned. Critical scholars were accustomed to remark that the daric was named after Darius I, who died in 486 B.C.,[19] and the fact that it was found in Palestine pointed to a period towards the end of the Persian regime. While the gold daric was indeed of Persian origin, there is no factual evidence that this coin (*'dharkonîm*) was named after Darius I. It is apparent from archaeological discoveries that coins were in wide circulation among the Greeks during the sixth century B.C., and it was from them that the Persians adopted the practice of minting coinage,[20] perhaps after the defeat of Croesus, king of Lydia, the traditional inventor of coinage, by Cyrus the Persian in 546 B.C. There is some ground for thinking that the gold daric first appeared during the reign of Nabonidus (556-539 B.C.), but even if the coin assumed its popular name in the period of Darius I, it would certainly have been in circulation in the Empire by the fifth century B.C. Thus the objection to an earlier dating-sequence for Chronicles, based upon the incidence of the gold daric, can be seen to have very little indeed to commend it.

C. The Historical Trustworthiness of the Book

Because of the particular standpoint from which Chronicles was compiled, as well as the association of this work in the Greek and other versions with the historical books of Samuel and Kings, it has become customary for liberal scholars generally to adopt a rather low view of the nature and historical trustworthiness of the books of Chronicles.[21] Part of

---

[18] *IOTT*, pp. 269ff. J. Morgenstern, *AJSL*, LV (1938), p. 56, *Universal Jewish Encyclopedia* (1943), X, p. 356, *HUCA*, XXII (1949), p. 40.

[19] So *IBOT*, p. 112; F. A. Banks, *Coins of Bible Days* (1957), p. 21.

[20] J. Weingreen, *DOTT*, p. 232.

[21] Cf. H. Ewald, *History of Israel* (1883), I, pp. 169ff.; K. H. Graf, *Die Geschichtlichen Bücher des AT* (1886), pp. 114ff.; J. Wellhausen, *Prolegomena to the History of Israel* (1885), pp. 171ff.; *DILOT*, p. 162; *IBOT*, p. 118; J. A. Bewer, *The Literature of the OT*, pp. 291ff., et al.

the misapprehension concerning these records has arisen because of a failure to realize that the overriding concern of the compiler was with a metaphysic of history rather than with a scrupulous cataloging of chronological sequences. As a result of this standpoint, the work was formulated along very different lines from those adopted by most modern historians.

Indeed, it should be noted at once that the writings of the Chronicler did not lay claim to be considered as history in the contemporary occidental sense of that term. As the Vulgate and English titles suggest, they constitute in effect a collection of somewhat eclectic records or annals of passing events, based upon a selected period in the history of Israel. So much of the misunderstanding in critical circles has arisen because the books have been thought to be something other than they actually claimed for themselves. To employ an analogy, it is therefore as improper to regard them as definitive chronological records of a particular era of Hebrew history as it would be to maintain that the chronicles of Pepys, Addison, or Steele were intended by their authors to constitute authoritative treatises on certain phases of English social history. This is not to say, however, that both kinds of material are consequently unhistorical or unreliable as sources for the corresponding periods under consideration. What is important, however, is the realization that these compositions need to be evaluated bearing in mind the purposes for which they were drawn up. When this is done, it will be seen that all these sources are patently valid in their own right.

This methodical excursus, which has been described by Elmslie as "the only instance in Hebraic philosophy of history presented on an immense scale"[22] is of very great importance both for the student of Hebrew history and the investigator of religious philosophy. The book of Chronicles confronted the post-exilic Jewish theocracy with the ontological significance of the divine commonwealth in the light of its own sacred history as no other attempt at historical evaluation had done. The work reflected to a limited extent certain facets of the contemporary religious and social situation in Judaea, as might well be expected of any such chronicle of events. Nevertheless, these factors were at best incidental to the true purpose of the Chronicler, which was to comprehend the rationale of historical events synthesized with reference to a particular religious standpoint.

The author evidently compiled his work against the background of life in the post-exilic theocratic community,[23] an institution that was religious rather than secular in structure, and in which the divine will was mediated to the people through an acceptable priesthood. It was the responsibility of the latter to maintain ceremonial holiness as a normative

---

[22] W. A. L. Elmslie, *IB*, III, p. 341.
[23] Cf. *BHI*, pp. 354f.; J. M. Myers, *I Chronicles* (1965), pp. lxxxviif.

feature of life by means of Temple worship and correct ritual observances, reflecting the ideals of Ezekiel and some of the post-exilic prophets in this regard. Under such conditions the elect were to live in harmony, governed by divine providence and liberated from the social tensions and disruptions that were characteristic of less exalted communities. Strict adherence to this pattern of social and religious organization was deemed imperative if the disastrous experience of the pre-exilic period was not to be repeated. It was with this in mind that Ezekiel had urged close attention to ritual procedures, not as a substitute for the righteousness of heart and life that had been demanded consistently by the prophets (e.g. Am. 5:14; Mic. 6:8; Hos. 6:6), but as a necessary safeguard against any further lapse into idolatry. The Chronicler was clearly in agreement with this prescription, for his metaphysic of divine grace and election demanded implicit obedience on the part of the theocratic community to the revealed will of God and a complete absence of corruption or slackness in liturgical worship as necessary prerequisites for divine blessing.

Part of the self-imposed task of the Chronicler lay in emphasizing the doctrine of divine retribution by referring to certain familiar events in pre-exilic Hebrew history, and at the same time in proclaiming, as the prophets generally had done, that God desired the sinner to repent and live a life of complete obedience to the divine will. He had as his basic conviction the proposition that the absolute moral standards of God as set forth in the Sinaitic enactments were to be binding upon those who considered themselves in Covenant relationship with Jehovah, for it was of fundamental importance that the character of the deity should be reflected by His Chosen People.

The Chronicler was painfully aware of the fact that, through ignorance and idolatry, the post-Mosaic generations had fallen away from this demanding way of life, and his entire outlook manifested the stern resolve that such a state of affairs should never recur in the life of the nation. Consequently he paid special attention to the Levitical priesthood, since it had aided and abetted the apostasy of the settlement and subsequent periods. But he was also concerned with the Davidic tradition, and on the basis of his conviction that Israel was the earthly representative of a deity who manifested His activity in all phases of historical development, the Chronicler sought to prove that the returned community in Judaea was the true successor of Davidic spirituality. As such the real glory of the Davidic religious tradition could only be realized when the ancient Law of God was obeyed implicitly against a background of ritual purity and exactitude.

In compiling his work the Chronicler drew upon a wide range of Biblical and extra-Biblical material. His chief sources in the canonical compositions were the Pentateuch, Joshua, the books of Samuel, and, particularly, the books of Kings, to which latter work frequent references seem to have been made (2 Chron. 27:7; 35:27; 36:8; cf. 1 Chron. 9:1; 2 Chron. 16:11; 20:34; 25:26; 28:26; 32:32; 33:18). Of the early genealogies (1 Chron. 1–9), only those involving the patriarchs could have been taken from the canonical books, since the deviation in the order and general arrangement of the balance is so great as to suggest that the author drew for his information upon old statistical compilations that had managed to survive the catastrophe of 597 B.C.

While the historical material of Samuel and Kings is reproduced in substantially the same form, it is very doubtful that the canonical works actually constituted the primary source of the information employed by the Chronicler. A careful comparison of parallel passages indicates that the sections in Chronicles frequently preserve numerous details not found in the corresponding portions of Samuel and Kings. In addition, the two types of material can be seen to represent differing standpoints, a fact which is further emphasized by the degree of variation in the arrangement of similar material. This situation might indicate that each had been derived from a common source, or perhaps that they were circulating as distinct variant forms of the same general literary tradition. The latter consideration need occasion no particular surprise in view of the evidence from Qumran relating to the state of the Hebrew text in the pre-Christian period, which shows that there were at least three distinctive types of Hebrew text in circulation among the Jews of the Second Commonwealth,[24] thereby pointing to an extended history of textual development and transmission.

There appear also to be indications of the fact that the Chronicler may have had access to the earlier sources utilized by the compilers of the historical writings. This can be illustrated by reference to the deeds of King Asa (2 Chron. 16:11ff.) where the source is mentioned and its contents are summarized. When this is compared with the corresponding section in Kings (1 Kgs. 15:23f.), which only mentioned the Book of the Chronicles of the kings of Judah, it becomes evident that the narrative in Chronicles has preserved certain facts not recorded in Kings. This might well indicate that the Chronicler drew upon the same source as that utilized by the compiler of Kings, but that he made a larger extract from its contents for the purpose of his own narrative.

In addition to the separate histories of the kings and kingdoms of Israel and Judah that he obviously cited (cf. 2 Chron. 25:26; 28:26; 32:32; 35:27; 36:8; 16:11; 20:34; 33:18), another similar source may have been the story or "midrash" of the book of Kings (2 Chron. 24:27), which was probably very similar to, if not actually identical with, the chronicles of the kings of Israel and Judah upon which the compiler of the canonical books of Kings also drew. The term "midrash" in later Judaism signified a learned and intensive adaptation of the Biblical

24 Cf. *BASOR*, No. 141 (1956), pp. 9ff.

narratives, but this sense was most probably not the one understood by the Chronicler, who was merely thinking in terms of a "study," "excursus," or "work" containing material not found in the canonical sources.[25]

Specifically extra-Biblical sources that the Chronicler utilized included what seem to be collections of narratives about the activities of prophets and seers (cf. 1 Chron. 29:29; 2 Chron. 9:29), as well as apparently independent compositions relating to the works of prophets (cf. 2 Chron. 12:15; 13:22; 24:30; 26:22; 32:32; 33:19) and a series of sources connected with King David (1 Chron. 23:27; 27:24; 2 Chron. 29:25; 35:4, 15). The genealogies were most probably derived in the main from material no longer extant, as has been remarked above, and almost certainly came from official lists. Some of them may have been of more importance than others, and this may be indicated by the fact that the best LXX manuscripts omitted 1 Chronicles 1:11-23, suggesting in turn that the verses in question were a later addition.[26]

In any discussion of the sources available to the Chronicler, the basic question must be whether or not he had at his disposal any document of significant proportions, other than Kings, which dealt with the history of Israel and Judah (cf. 2 Chron. 16:11; 27:7). If he did, he must have treated it differently from Kings, since there are no direct quotations from it, and such information as it contained was almost certainly recast in the literary style of the Chronicler. This may imply either that he regarded it as an inferior source from the standpoint of historiography, or that its contents were unsuitable for purposes of direct citation. Recent archaeological discoveries have tended to support the theory that he was able to draw upon a variety of subsidiary sources, some of them doubtless belonging to the pre-exilic period. Thus in connection with the events in the thirty-sixth year of the reign of Asa (2 Chron. 16:1-10), of which little is said in Kings (cf. 1 Kgs. 15:17), the discovery of the Benhadad *stele* in 1940 furnished decisive confirmation of the chronology supplied by the Chronicler.[27]

This carries with it the implication that the compiler of the work may have made use of certain pre-exilic annalistic sources that were either inaccessible when Kings was written, or else were considered unsuitable or unnecessary as sources for the period. Whatever the nature and extent of the extra-canonical material upon which the Chronicler drew for his own annals, there can be no doubt that the finished work is an invaluable

---

[25] Cf. A. Bentzen, *Introduction to the OT*, II, pp. 212f.; *IBOT*, pp. 113f.; the term occurs again in 2 Chron. 20:34.

[26] On the sources of Chronicles see C. C. Torrey, *AJSL*, XXV (1909), pp. 157ff., 188ff.; E. L. Curtis and A. A. Madsen, *A Critical and Exegetical Commentary on the Books of Chronicles*, p. 26; G. von Rad, *Festschrift Otto Procksch* (1934), pp. 113ff.

[27] W. F. Albright, *BASOR*, No. 87 (1942), pp. 23ff., No. 90 (1943), pp. 30ff.

guide to the religious attitudes and problems of the post-exilic theocratic community.

The priestly interests of the writer are evident from the manner in which he handled his sources to give prominence to Temple worship, liturgical procedures, priestly ministrations, and religious reforms (cf. 1 Chron. 15–16, 22–29; 2 Chron. 11:13ff.; 13–15, 17, 19–20; 26:16ff.; 29–31; 33:10ff.; 35). In this general connection it is legitimate to remark that his concern to show that the returned community was the true successor of the Davidic spiritual tradition led the Chronicler to accord great importance to the ceremonial institutions of David and Solomon, and in general to treat them as rather idealized personages.

While the additions of the Chronicler are obviously important, the material that he omitted is of equal significance in any attempt to estimate his concept of historical method. Quite obviously he was writing for those who already knew the contents of Samuel and Kings, and for this reason he retained only as much of that material as was deemed necessary to furnish a proper framework for his philosophy of history. Since his concern was to trace the Davidic descent, the history of the northern kingdom was not of paramount importance, and accordingly it was omitted.

Because the narratives dealing with the conduct of Absalom, Amnon, Adonijah, and the apostate Solomon were not strictly relevant to the larger issue of presenting what the Chronicler regarded as historical material relating to Temple worship and the institutions connected with the theocracy, they too were passed over in silence. In this connection it should be noted that almost everything dealing with the private lives of David and Solomon was omitted, including those aspects that would have contributed favorably to the rather idealized picture of those rulers presented occasionally in the book of Chronicles. From this it will be obvious that such omissions were the result of source-control, and were not prompted by apologetic considerations, as is so frequently maintained.[28]

In his use of source material, therefore, it would appear that the Chronicler was guided by certain clearly defined principles, and that a proper degree of control over his primary and secondary sources of information is evident in consequence. In general it can be said that his additions were designed to exemplify Israel as the true Church of God, and to show that the Temple services and religious institutions of the post-exilic theocracy were legitimate and valid adjuncts of community life.[29] Similarly his omissions can be regarded as deliberate attempts to consider only those sources which would substantiate the authority of the two institutions with which he was primarily concerned, namely the

[28] E.g. *PIOT*, p. 795; *IBOT*, p. 117; C. C. Torrey, *Ezra Studies*, p. 231.
[29] *OTFD*, p. 328.

Davidic succession and the Temple at Jerusalem as the center of theocratic worship for Judaism. By exercising these principles of selection and control, the Chronicler was able to show the way in which the historical process achieved the objective which God had ordained for His people.

Questions relating to the historical value of the books of Chronicles go back as far as the Talmudic authorities, who preferred to regard the work as didactic or homiletical in nature, rather than as an actual historical treatise.[30] While Chronicles is clearly written from a special standpoint, it is a mistake to assume that the composition is of no historical value, as so many modern critics have done.[31] To adopt such a view is to misunderstand completely the purpose the author had in mind when he compiled his book, as Elmslie has pointed out.[32] His efforts were designed to instruct the oriental outlook of his people, and since the returned exiles and their descendants had long been familiar with the canonical historical sources, the lessons of spirituality that he had to teach, and the insights into the philosophy of history which he furnished, would not be lost upon his readers.

Specific criticisms concerning the historicity of Chronicles have included rejection of the high numbers contained in the narratives,[33] which have been observed to be generally larger than their counterparts in the books of Kings. In this connection it must be recognized immediately that the problem of the numbers in the books of Chronicles is by no means restricted to that composition, but has an application to other important areas of the Old Testament. Therefore the answers to this issue should be sought primarily in the way numbers were normally employed in ancient Near Eastern descriptive or annalistic literature, in the recognition that oriental peoples of antiquity frequently assigned symbolic and schematic categories to numbers. The latter were by no means unpopular with the Semites, and it is quite probable that the expression "480th year" in 1 Kings 6:1 actually involves a double cycle of twelve generations, each consisting of forty years' duration, compounded schematically and meant to be understood symbolically.[34]

Large numbers were frequently employed by annalists to describe the magnitude of a conquest, and this usually resulted in rather dispropor-

---

[30] W. H. Bennett, *JE*, IV, p. 60.

[31] E.g. W. M. L. de Wette, *Beiträge zur Einleitung in das AT* (1806), III, p. 83; C. H. Cornill, *Introduction to the Canonical Books of the OT*, p. 239; *DILOT*, p. 532; *PIOT*, p. 806; G. B. Gray, *A Critical Introduction to the OT* (1927), p. 2; *IBOT*, p. 118. A more cautious attitude has been adopted by B. W. Anderson, *Understanding the OT* (1957), p. 436; G. W. Anderson, *A Critical Introduction to the OT* (1959), p. 223.

[32] W. A. L. Elmslie, *IB*, III, p. 343.

[33] E.g. *PIOT*, pp. 788, 796; *DILOT*, p. 532; E. L. Curtis and A. A. Madsen, *A Critical and Exegetical Commentary on the Books of Chronicles*, p. 8.

[34] Cf. *IOTT*, pp. 293ff.; R. K. Harrison, *A History of OT Times*, p. 98.

tionate estimates of the situation when judged by factual occidental standards of computation. This is even the case in many instances where Near Eastern annals can be compared with accounts of the same incident in Biblical writings. Thus the annals of Sennacherib described the victory achieved over Hezekiah of Judah in 701 B.C. in exaggerated terms, and assessed the tribute exacted from him on that occasion at 30 talents of gold, 800 talents of silver, and a wide range of valuable booty.[35] By contrast the account in Kings scaled the numbers down to the point where Hezekiah merely paid 30 talents of gold and 300 talents of silver in tribute (2 Kgs. 18:14). Even here the problem presented by the numbers is compounded by the fact that the Hebrew annalist may have been just as anxious to reduce the amount of tribute paid as his Assyrian counterpart was to exaggerate it.

In antiquity round numbers were frequently employed to convey the concept of a particular period of time, which in actual fact need not always have been even approximately correct. Thus the seventh line of the Moabite Stone stated that Omri annexed all the land of Medeba and occupied it during his own lifetime and half that of his son, amounting to a period of forty years. By comparison with the corresponding time recorded for the activity of Omri in 1 Kings 16, however, it can hardly have been more than twenty-three years at the very most.[36] In other more familiar instances, a forty-year period was frequently synonymous with a generation, and forty days with a month.

Yet another difficulty in grappling with the problem of numbers in the Old Testament narratives consists in the well-known fact that numbers occurring in documents of great antiquity are peculiarly liable to scribal corruption in process of transmission. The ancient Near Eastern source known as the Weld-Blundell prism[37] listed antediluvian Sumerian kings and attributed reigns of greatly exaggerated length to them in the cities of Eridu, Badtibira, Larak, Sippar, and Ur.[38] Many centuries later the Babylonian priest Berossus, who served under Antiochus I Soter (281-261 B.C.), extended the list to ten rulers and more than doubled the length of their individual reigns.[39]

In the Old Testament narratives, to furnish but a few examples, the number 50,070 in 1 Samuel 6:19 (AV, RV) probably ought to be reduced to 70 (RSV),[40] and the 40 years of 2 Samuel 15:7 (AV, RV) should doubtless be four years, with the Greek, Syriac, and RSV readings. Again, there is an evident corruption arising from textual transmission with respect to the number of the offspring of Jacob, which in Genesis

---

[35] *ARAB*, II, sects. 240f.
[36] E. Ullendorf, *DOTT,* pp. 195ff.
[37] *ANET*, pp. 265f.
[38] C. L. Woolley, *The Sumerians* (1928), p. 21.
[39] *LAP*, p. 25.
[40] Cf. *AJ*, VI, 1, 4.

46:26 was estimated at 66, while in Exodus 1:5 and Deuteronomy 10:22 the number was given as 70. A fragment of Exodus discovered in the Qumran caves preserved a reading of 75 persons for Exodus 1:5, and this agrees with the reference in Acts 7:14. It is quite possible, of course, that two different manuscript traditions had survived in this connection, and that Stephen cited the one preserved at Qumran, since his figures differed from those of the LXX, the Bible of the early Christian Church, which followed the MT.

In general it can be said that the books of Chronicles furnish approximate numerical estimates in the form of round numbers, frequently designed, as has been remarked, to express the magnitude of the occasion. Thus the reference to the forces of Zerah does not imply that his enemy consisted of one million men (LXX "in thousand thousands") but merely that it was an unusually large military force. Some estimates in Chronicles which appear to be particularly inflated can be corrected or scaled down by reference to the books of Samuel and Kings (e.g. 1 Chron. 18:4 and 2 Sam. 8:4; 2 Chron. 3:15, 4:5 and 1 Kgs. 7:15, 26; 2 Chron. 13:3, 17; 17:14ff. are probably corrupt also). However, it is not always the case that the figures in Chronicles exceed their counterparts in Samuel and Kings. Thus 2 Chronicles 9:25 gives 4000 stalls for the horses of Solomon, whereas 1 Kings 4:26 has 40,000. Again, 1 Chronicles 11:11 has 300 as against 800 in 2 Samuel 24:13.

The fact that many of the numerical differences are to be found in the LXX version indicates that they existed before the text was crystallized by the tradition of the Massoretes. Insofar as numbers were represented in the Hebrew text by the use of alphabetic consonants, it is comparatively easy to understand how corruptions of the text could have crept in as the various books were transmitted. There seems little doubt also that the existence of independent textual traditions regarding the size of particular numbers has played a part in complicating the situation. Be that as it may, even the existence of isolated numerical corruptions or inconsistencies is insufficient to overthrow the general historical credibility of Chronicles, particularly if the numbers in question are epic or symbolic in character.

It could also be noted at this juncture that even the western world is not infrequently given to using numbers in a symbolic manner in order to express certain aspects of historical fact. To furnish but one example, when the Russian armies were defeated decisively by the Turks at the battle of Plevna on July 31, 1877, the Turkish military authorities officially recorded Russian losses in the field as comprising 30,000 men slain in battle. The fact that the casualties on that occasion did not exceed 7,000 soldiers killed in action does not of itself discredit the historicity of the victory. It merely implies that rather different principles of computation were being employed by the various estimating bodies involved.

Severe criticisms have also been levelled against those sections in the books of Chronicles which cannot be paralleled in Samuel and Kings. Torrey and Pfeiffer in particular have regarded the genealogies as largely artificial concoctions, designed to relate theocratic institutions to a Davidic, if not actually to a Mosaic, origin.[41] Thus the Ephraimite Samuel and Obed-Edom of Gath were supposedly transformed into Levites by the Chronicler at a time when Obed-Edom was, according to Pfeiffer,[42] a Philistine captain of David hailing from Gath, as well as the eponym of a guild of gatekeepers, the name of a musician, and the son of a rather shadowy figure known as Jeduthun, a term originally signifying a musical tone or mode. In this connection it should be noticed that Samuel was nowhere spoken of as a lineal descendant of Ephraim, for although his father Elkanah came from Ramathaim-zophim near Mount Ephraim (1 Sam. 1:1), he actually traced his descent from Levite stock.[43] The misunderstanding has arisen in this instance because Elkanah, the Levite, was designated an Ephraimite, since as far as his civil standing was concerned he belonged to the tribe of Ephraim, the Levites being reckoned as belonging to those tribes in the midst of which they were living. The reason why Obed-Edom was regarded as a Gittite was that he belonged to the city of Gath-Rimmon, which was a Levitical city of refuge (Josh. 19:45; 21:24; 1 Chron. 6:69). Nowhere in the historical books was Obed-Edom spoken of as a Philistine captain of David hailing from Gath, as Pfeiffer asserted. There is clearly a distinction between the Obed-Edom of 1 Chronicles 15:18, 24, who functioned as a gatekeeper for the Ark when it was being brought into Jerusalem, and the individual of the same name in 1 Chronicles 15:21, who was a member of the musical guild. Furthermore, the two men are distinguished in 1 Chronicles 16:38, although the text appears to be corrupt, and the explanatory gloss "the son of Jeduthun" should follow the first Obed-Edom rather than the second, the reference to his "sixty-eight brethren" being obviously to his musical companions. From the above comments it will appear evident that a proper reading of the Levitical genealogies in Chronicles shows that the lists are far from fictitious in character.

The association of musical functions with Jeduthun, as with Ethan the Ezrahite (1 Kgs. 4:31) and others in the period of the monarchy, has been illumined by archaeological discoveries in Canaan. These have demonstrated the extent to which native Canaanites participated in musical activities relating to worship and the way in which they were organized in terms of an orchestral guild, as mentioned in an earlier chapter. The Hebrew term 'ezrāh (1 Kgs. 5:11 Heb.; 1 Chron. 2:6; cf. Exod. 12:19, 48; Num. 9:14; Ps. 89:1) has been shown by Albright to

---

[41] C. C. Torrey, *Ezra Studies,* pp. 227ff. *PIOT,* pp. 798f.

[42] *PIOT,* p. 800.

[43] *Ramathaim-zophim* should more properly be rendered, "Ramah of the twin heights, of the district of Zuph."

mean "aboriginal," indicating the native Canaanite origin of at least some of the singers employed in the service of King David. It seems fairly clear in the light of such evidence that the Chronicler was drawing knowledgeably upon a well-attested tradition, particularly in the areas of personal interest such as the genealogies of the singers, which were furnished in unusual detail.

If these had merely been a concoction of the Chronicler, the lineage of such a guild would have been supplied in a complete form from Levi to the fall of Jerusalem in 587 B.C. As the narrative (1 Chron. 6:1ff.) stands, twenty-two generations were listed from the time of Levi to that of Heman, a contemporary of David, and only four generations from that period to the fall of Jerusalem (6:33ff.). This state of affairs points to the authenticity of the earlier list, and the fact that the Chronicler was entirely unwilling to fabricate material in order to cover that particular extent of time for which he had no detailed information.

The historical accuracy of other portions of Chronicles has been widely disputed from time to time, not least those sections that mention Manasseh's captivity in Babylon (2 Chron. 33:10ff.). Although there is no direct archaeological evidence for this event at the time of writing, it is known that Manasseh visited Nineveh about 678 B.C. at the command of Esarhaddon,[44] who had rebuilt Babylon after it suffered destruction at the hands of Nebuchadnezzar.[45] Manasseh was mentioned by name on both the prism of Esarhaddon[46] and the prism of Ashurbanipal,[47] and the period of history in question is all the more intriguing as far as the books of Chronicles are concerned because the author furnished no reason for the appearance of Assyrian army officers in Judah.

From the inscriptions mentioned above it is known that Egypt was conquered and made tributary to Assyria (cf. Nah. 3:8), and it is quite possible that Manasseh was suspected of being involved to some degree in these events, if he was not actually an active participant, since Judah was an Egyptian sphere of political influence. When Babylon, led by Shamash-shumukin, brother of Ashurbanipal, rose in rebellion against Assyria in 652 B.C.,[48] a four-year period of civil war ensued, and it may well have been at this time that Manasseh rebelled against Assyria also, since Ashurbanipal appears to have had to march against resurgent Semitic forces, probably including some Arab tribes, in Transjordan. Perhaps this battle even occasioned the lament over Moab that was preserved in Isaiah 15—16 and Jeremiah 48, although a precise association is not absolutely assured.

---

[44] *ARAB*, II, sect. 690.
[45] Cf. *ARAB*, II, sects. 646f.
[46] *ANET*, p. 291.
[47] *ANET*, p. 294.
[48] *ANET*, p. 298.

Since the Chronicler mentioned the presence of Assyrian forces in Judah, it seems most probable that Manasseh had joined in the rebellion in company with Edom, Ammon, and Moab. On being defeated he was taken to Babylon as a captive, and restored to his former position at a later date. As MacLean has remarked, there is no particular difficulty inherent in such a situation, for it can be paralleled by the capture of Pharaoh-Necho I of Egypt, who according to the Rassam cylinder was taken prisoner along with others as the result of an abortive rebellion against Ashurbanipal, and carried off to Nineveh.[49] Of all those who revolted he alone was released and reinstated in his former position. There would therefore seem to be no merit in denying the essential historicity of the narrative preserved by the Chronicler with respect to the Babylonian captivity of Manasseh. Instead, it can be recognized as embodying material that was either not available at the time, or was considered unsuitable for inclusion in the short account of Manasseh furnished by the books of Kings (2 Kgs. 20:21–21:18). If this event is as historical as it appears to be, there is little reason for denying the validity of the reformation attributed by the Chronicler to Manasseh on his return to Jerusalem, short-lived though the reforms themselves may have been.

As a survey of Hebrew history, written from a special philosophical standpoint, the book of Chronicles is without parallel among the Hebrew canonical writings. The closeness of association with the language of Ezra and Nehemiah, along with the fact that the conclusion of Chronicles is almost identical with the beginning of Ezra (2 Chron. 32:22f.; Ez. 1:1ff.), has led scholars to assume that the three works originally constituted one composition. When the division was ultimately made, it has been argued, a common portion was left in each book to mark the point of separation.[50] Furthermore, it has been suggested that Ezra-Nehemiah was admitted into the Hebrew canon prior to Chronicles, and that when the latter was included it was thought desirable to add a fitting conclusion, which accordingly was taken from the opening verses of Ezra.[51] Unfortunately the first of these suggestions does not explain why it should have been thought necessary to mark the point of separation in view of the subsequent position of Chronicles in the Hebrew Bible, and the second fails to show why the first few verses of Ezra should have been thought suitable for a conclusion of Chronicles, since the narrative could have been edited so as to terminate where Ezra began, and not to overlap somewhat.

[49] H. B. MacLean, *IDB*, III, p. 255; cf. *ANET*, p. 295.
[50] E.g. Curtis and Madsen, *A Critical and Exegetical Commentary on the Book of Chronicles*, p. 3.
[51] *IBOT*, p. 110.

D. THE AUTHORSHIP OF CHRONICLES

As has been pointed out above, there is no factual evidence for the rabbinic opinion that Ezra wrote Chronicles. Instead, it seems much more probable that Ezra, Nehemiah, and Chronicles constituted a series rather than a unity, for if the latter were the case, it would be difficult to see why only Ezra and Nehemiah were admitted to the canon before Chronicles, as was apparently the case, and why the remainder should have been placed after these works when finally accorded canonicity, rather than before them, as the narrative chronology would demand.

If the three works constituted a unity from the beginning and bore the *imprimatur* of Ezra upon them, it would be far from easy to see precisely how or why they became separated in the first place. Certainly the view that these compositions were divided because Ezra and Nehemiah were thought to constitute the logical continuation of the canonical histories of Samuel and Kings, whereas Chronicles merely supplemented the latter,[52] is incompatible with the theory of authorship by Ezra, since he would obviously have intended his work to comprise a unity, and as such to supplement existing historical material.

Probably the most satisfactory explanation of the situation is that, whereas Ezra and Nehemiah supplied the contemporary historical background, Chronicles was written to furnish the pre-exilic religious and historical foundation of the theocracy. Together the works comprised a series, and were linked together in the ancient Babylonian manner by means of a catch-line. This latter is the precise function of the concluding two verses of 2 Chronicles, and served both to insure the continuity of the material and to demonstrate that the three works were basically linked in series.

The nature and purpose of the catch-line as employed by cuneiform writers was seemingly unknown to the rabbinic authorities, otherwise they would most probably have preserved the order of the books as they are found in the English versions. While the use of this Babylonian scribal device might argue for Ezra as the author of Chronicles, it is hardly to be supposed that he alone in fifth-century B.C. Judaea was familiar with this ancient Mesopotamian literary mechanism.

❖ ❖ ❖ ❖ ❖

Despite the comments made above, it is a fact that the Hebrew text of Chronicles has been transmitted reasonably well, and as a whole is considerably less corrupt than some of the other Old Testament canonical books. Many of the textual errors are to be found in the lists of names, which would seem to indicate that the author was unable to correct them conjecturally by reference to the context. On occasions the Hebrew text of Chronicles appears to preserve a reading that had be-

---

[52] Curtis and Madsen, *A Critical and Exegetical Commentary on the Books of Chronicles*, p. 3.

come corrupted in Samuel and Kings. Thus the information concerning the death of Lahmi, brother of Goliath (1 Chron. 20:5), is more likely to be correct than its counterpart in Samuel (2 Sam. 21:19), since the latter is already itself corrupt.

The LXX version does not offer quite the degree of help in emending the Hebrew text of Chronicles as it does for many other Old Testament books, since it appears to have been made from a manuscript almost identical with the MT. Of course there are times when the LXX is helpful in this respect, but these are rather infrequent, and of a minor nature at best (e.g. 2 Chron. 2:50; 3:21; 5:13; 25:8; 26:5). On occasions the LXX agrees with Samuel or Kings against the text of Chronicles (e.g. 2 Chron. 33:20). In one unusual instance (1 Chron. 1:11-23) the LXX in B (Codex Vaticanus) omitted an entire section of the Hebrew genealogy. The presence of corruptions that cannot be corrected from the LXX points to a reasonably early stage of error in the processes of textual transmission, and raises questions as to the purity of the sources with which the Chronicler worked. In certain instances the LXX demonstrates complete ignorance of the significance of specific words, and resorts to transliteration instead of translation (e.g. 2 Chron. 3:16; 26:21). On occasions the smaller numbers supplied by the LXX seem to indicate either that the larger ones of the Hebrew have not been transmitted in their original form, or that the compiler was scaling them down in the interests of factual reality (e.g. 1 Chron. 5:21; 2 Chron. 22:2).

It ought to be remarked again that a degree of caution should be exercised in emending the text of Chronicles by reference to Samuel and Kings, since quite apart from the fact that specific passages in those sources may themselves contain textual corruptions, it is evident that the Chronicler made certain changes in his sources so as to elicit smoother diction or better sense. In the last resort the task of the textual critic as far as Chronicles is concerned is merely to restore the text as it proceeded from the hand of the Chronicler, a principle that has unfortunately been overlooked far too often by scholars and commentators generally.

The non-canonical material utilized by the compiler appears in a reasonably uniform Hebrew style of a fairly late character, and is presumably contemporary with, or slightly earlier than, the Chronicler himself. From indications of textual roughness in these sources it may be inferred that they were in rather mutilated condition when the Chronicler used them for his genealogies and descriptive sections. The greater degree of deference with which the material from Samuel and Kings was handled would suggest that the Chronicler felt more at liberty to amend his extra-canonical sources and to adapt them so that they would conform to his special purposes.

Of the other versions of Chronicles, the fragments of the Old Latin that can be extracted from the patristic writings are of some value in indicating the nature of the LXX text from which the Old Latin rendering was made. The Vulgate was translated from a text current in the fourth century after Christ, and because of its late date it is not particularly useful for textual purposes. Occasionally, however, there are instances where the Vulgate appears to have retained a correct reading, as contrasted with the LXX (e.g. 1 Chron. 26:26). In the Syriac-speaking Church Chronicles was not originally regarded as canonical, and when ultimately translated it manifested the features of a paraphrase rather than a translation. Because the text of the Peshitta version of Chronicles was largely accommodated to that of Samuel and Kings, it is of limited value for critical purposes. This situation was carried a stage further in the Arabic version, which is merely a translation of the Peshitta text.

Supplementary Literature

Barnes, W. E. *The Books of Chronicles.* 1899.
Harvie-Jellie, W. *I and II Chronicles.* 1906.
von Rad, G. *Das Geschichtsbild des chronistischen Werkes.* 1930.
Slotki, I. W. *Chronicles.* 1952.
Welch, A. C. *The Work of the Chronicler: Its Purpose and Its Date.* 1939.

Part Fifteen

THE APOCRYPHA

I. THE APOCRYPHAL BOOKS

Over the centuries the term "Apocrypha" has had a variety of meanings for different groups.[1] As employed in post-Reformation Protestant writings it has normally designated some fourteen or fifteen documents, consisting of books or parts of books that emerged in the main from the last two centuries preceding the birth of Christ and the first century of the Christian era. This corpus was but one small portion of the vast output of literature within Judaism during this period of manifest political and religious ferment. Quite possibly the *terminus a quo* of the Apocrypha may have to be placed at an even earlier date than the one just mentioned, since one of the compositions in this literary group may have been written as early as the end of the fourth or the beginning of the third century B.C.[2]

Many of these documents are valuable because they mirror with considerable accuracy the religious, political, and social conditions in Judaea following the close of the Old Testament period proper. After the death of Alexander the Great in 323 B.C., the empire he had established was divided up among his generals to form five separate provinces. Egypt was placed under the control of Ptolemy I, who acted initially as regent for the mentally infirm half-brother of Alexander the Great. On the death of his protégé in 317 B.C., Ptolemy continued to act as regent for the younger son of Alexander while at the same time consolidating his own power in Egypt. At the same time Judaea was incorporated into the Syrian territory over which Seleucus I Nicator ruled. But in 320 B.C. Ptolemy I invaded Syria and annexed Judaea to his own dynasty, so that by the time the Seleucid regime became firmly established in Syria in 312 B.C., Palestine had fallen under the control of Ptolemy. He proved to be a prudent ruler, who pursued the enlightened and tolerant policies of Alexander, thus speedily winning the confidence of the Palestinian Jews to the extent that many of them emigrated to Egypt, and swelled the numbers of those who had already settled there in previous centuries. In return for his consideration the

[1] *MTA*, p. 3.
[2] *BCIA*, p. 1.

1175

Jews accorded Ptolemy their complete loyalty, and under his successors the province of Judaea enjoyed a prolonged period of peace and prosperity.

It was the stated policy of the earlier Seleucids generally to adopt an attitude of conciliation and friendship towards the Jewish populace. Following the pattern established by Ptolemy, the emperor Nicator, who had fallen heir to a large portion of Syria and Babylonia following the death of Alexander, encouraged his Jewish subjects to migrate to Asia Minor, and as an added inducement offered them the privileges of citizenship throughout his vast empire. Unlike the members of the Ptolemaic dynasty, however, the successors of Nicator did not display the same enlightened attitude towards the Jews as that manifested by the founder of their regime, and many of the tribulations through which the Jews in Palestine subsequently passed were occasioned by the tyrannical rule of the later Seleucids.

During the reign of Ptolemy I a good deal of grace and prestige was brought to the office of High Priest in Jerusalem by the attractive and imposing personage of Simon I (ca. 300-287 B.C.), whom Josephus styled "the Just."[3] To him was attributed the program of Temple renovation undertaken at that time, along with the general repairs made to the fortifications that surrounded the city of Jerusalem. His virtues were lauded in one of the apocryphal writings, the book of Ecclesiasticus, and his influence was so great among the Palestinian Jews that in his lifetime the government of the nation by the High Priest assumed its most attractive form.

The reign of Ptolemy II (285-246 B.C.) was important for the interest he took in the history and culture of the Jewish peoples in his empire. It was during this period that a beginning was made on the enormous task of translating the sacred Hebrew Scriptures into Greek. This version, the LXX, derived its name from the tradition that Ptolemy II, acting upon the advice of his librarian, summoned seventy scholars from Jerusalem to undertake the work of translation. As far as the political interests of Ptolemy II were concerned, his activities were directed in the main towards conciliating the Palestinian Jews, and with this in view he constructed a number of cities that served as Ptolemaic spheres of influence, including Philotera, south of the Sea of Galilee, and Ptolemais, located near Mount Carmel on the site of the ancient Canaanite port of Accho. A fresh wave of migrations to Egypt took place under Ptolemy III (246-221 B.C.), and this made for a substantial increase in the size of Jewish communities in such cities as Alexandria. The Ptolemaic dynasty was at the peak of its influence during this period, and the benevolence of Egyptian rule, combined with the material prosperity

---

[3] *AJ*, XII, 2, 5.

of the age, furnished a powerful attraction for those Jews who were contemplating the prospect of residing in Hellenized Egypt.

During the reign of Ptolemy III an avaricious High Priest named Onias II decided to withhold the tribute paid annually to his suzerain. Josephus, the nephew of the High Priest, managed to thwart this plan, and as a reward for his services was given the office of tax controller in Judaea by order of Ptolemy. He held this important position for over twenty years, and during this period of administrative supervision he was able to effect a noticeable improvement in the financial condition of his country. It was at this time, however, that the first serious rumblings of discontent with Ptolemaic rule began to make themselves heard in Jerusalem. About 225 B.C. a small reactionary group began an intensive effort to influence the Jews in favor of political alliance with the Seleucid regime of Syria. This movement was particularly gratifying to the Syrians, since from a geographical standpoint Palestine was much nearer to Syria than Egypt. When Antiochus III came to the throne of Syria in 223 B.C., the reactionary group clamored for allegiance to his regime instead of to the Egyptians. This movement brought about a deterioration in relations between the Seleucid and Ptolemaic dynasties, which was not improved by the occupation of Palestine by the Seleucids in 218 B.C. The following year Ptolemy IV sent an expedition to Raphia, and after defeating Antiochus in battle recovered Palestine for the Egyptian regime. On his return Ptolemy marched through Jerusalem and perpetrated certain acts of desecration in the Temple. Continuing his journey to Alexandria, he punished the resident Jews for the disloyalty of their Judaean compatriots by depriving them of some of their privileges.

A period of political confusion followed the death of Ptolemy IV in 203 B.C., during which Antiochus once again invaded Judaea. An Egyptian force was dispatched to northern Palestine in order to check his advance, but it suffered defeat near Sidon in 198 B.C. Antiochus thereupon occupied Judaea, making it part of the province of Syria, and when Jerusalem capitulated without a struggle the incorporation of Judaea into the Seleucid regime was complete. Some segments of the populace followed the reactionary group in welcoming Antiochus as a liberator, and he in turn continued the tolerant policies that Seleucus I had shown towards the Jews. He appointed Syrian military governors to positions in Judaea, and imposed regular taxes upon the populace. Although he guaranteed the sanctity of the Temple and made adequate grants of money to subsidize the priesthood, his firm control over the territory of Judaea soon made evident the fact that little if anything in the nature of improvement had resulted from the repudiation of Ptolemaic rule. The internecine civil strife typical of the Greek period, coupled with the growing military power of Rome, exercised an important restraining effect upon the ambitions of Antiochus, which were further restricted when the Romans invaded Asia Minor about 197 B.C. and subsequently defeated a Seleucid expeditionary force at Magnesia in 190 B.C.

Antiochus III was killed during a revolt at Elymas in 187 B.C., and was succeeded by his son Seleucus IV (187-175 B.C.). His reign was marked by heightened tension between the various political and religious factions in Judaea occasioned by a dispute as to whether Temple revenues should be collected by a civil or an ecclesiastical official. One result of this quarrel was that Seleucus IV sent an envoy to plunder the Temple treasury so that he could discharge some of the heavy debts incurred by Antiochus III in his wars against Rome. This intention, which happily for the Jews was frustrated (2 Macc. 3:23ff.), increased the bitterness between the more orthodox Palestinian Jews and their liberal counterparts, who had already succumbed to the blandishments of Hellenism. The latter were endeavoring desperately to end the traditional separation between Jews and Gentiles, employing the language, habits, and traditions of the Greeks as catalysts to this end. The more orthodox Jews still clung to the ideal of Egyptian hegemony, and resisted the encroachments of Hellenism with great vigor, realizing that the moral degeneration, irreligion, and skepticism of Greek culture had nothing in common with the religious traditions of the Torah.

The orthodox party suffered a considerable setback with the accession of Antiochus IV Epiphanes (175-163 B.C.), whose avowed policy was the dissemination of Greek culture throughout his realm in order to unite the different peoples over whom he ruled and insure the general stability of the Seleucid regime. The character of this proud and extravagant ruler was reflected in the cynical play on words that altered his royal designation from Epiphanes (*illustrious*) to Epimanes (*madman*). Almost immediately after his accession he became involved in a quarrel between the High Priest Onias III and his younger brother Joshua, the latter being a prominent member of the Hellenizing party in Jerusalem, and known widely by his Greek name of Jason. The outcome of this dispute was that Jason replaced Onias as High Priest, and was given a mandate to accomplish the Hellenizing of Jerusalem with all expedition. A number of serious conflicts broke out between the Hellenists and the loyal Hasidim, and these ultimately spread to the Temple priesthood. After three years Jason was supplanted by another pro-Hellenist named Menelaus, who gave Antiochus an even larger bribe than Jason had done for the privilege of being High Priest.

Antiochus launched a military expedition against Egypt in 168 B.C., and was within striking distance of Alexandria when the Roman senate was informed of his actions. An envoy was dispatched immediately with instructions to Antiochus to withdraw his forces, and although his pride was gravely hurt by this action he was wise enough to avoid a costly conflict with Rome by capitulating to the senate's ultimatum. In the meantime Jason had heard a rumor in Jerusalem that Antiochus had been killed during the Egyptian campaign, and on the strength of this information he launched an attack upon Menelaus and his supporters. Rebuffed and threatened as he was, Antiochus determined to vent his rage upon Jerusalem, and in 168 B.C. a detachment of 20,000 men under the command of Apollonius entered the city on the sabbath day and began to eradicate all traces of Judaism. The Temple was profaned and the sacred books of the Law were burned. A Greek altar dedicated to the worship of Zeus was erected in the Temple courts, and the sacrificial rites of traditional Judaism were replaced by pagan rituals, in which the people were compelled to participate on pain of death. In 167 B. C. a royal decree abolished the institutions of circumcision, sabbath observance, and the reading of the Torah.

Those who actively resisted these measures soon found a leader in Mattathias, a priest at Modin near Jerusalem, who had gained some renown by killing an apostate Jew and a Greek officer on an occasion when they were endeavoring to make him participate in idolatrous sacrificial rituals. Mattathias organized a guerrilla campaign against the forces of Antiochus (1 Macc. 2:45), and persuaded his followers that self-preservation took precedence over sabbath observance. On his death in 167 B.C. his son Judas Maccabaeus succeeded him; and, emboldened by initial successes, he launched into systematic attacks against the Syrian forces. The soldiers of Antiochus were defeated at Beth-horon in 166 B.C., and suffered a further reverse the following year at Beth-zur. Taking advantage of the fact that the remaining forces of Antiochus were engaged in crushing a rebellion in Parthia and Armenia, Judas Maccabaeus marched on Jerusalem, occupied the city, reconstructed the polluted sanctuary and restored the daily sacrifice. During the next two years he consolidated his hold on Judaea and prepared for further attacks upon the armies of the Syrian regime. In 163 B.C. he attempted to expel the Seleucid garrison from the old city in Jerusalem, but suffered a defeat near Bethlehem when Syrian reinforcements arrived. However, intrigue in the Syrian empire compelled Lysias, the Syrian regent, to conclude a treaty with Maccabaeus, the terms of which guaranteed Jewish religious liberties. As a result of this expedient the fortunes of the orthodox party in Jerusalem were restored to a certain extent (1 Macc. 6:59).

When the followers of Judas Maccabaeus opposed the appointment of the Hellenist Eliakim as High Priest, a Syrian force was dispatched to Jerusalem to settle the dispute. After a battle near Beth-horon in 161 B.C. in which the Syrian leader was killed, fresh Seleucid reinforcements arrived and by sheer weight of numbers turned the tide of battle against Judas Maccabaeus, who perished in the fighting. This defeat, however, did not vitiate the guarantees given earlier by Lysias, and while there still remained a strong Hellenizing faction in Judaea, the majority of the populace supported the Maccabaeans, who became known increasingly by their family name of Hasmoneans. During the succeeding years the degree of intrigue within the Jerusalem priesthood was matched by unrest and internal weakness in the Syrian empire, so that when in 142 B.C. the Seleucid garrison in the old city of Jerusalem capitulated to the forces of Simon, the last surviving son of Mattathias, thereby enabling the Judaeans to shake off the role of tributary to the Seleucids, the triumph of the Hasmoneans was complete.

Under Simon the nation enjoyed a period of religious and economic revival, but his competent leadership came to an untimely end when he was murdered in 134 B. C. by his son-in-law Ptolemy. John Hyrcanus, the one surviving son, succeeded Simon and endeavored to maintain the independence of Judaea, but was finally compelled by Antiochus VII Sidetes (139-129 B.C.) to become tributary once again to Syria. It was during the regime of John Hyrcanus (134-104 B.C.) that the party of the Pharisees was first mentioned by name. Their origin was yet another result of the impact of Hellenizing influences upon contemporary Hebrew life and culture. While many Jews, particularly those outside Palestine, adopted a reasonably tolerant attitude towards a moderate degree of synthesis between Greek civilization and Hebrew religion, there were those who interpreted the slightest incursions of Hellenism as a dire threat to the very existence of the Torah and the stability of the Jewish way of life. The Pharisees were prominent among the latter group, and although they did not exhibit the characteristic conservatism of the Sadducees, who enjoyed the favor of the Hasmonean rulers until 76 B.C., they drew upon a considerable following in Judaea, derived mostly from the artisan and middle classes. By contrast the Sadducees, who came predominantly from the powerful priestly classes, claimed little popular support.

On the death of Antiochus Sidetes, John Hyrcanus launched a successful military campaign against the Edomites, and subsequently besieged Samaria, which fell into his hands after a protracted struggle. He capitalized upon the general debility of the Seleucid domain to extend the boundaries of his own kingdom to something akin to the proportions of the monarchy during the period of Solomon. Towards the end of his reign he broke with the Pharisees, who by this time had become heirs to the ideals of the Hasidim, and sought to accommodate himself to the Sadducees, whose aims were secular and political rather than religious. This change was precipitated by a petition from Eleazar, the head of a Pharisaic deputation to Hyrcanus, suggesting that he should resign from the office of High Priest and remain in his capacity of civil governor. Although the request was well intentioned, it gave the impression of placing the family affairs of Hyrcanus in a bad light, and had as one result not merely the rise to power of the Sadducees but a decided increase in tension between Pharisees and Sadducees.

The death of Hyrcanus was followed by a period of decline which culminated in the weak rule of Alexander Jannaeus (104-78 B.C.). He was an enthusiastic supporter of Hellenism, an attitude that naturally provoked the resentment of the Pharisees. When civil war finally broke out the latter sought the support of the Seleucids, who themselves, unfortunately, were too weak to be of much assistance. As a result the Pharisees were crushed, and cruel reprisals were exacted as a warning to future rebels. Recompense was forthcoming ultimately, however, for when Jannaeus died in 78 B.C., his widow Queen Alexandra came to terms with the Pharisees to the point where they began to assume the real rule in Judaea, thus reversing the earlier situation completely. The influence of the Hasmoneans declined with the accession of Aristobulus in 68 B.C., partly as a result of the fact that his position was undermined by the intrigue of Antipater, governor of Judaea, and by Hyrcanus II. The latter in particular attempted to usurp the position of Aristobulus, but was thwarted in his immediate objective by Roman intervention in 64 B.C. under Pompey, who deposed Antiochus XIII and made Syria and Phoenicia into a Roman province.

When Aristobulus resisted this movement he was ordered by Pompey to capitulate, and on refusing was besieged in Jerusalem for three months. After a desperate battle the city was captured and the leaders of the insurrection were killed unceremoniously. The Temple was not pillaged, however, and shortly afterwards the sacrificial ritual was resumed. Jerusalem was garrisoned by Roman troops, and the districts outside Judaea were incorporated into the newly formed province of Syria. Hyrcanus was permitted to retain the title of High Priest, but his authority was restricted to Judaea proper. He fell increasingly under the influence of Antipater, father of Herod the Great; and although the Hasmoneans made several abortive attempts to regain power between 57 and 54 B.C., they failed completely in their efforts to overthrow the Herodian dynasty. Before Antipater was murdered in 43 B.C. he established his younger son Herod the Great as governor of Galilee. Herod gained the backing of Rome to support his claim to be the lawful king of Judaea, which proved to be fortunate since he had lost some prestige as the result of a battle with the son of Aristobulus II in 41 B.C. Herod besieged Jerusalem in 37 B.C. and quickly reduced it, thereby bringing the political life of Judaea firmly under Roman supervision and dispelling for ever the Hasmonean hope of independence for the nation. Although Herod catered to the religious feelings of the Jews by enlarging the Temple, his unstable and volatile personality, coupled with numerous acts of brutality and violence during the thirty-three years of his reign (37-4 B.C.), earned him the general hatred of his subjects.[4]

His son and successor, Archelaus, reigned in Judaea from 4 B.C. to A.D. 6, but was no more popular with the Jewish people than his father had been. In the end his oppressive rule led to his deposition by the Roman authorities. Herod Antipas (4 B.C.-A.D. 39), who was mentioned by name in the Gospels (cf. Mk. 6:14ff.; Lk. 3:19; 13:31f.; 23:7ff.), inherited the Galilean and Perean portions of the kingdom, but as a consequence of his marital affairs he incurred the wrath of the Nabatean king, Aretas IV, who defeated him in battle in A.D. 37. Antipas was banished by the Romans in A.D. 39, and Galilee and Perea were added to the territories in the northeast of Palestine over which Herod Agrippa I (A.D. 41-44) ruled. When the latter died suddenly in A.D. 44 (Acts 12: 2ff.), his son, also named Agrippa, exercised a nominal rule over the northern area of Palestine. He was given the prerogative of appointing the Jewish High Priest, a function that he exercised between the years 48 and 66 A.D. He was unable to prevent the intrigue that led to the outbreak of the Jewish war against Rome in A.D. 66, although he himself remained loyal to the empire until his death about A.D. 93.

It may quite possibly have been the restrictions imposed by Roman rule that furnished much of the impetus for the political and religious intrigue of this period, as well as for the development of a number of communities or religious sects that sought to preserve what they regarded as the distinctive elements of the Jewish tradition. One such political group was the Zealot party, described by Josephus as the "fourth philosophy" among the Jews.[5] It was founded by Judas the Galilean, who led an uprising against Rome in A.D. 6 to signify his opposition to the payment by Jews of tribute to a pagan emperor, on the ground that this behavior constituted an act of disloyalty towards God, the true King of Israel. Though inspired by such notable Jewish precursors as Mattathias and Phinehas (cf. 1 Macc. 2:24ff.; Num. 25:11; Ps. 106:30f.), they made little headway against the imperial forces, and their revolt was soon crushed. However, for the next sixty years they engaged the Romans in intermittent skirmishes, meeting with indifferent success. They were active in another uprising against Rome in A.D. 46, and when it failed, two of the sons of Judas who had been taken captive were crucified by orders of the procurator Alexander.[6] Twenty years later a third son, Menahem, attempted to seize control of the anti-Roman movement, which by this time was at its height;[7] and his party fought

---

[4] Cf. A. H. M. Jones, *The Herods of Judaea* (1938), p. 151; C. F. Pfeiffer, *Between the Testaments* (1959), p. 110.

[5] *AJ*, XVIII, 1, 1ff.; *BJ*, II, 8, 1.

[6] *AJ*, XX, 5, 2.

[7] *BJ*, II, 17, 8f.

vigorously against imperial forces throughout the war of A.D. 66-73.[8] Even when the last Zealot stronghold, Masada, capitulated in A.D. 73, the remnants of the party continued to resist the occupying Roman forces in a desultory manner. During their period of political and military activity the Zealots appear to have lived in small communities scattered throughout Judaea, and most probably practiced some form of communal existence.

The cleavage between the religious parties of Judaism was brought into sharp focus by the Roman occupation of Palestine, and even before the end of the first century B.C. the more zealous members of the Pharisaic party had begun to separate into communities. One of these was the "third philosophy" mentioned by Josephus, and known to history as the Essenes.[9] From descriptions of their activities they pursued a communal existence, practiced celibacy and pacifism, engaged in agricultural and other manual work, and spent a good deal of time in the study of their sacred writings as well as in liturgical exercises.[10] According to Josephus, the Essenes were to be found in all the cities of Judaea including Jerusalem. He also furnished a detailed description of their initiation procedures, which were based on a three-year novitiate culminating in a series of solemn oaths. From the accounts given in Josephus the Essenes commenced their day with prayers addressed to the sun, but this record was at variance with that supplied by Hippolytus, who merely stated that the Essenes continued in prayer from dawn onwards and refrained from engaging in conversation until they had sung a hymn of praise to God. The practice described by Josephus may in point of fact have been restricted principally to a small sect associated with the Essenes and known as Sampsaeans, who derived their name from acts of worship paid to the sun as a manifestation of divinity.

Yet another separatist group was that whose remains were discovered near the Wadi Qumran in 1947. It is considered probable that the Qumran sectaries occupied their buildings between 100 B.C. and A.D. 66, though whether they were in continuous residence throughout that period is somewhat difficult to determine. Despite the fact that many scholars have followed J. T. Milik in identifying this community with the Essenes, there are certain notable differences in their way of life as compared with general Essene practice,[11] making it undesirable to consider them as Essenes in the strictest sense of that term.[12] A protest

---

[8] C. Roth, *Journal of Semitic Studies*, IV (1959), pp. 33ff.

[9] *BJ*, II, 8, 2ff.; cf. *AJ*, XVIII, 1, 5.

[10] Cf. Philo, *Quod Omnis Probus Liber Sit*, 75ff.; Pliny, *Hist. Nat.* V, 15ff.; Hippolytus, *Refut.* IX, 20, 13ff.

[11] R. K. Harrison, *The Dead Sea Scrolls*, pp. 95ff.

[12] On the etymology of the name "Essenes" see G. Vermès, *Revue de Qumran*, II (1960), pp. 427ff.

against the general view that the Qumran sectaries were Essenes was made by Rabin, who argued that they were basically Pharisaic in character.[13] Similar in nature was the objection raised by Roth, who equated them with the Zealot partisans of the first century after Christ.[14] Assigning the Dead Sea brotherhood to the first century of the Christian era also, but regarding its members as Ebionites rather than Jewish sectaries, was J. L. Teicher.[15] Still another suggestion as to their nature and provenance was made by Marcus, who maintained that they were Gnosticizing Pharisees.[16] Certainly they constituted a small sectarian body, perhaps even unique in kind, that had withdrawn from the mainstream of Jewish life and was utilizing the disciplines of communal work, worship, and study to foster the expectation of the Messiah. Their writings indicate that they looked for the rise of three figures, a prophet similar to Moses, the Davidic Messiah, and a great Aaronic priest, who would emerge at the end of the age in order to communicate the will of God to the people and usher in the new era of righteousness. Throughout their existence the Qumran sectaries refused to acknowledge the rule of the Jerusalem High Priests, partly because of their moral inadequacy for the exalted office that they occupied, and partly because they were not of the Zadokite line of priests, which had been deposed by Antiochus Epiphanes. Instead, the brotherhood maintained its own structure of Zadokite priests and Levites, in readiness for the time when the old Jerusalem would be renewed and ritually correct sacrificial worship would be conducted in a cleansed Temple.

Certain of their ceremonial procedures had much in common with those of the various Essene groups in Palestine, and in particular their baptismal practices were in harmony with those in current use during the first century B.C. among sectarian bodies. In addition, the community at Qumran also partook of a ceremonial meal somewhat similar in character to the sacramental repast of subsequent generations of Christian believers. There are reasons for the belief that this meal may have been intended by the sectaries to represent an anticipation of the messianic banquet, which they expected to constitute an important initiatory feature in the dawning of the new era of divine grace.

It was from this uncertain and troubled situation in the realms of politics and religion that the writings constituting the Apocrypha emerged. The term itself is the neuter plural of the Greek word

---

[13] C. Rabin, *Qumran Studies* (1957), pp. 59f., 69f. For a criticism of this position see J. M. Baumgarten, *JBL*, LXXVII (1958), pp. 249ff.

[14] C. Roth, *The Historical Background of the Dead Sea Scrolls* (1958), p. 12 *passim*. For a study of this theory see R. de Vaux, *RB*, LXVI (1959), p. 102, and H. H. Rowley, *VT*, IX (1959), pp. 379ff.

[15] J. L. Teicher, *JJS*, II (1951), pp. 67ff., 115ff.

[16] R. Marcus, *JBL*, LXXIII (1954), p. 161.

ἀπόκρυφος, meaning "concealed" or "hidden." Applied to literary productions it designates those compositions intended to be kept from the profane gaze of the public because of the esoteric wisdom which they contained. Thus a magical book attributed to Moses, which may be as early as the first century of the Christian era, was designated by this term.[17] Some Greek Gnostic writings were venerated in a similar manner,[18] while certain apocalyptic works from Jewish authors of an even earlier date might be said to have partaken of this character also.[19] In 4 Esdras a distinction was made between the twenty-four canonical books, which were to be published for the benefit of worthy and unworthy alike, and the seventy or so esoteric works, which were to be preserved for the wise and tutored on the ground that they contained a more profound form of instruction (4 Esdr. 14:44ff.).[20] Following this commendatory fashion, Gregory of Nyssa even went so far as to include the New Testament book of Revelation in the category of that which was apocryphal.[21]

However, in the early Christian era the term came to be applied to writings that were withheld from general circulation owing to doubts either about their authenticity or their general value for faith and practice.[22] From the time of Origen an even more unfavorable sense of the word "apocryphal" interpreted it as describing that which was false, spurious, or heretical.[23] Thus according to the approach of the particular individual concerned, the term could have either an honorable or a derogatory sense, and could designate writings not included as well as books deliberately excluded from the Scriptural canon.

Although the period between 200 B.C. and A.D. 100 was marked by the production of a great many Jewish writings, large numbers of these were regarded as "outside books" in the best sense of the term. Since it was only towards the end of that period that the concept of a closed canon was implemented, the Jewish authorities did not regard in too serious a light the problem of the canonicity of these compositions. Technically they were known as "writings which do not defile the hands"[24] and enjoyed considerable popularity, as has been shown by the large number of Hebrew and Aramaic copies of such works circulating in Palestine, some of which were even recovered from Qumran. This vast corpus of literature is sometimes known as "Pseudepigrapha," since some of the books were issued under the names of ancient Hebrew

---

[17] Μωυσέως ἱερὰ βίβλος ἀπόκρυφος (Ed. Dieterich, Abraxas, 169).
[18] Cf. Clement of Alexandria, Stromateis I, 15.
[19] Cf. Dan. 12:4; 1 Enoch 1:2, 93:10; The Assumption of Moses, 1:16f.
[20] Cf. JE, II, p. 1; APOT, I, p. viii.
[21] Oratio in suam ordinationem, III, 549.
[22] Cf. Origen, Comm. in Matt. X, 18; XIII, 57.
[23] Origen, Prolog. in Cant. Cant. XIV, 325.
[24] JE, II, p. 1.

notables, but the term is misleading, and should properly be replaced by "Apocrypha."[25]

From the evidence furnished by the Qumran discoveries it is clear that the sectaries made little serious attempt to distinguish the canonical Scriptures from other works of a similar character. This is undoubtedly a reflection of current practices in Judaism, where the Law and Prophecy had already acquired their traditional sanctity, while the third division of the Hebrew Scriptures was moving rapidly towards a firm literary fixity by about 300 B.C. Between that time and the end of the first century of the Christian era it was possible for a number of apocryphal works to have been commonly regarded as Scriptural. But after the fall of Jerusalem in A.D. 70 the apocalyptic writings of Judaism fell into increasing disrepute, and when Christian interpolations began to appear in Jewish apocryphal works, the designation of the "outside books" became a matter of some concern. A canon of Scripture for use by the faithful was perhaps drawn up by the rabbis towards the end of the first century after Christ at the Council of Jamnia. Although the nature of the occasion has been the subject of scholarly debate, it seems clear that from the beginning of the second century the excluded literature was no longer of particular concern to the Jews, especially since there was by that period a substantial body of rabbinic literature to replace it. Indeed the Midrash Qōheleth warned that confusion would only result if more than the canonical Scriptures were read,[26] and apart from Ecclesiasticus, which survived in Hebrew literature until the twelfth century A.D., the apocryphal writings of Judaism were generally considered to be at best unsuitable for devotion, and at worst a positive danger to faith. In consequence of this attitude it can be remarked that the fact that this corpus has survived at all is due to the interest and activity of the Christian Church, many of whose members found these compositions both interesting and enlightening.

At the beginning of the Christian era the Church felt no particular inclination to proscribe those works that were not included in the Hebrew Scriptures, and there is little doubt that familiarity with such writings led to their being referred to occasionally within the general context of Scripture. However, there is no instance in the New Testament where any of the writers cited an apocryphal composition as though they recognized it as inspired Scripture or as in any way connected with matters of spiritual authority.[27] Even C. C. Torrey, who compiled a substantial list of what he deemed to be New Testament allusions to, or quotations from, the Apocrypha was compelled to concede that, in gen-

[25] Cf. C. T. Fritsch, *IDB*, I, p. 163.
[26] *Midr. Qoh.* XII, 12.
[27] G. D. Young in C. F. H. Henry (ed.), *Revelation and the Bible*, p. 175.

eral, the apocryphal literature was left unnoticed by the New Testament authors.[28] When the latter quoted from the Old Testament by way of the LXX, which preserved the apocryphal writings, they never cited material from any book that was not part of the Hebrew canon. The fact that the Alexandrian translators of the Hebrew Bible chose to preserve for posterity certain extra-Biblical compositions need not in itself necessarily imply that such writings were regarded as of equal inspiration and authority with the Hebrew Scriptures. From the contents of certain fourth- and fifth-century Biblical codices it would appear that there was no rigidly determined order of canonical books; that some "outside books" were incorporated into the canon; and that there was no definite tradition in the Greek manuscripts regarding which extra-canonical works were to be included.

These considerations can be illustrated by reference to Codex Sinaiticus (fourth century), Codex Vaticanus (fourth century), and Codex Alexandrinus (fifth century), whose contents will exemplify the diversity of usage in antiquity:

Codex Sinaiticus

Portions of Genesis and Numbers; 1 Chronicles 9:27–19:17; 2 Esdras (Ezra and Nehemiah) 9:9 to the end; Esther; Tobit; Judith; 1 Maccabees; 4 Maccabees; Isaiah; Jeremiah; Lamentations; Joel; Obadiah; Jonah; Nahum; Habakkuk; Zephaniah; Haggai; Zechariah; Malachi; Psalms; Proverbs; Ecclesiastes, Song of Solomon; Wisdom; Ecclesiasticus; Job.

Codex Vaticanus

Genesis to Deuteronomy; Joshua; Judges; Ruth; 1-4 Kings; 1 and 2 Chronicles; Ezra–Nehemiah; Psalms; Proverbs; Ecclesiastes; Song of Solomon; Job; Wisdom; Ecclesiasticus; Esther; Judith; Tobit; Hosea; Amos; Micah; Joel; Obadiah; Jonah; Nahum; Habakkuk; Zephaniah; Haggai; Zechariah; Malachi; Isaiah; Jeremiah; Baruch; Lamentations; Letter of Jeremiah; Ezekiel; Daniel.

Codex Alexandrinus

Genesis to Deuteronomy; Joshua; Judges; Ruth; 1-4 Kings; 1 and 2 Chronicles; Twelve Minor Prophets; Isaiah; Jeremiah; Baruch; Lamentations; Letter of Jeremiah; Ezekiel; Daniel; Esther; Tobit; Judith; 1 and 2 Esdras; 1-4 Maccabees; Psalms; Collected Odes; Job; Proverbs; Ecclesiastes; Song of Solomon; Wisdom; Ecclesiasticus.

Insofar as the early Christians included apocryphal writings in their lists of the Scriptures they appear to have been following the traditions of the Alexandrian canon rather than that of the Palestinian Jews. The works commonly designated by the term "Apocrypha" and which, with one or two exceptions, were included in the LXX version, can be listed as follows:

[28] *TAL*, p. 18; C. C. Torrey, *IB*, I, p. 393.

1 Esdras
2 Esdras
Tobit
Judith
The Additions to Esther
The Wisdom of Solomon
Ecclesiasticus
Baruch
The Letter of Jeremiah

Additions to the Book of Daniel
   (a) The Prayer of Azariah and The Song of the Three Young Men
   (b) Susanna
   (c) Bel and The Dragon
The Prayer of Manasseh
1 Maccabees
2 Maccabees

These works comprise additions to the LXX form of the canonical Hebrew Scriptures, and while many of them were unquestionably written in Hebrew or Aramaic, with the exception of the Wisdom of Solomon and 2 Maccabees, they were all translated into Greek at an early stage, a circumstance prompted by the popularity of such compositions in the intertestamental period.[29]

Some variation in the content of the Apocrypha as outlined above should be noted, however, since, for example, many manuscripts of the LXX included the quasi-historical books designated 3 and 4 Maccabees. Such diversity was further reflected in the fact that not all Christians of the early period recognized the apocryphal books in a uniform manner. Bishop Melito of Sardis (A.D. 170) drew up a list of the Old Testament writings that was identical with the Hebrew canon, except that it omitted Esther. Origen, who used the Greek Bible that included the Apocrypha, also followed the order of the Hebrew canon, apart from excluding Esther from his list. He further linked with the prophecy of Jeremiah a document called the "Epistle," which may be a reference either to the Letter of Jeremiah or to the Book of Baruch itself. Augustine, who used a Latin text that included the Apocrypha, regarded these works as of equal authority with the rest of the canonical Scriptures.[30] On the other hand Jerome, who was familiar with the Hebrew canon, declared as apocryphal all those writings that found no place in the list of Hebrew Scriptures. When he prepared the Old Testament portion of the Vulgate about A.D. 391, he translated from the Hebrew rather than from the LXX or Old Latin texts, and in his Prefaces to the various books he distinguished between the canonical writings of the Hebrews and those compositions that were of value for devotional use. In the end, however,

---

[29] Cf. R. H. Charles, *Religious Development Between the Old and the New Testaments* (1914), pp. 8f.
[30] Cf. *De Civitate Dei*, XVIII, 36.

the Vulgate included those works which are now commonly regarded as the Apocrypha despite the reservations of Jerome on the matter.[31] Thus the Apocrypha proper could be described as constituting the excess of the Vulgate over the Hebrew canon, derived by way of the LXX.

While there were some medieval scholars who inclined to the views of Jerome, the prevailing opinion concerning the authority and inspiration of the Apocrypha coincided with that of Augustine. A distinction was drawn between the canonical Hebrew Scriptures and the "uncanonical" writings, which included the bulk of the Apocrypha, in the work of Nicholas of Lyra (d. ca. A.D. 1340), an eminent Christian scholar of Jewish parentage who wrote a series of commentaries on the Bible. John Wycliffe in 1382 followed Jerome in rejecting as "without authority of belief" those writings which stood outside the classical Hebrew canon.

Of the early Reformers Andreas Bodenstein, who became known as Karlstadt after the name of his birthplace, regularized the use of the term "Apocrypha" to designate the excess of the Alexandrian over the Palestinian Jewish canon of the Old Testament in his *De Canonicis Scripturis Libellus* (1520), following Jerome, who had first used the term in this sense in his preface to the Vulgate translation of Samuel and Kings, the celebrated *Prologus Galeatus*. Bodenstein held that the books of Wisdom, Ecclesiasticus, Judith, Tobit, 1 and 2 Maccabees had some value, in that they were also hagiographa, but that others, including 1 and 2 Esdras, Baruch, and the Prayer of Manasseh, were clearly apocryphal. Martin Luther, a fellow-student of Bodenstein, was in substantial agreement with these conclusions, and in his 1534 German version of the Bible he collected the "outside books" that were extant in the Greek and Latin manuscripts of the Old Testament with which he worked, and relegated them to a section at the end of the canonical Old Testament, describing them as "Apocrypha." "These books," he held, "are not to be regarded as equal in esteem with the Sacred Scriptures, but yet are useful and valuable for reading."

This declaration was probably the nearest that the Church had come to that time to making any official pronouncement upon the nature and value of the books of the Apocrypha. The stand taken by Bodenstein and Luther established the inferior position of the Apocrypha in relation to the Old and New Testaments, and the Roman Catholic Church was quick to respond to the challenge. In 1546 the Council of Trent followed the canon of the Council of Hippo (A.D. 393) and that of Augustine, which declared all the Apocrypha to be canonical with the exception of 1 and 2 Esdras and the Prayer of Manasseh. In the official Vulgate of 1592, however, they were printed as an appendix following the New Testament, which helped to atone for their earlier omission. Because the

---

[31] Cf. H. F. D. Sparks in H. Wheeler Robinson (ed.), *The Bible in Its Ancient and English Versions,* p. 112.

books of the Apocrypha were now accorded the status of articles of belief, the Council of Trent pronounced the man anathema who did not
accept as canonical the entire books with all their parts as read in the
Catholic Church.[32]

Of the printed Bibles of this general period the Zurich Bible, produced
by the Swiss Reformers, included the apocryphal books and prefaced
them by the comment that they were not reckoned as Biblical by the
ancients, nor found among the Hebrews. The translation by Coverdale in
1535 followed the Continental Reformers in separating the apocryphal
books from the Old Testament canon. Matthew's Bible, published in
1537, also adopted the position taken by Coverdale, but included the
Prayer of Manasseh in the Apocrypha and removed Baruch from its
position following the book of Jeremiah, placing it after Ecclesiasticus.
In 1599 an edition of the Geneva Bible was issued without the Apocrypha, but this appears to have been accidental.[33]

Some representatives of the Reformed Churches who attended the
Synod of Dort in 1618 urged that certain apocryphal books of a legendary nature be excluded from future printed editions of the Bible, but the
Synod was unwilling to accede to this request. Other representatives
present then urged that the Belgic Confession, drawn up in 1561 for the
Protestant Churches in Belgium and the Netherlands and later adopted
by Reformed Churches elsewhere, be made the standard for distinguishing between the canonical books of the Old Testament and the contents
of the Apocrypha. In particular they pointed to Article VI, which stated
that, as far as the Apocrypha was concerned,

> the Church may read and take instruction from, so far as they agree with the
> Canonical books; but they are far from having such power and efficacy as that
> we may from their testimony confirm any point of faith or of the Christian
> religion; much less to detract from the authority of the other sacred books.

Even this device failed, and although the Synod sanctioned the publication of the Apocrypha as part of Scripture, it recognized the arguments
put forward in opposition to the extent of enacting the provision that the
books should be printed in smaller type, be accompanied by explanatory
notes pointing out doctrinal divergences from the canonical writings, and
be placed at the end of the Bible after the New Testament.

The King James Bible of 1611 followed normal custom in printing the
Apocrypha as a separate work and inserting it between the Old and
New Testaments. Subsequent issues of the Authorized Version, however,
were frequently printed without the Apocrypha.[34] The Westminster

---

[32] ". . . libros ipsos integros, cum omnibus suis partibus, prout in ecclesia catholica
legi consueverunt et in veteri vulgata Latina editione habentur, pro sacris et canonicis,
anathema sit."

[33] BCIA, p. 144.

[34] MTA, p. 197.

Confession of 1648 marked the final stage in the setting aside of the apocryphal literature from the standpoint of doctrine and authority. It decreed that

> the books commonly called Apocrypha, not being of Divine inspiration, are no part of the Canon of Scripture, and therefore are of no authority in the Church of God, nor to be in any otherwise approved, or made use of, than other human writings.

Some attempt to bridge the gulf between the widely divergent opinions of individuals and ecclesiastical bodies in antiquity regarding the value and authority of the Apocrypha was made by the formularies of the Church of England. Taking a position similar to that of Rufinus (d. A.D. 410), the Thirty-Nine Articles regarded the apocryphal books as ecclesiastical in nature, and of value for moral purposes. Thus Article VI stated,

> ...and the other books (as Hierome saith) the Church doth read for example of life and instruction of manners; but yet doth it not apply them to establish any doctrine.

This was a typically Anglican compromise, since the Apocrypha had fallen into disuse without official ecclesiastical approval or any formal statement regarding its value for doctrine or faith. Subsequently Article XXXV recommended two books of Homilies for their doctrinal content, although in these compositions passages were quoted freely from the Apocrypha as from the canonical writings, a situation that approximated somewhat to that in the early centuries of the Christian era.[35]

At the beginning of the nineteenth century the ultimate point in the dissociation of the Apocrypha from the Biblical compositions was reached when the British and Foreign Bible Society in London decided not to print the Apocrypha as part of its Scriptures. From its organization in 1804 the Society had followed the practice of subscribing funds to affiliated Societies on the continent of Europe, all of which circulated the Apocrypha in conjunction with the Old and New Testaments. Discussion of the matter broke out into the open when this policy was opposed by Scottish Presbyterians and by some evangelicals who supported the auxiliary Societies; and as a result the entire question was aired thoroughly for over a decade. The Edinburgh Bible Society issued a statement denouncing the Apocrypha as "replete with instances of vanity, flattery, idle curiosity, affectation of learning and other blemishes; with frivolous, absurd, false, superstitious and contradictory statements."[36] After a good deal of discussion, which unfortunately was

---

[35] Cf. W. O. E. Oesterley, *An Introduction to the Books of the Apocrypha* (1935), pp. 125ff.

[36] *Statement . . . Relative to the Circulation of the Apocrypha* (1825), append. p. 8.

marred by bitterness, the Bible Society decided in 1827 that the circulation of the Apocrypha was at variance with its basic principles. As a result the Society discontinued its subsidies to those affiliates that thereafter printed and distributed the Apocrypha as part of the Scriptures. This policy had embarrassing repercussions shortly before the coronation of King Edward VII in 1901, when the presentation Bible was supplied by the Bible Society. According to British tradition, the Bible that the newly initiated monarch kisses prior to signing the coronation oath must contain the Apocrypha.[37] At the last moment the presentation Bible was found to be deficient in this respect, and another copy that included the Apocrypha was hurriedly secured.

During the middle of the nineteenth century, controversy over the Apocrypha flared up once more, on this occasion in Germany. As the result of an essay competition set by a Bible Society in Karlsruhe in 1851, the two winning dissertations catalogued the defects of the Apocrypha in some detail, and recommended that the corpus be dispensed with in future printed editions of the Scriptures. This stand provoked a whole series of addresses, dissertations, and books, during which scholars undertook an exhaustive textual and critical investigation of the apocryphal writings.[38] The general consensus of scholarly opinion was that the Apocrypha should in fact be retained in published editions of the Scriptures, a stand which was endorsed by even the most conservative of the investigators.

In the Greek Orthodox Church some if not all of the apocryphal books have long been regarded as canonical, whereas the two divergent views which existed in the early Christian period have been perpetuated by the Roman Catholic Church on the one hand and by Protestant bodies on the other. Declaring itself supremely authoritative in all matters involving the canon of Scripture, the Roman Catholic Church has pronounced the Apocrypha canonical, and of equal value for doctrine with the Old and New Testaments. This stand has led to some doctrinal embarrassments, as for example in the teachings concerning purgatory, the very concept of which is expressly repudiated by the Book of Wisdom (3:1ff.). The Protestant Churches have emphatically rejected the Roman Catholic position concerning the inspiration and authority of the Apocrypha, maintaining that the Old Testament and New Testament are alone to be regarded as inspired Scripture.

[37] *MTA*, p. 202 n. 20; cf. E. J. Goodspeed, *The Story of the Apocrypha* (1939), p. 7.
[38] Cf. O. F. Fritzsche and C. L. W. Grimm, *Kurzgefasstes exegetisches Handbuch zu den Apokryphen des AT*, 6 vols. (1851-60); O. F. Fritzsche, *Libri apocryphi Veteris Testamenti Graece* (1871); O. Zöckler, *Die Apokryphen des AT nebst einem Anhang über die Pseudepigraphen-litteratur* (1891); E. C. Bissell, *The Apocrypha of the OT* (1880); H. B. Swete, *The OT in Greek According to the Septuagint* (1899). Cf. A. Rahlfs, *Septuaginta* (2 vols., 1935).

The compromise position adopted by the Church of England was carried to its logical conclusion in the Lectionary contained in the Book of Common Prayer. From the first edition of Edward VI in 1549, the Lectionary has always contained a series of lessons from the books of the Apocrypha. This pattern has been followed to a greater or lesser degree by the member churches of the Anglican communion, despite certain modifications resulting from local revisions of the Book of Common Prayer.

In supplying the world with an entirely unexpected cache of inter-testamentary literature, the caves of Qumran have also pointed to the immense importance of the classical apocryphal writings for any understanding of the period that followed the death of Alexander the Great and culminated in the destruction of the Jewish state as such. These multifarious documents reflect clearly the nature of the transition brought about by the Hellenizing policies of the various Seleucid rulers, and in the intellectual and moral field they demonstrate the manner in which such mediatorial concepts as those of angelic beings and wisdom secured a place in both Jewish and Christian belief.

For the Christian in particular these sources furnish a graphic illustration of the spiritual barrenness of contemporary religious life, and justify the incidence of the Incarnation in the manner envisaged by St. Paul when he recorded that God sent forth His Son when the fulness of the time had come (Gal. 4:4). Quite aside from historical, political, religious, and sociological considerations, there are aesthetic values to which one can appeal in any move for the retention of the Apocrypha as legitimate material for edification and instruction. As Brockington has shown, the Apocrypha is a kind of literary picture gallery hung with paintings of various sizes and merit, but all of them unique in character, and as they age becoming increasingly valuable and irreplaceable.[39] While the books at best do no more than hover on the fringe of canonicity, they are nevertheless an important and lasting record of men and nations in conflict over political, moral, and spiritual values, and as such their message transcends the boundaries of their own day.

[39] *BCIA,* p. 157.

II. THE FIRST BOOK OF ESDRAS

Alone of all the books of the Apocrypha, this work consists to a large extent of a somewhat divergent account of happenings already recorded in several of the Old Testament canonical writings. In the LXX the book was entitled Esdras *alpha*, and corresponded to 3 Esdras in the Vulgate version, while in the Lucianic recension of the LXX it was designated 2 Esdras. The book furnished a parallel account of events recorded in 1 and 2 Chronicles, Ezra, and Nehemiah, along with one notable addition known as the *Debate of the Three Soldiers* (3:1–5:6). On comparison it appears that 1 Esdras 1:1-20, 23-25 is parallel to 2 Chronicles 35:1–36:23; 1 Esdras 2:1-11 parallels Ezra 1:1-11; 1 Esdras 2:12-26 corresponds to Ezra 4:7-24; 1 Esdras 5:7-71 parallels Ezra 2:1–4:5; 1 Esdras 6:1–9:36 is the equivalent of Ezra 5:1–10:44, while 1 Esdras 9:37-55 records events mentioned in Nehemiah 7:72–8:12, breaking off in the middle of a sentence describing the public reading of the Torah by Ezra. Thus the book covers by selection the history of Israel from the late pre-exilic period to about 444 B.C., when Ezra promulgated the Law in the restored Jewish state.

In view of the manner in which 1 Esdras drew upon material from the canonical Old Testament books, the nature of the relationship between it and them has been a matter of considerable speculation among scholars. One significant aspect of the question is the fact that the LXX already had a translation of 1 and 2 Chronicles, Ezra and Nehemiah entitled *1 and 2 Paralipomenon and Esdras,* the latter book (i.e. Ezra-Nehemiah) being designated Esdras *beta* in order to distinguish it from the apocryphal work. The problem was further compounded by the fact that Josephus, living in the first century after Christ, preferred to use 1 Esdras as his authority for the period covered instead of the canonical writings of Ezra and Nehemiah. There is no question as to the immense popularity of the intertestamental writings generally in their day and age, and it may be that the style of the Greek of 1 Esdras commended the work to Josephus as a valuable historical source. The LXX version of Ezra and Nehemiah adheres closely to a Hebrew original, and the resultant literalistic and mechanical rendering of the canonical writing might have made it less preferable to Josephus and others as a literary

1194

composition when contrasted with the freer and more idiomatic style of 1 Esdras.

In their attempts to solve the problem of the relationship between 1 Esdras and Ezra-Nehemiah, scholars have suggested that the latter corpus was derived from the former; that 1 Esdras constituted a revision or modification of Ezra and Nehemiah, or that both reached back to a common original no longer extant. It can be observed at once that 1 Esdras is clearly not a translation of the MT of Ezra and Nehemiah, although it was most probably based on a closely related text belonging to one of the families now known to have been circulating in Judaea in the immediate pre-Christian period. A comparison of 1 Esdras with the LXX version of Ezra and Nehemiah shows that, while the two documents are probably independent translations from the Hebrew original, they do not reflect a usage of the same text. 1 Esdras appeared to follow a literary tradition for which, in at least some instances, there seems to be good textual evidence. The contrast of readings and the variation in chronology involving the Persian kings also point to a version of the Hebrew that was somewhat different from the MT. While 1 Esdras may perhaps be slightly earlier than Esdras *beta*, there is little question that the canonical books of Ezra and Nehemiah were already extant, making it highly improbable that Ezra and Nehemiah were derived from 1 Esdras.

The First Book of Esdras rearranged the chronological material found in the canonical histories in the interests of a continuous narrative, and it may be that this motive furnished sufficient justification for the existence and popularity of the work. The gap of about fourteen years between the end of Ezra and the beginning of Nehemiah was closed by making the contents of Nehemiah 8 follow the end of the Ezra narratives. This expedient, however, omitted a good deal of important information contained in Nehemiah 1:1–7:27a, and it is doubtful whether in fact the rearrangement represents any significant improvement upon the chronological sequences of the canonical writings. Elsewhere there are numerous errors of fact, inconsistencies, and repetitions of events, which combine to make it an unsatisfactory piece of historical writing. By way of illustration it can be remarked that the narrative passes from the reign of Cyrus to that of Artaxerxes, returns to the period of Darius, and then reverts to Artaxerxes, a procedure that does not serve the interests of the chronology very adequately.

While the book gives evidence of being a direct translation from a Semitic original rather than constituting a revision of an extant Greek source, the relationship between the Hebrew Ezra-Nehemiah, the LXX Esdras *beta*, and the apocryphal 1 Esdras is still far from clear, despite the scholarly speculation mentioned above. It may be that behind 1 Esdras there lies an ancient Hebrew text that rivals the MT in its intrinsic value. The difficulty with such a view is that it is impossible to be absolutely sure that 1 Esdras was compiled directly from the Hebrew whether from a text related to the MT or not, a situation that i complicated by the lack of general agreement among scholars regarding the suggestion that the deviations in 1 Esdras are the result of using different Hebrew text. If 1 Esdras was by some chance compiled from Greek sources, it might well have been based on a manuscript other than the LXX Esdras *beta*, which was probably not the only Greek version of Ezra-Nehemiah extant at the time.[1] Certain agreements between Esdras and the LXX Esdras *beta* as against the Hebrew of Ezra and Nehemiah have led to the suggestion that behind Esdras *beta* lay the MT proper, and that 1 Esdras drew upon an even older text from which a Greek translation had been made. This latter would then constitute working prototype of 1 Esdras in an unrevised form. However, this source has not survived, and it must be regarded as at best highly dubious that it ever existed.

The date of the composition is as doubtful as some of the questions relating to its origin. Evidence for the priority of 1 Esdras over the LXX Esdras *beta* consists principally of the position that it occupied in th contents of the major manuscripts, as well as the fact that Josephus preferred it as a source for his *Antiquities*. The latter consideration however, need have little bearing upon the date of the version, since Josephus may well have been governed by interests other than securing the most ancient Greek texts available for use as historical sources. Esdras would thus appear to be the work of a compiler who based his composition upon some form of 1 and 2 Chronicles, Ezra, and Nehemiah, to which he added a story from a source as yet unknown. This interpolation, the Debate of the Three Soldiers, was probably an adaptation of an old Persian tale,[2] and it may have been included in the narrative in order to identify the hero of the incident with Zerubbabel the celebrated builder of the Second Temple (1 Esdr. 4:13).[3] Torrey considered the story to have been a translation from a Hebrew and Aramaic original, and in this he was followed by Browne, who posited strictly Aramaic source.[4] Rudolph, on the other hand, upheld a Greek origin for the story, maintaining that the statement concerning truth was added just prior to the time when the story was circulated among the Jews.[5]

While the date of the compilation or translation of 1 Esdras cannot be fixed with any accuracy, there are certain considerations that might require it to be relegated to the work of an Alexandrian Jew during th

---

[1] N. Turner, *IDB*, II, p. 141.

[2] *HNTT*, pp. 252f. Cf. F. Zimmermann, *JQR*, LIV (1963-4), pp. 179ff.

[3] Cf. R. C. Dentan, *The Apocrypha, Bridge of the Testaments* (1954), p. 46.

[4] C. C. Torrey, *AJSL*, XXIII (1907), pp. 197ff., *Ezra Studies*, pp. 26ff., 58ff., *TA* pp. 48ff. L. E. Browne, *Early Judaism* (1929), p. 29.

[5] R. Rudolph, *ZAW*, LXI (1945-48), pp. 176ff.; similarly, *OTFD*, p. 390.

econd century B.C. In 1 Esdras 4:10a, 59f., there seems to be some
ague reminiscence of the LXX of Daniel 2:23f., 37, which, if it does not
ctually suggest that 1 Esdras and Daniel were translated by the same
and,[6] might at least imply that the Greek versions of these books
merged from the same general period. Certainly the final form of 1
'sdras must have been in circulation prior to A.D. 100, since Josephus
mployed it as a source. If the work was translated from Hebrew, the
riginal would almost certainly be pre-Maccabean. In its present state it
; somewhat fragmentary, though whether it constitutes an extract from
 larger work, or whether it has survived as an incomplete form of a
nore comprehensive original, is difficult to state. There seems little
eason to question the view of the majority of scholars that 1 Esdras was
ompiled about 150 B.C.

To add to the difficulties of an already complicated situation, further
roblems are encountered in any endeavor to assess the purpose of
/riting of what Dentan has styled "a pathetic orphan among books,"
-hose history is a problem, whose nature is obscure, and whose very
ame is uncertain.[7] It could hardly have been intended as a definitive ac-
ount of events after the edict of Cyrus permitted the captives in
;abylonia to return home, since the canonical books of Ezra and Nehe-
niah took care of that. Nor would the errors and contradictions in the
-ork commend it as a reliable source to any serious student of Jewish
istory. While the aim of the compiler may have been to glorify the
-orship of God as envisaged in the restored Temple and to give proper
redit to the work of Ezra in this regard, the inclusion of pagan folklore
night easily have detracted from the value of the composition as far as
ne pious Jew was concerned. If 1 Esdras was intended for circulation as
 popular work dealing with certain religious aspects of the exilic and
ost-exilic period, principally the history of the Jewish Temple and its
ultus, it may have been sufficient in the mind of the author for religious
onsiderations to be promoted at the expense of historical accuracy and
iternal consistency.

The book commenced with an account of the Passover celebration
uring the reign of Josiah, after which the events transpiring after the
attle of Megiddo were narrated. The description of the fall of
erusalem and the deportation of the exiles to Babylon concluded the
rst chapter, which corresponds closely to 2 Chronicles 35:1–36:21. It
nay be that this material prefaced 1 Esdras in order to demonstrate that
he exile was part of the divine plan and to furnish some historical
·ackground for the narratives about Zerubbabel and Ezra. Chapter 2
nentioned the decree of Cyrus and the manner in which the Jews
esponded to it. This particular section corresponds to 2 Chronicles

---

[6] Cf. N. Turner, *IDB*, II, p. 142.
[7] R. C. Dentan, *The Apocrypha, Bridge of the Testaments,* p. 44.

36:22f. and Ezra 1:1-11, and was followed by another one, simil; in content to Ezra 4:7-24, describing the frustrations encountered b those who were attempting to rebuild the walls of Jerusalem and recon struct the Temple. While this passage was probably intended to bring th narrative down to the work of Zerubbabel in the reign of Darius, ther are certain unfortunate historical errors present that appear to hav escaped the notice of the author or compiler. Thus from the account in Esdras it appears that Artaxerxes I (464-423 B.C.) preceded Darius (522-486 B.C.), which is incorrect. Presumably the narrative section i 2:15-26 was designed to explain the reason for the delay in the constru tion of the Second Temple until the second year of Darius, despite th instructions of Cyrus.

The central portion of 1 Esdras contains material for which there is n parallel in the Old Testament writings. It consists of a story (3:1–5:6 describing a competition between three soldiers of Darius, the third whom was identified with Zerubbabel by means of what is almo certainly an explanatory gloss (4:13). The soldiers were passing th time after a sumptuous banquet given for the nobles of the Persia empire by debating what constituted the most powerful thing in th world, on the assumption, presumably, that Darius would honor the mo profound answer. The first soldier proposed wine, the second suggeste the person of the king, and the third offered as his opinion the observ tion that while women are the strongest, truth was the victor over things. At a subsequent gathering the soldiers were invited to defer their ideas on the matter, at the end of which the third soldier w applauded as the winner of the debate. On being asked by Darius name his reward, the soldier requested the sanction of Darius for th return of the Temple treasures and the reconstruction of the Temp itself.

It is probable that this story was adapted from some facet of ancie Near Eastern folklore in order to give prominence to Zerubbabel. Edit rial connections with what follows may perhaps be seen in 4:43-4 57-61, while in 4:47 Darius was substituted for Cyrus in the narrative Ezra 3:7. The provenance of the story itself is most probably Persia rather than Greek, despite the reference to truth, though whether bears any real relationship to the Aramaic *Wisdom of Aḥikar,* as su gested by Pfeiffer,[8] is a matter of some debate. Certainly the work Aḥikar was familiar to the Jewish colony in Elephantine, and in nature resembled the Assyrian wisdom literature as well as certain portions the canonical book of Proverbs. These considerations would seem point to a Persian rather than a Greek origin for the tale.[9]

[8] *HNTT*, p. 252. Cf. A. T. Olmstead, *JAOS*, LVI (1936), p. 243.
[9] Cf. A. Cowley, *Aramaic Papyri of the Fifth Century B.C.*, pp. 206f.

The remainder of 1 Esdras continued the narrative of the return and the reconstruction of the Temple, followed by the promulgation of the Torah under Ezra. The material in this section was based upon the parallel passages in the canonical writings. The author recorded three different times when the exiles returned to Jerusalem, the first being under Sheshbazzar in 538 B.C., the second under the leadership of Zerubbabel in 520 B.C., and the third supervised by Ezra in 397 B.C. On each occasion the returning exiles were recorded as bringing with them the sacred Temple vessels that had been carried to Babylon in 587 B.C., a situation that presents certain obvious difficulties.

As Metzger has stated, the inconsistencies and historical errors of the book can only lead to the charitable verdict that the author was more concerned with the moral and spiritual issues of his subject than with an accurate chronology of events.[10] In particular, the recounting of the debate among the three soldiers furnished him with an excellent opportunity for moralizing, and it is not without good reason that the climax of the discussion, enshrined in the aphorism "great is Truth, and mighty above all things" (Vulgate, *Magna est veritas, et praevalet*), has attained the stature of a proverb. Augustine went even further, and in the light of the Johannine proclamation of Christ as the way of truth and life (John 14:6) understood 1 Esdras to be prophetic of the person of Christ.[11]

Finally it may be remarked with Brockington that the very fact that 1 Esdras is extant is an interesting commentary on the state of literary activity in Israel, which, within about two or three centuries, witnessed no less than three attempts to chronicle the sequence of events after the decree of Cyrus had been promulgated in 538 B.C.[12] Of these Esdras *alpha*, the 1 Esdras of the English Apocrypha, was employed as a preferred source by a noted Jewish historian in his description of the happenings in that eventful era.

Supplementary Literature

Ball, C. J. *The Variorum Apocrypha*. 1892.
Bayer, F. *Das dritte Buch Esdras und sein Verhältnis zu den Büchern Ezra-Nehemia*. 1911.
Cheyne, T. K. *Jewish Religious Life After the Exile*. 1898.
Lupton, J. H., in H. Wace (ed). *The Apocrypha*. 1888.
Tedesche, S. S. *A Critical Edition of 1 Esdras*. 1928.

[10] *MTA*, p. 18.
[11] *De Civitate Dei*, XVIII, 36. The underlying Semitic idiom of hendiadys in John is seldom noted by translators.
[12] *BCIA*, p. 18.

III. THE SECOND BOOK OF ESDRAS

The second book of the English Apocrypha was known in the Greek canons as "Esdras the prophet" (Ἔσδρας ὁ Προφήτης) or "The Apocalypse of Esdras" (Ἔσδρας Ἀποκάλυψις). In the Latin Church it was designated 4 Ezra,[1] while the Vulgate more specifically described chapters 3–14 as 4 Esdras, chapters 1–2 as 5 Esdras, and chapters 15–16 as 6 Esdras. The reason for this subdivision apparently consisted in the fact that 2 Esdras comprised a Jewish apocalypse to which certain Christian material had been prefaced, and which had been concluded by a further section originating either in Christian or Jewish circles. Some oriental versions of 2 Esdras lack the interpolated material, while the text of the work has been preserved most faithfully by the Latin version, which was derived from a Greek translation of a lost Hebrew original. The close resemblance of the composition to certain parts of the New Testament made for its widespread usage in the Early Church, and resulted in the Greek version's being rendered into Syriac, Ethiopic, Arabic, Armenian and Georgian. The work was also quoted by certain of the patristic writers, beginning about A.D. 200 with Clement of Alexandria.[2]

As with 1 Esdras, the problems of compilation and transmission associated with 2 Esdras are very involved. The central section, known as the Ezra-apocalypse, was probably written in Aramaic by an unknown Jew at the end of the first century after Christ, since the author appears to have witnessed the destruction of Jerusalem (2 Esdr. 5:35; 10:45).[3] In such an event the work may well have been compiled in Palestine although the exact place of origin is unknown. The middle of the second century saw the addition of the first two chapters of the extant book, and it is thought probable that as much as a century later the final two chapters were appended. Apart from a few fragments in the Oxyrhynchus Papyri,[4] the Greek text of 2 Esdras has perished with the Hebrew

---

[1] Cf. *APOT*, II, pp. 542f.

[2] *Stromateis*, III, 16.

[3] Cf. *APOT*, II, p. 552. On the original Hebrew text see A. Kaminka, *Monatsschrift für Geschichte und Wissenschaft des Judentums*, LXXVI (1933), pp. 76f.

[4] *Papy. Oxyrhyn.* VII, 1010.

1200

r Aramaic original. An interesting feature of the medieval Latin ver-
ions was that they preserved chapter seven in such a way as to indicate
textual hiatus between verses 35 and 36, following a ninth-century
manuscript, Codex Sangermanensis. In 1874 the omission was rectified,
when R. L. Bensly discovered another ninth-century manuscript named
Codex Ambianensis, which contained the missing section. The AV had
followed the medieval Latin practice of omission, but the English revi-
ion of the Apocrypha in 1895 utilized the discovery of Professor Bensly
and included the section previously left out.[5] That this additional mate-
ial was not unknown to textual scholars has been shown by Metzger,
who pointed out that eighteenth-century Bibles published in Westphalia
and Pennsylvania contained this lost section.[6] Obviously there were good
easons why this section was excluded from medieval Latin manuscripts,
one of the most pressing being that the passage contained an emphatic
denial of any value attaching to prayers for the dead (7:105), an
attitude diametrically opposed to Roman Catholic dogma.

On the basis of the available evidence there would seem to be a
variety of sources from which 2 Esdras was compiled. The first two
chapters, as has been remarked above, were of Christian origin and may
possibly have been composed by a convert from Judaism about A.D.
150. The Ezra-apocalypse itself, consisting of chapters 3–14, can be
subdivided as follows:

1. the Salathiel apocalypse (ch. 3–10)
2. the eagle vision (ch. 11:1–12:39)
3. the vision of the Man from the Sea (ch. 13)
4. the legend of Ezra the Scribe (ch. 14)

Chapters 15 and 16, which constitute an appendix to the Ezra-
apocalypse, may have originated in Jewish or Jewish-Christian circles as
late as A.D. 270. Such a delineation of sources is of interest if only
because it shows that the central portion of the work is one of the latest
in the entire Apocrypha, and that the majority, if not all of the New
Testament books antedated its final form, which was probably in circulation somewhat after A.D. 100. The nature of this composite work is such
as to make Palestine a more preferable place of origin than Alexandria or
Rome.

2 Esdras commenced with a lengthy genealogy of Ezra, the alleged
author, and this was apparently inserted for the purpose of demonstrat-
ng his priestly descent from the line of Aaron. Ezra then informed his
hearers of his mission to convict the Jews of their sin and announce the
choice of the Gentiles, who would become believers and would participate in the joyful advent of the Saviour (2 Esdr. 1:30; cf. Matt. 23:27;
2 Esdr. 1:37; cf. John 20:29). The second chapter concluded with an

5 Cf. B. M. Metzger, *JBL*, LXXVI (1957), pp. 153ff.
6 *MTA*, pp. 23f.

account of Ezra's experience of a vision of the risen saints standing in a great number on Mount Zion and receiving palms, symbolic of victory from the Son of God (2 Esdr. 2:42; cf. Rev. 7:9; 14:1). In what is probably a redactional addition, the final sentence of the chapter enable an easy transition to be made to the principal apocalyptic section.

Here the reader is introduced to a type of literature reflecting a form of religious thought whose roots probably reach back to the Zoroastriar religion of ancient Persia. Apocalyptic writings, whether those of the canonical Biblical books or of the Apocrypha, purported to reveal the future, and such works were as popular among the Jews prior to A.D. 70 as they were among the early Christians. Because of their Persian roots apocalyptic themes tended to enshrine a cosmic metaphysical dualism related both to the present age, which was deemed to be under the influence of the powers of evil, generally identified with Satan, and also to a future period of blessed perfection during which the overall control of God would remain unchallenged.[7] In addition to these features there was, as Frost has pointed out, a deterministic pattern that was characteristic of apocalyptic,[8] and the revelation itself was couched in symbolic imagery. It was further marked by obscure allusions to the world powers and to eschatological events in connection with which the advent of the righteous age would be ushered in. The nature of apocalyptic literature was such that the hidden meaning was clear enough to those who were initiated into the mysteries of this kind of religious thought, but concealed by the very form of the composition from the gaze of those who were unacquainted with the subtleties of the situation. It is important to recognize with Rist that the basic pattern of ancient apocalypticism consisted of dualistic and eschatological elements, upon which were superimposed at a subsequent period such concepts as the purely visionary factors, the personage of a Messiah, some measure of angelology, demonology, or both, and an admixture of other ingredients such as numerology, animal or plant symbolism, and facets of astral beliefs.[9]

All apocalyptic writers shared the common conviction that the inhabitants of the earth were inextricably caught up in the struggle between the two opposing and irreconcilable powers of good and evil. The monotheism of traditional Israelite faith prevented Jewish and Christian writers from contemplating the kind of philosophical dualism envisaged in Iranian thought, and their general view was that Satan was an inferior being who ruled only because God allowed such a state of affairs. In 2 Esdras the inherent dualism was further weakened by the concept that the evil *yēçer* was the principal cause of wicked deeds among human beings (2 Esdr. 3:20ff.). Since these sinful tendencies were inherited, it fol-

---

[7] Cf. *APOT*, II, pp. 554ff.
[8] S. B. Frost, *OT Apocalyptic* (1952), p. 20.
[9] M. Rist, *IDB*, I, pp. 157ff.

lowed that the entire human race was in bondage to the powers of evil, and that the situation promised to become worse rather than better. Thus it could hardly occasion surprise that the few surviving righteous persons who lived according to the precepts of the Torah would be subjected to oppression and persecution by their wicked contemporaries. The only hope of the righteous was that God would intervene with power and crush the might of the adversary, thereby inaugurating a new age of grace in which God alone, as supreme ruler, would reward His faithful followers with rich spiritual blessings.

Because the concept of apocalypse was modified to some extent through its derivation from a Greek word meaning "revelation," the disclosure was sometimes, though not uniformly, furnished in the context of a vision. Frequently, however, this latter merely constituted a literary device employed by the author to secure the attention of his readers and convey to them a sense of his own authority in the matter of the revelation itself. Where the author felt a sense of personal inadequacy in this regard he generally resorted to pseudonymity, and issued his works under such notable names of Hebrew history as Abraham, Moses, Solomon, and the like.[10]

The presence of a Messiah in Jewish apocalyptic sources was generally considered to be of secondary importance, an attitude quite different from that enshrined in such Christian apocalypses as the book of Revelation. However, certain Jewish writings gave great prominence to the Son of Man, as in Daniel 7:13 and the Similitudes of Enoch 46, 48, 62, 63, and 69. Where there was a messianic interval, as in 2 Esdras 7:28f., the personage of the Messiah was an obvious necessity. Even under such conditions, however, comparatively little mention was made of the functions of the Messiah. On occasions the messianic figure was balanced by a corresponding "antichrist," and both were very frequently supported by large numbers of angels and demons, although it should be noted that not all apocalyptists were attracted by this trend.

One of the more bizarre features of the apocalyptic writings was the use of animal and plant symbolism, whether in relationship to messianic passages such as 2 Esdras 11 or not. The beast of Daniel and Revelation, and the four living creatures of Ezekiel, constitute obvious examples of this tendency. Again, despite the popularity of this form of symbolism, not all apocalyptic writings emphasized it, and some ignored it completely.

The determinism of apocalyptic thinking was accompanied by a certain degree of pessimism that maintained the absolute impossibility of any prospects of improvement or betterment in the existing world situation. But as Rowley has pointed out, this attitude did not comprise pessimism in its most characteristic sense, but was instead the manifesta-

10 Cf. L. H. Brockington, *JTS*, IV (1953), pp. 15ff.

tion of a rather realistic approach towards affairs as they actually were, in the conscious appreciation that good could never emerge from evil.[11] By contrast there was inherent in the nature of apocalypticism a resolute optimism that the best has yet to be, and this was reinforced by the conviction that through a conscious exercise of divine power in the future, evil would be banished from the world and would be replaced by an established pattern of goodness. It may well have been the feeling that nothing could be done to improve the immediate situation that accounts for the almost complete lack of ethical and social teachings in the apocalyptic writings generally. Whereas the canonical Hebrew prophets proclaimed divine judgment upon an obstinate and wayward Israel, the apocalyptists were convinced that Israel was righteous, and that therefore her sufferings were entirely unmerited. Only when the present world order was reversed by divine intervention would Israel be vindicated, and her fundamental righteousness be made plain for all to see. From this point of view, therefore, there was not the same degree of moral or ethical urgency as that called for by the circumstances that confronted prophets such as Amos, Micah, and Hosea.

Against such a background it is now possible to examine the principal section of 2 Esdras. The first subdivision, the Salathiel apocalypse, identified the visionary with Ezra (2 Esdr. 3:1ff.), which is, of course, merely a literary fiction, for it was consistent with the nature of apocalyptic that the real author should be concealed behind a pseudonymous designation. In 2 Esdras Salathiel was employed in this connection originally, and in subsequent editing an explanatory gloss was most probably added, identifying Salathiel with Ezra. Since the former (Shealtiel) was a well-known member of the Jewish royal family and the father of Zerubbabel (Ez. 3:2; 1 Esdr. 5:5), it is clear that he could not have been the same person as Ezra, who lived nearly a century later. Most probably the references to Ezra were inserted when chapter 14, which deals with the literary activity of Ezra, was attached to the Ezra-apocalypse. There is no known reason why the author of the latter should have chosen the name Salathiel in preference to another and more familiar one from the events of Hebrew history. On the other hand it may be that not all apocalyptic writers sought to commend their work by issuing it under some prominent Hebrew name, despite frequent assertions to the contrary, and that some were quite content to employ a comparatively unknown designation. A comparison of 2 Esdras with a related pseudepigraph, 2 Baruch, fails to throw any light on this particular issue.

The first vision (3:1–5:19) showed Ezra bewailing the fate of the exiles and pondering on the problem of evil. In particular he was perplexed by the fact that those who were punishing Israel had committed even greater sins than those of their victims. The answer fur-

---

[11] H. H. Rowley, *The Relevance of Apocalyptic* (1944), p. 163.

ished by the angelic being Uriel stressed that the limitations of the human mind precluded an understanding of the divine plan for Israel, but that the coming age of righteousness would witness the vindication of the Chosen People. In response to an impatient inquiry, Uriel stated that the new age would dawn when the predetermined number of the righteous had been completed.

The second vision (5:20–6:34) dealt with an analogous problem, namely why Israel, the chosen of God, should have been delivered to an iniquitous nation to be humbled by punishment. The additional question was raised as to what would constitute the fate of those who died before the present age of travail gave way to the glorious future of divine rule. The answer was that the processes of history are inscrutable, and that responsibility for initiating the end of this age must rest with God alone. Those mortals who were so unfortunate as to fail to survive in order to enjoy it would be given appropriate status in the new era of grace. This period would be ushered in by means of clearly recognizable signs, including a time when men would be converted to the true saving faith.

The third vision (6:35–9:25) asked in a protracted manner why it was that the Jews had not already inherited the earth, since in the last analysis it had been created for their sake. The return of the angel Uriel to Ezra (7:1-17) was followed by a discussion of the numbers of those who were to be saved, along with a lengthy description of such eschatological matters as final judgment and the fate of the wicked. A promise was given of a messianic reign that would last four hundred years, and after that time a break in human existence would ensue, to be followed by the resurrection and final judgment (7:28-35). It is at this point that Israel would enter upon her spiritual inheritance, while the wicked, who had not travelled the narrow road leading to the kingdom, would be destroyed. This latter prospect caused Ezra in his vision to intercede for the lost mass of humanity (7:132ff.), and as a result he was upbraided for appearing to esteem the creature more highly than the Creator. As with the first and second visions, the third concluded with a list of premonitory signs heralding the coming judgment.

The fourth vision (9:26–10:59) revealed the concern of Ezra for Israel because the nation was destined for severe punishment. His vision included the figure of a woman who had been sorely bereaved under the most distressing circumstances. Ezra reproved her for her undue self-concern, reminding her that the grief of Israel for Jerusalem was of a far greater order. At this the woman became transfigured and vanished, leaving behind a glorious city, the heavenly Zion (10:29ff.). In explanation Ezra was informed that the present sorrow of Israel would soon terminate, and would be followed by the building of the new Jerusalem.

The fifth vision (11:1—12:51) was an allegorical one involving symbolic animals. One of these was a three-headed, twelve-winged eagle that arose from the sea and was rebuked for its oppression by a fierce lion who emerged from a wooded area. At this juncture the wings and heads of the eagle disappeared, and finally the body itself was burned up. The interpretation of this vision was that the eagle represented the last of the four world empires described in Daniel (Dan. 7:3), namely Imperial Rome, with the three heads probably being intended to signify Vespasian, Titus, and Domitian,[12] while the wings may have been former rulers of Rome or generals aspiring to that position. The lion symbolized the Messiah, whose function, among other things, was to punish the wicked at the end of the age and deliver the faithful remnant of Israel in accordance with the vision of Daniel.

The sixth vision (13:1-58) also contained a symbolic figure, that of a powerful man arising from the sea and annihilating his enemies by fire. Subsequently a peaceful crowd gathered around this man, and by way of interpretation Ezra was informed that the multitude represented the ten captive northern tribes of Israel whose fortunes were being restored. The man was the pre-existent Messiah, and his emergence from the sea indicated symbolically that nobody knew precisely when the Son of God was destined to make His appearance.

The final vision (14:1-48) differed to some extent from its precursors. Ezra was informed of his imminent departure from the midst of human society, and in some despair he pleaded to be permitted to rewrite the Books of the Law, which had been destroyed previously. Inspired by God he dictated the divine books to five scribes within a forty-day period, producing in all ninety-four books. Of these, twenty-four, constituting the books of the Old Testament, were intended for immediate publication, while the remaining seventy, which were more esoteric and consisted of the Apocrypha and other extra-canonical writings, were to be reserved for the use of the initiated members of the populace. Finally, Ezra was transported to the realm occupied by all those who shared a like mind and spirit.

At this point the oriental manuscripts terminate, but some of the Latin manuscripts contain chapters 15 and 16 as an appendix to the work. In these non-apocalyptic sources Ezra was promised that the tyranny of Rome would soon be ended (15:1-27), and that the nations which had oppressed Israel at an earlier period, such as Egypt, Syria, Babylon, and Asia, would themselves receive punishment (16:1-39). A warning was also issued to the faithful, telling them of the difficulties that they would encounter on the earth as the result of human wickedness (16:40-51). They were to engage in a realistic spiritual self-appraisal, and were encouraged by the assurance that evil would soon be removed from the

---

[12] *BCIA,* p. 24 n. 1.

face of the earth and God would emerge triumphant with His people (16:68-78).

By its very nature 2 Esdras presents certain bizarre factors for the modern reader, reaching back as it does to an age in which elaborate symbolism and visionary interludes were accepted features of insight concerning the future. Despite the strange and perhaps even alien form that some of the visions assume, and the tedious repetition that was so much a part of the Semitic mind, 2 Esdras contains an obvious mastery of literary expression deserving more than a passing glance. In common with much other ancient Near Eastern literature, the passages that describe, for example, the majesty of the Creator on the one hand or the pathos of the sorrowing on the other, are marked by dynamic poetic cadences which reflect most creditably upon the original author.

What is also of interest is the fact that the book as a whole comes to grips, as other ancient Near Eastern writings had also done, with the perennial problem of evil and the suffering of the innocent.[13] Although 2 Esdras is unable to attain to the levels of spiritual insight characteristic of the book of Job, it nevertheless insists that faith in the justice and providence of God is a prerequisite to any understanding of the problem of evil. Despite the sober outlook frequently found in apocalyptic writings, the book is essentially a theodicy fulfilling the purpose of endeavoring to justify to man the workings of the Divine.

Supplementary Literature

Bensly, R. L. *The Missing Fragment of the Fourth Book of Ezra.* 1875.
Gry, L. *Les dires prophétiques d'Esdras* (2 vols.). 1938.
Kabisch, R. *Das vierte Buch Esra auf seine Quellen untersucht.* 1889.
Porter, F. C. *The Messages of the Apocalyptic Writers.* 1909.
Violet, B. *Die Ezra-Apokalypse. I: Die Ueberlieferung.* 1910.
————. *Die Ezra-Apokalypse. II: Die Apokalypsen des Ezra und des Baruch in Deutscher Gestalt.* 1924.

[13] Cf. W. Mundle, ZAW, XLVII (1929), pp. 222ff.

IV. THE BOOK OF TOBIT

This pious romance concerning the fortunes of a righteous captive of the northern dispersion was one of the most popular of its kind in the intertestamental period. Although it contains obvious elements of folk-lore from various sources, the skill of the author enabled the pagan sources to be subordinated to the larger purpose of furnishing specifically Jewish moral and religious instruction in the form of an adventure.

The popularity that the composition enjoyed can be gauged from the fact that it was transmitted in three recensions of the Greek text[1] as well as in the Latin, Syriac, Hebrew, and Ethiopic versions. The Old Latin occurred in four manuscripts, and was closely akin textually to the Codex Sinaiticus recension.[2] The Vulgate was also of the same general type, although it is possible that an Aramaic text of Tobit was known to Jerome in addition to the Old Latin. Fragments of Tobit in Hebrew and Aramaic were found among the manuscript deposits in the Qumran caves,[3] and it is of some interest to note that they also agreed substantially with the textual traditions of Codex Sinaiticus and the Old Latin.

The varied form of the Greek recensions has naturally raised some questions as to their relationship. It seems probable that there are two principal editions of the Greek text, represented by Codex Sinaiticus on the one hand, and by Codices Vaticanus and Alexandrinus, supported by one other uncial and several minuscule manuscripts, on the other. A third subsidiary type, based principally upon Codex Sinaiticus, occurs in a few minuscules. While the two main types exhibit considerable agreement in matters of vocabulary and the general construction of sentences, there are distinct differences in text and content of a kind that may suggest that both were derived from an even earlier Greek source. The Sinaiticus account is considerably longer than that found in Vaticanus and Alexandrinus, but this feature may merely be due to an

---

[1] One represented by Codices Vaticanus and Alexandrinus, another by Codex Sinaiticus, and a third by the cursives 44, 106, 107, and 610. Cf. J. Rendle Harris, *American Journal of Theology*, III (1899), pp. 541ff.

[2] *APOT*, I, pp. 175ff.

[3] J. T. Milik, *BA*, XIX, No. 4 (1956), p. 88, *Ten Years of Discovery in the Wilderness of Judaea* (1959), p. 31.

independent scribal expansion of the text. Codex Vaticanus has been thought to constitute an improved edition of the longer form, and is probably more satisfactory in that it fills in certain lacunae present in Tobit 4:7b-18 and 13:8-11a of the Sinaiticus version. That the latter is earlier than the other principal edition of Tobit in Greek has been adduced from its more accurate list of Assyrian kings, its attention to geographical detail, and its reflection of an earlier theological standpoint concerning questions of tithing and fasting.[4] The Sinaitic codex appears to be closer to the style of a Hebrew or Aramaic composition and may perhaps have depended to some degree upon a Semitic original.

The question of the language in which Tobit was first written is naturally involved in any discussion of the priority of extant texts. The only external evidence was supplied by Origen in his letter to Africanus and Jerome's preface to the book in the Vulgate, but this still leaves the matter entirely open, since Origen professed not to know of a Hebrew text whereas Jerome did. On the whole, internal evidence has been interpreted subjectively by scholars to favor either a Greek or Aramaic original.[5] When Milik first examined the Qumran fragments of Tobit he inclined towards an Aramaic precursor of the Greek version, but this view need not necessarily be valid, since although the Elephantine papyri have shown that Aramaic would have been commonly used from the fourth century B.C. onwards by Jewish writers whether in Palestine, Egypt, or Mesopotamia, the persistence of Hebrew as a living language among the Qumran sectaries might well imply that a religious composition of the character of Tobit would be transmitted in Hebrew rather than Aramaic. Zimmermann followed Pfeiffer and Simpson in leaving the question of the original language quite open,[6] although he favored the existence of a Hebrew form of the text intermediate between the Aramaic and Greek recensions.

The nature of the original language of Tobit has in turn a bearing upon the place of composition of the work. Once more this is a problematical issue, since the book itself affords peculiarly little in the way of evidence. It appears to have been written at least in part in the first person by the alleged author, who claimed to have been taken captive to Nineveh under Shalmaneser V in 722 B.C. Yet it also hints at a knowledge of events occurring in the kingdom of Judah (Tobit 14:4f., 15) and mentions certain features that are normally associated with the Greek period (cf. 2:12; 5:14), as well as reflecting post-exilic religious developments (1:7). The book could thus have been written against a general Palestinian background, although this has been considered less likely by

---

[4] A. Wikgren, *IDB*, IV, p. 659.
[5] Cf. *APOT*, I, pp. 181f.
[6] F. Zimmermann, *The Book of Tobit* (1958), pp. 36f. *HNTT*, pp. 272f. *APOT*, I, p. 182.

some scholars than a Mesopotamian or even an Egyptian cultural milieu. While the incidence of demonology and magic might possibly point to Mesopotamia as the place of origin, the fact that the author was guilty of certain errors connected with the history and geography of the Near East makes this supposition unlikely.

Examples of this kind of inaccuracy consist in the assumption that it was Shalmaneser V who conquered Naphtali and Zebulun in 734 B.C. whereas it was actually his predecessor Tiglathpileser III who accomplished this feat (2 Kgs. 15:29); that Sennacherib was the son of Shalmaneser (Tobit 1:15), whereas in point of fact he was the son of Sargon II (although in this instance it may be that Tobit was following the traditional Semitic usage of "son" to mean "descendant"); and that Nineveh was reduced by Nebuchadnezzar and Assuerus (Tobit 14:15) instead of by Nabopolassar and Cyaxares as history shows.[7] In matters of geography the author falsely stated that the Tigris was situated between Nineveh and Ecbatana, although it may have been that he was actually describing one of the many tributaries of that river. It is also possible that he may have thought that Nineveh stood on the site of Seleucia, and therefore described the location accordingly.[8] Again, the writer regarded Rages as being a one-day journey from Ecbatana, whereas in point of fact the distance would require nearly two weeks by camel-caravan.

Some scholars including Löhr, Simpson, and Goodspeed followed Nöldeke in supposing that Egypt was the home of the author of Tobit, on the basis of the supposition that the work was originally written in Greek.[9] If, however, the historical and geographical errors and inconsistencies militate against a Mesopotamian background they are even more direct evidence against Egypt as the place of writing. The use of the extra-canonical *Story of Ahikar* by the author of Tobit has also been urged in favor of an Egyptian compositional milieu. Since the most primitive form of this story was Aramaic, it might indicate that Tobit also was written in Aramaic originally, and not in Greek as some scholars have supposed. Ahikar was depicted by Tobit as being his nephew and occupying a prominent office in the State and who, according to the northeastern version, adopted a wayward nephew named Nadan. The latter lived riotously, and finally procured a charge of treason against his uncle, thus securing his imprisonment. However, he was saved from immediate execution, and when Sennacherib stood in urgent need of wise counsel during a period of difficult relations with the pharaoh of

[7] Cf. C. C. Torrey, *JAOS*, LXVI (1946), p. 8.

[8] Cf. C. C. Torrey, *JBL*, XLI (1922), pp. 237ff.

[9] M. Löhr in E. Kautzsch (ed.), *Die Apokryphen und Pseudepigraphen* (1900), I, p. 136. D. C. Simpson in *APOT*, I, pp. 185ff. E. J. Goodspeed, *The Story of the Apocrypha*, p. 13. Th. Nöldeke, *Monatsberichten der Berliner Akademie* (1879), p. 62.

Egypt, Ahikar was able to resolve his problems satisfactorily, and gain the royal ear for more personal matters. In consequence of this his dissolute nephew was exposed, and Ahikar was vindicated as a righteous man. Although the *Story of Ahikar* was well known in Egypt, it probably originated in Babylonia in the seventh century B.C., so that dependence upon such a source can hardly be used as a conclusive argument to predicate Egyptian provenance for Tobit.

Be that as it may, some scholars have envisaged a further indication of an Egyptian background for the composition in the reflections that Tobit contains of the *Fable of the Grateful Dead* and the *Tractate of Khons*, the latter being extant as early as 500 B.C. Whatever factual content there may be in such allegations, it is simply a matter of observation that it is far from easy to argue from the internal evidence to a specific locale of composition, since the author has woven the various sources of his book together with great skill. Perhaps Tobit was written in a community of Jews such as that at Alexandria where there were wide literary interests in the Greek and Roman periods. Pfeiffer pronounced firmly in favor of Judaea, or more specifically Jerusalem, as the place of origin of the composition, although he conceded that the work echoed some of the feelings of the Jewish Diaspora.[10]

The date of composition is perhaps the least perplexing of the issues involved in a consideration of Tobit. It contains no references to the Maccabean revolt, so that presumably it can be assigned to a *terminus ad quem* of ca. 180 B.C. Some Roman Catholic scholars have dated Tobit as early as the seventh century B.C.,[11] but the majority of writers in the present century have favored a date of composition between 200 and 175 B.C.[12] The fragments from Qumran are not particularly helpful in this matter, since the date assigned to them has ranged from the sixth century B.C. down to A.D. 70.

The purpose of the author appears to have been that of weaving together certain ethical aspects of current pagan tales with other maxims concerning morality in order to inculcate an attitude of piety towards God and a desire for proper behavior in human society. Unlike many of his contemporaries Tobit abhorred apostasy, and as an antidote to this tendency he emphasized fidelity to the Mosaic Torah. He showed that a correct perspective of humility and faithfulness towards God would be reflected in sobriety of conduct, justice, and honesty. In more practical terms he was able to demonstrate the importance for life of tithing, marriage obligations, acts of charity, religious duties, and respect for the dead. One of his most memorable ethical enunciations was the negative

---

10 *HNTT*, p. 275.

11 E.g. C. Gutberlet, *Das Buch Tobias* (1877).

12 So J. T. Marshall, *HDB*, IV, p. 788; D. C. Simpson, *APOT*, I, p. 185; J. Goettesberger, *Einleitung in das AT* (1928), p. 178 n. 3; W. O. E. Oesterley, *An Introduction to the Books of the Apocrypha*, p. 169; *TAL*, p. 85.

form of the Golden Rule: "What you hate, do not do to anyone" (Tobit 4:15).

The book itself opened with a description of the piety of Tobit, who at a later period was described as accompanying his wife and son into exile during the reign of Shalmaneser. Even in captivity he resisted impure pagan influences, and gave succor to his fellow Israelites during the oppressive rule of Esarhaddon (RV, Sarchedonus). The latter appointed Aḥikar, the nephew of Tobit, to be keeper of the signet, and it was he who recalled Tobit from self-banishment. Some time after this Tobit became blind through an accident, and his wife was compelled to earn the living. Despite his affliction Tobit remained faithful to God and continued his life of piety. Meanwhile, at Ecbatana in Media, Sarah the devout kinswoman of Tobias prayed earnestly for death as a relief from her condition of suffering and privation occasioned by the premature death of seven husbands. The third chapter dealt with the way in which God responded to the pleas of both Tobit and Sarah, and described the mediating offices of the archangel Raphael who was sent to accompany Tobias, son of Tobit, to Media in order to bring back Sarah as his wife.

After reciting several moral precepts Tobit sent his son Tobias along with a companion, who was actually the archangel in disguise, to Media. On arriving there they caught a fish from the River Tigris and brought its entrails to the kinswoman of Tobit. On the bridal night the heart and liver of the fish were burned in order to drive away the demon Asmodeus,[13] the real cause of the affliction of Sarah, into Egypt. Tobias and Sarah returned to Tobit, who was subsequently cured of his blindness by the application of fish-gall (11:1-18). Raphael then revealed his true identity and discoursed at some length on such matters as almsgiving and charity. After a prayer of rejoicing in chapter 13, Tobit foretold the fall of Jerusalem (587 B.C.), the restoration of the city, and the fall of Nineveh as prophesied by Jonah. Tobit then died, and his son Tobias lived on to a ripe old age.

Although the book is completely unhistorical it furnishes a useful glimpse of traditional Jewish piety in the second century B.C. It demonstrates faith in the providence of God, and contrives to subordinate the various elements of apocalypticism in favor of emphasizing certain fundamental moral and religious truths, not least of which were various aspects of the divine character. The narrative also throws interesting light upon the developing doctrine of angels, spirits, and demons during the intertestamentary period. Finally, Tobit himself is seen to be the precursor and exemplar of the later orthodox Jews who sought to establish the pattern of their lives upon the basis of what have been called the

[13] Cf. P. Haupt, *JBL*, XL (1921), pp. 174ff.

"three pillars of Judaism," namely almsgiving, fasting, and prayer (Tobit 12:8; cf. 1:16; 11:14; 12:9; 2:4; 3:1ff.; 6:17; 8:5ff.).

Supplementary Literature

Conybeare, F. C., J. R. Harris and A. S. Lewis. *The Story of Ahikar.* 1913.

Gerould, G. H. *The Grateful Dead.* 1907.

Möller, J. *Beiträge zur Erklärung und Kritik des Buches Tobit.* 1907.

Neubauer, A. *The Book of Tobit.* 1878.

Pautrel, R. *Le Livre de Tobie.* 1957.

V. THE BOOK OF JUDITH

This dramatic story enshrined the adventures of a patriotic Jewess named Judith, who through guile and daring brought about the death of the enemy leader and saved her people from imminent destruction. It can be considered as one of the best examples of its kind to emerge from the intertestamentary period, and drew in part for its inspiration upon the activities of other notable women in previous historical eras who, by their counsel or cunning, had managed to stave off the forces of destruction (cf. Judg. 4:4ff.; 5:24ff.; 9:53; 2 Sam. 20:14ff.).

So popular was the underlying theme that the book was generally accorded the stature of historicity by the early patristic writers. Following the decision of the Council of Trent, which regarded the composition as canonical, some modern Roman Catholic scholars have supported the historicity of its contents,[1] although others have come to regard it as allegorical or legendary in nature.[2] Luther adhered to the view that the book was a religious allegory, and few subsequent Protestant scholars have questioned his opinion,[3] with some Jewish and Christian writers admitting that at the most there may be only a slight historical content or some allusion to historical events in the book of Judith.[4]

The extensive circulation of the work in antiquity is evident from the fact that no less than four different forms of an early Greek version have survived among the manuscripts,[5] all of which go back to an original Hebrew text which is no longer extant.[6] Where the work contains quotations from the canonical Old Testament books it is evident that they correspond to the LXX in form. The Syriac and Old Latin versions were

[1] E.g. P. A. Raboisson, *Judith: la véracité du livre de ce nom* (1898).

[2] E.g. A. Scholz, *Das Buch Judith eine Prophetie* (1885); F. Lenormant, *La divination chez les Chaldéens* (1874), pp. 153f.

[3] Only O. Wolff, *Das Buch Judith als geschichtliche Urkunde verteidigt und erklärt* (1861), defended its historicity.

[4] E.g. L. Herzfeld, *Geschichte des Volkes Israel* (1847), I, p. 319; H. Graetz, *Geschichte der Juden* (1866), IV, p. 132; H. Winckler, *Altorientalische Forschungen* (1900), II, pp. 266ff.

[5] These are: (1) the LXX, representing the tradition of the great uncials; (2) Codices 19, 108; (3) Codex 58; and (4) Codices 106, 107.

[6] Cf. F. Zimmermann, *JBL,* LVII (1938), pp. 67ff.

made from a Greek manuscript closely resembling Codex 58, but the Vulgate version, based according to Jerome on an Aramaic manuscript, has not preserved as good a text. The oldest extant portion of the work was found in Cairo in 1946, and consisted of a few verses from chapter 15. It was assigned to the middle of the third century after Christ on palaeographic and other grounds.

Although the chronological sequences mentioned in the book purport to cover a period of several centuries, the actual events probably took place within the space of a few months. The historical scene was set in a period shortly after the return of the Babylonian captives to Judaea, as contrasted with the time of the actual composition of the book, which is considerably nearer the Maccabean period. In the composition the Jews were represented as apparently free from foreign domination, and living under the control of a High Priest and a council of elders. The attempt by the author to locate Bethulia in the uplands of Ephraim would have placed it in fact within the territory of the Samaritans, who were nowhere mentioned in the book. If Bethulia is to be identified with Shechem,[7] which John Hyrcanus overthrew in 128 B.C., it may be that the book was written prior to the fall of the city in an attempt to persuade the Samaritans to ally with the Jews against the Hellenists.[8] If this was actually the motive for the compilation of the story it is all the more surprising that the Samaritans were not mentioned at all, and that their sacred center was referred to under a pseudonym. Since Galilee and the coastal plain were only annexed during the reign of Alexander Jannaeus (102-76 B.C.), the implication that this territory stood outside Judaea proper might well point to a date of composition around 150 B.C.

From the contents of the book scholars have sought to place its origin in various eras of Jewish history, ranging from the seventh century B.C. to the second century of the Christian era.[9] However, to take at face value the historical situations that the composition purports to describe is extremely precarious, since the author is guilty of a great many errors and anachronisms. Thus Nebuchadnezzar was held to have ruled in Nineveh, despite the fact that this city fell in 612 B.C., some seven years before Nebuchadnezzar became king of Babylon. The same monarch was also credited with an impossibly long reign, extending to the time when the Jewish Temple was rebuilt and affording the king an extra half-century of life. The ruler of Media, under the fictitious title of Arphaxad (Judith 1:1, 5, 13, 15; cf. Gen. 10:22), was given an even longer rule by the author, which in all amounted to about one hundred and fifty years. Further evidences of internal unreliability concern the

---

[7] Cf. C. C. Torrey, *JAOS*, XX (1899), pp. 60ff.; *TAL*, pp. 91ff.
[8] Cf. P. Winter, *IDB*, II, p. 1025.
[9] Cf. *HNTT*, pp. 293ff.

stories of Holofernes and his forces, who were made to perform impossible feats of maneuverability and conquest, as well as the matter of geographical locations, some of which clearly defy any identification (e.g. Judith 1:6, 9; 1:21ff.; 4:6; 10:10).[10] Perhaps the most assured guide in the matter of dating is the consistent pietistic emphasis manifested by the book, which marks it as a product of Palestinian Judaism *ca.* 150 B.C., at a time when the characteristic doctrines and practices of Pharisaism were beginning to gain the ascendancy.

Whether based on an actual deed of valor or not, the book recounted the courage of a young Jewish widow who employed considerable cunning, deceit, and enterprise in her objective of overthrowing the forces of Nebuchadnezzar. The composition in its extant form falls naturally into two parts, the first of which (1–7) furnished the alleged historical setting of the incident, while the second (8–16) supplied the remainder of the narrative and the account of the closing years of the life of Judith. The first section opened with the decision of Nebuchadnezzar, "king of the Assyrians [*sic*], the Great King, the Lord of the whole earth" to punish those vassal states that had not assisted him in his war against Media. Holofernes, the commander-in-chief, subdued all (3:1-10) except the Jews of Judaea, who determined to block his advance against Jerusalem (4:1-15). Holofernes summarily rejected the advice of Achior, leader of the Ammonites, from whom he had sought military intelligence, and directed his forces against the fortress of Bethulia. He cut off their water supply (7:1-18) and besieged the site for thirty-four days, at which point the morale of the defenders sank to a low ebb and a plan of surrender was discussed (7:19-32).

During this period of crisis the alluring widow Judith encouraged the people to continue in faith (8:1-25), and rejected their appeal that she in her piety should pray for rain in favor of her own plan for deliverance from the enemy (8:28-36). After an extensive and prayerful preparation (9:1-14), Judith adorned herself in her richest attire, and going over to the tent of Holofernes gained his confidence and promised to help him conquer Judaea (10:14–11:19). Holofernes began to entertain a passion for Judith, and capitalizing upon this situation she was able to behead him when he was overcome with wine and lust. Returning to Bethulia she displayed the severed head (13:11ff.) and stimulated the defenders to an attack upon the Assyrians (14:11). The enemy fled in complete disorder and Judith was honored in the ensuing victory. Hymns of praise were sung (15:8–16:17) and trophies of the battle were dedicated to the Lord. The book concluded with an account of the later years in the life of Judith, and of the peace that ensued throughout Judaea during that period.

[10] Cf. *MTA,* pp. 50f.

The purpose of the story was quite clearly to demonstrate that faith in God was warranted even in the very worst of circumstances, and served as an admonition to the reader to show the same kind of courage under adverse conditions as that manifested by Judith.[11] It is the sort of tale which fits most readily into the time of the Maccabean uprising against incursive Hellenism under Antiochus Epiphanes. Despite the obvious errors and inconsistencies in the book, there is an important theological undertone in the composition which ought not to be neglected. The heroine exemplified the legalistic Pharisaic piety of the Maccabean era to a nicety in her rigorous compliance with the requirements of ritual procedure. She observed the feasts of the new moon and the sabbath along with their eves (Judith 8:6), as required by later Pharisaic teachings, and abstained from food at the appropriate intervals. But over and above the ritual correctness of Judith was her awareness that the difficulties experienced by Israel were the direct result of sin (Judith 5:17f.; 11:10); that salvation would only come through trust in and obedience to the divine will, and that God often employed the weak to confound the strong (Judith 9:10). The Pharisaic background of the theology of Judith, however, is seen most clearly in the concept that obedience to God, which constitutes righteousness, consists in the strict observance of those precepts laid down by the Law.

Though there are elements in the book that would seem entirely out of character in less troubled times, the composition is in general harmony with the ancient traditions regarding other intrepid Hebrew women. As a tract for the times, Judith may well have served to rekindle the spirit of patriotism among orthodox Jews, and inspire those who were struggling with the insidious forces of Hellenism to new heights of moral and spiritual endeavor.

Supplementary Literature

Charles, R. H. *Religious Developments Between the Old and New Testaments.* 1914.

Grintz, J. M. *Sepher Yehudith.* 1957.

Scholz, A. V. *Kommentar zum Buche Judith.* 1887.

Stummer, F. *Geographie des Buches Judith.* 1947.

Stummer, F. and V. Hamp, *Tobias, Judith, Ester, Baruch.* 1950.

---

11 *APOT*, I, p. 247.

VI. THE ADDITIONS TO THE BOOK OF ESTHER

This material, entitled in the AV and RV "The Rest of the Chapters of the Book of Esther which are found neither in the Hebrew nor in the Chaldee," constitutes six additional sections that add considerably to the dimensions of the LXX version of Esther. Taken together the supplementary passages do not in fact constitute a separate continuous narrative, and it is only when they are considered as distinct elements that were meant to be inserted at various points in the LXX text that their true nature is apparent. The fact that they have been collected together in the English Apocrypha and enumerated as though they followed Esther 10:3 as continuous material is completely misleading.

Although Esther is apparently the only canonical Old Testament work that does not seem to have been represented in the manuscript deposits at Qumran, it was nevertheless a popular and widely circulated work in its own right. The Hebrew text of Esther was translated into Greek by a person named Lysimachus, probably during the second century B.C., and at six different places the LXX narrative was supplemented by the insertion of episodes that had no counterpart in the Hebrew, all of which amounted to approximately one hundred and five verses. While these additions may not have been the work of one author, they all appear to have been written originally in Greek, since they contain too few Semitisms to require a Hebrew original.[1] Normally designated by the letters A to F, the supplementary passages were inserted into the narrative as follows: A before 1:1; B following 3:13; C and D after 4:17; E following 8:12, and F after the concluding words of Esther 10:3. From a date given in 11:1 either the Greek translation of Esther or the expanded version itself could have been made in 114 B.C. Certainly by the time of Josephus the *Additions* were already a part of Esther, and in his *Antiquities* he made use of all of them except A and F.[2]

The augmented form of Esther passed into the Old Latin version, but when Jerome prepared the Vulgate he translated from the canonical

---

[1] *APOT*, I, p. 665. Cf. *HNTT*, p. 308; J. M. Fuller in H. Wace (ed.), *The Speaker's Commentary, Apocrypha I* (1888), pp. 361ff.

[2] *AJ*, XI, 6, 1.

Esther and relegated the additions to an appendix, along with explanatory notes. At a later time these comments were omitted in printed editions, resulting in an incomprehensible section from 10:4—16:24, which was printed as though it were a unity.[3]

The sections in summary as related to the text of the canonical book of Esther are as follows:

A. 11:2—12:6. *The Dream of Mordecai*

This section prefaced Esther, and recounted a vision that Mordecai, a Jewish official in the city of Susa, experienced in the second year of the reign of Artaxerxes the Great. Amid scenes of tumult two dragons commenced fighting, upon which pagan nations prepared to attack the Jews. By way of deliverance there came a river and a great light. On awaking Mordecai overheard two eunuchs plotting to assassinate the king. When he reported this he received a rich reward, but the jealousy of Haman, who may have been in league with the conspirators, was aroused.

B. 13:1-7. *The Edict of Artaxerxes*

This section purports to be a copy of the letter mentioned in Esther 3:13, which had been sent to all the governors of the provinces commanding the extirpation of the Jews.

The date of the massacre was stated to be the fourteenth of Adar, which is at variance with Esther 3:13; 8:12; 9:1, which correctly recorded that the thirteenth day of Adar was to be the specified day of slaughter. This insertion was followed by Esther 3:14—4:17.

C. 13:8—14:19. *Prayers of Mordecai and Esther*

This section recorded the supplication of Mordecai (13:8-18) and also of Esther (14:1-19) to God on behalf of their people. Mordecai insisted upon refusing to bow down before anyone except God, and prayed that the Almighty Lord would spare His people. Before commencing her prayer Esther removed her rich attire, and garbed in mourning she recalled the divine promises of earlier days. She sought courage and eloquence for herself so as to thwart the plan of destruction and be used to save her people from death.

D. 15:1-16. *Esther Before the King*

Three days later Esther went to the king in ceremonial array, and approached the royal presence in great trepidation. When rebuked she fainted, but was revived by the king and was permitted to state her petition.

This section elaborated on the contents of the canonical Esther 5:1-2, which it displaced in the Greek form of the book. It was followed by Esther 5:3—8:12.

E. 16:1-24. *The Counter-Edict*

A copy of the royal letter furnishing the text of the edict countermanding the one mentioned in B. It permitted the Jews to retaliate in kind on the thirteenth of Adar.

[3] *MTA,* p. 56.

Then follows Esther 8:13–10:3.

F. 10:4–11:1. *The Epilogue*

An interpretation of the dream of Mordecai as described in A. He recognized that the river was Esther, while the two dragons represented Mordecai himself and Haman. The divine plan for Jews and Gentiles was appropriately fulfilled, and was to be commemorated in the Feast of Purim.

A colophon (11:1) concluded the additions, stating that in the fourth year of Ptolemy and Cleopatra[4] the letter concerning Purim had been brought in translated form to Egypt.

As contrasted with the canonical book of Esther, in which there is an absence of references to God, and a minimum of allusions to Jewish religious rites and ceremonies, the Additions are characterized by open expressions of devotion, faith, and prayer to God. The Prayers of Mordecai and Esther (Addition C) may well have been intended to furnish an already popular work with those religious elements that would make it even more acceptable to its readers. From the standpoint of the patriotic Jew, the Additions would reinforce the anti-Gentile character of the canonical Esther, while the inclusion of the two royal edicts would add to its historical appearance and trustworthiness. By the manner in which they introduced a new theme, Additions A and F may be regarded both as a literary attempt to embellish the original narrative and to deepen the religious tone of the book as a whole.

Supplementary Literature

Jacob, B. *Das Buch Esther*. 1890.
Scholz, A. *Commentar über das Buch Esther*. 1892.
Streane, A. W. *The Book of Esther*. 1907.

[4] For various interpretations of this date see B. Jacob, ZAW, X (1890), pp. 274ff.; E. Bickermann, *JBL*, LXIII (1944), pp. 339ff.

VII. THE WISDOM OF SOLOMON

Of all the literature reflecting the Jewish concept of *hokhmāh*, the book of Wisdom is one of the most notable. It has its roots in the ideology and teachings of the ancient Hebrew sages as represented in certain writings of the Old Testament and in such books of the Apocrypha as Ecclesiasticus, but it is considerably further removed than these compositions from the original idea of wisdom as expounded in early Semitic circles, due predominantly to the influence of Greek thought.

Probably the first reference to the title of the book was contained in the Muratorian Canon (A.D. 200), where it was spoken of as *Sapientia . . . ab amicis Salomonis in honorem ipsius scripta.* Of the patristic writers, Epiphanius spoke of it as Πανάρετος Σοφία, the "All-Virtuous Wisdom," while Clement of Alexandria in *Stromateis* and Origen entitled it Ἡ Θεία Σοφία, the "Divine Wisdom."[1] Augustine styled it *Liber Christianae Sapientiae,* the "Book of Christian Wisdom," whereas Jerome's preface to the work entitled it "The Wisdom of Solomon" and characterized it as pseudepigraphic. In regard to this designation Jerome was following the original Greek title in one or other of its variant forms.[2] The Old Latin version of the work simply bore the title, "Book of Wisdom," which many modern writers have found to constitute an acceptable designation. The popularity and widespread use of the composition in the early Christian era appear evident from the extent to which it was translated into other languages including Syriac, Aramaic, Sahidic, Arabic, and Armenian.[3]

For purposes of circulation the book purported to have been written by Solomon, but it is doubtful if this literary artifice was even meant to be taken seriously. From a very early date the pseudonymous character of the work was recognized, but this does not appear to have occasioned much disturbance, since the revered name of Solomon was in any event recognized as an appropriate symbol for all that pertained to wisdom in

---

[1] *Epist. ad Rom.* VII, 14; *Stromateis* IV, 16.

[2] Codex Sinaiticus read Σοφία Σαλωμῶντος; Codex Alexandrinus had Σοφία Σολομῶντος, while Codex Vaticanus read Σοφία Σαλωμῶνος.

[3] J. Reider, *The Book of Wisdom* (1957), pp. 7f.

Hebrew life. Chapters 7 to 9 make a bold claim to have been written by Solomon himself, but this also may have been a literary device employed by the author to correct certain misrepresentations of Solomon found in Ecclesiastes, which he considered either erroneous or inadvertent.

So effectively has the author concealed his identity behind the pseudonym that a wide variety of opinion has resulted from attempts to uncover him. The compiler of the Syriac recension was aware of the problem, for the title of the book read as follows: "The book of the Great Wisdom of Solomon, son of David; of which there is a doubt whether another wise man of the Hebrews wrote it in a prophetic spirit, putting it in the name of Solomon, and it was received." Jerome attributed the work to Philo on the grounds that it was redolent of Greek eloquence rather than Hebrew piety, and in this contention he was followed, among others, by Luther. Augustine attributed the authorship to Ben Sira, but later on he changed his mind in this regard.[4] In more recent times it has been suggested that the author was an Essene, or perhaps a member of the Egyptian group known as the Therapeutae.[5] Regarding the foregoing suggestions, it is highly improbable that Philo was the author, for although the book of Wisdom may exhibit certain similarities to his work, it does not display the precision found in the writings of Philo, and in addition it is basically rhetorical rather than philosophical. Furthermore, the concept of the Logos, fundamental to the speculative system of Philo, is completely lacking in the book of Wisdom, which never identifies divine wisdom with the Logos. There are important theological differences also, for whereas Philo did not accept the concept of resurrection, the book of Wisdom did. Again, the elaborate trichotomy of the soul that occurred in the work of Philo was absent from the book of Wisdom.

The problem of authorship has been compounded in more recent times by certain critical assumptions to the effect that the book in itself is not to be considered a literary unity. Thus chapters 1–9 have been held to be the work of an author different from the one who composed chapters 10–19.[6] A slightly different division of the text was proposed by Eichhorn and followed by Gärtner, Holmes, and Torrey.[7] Lincke suggested an unusual solution to the problem, supposing that 1:1–12:18 had been written by a Samaritan, while 12:19–19:22 had been the work

---

[4] De Doct. Christ. II, 8. Retract. II, 4.

[5] Cf. A. F. Gfrörer, Philo und die jüdisch-alexandrinische Theosophie (1830), 2 vols.

[6] E.g. C. Gutberlet, Das Buch der Weisheit (1874); F. W. Farrar in H. Wace (ed.), The Speaker's Commentary, Apocrypha I (1888), pp. 403ff. C. H. Toy, EB, IV, cols. 5336f.; E. H. Blakeney, The Praises of Wisdom (1937).

[7] J. G. Eichhorn, Einleitung in die apokryphischen Schriften des AT (1795), pp. 86ff. E. Gärtner, Komposition und Wortwahl des Buches der Weisheit (1912), pp. 61ff. S. Holmes in APOT, I, p. 521. TAL, p. 98.

of an Alexandrian Jew.[8] Goodrick divided the work up into three principal sections consisting of chapters 1–6, 7–9, and 10–19; and in this he was followed with slight modifications by Pfeiffer.[9] The arguments for composite authorship have emphasized the differences in character between the earlier and later chapters of the book; the lack of allusions to wisdom and the concept of the immortality of the soul in chapters 14–19, and a number of important linguistic variations that are particularly evident in the choice of words and the use of particles.[10]

On the other hand it may be argued in favor of the unity of the work that there is a generally consistent pattern of vocabulary and rhyming structure evident throughout the book, that certain unusual terms and expressions appear consistently in both sections,[11] and that the use of Greek philosophical doctrines beginning with the Stoic concepts of the world-soul at the commencement and the metabolism of the four elements at the conclusion of the work makes for a pattern of internal regularity.

Even those scholars who have seen several divisions in the book have nevertheless been convinced as to the basic unity of authorship of Wisdom. Grimm, Siegfried, Bois, and Feldmann in particular were emphatic upon this matter.[12] Goodrick gave expression to the possibility that the author may have written the book of Wisdom at an early period when he was irritated by apostasy and persecution, and that subsequently he colored his work by means of philosophical concepts that he had encountered in the intervening years.[13] C. F. Houbigant, who was followed in this regard by Eichhorn, suggested that one and the same writer may have composed different portions of the book under varying conditions and perhaps even with divergent objectives in view.[14] Whatever the history of composition of Wisdom, it was known as a unity by the beginning of the Christian era. Whoever the author or authors may have been, the extant work constituted a Jewish apologetic written for the benefit of those whose canons of thought were primarily Greek. Whether they were Greek-speaking Jews or Greeks by race is completely unknown. It has been suggested that the rulers mentioned in 1:1; 6:1ff; and elsewhere were Jewish apostates who owed their positions to their ready conformity to Greek customs and ideals, and that it was to these

[8] L. Lincke, *Samaria und seine Propheten* (1903), pp. 119ff.
[9] A. T. S. Goodrick, *The Book of Wisdom* (1913), pp. 37ff. *HNTT,* p. 313.
[10] Cf. *APOT*, I, pp. 522f.
[11] Cf. J. Reider, *The Book of Wisdom*, p. 21 n. 105.
[12] C. L. W. Grimm, *Das Buch der Weisheit erklärt* (1860), pp. 9ff. K. Siegfried in E. Kautzsch (ed.), *Die Apokryphen und Pseudepigraphen des AT,* I, p. 479. H. Bois, *Essai sur les origines de la philosophie Judéo-Alexandrine* (1890), pp. 211ff. F. Feldmann, *Biblische Zeitschrift,* VII (1909), pp. 140ff.
[13] A. T. S. Goodrick, *The Book of Wisdom*, pp. 37ff.
[14] C. F. Houbigant, *Biblica Hebraica* (1753), III, preface to the book of Wisdom.

individuals that the early material in the book of Wisdom was addressed.

The general content of the work would seem to point to some Jewish center in a Hellenistic city as its place of origin. The most probable location would be Alexandria, and it may be that the references to the Exodus, Egypt, and the Egyptians were designed to exercise a local appeal. On the other hand, as Hadas pointed out, the opening chapters appear to conform to conditions in Palestine better than in other locations, and it is not entirely outside the bounds of possibility that the early chapters may have emerged from some such pietistic group as that which settled at Qumran.[15] In the light of the available evidence it would seem best to regard the work as having been written for a Jewish community educated according to the Greek tradition, and to interpret its familiarity with the Hellenistic environment of Egypt as pointing to Alexandria as its place of origin. This supposition would account for the great emphasis laid by the writer upon such matters as literary form, linguistic harmonies, and syntactical niceties.[16]

If the work was in fact a product of Hellenistic Judaism, whether Alexandrian or Palestinian, it may have been composed because the author was grieved at the lack of fidelity shown by the Jews towards the ancient concepts of the Torah, and was concerned at the extent to which apostasy and idolatry were going hand in hand among the Jews. That apostasy both in Palestine (cf. 1 Macc. 1:11f., 43ff.; 2 Macc. 4:10) and Egypt (3 Macc. 2:31)[17] occurred during the Maccabean period and later is a matter of historical record. Hence the book of Wisdom, and in particular the first five chapters, may have been compiled to illustrate the barrenness of contemporary materialistic emphases and to remind the reader of the penalties attached to apostasy. If the work was intended to correct the misrepresentations of Ecclesiastes, as some scholars have maintained, the author certainly succeeded in setting up a virtuous and orthodox Solomon against the quasi-Epicurean monarch of Ecclesiastes by demonstrating the fact of the divine wisdom in the ordering of the cosmos as well as establishing the necessity of morality in human society and the reality of retribution after the death of the body.

As with other facets of the book, the questions attaching to a consideration of the date when Wisdom was compiled have occasioned some controversy among scholars. A period of composition at the beginning of the second century B.C. was suggested by Friedländer, whereas Deane assigned the work to a period between 217 and 145 B.C.[18] Grimm favored a date between 145 B.C. and the time of Philo, ca. 50 B.C., and

---

[15] M. Hadas, *IDB*, IV, p. 862.
[16] *OTFD*, p. 411; *HNTT*, pp. 330ff.
[17] Philo, *Vita Mosis*, I, 6.
[18] M. Friedländer, *Griechische Philosophie im AT* (1904), pp. 182ff.; W. J. Deane, *The Book of Wisdom* (1881), p. 32.

in this conclusion he was followed with some variations by Gfrörer and Siegfried.[19] Heinisch and Focke held that the work originated in the period 88-30 B.C.,[20] while Holmes narrowed the date to between 50 B.C. and 30 B.C. for the first portion of the book, and assigned the later chapters to the period 30 B.C.-A.D. 10.[21] Farrar and Goodrick placed the compilation of the work in the middle of the first century of the Christian era, thinking that it was the product of an era of persecution, possibly that of Caligula (A.D. 37-41).[22] A *terminus a quo* can be established by the fact that the book of Wisdom appears to be later in origin than Ecclesiasticus, since no direct quotation from the former occurs in the latter.[23] The book of Wisdom is also later than the LXX version of the Prophets and the Sacred Writings (*ca.* 150 B.C.), which are quoted in Wisdom in a form different from that of the Hebrew Scriptures. The denunciation of idolatry would help to fix the *terminus ad quem,* particularly if Egyptian theriolatry was being envisaged by the author, in terms of the commencement of Roman rule in Egypt about 30 B.C. If the book of Wisdom preceded Philo, as might be implied by the omission of references to the Alexandrian doctrine of the Logos, the lowest limit of writing may perhaps have been *ca.* 50 B.C. In support of this contention it may also be noticed that the author ignored the Philonic tradition of the allegorical interpretation of Scripture, preferring instead to employ midrashic procedures. The most probable interval during which the book of Wisdom was composed, whether by one or more hands, would thus appear to be the century from 150 B.C. to 50 B.C.

The original language of the book has also been the subject of a great deal of scholarly discussion. The attribution of the work to Solomon led naturally to the assumption that it was first written in Hebrew, and this was the view commonly held by the Church Fathers of Alexandria as well as by certain medieval Jewish commentators. Houbigant was the first modern scholar to question this assumption, and in his preface to the book of Wisdom, which appeared in the third volume of the *Biblia Hebraica* of 1753, he suggested that only the first nine chapters were genuinely Solomonic, and thus written in Hebrew. He held that the remainder of the work had been composed in Greek, perhaps by the

---

[19] C. L. W. Grimm, *Das Buch der Weisheit erklärt*, pp. 34f. A. F. Gfrörer, *Philo und die jüdisch-alexandrinische Theosophie*, II, pp. 200ff. K. Siegfried in E. Kautzsch (ed.), *Die Apokryphen und Pseudepigraphen des Alten Testaments*, I, p. 479.

[20] P. Heinisch, *Das Buch der Weisheit*, pp. xx—xxiii. F. Focke, *Die Entstehung der Weisheit Salomos* (1913), pp. 74ff.

[21] S. Holmes, *APOT*, I, pp. 520f.

[22] F. W. Farrar, *The Wisdom of Solomon* in H. Wace (ed.), *The Speaker's Commentary, Apocrypha I*, p. 422. A. T. S. Goodrick, *The Book of Wisdom*, pp. 5ff.

[23] For similarities compare Ecclus. 4:11ff.; 6:18ff.; 15:1ff., with Wisdom chapters 6 and 8. Also Ecclus. 23:25 and Wisdom 4:3; Ecclus. 1:26 and Wisdom 6:18; Ecclus 33:10ff. and Wisdom 15:7f.

same person who had translated the balance of the book from Hebrew into Greek. Focke reduced the alleged original Hebrew content to the first five chapters only,[24] and it was upon this conclusion that Peters based his investigation of the work.[25] S. Margoliouth argued from the Greek expressions to an underlying Semitic original of Palestinian origin, a position that was conclusively refuted by Freudenthal.[26] At least two scholars remained unconvinced by this demonstration: Speiser and Purinton argued subsequently for a Hebrew original of the first ten chapters, basing their conclusions in part upon an alleged mistranslation from Hebrew.[27] Another notable objector was C. C. Torrey, who followed Purinton in his general conclusions.[28] However, as Deissmann showed at the beginning of the twentieth century, there are certain Hebraic forms that constitute an essential part of Hellenistic Greek. These have resulted in the first instance from contacts with Semitic peoples, but at the same time they do not necessarily require a Semitic precursor when they appear in written documents.[29]

Certainly the evidence adduced by Grimm would constitute a strong argument for an original Greek form of the book of Wisdom, which might look to Alexandria for its place of composition.[30] Quotations from Isaiah 3:10 (Wisdom 2:12) and 44:20 (Wisdom 15:10) and Job 9:12, 19 (Wisdom 12:12) followed the LXX rather than the Hebrew, and this fact alone would seem to militate against an original in Hebrew unless, of course, the author was following a manuscript tradition different from that perpetuated by the Massoretes. Even more significant is the contention that some of the least Hebraic concepts are to be found in the first ten chapters of the book of Wisdom, whose Hebrew origin most of the protagonists concerned have been attempting to demonstrate.

While there are no direct quotations of the book of Wisdom in the pages of the New Testament, there is some ground for the assertion that Paul and John were perhaps familiar with its contents. In that event a date well before the middle of the first century A.D. would seem to be required for the composition of the book in its extant form. Passages in the New Testament that allegedly reflect the contents of Wisdom include the Johannine teachings concerning the Logos (John 1:1, 18; cf. Wisdom 8:3; 9:4; John 1:3, 10; cf. Wisdom 7:21; 8:6; 9:1, 9; John 5:2; cf. Wisdom 8:4; 9:9ff.), certain sections in the Pauline epistles (Rom.

[24] F. Focke, Die Entstehung der Weisheit Salomos, pp. 82f.

[25] N. Peters, Biblische Zeitschrift, XIV (1916), pp. 1ff.

[26] S. Margoliouth, JRAS, XXII (1890), pp. 263ff. The Expositor, VI (1900), pp. 141ff., 186ff. J. Freudenthal, JQR, III (1891), pp. 722ff.

[27] E. A. Speiser, JQR, XIV (1923-24), pp. 455ff. C. E. Purinton, JBL, XLVII (1928), pp. 276ff.

[28] TAL, pp. 98ff.

[29] A. Deissmann, Die Hellenisierung des semitischen Monotheismus (1903).

[30] C. L. W. Grimm, Das Buch der Weisheit erklärt, pp. 5ff.

1:18ff.; cf. Wisdom 11, 13, and 15; Rom. 2:4; cf. Wisdom 11:23; 12:10, 19; Rom. 9:21; cf. Wisdom 15:7; 2 Cor. 5:5, 7; cf. Wisdom 9:15; Eph. 6: 11-17; cf. Wisdom 5:17ff.), references in Hebrews (Heb. 1:3; cf. Wisdom 7:25f.; Heb. 12:17; cf. Wisdom 12:10), portions of the letters of James (3:17f.; cf. Wisdom 7:22f.) and Peter (1 Pet. 1:6f.; cf. Wisdom 3: 5f.), and a possible allusion in chapters 8 and 9 of Revelation (to Wisdom 11:16-19). Certain restrictions of style and misunderstandings of Greek terms have led scholars to the general conclusion that the author was writing in a foreign language with which he was not thoroughly conversant. This proposition constituted an important part of the argument presented by Grimm in relation to the original language of the book, and would seem in general to justify the contention that the work was first written in Greek, probably by an Alexandrian Jew.

As Metzger has pointed out, the author of the book of Wisdom may have had several classes of people in mind when composing his work.[31] In view of widespread religious apostasy he may have been endeavoring to rekindle zeal for the God of Israel and the sacred Torah among his Jewish contemporaries, as well as furnishing at the same time an apologetic background for current Jewish faith and practice. His outreach may even have extended to the Gentiles in his attempt to demonstrate the fundamental truths of Judaism and expose the follies and superficialities of idolatry.

The book commenced with the appeal of the writer, under the guise of King Solomon, for earthly rulers to seek wisdom, in the conviction that, whereas evil deeds and impious speech culminated in spiritual death, righteousness was immortal (1:6-15). Apostasy was nothing less than a covenant with death, and marked out its adherents as associates of the devil (2:24). The suffering experienced by the righteous constituted a preliminary chastening in preparation for the blessedness of eternity, where the saints would rule over nations in the divine kingdom (3:1-9). From the observation that the wicked are unhappy and often frustrated even in this life, the author argued that true happiness consisted in being humble in prosperity and giving assistance to the poor (3:17–4:10). In any event the premature decease of the righteous was a far more preferable thing than the prolonged existence of the wicked, since they attained to eternal felicity all the more quickly. In the day of judgment the ungodly, in their anguish and sorrow, would be compelled to recognize the folly and inadequacy of their sinful lives (4:20–5:23).

Without wisdom, therefore, earthly rulers cannot properly discharge their great responsibilities. True kingship will emerge when wisdom is enthroned (6:12-21), and the author reveals that the traditional Solomonic wisdom was divinely bestowed as the result of prayer (6:27–7:14).

---

[31] *MTA,* p. 68; cf. *HNTT,* p. 334.

After enumerating the characteristics of wisdom the author explains how, by mentioning the four cardinal virtues of Plato and the Stoics (8:7), the qualities of wisdom and knowledge are communicated to the human mind. Thus "Solomon" prays that he will be given the greatest gift available to humanity (8:17-21). The prayer that follows constituted an expanded form of the shorter accounts in 2 Kings 3:7ff. and 2 Chronicles 1:8ff., and contains the hypostatization of wisdom as a celestial figure that is characteristic of the first nine chapters of the book.

A marked change of style occurs at this point, with the concept of the activity of wisdom in Hebrew history comprising the dominant theme of subsequent passages. The exalted rhetoric of earlier chapters degenerates into verbose narrative that frequently borders upon the dull and commonplace, with only occasional sections being written in the literary style and spirit of the first portion of the book of Wisdom. The point that the author seeks to prove is that, through wisdom, Israel has experienced divine providence in mighty acts of deliverance, and that God has punished the enemies of His people by the very things which worked so remarkably for the benefit of Israel (11:5).

Thus it was wisdom that guided the fortunes of the patriarchs, and through Joseph and Moses respectively encouraged the children of Israel to flourish in Egypt and be delivered from their enemies (10:1-21). It should be mentioned at this juncture that as a stylistic device the author never actually mentioned any Old Testament personality directly by name, but merely alluded to his presence and activity within the context of the narrative itself. The writer went on to show the way in which one receives punishment by means of those things through which he commits sin, illustrating his thesis by reference to the Egyptians (11:15-26) and Canaanites (12:1-11), although at the same time he stressed that God desired true repentance on the part of the sinner.

Polytheism generally was the next object of attention, with the veneration of wild beasts and idols receiving scathing denunciation (13:1-19). The gods were nothing more than deified human beings (14:12-21), and from such worship emerged all those vices which worked for the enervation of society. By contrast the Israelites had kept true to God because they knew His mercy, whereas their enemies deluded themselves into thinking that the creations of their hands were in fact deities (15:7-19). False objects of veneration were used by God to punish the Egyptians (16:1-4) and even the Israelites on one notable occasion (16:5-14), while the principle that what was friendly to Israel became inimical to her enemies was illustrated by reference to the plagues of Egypt (16:15–18:4). This is a tedious and sometimes rather boastful section, which most probably drew upon Jewish legends for its details. The subjugation of Egypt was elaborated by the account of the crossing of the Red Sea, in which miraculous phenomena were multiplied by the imaginative account of the writer (18:5–19:19). At this point the book ended abruptly without reaching any final conclusion, as though the author had grown tired of his literary and apologetic endeavor.

While the theological concepts expounded by the book were derived principally from the Old Testament, they were modified in a rather important manner by the Hellenistic speculations that were current at the time of writing. This resulted in an amalgam of Jewish religion and Hellenistic philosophy in which the Old Testament idea of wisdom was buttressed and transformed by Stoic speculation and the *Logos* doctrine of Heracleitus. Although this process was based upon the tacit recognition that the Hebrew Scriptures were superior in morals and ethics to anything which Greek culture had to offer, the reconciliation of the two led to the interpreting of the Old Testament narratives in an allegorical fashion, and ultimately to their crystallizing into universal and abstract principles, some of which had much in common with certain elements of Greek speculative thought. Thus the concept that matter was eternal was adopted from Plato and enshrined in Wisdom 11:17, as was the theory that matter was evil and that the soul, which had pre-existed (8:19f.), was imprisoned temporarily in the body (9:15). The four cardinal virtues (8:7), as already mentioned, and the idea of a world-soul (7:24; 11:7; 12:1) were Stoic tenets, as were also some of the attributes of wisdom (7:22ff.).

Of the characteristic teachings of the book, the doctrine that the individual soul enjoyed pre-existence was given prominence by the author. This was strictly Platonic in origin, and was enunciated so unmistakably in the book of Wisdom that only a very few scholars have been bold enough to deny it.[32] The concept of the immortality of the soul, only vaguely hinted at in the Old Testament (Job 19:25; Isa. 26:19; Dan. 12:2), but prominent in Platonic speculation,[33] was also firmly expressed in the book of Wisdom (1:12f.; 3:1). Though rejected by the Sadducees it was adopted in Pharisaic circles and given emphasis in the Mishnah.[34] The resurrection of the soul and not of the body was stated as a doctrine in Wisdom, and in particular the souls of the righteous were spoken of as enjoying security in the hand of God, and being at peace (Wisdom 3:1ff.). In view of the fact that the book of Wisdom was recognized as canonical by the Council of Trent in 1546, and was employed as a source in Roman Catholic liturgies, it is surprising to encounter a passage of alleged Scripture so emphatic in its repudiation

[32] E.g. M. J. Lagrange, *RB*, IV (1907), pp. 85ff.; F. C. Porter, *American Journal of Theology*, XII (1908), pp. 53ff. and in *OT and Semitic Studies in Memory of William Rainey Harper* (1908), I, pp. 208ff.; F. Feldmann, *Das Buch der Weisheit*, p. 19.

[33] E. Zeller, *Outlines of Greek Philosophy* (1896), p. 155. Cf. S. Lange, *JBL*, LV (1936), pp. 293ff.

[34] *Sanhed*. X, 1.

of the doctrine of purgatory, which, it is said, is also based on Scripture.

That the world was created out of eternal formless matter was a belief taught both by Plato and the Stoics,[35] and this concept was enshrined accordingly in the book of Wisdom, despite the tradition of Genesis which clearly envisaged *creatio ex nihilo*. The theory of Euhemerus that idolatry took its rise from the worship of deceased heroes was also propounded in Wisdom (14:15). The idea of divine providence as conceived by Pythagoras and Plato also found approval in the mind of the author (Wisdom 6:7; 14:3; 17:2), who for the first time in the Greek Bible employed the technical term *pronoia* in order to designate it. Though a thoroughly Semitic concept in its own right, the idea of wisdom was colored by distinctly Greek notions, as, for example, in the enumeration of the attributes of wisdom (Wisdom 7:22f.). Throughout the work wisdom was personified to the point where it was regarded hypostatically and favored with omnipotence and omniscience. As such it constituted an emanation from God rather than a creature (Wisdom 7:25f.), and was deemed to have existed prior to the forming of the world. At creation wisdom was held to have participated in the work of the Deity (7:22), and subsequently to have become an intermediary in the dealings of God with men (cf. 7:27). By its stress upon individual immortality the book showed that the rewards for good and evil need not be experienced in this life. The suffering of the righteous was regarded as a necessary factor of existence in order to prove them worthy of immortality and happiness in the divine kingdom, for which righteousness was emphasized by the author as a necessary prerequisite.

Although certain passages in the book of Wisdom (e.g. 2:12ff.; 14:7; 18:15) were interpreted in messianic terms by the early Christians, there is little actual reference in the work to traditional messianic ideas, particularly in the later chapters of the book. The avowed purpose of the writer seems to have been the encouraging of the faithful by demonstrating the ubiquitous nature and activity of God, as contrasted with the temporary and only apparent dominance of evil. Despite the blandishments of pagan culture, the Jews could thereby feel encouraged to adhere firmly to their ancestral faith.

Supplementary Literature

Bückers, H. *Die Unsterblichkeitslehre des Weisheitslinches.* 1938.
Blakeney, E. H. *The Praises of Wisdom.* 1937.
Emerton, J. A. (ed.). *The Peshitta of the Wisdom of Solomon.* 1959.
Fichtner, J. *Die Weisheit Salomos.* 1938.
Gregg, J. A. F. *The Wisdom of Solomon.* 1909.
Geyer, J. *The Wisdom of Solomon.* 1963.
Oesterley, W. O. E. *The Wisdom of Solomon.* 1917.

[35] E. Zeller, *Outlines of Greek Philosophy,* p. 147.

VIII. THE BOOK OF ECCLESIASTICUS

Although this book never achieved canonicity among the Jews, it was one of the most highly esteemed compositions to emerge from the intertestamental period. It was occasionally quoted by the rabbis as though it was in fact Scriptural, and as its title "Ecclesiasticus" indicates, it was greatly valued in Christian circles as a book to be read in church. The place of the composition in the larger corpus of the Wisdom Literature, however, was indicated by its alternative title, "The Wisdom of Jesus the Son of Sirach," which, as it happens, furnishes the identity of the only known author of an apocryphal book. This Jesus, the son of Sirach, the son of Eleazar of Jerusalem (Ecclus. 50:27, 51), is generally known to scholarship for convenience as Ben Sira, following the Hebrew usage.[1]

The author evidently belonged to that body of expositors of the Torah known as the Scribes (cf. Ecclus. 10:5; 38:24f.; 44:4), a conclusion arrived at from a consideration of his attitude towards the Law and the Scribes generally. At some time during his life he had travelled in foreign countries (Ecclus. 34:11), and had acquired some experience in the diplomatic service of his country (Ecclus. 39:4). During the period when he compiled his book he most probably conducted an educational institution in Jerusalem, where he instructed the youth in moral and religious precepts after the manner of the oral tradition favored by the ancient Hebrew sages. In an understandable desire to give his teachings a more permanent form he committed them to writing in Hebrew, employing the canonical book of Proverbs as a model. He did not follow any organized sequence of argument or narrative, with the result that his work consisted principally of religious maxims and proverbs, supplemented by an occasional dissertation upon some selected theme that might be thought to be of interest or importance to his readers.

Although Ben Sira lived at a time when the impact of Hellenistic culture was making serious inroads into traditional Judaism, his work gave no indication whatever of the influence or activity of Greek thought. While his precepts were in line with orthodox Hebrew doctrine,

---

[1] For the variant name forms see *HNTT*, p. 352 n. 1.

he himself inclined theologically to the later Sadducean point of view. Thus he laid great emphasis upon the Torah and the worship of the Temple, while displaying noticeable reticence about such matters as the resurrection of the body or belief in a life beyond the grave.

The book is generally thought to have been compiled about 180 B.C., and this conclusion rests in part upon the eulogizing of Simon son of Onias (Ecclus. 50:1ff.), which gives the impression that he had only recently taken office. Of two High Priests bearing the name "Simon son of Onias" as mentioned by Josephus, one of them, Simon I the Just[2] held office *ca.* 300 B.C., while the other, Simon II, was High Priest about a century later.[3] Even Josephus was somewhat confused about these two persons, however, and while it is probably too much to say that Simon I was nothing more than a figment of rabbinical imagination,[4] it seems likely that the person responsible for the construction of the Temple at Leontopolis in Egypt about 163 B.C. was a descendant of Simon II, whose son Onias III was deposed early in the reign of Antiochus Epiphanes. Thus the book was probably composed between 195 B.C., the approximate date of the death of Simon II, and 171 B.C., when Antiochus removed Jason, the successor to Onias III, the last legitimate Zadokite priest, and placed Menelaus in his stead, a turn of events of which Ben Sira appeared to know nothing. This general dating can be sustained from the Prologue to the Greek translation of Ecclesiasticus, written by the grandson of Ben Sira. In this he stated that he went to Egypt in the thirty-eighth year of Euergetes, and that he subsequently began to translate the book into Greek. The reference to Euergetes would be less likely to allude to Ptolemy III Euergetes (247-221 B.C.), who did not rule long enough to reach his thirty-eighth year as pharaoh, than to Ptolemy VI Euergetes (170-117 B.C.). It would thus appear that the translator arrived in Egypt in 132 B.C., and that his grandfather lived and wrote prior to the persecutions under Antiochus Epiphanes in 168 B.C., no mention of which is found in Ecclesiasticus.

The problems connected with ascertaining the original language of the book are rather complex. The Prologue stated that the Greek text was a translation from a Hebrew original, but for many centuries no trace of such a source was to be found. It was only in 1896 that a parchment fragment containing Ecclesiasticus 39:15—40:7 came to light, after which several additional fragments from the same manuscript, as well as from other manuscripts of the same work, were discovered and pub-

---

[2] *AJ*, XII, 2, 5; XII, 4, 1.

[3] *AJ*, XII, 4, 10. Cf. 3 Macc. 2:1.

[4] G. F. Moore, *Jewish Studies in Memory of Israel Abrahams* (1927), pp. 348ff. His opinions were opposed by H. Englander, *The Hebrew College Jub'lee Volume* (1925), pp. 145ff.; S. Zeitlin, *The Proceedings of the American Society for Jew:sh Research,* III (1932), pp. 145f.

ished.[5] They were found to have originated in the same location, the *genizah* of the Ezra synagogue in Cairo, and between them they represented almost two-thirds of the Hebrew text. A small fragment of the book (Ecclus. 6:20-31) was also recovered from 2Q,[6] and on examination it was found to exhibit certain textual differences from the other Hebrew manuscripts. In 1965, a first-century B.C. fragment of five chapters of the Hebrew original was recovered from Masada by Y. Yadin.[7] The many interpolations, omissions, and transpositions that characterize the extant Greek manuscript sources indicate that there were two distinct manuscript groups underlying Ecclesiasticus. One of these possibly represents a translation of the original Hebrew text, while the other may constitute a rendering of a Hebrew source that subsequently underwent revision. Two Syriac versions of Ecclesiasticus are extant, one having been made from a Hebrew original and the other from a Greek translation. The processes of copying and transmission are clearly reflected in the slight textual changes occurring in the Greek, Hebrew, and Syriac manuscripts. Until recently scholars were divided as to the worth of the Hebrew fragments, to at least one of which the Qumran scrap is related textually, with some maintaining that they went back to the original Ben Sira text while others thought that they were translated from the Greek and subsequently modified through contact with other versions.[8]

In any discussion of the subject it should be noted that the form of the teaching contained in the book of Ecclesiasticus was conducive to insertion, omission, and supplementation, since it consisted, as did the canonical book of Proverbs, of rhythmical patterns involving couplets of parallel lines. This structure, along with the general absence of plan or narrative content, would make possible a significant degree of variation in the text of both the primary and secondary versions, a situation that presents problems in any attempt to determine the nature of the original text of Ecclesiasticus.

Of the translations from the Greek, the oldest and most important was that of the Old Latin. However, it was made from a Greek text that was in worse condition than any of the extant Greek versions, and although the Old Latin rendering preserved the chapters of Ecclesiasticus in the correct order of contents, the work was marred in other respects by scribal errors and arbitrary alterations, the latter being presumably made on the basis of different Greek texts. Jerome did not revise the Old Latin

[5] *APOT*, I, p. 271.

[6] J. T. Milik, *Ten Years of Discovery in the Wilderness of Judaea*, p. 32.

[7] Y. Yadin, *Christian News From Israel*, XVI (1965), p. 30.

[8] Cf. W. B. Baumgartner, ZAW, XXXIV (1914), pp. 161ff.; J. Marcus (ed.), *The Newly Discovered Hebrew of Ben Sira* (1931), JQR, XXI (1930-31), p. 223; A. Büchler, *JQR*, XIII (1922-23), pp. 303ff., 461ff., XIV (1923-24), pp. 53ff.; M. H. Segal, JQR, XXV (1934-35), pp. 91ff., *Sepher Ben Sira Ha-shalem* (1953); *APOT*, pp. 272ff.

version of Ecclesiasticus when compiling the Vulgate, and as a result he perpetuated some ancient elements in the text that otherwise might have been removed. The title "Ecclesiasticus" was derived from the Latin version, signifying the most important of the "Church Books" read in divine worship without having been accorded full canonicity at that period. Other versions of Ecclesiasticus included the Coptic, Ethiopic, Armenian, Georgian, and Arabic renderings.

The book itself consists of a motley collection of practical precepts covering a great many areas of everyday life, and by nature stands firmly in the tradition of the ancient Hebrew sages. Because of its agglomerate nature it is difficult to detect any overall plan for the work, despite the fact that similar sayings were frequently grouped together. Within the larger collection of material it is possible to discern the presence of didactic poems concerning wisdom (Ecclus. 1:1-20; 4:11-19; 14:20–15:8; 51:13-29),[9] along with hymns (39:12-35; 42:15–43:33), prayers (33:1-13; 36:16-22), and sections that constitute the praise of the Fathers (44:1–49:16). The contents of Ecclesiasticus may have been based largely upon lecture notes that were rewritten in verse by Ben Sira prior to the publication of the book in its extant form. The rather general nature of the arrangement of Ecclesiasticus has led scholars to divide the work into a number of small sections,[10] but by far the most natural division is that which has envisaged the book as falling into two main parts consisting of chapters 1–23 and 24–50.[11] Whether these were ever issued separately in antiquity is open to serious doubt, since the work has always been known as a unity.

The dependence upon the structure of the canonical book of Proverbs as a model for the author is seen in the fact that Ecclesiasticus 1:1-20 and 24:1-34 constitute discourses in praise of wisdom, as do the opening chapters (1–9) of the book of Proverbs. In addition, the concluding section of Ecclesiasticus contains, like Proverbs 31:10-31, an alphabetic acrostic composition that serves as an appendix. The allegorical allusion that commences the second section of Ecclesiasticus (24:30-34) appears to indicate that the author had originally only planned a comparatively small-scale work, but that subsequently his material grew to the point where, augmented by the Torah, it became first a river and then a sea, encouraging him to pour out his teachings once more for the edification of the reader. The character of the second section differs from that of the first in that short moralizing essays tend to be repeated by longer poetical works that Ben Sira may have composed independently at an earlier

[9] The last poem constitutes an acrostic poem after the pattern of Psalms 25, 34, 37, 111, 112, 119; Lam. 1–4; Prov. 31:10-31.
[10] Cf. R. Smend, *Die Weisheit des Jesus Sirach erklärt* (1906), pp. xxxff.; O. T. Fritzsche, *Exegetisches Handbuch zu den Apokryphen* (1859), V, p. xxxii.
[11] *HNTT*, p. 353.

period. The doxology with which the work concluded, and which survived only in the Hebrew and Syriac forms, may have been added posthumously either by a disciple or an admirer of Ben Sira.

The prologue, as has been remarked above, enabled the translator to identify and commend the work of his grandfather, and like many later prefaces craved the indulgence of the reader with regard to imperfections in the translation. The first main section opened with a poem in praise of wisdom, stating that this gracious attribute was of divine origin and was rooted in the fear of the Lord (1:1-20). The following section dealt in rather broad terms with pride and hypocrisy (1:22–4:10), showing the place of humility in the life of the truly pious individual, and emphasizing in Sadducean fashion the importance of almsgiving as an atonement for sin (compare Ecclus. 3:3, 30 and Mark 12:33). A further discourse on the nature of wisdom (4:11–6:17) dilated upon the joy experienced in serving her interests. Such attributes as insincerity, sinful shame, and reliance upon wealth were to be avoided, while quickness of listening and slowness of response were commended as proper virtues for individual cultivation (Ecclus. 5:11; cf. Jas. 1:19). The search for wisdom should constitute a lifelong concern (6:18–8:7), and ought to be marked by justice and kindness as well as by the absence of either political ambition or religious formalism (cf. Ecclus. 7:14 and Mark 11:25; 7:34 and Rom. 12:15; 8:5 and Rom. 3:23).

The traditional lore of the Hebrew sages was reflected in the next section (8:8–10:29), which laid great emphasis upon wisdom, humility, and charity. Such an attitude of mind (10:30–14:19) will raise the humble to positions of prominence and authority. The wise man will avoid dissipating his energies, lest death should come prematurely and anticipate his ambitions (Ecclus. 11:19; cf. Lk. 12:16ff.). Meditation upon wisdom leads to happiness (14:20–18:26), and will circumvent human waywardness, which is the result of an evil choice (15:11-12; cf. Jas. 1:13). The divine ordering of the cosmos has placed man in a position of great responsibility, but because human beings are frail in their spiritual and moral constitution they need the constant assurance of the mercy and forgiveness of God.

A cautious approach to life, manifested in both words and deeds, is the mark of a wise man (18:27–20:26). Prudence and self-control will combine with insight to produce a God-fearing individual. The way of the sinner is contrasted with that of the wise man (20:27–23:27), and the fate of the former is shown to be the pit of Sheol (Ecclus. 21:10; cf. Matt. 7:13). The wise man will avoid the excesses of the foolish, and will behave circumspectly at all times.

The second principal section (24:1–42:14) commenced with a poem in praise of wisdom (24:1-22), and this was followed by a discourse upon married life (25:1–26:27). A subsequent passage (26:28–29:28) dealt discursively with honesty and dishonesty, matters involving human character, and practical issues such as forgiveness (28:2; cf. Matt. 6:12), lending to the needy (29:10; cf. Jas. 5:3), and the merits of the simple life. Advice relating to questions of living in general, and to the care of the body in particular (30:1–35:13), occupied an important place in the second major section of Ecclesiasticus, reflecting some of the excesses of contemporary Hellenistic culture. Within this division of the work the proper use of the Torah was outlined (32:14–33:18), in relationship to human traditions on the one hand, and to the wisdom of the ancient Hebrew sages on the other. Diverse comments on family life, travel, and true piety (33:19–36:17) were followed by other remarks concerning such matters as friends, divine guidance, and bereavement (36:18–38:23). The place of the Scribe in the community as the student of the Torah evoked sympathetic treatment from Ben Sira (38:24–39:35), and the dependence of such an individual upon divine wisdom was commended. Suffering and mortality were then discussed (40:1–42:14), and by way of conclusion the author arrived at the conviction that the only permanent thing was a good name.

Following this were three lengthy poems and certain appendices. The first poem (42:15–43:33) dealt with the omniscience and graciousness of God the creator; the second, embracing chapters 44 to 49, consisted of the "Praise of the Fathers" (cf. Heb. 11:4–12:2). The final composition lauded Simon II (50:1-24), and related the development of Temple worship and the general prosperity of Jerusalem in his day. Not all the appendices that constitute chapter 51 occur in the Greek manuscripts, for after 51:12 there followed a short liturgy found only in the Hebrew. This was also the case with an alphabetical acrostic psalm, which survived with some variation in the Syriac versions.

While there are certain rather obvious Sadducean precepts inherent in Ecclesiasticus, the work as a whole reflected the earliest traditions of the Hebrew sages, and is therefore representative of orthodox Judaism in a general sense. Thus Israel is believed to reside under the covenanted mercies of God, and has her life enriched by the divine gift of wisdom. The evil impulse or *yēçer hā-rāʿ* in man leads him to choose evil rather than good, and so is the real cause of sin. The Torah instructs men in the way in which iniquity can be avoided, and extends the assurance that a compassionate Deity is willing to forgive the truly penitent sinner. For Ben Sira, salvation seems to depend upon proper observance of the Law, as in later Pharisaism, but Ecclesiasticus contains no belief in a future life nor any doctrine of resurrection, a position that was in general accord with Sadducean tenets.

The book is of value as constituting the last great example of Hebrew Wisdom Literature, as well as for the manner in which it furnishes a remarkable mirror of the life and times of the author. While there are certain inconsistencies in the teachings of the writer, these may merely be due to his native background and his moral presuppositions.[12] His characteristic emphasis lay in the identification of wisdom with the Torah, which represents a distinct advance upon the position maintained in Proverbs. Ecclesiasticus indicates clearly that its author was a learned scribe, a skilled teacher, a devoted servant of his people, and a faithful follower of his God.

Supplementary Literature

Hart, J. H. A. *Ecclesiasticus. The Greek Text of Codex 248.* 1909.
Hughes, H. M. *The Ethics of Jewish Apocryphal Literature.* 1909.
Levi, I. *L'Ecclésiastique ou la Sagesse de Jésus fils de Sira.* 1898-1901.
Oesterley, W. O. E. *The Wisdom of Ben-Sira.* 1916.
―――― and G. H. Box. *Translations of Early Documents.* 1916.

[12] Cf. T. A. Burkill, *IDB*, II, p. 21.

IX. THE BOOK OF BARUCH

Of a number of books attributed to Baruch, son of Neriah and secretary to the prophet Jeremiah (Jer. 32:12; 36:4; 51:59), only one was included in the LXX. The Vulgate titled the composition "The Prophecy of Baruch," and there, as in the AV, the *Epistle of Jeremy* was added to form a sixth chapter of the work. Baruch is the only apocryphal writing to be based consciously upon the pattern established by the Old Testament prophets, and in actual fact it constitutes little more than a mosaic of verses extracted from the canonical writings of Isaiah, Jeremiah, Job, and Daniel.

Purporting to have issued from the period of the Babylonian captivity, the book was addressed to the deported Jews in Mesopotamia, where it was read aloud at gatherings of the faithful. At a later time it was sent to Jerusalem to become incorporated into the liturgy. The work falls into three principal parts prefaced by a title, which appears to furnish an explicit date for the composition of the book. The first section commenced with a confession of sins (1:15–2:10), based on the ninth chapter of the canonical book of Daniel, and this was followed by prayers for mercy and pardon (2:11–3:8), which drew heavily for their inspiration upon portions of the Pentateuch and the prophetical writings.

The second section (3:9–4:4) departed from the prose of the earlier passages to indulge in a poetical style of considerable merit. It commenced with a homily on wisdom, based on Job 28 and 29, in which true wisdom was identified with the Torah and regarded as the divine gift to Israel alone. The final division of the book (4:5–5:9) embodied words of consolation for the exiles, inspired by the content of Isaiah 40–45, which assured them that they would be brought back to their homeland in triumph and urged them to seek God in their captive state in a spirit of penitence and faith. A good deal of literary skill underlies the representation of Jerusalem as a sorrowing widow bereft of her offspring, and the cantos of consolation have elements in common with the dirges of Lamentations.

1238

While some Roman Catholic scholars have upheld the unity of the book of Baruch,[1] others, along with many Protestant writers, have adhered to a theory of composite authorship.[2] Though as many as four contributing authors have been envisaged by certain scholars,[3] some have recognized in the composition the activities of three,[4] or, following Ewald, two principal writers.[5] However, the essential unity of each of the parts thus derived has been questioned at various times by different writers, making for an extremely subjective analysis of the work.[6]

Although Baruch was read widely by the Jews of the Diaspora and subsequently incorporated into the liturgy of the synagogue (cf. 1:14), its influence survived considerably longer in Christian circles. Thus in the Prologue to his translation of the prophet Jeremiah, Jerome recorded that the Jews no longer read or possessed the book of Baruch, although in this connection it may very well be that Jerome was thinking of Palestinian Jews only. On the basis of synagogue usage it is highly improbable that any language other than Hebrew was employed for the original composition, contrary to the views of the older critics that the work was first written in Greek.[7] If this consideration applies to the prose sections it is doubtless equally true of the poetic passages also. While there are certain parallels in phraseology between Baruch 4:36—5:9 and the eleventh chapter of the pseudepigraphal *Psalms of Solomon* (*ca.* 50 B.C.),[8] it seems evident from the underlying parallelisms and from certain mistranslations in the Greek that the original work in its entirety was composed in Hebrew. The Greek version of Baruch depends to a considerable extent upon the LXX of Jeremiah and Daniel, and it has been suggested that the Greek translator of Baruch was identical with the person who rendered the second half of the canonical Jeremiah into the Greek of the LXX version.[9]

Taken at face value (1:2), the book could be dated in 582 B.C., or some five years after the fall of Jerusalem in 587 B.C. However, the chronological statement is far from clear, and the fifth year has been taken as that following the captivity of Jehoiachin in 587 B.C.[10] since the Temple still appeared to be intact (1:7, 10, 14; 2:16). Again, some critics

---

[1] E.g. E. Kalt, *Das Buch Baruch* (1932).
[2] E.g. W. Stoderl, *Zur Echtheitsfrage von Baruch 1-3, 8* (1922); P. Heinisch, *Theologie und Glaube*, XX (1928), pp. 696ff.
[3] E.g. J. T. Marshall, *HDB*, I, p. 251.
[4] E.g. *HNTT*, p. 413 n. 6.
[5] Cf. E. Schürer, *Geschichte des jüdischen Volkes im Zeitalter Jesu Christi*, III, p. 461.
[6] *AAT*, p. 260; O. C. Whitehouse in *APOT*, I, p. 570; J. J. Kneucker, *Das Buch Baruch* (1879), pp. 37ff.
[7] Cf. *APOT*, I, p. 571.
[8] Cf. *APOT*, I, pp. 572ff.
[9] Cf. J. J. Kneucker, *Das Buch Baruch*, p. 83.
[10] So J. J. Kneucker, *Das Buch Baruch*, pp. 10ff.; cf. Baruch 1:9; Ezra 1:2.

have amended the "fifth year" to the "fifth month," on the basis of 2 Kings 25:8.[11] Whatever the true significance of the chronological note, there are reasons for believing that the work was actually compiled at a considerably later period. In the first instance there is no evidence whatever that Baruch was ever in Babylon, particularly since he was mentioned elsewhere (Jer. 43:6f.) as going down to Egypt with Jeremiah.[12] On the other hand, the name of Baruch would constitute an extremely valuable pseudonym for circulating a document allegedly connected with the early days of the exile in Babylonia. The author followed Daniel (5:2) in making Belshazzar the son of Nebuchadnezzar, but this is in accord with the literary dependence of the author upon Daniel 9:4-19 in the prayer of confession (Baruch 1:15–2:19).

The *terminus ad quem* can be fixed approximately by reference to the latest of the authors that the book reflects, that is to say, the *Psalms of Solomon*. If Baruch is later than this compilation, and if the portion of the work which corresponds to the eleventh chapter of the *Psalms of Solomon* was written in Greek, then the book could well have been compiled between 70 B.C. and A.D. 70. However, such a dating seems rather late, even on the critical assumption of a Maccabean date for Daniel. If the entire book was originally written in Hebrew and subsequently translated into Greek, this could have been completed by the middle of the second century B.C. at the latest, making the relevant chapter of the *Psalms of Solomon* dependent upon Baruch, unless, of course, that section also was originally written in Hebrew. Uncertainty regarding the language in which the third portion was written makes for difficulties in any attempts at dating, while in other respects the internal evidence is far from helpful.

The religious teaching of the book is concerned exclusively with the sin, punishment, and forgiveness of Israel. The author appeared to agree with the synthesis of Ben Sira that identified wisdom with the Torah (Baruch 4:1), although the ode to wisdom seems to be out of place in a composition which is basically penitential in nature. Furthermore, the contents of the poem exhibit theological tendencies that are at some variance with the remainder of the book.[13] Of considerable importance is the emphasis upon sin as constituting rebellion against God, and which as a result can only evoke divine anger and punishment. This, along with the fact that the nation is treated as a unit, would place the theological perspective of the book in the general era of Jeremiah and Ezekiel. The eschatology of the work shows no interest whatever in

[11] E.g. W. O. E. Oesterley, *An Introduction to the Books of the Apocrypha*, pp. 256f.
[12] Cf. *AJ*, X, 9, 6.
[13] *HNTT*, pp. 423f.

immortality or the personage of a Messiah, but is distinctly terrestrial, and envisages the restored fortunes of a chastened, though still material, nation in a renewed homeland.

Supplementary Literature

Ferrar, W. J. *The Uncanonical Jewish Books.* 1925.
Harnell, R. R. *The Principal Versions of Baruch.* 1915.
Thackeray, H. St. J. *The Septuagint and Jewish Worship.* 1921.

X. THE LETTER OF JEREMIAH

This document, described in the AV and RV as "The Epistle of Jeremy," was placed in different positions in the various editions of the Apocrypha. In the Greek Codices Vaticanus and Alexandrinus it occurred after Lamentations, and this practice was followed by the Syriac Hexapla and the Arabic version. Other Greek and Syriac manuscripts, however, attached it to the apocryphal Book of Baruch, and it was found in this position in the Vulgate also. All English translations of the Apocrypha, as well as the Luther version of the Scriptures, printed it as the sixth chapter of the Book of Baruch. The RSV, however, departed from this tradition and regarded it as an entirely separate work.

The opening sentence describes the composition as the "copy of the Epistle that Jeremiah sent to those who were to be led captive to Babylon by the king of the Babylonians, to make known unto them in accordance with what had been commanded to him by God" (cf. Jer. 29:1ff.). Contrary to this laudable explanation, however, the document is not a letter at all, nor was it ever sent by Jeremiah to those about to be carried in captivity to Babylon. It was in fact a pamphlet, written to demonstrate the powerlessness of idols and the utter futility of venerating them. The sentiments that it expressed were based upon prophetic themes (cf. Isa. 44:9ff.; Jer. 10:1ff.; 11:10), and the general structure of this combined pastoral and prophetic document points to the original letter of Jeremiah as a model.

The third verse of the tractate has been taken as furnishing some sort of *terminus a quo*, where the captivity of the Jews was computed at some seven generations, thus suggesting a date about 300 B.C. as the earliest period of composition. The reference in 2 Maccabees 2:2 has been adduced as the earliest allusion to the letter of Jeremiah, but there is no foundation in fact for this.[1] While the familiarity with cultic worship in Babylonia might indicate that the writer was a Jew of the eastern Diaspora, it is well known that after 300 B.C. there were periodic lapses by the Jews into alien cult-worship, so that the "letter" could in fact have been written at any time between that date and the days of

---

[1] Cf. *AAT*, p. 267; H. L. Strack, *Einleitung in das AT* (1906), p. 173.

Hyrcanus. In the nature of the case it is impossible from the available evidence to arrive at any satisfactory conclusion with respect to the date of its composition.

Hebrew has commended itself to some authorities as the original language of the work, largely on the basis of indications of translation in the Greek text.[2] C. C. Torrey defended the theory of an Aramaic original for the document on the assumption that the reference in 2 Maccabees 2:1f. to instruction given by the prophet Jeremiah to those who were being deported, along with the advice to refrain from idolatrous contacts, were in fact allusions to this letter, and in this he was followed by Pfeiffer.[3] On the ground that the composition and style were of superior quality, other scholars argued persuasively for a Greek original, but as Tedesche has pointed out, this eventuality is improbable if a date at the end of the fourth century B.C. is favored.[4] However, even after careful scrutiny of the text, it is impossible to decide whether the original was written in Hebrew or Greek, so that this matter can throw no light at all upon the date of composition.

The declamatory style of the document might lead the reader to suspect some kind of systematized denunciation, based upon logical and compelling arguments. Unfortunately such is by no means the case, for the pamphlet discourses on a number of themes linked together in a mechanical fashion by means of a phrase expressing what the author believed to be a conclusive demonstration of the futility of idolatry (vv. 16, 23, 29, 30, 40, 44, 49, 52, 56, 64, 69). This refrain has the effect of dividing the homily up into a dozen or so small sections. The document has every appearance of being a characteristic Hellenistic-Jewish attack upon idolatry, and only on one occasion, in verse 41, was a particular deity named. The author mentioned only two religious practices typical of Babylonian cult-worship, but the implication that he was condemning all idolatrous customs is abundantly clear. The writer followed the lead given by Jeremiah in censuring those rites and ceremonies in which women played prominent parts (verses 41-43), and this had the effect of constituting a particular denunciation of the Babylonian Tammuz rituals.

The document commenced by informing the exiles that they were to remain in Babylonia for as long as seven generations, and that during their sojourn they must resist the blandishments of idol-worship (verses 1-7). The idols mentioned are declared to be merely the work of human hands, and as a result are completely powerless (verses 8-16). They suffer from precisely the same limitations as other inanimate objects, and are helpless in the face of human abuse of the offices attributed to them

---

2 Cf. *APOT*, I, p. 597.
3 *HNTT*, p. 430.
4 S. Tedesche, *IDB*, II, p. 823.

(verses 17-29). Being nothing more than the products of human creativity they have no innate freedom of expression, and thus are no better than stones from a mountain-side (verses 30-40). They even have to suffer the embarrassment of being hidden for safety in times of calamity, so helpless are they (verses 40-59). Unlike the divinely dispatched elements of the cosmos, idols are utterly useless. They cannot provide for themselves, like animals, and are no whit better than scarecrows which have been defiled by the birds (verses 60-73).

In the quality of its sarcasm this scathing attack upon that kind of idol-worship which was so typical of Babylonia compares favorably with any of the denunciations of paganism delivered by the canonical prophets. Whether this document was intended for the edification of the Diaspora as a whole, or for some particular Jewish community, perhaps in Babylonia[5] or elsewhere, is difficult to determine. It can be said, however, that the work was but one of a number of similar onslaughts against heathenism during the Hellenistic period, when pagan gods were held up as objects of ridicule and their powerlessness, which at that time was widely if tacitly acknowledged, was exposed for what it was.

Supplementary Literature

Naumann, W. *Untersuchungen über den apokryphen Jeremiasbrief.* 1913.

Thackeray, H. St. J. *Some Aspects of the Greek Old Testament.* 1927.

[5] *APOT*, I, p. 596.

XI. THE ADDITIONS TO THE BOOK OF DANIEL

The canonical book of Daniel, like Esther, contains in the ancient Greek and Latin versions a number of supplementary passages not found in the original Hebrew and Aramaic text. As well as numerous insignificant textual accretions, there are three major additions to the book, generally known as "The Prayer of Azariah and the Song of the Three Young Men," "Susanna," and "Bel and the Dragon." These narratives survived in two Greek recensions, one of which was the LXX text, preserved in a ninth-century manuscript in Rome, and the other constituting the revision of the LXX by Theodotion, about A.D. 175, undertaken on the basis of the Hebrew text. This version became an acceptable substitute for the LXX of Daniel in the Greek Bible of the Early Church, and it was against the background of this practice that versions into Latin, Syriac, Coptic, Arabic, Armenian, and Georgian were made.

There was some degree of divergence among the ancient versions in the matter of locating the additional portions within the text of the book of Daniel. In the Vulgate the Prayer of Azariah and the Song of the Three Young Men constituted part of the third chapter, with the story of Susanna following the final chapter of the prophecy and designated as chapter thirteen. The sequence was completed by the addition of Bel and the Dragon as a fourteenth chapter. In some Greek manuscripts, however, the tale of Susanna was moved to the beginning of Daniel, being prefixed to the first chapter, with the Prayer of Azariah and the Song of the Three Young Men inserted to form part of the third chapter, as in the Vulgate. Other Greek manuscripts included portions of these additions in a group of Odes, following the canonical Psalter. Bel and the Dragon was placed as an appendix after the twelfth chapter of Daniel in certain Greek manuscripts, while in others it was preceded by a title to show that it was a separate and distinct composition.

These Additions were popular ingredients of early Christian lore, and since the Greek versions seldom gave any indication that the sections were not part of the original Hebrew text, the Church Fathers frequently cited these passages as Scripture. Because Jerome worked from the Hebrew canon he rejected them as unauthentic in his preparation of the

Vulgate, and in his Preface to the book of Daniel he pointed out that they were no part of the original Hebrew or Aramaic text of that book.[1]

Whereas the supplementary material associated with Esther was written with a view to enlarging the book, the additions to Daniel were most probably in circulation originally as independent stories composed in Hebrew, Aramaic, or perhaps even Greek, which, because of their general affinity with the narratives of Daniel, were included in Greek recensions. The Prayer of Azariah in particular seems to have had a Semitic language as its original, with the liturgical passages in verse (Dan. 3:26-45, 52-90 LXX) possibly having been composed in Hebrew and the prose sections (Dan. 3:24-25, 46-51 LXX) in Aramaic. It appears unlikely in the light of the available evidence that the narratives of Susanna and Bel and the Dragon were originally written in Greek,[2] despite the presence of two puns on Greek words in Susanna, a circumstance that was employed as an argument for a Greek original of the work from the time of Origen.[3]

The source and date of these three principal additions to Daniel are far from easy to determine, since the available internal evidence is by no means conclusive. The Prayer of Azariah was almost certainly in circulation in the middle of the second century B.C., and it is highly probable that it was actually composed in Jerusalem, while the Song of the Three Young Men may have originated as early as the preceding century. The fact that Josephus gave no indication that he was familiar with either composition need throw no light upon the date of compilation, since it may merely imply that the copy of Daniel with which he was familiar did not contain the Additions.[4] There seems little reason to doubt that both the Prayer and the Song were originally separate compositions, and that they were subsequently brought together by a later editor.

The story of Susanna was given no geographical location in the LXX version, but the translation of Theodotion placed the incident in Babylon. If, however, the tale was originally written in Greek, Egypt would seem a more probable place of origin. Since the incident narrated was in the nature of a popular story, however, the place and time of composition need have no particular relationship to the location of the alleged original happenings. Susanna was probably issued in its extant form during the second century B.C., whether in Greek or Hebrew. If the latter, the most natural place of origin would be Judaea.

Bel and the Dragon was actually a composite of two individual stories, perhaps written in the first instance as entirely separate works and quite

---

[1] *PL*, XXVIII, 1291.

[2] *HNTT*, p. 449.

[3] Verse 54, σχῖνος, mastic tree, σχίζειν, to cut in two; verse 58, πρῖνος, holm-oak, πρίειν, to saw in two. Cf. *AAT*, p. 228; J. T. Marshall, *HDB*, IV, p. 632.

[4] *AJ*, X, 10, 5.

possibly composed in a Semitic language. The Babylonian background and the ridiculing of heathenism have much in common with the Letter of Jeremiah. The motif of the second story reached far back into the mythological past of ancient Mesopotamia, and may even be based upon the ancient legend of the conflict between Marduk and Tiamat.[5] Nevertheless, the gross caricature of such a situation as was presented by the author might easily be construed as a sarcastic attack upon pagan mythology. Most probably the composition arose in the middle of the second century B.C., or perhaps as late as the beginning of the first century B.C., in a Palestinian Jewish milieu.

A. THE PRAYER OF AZARIAH AND THE SONG OF THE THREE YOUNG MEN

This is the only addition that can be regarded as supplementing the narratives of Daniel in any strict sense. Following the description in the third chapter of the canonical book of the events leading to the casting of three Jews—Shadrach, Meshach, and Abednego—into the fiery furnace for refusing to comply with the royal commands, the interpolation commenced with an introductory sentence, probably inserted by the editor in the form of an explanatory gloss. Then Azariah (the Hebrew form of Abednego) began to pray to God and in process of this commended His justice, even though God had brought punishment upon His people for their sins (verses 2-10). Azariah recognized that God would not destroy the Jews completely because of His Covenant with them (verses 11-13), and that the divine purpose would be served adequately by humiliating them for a season (verses 14-15). When they manifested penitence and contrition of spirit, they would be restored to their former state and their oppressors would be dispersed (verses 15-22).

This short section was then followed by a narrative passage relating that, in answer to the prayer of Azariah, which, it should be noted, made no mention whatever of the fiery ordeal (verses 23-25), God sent an angel who drove the flames out of the furnace and created a pleasant wind inside it (verses 26f.). Remaining unharmed as a consequence of this intervention, the three men then sang a hymn of praise to God (verse 28).

In the AV and RV The Song of the Three Young Men was entitled "The Song of the Three Holy Children," following the tradition of some Greek manuscripts.[6] It can be divided conveniently into three portions comprising verses 29-34, 35-65, and 66-68. The first of these consisted of an ascription of praise to the Deity in which His majesty and exaltation were lauded. The second section was in the form of a liturgical hymn in which the singers called upon the animate and inanimate aspects of

---

[5] As suggested by H. Gunkel, *Schöpfung und Chaos in Urzeit und Endzeit* (1895), pp. 320ff. Cf. S. N. Kramer, *Sumerian Mythology*, pp. 76ff.

[6] *APOT*, I, p. 625.

divine creativity to join in praising and adoring God. The second half of each line contained a refrain, the idea for which probably came from Psalm 136 (135 LXX; cf. Pss. 148, 150), and this phrase occurred in all some thirty-two times. There is a high degree of solemnity and dignity of worship engendered by this canticle of praise, and in consequence it is hardly surprising that it has been preserved as a valued element in the corpus of Christian liturgical devotion, appearing in the litany of the early and medieval Church, in the Roman Catholic offices of the Mass and Lauds, and in the Anglican Prayer Book as an alternative to the *Te Deum Domine* in Morning Prayer under the title, *The Benedicite*, or, in its Latin form, *Benedicite, omnia opera Domini*. The third section (verses 66-68) was linked to the preceding song, and also to the Prayer of Azariah, by the mention of the three individuals in verse 66a. Quite probably this was no part of the original composition, but was employed by a later redactor as a device for connecting the Prayer and the Song in view of their ostensible suitability for inclusion in the Greek version of Daniel.

Whether the Prayer of Azariah originated earlier than the second century B.C. or not, there is little doubt that the furnace of affliction through which the Jews passed during the rule of the Seleucid Antiochus Epiphanes must have given considerable impetus to the sentiments which the work contained. In that event, the praises represented by the Song of the Three Young Men would be particularly appropriate during the period when the persecutions of Antiochus had finally come to an end. From a theological standpoint the Prayer and the Song reflect the religious traditions of the immediate pre-Pharisaic period. God was acknowledged as the one supreme Lord of heaven and earth, while the transgressions of the people were described in the most general terms. In line with the observations of the prophets it was conceded that the calamities that had overtaken the nation constituted just punishment for the iniquities of the people in departing from God and violating the precepts of the Torah. The non-sacrificial type of worship envisaged by Jeremiah and Ezekiel found expression in the Prayer of Azariah, where the priestly or ritualistic approach to sacrifice was superseded by the non-material concepts of the prophets, with penitence and contrition forming an acceptable substitute for the traditional sacrificial offerings (verses 16f., cf. Ps. 51:17; Isa. 57:15).

B. THE STORY OF SUSANNA

This composition was without question the most popular and widely circulated element of the Additions to Daniel, and is one of the finest examples of the short story genre. It appears to have enjoyed a certain amount of variation in content, since in the LXX it was inserted in a shorter form at the end of the canonical book of Daniel, while in the

1248

version of Theodotion it occupied a position at the commencement of the book in a longer recension.

The story described the adventures of Susanna, the beautiful wife of a prominent Babylonian Jew. This lady was of marked piety, grounded from her youth in the teachings of the Torah. Her husband, Joakim, was accustomed to lend the privacy of his estate to the Jewish elders and judges of Babylon in order that they might hold court. Two elderly jurists, who were characterized by reference to a Scriptural passage that spoke of iniquity coming forth from Babylonian judges (Susanna 5; cf. Jer. 23:15 LXX; Jer. 29:21ff. Heb.), conceived a passion for Susanna, having seen her walking in the garden from time to time after the court had concluded. Accordingly these two men planned to assault Susanna when she was alone, and they chose a day for this when she was bathing in the garden pool with the doors of the enclosure shut to guard against intrusion.

Seeing that she was alone, the two men demanded that she submit to them, or as an alternative be accused of consorting carnally with another man. Since the penalty for either offense was death, Susanna chose to call for help, and bear the accusation of associating immorally with a young man. The following day she appeared in judgment at her own home before the two lecherous elders, who repeated their false indictment and followed the established ritual procedure of the Law in such a case (Lev. 24:14).

As Susanna loudly protested her innocence she was heard by a young advocate named Daniel, who demanded an opportunity of interrogating the witnesses. The right of appeal being granted, Daniel faced the two accusers separately, and by astute questioning exposed their false and malicious charges. As a result of his intervention Susanna was discharged honorably and the elders were put to death for their crime (cf. Deut. 19:18ff.). The relatives and friends of Susanna glorified God for the deliverance of an innocent woman, and after this episode the reputation of Daniel was greatly enhanced.

It is most probable that the tale was widely circulated in secular society before it was ultimately adapted for the needs of Jewish readers. The basic theme of an innocent woman and an adroit attorney was by no means unknown in the ancient Near East, and Duschak considered that it went back in a Semitic form to exilic times.[7] Ewald and others discovered in the narrative the echo of a Babylonian myth,[8] while Fritzsche presented the view that the story was a Jewish form of an earlier legendary Babylonian incident.[9] Evidences of Haggadic interpre-

---

[7] M. Duschak, *Mosaisch-talmudische Strafrecht* (1869), pp. 94f.

[8] H. Ewald, *Geschichte des Volkes Israel* (1864), IV, p. 636; A. Kamphausen, *EB*, I, col. 1014.

[9] O. F. Fritzsche, *Exegetisches Handbuch zu den Apokryphen* (1851), I, pp. 118, 132f.; cf. L. Ginzberg, *Legends of the Jews* (1913), IV, pp. 336f.

tation of Jeremiah 29:21ff. have been discerned by some scholars in the extant narrative,[10] but it should be noted in this connection that the theme of an innocent woman wrongly accused is not a feature of the Jewish Haggadah. Other mythological interpreters have made recourse to various Greek literary materials in an attempt to discern the origin of the story of Susanna against a background of Aegean culture, but these attempts, ingenious as they are, appear unconvincing.[11] A twofold folk-lorist motif, that of an innocent woman wronged and a clever young advocate, has been suggested as the basis of the story, on the assumption that the narrative is to be interpreted purely as a folk-tale.[12]

The meaning of this composition has been variously understood by scholars. C. H. Toy suggested that it was a pure folk-tale, and was circulated as such without any ulterior motive whatever.[13] Other critics have seen the work as a didactic book that was written with deliberate moral and religious precepts in view. From the story, therefore, it may be gathered that God does not desert an innocent person who is falsely accused of criminal behavior,[14] and that models of probity and righteousness for both men and women are furnished by the narrative.[15] It is also worth noting that the book may well be continuing the criticism of the structure and functioning of patriarchal social organization that was begun in Job (32:9).

The juristic theory of interpretation as favored by Duschak was elaborated by Brüll, who regarded the story of Susanna as actually comprising a polemical Pharisaic tractate that attacked the Sadducees for certain irregularities in legal procedure condoned by them during the reign of Alexander Jannaeus (103-76 B.C.).[16] According to Brüll the work itself was composed during the rule of Alexandra, widow of Jannaeus (76-67 B.C.), to promote the political interests of the Pharisees and bring disrepute upon the Sadducees. It seems doubtful, however, that such a legalistic concept of interpretation was in the mind either of the editor of the LXX version or of Theodotion. The former appeared primarily concerned to point out that young men who revere God are filled with knowledge and discernment (verse 63), while the latter seems to have regarded the narrative as indicating the commencement of a growing

---

[10] E.g. N. Brüll, *Jahrbuch für Jüdische Geschichte und Literatur*, III (1877), pp. 5ff.; C. J. Ball in H. Wace (ed.), *The Speaker's Commentary, Apocrypha II*, pp. 325ff.; J. T. Marshall, *HDB*, IV, p. 631.

[11] Cf. K. Fries, *Orientalische Literaturzeitung*, XIII (1910), pp. 337ff.; W. Schultz, *Memnon*, IV (1910), pp. 137f.; E. Siecke, *Memnon*, V (1911), pp. 123ff.

[12] Cf. H. Gunkel, *Das Märchen im AT* (1921), p. 126.

[13] C. H. Toy, *JE*, XI, p. 603.

[14] So *AAT*, pp. 227f.

[15] A. Bertholet in K. Budde (ed.), *Geschichte der althebräischen Litteratur* (1909), pp. 384f.

[16] N. Brüll, *Jahrbuch für Jüdische Geschichte und Literatur*, III (1877), pp. 1ff.; cf. *Pirke Ab.* I, 9.

reputation in Babylon for Daniel (verse 64), but hardly as one who was assuming the role of a reformer of current judicial procedures.

From a theological standpoint the story of Susanna did not give expression to any specifically new doctrines. Against the background of accepted theism the narrative showed that the divine will was given normative expression in the Torah of Moses, and that injustice was unequivocally condemned by the written Word. Her experience of God led Susanna to choose death rather than sin, but in making this decision she was actually placing her entire confidence in the divine ability to answer prayer and vindicate the innocent suppliant. By contrast, however, the deceitful wicked were unmasked and exposed, despite their hypocritical pretensions to justice and religion. This would appear to indicate that gross injustice was but one of the fruits, not of the religious life, but of inherent atheism.

The popularity of the story led to many allegorical interpretations in the early Christian era, as well as a good deal of representation in pictorial art.[17] But as Kay has remarked, allegorical and apocalyptic interpretations have been derived by way of students of the story, and not from the narrative itself.[18] During the medieval period there arose a number of paraphrases and poetic versions of Susanna, one of the more interesting of which was prepared in 1622 by Robert Aylett for the edification of "Our Judges in Westminster Hall."

C. BEL AND THE DRAGON

These two tales, like that of Susanna, were handed down in two Greek recensions, the LXX and the version of Theodotion, and placed at the end of Daniel. The LXX version carried the title "Part of the Prophecy of Habakkuk the son of Jesus of the tribe of Levi." In the Vulgate these two stories constituted chapter fourteen of the book of Daniel, though Jerome rightly regarded them as *fabulas* in his preface to Daniel.

Like the Letter of Jeremiah, these stories inveighed against idolatry and ridiculed heathen cult-worship by utilizing as forceful arguments those Old Testament passages which demonstrated the inanimate nature of idols and their utter helplessness.[19] But, as with the story of Susanna, the underlying truth was presented in the form of a short narrative in which all the elements of artistic fiction were present. In brief compass these two tales manage to reveal a central plot, the interplay of emotional conflicts, an unfolding of individual character, struggle, climax, and a satisfying conclusion.

The first of these stories involved the Babylonian deity Bel, otherwise known as Marduk, the patron god of Babylon from about 2275 B.C., and

[17] Cf. *MTA*, pp. 112f.
[18] D. M. Kay, *APOT*, I, p. 646.
[19] For a list of such passages cf. R. H. Pfeiffer, *JBL*, XLIII (1924), p. 239.

for many centuries thereafter venerated as one of the most powerful members of the Babylonian pantheon. Innumerable cuneiform inscriptions from the Neo-Babylonian period (626-538 B.C.) attest to the worship of Marduk, and it was at the beginning of this particular phase of Mesopotamian history that by the command of Nebuchadnezzar II the temple known as Esagila, the shrine of Bel, was restored as part of a program involving the renovation of ancient Babylonian religious sites. The resultant building became one of the greatest edifices of the day, and in its completed form rivalled the neighboring *ziggurat* of Babel in majesty and dimensions.[20]

The story of Bel narrated the way in which Cyrus worshipped the deity, whereas Daniel, an honored companion of the king, venerated his own God. Cyrus believed superstitiously that the daily rations of food allocated to Bel, consisting of twelve bushels of fine flour, forty sheep, and fifty gallons of wine, were actually consumed by the deity himself.[21] In order to demonstrate the fundamental error of this supposition, Daniel persuaded Cyrus to seal up the sanctuary of Bel where the offerings were placed. Daniel, however, had apparently been indulging in a private investigation of the matter, and strewed the floor with a coating of fine ashes before the sanctuary was sealed. During the night the priests emerged from a concealed entrance beneath the table on which the o_ering had been placed, and consumed them according to their usual practice. The following morning the seal on the sanctuary remained still unbroken whereas the food was gone, an apparent vindication of the beliefs of Cyrus (verse 17). On closer inspection at the request of Daniel, however, the footprints of the offenders were clearly discerned in the deposit of fine ash, and as a result of this discovery the culprits were exposed and put to death. The important consequence of this for the Jewish reader was that the king permitted Daniel to destroy the *ziggurat* and the image of Bel (verses 18-22).

The author of the story was evidently aware that the temple of Bel lay in ruins at the time of writing, and this would help to furnish something of a *terminus a quo* for the story itself. Xerxes I (486-464 B.C.) was responsible for the overthrow of the shrine, and according to Herodotus he carried off as a trophy the golden image of the deity, represented as seated upon his throne.[22] Strabo narrated that when Alexander the Great entered Babylon in 332 B.C. he found the temple of Marduk already in ruins.[23] This would seem to point to a date not earlier than

[20] *LAP*, p. 186.

[21] For a discrepant Babylonian account of the quantity of food offered see S. Langdon, *Die Neubabilonischen Königsinschriften* (1912), p. 91, translated from H. C. Rawlinson, *The Cuneiform Inscriptions of Western Asia* (1861), I, p. 65, col. 1, lines 13-28.

[22] *Hist.* I, 183.

[23] *Geog.* XVI, 1, 5.

the fourth century B.C. as one outside limit of composition of the tale.

The other narrative, which may well have arisen from a different hand, but united with Bel by a later editor because of the general similarity of subject-matter, dealt also with the prowess of Daniel. On this occasion, however, it was the worship of a dragon which was involved. When the king suggested to Daniel that he ought to venerate the beast, since it was obviously alive, Daniel refused and was given permission by the king to try to destroy it. As far as the monarch was concerned this was an impossible task, for he believed implicitly in the immortality of the dragon whose divinity was thus being so abruptly challenged. Daniel employed the art of the apothecary in order to concoct a mixture of fat, hair, and pitch, which he boiled and made into cakes. These he subsequently fed to the unsuspecting dragon, which according to the narrative burst open immediately (verses 23-27).

This turn of events so provoked the Babylonians that they began to accuse the king of having become a convert to Judaism. They demanded the life of Daniel as a recompense, and failing this they stated that they would revolt against the royal house and overthrow it. Daniel was accordingly handed over to the people, and was thrown into a den of seven hungry lions (verses 28-32). A change of scene in the narrative saw the prophet Habakkuk coerced into leaving Judaea, feeding Daniel, and returning home (verses 33-39). On the seventh day the king found Daniel alive and well, whereupon he took him out of the den and commanded his persecutors to be thrown to the lions instead (verses 40-42).

Though there are obvious points of similarity to the events narrated in the sixth chapter of Daniel, there are some rather different overtones present that have elements in common with ancient Near Eastern mythology. The dragon claimed a long history as a symbol of Mesopotamian religion,[24] going back in Sumeria to at least the third millennium B.C.[25] Of those who suggested that the tale of the dragon had been inspired by the ancient Babylonian story of the slaying of Tiamat by Marduk, Gunkel was by far the most vehement,[26] and this resulted in his overstating the resemblances between the two sources.[27]

Like the story of Bel, that of the dragon was designed to ridicule the stupidities of pagan worship, and in consequence it could have had its rise at any time within the Greek period. Both narratives appear to suit the religious climate of the time between 150 and 100 B.C. in Judaea, and this date would seem to supply a satisfactory *terminus ad quem* for

---

[24] T. H. Gaster, *IDB*, I, p. 868, *Thespis*, pp. 137ff., 257ff.; *Baba Bathra* 74*b*.
[25] S. N. Kramer, *Sumerian Mythology*, pp. 77ff.
[26] H. Gunkel, *Schöpfung und Chaos in Urzeit und Endzeit*, pp. 320ff.; cf. C. H. Toy, *JE*, II, p. 650; J. T. Marshall, *HDB*, I, p. 267.
[27] Cf. T. W. Davies, *APOT*, I, pp. 653f.

the two documents, whether or not they were originally separate compositions, as was most probably the case.

Despite the views of the earlier scholars that these tales were originally written in Greek, there are sound reasons for adhering to a primary Semitic form for Bel and the Dragon. The fact that Theodotion introduced into his text certain Hebraic expressions that were lacking in the LXX recension would seem to imply that he had a Hebrew text readily available from which, presumably, he corrected the LXX readings. In addition, considerations of syntax would appear to prefer a distinctly Hebrew rather than either a Greek or an Aramaic original.[28]

As with the story of Susanna, so in Bel and the Dragon, certain familiar folk-tales and sagas were made to serve the ends of Jewish authors whose primary concern was to show the supreme dominance of God, and the telling effect of His power as compared with other iniquitous forces. In Bel and the Dragon, however, the revered themes of pagan religion were turned inwards by the skill of the authors in order to present a dramatic and forceful attack upon heathen deities, which among other things demonstrated the stupidity of worshipping powerless creatures. Precisely how certain legends concerning Daniel became associated with traditions involving Habakkuk in the story of the dragon is difficult to explain. While Habakkuk was mentioned by name both in the LXX, the Peshitta, and in the version of Theodotion, it was the last two only that specifically located him in Judaea (verse 33) and spoke of him as "the prophet." These additions would be more understandable if Theodotion had actually compiled his version in the light of a Hebrew form of the dragon story.

Supplementary Literature

Bludau, A. *Die alexandrinische Übersetzung des Buches Daniels.* 1897.
Daubney, W. H. *The Three Additions to Daniel.* 1906.
Oesterley, W. O. E. *An Introduction to the Books of the Apocrypha.* 1935.
Scholz, A. *Esther und Susanna.* 1892.

[28] *Ibid.*, pp. 655f.

XII. THE PRAYER OF MANASSEH

This short prayer, entitled in the AV and RV "The Prayer of Manasses king of Judah, when he was holden captive in Babylon," and in the Greek and Latin manuscripts "The Prayer of Manasses," is probably the best single piece of literature in the entire English Apocrypha. It constitutes a model of liturgical form and construction, and breathes the pure air of genuine religious piety. The composition looked for its origin to the incident recorded in 2 Chronicles 33:11f., 18f., according to which Manasseh repented and prayed to God when held as a captive in Babylonia. His prayer was preserved for posterity in the Acts of the Kings of Israel, and also in the history of Hozai.

This prayer first appeared in extant literature in the third century after Christ in Syriac as part of the *Didascalia* (II, 21), a manual of ecclesiastical procedures subsequently incorporated into the *Apostolic Constitutions*. At a later time it was found to have occupied various places in the text of the Bible. The Targum of Chronicles supplemented the reference in 2 Chronicles 33:11 by a story that narrated the methods employed when Manasseh was tried by ordeal in Babylon, and made it clear that he only turned to God for help after calling in vain upon the idols that he had revered previously.[1]

At least one modern author revived the medieval opinion that the prayer was formerly an integral part of the Chronicles narrative,[2] despite the uniform witness of the major Greek codices, several of which assigned it to a position among the fourteen Canticles or Odes that formed a poetic appendix to the Psalter. The manuscripts of the Vulgate generally attached the prayer to the end of 2 Chronicles in the medieval period, while versions such as the Syriac, Armenian, Ethiopic, and Old Slavonic varied in their usage in this regard, some of them placing it at the end of the Psalter and others utilizing it as a conclusion of 2 Chronicles. In his version, Martin Luther assigned it to a position at the

---

[1] Cf. C. J. Ball in H. Wace (ed.), *The Speaker's Commentary, Apocrypha II*, p. 371.

[2] H. H. Howarth, *Proceedings of the Society of Biblical Archaeology*, XXXI (1909), pp. 89ff., cf. Thomas Aquinas, *Summa Theol.* III, 984, 10.

end of the Apocrypha as a whole, while in the English version it was located immediately before 1 Maccabees. All official printings of the Vulgate since the Council of Trent relegated the Prayer of Manasseh to an appendix following the New Testament. By contrast, in the Geneva Bible of 1560 it was placed between 2 Chronicles and Ezra, with its title, "The Prayer of Manasseh, apocryphe," entered in the table of contents after 2 Chronicles. It also occurred in this position in the Modern Greek Bible, issued in 1876 at St. Petersburg.

Though the prayer contains thirty-seven *stichoi*, it has become customary to follow the division of this penitential psalm into fifteen verses, as adopted by Fritzsche in his *Libri apocryphi Veteris Testamenti Graece* of 1871. Its pattern was characteristic of Jewish liturgical forms from 400 B.C, and this fact may assist in determining the date of its composition. Clearly the prayer must have been held in considerable esteem to have been included in the Codex Alexandrinus, and whether the liturgical canticles in that manuscript were transcribed from an even earlier source or not, it appears evident that a significant interval of time must have elapsed between the date when the prayer was composed, its survival in Hellenistic sources, and the period of its use in the *Didascalia* and the *Apostolic Constitutions*. However, the position of the prayer in the *Didascalia*, placed as it was among several passages cited from the LXX of Kings and Chronicles, may suggest that the latter furnished the framework into which the prayer was set, with the implication that the latter was compiled at a later period than that in which the translations of the canonical works were made. Though positive indications of a specific date for the composition of the prayer are far from evident, it seems most probable that it was written between 250 and 150 B.C.

Equally uncertain is the nature of the original language in which this petition for forgiveness was drafted. The concepts that it embodied appear to be in much closer harmony with the traditions of Palestinian Judaism than the speculative approach of the Alexandrian intelligentsia. The shortness of the text itself makes for difficulty in determining the language of origin, though the presence of Semitisms as well as the use of the LXX[3] might point to a Hebrew or Aramaic original.[4] The majority of scholars have argued for Greek as the language of composition,[5] basing their reasoning upon such considerations as the flexibility of style and the simple nature of the vocabulary employed in the prayer.

[3] Cf. *TAL*, pp. 68f.

[4] So H. H. Howarth, *Proceedings of the Society of Biblical Archaeology*, XXXI (1909), pp. 91ff.; L. Couard, *Die religiösen und sittlichen Anschauungen der alttestamentlichen Apokryphen und Pseudepigraphen* (1907), p. 5; *HNTT*, p. 459.

[5] E.g. O. F. Fritzsche, *Exegetisches Handbuch zu den Apokryphen*, I, p. 157; *AAT*, p. 241; H. E. Ryle, *APOT*, I, p. 615. Cf. N. D. Coleman in C. Gore, H. L. Goudge and A. Guillaume (ed.), *A New Commentary on Holy Scripture Including the Apocrypha* (1928), p. 124.

The petition itself began with an introductory ascription of praise to the Almighty Lord, who manifested His glorious majesty both in creation (verses 1-4), and in the granting of repentance to sinners (verses 5-8). This was followed by a personal confession that outlined the spiritual despondency and sense of guilt entertained by the author. Such a recognition of sin led to supplication for forgiveness (verses 11-13) based on confession and contrition. The composition concluded with a petition for grace, followed by a doxology (verses 14-15).

The prayer may be said to represent what the author imagined Manasseh to have uttered as he implored divine mercy during his period of distress. The ascription of the work to Manasseh is completely unhistorical, although the tradition of his visit to Babylonia as recorded in Chronicles certainly deserves more than the cursory rejection accorded to it by many critical scholars. The long reign of this cruel monarch, at first probably as co-regent with his father from 696-686 B.C., and then as sole ruler from 686-641 B.C. (2 Kgs. 21:1; 2 Chron. 33:1),[6] was notorious for the introduction of illegal altars into the Temple precincts, and for the practice of offering human sacrifices in the valley of the sons of Hinnom. To the present, however, there is no firm archaeological evidence for the captivity of Manasseh in Babylon (2 Chron. 33:10ff.), although Assyrian sources contained a reference to a visit made by him to Nineveh about 678 B.C. at the command of Esarhaddon.[7]

It is known that Esarhaddon did in fact rebuild Babylon, which had suffered destruction under Nebuchadnezzar,[8] and in addition that the name "Manasseh, king of Judah" appeared not merely upon the Prism of Esarhaddon, but also in the form *Mi-in-si-e-shar Ia-u-di* on the Prism of Ashurbanipal along with twenty-one other tributaries of Assyria.[9] A parallel to the deportation of Manasseh to Babylon and his subsequent release can be seen in the treatment accorded to Pharaoh Necho I by Ashurbanipal, as preserved on the Rassam Cylinder.[10] Thus the tradition of the captivity of Manasseh as recorded by the Chronicler may well rest upon solid, if as yet incompletely demonstrated, historical foundations. It is now known that during the reign of Manasseh there occurred a revolt against Assyrian suzerainty in support of the insurgent Shamash-shum-ukin, the viceroy of Babylon. In an attempt to be free from the Assyrian yoke it may be that Manasseh joined in the revolt, only to be subjugated by his Assyrian overlord.[11]

[6] Cf. *MNHK*, pp. 156ff.
[7] *ARAB*, II, sect. 690.
[8] Cf. *ARAB*, II, sects. 646f.
[9] *ANET*, p. 294.
[10] *ANET*, p. 295.
[11] Cf. *ANET*, p. 298.

From 4Q a fragmentary *Prayer of Nabonidus*[12] was recovered, containing an experience similar to that recounted in the Prayer of Manasseh. It stated that Nabonidus was smitten by God with a severe illness, and that upon confession of his sins he was absolved and comforted by a Jewish priest from among the Babylonian exiles, who interpreted for him in part the significance of the affliction. It seems most probable that this fragment should not be connected with the fourth chapter of Daniel, nor yet regarded as proof of the contention that the extant text of that section related to Nabonidus rather than Nebuchadnezzar.[13] Instead, as mentioned in an earlier chapter, it may be considered to comprise a hitherto unknown member of a literary group, of which the Prayer of Manasseh was one, produced by some pietistic group or party in post-exilic Judaea.

The theological emphases of the Prayer of Manasseh conflict somewhat, inasmuch as the universal creator of the entire world was regarded as the God of the Jews alone. More specifically He was the Deity of the sinless patriarchs and of their spiritual followers, who adhered strictly to the tenets of the Mosaic Torah. This position anticipated the contention of Paul (Rom. 9:6f.) that all Israel constituted the true Israel. The concept of sin was restricted principally to the practice of idolatry, and pardon was held to follow true repentance and the complete abandonment of idolatrous worship. Nevertheless the infinite compassion of the Deity for the sinner and the emphasis upon the efficacy of true repentance, are permanent religious themes that were given a high degree of expression in the prayer. The sincerity of its thought and the depth of religious expression enshrined in the composition have rightly earned it a lasting place in the literature of spiritual devotion. Bishop Lancelot Andrewes incorporated the principal sections of it into his *Devotions*.

Supplementary Literature

Johnson, N. B. *Prayer in the Apocrypha and Pseudepigrapha: A Study of the Jewish Concept of God.* 1948.

Wicks, H. J. *The Doctrine of God in the Jewish Apocryphal and Apocalyptic Literature.* 1915.

[12] J. T. Milik, *RB*, LXIII (1956), pp. 407ff.
[13] Cf. D. N. Freedman, *BASOR*, No. 145 (1947), pp. 31f.; S. Smith, *Babylonian Historical Texts Relating to the Capture and Downfall of Babylon* (1924), pp. 36ff.

XIII. THE TWO BOOKS OF MACCABEES

As early as the late second century of the Christian era the title "The Things Maccabean" was employed as a designation of both 1 and 2 Maccabees of the English Apocrypha.[1] It may, however, have been used originally for 2 Maccabees only, since the surname Maccabaeus distinguished Judas, whose exploits were recounted in that work, from his brothers and successors mentioned in 1 Maccabees as well as 2 Maccabees. Nevertheless, so famous did the title "Maccabees" become that it was ultimately used as the designation of no less than four compositions purporting to describe in one way or another the personalities and events of the Hasmonean and related periods.

It is interesting to note that the term "Maccabee" did not occur in Semitic writings until long after the beginning of the Christian era, since it was customary to follow the Talmudic tradition using the family designation of "Hasmonean."[2] This was apparently derived from Hashmon, the name of an ancestor of Mattathias, who may perhaps have been referred to on one occasion in 1 Maccabees (2:1), if the suggestion first made by Wellhausen that Simeon was in fact an error for Hashmon is correct.[3] The origin of the name "Maccabaeus" has also been matter for some scholarly speculation, since the Greek spelling could presuppose an original *mqb*, as in the Syriac version, or *mkb*, as in the Latin name "Machabaeus," both of which are quite legitimate. If the former, the name may have meant "The Hammerer," from Old Testament references to a small hammer (מקבה, Judg. 4:21; 1 Kgs. 6:7; Isa. 44:12; Jer. 10:4), although some scholars have interpreted it in terms of leadership,[4] or offensive ability.[5] With the spelling *mkb*, the name has been understood

---

[1] Τὰ Μακκαβαϊκά. Origen, as recorded by Eusebius, *Hist. Eccl.* VI, 25, 2, transcribed it as Τὰ Μακκαβαϊκά.

[2] בית חשמנאי. Cf. *AJ*, XIV, 16, 4; XX, 8, 11.

[3] J. Wellhausen, *Die Pharisäer und die Sadducäer* (1874), p. 94n. Cf. C. C. Torrey, *JBL*, LXII (1943), p. 5; *AJ*, XII, 6, 1. Josephus, *BJ*, I, 1, 3, referred to Hashmon as the "father" of Mattathias, but this may merely be common Semitic usage for "ancestor."

[4] *AAT*, p. 64.

[5] C. J. Ball in H. Wace (ed.), *The Speaker's Commentary, Apocrypha I*, p. 248n.

acrostically,[6] as a contraction of some such Hebrew phrase as "what is like my father?",[7] or else as a title, "The Extinguisher."[8]

A. FIRST MACCABEES

Although 1 Maccabees contains no direct information about its author, it is clear that he was an orthodox Jew familiar with the geography and topography of Palestine. In matters of politics and doctrine alike he appears to have pursued a non-partisan policy, steering an adroit course between the fanaticism of the Pharisees and the conservative outlook of the priestly Sadducean families. Out of deference to the latter the author seems to have avoided controversial topics such as the belief in life after death, and to have spoken approvingly of the Jewish High Priesthood in Jerusalem, which even in the days of Jesus Christ was monopolized by the Sadducees. At the same time he emphasized loyalty to the principles of the Torah, and supported the aspirations of the Pharisees by representing all the sons of Mattathias as zealous champions of the Law and dire opponents of paganism.

If the final two verses of the book are genuine (1 Macc. 16:23f.), as seems probable, the author compiled the work during the reign of John Hyrcanus (134-104 B.C.), either at the beginning of that period,[9] during the middle of his rule,[10] or else towards 110 B.C.[11] It has been suggested that the author wrote 1 Maccabees as an unofficial history of the Maccabean rebellion,[12] but it appears more probable that the compiler was merely an admirer, and not a member[13] of the Hasmonean line, since his work seems to reflect a growing discontent with Hasmonean rule generally, an impression that would perhaps not have emerged had the author been related in some way to Simon. In actual fact his admiration for the Hasmoneans was by no means unqualified, since he regarded their leaders as merely victorious agents of God, who alone was responsible for the deliverance of Israel (1 Macc. 5:62). The writer also made it clear that it was the followers of Mattathias, and not the leader himself, who arrived at the decision to fight defensively on the sabbath (1 Macc. 2:40f.), while elsewhere he subordinated the interests of the ruling dynasty to the fate and destiny of Israel as a whole (cf. 1 Macc. 4:59; 5:16; 7:48f.; 14:27ff.). He approached history from substantially the same

---

[6] F. Delitzsch, *Geschichte der jüdischen Poesie* (1836), p. 28.

[7] Cf. H. Bévenot, *Die Beiden Makkabäerbücher* (1931), p. 3.

[8] S. J. Curtiss, *The Name Machabee* (1876), pp. 10ff. Cf. S. Zeitlin and S. Tedesche, *The First Book of Maccabees* (1950), pp. 250ff.

[9] So C. C. Torrey, *EB*, III, cols. 2859f.; *TAL*, p. 74.

[10] W. O. E. Oesterley, *APOT*, I, p. 60; E. Bickermann, *Der Gott der Makkabäer* (1937), p. 146.

[11] W. H. Brownlee, *IDB*, III, p. 205.

[12] E. Bickermann, *Der Gott der Makkabäer*, p. 145.

[13] As suggested in S. Zeitlin and S. Tedesche, *The First Book of Maccabees*, p. 27.

point of view as that of the Chronicler in regarding Israel as the holy congregation of God and seeing in the general trend of events the unmistakable indications of divine overruling.

For the writer the Jewish state under the High Priest constituted an island of spiritual enlightenment in the midst of a vast ocean of paganism. Israel was the pivot upon which the foreign policies of the Near Eastern nations turned (1 Macc. 10:4ff.; 11:3ff.; 14:10ff.), and in the last analysis there could not be the slightest doubt as to the outcome of her immediate temporal struggles, since she rejoiced in the protection of an invincible Deity. For this reason the writer could advocate a full recompense for the Gentiles (2:68), and a withdrawal into the confines afforded by the rigorous observance of the Law. The book exhibits clear instances of the manner in which Jewish religious security felt itself threatened by the encroachments of pagan Hellenism, as for example in the way in which all those calamities befalling Israel were depicted either as the result of Gentile scheming or of native Jewish apostasy (1 Macc. 3:10; 5:1; 7:23; 13:17).

With regard to the latter topic the author was particularly vehement, denouncing his disloyal compatriots and exposing their plans to overthrow the faithful congregation (1 Macc. 3:15; 6:21ff.; 7:10; 9:58; 11:21). Quite evidently he believed that his task as a chronicler was to record the continuing providence of God for Israel in the Greek period, just as the canonical books of Ezra, Nehemiah, and Chronicles had done for the Persian era. Thus he presented an analogous form of "salvation history" in which faith in God and loyalty to the Torah were the predominant considerations in any view of ultimate victory over those who would compel Israel to substitute the culture of pagan Hellenism for the Sinai Covenant and the Torah of God.

While there is no trace of a Semitic original extant, there is very little doubt that 1 Maccabees was first written in Hebrew. This appears evident from the fact that Origen gave the book the obscure title "Sarbeth Sabanaiel,"[14] and also that Jerome, in his *Prologus Galeatus* explicitly stated that Hebrew was the language in which the book had been composed.[15] Whether Jerome meant classical Hebrew or Palestinian Aramaic, however, is impossible to determine. Most probably the former was envisaged, since there are syntactical and other indications to show that the Greek was evidently translated from Hebrew.[16] The Greek version may have been made by an Alexandrian Jew who on occasions failed to understand the significance of the original text correctly, and

---

[14] Σαρβὴθ Σαβαναιέλ, perhaps a transcription roughly equivalent to the Aramaic title ספר בית חשמנאי, "The Book of the House of the Hasmoneans."
[15] "Machabaeorum primum librum hebraicum repperi."
[16] *APOT*, I, p. 61.

elsewhere committed certain errors of translation.[17] The extant Greek text displays numerous instances of Semitic idioms as well as a familiarity with the LXX, and in all probability was in circulation not later than a century after the original work was composed.

In contradistinction to the opinions of Zeitlin, who maintained that the familiarity of the author with the history of the period enabled him to dispense with literary sources,[18] there are clear indications that specific written material formed the background of, if not actually the basis for, the compilation of 1 Maccabees. Thus, what appears to be the text of an alliance between the Romans and the Jews occurred in chapter eight, and despite the doubts cast upon its genuineness because of the presence of alleged inconsistencies,[19] it has the appearance of substantial authenticity.

A further documentary source consisted of the letter purporting to have been written by Jonathan to the Spartans (1 Macc. 12:6ff.), the intention of which is far from clear, since its contents expressed a desire for friendship and repudiated foreign alliances at the same time. Less likely to be genuine is the letter of the Spartans to Onias (12:20ff.), which occurred as an appendix to the letters of Jonathan, since it has no bearing at all upon the central issues of the Maccabean struggle, and may conceivably have been of Jewish origin.

Of literary sources that may be credited with some confidence to foreign rulers, the letter from the Spartans to Simon (14:20ff.), while exhibiting certain internal inconsistencies,[20] appears on the whole to have made some use of an official document. The letter from Lucius, the Roman consul, to Ptolemy Euergetes of Egypt (15:16ff.; cf. *AJ*, XIV, 8, 5), proclaiming the friendship existing between the Romans and the Jews, breaks up the trend of the narrative in an obtrusive fashion, indicating that it was most probably interpolated by the compiler. From the account of the letter furnished by Josephus it would appear to be an authentic document, although it should be noted that the events relating to the letter mentioned by Josephus actually occurred during the reign of Hyrcanus II (63-40 B.C.).

Letters from Syrian rulers to Jewish leaders that have been incorporated into the text of 1 Maccabees included a message from Alexander Balas to Jonathan (10:18ff.), the general purport alone being recorded

---

[17] Cf. H. W. Ettelson, *The Integrity of 1 Maccabees* (1925), pp. 249ff.

[18] S. Zeitlin and S. Tedesche, *The First Book of Maccabees*, p. 27.

[19] Cf. H. Willrich, *Juden und Griechen* (1895), pp. 70ff.; J. Wellhausen, *Israelitische und Jüdische Geschichte* (1914), pp. 250ff.; *APOT*, I, p. 64. The use of metal for documents (cf. 14:27ff.) in the first century of the Christian era was clearly illustrated by the Qumran discoveries; cf. *BA*, XIX, No. 3 (1956), pp. 61ff.

[20] *APOT*, I, p. 64.

by the author; a letter from Demetrius I to the Jewish nation (10:25ff.) seeking to offset the proposals of Alexander Balas, which does not convey the impression of genuineness in matters of detail;[21] a letter from Demetrius II to Jonathan, enclosing a message to Lasthenes (11:30ff.), which seems to have constituted an authentic document deliberately elaborated by the author in order to suit his particular historical approach; a letter from Antiochus VI to Jonathan (11:57), which was probably a genuine document presented in summary form; the letter from Demetrius II to Simon (13:36ff.), which was in all probability a copy of the original document, and the letter from Antiochus VII to Simon (15:2ff.), which may have been an adaptation or elaboration of an original composition. The archives of the chief priest in the Temple treasury (14:23) may well have been the repository for such genuine letters as were of foreign origin or were addressed to the Jewish nation as a whole, to which the author of 1 Maccabees could have had ready access.

There are some indications that the writer drew upon a biography of Judas Maccabaeus for some of his material, since, as Brownlee has indicated,[22] the fact that half the book was devoted to only seven years (166-160/59 B.C.) in the life of Judas, whereas the remainder covered a twenty-five-year interval (160/59-135 B.C.) and dealt with his brothers Jonathan and Simon, would seem to suggest a special documentation for the period of Judas himself. The existence of such a record of events may even have been hinted at by the author of 1 Maccabees (9:22). Again, the structure of the narratives in the second chapter relating to Mattathias appears to indicate that the author drew upon a distinct tradition concerning this dynamic personality, for the way in which he described the resistance of Mattathias to pagan sacrificial rites (2:1ff.) and his final testament to his sons (2:49ff.) would seem to constitute a deliberate interpolation into the Judas source from a well-authenticated tradition.

If Jonathan and Simon, the brothers of Judas, followed the usual practice of keeping official annual chronicles of significant events upon becoming High Priest (cf. 16:23f.), those documents would constitute invaluable detailed sources relating to the deeds of their respective authors. In addition, the fact that the book is interspersed with poetic material (cf. 1:24ff., 36ff.; 2:7ff.; 3:3ff., 45, 50ff.; 7:17, 37f.; 14:4ff.)[23] might imply that some of these elements at least were composed by the author himself, with the remainder being possibly borrowed from a corpus of Maccabean psalms.

[21] *APOT*, I, p. 63.
[22] W. H. Brownlee, *IDB*, III, p. 204.
[23] T. K. Cheyne, *The Origin of the Psalter* (1891), p. 23; E. Bickermann, *Der Gott der Makkabäer*, p. 146.

Despite the uncertainty of specific sources,[24] as mentioned above, the book is, on the whole, a reasonably trustworthy account of the events it purports to describe. The chronology of 1 Maccabees was based upon the Seleucid era (1:10),[25] reckoned, as Josephus commented,[26] "from the time when Seleucus, surnamed Nicator, occupied Syria." This period commenced with the battle of Gaza in 312 B.C.; and in accordance with Seleucid and pre-exilic Hebrew custom, the year began in the autumn. This arrangement conflicted with the post-exilic Jewish tradition, which followed the Babylonian pattern of commencing the year in the spring, a fact that naturally complicates the dating scheme of 1 and 2 Maccabees.[27] Thus 1 Maccabees 6:1 placed the death of Antiochus IV Epiphanes in 149 B.C., whereas 2 Maccabees 9:1ff. and 11:23ff. assigned it to 148 B.C. 2 Maccabees appears to have followed the practice of calculating the commencement of the Seleucid era from the autumn of 311 B.C.,[28] while the chronology of 1 Maccabees counted the fractional interval between the summer of 312 B.C. and the seventh month Tishri as a year, thus commencing the second year of the Seleucid regime on the first of Tishri, 312 B.C.

Although many scholars have conceded that the author of 1 Maccabees employed great skill in weaving his own experiences together with eyewitness accounts and literary sources of uneven value, and also in some instances of dubious provenance, to formulate a narrative that can be regarded as a reasonably accurate representation of the history of the period under consideration by and large, the genuineness of the concluding chapters of the work has been questioned seriously in some quarters, and this attitude has thrown some doubt upon the integrity of the work as a whole. The problem stems from the fact that Josephus did not employ 1 Maccabees as an historical source in the compilation of his celebrated *Antiquities* from the time that Simon was elevated to the office of High Priest,[29] and this has cast doubts on the authenticity of the material from 13:43 to 16:24.

While there are certain internal contradictions in chapter 14, as indeed elsewhere in 1 Maccabees, the reasons why Josephus discontinued his use of the work as a source most probably subsist in the methodology of that renowned Jewish historian, and not necessarily in the intrinsic historical merits of the concluding chapters themselves. It seems proba-

[24] For scholarly opinion concerning the value and origin of these sources see *HNTT*, pp. 487ff.

[25] Cf. S. Zeitlin and S. Tedesche, *The First Book of Maccabees*, pp. 252ff.

[26] *AJ*, XIII, 6, 7.

[27] Cf. *AJ*, III, 10, 5.

[28] So S. Zeitlin and S. Tedesche, *The First Book of Maccabees*, p. 253, as against W. H. Brownlee, *IDB*, III, pp. 204, 207; E. Mahler, *Handbuch der jüdischen Chronologie* (1916), pp. 137ff. Cf. *HNTT*, pp. 480ff.

[29] *AJ*, XIII, 6, 7.

ble that Josephus preferred to rely upon his earlier work, the *Wars of the Jews*, for his narrative of the course of events subsequent to the assumption of the High Priestly office by Simon, for which he had drawn upon literary sources that apparently did not include 1 Maccabees. While Josephus followed the latter closely as far as the first thirteen chapters of the book are concerned, it should be noticed that he was seldom reluctant to elaborate or amplify the material with which he was dealing, even to the point of putting in the mouths of his speakers those sentiments which in his opinion would have been appropriate to the particular occasion. Thus the recension of 1 Maccabees available to Josephus most probably did not contain the speech of Mattathias to his sons, since 1 Maccabees 2:50-68 is an editorial interpolation. Nothing daunted, Josephus remedied the deficiency in a speech which represented Mattathias as exhorting his sons to preserve at all costs the theocratic form of government, which was in danger of collapsing. In addition to this theme, Josephus introduced another concept, namely the emphasis upon immortality.[30]

Elsewhere Josephus altered the tenor of the speeches recorded in 1 Maccabees,[31] and as a service to his Greek readers he modified certain Semitic titles. Bearing these considerations in mind, therefore, it seems fairly clear that in point of fact there are insufficient grounds for repudiating the substantial genuineness of the final chapters of 1 Maccabees, and also for the view that would destroy the integrity of the composition by suggesting, as Zeitlin did, that chapters 14—16 were written considerably later than the first thirteen chapters, possibly as part of another book, and that the two sections were unified during the first decade after the destruction of the Temple.[32]

With few exceptions, the narrative of the work pursued a normal chronological pattern, describing the Jewish struggle for religious and political liberty from the accession of Antiochus Epiphanes in 175 B.C. to the death of Simon Maccabaeus in 134 B.C. The central figure in the drama of liberation was Judas Maccabaeus, whose military and political exploits were dealt with at considerable length. After a brief introduction (1:1-9) in which reference was made to the conquests of Alexander the Great, the division of his empire, and the origin of the Seleucid kingdom, the first principal section of 1 Maccabees (1:10-64) described the nature of the causes that precipitated the Maccabean struggle. Here Antiochus IV was vividly portrayed as a sadistic egotist, whose single aim was the imposition of Hellenistic culture upon his subjects by a variety of means. But despite his forcefulness and ingenuity, these

[30] *AJ*, XII, 6, 3. For comments on the methodological techniques of Josephus see R. J. H. Shutt, *Studies in Josephus* (1961), p. 26 *passim*.

[31] Cf. *AJ*, XII, 7, 3.

[32] S. Zeitlin and S. Tedesche, *The First Book of Maccabees*, p. 32.

measures only proved to be totally abhorrent to the Jewish populace, and their main effect was to provoke resentment and hostility towards his regime.

The second chapter introduced the principal figures of resistance to the plans of Antiochus, in the personages of Mattathias and his five sons, who made the first concrete gestures of defiance at Modin (2:1-70). This move quickly developed into organized resistance in the form of guerrilla warfare, which was waged with equal vigor against the soldiers of Antiochus and apostate Jews.

The main section of 1 Maccabees (3:1—16:24) recounted the doings of three sons of Mattathias, namely Judas Maccabaeus (3:1—9:22), Jonathan (9:23—12:53), and Simon (13:1—16:24). After his father died, Judas gained certain initial successes (3:10—4:35), the result of which was the reoccupation of Jerusalem, the rededication of the defiled Temple, and the restoration of the daily sacrifice. Though successful in repelling Edomite and Ammonite attacks against Jewish forces in Transjordan, Judas experienced some military setbacks in Judaea, including the loss of Eleazar at Bethzur (5:9—6:54). Warlike preparations against the Seleucids from other quarters led to the enactment of a treaty between Judas Maccabaeus and Lysias, the commander of the Syrian forces (6:55-63). As the result of intrigue, Alcimus was reinstated in the office of High Priest, and Judas appealed to Syria with qualified success (7:21-50). A treaty of non-aggression was signed with the Romans (8:1-32), but not long afterwards Judas was killed at the battle of Berea in 160 B.C. (9:1-22).

The leadership of Jonathan (9:23—12:53) lasted from 160 B.C. until 143 B.C., during which time he avenged the death of his brother John (9:32-49), secured an interval of peace after defeating Bacchides (9:58-73), and succeeded to the office of High Priest during a religious dispute (10:1-21). Subsequent sections narrated his relations with the Seleucid regime (11:1-37), his embassies to Rome and Sparta (12:1-53), and his death by treachery at the hands of his ally Trypho in 143 B.C. (12:39-53).

Simon Maccabaeus (13:1—16:24) succeeded Jonathan and was able at last to secure political independence for the Jewish people (13:1-42). His capture of the citadel in Jerusalem enabled him to appoint his son John Hyrcanus as commander (13:43-53), and at a later time he renewed the alliance made previously with Rome and Sparta (14:16-24). So outstanding was the leadership of Simon that a special eulogy in his honor was included in the text (14:4-15), listing his conquests and noting the security and stability that were characteristic features of his rule. Public recognition of his services included the proclaiming in the Temple of a formal decree which declared that Simon and his successors should occupy the office of the High Priesthood and be constituted the civil and military rulers of the Jewish people for the future. However, this happy situation was beclouded in 138 B.C., when Antiochus VII revoked Simon's right to coin money in his name, a privilege that he had previously conceded to him (15:1-9), and demanded that the latter become tributary (15:10-31). Being reluctant to comply with this directive, Simon offered resistance in the persons of his sons Judas and John (16:3), who were successful in routing the forces of Antiochus (16:4-10). Simon and two of his sons, Mattathias and Judas, were treacherously murdered by Ptolemy, an army commander (16:11-16), whereupon John Hyrcanus, a surviving son, succeeded to the position and authority of Simon (16:17-24), and ruled until 104 B.C.

The book thus constituted a record of the fortunes enjoyed by a vigorous minority group fighting for civil and religious principles, and ultimately achieving their aim of freedom and independence. Quite aside from the intrinsic merits of such a standpoint, 1 Maccabees is of great importance to the historian as one of the few extant sources dealing authoritatively with the turbulent period of Jewish history that immediately preceded the dawn of the Christian era, and as such it furnishes valuable information regarding the origin of such politico-religious bodies as the Sadducees, Pharisees, and Zealots.

From a religious standpoint, 1 Maccabees was characterized by an outlook that recorded the history of the Jews in a sober, factual manner as the outworking of events through human agencies under divine control. The author emphasized the holiness of God and the necessity for implicit obedience to the principles of the Torah, since in any event a vital faith and a proper relationship of the human spirit to God were of far greater consequence than large armies. Clearly the blood of the Old Testament prophets flowed vigorously in his veins, and resulted in his giving special emphasis to the extent to which conscious human action, under divine inspiration and guidance, could exercise an important function in determining the course of affairs in life. Unflinching patriotism, the sterling virtue of the heroes of 1 Maccabees, was based upon unswerving trust in the ability of God to bring salvation out of apparent defeat, and it is hardly surprising that the book has furnished a continuing fount of inspiration for Jews throughout many centuries. The most obvious indication of this was the incorporation into the Jewish festal calendar of the Hanukkah celebrations, during which the exploits of the Maccabean heroes are recalled in a simple but expressive ritual.

B. SECOND MACCABEES

In the transition from 1 Maccabees to 2 Maccabees the reader passes from a fairly credible and objective historical account of the Maccabean period to a theological treatise that differs not merely in scope, but also in the way in which the material occurring in 1 Maccabees is handled by the compiler. Whereas the author of 1 Maccabees dealt in a comparatively factual and impersonal manner with his sources, the writer of 2

Maccabees outdid the best ambitions of the Chronicler in demonstrating how the omnipotence of God was brought to bear consistently upon the fortunes of His people as a result of proper and timely supplication.

The events narrated in 2 Maccabees occupied a period of only approximately fifteen years, beginning shortly before the accession of Antiochus V and ending about 160 B.C. Thus the main section of the book (4:7–15:36) covered much the same ground as the first seven chapters of 1 Maccabees, though it did so by rewriting the more prosaic narratives of that work in the florid and rather rhetorical forms of expression characteristic of the Alexandrian school at that particular period. Quite obviously the writer had been well grounded in Greek culture, and his literary style indicates that his work was composed in the Greek language. This unknown Alexandrian Jew stated at the outset (2 Macc. 2:23ff.)[33] that his work comprised a summary or *epitome* of a larger history in five volumes, written by a certain Jason of Cyrene. For this reason he is frequently referred to by scholars as the "Epitomist." He mentioned that the history of Jason, which was no longer extant, had dealt with Judas Maccabaeus and his brothers (2 Macc. 2:19ff.), the purification of the Temple, the struggles against Antiochus IV and his son Eupator, and the divine manifestations in support of the loyal followers of Judas Maccabaeus. Precisely who this Jason was is unknown, and it is pure conjecture to identify him with the individual of the same name who was dispatched on an embassy to Rome (1 Macc. 8:17). Only a very few scholars have dismissed the reference to the contents of a multi-volume history as fiction,[34] and for the most part the discussion has centered around the extent to which 2 Maccabees embraced the total content of this work, as well as the nature and provenance of the material that cannot be attributed to Jason.

As regards the latter, the prologue (2:19-32) and the epilogue (15:37-39) can obviously not be regarded in any sense as the work of Jason, since they were written by the Epitomist himself in the first person. Again, the letters to the Egyptian Jews (1:1–2:18) were obviously inserted either by the Epitomist or by a later editor. Much discussion has centered upon these letters in the past,[35] and as many as three separate documents have been identified. It seems probable, however, that only two letters (1:1-9; 1:10–2:18) can be distinguished, and it may be, as Torrey suggested, that they were originally written in Aramaic and translated into Greek by the Epitomist prior to being inserted into 2

---

[33] For the view that the author was Antiochean see S. Zeitlin and S. Tedesche, *The Second Book of Maccabees* (1954), p. 20.

[34] E.g. W. H. Kosters, *Theologisch Tijdschrift,* XII (1878), pp. 491ff.; A. Kamphausen in E. Kautzsch (ed.), *Die Apokryphen und Pseudepigraphen des AT,* I, pp. 81ff.

[35] Cf. the bibliography in *HNTT,* pp. 507f.

Maccabees.[36] The first of these was probably written in 124 B.C., and cited an earlier letter (1:7-8) written in 143 B.C., while the second, which appears to be composite in nature, bore no indication of a date but may have been written about 165 B.C., prior to the first observance of the Festival of Purification at the actual rededication of the Temple. The composite character of this document may be indicated by the presence of an internal digression consisting of legendary material relating to the altar (1:18b—2:15), and the entire letter may even be spurious, since it presented an account of the death of Antiochus IV that varied significantly from other descriptions of his decease.

As far as the original content of the history of Jason is concerned, it has been argued that the official documents contained in chapter eleven, whether genuine or spurious, were not incorporated either in the work attributed to Jason or in the original draft of 2 Maccabees.[37] Other scholars, however, have seen them as the work of Jason in one form or another.[38] As a result of the subjectivity of approach the various opinions expressed must inevitably be regarded as inconclusive. Similarly there is insufficient factual evidence available for the positive exclusion of such passages as the stories of the martyrs,[39] or the seventh chapter of the book.[40]

On the other hand, the history of Jason may well have been continued beyond the point at which 2 Maccabees concluded in narrating the death of Nicanor in 161 B.C. If the Epitomist is to be taken literally in his statement (2 Macc. 2:19) that Jason related the doings of Judas Maccabaeus and his brethren, this would imply that the multi-volume history went considerably beyond the death of Nicanor and concluded at some point after the death of Simon in 134 B.C., thus exceeding the limits of 2 Maccabees considerably. But if consideration is to be given to a contradictory statement of the Epitomist (2:20) in which the wars against Antiochus Epiphanes and his son Eupator were alone mentioned, these would cover somewhat less than the contents of 2 Maccabees, since they terminated in 162 B.C. Niese maintained that the history of Jason did not extend beyond the limits of 2 Maccabees,[41] while Bévenot and Moffatt went so far as to detect the terminal verses of

---

36 *TAL*, pp. 78f.; C. C. Torrey, *ZAW*, XX (1900), pp. 225ff.; *ibid. JAOS* (1940), LX, pp. 119ff.

37 Cf. R. Laqueur, *Kritische Untersuchungen zum zweiten Makkabäerbuch* (1904), pp. 38ff., 75; W. Kolbe, *Beiträge zur syrischen und jüdischen Geschichte* (1926), pp. 108ff.

38 Cf. E. Meyer, *Ursprung und Anfänge des Christentums* (1921-23), II, p. 460; H. Willrich, *Urkundenfälschung in der hellenistisch-jüdischen Literatur* (1924), pp. 35f.

39 As suggested by D. M. Sluys, *De Maccabaeorum libris I et II quaestiones* (1904), pp. 77f.

40 So B. Niese, *Kritik der beiden Makkabäerbücher* (1900), p. 38.

41 *Ibid.*

the five books in the text of 2 Maccabees (3:40; 7:42; 10:9; 13:26; 15:37).[42] On the other hand, André and Meyer extended the history into the lifetime of Simon,[43] while Schlatter took the work of Jason up to the time of John Hyrcanus.[44]

Any estimate of the extent to which the history of Jason conformed to the literary dimensions of 2 Maccabees ought to take into consideration the techniques employed by the Epitomist in adapting this historical material to his own purposes. He described the procedure in terms of omitting the tedious and uninteresting elements in the narratives of Jason, and embellishing that which was retained in order to enhance its literary style (2 Macc. 2:23ff.). On such a basis it would hardly be surprising to discover that certain incidents such as martyrdoms were described in a manner calculated to evoke the utmost in emotional response from the reader. By contrast, other incidents (e.g. 2 Macc. 13:22ff.) appear to be so obviously condensed that they must have existed in a considerably longer form in the original work. In some cases entire episodes of the history were omitted, as in the fourteenth chapter, where no mention was made of the expedition of Bacchides to install Alcimus as High Priest (1 Macc. 7:5ff., 25; 2 Macc. 14:4ff.), while elsewhere the author merely recorded the subsequent dispatch of Nicanor to reinstate Alcimus in his office (2 Macc. 14:11ff., parallel to 1 Macc. 7:26ff.).

But since the *epitome* proper can be subdivided into five sections (chapters 3; 4–7; 8:1–10:9; 10:10–13:26; 14:1–15:36) without undue violence to the text, it may be that these portions corresponded roughly to the fivefold division characteristic of the work of Jason. The sources employed by the latter probably included some biographical description of the career of Judas Maccabaeus, since the doings of this hero as described in 2 Maccabees agreed in considerable detail with what was recorded of him in 1 Maccabees. It is very doubtful, however, that Jason knew of 1 Maccabees as a written document, as Willrich once suggested,[45] and this factor would seem to imply that Jason had access to some other source dealing with the exploits of Judas Maccabaeus. Quite possibly the five-volume history also depended for certain information upon a chronicle of the Seleucid regime similar to, though not necessarily identical with, the one utilized by the author of 1 Maccabees. Discrepancies in such details as the number of soldiers fighting in battles, for example, would indicate that Jason had followed a somewhat diverse tradition of the Seleucid regime from that of 1 Maccabees,

[42] H. Bévenot, *Die beiden Makkabäerbücher*, p. 10. J. Moffatt, *APOT*, I, p. 125.
[43] *AAT*, p. 109. E. Meyer, *Ursprung und Anfänge des Christentums*, II, pp. 456f.
[44] D. A. Schlatter, *Jason von Kyrene* (1891), p. 50.
[45] H. Willrich, *Juden und Griechen* (1895), pp. 68, 76, later retracted in *Judaica* (1900), p. 134.

although the possibility that the Epitomist was responsible for certain differences between 1 and 2 Maccabees should never be overlooked.

If the documents quoted by the Epitomist are genuine (2 Macc. 9:19ff.; 11:16ff.), it seems clear that Jason must have had access to a repository of documents in the Temple archives. This contention receives additional support from the fact that the author held the Temple to be of paramount importance, for it was his ostensible aim to glorify the Second Temple as the abode of God in the midst of Israel. On this basis it is at least probable that Jason obtained information from such a source about Onias, Jason, and Menelaus, presumably from chronicles or annals of the pre-Hasmonean priestly line. The fact that 2 Maccabees contained considerable supernatural phenomena, however, need not indicate more than that existing oral traditions, or at best limited written ones, concerning the pre-Hasmonean priests, were embellished by the addition of miraculous occurrences inserted from the special standpoint of the Epitomist. If such were actually the case, the line of demarcation here, as indeed elsewhere, between the work of Jason and the adaptations of the Epitomist will be far from distinct.

The integrity of 2 Maccabees must therefore be more than a matter for merely passing concern, since it also involves certain internal disarrangements. Quite aside from the Jason source, the Epitomist must have employed traditions, not merely in the introductory section of 2 Maccabees (1:1–2:18) but also in other places in the *epitome* itself (e.g. 10: 32f.; 12:2f.), which came from diverse quarters, and may even have had affinities with extra-Biblical writings. In this latter connection there is more than a casual relationship between 2 Maccabees and the Qumran War Scroll (1QM), an ancient military manual that contained the strategy for an apocalyptic battle between the "sons of Light" and the "sons of Darkness."[46] The battle-slogans carried on the banner of the "sons of Light" were very similar to those coined by Judas Maccabaeus (2 Macc. 8:23; cf. 12:11; 13:13, 15, 17; 15:7f.). In both documents the Temple was given considerable prominence, and the avoidance of fighting during the sabbatical years was another feature found in each composition (2 Macc. 11:1ff.; cf. 1 Macc. 6:49ff.). Nevertheless, these similarities need do nothing more than reflect the Hasidean interests of the author, and do not in themselves imply direct dependence upon a written document by the compiler of 2 Maccabees.

More difficult to resolve is the problem connected with the disarrangements evident in the historical sequences. It is recognized that 2 Maccabees is not in any sense a sequel to or continuation of 1 Maccabees, since it is, as Luther remarked, another book dealing with the Maccabean era

---

[46] The War Scroll was published under the title "The War of the Sons of Light with the Sons of Darkness" by E. L. Sukenik (ed.), *The Dead Sea Scrolls of the Hebrew University* (1955), pp. 35f. and pls. 16-34.

rather than being *the* second book (*"ein anders Buch und nicht das ander Buch Maccabeorum"*). Nevertheless, it purported to be a serious historical study,[47] albeit from a specialized theological standpoint, and therefore the work might be expected to conform to at least some canons of accuracy and order. The most glaring error in this respect consisted in dating the death of Antiochus IV Epiphanes before the cleansing of the Temple by Judas (cf. 1:11ff.; 9:1–10:9), and this was followed closely by the statement that the seven brothers were killed in the presence of Antiochus IV, whereas the king was in fact visiting Antioch at the time (5:21; cf. 6:1). Other contradictions and errors include the reference to Philip's fleeing to Egypt immediately after the death of Antiochus Epiphanes (9:29; cf. 13:23), and the assertion that Antiochus received full authority as ruler at his accession (10:11; 11:15ff.; cf. 13:2).

With regard to the death of this notorious ruler there would appear to be a dislocation in the text of 2 Maccabees, since 10:9, which consisted of a concluding comment on his passing, should stand logically at the end of 9:29. A similar error in sequence occurred in 8:30-33, where a description of the conflicts between Timothy and Bacchides intervened to break the continuity of the narrative describing the defeat of Nicanor (8:23-29, 34-36). Again, the entire account of the activities of Lysias subsequent to the death of Antiochus (11:1ff.) indicates that the Epitomist, or the sources upon which he drew for his information, confused completely the two defeats of Lysias.

If the text of 2 Maccabees is rearranged with a view to restoring it to what may be considered as its original form, it becomes apparent that the questionable passages were securely incorporated into the narrative, so that any attempt at disturbance would only serve to destroy the integrity of the text as it now stands. Thus, as Brownlee has pointed out, to assign the events of the Seleucid year 148 to the reign of Eupator in chapter eleven would be to place the death of Antiochus IV Epiphanes in 147 B.C., and to shorten the period involving the desecration of the Temple from three years (1 Macc. 1:54ff.; 4:52) to two years (2 Macc. 10:3).[48] Since the dislocations apparent in the book are in harmony with its literary balance, they may have been the work of the Epitomist rather than of Jason or a later editor of 2 Maccabees. On the other hand, the general traditions regarding the death of Antiochus were well known, and it is doubtful that the Epitomist would have included such a variant account of his own accord, so that this might indicate that it was already present in the work of Jason.

There would seem to be, therefore, little need for blaming the disarrangements upon anyone other than the Epitomist. As Pfeiffer has re-

[47] Thus Hellenistic titles were used correctly, and details of Seleucid history as in 2 Macc. 4:21, 25; 5:22f.; 8:8; 9:29; 10:13f.; 13:25 were accurately recorded.
[48] W. H. Brownlee, *IDB*, III, p. 208.

marked, he evidently proceeded with great freedom and with more concern for public recognition of his literary abilities than for an objective, concise presentation of the historical material attributed to Jason.[49] He clearly showed little desire to indulge in accurate historical research (2 Macc. 2:28), and during the process of condensing the statistics and detail presented in the compilation of Jason he took the liberty of rearranging the order of events with unfortunate results, furnishing exaggerated accounts of atrocities and miracles, and in general superimposing his own religious concepts upon the structure of the historical situation. Nevertheless, the Epitomist performed a valuable service in preserving the bulk of a work that is no longer extant. His condensation was admittedly meant for popular consumption, and the gratitude with which it was received is reflected by the fact that the Greek text of 2 Maccabees was subsequently translated into Latin, Syriac, Coptic, and Armenian.

Aside from the probable dates to be assigned to the letters written to the Egyptian Jews (1:1–2:18), any dating of 2 Maccabees as a whole must take cognizance of the two stages by which the work arrived at its extant form. Unfortunately there is no evidence as to the time when Jason of Cyrene wrote his history, since the early reference to him and his work was the one made by the Epitomist, who claimed to have abridged the history of Jason. If he is not to be identified with the Jason who was sent on an embassy to Rome, he may perhaps have been a nephew of Judas Maccabaeus (cf. 1 Macc. 8:17) or possibly a contemporary of Philo Judaeus. As Pfeiffer has indicated,[50] his avowed intention of glorifying Judaism generally and the Temple cultus in particular, was given literary expression in an agglomeration of fact, drama, fancy, and faith, an approach that was characteristic of Hellenistic historiography, and that was reflected in the work of analogous historians who wrote in the immediate pre-Christian period, such as Polybius.[51] In the last resort it must be regarded as hazardous to do more than indicate a general period for the composition of the history of Jason, since so much of the form, style, rhetorical flourish, historical error, and detailed knowledge of Hellenistic literature evidenced by 2 Maccabees may well be the work of the Epitomist.

From a reference in the epilogue (15:37) to the fact that Jerusalem had been in the possession of the Jews for some time, it might appear that 2 Maccabees was compiled later than the period of John Hyrcanus I, and certainly not as early as the beginning of the second century B.C., as Clement of Alexandria claimed.[52] It must be stated in connection with

[49] *HNTT*, p. 521.
[50] *HNTT*, p. 518.
[51] Cf. *APOT*, I, p. 129.
[52] *Stromateis* V, 14.

patristic testimony, however, that 2 Maccabees was not known as such by Clement of Alexandria,[53] Origen,[54] or Cyprian.[55] The earliest references to it as a separate work occurred in Eusebius' *Praeparatio Evangelica* and Jerome's *Galataean Prologue*. Hippolytus speaks of a separate first Book of Maccabees in his *Commentary on Daniel*. Clement of Alexandria designated the first book as "Maccabees" (τὸ [βιβλίον] τῶν Μακκαβαϊκῶν) whereas he described 2 Maccabees as the *Epitome* (ἡ τῶν Μακκαβαϊκῶν ἐπιτομή), which presumably opened the way for the recognition of 2 Maccabees as a separate composition.

Zeitlin urged a date in the period of Agrippa I (A.D. 41-44) as the most probable time of composition,[56] on the ground that the circumstances of that era would have furnished the most satisfactory situation for the compilation of 2 Maccabees. He also suggested an Antiochene provenance because of basic differences in national allegiances and outlook between the Jews of Antioch and those of Alexandria. Despite the assumption that some of the martyrdoms described by the author (7:3; cf. 6:8) may have occurred in Antioch, thereby suggesting that city as the place where 2 Maccabees was compiled, the prefixing of the main treatise by letters addressed to the Jews in Egypt would seem to support the general contention of scholars that the book was written in Egypt, no doubt by an Alexandrian Jew who was in accord with the traditions and objectives associated with the writings of Jason. Postulated affinities with Daniel on the one hand,[57] or with the Hasidim on the other are inconclusive in any attempt to establish a date either for the history of Jason or for the extant 2 Maccabees. The most that can be said is that the latter was probably in circulation by the middle of the first century of the Christian era. In such an event, the history of Jason may have been compiled somewhat after 130 B.C.

As indicated earlier, 2 Maccabees falls into five principal parts, preceded by two letters to the Jews in Egypt concerning the Purification Festival (1:1–2:18), after which occurred the preface to the history proper, in which the Epitomist described his condensation and embellishment of the work of Jason (2:19-32). The causes of the Maccabean rebellion were then set out as a beginning for the main historical section of 2 Maccabees, commencing with the unsuccessful attempt at plundering the Temple made by Heliodorus, envoy of Seleucus IV (3:1-40). The evil intrigues of Simon with the Hellenizing priests Jason and Menelaus, as well as with the Seleucid regime, were described in a depressing fashion (4:1-50). Celestial phenomena warned of the wrath to come (5:1-4), which was precipitated when Jason attempted to regain the

---

[53] *Stromateis* I, 21.

[54] Cf. *Contra Cels.* VIII, 46.

[55] Cf. *Sicut Eleazar in libro Macchabaeorum profitetur et dicit*, VIII.

[56] S. Zeitlin and S. Tedesche, *The Second Book of Maccabees*, pp. 27ff.

[57] Cf. W. H. Brownlee, *IDB*, III, p. 209.

office of High Priest. Antiochus, who was in Egypt, interpreted this action as an attempt at revolt and marched against Jerusalem, pillaging the city and profaning the Temple. Judas Maccabaeus escaped to the mountains accompanied by a few followers (5:5-27), and thereafter forceful Hellenizing of the remaining populace resulted in much inhuman behavior, acute suffering, and a great many martyrdoms (5:28—7:42).

Chapters 8—15 correspond roughly to 1 Maccabees 3—7, narrating the rise of the Maccabeans and the way in which God used the heroic stand of those leaders, to the point where the death of Antiochus IV brought deliverance and freedom of worship to the ancient people of God (8:1—10:9). Subsequent narratives, liberally interspersed with descriptions of awesome celestial phenomena, demonstrated the way in which God supported the forces of Judas Maccabaeus against Timothy (10:24-38) and Lysias (11:1—13:26) during the reign of Antiochus V. A final important section (14:1—15:36) narrated the manner in which God showed His saving power in the defeat of Nicanor and the Syrian forces. By way of conclusion, an epilogue (15:37-39) noted that the author had combined historical fact with rhetorical style for the benefit of his readers who would want to peruse the work aloud.[58]

Any estimate of the worth of 2 Maccabees must ultimately be theological rather than purely historical or chronological in nature. The facts of history were clearly subordinated to the purpose of demonstrating the overall providence of God for His people. Reflecting Pharisaic attitudes, the author emphasized the ways in which God had ordained the affairs of His Chosen Nation, and by His power had forestalled the violation of His sacred Temple. The doctrine of providence and retribution was worked out with considerable care, one prominent feature of which was the artistry of the writer in showing just how appositely and appropriately the punishment fitted the crime (cf. 4:38; 5:10; 9:5f.; 13:4). Even though the sufferings of the martyrs were due to the sins of the nation as a whole (cf. 4:16f.; 5:17ff.; 6:12; 17:7), the author was not slow to point out that they were efficacious in expiating the righteous anger of God against their fellow Israelites (cf. 8:33ff.). The divine chastening, though severe, was far preferable for the Jews than the most drastic form of punishment as exhibited in the case of pagan nations, namely being left alone by God. The writer regarded as common occurrences the activity of agents in the unseen world functioning on behalf of mortal men (cf. 3:25; 5:2; 10:29; 13:2), and was firm in his enunciation of a doctrine of bodily resurrection, a feature characteristic of Pharisaic belief.

Not only did he emphasize survival after death, but he also stressed that upon the decease of the body the righteous would enjoy eternal life (7:36) in a restored physical state (7:11ff.; 14:26) in conjunction with

---

[58] For comments on the ancient practice of reading aloud see *MTA,* p. 145 n. 1.

the other members of the family(7:6ff.). This treatment was in diametric opposition to that accorded the wicked, who could expect nothing more than sustained punishment for their misdeeds. The references to the offerings of prayers and sacrifices for the dead (12:43ff.), and the intercession of the saints (15:11ff.) were to practices that had no theological or practical basis in the canonical Hebrew Scriptures, but which were employed subsequently for dogmatic reasons by the Church of Rome.

There can be little doubt that 2 Maccabees exerted an important influence upon the outlook of the Christians in the primitive Church, and it may be within the bounds of possibility that certain of the New Testament writings reflected the contents of this composition to a limited extent. Thus the passage in 2 Maccabees concerning the martyrdoms (6:10–7:42) was probably the subject of the allusion in Hebrews 11:35, while the reference in Hebrews 11:38 to the martyrs "wandering over deserts and mountains, and in dens and caves of the earth" appears to be a pointed allusion to some of the tribulations and atrocities described in 2 Maccabees (e.g. 5:27; 6:11; 10:6). Similarly the description in Revelation 21:8 of the cowardly and unbelieving seems to reflect the influence of 2 Maccabees (8:13).

Doctrinally, the expiatory suffering of Christ has been taken as being foreshadowed by the tragic experiences of the martyrs, who maintained that their sufferings had an atoning value (7:37; 8:3), but this argument could be used in connection with any person in the Old Testament period who had died as a witness to his faith. The functions of angelic beings and celestial messengers as evidenced in the New Testament can also be somewhat better understood through a consideration of the way in which the Epitomist stressed the supra-mundane character of the struggle of the people of God for their very existence. The eschatology of the messianic kingdom as reflected in 2 Maccabees has very little in common either with what is found in the canonical prophets or with the expectations of the Qumran community,[59] and in fact was typically Pharisaic in nature.

Supplementary Literature

Abel, F. M. *Les Livres Maccabées.* 1949.

Browne, L. E. and M. Black. *From Babylon to Bethlehem.* 1951.

Dancy, J. C. *A Commentary on 1 Maccabees.* 1954.

Fairweather, W. and J. C. Black. *I and II Maccabees.* 1897.

Farmer, W. R. *Maccabees, Zealots and Josephus.* 1957.

Keil, C. F. *Commentar über die Bücher der Maccabäer.* 1875.

Oesterley, W. O. E. *The Jews and Judaism During the Greek Period.* 1941.

Penna, A. *I e II Maccabei.* 1953.

[59] Cf. 1QS, IX:11, *CDC*, IX:10B, XV:4; J. M. Allegro, *The Dead Sea Scrolls*, pp. 148ff.

XIV. EPILOGUE

By way of epilogue to the Apocrypha, it can be stated that the pervasive influence of this literature through the centuries is obvious. Artists have drawn freely upon its themes for subject matter, as have composers, dramatists, and poets. Ecclesiastical dogmas have received their inspiration from these source materials, and their impact has also been felt in the liturgical forms, homilies, and meditations of various religious bodies. It is even asserted on good authority that a verse in 2 Esdras (6:42; cf. 6:47ff.) played a part in encouraging Christopher Columbus to set out upon the voyage of discovery that culminated in the finding and partial exploration of the New World.[60]

In the realm of music a number of familiar hymns seem to exhibit some dependence upon the Apocrypha, including the celebrated *Nun danket alle Gott*, written by Martin Runkart about 1636, which leans heavily on the doxology in Ecclesiasticus 50:22ff. Handel drew upon these writings for inspiration in composing the oratorios *Susanna*, *Judas Maccabaeus*, and *Alexander Balus*. A considerable number of proverbs in common use may well have had their origin in the Aprocrypha,[61] as well as such familiar names as Susan, Toby, and Edna.

Despite the nature of this impact upon the culture of the western world, there can be little doubt that the books of the English Apocrypha are of very uneven value. A bright devotional jewel such as the Prayer of Manasseh is more than a little beclouded when set against the mythological absurdities of Bel and the Dragon, or some of the theological crudities of 2 Maccabees. The canonization of the bulk of the Apocrypha by the Roman Catholic Church led to a spate of pious invention during the medieval period upon material that already partook of the nature of myth and legend, an activity that was also fostered in other unreformed Churches of the East.[62]

It is a matter of common agreement that the apocryphal literature supplies extremely important information concerning the religious, histo-

---

[60] *MTA*, pp. 205, 232ff.
[61] Cf. *MTA*, p. 231.
[62] *MTA*, pp. 149f.

1277

rical, cultural, and social development of Jewish life in the intertestamental period. That these writings also contain moral and spiritual insights that are in general harmony with the theological themes found in the canonical Hebrew Scriptures is also clearly evident, as is the manner in which certain New Testament concepts such as angelology, demonology, immortality, and the like are shown to have emerged in and through the doctrinal corpus of Pharisaism. But to do more than regard the apocryphal writings as a sample of the literature current in the period that separated the Old and the New Testaments and reflecting the trends and events that characterized that turbulent era of history is to run the risk of imposing serious limitations upon critical judgment regarding the ultimate value of these documents for history and faith alike. The most serious of such restrictions is incurred when the apocryphal books are deemed to constitute part of the Scriptural record, and held, as in the Roman Catholic Church, to be of equal canonicity, inspiration, and authority with the Old and New Testaments. The fact that such a position was adopted at all resulted in the main from dogmatic considerations, and a procedure such as this can have embarrassing consequences, as has been pointed out earlier, when questions of internal doctrinal consistency within the Scriptural corpus arise.

While the Western Church was undoubtedly well advised to regard the contents of the Apocrypha as constituting documents of a certain moral and historical utility, there can also be no question whatever as to the correctness of the stand taken by certain patristic authors in distinguishing between canonical and ecclesiastical writings in the Church. In this connection the criteria that are deemed to constitute canonicity must ultimately be related to the attitudes existing among the Alexandrian and Palestinian Jews, rather than to the approach of the Christian Church in Alexandria, Antioch, or elsewhere regarding those writings which should be considered canonical. Accordingly it should be observed that the Jews merely gave clearer definition to a situation that had been accepted in substance for some time previously in excluding from the category of Scripture certain compositions that the early Christian Church chose to perpetuate. Such being the case, it is merely a question of indulging in historical research as to the content of the Jewish canon of Scripture in order to determine whether or not the apocryphal writings can be legitimately considered part of the corpus of Scripture.

INDEXES

INDEX OF SUBJECTS

INDEX OF ANCIENT AUTHORS

INDEX OF MODERN AUTHORS

Niese, B., 1269n.
Nöldeke, T., 33, 203n., 241n., 248n., 1040n., 1077n., 1098n., 1144n., 1210n.
Norlie, O. M., 981n.
North, C. R., 68n., 77n., 228n., 300n., 370n., 484n., 486n., 487, 490, 642n., 697, 768n., 778n., 795n., 800, 947n., 994n., 1155n.
Noss, J. B., 354n.
Noth, M., 49, 57f., 61, 66n., 67, 70, 72, 79n., 81, 111n., 121n., 160n., 165n., 175n., 176, 177n., 181n., 184n., 222n., 238, 245n., 249n., 305ff., 314n., 316n., 320n., 325, 332ff., 336n., 345, 378, 434n., 437, 556n., 563, 574, 588, 613, 667f., 670n., 671, 673n., 676, 679, 680n., 683, 686n., 690n., 691n., 697, 704n., 712n., 731, 743n., 871n., 874n., 931n., 939n., 944n., 945n., 987n., 1013n., 1109, 1146n., 1156
Nötscher, F., 804n.
Nougayrol, J., 1025n.
Nowack, W., 36n., 59n., 504, 868n.
Nyberg, H. S., 66ff., 210n., 486, 505, 761, 863n., 867n., 1108

Obbinck, H. Th., 412n., 752n.
Obermann, J., 399n.
O'Callaghan, R. T., 166n., 310n.
O'Connell, P., 74n.
Odeberg, H., 767n., 1084
Oeder, G. L., 823
Oehler, G. F., 424f., 427
Oestborn, G., 68n., 402n., 440n., 487n., 872n.
Oesterley, W. O. E., 69, 76n., 281, 304, 343n., 355n., 368n., 383, 387n., 392f., 489n., 600n., 698, 725, 795f., 812ff., 826n., 830, 866, 869, 872, 875, 879, 886, 894, 900, 917, 934, 967n., 970n., 993f., 1006n., 1014, 1017n., 1052n., 1054n., 1056, 1060, 1066, 1133, 1140n., 1144, 1191n., 1230, 1237, 1240n., 1254, 1260n., 1276
Oestreicher, T., 44
Oettli, S., 1060, 1068n.
O'Leary, D., 248n.
Olmstead, A. T., 69, 186n., 342n., 345, 347n., 833n., 1013n., 1088n., 1096, 1121n., 1138, 1139n., 1142n., 1198n.
Olshausen, J., 967n., 1003
Oman, J., 465n.
Oort, H., 922
Oppenheim, A. L., 1119n.

Oppenheim, M. von, 96, 155n., 340n.
Orelli, C. von, 804n., 821, 864n., 897, 951
Orlinsky, H. M., 73, 219n., 230n., 231n., 233n., 235, 247n., 249n., 250, 252, 253n., 304, 315n., 485n., 532n., 691n., 833n., 834
Orr, J., 29, 78, 175n., 465n., 470n., 504
Osgood, H., 499n.
Ottley, R. L., 361n., 852n.
Ottley, R. R., 798n.
Otzen, B., 952n.
Oudenrijn, M. A. van den, 711n., 744n.
Owen, G. F., 112n.

Packer, J. I., 464n., 470
Pallis, S. A., 52, 370n.
Palm, A., 1075n.
Palmer, A. S., 686n.
Pap, L. I., 994
Parker, R. A., 172f., 174n., 733n., 845
Parrot, A., 78n., 89n., 100n., 101n., 105n., 157n., 164, 311n., 558n.
Parsons, J., 238n.
Parsons, T., 54n.
Paterson, J., 804f., 831n., 863n., 993
Paterson, W. P., 600n.
Paton, L. B., 32, 1090n., 1091n., 1093n., 1100n.
Patterson, C. H., 1046
Patton, J. H., 334n., 970n., 998n.
Paulus, H. E. G., 484f., 951
Pautrel, R., 1213
Payne, D. F., 453n., 555n.
Payne, E. A., 652n., 756n., 810n.
Payne, J. B., 76n., 479, 854n.
Peake, A. S., 40, 46, 51, 69, 100n., 344n., 485n., 564n., 803n., 896n., 1056n., 1071
Pearson, A. T., 850n.
Pedersen, J., 48, 65ff., 370n., 440n., 441n., 525n., 573f., 641, 646n., 684n., 745n., 866n., 895, 896n.
Peet, T. E., 56n., 175n., 1025n.
Penna, A., 1276
Perkins, A. L., 157n.
Perles, F., 255n., 972n.
Perowne, J. J. S., 967n.
Perowne, S., 726n.
Perring, B., 451n.
Petermann, H., 222n.
Peters, C., 241n.
Peters, J. P., 361n., 990n.
Peters, N., 247n., 903, 1226n.

1300

1304

INDEX OF THE OLD TESTAMENT

INDEX OF THE APOCRYPHA

INDEX OF THE NEW TESTAMENT